SAVAGES
and
SCIENTISTS

The Smithsonian Institution
and the Development of
American Anthropology
1846–1910

Curtis M. Hinsley, Jr.

Smithsonian Institution Press, Washington, D.C., 1981

Cover: Insignia for the Bureau of American Ethnology,
designed by William Henry Holmes in 1879.

Photographic Credits
Department of Anthropology, National Museum of
Natural History, Smithsonian Institution: p. 73
National Anthropological Archives, National Museum of
Natural History, Smithsonian Institution: Cover, pp. 90, 96, 124,
144, 163, 165, 173, 176, 191, 198, 209, 241, 269, 288
National Museum of American Art, Smithsonian Institu-
tion: pp. 45, 93, 106, 168, 235, 278

Library of Congress Cataloging in Publication Data
Hinsley, Curtis M
Savages and scientists.
Bibliography: P.
Includes index.
1. Anthropology—United States—History.
2. United States. Bureau of American Ethnology—
History. 3. Smithsonian Institution—History.
I. Title.
GN17.3.U6H56   301'.0973   80-20193
ISBN 0-87474-518-7

Contents

Abbreviations Used in the Notes

AES   American Ethnological Association
APS   American Philosophical Society
AR   Annual Report
ASW   Anthropological Society of Washington
BAE-IN   Records of 1903 Investigation of the Bureau of American Ethnology
BAE-LR   Bureau of American Ethnology Letterbooks
BP   Franz Boas Papers, American Philosophical Society
CNAE   Contributions to North American Ethnology
FMA   Field Museum Archives
FWP   Frederick Ward Putnam Papers, Harvard University Archives
GP   Gifford Pinchot Papers, Library of Congress
GPO   Government Printing Office
HUA   Harvard University Archives
LC   Library of Congress
LHM   Lewis Henry Morgan Papers, Rush Rhees Library, University of Rochester
MNCA   Museum of Navaho Ceremonial Art, Santa Fe, New Mexico
MP   W J McGee Papers, Library of Congress
NAA   National Anthropological Archives
OHS   Ohio Historical Society
PMA   Peabody Museum Archives
PSW   Philosophical Society of Washington
SI   Smithsonian Institution
SIA   Smithsonian Institution Archives
SIL   Smithsonian Institution Libraries
SW   Southwest Museum, Los Angeles, California
TASW   Transactions of the Anthropological Society of Washington
USNM   United States National Museum
WDW   William Dwight Whitney Papers, Sterling Library, Yale University
WHH   William Henry Holmes, "Random Records of a Lifetime," Library of the National Museum of American Art, Smithsonian Institution
WSHS   Wisconsin State Historical Society

Unless otherwise indicated, the date of publication for all SI, USNM, and BAE annual reports is the year following the date in the report title. Place of publication is Washington, D.C.

Preface

Between the Civil War and the First World War the United States underwent fundamental social reorganization. Patterns of daily work and community life before 1860 had been predominantly local and personal. If small communities restricted acceptable behavior, within those horizons they also provided a sense of comfort, coherence, and control. With faith, the world was manageable; men and women could cope. The rapid appearance in the second half of the nineteenth century of giant corporate structures, masses of laboring poor, urban filth, and rural poverty—the negative social and economic indices of modern growth—permanently destroyed antebellum America. Personal rootlessness, impotence, and retreat to the thin securities offered by industrial and farm unions, professional groups, and embattled family circles became the signs of a maturing industrial society. The organizational revolution of the second half of the century was a response to the dislocation that affected all facets of American life. It offered new personal identity and group leverage against impersonal, unpredictable economic forces.

The search for order and control was a central dynamic of Victorian America. In a remarkably short time it significantly altered the intellectual structures of the country. The curriculum of the antebellum college, neatly separated into moral and natural philosophy, had attempted to incorporate by addition the burgeoning physical and natural sciences.[1] After the Civil War, however, this curriculum rapidly divided into the recognizably modern disciplines of the sciences, humanities, and, after 1890, the social sciences. As the United States metamorphosed into an organizational society, it thus became a nation of scientific expertise as well. The new scientific professions of the post-Civil War era claimed to be neutral instruments serving the general welfare; in actuality, as Samuel Hays has observed, they "represented particular, not universal, values, rooted in particular perspectives . . ." They successfully preached a new ideology of science.[2]

In its roots, the professionalization of American science was attitudinal, a change first in consciousness and self-definition. Proliferation of professional organizations and journals was the outward sign of altered needs, motivations, and identities. This is not to deny the structural dynamics and shaping effects of the process. The critical need in American science between 1860 and 1920, according to Nathan Reingold, was certification of the unprecedented number of investigators and contributors who were flooding the new disciplines. From this perspective, professionalization was a response to a social and structural problem—a human sorting process.[3] One can "mark the beginning of modern academic science in the United States," Charles Rosenberg judges, "at that moment when American investigators began to care more for the approval and esteem of their disciplinary colleagues than they did for the general standards of success in the society which surrounded them."[1] Momentum varied with the field, but the general pattern and direction of change was the same across the sciences. But if the history of anthropology in this period is indicative, the process was neither smooth nor painless. Wrenching changes in self-perception and purpose were involved in the shift from local to national horizons, from inclusive to exclusive audiences, from amateur to professional identities. The American sciences did not come to organizational maturity without severe growing pains and heavy costs.

The present study traces the development of anthropology in Washington, D.C., from the founding of the Smithsonian Institution in 1846 to the death of John Wesley Powell and the decline of his Bureau of American Ethnology at the turn of the century. A combination of institutional, biographical, and intellectual history, it is the story of a search for scientific rigor and respectability in a field that was unusually ill-defined and professionally porous. Because American anthropologists of the previous century were moralists and citizens before they were scientists, the narrative of their struggle to find purpose in American society also illuminates the deep religious and political concerns of their culture.

Why, after all, study the American Indian? The question haunted and harassed anthropologists one hundred years ago, and in the exploration of this challenge lies the logic of the present study. For the fact is that nineteenth-century men and women did spend years in devoted study of aboriginal cultures in the Americas and around the world. They did so in the face of public skepticism. Historians of the time established national mythology and told edifying tales; political economists debated burning issues of commerce, manufacture, and government policy; chemists and engineers added visibly to the store of useful knowledge. But the self-appointed students of mankind persisted without clear purpose in a society that honored utility. Anthropology had to be taken on faith.

Why did they bother? The argument presented here is that anthropology was reflexive, an exercise in self-study by Americans who sensed but were unable to confront directly the tragic dimensions of their culture and of their own lives. The utility of anthropology was moral. The study of humanity has always been implicitly a moral, reforming enterprise, but in the previous century it was explicitly so, especially for individuals to whom biblical truths and religious orthodoxy appeared no longer personally persuasive or socially effective. Born into an increasingly secular world of chance and diversity, they found solace as well as aesthetic pleasure in the vision of a progressively evolving humanity. Beneath the appearance of chaos, their science would surely reveal unity and purpose in human affairs. After a long history of divergence, dissension, and misery, mankind would ultimately reunite in a single world brotherhood. Perhaps the words of Walt Whitman at the close of the Civil War would at last be realized:

I see not America only, not only Liberty's nation but
    other nations preparing,
I see tremendous entrances and exits, new combinations,
    the solidarity of races,
I see that force advancing with irresistible power on the
    world's stage,
(Have the old forces, the old wars, played their parts? are
    the acts suitable to them closed?)
Are all nations communing? Is there going to be but one
    heart to the globe?
Is humanity forming en-masse?[5]

The Smithsonian Institution dominated American anthropology from its founding in 1846 until the emergence of university departments after the turn of the century. Joseph Henry committed the prestige and resources of the young Institution to studies in linguistics, archaeology, and ethnology as part of his program to diffuse among Americans not only scientific knowledge but the pious experience of doing science. Anthropology offered one route to a nobler, more tolerant humanity. With the founding of the Bureau of American Ethnology in 1879, John Wesley Powell carried forward Henry's intentions and added a rationale for anthropology as a tool of public policy. Powell provided the first full-time employment for would-be anthropologists and adopted an elaborate theoretical framework of social and mental evolution for organizing the data that poured into the Bureau offices. Quite unintentionally, he also nurtured strains of exclusiveness and professional identity in his organization. "Anybody can go out and collect. But the main work," stated James Mooney in 1903, "is the investigation. What I mean is that I am not primarily collecting material for grammars and dictionaries. I am studying everything else they have . . ."[6]

Powell's death in 1902 marked the end of Smithsonian dominance in American anthropology; by the First World War the growth of university departments, under the guidance of Franz Boas, had permanently altered the institutional and intellectual paradigms of the profession. Just as Powell struggled to keep the BAE free from political interference, Boas's move to the university was a reach for autonomy. He sought to insure reliable financial support and minimize external influences over what he hoped would become a critical social science. He attempted, in other words, to establish a self-regulation in science analogous to that in other areas of modern corporate life. While Boas himself always remained a nineteenth-century moralist, the drive to university autonomy for anthropology created a sense of separateness that would have been alien to earlier American anthropologists. The shape and substance of nineteenth-century anthropology reflected specific commitments: to individual initiative; to a homogeneous, comfortable population; to uplift of the public through science. The decline of government anthropology and the ascendancy of a university science meant the displacement of these commitments by others: appeal to a restricted audience of trained colleagues rather than to a broad public; consciousness of value judgment in science; and, above all, perpetuation of the community of inquirers.

History is not progressive, and the course of American anthropology has been especially marked by compounded irony. It suggests in fact a balance sheet, not a success story. Thus, in 1846, Henry Rowe Schoolcraft exhorted Americans to relive the deeds of the "hardy and vigorous" American aborigines, pointing especially to their "strong, efficient, and popular" government as a model for the United States. The anthropologist, Schoolcraft predicted, would instill in his fellow citizens the virtues of the fiercely independent Indian, in this way completing the aboriginal destiny: for "it has been given to us, to carry out scenes of improvement, and of moral and intellectual progress, which providence in its profound workings, has deemed it best for the prosperity of man, that *we*, not *they*, should be entrusted with. We have succeeded to their inheritance. . . ."[7] For the rest of the century Schoolcraft and his followers looked to the government in Washington to bring about those "scenes of improvement." But by the painful years of the First World War, the trend toward organization and coordination that had seemed inevitable and welcome after 1865 now cast a dark shadow over scientific freedom. "Personally I must confess," Berthold Laufer confided to Boas in 1919, "that I do not believe in the organization of science, as it is now conceived in many quarters; organization has a disagreeable taste of militarism, bossism, and slavery, all of which are detestable. The true progress of science, in my estimation, rests on the freedom of the individual and the free development of his faculties."[8] Laufer's words suggest that the central institutional dilemmas of nineteenth-century anthropology have only been inherited in new forms, and they speak to all science: How do we protect the freedom of the individual and yet establish system in science? How do we harness the powers of organizational life without dimming the light of individual genius?

The history of anthropology, I am convinced, should not be left to anthropologists. Still, the historian who presumes to impose his judgment in this field is well advised to tread circumspectly and respectfully, and needs patient friends to overcome disciplinary myopia. In this regard I have been unusually fortunate. In the early stages of this study at the University of Wisconsin-Madison, Paul Conkin and Victor Hilts provided inspiration, encouragement, and close criticism. Nathan Reingold introduced me to Joseph Henry and to the history of science at its best; William Sturtevant has proved a resourceful critic and enthusiastic supporter; and throughout the months of writing and rewriting, George Stocking has served as a model and standard for my efforts in this field. In addition, the following individuals devoted precious time to reading and commenting on all or parts of the manuscript at various stages: Anthony Aveni, Nigel Bolland, Hamilton Cravens, Regna Darnell, Bernard Fontana, Don Fowler, Richard Frost, Ives Goddard, Arthur Molella, and Herman Viola. I owe a special debt to Ruth Selig of the Smithsonian Institution for her faith in the manuscript at a critical juncture.

The library and archival staffs of the following institutions were without exception cordial and unstinting in aiding my research: the American Philosophical Society; Field Museum of Chicago; Harvard University; Library of Congress; Museum of Navaho Ceremonial Art in Santa Fe; National Museum of American Art, Smithsonian Institution; Peabody Museum of Archaeology and Ethnology, Harvard University; Smithsonian Institution; and the Southwest Museum. Over the years, Paula Fleming and Jim Glenn of the National Anthropological Archives have graciously responded to my innumerable requests.

A predoctoral fellowship at the Joseph Henry Papers, Smithsonian Institution, during 1973–74, provided idyllic conditions for the original research, and I wish to record here my deep gratitude to the Institution and to the staff of the Joseph Henry Papers. It was a year I shall always recall happily. Further research was aided by grants from the Colgate University Research Council and, in 1977, from the American Council of Learned Societies.

Rebecca, my wife, has been my conscience, guide, and friend, always.

Notes

1. Stanley M. Guralnick, *Science and the Ante-Bellum American College*, Memoirs of the APS 109 (Philadelphia: APS, 1975).
2. Samuel P. Hays, Introduction to Jerry Israel, ed., *Building the Organizational Society* (New York, 1972), pp. 1–2.
3. Nathan Reingold, "Definitions and Speculations: The Professionalization of Science in the Nineteenth Century," in A. Oleson and S.C. Brown, eds., *The Pursuit of Knowledge in the Early American Republic* (Baltimore, 1976), pp. 33–69.
4. Charles E. Rosenberg, "Science and American Social Thought," in David D. Van Tassel and Michael G. Hall, eds., *Science and Society in the United States* (Homewood, Ill., 1968), pp. 154–55.
5. Walt Whitman, "Years of the Modern," in *Walt Whitman: Complete Poetry and Selected Prose and Letters*, ed. Emory Holloway (London: Nonesuch Press, 1938), pp. 438–39.
6. Testimony of James Mooney, BAE-IN, p. 971, NAA.
7. Henry Rowe Schoolcraft, *An Address, delivered before the Was-Ho-De-No-Son-Ne, or New Confederacy of the Iroquois, at its third annual council, August 14, 1846* (Rochester, 1846), pp. 28–29.
8. Laufer to Boas, 28 January 1919, FMA.

Part 1

Anthropology at the Smithsonian Institution 1846–1880

I

"Magnificent Intentions": Washington, D.C., and American Anthropology in 1846

In the closing years of the nineteenth century, aging, well-traveled American men of letters were fond of looking back, with condescension and nostalgia, to an unformed, innocent antebellum America. Reliving his first visit to Washington in 1849, Henry Adams remembered a sleepy, isolated outpost where "the brooding indolence of a warm climate and a negro population hung in the atmosphere heavier than the catalpas." The early national capital had lacked physical, social, and moral structure: here "the want of barriers, of pavements, of forms; the looseness, the laziness; the indolent Southern drawl; the pigs in the streets; the negro babies and their mothers with bandanas; the freedom, openness, swagger, of nature and man" had lulled and soothed tight Boston nerves. Even twenty years later, amid the chaos and crush of the first Grant administration, Washington still seemed "a mere political camp" to Adams. His fellow Bostonian, Edward Everett Hale, recalled the capital city of the 1840s as a "mud-hole" where "everything had the simplicity and ease, if you please, of a small Virginia town." The capital was so isolated from the larger society that the visitor of the forties seemed to come "out of America into Washington."[1]

Visiting Europeans reserved special spleen for the capital city. Here in "the headquarters of tobacco-tinctured saliva" Charles Dickens noted in 1842 the "spacious avenues, that begin in nothing, and lead nowhere; streets, mile-long, that only want houses, roads, and inhabitants; public buildings that need but a public to be complete; and ornaments of great thoroughfares, which only lack great thoroughfares to ornament." With little trade and a meager permanent population, Washington seemed to Dickens only a "City of Magnificent Intentions." Anthony Trollope, following in the footsteps of his famous mother, commented no less caustically. He arrived in the first, dismal winter of the Civil War to find a pretentious failure of a city, three-fourths of it "wild, trackless, unbridged, uninhabited, and desolate." Trollope saw little nobility of taste in the sparse government structures, still less in the "bastard gothic" architecture of the Smithsonian "Castle." But it was the sight of the unfinished stump of the Washington Monument on a bleak Sunday afternoon that evoked a summary judgment of the city and the nation:

> There, on the brown, ugly, undrained field, within easy sight of the President's house, stood the useless, shapeless, graceless pile of stones. It was as though I were looking on the genius of the city. It was vast, pretentious, bold, boastful with a loud voice, already taller by many heads than other obelisks, but nevertheless still in its infancy,—ugly, unpromising, and false.[2]

Jibes of European and American cosmopolites notwithstanding, antebellum Washington was not so much a swampy wilderness as a study in American contrasts. Here the unfinished dreams of civic and national splendor and the boisterous, brutal realities of American politics, commerce, and racial conflict coexisted in "a curious combination of sophistication and small-town simplicity."[3] Washington shared in the revival of the national economy following the panic of 1837, and local business prospered as more government officials brought their families to live in the capital during the 1840s. But Washington, like other American cities, was also plagued by widespread poverty, restlessness among low-paid workers, grossly inadequate sanitary facilities, and a distressing level of lawlessness. Furthermore, despite the general prosperity of the official city, trade remained largely local. By the end of the thirties it was apparent that the earlier dream of local merchants and investors of a major commercial metropolis on the Potomac was not to be realized. With or without the highly touted Chesapeake and Ohio Canal, Washington would never rival Baltimore or Philadelphia in manufacture or national trade.[4]

In the midst of prosperity, moreover, the capital had a unique racial situation that produced ambivalent feelings among Whites, northern or southern. Until its abolition in 1850, a lively slave trade existed in the District; indeed, as James Renwick's Smithsonian building began to rise on the Mall in the late forties, construction workers could view across the street from its rear entrance the slave pens of two of the major traders of the District. In 1840, the Black population of the District comprised nearly a third of the total; over the next decade the general population increased by twenty percent. The Black population increased somewhat more slowly, dropping to twenty-seven percent of the District by 1850. But within the Black populace, a significant change occurred, as the number of free Blacks increased by seventy percent during the decade; in 1850, the Black free/slave ratio had reached nearly four to one. The established free Black community of Washington continued to draw from outside.[5]

The response of Whites in Washington was revealing. As the issue of slavery extension began to arise in the late forties, the capital was caught between the sensitive national debate and equally delicate local conditions. By 1848 the slavery issue was the "all-absorbing topic of the day."[6] But interest focused chiefly on the District slave trade, and after its abolition two years later, the city relapsed into a strange quiet. By a kind of tacit agreement, Constance Green has suggested, Washingtonians decided to "say nothing, do nothing, that might upset the precarious sectional balance." The capital was "like the stillness at the eye of a hurricane" throughout the prosperous, turbulent 1850s.[7]

Growing scientific and artistic reputation perhaps made it easier to ignore political tempests. If the vision of commercial greatness had evaporated by midcentury, there had always been an older dream, shared by presidents Washington, Jefferson, and John Q. Adams, of "a cultural capital" spreading enlightenment to the nation by roads, canals, and rivers.[8] This vision of Washington as the source and sponsor of internal cultural improvements took several major strides toward realization in the forties, with the firm establishment of the Coast Survey under Alexander Dallas Bache; the Naval Observatory; and the Smithsonian Institution. In 1848 a newspaper correspondent could observe that "if there be one question set at rest in this community, it is that public opinion has decided that the national metropolis shall be distinguished for the cultivation of the mind."[9] Perhaps science and art would bring glory to Washington.

Early efforts provided little ground for optimism. The federal scientific agencies of the early republic did not owe their existence to any commitment to science as such—President Adams's call in 1825 for vigorous support of science met with no positive response in Congress but resulted from either practical needs or the exigencies of exploring and taming the continent. Local scientific societies also fared poorly. William Stanton has observed that, until the 1840s, Washingtonians "had founded a dreary train of institutions—the United States Military Philosophical Society, the Metropolitan Society, the Columbian Institute, the American Historical Society, to name only those of most imposing mien—only to see them crumble through apathy and neglect."[10] The Columbian Institute, founded in 1816, received a charter and five acres of swamp from Congress, but little else. The Institute membership, mainly of local businessmen, civil servants, and military men, managed to limp along through the next two decades, until its records and property were absorbed by the National Institution for the Promotion of Science in 1840.

In its brief burst of activity in the early 1840s, the National Institute (as it was called after 1842) demonstrated both the possibilities and limits of Washington science. The Institute, founded in 1840, resulted directly from two contemporary events: the prolonged public debate over Englishman James Smithson's bequest of $500,000 to the United States to found in Washington an institution "for the increase and diffusion of knowledge among men"; and the United States Exploring Expedition under Charles Wilkes, the country's first such large-scale effort, which began its four-year voyage in 1838. Joel R. Poinsett, who had been secretary of war under Martin Van Buren and was an amateur scientist from South Carolina, had successfully launched the Wilkes Expedition in the face of congressional apathy. Two years later, when the first crates of materials began to arrive in Philadelphia and Washington, Poinsett saw that some organization would be necessary to care for the specimens in order to prevent their dispersal and destruction. But Poinsett also had his eye on the Smithsonian funds. He hoped that the Englishman's money would support a national museum, for which the Wilkes materials, along with the National Institute's own circulars, would provide the basic collections. Between 1840 and 1845, Poinsett, Francis Markoe, and J. J. Abert— all government officials—lobbied to establish the Institute as the heir to the Wilkes collections and the Smithsonian monies. Like its ill-starred predecessor, the Columbian Insitute, the National Institute received a charter but little money from Congress. Ultimately it lost both the collections and the Smithsonian funds, but its failure exposed central issues in the politics of antebellum American science.[11]

The debate over the Smithson bequest revolved around several alternative institutions, including a library, university, observatory, and an agricultural experimental station. Poinsett argued for a "National Museum, with Professors who shall perform the double office of Curators and Lecturers," as an important component of a respectable national culture.[12] After the arrival of the first massive shipment of 50,000 specimens, Congress appropriated $5,000 for their care, and the Institute hired as curator Dr. Henry King, a geologist and mining expert employed in the Ordnance Bureau. The secretary of state made the new Patent Office Building, with its spacious hall, available for display of the treasures. Here King valiantly attempted to organize the swelling Wilkes materials, which soon crowded out the Institute's own growing collections. But when the ships came home in 1842, Wilkes, Charles Pickering, and others of the Expedition's scientific staff, far from showing gratitude for the Institute's labors, complained of the disastrous incompetence of King and the museum-keepers. Wilkes and Pickering argued to a parsimonious Congress that, with the gathering completed, the scientific enterprise was barely under way; preservation, research, and publication now required further public outlay, and these functions must be performed by the scientists familiar with their own collections. They had little patience with the amateurs of the Institute, who saw themselves as a "clearing-house for natural history."[13]

The Wilkes Expedition presented serious issues of private and public interests in science. The Institute men noted, for instance, that the Expedition's zoologist, Titian Peale, had labelled many valuable pieces as his private property, and they suspected that several barrels had been emptied in his Philadelphia museum before coming on to the capital. On the other hand, both Congress and the Expedition scientists expressed concern that the Institute, a private group of "friends of science," should control and possibly damage public collections.[14]

The dispute, furthermore, involved divergent conceptions of "museum." The Institute men clearly envisioned a museum chiefly as an institution of preservation and display, not without a certain element of public entertainment, while the Expedition scientists saw the museum essentially as a locus of study and the collections as a permanent research base, an extension of the Expedition itself. When they ruefully recorded that Dr. King had dismembered their specimens and otherwise violated their collections, behind the charge lay a perception of the museum as an ongoing scientific enterprise. Within such a vision, it is worth noting, lay a significant concept of the specimen as scientific property. Legally, of course, the collections belonged to the government; but, in a second and increasingly important sense, they were peculiarly the property of the collector-scientist, for only he knew them in their entirety and could elicit their full meaning for the public. The problem was both philosophical and proprietary, for it involved the very definition of a scientific object.

The appreciation of the scientist's unique, continuing interest in the objects of his study distinguished the Expedition staff from that of the amateur Institute. Similarly, the clue to the ultimate failure of the National Institute lies in the two chief complaints lodged against it: ignorance and unworthy purposes. Despite King's ineptitude, the second complaint was more crucial. The Institute men showed primary concern for national greatness as exhibited in collections of exotic objects—a kind of scientific and cultural boosterism— but little sympathy for patient, loving understanding of the specimens themselves. Externally oriented showcases could only undermine quiet, internal scientific growth—so the American experience seemed to indicate. In 1829, one John Varden had opened to the public a commercial enterprise, the "Washington Museum of Curiosities," complete with stuffed birds and Egyptian mummies. When the free National Institute drove him out of business, he sold out to it—and promptly became its assistant curator.[15] The Varden case was symbolic and instructive. The Institute men lacked an essential respect for the natural world, a nineteenth-century form of piety that set the true scientist apart from the amateur or the pandering commercial popularizer.

The attitudinal gulf was real and determinative. Through much of the nineteenth century, the number of men who shared serious scientific aspirations exceeded the capacity of the society to provide opportunities for full-time pursuit of those interests.[16] As Alexis deTocqueville perceived at the time, organization for power and promotion of individual and group interest was a central dynamic in American life; but historically this has occurred unevenly. Scientific (like artistic) interests came relatively late to organizational maturity. Consequently, members of the scientific community of mid-century were often forced to rely as much on personal judgments of character as on formal organizational affiliation for identity and mutual recognition.

This was especially true in the disparate collection of studies that comprised anthropology.

In August 1846, the New Confederacy of the Iroquois assembled around the light of their "emblematic council fire" in Rochester, New York, to hear the respected ethnologist Henry Rowe Schoolcraft. In a stirring paean to American distinctiveness, Schoolcraft urged Lewis Henry Morgan and the other young men of Rochester to devote themselves to the study of America's "free, bold, wild, independent, native race." America was unique. Without European patronage, Americans depended exclusively on "personal exertions, springing from the bosom of society" for the pursuit of history, literature, and science. Morgan's New Confederacy was such a voluntary effort, a "brotherhood of letters" to advance historical research, promote antiquarian knowledge, and cultivate polite literature.

The time had come, said Schoolcraft, to develop an American scientific and literary tradition: "No people can bear a true nationality, which does not exfoliate, as it were, from its bosom, something that expresses the peculiarities of its own soil and climate." In constructing its "intellectual edifice" America must draw "from the broad and deep quarries of its own mountains, foundation stones, and columns and capitals, which bear the impress of an indigenous mental geognosy."

The native American Indians had borne this distinctive "mental geognosy," and the present tribes, "walking statues" of their progenitors, were monuments far more worthy of study than the antiquarian remains of the Old World. The White man had superseded the Red in America, which obliged him to preserve the memory of the aborigine. After all, Schoolcraft reminded his audience, "their history is, to some extent, our history," a past full of deep tragic and poetic events. "The tomb that holds a man," he concluded, "derives all its moral interest *from* the man, and would be destitute of it, without him. America is the tomb of the Red man."[17]

Eight days after his address in Rochester, Schoolcraft sent to the Board of Regents of the new Smithsonian Institution a "Plan for the Investigation of American Ethnology," presented at its first meeting in September. In a far less effusive style than the Rochester speech, the veteran ethnologist proposed several major areas of activity for the Institution: support for a "Library of Philology"; archaeological investigation, particularly of the ancient earthworks of the Mississippi Valley; and material collections from living tribes to create a "Museum of Mankind."

Schoolcraft soberly outlined a field of inquiry open for exploitation and ripe for the application of scientific techniques. After a brief, tantalizing reference to the mysteries of the continent, he urged "the scrutiny of exact observation and description . . . under the lights of induction and historical analysis . . . to enable us to appreciate and understand our position on the globe." As investigators applied scientific method to ethnology, the boundaries of mystery and conjecture would certainly recede before established facts. Schoolcraft's optimism embraced various subfields of the science of man: physiology, history, archaeology, geography, and geology. But he stressed language as a "more enduring monument of ancient affinities than the physical type" and called attention to the study of mythology.[18]

Taken together, Schoolcraft's prospectus to the Smithsonian and his Rochester address of the preceding week reflect the undefined state of anthropology in 1846. Inspired in part by a romantic attachment to the natural wonders and vast beauty of America, but embracing a wide range of both established and developing branches of inquiry, the study of man in America stood somewhere between the amateur enthusiasm of Rochester and the scientific standards soon established at the Smithsonian, between a past marked by speculation and an anticipated future of scientific precision.

Created by the conflux of several distinct traditions, mid-century anthropology comprised a series of questions, pursued through methods that cut across various fields and traditions. In Joseph Henry's words, anthropology enjoyed a unique status as a "common ground" for students of the physical sciences, natural history, archaeology, language, history, and literature. All could contribute; all could draw intellectual enlightenment and moral inspiration.[19] Furthermore, if anthropology was institutionally and methodologically fractured, the inquiry nonetheless addressed issues that were crucial to American national and cultural identity.

"Great question has arisen from whence came those aboriginals of America?" Thus Jefferson expressed, in his *Notes on the State of Virginia* of 1784, the central historical question that impelled American anthropology until the Civil War. To be sure, for most Americans the significance of the question was never apparent. John Adams wrote his blunt opinion to Jefferson in 1812:

Whether Serpents Teeth were sown here and sprung up Men; whether Men and Women dropped from the Clouds upon the Atlantic Island; whether the Almighty created them here, or whether they immigrated from Europe, are questions of no moment to the present or future happiness of Man. Neither Agriculture, Commerce, Manufactures, Fisheries, Science, Literature, Taste, Religion, Morals, nor any other good will be promoted, or any Evil averted, by any discoveries that can be made in answer to those questions.[20]

In part Adams predicted accurately, for anthropologists struggled for decades to find an acceptable utilitarian rationale. But in a more important sense, his skepticism was misplaced. Between the Revolution and the Civil War, Americans groped for an understanding of their republican experiment, their civilization, and their destiny. The creed that gradually emerged from this introspection placed the new nation outside the ravages of human history, freed from the burdens of corrupt European institutions, as a new, perhaps final hope and home for man. Schoolcraft succinctly expressed this providential vision in 1846, when he described America as "a region destined for the human race to develope itself and expand in . . . a seat prepared for the re-union of the different stocks of mankind."[21]

Integral to the national teleology was a picture of the American continent waiting through the ages, pristine and nonhistorical, for the White man's arrival in order to play out a providentially assigned role. The freshness of America lay in the continent's great natural age without historical and moral blemish. It possessed, in other words, no human burdens, since before Columbus the continent had never known civilized institutions.[22] Accordingly, Americans lent no moral significance to Indian "history," which was, as they saw it, not history at all, but the meaningless meanderings of a benighted people. In retrospect it is apparent that the American Indians presented nineteenth-century White Americans with the challenge and opportunity of expanding accepted notions of history so as to embrace radically different human experiences. This proved impossible. Instead, the anthropologist commonly functioned as a variant of the historian, studying and justifying his own history and civilization through the Indian. In the end, few escaped the degradation of denying peoples the integrity of their own histories.

Jefferson's query suggested a second purpose, however, more religious than political in import. George Stocking has identified in British ethnology of the early nineteenth century a central goal: "to show how all the modern tribes and nations of men might have been derived from one family, and so far as possible to trace them back historically to a single source."[23] Like their contemporaries in various fields of natural history, students of anthropology in England and the United States were engaged in a strenuous effort to contain the exploding diversity of the human world within the explanatory framework of the Mosaic account. Defense of monogenism—original human unity in divine creation and descent from a single pair—lay at the religious core of American anthropology into the twentieth century, especially in Washington circles. In service of this goal, Joseph Henry generally excluded from the Smithsonian discussion of physical anthropology as politically explosive and morally repugnant.

For American no less than for British ethnologists, the study of man was a historical and geographical search of deep religious import. Furthermore, as discussed below, while the historical orientation lost ground in succeeding decades to systems of evolutionary classification, beneath these developments the central concern with human unity persisted. In the American context, the significance of Native Americans to White historical identity and national destiny, and the progressive annihilation of these peoples, compounded and complicated the religious impulse in anthropology, lending an urgency to

Indian studies that emerged in Americans' frequent expressions of "salvage ethnology": a unique blend of scientific interest, wistfulness, and guilt.

In their national and religious quest, American investigators at mid-century followed three distinct routes: archaeology, philology, and physical anthropology. The lack of consensus on method, untapped sources of data, and the relative lack of institutional structures and professional criteria created a sense of openness and lively competition that would characterize the subfields of anthropology in this country to the end of the century.

Americans had first encountered the earthworks of the Ohio and Mississippi River valleys in the 1780s, but it was not until after the War of 1812 that Caleb Atwater, of Circleville, Ohio, undertook a systematic investigation.[24] The American Antiquarian Society published his results in 1820. Atwater saw in the earthworks evidence of early occupation by a sedentary, law-abiding people. He hypothesized a migration from northern Asia at a remote period; a long, fixed abode in North America; and movement southward to found the ancient civilizations of Peru and Mexico. A subsequent migration from southern Asia by ancestors of the modern Indians supposedly superseded these original occupants of the American continent.[25]

Less systematic, more speculative observers followed Atwater. Most attempted to account for the differences between the supposed high civilization of the ancient Americans and the more primitive condition of the historical Indians by positing waves of migration and displacement. James H. McCulloh was among the more cautious in arguing against affinities based on the superficial artifacts of the mounds, which might be simply the products of a common human nature. McCulloh's *Researches*, a compilation of the work of others, concluded that ancestors of the present Indians came from the south and built the mounds. Despite disagreements over the identity of the mound-builders, most archaeological investigators agreed that the ancient inhabitants of America had originated elsewhere; and that "physical, moral, and traditionary evidence" pointed to Asia.[26]

Thomas Jefferson provided one of the first accounts of opening a mound, but he predicted that language would ultimately offer "the best proof of the affinity of nations which ever can be referred to." Schoolcraft, too, writing in his diary in 1823, observed that "Philology is one of the keys of knowledge which, I think, admits of its being said that, although it is rather rusty, the rust is, however, a proof of its antiquity. I am inclined to think that more true light is destined to be thrown on the history of the Indians by a study of their languages than of their traditions, or any other feature."[27] As the mounds explorers displayed more imagination than rigor, the predictions of Jefferson and Schoolcraft took on credibility. In the late 1840s, John R. Bartlett expressed a common judgment of archaeological labors when he wrote that "the practical investigations made from time to time by various individuals, have not been sufficiently thorough and extensive, nor have they developed sufficient data to warrant or sustain any definite or satisfactory conclusions."[28] Not until the 1860s would archaeology begin to attain the theoretical respect and academic establishment that philology had enjoyed since the eighteenth century. Faced with the "bewildering visions" of migrations,[29] a number of individuals turned hopefully to philology for the solution to the puzzle of American man.

In 1819 Peter Stephen Duponceau first announced his discovery that all American Indian languages appeared to demonstrate a uniform grammatical structure and underlying plan of thought, which he labeled "polysynthesis."[30] In Duponceau's view, the polysynthetic form permitted expression of many ideas in few words by consolidating the most significant sounds of simple words into compounds rich in meaning, and by combining various parts of speech into verbal forms to express "not only the principal action, but the greatest possible number of the moral ideas and physical objects connected with it."[31] Duponceau seemed to have penetrated to the "vital principle" controlling American Indian languages, a fact which, he hoped, would raise American philology out of the miasma of vocabulary comparisons to a respectable place beside European comparative philology. In America, grammatical structure would become the "true key to the origin and connection of the varieties of human speech."[32]

Duponceau's polysynthesis was more than a description of linguistic connection. He implied as well a single stage of mental development, thus subtly moving the question of Indian identity from the realm of historical affinity to one of developmental stages. The change was further encouraged by the tendency of philologists to borrow the prestige of natural-science method and terminology. Thus, when John Pickering adopted Duponceau's theory a few years later, he stressed the unity of form, noting that the languages exhibited a "uniform system, with such differences only as constitute varieties in natural objects."[33]

Albert Gallatin, Swiss-born statesman and student of Indian languages, similarly accepted polysynthesis as a demonstrated characteristic of American languages, but made allowance for exceptions, such as Basque in Europe, and held out the possibility of undiscovered connections across the oceans. To Gallatin, common structure indicated common origin, while diversity in vocabulary suggested a long time-span since dispersion across the continent— a principle that Jefferson had espoused. Gallatin speculated that the first inhabitants of America arrived at a remote time, "probably not much posterior to that of the dispersion of mankind." As he saw it, American languages showed clear signs of primitive origins; their form derived from "natural causes," indicating that the Native Americans had not degenerated from a higher state, as Schoolcraft and the mounds explorers maintained. Gallatin thus contributed another support to a paradigm of progressive development, though not yet of evolution.[34]

By mid-century the discovery of a single "antique plan of thought" in the structure of aboriginal tongues seemed destined to exert a significant influence on ethnology. With obvious satisfaction, the popular historian George Bancroft announced that a "savage physiognomy" characterized all Indian dialects; each was "almost absolutely free from irregularities, and is pervaded and governed by undeviating laws." The unreflecting American savage, like the bee building geometrically perfect cells, demonstrated "rule, method, and completeness" in his language. Far from indicating degeneration, the aboriginal tongues of America showed unmistakable signs of being "held in bonds of external nature." The Indian thought and spoke in terms of concrete experience, apparently lacking powers of abstract expression. Linguistic evidence showed, said Bancroft, that the American aborigines were still in "that earliest stage of intellectual culture where reflection has not begun."[35]

Bancroft conveyed to a wide audience the optimism (and ethnocentrism) of students of American languages at mid-century. They saw a certainty and regularity lacking in other approaches to anthropology. The precision, it should be noted, did not derive from the fact that language was a human phenomenon. Quite the opposite: linguistic regularities occurred in spite of man's efforts, indicating the operation of general principles of divine origin. Just as men could cultivate and adorn but not fundamentally alter the geology of the earth, so "language, in its earliest period, has a fixed character, which culture, by weeding out superfluities, inventing happy connections . . . and through analysis, perfecting the mastery of the mind over its instruments, may polish, enliven, and improve, but cannot essentially change."[36]

The work of the philologists pointed strongly toward aboriginal American unity and threw into question the ancient civilizations imagined by archaeologists. Both groups agreed, though, that the first inhabitants of America, whoever they were and whenever they had arrived, had migrated from somewhere else; thus they supported the orthodox view of the unity of mankind. As Bancroft summarized their findings, the "indigenous population of America offers no new obstacle to faith in the unity of the human race."[37]

Others were less sure. In the two decades prior to the Civil War, researchers in physical anthropology—notably Samuel George Morton, George Robins Gliddon, and Josiah Clark Nott—aided by the impressive scientific support of Louis Agassiz and the explorations of Ephraim George Squier, demonstrated that Native Americans, with the exception of the Eskimo, possessed a uniform and apparently unique physical type. This "American School" of anthropology directly challenged the Mosaic account by hypothesizing an indigenous, isolated American race, created in and fitted to the climate of America.[38]

Physical anthropology as systematic scientific inquiry in America began with Morton, a Philadelphia physician and anatomist. In the 1830s he began assembling a collection of crania, mainly of North American natives, that was unsurpassed and totaled nearly 1,000 by his death in 1851. In 1839 he published *Crania Americana*, based on his skull collection. This landmark in physical anthropology, the result of a decade of work, exhibited a consistency, precision, and thoroughness that established Morton as the leading American authority in the field.[39]

Morton hoped to determine "whether the American aborigines of all epochs have belonged to one race or to a plurality of races."[40] His conclusion was straightforward: the American Indian peoples, excluding the Eskimo tribes, belonged to a single race. This race Morton divided into two families, the Toltecan and Barbarous (American). The culturally superior Toltecan had built the North American mounds and also established the semi-civilizations of Central America; the historical Indians had descended from the inferior Barbarous (American) branch. In other words, Morton denied racial separation of the mound-builders from the modern American Indians but distinguished between two "families" in terms of cultural development. He emphasized that physically, morally, and intellectually this "separate and peculiar" race of America exhibited no connections with the Old World; even if apparent connections were discovered in the arts and religions, he maintained, the "organic characters" of the Indians would prove them a single, distinct race.[41]

Morton's strength lay in an unprecedented number of cranial measurements; but in fact he relied on only one or two indices, notably the formation of the occipital portion of the skull, in determining an ideal dominant type of American cranium. Repeatedly he noted exceptions and wide variation, but in his conclusions he either ignored them or attributed them to cultural factors.[42] Morton's opinions underwent little modification; he repeated them in his *Inquiry* of 1842, his "Account of a Craniological Collection" in 1848, and his "Physical Type of the American Indians," contributed posthumously to Schoolcraft's *Indian Tribes* in 1852.[43]

Morton's work provided the empirical base for polygenist arguments in the searing slavery-related controversies of the antebellum decade. The polygenist implications of Morton's theories required only time and encouragement to emerge fully. They received both. Louis Agassiz found in Morton important confirmation of his own theories of uniform distribution and local diversity that he found characteristic of the natural history of the New World. Nott and Gliddon drew heavily on Morton in introducing the basics of polygenist doctrine to a popular audience. Their ambitous *Types of Mankind* marshaled the evidence of Morton, the archaeologists, and the philologists to drive their points home. The languages of America, uniform in structure but diverse in vocabulary (as Gallatin had argued), indicated great age and common origin. The mounds similarly suggested long occupation of the continent. But phys-ical anthropology was conclusive: "American crania, antique as well as modern, are unlike those of any other race of ancient or recent times." Other ethnological data—an increasing number of fossil human bones; the apparent lack of alphabet, domestication practices, indigenous agriculture, astronomy, or calendar systems—all seemed to confirm the antiquity, unity, and isolation of the Native Americans.[44]

The work of Nott and Gliddon circulated widely, but it stimulated more vituperation than research and consequently discredited physical anthropology for decades. As Samuel F. Haven, librarian of the American Antiquarian Society, noted in 1856, Morton's theories had become hopelessly enmeshed in "polemical associations."[45] Because of the theological and political complications, physiologists busied themselves in other pursuits, and Morton at his death in 1851 left no disciple to carry on his researches. The Academy of Natural Sciences in Philadelphia inherited his collection of crania.[46]

The National Institute had a "special duty," Joel Poinsett wrote in 1841, to "inquire into the history of the people we have dispossessed." But the structure of the Institute hampered the inquiry: philology was subsumed under the department of geography; physical anthropology fell under natural history; and the department of American history and antiquities embraced all studies of "the Indian races, now fading from the earth; their mounds and pyramids, and temples and ruined cities," as well as questions of their origins and subsequent "degeneration."[47] The fractured anthropology of the Institute epitomized the methodological and disciplinary confusion that both plagued and enriched the inquiry. But within the flux of theory and observation, certain long-term, significant trends emerged. Interwined in the anthropology of the first half of the century were two distinct traditions of reaction to the phenomena of human variety, each a function of individual temperament and intellectual and religious commitment. For pious Christians fully committed to human unity through the biblical account, historical inquiry backward through time promised to reconcile present diversity with single creation. One suspects that classical philology derived much respect as a humanistic discipline from recognition of this potential service. Others, less satisfied with historical connections than with the categories of the powerful natural sciences, sought to order man rather than track men. Indeed, the development of Duponceau's idea of polysynthesis illustrates the ease with which questions of historical affinity transformed themselves into categories of mental and moral development. Whether one followed Morton or the philologists, the North American aborigines emerged as distinct and uniform, due either to "savage physiognomy" of thought and language or to autochthonous creation.

Morton's school, and physical anthropology generally, fell into disrepute in the second half of the century. The reasons were as much political as scientific. As noted earlier, during the 1850s Joseph Henry consistently steered the Smithsonian away from racial debates, even refusing to permit abolitionist lectures at the Institution. Personally he maintained a discreet silence on such matters, and the Smithsonian largely ignored physical anthropology through the rest of the century.[48] The policy was more than a function of local racial conditions, though these may have heightened sensitivity. The polygenist controversy nearly tore apart the American Ethnological Society of New York during the fifties. Ephraim Squier reported that "the question of human unity could not be discussed without offense to some of the members and its casual introduction was made a ground of impassioned protest."[49] Henry could not afford such bickering. His attempt to establish a nationwide scientific network and to bring together in common effort both missionaries and atheistic polygenists like Squier, required absolute neutrality.

With racial categories discounted and even institutionally suppressed, historical speculations of archaeologists suspect for lack of theoretical grounding (and control in the field), and masses of observations and data annually accruing, developmental schemes emerged in the middle decades of the century—independently of Darwinian biology—as a means of meeting both the commitment to unity and the observed diversity. The work of Lewis Henry Morgan, the dean of nineteenth-century American evolutionism, is particularly instructive in this regard. Morgan's career (1851-1881) spanned the decades during which American anthropology moved from primarily historical inquiry into the origins and early relationships of the different peoples of the globe, to "scientific" classifications, or rankings, of humanity in evolutionary stages of social, mental, and moral development. Morgan's own career, from *Ancient Society* (1851) to *Systems of Consanguinity and Affinity of the Human Family* (1871) to *Ancient Society* (1877), marked milestones in this transition from history to stage classification.[50]

While *Ancient Society* has been justly remembered as the full statement of Morgan's three-stage model of social and mental development (savagery, barbarism, civilization), it was *Systems of Consanguinity*, his massive empirical work on kinship published by the Smithsonian, which established Morgan's inquiry as a science and himself as an institution. Morgan conceived *Systems of Consanguinity* as a survey in the tradition of comparative philology but rooted in what he hoped would prove less mutable human phenomena than language: ideas of kinship. Philologists had reduced mankind to a number of linguistic families, but they had been unable to take the final step, to the "vital question" of origins. Ultimately, Morgan hoped, his "new instrument in ethnology" would prove to be "the most simple as well as the compendious method for the classification of nations upon the basis of affinity of blood."[51]

The vitally important truth about *Systems of Consanguinity* is that Morgan did not find the unity he had presumed and sought. Faced with two apparently distinct concepts and systems of kinship, he adopted a developmental explanatory framework in order to preserve a presumed original human unity. In effect, Morgan moved from a vision of man in historical and geographical migration and contact to a comparatively rigid, static construction devoid of historical fluidity.

Morgan's schema of human development, further elaborated in *Ancient Society*, did embrace notions of change and progress, but these were, like Schoolcraft's visions, strongly teleological and bound to a system of unfolding ideas rather than to the immediate historical experiences of peoples. Morgan's legacy to the next generation—Powell and the Bureau of American Ethnology—was the subordination of historical probings to the greater explanatory power and aesthetic satisfaction of ordering man in value-laden stages. Following Morgan's lead, Powell grounded BAE anthropology in the principle that the American Indians must be understood not as a racial type but as representatives of a single stage of human development. In escaping the tyranny and politics of racial typing, and in the name of science, Powell also denied history to the American aborigines. The resulting flatness of historical perspective was costly for all fields of anthropology, but especially so for archaeologists, who did not discard such assumptions and begin to develop concepts of cultural micro-change and methods of tracing cultural forms through space and time until the twentieth century.[52]

The divergent roots of anthropology in the traditions of the humanities and natural sciences, which by 1850 already reached down deeply, produced an inquiry whose unity lay not in method but in subject matter and in purposes that transcended the inquiry itself. With few exceptions, Native Americans constituted the subjects of American anthropology through the nineteenth century. This occasions no surprise, since the natives of the Western Hemisphere, and of the North American continent particularly, posed critical historical and providential questions for White Americans. The central, nagging, political and religious dilemmas were these: Are these people in any sense our brothers? By what right can we claim this land as our own?

Over the middle decades of the century, the various approaches to these problems lost or gained prestige and followers as a result of various factors: new theoretical breakthroughs (especially if originated in Europe); domestic political and racial currents; the growing status of the natural and physical sciences in general in this country; and individual and institutional decisions. Broadly sketched, physical anthropology declined for nearly a half-century as a method; while in archaeology (and to some extent linguistics), the purpose of inquiry shifted away from historical questions to "scientific," formally nonracial classifications of mankind that nonetheless in essence preserved the moral placement system of discredited racial categories. The Smithsonian was a critical institutional focus of these developments, and decisions of Joseph Henry were often determinative. His decision to support ethnology (the general term for anthropological work at the time) as part of his program of providing the experience of science to a wide section of the American citizenry provided tremendous stimulus in numerous directions.

Notes

1. Henry Adams, *The Education of Henry Adams: An Autobiography* (Cambridge, 1961), pp. 44–45, 256; E. E. Hale, *Tarry at Home Travels* (New York, 1906), pp. 377, 381, 387.

2. Charles Dickens, *American Notes* (Philadelphia, n.d.), pp. 111–12, 116; Anthony Trollope, *North America* (New York, 1862), pp. 301–2, 306, 314–15.

3. Constance McLaughlin Green, *Washington: Village and Capital, 1800–1878* (Princeton, 1962), p. 148.

4. Ibid., pp. 152–66.

5. Ibid., pp. 21, 175–80.

6. Ibid., p. 177.

7. Ibid., p. 180.

8. A. Hunter Dupree, *Science in the Federal Government: A History of Policies and Activities to 1940* (Cambridge, 1957), p. 40.

9. Quoted in Green, *Washington,* p. 170.

10. William Stanton, *The Great United States Exploring Expedition of 1838–1842* (Berkeley, 1975), p. 290.

11. For treatment of the National Institute see Stanton, *Exploring Expedition,* pp. 281–304; Sally G. Kohlstedt, "A Step Toward Scientific Self-Identity in the United States: The Failure of the National Institute, 1844," *Isis* 62 (1971); and George Brown Goode, "The Genesis of the U.S. National Museum," USNM, *AR for 1891* (Washington, D.C., 1891), pp. 273–380.

12. Stanton, *Exploring Expedition,* p. 292.

13. Ibid., p. 297.

14. Ibid., pp. 295–96.

15. Ibid.

16. Nathan Reingold, "Definitions and Speculations: The Professionalization of Science in America in the Nineteenth Century," in A. Oleson and S. C. Brown, eds., *The Pursuit of Knowledge in the Early American Republic* (Baltimore, 1976), pp. 33–69.

17. Henry Rowe Schoolcraft, *An Address, Delivered before the Was-Ah Ho-De-No-Son-Ne, or New Confederacy of the Iroquois, at its Third Annual Council, August 14, 1846* (Rochester, 1846), pp. 3–7, 29. For similar but less poetic sentiments, see Schoolcraft's "Incentives to the Study of the Ancient Period of American History," an address to the New-York Historical Society, 17 November 1846 (New York, 1847).

18. Henry Rowe Schoolcraft, *Plan for the Investigation of American Ethnology: to include the facts derived from other parts of the globe, and the eventual formation of a Museum of Antiquities and the peculiar Fabrics of Nations: and also the collection of a library of the Philology of the World, manuscript and printed* (New York, 1846), pp. 5, 12–13. Schoolcraft's *Plan* was reprinted in the SI, *AR for 1885* (pp. 907–14), with the note that although it was never officially adopted by the Institution, "even after the lapse of forty years it possesses sufficient interest and suggestiveness to justify its publication."

19. SI, *AR for 1860.* p. 38.

20. Adams to Jefferson, 28 June 1812, in *The Adams-Jefferson Letters*, ed. Lester J. Cappon (New York, 1959), pp. 308–09.

21. Schoolcraft, *Address*, p. 34.

22. Fred Somkin, *Unquiet Eagle: Memory and Desire in the Idea of American Freedom, 1815–1860* (Ithaca, 1967).

23. George Stocking, "From Chronology to Ethnology: James Cowles Prichard and British Anthropology, 1800–1850," in J. C. Prichard, *Researches in the Physical History of Man*, ed. Stocking (Chicago, 1973), p. XCIV.

24. The history of interest in the earthworks of North America, and of the theories adduced to account for them, has been treated extensively in several works, notably Robert Silverberg, *Mound Builders of Ancient America: The Archaeology of a Myth* (Greenwich, Conn., 1968); and Leo Deuel, *Conquistadores Without Swords: Archaeologists in the Americas* (New York, 1967). A recent regionally oriented survey is James E. Fitting, ed., *The Development of North American Archaeology* (Garden City, 1973). For further background, see Lee Eldridge Huddleston, *Origins of the American Indians: European Concepts, 1492–1729* (Austin, 1967). Gordon Willey and Jeremy Sabloff's *A History of American Archaeology* (San Francisco, 1974) places the archaeology of this period in historical and professional context. The most thorough account of the subject, however, remains unpublished: Thomas C. Tax's "The Development of American Archaeology, 1800–1879," Ph.D. diss. (University of Chicago, 1973). I have relied especially on Samuel F. Haven's valuable historical review, *Archaeology in the United States*, published as part of vol. 8 of Smithsonian Contributions to Knowledge (Washington, D.C., 1856).

25. Caleb Atwater, "Description of the Antiquities of Ohio and Other Historical States," *Transactions and Collections of the American Antiquarian Society* 1 (Worcester, Mass., 1820).

26. James H. McCulloh, *Researches Philosophical and Antiquarian Concerning the Aboriginal History of America* (Baltimore, 1829); see also John Haywood, *The Natural and Aboriginal History of Tennessee, up to the first Settlements by the White People* (1823); Constantine S. Rafinesque, *Ancient History, or Annals of Kentucky: with a Survey of the Ancient Monuments of North America, and a Tabular View of the Principal Languages and Primitive Nations of the Whole Earth* (Frankfort, 1824); John Delafield, Jr., *An Inquiry into the Origin of the Antiquities of America* (New York, 1839); William Henry Harrison, *A Discourse on the Aborigines of the Valley of the Ohio* (1838); and Alexander W. Bradford, *American Antiquities and Researches into the Origin and History of the Red Race* (New York, 1843). Some of these popular expositions enjoyed wide circulation; according to Haven (*Archaeology*, p. 41), one book on the "Moundbuilder Race" (by Joseph Priest) sold 22,000 copies by subscription in thirty months.

27. Thomas Jefferson, *Notes on Virginia*, in *Basic Writings of Thomas Jefferson*, ed. Philip Foner (Garden City, 1944), pp. 116–19; H. R. Schoolcraft, *Personal Memoirs of a Residence of Thirty Years with the Indian Tribes on the American Frontiers* (1851; reprint ed., New York, 1975), p. 176.

28. John R. Bartlett, "The Progress of Ethnology, an Account of Recent Archaeological, Philological, and Geographical Researches in Various Parts of the

Globe, tending to elucidate the Physical History of Man," *Transactions of the American Ethnological Society* 2 (New York, 1848): 4.

29. Haven, *Archaeology*, p. 97.

30. Peter Stephen Duponceau, "Report of the Historical and Literary Committee to the American Philosophical Society, January 9, 1818," *Transactions of the Historical and Literary Committee of the American Philosophical Society* 1 (Philadelphia, 1819): xi–xvi. Quoted in Mary Haas, "Grammar or Lexicon? The American Indian Side of the Question from Duponceau to Powell," *International Journal of Anthropological Linguistics* 35: 239–55. The discussion here is based on Haas's article.

31. Duponceau, "Report," p. xiv; quoted in Haas, "Grammar or Lexicon?" p. 240.

32. Haven, *Archaeology*, pp. 56, 54.

33. John Pickering, "Indian Languages of America," *Encyclopedia Americana* 4 (appendix): 581; quoted in Haas, "Grammar or Lexicon?", p. 241. See also Haas, p. 242; and Regna D. Darnell, "The Powell Classification of American Indian Languages," *Papers in Linguistics* (July 1971), pp. 73–76.

34. Albert Gallatin, "A Synopsis of the Indian Tribes within the United States East of the Rocky Mountains and in the British and Russian Possessions in North America," *Transactions and Collections of the American Antiquarian Society* (Cambridge, 1836), p. 6. Quoted in Haas, "Grammar or Lexicon?", p. 243.

35. George Bancroft, *History of the United States*, 14th ed., vol. 3 (1854), pp. 254–66.

36. Ibid., pp. 256, 264–65, 318. Schoolcraft also found ground for optimism in the slow mutability of language; see his "Incentives," p. 23.

37. Ibid., p. 318

38. The following discussion is based on William Stanton, *The Leopard's Spots* (Chicago, 1960); George M. Fredrickson, *The Black Image in the White Mind: The Debate on Afro-American Character and Destiny, 1817–1914* (New York, 1971), pp. 71–96; Paul A. Erickson, *The Origins of Physical Anthropology*, Ph.D. diss. (University of Connecticut, 1974), p. 66–80; Haven, *Archaeology*; Daniel Wilson, "Lectures on Physical Ethnology," SI, *AR for 1862–63*, pp. 240–302; and Aleš Hrdlička, "Physical Anthropology in America," *American Anthropologist*, n.s. 16 (1914): 508–54.

39. Samuel George Morton, *Crania Americana, or a Comparative View of the Skulls of the Various Aboriginal Nations of North and South America. To Which is Prefixed an Essay on the Varieties of the Human Species* (Philadelphia, 1839).

40. Hrdlička, "Physical Anthropology," p. 515.

41. S. G. Morton, "Account of a Craniological Collection," *Transactions of the American Ethnological Society* 2 (1848): 219.

42. For a critical account of Morton's work and conclusions by a near-contemporary, see Daniel Wilson, "Lectures," pp. 240–65. On reexamination of Morton's collection, Wilson denied the existence of Morton's ideal type—the rounded, brachycephalic "Peruvian" head—among the North American skulls.

43. S. G. Morton, *An Inquiry into the Distinctive Characteristics of the Aboriginal Race of America* (Boston, 1842; Philadelphia, 1844); H. R. Schoolcraft, *Indian Tribes* 2 (Philadelphia, 1852): 316–30. See also, in Schoolcraft, Morton's "Unity of the Human Race," vol. 3, pp. 374–75.

44. J. C. Nott and G. R. Gliddon, *Types of Mankind, or Ethnological Researches, based*

upon the ancient monuments, paintings, sculptures, and crania of races, and upon their natural geographical, philological, and Biblical history (Philadelphia, 1854); quoted in Haven, *Archaeology*, p. 85.

45. Haven, *Archaeology*, p. 81.
46. Hrdlička noted ("Physical Anthropology," pp. 524–26) that Joseph Leidy and J. Aitken Meigs, both of Philadelphia, considered picking up the mantle of the great Morton, but while each contributed in his own way to the advancement of physical anthropology and anatomy, Meigs and Leidy went in other directions. Of Leidy's more than 500 publications in natural science, Hrdlička found only thirteen related directly to anthropology.
47. Joel R. Poinsett, *Discourse on the Objects and Importance of the National Institution for the Promotion of Science, Established at Washington, 1840, Delivered at the First Anniversary* (Washington, D.C., 1841), pp. 19–20, 42–43. On the formation and early activities of the various departments, see the *Bulletins* of the Institute, 1840–42.
48. Green, *Washington*, p. 287.
49. Robert E. Bieder and Thomas G. Tax, "From Ethnologists to Anthropologists: A Brief History of the American Ethnological Society," in John V. Murra, ed., *American Anthropology: The Early Years* (St. Paul, 1976), p. 17.
50. George W. Stocking's essay, "Some Problems in the Understanding of Nineteenth Century Cultural Evolutionism," in Regna Darnell, ed., *Readings in the History of Anthropology*, (New York, 1974), pp. 407–25, has been suggestive for the following discussion.
51. L. H. Morgan, *Systems of Consanguinity and Affinity in the Human Family*. Smithsonian Contributions to Knowledge 17 (Washington, D.C., 1871), pp. 9, 506.
52. Willey and Sabloff, *History of American Archaeology*, p. 88.

II

Promoting Popular Science: Archaeology and Philology at the Smithsonian Institution, 1846–1878

"The most prominent idea in my mind," Joseph Henry wrote in 1847, "is that of stimulating the talent of our country to original research—in which it has been most lamentably difficult [*sic*]—to pour fresh material on the apex of the pyramid of science, and thus to enlarge its base . . ."[1] Anthropology occupied a prominent place in Henry's vision. In the "Programme of Organization" outlined before his election as first Secretary of the Smithsonian Institution in 1846 and approved by the Regents the following year, Henry proposed to increase knowledge of man in North America through surveys and explorations of mounds and other remains. In addition, the Smithsonian should help diffuse discoveries relating to "particular history, comparative philology, antiquities, etc."[2]

From the beginning, Henry rejected arguments to limit Smithsonian support to fields of science having "immediate application to the practical arts of life." To do so would violate the memory of James Smithson, who had been "fully impressed with the important philosophical fact, that all subjects of human thought relate to one great system of truth." Some fields that held little hope of generalization nonetheless "could hardly fail to produce results of importance in a practical and a theoretic point of view." He specifically mentioned ethnology as one such undeveloped but promising field.[3]

Henry's support for anthropology must be understood as part of a broader scientific promotion. The creation of a national system of scientific correspondents, one of Henry's remarkable achievements as Smithsonian Secretary, accompanied his plans for a continental, even hemispheric coordination of meteorological observations. Both Henry and his assistant secretary, Spencer F. Baird, assumed that their observers would report to the Smithsonian on a variety of scientific topics. He had "long dreamed of some central association or influence," Baird wrote to Henry in 1849, "for gathering, digesting, and publishing scientific information in all fields.[4]

Their program was suited to a sparsely populated continent and an early stage of scientific organization. In the middle of the nineteenth century, being a scientist in America was still as much a matter of character and integrity as one of specific academic or laboratory training. A man could be taught to use the latest instruments of physical science, Henry believed, but dedication to the pursuit of truth and willingness to forego the public acclaim that frequently rewarded the fraud or popularizer were qualities that transcended the expertise of separate branches of science. Henry sought to build a system of trustworthy observers whose reports, systematized by instructions and instruments from the Smithsonian, would form the factual basis for scientific knowledge of the American continent.

A physicist without any personal experience in anthropology, Henry was ambivalent about the independence of a field that he always viewed as burdened with unwarranted speculation and consequently in need of purging and guidance. On the one hand, he seems to have turned to anthropological questions as "a kind of middle ground between literature and science, on which men of letters and the investigators of nature may meet with mutual interest," as he advised John Fries Frazer in 1855. On the other hand, Henry recognized degrees of anthropological expertise and warned away interlopers. In the same letter to Frazer cited above, Henry admonished his friend that "however the world may give you credit for knowledge in the line of physical science, you are no authority in the line of ethnology." In the course of his secretariat Henry watched with pride as anthropological studies grew in popularity and, he claimed, in precision. "We have passed," he told one correspondent in 1868, "from the period of pure speculation in regard to [ethnology], into that of the active collection of materials preparatory to the next—that of deduction and generalizations."[5] While some of his colleagues, and perhaps some of the Regents, refused to accept such studies as serious science, Henry saw an opportunity for the Institution to guide the development of a promising field by enlisting the support of a broad network of correspondents and by applying to it the standards of proof of the physical sciences.[6]

Because of its status in 1846 as a field on the fringes of science, anthropology presented an unusual opportunity for making a science, for drawing a clear line between speculative popularization or commercial humbuggery, and the sober search for truth. In this enterprise Henry was a willing and forceful participant; he lost no opportunity to elevate the true investigator and denounce the pretender. To some extent the crusade against amateurism and speculation was simply a matter of giving proper credit. Printing unverified theory, to Henry, was equivalent to "throwing dice for discovery"; only zealous, persevering research deserved recognition.[7]

Henry demonstrated his determination to purge anthropology of speculation with the first volume of the series of Smithsonian Contributions to Knowledge: *Ancient Monuments of the Mississippi Valley*, by Ephraim George

Squier and Edwin H. Davis.[8] Publication in 1848 of this 300-page, lavishly illustrated volume was a landmark in the development of American anthropology, at once symbolizing the commitment of the Smithsonian to the science and reflecting the growing popular interest in America's ancient inhabitants. For Henry the significance of *Ancient Monuments* lay in the rigorous scientific standards it established. He realized his support for ethnological investigations was not altogether expected or shared. He was pleased, he confided to Elias Loomis, to publish an archaeological paper first, "because it will show that I am not inclined to devote the funds entirely to the advance of Physical science."[9]

Squier and Davis submitted their paper to Henry in early 1847. The paper arrived with strong recommendations from the American Ethnological Society of New York, several members of which had been avidly following the Ohio work for some time. Indeed, only financial restrictions had prevented the Society from printing the work itself. Henry responded enthusiastically. Concerned that Squier was considering a commercial outlet, the Secretary urged him to publish with the Smithsonian. Squier's own scientific reputation, he wrote, depended on the appearance of his researches in the transactions of a respectable scientific institution, in which it might receive "that commendation which it is the privilege of only the learned few to grant . . ." Commercial publication, he continued, constituted an appeal to the public that would most certainly "produce a prejudice against the work in the minds of those who are best qualified to appreciate its merits and on whose judgment its character must ultimately depend."[10] Henry convinced the authors. He then formally submitted the work to the Ethnological Society for review and approval. Since the review committee consisted of the same individuals—Edward Robinson, John R. Bartlett, William W. Turner, Samuel G. Morton, and George P. Marsh—who had already expressed a lively interest in the paper, approval was assured.[11]

In the year between acceptance and publication of *Ancient Monuments*, Henry severely edited the memoir, which meant excising what he considered unjustified speculation. Squier added new material, mainly reports and drawings from earlier works and remarks suggesting connections between the moundbuilders of North America and the ancient civilizations of Central America. Henry strongly disapproved and sharply rebuked Squier: "Your labours should be given to the world as free as possible from everything of a speculative nature and . . . your positive addition to the sum of human knowledge should stand in bold relief unmingled with the labours of others," he admonished. Enlisting the impressive scientific support of Morton, Marsh, and Alexander Dallas Bache, the Secretary warned against including any theoretical matter, "except in a very subordinate degree." Full theoretical exposition would have to wait.[12]

By editing, and threatening to withdraw support, Henry imposed his standards on *Ancient Monuments* and established a dominant tone of caution in the memoir. "It has been a constant aim in the preparation of this memoir," the authors announced, "to present facts in a clear and concise form, with such simple deductions and generalizations alone, as may follow from their careful consideration." They had no hypothesis to sustain, but only a desire to arrive at truth, with the result that "everything like mere speculation has been avoided."[13] The result was impressive. *Ancient Monuments* seemed a model of Baconian induction; Squier and Davis had let the facts speak for themselves, John Bartlett observed, and "out of confusion, system began to develope itself, and what seemed accidents, were found to be characteristic." Few disagreed.[14]

Henry's admonitions to Squier and Davis reflected his concern for the reputations of the Smithsonian, the authors, and the science. He realized that if anthropology in America were ever to transcend the realm of hobbyists, students had to forego the lures of public acclaim and subject their methods and results to the scrutiny of the small group of persons—the "learned few"—capable of judging their work in the "regular channels of scientific communication."[15]

But excising unfounded speculation was only half the battle. New rigor and system in data-gathering were badly needed. To this end Henry, a physicist, envisioned applying the methodological system and accurate instrumentation of the physical sciences wherever possible.[16] The Secretary's correspondence with Increase A. Lapham of Wisconsin, one of his most active and enterprising contacts over thirty years, illustrated his efforts to introduce precision in ethnology. In 1850, Lapham requested two barometers for field work on the Indian mounds of Wisconsin, apparently to obtain as complete a picture as possible of the elevations and environments of the mounds. Despite limited funds and the difficulty of shipping the delicate instruments, Henry loaned the barometers. He took the opportunity to remind Lapham that the value of his work depended on "minute accuracy" and strict induction: "We are as yet only collecting the bricks of the temple of American antiquities," he wrote, "which are hereafter to be arranged and fashioned into a durable edifice; it is therefore of the first importance that our materials should be of the proper kind."[17]

It should be emphasized that Henry did not belittle theorizing in itself; he opposed unwarranted, unverified speculation that had no roots in observation and often came from wrong motivations. The insistence on a rigorously inductive ethnology, purged of speculation and based on systematic observation, derived from Henry's perception that diffusion of scientific knowledge had been accompanied by the spread of crank ideas as well, and that Americans were generally unable to discriminate between them. As a result, the fraud often basked in public acclaim, overshadowing the modest, honest scientist. Self-denial and social oblivion were not, of course, necessary elements in Henry's definition of a scientist; but popular recognition was so rare that, as he warned Squier, the scientist who voluntarily sought acclaim soon aroused suspicion among his fellow investigators.

The spread of misleading theory was not necessarily deliberate or malicious; sometimes it merely reflected "defective scientific training" of powerful and original minds. It was, alas, all too easy to stray from "the narrow path . . . to real advance in positive knowledge." But while unwitting detractors saddened Henry, he despised the deliberate deceivers, and the Smithsonian became an important instrument in his lifelong crusade against scientific fraud. Indeed, one of the "germs" of the operations of the Institution, he noted to himself in 1848, was that its reports should "expose popular fallacies and attempt to put down quackery."[18] Above all the Smithsonian must remain free from any taint of excessive speculation or commercial appeal; in 1869 Henry wrote with apparent relief that the Institution had not been touched by the recent Cardiff Giant hoax, and he bitterly reproached the perpetrators of such "unblushing deceptions" for their "bad effect on the morals of the community."[19]

Science was a moral enterprise to Joseph Henry. His enthusiasm for anthropology is fully comprehensible only in the light of his convictions about the mission and needs of science in American society. No country in the world owed more to science than did America, and yet none encouraged and supported it less. "The blindness of the public," Henry admonished a New York audience in 1874, "to the value of abstract science and to the importance of endowments for its advancement is truly remarkable."[20] Americans, he thought, did not recognize or treasure the scientific life because they had not personally experienced the intellectual and spiritual stimulation of contemplating nature.

Not that everyone was capable of becoming a first-rate scientist. Henry was more elitist than egalitarian in his science. He believed that "like the poet, the discoverer is born, not made," and like him must be left to "wait the fitting time of inspiration." Only a few could profitably dedicate their lives to the "high and holy office of penetrating the mysteries of nature."[21] But Henry did not exclude most people from active participation in science. There were many functions and many useful roles, particularly in a young science still gathering its basic materials from remote and unpopulated regions. While only the best scientific minds might perform the ultimate task of synthesis, many could participate in the exciting fact-gathering operations.

Of course, in most scientific activity inductive and deductive processes are not clearly separated; both occur simultaneously, with constant modification of even well-established generalizations in the light of new information. But at mid-century, anthropology appeared overwhelmingly inductive. The young science faced such a formidable task of collecting and classifying the vast materials of the American hemisphere that discovery of laws and regularities receded as a goal into the distant future. Despite his own vigorous speculations, Ephraim Squier appreciated with Henry that "no sciences are so eminently inductive as Archaeology and Ethnology . . . none which require so extensive a range of facts to their elucidation."[22]

The inductive needs of anthropology meshed well with the broader social functions of science in America as Henry perceived them. A wide network of correspondents sending information and specimens to Washington from every region of North America not only increased the factual foundation of ethnology; it also introduced the scientific experience to many persons in whom, "for lack of an awakening word," the love of science had lain dormant.[23] It is imperative to understand that under Henry and Baird the Smithsonian operated to diffuse not only specific knowledge but also the experience of the search for truth and the desire for the serious study of nature.[24] It is difficult to say which function was ultimately more important to the Secretary. Reporting on collections received from explorers in the Northwest Territory in 1867, the Secretary noted with pride that the Smithsonian had served as a stimulating and civilizing force for the inhabitants of the region, "enlivening their isolated and monotonous life by the incitements and facilities it has offered them for the study and observation of the phenomena and objects of nature."[25] Henry originally conceived the Smithsonian's series of Miscellaneous Collections, begun in 1861, as popularly palatable introductory materials on the various sciences, particularly natural history, for persons without access to libraries. However quixotic in retrospect, the blend of scientific erudition with popular enlightenment (beginning with expositions on entomology and conchology) was a serious effort to bridge a perceived social, intellectual, and moral gap in American society. To Henry it was apparent that "the objects of nature, like the specimens of high art, are the luxuries of the cultivated mind, and the awakening of a taste for their study affords an inexhaustible source of pleasure and contentment to the most numerous and the most important classes of the community."[26]

Joseph Henry appreciated the technological advances that accompanied increase in scientific knowledge, but for him the aesthetic and spiritual experience of contemplating order and beauty in the universe was the true, highest reward of science. He sustained a sincere faith in the benevolent influences of science, insisting that "it is not alone the material advantages which the world enjoys from the study of abstract science on which its claims are founded." Science offered "unbounded fields of pleasurable, healthful, and ennobling exercise to the restless intellect of man, expanding his powers and enlarging his conceptions of the wisdom, the energy, and the beneficence of the Great Ruler of the universe."[27] Henry's conviction of the pious, humbling effect of scientific pursuits never failed him, and throughout his life he attempted to spread that exquisite joy to an ever-larger circle.

Between 1848 and 1860, Henry followed Squier and Davis's *Ancient Monuments* with North American archaeological investigations in the Smithsonian Contributions to Knowledge. Henry planned systematic description of the mounds of the eastern United States—a strictly inductive process. The papers at least formally upheld the standard set by *Ancient Monuments*. In the preface to *Antiquities of Wisconsin,* Increase Lapham disclaimed theoretical ambitions; he was a mere surveyor, faithfully observing and recording the facts, "leaving it to others with better opportunities, to compare them, and to establish, in connection with other means of information, such general principles as may be legitimately deduced." Charles Whittlesey, a former member of the Geological Survey of Ohio, displayed even greater humility, claiming only the role of a "common laborer . . . bringing together materials with which some master workman may raise a perfect edifice." A few years later, Brantz Mayer, reviewing Mexican archaeology, warned against speculation in antiquarian studies, in which the "mythic confusion" of the aboriginal past might provide support for wild suppositions. In the present state of archaeology, all labors should form a "mass of testimony" for future researchers. Secretary Henry's hand was firm indeed.[28]

The appearance in 1856 of Samuel F. Haven's review of American archaeology—actually a review of American developments in all branches of anthropology to that time and prepared "by special request of the Institution"—marked the close of this period of broad mound surveys.[29] Under Henry's watchful editing, Haven prepared his synthesis of American archaeology with a judicious, critical eye, rejecting speculative migrations but allowing the possibility of Asiatic connection. He saw no evidence of a race of moundbuilders distinct from the historical Indians. Haven appeared "a spokesman for the new era" of factual, descriptive archaeology that Henry promoted.[30]

While observations and data mounted, however, no master craftsman appeared, and clear patterns failed to develop to give broader significance to the archaeology of America. Mayer noted in 1857 that twenty years of archaeological investigations in Mexico had produced no definite historical results.[31] Henry reminded an ambitious correspondent in 1861 that "at present our efforts in this country should be directed to the collection of facts, and the accurate delineation of ancient remains previous to attempting to solve the problem as to the origin of the inhabitants of this continent."[32] In actuality, Henry had begun seriously to doubt that archaeology would ever trace the origins of American man. But at this point he also became aware of recent European archaeological developments.

The decade of the 1860s marked the maturation of Old World archaeology, signified by the publication of John Lubbock's popular *Prehistoric Times* in 1865 and the Paris Anthropological Exposition two years later. The acceptance and adoption of the principles of uniformitarian geology, the establishment of the antiquity of man in Europe through the discoveries of Boucher de Perthes in France, William Pengally in England, and Christian J. Thomsen in Denmark, and the development and wide acceptance of the three-stage technological classification system—Stone, Bronze, and Iron Age—appeared to place Old World prehistory on a new scientific plateau.[33]

Henry immediately saw the relevance of Old World theory to American antiquities, and optimistically introduced them to the United States through the Institution's annual reports, beginning in 1860 with a comprehensive and authoritative report, "General Views on Archaeology" by Adolphe Morlot.[34] Morlot, professor of geology at Lausanne Academy and the man largely responsible for the adoption in Switzerland of the Scandinavian three-age classification, reviewed the latest developments in Old World prehistory and outlined its principles. Just as the geologist used present formations as a guide to past geological changes, so the student of man first examined the different peoples of the earth in their present states in order to understand the different degrees of civilization. Ethnology provided a contemporary scale of development that archaeology then traced in successive stages through time. Adoption of the geological model had resulted in that "great conquest" of the Scandinavian savants, the three-stage analysis of European prehistory. Morlot also reported on Stone Age kitchen-middens* and peat-bogs of Scandinavia, and the ancient lake-dwellings of Switzerland.

Morlot's paper stimulated new interest in collecting Indian relics in America. Henry published four more papers on Swiss archaeology and distributed both a circular requesting recent information relating to ancient mining in the much-discussed Lake Superior region, and George Gibbs's *Instructions for Archaeological Investigations in the United States*. Following the European example, Gibbs encouraged careful excavation of American shell heaps, mounds, caves, and mines, in the hope that "a similar investigation in America may take us back to a very remote period in aboriginal history."[35]

Swiss and Scandinavian researches provided the needed focus for American archaeology, and the tripartite classification of artifacts supplied a fresh framework. They replaced a search for migrations and historical connections that by 1860 had reached a dead end. Henry recognized as much. Americans had been searching in the mounds for the solutions to two distinct problems: the

---

*Piles of shells, bones, and stone implements assumed to be the refuse-heaps of Stone Age peoples.

historical roots of the American Indians and the stages of cultural development that the inhabitants of America had attained. It was critical, Henry believed, to separate the two inquiries in order to distinguish between traits that were attributable to a common humanity and those peculiar to specific peoples.

Even before the discovery of supposedly parallel European phenomena, Henry had gradually come to believe that similarities in material culture could not be accepted as evidence of contact. "That different peoples should make use of the same implements for assisting to effect results of a mechanical kind . . . is no sign that they had intercourse with one another, since these are natural products of the same kind of intellect, or the instinctive productions of man." Men possessed certain common wants and instincts that produced widespread similar products.[36]

The exception to Henry's psychic unity and parallel invention was language, which seemed a possible key to unraveling the histories of individual migrations. "The general structure[s] of distinct and original language," Henry wrote, "may be, and were probably, similar in some respects and identical in others, yet the words are arbitrarily chosen, and therefore are as different as the objects and the relative conditions of different races or tribes are." The study of language was "of the highest importance" in solving historical puzzles.[37]

The important consequences of European discoveries for American archaeology were to stimulate renewed activity but simultaneously to discredit archaeology as a historical tool and redirect the purpose of the work toward classifying artifacts and peoples in categories of material culture. Archaeologists in this country readily embraced the new categories and hastened to place their materials accordingly, leaving to the linguists the nagging problems of aboriginal origin and affinity. The distinction in method and purpose that thus emerged in the sixties proved to be extremely significant for American anthropology in the coming decades.

The career of Charles Rau, Henry's chief archaeological collaborator, illustrated both the personal and professional aspects of archaeology in Washington. Rau's biography reads simply. A lonely, ascetic German immigrant, Rau was born in Belgium in 1826, attended the University of Heidelberg, and in 1848 sailed to New Orleans. For twenty-seven years he taught German to school children in St. Louis, Belleville (Illinois), and New York City. In 1876 he finally obtained a position at the Smithsonian, and five years later became curator of the Department of Antiquities (later Archaeology) in the National Museum. Rau never married, and at his death in July 1887, his valuable personal library and archaeological collection came to the Smithsonian.[38]

Rau's career in this country was not happy. He detested teaching "brutish, half-savage, actually *lousy* Irish boys" in the seventh ward of New York City, a position he held only "by the grace of a few illiterate Irishmen."[39] But Rau consistently failed to obtain the respectable scientific position that he sought in archaeology or ethnology. Prior to the founding of the Bureau of Ethnology in 1879, few institutions in the United States provided employment in anthropology. Most practitioners either relied upon independent wealth or pursued careers that permitted time for anthropological studies as an avocation.[40] For an aspiring investigator like Rau, possessing considerable erudition but neither financial means nor influential friends, the situation in America was acutely frustrating. "For nearly twenty years," he wrote Henry in 1867, "I have been striving to obtain a respectable situation, but in vain." Rau blamed American antipathy to foreigners: "They treat me politely and eulogise me for the interest I take in American ethnology—but their sympathy extends no further."[41]

Rau applied for the few suitable positions that did appear, and each time he asked Henry for support. At the founding of the Peabody Museum in 1866, he eagerly sought Henry's recommendation for the curatorship. "To superintend and to classify on scientific principles a large archaeological collection would be the occupation to which nature, as it were, has destined me," he confided. When Jeffries Wyman received the appointment, Rau was crushed. Wyman was a fine anatomist but no archaeologist, he complained. Henry responded sympathetically: "As in every part of the world called civilized . . . modest merit is frequently overlooked while pushing incompetency is chosen."[42]

Rau continued to teach in New York until 1875, when his position was abolished, leaving him with the "odious" prospect of clerking in an office. Once again he appealed to the Smithsonian for help in realizing "the aim of my life," a major work on the North American Stone Age. Rau assured Baird that he planned a descriptive and comparative rather than theoretical work, dealing in some detail with modern applications of American implements in order to elucidate the uses of ancient specimens. His study would form an interesting Smithsonian publication, "especially at a time when archaeology . . . forms the favorite study of intelligent persons in all civilized countries."[43]

Rau's supplication underscored the humiliating position in which this aspiring student found himself for so many years of his life. He felt that he had much to contribute to the young science but so few opportunities that he had to promote himself as widely as possible. At times his anxiety led to friction with Henry over speed, quality, and distribution of his Smithsonian publications, but Rau had no alternative. "I cannot display my wares behind a window like a mechanic or a merchant," he informed Baird. "I need a field of action for showing what I can do. To whom could I apply for obtaining such a chance, but to men like Professor Henry and yourself?"[44]

Rau finally got his chance in 1875. After some hesitation Henry hired him to study, classify, and prepare the ethnological specimens in the National

Museum for the Centennial Exposition in Philadelphia.[45] It was only a one-year appointment, but Rau managed to stay on as a collaborator and assistant, eventually becoming curator of the Department of Antiquities.

The discoveries and developments in the typological, descriptive classifications of Old World prehistory found an earnest devotee and spokesman in Rau, whose papers in German and American publications provided a transatlantic conduit for joining Old and New World observations. Rau hoped to fit the vast quantities of American raw materials into a European theoretical framework. Thus, while his studies and collections were American in subject matter, he looked with admiration to his homeland for guidance.

Rau believed that the search for origins and migrations in the first half of the century had been hopeless and fruitless. Forsaking historical queries, he returned to the model of the eighteenth-century ethnologist William Robertson and the quest for universal patterns of development. Rau contended for "a certain law that regulates the march of civilization, and compels, as it were, the populations of different parts of the world to act, independently of each other, in a similar manner, provided there is a sufficient similarity in their external conditions of life."[46] The search for materials in North America to indicate parallels with European technological stages formed the major theme in Rau's work. In 1864 he published "Artificial Shell-Deposits in New Jersey" in the Smithsonian annual report. The New Jersey shore, he discovered, contained unstratified deposits of oyster, clam, and mollusk shells, bones, implements, and other remains that perfectly matched the European shell-heaps, furnishing "a striking illustration of the similarity in the development of man in both hemispheres."[47] Furthermore, Rau had reports of similar deposits in Long Island, California, Georgia, Massachusetts, and Newfoundland, convincing proof that "the condition of man is everywhere essentially the same, while the rude implements indicate a similarity of wants and identity of mental characteristics by which these wants are supplied."[48]

As early as the mid-sixties, Rau began planning a major work on American antiquities written in German for a European audience.[49] While he continued to contribute short articles to American and European journals, however, he altered this plan in favor of a paper on North America for domestic consumption. American archaeology, Rau observed, had developed into a totally new science in the twenty years since Squier and Davis had published *Ancient Monuments*. European discoveries had shed new light on America, and Rau proposed to "introduce new features by comparing the aborigines of this country with the primeval people of Europe," an undertaking requiring much "moral assistance." The paper, which Rau confidently felt would appear as a volume of the Smithsonian Contributions, would include a synopsis of European archaeological discoveries and systematic comparison of European and American stone, bone, horn, pottery, and metal products.[50]

Charles Rau, the German immigrant who became curator of the Department of Antiquities at the National Museum.

Rau as sketched by Frank Hamilton Cushing, the brilliant young scientist of the Bureau of American Ethnology.

In 1868 Rau made his proposal to Henry. At first the Secretary was enthusiastic, expecting a review of the state of American archaeology similar to Haven's a decade earlier. He suggested that Rau include instructions for archaeological explorers. But when Rau clarified his plans, Henry withdrew and in a shattering letter flatly rejected the project. The time was not ripe, he advised Rau, for an extensive work involving fresh investigations and comparisons. True, archaeology was currently enjoying a lively popular interest; but in 1868 Henry wanted only "sketches of progress, suggestions of hypotheses to direct lines of research, and instructions as to the method of making explorations, and the preservation of relics, etc." Rau could gradually acquire the materials for a summary treatment.[51]

The great treatise never appeared. In 1884 he issued his last and most original contribution to anthropology, *Prehistoric Fishing in Europe and North America*. Undertaken at the suggestion of Baird and ichthyologist George Brown Goode, *Prehistoric Fishing* was Rau's final statement on archaeological matters. He hoped it would "illustrate anew the parallelism in the technical progress of populations totally unknown to each other, and for which only the common bond of humanity can be claimed."[52] The recent discoveries of Charles C. Abbott in the Trenton gravels, described in *Primitive Industry*,[53] had confirmed Rau's belief in the antiquity of man in America. But by 1884 he had to concede that prehistory was considerably more complex in America than in Europe, due largely to the difficulty in discriminating between ancient and recent Indian products. He organized his European fishing utensils according to the traditional categories—Paleolithic, Neolithic, Bronze—but had to arrange the American tools according to function.

Charles Rau enjoyed only a brief career as full-time archaeologist. For fifteen years he struggled to obtain a position in America that would permit him to earn a living in anthropology; then he enjoyed a decade at the Smithsonian. He made no seminal contributions to either theory or field data in anthropology, devoting himself instead to the analysis of museum collections. Consequently, he is remembered today only as an early classifier, if at all. Yet between 1860 and 1880, probably no other man in the United States was more aware of developments in archaeology on both sides of the Atlantic. Drawing heavily on German and English theory, Rau sought order for American antiquities in European theories, and clues to the functions of ancient European relics in the modern uses of American implements. He helped apply European theory in America at the same time that he relayed American discoveries to European scholars. Anonymous and unemployed in his adopted country, Rau achieved some recognition in his native land.[54]

Rau's career reflected the state of archaeology in Washington and the United States in his lifetime. In personal terms, the study of any branch of anthropology provided a livelihood for only a handful; for others it was either an avocation or a struggle. More broadly viewed, anthropology in America, and particularly archaeology, still maintained a colonial relationship to Europe: Americans provided masses of new raw materials but relied heavily on European scholars for direction and organizing principles to fashion them into finished products. As the ambiguity of Rau's last work illustrated, by the 1880s American materials were simply refusing to fit Old World categories. The transatlantic relationship began to change rapidly after the 1876 Centennial, as Washington anthropologists turned their backs on European models to assert a new American independence and uniqueness. Rau died in 1887, just before Powell's Bureau of American Ethnology launched a withering attack on Paleolithic man in America.

The study of language, Schoolcraft advised the Smithsonian Regents in 1846, held the most promise of solving the puzzles of the origins and histories of the American aborigines. While the Regents preferred more tangible collections, Henry agreed with his friend.[55] Unlike the relics of the mounds or the artifacts of living tribes, language was not originally a "thing of man's device" but the "spontaneous production of human instinct" modified by the mental and physical peculiarities of specific peoples and environments. Divinely inspired but humanly altered, language straddled the realms of the universal and the particular. Herein lay its great promise. Eventually, it seemed, knowledge of linguistic principles would permit philologists to distinguish between similarities due to mental structure and those due to historical connection.[56]

Henry promoted American philology primarily through lectures, circulation of instructions, and collection of vocabulary lists. As early as 1849, the Secretary invited Pennsylvania naturalist and linguist Samuel Stedman Haldeman to discuss his views on phonetics, which were advanced for his time; the lectures of the 1857–58 season included a talk on "Comparative philology in some of its bearing upon ethnology" by Joshua H. McIlvaine of Rochester, mentor of Lewis Henry Morgan. Six years later, Yale philologist William Dwight Whitney delivered his "Lectures on the principles of linguistic science" for the first time at the Smithsonian. This landmark series, printed in the 1863 annual report, Whitney subsequently expanded into *Language and the Study of Language*, the first authoritative American textbook on linguistics.[57]

In 1847 and again two years later, Schoolcraft issued a comparative vocabulary list for missionaries, government agents, and soldiers to facilitate his massive information-gathering project. The American Ethnological Society followed Schoolcraft with its own circular in 1852.[58] Henry helped to distribute these, and a few years later the Smithsonian issued its own philological circular. In 1863, George Gibbs, with Whitney's aid, expanded his "Instructions for Archaeological Investigations in the U.S." (1861) to include directions for philological observations, rules for recording sounds, and a short vocabulary list. Simultaneously, Gibbs published a longer comparative vocabulary for the Institution. He improved upon earlier lists by Albert Gallatin and Horatio Hale, chiefly by expanding the number of words from 180 to 211, presented in four languages. Both the instructions and the vocabulary lists received wide dissemination, and after only two years Gibbs prepared a second edition of instructions, with new appendices and blank forms to facilitate "systematic records."[59] Gibbs's circular of 1865 served as the basis for the vocabulary gathering of the next twelve years; Powell used it in his early field work. In 1877, Powell expanded the Gibbs circular into his *Introduction to the Study of American Indian Languages.*[60]

Circulating instructions and vocabulary lists became the Smithsonian's means of connecting linguists established in eastern universities with observers in the western regions—explorers, soldiers, missionaries, and settlers. Whatever their other qualifications, these individuals rarely possessed linguistic training, and they faced formidable obstacles. Linguistic work in North America varied widely in thoroughness, depending on local conditions and the vigor and enthusiasm of the recorder; further, it involved a level of subjectivity that could only be partially reduced by standardizing vocabulary lists and orthography. The resulting frustrations were sometimes acute, as Gibbs indicated to W. D. Whitney in 1861: "I had rather puzzle out the rude spelling of an illiterate man than the over exactness of one correspondent whose work lies before me, every letter overloaded with dots and accents."[61] Whitney appreciated the dilemmas of subjectivity and professional division. "The 'personal equation' as the astronomers call it," he wrote in *Language,* "the allowance for difference of temperament, endowment, and skill, has to be applied, certainly not less rigorously, in estimating the observations and deductions of linguistic scholars than those of the labourers in other sciences." He divided linguists into the "facile and anticipative investigators," who furnished the better explorers; and the less ardent students, who made better critics. Each, he felt, had a legitimate place.[62]

The Smithsonian facilitated the flow of information: instructions and forms went from analysts to explorers, data traveled back from the field. To insure the scientific respectability of materials, Henry submitted them to recognized authorities for review. For this purpose he turned to a small circle of collaborators: in the 1850s, Edward E. Salisbury, the elder Josiah Willard Gibbs (unrelated to George), Cornelius Conway Felton, and, most frequently, William Wadden Turner. After Turner's death in 1859, the Secretary turned to Whitney, George Gibbs, and James Hammond Trumbull. All of the earlier group belonged to an academic tradition and each held a professorship in an established American institution: J. W. Gibbs and Salisbury at Yale, Felton at Harvard, and Turner at Union Theological Seminary. Of the latter group only Whitney held an academic post (at Yale). Henry particularly relied on William Turner and George Gibbs.

William W. Turner (1811–1859) came from England as a child in 1818. Both his parents died within ten years, leaving Turner with the care of two sisters. After first studying printing, he embarked upon a self-education program in Latin, Greek, Hebrew, and Oriental languages, aided by a professor of Hebrew at Columbia. Turner, always as much a bibliographer and bibliophile as an original scholar, worked at the Yale and Columbia libraries for three years before Union offered him a professorship in Oriental languages in 1842. He held this position until 1852, when he moved with his sisters to Washington to organize the Patent Office Library.[63]

In the small intellectual circle of antebellum Washington, the Turners found a congenial home. On Sundays and holidays Turner and his sisters were frequent visitors at the Spencer Baird household, where they were all "privileged inmates," and where Turner, Lucy Baird recalled, was one of the most intimate friends of the family. When Baird asked him to catalog the Smithsonian library in 1858, Turner brought along his sister Jane, who remained with the Institution for thirty years.[64]

Turner joined the American Oriental Society in 1846, and later he became a member of the Historical Society of New York and secretary of the National Institute. While he possessed minimal training and published little, through memberships and contacts Turner attained a position of respect in the thin ranks of American philology. At his premature death in 1859 he was "preeminently distinguished at Washington as the highest authority in all matters appertaining to the knowledge of the languages of the aborigines of America." Turner had "mastered easily and rapidly the principles of comparative philology which have become in the present period the surest guides in tracing the histories and affinities of different races." Henry mourned "a ripe scholar, a profound philosopher, and an honest man."[65]

In 1851 Henry asked Turner to explain his reasons for recommending publication of Stephen Riggs's Dakota dictionary and grammar. Turner's response revealed the motivations of students of North American languages. Scientific study of the aboriginal tongues, he explained, rewarded the comparative philologist by showing not only analogies with other languages of the world but fascinating peculiarities as well, by disclosing "new and curious phases of the human mind." Because every language was the "spontaneous growth" of the mind of the people speaking it, the study of Indian tongues, even without the literature, provided the same kind of "delight and instruction" that the naturalist enjoyed from a new species of plant or animal. Even the rudest forms of speech furnished more reason to admire the work of the "Great Fashioner."

Furthermore, the American languages held clues to pre-Columbian history. While sharing the common opinion that Indian myths and traditions were worthless for historical purposes, Turner thought comparison of vocabularies and grammars of "men without a history" provided the most reliable evidence of contacts. The professor urged that the Smithsonian give to the learned world a complete dictionary and grammar of each American language.[66]

The only group of men "qualified by education and sustained by motives of benevolence" to spend the necessary years studying the "mental idiosyncracies of our rude red brethren," Turner went on, were missionaries like Riggs and his fellow workers at the Dakota mission. The agents of the Bureau of Indian Affairs had shown no interest in ethnological matters. But Turner supposed that there were other competent persons who had simply never had the inducement—Henry's "awakening word"—to undertake such projects.[67]

The missionaries had indeed accomplished major work. Riggs's dictionary/ grammar, jointly sponsored by the Historical Society of Minnesota, the American Board of Missions, and the Smithsonian, represented the collective work of eighteen years among the Indians. The Choctaw dictionary/grammar of Reverend Cyrus Byington, which the good minister rewrote six times while the Smithsonian delayed publishing it for twenty years, represented more than thirty years' labor in evangelical and ethnological vineyards.[68] When he originally accepted the Choctaw work on behalf of the Smithsonian in 1852, Turner took the opportunity to remind Byington of some additional merits of such study. Byington had done the Choctaw people the immense favor, he told the reverend, of explaining their own language to them. This would enhance their own self-esteem and give "vigor and perspicacity" to the thought of future generations of Choctaw. Equally important, it would interest others in their welfare. As Turner sagely observed, "We care only for those about whom we know something."[69]

The last point was important. The familiarizing work of the missionaries advanced the tide of Christian fellowship that Turner saw growing in strength. Where men once looked selfishly to themselves and with hostility at others, Turner wrote eight years before the Civil War, they were now beginning to perceive God's same "wise harmony of plan" among the races of men as among the other natural wonders of nature. Anthropology not only Christianized the heathen Indian but cleansed the White of ignorance and prejudice:

This science cannot like some others be cultivated as a mere intellectual exercise, nor can any man long pursue it and cherish bitter & contemptuous prejudices against races less fortunately situated than his own; on the contrary a feeling of good will to all men is its necessary result.[70]

The year after Turner's death, George Gibbs IV arrived in Washington and quickly replaced him as Henry's chief linguistic advisor. In training and experience Gibbs and Turner were very different men. Whereas Turner was a product of scholarly cloisters and quiet libraries, Gibbs had spent twelve years in rugged Washington Territory as government official, surveyor, geologist, miner, farmer, and observer of Indians. Turner's knowledge came almost entirely from books; Gibbs's grew from frequent contact with the aborigines. But Gibbs was by no means an uneducated, illiterate mountain man. Like Powell after him, he embodied both the explorer and the scholar. Because his career reflected the peculiar patterns of American linguistic work—because he spoke the language of the explorer and the academic—he served appropriately as Henry's resident collaborator in the Institution's linguistic clearinghouse of the 1860s.

The eldest child of Laura Wolcott and Colonel George Gibbs III, George was born in 1815 into Federalist-Whig elegance on Long Island, New York. He attended George Bancroft's Round Hill School in preparation for West Point, but following a two-year European tour he studied law at Harvard instead.[71] After graduation in 1838 Gibbs practiced law in New York for a decade. But law never became more than a necessary means of livelihood to him, and he spent the greater part of his time collecting minerals and birds and writing the *Memoirs of the Administration of Washington and Adams*.[72]

By 1848 Gibbs had reached a dead end. Thirty-three years old, he had squandered his share of the diminished family estate in high living and liquor, and his legal career was in decline. While his brothers and sisters married, soldiered, and explored, Gibbs remained in New York City with his mother. Desperate to get away, deeply in debt, and infected by gold fever, he escaped New York by joining the "March of the Mounted Rifles" from St. Louis to the gold fields of Oregon.[73]

In the Northwest, Gibbs began to piece together a broken and aimless life. He fell in love with the region and became a close observer of its natural products, including its people. Like the rivers, mountains, and valleys of Washington Territory, which he came to know so well, the Indians were a natural wonder for Gibbs. To be sure, they were a danger and obstacle to settlement, but they were also an important ally in the struggle to survive in the rugged country. Like explorers before and anthropologists after him, Gibbs experienced an unresolved ambivalence toward Native Americans. On the one hand he could write with sincerity that "we too often give a general character to savage races, derived from a few, and those most probably the worst of their nation; forgetting that there may be as great diversity of disposition among them as among ourselves."[74] At the same time he measured the Indians by the only standards he found comfortable. While he watched their steady attrition from White disease and greed, Gibbs served as interpreter to treaty parlays and himself frequently visited young Indian maidens in their villages. Later, with apparently few second thoughts, he attributed the epidemic proportions of syphilis among the aborigines to their "erotic temperament," moral laxness, and fish diet.[75]

Gibbs never made a living panning for gold; but between 1854 and 1860, three survey commissions utilized his firsthand knowledge of the region. Most significant was his service as geologist, botanist, and naturalist on the Northwest Boundary Survey of 1857, for which he prepared a long report on the natural history of the Washington Territory. By 1860 Gibbs had erased his debts and emerged as a respected settler.

He began serious study of the aboriginal Northwest in the late 1850s. Simple word lists, he realized, served only limited functions; Gibbs emphasized instead collection of creation myths and other tales. Alone he could accomplish a restricted amount, but he also became a stimulus to others. When large numbers of Indians were transferred to local reservations in the mid-1850s, Gibbs saw potential ethnological treasures, and he enlisted the aid of bored Army doctors and officers.[76]

In his enthusiasm to broaden the geographical base of his inquiry, Gibbs even contacted the governor of the Russian colonies in Alaska, providing him with vocabulary blanks for each of the principal languages of Russian America. His plans were ambitious: a "complete collection of all languages west of the Rocky Mountains," including all dialects. His ultimate goal, though, was to trace migration routes, and thereby determine the geographical origins of the American Indians. By the end of his years in the West, Gibbs had established a general theory of westward movement from the Great Plains along the Columbia and Fraser river valleys to the Pacific. The buffalo country, he thought, had been the "nursery" of the "countless hordes who have gradually pushed themselves southward & westward." At the same time he believed firmly in a remoter Asiatic origin. Gibbs never resolved the issue.[77]

In early 1861 Gibbs returned to New York, intending to remain on the east coast temporarily. After a few weeks he moved to Washington, where he stayed ten years, first finishing up the Northwest Boundary work, then serving as secretary to the Hudson Bay Claims Commission, and finally moving, at Henry's invitation in 1867, into a study in the tower of the Smithsonian.[78] There he lived for three years. After the death of his mother in 1870, Gibbs married his cousin, Mary Kane Gibbs, and moved to New Haven. He died there two years later.

During Gibbs's decade in Washington, he brought his linguistic studies to partial fruition through his close contacts with Smithsonian officials. He found the Smithsonian ethnographic collections and linguistic library a vast new source of materials and enjoyed his near-monopoly of them.[79] At first he jealously kept his own field notes at his home in New York, but after 1862, when the Boundary employment ended, he sought closer affiliation with the Institution as an outlet for publication. Eventually his linguistic materials became the property of the Smithsonian and a major part of Powell's linguistic inventory in the Bureau.

Gibbs had three major projects in mind: an ethnological map of the region west of the Rockies, showing particularly the supposed Indian migration routes; publication of his fifty or more vocabularies and reconstruction of the historical connections they indicated; and a general ethnography, including mythologies and social organizations, of the Northwest Coast aborigines. The third project never got beyond his notebooks. The ethnological map did not become a reality until after his death, in the form of Powell's linguistic map of North America; and only a few vocabularies reached print.[80] Gibbs's failure to realize his dreams led one biographer to accuse him of "frittering away" his years in the Smithsonian tower recopying old vocabulary lists.[81] The judgment fails to appreciate the professional and scientific situation in which Gibbs operated.

Gibbs inherited a scientific tradition exemplified by the cosmography of Alexander von Humboldt: an attempt to treat regions as entities by correlating features of climate with soil, vegetation, and animal and human life. An ethnological map, from this perspective, was only part of a larger enterprise of thorough regional understanding. A synchronic environmental picture had to be the basis for reconstruction of Northwest Coast ethnology, Gibbs believed. This unified, comprehensive approach underlay Gibbs's proposal in 1865 for a "Smithsonian Atlas" of North America. With the close of the Civil War, he urged, the time had arrived to embrace "all departments of natural, physical, and social science" in a grand atlas of the continent, following natural rather than political boundaries. The scientific future of America, he argued, lay in comprehensive undertakings: "If the United States, as we all trust, is now to enter upon a new career of mental as well as physical advancement, it becomes us to anticipate the directions in which scientific inquiry can be pushed."[82]

Gibbs anticipated and encouraged a pan-American perspective in anthropology that would reemerge at the turn of the century under radically changed political conditions. He envisioned close cooperation with Russian and British authorities in the Northwest, and Mexican officials in the Southwest, but also insisted on supervision by an American, possibly an Army engineer with experience in survey work. He hoped for a "continental league of science & art, with its headquarters at Washington" as a "first step to an extended Americanism of which the future is boundless." Gibbs urged that the Smithsonian take the initiative by ignoring language differences and publishing Mexican as well as American work in archaeology.[83]

The blend of investigations that Gibbs called for throughout the hemisphere was possible in the fertile, wide-ranging mind of a single man but impossible to carry out without cooperation of experts in many fields—without organization. Interestingly, over the next fifteen years (the heyday of the western surveys), various individuals operating under government aegis, including Powell, attempted to carry out the kind of regional studies that Gibbs foresaw, but in each case emphasis drifted to one field or another, and the inevitable splintering of disciplines ensued. The unity of the Humboldtian holistic, regional approach broke down.

Problems peculiar to linguistic work also plagued Gibbs. In addition to the tedium of field work, the results were often difficult and expensive to set in type, since they involved designing new characters. This assumed consensus on orthography in the first place, but achieving agreement on a generally useful and yet accurate alphabet preoccupied Gibbs, Whitney, and Powell for years. Gibbs outlined the alphabet problem to Whitney soon after his arrival in Washington, when the experiences of the Northwest were fresh in his mind. What was needed, he told the Yale philologist, was a "field alphabet":

> Could one man of education and leisure visit successively each Indian tribe, or could even a number of such inquirers occupy different portions of the field, taking abundant time to weigh the niceties of sound, a complicated alphabet like that of Lepsius would be practicable . . . But the difficulty is that the men who collect vocabularies in Indian countries are seldom men of philological learning. They are officers of the army, Indian agents, and general explorers, often with very meagre orthographic acquirements, yet sufficiently competent to obtain useful vocabularies, and generally the contributors of the only ones.

To give such men a complicated alphabet would only confuse and dishearten them. A short, simple one was needed, relying on the good sense of the investigator to note unusual sounds. "Different capacities & degrees of training," he confessed, "will estimate these differently."[84]

Whitney did prepare a simplified alphabet for the Smithsonian, but in 1870 Gibbs still complained that most alphabets were "beyond the comprehension of any but their inventors" and presupposed wide knowledge and fine discriminations. He could only conclude that "the explanation, in writing, of unusual sounds is always a hazardous experiment."[85]

Joseph Henry shared only part of Gibbs's vision. Through the 1860s Henry planned for Gibbs to analyze the collected Smithsonian vocabularies, distribute them to others for discussion, and finally derive a linguistic map. But the project dragged on. In 1870, when he had 100 vocabularies, Gibbs proposed that the Smithsonian undertake an ambitious treatise on North American languages, embracing not only its unpublished materials but also earlier vocabularies that were sufficiently reliable and useful for reprinting. Gibbs offered to take responsibility for the Far West, leaving the rest of the continent to half-a-dozen collaborators.[86] Henry reacted cautiously. He favored distributing vocabularies to a small circle of investigators; the vocabularies would then be worked up with new information into a "general system." He referred the question to Whitney and Trumbull, making clear that he preferred to postpone any "treatise." Whitney and Trumbull concurred. Trumbull advised that vocabularies be distributed "to enable all who are interested in the subject to contribute to the work of comparison and discussion for which it might not be easy to find just now any one competent person." The treatise on American linguistics would have to wait for "the coming man."[87]

The caution of Gibbs's coworkers reflected a growing hesitancy to make any summary statement about the languages of America without much more data. Just as he cautioned Squier and Davis against speculation and urged Rau to delay his archaeological masterwork, Henry put off Gibbs's ambitious mapping plans. Whitney still saw confusion in American languages and urged patience. The search for Asian or any other connections was premature and "at variance with all the principles of linguistic science." The conservatism of the academic philologist must have distressed explorer Gibbs:

> Sound method [Whitney wrote in *Language*] . . . requires that we study each dialect, group, branch, and family by itself, before we venture to examine and pronounce upon its more distant connections. What we have to do at present, then, is simply to learn all that we possibly can of the Indian languages themselves; to settle their internal relations, elicit their laws of growth, reconstruct their older forms, and ascend toward their original conditions as far as the material within our reach, and the state in which it is presented, will allow. . . .[88]

Whitney, the stern voice of academic linguistics, aimed at very different goals than Gibbs sought. While hailing the "self-prompted study" of "self-denying men" in this "most fertile and important" science, Whitney deplored in the same breath the numerous investigators "with minds crammed with scattering items of historical information, abounding prejudice, and teeming fancies . . ."[89]

James Hammond Trumbull, self-taught Indian language expert from Connecticut, also found fault with the prevailing American linguistic methods. Collecting more Indian vocabularies, he said, was a scientifically useless enterprise. In the days of Gallatin, vocabulary gathering had helped to make sense of a chaotic mass of materials, but the work of Gallatin and the young Horatio Hale had been mere stepping stones. By the 1870s, it seemed to Trumbull, the real work of the linguist began where "the provisional labors of the word-collector" ended. Trumbull realized fully the futility of trying to match word-for-word correspondences between languages that differed fundamentally in their "plans of thought." He insisted instead on thorough knowledge of grammatical structures and analysis of Indian tongues into their basic components. Thus, while he deprecated mere word collecting, he contended that Indian languages could be studied by atomistic analysis. Where Duponceau and Schoolcraft had emphasized the unpredictable whim of the Indian in forming polysynthetic compounds, Trumbull saw order and regularity. The Indian no less than any other man, he insisted, always aimed at "extreme precision" in language. Only this fact made a science of American languages possible.[90]

The criticisms of Whitney and Trumbull exposed the gulf that separated them from Gibbs. The former settler also appreciated the complexity of Indian languages. But Gibbs was also impatient to determine the historical connections of various peoples and their relations to the environment. Whitney and Trumbull searched for the origin and laws, the philosophy, of language; looking to Indo-European models, they desired thorough understanding of speech. As Trumbull expressed his position, "absolute mastery of an Indian tongue is, for one to whom it is not vernacular, the work of a lifetime."[91] Gibbs would have agreed, but he never sought absolute mastery. To him, and to his successor Powell, language study was never more than a means to more important ends.

American Indian linguistics between 1840 and 1870 called forth differing motivations and encountered severe dilemmas. For William Turner, language study was a moral enterprise, closely joined to Christianizing efforts; for Gibbs, aboriginal tongues provided the only reliable key to the profound question of origins; for Whitney, language was a wonder, worthy of scientific study for its own beauty. All saw the need for system in observation and recording, and in the end they agreed that formal training was necessary. Two years before his death, Gibbs finally broke with the Hale/Gallatin tradition by proposing a flexible list of at least 1,500 words and phrases, rather than the 211 of his earlier circulars. Calling for "some new standard" for "an intelligent philology," he deplored the lack of sophisticated grammatical studies and suggested sending out manuals on "How to observe and what to observe" as a "stimulus . . . to the exertions of many who only require to know in what direction to employ their leisure and tastes."[92] Faith in the awakening word lived in George Gibbs as in Henry and Turner. He even proposed college courses to prepare future investigators. But in the end, the strength of Gibbs's salvage ethnology prevailed: in 1871 he advised Henry to halt the analytical and grammatical studies and gather more word lists—before the Indians all died out.[93]

Under Joseph Henry the Smithsonian Institution was a haven of science. The informal, family atmosphere that Henry and Baird created on the Mall contrasted sharply with the brutal political world of Washington in the decades surrounding the Civil War. Here natural scientists and wandering explorers found a temporary home and the leisure to study their collections, and aspiring young men like George Brown Goode and Frank Hamilton Cushing drank in the atmosphere of scientific congeniality. Naturalist Robert Kennicott was not exceptional in finding adjustment to Washington life greatly eased by the cozy circumstances at the Smithsonian during the winter of 1862–63:

> It's all very well to *talk* of the delights of the civilized world, but give me the comfortable north where a man can have some fun, see good dogs and smoke his pipe unmolested—D––n civilization. Not that I see it so much either for I live constantly here at the Smithsonian among a set of naturalists nearly all of whom have spent their lives in the wilderness.[94]

The comfort and informality were destined to be shortlived, because Henry's institution grew from demographic and professional conditions that were rapidly disappearing. In the middle years of the century, the sparsely populated national domain and the drive to diffuse the experience of science widely from Washington produced an enthusiasm for anthropology. The impressive richness of materials; the obvious, rapid, and steady annihilation of Native Americans before the onslaught of civilization; and the strong commitment to "facts" together contributed to making anthropology the Smithsonian's most public science. In 1877, the year before his death, Henry wrote with assurance that anthropology "is at present the most popular branch of science."[95]

[handwritten annotation: 'strong commitment to facts' / 'haven of science'.]

Notes

1. Henry to J. B. Varnum [draft], 22 June 1847, SIA.
2. SI, *AR for 1847*, pp. 175–76.
3. Ibid., pp. 179, 181–82.
4. Baird to Henry, 3 November 1849; quoted in William H. Dall, *Spencer Fullerton Baird* (Philadelphia, 1915), p. 191. "Every effort was made to enlist the services of occasional correspondents who wrote to the Smithsonian for information. A letter giving the particulars desired would perhaps have a postscript asking whether there were any Indian remains to be found in the locality . . . In a great many instances these letters bore important fruit . . ." (T. D. A. Cockerell, "Spencer Fullerton Baird," *Popular Science Monthly* [January 1906], p. 72). Henry and Baird did in fact use the meteorological network for anthropological inquiries. See, for instance, Henry's report (SI, *AR for 1860*, p. 42) on a circular, sent out in conjunction with the Academy of Natural Sciences of Philadelphia, on the physical characteristics of native-born Americans—one of the few instances of Smithsonian activity in physical anthropology in this period.
5. Henry to Frazer, 27 October 1855, Frazer Papers, APS. I am indebted to Nathan Reingold and Arthur Molella for this reference. Henry to Dr. Joseph Jones, 13 August 1868, Joseph Jones Papers.

6. Reaction to the acceptance of Squier and Davis's *Ancient Monuments*, for instance, was not entirely positive. "Those who consider no branch of knowledge of any value but such as relates to the immediate gratification of our physical wants, have objected to the acceptance of this memoir," Henry reported, but it was the first publication to meet his announced standards. "Besides this, it furnishes an addition to a branch of knowledge which is at this time occupying the attention of a large class of minds." (SI, *AR for 1847*, p. 188.) *Scientific American* (5 February 1848) registered disgust that Smithson's bequest was being squandered on "a useless and ambiguous science like Archaeology . . . ."

7. Joseph Henry Pocket Notebook, 1848, p. 35, SIA; SI, *AR for 1847*, p. 181.

8. Ephraim G. Squier and Edwin H. Davis, *Ancient Monuments of the Mississippi Valley: Comprising the Results of Extensive Original Surveys and Explorations* (Washington, D.C., 1848).

9. SI, *AR for 1877*, p. 22; Henry to Loomis, 5 June 1847, Loomis Papers.

10. Henry to Squier, 3 April 1847, Squier Papers.

11. Henry to Gallatin, 2 June 1847; Henry to Squier, 23 June 1847; and report of the AES committee, June 1847, all in SI, *AR for 1847*, pp. 185–87. The circumstances of the acceptance of the memoir bothered Henry, since if it became known that the reviewing committee had been chosen by "the author and his friends" rather than by the Secretary of the Smithsonian, it would set a poor precedent for Henry's future operations. Thus he advised "a little management" of the facts, and printed an edited version of his correspondence with the Ethnological Society. Henry to Squier, 23 June 1847, and Henry to Bartlett, 23 June 1847, Squier Papers.

12. Henry to Squier and Davis, 16 February 1848, Squier Papers.

13. Squier and Davis, *Ancient Monuments*, p. xxxviii. Three years later, Squier, in his second Smithsonian publication, again distinguished his own work from past efforts in ethnology: "Men seem to have indulged the belief that here nothing is fixed, nothing certain, and have turned aside into this field as one where the severer rules which elsewhere regulate philosophical research are not enforced . . ." *Aboriginal Monuments of New York* (Washington, D.C., 1851), p. 81.

14. John Russell Bartlett, "The Progress of Ethnology, An Account of Recent Archaeological, Philological, and Geographical Researches in Various Parts of the Globe, tending to elucidate the Physical History of Man," *Transactions of the American Ethnological Society* 2 (New York, 1848): 4. Samuel F. Haven, of the American Antiquarian Society in Worcester, Massachusetts, doubted the soundness of the work, though. Henry, disturbed to learn of Haven's opinion, appealed to him to explain his reservations, noting that "in regard to the character of a memoir on antiquities I must trust to others." Henry to Haven, 19 October 1847, Haven Papers.

15. Henry to Charles Rau, 10 December 1864, SIA.

16. Thomas Coulson, *Joseph Henry: His Life and Work* (Princeton, 1950), pp. 202–03.

17. Lapham to Henry, 12 March 1850 and 1 November 1851, Lapham Papers, OHS; Edward Foreman to Lapham, 29 March 1850, and Henry to Lapham, 22 November 1851, WSHS. In his desire to become "one of the men among whom

knowledge is to be 'increased and diffused' by your Institution," Lapham had written for advice and instruments as early as 1848. Lapham to Henry, 3 April 1848 and 2 March 1849, Lapham Papers, OHS.

18. SI, *AR for 1853*, pp. 20–21; Joseph Henry Pocket Notebook, 24 January 1848, SIA.

19. Henry to Charles Rau, 17 December 1869, SIA.

20. "Address of Prof. Joseph Henry," *Fifth and Sixth Annual Reports of the American Museum of Natural History* (New York, 1874), pp. 44–50 (quotation, p. 47).

21. Ibid., p. 47; cf. SI, *AR for 1847*, p. 181.

22. Ephraim G. Squier, *The Serpent Symbol* (New York, 1851), p. ix.

23. SI, *AR for 1846*, p. 23.

24. This point is central to understanding Henry's operations. I am indebted here to Arthur Molella's suggestions in his unpublished paper, "At the Edge of Science: Visionary Theorizers at the Smithsonian."

25. SI, *AR for 1867*, p. 44.

26. SI, *AR for 1861*, p. 26. In 1856 Henry observed with pleasure that the citizens of Chicago, apparently stimulated by Lapham's work, had founded a historical and antiquarian society. "Man is an imitative animal," he noted to Haven, "and the influence of our successful example sets many in operation." Henry to Haven, 27 October 1856, Haven Papers.

27. SI, *AR for 1859*, p. 17.

28. Increase Lapham, *Antiquities of Wisconsin*, Smithsonian Contributions to Knowledge 7 (Washington, D.C., 1855); Charles Whittlesey, *Ancient Works in Ohio*, Smithsonian Contributions to Knowledge 3 (Washington, D.C. 1852): 6; Brantz Mayer, *Mexican Archaeology and History*, Smithsonian Contributions to Knowledge 9 (Washington, D.C. 1857): 2.

29. Jesse Walter Fewkes, "Anthropology," in George Brown Goode, ed., *The Smithsonian Institution, 1846–1898* (Washington, D.C., 1897), p. 751. Between 1860 and 1872, when Joseph Jones's *Antiquities of Tennessee* appeared as part of vol. 22 of the Contributions, the Institution published countless brief accounts of excavations in its annual reports, but no major works on American archaeology.

    Haven originally intended a "purely historical (not speculative)" introduction to Lapham's memoir, as a "retrospective view" of the factual results of researches on the mound-builders. (Haven to Henry, 4 January, 7 July, and 20 November 1854, Haven Papers.) The project soon expanded, however, to a discussion of developments in philology and physical anthropology as well. Henry advised him to avoid discussion of the "vexed question" of the unity of the race. (Haven to Henry, 10 March 1855; Henry to Haven, 8 December and 17 December 1855; 3 April 1856, Haven Papers.)

30. Gordon R. Willey, "One Hundred Years of American Archaeology," in J. O. Brew, ed., *One Hundred Years of Anthropology* (Cambridge, 1968), pp. 29–53. For a fuller treatment of this period, see Gordon R. Willey and Jeremy A. Sabloff, *A History of American Archaeology* (San Francisco, 1974), pp. 42–87.

31. Mayer, *Mexican Archaeology*, p. 1. Twenty years later, Haven similarly observed that all the empirical advances of two decades in American archaeology had produced little "absolute progress" toward settlement of these "great questions."

(Haven to Henry, 20 January 1876, Haven Papers.)

32. Henry to T. Apoleon Cheny, 11 November 1861, Joseph Henry Collection, Princeton University Library.

33. Glyn E. Daniel has summarized this formative period in "Old World Prehistory," in Brew, *One Hundred Years*. pp. 58–59. For an extensive discussion, see Daniel's *A Hundred Years of Archaeology* (London, 1950).

34. SI, *AR for 1860*. pp. 284–343. Morlot's work enjoyed wide circulation and influence in Europe. See Daniel, *Hundred Years*, p. 79.

35. SI, *AR for 1861*, pp. 34–35, 392–96.

36. Henry, Extracts from Locked Book, 25 April 1862, SIA; SI, *AR for 1865*. p. 46. Such doubts were not original with Henry; see, e.g., E. G. Squier, *Aboriginal Mounds of New York* (Washington, D.C., 1851), p. 84.
    Henry also attributed analogies in social organization to a common human nature. The fact of different races having the same system of sexual promiscuity in remote times, Henry wrote William D. Whitney (in reference to Lewis Henry Morgan's work), "does not prove a unity of origin, but merely a unity of custom, arising from the brutal propensities of the species." (11 May 1869, Whitney Papers.) Henry refused to print an appendix on migrations to Morgan's *Systems of Consanguinity and Affinity in the Human Family* (Washington, D.C., 1871). Henry to Morgan, 8 April 1870, LHM Papers.

37. Henry Locked Book, 25 April 1862, SIA.

38. SI, *AR for 1888*. pp. 27, 91–92; *Dictionary of American Biography* 15 (1935): 388–89 (article by Walter Hough).

39. Rau to Henry, 25 February 1869; 29 November 1867; 6 March 1869, SIA.

40. Regna Darnell, "The Development of American Anthropology, 1879 to 1920: From the Bureau of American Ethnology to Franz Boas," Ph.D. diss. (University of Pennsylvania, 1969), pp. 2–4.

41. Rau to Henry, 29 November 1867, SIA.

42. Henry to Rau, 30 November 1867, SIA. For a recent assessment of Morton's unconscious "finagling" of his data, see Stephen Jay Gould, "Morton's Ranking of Races by Cranial Capacity: Unconscious Manipulation of Data May Be a Scientific Norm," *Science* 200 (5 May 1978): 503–09.

43. Rau to Baird, 1 January 1875, SIA. Henry consistently supported and encouraged Rau, who reported to his friend Carl Herman Berendt in 1876 that while he chafed under the direct supervision of Baird, "der alte Henry hat sich mir genenüber stets als Gentleman gezeigt . . . und wird sich ohne Zweifel in meinem Interesse bemühen." ("Henry has always been a gentleman to me . . . and will undoubtedly exert himself on my behalf.")

44. Rau to Baird, 1 January 1875, SIA.

45. Henry to Rau, 23 April and 10 May 1875, SIA.

46. Charles Rau, "Brooklyn Lecture on Archaeology," unpub. ms., p. 4, NAA; Rau, "On the Parallelism in the Development of Mankind, with Special Reference to the Red Race," unpub. ms., p. 1, NAA. The latter paper is the clearest statement of Rau's concept of parallel invention.

47. SI, *AR for 1864*, p. 374.

48. SI, *AR for 1865* (Washington, D.C., 1872), p. 50.

49. Rau to Henry, 26 October 1863, SIA.

50. Rau to George Gibbs, 30 May 1868, SIA.

51. Henry to Rau, 11 April and 6 June 1868; Rau to Henry, 28 April 1868, SIA. In 1875 and again in 1877 Henry asked Haven to prepare a new edition of his 1856 "master work," incorporating the results of the intervening decades. Haven's health did not permit him to accept Henry's offer. Henry to Haven, 3 March 1875; 26 November 1877; 12 March 1878; Haven to Henry, 20 January 1876, Haven Papers.

52. Smithsonian Contributions to Knowledge 25 (Washington, D.C. 1884): viii.

53. Charles C. Abbott, *Primitive Industry* (Salem, Mass., 1881).

54. See, e.g., reviews of Rau's work in *Archiv für Anthropologie* 13 (1880–81): 150–56, 157–62; also Rau to Henry, 3 February 1875, SIA.

55. The relationship between Henry and Schoolcraft is not entirely clear, but the two natives of upstate New York were apparently close friends for some time. When the Henrys moved to Washington, the Schoolcrafts and Henrys set up housekeeping together, an arrangement that proved most unsatisfactory to the two wives. After Schoolcraft's death in 1864, Henry actively aided his widow in assuring her an adequate income.

56. SI, *AR for 1851*, p. 13. For Henry's belief that languages indicate historical connections, see Henry Locked Book, 25 April 1862, SIA; and SI, *AR for 1865* (Washington, D.C., 1872), p. 46.

57. Henry Pocket Notebook, 1849, p. 14, SIA; SI, *AR for 1851*, p. 27; SI, *AR for 1857*, p. 37; SI, *AR for 1863*, pp. 42, 95–116.

58. Henry Rowe Schoolcraft, *Inquiries, Respecting the history, present condition and future prospects of the Indian tribes of the United States* (Washington, D.C., 1847). Schoolcraft's vocabulary list, reissued in 1849, totaled 350 words. *Indian Languages of North America*, American Ethnological Society Circular No. 1 (June 1852).

59. SI, *AR for 1867*, p. 36; George Gibbs, "Instructions for Archaeological Investigations in the U.S.," SI, *AR for 1861*, pp. 392–96; Gibbs, "Instructions for Research Relative to the Ethnology and Philology of America," SI Miscellaneous Collections 7, no. 160 (Washington, D.C., 1863); Gibbs, "Instructions relative to the Ethnology and Philology of America. Appendix A: Physical Characters of the Indian Races; Appendix B: Numerical Systems," in Smithsonian Contributions to Knowledge 15 (Washington, D.C., 1865). For a useful survey of circulars relating to ethnology, see Don D. Fowler, "Notes on Inquiries in Anthropology—A Bibliographic Essay," in T. H. H. Thoreson, ed., *Toward A Science of Man: Essays in the History of Anthropology* (The Hague, 1976), pp. 15–32.

60. SI, *AR for 1876*, p. 36; SI, *AR for 1877*, p. 24.

61. Gibbs to Whitney, 12 May 1861, Whitney Papers.

62. W.D. Whitney, *Language and the Study of Language* (New York, 1867), p. 324.

63. This account of Turner's career is based on "In Memoriam: Susan Wadden Turner and Jane Wadden Turner" (privately printed, 1898).

64. William H. Dall, *Spencer Fullerton Baird* (Philadelphia, 1915), p. 231; "In Memoriam," p. 9. See also Turner to Baird, 26 August and 23 September 1858, SIA, for evidence of their close personal friendship.

65. Felton to Smithsonian Regents, 4 February 1860, quoted in "In Memoriam," p. 14; Henry to John R. Bartlett, 7 November 1859, Bartlett Papers.

66. "Professor Turner's Letter on Indian Philology" (16 December 1851), SI, *AR for 1851*, pp. 97–98.

67. Ibid., p. 99.

68. J. W. Fewkes, "Anthropology," in G.B. Goode, ed., *The Smithsonian Institution, 1846–1896* (Washington, D.C., 1897), pp. 758–59; "Professor Turner's Letter," p. 97. Byington's Choctaw grammar was published by the American Philosophical Society in 1871; the dictionary, edited by John Swanton, was published by the BAE in 1915. Byington died in 1868.

69. Turner to Byington, 3 December 1852, Rhees Papers, SIA.

70. Ibid.

71. The following account of Gibbs's career is based upon Stephen Dow Beckham, "George Gibbs, 1815–1873: Historian and Ethnologist," Ph.D. diss. (UCLA, 1969); John Austin Stevens, "A Memorial of George Gibbs," SI, *AR for 1873*, pp. 219–25; and *Dictionary of American Biography* 8: 245–46. Stevens and Gibbs were intimate, lifelong friends. Their correspondence of the 1850s and 1860s is in the Gibbs Family Papers, WSHS.

72. George Gibbs, *The Memoirs of the Administration of Washington and Adams, edited from the Papers of Oliver Wolcott, Secretary of the Treasury* (New York, 1846). Gibbs's younger brother, Oliver Wolcott, was also denied admission to West Point, going instead to Columbia University to study chemistry. Alfred, the third son, finally attained West Point, eventually rising to major general. The entire family, including George, followed his career with enthusiasm.

73. Beckham, "George Gibbs," pp. 52–53. On Gibbs's move westward and his early years in the Northwest, see David I. Bushnell, Jr., "Drawings by George Gibbs in the Far Northwest, 1849–1851," Smithsonian Miscellaneous Collections 97, no. 8 (1938). The remarks on Gibbs's financial and personal dilemma derive from references and intimations in his correspondence to his family, 1850–53, in Gibbs Papers, WSHS.

74. Beckham, "George Gibbs," p. 99.

75. Ibid., pp. 102–03, 214; Gibbs, "The Intermixture of Races," SI, *AR for 1864*, p. 377.

76. Ibid., pp. 147, 193–94.

77. Ibid., pp. 194–95, 257.

78. Henry first invited him to take up residence at the Institution in 1861, but Gibbs declined. Beckham, "George Gibbs," p. 246.

79. Gibbs to Laura Wolcott Gibbs, 5 April 1861, Gibbs Family Papers, WSHS.

80. Beckham, "George Gibbs," pp. 232–33. The volumes for Shea were on Yakima, Chinook jargon, and the Lummi and Clallam dialects.

81. Ibid., p. 248.

82. George Gibbs, "A physical atlas of North America," SI, *AR for 1866* (Washington, D.C., 1872), pp. 368–69.

83. Gibbs to Baird, 10 and 22 February and 2 March 1863, SIA.

84. Gibbs to Whitney, 12 May 1861; Henry to Whitney, 1 August 1861 (Whitney Papers), in which the Secretary instructed Whitney to prepare an alphabet "especially adapted to the Indian dialects on this continent." Gibbs had included an alphabet in his 1863 "Instructions for Research Relative to the Ethnology

and Philology of America," SI Miscellaneous Collections 7, no. 160.

85. George Gibbs, "On the language of the aboriginal Indians of America," SI, *AR for 1870*, p. 367.

86. Henry Desk Diary, 8 April and 19 November 1868, and 25 January and 30 January 1870, SIA.

87. Henry to Whitney, 25 January 1870; Trumbull to Whitney, 31 January 1870, Whitney Papers.

88. Whitney, *Language*, p. 351.

89. Ibid., p. 353.

90. J.H. Trumbull, "On the Best Method of Studying the North American Languages," *Transactions of the American Philological Association* (1870): 78.

91. *Transactions of the American Philological Association* 3 (1872): 117.

92. SI, *AR for 1870*, pp. 364–67.

93. Beckham, "George Gibbs," p. 253.

94. Kennicott to Robert MacFarlane, 19 April 1863, Kennicott Papers, SIA.

95. SI, *AR for 1877*, p. 22.

III

An "Omnium Gatherum": Museum Anthropology at the Smithsonian Institution, 1846–1880

Joseph Henry was not a museum man—most of the time. Strictures against museum collections appeared regularly in his annual reports and correspondence, and his battle against museum advocates in Congress and on his own Board of Regents is well known.[1] The first Smithsonian Secretary repeatedly warned that "the formation of a museum of objects of nature and art requires much caution"; he frequently associated museums with gratification of "mere curiosity" rather than serious science.[2] In his last report (1877) Henry made a special effort to distinguish between the secondary, educational functions of the museum and the primary functions of the Smithsonian: support of original investigation and exploration, and publication and distribution of results.[3]

This familiar image of Henry as arch-opponent of the museum involves a chain of historical ironies. Despite his supposed museum antipathy, for assistant secretary Henry chose Spencer F. Baird, who came with his private collections in two railroad boxcars.[4] Henry lived and worked closely with Baird for twenty-five years, during which time the Smithsonian's natural history and anthropology acquisitions grew enormously. In 1857, after years of maneuvering for the proper conditions of transfer, Henry finally accepted the Wilkes materials from the Patent Office Building; similarly, twenty years later, rather than refuse the vast Centennial Exposition treasures offered to the Institution, at the time of his death Henry was engaged in obtaining from Congress a new museum building to house the objects. These decisions and policies did not arise from weakness or vacillation. As his firing of librarian Charles C. Jewett demonstrated, Henry firmly controlled Smithsonian affairs throughout his tenure; his tolerance for Baird's collecting impulses arose from confidence in his own position.

Henry and the museum thus require reassessment. In actuality, as one historian of science has argued, the view of Henry as a research scientist opposed to museum collections distorts this "very complex, ambiguous person" who actively collected art, books, artifacts, and natural history specimens "while complaining correctly that all these activities would severely hobble the Institution's research role."[5] In reconsidering Henry, it is important to note, first, that his stated resistance never applied to all collections, but only to the kind of "heterogeneous collection of objects of mere curiosity" that comprised most American museums of science and history and plagued the National Institute. He recognized the scientific value of limited collections as bases for research in natural history, and he accordingly accepted "special collections" to demonstrate specific theory. In addition, Henry believed that the Smithsonian could properly concentrate on North American materials, especially ethnological and archaeological materials, which were relatively inexpensive to preserve.[6] In fact, Henry's interests in natural history collections, and in the problem of geographical distribution of plants and animals, dated from his early years in Albany.[7] He recognized, moreover, the scientific integrity and importance of the taxonomic work of Baird and the naturalists, although he did tend to rank them below physical scientists.[8] Henry's position thus did not grow from antipathy toward natural history. Rather, two other factors caused his deep concern: the example of the National Institute and the political vulnerability of museums as institutions.

The act of Congress of 1846 creating the Smithsonian Institution provided for a building to house "objects of natural history, including a geological and mineralogical cabinet." At an early meeting the Regents confirmed these intentions by allotting $1,000 to advise U.S. consuls and other officials about procuring additions to the proposed museum and to encourage the Commissioner of Indian Affairs to collect items "illustrating the natural history of the country, and more especially the physical history, manners, and customs of the American aborigines." Reporting to the Regents in early 1847, the Smithsonian's committee of organization reiterated that "as important as the cabinets of natural history by the charter required to be included in the museum, your committee regard its ethnological portion"; they hoped to enlist the general public in building the anthropological collections.[9]

The shadow of the National Institute lingered over these early deliberations. As discussed earlier, from its inception the leaders of the Institute had placed priority on a national museum as the principal means of promoting "science and the useful arts," and the Institute model had considerable support within the original Smithsonian Board of Regents. Poinsett and his colleagues received tons of specimens from all parts of the continent, but no public funds for their care. As a consequence, the Institute's "National Cabinet" very quickly became a motley collection.

The confused state of the anthropological materials was typical of the Institute's "Cabinet." In 1841 and 1842, donations included such items as an "Indian pipe" (the Institute had many of these); "Bear-skin robe"; "A knife, said to have belonged to Wacousta, a celebrated Indian Chief"; "Skull of John Hicks, a noted Seminole Chief"; "Head-dress worn by Atahualpa, the last of the Incas"; and "39 Indian Arrowheads and White Oak acorns of three varieties." From Egypt, George Gliddon sent boxes of specimens, mainly pieces of stone, trees, shells, and bones. Among Gliddon's numerous gifts was "One piece of the sycamore tree under which tradition says 'Joseph and Mary sat' "—to which the budding Egyptologist and popularizer added: "The tree is old enough." In sum, as one observer noted, the Institute's antiquities amounted to a mixture of "natural science and bold adventure."[10]

Poinsett originally saw the museum as only a means of promoting science, not as a final goal. In the battles over the Wilkes collections and the Smithsonian bequest, though, the museum came to represent the material reason for the Institute's existence, and research programs waited for an indefinite future when the museum would presumably be in full operation. In 1841 John Pickering advised that the Institute encourage efforts by army officers to gather information about Indian languages. Brantz Mayer, secretary of the U.S. legation to Mexico, urged work in Central America. Preoccupation with museum care prevented the Institute from acting on these and other suggestions for research in science. The fresh image of the ill-fated Institute, "crushed to death by the weight of the collections and books" donated to it, surely figured largely in Henry's early conception of the Smithsonian.[11]

Beyond the National Institute precedent, however, Henry's resistance to museums was primarily political. His constant admonition that a large building and care for collections would bankrupt Smithson's bequest arose from his desire to keep Smithsonian science independent of political influence. He knew that a large museum would eventually require government funds, which meant annual trips to Capitol Hill and entrapment in Washington politics. "But now comes the danger," he wrote in 1877. Entering the political sphere, the Institution might "fall under political dominium." Henry had always recognized the danger. "Will [the Smithsonian] not be subject to party influences, and to the harassing questions of coarse and incompetent men?" his Princeton friend Charles Hodge had queried Henry in 1846. Knowing the risk, Henry nonetheless took it in the hope of establishing, against great odds, an independent scientific organization, free from the charlatanry and quackery of American politics and popular science. To be sure, the powers of Capitol Hill, of the "coarse and incompetent men" who ruled America, were awesome—"it will probably be found necessary to make a few oblations to Buncombe," Henry confessed—but these could be best resisted, he hoped, by minimizing financial dependence.[12] As the museum developed, it pushed Henry into the dependence he had feared, leaving his successors, Baird and Langley, without the luxury of a choice. Even before the end of the century, the oblations had become obligatory.

The Smithsonian did not actively encourage anthropological collecting before the Civil War. During the fifties, Baird amassed large numbers of mammals, birds, reptiles, fish, shells, and minerals from the exploring and surveying expeditions of federal departments, as well as from state governments, local scientific societies, and individuals.[13] Few anthropological specimens appeared among these acquisitions. In 1850 Ephraim Squier shipped five large "stone idols" and other items from Nicaragua to Washington, offering them as the nucleus of a "National Archaeological Museum." Henry agreed on the importance of such a museum but cautioned that it should be of "special objects and not an omnium gatherum of the ods & end[s] of creation."[14] For the next seven years Baird recorded only occasional Indian relics and artifacts.

Acquisition of the government (including Wilkes's) materials in 1857 augmented total Smithsonian collections by about twenty-five percent, and a considerable portion of the new treasures were anthropological.[15] William J. Rhees's *Guide to the Smithsonian Institution* (1859) claimed that the Institution possessed "one of the most extensive and curious ethnological collections in the world." The cases occupied the entire upper west gallery of the museum hall, one-fourth of total museum space. In contrast to the Secretary's emphasis on North American natural history, the anthropology drew from regions outside North America visited by Wilkes and other explorers, chiefly islands of the South Pacific. In fact, of fifteen display cases, only one featured North American groups. The contents of each display unit were determined by whatever items happened to have been collected, with haphazard results.[16]

By the time of the Civil War, then, if the Smithsonian's museum anthropology still displayed little scientific system, it at least showed sober intentions, particularly in comparison to the National Institute's "Cabinet." Portions of the latter still existed in the Patent Office in 1859, when Alfred Hunter published a *Popular Catalogue* to these collections.[17] Comparison of the guides to the two museums is instructive. Both, for instance, featured calumets, or peace pipes. But while Rhees's pamphlet briefly explained the supposed material and construction of the pipes, Hunter took the opportunity to lecture the public on Indian character:

> The disappearance of the original inhabitants of the Western continent is not the result of destruction, but a decaying atrophy, which nothing can avert, except the cataclysm of the Caucasian strain. The Indian . . . is a brute and bully to his women, a blackguard when in liquor, and more cruel and ruthless than all the bloodquaffing demons of Scandinavia when fortune gives him the upper hand.[18]

Hunter's prose reflected the confusion and arbitrariness in the Institute's museum. The display case adjacent to the Indian pipes contained the lower jaw of a sperm whale, insects from British Guiana, "remains of a Megetherium," coral, fossils, and crystal. In contrast to the chaos over at the Patent Office, the Smithsonian, while still far from systematic classification, had come some distance.

During the 1860s, and especially after the distractions of the Civil War, the Smithsonian's anthropological acquisitions increased rapidly for two reasons: European developments in archaeology, and trans-Mississippi expansion. The developments in Old World archaeology discussed in the previous chapter inspired Henry to a vigorous search for American antiquities, which he encouraged through circulars, correspondence, and his annual reports. Material results were gratifying: "Every state in the union," reported Baird in 1873, "has been represented to a greater or less extent in the form of stone-axes, pipes, pottery, etc." Henry was sanguine about the prospects of the archaeological specimens; no longer merely curiosities for "the wonder of the illiterate," by 1868 they promised to provide a basis for reconstructing the human history of North America. [19]

While collections from the eastern half of the continent came from shell heaps, mounds, and ploughed fields, explorers and agents in the western territories divested living tribes of clothing, implements, ornaments, and anything else they could be persuaded to sell or give away. The various territorial surveying parties of the post-war decade—under Hayden, Wheeler, King, and Powell—deposited their considerable ethnological treasures with Baird. [20] In addition, the assistant secretary combined efforts with other government agencies, such as the Department of Agriculture and the Bureau of Indian Affairs, to make maximum use of travelers, explorers, and agents in the West. Smithsonian archaeology, in other words, centered geographically east of the Mississippi (the shift to the Southwest would occur in Powell's Bureau during the 1880s); ethnological study and collection usually focused on the disappearing tribes from the Plains to the Pacific, with special attention to those already removed or settling in the Indian Territory. Geographically, institutionally, and paradigmatically, ethnology and archaeology in North America continued to suffer a debilitating separation. The absence or advanced decline of living cultures in the Northeast, Southeast, or Mississippi Valley, together with the general orientation of American archaeologists toward classification by technological stages, effectively removed the possibility of establishing historical depth and continuity in their studies. West of the Mississippi, the brutal, constant warfare against the dying tribes of the northern Plains, the Rocky Mountains, and the Southwest served strongly to confirm the popular image of the Indians as a nomadic, warlike race without proper home or history.

Within the quiet world of the Smithsonian, museum anthropology flowed with these broad cultural currents. Before 1880 all materials relating to Native Americans, whether archaeological or ethnological, came to the "ethnological division"; later the reorganization of the early eighties created departments of ethnology (Otis Mason), antiquities (Rau; later, Thomas Wilson), and arts and industries of civilization (George B. Goode), thereby formalizing the distinct purposes and conceptual divisions that had come to characterize the science of man in the museum. The museum thus confirmed in its structure the longstanding line between America's prehistory and the cultural status of the Indian, as well as the presumed wide gulf between the Indian and Anglo-Saxon civilizations. From the beginning, the logic was difficult to maintain, and almost immediately, in the eighties, the influx of large amounts of pottery, ancient and modern, from the sedentary, historical Pueblo peoples of the Southwest challenged the validity of the separation between archaeology and ethnology. To which division did the pottery belong? Significantly, Smithsonian officials postponed the dilemma by creating, under William Henry Holmes, a separate "Section of Aboriginal American Pottery."

The methods and personnel of this period, both in museum and field, emphasized broad coverage and freedom of movement, physically and intellectually. The men who built the early collections were naturalists and explorers, not ethnologists. Edward Palmer (1831–1911), listed regularly in the annual reports of the 1860s and 1870s as a major contributor to ethnology, exemplified the pattern. Palmer was primarily a botanical collector—"Plant Explorer of the West," his biographer has aptly suggested[21]—who spent the better part of almost every year of his adult life, between 1857 and 1910, roaming the western regions of North America. He collected for friends, patrons, and institutions in the East, largely leaving to them the work of classifying, labeling, studying, and exchanging the specimens he provided. The same was true of his auxiliary work in anthropology. Throughout his life Palmer revealed a consistent pattern of dependence: "anxious for opportunities to travel and collect, but without organizing ability to direct his own expeditions; sincere in his devotion to the prosecution of science, but not realizing his own limitations; willing to let his work as a collector speak for itself, and proud of his work, without understanding that the collections in themselves were not enough to make him the intellectual equal of such men as Henry and Baird."[22]

Abrasive and insensitive in personal affairs, Palmer established early a pattern of constant movement. He emigrated from England in 1849, and three years later attached himself as hospital steward to the La Plata exploring expedition to South America under Thomas Jefferson Page. Following his return in 1855, Palmer moved to Cleveland, back to England (where he briefly married), returned to New York and Cleveland, where for a short time he attended medical lectures, then proceeded on to Kansas in 1857. By 1860 Palmer was in Colorado, as always collecting plants and animals with every opportunity. On the basis of his meager medical experience, he served in the Union Army as an assistant surgeon in the campaigns in the Indian Territory, and due to his military connections he spent the years 1865–67 in Arizona as a surgeon at the various military posts recently established to control Apache outbreaks. He devoted most of his time here, however, to gathering and shipping eastward specimens of plants and seeds. The following year he moved again to the Indian Territory as agency doctor among the Kiowas and

Comanches, but his preoccupation with collecting and excessive disregard for his Indian patients caused his removal to the nearby Wichita agency, where presumably he indulged his collecting impulses without the burden of medical duties.[23]

Palmer made his first ethnological collections for Baird in 1867 in Arizona and continued this side interest during the next year in the Indian Territory. The Smithsonian ethnology catalogs list items from the Apache, Pima, Papago, and Comanche peoples, and Henry noted that Palmer's collections formed "very complete illustrations of the manners and customs of the tribes."[24] Palmer's methods among the harassed tribes of the region reflected his detached view of the Indians themselves, as shown in his account of one incident. An Apache child, wounded in an Army raid, had died. "The females of the camp," Palmer recounted, "laid it out after their custom & covered it with wild flowers and carried it to a grave. . . . They hid it so completely that its' body could not be found, as I had a wish to have it for a specimen . . . no persuasion could induce them to tell the secret, so I did not get the specimen."[25]

After a year of strenuous traveling through Utah, Arizona, and northern Mexico under the joint auspices of the Department of Agriculture, the Army Medical Museum, and the Smithsonian, Palmer settled for three winters in Washington (1871–73), spending the summers with Baird at Woods Hole, Massachusetts. Here he collected and prepared marine specimens at $60 (later $100) a month for Baird's U.S. Fish Commission; during the winter he performed similar curatorial work in the Smithsonian museum.[26]

Palmer's peripatetic services for the Smithsonian, the Peabody Museum of American Archaeology and Ethnology, and government agencies continued through the seventies and eighties—indeed, for the rest of his life. The year 1874 found him collecting for private patrons in Florida and the Bahamas. Between 1875 and 1877 he made botanical and ethnobotanical collections (and nearly starved) on Guadalupe Island, off the lower California coast; then, working for both Baird and the Peabody Museum in preparation for the 1876 Centennial, he undertook archaeological work in Utah and Arizona and collected on the Mohave Reservation and along the Gila and Colorado Rivers in southwestern Arizona.[27] After three more years of combined botany and archaeology, in 1880 Baird secured him a position in Powell's Bureau of American Ethnology, working under Cyrus Thomas's mounds survey.

Though the pay was sufficient ($125 a month), Palmer's three years in the BAE were unhappy ones. He was constantly in the Southeast, traveling among mounds between Tennessee and Arkansas, at the same time collecting artifacts for the National Museum and the New Orleans Exposition of 1884–85. Thomas and Powell gave him no formal credit for his work, and Palmer left the Bureau and the mounds with relief in 1885 to collect for three years in the more appealing region of Mexico.

Movement was the key to Palmer and his science. Placing himself at the service of sponsors—the Army, Smithsonian, Peabody, and private patrons—whose needs and interests matched or complemented his own, Palmer salvaged frenetically among Native Americans and among plants. He thus typified the scientist-explorers of post-Civil War anthropology, who collected materials with which others might build a science. The scientific results, however, followed the structure of the pursuit: Palmer's ethnological and archaeological collections (unlike his botanical work) were spotty and unsystematic: good, perhaps, for exciting public interest in museums, but unsatisfactory for scientific purposes, despite Henry's hopes. Furthermore, Palmer himself was opportunistic, but he was also powerless and dependent. From one perspective, he cut his own paths across North America, and certainly the sensations of physical freedom must have been very real and important to him. In a larger sense, though, he followed the well-worn cultural tracks of Army desolation and settler exploitation, contributing in his own way to both knowledge and annihilation.

From Palmer and others, the Smithsonian received massive amounts of material. As early as 1865 Baird began noting the backlog of anthropological materials, uncataloged and unarranged for lack of time and labor. Over the next decade the situation worsened as the anthropological specimens began to dominate the accession books. According to Baird's annual reports, in 1868 twenty percent of new materials were anthropological; by 1874 they had increased to one third.[28] The accessioning work—preparing, studying, drawing, classifying, and labeling—fell to a handful of individuals with more enthusiasm than training. Donors of large collections frequently stayed over the winter months in Washington, living in the Smithsonian quarters and organizing their materials. Robert Kennicott, for example, spent the winters of 1858–59 and 1862–63, following his trips to the Northwest and the Arctic, preparing his materials at the Smithsonian; as we have seen, Palmer similarly busied himself with museum tasks during the winters of his collecting years.

Baird's chief aide in anthropology in these years was, however, no explorer. Edward Foreman (1808–1885), in contrast to Palmer, spent his entire life near the city of his birth, Baltimore.[29] After receiving a medical degree in 1830, Foreman spent nearly twenty years as a professor at Washington University of Baltimore (1835–1853), in the same years avidly studying and collecting in local geology, paleontology, botany, conchology, and archaeology. He became an active corresponding member of the National Institute of the 1840s, to which he sent a collection of shells and advice on specimen exchange. Between 1849 and 1853, he served as Henry's and Baird's "General Assistant," in charge of the Smithsonian's correspondence and collections. He left the Smithsonian for a position in the Patent Office, where he stayed until the outbreak of the Civil War.

The years of war and its aftermath were scientifically barren ones for Foreman. A Confederate sympathizer, he moved out of Washington to Catonsville, Maryland, but prudently kept up contact with his close friend Baird. "Being deep in the cultivation of vulgar vegetables," he wrote to Baird in 1864, "I neglect all scientific pursuits, the more so, as there is not a soul within attainable distance who sympathizes with such avocations . . . the cursed war absorbs and brutalizes everything." At the close of the war Foreman found himself "in a state of literary and scientific destitution" (as he told Baird) and in 1867 announced himself ready to return to the Smithsonian in order to "proceed with the arrangement of the Smithsonian Ethnological Collections this winter ensuing . . ."[30]

Between 1867 and 1884, when he resigned in ill health, Foreman made entries for approximately 45,000 ethnological specimens in the Smithsonian accession catalogs (of an estimated total of 75,000 received in this period).[31] But Foreman was not satisfied with brief verbal descriptions, as he explained to Baird in 1878: "I have never, as intimated, in any instance omitted making sketches of objects received, knowing too well that they give the only certain data for making a proper return to owners;—the only safeguard against meddlesome and purblind officials."[32] Even if the motivation were less scientific than proprietary, Foreman's tiny, meticulous drawings—some 5,000 of them altogether—still provide valuable clues to artifact identity for students of the collections today.

Foreman's sketches are silent, poignant reminders of both his relevance and his irrelevance for modern museum anthropology. Foreman belonged to antebellum America: he was a Baltimore gentleman, a medical man, a naturalist—the kind of man who actively participated in the local scientific societies of nineteenth-century America. He, too, believed in Henry's "awakening word," and he happily bore testimony to "the great liberality and promptitude which I have invariably found to actuate naturalists, though personally strangers to each other. I have attributed these noble qualities as much to the gentle influences exercised by their quiet pursuits as [to] the wish to extend the humanizing results which always attend the cultivation of science."[33] But Foreman belonged among the fortunate few who established long-term institutional connections; the many who did not had to rest contented with tenuous ties. Not that Foreman's own Smithsonian situation was ever secure, even in the last years. On one occasion at the end of 1879, when Foreman was seventy-one years old, Baird informed him that due to museum overexpenditures he and several other assistants must be dispensed with for six months. "I hope this will not be any serious inconvenience to you," Baird commiserated, "as the step is absolutely necessary under the circumstances. Of course we will be obligated to get alone [sic] the best way we can, in regard to labeling the ethnological specimens . . ."[34]

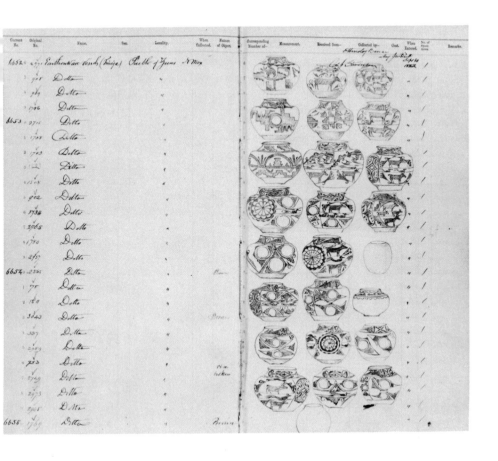

A sample page of Edward Foreman's drawings from the U.S.
National Museum Ethnology Accession Books, 1879.

The approach of the 1876 Centennial Exposition accelerated the trend, already strong, toward government support of the Smithsonian museum. Since the transfer of the government collections in 1857, Congress had annually appropriated $4,000 for their maintenance. In 1870, faced with ever-growing collections, Henry lobbied successfully for an increase to $10,000 for museum maintenance, and another $10,000 for construction of new facilities in the Smithsonian Building. Further increase of the maintenance allotment to $20,000 in 1872 signaled an important shift in congressional attitude toward the museum, as well as considerable financial relief for Henry and Baird.

The increased funding of the early seventies ushered in a decade of dynamics between the growing collections, financial support, organizational complexity, and specialization. In anthropology the unprecedented Centennial preparations included much collecting, in which Palmer, Foreman, and dozens of others participated, and which absorbed thousands of government dollars. The resulting acquisitions required, in turn, thousands more for new facilities and permanent museum workers. By 1877 the "division of ethnology" boasted three paid assistants: Rau, Foreman, and a young protégé of Baird's, Frank Hamilton Cushing. Equally important, the larger collections required and the larger staff permitted new distinctions: "After the arrival of the [Exposition] materials at Washington, 1876–1877, there appears to have been made a more marked division between archeological and ethnological material than had previously obtained, and the title of Dr. Rau was changed to 'Assistant, Archeology'," an early department history stated. More changes ensued. Rau and others who had previously served as assistants in 1880 became "curators," receiving for the first time specific letters of appointment defining their duties.[35]

By 1881, the final consequence of these rapid developments was a more efficient, formal, specialized "National Museum" for the education and enlightenment of the American people. Mass education had become primary during the seventies. In a sense, of course, Henry had always intended Smithsonian science as moral uplift, but in his final years he seemed increasingly to value the museum as an educational instrument. Here the visitor effortlessly received valuable impressions that served as the basis for further mental development. "It is truly surprising," he observed, "how tastes may be formed, how objects before disregarded may, when viewed as a part of a natural family, be invested with attractions which shall ever after render them sources of refined pleasure and unalloyed enjoyment." While the Smithsonian Institution should continue its scientific researches, Henry suggested, the "public museum" should "largely partake of the popular element." Supported by the U.S. government, the museum would appeal to Americans visiting their capital. Moreover, while adding to the attractions of Washington, the museum would draw to itself isolated private collections, "especially of anthropology."[36]

Henry's vision of the future National Museum included a major role for anthropology. He was especially proud of the archaeological series of North American implements amassed during his long tenure, supplemented by important collections from European excavations; and he was particularly anxious to see them arranged in good order, as a model of the developmental sequences that could be discovered in the history of any of the civilized arts of man. After years of patient, cautious accumulation, Henry finally felt that the archaeology of North America was sufficiently complete for preliminary description and exhibition. He devoted an entire new room to anthropology, "the branch of science attracting perhaps at the present time more attention than almost any other . . . ." To his old friend Asa Gray, Henry confided, "I shall make a grand display."[37]

In 1880, more than twenty years after his first guidebook, William J. Rhees published a *Visitor's Guide to the Smithsonian Institution and National Museum.* Because all the collections were about to be transferred to the new museum building (paid for by Congress), the guide was only temporary, and, as in 1859, "no attempt [was] made at a scientific classification or description of the specimens." But Rhees described well the scope of the collections. True to Henry's vision, "Anthropology Hall" occupied the entire second story of the central building—more than 150 display cases. Only Rau's archaeological series appeared in a systematic manner, while many ethnological items—baskets, bows, arrows, and dance masks—were simply shoved under display cases, where presumably visitors could examine them.[38]

Rau's classification of prehistoric archaeological specimens separated North American objects by materials; remaining anthropological exhibits, while somewhat disorganized, appeared geographically, and in some instances, according to specific tribes. Many cases, however, still retained vestiges of the chaos of National Institute days: Case 80 contained, among other oddments, a "tomahawk presented to Davy Crockett by the young men of Philadelphia," "Fragments of one of the bolts to which Columbus was chained in San Domingo," and an old English battle axe from Windsor Castle.[39] As Rhees's catalog illustrated, even after Henry's death the National Museum's anthropological collections were still in great part a congeries of archaeological relics, ethnological curiosities, and historical Americana badly in need of definition.

In evaluating anthropological activity in the early Smithsonian museum, it is possible to dismiss the period, the conditions, and the men as "amateur" or "preprofessional" and let it go at that; alternatively, there is strong temptation to romanticize the fluid structure, the personal freedom, and the absence of bureaucracy under Henry and Baird. To be sure, operations were highly personal, in part due to lack of funds for hiring a permanent staff—volunteers, temporary help, and personal friends do not conform readily to bureaucratic rigor—and in part because museum specialists were often not available. While the Smithsonian served as the repository for enormous, ever-accruing government collections, Baird could initiate and underwrite no anthropology projects of his own before the founding of the BAE in 1879 created a new source of·funds for research and (in Baird's opinion, at least) collecting. As a consequence, in field or museum, Baird's anthropology went forward as a "Nebenfach"—a side or auxiliary activity by individuals with broader interests. In some cases those interests were defined geographically, in others by lines of specialty, in still others by various combinations of the two, for these were simultaneously the final decades of a vigorous American surveying tradition and the early stages of a new, university-bred era of specialization.

The careers of men like Palmer and Foreman (and Charles Rau) point to the double edge that the Smithsonian Institution, and government agencies generally, presented to nineteenth-century Americans. The dilemmas lay not with the Smithsonian but with the inherent limitations of certain institutional structures, in particular with the difficulties of superimposing national horizons and networks upon a nation of predominantly local communities and loyalties. As Powell soon discovered in both his BAE and the U. S. Geological Survey, it was impossible to pursue national programs without treading on local toes.[40] Edward Foreman got a brief taste of American parochialism in anthropology on a trip to Cincinnati in 1875. Acting as representative of Baird and Henry, Foreman's objective was to review the private archaeological cabinets of prominent Cincinnati gentlemen and persuade them to loan choice specimens to the Smithsonian for its Exposition exhibits in Philadelphia. The Cincinnati men got over their disappointment at not seeing Henry or Baird, but Foreman could not overcome their jealous possessiveness: "All of the collectors freeze hard to their specimens and are unwilling to let them go out of their sight," Foreman reported. "Some were exhibited at the recent Cincinnati Exposition but the owners conveyed them to the Hall in person and brought them away when the show was over. They know & feel that Ohio has great claims to consideration on account of her antiquities, and are indignant at any instance of valuable specimens being carried out of the state and probably to foreign lands."[41]

Personal desire and expectation complicated formal institutional relationships. The Smithsonian unquestionably provided scientific stimulus and opportunity for thousands of Americans, as Henry hoped and intended. But merely by creating visions of possibilities that could not, under the circumstances, find more than partial fulfillment, Henry's institution set in motion across the country complex personal and professional dynamics of aroused interest, hopeful ambition, frustration, and resentment—as well as much gratitude.[42] The Smithsonian could not at the same time promote democratic participation and also discriminate among enthusiastic participants without dampening ardor. Even for those, like Palmer and Foreman, who attached themselves (however tenuously), the line between opportunity and exploitation is still difficult to draw, as it must have been for them at times. They were fortunate, but they were also used. The early Smithsonian—the institution and the science—in this as in many respects was riddled with ambivalence, leaving us finally with only rich images to ponder. Palmer, fifty years old, after thirty years in the field, digging unnoticed in the mounds of Tennessee and Arkansas; Foreman, in his seventies, meticulously recording entry after entry with an artist's hand: these are some of the lasting, haunting images of Smithsonian museum anthropology a hundred years ago.

Notes

1. See, e.g., Wilcomb E. Washburn, "Joseph Henry's Conception of the Purpose of the Smithsonian Institution," in Whitfield J. Bell, ed., *A Cabinet of Curiosities: Five Episodes in the Evolution of American Museums* (Charlottesville, Va., 1967), pp. 106–66.
2. SI, *AR for 1849* (Washington, D.C., 1854), p. 173.
3. Washburn, "Joseph Henry," pp. 143–44.
4. William H. Dall, *Spencer Fullerton Baird: A Biography* (Philadelphia, 1915), p. 220.
5. Nathan Reingold, "The New York State Roots of Joseph Henry's National Career," *New York History* 54 (1973): 143. Reingold's article is a persuasive presentation of Henry's consistent positions on science, research, and museums. For reappraisal of Henry in the cultural environment of early nineteenth-century America, see Arthur P. Molella and Nathan Reingold, "Theorists and Ingenious Mechanics: Joseph Henry Defines Science," *Science Studies* 3 (1973): 323–51.
6. SI, *AR for 1850* (Washington, D.C., 1854), p. 194; Henry to Louis Agassiz, 10 June 1865 (from Mary Henry typescript), SIA; Henry to Alexander Dallas Bache, 6 September 1846, SIA.
7. Reingold, "New York State Roots," p. 140; SI, *AR for 1856,* pp. 41–42.
8. See, e.g., Henry to Bache, 15 August 1864, quoted in Washburn, "Joseph Henry," p. 152. The entire letter is reproduced in Nathan Reingold, ed., *Science in Nineteenth-Century America: A Documentary History* (New York, 1964), pp. 216–217.
9. SI, *AR for 1846,* pp. 11–13, 19.
10. *Second Bulletin of the National Institute* (Washington, D.C., 1842); contributions are listed throughout; for Gliddon, see p. 232. See also Francis Markoe and J. J. Abert to George P. Marsh, 8 April 1844, with appended description of the Institute collections, in George Brown Goode, "The Genesis of the U.S. National Museum," USNM, *AR for 1891,* pp. 322–25. The observer was H. T. Tuckerman writing in the *Southern Literary Messenger* in 1849, quoted in Goode, "The Genesis," p. 236.
11. Pickering to Markoe, 1 September 1841; Mayer to Markoe, 11 September 1841, in *Proceedings of the National Institute* (Washington, D.C. 1841), pp. 107, 112–13; Goode, "The Genesis," p. 335.

12. Henry to J. P. Lesley, 12 January 1877; Hodge to Henry, 5 December 1846; Henry to J. B. Varnum, 22 June 1847; all quoted in Washburn, "Joseph Henry," pp. 145, 113, 112.

13. A. Hunter Dupree, *Science in the Federal Government: A History of Policies and Activities to 1940* (New York, 1957), p. 99.

14. SI, *AR for 1856*, pp. 22–23; Squier to Henry, 2 December 1850, in SI, *AR for 1850*, appendix II, pp. 78–80; Henry to Squier, 5 December 1850, Squier Papers.

15. Baird's list of the major new acquisitions appeared in SI, *AR for 1858*, pp. 52–53.

16. William J. Rhees, *Guide to the Smithsonian Institution and National Museum* (Washington, D.C., 1859), pp. 69–75.

17. Alfred Hunter, *A Popular Catalogue of the Extraordinary Curiosities in the National Institute Arranged in the Building Belonging to the Patent Office* (Washington, D.C., 1859).

18. Ibid., p. 23.

19. SI, *AR for 1873*, p. 45; SI, *AR for 1868*, p. 33.

20. For the western surveys, see William H. Goetzmann, *Exploration and Empire: The Explorer and the Scientist in the Winning of the American West* (New York, 1966); Dupree, *Science in the Federal Government;* William Culp Darrah, *Powell of the Colorado* (Princeton, 1951); Wallace Stegner, *Beyond the Hundredth Meridian: John Wesley Powell and the Second Opening of the West* (Boston, 1954).

21. Rogers McVaugh, *Edward Palmer: Plant Explorer of the American West* (Norman, Okla., 1956). The following discussion of Palmer is based largely on McVaugh's careful tracing of Palmer's career.

22. Ibid., pp. 11–12.

23. Ibid., pp. 15–40.

24. Ibid., pp. 34, 38; SI, *AR for 1867*, p. 45; SI, *AR for 1868*, p. 30.

25. Ibid., p. 30.

26. Palmer's position as "curator" in the SI, *AR for 1871* (Washington, D.C., 1873), p. 30, referred apparently to these routine labors.

27. McVaugh, *Edward Palmer*, pp. 60–71.

28. SI, *AR for 1868*, p. 54; SI, *AR for 1874*, p. 49.

29. The following discussion of Foreman's career derives from personal correspondence with Charles E. Ellis, a descendant of Foreman who has painstakingly reconstructed Foreman's life and work at the Smithsonian. I am indebted to Mr. Ellis for permission to utilize his materials and findings.

30. Quoted in Ellis to Robert Elder, 29 November 1973, copy in author's possession.

31. Estimated by Ellis, who has examined most of the surviving ethnology catalogs in the Anthropology Department Processing Laboratory, Smithsonian Institution.

32. Quoted in Ellis to Elder, 29 November 1973.

33. Quoted in Ellis to the author, personal correspondence, 16 March 1974.

34. Ibid. As General Assistant between 1849 and 1853, Foreman had received $100 a month, about a third less than Baird. His salary for the later period has not been determined; catalog records indicate that he continued to work after Baird's memorandum.

35. "Historical Sketch of the Division of Prehistoric Archeology" (ca. 1906), pp. 4–5, OTM Papers, NAA; the title of Rau's department, originally Archeology, changed to Antiquities in the mid-eighties, to Prehistoric Anthropology in 1888, and again to Prehistoric Archeology in 1897—changes that reflected the unclear status and function of American archaeology in this period.

36. SI, *AR for 1870*, pp. 33–36.

37. SI, *AR for 1873*, p. 35; Henry to Gray, 4 March 1874, Gray Papers.

38. William J. Rhees, *Visitor's Guide to the Smithsonian Institution and National Museum* (Washington, D.C., 1880), pp. 69–75.

39. Ibid., p. 59.

40. An outstanding and complex instance of jealousy and conflict in the 1880s between Powell's BAE and the Davenport (Iowa) Academy of Sciences is recounted in Marshall McKusick, *The Davenport Conspiracy* (Iowa City, 1970).

41. Foreman to Baird, November 1875, NAA.

42. From this viewpoint, the Smithsonian fire in 1865, which destroyed most of the records and correspondence of the Institution, could be viewed with mixed feelings, as William H. Dall *(Spencer Fullerton Baird, pp. 234–35)* noted:

Professor Henry had invariably replied to all his correspondents with extreme courtesy, no matter how absurd the proposition advanced or question asked. When the inventor of a scheme for perpetual motion sent his manuscript, he was politely informed of its receipt and that it would be carefully 'filed with the archives of the Institution.' This was usually sufficient for the vanity of the inventor. But later on someone, irritated at the non-appearance in print of his lucubrations, would write an angry letter inquiring the reasons therefor, and would be politely informed that all the valuable archives of the Institution had perished in the flames. The Professor once declared that the relief of mind thus afforded was almost worth the cost of the fire.

Part 2

Anthropology as
Government Science
1879–1910

IV

From Culture History to Culture Areas: Anthropology in the U.S. National Museum, 1881–1908

Chaos was a major social and intellectual concern of Victorian Americans. It took many forms: the personal threats of a precarious, seemingly whimsical economic system that distributed rewards without regard to individual merit; the social disruptions attendant upon mass immigration, disorderly urban growth, and the emerging class antagonisms of unregulated industrial capitalism; the cosmic chaos of a secular universe without guiding hand or final purpose. Historians have long pointed to reaction to Charles Darwin's biological evolutionism—specifically to his hypothesis of natural selection, which seemed to replace a world of design with one of chance occurrence—as a measure of commitment to the orderly, understandable cosmos of antebellum America. But for most people the personal and social chaos of unsettled daily life was more immediate and tangible than the chance variation and selection of the biological world. Responses to dislocation were weighty and deliberate: massive architecture and machinery, comprehensive philosophical systems, even oppressive clothing—all facets of the culture seemed to express a heavy-handed materialism aimed at concreteness and assurance, as if the culture, lacking a central mass, would fly apart. Assertion of control bespoke deep fear of fragmentation.[1]

The museum as an institution embodies imposed order. Not surprisingly, during its "golden years" between the Civil War and the First World War, American museum anthropology served anthropologists and their public as a bastion of certainties, as an important defense against racing change, social turmoil, and a world of more human variety than was previously imagined or, one suspects, desired. After the Civil War, museums, along with public schools, began to assume the moral and political functions of educating and socializing the mass public of an emerging industrial order. At the same time, museum focus shifted noticeably from the natural wonders of God to the artificial inventions of man, especially the material achievements of the Anglo-Saxon. While industrial museums and expositions displayed the superiority of civilization, museum anthropology made the same point by exhibiting the inferiority of other peoples. It contributed to the celebration of America's coming of industrial age by demonstrating relative racial and national accomplishment.[2]

American anthropologists belonged to a society caught in the paradoxes of its own progress. The celebration of civilized power that characterized American public expositions and museums between 1876 and 1917 could not completely hide a sense of loss and fear: loss of innocence and natural vigor, and fear that civilized man was also losing control over the products of his own genius. To some, indeed, mankind seemed to be "dragged on by an attractive power in advance, which even the leaders obeyed without understanding, as the planets obeyed gravity, or the trees obeyed heat and light."[3] Caught between a fading human past and an uncertain technological future, anthropologists in the nation's capital felt a particular responsibility to retrieve that past in order to take a hand in determining and shaping man's fate. The task seemed monumental and absolutely crucial to them. As Otis T. Mason, first curator of ethnology in the National Museum, explained in 1883, the anthropologist enjoyed a sense of involvement in vital affairs, for he or she participated in the universal quest for the "secrets of man's origin, progress, and destiny."[4]

Still, the secularization implicit in the shift from cabinets of natural wonders to museums of man's works was far from complete. The men who established anthropology in the National Museum saw their enterprise as a pious endeavor in an age of science and religious doubt; they called themselves scientists, but theirs was as often an aesthetic and religious exercise, and always a moral service to the nation. By displaying order in the tangible works of man through all ages and places, they would confirm cosmic purpose. The consequence of this stance was an anthropology that was constraining rather than expansive, classificatory rather than exploratory. The anthropologists of the early National Museum sought to contain the world within walls and categories; they sought old verities, not new truths.

The life of science, Joseph Henry had believed, at once humbled and ennobled the individual, instilling piety before the beauty of God's creation and raising the student of nature to spiritual heights. Otis T. Mason found such fulfillment. Mason approached the science of man with wonder, and his joy grew with time. The plenitude of the human mind endlessly enthralled him. Rooted in the animal but approaching the Creator with an inventive faculty, humankind required the methods of natural science but necessarily inspired religious awe. As the first curator of ethnology in the National Museum (1884–1908), Mason attempted throughout his life to find compatibility between the two.

Mason came from humble beginnings. He was eleven when his family arrived in 1849 in northern Virginia, leaving behind a trail of financial difficulties from Maine to New Jersey. Here he tended cows and studied surveying with a neighbor, but young Mason most admired the seminarians who came to preach on Sundays, and he dreamed of college. In 1856 his grandfather sent him to Columbian College (now George Washington University) in Washington, D.C. At Columbian he received the standard education in Scottish moral philosophy from the president of the college, Reverend George W. Samson, became interested in biblical and classical studies, participated in the college literary societies, and delivered the salutatory address at his graduation in 1861.[5]

Mason stayed on as the principal of Columbian Academy, the preparatory department of the college. Over the next twenty-three years he became a fixture at the school, teaching natural history, classics, history, English, mathematics, and geography to the boys who came to the nation's capital to be educated, and helping to introduce to the school the "general principles of Natural Science." The department was informal, even intimate; for many years the boarding students lived in the Mason household. Apparently in exchange for his loyal services to the college, Mason acquired additional academic credentials—A.M. and Ph.D.—from Columbian. By 1880 he was instructor of English and history in the college; four years later, when he left Columbian for the National Museum, Mason was listed as "Professor of Anthropology" in the prospectus for the Corcoran School of Science and Arts of Columbian University.[6]

Mason's life, Walter Hough wrote in 1909, was completely "bound up" with the Smithsonian Institution. In the early 1850s he had seen Henry perform a brief experiment at the Institution, an event he still recalled vividly half a century later.[7] But his interest in the eastern Mediterranean region drew him permanently into the Smithsonian and indirectly into American anthropology. Arriving at the Institution one day in 1869 to examine some Semitic inscriptions, Mason explained them as well as he could to Baird and Henry. But when he finished Baird recommended that he "give all this up. If you devote your life to such a subject as this, you will have to take the leavings of European workers. It will not be possible for you here in America to obtain the material for important researches; but—I give you the two Americas!" Mason later recalled that he was "born again that day."[8] The chance meeting had "opened the Western Hemisphere to my mind and changed the current of my life."[9]

Mason soon joined Baird's corps of "resident collaborators," devoting all spare time to North American ethnology. His forte and joy was classification: patient, careful search for similarities and distinctions among objects. As he handled and examined each specimen minutely and lovingly, his impelling motive was always his "ardent desire to say the last word" on specimens, leading him "to so thoroughly examine their structure and function that he was as familiar with them as were their original makers . . . ." Baird directed

Mason's activities closely, and the younger man responded dutifully: "My sole object is to put the collection completely under *your* thumb. And every word I write, every object I put in a tray is to that end."[10]

Mason worked conscientiously at his avocation. During his twelve years as collaborator, he absorbed the fundamentals of natural science taxonomy from Baird, applied them to the ethnological collections, and soon emerged as the Museum's anthropology expert. He began his own card catalog of North American Indian tribes, which he expanded in collaboration with Powell into an early synonymy, the "nest egg" of the BAE's *Handbook of American Indians North of Mexico* (1907–10).[11] In addition he edited the archaeological reports from correspondents that appeared in the annual reports between 1874 and 1883; by 1878 Baird considered him the Smithsonian's expert on such matters.[12] Finally, between 1873 and 1877, at Baird's request, Mason submitted monthly reports on anthropology to *Harper's Record of Science and Industry,* and later to *American Naturalist;* between 1879 and 1892, again at Baird's urging, he contributed comprehensive annual reviews of work in anthropology to the Smithsonian reports.

Mason was impressed with the great strides anthropology had taken in a few decades. Emerging from a recent past of speculation and drawing on the latest discoveries in the physical and natural sciences, anthropologists were assembling a complete, sophisticated view of man in nature and society. This maturation, Mason reasoned, resulted from significant changes in social and professional structure. Anthropology had become an open science. Previously its various branches had been dominated by individuals working for selfish, partial ends and generalizing from incomplete, private collections. "There are times in the settlement of a new country," Mason allowed, "when every man is his own carpenter, smith, and physician." But by the 1880s the day of the tyros had passed; the period of organization in American science was at hand, but it was to be an open organization.[13]

In part, Mason only expressed the fascination with centralization that was increasingly evident at the nation's capital in the closing decades of the nineteenth century. But he went further. The marvelous thing about the study of man, Mason observed, was that it offered something for everybody to investigate. Every person was a specialist, because there was an anthropological aspect to every walk of life, from mothers and schoolteachers to musicians and legislators. "Who may be an anthropologist?" Mason asked, and answered: "Every man, woman, and child that has sense and patience to observe, and that can honestly record the thing observed." Each had only to look into the historical and scientific aspects of his or her specialty to become a student of humanity and contribute to the growing science. Here there was "no priesthood and no laity, no sacred language . . . [here] you are all both the investigator and the investigated . . ."[14] Mason envisioned an open science embracing thousands, nurtured by the spirit of voluntarism and service that marked his own early years with the Smithsonian. Like many of his contemporaries, he assumed that anyone undertaking anthropology did so out of love. He reminded one correspondent that "we are working for the pleasure of it," and to another he urged patience and hard work:

> Very few of us walked a bee line into our present work. We just fell in love with it and by and by the doors opened . . . If you have a living income, stick to it, watch, and pray. I will have you in mind. Maybe the train will be delayed, but don't miss it when it does arrive. Write for the papers. Be seen about the societies. Take a hand in the drudgery. If Doctor [Roland B.] Dixon asks you to go a mile, go with him twain. When I was young and strong I served and result came."[15]

Mason realized, however, that broad participation and specialization led nowhere without coordination. Within Washington, Mason argued, the Bureau of American Ethnology, the National Museum, the Army Medical Museum, and the Anthropological Society of Washington had begun to centralize resources, making it possible for all to contribute. These central organizations, which characterized "modern anthropology," were accomplishing a "wonderful reformation" by turning the "rambling and disorganized labor" of previous years into "systematic and rational employment." With pride he noted the number of professions represented in the proceedings of the Anthropological Society and he appealed to all workers, even soldiers going to war zones, to collect items in their line.[16]

The goal of organized science was to coordinate disparate observations and distill generalizations. Mason approved heartily of local scientific societies as vehicles for joining the energies of many individuals with widely varying interests and a common desire to participate in science. Aside from the obvious social benefits, the presentation of a paper for criticism aided the author in grasping the subject.[17] More importantly, the voluntary society could guide local exploration that would otherwise be wasted. Just as Henry in the middle years of the century had looked to individuals like Increase Lapham for local scientific leadership and information in newly settled territories, Mason relied a few decades later on the young societies as "essential to a correct exploration of our entire country."[18] As in social, economic, and political affairs, in science all individuals were servants of one another, members in "a universal combine for mutual helpfulness."[19]

In 1873 Mason introduced culture history to Washington. Mason's principles of museum classification derived directly from the system of Gustav Klemm at the Museum of Ethnology in Leipzig. Walter Hough later observed that this "epochal synthesis" appeared at a "psychological moment" in the history of American anthropology; certainly the Klemm model did promise to give meaning and order for the first time to the Smithsonian's ethnology collections.[20] Klemm, like Mason, was concerned to replace local, partial collections with central repositories in order to facilitate comparative study. This was no simple matter of convenience, however. The only legitimate study of man, Klemm argued, was a composite history of human development through the familiar stages of savagery, barbarism, and enlightenment (or civilization). Beyond all "geographical, isothermal, chronological, tribal, linguistic and religious" divisions lay a single, continuous historical growth. This continuum was the ethnologist's proper, ultimate focus of study.[21] Klemm thus reformulated for students of material culture the beliefs in unity and teleological movement that, in various forms, had been staples of anthropological thought for more than a century.

At the same time, Klemm hastened to embrace the most recent teachings of natural science, and he incorporated into his "Kulturgeschichte" an important appreciation of physical environment. "Nature was the foundation of culture," Klemm and Mason agreed; man's dependence on nature and his progressive subjugation of it must both be recognized in a complete science of man. According to Klemm's prescription, the ethnologist must follow the lead of the naturalist and analyze his subject in all its geographical and developmental variety, then put all his observations together to present the larger historical picture. Nowhere were anthropology's distinct roots in natural science and moral philosophy more visible than in Klemm's attempt to combine the two traditions. In effect he presented to the ethnologist two functions, which he viewed as complementary: to examine minutely into the conditions of human need, creativity, and use in particular contexts; and to "study and seek to comprehend and exhibit the human race, in all its members, as a totality, in its origin, development, present condition, and future prospects, in all its tendencies and relations." The ethnologist must be naturalist first, philosopher second.[22]

Mason's career elaborated Klemm's theories. The central concept in Mason's version of culture history was invention. Man was the inventing or "artificializing" animal; ultimately, Mason wrote, the identity of the human species lay in this characteristic. Certain animals possessed inventive capacity in embryonic form, and some had possibly seen "the dawn of culture" in constructing habitations and storing food. To an extent they had begun the war on nature, but without fully awakened minds. But "the human animal has mastered all," Mason explained to Charles F. Lummis in 1906. "That is why I love, admire, and study him." Only restless, unsatisfied man translated needs into desires, then responded with inventions to fulfill them. Man's "superabundant brain" had always "held in trust the possibilities of the future, and stamped upon man the divine likeness."[23]

Mason defined invention broadly: as changes in materials and processes; as modifications in structure and function of artifacts; as changes in the inventor or society. The concept referred, in fact, not merely to mechanical devices but to cultural processes.[24] In the broadest sense, invention could be any series of actions toward some new end; social change might be defined, in fact, simply as a highly complex chain of inventions. In sum, the categories of invention encompassed all human activities. While Powell's Bureau of American Ethnology concentrated on language, religion, and folklore, Mason turned to the works of the hands for insight into the mind. The difference was one of approach, not purpose. "It has been the ruling thought of my life," he reflected in 1906, "that the people of the world have left their history most fully recorded in the works of their hands."[25] His "great idea," as he called it, was that "the true history of our race is written in things . . . the material expressions of the human mind." Culture history enabled the ethnologist to trace modern industries and institutions to their sources, to "put handles on stone implements, men and women into ancient ruins, and thoughts into empty crania."[26]

All people invented, but primitive man saw dimly and thought imperfectly. In his mind lay the germs of inventions that civilized man would elaborate more fully. Like most of his contemporaries, Mason saw the mind of primitive man as undeveloped, imperfect, and inefficient. This vision produced an ambivalent judgment in which such peoples received credit as human participants, but clearly inferior ones. Mason sought out and recognized early signs of aesthetic taste or ingenuity, and he insisted that those "in possession of our family records" deserved sympathetic understanding. But the "unbroken kinship of minds, savage and civilized, from first to last" did not imply equal valuation.[27] Among other distinctions, primitive man invented less spontaneously and playfully than his civilized brethren. Walter Hough explained:

> It is too easy to dream. The poets get weaving from the spider and fire from branches waving in the wind, but early man was not an Edison to seize the salient points of nature replete with what was to be. It is nearer to the earth to find that man got his knowledge of wood friction by a series of more or less conscious observations during a long period in working wood and vegetable fibres. This is conceived to have been a long process devoid of brilliant and analogical deductions, but advancing at times quite rapidly toward the goal.[28]

Mason and Hough, like Lewis Henry Morgan, were less interested in particular histories than in the "series of ever perfecting thoughts" for which the human mind was in fact no more than a constantly evolving agent of expression, and which had led man inexorably to a condition approaching "most nearly to the mind and life of the Creator."[29] On occasion Mason came close to bestowing divinity on nineteenth-century civilization. Fittingly, though, the exalted status was struggled for, the diadem had to be deserved.

Methodologically, continuity was critical. Like geology, a scientific an-

Walter J. Hoffman, posing as a Crow painter.

Frank Hamilton Cushing demonstrating pottery-making technique.

thropology could not admit discontinuities and cataclysms in the record. There were no wide gulfs between naturalism and the world of artifice, as shown by the fact that even in the nineties, "the crowning decade of the crowning century" (as Mason reflected on it), traces of "ancient ingenuity" still lingered among the civilized.[30] The continuous mental connection provided a one-way path to the primitive world, enabling the imaginative and dexterous ethnologist to relive, rethink, and reproduce the acts and artifacts of his untutored ancestors—in effect, to surpass the savage in his own pastimes. For Mason and his assistant Hough, meticulous attention to artifact structure and material was only the first, necessary step to rediscovery of the methods of manufacture. Mason's classic work on basketry exemplified the approach, but most of his shorter museum studies had the same purpose. For some— Frank Cushing comes to mind—the fascination with reproducing Indian life went a step further, to the dangerous presumption of showing skill by "improving upon" the aboriginal. Mason never went so far, but his logic was the same: a logic of superiority by virtue of evolutionary transcendence.

It is not difficult to see in Mason's insistence on continuity yet another instance of his debts to the natural sciences. In 1883 he referred to anthropology as "the application of the instrumentalities and methods of natural history to the study of man"; Franz Boas recognized a few years later that biological analogy was the "leading idea" in Mason's work.[31] In part this was a deliberate attempt to insure scientific respectability. "The older ethnologists," Mason recalled late in his life, "have had a struggle to get recognized as students of science," and so he took "a little grim comfort" in adopting acceptable terminology.[32] His attention to Klemm and long apprenticeship to Baird could only have confirmed the orientation.[33] "Culture history," he once proposed, "takes up the thread of human social groupings where biology drops it and traces its further weavings."[34] Like biological species, every tool, building, or garment had passed through a series of traceable transformations. For this reason Mason valued highly Hough's natural science training, and in his own "measuring, counting, and dissecting," Mason's first step with a specimen was to identify its geographic and ethnographic provenance, shape, structure, purpose, and unique properties, "just as a naturalist would [with] a plant or an animal . . ."[35] In the end, though, Mason's essential piety required that the implications of Darwinian biology, as he understood them, be closely restricted. The unfolding of culture, he insisted, was neither haphazard nor chaotic, but a gradual working out by human minds and hands, guided by "some pilot with his hand upon the helm in the industrial history of the globe . . . steering toward a light with which he was perfectly familiar."[36]

In establishing culture history in the Smithsonian's National Museum, Mason enjoyed the strong support of another young protégé of Spencer Baird, George

Brown Goode.[37] Like Mason, Goode came to the Smithsonian in the early
seventies. He organized and invigorated the new National Museum in the
eighties, and as assistant secretary of the Smithsonian under Baird and Samuel
Langley, he oversaw museum operations until his premature death, at forty-
five, in 1896. Scion of old-stock Virginians and New Englanders ("singularly
free from foreign mixture," Samuel Langley noted), Goode was born in 1851
in Indiana, received private tutoring as a boy, and at fifteen entered Wesleyan
College in Connecticut. After graduation he studied briefly under Louis
Agassiz at Harvard in 1870. The following year he met Baird, and the meeting
was the "turning point of his professional life." Baird immediately chose the
young man as his "chief pupil, his intimate friend, his confidential adviser,
and his assistant" in natural history. In 1873 Goode moved to Washington,
where he lived in the Smithsonian building with the Henry family and a
dozen other staff members. He never left.[38]

Apostle of scientific knowledge and public-spirited naturalist, Goode became an eloquent spokesman for the museum as a cultural instrument and index
of civilization. He shared Henry's concern over the low esteem of science in
America, but Goode blamed the scientists. They had become so involved in
their own pursuits that they had lost sight of the higher obligation of science to
the nation: to promote physical, mental, and moral welfare. In the United
States more than elsewhere it seemed critical that "accurate knowledge and a
scientific manner of thought" exist among the people. To George Goode,
science seemed destined to save the world. Through the unfolding of his
intellectual powers, man was gradually but surely approaching a God-like
destiny; and men of science above all had to assume the heavy responsibility, as
"the natural custodians of the treasured knowledge of the world," to share that
knowledge with the people.[39]

The ideal national museum, according to Goode, had three roles: to preserve
the "material foundations" of scientific knowledge; to encourage research; and
to educate the "popular mind."[40] Until 1876 the National Museum had
performed the first two and ignored the third, and Goode prepared to reor-
ganize it along educational lines. Whereas in the past museums had been the
private preserves of the fortunate few, limited in scope and interests, Goode
envisioned new functions. His "museum idea" foresaw a system of public
museums and libraries enriching the life of every community in the nation.
In democratic America these facilities would be adapted to "the needs of the
mechanic, the factory operator, the day-laborer, the salesman, and the clerk,
as much as to those of the professional man and the man of leisure." A network
of museums across the country would provide continuing adult education,
civilizing the masses and assuring America's front rank among the enlightened
nations of the world. It was an unabashedly patriotic and politically conservative endeavor, part of an effort to use museums, parks, and libraries as
"passionless reformers" with positive moral influence.[41]

Man in nature and society was the center of Goode's museums. The National

George Brown Goode, Samuel Langley, and Otis Tufton Mason installing Eastern Island images in the National Museum, 1888.

Museum, wrote one visitor of the early eighties, "takes man as its central pivot, and around this is to revolve everything that man has done in the past or in the present in the world he lives in."[42] But while the natural history departments presented little problem in exhibition technique, no satisfactory models existed among ethnological museums. Anthropology seemed to fall somewhere between science and art, a field not to be arranged according to either humanistic or strict natural science principles.[43] Ultimately Goode and Mason agreed upon a combination of methods for display: geographical, Klemm's developmental (also called synoptic or genetic), and according to materials. Looking to Leipzig and to the Pitt Rivers Museum of weaponry in Oxford, Goode and Mason organized their anthropology mainly along developmental lines, stressing the unity underlying apparent diversity of human phenomena throughout the world. Significant lessons could be taught, they believed, by placing all weapons, hats, boats, fire-making apparatus, or whatever, of all ages and all peoples, together in a single series in order to show the "natural history" of a particular idea from its earliest manifestations among primitive peoples to its fullest flowering among the advanced industrialized nations of the world. In Goode's words, "the series should begin with the simplest types and close with the most perfect and elaborate objects of the same class which human effort has produced."[44]

On July 1, 1884, after twelve years of unpaid service, Mason became curator of the Division of Ethnology in the reorganized National Museum. He had no idea how many specimens belonged to his division. In the first place, the Museum had recorded all ethnology and archaeology acquisitions together until 1881. The ethnology estimate had been 200,000 in 1882, but after personally examining the collections Mason revised it to 500,000. The figure was only a guess, but he started counting from there anyway.[45] Secondly, the boundaries between departments were unclear. Arts and industries was supposed to include "civilized" industries; ethnology contained the artifacts of "primitive" peoples. In practice the line was impossible to draw. On his first day as curator, Mason complained that his division received all the materials not wanted by Rau in archaeology or the curators of arts and industries; ethnology was squeezed between the prehistoric and the historic. For his part, Goode lamented that his arts and industries consisted of "all materials possessing anthropological significance, which are not elsewhere assigned." His heterogeneous collections were so intimately tied with ethnology, he confessed, "that it is impossible to make a definite division between them."[46]

Beginning with only one assistant, Mason worked steadily at the chaotic collections, but the huge backlog of uncataloged and unprepared materials prevented visible progress. In 1886 Walter Hough joined Mason, and the following year Lucien Turner came. But the ethnology force, never more than four or five, was severely hampered by the constant flow of new accessions, lack of space and funds, and the distractions of unending expositions. Some of the collections were in deplorable condition. "Between breakage and the moths," Mason told James C. Pilling, "things are fallen on evil times." Cushing's Zuñi materials were especially damaged and salvageable only by an expert, "such as Mr. Cushing himself."[47] In these circumstances volunteers provided a precious service. In every division the small salaried staff was supplemented by a corps of unpaid workers, students, military men, and collectors, assigned or invited to organize collections with which they had some familiarity. Furthermore, ties with other government bureaus continued to aid the curatorial staff in the 1880s. Half of the National Museum's twenty-seven curators and assistant curators in 1888 were detailed from the Geological Survey, the BAE, the Fish Commission, the Army, and the Navy.

Honorary curatorships (successor to Henry's resident collaborators) brought more help but also more collections. The Museum accepted private collections and in return made the donor an honorary curator or custodian for life, giving him access to the collections. Joseph D. McGuire was a case in point. McGuire, a local lawyer active in the Anthropological Society (and later in a semi-official capacity in the BAE as well), donated his archaeological collection and joined the Division of Prehistoric Anthropology. He received no salary but enjoyed "delightful standing and social attachment," stationery and mailing privileges, and an occasional opportunity to make money through lecturing or publishing—"in addition to his dignity."[48]

By 1900 all this was rapidly changing. The volunteer system flourished in the fluid milieu of a formative period, and that era was closing in the Museum. In 1897 Charles D. Walcott, succeeding Goode as Museum director, announced a new regime. The new director was astonished to discover that the Museum actually paid the salaries of only twenty-six of sixty-three scientific staff members. The system of unpaid workers had gone too far, Walcott thought; it lowered morale because volunteers were not sufficiently under the control of the regular staff. Worst of all, there were few young people in training to succeed senior officers.[49]

In the early years Mason needed all the help he could get, paid or gratis. He took every available moment for his own museum studies, which he considered preliminary to public display. Because he never went afield himself, Mason depended on the collections for his work, and they accordingly determined its focus and orientation. His first two museum studies, "Throwing-Sticks in the National Museum" and "Basket-Work of the North American Aborigines," both published in 1884, were intended as models for a monograph series to cover the collections of all primitive inventions. The articles mixed geographical and developmental approaches. On the basis of detailed examination of the structures of the throwing-sticks of the Arctic region, Mason distinguished thirteen regional types and attempted to correlate func-

Offices of the Department of Ethnology at the National Museum, c. 1890.

tions with structures. The study confirmed, he said, that the peoples of the Arctic were "driven" to modify this weapon with change of environment. But Mason also placed his artifacts on a developmental continuum, from the simple Anderson River model to the "most perfect" Norton Sound instrument, which appeared to incorporate all the features of the others.[50] The life histories of the Eskimo peoples, it appeared, were closely connected to the fauna of the region, for within the broad "generic similarities" of the Arctic, Mason found extreme differentiation in cultural phenomena. The study of basketry, which eventually grew into Mason's classic *Aboriginal American Basketry* (1902), exhibited his talent for studying the minutest techniques in the manual industry that he called "the savage art par excellence." Through detailed drawings of weaves and ornamentation and close attention to materials, shapes, structures, and presumed uses, Mason worked out typologies of form and technique. In many cases the types and terminology of his ethnological "comparative anatomy" are still considered useful.[51] In *American Basketry* he also outlined about a dozen regional varieties, defined by geography or tribe (depending on the precision and extent of Mason's collection).[52] As he continued his museum studies of primitive basketry, cradles, knives, bows and arrows, traps, and domestication of animals and plants, the unity theme gave way increasingly to the mystery of varieties and the influence of environment on their shaping.

The practical problem with ethnographic displays was lack of sufficient description for many of the Museum's older collections. When such "desultory" material did not portray the "total life history" of a tribe, the curator could best use it, Mason thought, in synoptic series illustrating the progress of the race, at least until the imperfect material could be "ennobled" with life and meaning by new artifacts from reliable sources. This the early BAE provided, along with firsthand observers to explain the functions of their pieces. Before 1880 the only regions of North America represented in the Museum in any depth were parts of the Northwest Coast and Alaska. The Bureau collections, reflecting Powell's interests and activities, came chiefly from three other regions: the Pueblos of the Southwest; the Southeast; and the Ohio Valley. In 1906 Hough estimated that the BAE had contributed a third of the Museum's ethnology, concentrated in these areas.[53]

Mason's first attempt at an "ethnic idea" in exhibits in 1886 involved Eskimo collections, which he had been studying for some time. The display was awkward. Mason tried to join rigid natural science categories with a dawning understanding of the fluidity and complexity of human phenomena. He set up a checkerboard arrangement of exhibits, dominated by the concept of the ethnographic region. While he defined fifteen regional or ethnographic areas, he cautioned that "it must be distinctly understood that these areas are wholly secondary to types and material." By walking along one axis of the checkerboard the visitor viewed a single cultural region in all its inventional variety; moving at right angles he could follow a single invention. Mason thought the educational advantages were obvious, for "with all the objects in the Eskimo collection being placed in their appropriate boxes," the visitor could easily learn that the people of a given area do or do not use a specific device.[54] The checkerboard plan had the merit of preserving at once the dignity and order that Goode insisted upon, the supposed rigor and clarity of natural science taxonomy, and the integrity of the ethnographic unit as Mason understood it. He hoped eventually to apply his scheme to other peoples and regions, and in 1888 he began serious work on his "ethnic series."[55]

Franz Boas first visited Mason's Eskimo collections in 1885, and he came away deeply disturbed.[56] Despite Goode's assurances that articles that belonged together "in a monographic way" would never be disturbed, Boas felt that the Museum's strongly developmental arrangements severely hampered study. In 1887 he addressed the issue in *Science.* The belief that connection exists between similar phenomena occurring among widely separated peoples, Boas began, lay at the heart of Mason's natural science model of ethnology. Mason offered three explanations for such similarities: migration of peoples; migration of inventions through passing contact; and the axiom (among Washington anthropologists) that like causes produce like effects, or that the human mind everywhere produces the same products "under the same stress and resources." To these principles, however, Boas added a fourth: unlike causes also produce like effects. Outside of a vague sense in which it could be said that all men act "suitably" to their environments, mental unity possessed no explanatory power because of the complexity of human mental processes. Occurrence of similar phenomena from unlike causes in fact appeared more likely to Boas.[57]

Boas's disagreements went deeper still. The attempt to classify human works into biological categories missed the whole point of post-Darwinian natural science. The focus of investigation should be the individual phenomenon "in its history and in its medium," not abstraction into a synthetic grouping determined by the special interests of the scientist. "By regarding a single phenomenon outside of its surroundings, outside of other inventions of the people to whom it belongs, and outside of other phenomena affecting that people and its productions," Boas lectured Mason, "we cannot understand its meaning." Mason's system taught only that man in different parts of the world has made similar inventions; it promoted no deeper understanding. The productions and individual styles of specific peoples must be studied as a whole—an impossible task when artifacts were distributed about the museum. "Classification is not explanation" in biology or ethnology, Boas concluded.[58]

From his established Washington post, Mason responded graciously to the young German immigrant. Dismissing the suggestion of unlike causes as ingenious but mistaken, he affirmed his commitment to the methods and instruments of biology as "an immovable foundation" for the science of man. Of course in ethnology as in biology there were "polyorganic units" that belonged together—the artifacts from a single burial mound, for example. But a museum curator drew on people with diverse interests in establishing his collections, and the exhibits had to reflect and appeal to those different minds.[59] The true value of synoptic exhibits, Mason later observed, lay in their appeal to unlearned men and women in all walks of life, who found "charming food for thought" therein.[60] Mason also took the opportunity to reaffirm the wisdom of his comparative approach, and he reminded Boas that every ethnologist going to study a specific people in depth should keep comparisons with other groups constantly in mind. In short, Mason conceded nothing.[61]

Boas again attempted to explain his position. The true nature of biological or ethnological phenomena lay in their full historical and social contexts, not in present appearances. In this light the tribal arrangement seemed to Boas the only useful system for museum study. "In ethnology," he remarked pointedly, "all is individuality." Taking aim squarely at Mason's entire structure, Boas confessed his deep conviction that the museum must demonstrate, through ethnically arranged exhibits, the all-important fact that "civilization is not something absolute, but that it is relative, and that our ideas and conceptions are true only so far as our civilization goes."[62]

At this point Mason turned to Powell for help. Powell's candid response included a surprising confession of ignorance. Addressing only the question of museum classification, the powerful head of Washington anthropology defended Mason's assumptions. Tribal organization in the museum was impossible because of the constant migrations, absorptions, and redivisions of the North American tribes through the historical period. Under modern conditions there were no stable, permanent tribal units to be represented, the Major argued. Nor could the archaeological artifacts of North America yet be safely assigned to specific tribes. But more than this, no classification of the peoples of North America could ever succeed. Physical anthropology had only established general varieties; all the work of the Bureau on language had provided only "imperfect" distinctions. Arts, institutions, opinions, religions, material products—these could be grouped, but not peoples. Powell did leave open the possibility of delineating "art regions" as potentially meaningful units, but the Bureau was only beginning to elaborate this concept in 1887. After nearly a decade in the Bureau, Powell had concluded that "there is no science of ethnology, for the attempt to classify mankind in groups has failed on every hand." "The unity of mankind," he answered Boas, "is the greatest induction of anthropology."[63]

The gap between Boas and the Washington scientists was unbridgeable in 1887. Mason and Powell stressed system and unity; Boas saw uniqueness and individuality. Though they all realized the potential of museums as educational facilities, Boas showed primary concern for the serious student of collections, while the Washington men served the mass public. But beyond this they differed on the very lessons to be taught: while Mason preached the unity of human cultural development in all its varieties, Boas was already implying cultural relativism and pluralism. The historicism and attention to cultures as complex, discrete phenomena that Boas urged seemed grossly unscientific to those who celebrated man's "ever increasing comprehensiveness," his ability to coordinate and systematize, as his "crowning glory."[64] And Boas's reproach to taxonomy would never impress a museum curator whose first thought after preparing a specimen was always "where to put it."[65] And yet over the next decade, as Mason approached the zenith of his influence in American anthropology, he began to focus on ethnographic regions, or culture areas, as he called them. Indeed, Mason had already begun to incorporate such schemes into his exhibits by 1887, as we have seen. His cultural history had always recognized regional variation in inventions as a problem for study. During the nineties, in response to a number of experiences and influences, he turned enthusiastically to ethnic "life-groups" as the central exhibit form for museum anthropology, supplanting the boring comparative cabinets of artifacts arranged row on row. But he did not do so singlehandedly. In order to grasp the complex background and the significance of this change in museum method, it is first necessary to consider the career of William Henry Holmes, the artist-anthropologist who designed and implemented the new life-group form in Washington.

William Henry Holmes (1846–1933) was an artist all his life. On his appointment at age seventy-five as the director of the National Gallery of Art, a student whom he had taught in his native Ohio a half-century before congratulated his former schoolmaster: "I have the feeling," he wrote, "that you have now reached the position for which nature intended you. For we always thought of our 'Teacher' as an artist."[66] The road to the National Gallery had been long and winding. It traversed geology, ethnology, and archaeology, and it passed through a series of prominent scientific institutions: the Hayden Survey, the National Museum, Chicago's Field Museum, and the Bureau of American Ethnology. But the meanderings and detours of Holmes's "lifetime devoted to science and art" nonetheless pointed finally in a single direction. The source of artistic creativity was the focus of Holmes's life. How do men define beauty? How do innate principles, social forces, or environmental factors combine to produce art as an individual and social phenomenon? These questions impelled and defined Holmes's anthropology, from the early surveys of the San Juan cliff-dwellers through the prolonged, bitter struggle over Paleolithic man in North America. Following Mason's prescription, Holmes probed the "anthropological aspect" of his own vocation; in so doing he inquired into the wellsprings of his own artistic soul.

Born in 1846, Holmes came to view himself as "an original predestined member of the [Smithsonian] family."[67] Fierce familial loyalty was not uncommon among the Institution's early scientific corps. But Holmes originally came to Washington in 1871 to study art, not science. At the art school of Theodore Kauffman he met Mary Henry, daughter of the Smithsonian Secretary, and in April he visited the Institution. While sketching a bird on this first visit, Holmes came to the attention of a visiting naturalist, and he soon found himself employed to draw fossil and mollusk shells for Fielding B. Meek and William H. Dall.[68] This led, in turn, the following year, to a position as artist on Ferdinand V. Hayden's U.S. Geological Survey of the Territories. Holmes remained with Hayden for six years as artist and geologist, exploring the Yellowstone region, the mountains of central Colorado, and the San Juan Valley in New Mexico and Arizona. During the 1875 season he took personal charge of the San Juan expedition; it was here, among the remains of the mysterious "cliff-dwellers" of the Southwest, that he first confronted the fascinations of North American archaeology.

Holmes's San Juan report (1876) gave early indications of his future style and emphasis in archaeology.[69] Like his pen-and-ink landscapes of the Colorado plateau country, that style was marked by precise observation, remarkable visual clarity, and close attention to form and process. Still, through the pages of the brief, fully illustrated report, Holmes's recently acquired geological sobriety contended with imaginative, romantic responses to the allures of the cliff-dwellers. For Holmes the 1870s were formative, unforgettable years of freedom and rapid growth; he loved the trans-Mississippi West. But emotion required restraint to yield scientific results. He fought that battle for years, resolving the issue only by harnessing his imagination to the service of a strongly inductive science. In 1876 he could barely control his wonder, and his struggle marks a significant personal milestone in the transition to a chastened, disciplined exploration of the Southwest. Approaching the ruins at Rio Mancos, Holmes found himself "led to wonder if they are not the ruins of some ancient castle, behind whose mouldering walls are hidden the dread secrets of a long-forgotten people; but a nearer approach quickly dispels such fancies, for the windows prove to be only the doorways to shallow and irregular apartments, hardly sufficiently commodious for a race of pygmies."[70] His journal reveals more explicitly that, just as they collected geological specimens, Holmes and his men sought precious archaeological booty. The result was an enterprise that combined serious observation, imaginative speculation, and something of the treasure hunt:

In one of the recesses and just by the side of the entrance-way, Dick (who was with me) came upon an object that made him shout with excitement and expectation. In scratching among the debris he came suddenly upon the top of a large earthen jar, tightly closed by a stone lid. 'Harry, I've got it' he cried, 'I have found it at last, here is their treasure. Here are the gold dubloons at last, buried in the wall. Ah! Ye don't believe it, just come and see.' Excitedly we cleared away the sand and raised the lid. The opening was deep and dark and to our chagrin, empty; only a little dirt, 'bah.' Well there must be others and they may be full. So to work we went and for an hour the dust flew and the loosened rocks rattled down the steep cliff and plunged into the deep gulches. Another large jar was brought to light, also empty of rubies and [of] gold dubloons and gorgeous trinkets there was not a sign. Besides large jars there was nothing but a bit of cane plaiting [,] fragments of what must have been very neat work. We left many of the rooms and recesses unexplored; for we had no implements and our fingers were already blistered.[71]

The public never saw Holmes's notebooks, but his San Juan report and W. H. Jackson's model of cliff-dwellings at the government exhibition in Philadelphia announced their discovery to the world. While he found neither gold nor rubies, Holmes came away from the canyon with something far more precious: an aroused imagination already pondering the secrets of America's human past:

From the top of the wall we looked out and down; there was the deep Canoma Valley. The cliffs above the trees slope below, and the winding thread of the Mancos in the green strip [at] the bottom. How secure; how impregnate [sic]; one man with loose rocks at his command could keep off the world. I had the feeling of being in an eagle's nest and was tempted to take wing and fly, but only screamed and then started at the perplexing echoes. We admired the skill with which these fortresses were built and the hardihood, and were amazed that such means of defense could have been conceived and carried out with the nearest water far below, and only these great jars to contain a supply. With their fields and flocks and the supply of water within the hands of an enemy . . . [they] must have perished or have crept down the cliffs to fight or yield to the foe. They are gone now indeed and have been for centuries and now like vandals we invade their homes and sack their cities. We, at least, carry off their earthen jars and reprimand them for not having left us more gold and jewels.[72]

Holmes's language in notebooks and final report is suggestive. That the "nearer approach" of clear-eyed science must supersede the distant visions of the romantic or the treasure-hunter would soon become an article of faith among government anthropologists. If science replaced the superior ancient races of earlier speculators with a race of physical or cultural "pygmies," if it forced attention from gold and rubies to the mundane treasures of ethnology—rush matting, stick bundles, potsherds—the adjustment was only a necessary step. Sober deflation prepared the ground for new standards of cultural evaluation.

As Holmes's San Juan report showed, the archaeology and ethnology of the Southwest, like the geology of the region, permitted and invited historical inquiry, and the area offered valuable clues to the processes of cultural change. The puzzle of relationships between past and present inhabitants confronted and fascinated every student of the Southwest, including Matilda and James Stevenson, Frank Cushing, John G. Bourke, Washington Matthews, Lewis H. Morgan, and Adolphe F. Bandelier. But in the context of Washington anthropology, ethnohistorical inquiry seemed to hold limited value. While it promised insight into past migration, contact, and affinity among specific peoples, scientific classification of mankind on the Morgan/Powell model required more permanent, universal standards and patterns than those provided by observing historical flux. To become a science, anthropology had to transcend history—so Powell believed. The problem permeated the Bureau of American Ethnology, but the resulting tension between developmental classification and attention to historical context seems to have been especially severe among students of the Southwest.

With the dissolution of the Hayden Survey in 1879, Holmes studied art in Europe for a year. On his return he joined Powell's Geological Survey, where he remained until 1889, when he moved over to the BAE. By then he had for several years been a museum anthropologist and a recognized expert on the evolution of decorative art. His studies of pottery of the eighties displayed the tension between historical questions and evolutionary classification. Specific intellectual influences are impossible to pinpoint, but it is apparent that by the early eighties Holmes had thoroughly absorbed the evolutionism of Morgan and Powell, and he framed his studies of primitive art accordingly. Holmes hoped to discover the origins of art: not particular historical precedents or influences on specific forms of cultural expression, but the general laws of aesthetic development. He explained change as development or growth, rejecting, in normal evidential circumstance, diffusion through borrowing or contact.[73] He firmly believed that degree of aesthetic progress, when correlated with like evidence from other fields of human activity, could serve as a reliable index of cultural status.

The debate over the origins of primitive art was widespread and prolonged in the second half of the nineteenth century. In the Washington context it took on special significance, for it touched on virtually all subfields of inquiry, from Cyrus Thomas's mounds survey to the issue that would embroil Holmes after 1889, the antiquity of man in North America.[74] Holmes emphasized technique and material as sources of decorative forms; he accordingly minimized the role of aesthetic ideas or simple spontaneity in the "early stages" of art. Geometric designs were originally suggested to the primitive artist by, for example, the imprint of a woven design on wet clay, or were transferred from one technical art to another, e.g., basketry to pottery. In explaining the appearance of ideographic forms, he hypothesized various series of stages— three stages for Pueblo pottery, a more complex series for Chiriqui work— moving, with mental and cultural growth, from purely nonideographic to pictorial designs. He also allowed for the possibility of degeneration from the higher delineative stage back into geometric design. In either case, Holmes agreed with Powell that such art forms had expressed tribal philosophy at a certain stage of development, and as such were useful in tracing the mental development of mankind. But a universal conjectural history, not specific tribal histories, was always Holmes's objective. As T.H.H. Thoreson has observed, "Holmes never contended that he was depicting the evolution of any particular design; his series were instead illustrative of what he called 'general tendencies' and 'general laws.' Empirical research was aimed toward filling in the gaps in the evolutionary sequence, while the only serious question (the core of the art question) lay in explaining how such a series did or could have come about."[75] In Holmes's words, "Investigations relating to the history of culture proceed on the theory that from the simplest possible beginnings in the manual arts advance was made until the highest round of the ladder was reached and that a study of the entire series must reveal the steps, the processes, and the laws of advancement."[76]

The emphasis on material and technique derived from the assumption that men in stages of savagery were highly vulnerable to the influences and suggestions of environment. Because they were more closely tied than barbarous or civilized peoples to their material world, there was little room for play, imagination, or free creativity in art or other activities. The life of primitive man as portrayed by Holmes and his colleagues was restricted and grim, to be sure. But more importantly, the vision led to a methodology that prescribed narrow treatment of artifacts. The approach might be called "reconstruction" or "reenactment" of the material conditions and techniques of invention. The first step in reconstruction, as described above, involved minute examination of artifacts to determine material and process of manufacture. Having analyzed the product, the anthropologist then proceeded to reenact the process (see illustrations of Hoffman and Cushing).

Reconstruction was the heart of Mason's museum work, and his best museum taxonomies, notably his work on North American basketry, emerged from this method. Hough, Hoffman, Cushing, and Holmes shared the basic assumption, which emerged in various forms in their work. On the positive side, the method produced the delineation of areal types that would eventuate in Mason's concept of culture areas. At the same time, though, it is clear that the men in the National Museum were "playing Indian" in a presumptuous manner. The danger and limitation in the method lay in assuming that demonstration of supposed conditions and techniques of invention constitutes a sufficient anthropology; that knowledge of structure or technical process is, in fact, knowledge of invention or creativity. But the Washington men saw only driven savages, not independently creative agents, in primitive art.

In two unpublished papers toward the end of his life, Holmes set forth his views on the evolution of aesthetics. He distinguished between two fundamental drives (exigencies of survival, desire for betterment) and the "major factors" in cultural advancement: religious beliefs and "the struggle for advantage through the increase of personal attractiveness." In early stages, he still believed, "religion has been a chief factor in shaping and advancing culture"; throughout North American aboriginal life the anthropologist finds that "every beautiful article is there because religion demanded it." Only in later stages does love of beauty emerge as a major creative factor: "In early art development the dynamic force was religion, but clinging to it, like a slender vine, was the esthetic impulse—the love of beauty for its own sake."[77]

Beneath Holmes's malleable personal exterior lay a set of rock-hard convictions about the progressive evolution of art—from geometric, nonideographic to delineative forms, from motives of religious superstition to refined sense of beauty, from imitation to spontaneity—that remained rigid and undisturbed for fifty years. (Not surprisingly, he held very conservative views of painting. A great admirer of Thomas Moran, he once noted that Moran's panorama of the Grand Canyon would someday be fully recognized, after "the lunacy of impressionism" had passed, as the greatest landscape in American painting.)[78] Having established as much, Holmes gave his attention only to the conditioning elements—physical environment and materials—that determined the rate of cultural progress and shaped specific styles. It is in this context that development of his museum life-groups in the 1890s must be understood.

Holmes's pottery studies made him central to Powell's organization of anthropology, but he achieved wide recognition in scientific circles as a result of his role in the debate over North American Paleolithic man during the 1890s.[79] To this bitter wrangle, which embroiled the major anthropological institutions of Boston and Washington in a test of scientific respectability, Holmes contributed a simple notion that rapidly achieved the status of scientific proof. The insight derived directly from the "reenactment" method of the Washington men. In accord with the growing orthodoxy among government investigators, Holmes rejected the effort to establish New World archaeological periods of technology to parallel those of western Europe. He thus began by assuming that Paleolithic man had never existed in North America, thereby placing the burden of proof on the proponents. Faced with

A realistic lay-figure group set up along Piney Branch in
Washington, D.C., by W. H. Holmes.

W. H. Holmes in "an ocean of paleoliths," which he demonstrated
to be "refuse of Indian implement making."

claims by Charles C. Abbott, George F. Wright, and others, from 1872 onward, of Paleolithic finds in the glacial gravels of New Jersey, in Minnesota, and elsewhere, Holmes in 1889 took to the field himself. At the Piney Branch site on Rock Creek, just outside the capital city, Holmes discovered a quarry site with thousands of "paleoliths" strewn over the ground. Reconstructing the scene in his mind and experimenting with the rude stone implements and products himself, he realized that the so-called paleoliths were the unfinished products and rejects of the primitive manufacturing process. In his published articles he not only presented the theory but demonstrated the step-by-step manufacturing process and the products at each stage.

For men who despised mystery and lauded simple, common-sense explanations, Holmes's breakthrough established him fully. Clarence Dutton, with whom he had worked in the early Geological Survey, spoke for his Washington admirers: "I have just been reading your article in 'Science' of Nov. 25th, on Modern Quarry Refuse and the Paleolithic Theory. It strikes me as about the most level headed article in the anthropologic 'racket' I have seen for many a year. Your simple statement of the facts is such as to carry conviction with it by the sheer force of good sense and to resist it looks like 'biting a file.' I wonder I never thought of that view of the situation before. We always do wonder when a simple sensible explanation comes forward to take the place of a complex overloaded hypothesis [,] and no better evidence is wanted of the strength of a hypothesis than its perfect simplicity and naturalness."[80] Over the years Holmes marshalled additional criteria for challenging every claim for Paleolithic man—uprooted trees, mud slides, the integrity of the investigator—but his simple demonstration and reconstruction at Piney Branch established his reputation as a man of scientific caution and perception.

Holmes was indeed formidable by the early nineties. His published reviews of Paleolithic finds were masterpieces of cautious, apparently open-minded treatment that nonetheless systematically destroyed every claim. Drawing on accepted geological and archaeological practice, he excused ignorant, misled discoverers while unmercifully castigating his serious opponents, such as George Wright and Charles Abbott. His paper on "Primitive Man in the Delaware Valley," read at the meetings of the American Association for the Advancement of Science and published in *Science* in 1897, demonstrates his style and tactics.[81] Granting that "pioneer investigators [are] struggling through a difficult period of inquiry," Holmes put forward the maxim of uniformitarian geology that the first step in knowing the past is understanding the present. He observed that the historic peoples of the Delaware Valley, the Algonkian stock, were Neolithic peoples who produced among their stoneware many unfinished objects. These could have intruded below the surface into "glacial gravels" through a variety of natural and human means:

"Every bank that crumbled, every grave dug, every palisade planted, every burrow made, every root that penetrated and every storm that raged took part in the work of intermingling and burial . . ." The student must consider these processes of past and present before "conjuring up shadowy images of other races." Blind adherence to European theories of a "uniform race on both sides of the Atlantic" and a desire to "establish a peculiar theoretic culture for America," as well as excessive attention to similarities of form, had interfered with respectable archaeological practice. But now, Holmes concluded, "It may be regarded as substantially proved that the glacial gravels proper contain no relics of art, and it would appear that now very few persons, indeed, expect them to yield any evidence whatever on the subject of human occupation."[82] The verdict was premature, but Holmes's reputation became firmly established in the process.

Holmes's museum orientation grew in part from such scientific debate. The antiquity issue impressed upon him again the importance of re-creating the conditions and techniques of invention and art. At the same time he was quick to recognize the desirable effects of drama, plot, action, and emotional involvement in the life-group approach to popular museum anthropology. Reflecting perhaps the growing influence of photography in anthropological field work at the time, Holmes's displays were intended as snapshots of primitive life long vanished.

The Smithsonian had experimented with life-size wax figures from the early seventies, and the government displays at Philadelphia had included figures of Swedish peasants, but the approach was still decidedly subordinate to the extensive showcases of primitive implements arranged by Rau and Mason. The Louisville and New Orleans fairs of 1884 and 1885 for the first time made serious attempts to portray specific peoples in an environmental situation. These exhibits showed the social life and industries of the Alaskan and Eskimo groups (at the time the strongest regional collections in the Museum). But the "ethnic series" still shared space with archaeological artifacts and models of American ship-building.

Chicago marked the critical change in technique and arrangement. Under Holmes's direction, the Smithsonian exhibits displayed an impressive number of life-size, realistic groups of North American aborigines working in pristine, pre-Columbian surroundings. The theme was environment, but the new element was the group, and the concept changed the displays from pieces of sculpture to "pictures from life." In a professionally important departure, ethnologists Cushing, Mooney, and Hoffman, along with Holmes, supervised the construction of the exhibits personally, contributing their invaluable direct field experiences. Though the lay groups would not supplant the more traditional showcases, Goode assured himself, they did possess certain limited and valuable functions. His only concern was to maintain "dignified, systematic order" in the exhibits.[83]

After Chicago virtually every government anthropology exhibit featured primitive peoples working and playing in appropriately naturalistic environments. At Nashville, people learned about the strong contrasts between Eskimo and Pueblo surroundings and life styles, and also saw a Kiowa camping circle. The Pan-American Exposition of 1901 displayed twelve groups of aboriginal folks of the entire Western hemisphere (along with thirteen series of inventions). At the St. Louis Exposition in 1904, W J McGee, outdoing them all, imported half-a-dozen groups of live "savages" from all over the world to set up housekeeping on fair grounds in the middle of America.[84]

Otis Mason never joined the debate over Paleolithic man, but between 1887 and 1896 logic and personal experience also pushed him steadily toward ethnographic exhibit techniques. Two events were particularly formative: his tour of European museums in 1889 and the publication of Powell's linguistic map and classification in 1891. The immediate purposes of the European tour were to study museum methods and to attend the Paris Exposition, but for Mason the journey answered the prayers of a lifetime. At Paris he reveled in meeting the great European savants of his day: Adolphe B. Meyer, Sir John Evans, Adolf Bastian, and Paul Broca. Meyer, director of the Dresden Museum of Zoology and Anthropology, so impressed the American visitor that he wanted to "grapple him to [his] soul with hooks of steel." Alfred H. Keane, his host in London, Mason considered a "great godsend" to anthropology as well as "the jolliest Englishman I ever saw . . ." The whole experience humbled Mason. "How my heart rejoices when I see the men whose thoughts have moved the world," he confided to his wife. "I ought to have taken this trip thirty years ago. My intellectual life has been in a bag."[85]

Exhibits even more than intellects overwhelmed him. In the Pitt Rivers collections at Oxford, Mason studied the developmental scheme, "the only one in which every piece has a raison d'être." Unlike the British Museum, where "they have a pen for each country and when they get a new specimen they turn it into the pen," at Oxford every specimen had its place. At the Musée Guimet in Paris and with Meyer in Dresden, Mason received further confirmation of his own methods, but he also began to appreciate ethnographic approaches. The British Museum's Polynesian collection, Mason reported, "made my mouth water"; and at the India Museum he was struck with the wax figures of working groups.[86]

Paris was a revelation. The entire exposition, which he thought the "most thoroughly anthropological" to that time, taught the history of human culture by means of models of habitations and working scenes displayed along the Seine. Mason reported enthusiastically on the twelve African villages with real villagers and the Tonkinese temple with Buddhist priests performing rites. The crowds thronged like children to the working scenes. Although the French showed "no caution" in displaying anthropological science in such groups, Mason had to admit their popular success. "It was an exposition," he wrote home, "whose presiding Genius was a teacher, a professor of history, whose scholars were the whole world."[87]

Mason returned convinced that "all that Europe will ever know of [the American Indian] will be what we tell her."[88] With this thought and renewed energy he began preparing the government exhibits for the Chicago World's Fair. Here he saw an opportunity to display fifty years of North American anthropology by the Smithsonian and government agencies.[89] Powell's map, the culmination of that work opportunely published in 1891, furnished the stimulus and organizing principle for his efforts. Mason's goal at Chicago was to honor Powell, the map, and American anthropology.[90] The linguistic map, Mason thought, focused the critical questions of American anthropology in 1893: To what extent does language coordinate with industries and other activities as a sign of kinship or race? What are the effects of climate and natural resources on arts and industries? He attempted to elucidate these problems by hanging an enlarged copy of the map (sixteen by twelve feet) in the center of his Chicago exhibits. Of Powell's fifty-seven stocks Mason chose sixteen "great families" and arranged the costumes and arts of each group in separate alcoves. He hoped thereby to present a "practical solution" to the central question of the connection between race, language, material culture, and systems of thought.[91]

In Chicago, Mason first expressed unambiguously an awareness of the complexity of cultural phenomena, particularly of the role of the physical environment in influencing cultural behavior. Environment promised to explain the vast diversity of human activities and social systems that the researches of the 1880s had unexpectedly discovered in North America. By 1893, BAE ethnologists had already begun to learn at firsthand of the "intimate connection between the practical activities of the people, their artistic productions, their philosophies, and their myths."[92] Consequently the analyses of phenomena into classes of activities that had organized research in 1879 were steadily yielding to a deepening sense of complexity and interdependence—and much confusion. The physical environment, stressed by Gibbs in the 1860s and by Boas again in 1887, became a critical tool that explained ethnographic diversity, gave coherence to the various activities common to an ethnic or regional unit (or in Mason's scheme at Chicago, a linguistic unit), and yet preserved the presumed racial and cultural unity of aboriginal North America.

Mason presented his case for environment at the International Congress of Anthropology during the Exposition. It was now clear, he argued, that the American aborigines were "practically" a single race, dispersed in the pre-contact era into many culture areas, which had developed hundreds of separate languages, social systems, mythologies, and philosophies. Each human product, as Mason analyzed it, contained "an element of intellectuality and an element of materiality," something of the people and something of the environment. This was as true of language and religions as of pottery and clothing, for just as ideas inhered in the works of the hands, so "there is solid material with the intellectual culture concepts . . ." Beliefs no less than arrows were influenced by environment. The distinctive features of all human products could only be understood in terms of the "patronage and directorship of the region."[93] In the spirit of the Congress of 1893, the slogan of which was "Men Not Things," Mason seemed to be moving slowly from his earlier concern with materials to environments, from the study of man to studying men, from culture to distinct cultures.

The following year Mason elaborated his culture-area concept further in his presidential address to the Anthropological Society of Washington. Drawing liberally on the earlier geographical and environmental studies of Karl Ritter, Arnold Guyot, and George P. Marsh, Mason turned from his preoccupation with man's conquest of nature to view human activities as shaped and modified by the forces of the earth. Taken as a whole, the earth, he said, was the mother of all men, the storehouse of material resources, the reservoir of tremendous potential forces, and man's first teacher. But the earth consisted of many "great isolated parts or patches," which Aristotle had called *Oikoumenai,* Adolf Bastian labeled geographical provinces, and Mason termed inventional or culture areas. Each region possessed a unique set of conditions shaping a certain kind of human life. Despite the mixings and migrations of North American aborigines in historical times, Mason felt certain that many of these separate culture areas could still be traced. Since distinct zoological and botanical regions produced distinct arts, the anthropologist encountering a people with unique industries must search the region for the resources that "endowed and patronized" those arts.[94]

Mason then outlined in greater detail eighteen culture areas of the Western Hemisphere, but with one significant addition: he reminded his audience that the emphasis on environment should not obscure the crucial fact that human ingenuity produced all art, for which environment provided only the occasion, the mold.[95] Furthermore, Mason was careful to point out that the establishment of ethnic units belonged to the "centrifugal period" of human history, during which small groups of men had spun out from major centers to develop their own cultural patterns in various degrees of isolation from one another. (Powell's vision of linguistic differentiation was analogous.) Mason went on to postulate a second, centripetal stage of industrial history, well under way in the 1890s, in which all men moved gradually from discrete, independent cultural units to an all-embracing world community, a single cosmopolitan cultural area. Already man had replaced the natural cultural regions of many parts of the world with his own artificial political boundaries. Eventually these unnatural boundaries would be swept away, too, and all arts and industries developed in isolation would mingle and blend into "the proper flow of true culture." As Mason saw the future, "non-progressive races [would be] extinguished or driven to the suburbs, the play of worldwide action left unincumbered [*sic*], the flow of world-embracing commerce unimpeded, and every desire of man will be gratified."[96]

In evaluating the development of an ethnographic and environmental orientation in the life-group exhibits of the National Museum, it is useful to recall Boas's axiom: unlike causes often produce like effects. Boas's arguments had probably convinced nobody in Washington in 1887. The new exhibit style derived not from Boasian philosophy but from currents within the Washington anthropological community, including sensitivity to positive public response. What did Goode, Mason, and Holmes intend to teach the public with the new techniques? Essentially the same lessons of the earlier taxonomic exhibits: the fundamental unity beneath the diversity of human experience, a unity demonstrated in man's psychic activity—his inventions— and a unity to be achieved finally in the approaching coalescence into a single racial, linguistic, and cultural community. Beginning as one, man would end as one. Nothing less could instill the public piety toward man's Creator and the belief in American destiny that were their ultimate concerns. Although Mason to some extent transcended the bald evolutionism of the Klemm model of "Kulturgeschichte," the life-group orientation that he and Holmes pioneered in Washington served rather than questioned the superiority of Victorian American culture. As Frederick W. Putnam learned in Chicago in the nineties, there was always a strong element of the midway and the sideshow in exposition anthropology, even with the highest scientific intentions.[97] The need to attract and entertain in order to educate the American populace decisively influenced museum anthropology. One historian has remarked that "without the proper control of scholarly texts subject to 'professional' standards, an exhibit could in fact feed the taste for racist exoticism that it was meant to curb."[98] But even with such controls the outcome would have been uncertain. Visitors might discover Mason's "charming food for thought," but they would hardly rise to Boas's central insight that "civilization is not something absolute, but . . . is relative, and . . . our ideas and conceptions are true only so far as our civilization goes."

Mason and Holmes freely admitted that "there are two ways to study a large museum, both excellent and each necessary to the full development of the other: one is ethnical, the other technical."[99] But here the similarity with Boas ended. Boas was steadily building in these years toward a concept of cultures as historical, accidental accretions, at the same time approaching the principle of divorce between race and culture that his immigrant head-form studies and subsequent work would confirm. The Washington museum men were moving in the opposite direction; or perhaps had stopped moving. In the nineties they embraced environmental concepts and exhibition techniques essentially to explain and apologize for the underdevelopment of most peoples of the world. Still seeking the unity of their science and of man in the face of an explosion of new observations and data, they celebrated variety in order to contain it and ultimately deny its import. Thus Holmes in 1903 explained recent developments in anthropology: "It is customary with anthropologists to regard the physical and cultural phenomena as constituting a single unit, *the correlation between race and culture being intimate and vital*, and it is a cherished idea to present this unit with the completeness and effectiveness that its importance warrants."[100] It is abundantly clear that Holmes's environmentalism supplemented and modified but never supplanted strong categories of race and evolution. The moral lesson could not help but emerge clearly in exhibits as well as writings, and it must have come through to the museum-going public:

> In the inevitable course of human history the individual races will probably fade out and disappear, and the world will be filled to overflowing with a generalized race in which the dominating blood will be that of the race that today has the strongest claim, physically and intellectually, to take possession of all the resources of the land and sea. The resultant race will not have of the native American blood even this one three-hundredth part, because they are decadent as a result of conditions imposed by civilization. As diagrammed by the ethnologist of the far future the career of the Indian will appear as a lenticular figure—beginning in nothing, ending in nothing—a figure of perhaps universal application by the historian of mundane things.[101]

In 1898 Mason suffered a stroke that paralyzed his right side and forced him into semiretirement. He continued in the Museum, but his public and social life otherwise stopped. For six years he attended no meeting of the Anthropological Society, and it was nine years before Hough read Mason's "Comparison of Malaysian and American Indian Basketwork" before the Society that he had cofounded twenty-eight years before. Further tragedy befell the aging curator with the deaths of his wife and, in 1904, of one of his three daughters. The latter event broke up his house in Washington, and he distributed his large anthropological library to the Smithsonian and elsewhere. His fragile health forced him to spend several weeks of each year recuperating from fatigue and conserving his remaining strength at a seminary, a sanitarium, or at the home of a surviving daughter.[102]

With characteristic optimism and enthusiasm, however, Mason persevered. Practicing a "rhythmic life," he immersed himself more than ever in his work. Unable to use his right hand for more than a few minutes at a time, he taught himself to write with his left to the beating of a clock. He arose regularly at four in the morning to write, and except for rest periods away from Washington he rarely missed a day at the Museum. [103] During the last years of his life, Mason closely regulated his extra-official life in order to give all his strength to his job at the Museum. It kept him busy. In 1902 Langley asked Mason to serve as acting head curator of the Department of Anthropology as well as curator of ethnology. [104] Despite doubts about his strength, Mason agreed; in May 1905, he became permanent head curator, retaining his divisional position. He kept both jobs until his death in 1908.

In the last decade of his life Mason abandoned North American anthropology for the greener fields of East Asia. In moving beyond the continental boundaries of the Western Hemisphere, he conformed to larger tendencies in the Museum, the BAE, and government science generally in the first decade of the new century. The American war in the Pacific and Caribbean opened the eyes of government scientists to the rich fields of exploration in these areas, and the Russo-Japanese War of 1904 focused attention on Northeast Asia as a territory promising rich harvests for science. [105] These themes all appeared in Mason's work at the time. He reminded Smithsonian officials of the possibilities for ethnology and physical anthropology in the Panama Canal work, in archaeological finds and the mixture of races among the workers. [106] The war in Manchuria inspired him to explain Japanese and Russian expansionism in terms of biology rather than politics. Although his effort here was a mélange of cultural, racial, and linguistic evidence, it represented a sincere attempt to apply anthropology to a current problem. He encouraged Americans sojourning in this "meeting-ground of the two great ruling types of mankind in Asia" to collect for the Museum. [107] The eastern Mediterranean, the "backbone of Asia" and Mason's original focus of study, caught his attention once again after thirty years. He also became interested in the question of ancient migration routes across the Pacific. [108]

But his heart, he told George Grant MacCurdy in 1907, was "now in Malaysia, with my proto-Americans." [109] Mason's new fascination with Southeast Asia grew from the collections that arrived regularly from world traveler William L. Abbott. Independently wealthy and violently allergic to civilization, Abbott had been combing the islands of southern Asia, as well as central Asia and the east coast of Africa, since 1890. His collecting ventures on the *Terrapin* lasted for months at a time, and on his brief returns to Singapore he shipped tons of materials to Washington. Until 1903 these consisted chiefly of natural history collections, but over the next five years he sent Mason large ethnological shipments.

The two men enjoyed a mutually satisfying relationship reminiscent of early Smithsonian days. Mason, never a field man and now confined to his office, took deep, vicarious pleasure and excitement in Abbott's adventures. North America was becoming too crowded with young, enthusiastic investigators anyway, and the old man welcomed the opportunity to explore virgin fields: "A lot of young men, God bless them, are rummaging the Western Hemisphere for ethnic fame," he wrote Abbott. "If I can quietly steal aboard the *Terrapin* in spirit and let them rage, that will suit my 72 pulse better. I would follow you anywhere," Mason offered, "but give me a night to think it over."[110]

Abbott loathed civilization as much as Mason rejoiced in it. "I never feel as if life were worth living in Europe," he wrote to Hough, "until the scorching wind from the desert strikes the ship in the Red Sea, east bound." Abbott delayed as long as possible returning from his "happy land" to the bad air and overheated houses of America and England. Even twenty-five days in "rotten" Singapore, with its hotels full of American women with shrill "catlike drawls," left him feverish and "crazy to get away and smell the water and the coral beaches again." After so many years in the East, the West seemed strange to him, and he avoided contact with any people, "black, white, or brown, except the jungle people or wild tribes."[111]

Abbott was a collector who "worked" his region, not an ethnographer. He considered himself a poor observer of men, and he refused to write up his travels or permit Mason to discuss them in describing the collections.[112] The ethnographical map of Southeast Asia showed thousands of isolated cul-de-sacs with little apparent intermixture. Abbott and Mason agreed that a mere passerby could not make scientific comments on ethnology. Abbott estimated that ten years' work would be required for a "decently thorough" investigation, and he had neither the time nor patience for it. Like Mason, he preferred to move on to untapped and untouched regions. The long fingers of Western culture were reaching, via Singapore, to even the remotest peoples. Abbott was determined to get to them first.

On the basis of Abbott's work, Mason became convinced that the indigenous "brown race" of southern Asia represented a stage of industrial development midway between the savages of North America and the early civilized societies of the West. The basketry and other arts indicated in complexity and refinement a high stage of manual industry, beyond those of aboriginal America. In every art and industry, Abbott's gifts seemed to fill gaping holes in Mason's culture history. Still, Mason recognized among the Malaysian pieces some specimens "touching the very bottom of primitive culture."[113] He halfheartedly pursued the idea of a Malaysian source for American Indians, or perhaps a common source for both peoples; at other times he wondered if Captain James Cook had introduced certain arts to the region. But Mason reached no firm answers, and published only a detailed examination and glossary of Malaysian basketry. *The Vocabulary of Malaysian Basketwork,* issued in 1908 on the day of his funeral, was impressively detailed and lavishly illustrated, like Mason's *Aboriginal American Basketry* four years previously. But once again Mason lost himself in the details of specimens.[114]

The significance of Mason's infatuation with Abbott and Malaysia lies in the fact that after thirty years he turned his back on American anthropology and on the promising concept of cultural areas. Mason was bored and dissatisfied with North American work. Boas had analyzed the reason back in 1887, when he observed that the historical scientist or cosmographer absorbed himself intently in the phenomena of a region, while the impatient, law-formulating scientist constantly extended the range of his study over new areas.[115] Mason fitted the latter description precisely. In 1904, encouraging Jesse Fewkes to pursue a thorough ethnological research of the Caribbean, Mason remarked revealingly that the region would open "a new and rich field as a relief from the overthrashed straw of our own native tribes."[116] Mason was suffering from intellectual malaise. The experience and reflections of his first ten years as curator had borne fruit in more sophisticated concepts of culture areas superimposed upon a strong sense of cultural development. But here Mason had stopped.

Perhaps it was the stroke; or perhaps the powerful impact of political and military events diverted him. More likely, though, Mason set his own limits. Recognition of the shaping influence of environment collided with Mason's deep convictions of man's God-like, independent creativity. Mason's college training in the certitudes of Scottish moral philosophy warred constantly with the evolutionary naturalism dominant in America in his mature years. The result was tension between undeniable environmental influence on the vast array of human products, on the one hand, and Mason's strongly teleological notion of human unity, on the other. Most of the Washington anthropologists shared the dilemma. Mason's compromise was a constant search for specimens and data to fill up the rows of boxes that constituted his vision of human culture. Having begun his career in anthropology relying on constant acquisition of new material, after 1900 he turned with relief to fresh fields and vast raw materials, leaving America to younger scholars. His exhausting scientific pilgrimage was over.

The anthropology that Goode, Mason, and Holmes established in the National Museum in the last quarter of the century answered deep artistic and religious needs. Goode carried forward in his museum Joseph Henry's profound commitment to public moral education, although in the process he helped drive the Museum permanently into the very political dependence that Henry had so feared. Holmes and Mason devised the exhibit form for the lessons of that education. For Holmes the development of life-group exhibits provided an outlet for strong artistic and imaginative drives, at the same time permitting demonstration of the life of the primitive artist and inventor. The stress on naturalistic setting, material environment, and, in most cases, the immediate family as the relevant social group, fitted the purposes of men who as scientists recognized the varieties of human life, past and present, but who as moralists of their age insisted on original unity, purpose, and progress in history, and at least the reflection of divinity in man. They adopted the rhetoric of evolutionary naturalism, but their purposes were deeply pious.

In the beginning, Mason wrote in a poem of his youth, the Angel of Beauty had created the world and the soul of man in intimate compatibility. At first there had been only a "shadowy forecast" of God's purpose. When He spoke, "each material and ethereal thing/Became a word; the form articulate/Of his intention and predestining." Mason never deserted that vision of God's design, and he carried his own natural theology over into a secular, scientific twentieth century. To those in the industrial age who claimed that science had eclipsed art, that great aesthetic triumphs belonged to the past, the men of the National Museum responded with a strong affirmation of the indissoluble link between science and art, and of man's undying, God-implanted love of beauty:

Take knowledge, culture, every hot desire;
Give us of soul-stirred sorrow no surcease;
Try us till tried in the refining fire,
But give, oh! give us Beauty's smiling face. [117]

Notes

1. The general orientation presented here owes debts to Robert H. Wiebe, *The Search for Order, 1877–1920* (New York, 1967); Paul F. Boller, Jr., *American Thought in Transition: The Impact of Evolutionary Naturalism, 1865–1900* (Chicago, 1969); and Paul A. Carter, *The Spiritual Crisis of the Gilded Age* (DeKalb, 1971).

2. On American museum anthropology between 1860 and 1920, see Donald Collier and Harry Tschopik, Jr., "The Role of Museums in American Anthropology," *American Anthropologist* 56 (1954): 768–79; William C. Sturtevant, "Does Anthropology Need Museums?" *Proceedings of the Biological Society of Washington* 82 (1969): 619–50. I am grateful to Ira Jacknis for permission to consult his unpublished study, "Franz Boas and Museums of Anthropology in America, 1880–1920," which has influenced my analysis.

3. Henry Adams, *The Education of Henry Adams: An Autobiography* (Boston, 1961), pp. 338, 343–45.

4. Otis T. Mason, "What is Anthropology?" (Washington, D.C., 1883), p. 5.

5. For Mason's early years, see Walter Hough, "Otis Tufton Mason," *American Anthropologist* 10 (1908): 661–67; Mason to William J. Rhees, 1 November 1904, Rhees Papers, Huntington Library; Mason to Charles Hallock, 28 July 1899, in Hallock, "Smithsonian Gleanings: Scientific Work and Professional Correspondence, 1860 to 1912," SIL Manuscripts; Mason to Sallie Mason (daughter), 27 September 1889, in "Letters from Europe," SIA.

6. For Mason's career at Columbia, see Elmer Louis Kayser, "Columbian Academy, 1821–1897: The Preparatory Department of Columbian College in the District of Columbia," *Records of the Columbia Historical Society* (1971), pp. 150–63. See also the catalogs of Columbian College (after 1873, Columbian University) and the catalogs and prospectuses of Columbian College Preparatory School, 1861–84, in George Washington University *Bulletins*, GWU Archives. Quotation from GWU *Bulletin* 51 (1871): 45. The Corcoran prospectus appears in *Bulletin* 64 (1884). As early as 1873, the new university had planned to include in its new school of sciences a course in "Ethnology, Archaeology, and Anthropology." In 1884, the catalog listed a course in anthropology for the first term of the fourth year, but there is no evidence that the course was ever offered, or that Mason taught anthropology at Columbian.

7. USNM, *AR for 1909*, p. 62; Mason to Dr. Willis Moore, 18 February 1906, Mason Papers, NAA.

8. The story of Mason's conversion to American studies appears in T.D.A. Cockerell, "Spencer Fullerton Baird," *Popular Science Monthly* 68 (1906): 79–80. Mason made frequent reference to this critical meeting, usually assigning it to the early 1870s. See also Mason to G. T. Emmons, 9 May 1908, Mason Papers, NAA.

9. USNM, *AR for 1902*, p. 32. The statement comes from Mason's "autobiography," according to this necrology. I have been unable to find any trace of an autobiography, or any reference to it in Mason's papers.

10. Hough, "Otis Tufton Mason," p. 663; Mason to Baird, 26 August 1874; Baird to Mason, 14 July and 23 July 1874; Mason to Baird, 31 July 1874 and 18 July 1878, SIA. Although Baird took a personal interest in the ethnological collections, he apparently made little headway in classification. He reported in 1874 that the Institution had distributed 2,069 ethnological specimens, of 1,950 different "species."

11. Mason to John G. Henderson, 8 June 1907; Mason to F. W. Hodge, 31 January 1907, Hodge-Cushing Papers, Southwest Museum, Los Angeles.

12. Some of the original letters, with Mason's editorial comments, are in NAA (Series 2431, Archeology); Baird to Leslie Bessett, 22 July 1878, SIA.

13. O. T. Mason, "The Scope and Value of Anthropological Studies," *Proceedings of the American Association for the Advancement of Science* (1883), pp. 370, 378–79.

14. Mason, "What is Anthropology?" pp. 3–4, 13, 20.

15. Mason to W. F. Sands, 7 October 1905; Mason to Arthur P. Rice, 18 May 1906, NAA.

16. Mason, "What is Anthropology?" p. 5; "Scope and Value," pp. 376, 379; Mason to William V. Judson, 4 March 1904, and to Richard Rathbun, 16 March 1904, NAA.

17. Mason to Rathbun, 28 October 1905, NAA. Others who shared Mason's opinion were Lester Ward, who presented early drafts of *Dynamic Sociology* to early meetings of the Anthropological Society of Washington, and Powell, who first tried out virtually all his major works on the Society members.

18. Mason to E. W. Hensinger, 24 March 1905; Mason to Daniel G. Gillette, 10 March 1905, NAA. His advice included the suggestion that the ASW found a school of anthropology by upgrading the old Saturday Lectures at the

Smithsonian and inviting public school teachers. Mason to W J McGee, 9 February 1893, McGee Papers, LC.

19. O. T. Mason, "The Birth of Invention," in SI, *AR for 1892*, p. 610.

20. O. T. Mason, "The Leipsic Museum of Ethnology," SI, *AR for 1873*, pp. 390–409; Walter Hough, "Historical Sketch of the Division, Ethnology," ms., pp. 33–34, NAA. Mason's discussion of Klemm's system was condensed from "Extra-Beilage zu No. 104 der wissenschaftlichen Beilage der Leipziger Zeitung" and "Erster Bericht des Museums für Völkerkunde in Leipzig, 1873."

21. Mason, "Leipsic Museum," pp. 392–96, 401.

22. Ibid.

23. Mason, "Birth of Invention," p. 604; Mason to Charles Lummis, 4 June 1906, NAA.

24. Walter Hough, "Otis Tufton Mason," *Encyclopedia of the Social Sciences* 5 (1930).

25. Mason to J. S. Warmbath, 4 June 1906, NAA. Mason encouraged folklore and linguistic work by local societies like the ASW: "If it is possible . . . to reconstruct the material history of a region by means of its monuments and relics, so from its lore we may by patient study reconstruct its intellectual history." (Minutes of ASW meeting, 2 February 1886, ASW Papers, NAA.)

26. Mason to "Mr. Willard-French," 21 September 1904; to Albert G. Bauersfeld, 14 June 1904; to R. D. Cambiaso, 1 November 1906, NAA.

27. O. T. Mason, "Culture History" ms., NAA, unnumbered and "Not Assigned" notes; untitled paper in "Evolution of Inventions" notebook, pp. 10–11, NAA; "Scope and Value," p. 381; "Birth of Invention," p. 605; Mason to Blanche Nevin, 11 February 1906, NAA.

28. Hough to J. W. Fewkes, 5 January 1920, USNM Papers, NAA.

29. Mason, "Culture History" ms. notes.

30. Ibid; see also his notebooks on "Evolution of Inventions," NAA.

31. Mason, "Scope and Value," p. 367; *Science* 9, no. 224 (20 May 1887), p. 485.

32. Mason to M. L. Kissell, 13 February 1908, NAA.

33. Mason's clearest statement of his debts to Klemm and natural history appears in "The Educational Aspect of the United States National Museum," *Johns Hopkins University Studies in Historical and Political Science* (1890), pp. 505–19.

34. Mason, "Culture History" notes.

35. Mason, "What is Anthropology?" p. 13; Mason to Edgar A. Mearns, 1 November 1907 and to W. L. Abbott, 6 March 1907, NAA; "Educational Aspect," p. 505; USNM, *AR for 1884*, p. 57; Mason to Constance Goddard Davis, 13 April 1904, NAA.

36. Mason, unnumbered notes in "Culture History" notebooks.

37. Discussion of Goode's career is based on Henry Fairchild Osborn, "Goode as a Naturalist," *Science*, n.s. 5, no. 114 (5 March 1897), pp. 374–79; Samuel P. Langley, "Memoir of George Brown Goode, 1851–1896" (Washington, D.C., 1897), a thorough and touching memoir read before the National Academy of Sciences, 21 April 1897; "Goode Memorial Meeting," *Science*, n.s., vol. 5, no. 114 (5 March 1897), pp. 365–72; William Van Zandt Cox, "George Brown Goode: A Memorial Sketch," *American Monthly Magazine* (January 1897), pp. 1–11; and Paul H. Oehser, *Sons of Science: The Story of the Smithsonian Institution and its Leaders* (New York, 1949), pp. 92–105.

38. Langley, "Memoir," pp. 4, 6–7.
39. Osborn, "Goode," pp. 375, 378–79.
40. George Brown Goode, "The Organization and Objects of the National Museum" (USNM Circular 15), in *USNM Proceedings* 4 (1881), appendix 4. Goode presented his organizational scheme for the first time in this and two other circulars (Nos. 1 and 13), all appearing in the appendix to this volume of the *Proceedings*.
41. George Brown Goode, "Museum-History and Museums of History," *Papers of the American Historical Association* 3 (1887): 261–63; Goode, "The Principles of Museum Administration," in *Annual Report of the Museums Association of Great Britain* (1895), p. 71.
42. Barnet Phillips, "Two Letters on the Work of the National Museum" (reprinted from *New York Times*), USNM, *AR for 1884,* appendix 2.
43. Goode, "Museum-History," p. 512.
44. USNM, *AR for 1884,* p. 54. The Pitt Rivers Museum opened in Oxford in 1884; from 1874 to 1878 it was located in the Bethnal Green Branch of the South Kensington Museum. (Beatrice Blackwood, "The Origin and Development of the Pitt Rivers Museum," in *The Classification of Artifacts in the Pitt Rivers Museum, Oxford.* Pitt Rivers Museum Occasional Papers on Technology 11 [Oxford, 1970].)
45. The 500,000 figure was inflated. Twenty years later, Hough estimated the ethnology specimens at about 193,000. (Hough, "Historical Sketch of the Division of Ethnology," ms., NAA.)
46. "Diary of O. T. Mason in the National Museum, 7/1/84—5/23/91," NAA, entry for 1 July 1884; USNM, *AR for 1884,* p. 53.
47. Mason to Pilling, 27 August 1884; to Powell, 27 September 1884, BAE-LR, NAA.
48. Mason to Edward Lovett, 23 April 1904, NAA.
49. USNM, *AR for 1897,* p. 10.
50. O. T. Mason, "Throwing-Sticks in the National Museum," USNM, *AR for 1884,* part 2, pp. 279–91.
51. O. T. Mason, "The Eskimo of Point Barrow," *American Naturalist* 20 (1886): 197–98. Personal communication from W. C. Sturtevant.
52. O. T. Mason, "Basket-Work of the North American Aborigines," USNM, *AR for 1884,* part 2, pp. 291–316; cf. Mason, *Aboriginal American Basketry: Studies in a Textile Art Without Machinery,* USNM, *AR for 1902,* pp. 171–548.
53. Walter Hough, "History of the Division of Ethnology," handwritten ms., unnumbered pages, NAA.
54. USNM, *AR for 1886,* pp. 89–90.
55. Mason, "Diary," 21 September 1888. Mason's elaborations of his checkerboard scheme underscored order. To William DeC. Ravenal, assistant to Langley, he explained it with detailed drawings: "Supposing there are six great divisions of men and six ways of supplying wants. You will then have 36 exhibits, and if they were laid out in a vast room checker fashion you could study the ethnology of mankind by going from north to south, or activities of all mankind by moving east to west. This would represent any epoch of the world. And

if you had a building of several stories, each one would represent a grade of culture and these would constitute the synoptic series of *all activities* of *all peoples* in *all ages*, 216 exhibits in all." (Mason to Ravenal, 13 May 1905, NAA.) It is interesting to note that in the 1960s, Bernard Fagg planned a new building for the Pitt Rivers Museum, a circular structure with concentric bands devoted to major artifact types, and wedge-shaped sections for major cultural and geographical areas. Exhibition areas and underground storage areas were both to be so arranged. (Personal communication from W. C. Sturtevant.)

56. The Mason-Boas debate described below has been discussed from a somewhat different viewpoint in John Buettner-Janusch, "Boas and Mason: Particularism versus Generalization," *American Anthropologist* 59 (1957): 318–24. For an incisive and suggestive treatment of the event, however, see George W. Stocking, Jr., ed., *The Shaping of American Anthropology, 1883–1911: A Franz Boas Reader* (New York, 1974), pp. 1–20. According to Mason's diary, Boas visited the Museum on December 3–5, 1884, and January 7–13, 1885.

57. Franz Boas, "The Occurrence of Similar Inventions in Areas Widely Separated," *Science* 9, no. 224 (20 May 1887), pp. 485–86.

58. Ibid.

59. O. T. Mason, "The Occurrence of Similar Inventions in Areas Widely Apart," *Science* 9, no. 226 (3 June 1887), p. 534.

60. Mason to William DeC. Ravenal, 13 May 1905, NAA.

61. Mason, "Occurrence," p. 534.

62. Franz Boas, "Museums of Ethnology and their Classification," *Science* 9, no. 228 (17 June 1887), pp. 587–89.

63. J. W. Powell, "Museums of Ethnology and their Classification," *Science* 9, no. 229 (24 June 1887), pp. 612–14.

64. Mason, "The Birth of Invention," p. 603.

65. Mason, "Educational Aspect," p. 515.

66. Melvin Grove Kyle to Holmes, 9 August 1920, in WHH 14: 167.

67. Ibid., 1:8.

68. John R. Swanton, "William Henry Holmes," *National Academy of Sciences Biographical Memoirs* 17 (Washington, D.C., 1937): 224.

69. W. H. Holmes, "Report on the Ancient Ruins of Southwestern Colorado, Examined During the Summers of 1875 and 1876," in *Tenth Annual Report of the United States Geological and Geographical Survey of the Territories* (Washington, D.C., 1878), pp. 381–408.

70. Ibid., p. 390.

71. "Field Notes of W. H. Holmes in Charge of the San Juan Division of the Geological Survey of the Territories, 1875," in WHH 4: 23–24.

72. Ibid., p. 30.

73. Powell had set forth the appropriate guidelines in "On the Limitations to the Use of Some Anthropologic Data," in BAE, *AR for 1879–80*, pp. 71–86.

74. Timothy H. H. Thoreson, "Art, Evolution, and History: A Case Study of Paradigm Change in Anthropology," *Journal of the History of the Behavioral Sciences* 13 (1977): 109.

75. Ibid., pp. 112, 113.

76. W. H. Holmes, "The American Man and His Culture," ms., n.d., series 4695, p. 4, NAA.

77. Ibid., p. 5; W. H. Holmes, "The Story of the Human Race. Notes for Lecture by Dr. Holmes, Dec. 5, 1916,"Series 4695, pp. 5–6, NAA.

78. WHH 2: 97–98.

79. The complex story of the debate over Paleolithic man between 1875 and 1900 has never been told in depth. For a brief account of Holmes's fieldwork and theoretical position, see Virginia H. Noelke, "The Origin and Early History of the Bureau of American Ethnology, 1879–1910," Ph.D. diss. (University of Texas at Austin, 1974), pp. 126–33.

80. Dutton to Holmes, 10 December 1892, in WHH 6: 51.

81. W. H. Holmes, "Primitive Man in the Delaware Valley," Science, n.s. 6, no. 153 (3 December 1897), pp. 824–29.

82. Ibid., pp. 824–26, 828.

83. USNM, AR for 1884, pp. 51–52.

84. USNM, AR for 1893, pp. 52–56. Importation of natives and use of model villages as outdoor exhibitions at international expositions are discussed and illustrated in P. H. Pott, Naar wijder horizon: Kaleidscoop op ons beeld van de Buitenwereld (The Hague, Mouton & Co., 1962).

85. Mason to Sallie Mason (daughter), 3 August 1889; to Goode, 3 August, 16 August, and 5 September 1889; to Sallie (wife), 7 September 1889; to New York Examiner, 26 August 1889; all in "Letters from Europe. Written by O. T. Mason to Dr. Goode and the Mason Family, July 17–Oct. 7, 1889," SIA.

86. Mason to Goode, 31 July, 1 August, 3 August, 8 August, 31 August, and 5 September 1889; "Letters from Europe."

87. Mason to Goode, 31 July, 3 August, and 16 August 1889; Mason to New York Examiner, 26 August 1889; "Letters from Europe." Mason, "Anthropology in Paris," American Anthropologist, o.s. 3 (1890): 34.

88. Mason to Goode, 31 August 1889; "Letters from Europe."

89. USNM, AR for 1891, p. 139: O. T. Mason, "Ethnological Exhibit of the Smithsonian Institution at the World's Columbia Exposition," Memoirs of the International Congress of Anthropology (Chicago, 1894), p. 211.

90. Mason to McGee, 21 May 1893, NAA. An untitled ms. in Mason's papers, NAA, discusses the history of American anthropology and the critical questions of the early 1890s and presents an outline of ethnogeographic units of North America. This ms. expresses more clearly than his published statements Mason's sense of accomplishment that the Powell classification provided, e.g.: "Only those who have for themselves undertaken to bring order out of this chaos realize the importance of this achievement." (Page 9 of unnumbered pages)

91. USNM, AR for 1892, pp. 101–02; Mason, "Ethnological Exhibit," p. 211.

92. Ibid., p. 210.

93. Ibid., pp. 214–15.

94. O. T. Mason, "Technogeography, or the Relation of the Earth to the Industries of Mankind," American Anthropologist, o.s. 7 (1894): 137–53.

95. O. T. Mason, "Influence of Environment Upon Human Industries or Arts," SI, AR for 1895, pp. 639–65, esp. 662–63.

96. Mason, "Technogeography," pp. 153–61.

97. Ralph W. Dexter, "Putnam's Problems Popularizing Anthropology," *American Scientist* 54 (1966): 315–32.

98. Jacknis, "Franz Boas," p. 4.

99. O. T. Mason, review of Stewart Culin's *Korean Games*, in *American Anthropologist*, o.s. 9 (1896): 22–23.

100. Holmes to Richard Rathbun, 7 October 1903, Holmes letterbooks, NAA. Emphasis added.

101. WHH 9: 157–59.

102. Mason's personal life is gleaned from casual comments throughout his correspondence, in USNM Letterbooks, NAA. See, e.g., Mason to Ella F. Hubby, 28 September 1904; to C. H. Robinson, 16 December 1904; and to A. L. Kroeber, undated but presumably early 1906. Holmes's later career is treated in Chapter. IX.

103. Mason to Alice M. Earle, 2 October 1906; to David M. Ritchie, 23 January 1906, NAA.

104. Walcott's museum plan, instituted in 1897, reversed earlier terminology, creating three "departments"—anthropology, geology, and biology—each of which consisted of several "divisions."

105. See, for instance, Holmes and Mason's "Instructions to Collectors of Historical and Anthropological Specimens," *USNM Bulletin* 39, part Q (Washington, D.C., 1902), "especially designed for collectors in the insular possessions of the United States."

106. Mason to Richard Rathbun, 7 August 1904, NAA.

107. Mason, "The Races at War in the Far East," notebook and unpublished ms.; Mason to William V. Judson, 4 March 1904; and to Rathbun, 16 March 1904, NAA.

108. Mason to Frederick W. True, 1 October 1904; to Raphael Pumpelly, 4 October 1904; to the consul general to Ecuador, 8 December 1903; and to Zelia Nuttall, 4 June 1906, NAA.

109. Mason to George Grant MacCurdy, 12 January 1907, NAA.

110. Mason to Abbott, 27 June and 25 October 1904; 29 April 1905, NAA. Correspondence to Abbott is in the Mason Letterbooks, NAA; correspondence from Abbott to Mason and other Smithsonian officials is in the William L. Abbott Papers, NAA.

111. Abbott to Mason, 15 May 1903; 30 March, 14 May, and 28 September 1904; Abbott to Hough, 4 October 1907, NAA.

112. Abbott to Mason, 30 March 1904; 14 April 1907, NAA.

113. Mason to Abbott, 29 April 1905; to Rathbun, 17 January 1905, NAA.

114. Mason to Abbott, 23 September 1907, NAA; O. T. Mason, "Vocabulary of Malaysia Basketwork: A Study in the W. L. Abbott Collections," *USNM Proceedings* 35 (Washington, D.C., 1908): 1–51.

115. Boas, "The Study of Geography," p. 137.

116. Mason to Fewkes, 1 July 1904, NAA.

117. O. T. Mason, "The Spirit of the Beautiful," delivered before the Enosinian Society of Columbian College, 22 June 1863 (Washington, D.C., 1863), pp. 9, 10, 17–18.

John Wesley Powell in his final years, c. 1900.

V

Spencer, Morgan, and Powell: The Intellectual Framework of the Bureau of American Ethnology

"For the young men whose lives were cast in the generation between 1867 and 1900, Law should be Evolution from lower to higher, aggregation of the atom in the mass, concentration of multiplicity in unity, compulsion of anarchy in order . . ."[1] Thus Henry Adams summarized the intellectual tenets of the tumultuous decades of the late nineteenth century. John Wesley Powell would have found little to disagree with in Adams's statement. Like many others of the generation that fought as young men in the Civil War, Powell struggled all his life to compose a philosophy that at once embraced the powerful truths of evolutionary science, preserved unity and purpose in a changing cosmos, and bolstered the faith in human dignity and autonomy that he inherited from an antebellum Methodist childhood. His anthropology is understandable only by recognizing the force of these commitments. Throughout his scientific career, Powell sought a single causal principle, a scientific God, to explain all phenomena. The monistic tendency had two consequences for his programs. First, it tended to blur distinctions between the subject matter of diverse sciences; his anthropology was laced with borrowings from biology, physics, anatomy, and elsewhere. Secondly, the inclination to stress a general "scientific method" of thought rather than expertise in a specific discipline explains the temerity with which Powell borrowed men from all walks of life and applied their talents in the Bureau.

The unifying, reductionist proclivity was very strong in Powell. But he also revealed a contrary tendency, partially in reaction to Charles Darwin and Herbert Spencer (as he understood them), to set man apart from the rest of the world as a separate, qualitatively different object of study. The assertion of human uniqueness within universal evolution was an attempt to free man from the determinism Powell perceived in Darwin and from the passivity he saw as man's lot in Spencer's cosmic evolutionism. Powell may have been mistaken in both perceptions. Still, in establishing the "New Ethnology" in Washington he specifically rejected biological analogy as a false guide to the human world, and he discounted physical anthropology as a means to a useful classification of peoples.

125

Like Otis Mason, Powell celebrated the human mind; it was always the primary focus of his inquiry. Mind became for him the generative force in man's evolution, the process behind the human products and activities that anthropologists studied. Man's mind set him above the rest of the universe. Powell intended to trace the development of mind from the most primitive savages to Washington scientists. Material culture, kinship systems, languages, folklore—all were inherently interesting, but they were ultimately only the data of the science, the outward manifestations that revealed the operations of an underlying agency.

Herbert Spencer exerted a profound influence on Powell. Though he rarely cited Spencer or anyone else in his writings, Powell always had the English philosopher before him as a model and challenge. Spencer's massive *Synthetic Philosophy*, which began to appear in the 1860s and to receive critical attention in the United States in the next decade, attempted to embrace all existence in a single framework. He hoped to subordinate all knowledge to a supreme, cosmic law of evolution, positing a single, unknowable force behind all phenomena. Drawing especially on the powerful axioms of nineteenth-century physics—the persistence of force, the indestructibility of matter—Spencer sought a law applicable to every field of scientific investigation.[2]

The universe, Spencer claimed, was in constant change, leading at any one time in one of two directions: toward integration of matter (evolution) or disintegration of matter (dissolution). Evolution involved not only the integration of matter but, equally important, increasing heterogeneity and differentiation of parts and functions. This was a single process of the whole universe and its parts, determining at once geological change, biological evolution, the development of human society, and the growth of the mind.

Spencer defined progress simply as increasing differentiation from homogeneous to heterogeneous structures. Progress so defined was apparent, for example, in the development of the solar system from a nebular mass to an ordered planetary system; in the gradual differentiation of the parts of the earth; in races of men diverging from a common ancestry; in the accelerating divisions of labor and other functions in human societies; and in the historical development of dialects and languages from a few mother tongues.

At the outset Spencer conceded that the ultimate cause of universal evolution was unknown and unknowable, although men would always compose theories about it. Such conjecture belonged to the realm of religion, which unlike science possessed no substantive knowledge but was merely a healthy and necessary awareness of the boundaries of human cognition. By positing the existence of an Unknowable beyond the limits of cognition, and by arguing for the compatible, complementary nature of science and religion, Spencer disarmed potential clerical critics and imposed a certain humility on those who applauded positive human knowledge.

Biological interpretation of human society became a distinctive feature of Spencerian thought. Social forms developed according to natural laws, not by man's design. Social structures revealed the same patterns of growth, specialization of functions, and interdependence of parts that plants and animals displayed. Spencer's profound respect for the laws governing man, and his disenchantment with social reform efforts in England, led him to discount attempts at social guidance based on partial knowledge or special interest. He saw only arrogant foolishness in the panaceas of those who would use government to shape society according to their visions. The purpose of social science, as he explained in *The Study of Sociology* (1872), was not to aid in calculating needs and remedies but to teach the futility of ill-considered plans. Schemes that ignored the complexity of society brought only disaster and retrogression. Sociology must remind men of their limitations and fit them to their fates. In this sense the presumptuousness of the *Synthetic Philosophy* was illusory; Spencer's work, read carefully, is a monument to humility in an age of arrogance.

Powell knew Spencer's work well, and he grew to dislike the Englishman intensely. They shared the desire to synthesize knowledge, to be sure. But Spencer's Unknowable was, to Powell, an abomination, an insult to the human mind, and a throwback to the metaphysical speculations that had plagued mankind for most of its history. Powell was fond of repeating the well-worn axiom that research proceeds from the known to the unknown. To contend that the unknown is ultimately unknowable, that the human mind faces final limits to its penetration into the secrets of the universe, seemed only the "despondency of unrewarded mental toil." Spencer's metaphysics, said Powell, amounted to no more than the "spectral imaginings that haunt the minds of introverted thinkers as devils possess the imaginations of the depraved."[3]

Powell both judged Spencer severely and often caricatured him. In Spencer's "intoxication of illusion facts seem cold and colorless," and like a "wrapt dreamer" the philosopher "imagines that he dwells in a realm above science" where "feverish dreams are supposed to be glimpses of the unknown and unknowable." Writing from his easy chair, wrapped warmly in his own imaginings, Spencer threatened the empirical science that Powell saw as America's glory. The Spencerian philosophy was a prime example of what happens when hypotheses dominate inquiry. "When an hypothesis gains such control over the mind that phenomena are subjectively discerned, that they are seen only in the light of the preconceived idea," Powell wrote in a thinly disguised attack on Spencer, "research but adds to vain speculation. A mind controlled by an hypothesis is to that extent insane; the rational mind is controlled only by the facts, and contradicted hypotheses vanish in their light."[4]

Hypothesis was a necessity in scientific inquiry, of course. Progress was impossible without it. "Men do not go about the earth indiscriminately discerning and grouping," Powell observed.[5] Proper discernment involved seeing phenomena in relation to other objects, and this required direction. Generations of philologists, for instance, had recorded linguistic data—sounds and words—with considerable precision, resulting in masses of unorganized data. But scientific research, Powell insisted, "is not random observation and comparison, but designed discernment and classification; it is research for a purpose, and the purpose is the explanation of imperfectly discerned phenomena."[6]

Darwin had taught that pure induction and pure deduction were equally fruitless.[7] Some facts possessed value for some purposes; some did not. While the fool collects facts, the wise man selects them, suggested Powell: "The true scientific man walks not at random throughout the world making notes of what he sees," but chooses a narrow field of specialization, using and discarding hypotheses as required. Both deductive and inductive methods had been superseded by the method of working hypotheses.[8]

Powell's call for an improved inductive science was hardly new. Even in the early nineteenth century, the supposed heyday of "pure Baconianism" in America, it is doubtful that scientists ever rigorously denied selecting among data. As Nathan Reingold has observed, neither the supposed anti-intellectualism nor the emphasis on taxonomy of early American science necessarily implied data-grubbing without theory.[9] The terms "Baconianism" and "pure Baconian induction," as employed by the Washington scientists, assumed the use of hypotheses. The critical distinction for them was that hypotheses be discarded readily, willingly, in the face of contrary facts.

Powell maintained that Spencer's fundamental mistake lay in his notion of force. Force was Spencer's term for the unconditioned, unknowable reality. Although man could never comprehend this reality, he did experience its effects as matter and motion. By "intrinsic force" a body manifests its existence; by "extrinsic force" it moves. Both manifestations, said Spencer, are received in human consciousness, which necessarily posits from them the existence of an Unknowable.[10]

This was dangerous nonsense to Powell. It was an unfortunate fact of life that men loved mystery over scientific truth, he recognized sadly; "in the revelry developed by the hashish of mystery, the pure water of truth is insipid." The "intellectual intoxication" of metaphysics apparently held far greater attraction than the simple truths of science, yet Powell claimed to find a "spirit of sanity" in the true and simple.[11] The steady progress of science, he answered Spencer, had gradually resolved all the mysterious "forces" of metaphysics into understandable antecedent motions. Only gravity, chemical "affinity," and magnetism remained unexplained, and Powell felt certain that these too would eventually prove to be merely other modes of motion.[12] Powell thus resolved Spencer's mysterious forces into forms of motion and believed he had removed a major metaphysical obstacle from science. In actuality, his own concept of "motion," if not unknowable, was remarkably obscure.[13]

At the very foundation of Spencer's philosophy Powell saw unacceptable passivity and vulnerability to inscrutable forces. Spencer contended that homogeneous phenomena, from stars to societies, are inherently unstable and soon develop heterogeneous features. It was the agency of change in this scheme that marked the attitudinal gap between the two men. Spencer contended that outside forces acted upon certain parts of the homogeneous mass to cause differentiation. The agency thus seemed to lay with outside forces, not within organisms.

Spencer's unknowable forces and his derivative social theories equally sickened Powell. The first reeked of metaphysics and the second belittled man. The point of Powell's philosophical excursions was to show that the generative mechanism of evolution came not from without but from within. Motion, he was fond of saying, was the first and only property of matter.[14] Applied to man, this meant that the motivating force in evolution was the human mind, the highest organization of motion. Spencer's false philosophy taught that man, subject to forces beyond his control, could do nothing. Such doctrines, Powell told a meeting of the Anthropological Society of Washington in 1881, would "neutralize nine-tenths of the legislation of the world."[15] The hero of the Grand Canyon feared that if such an attitude became prevalent, "modern civilization would lapse into a condition no whit superior to that of the millions of India. . . . When man loses faith in himself, and worships nature, and subjects himself to the government of the laws of physical nature," Powell exhorted, "he lapses into stagnation, where mental and moral miasm [*sic*] is bred."[16]

Powell never questioned the validity of biological science itself. Biology under the genius of Darwin and Thomas Henry Huxley accounted for the highest attainment of the century. It was thus hardly surprising that the best scientific minds of the time were engaged in biological research, he noted, for evolutionary biology had provided an attractive vision of the future. "The philosophy of biology," Powell found, "satisfies the reason." Had scientists discovered either degeneration or endless cyclical movement in life, "the gift of science to man would have been worthless." But biology had instead discovered steady progress to a higher life, and Powell rejoiced that "science has discovered hope."[17] Furthermore, the biologists themselves did not misapply their principles; rather it was those on "the verge of science" who spread pernicious errors through the press. Consequently, Powell lamented, " 'The Survival of the Fittest' is inscribed on the banner of every man who opposes any endeavor to ameliorate the condition of mankind."[18]

Darwin must not be misread, Powell insisted.[19] The explorer of the Colorado knew from first hand that the natural world teemed with abundant life; he had been studying the flora and fauna along with the geology of the trans-Mississippi region since before the Civil War. But Darwin and Wallace had clarified the nature of competition among plants and animals. Powell fully concurred with their observation that the life of the few was secured at the cost of the many. The "wanton superfluity" of nature introduced plants and animals to a world of fierce competition where only the lucky and the well-adapted—the "favorites of surrounding circumstances"—survived.[20] Results were mixed. Graceful, perfumed flowers proliferated and became even more beautiful through the agencies of insects and birds; but at the same time noxious and thorny plants also prospered. Progress of the few by the death of many resulted in "hardness, bitterness, piercing cruelty, and deadly poison . . ." And if the floral realm created such products, animal evolution by claw and fang, Powell showed, "has cost the world a hell of misery."[21]

Powell readily translated the observations of nature into moral lessons. Tender and hard fruits growing on the same hillside, the beautiful and the ugly coexisting in the same forest—all demonstrated that, by his standards of taste at least, "good and evil flourish in the same soil." Competition among animals gave rise to anger, hatred, ferocity, fear, and pain, as well as the delicate and lovely marvels of the faunal world: "So good and evil dwell together."[22] The world of nature was a wasteful, extravagant process unworthy of man.

Man had irrevocably altered the mechanism of evolution. Powell and his colleagues in Washington science argued strenuously that the population theories of English clergyman and mathematician Thomas Malthus, which Darwin had employed so brilliantly, had application solely to the biological realm; their original application to man, in Malthus's *Essay on the Principles of Population,* had actually been quite wrong.[23] In rejection of Malthus lay a statement of the physical and attitudinal gulf separating the Old and New Worlds. Certainly the English theoretician, writing at the close of the eighteenth century in a rapidly industrializing island nation, and the explorer of the wide expanses of North America saw very different human futures. Where Malthus projected population pressures on relatively dwindling food supplies, Powell anticipated no lack of food, only possible maldistribution.

Wallace Stegner suggested that Powell's broadest philosophical positions must be seen in terms of "ultimately regional roots," a midwestern boosterism and optimism that saw bounteous nature and open spaces.[24] This is an important insight. To be sure, Powell's *Report on the Lands of the Arid Region of the United States* (1878) and his subsequent fight for the Irrigation Survey and a rational land-use policy in the West fully demonstrated his prescient doubts that portions of the continent could sustain unplanned settlement.[25] But in more sanguine moments, and for different audiences, he could express a confidence that emerged from the heart of North America:

Men are not crowded against plants, men are not crowded against beasts, and men are not crowded against one another. The land is yet broad enough for all. The valleys are not all filled, the hillsides are not all covered. The portion of the earth that is actually cultivated and utilized to supply the wants of man is very small; it compares with all the land as a garden to a plain, an orchard to a forest, a meadow to a prairie. Nature is prodigal of her gifts. The sweet air as it sweeps from zone to zone is enough to fan every cheek; the pure water that falls from the heavens and refreshes the earth and is again carried to the heavens on chariots of light is more than enough to refresh all mankind; the bounteous earth spread out in great continents is more than enough to furnish every man a home; and the illimitable sea has wealth for man that has not yet been touched. [26]

Vestiges of brutal competition did linger among civilized men as degrading crime, or in organized form as warfare. But far from improving the race, argued the Civil War veteran, crime on the individual level and warfare as a collective activity selected out the best and healthiest for destruction, leaving behind the deformed and weak to propagate. To the extent that man fell individually or collectively under the laws of biological evolution, he degraded himself to the level of the beast. [27]

Fortunately, throughout the centuries man had increasingly freed himself from the despotism of biology and transferred the struggle for existence from himself to the products of his genius. In the process he had changed the cruel law of evolution into an agency of human improvement. The key was man's inventive mind. Invention, as Washington anthropologists employed the term, embraced all products of man's mind. [28] Every invention of civilized man, from the reaper to representative government, stood as the culminating product in a long series of predecessors. In each line of invention there had been a few successful efforts—ideas, institutions, or technological improvements that served man adequately for a time—but far more failures. This occurred because man, like nature, created abundantly:

Man invents more devices than he can use; of the many only the few are selected consciously and intelligently because they are the best. And all these inventions are made not because men struggle with nature for existence, but because men endeavor to secure happiness, to improve their condition; it is a conscious and intelligent effort for improvement. Human progress is by human endeavor. [29]

In all times and places men invented rival concepts and instruments, which competed with one another for adoption. Man picked the most useful, discarding the rest. Human evolution resulted solely from this process of human selection, Powell insisted; natural selection played no role beyond the animal stage.

Perhaps it was the proximity to the Patent Office that made man's inventive capacities so enthralling to Powell and his Washington colleagues.[30] Powell had a tentative explanation for human inventiveness. He observed that with evolution from lower to higher organisms, plants and animals produced fewer offspring, until, at the highest civilization, reproduction reached a minimal rate. At the same time inventive capacity increased enormously through the various grades of higher animals and races of man. Spencer had argued similarly in *Principles of Biology* that as the race progresses, fewer offspring will be produced; in his words, "individuation and reproduction are antagonistic." This led Powell to conjecture that "the marvelous powers of reproduction are transferred from the body of man to the soul of man, and he multiplies his intellectual creations at an amazing rate."[31]

Powell put theory to practice. As numerous contemporaries recalled, he gave freely of the "offspring" of his mind, merely stating his thoughts for the world to accept or reject. Grove Karl Gilbert, geologist in the Survey, recalled that "the fruits of his study were cast forth as simple seeds, to germinate or perish, according to their worthiness or unworthiness, or as the accident of their environment might determine."[32]

Chance variation and survival by struggle resulted in the proliferation of varieties and species of plant and animal. According to Powell's scheme, primitive man, originating at a single locus, or possibly a small number of centers, had also followed biotic laws, differentiating into varieties characterized by skull, skeletal, skin, hair, and other physical peculiarities. Races of men had formed early. Had the trend continued, distinct species would have resulted. But at some critical point in human history, differentiation was checked and man assumed control of his evolution. From this point, which occurred at different times for different peoples, man began the long, slow return to homogeneity through cultural evolution.

Both polygenists and monogenists had a place in Powell's conjectural history. He conceded the possibility of a common biological origin but posited a multitude of cultural origins. From a condition of dispersal and variety (Spencer's heterogeneity), man had steadily moved back toward the interdependence and solidarity of his "pristine homogeneity."[33] The return to unity came about in various ways. Useful arts and inventions spread rapidly to appropriate peoples, thereby creating common bonds; through conquest and in other ways, social institutions also dispersed. More difficult was the spread of dominant languages, opinions, and higher methods of reasoning, but Powell claimed to perceive in his lifetime a tendency toward "homogeneity of tongue" and the global spread of scientific philosophy. Equally promising, men all over the world were intermarrying, as the American experience exemplified. While the "synthetic chemistry of social life" was bleaching black Americans, the American Indian was rapidly fading as a distinct race as well. Powell predicted that within three generations there would be no pure Indian or Negro blood in North America: "Civilization overwhelms Savagery, not so much by spilling blood as by mixing blood, but whether spilled or mixed, a greater homogeneity is secured."[34]

> I have many facts which fit perfectly into the system which you have laid out: the bearing of these facts I did not understand before. Had I more fully appreciated your system, I believe I could have given you much additional data . . . After reading your book, I believe you have discovered the true system of social and governmental organization among the Indians.[35]

Powell never stated his debt to Lewis Henry Morgan more explicitly than in the above passage of 1877, but he envisioned BAE anthropology as the fulfillment of the work begun so promisingly with *Ancient Society*. Morgan's famous three-stage scheme of social development—through savagery, barbarism, and civilization—was handy, current, and authoritative when Powell founded the Bureau in 1879. Above all it was a system, and as many observers have noted, Powell owed a large intellectual debt to the Rochester sage.

Morgan, like so many others, had accepted Darwinian natural selection on his own terms. Man, he agreed, began at the bottom of the scale and slowly worked his way up, but Morgan's scale was quite different from Darwin's. Men and animals, according to Morgan, began as separate creations of God, endowed with all the same faculties but to different degrees, so that man subsequently progressed more rapidly. Thus, when Morgan used his favorite phrase, "Man works himself up," or when he discussed mental similarities between man and the "mutes," as in his classic study of *The American Beaver and His Works* (1868), he never intended to lower man to original identity with animals. Morgan's evolutionism was actually tied closely to eighteenth-century models that embraced an idea of material progress but not change in mental structures. For Morgan it was ideas, not mind itself, which grew and developed over time. Furthermore, as discussed previously, his work on the development of human society originally grew from strongly historical interests, and he moved to theories of developmental stages only under great pressure to organize his data.[36]

Morgan saw human history as the product of "unrecognized social processes and conscious decision," in which the growth of ideas, especially concepts of property, played a critical role.[37] "Historians, out of a certain necessity," he wrote in *Ancient Society* (1877), "give to individuals great prominence in the production of events; thus placing persons, who are transient, in the place of principles, which are enduring. . . . It will be recognized generally that the substance of human history is bound up in the growth of ideas, which are wrought out by the people and expressed in their institutions, usages, inventions, and discoveries."[38] The emphasis on the elaboration of ideas marked a strong teleological strain in Morgan. Indeed, he claimed to see "unconscious reformations" toward a future social ideal that humanity was approaching. For Morgan, history ultimately "was enacted *through people* with a common 'principle of intelligence' seeking ideal standards invariably the same."[39] The history of society was, in short, all part of the grand plan of the "Supreme Intelligence."[40]

Ancient Society traced that plan. Morgan followed man's cultural growth through savagery and barbarism (each subdivided into lower, middle, and upper planes) to civilization. The divisions were neither new nor unique, but he also proposed an explanation of the mechanics of human progress. The "real epochs of progress," he advised Joseph Henry in 1873, "are connected with the arts of subsistence which includes the Darwinian idea of the 'struggle for existence.' "[41] Without enlarging the basis of subsistence, man could not have propagated and dominated the globe; it followed that "great epochs of human progress have been identified, more or less directly, with the enlargement of the sources of subsistence."[42]

Morgan defined his "ethnical periods" through subsistence arts, then correlated social and political institutions to the fundamental classification. In lowest savagery, man had lived for centuries by digging roots and gathering berries; eventually he acquired fire, and in upper savagery he invented the bow and arrow and hunting. Domestication of animals, cultivation of grains, and pottery-making marked the beginning of lower barbarism; iron smelting closed upper barbarism and ushered in civilization.

Each level possessed its characteristic forms of government, family, and property—the three institutions treated in *Ancient Society*. Human government, he said, had followed two successive plans: kinship organization, based on gentes, phratries, and tribes; and later, political organization, founded upon territory and property relationships. Under the first, government was personal; under the latter it became territorial. Without a concept of individual property, the earlier arrangements had no class distinctions—they were essentially democratic. But with progress in subsistence arts and consequent acquisition of land and personal property, the communal arrangements of this early "gentile society" gave way to political relationships based on property and territorial rights.

Concomitant changes had occurred in family structures. Drawing on his extensive kinship work, Morgan outlined five stages of family organization, from consanguine (group marriage between brothers and sisters) to monogamous (insured paternity and exclusive inheritance of property). Since in the earlier stages of promiscuity descent could be reckoned only through the mother, he reasoned, the family was everywhere originally matriarchal.

The growth of ideas of property from their origins in savage minds caused and accompanied changes in inventions and social institutions. Morgan meant by "property" a single, growing force among all men, a divinely implanted principle that took various forms. Consequently, Morgan did not distinguish the nuances beneath the general term. It is clear, however, that he deplored the vast accumulations of private wealth, in individual and corporate forms, that alienated man from man and threatened social harmony. He called for return to the communal ownership pattern that had supposedly characterized savage society. With their meager belongings, common lands, and houses, the men of savagery barely knew individual property. But by the upper status of barbarism the various improvements in inventions gave rise to enough individually owned property to require laws regulating ownership, and what had been only "a feeble impulse" among savages grew to a "tremendous passion." The foundations of the economic inequalities of civilization—personal wealth, family inheritance, aristocracy—had been laid.[43]

He observed the results in American civilization with deep uneasiness. During his career as lawyer and land investor he had watched lumbering and mining interests ravish the upper Michigan forests, and he came to deplore the brutal Indian wars and the growing rapacity of American economic enterprise.[44] Although he believed the United States had largely abolished class distinctions, Morgan never saw his own society as the apex of evolution. Here lay his hope, for surely society would continue to change in the future as in the past. That change, Morgan predicted, would involve a return to democratic, communal principles and a rejection of individual property as a basis for social relationships. Democracy, "once universal in a rudimentary form," would return in a fuller and more perfect flowering.[45] Toward the end of *Ancient Society* Morgan delivered an inspiring declaration of faith in man's ability to transcend the thralldom of individual property. Property, he pronounced, has become "an unmanageable power," and "the human mind stands bewildered in the presence of its own creation." But human intelligence would surely master property and usher in a glorious future of peace and harmony:

A mere property career is not the final destiny of mankind, if progress is to be the law of the future as it has been of the past. The time which has passed away since civilization began is but a fragment of the past duration of man's existence; and but a fragment of the ages yet to come. The dissolution of society bids fair to become the termination of a career of which property is the end and aim; because such a career contains the elements of self-destruction. Democracy in government, brotherhood in society, equality in rights and privileges, and universal education, foreshadow the next higher plane of society to which experience, intelligence and knowledge are steadily tending. It will be a revival, in a higher form, of the liberty, equality, and fraternity of the ancient gentes.[46]

By the middle of the 1870s, when Powell was doing his field work, Morgan was the recognized dean of American anthropology. *Ancient Society,* his enduring theoretical contribution to the science, confirmed his eminent position. "It is not one of the least results accomplished by Mr. Morgan," Powell wrote in 1880, a year before Morgan's death, "that he has gathered about him living disciples who are reaping harvests from fields planted by himself." Powell stood foremost among those followers. Morgan had "laid the foundation for the science of government as it is finally to be erected by the philosophy of evolution," Powell announced.[47] Without accepting all his assumptions, Powell found a kindred spirit in Morgan. Morgan's critical views on private property and his optimistic vision of future social organization matched Powell's own concerns about western land development. Perhaps Morgan's most important lesson for statesmen, wrote Powell, was that "government by the people is the normal condition of mankind"; despite occasional lapses and setbacks, democracy would prevail by natural selection. "Hope for the future of society," Powell concluded happily, "is the best-loved daughter of Evolution."[48] For his part, Morgan enjoyed Powell's comments and agreed that his book was "a tremendous thrust at privileged classes . . ."[49]

The two ethnologists shared as well a respect for the primitive peoples they studied, which, while not free of ethnocentrism, did encourage sympathetic treatment. Morgan's humanism lay partly in his belief that relative progress among men was largely accidental. Environmental conditions and chance inventions played major roles in advancing one people rather than another. *Ancient Society,* in fact, closed not with the ringing declaration for the future cited above, but with the peculiarly diffident reminder that civilization, while probably inevitable in God's plan, was at least in its timing the consequence of "a series of fortuitous circumstances." Civilized man owed his present condition, Morgan lectured the public, to "the struggles, the sufferings, the heroic exertions, and the patient toil of our barbarous, and more remotely, of our savage ancestors."[50]

Morgan's emphasis on the central role of human intelligence in conquering nature struck a sympathetic chord in Powell, and he was fascinated with the way in which Morgan correlated social institutions with notions of property and subsistence arts. "In the lower stages of culture," Powell later wrote, "all progress rests upon the arts of life." To discover the "efficient agency" in human development from one stage to the next, the anthropologist must look to man's "art-inventions," particularly those of subsistence.[51] Here lay the cornerstone of a scientific anthropology.

Powell wanted to do for the science of man what Darwin had done for biology: formulate a powerful guiding theory of (human) evolution buttressed by an unassailable mountain of empiricism. Morgan made a critical contribution with his development stages marked by characteristic, correlated forms of inventions in material goods, ideas, and institutions. Here the student could see the unity of the human mind in its full clarity, as it created essentially similar products across the spectrum of human needs at each point in evolution. Methodologically, this was a breakthrough for Powell. If Morgan's scheme could be expanded from arts of subsistence, family, government, and property to include the full range of man's creations, the anthropologist operating with only the remnants of a given tribe could rebuild its life entirely, like the paleontological reconstructions of Georges Cuvier. Further, with the full panoply of man's inventions at each stage spread before him, the student of man could then proceed to examine by inference the development of the magnificent agency that had created them: mind. This was Powell's final destination, to which Morgan opened a way.

Correlating the different categories of human activities thus became a prime feature of the New Ethnology, as Powell termed Bureau anthropology. Past investigators had examined languages, material arts, kinship, and social institutions without seeing them in relation to each other. But study of any single field of human activity without discovering relations to all others amounted merely to collecting curiosities:

All the grand classes of human activities are inter-related in such a manner that one presupposes another, and no one can exist without all the others. Arts are impossible without institutions, languages, opinions, and reasoning; and in like manner every one is developed by aid of the others. If, then, all of the grand classes of human activities are interdependent, any great change in one must effect corresponding changes in the others. The five classes of activities must progress together. Art-stages must have corresponding institutional, linguistic, philosophic, and psychic stages.[52]

Morgan had taken the first step by connecting certain institutions and economic factors in a causal sequence. But his work was imperfect, Powell found, because he never explained the interdependence satisfactorily, and because he largely ignored language and mythology, Powell's personal areas of interest.[53]

Powell's stress on man as a subject with multiple aspects requiring simultaneous, coordinated study came partly in reaction to the unsatisfactory racial classifications of physical anthropologists. Beyond the primary division into four or five races, physical features had been found useless in distinguishing tribes, so that the student of man had to go beyond biological criteria in order to investigate men in groups. As Powell never tired of saying, the study of man is demotic, not biotic. This became, in McGee's words, "the germ of a rejuvenated ethnology, i.e., a science of races based on human rather than animal attributes."[54] Both primitive and civilized peoples were to be most profitably studied as groups, "in which each individual reflects and is molded by the characteristics of his associates . . ."[55]

By extending Morgan's initiative and attempting to raise the "New Ethnology" above the methods of biology, Powell took American anthropology

one important step toward a holistic approach to human society. In a rudimentary way he saw that the material arts, social institutions, customs, beliefs,
and languages of groups of people are interconnected in various complex ways,
and to some extent he permitted Bureau ethnologists to explore these interconnections. But the advance should not be overestimated. Powell operated
within specific intellectual confines. The correlations and interconnections
referred to stages of culture, not to specific cultures. The goal was to discover,
for example, how savage subsistence arts are related to savage linguistic
behavior in general, without application to a given tribe. The experiences of
particular societies constituted only the data of Powell's anthropology, not
the final scientific object. Consequently, Powell had no compunctions about
dismantling an ethnographic study into components and reassembling them
with data in the same "lines" of activity from other peoples. At heart, Powell
remained always comparative.

The dichotomy between ethnographic completeness and "lines" of study
appeared in Powell's own early field work of the 1870s. While he emphasized
language and mythology, Powell's interests extended to most aspects of social
life: kinship terminology, ceremonialism, curing practices, material culture;
he even noted treatment of children, the aged, and the insane.[56] But Powell
took great liberties with his data, abstracting, for example, the stylized songs
and chants from his Southern Paiute tales.[57] And while he apparently intended
to write up his notes on the various tribes of the Numic peoples into an
ethnographic summary, over the years he actually used his field notes, particularly his observations on psychology, in a highly selective manner.[58] The
burdens of administering two agencies explain in part his failure to produce
integrated studies, but full ethnographies were simply less important to
Powell than applying the data to a larger developmental picture.

Powell's evolutionary anthropology, as he imposed it on the Bureau of
American Ethnology, envisioned lines of human activity running from savagery to civilization (he later added "enlightenment" as a fourth stage). The
intention was, first, to draw correspondences across categories at each stage
of development. Secondly, since the "culture-grades" in fact represented stages
of mental growth, the array of inventions at each level would presumably
provide sufficient data for inferring the nature of mental operations at that
point. For instance, a brief summary of Powell's vision of savagery was as
follows: The savage has extremely rude tools and methods for obtaining food,
shelter, and clothing; kinship is vague, determined in the female line; he has
spoken language, gesture speech, and picture-writing, but no hieroglyphic
or alphabetic writing; he attributes animal characteristics to inanimate objects,
and deifies animals. Lack of conventional characters in writing, and inability
to perform simple arithmetic without counting on the fingers, provided firm
evidence for Powell's general conclusion: the savage mind had only "slightly

developed" capacities for "perception" (defined as instantaneous trains of inductive reasoning). But during barbarism the gradual accumulation of wealth, stimulated by improved arts of subsistence, led to an ability to perceive simple numerical relations. And the development of arithmetic issued, Powell theorized, in "a nicer discrimination of phenomena" generally and new systems for grouping them.[59] At the same time, as man domesticated animals the mysteries of animal life were dispelled and zootheism faded; conversely, with the growth of agriculture, meteorological factors became all important to man's survival, and he became increasingly physitheistic (worshipping natural phenomena). By such reasoning Powell developed a close causal chain across the fields of culture and mind, without any mysterious gaps, running from animal-like existence to civilized society. It was, McGee summarized, a "comprehensive anthropology, broad enough to touch every human ideal and passion and law and motive . . . "[60]

Powell's views were well established by the early 1880s; subsequent statements merely elaborated them. From his geological studies of the seventies he had carried over a fertile idea: that phenomena must be analyzed in terms of the agency or process that produced them, not in terms of apparent similarities. This principle was the "keynote" of both his geology and his anthropology.[61] When he turned to primitive peoples, he saw that the multitude of human products "are best interpreted in terms of agency, the agency in this case being human thought."[62] Mental power was the driving force in human affairs. Fully appreciating the analogy, linguist Frederick Max Müller once referred to BAE anthropology as "intellectual geology."[63]

It is difficult to recapture the sense of empirical chaos in both geology and anthropology by the end of the 1870s in the United States. A long apprenticeship to European savants was ending, but the search for organizing principles was almost desperate. This partly accounts for the contemporary impact of Morgan and the feeling of revelation in Powell's discussions of mind as the agent in human evolution. The overarching principles and the confidence and direction that Powell instilled in the Bureau provided at least the appearance of scientific unity in a young, politically vulnerable organization. But as following chapters illustrate, the Bureau was a collection of individual personalities, not a disciplined school of believers; if the intellectual framework was formally adopted, it was not always privately absorbed. The freedom provided by Bureau salary and support was more determinative than Powell's evolutionary designs. Of course each case was distinct: James Mooney paid little attention to Powell's philosophical musings, while W J McGee carried them to an extreme degree that warped his own field observations and in the long run exposed fallacious assumptions. In every instance, though, Powell offered patronage and protection for anthropology that could not be found elsewhere in nineteenth-century America. Institutional support required a clear statement of purpose and a systematic, comprehensive framework for the science of man. Powell provided both.

Notes

1. Henry Adams, *The Education of Henry Adams: An Autobiography* (Boston, 1961), p. 232.
2. Herbert Spencer should be experienced firsthand. The account presented here is based chiefly on *First Principles* (New York, 1880 [reprinted from 5th London edition]).
3. J.W. Powell, "The Three Methods of Evolution," *Bulletin of the Philosophical Society of Washington* 6 (Washington, D.C., 1883): xxxiv.
4. J. W. Powell, *Truth and Error* (Chicago, 1898), p. 8; Powell, "Three Methods," p. xxxiv.
5. J.W. Powell, "Human Evolution," *TASW* 3 (Washington, D.C., 1883): 203.
6. Powell, "Three Methods," p. xxxiv.
7. J. W. Powell, "Darwin's Contributions of Philosophy," *Darwin Memorial Meeting of Biological Society of Washington* (Washington, D.C., 1882), pp. 60–70.
8. Ibid., pp. 67–69. For a similar discussion, see Powell, "Human Evolution," pp. 203–05. The classic contemporary statement on the use of hypothesis, respected by Powell and his Washington circle, was Thomas C. Chamberlin's "The Method of Multiple Working Hypotheses," *Science,* o.s. 15 (1890): 92–96; later expanded in *Journal of Geology* 5 (1897): 837–48.
9. Nathan Reingold, "American Indifference to Basic Research: A Reappraisal," in George H. Daniels, ed., *Nineteenth-Century American Science: A Reappraisal* (Evanston, Ill., 1972), p. 47.
10. Spencer emphasized that the two major manifestations of force—matter and motion—were received by human consciousness in terms of effort (muscle strain), reflecting his own early interest in psycho-physics (*First Principles,* pp. 159–61). Spencer was not always certain that the distinction between the two modes of force could be rigidly maintained, but "the forms of our experience" justified the separation (*First Principles,* pp. 162–64). Spencer revealed finer sensitivity to the subjectivity of human observation than his critic Powell. Indeed, awareness of cultural and personal idiosyncrasy was a powerful motivation in Spencer's attempt to build a philosophy that would transcend such considerations. His personal isolation and estrangement from society, to a great extent self-imposed, might be seen as part of Spencer's attempt at cultural transcendence.
11. Powell, *Truth and Error,* pp. 4–5.
12. Powell, "Three Methods," pp. xxviii–xxix.
13. If Spencer's notion of force was not recognizable to physicists, neither was Powell's concept of motion, nor other terms he lightly borrowed from the physical sciences. When confronted by physicists and pressured for explicit definitions, the Major came off badly. See, e.g., the series of exchanges in 1896

between Powell and "M" in *Science,* n.s. 3: 426–33, 513–14; 595–96; 631; 743–45. "M," apparently a physicist, gave up in exasperation.

14. Powell, "Three Methods," p. xl.

15. Smithsonian Institution Miscellaneous Collections 25 (Washington, D.C., 1883), p. 42.

16. Ibid., pp. li–lii.

17. Powell, "Darwin's Contributions," p. 66.

18. Powell, "Human Evolution," pp. 207–08.

19. Powell's most complete statements on the nature of biological and human evolution appear in "Three Methods" (1883), "Human Evolution" (1883), and "Competition as a Factor in Human Evolution" (*American Anthropologist,* o.s. 1 [Washington, D.C., 1888]: 297–321). The following discussion is based chiefly on "Competition," Powell's most vigorously anti-Spencerian statement of the period. The major themes can be found throughout Powell's writings in the 1880s.

20. Powell, "Competition," pp. 298–99.

21. Ibid., pp. 300, 304.

22. Ibid., pp. 300–01.

23. This discussion leaves aside the question to what extent Darwin was indebted to Malthus (as opposed to William Paley or Charles Lyell) in the development of his idea of struggle. After 1859 both Darwin and A. R. Wallace credited Malthus with the original insight into population pressures, and the Washington men of the 1880s saw that they must address Malthus. See Loren Eiseley, *Darwin's Century: Evolution and the Men Who Discovered It* (Garden City, 1958), pp. 178–82.

The Anthropological Society of Washington was a hot-bed of anti-Malthusian and anti-Spencerian forces, led by Powell, Lester Frank Ward, and James C. Welling. Here Ward first tried out chapters of his *Dynamic Sociology* amid general agreement that Spencerian evolution amounted to "a green sickness or mental chlorosis." (*TASW,* meeting of 9 May 1882, p. 13. See also Welling's "The Turning Point of Modern Sociological Science" and discussion, ibid., 7 November 1882, pp. 15–33; and his "The Law of Malthus Inductively Investigated," 1 February 1887, after which Powell repeated his conviction that "Population has hitherto been limited through ignorance and injustice.") At the ASW meeting of 21 December 1886, geologist Clarence Dutton presented a Malthusian analysis of Henry George's *Progress and Poverty* and was sharply attacked by Ward.

24. Wallace Stegner, *Beyond the Hundredth Meridian: John Wesley Powell and the Second Opening of the West* (Boston, 1954), pp. 8–21.

25. Ibid., pp. 202–38, 294–350.

26. Powell, "Competition," pp. 301–02.

27. Ibid., pp. 302–03.

28. Powell sometimes used the term "human arts" synonymously with "activities" and "inventions."

29. Powell, "Competition," p. 308.

30. The Patent Office was well represented in the ASW membership, and several papers focused on man's material inventions.

31. Powell, "Competition," p. 53. It is impossible to say if the Washington scientists took seriously this inverse correlation between biological and mental progeny. Two points are certain, however: the widely held fascination and admiration for invention, and the growing concern over low production among the "Aryan stock." In this context Powell's explanation, backed by Spencer's earlier statements, was plausible and flattering.

32. Quoted in "John Wesley Powell Commemorative Meeting," *Proceedings of Washington Academy of Sciences* 5 (1903): 116.

33. J. W. Powell, "From Savagery to Barbarism," *TASW* 3 (Washington, D.C., 1885): 193.

34. Ibid., pp. 193–94.

35. Powell to Lewis Henry Morgan, 23 May 1877; as quoted in Virginia Noelke, "The Origin and Early History of the Bureau of American Ethnology, 1879–1910," Ph.D. diss. (University of Texas at Austin, 1974), p. 52.

36. George W. Stocking, Jr., "Some Problems in the Understanding of Nineteenth Century Evolutionism," in Regna D. Darnell, *Readings in the History of Anthropology* (New York, 1973), pp. 420–23; L. H. Morgan, *Ancient Society: or Researches in the Lines of Human Progress from Savagery through Barbarism to Civilization,* ed. Eleanor Burke Leacock (Cleveland, 1963), p. IViii.

37. Morgan, *Ancient Society,* p. IIxvi.

38. Ibid., p. 311.

39. Ibid., p. IViii. Emphasis added.

40. Ibid., p. 563.

41. Quoted in Carl Resek, *Lewis Henry Morgan: American Scholar* (Chicago, 1960), pp. 136–37.

42. Morgan, *Ancient Society,* p. 19.

43. The preceding summary is based on Resek, *Lewis Henry Morgan,* pp. 137–40.

44. Ibid., pp. 144–45.

45. Morgan, *Ancient Society,* p. 351.

46. Ibid., pp. 561–62.

47. J. W. Powell, "Sketch of Lewis H. Morgan," *Popular Science Monthly* (November 1880), pp. 120–21.

48. Ibid., p. 121.

49. Quoted in Resek, *Lewis Henry Morgan,* p. 143.

50. Morgan, *Ancient Society,* p. 563.

51. Powell, "Savagery to Barbarism," p. 184.

52. BAE, *AR for 1881,* p. iii; Powell, "Savagery to Barbarism," pp. 175–76. The emphasis on viewing objects or phenomena in relation to others became an obsessive concern in Powell's later philosophical ruminations; in his eyes one of the most important lessons of his philosophy of science was the insistence that true understanding of phenomena lay in seeing their relations to others. In *Truth and Error* he expressed the idea in terms of physics—motion, speed, position—but it originally grew from his early disenchantment with biological taxonomies. He was not consistent regarding the number of categories, usually but not always referring to five areas of human "activities" or "humanities."

53. Powell, "Savagery to Barbarism," p. 174.

54. Quoted in "Powell Commemorative Meeting," p. 120.

55. BAE, *AR for 1894*, p. xviii.

56. Powell's collections, in the U.S. National Museum, have been examined in Don D. Fowler and John Matley, "Material Culture of the Numa: The Powell Collection, 1868-1876," Smithsonian Contributions to Anthropology (Washington, D.C., 1975).

57. Don D. Fowler and Catherine S. Fowler, "Anthropology of the Numa: John Wesley Powell's Manuscripts on the Numic Peoples of Western North America, 1868–1880," Smithsonian Contributions to Anthropology 14 (Washington, D.C., 1971): 17, 19.

58. See, for instance, the first chapter of *Truth and Error*.

59. Powell, "Savagery to Barbarism," pp. 190–91.

60. Quoted in "Powell Commemorative Meeting," p. 121.

61. Ibid.

62. Ibid., p. 122.

63. *Journal of the Royal Anthropological Institute* 21 (1891–92): 211.

The BAE insignia, designed by W. H. Holmes in 1879,
showing cliff dwelling, pictographs, and cloud-and-rain symbol in the sky.

VI

Toward an Anthropological Survey: The Early Years of the BAE, 1879–1893

Inequality was an inescapable social fact in post-Civil War America. The discovery of defeated, impoverished, excluded multitudes, immigrant or aboriginal, within an increasingly rigid, differentially prosperous class society came as shock to a nation that still held to a creed of open opportunity. For most, the answer lay where it always had, in exhortation to self-mastery—from the novels of Horatio Alger to the Dawes Act of 1887—even as this steadily faded as a realistic option for masses of people. For some concerned middle-class Americans, however, the experiences of war and the disorganized postwar condition of the country, North and South, gave additional impetus to systematic, institutional study and treatment of social problems. The embryonic forms of political science, economics, and sociology that emerged in these decades came partially as response to concern over the dispossessed. They were at once a political threat, an economic failure, and a moral disgrace.[1]

Perhaps because anthropology arrived late to academic respectability, its history has seemed unique and complex among the early social sciences.[2] But study of the North American Indian shared with political economy and sociology a common source in both the recognition of less fortunate, possibly doomed peoples, and interest in their political and moral meaning for the nation. Language is indicative in such matters. Arguing in 1862 to establish the Massachusetts State Board of Charities for the care of Irish-American poor, Samuel Gridley Howe set forth the alternatives: "We have here this foreign element among us; we cannot get rid of it if we would; and we should strive to fuse it into our common nationality as fast as possible. We strengthen our state by homogeneity; we weaken it by the contrary course."[3] Howe expressed the dawning awareness of ethnic heterogeneity and social and economic inequality that not only spurred the growth of the social sciences as promising academic disciplines, but underlay the drive for scientific understanding of the American Indian as a domestic social problem as well. Lot M. Morrill, Republican senator from Maine, reminded his colleagues in 1867 that "we have come to this point in the history of the country that there is no place beyond population to which you can remove the Indian . . . and the precise question [now] is, will you exterminate him, or will you fix an abiding place for him?"[4] Seven years later, reporting to Congress on the destitution of the Indians of the Colorado and Utah territories, John Wesley Powell employed strikingly similar terms: "There is now no great uninhabited and unknown region to which the Indian can be sent. He is among us, and we must either protect him or destroy him."[5]

Between 1860 and 1890, American demography and identity embraced the entire continent. As a consequence, in these years the Indian ceased being a subject of foreign policy and became a focus of domestic concern for the United States. The gradual shift of responsibility for Indian affairs from the War Department to the Department of Interior at once symbolized and institutionalized this critical alteration in perception. At the same time, one senses, observers and policy-makers of Powell's generation suffered a loss of alternatives as the immense industrial might of American civilization proceeded westward. The phrases of Howe, Morrill, and Powell were echoed endlessly in public statements of the postwar decades, but they amounted to a litany of limited options. In the aftermath of the slavery controversy and the distractions of war, it seems, the Indian question had finally been reduced to a bare choice: civilization or extermination.[6] These were the polar points of a debate carried forward with all the rigid clarity of Victorian certainty.

The mobilization for war and the permanently altered political balance in Washington of the 1860s released irresistible dynamics of expansive economic power that flowed through the following years. These unchallenged forces determined the deep currents of American history for the rest of the century. For the Indian cultures of the trans-Mississippi West, the result was final, massive tragedy; but it was tragic for others, too. Strong military presence and territorial scientific explorations in the West during the seventies served to provide the necessary preconditions for settlement and exploitation: familiarity with the land and a measure of peace and security. To be sure, the men who, like William Henry Holmes, served under Wheeler, King, Hayden, and Powell in the Survey years breathed deeply the invigorating airs of freedom and power, certain that "they held under their hammers a thousand miles of mineral country with all its riddles to solve, and its stores of possible wealth to mark. They felt the future in their hands."[7] But the future lay in other hands, as Powell subsequently discovered in the fights over his Irrigation Survey. Scientific pathfinders like Powell achieved the dubious stature of the explorer and pioneer. Latter-day Leatherstockings, they were themselves doomed to pass away before the destructive progress they heralded, enjoying only an ephemeral heroism.

By the last third of the nineteenth century, the basic directions of American growth were no longer open to question, and they spelled destruction for aboriginal cultures. Social evolutionism was one way of dealing with discrete, unequal human fates. Evolutionary modes of thought imbued the economically inevitable with a veneer of moral grace as Americans turned to science to assure the rightness and acceptance of current trends. Understandably, identity as a scientist in Victorian America provided not only desirable status but the illusion of individual power to shape human affairs. The fascination with science and the scientist may be seen, in fact, as an important part of an effort to discover motivation and cause other than economics to justify the vulgar prosperity and hidden misery of American society: if the transcendent Yankee was still alive in Gilded Age America, then the task of the social scientists was to uncover proof of his existence. This need was as old as the Puritan settlements; only the language was new.

The choice between extermination and civilization of the Indian was, from this viewpoint, merely one outgrowth of a driven, unilinear society. It was of course a choice only for the White man—the Indian no longer enjoyed choice—between barbaric power and various milder forms of domination. That is precisely the point: the parameters were established and unalterable after the Civil War, leaving only issues of style and procedure open to discussion. Powell's Bureau of American Ethnology was originally founded to address such questions.

In March 1879, Congress passed the civil sundry bill for the next year, which consolidated the Wheeler, Hayden, King, and Powell surveys into the United States Geological Survey. As a result of Powell's personal lobbying, and almost as an afterthought, the bill also established the Bureau of American Ethnology (BAE), with an initial appropriation of $20,000 "for completing and preparing for publication the *Contributions to North American Ethnology*, under the Smithsonian Institution."[8] The BAE was Powell's personal creation, the culmination of his experiences in science, politics, and exploration during the 1870s; it emerged from the Survey tradition and in every important respect continued the patterns of structure, procedure, and purpose of the Survey years. The BAE was to be a permanent anthropological survey.

The roots of the Bureau lay in the seventies, when Powell did his only extended anthropological fieldwork, gradually realized the need for a government-sponsored bureau for anthropology, and formulated the general research plans that dominated the BAE until his death in 1902. The story of Powell's early exploits in geology has been told from various perspectives; it is sufficient here merely to present the background relevant to the Bureau and to clarify Powell's arguments for its existence.[9]

In 1870, following his successful first descent of the Colorado, Powell's Geographical and Topographical Survey of the Colorado River of the West and its Tributaries was commissioned with an appropriation of $12,000. A clerical error may have sent the Survey to the Smithsonian rather than the Interior Department, but Powell worked well with Joseph Henry, as he acknowledged in the first volume of *Contributions to North American Ethnology:*

> For the last ten years I have habitually laid before Professor Henry all
> of my scientific work, and have during that time received the benefit
> of his judgment on these matters, and to a great extent I am indebted
> to him for advice, encouragement, and influence. [10]

In 1874 Powell's survey, now renamed the Geographical and Geological
Survey of the Rocky Mountain Region, went back to the Interior Department,
where it remained until 1879. During these years Powell was deeply involved
in geology, but his personal interests shifted steadily to anthropology, and
the Rocky Mountain Survey began to gather together the corps that would
constitute the original BAE. Powell had time for only sporadic work among
the Numa, but even when he could not go to the field, as in 1876, he worked
on materials in Washington. At one point he brought Richard Komas, a
Northern Ute, to attend school at Lincoln University in Pennslyvania, and
employed him as a clerk in the Washington office. [11]

Between 1873 and 1878 Powell developed his essential argument for a
government-supported scientific bureau of anthropology. In 1873 he was appointed Special Commissioner of Indian Affairs to investigate the condition
of the Numic peoples of the Great Basin territory. [12] On arrival in Salt Lake
City he heard rumors of an impending Indian uprising but soon discovered
that the Indians were far more terrified than the White settlers. Whites had
spoiled former hunting areas and occupied all the best land, forcing the
Indians to scatter into small groups and eke out subsistence through nut and
berry gathering, root digging, and begging. The settlers had nothing to
anticipate but annoyance from such demoralized creatures, Powell concluded:
"Nothing then remains but to remove them from the country, or let them
stay in their present condition, to be finally extinguished by want, loathsome
disease, and the dissent consequent upon incessant conflict with white men." [13]

It was an old story, repeated with each wave of settlement westward; George
Gibbs had experienced similar, sad progress in the Northwest in the 1850s.
But in the canyon country there was so little arable land in the first place,
and already so many Whites, that the Indians' situation was critical. Powell
recommended sending them away to established reservations, totaling 10,000
square miles, of which "only a small portion . . . is fit for agricultural
purposes, much of it being sandy desert and mountain wastes." The Numa
would relinquish in exchange 410,000 square miles of homeland. [14]

The trade was worth it, Powell thought, if the reservation arrangements
were handled in the proper spirit. He reported that the Indians fully appreciated the hopelessness of their situation and desired only the necessary tools,
training, and cattle to become self-sufficient farmers. At the same time that
he banished the Numa to already crowded reservations of sand and rock,
Powell clung to past dreams and made careful recommendations for their

education to civilization. His "Suggestions on the Management of these Re-servations" expressed a sympathetic but firm attitude toward childlike folk. Above all the Indians must be taught self-sufficiency and work, receiving goods only in compensation for labor. Powell advised giving fabrics rather than ready-made clothing and teaching the women to sew; discouraging nomadic behavior by providing houses rather than tents; and giving each family a cow as a first personal possession, for "as soon as an Indian acquires property, he more thoroughly appreciates the rights of property, and becomes an advocate of law and order."[15]

Powell's concern was sincere. He gave close attention to reservation con-ditions because he viewed them as the only hope for Indian survival in the White world. Transition to agrarianism seemed the sole alternative to total dependence on government goods, once the environmental base of old patterns was gone. But when he turned to the central question of inquiry: "What division of the roaming tribes do their linguistic and other affinities dictate?" Powell had to admit ignorance.[16] The names by which tribes were known to Whites were not the same as those used by tribes for each other, and they gave no indication of historical relationships. The point was highly practical, for if hostile tribes were settled together they would merely fight and scatter again, at great expense to the government. Efficiency and humaneness de-manded a system based on intelligence and scientific knowledge.

The bitter Indian wars of the mid-seventies confirmed Powell's fears. At the same time, the appearance of Lewis Henry Morgan's *Ancient Society* in 1877 gave both renewed hope and a usable framework for a scientific eth-nology. In his 1878 report to the Secretary of the Interior, Powell expressed a new sense of urgency. The rapid destruction of the North American abo-riginal population meant that habits, customs, and languages were disap-pearing at an alarming rate. "In a few years," he warned, "it will be impossible to study our North American Indians in their primitive condition, except from recorded history." He urged "utmost vigor."[17] Drawing from Morgan's scheme, Powell lectured on the attributes of savage society, focusing on the distinction between communal and private property. The personal rights of property recognized in civilization, he instructed the politicians, were "in-tensely obnoxious" to the Indian, who saw them as an evil for which the White would eventually be punished by the gods. The point was simple: savagery was a distinct stage of social development, with its own complete system of institutions, customs, and beliefs. The studies of the 1870s had already revealed the "fundamental fact" that the aboriginal peoples of America, while organized in distinct groups, shared a common cultural stage, "so that the tribes of any district can not be successfully studied without observation among the tribes of other districts . . ." The complex of savagery had to be understood and overthrown before one could introduce civilized notions and habits. In summary, Powell urged, we must either deal with the Indian as he is, looking to the slow but irresistible influence of civilization . . . to effect a change, or we must reduce him to abject slavery. The attempt to transform a savage into a civilized man by a law, a policy, an administration, or a great conversion . . . in a few months or in a few years, is an impossibility clearly appreciated by scientific ethnologists who understand the institutions and social conditions of the Indians.[18]

Powell's report of 1878 presented the logic of the early BAE. In the first place, Morgan had demonstrated that the American Indian must be understood not as a racial category but as a savage stage of human culture. Understanding of the Indian thus required total comprehension of savagery, which could only be accomplished through centralized, systematic study of aboriginal populations. At the same time, however, Powell aimed at a second, distinct goal: tracing of historical migrations and contacts between tribes and stocks. Thus at the founding Powell blended the historical and classificatory orientations that had coexisted for decades within American anthropology. He thereby built into the Bureau a dichotomy of purpose that would both enrich and plague its operations for the rest of the century.

Furthermore, to the politicians Powell stressed the potential utility of anthropology:

In pursuing these ethnographic investigations [he reported in 1878] it has been the endeavor as far as possible to produce results that would be of practical value in the administration of Indian affairs, and for this purpose especial attention has been paid to vital statistics, to the discovery of linguistic affinities, the progress made by the Indians toward civilization, and the causes and remedies for the inevitable conflict that arises from the spread of civilization over a region previously inhabited by savages. I may be allowed to express the hope that our labors in this direction will not be void of such useful results.[19]

But he also emphasized that there were no panaceas in Indian policy; permanent solutions must await the scientists.[20] Not that Powell urged passivity. On the contrary, through the BAE and as director of the U. S. Geological Survey from 1881 to 1894, he fought two of the most powerful, complementary dynamics in American culture: unplanned settlement, with its destructive impact on Indian peoples and the natural environment; and well-intentioned but ignorant efforts to "save" the Indian through conversion to Christianity and civilization. He questioned both the ruinous expansion and the belief in quick solutions that only eased consciences. Powell revolted against a world of easy solutions. Man must act, he preached; he must take control, but only on the basis of full, final scientific knowledge.

Under the circumstances it was probably inevitable that when Powell announced his intention to "organize anthropologic research in America," the statement contained divergent purposes. On the one hand, he would vigorously pursue the search for historical connections and the mapping of aboriginal America as aids to informed policy. This more than any other single purpose was the focus of BAE activities until the publication of the Powell linguistic map and classification of 1891, when the survey impulse finally expired. From that point the Bureau began to lose direction and to drift. On the other hand, Powell intimated at the founding even more grandiose plans: nothing less than a complete science of man. Deeply influenced by Morgan's model and Spencer's comprehensive approach, Powell foresaw a central organization that would found a "New Ethnology" of final, positive knowledge to explain and justify the wide disparities in human conditions, past, present, and future. Science was still a deeply moral enterprise. In 1878 the Secretary of the Interior had announced that "The 'Indian frontier' has virtually disappeared."[11] A year later Powell's new Bureau began to explore the political and moral import of that event.

The founding of the BAE profoundly altered the context, force, and direction of nineteenth-century American anthropology, but the precise nature of those alterations has never been specified. After the Boasian "school" of cultural anthropology rose to dominance in the 1920s and '30s, Robert H. Lowie and others established their own professional and tribal identity in part by drawing a clear line between the amateur proponents of unilinear evolutionism of the late nineteenth century, and the wave of Boas-trained students that formed the profession of anthropology after the turn of the century. The division was presumed to be at once institutional, attitudinal, and theoretical; the break seemed complete. Recent studies, often employing the insights and terminology of Thomas Kuhn, still emphasize major institutional and intellectual paradigm changes from the Bureau to Boas, but with awareness that such metamorphoses are fuzzy, gradual, and partial. Indeed, the stress now lies on continuities.[22] In order to address the issue of the Bureau's status in the professionalization of anthropology, the question must be rephrased so as to place the institution in historical context: In what ways did the BAE mark the culmination of certain trends in nineteenth-century science, including anthropology? On the other hand, in what ways did Powell's organization, by intention or otherwise, foster patterns of research, communication, personal identity, or institutional growth that are recognizably "professional" in a modern sense? The final judgment here is that Powell's organization was root-and-branch a nineteenth-century institution—the product of conditions and assumptions of another age—and that to view it as an early form or precursor of modern professional social science ignores Powell's deeply held commitments to the contrary. Powell never intended to "professionalize" anthropology, though he did hope to organize and systematize research. Powell drew simultaneously on two anthropological traditions, one from the natural sciences, the other deriving from the broad realm of eighteenth- and early-nineteenth-century moral philosophy. The first of these—the natural-history exploring, surveying tradition that came to him through such men as Humboldt and Gibbs—dominated American natural science to the Civil War and reached its peak in the western territorial surveys of the seventies. The scientific premium of the survey lay on discovery and description. Within this tradition there was a further division between those who, like George Gibbs, stressed holistic understanding of a region, and those who spread their nets more widely but selectively, such as Edward Palmer, botanist and ethnologist. In other words, the tradition embraced a broad continuum: from areal concentration to expertise in a specific line of work. While local scientific societies sustained (as they still do) the tradition of holistic inquiry defined by locality, by the end of the century powerful economic and cultural forces were determining its demise. One signal of the trend on the national level was the emergence of the BAE from the territorially defined Powell Survey.

The survey tradition centered on the individual for initiative and execution. In fact the American mythology of the lone trailblazer probably found more correspondence with reality among naturalists than among, say, commercial entrepreneurs. But the limits of this structure became apparent with the swelling ambitions of men like Gibbs and Powell. For a time the Smithsonian of mid-century provided one institutional solution to men whose visions exceeded their personal powers: Joseph Henry's distribution of circular questionnaires brought information more systematically while stimulating new exertions among the growing circle of correspondents. The intention, and effect, was to increase rather than limit participation in a guided scientific endeavor. But circulars provided, it turned out, insufficient control over personal idiosyncracy, and in retrospect the next developments seem obvious and inevitable: first, the personally led expedition with hand-picked men; following that, the permanent bureau of research filled with tested and trustworthy companions. The developments follow logically: frustration with unsystematic data led to increasingly elaborate circulars with detailed instructions; similarly, desire for personal influence in molding the scientific results created ever-more-rigid organizational structures. Finally, the sheer vastness of the undertakings induced a new appreciation of team effort.

But that is less than half the picture. Powell's commitments to individual freedom and autonomy warred constantly with the very structures he was creating. Here lay a deep paradox for Powell: system in science threatened to destroy individual genius. It was more generally the dilemma of a society that placed ever-greater value on efficiency and coordination in production, whether scientific or industrial—never mind the costs to the quality of the scientific (or industrial) experience. But Powell did mind, for like Joseph Henry he remembered and treasured his own scientific and spiritual awakening, and he wished the same for as many others as possible.

To Powell the individual was always prior to the organization, for only the individual perceived new needs and initiated new programs. Organizations, because they were no more than the extensions of the individual, were inherently limited. W J McGee best expressed this viewpoint in 1888 to Eugene W. Hilgard, an agricultural chemist. Agricultural geology, he predicted, would be the geology of the coming generation, but first the prophet of the science must arise and awake the people from torpor; until then, nothing could be expected from organized science. McGee reminded Hilgard that neither the state nor the federal surveys could "give inspiration or furnish brains to employees; the inspiration and the brain must precede the organization and give character to it; and the organization can only furnish means to ends already clearly perceived." It was necessary first to have "the genius of a born leader among thinking men" directed to clear goals.[23] In the Bureau this vision created loose arrangements in which individual personalities sometimes determined whole projects, and it led to accusations of poor planning. But the organized science of Powell and McGee was to be a conscious extension rather than a harnessing of nineteenth-century independence and individual effort.

It was not always perceived that way. The first generation of Americans to work in large, relatively impersonal structures (whether industrial, academic, or governmental) sometimes experienced severe problems of adjustment. The slow spiritual decay of the white-collar clerk world of Victorian America has yet to be examined by historians, though the Bartleby figures were legion by 1900. From the outside, such organizations appeared cold, unappreciative, and exclusive; from the inside, they could seem cold, unappreciative, and expropriative. Powell struggled for a balance between necessary bureaucracy and individual recognition and visibility, and he generally succeeded. For instance, both the BAE and his Geological Survey issued separate monograph series of lavishly illustrated papers by individuals. Additionally, the annual reports contained long monograph appendices, and the body of each report was organized around individual work. Administrators took care to outline the field and office work of each subordinate month by month. In the BAE reports it is sometimes possible to follow the monthly movements of individual personnel over stretches of years.

Still, Powell's structure of science was no simple democracy of discoverers. The legacy of Lewis Henry Morgan, which Powell self-consciously inherited, placed him clearly in the second anthropological tradition referred to above, one with very different implications for the purpose and structure of the science. Morgan's science of man, like that of contemporaries Herbert Spencer,

Edward B. Tylor, and Henry Maine, stood in the tradition of conjectural, reasoned histories of mankind, which had recent (though disrupted) roots among the French and Scottish moral philosophers of the eighteenth century. In contrast to the believer in the natural-science survey, the conjectural historian sought an all-embracing account of man's mental, social, and moral evolution based on comparative observations and organized in various series of stages. Where the naturalist/explorer emphasized descriptive taxonomy and (some of them) regional holism, the goal of the comparative method was boundless, overarching synthesis—universal laws of human development.

The nineteenth-century moral philosophers (including Morgan and Powell) who built grand conjectural structures of human development aimed in the end at a predictive science of man; they looked to the past mainly for clues to the future. The relevant point for present purposes is that in the scientific structure of this tradition, the generalizing savant stood apart from the mass of data-collectors, whose labors constituted only the essential first stage of science. The scientific enterprise was consequently divided into two classes of functions: the lower, preliminary work of exploration, observation, and collection; and the higher tasks of synthesis. Every man had a potential role as a scientist of some order, but some individuals were more complete scientists than others. When Otis T. Mason claimed that "every man, woman, and child" could be an anthropologist, he tacitly assumed a hierarchical, deferential community.

There were, in short, degrees of individual completeness in Bureau science. Furthermore, these degrees were determined not by depth of training in a specific field, but by character, integrity, and breadth of exposure across the sciences—precisely the subjective, loose criteria against which proponents of university training would do battle. "Worthy has been the work of specialists in the extension of knowledge, during the past half-century," McGee observed, "but nobler still have been the tasks of the fewer searchers who have been able to span two or more specialties, and to simplify knowledge by coordination."[24] To the extent that professionalism meant specialization, it was of secondary value. On his Colorado expeditions Powell had permitted his men to make their observations but reserved to himself responsibility for drawing the major conclusions.[25] Similarly, in the Bureau he established the general directions, entrusting the details to "selected persons skilled in their pursuits."[26] But the teamwork of the Bureau was not the cooperation of professional equals; while enjoying wide latitude in pace and choice of work, some men still worked for others. They did not entirely control their science.

Not that the ethnologists were discouraged from drawing their own conclusions. For the official record, at least, McGee noted that they "were always encouraged to seek relations and educe principles, and to publish under their own names such results of their work *as were not inconsistent* with those of other investigators; for it was recognized that research is best promoted by encouraging the investigator."[27] And Powell observed in 1890 that

> the ethnologists who, as authors, prepare the publications of the Bureau, personally gather the material for them in the field, supplementing this material by a study of all the connected literature and by a subsequent comparison of all ascertained facts. The continuance of the work for a number of years by the same zealous observers and students, who freely interchange their information and opinions, has resulted in their training with the acuteness of specialists . . .

But this was an unanticipated development for the director, and the results went "far beyond the expectations entertained when the Bureau was originally organized."[28] When the progress of research permitted the comparison and grouping of phenomena, Powell did the synthesizing, gradually using the materials of his staff as "building blocks in his synthetic history of mankind."[29] In part the practice reflected Powell's sense that the science of the Bureau must present a united front to Congress, as McGee intimated; he thus guarded against misreading of the monograph studies by politicians and the public. At the same time, though, he once explained to Samuel Langley that his staff members were "learners" whose papers "contribute[d] to the data and simpler principles" of anthropology but required elaboration to yield significant generalizations.[30]

The nature of individual scientific roles and team effort in the early Bureau is best illustrated by first reviewing the collaborative projects that formed the central focus of the 1880s, then examining the individual careers of some of Powell's colleagues. In 1879 Powell launched three group projects "of a generally practical or economic character":[31] a linguistic classification; a synonymy of tribal and stock names; and a history of treaty relations between the federal government and the Indian tribes. The treaty study, referred to as a "Historical Atlas of Indian Affairs," anticipated future questions over land titles in the western territories. It became the personal project of Charles C. Royce, a part-time staff member. Although Royce finished it (and left the Bureau) in 1885 and Powell promised its appearance "as rapidly as possible," the work lay untouched until 1895, when Cyrus Thomas brought it up to date. The authoritative *Indian Land Cessions in the United States* finally appeared in 1899.[32]

While the treaty study developed as an individual project, the synonymy and language classification were the products of many minds and hands. The synonymy arose from Powell's conviction that the first task in any science is to achieve consensus on terminology. His experience in the Great Basin had demonstrated the need to order all the names used historically for each tribe or language group, in order to clear the way for further study and reveal historical affinities. As he noted in the first BAE annual report, "to follow any tribe of Indians through post-Columbian times is a task of no little difficulty. Yet this portion of history is of importance, and the scholars of America have a great work before them."[33] In theory this step should precede new research, but as it turned out the synonymy work proceeded concurrently with other Bureau interests, in a decidedly subordinate position. Fresh field work always seemed more urgent.

Otis Mason had begun a synonymy around 1873 as a card catalog. "I could not take one step without it," he remembered. With the founding of the Bureau he offered it to Powell, who suggested that Mason continue it under his direction.[34] Mason refused; Powell then asked Garrick Mallery to keep the synonymy up to date and expand it, but Mallery was less than enthusiastic and soon returned to his studies of sign-language and pictography. Eventually, though, Powell got the entire staff involved in the work, which became enmeshed with individual projects and with Powell's main goal, the linguistic classification. At first, it seems, Powell thought that the confusion over tribal names had to be clarified for progress in any field: anthropology simply had to have a "code of nomenclature rules similar in scope to those prevailing among zoologists."[35] During the first years, however, Powell and Henry W. Henshaw gradually came to the opinion that a synonymy was itself impossible without prior division of North American tribes into linguistic stocks.[36] Until 1885, when they completed the preliminary classification, the synonymy was placed on a back burner.

Powell's problem was a classic dilemma in the history of science: categories are necessary simply to deal with data; but the categories themselves easily become sources of distortion because shaping and selecting shade so easily into warping. For a man as sensitive as Powell to the charge of violating the inductive process, the problem was acute, and his shifting search for a firm ground in ethnology was readily apparent in these years. In addition, his staff was somewhat recalcitrant to work on the synonymy. The first half dozen years of the new Bureau were a period of excitement and productivity for the staff, who were busily extending and deepening studies begun during the seventies.

The synonymy received a flurry of attention around 1886, due mainly to the arrival of James Mooney at the Bureau, and the completion of the preliminary classification. Since boyhood, Mooney had been running his personal BAE in Indiana, and he arrived in Washington with an advanced synonymy (as well as a treaty study and linguistic work). According to a recent biography of Mooney, "Henshaw and Mooney spent several weeks [in 1885] on Mooney's synonymy and regrouped the almost 2,500 tribal names into linguistic categories."[37] The result was their landmark "List of Linguistic Families of the Indian Tribes North of Mexico, with Provisional List of the Principal Tribal

Names and Synonyms," a fifty-five-page booklet that Powell printed and that remained the guide to BAE linguistic and synonymy work until 1891.

On the strength of the Mooney-Henshaw guide, Powell returned to the synonymy, instructing the staff to suspend individual work. He placed Henshaw in charge of what was already becoming a "vast and complicated undertaking."[38] Henshaw was to take the immensely complex tribes of the Northwest Coast and California; Albert S. Gatschet's attention was divided between the southeastern region and the Pueblo and Yuman peoples; James Owen Dorsey handled the Athapaskan stock, in addition to his specialties, Caddoan and Siouan; Garrick Mallery and James Mooney undertook the most complicated (in terms of historical literature and nomenclature), the Algonquian and Iroquoian; Walter J. Hoffman aided Powell with the Shoshonean; and Jeremiah Curtin worked mainly in California but helped all around.[39]

At the end of fiscal 1886 Powell estimated that work on half of the linguistic families was finished; but a year later he again dropped the synonymy and each man returned to private endeavors. Henshaw continued to help Powell with the linguistic map and classification that, the director now reminded his readers, "properly precedes and forms the basis of the volume on synonymy."[40] The brief flurry of the preceding year had apparently been a false start. Still, in 1888 J. Howard Gore, member of the Anthropological Society of Washington and friend of Powell, announced that the synonymy was "far advanced toward completion" and would reach a thousand pages.[41] In 1890 the director announced that Henshaw was engaged in a "final revision" of the synonymy, but developments further delayed its appearance.[42] At this point Henshaw's health failed. He was transferred to field work in California; in 1893 he obtained an indefinite leave of absence and moved to Hawaii.

Henshaw's departure left the synonymy dangling. But more than this, the project itself continued to change character, as reflected in the variety of names attached to it: Dictionary of Indian Tribes, Dictionary of Tribal Synonymy, Tribal Synonymy of the American Indians, and finally, in 1895, Cyclopedia of the American Indians. Powell confessed in 1894 that "the work is of such character as not soon to be completed, since each new investigation yields additional information."[43] That was precisely the chief dilemma of the Bureau's first twenty years: how to undertake exciting, fresh research and also achieve the final synthesis of definite knowledge that was the goal of Powell's science. Reviewing the history of the synonymy project in 1895, he recognized that the constant influx of new information from the field had permanently altered the nature of the project, so that "the synonymy proper diminished relatively, while the body of general information became greatly expanded." The work had become a "great cyclopedia."[44]

After 1893, Frederick Webb Hodge gradually assumed more control of the project, and between 1896 and 1901 he and Cyrus Thomas devoted their attention to it, aided occasionally by others. Thomas, fresh from work on Royce's *Land Cessions*, pursued the assignment vigorously, finishing the Algonquian and Siouan stocks. But in 1901 Langley transferred Hodge to the Smithsonian, Thomas returned to his Mayan calendar studies, and James Mooney reluctantly inherited the synonymy.[45] It still lay in his file drawers when Powell died.

In the last years Langley repeatedly urged Powell and McGee to make haste with the Cyclopedia in order to mollify congressional critics. After Powell's death, Langley took tight control of the Bureau through Holmes, and he pushed the project, now finally renamed *The Handbook of American Indians North of Mexico*, at the expense of Bureau field research. Hodge became general editor of the greatly expanded work that included, in addition to synonymies, essays on every aspect of anthropological science and Indian life. He moved back to the Bureau, marshaled the entire staff, and hired outsiders to contribute essays. The work was largely finished by 1905 and began to appear in 1907, one year after Langley's death.

"What happened to it was what happened to the Bureau in other respects: men died, that was the chief difficulty," McGee said of the synonymy in 1903. Henshaw left; Dorsey, Pilling, Mallery, and Hoffman died; Mooney's Kiowa work was too important to suspend; and Langley distracted Hodge with other duties.[46] But the fate of the synonymy owed more to deep-running dichotomies of purpose and less to individual careers than McGee indicated. Virtually every annual report of the BAE between 1880 and 1900 began by explaining that individual researches were constantly interrupted by the higher demands of the collaborative projects, and year after year Powell promised the Synonymy or Cyclopedia to Congress and the public. But with the exception of the 1886–87 period, the project never received concentrated effort. Increasingly it came to be seen as a hindrance to individual research.

The linguistic map and classification of 1891, which fulfilled a vision shared by Jefferson, Gallatin, and Gibbs, proved to be the single most lasting and influential contribution of the early Bureau to American anthropology. From the beginning, linguistics was the heart of Powell's "New Ethnology," his clearest window into the mind of primitive man. And yet his emphasis on language is initially puzzling, given his background in geology and natural history and his own mediocre linguistic abilities. It was Joseph Henry who first suggested Indian studies to Powell as a proper field of inquiry, but the inspiration behind his work probably came from Gibbs and William Dwight Whitney. Gibbs, as we have seen, envisioned a continental map and took important steps in that direction by collecting hundreds of vocabularies.[47] Whitney's influence on Powell was subtler but perhaps stronger.

"Of the different attempts between the years 1860 and 1870, which *for the first time* began to extract from the mass of results accumulated by comparative grammar some generalizations about language, all were frustrated or without general value, except that of Whitney. . . ."[48] In these words Ferdinande de Saussure in 1909 recalled the powerful impact of Whitney on the transatlantic linguistic community of the latter nineteenth century. The power derived from Whitney's insistence, in his works on general linguistics *Language and the Study of Language* (1867) and *Life and Growth of Language* (1875), that language must be studied as a natural phenomenon obeying traceable laws, not as a semi-divine gift, and that it is deeply embedded in human institutions. He treated linguistics as a "cultural fact."[49] But the scientific analog that Whitney most frequently employed to describe linguistic change and growth was the same one that so deeply affected Powell's ethnology: uniformitarian geology.

> There is no way of investigating the first hidden steps of any continuous historical process, except by carefully studying the later recorded steps, and cautiously applying the analogies thence deduced. So the geologist studies the forces which are now altering by slow degrees the form and aspect of the earth's crust, wearing down the rocks here, depositing beds of sand and pebbles there, pouring out floods of lava over certain regions, raising or lowering the line of coast along certain seas; and he applies the results of his observations with confidence to the explanation of phenomena dating from a time to which men's imaginations, even, can hardly reach. The legitimacy of the analogical reasoning is not less undeniable in the one case than in the other.[50]

Whitney demonstrated the possibility of a humanistic study that was at once a moral and historical science. Indeed, his great appeal as a scientist, for Powell as for others, lay in his pervasive developmental historicism. For Whitney, Michael Silverstein has written, "explanation must be in terms of how the particular items get there, that is, in terms of how they arise, spread, and become productive, and run their course to obsolescence and atavism. Furthermore, this historical explanation deals with change that is gradual and regular; it is free from catastrophes, such as the floods and crumbling towers invoked by defenders of Mosaic chronology."[51] From this perspective, Whitney's and Powell's visions of scientific purpose—to abolish mystery from the science of man—were identical.

The fact that Whitney's European contemporaries explicitly acknowledged his influence has led to the judgment that he found less appreciative reception in the United States.[52] It seems likely, however, that in a number of particulars and, more importantly, in a general confidence in linguistics as a reliable basis for anthropology, Powell was a clear disciple of Whitney. In his conviction that grammar illustrates a unilinear evolution to highly inflective forms, and in his initial assumption (later rejected) that the American Indian languages could be traced back to a common ancestor, Powell could find authority in Whitney. Powell relied on lexical rather than grammatical data for his classification because grammar, Whitney taught, was partly adventitious, partly a phenomenon and index of stages of growth. Powell introduced the map and classification in words that showed his debt to Whitney:

> Grammatic stucture is but a phase or accident of growth, and not a primordial element of language. The roots of a language are its most permanent characteristics, and while the words which are formed from them may change so as to obscure their elements or in some cases even to lose them, it seems that they are never lost from all, but can be recovered in large part. The grammatic structure or plan of a language is forever changing, and in this respect the language may become entirely transformed.[53]

During the seventies both Henry and Powell looked to the Yale professor for aid and approval of their linguistic program. In early 1873, Henry spoke with Whitney and Trumbull "as to the charge of our ethnology now that George Gibbs has departed this life."[54] Powell was the apparent successor, but three more years passed before the Smithsonian Secretary, responding to Powell's initiative, turned over to him the Institution's collection of 668 North American language vocabularies.

Powell's first move was to revise Gibbs's "Instructions" of 1865, which had proved such a useful stimulus. With help from Whitney he enlarged the alphabet and vocabulary list by adding phrases and simple sentences to demonstrate grammatical structure, as Gibbs had intended.[55] During the summer of 1877 Powell and Whitney corresponded about a general alphabet for Indian languages. Their relationship exposed both Powell's respect for academic linguistics and his sensitivity to the lessons of field experience. Like Gibbs, he was a man straddling two worlds. While bowing to Whitney's "superior judgment" in linguistic questions, Powell wrote that he was anxious to test the alphabet "by practical use this summer in my own hands" and to make changes "as experience suggests." He urged a simple alphabet for cheap printing and wide circulation among the "general literature of the country"; Whitney's proposals offered, he objected, "no general plan which can be easily learned and remembered" by field workers.[56] For his part, Whitney simply reminded Powell that "you have no good reason for regarding and treating me as an authority in these matters . . . questions of alphabetizing are questions of expediency and compromise."[57]

Powell's ambivalence toward Old World linguistics came through in his correspondence with Whitney. Following Schoolcraft and Gibbs, he saw that mythology and belief systems remained hidden without knowledge of the languages in which they are expressed.[58] But the study of language in America must differ somewhat in purpose and method from the work of Greek and Sanskrit scholars, Powell reasoned. While they might look admiringly at the symmetry and complexity of Old World tongues, the American linguist could never adopt such a posture. The modern anthropologist, Powell exclaimed in 1884, "no longer looks into antiquity for human perfection, but he looks into the future of the world's history for the establishment of universal justice . . ."—and, he might have added, for models of language. "So we may laud the ingenious grammatic devices of ancient languages, but who would make Greek the vernacular of civilization?"[59] Powell studied languages not for themselves but for what they revealed about man's mental growth, past and future.

Always the surveyor and mapper, Powell set out to organize the linguistic diversity of North America. For this purpose he required simple instructions and a corps of workers, not the complex instruments of academics. After Powell received the Smithsonian vocabularies in 1876, the Rocky Mountain Survey veered noticeably toward ethnology. The materials in Powell's charge were hopelessly unsystematic. Because "those engaged in the work needed constant direction and were frequently calling for explanations," the following year he issued the *Introduction to the Study of Indian Languages,* a manual for the field.[60] But he soon grew dissatisfied with the first edition because the alphabet, prepared by Whitney, was too complicated, the word lists were too short, and the instructions were unclear. In 1880 he issued a much bulkier edition, including his own alphabet, fifty pages of "hints and explanations," 150 pages of vocabulary lists organized in thirty schedules, and four Morgan kinship charts in the cover pocket. Powell had created a portable course in ethnology for the untutored but zealous traveler.

It is worth noting that in the second edition Powell arranged the vocabulary schedules according to his newly established categories of human "activities," in order to connect the language study with other aspects of culture. He hoped thereby to involve the collector more deeply with specific peoples so as to extract maximum meaning from the data. The ideal was not simply a smattering of significant words to establish affinities with other tribes, but greater depth:

> It has been the effort of the author to connect the study of language with the study of the other branches of anthropology, for a language is best understood when the habits, customs, institutions, philosophy—the subject-matter of thought embodied in the language are best known. The student of language should be a student of the people who speak the language; and to this end the book has been prepared . . .[61]

The 1880 *Introduction* thus struck two themes: extensive coverage and intensive knowledge. In phrases that echoed the mythology of the beckoning American frontier, Powell's scientific virgin land called to potential students: "The field of research is vast: the materials are abundant and easily collected; reward for scientific labor is prompt and generous."[62] The vast open spaces of anthropological science invited personal investment.

Between 1880 and 1885, on the basis of vocabulary materials gathered by predecessors, collaborators, and the BAE (mainly Dorsey and Gatschet), Powell and Henshaw gradually filled in the linguistic map of North America. Henshaw appeared as the author of the 1885 classification—substantially the same as the better-known 1891 publication, for which Powell assumed major credit and responsibility.[63] Because the classification was a long-term, cooperative effort, and because Powell did not publish evidence for linguistic connections, assigning specific responsibility for the map and stock groupings has been difficult.[64] Still, the general outline of operations is clear, and it suggests the nature of the inner dynamics of the early Bureau.

If there was a Bureau inner circle around Powell—perhaps equivalent to the "Great Basin Lunch Mess" over at the Geological Survey offices of the time[65]—it consisted of James Pilling, James Stevenson (until his death in 1888), Garrick Mallery, and Henry Henshaw. By contrast, James Owen Dorsey and Albert S. Gatschet never enjoyed the director's full esteem, though he valued their talents and integrity.[66] Gatschet in particular became the "laboring work-horse and philologist clerk for Powell and Henshaw," with little of his own to show for it.[67]

Henshaw was the central staff figure in both the classification and synonymy work. A veteran of the Wheeler (Army) Survey, on which he had worked with Harry C. Yarrow and others, Henshaw was an avid naturalist and ornithologist. Chronically weak health, which had prevented him from matriculating at Harvard as a young man, plagued him all his life—a life lived alone for eighty years. Henshaw recalled that "it was Major Powell's opinion that a biologic training was a prerequisite to a successful career in anthropology, and this opinion he held to the last."[68] Powell looked to him to establish a respectable scientific nomenclature for anthropology, and it was probably Henshaw who determined on borrowing from biology the law of priority as the organizing principle for Amerindian linguistics (beginning with Gallatin's 1836 *Synopsis of the Indian Tribes*).[69] (William H. Dall, a naturalist whose work appeared in the first volume of Powell's *Contributions to North American Ethnology*, may also have influenced Powell's model.) Powell ambiguously credited Henshaw with the "final form" of the classification, and his reliance may have been more general than appears. C. Hart Merriam, a close friend for much of Henshaw's life, claimed that Powell intended him to be the next director of the Bureau.[70] Whatever Powell's intentions, Henshaw's health declined precipitously in the early nineties, and W J McGee replaced him as Powell's administrative officer, amanuensis, and presumptive heir.

Dorsey and Gatschet did the field work, aided to some extent by Jeremiah Curtin in California. Contrary to his own advice in the 1880 *Introduction*, Powell often assigned his men to groups with whom they had no familiarity. To some extent this was inevitable, given the massive undertaking. But in

Henry Weatherbee Henshaw, who served as Powell's linguistic
coordinator until 1892.

one instance, at least, he rejected Gatschet's separation of two Oregon languages—the conclusion from a prolonged study in the region—on the basis of a short reconnaissance by Dorsey.[71] Despite his European linguistic training, Gatschet was considered an astute observer and collector, but little more. While he and Dorsey collected, Powell and Henshaw compared. In his reports the director credited the vocabulary gathering expeditions in detail but remained silent about his own methods and criteria. Both scientific roles were necessary, but the higher functions involved less accountability to the public or Congress.

The linguistic work exemplified the unusual combination of openness and exclusiveness, even secrecy, that marked BAE work. It also illustrated the extent to which Dorsey and Gatschet, and in various ways all the BAE ethnologists, were incomplete scientists. The development of a "professional" consciousness, in Washington and elsewhere, required the transformation of this pattern into the modern concept of the field anthropologist, competent through training to collect and analyze his own observations. This development could not occur within the institutional structures of government anthropology. In Washington in the 1880s, functions were parceled out among different men.

To the early Bureau Powell brought men whom he knew and trusted. The major figures in this core of BAE founders were James C. Pilling, James Owen Dorsey, Albert S. Gatschet, and Garrick Mallery. For each of them the Bureau presented opportunity to expand researches already in progress. These individual projects, along with Powell's attempts at larger joint efforts, shaped the original BAE.

Perhaps closest to Powell as friend and amanuensis was James Pilling. A patient, painstaking, thoroughly upright man, Pilling was by all accounts admirable but not lovable, pleasant but cold—an unexciting personality. Those who failed to appreciate the value of his services could easily detest his plodding, filing-system mentality. The brilliant Clarence King was one such: "Do you want to do Powell a favor?" he advised a colleague. "Poison Pilling."[72]

Pilling's personality and methods produced a prodigious amount of work, however. A native of Washington state, Pilling attended Gonzaga College and taught himself the commercially valuable art of stenography. At age twenty he was a stenographer for congressional committees and commissions, and in this way came eventually to join Powell's Rocky Mountain Survey in 1875. For nearly four years he was "almost continuously" among Indians, faithfully recording Powell's vocabularies and stories. The two men formed a bond, as Powell fondly recalled:

Through many of the years of active life James and I were associated, in the office and in the field. Field work led us into the wilderness of

James Pilling, faithful clerk to Powell, in his library.

mountain and canyon, of forest and desert, away from the comforts and conveniences of civilization, where life itself was preserved by a constant struggle. In all this experience my boon companion never failed nor faltered, always doing more than his share in the struggle for existence and in the effort necessary to fill life with joy. He never rested from his labor when labor could be of value; he never lost courage, and courage was always in demand.[73]

Powell took care of his own, and he brought Pilling to the Bureau in 1879 as clerk and friend. When he succeeded Clarence King as director of the Geological Survey two years later, he eased the burden on BAE appropriations by moving Pilling, along with photographer Jack Hillers, executive officer James Stevenson, and himself, to the Survey payroll. Pilling became chief clerk of the Survey as well as clerk of the Bureau, retaining and expanding his bibliographical duties. These soon became all-consuming. His career project, begun in 1877, was nothing less than complete bibliographies of the literature on all the Indian languages of North America. If he did not know it in the beginning, Pilling soon realized that he could never complete such a massive task; in 1881 he wrote that "if I ever print my Bibliography I should like to insert a note telling why the work was never finished."[74]

Pilling persisted. Through the first decade of the Bureau, in tandem with the linguistic classification and the synonymy, Pilling's bibliographies grew steadily to thousands of titles. The meticulous file man received help from the entire Bureau staff and from interested individuals outside Washington who recognized the value of reference works.[75] The bibliographies remained Pilling's individual devotion, and he gave the last fifteen years of his life to them. He scoured the private and public libraries of the United States and Canada; when he went to Europe on personal matters, he spent most of his time in libraries and bookstores. In the process he established for the Bureau one of the finest ethnological libraries in the world.[76]

In 1885 Pilling sent out 100 copies of the 1,200-page *Proof-Sheets*, his preliminary bibliography, to collaborators for criticism and use.[77] But as new titles and information arrived almost daily, Pilling's work grew from a single volume to a series of large BAE *Bulletins*. The first linguistic stock completed was the Eskimo, which appeared as the Bureau's initial *Bulletin* in 1887. Eight more stock bibliographies had followed by Pilling's death in 1895.

After the death of his friend, Powell wrote somewhat ambiguously to Pilling's widow that the bibliographic work constituted a "monument to wisely directed labor."[78] Pilling's bibliographic labors indeed derived directly from Powell's larger purposes. The developing linguistic classification defined the categories of the bibliography, which progressed accordingly. More important, the history of Pilling's work typified the experience of the early Bureau. As Wallace Stegner has noted, despite the constant search and acquisition of new materials, "the aim was utter definitiveness, completion."[79]

The daily activities of the Bureau's office and field staff constantly frustrated the larger synthetic goals of Powell's anthropology. Originally envisioned as a definitive "pre-chore," a cornerstone of future research, Pilling's bibliographies emerged as a partial product. Pilling published only nine of fifty-eight language stocks, but they were the stocks with the largest, most scattered literature. A preparatory task grew into a major library research project and an unfinished but monumental personal accomplishment.

Pilling's drive to completeness also characterized the labors of another original member of Powell's staff, Colonel Garrick Mallery. A Pennsylvanian who traced his lineage back to the first decade of Puritan settlement, Mallery graduated from Yale in 1850, received a law degree from the University of Pennsylvania three years later, and at the onset of the Civil War had established a legal career in Philadelphia. In 1861, however, he abandoned the law to volunteer in the Union army. A year later he was severely wounded, captured, and exchanged; he returned to active duty in 1863. At the end of the war, Mallery accepted a commission in the regular army. After serving as secretary of state and adjutant general during the military occupation of Virginia, he worked for six years in the office of the chief signal officer, where he undertook meteorological researches. In 1876 he received command of Fort Rice (Dakota Territory), but his war wounds finally forced his retirement from the army in 1879.[80]

"Old habits of the Civil War left their mark of military drill on everyone who lived through it," Henry Adams perceived.[81] Major Powell's Bureau bore a few such marks. Among Washington circles of scientists and politicians who celebrated Civil War heroism and literate gentility, Mallery's "rugged manliness," educational and legal background, and conversational ease assured immediate and hearty acceptance. He seemed, in fact, the epitome of American Anglo-Saxon manhood: gallant soldier, broad scholar, man of science, genial companion, affectionate husband, staunch friend, and "high-bred gentleman," in the words of a lifelong friend.[82] As witty contributor to the Literary Society of Washington, president of the Philosophical Society of Washington, and BAE ethnologist, Mallery enjoyed great esteem in the capital until his death in 1894.

Mallery's interest in the North American Indians stemmed from his time in the Dakotas, where he found a "rude and interesting native picture record" that he analyzed as a primitive calendar. The following year he published "A Calendar of the Dakota Nation" as part of Ferdinand Hayden's survey of the territories.[83] It immediately attracted attention, and within two months Powell had obtained Mallery's transfer to the Rocky Mountain Survey. Mallery stayed with Powell for the rest of his life. When the founding of the Bureau coincided with his forced resignation from the military, the Colonel joined up with the Major.[84]

Colonel Garrick Mallery, lawyer, soldier, and stalwart scientist
of the BAE.

Over the next fifteen years, the Colonel, like Pilling, committed himself with rare devotion to a project that became an obsession: North American sign languages and picture-writing. And like the bibliographies and the synonymy, Mallery's pursuit became an uncompleted lifetime project because the data always outran the synthesis. But in the process Mallery, working through correspondents and his field researcher, Walter J. Hoffman, collected vast amounts of data on sign language, pictographs, and other forms of early Indian writing that would otherwise have disappeared unrecorded. His Bureau publications, lavishly illustrated with hundreds of color drawings, still remain a mine of information on phenomena that have since vanished.[85]

Between 1879 and 1894 Mallery worked steadily at his task. A preliminary goal was reached early with the publication of his *Introduction to the Study of Sign-Language* (1880), the third of Powell's proposed series of manuals for students and collaborators.[86] The same year, in accord with Powell's mode of operation, Mallery privately circulated to some correspondents a "Collection of Gesture Signs and Signals of the North American Indians, with some comparisons." These private and public stimuli produced a flood of data from across the country and overseas. Mallery immediately began synthesizing it into his *Sign-Language among the North American Indians for the first annual report*.[87] Although intended as tentative, *Sign-Language* was soon hailed as definitive. He then turned his attention to his original interest, pictographs; the results were another "preliminary paper" on pictographs (1886), and ultimately the 800-page *Picture-writing* opus of 1893.

Mallery carried forward the pattern of science-by-correspondence that Henry had found appropriate to the early Smithsonian, and Powell judged his methods and results as the best example of the fundamental plan behind the Bureau.[88] With the exceptions of two field trips in the late 1880s, Mallery remained an office worker, an editor of raw data. As Powell remarked of his work on pictography, the "primary authors" were unknown aborigines, for whom Mallery served as "discoverer, compiler, and editor."[89]

Within the Bureau framework, Mallery's purpose was clear: to discover the laws regulating early stages of linguistic evolution.[90] Gesturing and pictography, Powell believed, represented the typically "vague and indefinite, or chaotic" but unceasing efforts of primitive men to communicate through "thought symbols." The Indians of North America, "still groping blindly and widely for definite methods" at the time of White contact, illustrated among themselves the modes of picture-writing.[91] Mallery's efforts were expected to shed light on this early mental development.

The educated, stalwart Army colonel provided Powell with an unimpeachable investigator, a man of credentials in an area that invited speculation. Some investigators, Powell reminded his readers, had imagined "in the nebulous light of hieroglyphic symbols" connections between the Indians and other races of men, or had seen mysterious religious meanings in the aboriginal pictographs. Mallery had introduced a refreshingly objective and practical view:

> There was in him no bias toward a mystic interpretation, or any pre-determination to discover an occult significance in pictographs. . . . The probability appeared, from his actual experience, that the interpretation was a simple and direct, not a mysterious and involved process . . .[92]

While fully appreciating the poetic and imaginative features of primitive pictography, Mallery avoided "mystic symbolism" as a canon of interpretation; he presented facts "simply as facts."[93] Thus Powell celebrated with Mallery the new empirical age of post-Civil War America. Mallery turned to poetry himself to describe the new order:

> But now the cosmologic drama's o'er,
> Mithra's a myth, Great Pan pans out no more.
> Our world gives little scope to doctrine mystic—
> 'Tis wary, doubting, stern, and realistic;
> Takes every axiom on strict probation,
> And calls for propter hoc and demonstration.[94]

Mallery drew from his empirical rigor (if not from his poetry) an optimistic vision of human history. Herbert Spencer had argued that human militancy had paralyzed men with fear; gestures of greeting were signals of defense-lessness and terror. Reviewing collaborators' reports, Mallery answered that such salutations are in fact exchanged with greater frequency as civilization advances, "thus denoting a mutual sentiment or sympathy." "The history of salutations," he concluded, "illustrates the transition from egoism to altruism."[95]

In his vice-presidential address to the American Association for the Advancement of Science in 1889, the ethnologist turned to the implications of his work for the future of the American Indian. "Israelite and Indian: A Parallel in Planes of Culture" was an extended argument for psychic unity and against transoceanic contact. He went on to argue, as Powell had been reiterating for a decade, that study of the Indian was fruitless as long as anthropologists viewed the aborigines as a racial division of man rather than a stage of development. The Indians were not a people uniquely resistant to civilization, nor were they more naturalistic or spiritualistic than any people in their culture status. With "reasonable opportunities" the Indian would progress to civilization and Christianity.[96] The ineluctable trend to human unity would embrace all people, and "both Israelite and Indian will be lost in the homogeneous ocean which mankind seems destined to swell."[97]

In the obituary of his staunch friend, Powell especially noted his "scholarly taste" and "strong power of philosophic comparison."[98] The joining of the aesthetic and the intellectual reveals much about the wide respect that Mallery enjoyed. His scientific credentials lay in his Army virility, good taste and manners, elegant writing style, dedication to work, and adherence to a general evolutionary persuasion. A genial and witty raconteur, Mallery was a favorite at the gentlemanly literary and scientific societies of the capital. Because he embodied the ideal combination of soldier-scientist-litterateur, he lent important prestige to Powell's young anthropological research center at a time when the credibility of the science still lay in such general attributes. At Mallery's death in 1894 (within a few months of Pilling's and Dorsey's), Major Powell felt a deep personal and institutional loss.

Powell's feeling of loss is understandable, for the philosophical affinity between the two men was abundantly clear. Mallery, though, possessed a sensitive intelligence that was confined by his manners, moralisms, and philosophical categories. Powell shared the evolutionary worldview, and until his final years at least, it empowered him to great institutional and intellectual feats. But the structures that invigorate some men stifle others, and with Mallery there is a distinct sense of lost possibility. For example, in 1877 he delivered a paper before the Philosophical Society of Washington in which he convincingly refuted wishful assertions that North American Indians had worshipped a single God or Great Spirit. Mallery explained:

> Doubtless in councils and other intercourse with Christians, Indian speakers employed the words *Manito, Taku Wakan,* and the like, in a sense acceptable to the known prejudices of their interlocuters, but that was through courtesy and policy, much as the strictest Protestant would once have found it convenient if not necessary, when at Rome, to speak respectfully to the Pope. The adoption of expressions as well as of ideas which were understood to be agreeable to or expected by the whites, is well illustrated in the use by western Indians of the terms "squaw" and "papoose," which are not in their languages, but are mere corruptions from the Algonkin. As all travelers insisted upon those words to signify woman and child, the tribes, as successively met, complied . . .[99]

Mallery's observations are commonsensical and yet astute, for he displays insight into patterns of accommodation and acculturation that was rare in his generation. But such insight came, could only come, in flashes, without elaboration and further pursuit. Similarly, the overriding conviction of human progress hid from him, perhaps mercifully, the tragic complexity behind his observations. But in those moments of insight lay the Colonel's true scientific, humanistic credentials.

William Turner advised Henry in 1851 that the only men suitably motivated to study the "mental idiosyncracies" of American Indians were the dedicated missionaries who spent long, arduous years at their posts.[100] The career of

James Owen Dorsey, a member of the Bureau from its founding until his death in 1895, demonstrated that the missionary spirit lived on, although attenuated and secularized, to the end of the century. If Pilling contributed the punctiliousness of the librarian, and Mallery the robust vigor of the Army man, the early Bureau found in Dorsey a sympathetic patience and a desire to understand in order eventually to save the Indian. Through all his immersion in the details of Indian linguistics and mythology, Dorsey always retained "in some measure his evangelical functions."[101] It was not an easy position to hold in the Bureau.

Born in Baltimore in 1848, Dorsey displayed a talent for languages even as a boy. He joined the Theological Seminary of Virginia in 1867 and became a deacon in the Episcopal church in 1871. Immediately Dorsey began missionary work among the Ponca Indians, a Siouan tribe of present-day Nebraska. After twenty-seven months he interrupted this work due to serious illness.[102]

When he left the Poncas in 1873, Dorsey was already speaking to the Indians without an interpreter and working on grammars and dictionaries of the Ponca language. Joseph Henry, an old family friend, aided and censored his work. Using a copy of Riggs's Dakota dictionary on loan from the Smithsonian, Dorsey examined the Indian tongues according to the categories of classical languages, carefully noting supposed similarities between Hebrew and Siouan tongues.[103] Since he was anxious to obtain Smithsonian support for publishing, he offered to send periodic accounts of his investigations and hoped for helpful suggestions from Henry's "philological collaborator." Others in the same line of work had only single informants, while he had 730 natives, Dorsey reminded one correspondent. Besides, other investigators operated from "improper motives."[104] However noble his motivations, Dorsey's early work, particularly the Hebrew connections, did not impress Smithsonian officials:

> But I would at the same time strongly advise to admit nothing but the bare materials without any kind of "comparisons" or would-be philological remarks. The work ought to be simple, clear, plain, and written in sober style. . . . Thus Mr. Dorsey will have to avoid in his work all sorts of digressions and everything else that savors of eccentricity and enthusiasm, especially those very crude and immature comparisons with Hebrew![105]

Dorsey returned eastward to a Maryland parish for five years in the midseventies, but neither his linguistic proficiency nor his mission was forgotten. When Powell began assembling his corps of ethnologists for the Rocky Mountain Survey in 1877, Henry recommended Dorsey. That year Powell engaged Dorsey to develop a grammar and dictionary of Ponca; in July 1878, Powell dispatched him to the Omaha reservation in eastern Nebraska for further field

Reverend James Owen Dorsey, linguist and ethnologist of the
Siouan peoples.

study. Dorsey stayed there nearly two years and returned as a member of the new Bureau.

Dorsey was hired as an expert on the Siouan languages and tribes, particularly the Omahas, Poncas, Quapaws, and Kansas. At the founding of the BAE, the Siouan family was known in greater detail than any other North American stock. The Bureau recognized eight Siouan languages, subdivided into twelve dialects. Of these, Dorsey devoted most of his attention to the four dialects he recognized in the language he called Cegiha: Ponca, Kansas, Osage, and Quapaw.

Dorsey's field experience among the Omahas and Poncas in 1871–73 and in 1878–80 provided the foundation for all his subsequent Siouan work; with only three exceptions he thereafter confined his work to Washington. In 1883 he traveled to Canada to investigate Tutelo, which Horatio Hale had recognized as a Siouan tongue; and to the Indian Territory to work with Quapaw speakers. Two years later, at Henshaw's insistence and very reluctantly, he undertook a four-month investigation of the linguistic groups of Oregon; and in 1892 he spent two months in Louisiana living with the last surviving speakers of Biloxi, which Gatschet had discovered as Siouan in 1887.[106]

Dorsey repeated the pattern of Powell and Mallery: intense early field work succeeded by an office career of collating and synthesizing, with only sporadic returns to the field. At times he struck a compromise of sorts by working with individual informants in Washington. This practice produced particularly fruitful results in 1887, when the Bureau hired George Bushotter, a Dakota who spoke Teton dialect, to record myths and legends. Over a six-month period Bushotter provided Dorsey with 258 manuscripts, as well as illustrative sketches, to which Dorsey added editorial notes and translations. The following year, John Bruyier, from the Cheyenne River Agency, worked on some of the Bushotter texts, demonstrating for Dorsey the differences between Teton among his people and the dialect of Bushotter's folk at the Pine Ridge and Lower Brulé reservations. In subsequent years Dorsey undertook similar informant work at his Washington office.[107]

Franz Boas once wrote that Dorsey's record of Ponca and Omaha literature, while severely limited, gave "deep insight into the mode of thought of the Indian," and he recommended Dorsey as a model, albeit an imperfect one, for linguistically based ethnography. In Boas's opinion, Dorsey largely ignored material culture and major aspects of ritual and social organization, but his work was still the best in 1906.[108] In actuality Dorsey did address many of these subjects. His publications included studies of dwellings, furniture, implements; migrations and war and mourning customs; kinship and marriage and social arrangements; as well as various collections of myths, stories, letters, dictionaries, and grammars. In his early work he even took notes on ethnobotany.

Dorsey always remained a student and active supporter of the interests of the peoples of the northern Plains. More than any other member of the original BAE, he resisted the strong surveying tendency by returning again and again to the languages, myths, rituals, and social arrangements of the Siouan peoples. He helped the Poncas write letters requesting improvements in reservation conditions, attended their councils, and personally wrote to the Commissioner of Indian Affairs on their behalf, all the while avidly attending to their language and social life. He observed sensitively and gathered his knowledge "without any force or artifice at all."[109]

This intimacy made possible a high standard in field method for the Bureau, and at least one novice, James Mooney, found a model in Dorsey's modest, sympathetic temperament.[110] Dorsey remarked acutely on the inconsistency of speakers of any language, noting that individuals change linguistic habits with age and that dialects are constantly in flux through contact. Thus, any grammar was an ideal, not a description of reality. In both his vocabulary work and grammar analysis, Dorsey resisted the imposition of Indo-European categories, insisting on the integrity of native systems.[111]

While he obediently adopted Morgan-Powell structures and terminology, Dorsey refused to theorize from his data, which as often as not contradicted Powell's expectations. Thus, Powell anticipated a process of differentiation in government functions among the Omaha; Dorsey's *Omaha Sociology* announced steady consolidation. As one historian has aptly concluded, "Dorsey's reports are an excellent example of how Powell's insistence on extensive field work by good observers did not function to prove Powell's theories, but instead provided information damaging to what the Director believed should be found."[112] Nonetheless, Powell managed to mold Dorsey's findings into appropriate shapes. At first Dorsey's investigations displeased the director, who ordered him to undertake a "special study" of anthropology—which meant reading Morgan's *Ancient Society*.[113] Although the "crude Hebraic comparisons" of his linguistics had long since disappeared, the former missionary was still inclined to see civilized notions of monotheism in primitive religions.[114] Once accommodated to the Morgan/Powell framework, though, Dorsey's empirical work yielded far-reaching conclusions for the director. When Dorsey's *Study of Siouan Cults* appeared in the 1890 report, Powell found "many important conclusions" standing "in the background" awaiting elucidation. Chief among them was confirmation of Powell's vision of primitive belief, in which supernatural powers are attributed to organic and inorganic objects. Dorsey had found that "it is safer to divide phenomena as they appear to the Indian mind into the human and superhuman, as many, if not most natural phenomena are mysterious to the Indian."[115] To Powell the iconoclastic lesson was clear. For three centuries, hasty observers had written of Indian belief in a single "Great Spirit." Taking this as a sign of

ANDRÉE

Albert Samuel Gatschet, Swiss-born linguist and student of
American Indian languages.

preparation for Christianity, generations of missionaries had sought to impose their God on it. Now the work of missionary Dorsey had finally exploded the myth: the savage mind knew no such concept.

While never a member of Powell's inner group, Dorsey was popular in the Bureau and was valued as an ethnologist and as a model of scientific method. From Powell's viewpoint he embodied the conflict between science and religion—an integral part of Powell's vision of mental evolution—in which empirical experience ultimately would override prejudice and superstition. His own career demonstrated the importance of prolonged, repeated, first-hand observations; perhaps the director viewed Dorsey's fieldwork as a kind of mental health cure on the Plains. Independent of untrustworthy interpreters, cautious, competent, Dorsey could present Indian beliefs with "unsurpassed fidelity."[116] He was a clear advance over deluded, pioneer missionary-ethnologists. As with Mallery, though, it is difficult to accept the contemporary Powellian evaluation of Dorsey. He did not embody conflict; rather, he combined deep human concern with stubborn attention to experienced truth. In sum, Dorsey brought forward the best of the American missionary tradition to the very edge of modern field ethnography. Perhaps Turner was correct after all: a truly human anthropology must retain within it something of the purged, sober mission.

In 1972 the following note was found among Albert S. Gatschet's notes for the synonymy: Every day from nine to ten, A. M.:

> Black the shoes.
> Fill bottles with coal oil.
> Clean & fill the lamp.
> Empty the waste-basket.[117]

That note might have served as the linguist's epitaph.

Gatschet personified the contradictory impulses of Washington anthropology. While he dispersed his energies at Powell's request over more than a hundred languages, he kept trying to return to his favorites, the Klamath Indians of Oregon. His linguistic ethnography of the Klamath, Boas judged in 1903, included "at the present time by far the best grammar of an American language in existence. If he had done nothing else but that he would have justified his work."[118]

Gatschet did much else. Between March 1877, when he joined Powell's Rocky Mountain Survey, and his forced retirement from the Bureau because of ill health in March 1905, he was an accomplished linguist and an indefatigable worker. A native of Switzerland, Gatschet attended the universities of Bern and Berlin, studying philology and theology. He emigrated in 1868 to New York, where he taught languages and contributed articles to scientific journals in both Europe and America. In 1872 Oscar Loew, a German botanist and linguist, returned to New York from the Wheeler Survey of the Southwest with sixteen Indian vocabularies, which he asked Gatschet to examine. To the countryman of Gallatin and Agassiz the experience opened a new world. His analyses appeared in the 1875 and 1876 reports of the Wheeler Survey, where Powell first saw Gatschet's name and work.[119] In March 1877, he accepted the Major's offer of a position on the Rocky Mountain team, with the understanding that he could publish any linguistic materials that he discovered in the manuscripts of the Smithsonian or in Powell's Survey.[120]

Gatschet's first assignment sent him to the Pacific coast to gather statistics on the tribes of Oregon and Washington Territory for the Bureau of Indian Affairs. Although the project was of a census nature, it marked the beginning of his Klamath studies.[121] His "Linguistic and General Researches among the Klamath Indians" appeared in the first report (1880). Like most of the first Bureau publications, it was a progress report. Using the language and texts as a basis, Gatschet ranged widely into the culture, embracing "mythic, ethnic, historic tales, grammar, and dictionary."[122]

Powell praised the Swiss immigrant for his unique ability to combine field experience with "high linguistic attainments of a general character." Here again Powell derived generalizations from Gatschet's painstaking Northwest work.[123] But the director had other priorities as well, and they soon began to impinge on Gatschet. In 1881 his detailed study of the Klamath language was already "in press," but it did not appear for nine more years, as Powell placed heavier burdens of the synonymy and the linguistic map on his linguist.

Between 1882 and 1890, Gatschet's career was marked by short, often fruitless foraging expeditions through the Southeast in search of remnant linguistic groups. There were a few startling discoveries, such as Biloxi; but the annual reports record some meager harvests. During the winter of 1881–82, for example, Gatschet traveled to South Carolina, where he located twenty surviving speakers of Catawba; then to New Orleans to record words and sentences from Choctaw speakers. He next spent two weeks with a small group of Chitimacha Indians, recording some 2,000 terms; and concluded his season with a vain search for three other groups. On his return Gatschet spent the rest of the year and the following two on Klamath.[124] In 1885, when Powell again superimposed the synonymy on his staff, Gatschet returned to the field: six weeks among Apaches in Texas, where without an interpreter he could not get trustworthy results; two months among reservation Kiowa and Comanches, where "the circumstances necessitated careful and numerous revisions of everything obtained"; and another month with the long-sought Atakapa of Louisiana, where he found the "sonorous, but strongly nasal" language spoken by "a few women living at the town." Other tribes visited on this sweep included Creek, Yuchi, Modoc, and Shawnee. Two he failed to locate.[125]

By 1888 Gatschet had rewritten the morphology of Klamath three times but was still digesting material for his region of the synonymy (eastern Florida to the Rio Grande). In 1890 he finally completed the Klamath grammar and wrote the last section, an "Ethnographic Sketch." It took another year to prepare the entire monograph for printing.[126]

As the Klamath work was emerging, Gatschet returned to ten years of unfinished notes on other tribes. But Powell had other plans. Gatschet, now approaching sixty, received the unenviable assignment of phonetically comparing the eastern and western dialects of the Algonquian family, a total of some forty to fifty dialects. It was an entirely new field for the aging linguist, and he spent the rest of his career, until 1905, diligently at work on it. He never produced another major study.

Judgments of Gatschet's work have varied widely. John R. Swanton, who joined the Bureau in 1901 (as successor to Dorsey) and knew Gatschet in his years of decline, suggested that while Dorsey became involved in the "mentality" of his subjects, Gatschet was purely a linguist.[127] Swanton was wrong. Gatschet was primarily a linguist in the sense that he, like Powell, viewed language as the key to ethnological study, and he devoted the larger proportion of his time to lexical and morphological analysis. But his Klamath work— as well as *Migration Legend*, which includes ethnographic materials from Creek, and which Swanton used heavily—demonstrates that his interests ranged well beyond language. The most qualified contemporary judge, Boas, was ambivalent. As we have seen, he highly praised Gatschet's work, but he also doubted that Gatschet could write the kind of analytical grammar that Boas envisioned for his *Handbook of North American Languages*. He avoided confronting his old friend while planning the project.[128]

Clearly Gatschet did not produce the major works that might have been expected from nearly three decades of labor. Regna Darnell has pointed out perceptively that standards changed in the Bureau between 1879 and 1895: the scattered bits and pieces of languages that filled out the linguistic map in 1891 had little value subsequently. But, as Boas knew quite well, Gatschet more than any other Bureau member was used for the director's ends and distracted from his own preferred work. Defending the old man's failure to publish, Boas reminded an investigating committee that Gatschet had been a tool to satisfy Powell's salvaging and surveying impulses:

By 1893 [Boas testified], Gatschet had accumulated such a vast amount of material that the only right thing for him to do would have been to sit down and write it out for publication. And he himself would have been only too glad to have had an opportunity to do so. His lack of publication is only a result of the policy of Major Powell, who wanted him to gather material for his general volume on the languages of the American Race.

Gatschet, concluded Boas, "has been by far the most eminent American philologist, away ahead of all of us."[129]

Gatschet was retired by the Bureau in 1905 and lived his last two years in poverty. Boas and others attempted unsuccessfully to ease the end with a pension from the new Carnegie Institution. Speaking of his former colleague, Otis Mason summarized his feelings: "For thirty years I have intimately known this scholar with an eye single to his researches concerning American Aboriginal languages. No other thought entered his mind. His permanent results are enormous."[130] Six months later Gatschet was dead.

Gatschet's dilemma was that of the early Bureau. He could not simultaneously produce the integrated studies of specific cultures that only years of concentrated exposure would have made possible, and also fill out Powell's map and synonymy. He bent to Powell's purposes partly because they suited his style, if not his scientific interests. A contributor but never fully an insider in Powell's organization, Gatschet preferred to work alone, methodically, thoroughly, honestly, and he was largely left alone. James Mooney warmly saluted the Bureau linguist, who "secure in his own honor . . . made no attempt to build up a reputation at the expense of other men, but gave to each his due credit.[131]

"When brought into close contact with the Indian, and into intimate acquaintance with his language, customs, and religious ideas," Powell lamented in 1891, "there is a curious tendency observable in students to overlook aboriginal vices and to exaggerate aboriginal virtues. It seems to be forgotten that after all the Indian is a savage . . ."[132] In this remarkably revealing statement Powell confessed to an unanticipated paradox. The tendency to subjective attachment, which resulted from prolonged exposure to specific peoples and which (Powell claimed) was particularly strong among students of language, warped scientific judgment as surely as did earlier negative estimates of the Indian based on prejudice. After more than a decade of Bureau activity, its director feared a loss of philosophical detachment.

Powell had always taken upon himself to keep before the Congress and the public the "great truths" of anthropological science; his entire scientific structure reflected this purpose and vision of his own role. Primary among these truths was the assertion that "the mind of man is everywhere practically the same, and that the innumerable differences of its products are indices merely of different stages of growth or are the results of different conditions of environment."[133] But why did Powell feel compelled at this time to restate his tenets of psychic unity and unilinear evolutionism and to remind his readers that "after all the Indian is a savage"?

The underlying moral and political question of BAE anthropology was the justice of the Indian's fate. This is not to suggest that the Bureau ethnologists operated under a cloud of guilt and penitence; on the contrary, with the possible exception of Charles Royce among the early staff, no man would have denied that the North American aborigines in one sense or another deserved their doom.[134] Powell and his associates worked not to question the outcome of history but to demonstrate why it had to be so, and possibly to ameliorate the process through science. By 1890 the general outline of human history and the major factors in determining the disparate fates of man seemed to be clear: Man had begun as one, but through a long period of prehistoric time had dispersed over the globe. From the point of dispersion, environmental influences had acted to determine differential rates of invention and growth and had gradually instilled permanent differences among races of men. Thus racial differences, while originally environmental, were nonetheless persistent and determinative of further growth or stagnation. However, since the beginning of European expansion and communication, the process of human differentiation had been reversed; the twentieth century would see the physical and cultural integration of all peoples in a global community.

This was essentially Morgan's optimistic prediction, which Powell, McGee, Mason, and Holmes elaborated in their own ways. Architectonically it also owed much to Spencer's suggestion of universal, alternating phases of integration and differentiation in all phenomena. But the emphasis on return to an egalitarian world fellowship demonstrates a spirit that was peculiarly American—and wishfully romantic.

Ill-equipped or unwilling to face the realities of growth, power, and destruction in their own society, Powell and his followers sought to rise above immediate experience by appeal to the categories of scientific understanding. In short, the insistence on the large vision, the "great truths," over immediacy and sentimental attachment was an appeal and escape from history to scientific abstraction. However tragic Indian-White relations may seem to the untutored, Powell wrote more than once, the scientific ethnologist, seeing the larger picture of past and future, knows better:

> Despite the pitiably frequent cases of personal and temporary injustice to the weaker race, the general policy has been guided by a deep-grounded recognition of the principles of justice and right on the part of both peoples . . . that the recognition of the rights of the aboriginal landowners has grown stronger and firmer with the passing of generations from the first settlement to the present, that the sympathy for the weaker race has increased with mutual understanding, and that the justice shown the red man is more richly tempered with mercy than during any earlier decade.[135]

In the light of such personal and social needs, the two-tiered structure of divided functions in the Bureau becomes intelligible. Like Henry before him and like his contemporaries Goode and Mason, Powell believed deeply in the moral education of the public. Despite appearances to the contrary, the story of man must be one of progress, and civilized man must stand at the apex. If not, then all was folly and absurdity and a cruel delusion. Powell depended on his staff to lay the empirical foundations of the New Ethnology, but the conclusions were predetermined by prior commitments. For this reason the Bureau men only controlled their data and observations to the degree that they concluded rightly. There was indeed, as John Swanton noticed, a "party line" in the Bureau.[136] But he and subsequent critics failed to appreciate the serious purposes beneath the Procrustean bed of Morgan/Powell evolutionism; belonging to a later generation, they could never understand the assurance and the hope it gave to men whose world was kaleidoscopically turning.

Notes

1. On the development of the social sciences after the Civil War, see Mary O. Furner, *Advocacy and Objectivity: A Crisis in the Professionalization of American Social Science, 1865–1905* (Lexington, 1975); Thomas J. Haskell, *The Emergence of Professional Social Science: The American Social Science Association and the Nineteenth-Century Crisis of Authority* (Urbana, 1977); and Hugh Hawkins, "The Ideal of Objectivity among American Social Scientists in the Era of Professionalization, 1876–1916," in Charles Frankel, ed., *Controversies and Decisions: The Social Sciences and Public Policy* (New York, 1976); also, Burton J. Bledstein, *The Culture of Professionalism: The Middle Class and the Development of Higher Education in America* (New York, 1976). Chapter 8 is especially suggestive.

2. Furner and Haskell specifically exclude anthropology from their studies.

3. Quoted in Haskell, *Emergence of Professional Social Science*, p. 97.

4. *Congressional Globe*, 40th Cong., 1st Session, 1867, p. 672; as quoted in Robert Winston Mardock, *The Reformers and the American Indian* (Columbia, 1971), p. 28.

5. Quoted in Don D. Fowler and Catherine S. Fowler, "Anthropology of the Numa: John Wesley Powell's Manuscripts on the Numic Peoples of Western North America, 1868–1880," Smithsonian Contributions to Anthropology 14 (Washington, D.C., 1971): 119.

6. Cf., Mardock, *Reformers and the American Indian*, Chapter 6: "Civilization or Extermination?" Mardock sees 1867 as the year of emergence of a humane peace policy, while 1876–79 were the "critical years" for removal and reservation policy (pp. 150–67).

7. Henry Adams, *The Education of Henry Adams: An Autobiography* (Boston, 1961), p. 309. The most complete account of the post-Civil War survey tradition is William H. Goetzmann, *Exploration and Empire: The Explorer and the Scientist in the Winning of the American West* (New York, 1966).

8. The original name was Bureau of Ethnology; "American" was added in 1894. The bill passed March 3, 1879 (U.S. Statutes 20:397). For background on the

consolidation movement and Powell's role in it and in the establishment of the Bureau, see William Culp Darrah, *Powell of the Colorado* (Princeton, 1951), pp. 237–54.

9. The major sources are Darrah, *Powell of the Colorado*; Wallace Stegner, *Beyond the Hundredth Meridian: John Wesley Powell and the Second Opening of the West* (Boston, 1954); Thomas G. Manning, *Government in Science* (Lexington, 1967), a history of the first twenty years of the Geological Survey; and A. Hunter Dupree, *Science in the Federal Government: A History of Policies and Activities to 1940* (Cambridge, 1957), pp. 195–255.

10. *CNAE* 1 (Washington, D.C., 1877): ix.

11. Fowler and Fowler, "Anthropology of the Numa," pp. 12–13. See this discussion for a detailed account of Powell's itinerary and fieldwork between 1868 and 1880. The ethnological work had to be squeezed into spare moments. The work with Komas went slowly, as Powell complained to James Hammond Trumbull in 1876 (ibid., p. 119).

12. Ibid., p. 11. Powell's report is reproduced in this volume, pp. 97–119. Powell elaborated his statements before a congressional committee the following year.

13. Ibid., pp. 97–99.

14. Ibid., p. 116.

15. Ibid., pp. 117–18.

16. Ibid., pp. 99, 101.

17. Quoted in Darrah, *Powell of the Colorado*, p. 256.

18. BAE, *AR for 1895*, p. lxxxvi; Darrah, *Powell of the Colorado*, pp. 255–56.

19. *Report of the Secretary of the Interior for 1877*, vol. 1 (Washington, D.C., 1877), pp. 797–98.

20. I have dealt at length with the issue of utility in "Anthropology as Science and Politics: The Dilemmas of the Bureau of American Ethnology, 1879 to 1904," in Walter Goldschmidt, ed., *The Uses of Anthropology* (Washington, D.C., 1979), pp. 15–32. Passages from that article are reproduced here.

21. *Report of the Secretary of the Interior for 1877*, vol. 1 (Washington, D.C., 1877), p. ix.

22. See, esp., Regna D. Darnell, "The Professionalization of American Anthropology: A Case Study in the Sociology of Knowledge," *Social Science Information* 10, no. 2 (1972), pp. 83–103; C. M. Hinsley, "Amateurs and Professionals in Washington Anthropology, 1879 to 1903," in John V. Murra, ed., *American Anthropology: The Early Years* (St. Paul, 1976), pp. 36–68; and Timothy H. H. Thoreson, "Art, History, and Evolution," *Journal of the History of the Behavioral Sciences* 13 (1977): 107–25.

23. McGee to Hilgard, 17 July 1888, MP.

24. W J McGee, "Fifty Years of American Science," *Atlantic Monthly* 82 (1898): 320.

25. Stegner, *Beyond the Hundredth Meridian*, p. 146.

26. BAE, *AR for 1890*, p. xxi.

27. W J McGee, "The Bureau of American Ethnology," in George Brown Goode, ed., *The Smithsonian Institution, 1846–1896* (Washington, D.C., 1897), pp. 371–72. Emphasis added.

28. BAE, *AR for 1890*, pp. xxi–xxii.

29. Stegner, *Beyond the Hundredth Meridian,* p. 269.

30. Powell to Langley, 7 April 1900; as quoted in Virginia Noelke, "The Origin and Early History of the Bureau of American Ethnology, 1879–1910," Ph.D. diss. (University of Texas at Austin, 1974), p. 69.

31. BAE, *AR for 1885,* pp. 1–1i.

32. Charles C. Royce, "Indian Land Cessions in the United States," BAE, *AR for 1897* (Washington, D.C., 1899), pp. 521–964 (with introduction by Cyrus Thomas). Powell had hired Royce, who had been working independently, in 1879, without any authorization for entering the field of historical relations. Royce stayed two years, left the Bureau in 1881, returned again in 1883, and resigned permanently in 1885.

   The delay in publication has never been satisfactorily explained, but it was probably due to the political sensitivity of the issue. See my remarks in "Anthropology as Science and Politics," pp. 22–23.

33. BAE, *AR for 1880,* p. 76.

34. Mason to John G. Henderson, 8 June 1907, Otis T. Mason Papers, NAA; Mason to F. W. Hodge, 31 January 1907, Hodge-Cushing Papers.

35. BAE, *AR for 1866,* p. xxxv; BAE, *AR for 1885,* p. xliv.

36. BAE, *AR for 1886,* p. xxxv.

37. BAE, *AR for 1885,* p. xliii; BAE, *AR for 1886,* pp. xxxiii, xxxv. Powell and Henshaw were both impressed by Mooney's classification and synonymy work. See William L. Colby, "Routes to Rainy Mountain: A Biography of James Mooney, Ethnologist," Ph.D. diss. (University of Wisconsin, Madison, 1977), pp. 42–44.

38. BAE, *AR for 1885,* p. xlv.

39. BAE, *AR for 1886,* p. xxxv.

40. BAE, *AR for 1887,* p. xxix.

41. J. Howard Gore, "Anthropology at Washington," *Popular Science Monthly* 35 (1889): 790.

42. BAE, *AR for 1890,* p. xxxi.

43. BAE, AR for 1891, pp. xxxii, xxxv; BAE, *AR for 1894,* p. lxxxix; BAE, *AR for 1895,* p. lxxi; BAE, *AR for 1894,* p. lxxix.

44. BAE, *AR for 1895,* p. lxxi.

45. Hodge moved to the Smithsonian as acting curator of exchanges and assistant in charge of the office of the Secretary (Langley to Hodge, 31 January 1901, Hodge Papers, SW).

46. BAE-IN, pp. 248–51.

47. The idea of a linguistic map was not new with Gibbs. See Regna D. Darnell, "The Powell Classification of American Indian Languages," *Papers in Linguistics* 4, no. 1 (July 1971), pp. 73–76; and Mary Haas, "Grammar or Lexicon? The American Indian Side of the Question from Duponceau to Powell," *International Journal of Anthropological Linguistics* 35 (1969): 239–55. Gibbs's contribution has generally been ignored. Responding to Lewis Henry Morgan's "Suggestions Relative to an Ethnological Map of North America" (SI, *AR for 1861,* pp. 397–98), Gibbs outlined his concept of an "ethnological atlas" in letters of November and December 1862, to Joseph Henry, printed in SI, *AR for 1862,* pp. 87–93.

48. As quoted by Roman Jakobson, "World Response to Whitney," in Michael Silverstein, ed., *Whitney on Language: Selected Writings of William Dwight Whitney* (Cambridge, 1971), p. xxix.

49. Ibid., p. viii.

50. As quoted in ibid., p. xi.

51. Ibid., p. x.

52. Jakobson, "World Response," pp. xliii–xliv.

53. Powell, "Indian Linguistic Families," p. 12.

54. Henry Desk Diary, 15 April 1873, SIA.

55. SI, *AR for 1876*, pp. 35–36.

56. Powell to Whitney, 17 July and 27 August 1877, WDW Papers.

57. Whitney to Powell, 25 July 1877, NAA; as quoted in Regna D. Darnell, "The Development of American Anthropology, 1879–1920: From the Bureau of American Ethnology to Franz Boas," Ph.D. diss. (University of Pennsylvania, 1969), p. 65.

58. See, for instance, Powell's remarks in BAE, *AR for 1880*, p. xv.

59. "Address by Hon. John W. Powell," at inauguration of Corcoran School of Science and Arts (Washington, D.C., 1884), pp. 10,11.

60. *Introduction to the Study of Indian Languages*, 2d ed. (Washington, D.C., 1880), pp. v-vi.

61. Ibid., p. vi.

62. Ibid., p. viii.

63. J. W. Powell, "Indian Linguistic Families of America North of Mexico," BAE, *AR for 1885* (Washington, D.C., 1891), p. 142; Henry W. Henshaw and James Mooney, *Linguistic Families of the Indian Tribes North of Mexico, With a Provisional List of the Principal Tribal Names and Synonyms* (Washington, D.C., 1885); Regna D. Darnell, "The Powell Classification of American Indian Languages," *Papers in Linguistics* 4, no. 1 (July 1970), p. 79. See Darnell's Table I (pp. 100–08) for a list of changes between 1885 and 1891.

64. Darnell, "Powell Classification," pp. 82–85. For fuller discussion of the recent debate over authorship and additional references, see Darnell, "Development of American Anthropology," pp. 83–95.

65. Darrah, *Powell of the Colorado*, pp. 323–24; Thomas G. Manning, *Government in Science: The U.S. Geological Survey, 1867–1894* (Lexington, 1967), pp. 113–14.

66. See discussion of these men, below.

67. Colby, "Routes to Rainy Mountain," p. 49.

68. Henry W. Henshaw, "Autobiographical Notes," *The Condor* 22 (1920): 10.

69. Powell, "Indian Linguistic Families," pp. 8–10. Gatschet proposed a binomial, taxonomic linguistic classification that Powell found appealing. Powell noted ("Indian Linguistic Families," p. 23) of Gatschet's 1877 article on "Indian Languages of the Pacific States and Territories" (*Magazine of American History* 1) that Gatschet "advocates the plan of using a system of nomenclature similar in nature to that employed in zoology in the case of generic and specific names, adding after the name of the tribe the family to which it belongs; thus, Warm Springs, Sahaptin." Both the rule of priority and such taxonomic schemes no longer find application in linguistics, since languages do not conform to bi-

ological models. In no field of anthropology was the model of zoology clearer than in BAE linguistics.

70. Letter, 29 August 1930, printed in *American Anthropologist,* n.s. 33 (1931): 104.

71. Darnell, "Powell Classification," p. 83.

72. Quoted in Stegner, *Beyond the Hundredth Meridian,* p. 364.

73. Powell to Mrs. Pilling, 12 August 1895, reproduced in "James Constantine Pilling, 1846–1895" (privately printed memorial, 1895).

74. Pilling to Daniel Shea, 11 April 1881, NAA, quoted in Darnell, "Development," p. 63.

75. Ibid., 63–64.

76. Stegner, *Beyond the Hundredth Meridian,* pp. 263–64. In a personal communication to the author, William Sturtevant offered the following estimate of Pilling: "He was a very meticulous, accurate, and critical bibliographer. He included as much ms. material as he could locate, and all sorts of printed material—texts such as biblical translations, and letters and newspapers written in Indian languages, as well as brief vocabularies, grammars, etc. etc. He also included extremely useful brief biographies of many of the important authors. The results have been constantly and continuously referred to by generations of North Americanists. Bibliographic tools rarely get cited in publications, but they are used and save future scholars endless work and prevent ignorant errors."

77. J. C. Pilling, *Proof-Sheets of a Bibliography of the Languages of the North American Indians* (Washington, D.C., 1895).

78. Powell to Mrs. Pilling, 12 August 1895, in "James Constantine Pilling."

79. Stegner, *Beyond the Hundredth Meridian,* p. 264.

80. Robert Fletcher, "Brief Memoir of Colonel Garrick Mallery, U.S.A." (Washington, D.C., 1895, privately printed [copy in Smithsonian Institution Libraries]); John Wesley Powell, "Garrick Mallery," SI, *AR for 1895,* pp. 52–53.

81. Adams, *Education,* p. 366.

82. Fletcher, "Brief Memoir," p. 11.

83. Frederick Starr, "Anthropological Work in America," *Popular Science Monthly* 41 (1892): 301; Garrick Mallery, "A Calendar of the Dakota Nation," *Bulletin of the U.S. Geological and Geographical Survey of the Territories* 3:1 (Washington, D.C., 1877).

84. BAE, *AR for 1883,* pp. lii–liii; BAE, *AR for 1889,* pp. xxvi–xxvii.

85. Mallery's major publications were: *Sign-language among North American Indians, compared with that among other People and Deaf-mutes,* BAE, *AR for 1880,* pp. 263–552; *Picture-Writing of the American Indians,* BAE, *AR for 1889,* pp. 1–807.

86. Garrick Mallery, *Introduction to the Study of Sign-Language among the North American Indians as Illustrating the Gesture-speech of Mankind* (Washington, D.C., 1880).

87. The dates are confusing because of publication delays. *Sign-language* appeared in the 1880 report, but the report was not issued until 1881, which gave Mallery additional months to prepare his paper. Delays subsequently became more severe. Thus, for instance, Mallery's *Picture-writing* was part of the 1889 report, but did not appear until 1893. Bureau reports for the intervening years,

moreover, show that Mallery was still working on his report throughout this time. In addition to the normal delays of publication and government bureaucracy, Powell's desire to mollify Congress probably led him to promise reports before they were finished. Constant acquisition of new materials also led to unending revisions.

88. BAE, *AR for 1880*. p. xxv.
89. BAE, *AR for 1893*, p. xxxi.
90. BAE, *AR for 1889*, p. xxx; Darnell, "Development," p. 132.
91. BAE, *AR for 1893*, pp. xxxi–xxxii.
92. BAE, *AR for 1883*, p. lv.
93. Ibid, p. lvi.
94. Garrick Mallery, "A Philosophic Phantasy," read before the Philosophical Society of Washington, 18 February 1893 (privately printed, n.d.).
95. Garrick Mallery, "Greeting by Gesture," *Popular Science Monthly* 38 (1891): 644.
96. Garrick Mallery, "Israelite and Indian: A Parallel in Planes of Culture,"*Popular Science Monthly* 36 (1889–90): 52–76, 193–213 (quotations pp. 207, 210). In Mallery's (and Powell's) view, civilization had to precede Christianity: "Christianity, belonging to the plane of civilization and to that only, sits on a savage or barbarian as a bishop's mitre would on a naked Hottentot." (p. 208)
97. Ibid., p. 209. Mallery had expressed the same views in 1877, before his Bureau career began. See Mallery, "Some Common Errors Respecting the North American Indians," *Bulletins of PSW* II (Washington, D.C., 1875–1880), pp. 175–81.
98. SI, *AR for 1895*. p. 53.
99. Mallery, "Some Common Errors," p. 177.
100. "Professor Turner's Letter on Indian Philology: (12/16/51)," SI, *AR for 1851*. pp. 97–98.
101. BAE, *AR for 1890*, p. xliii; cf. Darnell, "Development," pp. 122–23, on Dorsey's double role as missionary and scientist.
102. "James Owen Dorsey," SI, *AR for 1895*, p. 53.
103. Dorsey to Henry, 18 March 1873; Dorsey to Rev. Joseph Packard, 24 March 1873, Rhees Papers, SIA.
104. Dorsey to Henry, 8 April 1873; Dorsey to Packard, 24 March 1873, Rhees Papers, SIA.
105. F.L.O. Roehrig to Henry, 18 March 1873, SIA; quoted in Darnell, "Development," p. 11.
106. Darnell, "Development," pp. 86–87; BAE, *AR for 1883*, pp. xli–xlii; BAE, *AR for 1885*, p. xxxvi; BAE, *AR for 1893*, p. xl.
107. BAE, *AR for 1887*, p. xxix; BAE, *AR for 1888*, p. xxxvii. Although the Bushotter interviews were the most extensive, subsequent informant work in Washington also lasted long periods. In 1889 Samuel Fremont (Omaha) stayed five months; Little Standing Buffalo (Ponca), two months; during 1890 George Miller (Omaha), three months; in 1891, an anonymous Quapaw visited for four months; and in 1894 Dorsey recorded Winnebago texts for an unspecified period from one Philip Longtail. On Dorsey's collaboration with

Bushotter, see Raymond J. DeMallie, "George Bushotter: The First Lakota Ethnographer," in Margot Liberty, ed., *American Indian Intellectuals: 1976 Proceedings of the American Ethnological Society* (St. Paul, 1978) pp. 91–102.

108. Franz Boas, "Some Philological Aspects of Anthropological Research," *Science* 23 (1906): 641–45. Reprinted in George W. Stocking, Jr., *The Shaping of American Anthropology, 1883–1911: A Franz Boas Reader* (New York, 1974), p. 185.

109. Noelke, "Origin and Early History," pp. 145–46.

110. Colby, "Routes to Rainy Mountain," pp. 49–51.

111. Darnell, "Development," p. 112.

112. Noelke, "Origin and Early History," p. 148.

113. BAE, *AR for 1882*, p. xxxv.

114. BAE, *AR for 1890*, p. xlvi.

115. Ibid., p. xlv.

116. Ibid., pp. xlv–xlvi.

117. From a note in BAE photograph files, NAA.

118. Boas testimony, BAE-IN, p. 943; A. S. Gatschet, "The Klamath Tribe and Language of Oregon," *Contributions to North American Ethnology* 2 [parts 1 and 2] (Washington, D.C., 1890).

119. A. S. Gatschet, "Report on the Pueblo Languages of New Mexico, and of the Moquis in Arizona: their affinity to each other and to the languages of the other Indian tribes," in *Annual Report of the U.S. Geological Survey West of the 100th Meridian for 1875* [Appendix LL of annual report of Chief of Engineers for 1875] (Washington, D.C., 1875); A. S. Gatschet, "Analytical Report upon Indian dialects spoken in southern California, Nevada, and on the lower Colorado River, etc.," in *Annual Report of the U.S. Geological Survey West of the 100th Meridian for 1876* [Appendix JJ of annual report of the Chief of Engineers for 1876] (Washington, D.C. 1876).

120. James Mooney, "Albert Samuel Gatschet, 1832–1907," *American Anthropologist*, n.s. 9 (1907): 561–62; Gatschet testimony, BAE-IN, p. 553; BAE, *AR for 1880*, p. xiii. Although both Dorsey and Gatschet joined Powell as "ethnologists," this description was intended mainly to distinguish them from the geologists, botanists, etc., on the Survey. The focus of their work was understood to be linguistic; in particular they were to compare the several hundred Powell and Smithsonian vocabulary lists (see Darnell, "Development" p. 318; Mooney, "Gatschet'" p. 562).

121. BAE, *AR for 1880*, p. xiii; Mooney, "Gatschet," p. 562.

122. BAE, *AR for 1880*, pp. xx–xxii.

123. BAE, *AR for 1881*, p. xxi; see, e.g., Powell's discussion of the development of separate modifiers through the "law of phonic change" and "economy," in BAE, *AR for 1880*, pp. xxi–xxii.

124. BAE, *AR for 1882*, pp. xxxi–xxxiii; BAE, *AR for 1883*, p. xlvii; BAE, *AR for 1884*, p. xxxiii.

125. BAE, *AR for 1885*, pp. xxxiv–xxxvi.

126. BAE, *AR for 1886*, p. xxxvi; BAE, *AR for 1889*, p. xvii; BAE, *AR for 1890*, pp. xxxii–xxxiii; BAE, *AR for 1891*, p. xxiv.

127. Swanton testimony, BAE-IN, p. 540; Darnell, "Development," pp. 112–13 (footnote).
128. Darnell, "Development," p. 287; Boas testimony, BAE-IN, p. 925.
129. Boas testimony, BAE-IN, p. 944. Boas considered Gatschet's assignment to Algonquian "the greatest mistake that Powell made" in administering the Bureau. (Boas testimony, original, unrevised copy, BAE-IN, p. 943.)
130. Mason to H. S. Pritchett, 26 September 1906, NAA.
131. Mooney, "Gatschet," p. 566.
132. Powell, "Indian Linguistic Families," pp. 35–36.
133. Ibid.
134. See remarks on Royce in Hinsley, "Anthropology as Science and Politics," pp. 22–23.
135. BAE, *AR for 1897* (Washington, D.C., 1899), pp. lvi–lvii.
136. John R. Swanton, "Notes Regarding My Adventures in Anthropology and with Anthropologists," ms., pp. 33–34, NAA.

VII

Heroes and Homelessness:
Reflections on
Frank Hamilton Cushing,
James Mooney, and BAE Anthropology

"The fate of our times," Max Weber wrote toward the end of his life, "is characterized by rationalization and intellectualization and, above all, by the 'disenchantment of the world.'"[1] Weber was not the only observer and critic who perceived that by 1900 western civilization could boast of great achievements but little mystery. Henry Adams thought that the American people "were wandering in a wilderness much more sandy than the Hebrews had ever trodden about Sinai; they had neither serpents nor golden calves to worship. They had lost the sense of worship. . . ."[2] Fairy tales were for children, myths were for savages. But if enlightened civilization yielded power over both nature and man, it left many dissatisfied souls.

At the emotional center of American culture stood the home. The stable, comfortable Victorian household protected stoutly against unpredictable social and economic forces outside, but it was an unexciting haven. As middle-class Americans slowly discovered, the age of science and industry left little room for imagination, mystery, and romance. If one can measure by tastes in magazine fiction, by the end of the century a large reading public was turning outward to far-flung scenes for vicarious excitements. A flaccid, neurasthenic society seemed to require exotic tonics, because there was little heroism at home. For people feeling acutely the confines of closing frontiers, the North American Indian emerged once again as a source of national reinvigoration.

As Richard Slotkin has brilliantly demonstrated, American literature and national mythology have been populated from the beginning by a series of intermediaries between savagery and civilization: captives, hunters, frontiersmen, Indian fighters, mountain men. In each case the mediating figure, through immersion in the wilderness and savage ways, returns to civilization with a gift, or boon, to his troubled people. From the forest and savagery he learns the secret of regeneration and prosperity.[3] By 1880, as the days of the frontiersman were rapidly fading, the heroic stature of boon-bringer passed for a time to the scientific explorer—the naturalist and ethnologist. The salvage

Frank Hamilton Cushing, young genius of the Bureau of
American Ethnology, c. 1879.

ethnology of these years was, therefore, potentially more than curiosity collecting, for the ethnologist offered a gift of romantic aboriginal cosmology to a callow, disenchanted people. Those who succeeded most fully in this quest were individuals who, like their predecessors on the fictional and actual frontiers of American history, were themselves homeless and partially estranged. A degree of alienation was both precondition and product of the quest.

It may be true that, as Susan Sontag observed, anthropologists have institutionalized homelessness as an integral part of professional training and identity. Conformist abroad and critic at home, the anthropologist struggles constantly with ambivalence toward his own society and those he studies.[4] Whatever the current situation in the profession, cultural distance was decidedly undesirable in the world of Powell's Bureau. Committed to the mores and values of contemporary American life, Powell hardly intended to institutionalize any degree of alienation in Washington. Yet the BAE, like the early Smithsonian, became a haven for some individuals to whom restlessness or idiosyncrasy permitted no comfortable home in society. In their searches for alternative modes of understanding, these individuals contributed, not to the professionalization of American anthropology, but to the richness of its heritage.

In 1880 the Southwest presented the most alluring ethnographic fields in North America. An invigorating climate; sedentary populations of artisans in weaving, pottery, and silver; mysterious, bird-like cliff-dwellers of the remote past; possible links between the high civilizations of Central America and the North American aborigines: these were some of the appealing aspects that fed a popular romance with the Southwest that blossomed into commercial exploitation with the new century. The lower canyon country of New Mexico and Arizona became the primary regional focus of Bureau work, and Powell displayed a particular proprietary interest in the pueblo peoples. Among those who worked in the region were Frank Hamilton Cushing, James and Matilda Stevenson, Washington Matthews, and Jesse W. Fewkes. Interests overlapped and ambitions often clashed, with Matthews, Cushing, and Army lieutenant John G. Bourke forming a cordon against what they considered the incursions of the Stevensons, Fewkes, and others. The Indian cultures of the region apparently fostered unusual attachment and possessiveness, and under the exposure of public popularity anthropology in the Southwest became heavily infused with personal style.

Frank Hamilton Cushing (1857-1899) certainly had style. Cushing was the precocious young genius of Bureau ethnology, and Powell doted paternally on this chronically ill, eccentric, and uncontrollable spirit. Cushing remains enigmatic.[5] Matilda Stevenson considered him a fool and a charlatan.[6] Powell and McGee called him a genius for his ability to enter fully into savage thought, while Boas stated that Cushing's genius "was his greatest enemy" and suggested that all his work would have to be done over.[7] Alfred Kroeber valued Mrs. Stevenson's sobriety above Cushing's flamboyance and judged their work accordingly. On the other hand, Claude Lévi-Strauss has seen in Cushing a brilliant, intuitive precursor of structuralism.[8] Cushing remains a live issue even today.

According to Cushing's own account of his childhood, at the family homestead in western New York the sickly, premature child spent years in social isolation and self-education into the ways of the woodland Indians. Avoiding formal schooling and "relieved of the constant waste of mentality through the friction of social relation," his mind followed its own channels.[9] The account may well be, like many such biographical statements of the period, a retrospective search for scientific roots. Its importance lies not in historical accuracy but in the fact that Cushing chose to portray his early life in a certain manner. Immediately in his reconstructed biography one faces the single consistent thread of Cushing's life: his insight that reality, whether the individual life or the group experience, is a psychological construct.[10] Each person structures his own world, and each group its collective experience, according to categories and patterns that must be understood and respected.

Cushing possessed a gift that was rare in his (or any) time: a tentativeness toward truth, values, and mores. Perhaps it was the excessive freedom of an unstructured or self-structured youth that encouraged levity and distance from his culture and branded him a wayfarer. His insistence on creating as well as discovering—that is, his free insertion of imagination in his work—placed Cushing on the fringes of any scientific community. He spurned institutional bonds, though he readily used individuals and organizations for his own purposes. He never valued institutional loyalty. In similar fashion he found little use for the language, channels, and forms of dialogue within established scientific circles. Not that he denied the importance of method in ethnology. In an early letter to Otis Mason he lamented that "America has no *Science* of Ethnology or Archaeology, and (I may add) that every Boer who has correctly or incorrectly described an arrowhead or a simple mound, is at once considered an archaeologist and styles himself, 'Professor.'"[11] Previous literature on the Zuñi pueblo, he told Baird soon after arrival in the Southwest, was "nothing," and he felt confident that "my *method must* succeed."[12] And at one low point in his career, when he thought he was dying in 1889, Cushing begged Bourke to "let the world know of my hard work and say that my method was the correct one in ethnological investigation. . ."[13] But Cushing was far too idiosyncratic to recognize the primacy of a scientific peer audience or to contribute in a major way to its creation. He knew personal friendships and bitter feuds, but he never developed a strong sense of professional community.

In 1874, when he was seventeen, Cushing sent a brief report of his New

York arrowhead collections to Baird, who printed it in the Smithsonian report. The following year Cushing entered Cornell University to study with naturalist Charles Hartt, but soon left for Washington. At Baird's invitation he lived in the Smithsonian towers and assisted Charles Rau with the Philadelphia Centennial collections.[14] Cushing found Rau irascible, and the old German's method of classifying implements did not satisfy Cushing's growing conviction that the anthropologist must understand motive through ethnographic data, and method through personal experiment.[15] The only way to grasp the subtle influences in aboriginal art, he wrote some years later, is "through experiments with original materials with one's own hands, limited in action to the appliances of the original local stone age conditions in each given case, and in almost blind submission to their influences and promptings."[16] "Blind submission" to nature's promptings was as alien to Charles Rau's neat, controlled cabinets as it was illicit in American society generally.

After the Centennial, Cushing remained in touch with Baird, but the Smithsonian could not take him on and he had to wait three years for a field opportunity.[17] The first BAE expedition, under Powell's compatriot of the seventies, James Stevenson, left for the Southwest in August 1879, to make "as careful a study as circumstances will permit of the Pueblo Ruins and caves of that district of country. . ."[18] The expedition was impelled by persistent concern, expressed through Congress to Baird, that foreign emissaries were ransacking the Southwest of its archaeological and ethnological treasures. In 1876 Ephraim G. Squier had advised the Peabody Museum (somewhat prematurely, as it has turned out) that foreigners had already turned Mexico into an ethnological wasteland, and now the southwestern United States seemed similarly threatened.[19] The BAE/Smithsonian venture became a perennial "Ethnological campaign" against such intruders.[20] Accordingly, the emphasis lay on material collections, after which the expedition might turn its attention to "language, customs, and habits, mythology, government, architecture, etc., etc.—"[21]

Spencer Baird's central role in Cushing's Zuñi experience has been obscured by time and by the romanticization of Cushing. Cushing joined the Stevenson expedition as the representative of Baird and the National Museum, and he reported directly to Baird even after his transfer to the Bureau in 1882.[22] Baird had insisted on including a special investigator of a single pueblo on the Stevenson reconnaissance group, and he recommended Cushing. He also requested regular reports from his man. For his part, Cushing viewed himself somewhat as a bird thrown out of the nest: he was determined to fly or die in the attempt. He would, Cushing assured Baird, "obey orders like a private"; after nearly a year at Zuñi, he confessed that "On the whole, then, I am *far* from sorry you have decided to keep me down here 'till I've done something."[23] Initially at least, the Zuñi experience was as much exile as involvement. In either case, Cushing's infatuation with the Zuñis was neither immediate nor reciprocal. At an early date he reported to Baird that "it is solely with the wish to make my visit to this Pueblo of a little scientific use, that I would *consent* even to remain here." Inability to communicate, constant physical discomfort, "disgusting" food made his first weeks utter misery.[24]

Still, it was Cushing's decision to stay at Zuñi when the rest of the Stevenson party moved on, and both Baird and Powell acceded to his wishes with apprehension. At first neither Cushing nor his superiors had a clear notion of the length of time that would be involved in his Zuñi work. "I think very well of leaving Cushing in pueblo country to complete his investigations," Baird informed Stevenson. "It will be difficult for him to get so completely on the inside track of this people again, as he appears to be now." To Putnam, who was watching with reserved approval from the Peabody Museum in Cambridge, Baird wrote that "It gives us great pleasure to have the endorsement of such eminent critics as yourself for our action in keeping Mr. Cushing in the Zuñi country for so long a time and of our intention of maintaining him in that service as long as may be necessary."[25] The Cushing experiment was being observed from the East with great interest.

As his stay lengthened into years and stories filtered back to eastern newspapers about the "White Indian," rumors arose questioning Cushing's moral state. The Smithsonian and the Bureau stoutly defended him, and Cushing fought back effectively through a series of popular articles in *Century Magazine* on "My Adventures at Zuñi," as well as by bringing back to the pueblo, in 1882, a White bride. The ambivalent nature of his undertaking—both the appeal and the revulsion—as seen from the bounds of his own culture was significant in determining the nature of Cushing's work and the timing of decisions. He had to balance carefully between two cultures.

He gradually came to sense the deep complexity of Zuñi life. It was like a veil lifting slowly before his eyes, as he told Baird:

> As gradually their language dawns upon my inquiring mind not the significance of these ceremonials alone but many other dark things are lighted up by its meanings. They are the people who built the ruins of Cañon Bonito. In their language is told the strange history of these heretofore mysterious remains each one of which has its definite name and story. The handworks on the rock face and the pictograph of a 'Primitive civilization' in the light of this language and tradition reveal their mysteries at once with their proof . . . Perhaps not a more conventional people may be found than these pueblos.

The secret of his success, Cushing continued, was his method: he observed Zuñi ceremonies and customs with "unfeigned reverence," never laughing. As a result, he claimed, "they love me, and I learn."[26]

Cushing exaggerated his acceptance. He was hardly an object of veneration at Zuñi, despite his efforts to portray as much. There is in fact evidence that he forced his will and presence on frequently unreceptive people (though perhaps not as vigorously as Matilda Stevenson, who ultimately had to guard her living quarters).[27] Still, Cushing's inquiries steadily widened into questions of history and origins. In an important statement of early 1880, he outlined fifteen broad areas of research to Baird and Powell, and he reported his most important discovery to date: that the arts, industries, and ceremonies of the pueblo peoples were governed by rigid rules, measures, and patterns, "formulas" as he called them, transmitted through generations by means of "ancient talks." These were the keys to understanding past history and current practices, he thought. Now deeply absorbed in Zuñi life, Cushing estimated another year and a half would be required for thorough knowledge of the language, prayers, and ancient instructions.[28]

Powell and Baird were excited with Cushing's progress. Powell's annual reports devoted considerable space to detailing the Zuñi experiences. Clearly here was an exceptional ethnologist, whose "devotion, energy, and tact" had gained him admission to the Order of the Bow and the position of "Assistant Chief" of the pueblo, the director reported. While biding his time to gain entrance to the "ancient epic rituals," Cushing explored the cemeteries, ruins, caves, shrines, and grottoes of the valleys with great material and theoretical profit. By the time of his return in March 1884, Cushing was convinced that he had located the seven lost cities of Cibola of the Spanish chroniclers— demonstration, he argued, of the reliability of Indian stories and traditions when properly interpreted.[29]

However sincere his enthusiasm, Cushing overestimated his advance in understanding the Zuñis, and his very presence was a disrupting factor in the pueblo. As a Bow Priest the ethnologist gained access to the sacred as well as the secular organization of the tribe, and he considered his admission "the greatest of all the achievements of my life perhaps; for it breaks down the last shadow of objection to my gaining knowledge of the sacred rites. . . ."[30] By virtue of his office, though, Cushing aligned himself with the traditional tribal leadership in battles against other Zuñi families and "progressive" White influences, such as missionaries, traders, politicians, and Army personnel. The roles of ethnologist and tribal spokesman were incompatible for him. Cushing's life at Zuñi was consequently marked by disputes over horse stealing, lost Army mules, missionary influence, and land claims of Whites.

One such dispute caused the Bureau anguish and probably led to Cushing's recall to Washington in 1884. The son-in-law of John H. Logan, senator from Illinois and candidate for vice-president, had filed a claim for some 800 acres of the Nutria Valley, which had mistakenly been omitted from the 1877 Zuñi Reservation boundaries. When Cushing led the tribe's successful fight to reclaim the land, an infuriated Logan visited Zuñi in 1882, declared Cushing a fraud, and launched an attack against the ethnologist and the Bureau.[32] Significantly, the main focus of attack was his supposed moral degradation through prolonged exposure to Indians. Responding to criticism of his lifestyle, Cushing reassured Baird that his methods were "the results of my deliberate and best judgment," and that his relation with the Zuñis had always preserved his honor.[33] In an unpublished "interview" with himself in June 1883, Cushing again addressed this sensitive issue. He found himself "sincere in his motives, honest in his assertions, and in spite of his undeniable but voluntary and acknowledged 'degradation' to have retained fully his moral character and self-respect. . ."[34] The Logan dispute revealed not only the political pressures that could be brought to bear on Powell's organization but also the vulnerability of Cushing's style of field work in the 1880s, not least due to the self-doubts that critics could instill in an introspective ethnologist.

Politicians were not Cushing's only source of friction. He and the Stevensons competed more than they cooperated, and Cushing's growing fame added to the animosity. Washington Matthews, who was an Army man, the first careful student of Navaho life, and a staunch friend of Cushing's, cordially disliked both James and Matilda Stevenson, and he wrote to Cushing in caustic phrases of their attitudes and methods:

> "Colonel"! Stephenson [sic] came down on us a week ago with half a dozen tenderfeet, including professor Gore Harry Biddle, the son of a Virginia senator, a young Mr. McElhone, brother of a potent newspaperman, Mr. Mindelieff [sic], an artist, and several other "judicious" appointments. Stephenson staid with us, and we blew your trumpet all the time he was here & he kept rather "mum." A portion of the party are gone to Zuni to get materials to make an immense model of the Pueblo, the biggest model they have yet made. . . . Stephenson has gone to Santa Fe for some inscrutable purpose and expects to bring Powell back with him in a few days. Mrs. Stephenson came to Crane's Ranch and stopped there, so we have not seen her fair face nor listened to her gentle voice. Perhaps she wanted an invitation to [Fort] Wingate but she didn't get one.[35]

The ill-feeling toward the Stevensons, which Cushing certainly shared, centered on their high-handed manner with the Indians, their supposed failure to give proper credit to informants, their essential lack of respect for the pueblo peoples, and their political connections. Matthews particularly resented the financial support that they enjoyed through the Bureau and their presumptuous claims of knowledge based on short visits. "I suppose that you have heard that the Stevensons poached on my preserve last fall," he confided to Cushing in 1886. "They went there to duplicate my work, with a stenographer and far more means and materials than had ever been placed at my disposal. . ."[36] After Cushing's recall, the Zuñi field was open to his competitors: "There will, I think, be no necessity for your bringing in your

Victorian America meets the Southwest: Matilda Stevenson
in Taos country; interior of Stevenson's Washington home.

Indians from Zuñi or for your coming out here again," Matthews informed him with sarcasm. "I saw Col. Stevenson at Wingate. He assured me that Mrs. Stevenson had learned to talk both Zuñi and Spanish fluently and was obtaining no end of valuable information from the Indians. From the way she is working I think she will get all that is worth getting before long. The Indians are just unbosoming themselves to her. Col. S. too has explored a number of caves around Zuñi and made wonderful discoveries. . ." In 1891 Matilda was still "working her sponge for all it was worth."[37]

Bourke, Matthews, and Cushing believed that they had come to the South-west not merely to take but to exchange with mutuality and sympathy. To be sure, there is no question that Cushing bullied the Zuñis for information, especially at first; and both Bourke and Matthews felt acutely the constrictions of Army duties on their scientific ambitions—jealousy played a role in their judgments of the Stevensons and, later, of Jesse Fewkes. But more impor-tantly, they reacted against invasion and exploitation by mere passersby, observers who could not, they felt, understand complex secrets that were revealed only with time and patience. "Got into the medicine-lodge and saw things I never dreamt of. Would you imagine that the rascals, who have neither ornamented robes, skins, or pottery, or carven idols, have nevertheless a complete system of pictographic myth symbolism?" Thus Matthews an-nounced his discovery of Navaho sand-painting to Cushing in 1884. Eight years later he reported another personal breakthrough:

> I have made great strides in my knowledge of Navajo rites &c within the past years (But this is *private* to *you*), particularly during the past winter, & I have gained a position among the shamans that I had never hoped to get. Now they *urge* information and opportunities on me— nothing is witheld; I have been baptized and confirmed & have partaken of the Lord's supper (or its undoubted analogue) with them, and they urge on me a final ceremony of consecration which I doubt if my con-stitution will stand. But I keep all this quiet.[38]

Intimacy always carries a heavy burden of responsibility, and for some individuals it is difficult to glimpse the sacred and secret without also sharing veneration for it. It seems that for Cushing and Matthews, at least, profound ethnological experiences brought awareness of possible violation and betrayal of the Zuñis and Navahos. This was an especially painful dilemma for men who sensed the barrenness and irreverence of their own civilization. In order to bring regenerating knowledge to their own people, they necessarily violated trusts to others. The dilemma was insoluble, and it may have contributed to Cushing's reticence in publishing.[39]

On the 1879 expedition Cushing complained to Baird that while Stevenson was a good business manager (he served as executive officer of the Bureau and the Geological Survey), he treated Cushing like a boy. Subsequent experiences

confirmed Cushing's misgivings about the Bureau, which he shared with
Matthews and Bourke. At one point in 1881 he decided to seek an Army
commission in order to "cultivate arms as a profession, & science as a recreation
I love." Despite Bourke's support and the endorsement of General Philip
Sheridan, the appointment never materialized.[40] Bourke, who at the time was
considering retirement from the Army in order to devote himself to Apache
studies, suspected that the Bureau had blocked Cushing's appointment. The
problem, Bourke advised his friend, was that Cushing's excellence had alienated the BAE corps. He consequently could expect little help, because his
reputation "will destroy or dim that of many an old plug who has grown fat
and greasy. . ."[41] "You haven't a friend too many," he warned Cushing;
without them he could be destroyed by the BAE:

> A congregation of penny-dips will not be disposed to let an electric light
> enter among them. You know well that I have always distrusted those
> people and that in our conversations long ago we both concluded not
> to lean upon them too much.

Bourke advised him to locate a good cattle ranch near Zuñi, "near enough
so that you can have their protection and they your counsels," possibly financed
by "N.Y. and Boston capitalists."[42] At the same time Cushing should cultivate
a "European reputation" with Edward B. Tylor, Spencer, and others:

> America offers no suitable field for you. Very few of our people care for
> the Indians and nearly all of them manifest a suspicion of a man who
> presumes to consider their manners, customs, and ideas worthy of note
> and preservation.[43]

Integrity intact but harboring doubts about the Bureau, Cushing was
ordered to Washington in January 1884, to write up four and half years of
field work. He spent more than two years in the capital but never began the
expected work. Powell pushed him to complete his Zuñi linguistics in preparation for a full study of mythology and social arrangements. The only
immediate result for the BAE was a brief study of pueblo pottery.[44]

Cushing's frail health gave way under office rigor in late 1886, when he
took an indefinite leave of absence from the Bureau and returned to the
Southwest. But he did not return alone. Perhaps remembering Bourke's
advice, Cushing had located a rich Boston capitalist, and he went back to the
arid country as director of the Hemenway South-Western Archaeological
Expedition, endowed by Boston blueblood Mary Hemenway. Cushing's interests had been moving for some time from ethnology to history and archaeology, and the Hemenway project offered him the opportunity to follow
his imagination wherever it led. For two years he combed the Arizona ruins
that had increasingly fascinated him and that held, he was convinced, keys
to the past civilizations of the region, and perhaps of North and Central

America generally. Cushing produced glowing reports of significant finds, but it was all fragmentary. In 1889, just as the expedition might have been expected to reach significant results, Cushing collapsed again and was forced to return to the East, and Mrs. Hemenway replaced him with a Harvard-trained naturalist, Jesse Walter Fewkes.

Fewkes's appointment infuriated Cushing and initiated a decade-long feud. Confined to his New York homestead, unable or unwilling to produce the final report on the expedition, Cushing fumed against his successor. Fewkes had taken his manuscript data; had accused him of mismanagement, intemperance, and insanity; and had published without giving proper credit, Cushing railed.[45] Matthews comforted Cushing, reminding his friend that "the Codfish" (Fewkes) was completely unqualified for the Hemenway:

> Our Boston friend, while in Zuñi never spoke a word of Zuñi and didn't know a word of Spanish. He never employed either Graham or 'Nick' the only English-speaking men in Zuñi, yet he learned everything about them in two months. What a pity it is we have not a few more such brilliant lights in Ethnography![46]

William T. Harris, mediator between Cushing and Mrs. Hemenway, patiently reminded Cushing of the real issue: he had produced only fragments from an investment of $100,000. As of June 1891, there were no hard accusations against him, only "hard suspicions." All Mrs. Hemenway wanted was the final report. In response to Cushing's threat to abandon the work altogether, Harris explained his moral obligation and exposed his shortcomings as a scientist in painfully clear language:

> If you give up that work it seems to me that you will make the greatest mistake of your life. Because you see all your special articles on various themes hinge upon the validity of your work of simple observation and inventory. You have nothing to show on that side that is published and secondly you cannot defend yourself from the almost universal charge that is made and will be made against your work, that it is visionary, rather than scientific. You have left the results of the South-West Expedition in such a form that a scientific report upon it made by specialists would undoubtedly prove that you had abused the trust placed in you by Mrs. Hemenway, and had taken no care to save the results of your investigations, step by step, just as such results are saved by scientific expeditions.
>
> You know what the astronomers call the personal equation. In dealing with the religious and philosophical ideas of a lower people we must be very careful not to read into their poems ideas which have come to consciousness only with modern nations. There will be the suspicion that you have consciously or unconsciously modified the data given you by

the natives and this will seriously diminish the credit which your articles should have. But if you prove your right to be trusted as to data, you must prove it by writing minute and clear histories or records of your discoveries.[47]

The early years of the Hemenway Expedition under Cushing (it continued until the patroness's death in 1894) were a turning point in his career and in Southwestern archaeology. Highs and lows were inseparable with Cushing. At the moment of his greatest promise and in a position of critical leadership, he suffered dreadfully from heat and his various bodily ills, which had worsened. The expedition was bedevilled by relic-hunters who destroyed bones and artifacts, and Cushing had difficulty keeping order and momentum. He was completely unfit as a leader. Frederick Webb Hodge, who accompanied the expedition and later became both a brother-in-law and harsh critic of Cushing,[48] recalled that the director, perhaps because he was so ill, took few field notes but "depended largely on long accounts written in letter form to Mrs. Hemenway and to Sylvester Baxter." Baxter was a Boston journalist who served as home secretary and popularizer of the expedition back East. These reports "contained a great deal of bunk"—hypotheses and ambitious plans.[49] According to Hodge, Cushing simply failed to function well:

> The location of artifacts on the maps was done at Cushing's insistence, as he made no notes himself and he thought that by locating the 'finds' on the maps his memory would be aided when the time came to write the final report. Illness prevented Cushing, at times, from visiting the diggings from Camp Hemenway nearby; at other times he fiddled away his time in making flags for the tents and other useless trifles. Sometimes weeks passed without the laborers having any supervision excepting that given by the intelligent Mexican laborer Ramon Castro. Cushing was jealous of note-taking by anybody but himself.[50]

The digging was not thorough, and Cushing's interpretations of the finds were often based on his imagination. Thus, for instance, he explained "ultra mural" houses (structures beyond the pueblo walls) in terms of a supposed caste system, whereas it was, Hodge argued, "more reasonable to suppose that they were merely shelters occupied when the farming work was in progress, as in the case of Zuñi today."[51] Partly as a result of Cushing's slipshod methods, the Hemenway Collection, now in the Peabody Museum of Harvard, still awaits thorough study. He never wrote a final report.

The famous incident of the jewelled frog perhaps indicates Cushing's state of mind at Camp Hemenway. Having seen a shell frog from the ruins of southern Arizona in the possession of a Phoenix businessman, Cushing secretly "improved" a plain, frog-shaped shell found at Los Muertos to look like an aboriginal product. Some years later Hodge told the story of Cushing's deception:

> Some days later he appeared [from his tent] holding in his clenched hand a beautiful mosaic frog. That he had intended to palm it off as a specimen found in the ruins, I have no doubt. When he opened his hand and showed the object to me, I did not exclaim, but spoke of it casually as his own handiwork, as if he was aware that I knew he had made it, whereupon he said, "But it looks too new." This, coupled with the secrecy with which the frog was manufactured, confirmed my belief that he had intended to represent it as of Indian manufacture, but on account of its newness had abandoned the idea and thought of preserving it only as a model.

> Some time later, Prof. Edward S. Morse visited Los Muertos. . . . It was, I believe, in the evening of the day of his arrival that Cushing brought out the frog, and showed it to Morse, first holding it in his closed hand as before. As soon as Morse put eyes on it, he exclaimed. 'Great Lord, Cushing, where did you find that?' Cushing responded, nonchalantly, 'In a jar in Ruin III.'

> In his own belief, Cushing had won, for if the frog could deceive Morse, it would deceive anyone. The result was that Morse took the frog to Boston and showed or gave it to Mrs. Hemenway, never suspecting that the object was anything but genuine. It was thus that the frog found its way into the Hemenway collections.[52]

Cushing's own account naturally presented a different perspective on the matter. Responding in 1898 to Putnam's request for a statement as to the genuineness of the frog, Cushing struggled to explain how he worked on the specimen step by step with primitive materials and methods. He wrote in part:

> When I had completed these preliminary operations I mistakenly endeavored to solidify the more fragile parts by gently heating the entire surface,—by which the work coalesced in such manner that the portions restored were almost indistinguishable from the others. Then hoping to bring out the difference again, I cautiously rubbed the surface on a piece of suspended buckskin, using as the safest buff I could find the fine loam of the ruins. This did not accomplish what I intended & I frankly acknowledge it was a mistake, but a conscientious mistake. . .

> Since this was the first recognizable specimen of its kind that had to my knowledge been found; since I used such care in its restoration, and since subsequently another specimen identical with it in general and in several specific characteristics has been found . . . , you may without hesitation

exhibit this example not only as the first type specimen, but also, as accurate and authentic.[53]

The entire performance, from the specimen reconstruction (told with some pride, one senses) to the final confession of conscientious error and claim of authenticity, was pure Cushing.

The Hemenway expedition was at once the greatest opportunity, trial, and failure of Cushing's life, and he never entirely recovered from its impact. The heightened self-pity and martyrdom of his later years found expression in another confession to Putnam:

> In the vain efforts of a sick man, to meet the demands or desires of friends and fellow workers, my efforts too often become scattered, my sense of proportion or relative importance distorted, and my power to do any special & practical work, any one thing as it should be done, deferred or hazarded.
>
> It is this, my dear sir, [that has] led men . . . to pronounce me a false claimer, a vain speculator, a fraud, a drunkard, a pretender to the illness that is my mortal scourge and slow living death. And these men have no pity in judgement and they are such as would undo you and me alike if they could.[54]

Ignoring Harris's advice, Cushing abandoned the Hemenway work and returned to the BAE and his pending Zuñi materials. Between 1892 and 1894 he produced the beautiful *Outlines of Zuñi Creation Myths* and a series of shorter pieces, along Powellian lines, on the development of mental concepts and manual agility. From a scholarly viewpoint these were the most disciplined and productive years of Cushing's life.[55]

The prolonged office work again proved burdensome and depressing to Cushing. In 1894 Powell secretly arranged with William Pepper, Cushing's personal physician and provost of the University of Pennsylvania, to send Cushing to Florida for a rest and archaeological reconnaissance.[56] The health trip produced scientific bonanzas. As before at Zuñi and Camp Hemenway, the first reports glowed with the enthusiasm of fresh discovery. Cushing's early observations in the coastal shell mounds occupied two pages in the Bureau's 1895 report, and the data led to far-reaching hypotheses:

> Some of these pile-dwellings appeared to Mr. Cushing to stand in definite relation to certain of the shell mounds, particularly those of definite form, and through this relation he is able to gain some insight into the origin and development of mound building among the American aborigines, this insight being in part due to his intimate acqaintance with Indian modes of thought.[57]

The above statement, which seemed to promise a major insight into North

American aboriginal mound building, was based on a preliminary survey of the site that lasted less than one day in May 1895.[58]

The full expedition, partly financed by Phoebe Hearst and consisting of Cushing, his wife, and seven workers, arrived in late February 1896, and excavated for two months. Cushing returned to Washington in May; the fifty-nine boxes and eleven barrels of relics arrived somewhat later in Philadelphia for his reconstruction and analysis. Cushing never returned to Florida.

He also never finished classifying and arranging the collections, which remain unique in Florida archaeology.[59] Instead, Cushing became embroiled in a nasty dispute with Bureau photographer William Dinwiddie, who in the summer of 1896 accused the ethnologist of falsifying another shell specimen. Cushing's aides on the expedition all vouched for the authenticity of the find and for his honesty; Powell and the Bureau rallied around him; and Dinwiddie was fired for insubordination.[60] Cushing and his friends saw the episode as another attack on his character. "So after all the hub-bub," Matthews reflected, "the only one to suffer as a result of 'the Cushing slander' is poor little Dinwiddie, with his wife and children, he was only a catspaw for more designing men. . ."[61]

The Dinwiddie affair dragged on for months, disturbing the clear Key Marco waters and sapping Cushing of his limited energy; or so he claimed to Pepper. He hoped to complete the Key Marco report by early 1898, but chronic illness and the inconvenience of traveling to Philadelphia to examine the collection delayed the work. In October 1898, the collection moved to Washington, but Cushing died five months later.[62]

In each of the major phases of his career—Zuñi, Hemenway, the Pepper Expedition—Cushing left promising insights or discoveries unfinished. In each case, too, he experienced incapacitating illness and acrimonious personal relationships. At the time of his sudden death he was busily planning, with Powell's doting approval, yet another undertaking, this time with Powell, in the shell-heaps of Maine. So, had he lived, the pattern would have continued. Cushing could not be tied to institutions or individuals, but used them even as he depended on them—Baird's Smithsonian, Powell's Bureau, Hemenway's Expedition, Pepper and Stewart Culin's University Museum—to pursue his own erratic course. He lived for the great moments of discovery; they were a necessity for him. Cushing had no time for the deadening chores of scientific polish and proof. The flash of brilliance, promising insight, far-reaching theory—then Cushing was moving on, leaving the litter of his research strewn across the Southwest and elsewhere for others to pick up, if they could. Here was genius of a sort, but its credentials came increasingly under question, as William Harris informed Cushing. When Harvard-trained Fewkes succeeded self-taught Cushing on the Hemenway project, the change symbolized a generation's experience. Brilliant intuition alone went only so far.

Two years before his death, Cushing explained to the Board of Indian Commissioners "the need of studying the Indian in order to teach him." His address summarized the Bureau's reform philosophy: that Indian policy must be based on accurate knowledge rather than sentiment, fervor, prejudice, or ignorance. The BAE, Cushing explained, was not devoted to anthropology as a science alone, but aimed to understand the Indian's

> very nature, his mood of mind, his usages, his attitude, all in order that we may be better able to treat him as a subject or ward, and to aid him to overcome in his sadly unequal struggle with an advancing and alien civilization, so that he may be fitted to survive among us and not be further degraded or utterly destroyed.[63]

In order to understand the Indian, Cushing instructed, we must go to him as brothers, fully comprehend his inmost nature, study his past, "learn how he came to be what he is, and thus learn how to make him other than what he is." Rather than bludgeon the aborigine with Christianity and civilization, Whites must not immediately require the Indian to abandon his traditions, but wean him away through understanding and example:

> Of all the people on this continent, not excluding ourselves, the most profoundly religious—if by religion is meant fidelity to teachings and observances that are regarded as sacred—are the American Indians. . . For with them, sociologic organization and government and the philosophy and daily usages of life are still so closely united with religion, that all their customs, which we consider as absurd and useless, grow from it as naturally and directly as plants grow from the soil. . . . It is, then, most dangerous to tell the Indians of the baselessness of their beliefs, the uselessness of the customs and ceremonies founded upon them. Why strike at the very root of the life whereby they maintain their communities, by striking at these things before the appointed time?

Only through "searching knowledge," Cushing advised, could the government representatives teach "these latter-day barbarians, as we style them."[64] Sudden transitions tragically destroyed the revered traditions of Indian life, traditions that are loved "in a way that passes our comprehension, for we are weaned from love of our traditions":

> We do not want to go to them, then, and weaken their sense of morality founded on the traditions they believe, and so venerate, by saying that these are wrong, for we never in a lifetime, with the utmost effort and labor, can blot out of their minds what their fathers and mothers have taught them when young, of reverence for these traditions, and replace it with equally influential reverence of our own.[65]

It was reverence and mystery that Frank Cushing sought, at Zuñi pueblo, in the buried secrets of Los Muertos, among his imagined Key-dwellers of western Florida. Today Cushing is remembered and valued chiefly as a precursor in need of refinement and discipline. But Cushing's message to his own age speaks even more directly to ours. His message was this: A truly rich culture must not deny or eradicate the deep mythological and imaginative wellsprings of the soul. Beneath the vast cultural diversity of mankind lies a spiritual commonality, a level of intuitive communication.[66] The poetic and artistic powers of man exist independently of positive rational knowledge, and they constitute an equally valid, necessary, and deeply satisfying mode of dealing with the cosmos. The scientific world of observation and deduction that was in the making with such fanfare by anthropologists and others during Cushing's lifetime was tragically limiting and impoverished, despite its unprecedented yield of power. He realized as much. The institutional and personal storms that marked his life attested to his unfitness for the new century he never saw. The heartfelt eulogies by fellow anthropologists at his early death revealed that they too felt an irreplaceable loss, as if a part of themselves had been suddenly snatched away.

James Mooney (1861-1921) was an Irish Catholic and a journalist. His ethnic heritage and early newspaper career determined the deepest patterns of his anthropology. Even as a child of Irish immigrants in Richmond, Indiana, Mooney was conscious of separation from the mainstream of American culture. His estrangement grew with time. From the age of eight until he joined the Bureau of Ethnology, at twenty-four, in 1885, Mooney worked for a newspaper in his home town. Like his Irish sensibility, Mooney's journalistic bent never left him. Throughout his career in anthropology he was associated and concerned with politically and culturally oppressed peoples—Irish or Native American—and he was fascinated by modes of communication. From these roots came the central questions of his anthropology: How do oppressed people transmit the binding elements of their culture from one generation to the next? How do those who are defeated and dispersed nonetheless preserve identity and tradition?

Political consciousness came to Mooney as a birthright. While most of his colleagues explained the demise of the American Indian in racial or developmental terms, human fate for Mooney was the product of history and relative power. Although in early writings he occasionally adopted the rhetoric of evolutionism, Mooney did not take decline and subordination as signs of mental or cultural inferiority. Misfortune brought forth no judgment from him because as a Catholic Irishman he knew that "failure" said nothing about inherent worth. Social and political disintegration was a historical fact, not a moral state.[67]

Mooney realized no less than Powell that Indian cultures in their pristine, precontact forms were fast disappearing; consequently, there was a strong element of urgency and salvage in his work. However, perhaps because of his historical perspective and Irish nationalist sympathies, Mooney came to see Indian cultures as living and changing, struggling to survive under extremely demoralizing conditions. As he poignantly demonstrated in his monograph on the ghost-dance (1896), the aboriginal cultures of North America were human responses to hopelessness, misery, and social chaos.[68] Mooney was one of the first to recognize in Indian degradation the trauma of acculturation and adjustment to loss of power.

To a degree that was exceptional in his generation, Mooney's ethnology was grounded in painstaking historical reconstruction. His library and bibliographic research elicit admiration and gratitude from students even today; his major monographs on the Cherokee, the Ghost Dance, and the Kiowa are indispensable classics. But the Cherokees still consider Mooney their outstanding historian not merely because he told the story of their trials drawing on both Indian and White materials and memories, but also because he saw that history exists in the mind of the present as much as in documents. The persistent strength of oral tradition and unwritten knowledge comes from the deep roots they take in the personality and daily habits of the individual. Mooney discovered first among the eastern Cherokees what Cushing found in Zuñi pueblo: that the past lived vibrantly in the present and still controlled central aspects of aboriginal cultures. Mooney, like Cushing, sought to isolate the most secret keys that defined the past and determined present behavior. He would later locate such keys in the heraldry of the southern Plains peoples; among the Cherokees of the North Carolina mountains, he found them in sacred "formulas" of healing, love, and hunting. In these formulas, Cherokee history lived on. Perhaps Mooney's greatest contribution was to expand and redefine history so as to embrace Indian experience, and to incorporate this into his ethnology.

As a boy Mooney loved lists. When he was ten he wrote down names of sewing machine manufacturers and kept statistics on European languages. A short time later he began to direct his energies toward American Indians, gathering information on tribal names, languages, migration histories, boundaries, and treaty relations. In a fashion remarkably similar to Powell's program, by age sixteen Mooney had developed, on his own in Indiana, a large map of the tribes of North America.[69] In 1882 Mooney first applied to the Bureau, but Powell rejected him because of his lack of linguistic experience and the shortage of funds at the Bureau. He was turned down again the following year, and again in 1884. Finally in 1885 he traveled to Washington for a personal interview. This resulted in an unsalaried opportunity to prove himself.[70]

Mooney made immediate, significant contributions to the Bureau synonymy; his arrival in fact stimulated a flurry of activity for a year or so.[71] But the tentativeness of his hiring seems to have persisted; he never shared

James Mooney, newspaperman, student of Cherokee and Plains ethnography.

Powell's favor or joined the inner circle at the Bureau. He worked with Mallery on the synonymy but became friends with Gatschet and Matthews. It was Matthews who did the most to shape Mooney. Despite his Army affiliations and friendship with the favored Cushing, Matthews was no confidante of Powell's; as we have seen, he felt slighted and unappreciated at the Bureau. After Matthews's death in 1905, his wife, Caroline, wrote to Charles Lummis that the failure of the Bureau to provide an obituary of her husband was perfectly consistent: "The Bureau of Ethnology has ignored him as it always has done in the past. . ."[72] But Mooney was fortunate that in 1885 Matthews was stationed for a period in Washington and working in the Bureau. As sons of Irish immigrants to the Midwest (Matthews grew up in Iowa), the two men shared an important ethnic and religious bond. Mooney, who eventually did write Matthews's obituary in the *American Anthropologist*, attributed his success as an ethnologist to his Irish heritage:

> By a faculty of mingled sympathy and command he won the confidence of the Indian and the knowledge of his secrets, while by virtue of that spiritual vision which was his Keltic inheritance, he was able to look into the soul of primitive things and interpret their meaning as few others have done.[73]

Matthews offered Mooney four points of guidance for field work: learn the language; be authoritative but sympathetic; record everything precisely; and avoid preconceptions.[74] Mooney apparently listened carefully. His first field trip, to the eastern Cherokees in the North Carolina hills, was originally commissioned to examine remnant dialects for the linguistic map. But Mooney immediately envisioned much wider purposes. In his first seasons (1886 and 1887) he established the field methods that always characterized his work. Like Cushing and Matthews, he emphasized patience, indirection in questioning, and mutuality of exchange.

Mooney's field success was attributable in part to the fact that he astutely but sympathetically took advantage of the social disintegration and economic poverty of the Cherokees. He began with material culture, inquiring about purchase of artifacts, expressing interest in manufacturing techniques, gently probing into sources of daily habits and customs. Severe economic hardship may have facilitated purchase of articles (including written formulae for the BAE) among these people, as among most other Native American groups by the second half of the century. Mooney further demonstrated serious purpose by working assiduously on the complicated Cherokee language. He soon discovered that the combination of sincere interest and calculated flattery usually, but not always, opened the way to establishing the individual informant relationships that he enjoyed and utilized to such profit.[75]

Mooney found the Cherokee men of knowledge secretive, proud, and competitive; furthermore, "at present each priest or shaman is isolated and independent":

> It frequently happens, however, that priests form personal friendships and thus are led to divulge their secrets to each other for their mutual advantage. Thus when one shaman meets another who he thinks can probably give him some valuable information, he says to him, "Let us sit down together." This is understood by the other to mean, "Let us tell each other our secrets." Should it seem probable that the seeker after knowledge can give as much as he receives, an agreement is generally arrived at, the two retire to some convenient spot secure from observation, and the first party begins by reciting one of his formulas with the explanations. The other then reciprocates with one of his own, unless it appears that the bargain is apt to prove a losing one, in which case the conference comes to an abrupt ending.[76]

The key to Mooney's Cherokee work was his ability to penetrate and participate in this system of knowledge exchange. Gaining trust to enter this exclusive circle of knowledge required time and sensitivity; and, of course, Mooney had to have something to give as well. Matthews's success among the Navaho shamans in the same period was due largely to his standing as a physician, which permitted a cross-cultural exchange of privileged information: his anthropology was in part professional dialogue. Mooney did not formally possess similar expertise, but he had amassed a large store of Irish lore, stories, and medical remedies. With these he was able to claim a place of respect within the dwindling circle of Cherokee medicine men.

If cooperation and exchange faltered, however, Mooney had other methods at his disposal. The independence that derived from social disintegration also led to jealousy and vanity among the Cherokee men of knowledge. Mooney played on these feelings. He acquired his first book of written Cherokee formulas, the Swimmer manuscript, by appealing to his informant's pride:

> Mooney reminded Swimmer that there were only a few men of knowledge left and that the only purpose of recording myths was to let the world know how rich the Cherokee culture had been. If Swimmer could not give him complete information, perhaps someone else within the tribe could. Mooney also told him that shamans from other tribes sent songs and myths of a similar nature to Washington. . . . Swimmer said he knew as much or more than any medicine man in his tribe, and he would tell all he knew to prove it.[77]

Mooney succeeded handsomely as an ethnologist, and his success complicated relations in the Bureau. His early years in Washington, until about 1890, were, like Cushing's years at Zuñi, a period of struggling self-assertion.

One suspects that his preference for the field, like Cushing's long absences from Washington, reflected desire for physical and intellectual autonomy as much as commitment to preserving Indian cultures. Powell was a formidable, powerful figure in the eighties, a man of heroic proportions. It was no simple matter for a young man to declare independence or to differ openly, even with a director committed to individual fulfillment. As a result, the Bureau annual reports sometimes contained muted arguments between Powell and his ethnologists, as he sought to correct rather than censor wayward notions.

Mooney soon began to test his tether. Powell was certainly impressed with the Cherokee results, particularly the unique written formulas Mooney had acquired for the Bureau. But signs of potential and profound rift emerged early. Powell's brief remarks introducing Mooney's *Sacred Formulas of the Cherokees*, in the seventh annual report, damned the work with faint praise. Attempting to place aboriginal zootheism in its proper developmental niche, the director reminded the reading public that "zoic mythology degenerates into folk tales of beasts, to be recited by crones to children or told by garrulous old men as amusing stories inherited from past generations. . ." By so displaying his commitment to civilized rationality, Powell implied that Mooney's discoveries had little value other than as "vestiges" of earlier systems.[78]

Mooney understandably estimated his own work more favorably (as do most others today); but his evaluation was grounded in a different perspective and purpose. Mooney's vitality and sympathy at this early point are best conveyed in his own words:

> The formulas contained in these manuscripts are not disjointed fragments of a system long since extinct, but are the revelation of a living faith which still has its priests and devoted adherents, and it is only necessary to witness a ceremonial ball play, with its fasting, its going to water, and its mystic bead manipulation, to understand how strong is the hold which the old faith yet has upon the minds even of the younger generation.

> It is impossible to overestimate the ethnologic importance of the materials thus obtained. They are invaluable as the genuine production of the Indian mind, setting forth in the clearest light the state of the aboriginal religion before its contamination by contact with the whites. . . .

> These formulas furnish a complete refutation of the assertion so frequently made by ignorant and prejudiced writers that the Indian had no religion excepting what they are pleased to call the meaningless mummeries of the medicine man. This is the very reverse of the truth. The Indian is essentially religious and contemplative, and it might almost be said that every act of his life is regulated and determined by his religious belief. It matters not that some may call this superstition. The difference is

only relative. The religion to-day has developed from the cruder super-
stitions of yesterday, and Christianity itself is but an outgrowth and
enlargement of the beliefs and ceremonies which have been preserved
by the Indian in their more ancient form.[79]

The reference to Christianity was an early sign of Mooney's movement
toward a cross-cultural perspective based on the suspicion that cultural phenomena are functions of social, economic, and political conditions rather than
indices of mental growth. It is important to note, however, that Mooney's
position emerged within the intellectual atmosphere of the BAE. Powell's
system of mental evolutionism was always flawed and open to radical
challenge. While Powell chose to emphasize the gulfs and distances separating
savage and civilized men, other observers, including some members of his
own staff, formally embraced the stage-sequence framework but were nonetheless struck, not by the disparities, but by the similarities in belief and
behavior among all men. Why were they impressed in such a manner? As
in Mooney's case, personal temperament and prior experience deeply influence
basic perspective in anthropology, shaping the personal politics of the
science. As he grew older Powell increasingly accented the great psychic and
social leaps at critical points in his conjectured human development, while
Mooney, with equal legitimacy and oftentimes similar language, pointed to
continuity and behavioral kinship among men. He was exploring the possibility that Indian cultures represented not simpler, undeveloped human experiences, but full, complex models that were in no meaningful sense distinct
from civilization.

This awareness, which dawned in the Cherokee work, became possible only
when Mooney viewed the Cherokees as more than a dying cultural remnant.
Nineteenth-century ethnology was built on the assumption of Indian decay,
and the BAE had been founded within that tradition. As long as he pursued
the professed institutional purposes of the Bureau—salvaging linguistic and
material pieces—the intellectual perimeter of Mooney's work would be confined. But Mooney bent the institution to his personality and desires, and
he was inclined to see vigor, not decay. However gradual the personal process,
the result was a perceptual switch that set Mooney on a path diverging widely
from Powell's.[80] By 1900, when he published *Myths of the Cherokee*,[81] Mooney
had long since abandoned Powell's developmental approach to mythology in
favor of ethnohistorical questions. His biographer has stated that it "made
more sense to him to study myth exchange within the context of tribal trading
and raiding patterns."[82] In the face of Powell's strong predilection for viewing
Indian mythology as a system of thought rather than a historical product,
and considering Mooney's subordinate status in the Bureau, his historicism
required courage and conviction. Why did this approach seem more reasonable
to him; what factors determined Mooney's preference?

In pursuing Mooney's anthropology to its sources, it is instructive to consider briefly the contrasting career of Jeremiah Curtin, the myth-collector who worked for the Bureau at intervals during the eighties and nineties. Curtin (1835-1906), born in Wisconsin territory and educated at Harvard during the Civil War, omnivorously studied languages and recorded folktales and myths around the world, from the Modocs and Wintus of California to the Irish and the Slavs. Despite a common Irish heritage, midwestern roots, mutual interest in both Celtic and American Indian mythology, and overlapping sojourns at the Bureau, Curtin and Mooney curiously never developed any professional or personal relationship. Age may have been a factor, since Curtin was a considerably older man, but then, so was Washington Matthews. The breach between Curtin and Mooney was deeper than age.

Curtin saw globally: "Not greatness dwarfs men," but littleness, petty surroundings, petty associates, petty interests dwarf."[83] Externally at least, Curtin was certainly not petty. He could never be tied to focused study or a single spot; he never owned a home and, except for brief periods of BAE office work, rarely stayed in one place more than a few months. For decades his faithful wife accompanied him everywhere as companion and secretary. Unquestionably a talented polyglot—he knew dozens of languages with various degrees of proficiency—Curtin skimmed a score of cultures, enduring terrible privations and enjoying cosmopolitan luxuries. So did his wife.

When he was in Washington, Curtin was a favorite of Powell's; he dedicated Creation Myths of Primitive America (1898) to the one-armed explorer through whom, he said, "the world has learned more of the great primitive race of our country than it learned from the discovery of the continent till the day when the Bureau was founded."[84] It is evident from his published statements that Curtin accepted Powell's theories and purposes. He had little interest in aboriginal histories. The myths of the American Indians, he believed, together formed a coherent system that was characteristic of a primitive plateau of mentality.[85] They had "philosophies of life and systems of religion which resembled one another, but were greatly varied in detail; the underlying ideas were mainly the same, but the working out varied from tribe to tribe." Curtin saw the Western Hemisphere as an extensive "museum of the human mind in its earlier conditions." He valued Indian mythology as a "treasure saved to science by the primitive race of America," not as a living presence or means of further inquiry.[86]

Curtin's field practice fitted his purposes. He claimed, like a successful ethnologist, to have been "adopted" by the Seneca, but the honor was a meaningless gesture that occurred on his first day at the reservation near Versailles, New York. In Curtin's words, "Then I ate an ear of corn and I was an Indian. . . . After receiving the congratulations of the crowd, I went back to Versailles, leaving the Indians to partake of their feast."[87] Curtin did subsequently return to the Seneca and in time developed relatively stable informant relations with people who were already highly acculturated into local White society. Among the Modocs, Klamaths, and Wintus of the west coast, however, Curtin was more a detached consumer than a committed investigator: "Whenever one Indian failed me, I sent for another and, while waiting, I kept my nerves steady by reading Persian," he wrote of one visit.[88] In sum, Curtin was never really more than a sojourner anywhere, even in Washington: "In the Bureau (in 1885-86) I was occupied with the Alaskan work but I found time to read Hebrew and Persian, and with the assistance of Smith, a Cherokee Indian, I learned the Cherokee language. Evening hours were given to study."[89]

The contrasts between Mooney and Curtin—in personality, method, experience, and basic concerns—point to the complexity in the shaping of an ethnologist. Curtin was restless and homeless, but he was not alienated from or critical of his civilization. While at Harvard he had easily adopted the style and values of mid-century Boston as it entered its "New England Indian Summer": he wrote with polish but no passion; he traveled widely, but his nerves were numbed to the pain and sorrow of Indian fate. His goal was to contribute to the library of humanist knowledge, not to participate in history or pass judgment on it.

Mooney came to the BAE with a critical edge that was soon sharpened by work among a defeated but persistent people. The remarkable fact is that Mooney, perhaps because he lacked a thorough grounding in Powellian philosophy or a variant evolutionism, saw the persistence in Cherokee defeat. Mooney's own persistence and struggle may have been determinative. For him, nothing came easily. A shy and reticent man, he did not possess the flair or ease of Curtin. To him the human world was enigmatic, an accidental series of affairs, anything but a progressive rise to civilized reason. The measure of Mooney's growth was an increasing tentativeness toward knowledge. "I am not infallible or omniscient," he reminded Matthews in 1897, "& every field trip serves only to convince me more than before that at the best a white man can only hope to gather scraps around the edge of his Indian subject."[90]

In 1890 Mooney turned to the Plains region and shelved his Cherokee notes for nearly a decade. The switch was occasioned by an outbreak of the ghost-dance among the Arapaho, Cheyenne, and other tribes from the Mississippi to California, but Mooney's work in the Southeast had already led him to the Indian Territory to study the western Cherokee. On the basis of linguistic and historical evidence, Mooney had argued, following Horatio Hale's suggestion, that the Tutelo and related groups of the Southeast were survivors of the parent stock of western Siouan tribes, who at some point had been driven out of the Southeast by Algonquian and Iroquoian interlopers. Mooney's case was largely circumstantial and hotly debated, but it indicated his growing historicism and drew his attention westward.[91]

His famous memoir on *The Ghost Dance Religion and the Sioux Outbreak of*

1890, which appeared in the Bureau's 1893 annual report (published in 1896), marked his maturity as reporter, historian, and ethnologist; it has remained the major source of his enduring reputation. The ghost-dance had been misrepresented by agents of the Bureau of Indian Affairs and by eastern newspapers as preparation for war. Mooney soon discovered that the fears were unfounded and that the dance pointed to deep historical and ethnological puzzles:

> In the fall of 1890 the author was preparing to go to Indian Territory, under the auspices of the Bureau of Ethnology, to continue researches among the Cherokee, when the Ghost dance began to attract attention, and permission was asked and received to investigate the subject also among the wilder tribes in the western part of the territory. Proceeding directly to the Cheyenne and Arapaho, it soon became evident that there was more in the Ghost dance than had been suspected, with the result that the investigation, to which it had been intended to devote only a few weeks, has extended over a period of more than three years, and might be continued indefinitely, as the dance still exists (in 1896) and is developing new features at every performance.[92]

Mooney observed and participated in the ghost-dance during three field seasons (1891–93), chiefly among the Arapaho, Sioux, Kiowa, and Cheyenne. He carefully wrote down a multitude of songs, and in 1893 became one of the first ethnologists to use a gramophone in the field. Because the songs contained the structure of the religion, he argued, analysis of their symbolism would yield insights into the mythology and customs of each tribe. At the ceremonies Mooney carefully watched face and body movements, the gestures of the medicine-men, and the symptoms and timing of trances. His research into the history of the spread of the ghost-dance, and his pilgrimage, at the end of 1891, to Wovoka, the Paiute prophet who lived on Walker Lake reservation in Nevada, convinced Mooney that the dance was a ceremony of peace and brotherhood, a movement of cultural revitalization among desperately poor, nearly hopeless peoples. Wovoka's written statement of religious principles, as Mooney analyzed it, contained the basic elements of every religion: ethical precepts, a spiritual mythology, and exhortation to ritual observance. The ghost-dance religion was a "revolution" that came "but once in the life of a race."[93] While each of the tribes interpreted Wovoka's message according to its own myths, they all shared the messianic faith as "the only viable alternative in a world of insufferable oppression."[94]

The massacre at Wounded Knee, which occurred as Mooney was preparing for the field in the last days of 1890, and the stunning ignorance and corruption of BIA agents, moved Mooney to anger that he transformed into poignant descriptive passages. After reviewing the evidence and official reports of Wounded Knee, he concluded in a balanced tone "that the first shot was fired by an Indian, and that the Indians were responsible for the engagement; that the answering volley and attack by the troops was right and justifiable, but that the wholesale slaughter of women and children was unnecessary and inexcusable."[95] Even less forgivable was the failure to send a medical or burial team to the site for three days. Mooney described the scene:

> The bodies of the slaughtered men, women, and children were found lying about under the snow, frozen stiff and covered with blood. . . . Almost all the dead warriors were found lying near where the fight began, about Big Foot's tipi, but the bodies of the women and children were found scattered along for 2 miles from the scene of the encounter, showing that they had been killed while trying to escape. . . . A number of women and children were found still alive, but all badly wounded or frozen, or both, and most of them died after being brought in. Four babies were found alive under the snow, wrapped in shawls and lying beside their dead mothers, whose last thought had been of them. They were all badly frozen and only one lived. The tenacity of life so characteristic of wild people as well as of wild beasts was strikingly illustrated in the case of these wounded and helpless Indian women and children who thus lived three days through a Dakota blizzard, without food, shelter, or attention to their wounds. It is a commentary on our boasted Christian civilization that although there were two or three salaried missionaries at the agency not one went out to say a prayer over the poor mangled bodies of these victims of war.

> A long trench was dug and into it were thrown all the bodies, piled one upon another like so much cordwood, until the pit was full, when the earth was heaped over them and the funeral was complete. . . . Many of the bodies were stripped by the whites, who went out in order to get the "ghost shirts," and the frozen bodies were thrown into the trench stiff and naked. They were only dead Indians. As one of the burial party said, "It was a thing to melt the heart of a man, if it was of stone, to see those little children, with their bodies shot to pieces, thrown naked into the pit."[96]

Powell valued Mooney's ethnological labors, but he was undoubtedly pleased that it did not appear in print until 1896. While Mooney was in the field in early 1891, *Illustrated American* and several eastern newspapers began a campaign for an official investigation into the roles of the army and Bureau of Indian Affairs in recent events, especially Wounded Knee. The editors of *Illustrated American,* circulating a petition in Washington, called on both Powell and Mason. Both refused to sign. Mason, according to the magazine, replied that "we never express ourselves vehemently upon political matters. It isn't healthy to do so." *Illustrated American* also reported its meeting with Powell:

I next visited Major Powell, the head of the Geological Survey, and one of the best posted men on Indian affairs in this country. He refused to sign the petition on the ground that it would embroil him in a controversy with the Secretary of the Interior. (And, by the way, all these department heads seem to be in mortal dread of Secretary Noble.) Major Powell further said that he had no doubt that the Sioux had suffered to an extreme degree. He heartily wished that the appeal to Congress should be successful.[97]

Powell had good reason to be circumspect, since he was under heavy attack from critics of the Geological Survey, who would force him to resign from the Survey two years later. But more disturbing than Mooney's accusation of Army "butchery" at Wounded Knee and his transparent Indian sympathies were his speculative cross-cultural comparisons between the ghost-dance and other religious movements of revitalization among the oppressed, including early Christianity. This aspect of Moooney's work, which presaged theoretical and comparative work in cultural deprivation in the twentieth century, was unwelcome heterodoxy in Langley's Smithsonian and Powell's Bureau. Mooney's suggestion that Christian doctrine might be founded on dreams and visions appalled Langley, who admonished Powell that "such words . . . had better have been left unwritten. They give the ill-wishers of the Bureau a powerful means of attack, if attention is called to them, which I trust it will not be."[98] Powell agreed and regretted that Mooney's statements in an official government publication might "provoke hostile criticism."[99] Characteristically, in his introduction to the annual report the director repaired the damage as best he could:

It may be observed that caution should be exercised in comparing or contrasting religious movements among civilized peoples with such fantasies as that described in the memoir; for while interesting and suggestive analogies may be found, the essential features of the movements are not homologous. Most of the primitive peoples of the earth, including the greater part of the American Indians, represent the prescriptorial stage of culture. . . . while white men represent the scriptorial stage. Now, the passage from the earlier of these stages to the later, albeit partially accomplished among different peoples, probably marks the most important transition in the development of human culture or the history of the race; so that in mode of thought and in coordination between thought and action, red men and white men are separated by a chasm so broad and deep that few representatives of either race are ever able clearly to see its further sides. . . . Thus, many of the movements described in this chapter were among people separated from the ghost dance enthusiasts by the widest known cultural break as well as by the widest known break in fiducial development; and whatever the superficial resemblance in the movements, there is a strong presumption against their essential homology.[100]

The experiences of the early nineties drove Mooney further away from the "party line" of the Bureau. His meticulous research, mainly in official government documents, protected him from reprisal from those outside the Bureau who objected to his account of Wounded Knee, but within the BAE Mooney seems to have become increasingly isolated. At the World's Fair in Chicago in 1893 he clashed with Cushing over display techniques, and in the field he began to find the Bureau's procedures irksome and constricting. At one point he exploded to Henshaw:

> I have spent the last two weeks in a dirty tepee, sleeping on the ground and living on crackers and coffee, because I wouldn't eat a sick colt. I come back to find my vouchers returned and no money and [have] to dodge the traders and stand off a mob of wild Indians. . . . When I return I must have money . . . from some source and after that I can sit down and make vouchers to suit all the red tape requirements of the treasury.[101]

The trajectory of Mooney's career pointed to intensive history and ethnography of specific cultures at the very time that Powell, with the aid of W J McGee, was beginning his final, rigid evolutionary synthesis. Mooney, intellectually (and often physically) isolated and possessed by a sense of urgency to record the disappearing way of life of the southern plains, spent two-thirds of his time in the field, usually among the Kiowa, over the next decade. Finding in the Kiowa the most conservative tribe of the region, in 1893 he started the most intensive, prolonged field study of his life. He focused on two points: discovery and analysis of Kiowa calendar counts, and reproduction and study of the symbolism of Kiowa heraldry (tipi and warrior shield designs). The dual emphasis had a logic. The calendar studies offered insight into the Kiowas' view of their own recent history; in 1898 Mooney published *Calendar History of the Kiowa Indians*, now recognized as a meticulously researched classic. The heraldry studies that Mooney extended to the Cheyenne and others but never completed, were a promising window into social organization and the world of dreams and visions.[102]

McGee, who acted as ethnologist in charge of the Bureau after 1893, had little understanding or patience with Mooney's ethnohistorical interests, and he grew progressively annoyed with Mooney's political and personal activities on behalf of his Indian friends. McGee wanted published work; he saw no reason why an ethnologist could not go to the field and make his observations one year and write them up the next, as he did with the Seri Indians in 1894 and 1895.[103] When Mooney complained of illness in a difficult 1895 season, McGee advised him that if his health did not "permit effective operations," he should stop wasting Bureau money. Hurt and angry, Mooney retorted that

"During all these months that I have been almost fighting for my life to carry through to completion a piece of work that might bring credit to the bureau . . . an occasional expression of official concern might have served to brace up failing energies, but this goes far to kill what strength is left."[104] He returned to Washington early, as McGee ordered.

Mooney came to despise McGee for his arrogance and ignorance. But quite aside from personalities, well before the turn of the century Mooney realized that the framework of social and mental development into which Powell and McGee insisted on placing his studies was sterile. He saw, furthermore, that Powell's program for anthropology no longer served a useful purpose and must give way to fresh ideas. In 1903 Mooney received an opportunity to state views orally that he would certainly have hesitated to commit to writing. Testifying before the Smithsonian committee looking into practices in Powell's Bureau, Mooney was initially reticent, but when requested to state his personal views on organizing research he summarized nearly two decades of experience.

The era of the survey was over in anthropology, Mooney observed. Linguistic stock classification, he contended, bore little relation to environmental/cultural types, which was a far more meaningful classification for study and museum display.[105] Given the small corps of ethnologists available, Mooney judged, to undertake to study every tribe would only result in "a lot of bad work."[106] His plan was to map out the major type areas and concentrate on typical "study tribes" for each group, as he had done with the Cherokee for the southeastern woodland type, and the Kiowa for the southern plains. He estimated that about thirty such "broadly defined types" could be established north of Mexico. Mooney's description of the plains type revealed the importance he placed on environment and his broad scope of interrelationships:

For instance, we will take the plains, stretching, say, from the Saskatchewan down to the Rio Grande, generally a timberless region, occupied originally by the buffalo as the principal game animal; and the Indians consequently were nomadic in their habits. They could not manufacture anything that was easily breakable, and for that reason did not have pottery . . . and they did not have the wood carving of the Pueblo tribes, and they did not do much basket work, for lack of material. They depended on the buffalo, and had to follow him, so they had to have portable houses, and could not build stone or adobe houses. They had the tipi, and it was made of skin. They developed certain arts all along that line; and along with the tipi as the center of the house life they had certain other things that belonged to the same kind of hunting and nomadic life. They did not have agriculture, and as they did not have that, they did not have certain of the arts and objects that sedentary tribes had. They did not have the Green Corn Dance that belonged especially to agriculture, but they did have certain things that the tribes to the east and the west of them did not have.[107]

The work must be done quickly, Mooney told the committee. Defending his practice of spending so much time in the field, Mooney confessed that his notes would be of limited use to another student, since they were "short-hand notes, to be interpreted from my own knowledge and experience, for final writing."[108] But the field work could not wait: "I do not think much of the desk ethnologist, on general principles, and I know from being out there—well, being with any tribe—how rapidly this thing is passing away."

Now, for instance, I have just come from one great ceremonial, and I have seen it four times. I saw it ten years ago for the first time, and I have seen it twice since, and then this last time. It would be impossible to make anybody in the east realize the difference between that ceremonial the first time I saw it and this last time. And I can judge from that that in five years it will be wiped [out]; it will not be there at all; it will have vanished.

Now I am most of my time with the Kiowas. I hope to work them up as a complete tribal study. I picked them out about twelve years ago, after having seen a great many tribes, as being the best study tribe upon the plains, and the most conservative—as being the most Indian. I have been with them on this last trip, for a year and a half, and in all that time I have not seen one man in Indian dress in that tribe. When I went to them there were not half a dozen families in the tribe living in houses. They were all in tipis and in tipi camps. . . . There were not a dozen men who ever wore a hat. They had feathers in their hair, and they painted their faces whenever they went any place. The man with whom I made my home—I lived in tipis then for several years during the time I was with them—had eight rings in one ear and five in the other. He lived in a tipi and under an arbor in summer, always had his full buckskin on when it was time for buckskin; and he never went to a military post, or to a dance, or to anything else, without spending a couple of hours at least to dress and paint up. Now he is in a house, and has chickens and a corn field, and stoves and clocks and beds; and he has taken out his rings and cut his hair, and he looks like a dilapidated tramp.

Now, that sort of thing is going on everywhere, and I do not think an ethnologist can afford to spend much time in the office under such circumstances. When a man gets broken down he can afford to sit at a desk; but I believe it is better to take the chances of having some of this note material lost, and to spend this present time in investigation.[109]

When Mooney described to the committee the indirect, cumulative nature of field note-taking, his terms exposed clearly the chasm that separated his anthropology from the natural-science tradition of Powell and the early Bureau. People, Mooney had found, simply could not be observed and described in the same manner as birds or geological deposits:

A man investigating another kind of a subject perhaps, some natural science, is making his own investigations, in his laboratory; he is alone, and as he discovers a fact he can note it there. But I am talking to an Indian—well, say I am talking to an Indian about his shield, and he tells me that this shield was dreamed by a certain man. Then I get a dream origin for my myth note-book; I get a name with a translation for my—well, for my dictionary, if you please, or glossary, and I get a statement on name giving for some other investigation, and before I am done with it, he may mention a plant, and some use for that plant, and there may be some origin for that, and after an hour's talk with him, I have probably struck a dozen threads for investigation; and that would all be on two or three pages. And the rest of those same lines or threads would be on other pages in other notebooks. Now, when it comes to writing those out for the final publication, it must be all overhauled, and all the material from the different places put together. In that way, as you can see, each one of these things will be scattered all through the note material.[110]

Mooney was not alone with the insights of his field experiences. He had learned from Dorsey and Matthews; Cushing, too, had sensed the depth of Zuñi life. Matilda Stevenson, whom Powell detested but tolerated in the Bureau because of her political connections, steadily deepened her knowledge of Zuñi and Zia pueblos over several decades. By all accounts an insensitive field worker,[111] Stevenson nonetheless came to see the importance of prolonged exposure. She had written her BAE monograph *The Zuñi Indians*,[112] she explained in 1903, because

I felt the need of some definite publication, a sort of foundation of some tribe, and my aim in the Zuñi work was to probe to the very core of their philosophy, their religion, and sociology and to make such a book as would be of positive value to the student of ethnology . . . I hoped to get something that the student could take hold of and read and then start on any line of study he might desire. It takes a good part of a life to get a work like that. . . . No one can pursue a profound study in any special line in ethnological work without having a foundation to go upon, because their religion, their sociology, their whole life, is so entangled, so gnarled together, that you cannot study one line without the other unless you are familiar with their life.[113]

At the founding of the BAE, vocabulary lists and circulars of inquiry had still been basic methodology. They had introduced system and consistency but had discouraged flexibility in the field—the flexibility that Mooney had in mind when he stated that "The Indian is an uncertain quantity. You get him in one place and in another place. He is not a man whom you can talk with right straight along."[114] Years in the field, made possible by the institutional freedom of the Bureau, had taught Mooney a patient willingness to let specific conditions determine the immediate direction of inquiry. But flexibility was not capitulation. As we have seen, Cushing suffered accusations of having become a savage, and Mooney's sympathy with Indian political concerns created considerable friction. Yet neither man "went native," and in most respects, such as Mooney's aversion to sexual or scatological references in print, both adhered to contemporary American mores. What set them apart was their gradual realization that just as grammatical categories must be altered in learning Indian languages, the anthropologist must suspend, not abandon, inherited notions of social organization, scientific knowledge, artistic beauty, even moral categories, if he is to come to understand another people. This was a difficult and troublesome stance, for it involved willingness to doubt and surrender, albeit temporarily, the hard-won certainties of industrial civilization. As Henry Adams remarked of the 1890s, "one could not stop to chase doubts as though they were rabbits."[115]

By the new century the BAE had inadvertently spawned, in certain individuals, a critical perspective and an ethnographic emphasis that had been largely unknown only twenty years before. There is an understandable temptation to see in Mooney or Cushing forebears of modern professional anthropology, particularly when they appear against a background of nineteenth-century evolutionary enthusiasts. In a recent study of Cushing, Joan Mark credits him with developing "an American science of anthropology" and argues for his priority in conceiving and developing, in his Hemenway years, the culture concept usually attributed to Boas.[116] Cushing did use the term "cultures" in his writings of the 1890s, in contexts which leave little doubt that he meant integrated, holistic, historically determined phenomena. But for Cushing (and Mooney), intellectual discoveries had no direct bearing on the structures of scientific institutions. They did not perceive that certain avenues of inquiry, especially in the social sciences, must be guaranteed freedom from external interference in order to proceed. Similarly, Cushing never followed his concept of culture to its clear institutional implication: that anthropologists must be trained to recognize and allow for the cultural and personal bias of their observing. The element lacking (from current perspective) in Mooney and Cushing, the blind spot that places them in their own time, was their inability to see the intimate linkage between intellectual life and the institutional structures in which it necessarily takes place.

The structures of nineteenth-century anthropology no less than those of today permitted favorable conditions of growth for some inquiries, while others withered for lack of nourishment. Boas realized as much, and between 1896 and 1905 he stated clearly the limitations and possibilities, as he saw them, of the government bureau and the museum as institutional forms for anthropological science.[117] Over the following decade he brought about the major alterations in both the intellectual and institutional contours of American anthropology that would establish his dominance in the profession by 1920. But the driving force in the Boasian revolution, and the reason that one could speak of a "profession" by 1920, came precisely from that combination of institutional and intellectual structure: through the university department Boas consciously institutionalized a new constellation of ideas capable of being tested and elaborated by a subsequent generation of trained students.

Intimacy between institutions and ideas is a fundamental condition of modern intellectual life.[118] Beyond the annual meetings and journals of communication, the professional condition means that the survival and development of ideas depend heavily on the barrenness or fertility of institutional soil. And, as Boas quickly learned, institutions by their very natures offer widely varying conditions for growth. Because they possessed little institutional perspective, Mooney and Cushing, for better or worse, were not "professional" anthropologists. To the limited extent that they concerned themselves with perpetuating theory or method through testing and refinement, they relied, like Powell, on example rather than on training others to follow them. As Mooney confessed, he was willing to take the risk of leaving behind piles of undigested, possibly unusable field notes. Of equal importance, their audience was the American nation, not a well-defined academic peer group. As Joan Mark has perceptively observed, Cushing "gloried in the cleverness of the Zuñi people, and implicitly in his own cleverness, in being able to follow along and trace the interconnections in their culture. He was an insider telling the rest of the world something it did not know. For later anthropologists the approach was more often that of scientists telling one another things about a group of people which the people did not know about themselves."[119]

The cases of Mooney and Cushing demonstrate that professionalism, in Washington anthropology or elsewhere, did not come naturally or without a cost. The national moral service that Joseph Henry had foreseen for American anthropology remained a possibility for Cushing, Mooney, and their colleagues. They could not make the adjustment to a more rigorous, constructed professional audience and its horizons. If they were not anthropologists of the sort that we would recognize today, it was only because they held to grander goals. Professionals, no, but they were exceptional, committed men.

Notes

1. Max Weber, "Science as Vocation," in H. H. Gerth and C. Wright Mills, eds., *From Max Weber: Essays in Sociology* (London, 1948), p. 155.
2. Henry Adams, *The Education of Henry Adams: An Autobiography* (Boston, 1961), p. 328.
3. Richard L. Slotkin, *Regeneration Through Violence: The Mythology of the American Frontier, 1600–1860* (Middletown, Conn., 1974).
4. Susan Sontag, "The Anthropologist as Hero," in E. N. Hayes and T. Hayes, eds., *Claude Lévi-Strauss: The Anthropologist as Hero* (Cambridge, 1970), pp. 188–89.
5. I have borrowed this point from Joan Mark, "Frank Hamilton Cushing and an American Science of Anthropology," *Perspectives in American History* 10 (1976): 482.
6. Notation on reverse of a photograph of Cushing presented to the Southwest Museum by F.W. Hodge in 1950. I am indebted to William Sturtevant for this reference.
7. Boas quoted in Neil Judd, *The Bureau of American Ethnology: A Partial History* (Norman, Okla., 1967), pp. 62–63; F. W. Hodge to E. DeGolyer, 3 April 1946, Hodge-Cushing Papers.
8. Alfred Kroeber, "Frank Hamilton Cushing," *Encyclopedia of the Social Sciences* II (New York, 1930–35): 657; Mark, "Frank Hamilton Cushing," p. 485.
9. "Necrology: Frank Hamilton Cushing," BAE, *AR for 1900*, p. xxxv. The author was almost certainly McGee, but materials in Cushing's papers indicate that the oft-repeated stories of Cushing's childhood originated with him.
10. See Mark, "Frank Hamilton Cushing," pp. 484–86.
11. Cushing to Mason, 30 September 1876, Hodge-Cushing Papers.
12. Cushing to Baird, 29 October 1879, NAA.
13. Bourke Diary, 30 May 1889; as quoted in Robert Poor, "Washington Matthews: An Intellectual Biography," M.A. thesis (University of Nevada-Reno, 1975), p. 45.
14. F.H. Cushing, "Antiquities of Orleans County, New York," SI, *AR for 1874*, pp. 375–77; Baird to Cushing, 3 December 1875, SIA.
15. Cushing to Lucien Turner, 15 May 1879, Hodge-Cushing Papers.
16. F.H. Cushing, "The Germ of Shore-Land Pottery," *Memoirs of the International Congress of Anthropology* (Chicago, 1893), p. 234.
17. See, e.g., Baird to Cushing, 12 July 1878, NAA, for an example of their continued close contact.
18. Powell to James Stevenson, 4 August 1879, M. C. Stevenson Papers, NAA.
19. Squier to Robert Winthrop, 15 February 1875, Peabody Museum Papers, HUA.
20. The phrase was Baird's. Baird to "Dear James," 10 July 1883, M. C. Stevenson Papers, NAA.
21. Powell to Stevenson, 8 September 1880, M. C. Stevenson Papers, NAA.

22. Despite Powell's claim that he "first sent Mr. Cushing to Zuñi" (BAE, *AR for 1898*, p. xlvii), it was Baird who guided Cushing's course in the early years.

23. Cushing to Baird, 18 July 1880, NAA.

24. Cushing's severe gastrointestinal problems plagued him for years. In 1883, E. N. Horsford, a Boston admirer, offered to pay Cushing's fare back to Washington and begged Powell to let him return: "Cushing has repeatedly written me of his terrible suffering from dyspepsia. . . . I see a little of the martyr spirit which alarms me. We cannot afford to indulge in such sacrifice." (Horsford to Powell, 19 November 1883, NAA).

25. Baird to Stevenson, 8 September 1880, M. C. Stevenson Papers, NAA; Baird to Putnam, 8 April 1882, Peabody Museum Papers, HUA.

26. Cushing to Baird, 9 October 1879, NAA.

27. Triloki Nath Pandey, "Anthropologists at Zuñi," *Proceedings of the American Philosophical Society* 116, no. 4 (1972), pp. 322–28.

28. Cushing to Baird and Powell, 18 February 1880 (draft), NAA. This important letter included Cushing's list of fields for study at Zuñi: language (prerequisite); industrial and art "formulas"; religious instructions, prayers, and songs; religious materials (masks, etc.); plume sticks; astronomic monuments; "Zuñi culture compared to other indigenous American Civilizations"; gesture language survivals; kinship patterns; ancient ruins; primitive condition of the Shiwe; origin of current mythological usages; "effects of natural phenomena and physical environment on nature belief"; philosophy of games; recording oratory, folklore, and mythology.

29. BAE, *AR for 1884*, pp. xxv–xxix, xxxii–xxxv.

30. Cushing to Baird, 4 December 1881, as quoted in Pandey, "Anthropologists at Zuñi," p. 323.

31. Ibid., p. 326. The most complete recital of these events occurs in Raymond Stewart Brandes, "Frank Hamilton Cushing: Pioneer Americanist," Ph.D. diss. (University of Arizona, 1965). Brandes's work, the only full-length study of Cushing, is valuable for basic facts and anecdotal material. See also Bernard L. Fontana, "Pioneers in Ideas: Three Early Southwestern Ethnologists," *Journal of Arizona Academy of Science* 2 (1960): 124–29.

32. Pandey, "Anthropologists at Zuñi," pp. 325–26.

33. Cushing to Baird (draft, n.d.), NAA.

34. Ms. "Interview," 9 June 1883, Hodge-Cushing Papers; as quoted in Pandey, "Anthropologists at Zuñi," p. 326, and in Brandes, "Frank Hamilton Cushing," p. 107.

35. Washington Matthews to Cushing, 8 August 1881, Hodge-Cushing Papers. Reference courtesy of Robert Poor.

36. Matthews to Cushing, 17 August 1886, Hodge-Cushing Papers. Reference courtesy of Robert Poor.

37. Matthews to Cushing, 4 November 1884, Hodge-Cushing Papers; and Matthews to Cushing, 18 November 1891, Hodge-Cushing Papers.

38. Matthews to Cushing, 4 November 1884, Hodge-Cushing Papers; Matthews to Cushing, 5 April 1892, Hodge-Cushing Papers. Reference courtesy of Robert Poor.

39. As suggested by Philip Phillips in his introduction to Cushing, *Exploration of Ancient Key Dwellers' Remains on the Gulf Coast of Florida* (New York, 1973). However, Cushing failed to produce consistently, in instances where this consideration played no part.

40. Cushing to Bourke, 13 August 1881; Sheridan to Bourke, 8 June 1882, Hodge-Cushing Papers.

41. Bourke to Cushing, 7 June 1882, Hodge-Cushing Papers.

42. Bourke to Cushing, 25 November 1882 and 30 June 1884, Hodge-Cushing Papers.

43. Bourke to Cushing, 30 September 1884, Hodge-Cushing Papers.

44. BAE, *AR for* 1885, p. xlvii; F.H. Cushing, "A Study of Pueblo Pottery, as Illustrative of Zuñi Culture Growth," BAE, *AR for 1883*, pp. 467–521.

45. Cushing to "My Dear Friend," 27 August 1891 (draft), Hodge-Cushing Papers.

46. Matthews to Cushing, 7 January 1891 and 23 July 1889, Hodge-Cushing Papers.

47. Harris to Cushing, 9 November 1891, Hodge-Cushing Papers.

48. On Hodge's hostility, see Mark, "Frank Hamilton Cushing," p. 481, fn.

49. Hodge to Emil W. Haury, 5 October 1931, and handwritten notes, PMA.

50. Ibid.

51. Ibid.

52. Ibid.

53. Cushing to Putnam, 4 January 1898 (copy of letter of June 1897), PMA.

54. Cushing to Putnam, 4 January 1898, PMA.

55. Brandes, "Frank Hamilton Cushing," pp. 161–67, discusses this period.

56. The Florida excursion is treated in F. H. Cushing, *Exploration of Ancient Key Dwellers' Remains on the Gulf Coast of Florida*, ed. with intro. by Philip Phillips (New York, 1973); in Brandes, "Frank Hamilton Cushing," pp. 167–205; and in Marion Spjut Gilliland, *The Material Culture of Key Marco Florida* (Gainesville, 1975). Gilliland presents a judicious account of the Cushing expedition, including the Dinwiddie accusation against Cushing, discussed below. She concludes that Cushing was innocent and the painted shell was genuine (p. 183).

57. BAE, *AR for 1895*, p. lvii.

58. Gilliland, *Material Culture*, p. 4.

59. Cushing, *Key Dwellers' Remains*, p. xvii.

60. Gilliland, *Material Culture*, presents the case and reproduces relevant documents. Dinwiddie had made slanderous statements about other Bureau staff members as well (McGee to Powell, 27 October 1896, copy in BAE-IN, NAA).

61. Matthews to Cushing, 21 January 1897, Hodge-Cushing Papers. Reference courtesy of Robert Poor.

62. Gilliland, *Material Culture*, p. 5.

63. F. H. Cushing, "The Need of Studying the Indian in Order to Teach Him," *28th Annual Report of the Board of Indian Commissioners* (Washington, D.C., 1897 [reprinted by A. M. Eddy, Albion, New York, 1897]), pp. 3–4.

64. Ibid., pp. 9–10.

65. Ibid., p. 12.
66. Mark, "Frank Hamilton Cushing," p. 482.
67. The major source for this discussion of James Mooney is the recent, thorough biography of Mooney by William Colby: "Routes to Rainy Mountain: A Biography of James Mooney, Ethnologist", Ph.D. diss. (University of Wisconsin-Madison, 1977). I am deeply indebted to Mr. Colby for permitting me to use his unpublished study and other materials.

   "The nineteenth-century Irish saw themselves as the victims of history," Arthur M. Schlesinger, Jr., writes in *Robert Kennedy and His Times* (New York, 1978). "Memories of dispossession and defeat filled their souls. They had lost their national independence, their personal dignity, their land, even their language, to intruders from across the sea" (p. 3).
68. James Mooney, *The Ghost-Dance Religion and the Sioux Outbreak of 1890*, BAE, *AR for 1893*, Part 2 (Washington, D.C., 1896).
69. John R. Swanton, "James Mooney," *American Anthropologist* 24 (1922): 209.
70. Colby, "Routes to Rainy Mountain," p. 42.
71. See the discussion in Chapter VI.
72. Caroline Matthews to Charles F. Lummis, 22 May 1905, CFL Papers. Reference courtesy of Robert Poor.
73. James Mooney, "In Memoriam: Washington Matthews," *American Anthropologist* 7 (1905):520.
74. Colby, "Routes to Rainy Mountain," p. 52.
75. Ibid., p. 76.
76. James Mooney, "Sacred Formulas of the Cherokees," BAE, *AR for 1886* (Washington, D.C., 1891), p. 309.
77. Colby, "Routes to Rainy Mountain," pp. 81–82, 84.
78. BAE, *AR for 1886* (Washington, D.C., 1891), pp. xxxix–xl.
79. Mooney, "Sacred Formulas," pp. 309, 318–19.
80. On the "gestalt" switch as analog to the process of scientific discovery, see Thomas Kuhn, *The Structure of Scientific Revolutions* (Chicago, 1962).
81. James Mooney, *Myths of the Cherokee*, BAE, *AR for 1898*, Part 1 (Washington, D.C., 1900), pp. 3–548.
82. Colby, "Routes to Rainy Mountain," p. 172.
83. Jeremiah Curtin, *The Memoirs of Jeremiah Curtin* (Madison, 1940), p. 383.
84. Jeremiah Curtin, *Creation Myths of Primitive America in Relation to the Religious History and Mental Development of Mankind* (Boston, 1898).
85. Ibid., pp. xi–xxxix, presents Curtin's synthesis of American creation myths. It is of interest that Curtin, a prolific writer, noted in his *Memoirs* (p. 687) that he struggled to compose this introduction.
86. Curtin, *Memoirs*, pp. 637–38, 502.
87. Ibid., p. 319.
88. Ibid., p. 367.
89. Ibid., p. 382.
90. Mooney to Matthews, 4 July 1897, Matthews Papers, MNCA.
91. James Mooney, "Siouan Tribes of the East," *BAE Bulletin* 22 (Washington, D.C., 1894). For an assessment see Colby, "Routes to Rainy Mountain," pp. 133–35.

92. Mooney, *The Ghost-Dance,* p. 653.

93. Colby, "Routes to Rainy Moutain," p. 232.

94. Ibid., p. 200.

95. Mooney, *The Ghost-Dance,* p. 870.

96. Ibid., pp. 876-79. Robert Underhill, historian of the Puritan slaughter of the Pequot Indians in May 1637, recalled that the Pequots "brake forth into a most doleful cry; so as if God had not filled the hearts of men for the service, it would have bred in them a commiseration towards them." (Larzer Ziff, *Puritanism in America: New Culture in a New World* [New York, 1974], p. 91.) The cant of conquest has a haunting echo.

97. I am indebted to William Colby for providing this information.

98. Langley to Powell, 25 May 1897, NAA.

99. Powell to Langley, 26 May 1897, SIA.

100. BAE, *AR for 1893* (Washington, D.C., 1896), pp. LX–LXI.

101. Mooney to Henshaw, 8 June 1891, NAA; as quoted in Colby, "Routes to Rainy Mountain."

102. James Mooney, *Calendar History of the Kiowa Indians,* BAE, *AR for 1896* (Washington, D.C., 1898), pp. 129–445; Colby, "Routes to Rainy Mountain," pp. 321–22. John C. Ewers has recently evaluated Mooney's Kiowa field work, especially his oral history, in his introduction to the Smithsonian Institution Press reprint of the *Calendar History* (Washington, D.C., 1979). John C. Ewers's *Murals in the Round: Painted Tipis of the Kiowa and Kiowa-Apache Indians; An exhibition of tipi models made for James Mooney of the Smithsonian Institution during his field studies of Indian history and art in southwestern Oklahoma, 1891–1904* (Washington, D.C., 1978), an exhibition catalog for the Renwick Gallery of the National Museum of American Art, presents the first sizable publication of Mooney's tipi data.

103. McGee's career is the subject of Chapter VIII.

104. As quoted in Colby, "Routes to Rainy Mountain," p. 320.

105. Mooney Testimony, BAE-IN, p. 968.

106. Ibid., p. 969.

107. Ibid., p. 970.

108. Ibid., p. 973.

109. Ibid., pp. 974–75.

110. Ibid., pp. 983–84.

111. See, e.g., the account of Stevenson in Pandey, "Anthropologists at Zuñi." It should be noted, however, that Stevenson bore burdens, as the pioneer woman field anthropologist in the Southwest, that none of her male contemporaries shared or recognized. Merely being taken seriously as a scientist was a major accomplishment for a woman in the Bureau. Stevenson's "pushiness" undoubtedly grew in part from intense pressures. For sympathetic portraits, see Nancy O. Lurie, "Matilda Coxe Stevenson," in *Notable American Women, 1607–1950* 3 (Cambridge, 1971): 373–74; and Lurie, "Women in Early American Anthropology," in June Helm, ed., *Pioneers of American Anthropology: The Uses of Biography,* American Ethnological Society monographs, No. 43 (Seattle and London, 1966), pp. 29–81.

112. Matilda Coxe Stevenson, *The Zuñi Indians: Their Mythology, Esoteric Fraternities,*

and Ceremonies, BAE, *AR for 1902* (Washington, D.C., 1904), pp. 1–608.

113. Testimony of M. C. Stevenson, BAE-IN, p. 353.

114. Mooney Testimony, BAE-IN, p. 982.

115. Adams, *Education,* p. 232.

116. Mark, "Frank Hamilton Cushing," passim. For a balanced, closely researched essay on Cushing, see Jeese Green's introduction to his edited *Zuñi: Selected Writings of Frank Hamilton Cushing* (Lincoln, Neb., 1979). Green's full notes display painstaking research and address many of the events discussed earlier in this chapter. By contrast, John Sherwood's recent article on "Frank Cushing, Boy Wonder of the Smithsonian's Old Bureau of Ethnology" (*Smithsonian* 10, no. 5 [1979], pp. 96–113), merely rethreshes old straw.

117. See Chapters VIII and IX.

118. George W. Stocking has begun to investigate and elaborate this point for twentieth-century American anthropology in "Ideas and Institutions in American Anthropology: Toward a History of the Interwar Period," intro. to Stocking, ed., *Selected Papers from the American Anthropologist, 1921-45* (Washington, D.C., 1976), pp. 1–50.

119. Mark, "Frank Hamilton Cushing," p. 484.

VIII

Fin-de-Siècle: The Rise and Fall of William John McGee, 1893–1903

As the nation neared the end of the nineteenth century, severe dislocations and sharp contrasts marked American public and private life. At Chicago in 1893 the White City rose in splendor on the shore of Lake Michigan to celebrate (a year late) 400 years of conquest, expansion, and progress, while a few blocks away the nation's worst depression already gnawed away at the masses of urban poor. The World's Fair lasted less than a year; its anthropology collections would form the nucleus of Marshall Field's ambitious Columbian Museum. The depression lasted until 1897, leaving a different legacy: sober realities of suffering and inequality that even the jingoistic distractions of the Spanish-American War could not conceal. If Chicago was America, the state of civilization was brutally clear: personal exertion and private charity had failed to sustain a free, mobile society. People, millions of them, were caught. Henceforth new commitments and new social forms would be required to preserve stability—never mind equality. "For a hundred years, between 1793 and 1893," Henry Adams reflected, "the American people had hesitated, vacillated, swayed forward and back, between two forces, one simply industrial, the other capitalistic, centralizing, and mechanical." Now they "slipped across the chasm."[1]

For his own part, Adams learned to ride a bicycle.[2] The release of the outdoors in the nineties—bicycling, sports, naturalist clubs, wilderness fiction—came as an antidote to cluttered parlors and closed frontiers.[3] But it was also, perhaps, a sign of altered possibilities. If effective economic and political freedoms were diminished, personal freedoms would fill the void; if few individuals owned their productive lives, many could buy into the life of consumption. Thus, beneath the apparent incongruities and paradoxes of the decade lay the coherence of modern life, a complementarity between immense power and impotent individuals—individuals, like Adams, "landed, lost, and forgotten, in the centre of this vast plain of self-content."[4]

W J McGee has been largely forgotten in American anthropology today. Yet in his ten-year career as anthropologist, from 1893 to 1903, he rose to the height of the profession in this country. At the time of his abrupt departure

231

from Washington in 1903, Alice Fletcher spoke of him as "a man of growing power" in anthropology, and Franz Boas saw in him "the main stay" of sound government anthropology.[5] Fletcher and Boas valued McGee because he played a central role in establishing anthropology as a respectable scientific pursuit at the turn of the century. He vigorously promoted the science, wielding influence less by original contributions than by position—his close relationship to Powell, marriage to Anita Newcomb, and incessant activity in local and national scientific societies. Throughout his career McGee boosted government science: in the eighties, Survey geology; in the nineties, BAE anthropology; from 1907 to his death, Interior Department conservation.

McGee was a master of synthesis. One contemporary wrote that his great strength was "the skillful use of the results of others." John Swanton made the same point less charitably, recalling that McGee "did not impress me as a profound thinker but as intensely desirous to win scientific consideration, and while aping originality . . . desperately feared to depart from the 'party line' of his day . . ."[6] Swanton was accurate but not entirely to the point. McGee served an idea of science, not a specific field; he valued generalization based on broad experience over specialization. As one colleague lamented in 1916, he belonged to a dying breed, "whom there seems to be a tendency to crowd out now . . ."[7]

McGee arrived in Washington in 1883 from a rural Iowa upbringing that included less than eight years of schooling, many seasons of farming, and brief experiments in blacksmithing, inventing, and surveying.[8] Born prematurely and seemingly subject to every possible disease, McGee grew up as "a very sickly, delicate child" on his parents' small farm outside Farley, in eastern Iowa. Triumph over childhood infirmities that led to adult robustness later became a part of the McGee legend. So did self-education. During later years of fame McGee elaborated a "self-made" image, claiming to have taught himself German, Latin, higher mathematics, and law. This was fabrication. The simple fact is that throughout his boyhood and adolescence his work was the farm, and he had little access to even a small library.[9]

In many ways, McGee never left Iowa. Until late in life he retained his state residency, cultivated the powerful Iowa politicians in Washington, who provided him with an important power base, and capitalized on the image of self-made country boy. But he always held in tension contradictory sentiments about his poor roots, making virtue of an undeniable biography, building grand systems of scientific philosophy while telling his daughter nostalgic tales of elementary school foot-races and of taking the hay wagons to town in the hot midwestern summers. Like his friend and fellow Iowan, novelist Hamlin Garland, McGee straddled two worlds: that of the "old red schoolhouse on the hill" and that of Washington science.[10] It was his personal tragedy that McGee never found peace or acceptance in either. By 1912 he was exiled from both. Having cut communication with his Iowa relatives and his wife and children, he passed away alone in a room at the Cosmos Club in Washington.

McGee's early work was on glacial geology. It was audacious, characterized by a slim foundation of careful, even brilliant observation and a large super-structure of theory. He moved easily from present formations to imaginative reconstruction of earlier processes and structures. His geology always contained a distinctly romantic streak; his visionary faculty seemed irrepressible. Powell recognized a kinship, brought him to Washington in 1883, and entrusted major projects to him: a thesaurus of American geological formations and a preliminary geological map of the United States. Their relationship was solidly built on tacit understanding: "McGee, I know what I want; you know what I want. Figure a way to do it before next March."[11]

McGee always figured a way. Learning rapidly and working furiously at his administrative tasks and his own research in the U. S. Geological Survey, within a short period he was exuding self-confidence, influence, and success from Washington. It seemed to one friend that "your fly-wheel is running more smoothly now even than when you used to . . . study panoramic geology at the rate of 40 miles per day; or face highwaymen on dark roads, unarmed, on principle; or make [map] sections for [Israel] Russell in Salt Lake and sub voce swear yourself into a seriously hyperaemic condition."[12] McGee's driving ambition and political malleability fitted him well to government organization. He fully realized that adjustment was the key to power in organizational science.

He adjusted in various ways. In 1888 he married Anita Newcomb, second daughter of Simon Newcomb, America's foremost astronomer and a powerful influence in the capital. Anita's mother opposed the marriage and her father simply ignored his son-in-law.[13] If McGee needed further motivation, this rejection surely provided it. Anita became a driving force behind his career for the next fifteen years.

In the early years, "Beauty" and "Don," as they affectionately called one another, made the requisite efforts, molding their life together around in-dividual needs and capacities. Anita devotedly accompanied him to the fields of Iowa in 1888, where she examined his genealogy while he displayed his new wife and prepared his old Iowa survey for publication. Subsequently she represénted him at professional meetings and joined expeditions in the Po-tomac region. For his part, McGee realized that his wife, as one historian has observed, had "more intellectual than domestic capacity."[14] He encouraged her to pursue medicine and anthropology. She entered Columbian University's School of Medicine and emerged as an M.D. in 1892—a singular achievement for a woman at the time. In the same year she joined the Anthropological Society of Washington and remained a member until 1905.[15]

Participation in scientific societies further enhanced McGee's social status in the capital. He considered such gatherings indispensable to American science. Much of the "substantial scientific progress" of the country came from local societies, contended McGee, for they occupied a critical position between the general populace and organized science; they formed an "intermediate link" between the increasingly isolated specialist and the layman.[16] Specialization bothered McGee deeply, but he responded ambivalently. He defended his own practice of coining new terms because, he argued, new ideas required them. This might be a mistake, he confessed, because science was after all the servant of man; but he was often too busy to reach back to the "cradle terms" of English for the sake of the public.[17] In McGee's view, "specialists grow up through the indifference of the masses and their inability to keep pace with the investigator." At the same time, the knowledge of the specialist was "soon blasted by the poison of its own egoism, unless the richer part of its substance is guided toward the general mass of society."[18]

Ideally the scientific society, embracing educated and intelligent laymen as well as experts, should counteract specialization by diffusing knowledge in reasonably sophisticated form. It might also serve as a badge of membership for men lacking family background.[19] Upon arrival in Washington, McGee lost no time in applying to the array of organizations in the capital. He immediately joined the Anthropological Society, and over the next two decades he delivered twenty-two papers and served as an officer for fifteen consecutive years.[20] But the ASW was only the beginning. Sensing new needs and opportunities, McGee became a driving force in the National Geographic Society, the Geological Society of America, the Columbian Historical Society, and the American Anthropological Association. When the ASW fell on hard times in 1898, McGee and Boas personally took over joint ownership of the *American Anthropologist* and kept it afloat until the founding of the national association four years later.[21] At the founding of the Washington Academy of Sciences in 1898, McGee was the only person belonging to all twelve constituent societies.

Despite the multiple memberships, McGee never felt accepted in Washington. His daughter remembered that "for years my environment had no more use for my father than if he had been a coal-heaver."[22] Marriage into the Newcombs was a major step, to be sure, and in Anita he gained a source of encouragement and further status. But he also brought upon himself expectations that his salary, always anomalously high for a government employee and sufficient for a comfortable life, could never fully satisfy. Not that Anita whipped her husband along in his career. The challenges were always self-imposed with McGee. He loved Anita as he loved science; his doctor wife became a symbol of the social and scientific attainment he never completely knew. He was always impelled to continue proving his worth to his wife and her family, to Washington, and perhaps to himself.

Success and time hardened McGee. By the early nineties he was a powerful force in Washington society. Yet in these years of promise a strident tone

An outing to the soapstone quarry in west Washington, D.C.:
W J and Anita McGee to the left; Otis Mason, center, with stick;
geologist Rollin D. Salisbury to far right, with umbrella.

had already entered his work. Having served his apprenticeship in science, he was now prepared to judge others. His Iowa survey, published in 1890, along with his work on the Potomac region, served as accreditation. The publications, the marriage, the societies—all announced his arrival. But along with them came intemperance and haughtiness, signs of the officious government scientist.

Under intense fire from congressional critics and western mining, timber, and land entrepreneurs, Powell resigned as director of the U. S. Geological Survey in 1893. He retired to the Bureau, bringing along McGee as protégé and heir apparent. The following year Powell underwent a second operation on his painful right arm; he had begun the slow decline to his death in 1902. During these years McGee, operating as "ethnologist in charge," directed the Bureau of American Ethnology. Powell's demise marked McGee's ascendancy in Washington science.

Institutional relations had always been highly personal on the Mall. Powell's friendships with Spencer Baird, Smithsonian Secretary from 1878 to 1887, and with Baird's successor (1887–1906), Langley, were critical in determining Bureau autonomy. Powell had accepted Henry's advice, encouragement, and support as a protégé. With Baird positions were more equal. Powell respected Baird as a brilliant scientific organizer, a fine zoologist and, most importantly, a man who "knew how to marshal significant facts into systems, and to weld them into principles."[23] But Powell also considered the BAE a personal enterprise, placed within the Smithsonian only to insure its independence. He stoutly resisted external control over personnel, appropriations, or research priorities.

The battle for autonomy centered perennially on the "Secretary's reserve." Powell's original plans for the BAE did not involve expeditions for the U.S. National Museum, but Baird maintained that the Bureau must also serve as a collecting arm of the Museum. In November 1879, he announced that he was setting aside one fourth of the BAE's $20,000 appropriation for purchasing or discovering material for the Museum.[24] Baird's motives were scientific and political, as Langley later explained:

> It is a recognized fact among all the natural sciences that objects and specimens are as necessary to researches as explorations and notes in the field. This fact was pointed out by Secretary Baird to Major Powell, but, as he was largely interested in linguistics, and was disposed to sacrifice other things to his favorite studies, the collecting of material was largely disregarded, until Secretary Baird insisted, as he told me, upon his view of the wishes of Congress to have some objects well worthy to show as part of the results of the explorations.[25]

The Secretary's reserve remained an informal arrangement, and thus a bone of contention, year after year. As BAE appropriations increased and stabilized at $40,000 from 1883 to 1892, the $5,000 reserve represented a smaller bite of the total. But Powell's research ambitions grew even faster than the funding, so that the reserve became more rather than less irritating. It was an encroachment, a reminder of dependence. In July 1883, for instance, Baird instructed Powell regarding funds for the coming year. He told the director that Congress was "extremely impatient" for material collections, since foreign governments were rapidly "sweeping the localities" of North America for treasures. While Baird complained of the large BAE salaries, he informed Powell of his decision to hire James G. Swan for Northwest Coast work, taking $3,600 of Bureau money—a generous year's salary at the time. His own expenditures, "without the formalities of reference to the director of the Bureau of Ethnology," the Secretary needled Powell, had been "very productive, and will compare favorably with the result of outlays of a similar amount by the Bureau."[26] For the remainder of Baird's tenure, Powell grudgingly tolerated the reserve, working around it but never accepting its validity.

Astronomer Samuel P. Langley came to the Smithsonian from Allegheny Observatory in Pittsburgh less than a year before Baird's death. When he became the Smithsonian's third Secretary in 1887, Washingtonians hardly knew him. They knew little more of him at his death nineteen years later. Fifty-three years old, unmarried and without family ties, Langley arrived alone and lived a lonely life in the capital. Reserved, shy, socially inept, belonging to an older generation, Langley was generally perceived as cold and aloof. He had few friends; according to one of them, "his hunger for real friendship and affection was pathetic."[27]

Powell was one of those few, cherished friends. In the last decade of his life he and Langley vacationed together and exchanged papers on their philosophies of science.[28] When Powell and Holmes traveled to Cuba in 1900, Langley asked them repeatedly to join him in Jamaica, where he was studying the flight of turkey buzzards.[29]

The intimacy with Powell interfered with Langley's control of the Bureau. In 1891 he proposed to assume direct supervision of Bureau personnel and appropriations. Powell lashed out to defend his prerogatives:

> To take from the director the planning of the work, the appointment of employees, and the disbursement of moneys, and to have these duties assumed by the secretary of the Smithsonian, would place the secretary in the position of performing the duties of a Bureau officer, and the director of the Bureau of Ethnology would be but a chief of division, or clerk, to carry out his plans. I regret that you should consider it necessary to pursue this course. So far as I know, up to the present time the work has been carried on without criticism, the accounts have all

been settled in the treasury promptly, the publications of the Bureau have been well received by the scholars of America and of the world, and the service has inspired the confidence of the Congress.[30]

One month after joining the BAE, McGee challenged Langley's authority to set aside the reserve, thereby reopening an old wound.[31] Over the next decade Langley grew to despise and distrust the new ethnologist. While Powell lived, the tense and suspicious relations between the Smithsonian staff and the BAE did not erupt into open conflict, despite accusations of shoddy business methods in the Bureau. Langley fostered an exterior of amiable scientific neutrality. But it was an uneasy, unstable condition.

McGee came to the Bureau simply as an ethnologist, but the title did not match his self-image, salary, or ambition. Accordingly, in September 1893, he began signing correspondence as "ethnologist in charge." The new title went unchallenged but not unnoticed; it became a small but significant irritant in Bureau/Smithsonian relations in coming years.

As an ethnologist, McGee once again had to apply himself assiduously. For six months he studied Powell's principles of sociology and mental evolution. His first article, "The Siouan Indians: A Preliminary Sketch," which appeared in the 1894 annual report as an introduction to Dorsey's posthumous *Siouan Sociology,* demonstrated that he was a good disciple.[32] "Siouan Indians" was a model of Powellian anthropology in approach and conclusions. Drawing heavily on Dorsey's notes, McGee first demonstrated mastery of the literature on the Siouan stock. He then reviewed the Sioux according to the standard categories: language, arts and industries, social institutions, beliefs, physical traits. His summary elaborated Powell's theories and placed the Siouan stock in its "proper" place among North American tribes and human development generally. He offered little that was new, but forcefully restated Powellian orthodoxy.

After 1893 Powell indulged his interest in the origins of human institutions to an obsessive degree, and McGee suited his fieldwork to those concerns. Having completed his office and library apprenticeship in anthropology in his first year, McGee prepared in the fall of 1894 to gain his spurs in the field. Taking $2,000 from the Secretary's reserve, he organized an expedition to the Southwest to collect artifacts from the Papago and neighboring tribes, and from the cliff ruins of Arizona and New Mexico.[33] He left Washington in mid-October, outfitted in Tucson, and dropped south across the border into Sonora. McGee stopped briefly at numerous Papago villages, but spent a good deal of his time noting weed growth and local soil and water conditions.[34] The party lost a week in delays with Mexican officials. Since Mexican law prohibited collecting antiquities—the main purpose of the trip—McGee made small collections of modern Papago materials. The first half of the trip was an aimless trek through northern Mexico in search of primitive, unacculturated Indians.

The party arrived in Hermosillo at the end of the month, where they tarried several days. Here McGee heard for the first time of the wild, bloodthirsty Seri Indians, only a few miles away, along the coast of the California Gulf and on Tiburon Island.[35] At last he confronted a significant challenge: native inhabitants of the forbidding Sonora desert, never studied by White Americans and reportedly the most hostile people of North America. McGee expected to find here men and women living in near-bestial conditions, American examples of the heretofore-only-theorized primal savagery. His expectations, not surprisingly, were met.

With Mexican government permission to enter "Seriland," as McGee's men dubbed the desert region, the party proceeded westward to the coast adjacent to Tiburon Island, guided by an aging Mexican, Pascual Encinas, who as a young man had pushed the Seri off their lands. The McGee party finally located a temporary Seri settlement of about sixty individuals. They stayed for several days, but the interviewing occurred in one thirty-six-hour period.[36] McGee recorded a 400-word vocabulary, took numerous group and individual photographs, collected artifacts for the Museum, and observed Indian habits. McGee was back in Washington by the end of November, after forty days' absence, only a handful of which were actually spent in contact with Indians.[37]

The following year McGee returned to study the warlike Seri in depth. The expedition was ill-fated from the start, largely due to the leader's bravado and incompetence. The party left Tucson on November 9, 1895, by a slightly different route than the previous year and spent several days examining, drawing, and photographing ruins and collecting artifacts. McGee then headed directly for Costa Rica, where he had found the Seri rancheria the preceding year. The Seri had abandoned the site and reportedly moved out to Tiburon.

McGee decided to pursue. While Señor Encinas constructed a crude boat at his ranch, McGee explored and mapped parts of the nearby mountains in his vain search for the elusive Indians. McGee, Encinas, and company then "with much difficulty" hauled "la lancha *Anita*" across the narrow desert to Kino Bay on the Gulf of California. With ten days' food rations and five days' water supply, McGee organized his eleven-man party and headed up the coast to a point opposite Tiburon Island.

After five days of delay due to severe gales, part of the expedition crossed the strait "El Infiernillo." On returning for the rest of the party, however, two men encountered a gale and were blown twenty-five miles down the coast, where, as McGee reported, the *Anita* was "practically wrecked on a desert island." Four days later the men had worked their way back up the coast, met the returning ranchhands (from whom they obtained fresh water) at Kino Bay, and reunited with the three members of the party ("who had suffered much thirst") still waiting upcoast to cross to the island.

In the meanwhile McGee and his party on Tiburon were trying to stay alive by traveling inland for water and building a driftwood raft. When the boat finally reappeared, McGee set out across the island with renewed vigor in pursuit of the Indians. Most of the energy of the party was spent hauling water, with armed guards to protect against the "considerable and constant" threat of Seri ambush. McGee found some artifacts, including a balsa canoe-raft, and some deserted encampments, but he never contacted a single Seri.

When the men's shoes and moccasins were worn out, McGee called off the chase. But his problems were far from over. The party, "now practically barefoot," crossed to the mainland but found themselves without food or water, miles from Encinas's ranch, and "still constantly under the eyes of Seri warriors watching from a distance," presumably waiting to attack. At this point McGee set off alone for Kino Bay, twenty-five miles away, for help. But on reaching the rendezvous point he found it abandoned, and in eighteen hours trekked miles across the desert to the ranch. He returned with supplies to his waiting party and on the last day of 1895 they were all safely back at the ranch.

On January 3, 1896, his last day in Mexico, McGee made one final attempt at Seri ethnology: an interview with Fernando Kolusio, an outcast Seri who had lived for decades with Encinas. McGee closed five-and-a-half pages of notes with the following observation:

> Culusio [sic] was very small when he left the tribe; he is now old, somewhat deaf, and has nearly forgotten the language. It is my judgment that his information is practically worthless except when corroborated. So the inquiry is not continued. [38]

Thus ended the 1895 Seri expedition.

These expeditions constituted McGee's fieldwork in ethnology, and he relied on them for his anthropological credentials. It is, therefore, not unfair to ask what the Seri and Papago trips actually accomplished. The ethnological value of the second expedition was virtually nil. Despite McGee's attempts to picture a dangerous, heroic adventure among bloodthirsty savages, the hunt for the Seri emerges as a series of blundering, foolish decisions by an ignorant and glory-hungry greenhorn. Somehow the entire party survived in spite of McGee. Furthermore, his notebooks of the trip, replete with self-conscious comments on dwindling food supplies and romantic appellations (Camp Thirsty, Camp Disappointment, Camp Despair), clearly imitated Powell's first Colorado expedition. Down to naming the boats—"la lancha *Anita*" for Powell's *Emma Dean*—his performance was pathetically derivative. [39]

The first trip provided McGee's Seri information, gathered in a very brief period at an encampment of some sixty starving, miserably poor souls. From this he constructed a 300-page monograph, "The Seri Indians," which appeared after long delay in the 1896 BAE report. [40] "Rarely in the annals of

W J McGee in dangerous "Seriland," 1895.

anthropology has so much been written based on so little field work," Bernard Fontana wrote of it.[41]

What did McGee find? He found the savages he sought. On Powell's ladder of culture, McGee discovered, the Seri occupied a bottom rung, and he stretched his rich vocabulary to define their near-bestial state. Every facet of Seri life exhibited a preoccupation with animal life; they were "zoosematic in esthetic, zoomimic in technic, zootheistic in faith, and putatively zoocratic in government." Even their language seemed "largely mimetic or onomato-poetic."[42] Although he gathered extremely sparse data on language and my-thology, the "coincident testimony" of all other aspects of their lives consigned the Seri to "the lowest recognized plane of savagery."[43]

The most conspicuous fact of Seri life was isolation, in habitat and more importantly in thought. The fear and animosity that neighboring Papago Indians displayed toward them, the sullen dislike for Encinas (known locally as "conqueror of the Seri" and viewed by the Seri as a "hated trainer") made them resemble "a menagerie of caged carnivores" to McGee. Even in the face of Caucasian gifts and goodwill, the Indians showed only "curiosity, avidity for food, studied indifference, and shrouded or snarling disgust," although, he noted, they were cheerfully affectionate among themselves. McGee saw an "intuitive and involuntary" loathing for outsiders, a highly developed, inbred "race-sense" to match their beautiful bodies.[44]

For the Seri, McGee found, were a singularly attractive people; men and women of all ages appeared "notably deep-chested and clean-limbed quick steppers," not unlike "human thoroughbreds." As the published photographs and drawings of bare-chested women attest, McGee was struck by Seri beauty and grace. The animal-like physiques and movements resulted, he concluded, from the rugged environment and isolation from other tribes, which had permitted mutually reinforcing mind and body developments. Consequently the Seri were even farther away from their neighbors "in feeling than in features, in function than in structure, in mind than in body."[45]

The animal likeness emerged everywhere. Unable to photograph a Seri hunter in shooting position, McGee concluded that Seri archery was a fluid movement, not a static position, another sign of bestial behavior. The Seri habit of hunting pregnant animals revolted McGee and reminded him that "the very sight of pregnancy or travail or newborn helplessness awakens [in the savage mind] slumbering blood-thirst and impels to ferocious slaughter." Here one could see the roots of the shocking barbarities of Seri his-tory, "tragedies too terrible for repetition save in bated breath of sur-vivors..."[46] McGee had probably heard many such stories through the "bated breath" of Pascual Encinas and his Mexican ranch hands, who had fought a war of near-annihilation against the Seri for years. The second-hand, hearsay influence of McGee's hosts runs throughout his demeaning account.

The Seri, in sum, confirmed Powellian evolution. First, they demonstrated that human evolution was to be traced in the mind, not in physical features (although these provided useful supplementary evidence). While they possessed some animal affinities physically, this low group of savages demonstrated that "the nearest and clearest indications of bestial relationship are to be found in the psychical features"; the Seri possessed a "burgeoning yet still bestial mind."[47] Secondly, the Seri illustrated the impact of immediate physical environment on all institutions at such a low level of development. Powell could not have asked for a more complete validation of his philosophy.

In his anthropology as in his geology, McGee combined perceptive field observations with a fertile imagination. Some of his field data have stood the tests of subsequent students; his imaginative interpretations have not. Reviewing his work in 1931, Alfred Kroeber found his observations "excellent but slender in range," permeated with conjectures and doubtful assumptions.[48] Kroeber's judgment has been echoed more recently by Bernard Fontana, who finds McGee "an incredibly astute observer, a kind of human Kodak."[49] Speculations and value judgments aside, Fontana contends, McGee produced a valuable and on many points essentially accurate baseline ethnography of a little-studied people. Be that as it may, the point is that for McGee the speculations constituted the valuable part of the study. Furthermore, the pure data of the field diary and the ethnographer's preconceptions cannot be so easily separated. As Kroeber's Seri work clearly showed, McGee's assumptions about his subjects and his anxiety to place them clearly in a developmental sequence warped his observations.

Kroeber corrected McGee on three major points: the pedestrian habit and footspeed of the Seri, their absence of a tool sense, and hostility to aliens, particularly to racial mixture. Kroeber found that Seri tools, like all their material culture, lacked order and polish, but in contrast to McGee he credited the people with "excellent practical mechanical sense."[50] Most importantly, McGee had erred grievously in stressing Seri cultural isolation.[51] "They are strictly, indeed fiercely, endogamous, alien connection being the blackest crime in their calendar and invariably punished by death," McGee had claimed.[52] But McGee wrote in total ignorance of neighboring Pima and Yuma cultures. He never saw that the Seri must be understood as a problem in local ethnohistory, not as a people with "congenital deficiencies or abnormalities" resulting from isolation, or instinctive animal impulses hindering social development. In sum, Kroeber concluded, the Seri

relate culturally to other peoples much as might be anticipated from their geographical position and subsistence opportunities. The Seri problem consequently has to be removed from the category of those which hold out a hope or illusion of being particularly significant for the solution of basic questions or broad hypotheses. . . . The thorough study of this culture will involve much grinding physical hardship and possibly

244 / Savages and Scientists

some danger. It is to be hoped that when the work is undertaken, it will not be in a spirit of personal adventure, with emphasis on the external difficulties to be overcome, but with a serious desire and competence to secure facts and understanding.[53]

McGee, never even a mediocre linguist, could not begin to understand Seri tales and mythology. He was thus restricted to the visual. While sufficient for geology, this was crippling in ethnology. As Kroeber noted, it was in the social and religious aspects of Seri life, "where verbal communications are as important as observation," that McGee's work was most questionable.[54]

The Seri Indians served to establish McGee's credentials in his adopted science, at least as far as Washington anthropologists were concerned. But the Seri study was less important for McGee's personal growth than the fascination with desert life that he found in the Southwest. Two brief studies of desert ecology, "The Beginning of Agriculture" and "The Beginning of Zooculture," certify that his jaunts were not a total scientific loss. McGee's desert studies were highly perceptive. In the words of Clark Wissler, he "presented concisely the interrelations of plant and animal life as constituting a kind of community and then observed man in this setting."[55] He found that desert plants adjusted in various delicate ways to aridity, among them leaflessness, waxiness, and greenness. While plants made such adjustments, McGee observed, desert animals exhibited traits of cooperation with other animals as well as plants in order to withstand the rugged environment. Sometimes the cooperation involved only minor modifications in behavior and no "loss of individuality," as McGee put it. This arrangement he termed communality. Other adjustments involved intimate interdependence with other creatures, which he called commensality. In phrases reminiscent of Darwin's "tangled bank," McGee described the community of life centering on the saguaro cactus:

> The flowers are fertilized by insects . . . and the seeds are distributed by birds; for it is manifest that the finding of the plants by flying things is facilitated by their great stature. Moreover the flowers are brilliantly white in color and attractive in perfume, while the fruit is gorgeously red and sweetly sapid. Still further it is manifest that the typical placing of branches is the most economical possible at once for the pumping of water from below and for bringing the flowers and fruits at the extremities within easy sight of the cooperating insects and birds. So it would appear that the saguaro is a monstrosity in fact as well as in appearance—a product of miscegenation between plant and animal, probably depending for its form and life-history, if not for its very existence, on its commensals.

The lesson was clear: subhuman organisms in the desert displayed incipient social organization against the common environment. Moreover, this "sub-human communality" frequently resulted not only in solidarity but stronger "individuality" among plants and animals.[56]

Man represented the final step in a direction determined before him. By consuming seeds and fruits and redistributing the seeds of useful plants, the Papago "entered into the vital solidarity of the desert," partially conquering the soil and increasing the sum total of desert life. Although the modern Papago made no attempt to control water supply, McGee saw in the archaeological ruins of northern Mexico indications of a higher antecedent culture that had practiced irrigation. The beginning of environmental control thus began among the subhuman desert species, whereas with man, "strength lies in union; and progress in combination leads to solidarity." Agriculture was the final stage of this process. "So, whatever its last estate," McGee concluded, "in its beginning agriculture is the art of the desert."[57]

McGee's theories on the domestication of animals followed a similar logic and drew likewise on the Papago notes. Observing Papago toleration and use of vultures, quails, doves, coyotes, and cows, McGee analyzed various degrees of intimacy in the human-animal relations of the desert. In all cases, however, the arrangements were essentially collective, that is, between groups of people and groups of animals. Individual ownership was rare. McGee inferred that associations arose in mutual toleration and were mainly a collective phenomenon. Plant, animal, and human formed a continuum of intellectual development: the plant responded imperfectly, almost passively, to environmental pressures, displaying only the "germ of instinct"; instinctual animals showed the "germ of reason" in gathering together and cooperating more effectively; only man consciously bred and exterminated species for his benefit, multiplying "both vitality and mentality." Taken as a whole, southwestern desert life traced out a "comforting and promising course of development."[58]

The southwestern trips of 1894 and 1895 convinced McGee that social organization began in the arid regions of the world, where the forbidding environment forced all forms of life to cooperate in order to survive. Typically, this vision was both speculative and structured, at once founded upon yet divorced from observation. Once again the quest for origins led the ethnologist away from the immediate, sensible world to a misty past of imagined races of primeval animal-men. Just as for Powell the trips down the deepening canyons of the Colorado River had been journeys into the past, McGee traveled back in time in Sonora, hoping to find the roots of human society.

"Practically we bought the Seris out," McGee wrote to Holmes after his first trip.[59] It was a small collection from Indians who had almost nothing to give or sell. But if the collection was meager and the second trip a disaster, McGee returned with a heightened reputation as explorer and scientist. Between

1895 and 1900 he reached his zenith. As Powell withdrew, his protégé took control of the Bureau, dictating Powell's correspondence and composing the annual reports. "I knew it all," he testified. "I drafted every plan of operations, and wrote every report, and drafted every important letter, letters from Major Powell as well as from myself." Powell devoted his office time after 1895, McGee's stenographer remembered, almost entirely to *Truth and Error;* he did not dictate "more than the smallest percent" of the letters he signed. During the summers, when Powell was in Maine, "every particle of control" remained in McGee's hands.[60] To Powell's widow, McGee was poignantly explicit about the last years:

> In his office life I knew the condition better than anyone else, and sought in every way to have his best side kept outward. The fact remains that since the final operation on his arm in Baltimore [in 1894] the Major never wrote a report or any other important official paper; for while sometimes he was undoubtedly able to do so, he was oftener unable, and even in his best hours the strain of the work and the need for gathering half-forgotten details would have been injurious . . . during the later years of the Bureau he seldom saw the reports until they were shown to him in printer's proofs.[61]

Press clipping services solicited McGee—a sure sign of notoriety. He engaged in ceaseless activity in the social and scientific circles of the capital. Above all, McGee emerged as the dominant spokesman for Powellian evolutionism and his own vigorous championing of American science, technology, and mature nationhood. As vice president of section H of the AAAS (1897) and as three-time president of the Anthropological Society of Washington (1898–1900), McGee made good use of professional forums. He took these opportunities between 1897 and 1902 to bring together his thoughts on anthropology, science, evolution, and American life in a culminating *fin-de-siècle* performance.

The passing of the old century called forth nostalgia and celebration for the stunning accomplishments of recent decades, while the coming of the new century inspired anxiety and optimism. The Iowa farmboy knew nostalgia and anxiety well, but he subordinated them to an aggressive, positive vision of the future. With the sum of human experience laid before them, what had Washington anthropologists learned? What laws had emerged? History and science, especially anthropology, showed that the trend of human development was toward unity of all races and cultures, a single world community on the highest cultural plane. On the individual level, McGee discerned a trend toward greater strength: "Perfected man is overspreading the world."[62] At the same time, the races of the world were rapidly mixing. White and Red had produced some fine specimens of humanity; White and Black mixtures included such men as Frederick Douglass and Booker T. Washington. The difficulty in interracial mixing was its frequently illicit nature among the lowest representatives of either race, rather than among the "eminent Othellos and dignified Desdemonas" of the country. Mixture was fundamentally a class, not a race problem. To McGee it was apparent that "the predominant peoples of the world are of mixed blood," and that mixing would continue. The law of humanity was "convergence in brain and blood."[63]

The laws of the animal and plant realms so brilliantly elucidated by Darwin had no human application. Having uniquely overshadowed and controlled nature's forces, man no longer diverged into varieties in response to environmental stimuli. Darwin and Spencer notwithstanding, "when the entire field of man's experience . . . is surveyed, it becomes clear that the human genus is not dividing into species . . . but is steadily drifting toward unity of blood and equality of culture."[64]

Other fields confirmed the physical trends. Discriminating five stages of human mental development, McGee found that the sum of mental powers increased considerably with each successive stage. Psychology corroborated racial observations: "Thought is extending from man to man and from group to group and gaining force with each extension, and . . . all lines converge toward a plane higher than any yet attained."[65] The course of pre-Columbian history in North America showed a "series of convergent and interblending lines, coming up from a large but unknown number of original sources scattered along the various coasts of the continent." Evidence from all aspects of cultural life led to the same conclusion: Man had reversed the patterns of lower life to take control. The twentieth century would see human unity in blood and culture.

America stood at the head of advancing humanity, and the lessons of the national history indicated the future. The mingling of peoples had gone so far that the American had become "the world's most complex ethnic strain," and American culture embraced all others. The United States was a nation of strength; "The selection of the strong by pioneering has been repeated over and over again, and the prepotent progeny have gone back to vitalize the weaker vessels with little loss of their own vigor . . ."[66] What was the role of the anthropologist in this "prepotent" culture? Simply to put men in touch with the laws of their own nature so that they would aid the progress of humanity. As McGee pointed out in an 1897 address on "The Science of Humanity," man had always been a favorite theme of artists and scholars, but until recent years he had remained a "vast chaos of action and thought . . . that last citadel of the unknown."[67] But now the human body and brain, like all other material things, "will be controlled and reconstructed for the good and glory of intelligent Man."[68] The anthropologist would show the way to a fully human future.

But would the people follow? Science, as Joseph Henry believed, had no meaning without application to human need, and utility was also integral to McGee's concept of science. Fortunately, a generation after Henry's death McGee could rejoice that America had become, in its institutions and daily habits, a nation of science. It was a sign of the times that

most men of civilized and enlightened lands are coming to appreciate the coin of experience above the dust of tradition, and are gradually entering, whether intentionally or not, into the ways of Science. Only a generation ago the very name of Science was the symbol of a cult to one class of thinkers and a juggler's gaud to another class; today Science is an actual part of everyday life of all enlightened folk. [69]

For McGee, the fate of a disenchanted world rested in the hands of the scientist, who combined virtue and altruism. With an appreciative, scientific citizenry behind him, how could the scientist fail?

Yet if the new century looked bright for enlightened humanity, clouds were gathering on the horizon of McGee's own career. Samuel Langley had never wanted McGee in the Bureau to begin with. When Powell first proposed moving him from the Survey in 1893, Langley resisted, arguing that while McGee was a man of "uncommon force and ability," he was not qualified by temperament or training to administer a scientific bureau. Langley acquiesced only with the understanding that McGee would never succeed to the directorship. [70] "I did this at a time when Mr. McGee was nearly a stranger to me, on the testimony of his unfitness for that place," Langley confided in 1902. "Now that I have known him for ten years, I see no reason to change my opinion." [71]

Langley distrusted McGee's brand of science. While he wanted a socially relevant Bureau, the Secretary felt that McGee's pronouncements on current racial and social issues, which appeared more frequently every year, were hardly impartial. To Langley, the role of the scientist amounted to presenting data and results without interpretation, particularly without the musings in which McGee indulged at government expense. Where problems of philosophy were concerned, Henry Adams wrote, Langley "liked to wander past them in a courteous temper, even bowing to them distantly as though recognizing their existence, while doubting their respectability." [72] Unfortunately McGee crossed over and shook hands with them. In 1902 Langley informed Daniel Coit Gilman that after Powell's death he intended to purge the Bureau so that "in accordance with the well-established policy of the Smithsonian Institution, its scientific work shall be limited to the observation and recording of phenomena . . . and that its sanction shall not be given to theoretical or speculative work." [73]

Politics partially determined Langley's position. By the turn of the new century he was under heavy pressure to reform the BAE. In the eyes of most congressmen the original purpose and chief goal of the Bureau had been eminently practical: to furnish the national legislature with reliable scientific information for dealing with the American aborigines. Langley could point at least to Royce's *History of Land Cessions of the Indian Tribes,* finally published in 1899, as a utilitarian product. But practical work was more often promised than produced. The BAE had wandered far from such enterprises, congressmen complained, citing such papers as McGee's work on the Seri and James Mooney's "Myths of the Cherokees" as examples of wasting public funds.[74]

In early 1902, when Powell's death seemed imminent, Langley decided to take action. The time had come for the BAE "to begin a new career, and to show that in this new life it can be useful to Congress in the way that Congress wants." He blamed McGee for the declension in Bureau fortunes. "The possible death of Major Powell is so near a contingency, and the unfortunate affairs of the Bureau have aroused such opposition in Congress to its continuance," he wrote to his aide, Richard Rathbun, "that I am more disposed than heretofore, if possible, to say that Mr. McGee must not hope to occupy that position [the directorship] while I am responsible for his official acts."[75]

In February, Langley asked Holmes to take over the Bureau on Powell's death. Holmes balked, protesting that he could not do such a thing to his friend. McGee, he said, was Powell's chosen successor, a politically powerful midwesterner, and "the strongest man in Anthropology today in America, if not in the world . . ."[76] Shortly after this conversation, Joseph Cannon, chairman of the House Appropriations Committee and near-dictator of the House of Representatives, notified Langley that he would approve the upcoming BAE appropriations only if Langley would personally direct Bureau affairs and produce something to justify its existence. Further discomfited, Langley told Holmes that after Powell, the new relationship between the Smithsonian and the Bureau would "materially differ" from the old; he would place the BAE on the same footing as other divisions of the Smithsonian, something he had "foreborne to do." If the Bureau was to last, "its work must be popularized and shown to be practical," and it would have to be guided directly from the Smithsonian. Through the next months he vainly urged on McGee and Powell the importance of pursuing vigorously the long-delayed *Cyclopedia of Indian Tribes.*[77]

In early September, McGee traveled to Baddeck, Nova Scotia, on the pretext of a "general reconnaissance of the survivors of the Micmac, Molisit, and related Algonquin tribes" of upper New England, but in reality to lay future plans with Smithsonian Regent Alexander Graham Bell.[78] On September 15, Mrs. Powell summoned McGee to be with the old Major in his final hours; he passed away on September 23. Whatever private assurances the dying Powell may have given his protégé in Maine, McGee returned to Washington without an official blessing. The day after the funeral McGee requested his own promotion, and during the next two weeks McGee's numerous friends in politics and science flooded Langley's office with supporting letters.[79]

Langley appointed Holmes, and McGee declared war on them both. American anthropologists almost without exception sided with McGee, and in the weeks of late October and November they expressed their views clearly. On October 14, Alice Fletcher described the situation to Boas, who responded with a telegram and the first of many letters on McGee's behalf. Frederick Ward Putnam had already advised Langley that ethnologists were expecting McGee's appointment: "It would be a serious mistake if he is not appointed." George A. Dorsey at the Field Museum, Frank Russell at Harvard, and Stewart Culin at the University Museum in Philadelphia, expressed similar sentiments.[80]

McGee organized a lobbying effort aimed at the Smithsonian Regents to discredit Langley. During October, Regent Richard Olney, for instance, received protests from Boas, Russell, *Science* editor James McKeen Cattell, and professors of geology Albert Perry Brigham at Colgate, H. LeRoy Fairchild at Rochester, and Ralph S. Tarr at Cornell.[81] The campaign soon developed into a general attack on Langley's administration. To his friends outside Washington, McGee pictured Langley's decision as merely the latest move in a long-term scheme aimed at "the undermining and reduction, if not complete abolition" of the Bureau. "Matters are now in such shape," he wrote Russell, "that the Bureau can be retained and rehabilitated only by joint and determined efforts on the part of the anthropologists of the country . . ." The issue, according to McGee, boiled down to a single question: "Shall Major Powell's monument as the greatest scientific man in America be perfected, or shall envy and jealousy be permitted to scatter the stones?"[82]

In the course of the debate over the Powell succession, Franz Boas emerged as a spokesman for the still-inchoate but growing professional consciousness among American anthropologists. While most anthropologists probably shared Boas's reservations about Langley, Boas's vigorous support of McGee at this time requires its own explanation, for it was very personal and highly significant. Boas had arrived in the United States in the mid-eighties, but it was a full decade before he gained institutional stability at Columbia University. He served briefly as geographical editor for *Science*, undertook fieldwork on the Northwest Coast sponsored by the British Association for the Advancement of Science, and between 1889 and 1892 taught anthropology at Clark University. In 1893 he came to Chicago as chief assistant to Frederick Putnam at the Columbian Exposition. Having nowhere to go at the close of the Fair, he agreed to stay on to organize the inherited anthropology exhibits for the new Field Columbian Museum. He hoped to stay on in Chicago permanently, but he was displaced by William H. Holmes and resigned in the spring of 1894. It was a year and a half before the New York appointments, at Columbia and the American Museum, materialized.[83]

The Chicago experience was extremely bitter for Boas, but it taught him important lessons of politics and science, one of which was the limitations of the museum as an institution of scientific anthropology. Thus, when he began to develop his own plans for the future science, the Bureau was a major part of them. The BAE was the only institution in the country willing to underwrite and publish the work in linguistics and mythology that Boas considered integral to a complete science of anthropology. Museums, by contrast, seemed interested only in material collections. Since the early nineties, Boas had been talking with McGee and Powell about preserving full texts as the basis for future linguistic and ethnological work, and the Washington men had responded.[84] Between 1893 and 1903 the BAE supported a great deal of Boas's work by purchasing linguistic manuscripts and notebooks from him at a total cost of about $4,000. This support was critical not only for his livelihood but for Boas's personal scientific growth.

As Boas saw the issue, the Bureau had maintained a balance and fullness in American anthropology that aided harmonious and healthy progress. "The interests of anthropological science," he instructed Langley, "requires [sic] . . . that those lines of human activities that do *not* find expression in material objects—namely language, thought, customs, and I may add, anthropometric measurements—be investigated thoroughly and carefully." The Bureau was the only American institution dealing with the "general problems" of anthropology. Furthermore, other anthropologists working in museums, such as George A. Dorsey at Field, had similarly discovered that museum funds were simply not available for "purely theoretical work."[85]

Thus Boas approached McGee's dispute with clear preferences: he valued support for his linguistic and mythology work, and hoped for its continuance; he was fully prepared to befriend McGee against the man who had taken his place in Chicago; and he deplored the possible domination by the museum. While he avoided disparaging Holmes, Boas distinguished between the talents of a museum man and those of other anthropologists. Holmes's natural gifts led him to a thorough appreciation of visual objects, Boas admitted, but his interest in "that part of anthropology that deals with ideas alone" was slight. And it was precisely such matters that formed the BAE's principal work. Placing Holmes in charge would inevitably mean subordinating the Bureau to "museum interest."[86] Finally, with Holmes as head curator of anthropology at the National Museum and director of the Bureau, no good could possibly come to an already overworked man and understaffed museum.[87]

But the real issue lay beyond "museum influence" or the vitality of either institution. Langley, through his presumptuous interference with the Bureau succession and his disregard of the opinions of American anthropologists, struck at the integrity and independence of anthropology. In 1902 the status of the fledgling science remained so precarious that anthropologists felt such a blow keenly. By exercising his "personal inclination" without regard to the opinions of concerned scientists, Langley had introduced a dangerous element of uncertainty that threatened the very existence of the Bureau; and he had instilled, said Boas, "a feeling of general instability in the scientific service of the government which we hoped had been entirely overcome by this time."[88]

Furthermore, by appointing Holmes "chief" rather than "director," Langley had demonstrated his intention to control the Bureau. But in its stage of development at the turn of the century, American anthropology above all required individuals with generous conceptions of its needs and possibilities. Langley did not have them; whatever his other faults, Boas argued, McGee did possess such understanding: "It is easy to criticize McGee . . . because his mannerism, and his tendency to bring out the ultimate bearings of single observations, make easy points of attack. But all this has nothing to do with McGee's intelligent understanding of the work of the Bureau, nor with his administrative ability."[89]

Although Langley never abolished or intended to abolish the Bureau, Boas subsequently found his doubts justified. Langley insisted on gathering up the dangling threads of investigations that had been dragging along since the early days. It was time to clean house: to close off investigations and begin summing up the results of two decades of work on the American Indian. Boas was astonished at Langley's insistence on final results. Anthropologists could not simply decide that the final results were in, he answered, any more than Langley could submit the final report on his astrophysical work. The work of the Bureau, just like investigation in any other field of science, he explained to Charles D. Walcott, "should of course be such that with the advance of studies each line of research should be deepened and made more useful," not abruptly terminated. Anthropology was a continuing, ongoing experience; Langley's failure to comprehend that fact amounted to a "fundamental error of judgment."[90]

McGee's case was lost from the start, because Langley was determined not to promote him. Far from destroying the BAE, Langley believed, with some justification, that he was saving it from almost certain demise at the hands of politicians who were no longer awed by Powell and were now demanding useful results. Langley wanted, in short, to return the Bureau to its original role of 1879, as an informational arm of the Congress and the people. As he explained it to himself in a memorandum, "On [Powell's] death a new day begins for the Bureau—partly a reversion to the policy of his own vigorous years."[91] Until his own death four years later, Langley concentrated all BAE resources on the long-awaited *Handbook of American Indians* (formerly the *Cyclopedia*), which he intended as a practical manual for congressmen and constituents.

McGee made his final eight months in the Bureau utter misery for everyone. In Mexico he contracted typhoid, from which he never completely recovered. Nor did he ever recover from the decisions of Langley—that "frog nestled in the shelter of the Smithsonian," the "Senegambian in the woodpile," in McGee's rich phrases—or his deceitful friend Holmes.[92] For months he sniped at Holmes and contributed no work of his own. (He took fifty-seven days of sick leave in the first three months of 1903.)[93] He turned bitterly on his former friend, accusing him of adopting Langley's policy of "fair words and foul acts," and reminding Boas that "you saw Holmes' cloven foot in Chicago, but I see both of them and the forked tail as well."[94] For a time Holmes tried to placate McGee and serve Langley at the same time, but he soon became disgusted with McGee's attacks.[95]

The crisis came in the summer of 1903. In April, officials of the Bureau discovered evidence of forgery and embezzlement by Frank M. Barnett, a minor employee. Barnett was apprehended and tried, but his misdeeds led in July to a general inquiry by Smithsonian officials into the operations of the Bureau during the Powell/McGee tenure.[96] Throughout the sweltering Washington midsummer, Langley's investigating committee took more than 1,000 pages of testimony from Bureau anthropologists (including Boas, who held an unsalaried position as honorary philologist) and staff members.

The investigation ranged widely but returned again and again to McGee's shortcomings as administrator and scientist. Boas returned to New York after his testimony, convinced that the investigation was a witchhunt. The records tend to confirm his impression.[97] The committee combed McGee's correspondence since 1893. They were appalled to find letters relating to private affairs, stock transactions, real estate settlements, political affairs, and other matters unrelated to official business.[98] As if the letters were not sufficiently damaging, his own stenographer confirmed McGee's working habits in a vengeful letter to Matilda Stevenson, who happily turned it over to the Smithsonian committee. Her boss, Caroline Dinwiddie reported, spent a great amount of time on personal business at the cost of the BAE. "Over and over again I spent weeks of office time on articles which were published in *Harper's*, the *Atlantic Monthly*, *The Forum*, etc., for which he was paid magazine rates." She spared nothing: "In my judgment, such a man is absolutely unfit for an administrative office. His whole policy is autocratic in the extreme, and no man dares do independent work under his tutelage."[99] Clearly the Bureau under McGee had not possessed the spirit of "Barnum's happy family," as later claimed by a friendly Washington newspaper.[100]

A series of "mistaken enterprises and dangerously faulty methods" was laid at McGee's door. His fruitless trip to Nova Scotia at the time of Powell's death did not go unnoticed; nor his Mexico jaunt at government expense the following November.[101] His performance after October 1902, probably sealed his fate. Rathbun noted that his attitude toward the Smithsonian Secretary had been offensive, "disloyally outspoken and malicious," and had begun to spread to others.[102] Particularly irksome was his effort during the recent period to organize a Bureau of Archaeology and Ethnology under the International Archaeological Commission. McGee seemed to be preparing a place for himself elsewhere while still on the BAE payroll.

McGee defended himself, but without effect. In the Bureau, private and public often mixed, and individuals often made sacrifices for science, even to the extent of personally making up deficits, he explained.[103] As far as the "unofficial" work was concerned, McGee saw no conflict because he honestly saw no distinction between activities within and without the Bureau, between the so-called personal and public. A man's science was of a piece. It was essential, he believed, that every collaborator of the Bureau, "according to his powers and his lights," should be connected with "general scientific progress" in order to confirm "the character and standing of these men who are engaged in the researches relating to American Indians." McGee's profession of faith on this point is so enlightening that it bears repetition in full:

> I have thought it important that every scientific collaborator of the Bureau should be a member of the Anthropological Society of Washington, and I think that it is important that every collaborator of the Bureau should be a member of the newly established [American] Anthropological Association. I have thought that the reputation of the Bureau would depend to a considerable extent on the scientific standing of the several officers and collaborators and I have thought . . . that the scientific standing of the collaborators, determining that of the office, would depend upon the amount of work they did in connection with these voluntary scientific associations. It may be a fad on my part, but . . . one of which I am not at all ashamed, to hold that the scientific activity of this country of ours finds its best expression in the voluntary scientific associations . . . [which] have placed this country where it is in the scientific world today. . . . The fact that salaries are paid out of appropriations made by the government or paid in other ways is largely an incident in connection with the scientific development of the individuals who constitute the scientific element in this country, and it is for that reason that my policy has always been an extremely liberal one with respect to my own activity and the activity of other collaborators of the Bureau in general scientific work, in the maintenance of scientific societies, in making contributions very largely of a gratuitous character. . . . That has been my policy throughout.[104]

McGee set forth a conception of government science that stressed the development of the individual, not of an organization or a delimited body of knowledge. Because the organization derived from individual enterprise, the government's proper role was strictly supportive, not directive. To McGee, furthermore, everything he did outside his home was in the public interest; and yet his personal scientific growth was always involved, which ultimately benefited the public.[105] The 1903 investigation revealed, among other things, that this vision of government science was already under heavy attack from a new breed of functionaries who emphasized loyalty to the institution over either personal development or loyalty to science in general.

The committee's verdict was predictable. Although McGee was not fired, his position was abolished, and he resigned at the end of July, as expected. The blistering indictment found him guilty of unsystematic financial methods; carelessness and possible corruption in purchasing manuscripts, chiefly from Boas and Fletcher; gross negligence of the manuscript collections; and hostility toward Langley.[106] McGee left Washington under a heavy cloud.

Over the next four years McGee's personal life crumbled, as he and Anita permanently separated. He returned to government work in 1907, however, as a member of the Department of Agriculture. That summer, while camping in the California Sierras, he and Gifford Pinchot laid the plans for what became the conservation movement of the early twentieth century.[107] McGee fulfilled his scientific life in these years. Whitney Cross observed that "it was McGee, and neither Powell, Ward, nor any other of their fellows, who directly and specifically transmitted the common beliefs of the trio into the twentieth century conservation movement."[108] Powell's Irrigation Survey had been an early and abortive attempt to apply the lessons of science to an unruly political and social world. In the conservation movement McGee combined the lessons learned from Powell and his own experiences with desert and water into a final attempt to guide American society scientifically. "All the compensatory drives from a disease-ridden body, a ruined career, and a broken marriage," Cross concluded, "heightened his lifelong devotion to the general welfare for a final decisive stroke of public service."[109]

In the spirit of Morgan and Powell, McGee ended his life condemning wasteful American capitalism and turning to the model of aboriginal America for alternative modes of organizing society and resources. Pinchot recalled that McGee made him see that "monopoly of natural resources was only less dangerous to the public welfare than their actual destruction." Adopting the iconoclastic view of American history coming into vogue among progressive reformers, McGee preached that the dreams of the Founding Fathers had been subverted as "the People became in large measure industrial dependents rather than free citizens." This had occurred because the national habit of giving away land and resource rights to individuals had developed into an unprecedented "saturnalia of squandering the sources of permanent prosperity." In his dying years McGee called for a nobler patriotism, honesty of purpose, a warmer charity, a stronger sense of family, and "a livelier humanity, in which each will feel that he lives not for himself alone but as a part of a common life for a common world and for the common good . . ."[110] McGee never lost faith—the Iowa fields were there to the end. A champion of American individualism in science, technology, and commerce throughout his life, in the end he foresaw and demanded its demise in order to return to what the desert had shown him: that man, like all life, must band together for the common welfare. This was the lesson and promise of anthropology for the new century.[111]

Science meant order and system to Powell and McGee. It was synonymous with philosophy—they used the terms interchangeably—because scientific understanding transcended the flux and confusion of daily experience to provide perspective on events. Still, any theoretical framework must have some foundation in empiricism, and McGee extended Powell's system almost to the point of caricature. He became an easy target.

In McGee's demise were indications of a major cultural change. By the turn of the new century, the federal government no longer provided the environment for personal fulfillment as defined by Powell. At the same time, the insistence of Schoolcraft, Morgan, Gibbs, and Powell on an open science and on the general "scientific development of individuals" argued against the critical, exclusive university training that Boas would bring. Powell's institution, like its predecessors, sought to perpetuate and preserve an accepted, cherished style and set of American values, not evaluate them in order to consider alternatives.

Powell's Bureau of American Ethnology, like McGee, reached the political and historical limits of a tradition. American anthropologists of the nineteenth century had appealed to and placed faith in the same constituency that Joseph Henry strove to create and encourage in science: the intelligent, stalwart, presumably large middle section of Americans with moderate leisure and freedom from pecuniary pursuit. Their science amounted to a form of moral uplift; their middle-class helpers would serve as the leavening for a nation. Perhaps it was a myth, but men build institutions on myths. By the end of the century that democratic homogeneity was clearly crumbling, in Chicago and across the nation, under racial and social strife, taking with it the foundations of an institutional order. Not coincidentally, new criteria and groupings arose to provide identity, order, and purpose for anthropology.

Notes

1. Henry Adams, *The Education of Henry Adams: An Autobiography* (Boston, 1961), pp. 344–45.
2. Ibid., p. 330.
3. See John Higham, "The Reorientation of American Culture in the 1890s," in

John Weiss, ed., *The Origins of Modern Consciousness* (Detroit, 1965), pp. 25–48.

4. Adams, *Education,* p. 330.

5. Fletcher to Boas, 14 October 1902, BP; Boas to McGee, 3 August 1903, MP.

6. Charles Keyes, "W J McGee, Anthropologist, Geologist, Hydrologist," *Annals of Iowa,* series 3, vol. 2 (1913), p. 187; John R. Swanton, "Notes regarding my adventures in anthropology and with anthropologists," ms. (ca. 1944), pp. 33–34, NAA.

7. Remarks of Alfred C. Lane, quoted in *The McGee Memorial Meeting of the Washington Academy of Sciences* (Baltimore, 1916), p. 90.

8. On McGee's early years, see Emma R. McGee, *Life of W J McGee* (privately printed, Farley, Iowa, 1915); F. H. Knowlton, "Memoir of W J McGee," *Bulletin of the Geological Society of America* 24 (1912): 18–29; N. H. Darton, "Memoir of W J McGee," *Annals of the Association of American Geographers* 3: 103–10; Whitney R. Cross, "W J McGee and the Idea of Conservation," *Historian* 15 (1953): 148–62; *The McGee Memorial Meeting;* F. W. Hodge, "W J McGee," *American Anthropologist* 14 (1912): 683–86; and Anita Newcomb McGee to Gifford Pinchot, 5 June 1916, GP.

9. Remarks of Emma McGee, quoted in *McGee Memorial Meeting,* p. 90; *Life-History Album* belonging to Klotho McGee Lattin, p. 9, in which Anita McGee recorded the full list of McGee's illnesses; Anita McGee to Pinchot, 15 June 1916, GP.

10. "Stories told to Klotho McGee," typescript in author's possession. The schoolhouse reference occurs in McGee's biographical entry in the membership lists of the Explorers Club of New York, which he joined at its founding in 1905.

11. Quoted in William C. Darrah, *Powell of the Colorado* (Princeton, 1951), p. 316.

12. Willard Johnson to McGee, 10 June 1885, MP.

13. Personal interview with Klotho McGee Lattin, 31 December 1973.

14. Cross, "W J McGee," p. 152.

15. Ms. membership list, Anthropological Society of Washington Papers, NAA.

16. McGee to F. P. Venable, 25 March 1887, MP.

17. McGee to J. P. Lesley, 7 October 1892, MP.

18. W J McGee, "The Science of Humanity," *American Anthropologist,* o.s. 10 (1897): 246.

19. James Kirkpatrick Flack, *Desideratum in Washington: The Intellectual Community in the Capital City, 1870–1900* (Cambridge, 1975).

20. Membership and officer records, ASW Papers, NAA.

21. On McGee's role in founding the American Anthropological Association, see George W. Stocking, Jr., "Franz Boas and the Founding of the American Anthropological Association," *American Anthropologist* 62 (1960): 1–17.

22. Personal interview, 31 December 1973.

23. J. W. Powell, "The Personal Characteristics of Professor Baird," *Bulletin of the PSW* 10 (Washington, D.C., 1887): 71.

24. Don D. Fowler and Catherine S. Fowler, "John Wesley Powell, Ethnologist," *Utah Historical Quarterly* 37 (1969): 170; notes on "Reserve Fund," 13 January 1903, BAE-IN.

25. Langley memorandum, "The Bureau of Ethnology," n.d., BAE-IN.

26. Baird to Powell, 7 July 1883, copy in MP.

27. Cyrus Adler, "Samuel Pierpont Langley," SI, *AR for 1906,* pp. 531–32.

28. See, e.g., Powell to Langley, 20 December 1901, NAA.

29. W. H. Holmes, WHH 8, sections 1 and 2.

30. Powell to Langley, 11 June 1891, copy in BAE-IN.

31. Langley, "Memorandum," 2 August 1893, copy in BAE-IN. McGee presented four reasons against the reserve. Langley refused to discuss it.

32. W J McGee, *The Siouan Indians: a Preliminary Sketch,* BAE, *AR for 1894,* pp. 157–204; James Owen Dorsey, *Siouan Sociology,* ibid., pp. 205–44.

33. Powell to Langley, 9 August 1894, NAA.

34. Seri notebooks, 24 October and 25 October 1894, MP.

35. Bernard L. Fontana, "The Seri Indians in Perspective," in W J McGee, *The Seri Indians of Bahia Kino and Sonora, Mexico* (Glorieta, New Mexico, 1971 [reprint of the BAE, *AR for 1896*]), no pagination.

36. Ibid.

37. The 1894 trip is summarized from McGee's viewpoint in BAE, *AR for 1895,* pp. lxii–lxv. For a closer summary see Fontana, "The Seri Indians."

38. Seri notebooks, MP.

39. Ibid.

40. "The Seri Indians," BAE, *AR for 1896,* pp. 1–298 (with a comparative lexicology of Seri-Yuman by J.N.B. Hewitt, pp. 299–344). Government publication dates generally ran about two years behind the reporting fiscal year. McGee delayed the report at least one extra year for his Seri article—so long, in fact, that the report was prepared first and the bulk of his "Seri Indians" was later inserted with separate pagination.

41. Fontana, "The Seri Indians."

42. BAE, *AR for 1896,* p. 294.

43. Ibid., p. 295.

44. Ibid., pp. 130–33.

45. Ibid., p. 161.

46. Ibid., p. 203.

47. Ibid., p. 295.

48. Alfred Kroeber, "The Seri," *Southwest Museum Papers* 6 (Los Angeles, 1931): 18, 52.

49. Fontana, "The Seri Indians."

50. Kroeber, "The Seri," p. 25.

51. Ibid., pp. 24–28.

52. W J McGee, "Expedition to Papagueria and Seriland: A preliminary note," *American Anthropologist,* o.s. 9 (1896): 97–98.

53. Kroeber, "The Seri," p. 53.

54. Ibid., p. 48.

55. Clark Wissler, "W J McGee," in *Encyclopedia of the Social Sciences* 5: 652–53.

56. W J McGee, "Beginning of Agriculture," *American Anthropologist,* o.s. 8 (1895): 368–69.

57. Ibid., pp. 374–75.

58. W J McGee, "Beginning of Zooculture," *American Anthropologist*, o.s. 10 (1897): 228–29.

59. McGee to Holmes, 6 December 1894, MP.

60. McGee testimony, BAE-IN, pp. 125, 127; Caroline Brooke Dinwiddie to Matilda Coxe Stevenson, 21 February 1902, BAE-IN.

61. McGee to Emma Dean Powell, 19 November 1902, BAE-IN.

62. W J McGee, "The Trend of Human Progress," *American Anthropologist*, n.s. 1 (1899): 414.

63. Ibid., pp. 419, 421.

64. Ibid., p. 424. McGee elaborated these thoughts fully in "Man's Place in Nature," *American Anthropologist*, n.s. 3 (1901): 1–13.

65. Ibid., p. 435.

66. Ibid., pp. 445–47. For another statement of the same theme, applied to the Spanish-American War and its evolutionary significance, see McGee's "The Course of Human Development," *Forum* (1898): 56–65.

67. W J McGee, "The Science of Humanity," *American Anthropologist*, o.s. 10 (1897): 271.

68. Ibid., p. 272.

69. W J McGee, "Cardinal Principles of Science," *Proceedings of the Washington Academy of Sciences* 2 (1900): 7–8.

70. Handwritten note, addressed to R. R. Hitt, n.d., SIA.

71. Langley to Richard Rathbun, confidential note, 15 February 1902, BAE-IN.

72. Adams, *Education*, p. 377.

73. Langley to Gilman (draft), 24 November 1902, SIA.

74. Langley to Holmes, 19 November 1902; "Papers on the work of the Bureau by Secretary and others" and "Memorandum of conversation between Senator O. H. Platt and the Secretary," 11 November 1902, both in BAE-IN. Langley was fully aware of congressional opinion and shared much of the concern over the tendency to provide work of "purely scientific & abstract interest." Langley, "Memorandum of what I am saying to Mr. Cannon," n.d., BAE-IN.

75. Langley to Rathbun, 15 February 1902, BAE-IN.

76. Holmes, WHH 9, section 1: "Chiefship period, BAE, 1902–1910," in Library of the National Museum of American Art and the National Portrait Gallery, SI. The meetings took place on 13 and 14 February 1902.

77. Fragment of letter from Langley, 12 April 1902, SIA.

78. McGee to himself, 9 September 1902, commissioning his trip; unsigned memorandum noting that McGee went to Baddeck "ostensibly to study Indians. There is no record of any Indians having been visited"; McGee to Bell, August 1902; handwritten note of Anita N. McGee, 15 September 1902; all in BAE-IN.

79. McGee to Langley, 27 September 1902, SIA; Memorandum of S. P. Langley, 9 October 1902, BAE-IN. The complex maneuverings of October and November 1902, are well documented but not recounted here.

80. Fletcher to Boas, 14 October 1902, BP; Putnam to Langley, n.d., SIA. The Dorsey, Culin, and Russell correspondence is also in the Secretary's incoming correspondence for these years, SIA.

81. The letters to Olney are in the Secretary's incoming correspondence, SIA.

McGee also conferred with Boas and other anthropologists at the meeting of the Congress of the Americanists in New York during the week of October 21. McGee later denied any involvement in organized efforts on his behalf.

82. McGee to Russell, 29 October 1902; McGee to Henderson, 30 October 1902, BAE-IN. These letters later served as evidence of McGee's disloyalty to Langley. McGee's appeal to the memory of Powell was serious, for his veneration and love for his mentor were clearly sincere. (Although for his own purposes McGee could be ugly. To Stephen Peet, whom he had always treated rather shabbily, he complained in November 1902: "I have been carrying an invalid for ten years and working for two . . . [McGee to Peet, 17 November 1902, Peet Papers, Beloit College Archives].) McGee's hatred for the Smithsonian officials ran so deeply that he defiantly refused to hand over Powell's brain, in his possession, to the National Museum until June 1906—surely a powerful symbolic gesture! Richard Rathbun, for his part, so despised McGee that he advised against accepting it. Daniel S. Lamb received the Major's brain in the Army Medical Museum on June 15, 1906. (Rathbun to Adler, 29 May 1906, SIA.)

83. On Boas's trials in this period, see Curtis M. Hinsley and Bill Holm, "A Cannibal in the National Museum: The Early Career of Franz Boas in America," *American Anthropologist* 78 (1976): 306–16.

84. Boas to Powell, 18 January and 19 March 1893, NAA.

85. Boas to Langley, 15 October 1902, SIA; Boas to Bell, 18 June 1903, BP.

86. Boas to Alexander Graham Bell, 7 August 1903, BP.

87. Boas to Langley, 3 December 1903, SIA. Indicative of Boas's reputation with the Langley staff was the comment of Richard Rathbun to Cyrus Adler on this letter: "Our friend takes himself very seriously." See also Boas to Bell, 9 November 1902, BP.

88. *Science* (21 November 1902), p. 831.

89. Boas to Bell, 7 August 1903, BP.

90. Boas to Charles P. Bowditch, 17 December 1903; Boas to Charles D. Walcott, 7 December 1903, BP.

91. Langley, "Strictly private memorandum of what I am saying to Mr. Cannon," BAE-IN.

92. McGee to W. A. Croffut, 10 February 1904, MP.

93. "Memorandum of annual and sick leave had by W J McGee . . . up to 6/30/03," BAE-IN.

94. McGee to Boas, 21 December 1902 and 16 June 1903, BP.

95. Holmes, WHH 9, section 1.

96. The records of the 1903 investigation (BAE-IN) are in the NAA of the SI. The significance of the investigation for Washington anthropology generally is the subject of the following chapter. The discussion here treats only the impact on McGee.

97. Boas to McGee, 3 August 1903, and to Carl Schurz, 12 August 1903, BP.

98. Adler *et al.* to Langley, 24 September 1903, p. 39, BAE-IN. Hereafter referred to as Adler Committee report.

99. Caroline Brooke Dinwiddie to Matilda Stevenson, 21 February 1902, BAE-IN. This letter, written when Powell lay near death in February 1902, may have been solicited by Stevenson—who loathed McGee—as evidence against him.

100. *Washington Evening Times,* 16 October 1902.

101. McGee testimony, p. 621, BAE-IN.

102. Handwritten notes by Rathbun, n.d., and McGee testimony, pp. 787–88, BAE-IN.

103. McGee testimony, p. 660, BAE-IN.

104. McGee testimony, pp. 821–22.

105. It should be noted that the public/private distinction and the question of the proprietary rights of the individual in the scientific organization plagued Langley, too, as shown in an 1894 letter to George Brown Goode:

> It is equally recognized that a subordinate may, in the course of his official work, make original observations which, in a scientific sense are his, rather than the Institution's; and it probably never will be practicable to formulate a rule or system of rules which will discriminate satisfactorily in every case as to the moral right of publication of such facts, especially as it is, in the nature of the case, indeterminable what part of his work is really official, what is purely personal and independent, and what is due to the thought, method, or experience of his scientific mind.

But, he added, there must be an ultimate authority for "the necessities of administration." (Langley to Goode, April 1894, assistant secretary's incoming correspondence, 1881–1896, SIA.)

106. Adler Committee report, pp. 40–42. The committee placed entire responsibility for the shortcomings of the Bureau on McGee. As Boas pointed out, this was not completely just, since McGee had worked within limits set by Powell (Boas testimony, pp. 946–51). Boas concluded that "whatever was good went to the credit of Powell and whatever was bad went to the discredit of McGee" (p. 951).

107. Remarks of Joseph A. Holmes, quoted in *McGee Memorial Meeting,* p. 20.

108. Cross, "W J McGee," p. 156; Gifford Pinchot, *Breaking New Ground* (New York, 1947). For McGee's central role in the conservation movement, see also Samuel P. Hays, *Conservation and the Gospel of Efficiency: The Progressive Conservation Movement, 1890-1920* (Cambridge, 1959), pp. 102-07.

109. Cross, "W J McGee," p. 160. For a recent, thorough assessment of McGee's contributions to the conservation movement, see Michael J. Lacey, "The Mysteries of Earth-Making Dissolve: A Study of Washington's Intellectual Community and the Origins of American Environmentalism in the Late Nineteenth Century," Ph.D. diss. (George Washington University, 1979), pp. 284–342.

110. W J McGee, "The Conservation of Natural Resources," *Proceedings of Mississippi Valley Historical Association* 3 (1909–10); quoted in Roderick Nash, ed., *The American Environment: Readings in the History of Conservation* (Reading, Mass., 1968), pp. 41–45.

111. See, for instance, McGee's address, "Principles underlying water rights," closing the 19th National Irrigation Congress, 7 December 1911, in *Official Proceedings of the Congress* (Chicago, 1912), pp. 309–20. McGee insisted on the "essential principle of natural equity" that "All the water belongs to all the People" (p. 318).

IX

Crisis and Aftermath: Smithsonian Anthropology under William Henry Holmes, 1902–1910

Washington, D.C., in 1900 was the capital of American politics and, in some fields, science as well. No longer an isolated outpost in an unproven republic, in the years since the Civil War the capital city had blossomed into a consequential intellectual center; it had become a locus of ideas in action. Government science stood at its apex in substantive contributions and in reputation, not yet visibly overtaken by graduate schools, private research foundations, and industrial research laboratories. The magnet of scientific power would never again draw men so strongly to Washington, nor would the preeminence outlast the First World War; but the early years of the new century were a heady, inspiring moment for national scientific service.

President Theodore Roosevelt carried into his administrations (1901–08) a reassertion of national vigor and expansion of the executive branch that relied heavily on a community of scientists and on a belief in impartial government service. The community and the belief were both offspring of the post-Civil War decades of tumultuous demographic and economic growth. Roosevelt's chief institutional innovation, the federal regulatory agency, pre-supposed a corps of objective investigators; in most of the major domestic political disputes of the Roosevelt and Taft years—pure food and drug, conservation of natural resources, railroad and social welfare legislation—government scientists played central informational and catalytic roles.

Scientific men and women constituted the heart of Washington intellectual and social life as the century turned. For thirty-five years a fertile and flourishing intellectual community had gradually created a set of forums for discussion and enlightenment: the Philosophical, Literary, Anthropological, and Biological Societies of Washington formed the nucleus of this constellation of social groupings. In 1898, when thirteen societies joined to establish the "interlocking directorship" of the Washington Academy of Sciences, the capital seemed to arrive at intellectual maturity.[1]

Washington's intellectual community was built upon a substratum of common concerns and purposes. Powell, McGee, and sociologist/paleobotanist Lester Frank Ward were prominent in ignoring disciplinary boundaries to address what they saw as the fundamental issues of their day. "What was going forward in the intellectual lives of these men in the last decades of the century," one historian has recently observed, "was the interpretation of the social meaning of the doctrine of evolution. The whole experience had powerful moral and religious dimensions, and the basic question they dealt with was this: are cosmogenesis, biological evolution, and human social evolution driven by processes cognate to us all as moral beings, or are they indifferent and alien to us?"[2] The questions bequeathed by Darwin had evolved by the 1890s into a set of highly charged issues with direct political import: With what costs and benefits does man presume to alter the courses of nature and of human society? On what ground may man claim a hand in shaping his own fate? Washington was the appropriate scene of debate, for on the resolution of these questions hinged the very legitimacy of government science.

By the time of America's entry into the First World War, the question of the propriety of an activist government had been settled by economic and social developments, not by the arguments of Ward, William Graham Sumner, or Herbert Croly. Management efficiency and scientific expertise soon became the watchwords of a generation busily erecting an "organizational society" in which those who could claim status as scientists assumed important advisory roles in policy-making.[3] Not surprisingly, with the new century "every year brought more scientists into federal service." Scientific bureaus began to proliferate after 1900: the National Bureau of Standards, Bureau of Mines, Bureau of the Census, and the Forestry Service all appeared between 1901 and 1905. Under the powerful influence of figures like Charles D. Walcott and Gifford Pinchot, emphasis moved noticeably toward applied research for public utility, leaving basic work to the growing university departments or foundations like the Carnegie Institution of Washington (1902) and the National Geographic Society (1888).[4]

Washington cultural life was consequently weak in the arts and weighted toward the scientific. Still, Henry James considered the capital a "City of Conversation," somehow not entirely absorbed by politics.[5] The growing bureaucracies and international cares that came with the world war would undermine the social ease of nineteenth-century Washington, erasing the vestiges of southern small-town sleepiness that Henry Adams recalled. But in 1900 the city had reached a cultural apex. "More and more," an English visitor remarked, "Washington becomes the Mecca of the United States."[6]

The Smithsonian Institution, situated expansively on the Mall, shifted with political and scientific winds. Smithson's original bequest of $515,000, augmented over the years by private gifts, had risen in fifty years to more than $900,000, yielding in 1900 an annual private operating fund of some $60,000. This sum represented a mere fraction of the Institution's expenditures, however. Now embracing the ever-growing National Museum, the Astrophysical Observatory, the National Zoological Park, and the BAE, the

Smithsonian absorbed half-a-million dollars a year. The Museum, as Henry had anticipated, depended entirely on Congress for its annual sustenance of $250,000.[7]

The Smithsonian had never enjoyed true political neutrality under Henry or Baird, and the scope of its activity in an age enamored of science and aware of public service assured that the Institution would be exposed to national politics as never before. Between the Spanish-American War and the First World War, Smithsonian science generally and BAE anthropology in particular were caught in the throes of major social adjustments. Professing scientific impartiality for his Institution, Secretary Samuel Langley found it prudent to stress public service, even as the Smithsonian moved away from the central dynamics of American science. But Langley's notion of service bore little resemblance to Henry's nineteenth-century sense of moral uplift. Langley sought to apply science immediately to current concerns, and he desired to educate the museum public to a limited degree through entertaining, eye-catching exhibits. The change from Henry to Langley had occurred incrementally, but it involved abdication of a vital ethical element. Powell was a pivotal and fascinating example of the transformation. As we have seen, he originally promised useful functions for ethnology, then withdrew into esoteric interests, never again to emerge as a policy advisor in Indian affairs (although the course of his career was radically different in geology). Like Henry, he believed deeply in ultimate public enlightenment through doing as well as dispensing science. This dream was dead by the time of Powell's death. The hardening class lines of American science and society had already determined that the mass of Americans would merely consume, not experience their science.

The enormous growth of the Smithsonian; its consequent vulnerability to political pressures; the turn to applied research in government science in the Roosevelt years; and the use of the museum as public entertainment: these were some of the related historical trends that combined to push BAE anthropology for a time into Henry Adams's fin-de-siècle dead-water, "where not a breath stirred the idle air."[8] The timing was most unfortunate for the place of government anthropology in the emerging national profession. At the very period when Boas at Columbia and Putnam at Harvard were training a new generation of American ethnologists, linguists, and archaeologists, Langley and Holmes faced the apparent bankruptcy of Powell's scientific vision with little vigor of their own. While self-trained amateurs were rapidly passing out of acceptance, the Bureau had neither facilities nor philosophy for training men and women. Dependent on others for its staff, the Bureau became dependent on the outside for new ideas as well.

Broadly sketched, then, the fate of the Bureau after Powell had less to do with individual personalities than with deeply running social and scientific currents. The BAE was the victim of historical movements both within and beyond anthropology. On the one hand, a public sinking ever further into ignorance and impotence demanded titillation more than edification from tax-supported bureaus and museums of science. Politicians responded predictably, and among Washington anthropologists, the "museum interest," as Boas aptly phrased it, gained dominance over research in nonmaterial culture. On the other hand, the cadre of new university professionals in anthropology, abandoning a public voice, soon moved off into debates among themselves. The Bureau of American Ethnology, child of a past world, was left without respectable program or purpose.

Powell's scientific world crumbled in the summer of 1903. The torrent that washed away W J McGee's career in anthropology had been building for years, held back only by Powell's massive presence. During the eighties his structure had been useful in focusing work and framing questions. But beginning in the early nineties his health steadily deteriorated and he progressively withdrew from active participation in the Bureau. The last decade was a long, sad decline. Between 1890 and 1895, old and trusted collaborators departed and were replaced by McGee, who cared for Powell as he prepared to succeed him. By 1900, stagnation had overtaken the Bureau. No new projects appeared, and the valuable work that did continue grew from seeds sown much earlier (such as Mooney's work) or from Boas's efforts to revise BAE linguistics.[9]

The Smithsonian investigation in the summer of 1903 brought these political, professional, and personal matters to a head. The testimony of Boas, McGee, Fewkes, Stevenson, Mooney, and others revealed in detail the underpinnings and daily operations of Powell's organization. As they freely discussed their concerns about the Bureau's methods, they revealed that it had reached an untenable position in anthropology. By the end of July it was clear that in the new century Powellian science no longer satisfied either public or nascent professional needs. Four related issues emerged: lack of scientific planning; institutional loyalty; the appropriate role of the individual in science; and withholding of materials from publication. All of them touched on Powell's cherished assumptions.

The primary question, as committee chairman Cyrus Adler posed it, was "whether the work of the members of the scientific staff of the Bureau was being pursued in accordance with some general system so that it might . . . show definite results in a reasonable time; or whether it was being done upon individual opinion, according to individual tastes . . ."[10] In the early years, Frederick Webb Hodge answered, Powell had outlined the collaborative projects. Of these, two were long since finished and the third, the synonymy, was still limping along, hampered by the constant accumulation of new data and shuffled from one reluctant staff member to the next, an unwanted stepchild of Powell's fertile mind.[11] Outside of these general projects, pursued sporadically over the years, BAE anthropology amounted to private pursuits. Jesse Fewkes, who had joined the staff in 1897, complained that in his experience things has just "drifted along" without guidance. Investigations had always been determined more by personality than by problem: "If they could get a good man to do work in any field," he stated, "they got him, and he brought in his results, and they catalogued them under the different sciences." Correlation of effort was totally absent: "Anyone that wants to go out [in the field] makes a strong appeal and he goes out," Fewkes added. He contrasted the Washington work with the American Museum of Natural History's current program, the Jesup Expedition organized by Boas:

> Take the New York people. They start with a question of the trail of migration of the Indian from the Old to the New World via Behring Strait, the so-called Jesup expedition. Men are sent to different points to study. There is a correlated plan of effort to which the endeavors of these men are directed.

What the Bureau needed, he suggested, was "a certain definite plan," in which "we could work in harmony, and it would be much better."[12]

John N. B. Hewitt, a member of the Bureau since the mid-eighties, confirmed Adler's impression that the Bureau was not a "close corporation." "You could work in the same office with an ethnologist, ten of you in all, for ten years, and although you were speaking acquaintances, you do not seem to have collaborated very closely," Adler surmised. Hewitt agreed that "each man had his own work and stuck to it."[13] As a result, Matilda Stevenson summarized, Powell and McGee's organization had become not "a Mecca for scientific men to come to and to believe in," but "a place at which scientific men all over the country shrug their shoulders."[14]

Powell's tendency to accumulate materials without publishing them bothered the committee deeply. The hoarding was a result of his desire to release only final results—Powell's "determinate knowledge"—and it had infuriated contemporaries for years. A decade earlier, in fact, Otis Mason had described to Langley the resistance to Powell's Bureau from elsewhere in the country. Opponents at that time, as Mason saw it, included Putnam, Alice Fletcher, and Daniel Brinton, and their reasons for dissatisfaction included "the alleged exclusive spirit of the Bureau in reference to material in its possession and withheld both from publication and from the privilege of investigation."[15] At about the same time another critic had reminded the Washington men that the public and the scientific community had more interest in the scientific process than in the grand generalizations that arrogant government men chose to reveal.[16] This proprietary attitude had prevented respected anthropologists, such as Putnam and Brinton, from enjoying access to Bureau data. It had even kept the researches of some BAE personnel, such as Gatschet, from reaching the public.[17] Joseph H. McCormick, who worked with the Bureau on a part-time basis in the nineties, added that "the criticism that I find in travelling over the country by outside anthropologists is that by the time the material is published it is old and practically valueless, because it has been anticipated by other colleges and museums or something of that sort."[18] Boas deplored Powell's retention of material, which had resulted, he said, in large amounts of unfinished, possibly useless material. Boas's criticism was part of his general stance on the importance of publishing data. While government science should not be limited to publication of facts without "ultimately trying to draw the widest, and consequently most useful inferences," he suggested, at the same time no scientist had the right "to present the conclusions he has drawn without giving to the world the facts on which his conclusions are based."[19]

Boas's remarks to the committee exposed additional dilemmas in the young profession of anthropology. By the turn of the century, Boas, as previously discussed, was formulating his own plans for anthropology in the United States. The Bureau was pivotal for the future of linguistic work; indeed, during Holmes's tenure as BAE chief, Boas took complete charge of Bureau linguistics. But the previous arrangements between Boas and the Bureau for his linguistic work and that of his students encountered deep suspicion from Smithsonian officers. To the committee Boas defended his joint expeditions of the previous decade for the Bureau and the American Museum. The joint efforts, he argued, had provided linguistic material for the Bureau and ethnographic data for the Museum at minimum cost. For John Swanton's early Haida work, for example, the BAE paid only his salary of $700, while the New York museum took care of all field expenses. In return the BAE received a Haida grammar and a large collection of texts. The equivalent results by the BAE alone would have cost an additional $1,200, Boas estimated. Furthermore, the cooperation was a natural division of interests:

> I wanted to have full information on the social organization of the Haida, and to get this it was necessary to collect, in the original language, the whole history of the families. We cannot handle all these texts in New York; we have not the means of working out grammars; we cannot engage men to do philological work. Therefore, we could afford to turn over the philological work to the Bureau of Ethnology . . .[20]

The integrated nature of anthropology was uppermost in Boas's mind, and it required multiple approaches to cultural phenomena. This dissolved questions of institutional loyalty. The investigator cared only about the intricacies of the problem at hand, with no thought of the ultimate disbursement of his findings. In the cases of his own students Boas instructed them to collect certain things and to collect with everything they get information in the native language and to obtain grammatical information that is necessary to explain their texts. Consequently the results of their journeys are the following: they get specimens; they get explanations of the specimens; they get connected texts that partly refer to the specimens and partly refer simply to abstract things concerning the people; and they get grammatical information. The line of division is clear; the grammatical material and the texts go to the Bureau, and the specimens with their explanations go to the New York Museum. There is no conflict of any sort.[21]

Under close questioning Boas detailed his methods of working up linguistic materials. He proceeded by stages, during which the notecards moved back and forth between Washington and New York. At each point he "endeavored to put it in such shape that anyone familiar with linguistic methods might take it up, if for some reason or other I could not complete it."[22] Boas's sense of incompleteness and tentativeness in his science marked his testimony throughout.

Smithsonian officers found Boas's methods unorthodox. While he stressed an open-ended, unfinished science, with loyalty transcending local institutions, the committee asked for final products and exhibited a proprietary attitude. They were impatient with tentativeness and distrustful of divided allegiances. The constant recall of materials to New York for further work was particularly irksome. If these linguistic manuscripts were the property of the Bureau, they asked, why were most of them still with Boas? What had the Bureau paid for? The demand for complete materials to justify congressional appropriations indicated growing pressures and frustration with an apparently endless enterprise. It was a lack of understanding that undermined Boas's work with Washington, thus contributing to the isolation of Bureau anthropology over the coming years.

Amidst the swirling institutional change of this period, Boas was unquestionably the central figure, as even Cyrus Adler and his committee grudgingly recognized in 1903. In promoting his view of a broad-based science, Boas had first to reorient the attachments of anthropologists. This was to be, in fact, as important as any specific theoretical or methodological point inculcated by university training. Having suffered personally from the vagaries of local cliques and institutional myopia, Boas was convinced that the parochial pride and gentlemanly enthusiasms that had inspired much nineteenth-century American science must give way to wider horizons and higher intellectual standards. Local academies of science, he lectured Charles D. Walcott in 1902, had outlived their usefulness. Arguing for national publication series framed around disciplinary interests rather than local activities, Boas admitted that "The objection might be raised that by combining forces in this manner each academy would lose its individuality. Personally I should consider this

Franz Boas posing as a Kwakiutl hamatsa dancer for a National
Museum diorama, 1895.

a most desirable effect, but it is very probable that the emotional interest in the welfare of the local bodies may outweigh among many individuals the more general interest in the advancement of science."[23]

In this instance, as in his fight with McGee for exclusive membership in the new American Anthropological Association (which he temporarily lost to McGee's preference for an open organization),[24] Boas stood athwart deep historical patterns of his adopted country. Nor were these the only fronts on which he fought. Anthropology as he foresaw it required full cooperation between museums and those institutions, such as the BAE or university departments, with main interests in nonmaterial culture. But the hoped-for collaboration repeatedly failed—in Chicago, Philadelphia, Washington, New York. In each case personalities and unique conditions played roles, but with the exception of Harvard's Peabody Museum, where the university department grew from an established museum, the consequences were always the same.[25] On this issue Boas was stymied for years, and his frustration was a measure of the strength of the interests that he confronted. But he never abandoned the ideal of a university-museum complex. Writing to Berthold Laufer in 1918 regarding the establishment of an East Asiatic Institute, Boas described the situation he had known through much of his career:

It is, of course, perfectly clear that as long as we have a single professorship without any prospect for occupation for young people, we shall never make any headway, no matter how good a professor may be; neither will your museum work be effective, unless it is placed on a wider basis. My idea would be to take up the plan as we had it in mind about fifteen years ago or more, namely: outline an institution in which both university and museum work should be represented, and in which provision should be made that the young people to be trained will find useful occupation for a number of years until the country is well enough advanced in interest to take up the work in different centers.[26]

Laufer pursued his career at the Field Museum in Chicago, which provides an instructive illustration of the institutional flux and the prominence of Boas after the turn of the century. In Chicago the failure to meld university and museum anthropology was almost total.[27] The officers and trustees of the Field Museum were ambitious and hopeful that their museum in the midwestern capital would soon overtake other museums of natural history and anthropology, and they set out in 1894 to obtain the best collections that money could buy. Frederick Putnam had hoped that the Field would become "an everlasting memorial of the [1893] Exposition," particularly of his own department of anthropology at the fair, but by 1894 it was clear to him that the "grand opportunity for science [had been] made such a football" that local politics rather than science would dominate.[28] Putnam warned Edward H. Thompson, his archaeological agent in Yucatan, to avoid Chicago: "You need a quiet, conservative, scientific life in order to do your best work. In Chicago all would be drive and rush and largely sensational effects. That is what they are now after, and it is natural in a place which has started out with great hopes and plenty of money and a feeling that money will do anything. By and by they will realize that while money is an important factor in the work, it alone will not make a scientific institution."[29]

During the formative months of the Field Museum in early 1894, Boas outlined a plan of development for the department of anthropology. The Boas plan featured two points: increased collections from different continents to illustrate the main theme of the department, namely, human development under different environments; and completion of the American collections, which already constituted eighty percent of the total acquisitions and which Boas considered among the most valuable in the country. Boas was attempting, in short, to balance the educational and scientific functions of the Museum.[30] Over the next decade, first under Holmes (1894–97) and then under George A. Dorsey, the Boas plan guided the department's growth, but not in Boas's spirit. In 1897, for instance, Holmes instructed Dorsey to undertake an absurdly ambitious collecting trip for the Museum. Dorsey's itinerary took him to Montana, Washington, British Columbia, California, and the Southwest, all in the course of a few weeks. His purposes were diverse: "You are to endeavor in the first place to secure collections illustrating the physical characteristics of the principal Ethnic groups visited, and in the second to collect materials and data for the construction of certain culture groups illustrative of the great culture provinces into which your work may carry you." Holmes's further instructions made clear that the goal of Dorsey's reconnaissance bore little resemblance to Boas's call for in-depth, holistic study. Holmes, always as much artist as anthropologist, aimed at eye-catching synopses of peoples:

> The goal is the erection of Museum group exhibits representing at least four of the principal ethnic groups, viz: the hunter peoples of the great plains, the cedar-carving peoples of the Northwest Coast, the basket-making tribes of California, and the stone house builders of Arizona and New Mexico. The general idea of these Museum exhibit groups is that they should include life size models of the men, women, and children of the typical community selected to represent the group, and that these figures should be represented as engaged in some characteristic occupation and surrounded by such of their belongings as may be conveniently brought together and displayed.[31]

Dorsey, who succeeded Holmes as curator of anthropology and remained in that position until 1915, continued to dream of amassing the premier collections of North American aboriginal cultures.[32] Due to his Chicago appointment, which came at an early age, his training under Putnam (and later briefly under Boas), and his clear independence of Washington, Dorsey enjoyed a potentially powerful position in American anthropology. But like Holmes in Washington, Dorsey seems never to have asserted himself against the desires of the museum director and patrons; nor did he make overtures of cooperation toward Frederick Starr and the fledgling anthropology department at the University of Chicago.

Boas sensed Dorsey's tendency to drift. Dorsey deeply respected Boas and wished above all to be included among his inner circle. Boas's influence was "the greatest factor in our science today," he wrote on the occasion of the Boas *Festschrift* in 1907. "I for one believe that I fully realize what this means, but I can only come to a full realization of it all when I try to conceive what we were before you came among us and what we would have been had you not come. Every worker in anthropology is indebted to you, and the amount of his success may be measured by the extent of his indebtedness. It seems to me that I can wish for nothing higher than that your students may be worthy of their master."[33] If Dorsey expected to be recognized as one of those worthy students, he was disappointed. Berthold Laufer, who worked with Dorsey at Field Museum and whom Boas valued most highly among American workers in 1903,[34] once referred to Dorsey's "terrifying superficialness"; it was an estimation that Boas shared.[35]

The upstart nature of Chicago science annoyed Boas no less than it had Putnam. Moreover, there was his own humiliation in Chicago in 1894 to chill Boas's interest in Dorsey's museum. Introducing Fay-Cooper Cole to Boas in 1906, Dorsey explained that he was especially "desirous that he should receive the benefit of your instruction in linguistic methods, and in the second place, I am desirous that he should obtain the ability to define and investigate ethnological problems from your point of view." Cole dutifully arrived at Columbia at mid-semester and reported progress to Dorsey, but Boas was not impressed: "Of course, I shall do what I can for Mr. Cole, but he seems to be too much in a hurry, and expects to be able to do too much inside of the two months and a half of this term that remain."[36] The following year Dorsey arranged to spend two months studying linguistics with Boas, in connection with his Pawnee studies, as "sufficient proof, if any were needed, of my serious desire to have the benefit of some work with you." Although he came to New York, Boas was unreceptive. "I think that if you want to get familiar with linguistic methods," he advised the Chicagoan, "you have to allow more time for it than you seem to think necessary. It seems to me that Mr. Cole was altogether too hasty in his work and tried to cover too much in a very short time. Of course, the whole matter was new to him, and he may have the impression that he learned a great deal, but it is only a most elementary foundation that he got. If you simply want to know how we go about linguistic work, of course you can get that idea within a reasonable time, and I shall be very glad to do all I can to help you. I have, of course, my own researches on hand, and I shall not be able to give more than a certain limited time to you, unless I should want to take up the study of Pawnee myself."[37]

The relations with Dorsey and the Field Museum demonstrate that Boas was a tough taskmaster for his science, tolerating little frivolity where his students were concerned—and he chose those students himself. The outstanding quality of J. Alden Mason, he judged, was that "he appreciates how much he has to learn." Of William Mechling, who was a student at Harvard in 1916, Boas was uncertain "on account of the ease with which he was distracted from his work by amusements of various sorts." (Although Boas hastened to add that "I do not hold this particularly against him, because a good many young men who turn out very good later on have that characteristic.")[38] The frequent remarks about personality linked Boas with the world of Powell and McGee, indicating that there was still strong paternalism within Boasian professionalism. In Leslie Spier, Boas recognized and sympathized with a kindred spirit, and his comments are worth recording:

> He is very careful and painstaking, and knows something about biological, archaeological, and ethnological character. He has ideals and is true to them, even if his loyalty brings about discomforts. Connected with this is a certain unyielding position which is easily taken for conceit, but I feel that, as he grows older, he outgrows the difficulties which result from this peculiarity.

> He is without doubt the most independent and intelligent thinker that I have had for a long time. He still lacks the broad foundation that a man like [H. K.] Haeberlin had, but he is a serious student and absolutely truthful in his search for truth. He used to be rather difficult in his personal relations with other people, but his angles and corners are wearing off very rapidly and he is quite a different man now from what he used to be a few years ago. Some people think that he is conceited, but that is a very unfair judgment. It is rather shyness and intolerance of dogmatism that gives the impression.[39]

It is doubtful that Boas ever wrote more lucid descriptions of himself than these reflective passages on Spier.

Thus between 1900 and 1920, Boas's influence grew steadily through his own driving energies and those of his students, and new centers of activity, such as Chicago and Berkeley, claimed increasing attention and funds. Powell's Bureau, however, emerged from the 1903 investigation tarnished and demoralized. In the late summer, John Swanton described to Boas the uncomfortable conditions under Langley's "dictatorship":

> I think this atmosphere of suspicion, meanness, and political pulling and hauling about the worst for any young man of energy and high scientific ideals. I see a splendid field open to the Bureau, but until it

is headed by a real able sympathetic ethnologist I do not believe it can properly make use of its opportunities. Where editors and private secretaries flourish while scientific workers are backlisted [sic], where compilation is made to count for more than original research, and where talk runs on saving a hundred dollars [rather than] on solving ethnological problems, what scientific future can we look forward to and what inducements are there for scientists?[40]

The Powell-McGee Bureau appeared an inefficient, highly exclusive agency, molded by Powell's theories despite claims of inductive science. While jealously guarding materials from outsiders, the BAE had suffered from lack of a research program beyond the whims of individuals. Finally, it was irrelevant to public needs.

There was truth in the picture, for the Bureau had indeed been founded on the individual. Matilda Stevenson recalled that "my instructions were usually these from Major Powell: 'Go and do the best you can, you know best how to pursue your work and I know that you will accomplish all that is possible.'"[41] If this meant lack of planning, it was because Powell's early scientific career had confirmed his faith that the path to general truth lay in ever-greater accumulation of facts and that the scientist must follow his genius. He assumed that if one ethnologist died, any competent successor could work up the notes—thus his willingness to withhold materials for years. Again and again, early personal experiences seemed to determine the institutional forms and behavior of later years. McGee caught this important truth for his and perhaps every generation when, late in life, he wrote to Walcott: "You may recall that both Powell and I began scientific work at our own cost and not for salary; and we never got over the habit."[42]

In the wake of the investigation a number of blueprints for future Bureau anthropology appeared, all of them designed to return the agency to public purpose. By 1900 many influential Americans were deeply concerned about the quality of the "American stock" and the effects of mixing with Indians, Blacks, Orientals, and others, and they demanded that the government discover the scientific facts about race mixture. In early 1904, attempting to mollify congressional critics and avoid appropriation cuts, Langley and Alexander Graham Bell, a Regent of the Smithsonian, drew up an outline of future BAE work for Congress. Langley did not welcome active Smithsonian involvement in social questions, but encouraged by Bell, he proposed to expand agency activities to include studies of the peoples of Samoa and Hawaii, and he included an ambitious "Biological Study of the People of the United States." Langley voiced both a concern for the country's racial state and a faith in applied anthropology:

The ethnic elements of all nations and races are assembling in America, and are rapidly coalescing. It is the first occurrence of its kind known in history, and is the beginning of an era fraught with the deepest possible interest, historic, scientific, and national. It affords a great, and probably a last, opportunity to witness and record the intermingling of the racial elements of the world and the resultant physical, mental, moral, and pathologic interactions in all stages and in every phase. Shall the opportunity be neglected by the American Government? It is a self-evident fact that a knowledge of the elements with which a nation has to deal is the first essential to intelligent administration of these elements . . . Science can have no greater purpose than to lay the foundation for the future molding of the racial destinies of the United States—to so determine the results of the mingling of white, black, red, and yellow races on the longevity, fecundity, vigor, liability to disease, moral and intellectual qualities, and to so fully understand the operations of heredity and the effects of changing social and climatic conditions, as to frame and administer wise laws regarding these subjects, and to direct the policy of the thousands of institutions that deal with the racial welfare of the nation.[43]

Bell approved Langley's plan, but in revising the proposal he stressed the importance to the nation of the biological or, as he preferred, ethnological survey. Bell saw a "new people" gradually evolving in the United States, and he hoped that "the final result should be the evolution of a higher and nobler type of man—and not deterioration of the nation."[44]

In his last report as acting director of the BAE (1902), McGee had outlined his own "Applied Ethnology," which included a prominent place for laboratory and field work in physical anthropology. Noting that "the time is at hand for applying the principles of the New Ethnology to American aborigines as ethnic constituents of a growing citizenship," McGee observed that "many of the practical problems connected with immigration, Chinese exclusion, the occupation of Porto Rico, Hawaii, and the Philippines, and the education of the colored race can finally be solved only in the light of ethnologic principles. . . . These and other weighty considerations have led to the inauguration of researches in physical anthropology." He explained to Boas that he intended to develop beside the "purely scientific branch" of the Bureau a "practical branch" to determine "the citizenship value of both pure and mixed Indians." It was time "to utilize the principles developed during the formative period [of Bureau anthropology] and to apply them to the welfare of the nation." McGee prepared another outline, which Boas presented to the Smithsonian Regents on McGee's behalf in December, in which he pictured himself as the proponent of a socially relevant agency and reminded the Regents that "it was my purpose gradually to transform the Bureau from a special and purely scientific office to one of more general and practical character."[45] This had never come about, he contended, because Powell had argued that "We must leave something for McGee, and besides, I am an old man now, and I do not want to do it."[46]

Predictably, Boas presented the most ambitious program. He had a great stake in Bureau operations, and he tended to blame Powell rather than McGee for the Bureau's loss of direction and contraction in scope. Powell's antipathy to physical anthropology had kept the Bureau from developing into the "Ethnological Survey" of the American population (including Blacks, mestizos, and mulattos) that Boas also foresaw. In addition to work in physical anthropology, Boas emphasized investigations with "practical bearings," such as the effects of White education and missionary teaching on Indian amalgamation with White society.

In late 1903 he prepared a prospectus on the "Organization of the Bureau of American Ethnology," presented to the Smithsonian Regents late in that year. His program deserves attention. Boas defined two broad areas of activity for the Bureau: further study of the early, unwritten history of the American Indians, as Powell had pursued; and study of the "Effects of Social and Climatic Adaptation and of Race Mixture in America." Under Powell the purely scientific had received emphasis, while application had been largely ignored. Boas proposed to correct this imbalance with a reinvigorated Bureau.[47]

Physical anthropology was the heart of Boas's plan. For years he had promoted and directed anthropometric studies as an integral part of anthropology. In *Science* magazine Boas argued that "the physical and mental characteristics of Indian half-bloods, of negroes and mulattoes, and the effects of adaptation and amalgamation of the many European nationalities that settle in our country" were proper fields of work for the Bureau. And he told Bell that anthropologists had wished for years that the Bureau would be extended to include race mixture, so that reliable information would be available to guide legislation on race problems.[48]

To the Regents, Boas outlined a five-year, $800,000 program for the Bureau. (The annual BAE budget at the time varied between $30,000 and $40,000.) Comparing the Bureau to the American Museum of Natural History, he found that the BAE spent $6,000 working up every $1,000 of field work, while the corresponding office expense in New York was only $1,600. Since the large permanent staff at the Bureau meant high administrative expenditures, Boas advised that the Bureau start with a small core of young scientists and cooperate extensively with anthropologists employed by other institutions, just as he had worked with Powell. Bureau money should be confined to research and, unlike past practice, never be used to pay for specimens for the National Museum. By cutting the staff to a minimum, Boas estimated, general administration could be limited to about $21,000 a year.

But this was only the administrative budget. He divided Bureau activities into the "historical" work of the ethnologists and the "amalgamation of races" work of the physical anthropologists. Typically, Boas fitted his vision to his audience, matching urgency with large demands. Boas predicted that within twenty years the North American tribes would have disappeared altogether, so that the ethnological work was necessarily limited in time. He estimated that about 450 separate field trips (of unspecified length) would be necessary to record the ethnology of the vanishing tribes of North America. This work would be done by "special agents," not regular Bureau employees. Although fewer than ten trained men were available in 1903, Boas thought that a sufficient number could be trained within five years to cover everything. He proposed a similar program of special agents for archaeological work, noting that here, too, at least ten competent archaeologists could be trained in five years. The entire ethnological budget, including permanent BAE ethnologists, special agents, archaeologists, and administration, rose from $76,000 in the first year to $170,000 in the fifth.

This large allotment still did not include the work in physical anthropology, which was the "general anthropological survey" that Boas envisioned. While the historical work would eventually die out with its subject matter, Boas predicted that the work of the physical anthropologists "will prove to be beneficial in so many different lines, that its continuance and expansion will become necessary."[49] Here again trained men were not immediately available, so that in the first year only $12,000 would be required for this work. Boas anticipated that as the purely ethnological work decreased and eventually ceased altogether, the importance of the applied anthropology would grow and ultimately dominate the Bureau. In this way the Bureau would develop by 1920 into a complete, ongoing "Anthropological Survey" of the racial elements of the nation.

The Bureau of Ethnology never became an anthropological survey of the American people. Holmes proved to be a weak administrator who permitted the Bureau to slide under the supervision of Langley and, after Langley's death in 1906, of Charles D. Walcott, an old friend from Geological Survey and Chicago days. Bureau correspondence passed through the Institution's offices, and the BAE offices moved from the Adams building on F Street down to the Mall. Thus was the Bureau subordinated and disciplined to the larger institution, so that "airplane builders and geologists were now making final decisions in the field of anthropology." In her study of the Holmes years, Virginia Noelke has further concluded that while Powell "left the BAE without a clear definition or purpose," eight years later "Holmes left a scientific agency which had no important role in either the field of anthropology or in the [government] bureaucracy."[50] Unable to compete with foundations and universities for funds and trained personnel, the Bureau also had difficulty living up to political demands for applied science.

The dilemmas of the Bureau extended well beyond the shortcomings of Holmes. Even with more assertive leadership, the Bureau after Powell would

William Henry Holmes with a friend on the Washington Mall, summer of 1871; and in his office at the BAE, winter of 1904.

have been buffeted about by currents of professional change. While new people were in training with Boas and Putnam and soon with Kroeber, the BAE staff was aging. Mooney and Stevenson continued field work whenever possible, but John Swanton's unceasing linguistic and ethnological work represented the only infusion of fresh enthusiasm. Significantly, Swanton was a student of both Putnam and Boas. Holmes was not unaware of the problem, but he was powerless. He wisely freed Swanton for field work while most of the staff was manacled to the *Handbook*, and he bemoaned the lost opportunities caused by government restrictions:

> It is a constant regret to me that the Bureau is not able to add to its forces at least a few of the promising young students trained by . . . teachers in the field of anthropology, but the conditions under which our work is directed make this next to impossible.

To another correspondent Holmes specified one of those conditions when he noted simply that "few die and none resign in the Government service."[51]

Holmes was a tired man of fifty-six when he reluctantly assumed the reins of the Bureau. For this shy but proud man, the nasty dispute with McGee was a shattering climax to more than two decades of government science. His own archaeological field work was largely over by 1902, and he spent the rest of his long life (until 1933) defending opinions formed early on, notably his skepticism toward all claims for Paleolithic man in the New World. As Boas had anticipated, museum matters occupied most of Holmes's attention, and he traveled frequently on museum and exposition business. Part of 1904 was devoted to the International Congress of Americanists in Stuttgart and a subsequent tour of European museums reminiscent of Mason's tour of 1889. In 1908–09, Holmes traveled to Santiago, Chile, for the first Pan-American Scientific Congress. In the intervening years domestic fairs, such as the Jamestown Tercentennial of 1906 and the Alaska-Yukon-Pacific Exposition (Seattle, 1908), drained him further.

Honors came to Holmes now, and after years in the shadows of Powell and McGee he savored them. William H. Dall thought the recognition long overdue: "There is more or less human nature mixed up with all the affairs of man, and pure justice is strictly supernatural and not to be counted on here below," Dall wrote in congratulating Holmes on his election to the National Academy of Science in 1905. Holmes may have been, as his daughter-in-law claimed, "an avowed materialist," but he selected Dall's letter for inclusion in his scrapbook memoirs.[52] In Chile, too, he basked in honor at the Pan-American meetings: "I dined with the [Pedro] Moutts in Santiago Chile 1909; sat at his left and he pared a peach for me and ordered a special bottle of wine," Holmes inscribed on a photograph of the Chilean president.[53]

Holmes wished at long last to place archaeology in a central position within American anthropology.[54] New World archaeology, ethnology, and historical research had traveled separate paths through the nineteenth century, but a hope for synthesis had grown, especially with southwestern and Central American students, from the 1870s. Putnam had rejoiced to Morgan in 1876 that "the data exists for a better understanding than we have had before & that such men as Morgan & [Adolphe] Bandelier are living & ready for the work. My own work," he continued, "has been so entirely from objects & not from books that I find much in all you & he write that is confirmatory of what I do from specimens as to prove that careful work from both these sources will in time clear up much which is now dark and mysterious."[55] Bandelier, too, saw the necessity of multiple approaches, but he leaned to library and ethnological research, and he disdained archaeologists for their ignorance of the Spanish chroniclers and of living peoples: "It is my firm belief," he had advised Morgan, "that much more can be realized out of the aboriginal clusters in Mexico, Guatemala, and in Yucatan as they are found at this present day, than from any survey of Palenqué, Uxmal, and Chichen-Itza."[56]

Thus recognition of the desirability of collaboration had dawned, even as personal and institutional limitations prevented implementation. Discounting or choosing to postpone archaeological work, Powell had pursued the North American mounds survey partly as a result of congressional and Smithsonian pressures. By contrast, Holmes felt that as archaeology entered the twentieth century, it stood prepared to make essential, unique contributions to the science of man. To the assemblage in Stuttgart he announced that "when the results achieved [by archaeologists] are supplemented by the rich materials furnished by a study of the living peoples, they must go far toward illuminating the pages of the story of humanity which the Old World has been gradually but surely revealing."[57]

Holmes promoted Bureau archaeology in two ways: by continuing his crusade against claims for Paleolithic man in America, and by supporting Jesse W. Fewkes's work in the Southwest and the Caribbean. While he no longer took to the field himself, the Chief worked through others, notably Gerard Fowke, in explaining away signs of glacial or preglacial man in America. Holmes's determined efforts derived in part from his conviction, established years before, that Old World categories must not be imported and imposed on American prehistory. "So far as the use of the terms 'paleolithic' and 'neolithic' are concerned they may both be omitted from the literature of American archeology without loss if not to possible advantage," he stated in 1904. At the same time, he confessed, American scholars had failed to establish a convincing cultural chronology:

> Hundreds of ancient caves have been searched with only negative results; glacial gravels have been examined with great care but the returns are exceedingly meager; river terraces, and kitchen midden deposits, yield

nothing of particular value, and the results, when viewed as a whole, instead of enlightening the mind, fill it rather with confusion. It is within the bounds of possibility that this confusion may in a measure be due to the presence in America of an autochthonous race element.[58]

Holmes's blindness resulted from the focus of his vision: seeking major statements about New World race history, insisting on seeing widespread, disparate observations as a whole, he discouraged study of local microchange. While he was aware of new trends, he served old purposes.

Much the same can be said of Fewkes's archaeology in the Southwest and the Caribbean. Fewkes seems to have been widely disliked and distrusted; Cushing was only the first of his detractors. The antipathy may have been due in part to his loyalty to Langley, the Smithsonian, and the needs of the National Museum. While he was certainly never a mere pot-hunter, institutional bonds and his own inclinations did delimit his archaeology.[59] Because he followed Cushing and Bandelier in the Southwest and was familiar with developments at the Peabody Museum, Fewkes was sensitive to the possibilities of an approach to the prehistory of the Southwest such as both Putnam and Holmes had hoped to establish. Fewkes's article, "The Prehistoric Culture of Tusayan," published in 1896, in fact suggested such a program.[60]

But Fewkes was unable to follow through. After his discovery of the striking Sikyatki pottery in the mid-nineties, he continued southwestern research into Hopi ethnology and history with funds drawn by Langley from the Secretary's Bureau reserve. Then, following the Spanish-American War, he switched to the Caribbean for collecting and theorizing about the roots and spread of Antillean culture. Like the BAE flirtation with Hawaiian ethnology in these years (which produced minimal results), Fewkes's Caribbean foray followed the course of empire more than the logic of science. His work, while pioneering, was less than notable, and at times he elected to purchase collections rather than excavate deeply. After the establishment of Mesa Verde National Park in 1906, Fewkes assumed responsibility for preparing various sites for public visit, exclusively excavating major cliff dwellings and mesa cities.[61]

Despite indefatigable labors, Fewkes lacked focus or depth. In the nineteenth-century tradition of the Cyrus Thomas mounds survey, he undertook reconnaissance of large areas, addressing broad questions and amassing material collections. In contrast to Alfred V. Kidder's decades of work at Four Corners and Pecos, Fewkes did not excavate fully or consider local developments sufficiently. While the nature of his archaeology could produce occasional new discoveries, they were theoretically sterile.

Holmes pushed government anthropology in another important new direction, but here too the locus of innovation was the National Museum. Reversing Powell's priorities, he brought serious work in physical anthroplogy to Washington for the first time by hiring Aleš Hrdlička and setting up a division for him in the Museum. Over the following decades Hrdlička became a fixture in Smithsonian anthropology and a dominant force in his profession. The story of Holmes and Hrdlička lies beyond the scope of this discussion, but it should be noted that the two men built a firm rapport based on several commonalities: skepticism toward Paleolithic man, dislike of Boas and Germans generally, loyalty to the Smithsonian Institution, and stubborn scrappiness. In his dying days Holmes wrote to his old friend that "[I] miss you, miss you very much. . . . And those lunch hours were a tonic which there is nothing to replace." For his part Hrdlička recalled (to Frederick Hodge) stirring scientific battles and lamented that "one after another of the 'old guard' is passing away. . . . Ten years hence there will be hardly a soul left of our generation, but this is quite all right if only one could be more hopeful of some of the youngsters."[62]

The Holmes years, in sum, were a prolonged struggle to define new purpose and interest for the Bureau. The constant awareness of public scrutiny warped and inhibited its anthropology. Holmes extended the BAE reach to the Caribbean and the Pacific; he became a strong proponent of government preservation of antiquities and sought a major role for the Bureau in their management; he encouraged Swanton's field work and Fewkes's archaeology, while abdicating Bureau linguistics almost entirely to the man most capable of advancing it, Boas. Finally, he sought out and supported Hrdlička for the Museum. The Bureau was hardly moribund as a scientific agency, but it continued to drift.

The professional difficulties of Holmes's organization were distilled in the major publication and preoccupation of the Bureau: *The Handbook of American Indians North of Mexico*. The *Handbook* appeared in two large volumes (1907, 1910) under Langley's insistent direction and Hodge's dutiful, competent editing. As it finally emerged, the *Handbook* was not so much the culmination of Powellian anthropology as a testimony to changed times, both in Washington and in American anthropology. While referring to public utility Powell had intended his "cyclopedia" as a scientific tool for intelligent laymen. Langley appealed to the memory of the Major but ordered a handbook for politicians and their favored constituents in order to bolster appropriations and his sagging reputation. The volumes were immensely popular but—final irony for a bureau founded by Powell—so few were placed at the Bureau's disposal that requests had to be turned down.

The *Handbook* was a model of nineteenth-century popular science—a generation late. Drawing on virtually the entire anthropological community, Holmes and Hodge mixed invaluable synonymy, bibliography, history, census statistics, and respectable ethnography with occasional judgmental generalization. Of the Eskimo, for example, Henshaw and Swanton wrote: "In disposition the Eskimo may be described as peaceful, cheerful, truthful, and honest, but exceptionally loose in sexual morality." Elsewhere in the article the authors distinguished the several branches of the Eskimauan stock, as determined by Boas and others' meticulous work, and provided a full bibliography.[63]

Holmes described the *Handbook* as a "comprehensive treatise" that would give rise to a supplementary series of specialized handbooks, including Boas's *Handbook of American Indian Languages* (1911) and Holmes's *Handbook of Aboriginal American Antiquities* (1919).[64] The *Handbook of American Indians* did occasion some new research and summary of past years' work, especially among the Bureau staff, but the enterprise was fundamentally at odds with the developing profession of anthropology. It was not simply that the project kept the BAE staff at their desks for at least five years. More importantly, the *Handbook*, a reflection of Langley's attitude toward anthropology, assumed a contracting rather than an expanding, deepening field. The compilation, Hodge predicted, "will eventually represent a complete summary of existing knowledge respecting the aborigines of northern America."[65] Hodge was restating Powell's old dream of comprehensiveness and ultimate knowledge, but by 1906 this was an expectation that had been belied and undermined by the history of the Bureau itself. The image of anthropology as a terminal enterprise, dying out with its subject matter, directly contradicted the notions of continuity and an inquiring community being nurtured, at great personal expense and exertion, in Cambridge, New York, and elsewhere. Quite aside from its clear merits as a resource book in anthropology, the *Handbook* was a fascinating historical product of clashing suppositions and grinding institutional change.

Boas's estrangement from Washington anthropology grew after 1903, despite his position as Honorary Philologist in the Bureau; but it did not in itself condemn Smithsonian anthropology to backwardness or irrelevance. The alienation was, rather, indicative of deep differences of critical perspective within the American anthropological community. Those differences never surfaced for direct confrontation. In retrospect it is possible to watch Boas building his case piece by piece, in linguistics, racial studies, and ethnology, against the linked formal categories of nineteenth-century evolutionism.[66] If his critique was largely complete in its basic elements by 1896, its implications were not apparent to many at the time; nor was he in a position to present it forcefully. The Spanish-American War of 1898, Boas later claimed, was his "rude awakening," for it revealed the American nation to him as "a young giant, eager to grow at the expense of others, and dominated by the same desire of aggrandizement that sways the narrowly confined European states."[67] As the myth of American exceptionalism burst for Boas, his sense of urgency to combat American intolerance and ignorance increased. He became more strident and aggressive.

The consequences of American war and imperialism were thus radically different for Boas and for the Washington men. Finally established at Columbia University and the American Museum, Boas began two decades of academic entrepreneurship, deeply enmeshing himself in teaching, administrative machinations, and untiring promotion of anthropology. As his appeals to Morris K. Jesup, Phoebe Hearst, Archer Huntington, and others demonstrate, he was entirely pragmatic, perfectly willing to take advantage of the whims of America's capitalist elite to promote his science.[68] Just as Powell had worked twenty years earlier to carve out scientific autonomy within the only institution then capable of funding anthropology, the federal government, Boas now labored singlemindedly toward independent bases for a critical social science.

Boas's institutional drive followed directly from the deepest lessons of his anthropology and from his American experience. In the United States, he came to see, the strength of unreasoning tradition and emotional attachments still blinded men to the truths of humane intelligence: that "others may abhor where we worship," and that consequently self-restraint rather than self-assertion is the highest duty of the nation.[69] Under such discouraging conditions, Boas's moral science required an institutional base from which to promote rational inquiry free of economic indebtedness, political dependence, or cultural myopia. In short, the basic tenets of Boasian anthropology, the structures he worked to create, and his long crusade against racial, ethnic, and cultural intolerance formed a single fabric of activist, humane social science. In 1916 he stated once again the basic point of his dispute with Mason and Powell in 1887, but it was now confirmed by thirty years of personal and professional history:

> As a matter of fact, the number of people in our country who are willing and able to enter into the modes of thought of other nations is altogether too small. The American, on the whole, is inclined to consider American standards of thought and action as absolute standards, and the more idealistic his nature, the more strongly he wants to "raise" everyone to his own standards. For this reason the American who is cognizant only of his own standpoint sets himself up as arbiter of the world.[70]

For Smithsonian/BAE anthropologists, the expansionism and domestic issues of the Roosevelt years taught differently. As discussed above, Holmes no less than Boas encouraged an expanded scope for anthropology, first to Central and South America, then to the U.S. insular possessions. For Boas it was a question of combating American narcissism and provincialism with exposure to other cultures; his intentions had changed little since the 1893 Exposition. It is difficult to find any such critique in the scientific expansionism of Holmes or Langley. Their science in the public service, it must be said, came to mean loyalty to American ways.

As he reached the height of his career in the science of man, Holmes, it turned out, was no less prone than McGee had been to making grand pronouncements on human affairs of the past, present, and future. In his version of human evolution the role of physical environment was somewhat greater than it had been for Powell, thus removing some of the stigma of cultural backwardness. But his evaluation of aboriginal New World cultures was low, and his environmentalism lay as a thin veil over a racial hierarchy. The evolutionism that Holmes had adopted at an early point did not promote greater tolerance; rather it became another tool for legitimizing conquest and the submission of other peoples. The less fortunate peoples of the earth, he believed, owed their status not to inherent racial inadequacies but to traits acquired from specific environmental conditions. They were doomed in either case, of course, but they had been equal at the creation. This was a comforting thought for men who, like Holmes, still believed in the American ideals of freedom and individual opportunity. If men had begun biologically unequal to the struggle, thereby scientifically predestined to extinction or prosperity, human evolution lost all moral meaning. If, on the other hand, all men had begun with equal possibilities but in a cosmos of differing environments, some of which encouraged thrift and inventiveness while others retarded such progress, success and prosperity could be earned and justified. Holmes's anthropology was always a curious blend of biology, religion, and politics, and perhaps it offered reassurance to people in the midst of urbanization, social stratification, and ambivalent imperialism. Certainly it satisfied Holmes. He implied a stern but just creative force, and portrayed a world in which the hard-working, thrifty individual, like the hardy, tempered race, rightly succeeded. In Holmes the apology and explanation for Anglo-Saxon dominance at home and abroad, for the disappearance of "inferior" types everywhere, found a staunch scientific spokesman.

More than half a century separated Henry Schoolcraft's 1846 ethnological prospectus to the first meeting of Smithsonian Regents from the BAE blueprints of Boas, McGee, and Langley in 1903. In that interval immense changes took place in the intellectual and institutional scaffolding of American anthropology. Yet in retrospect the developments appear gradual, piecemeal; continuities more than discontinuities seem to characterize the overlapping generations of Schoolcraft and Henry, Morgan, Powell, even Boas.

Science in nineteenth-century America was a moral enterprise. The modern attitude of respect, even veneration, of scientific expertise in this country rests on its strictly secular, problem-solving function: the scientist possesses the treasured knowledge necessary for keeping social and technological machinery running more or less smoothly. Higher claims are accepted only at great risk. In the last century, by contrast, scientists of Joseph Henry's persuasion believed that they were entrusted with the moral conscience and future welfare of America. Surrounded by a grasping, impious culture, the scientist had a momentous task: to turn men back, as their clerical fathers and grandfathers had done, to nature and nature's God by exposing them to the brilliant order of the universe.[71] At the same time, appropriately, the public would presumably show respect and appreciation for the scientist as the modern shepherd. Not surprisingly, from this viewpoint the needs of society and scientist achieved a comfortable accord.

The role of the American scientific elite, then, embraced two tendencies that coexisted uneasily. The scientist must spread scientific experience among the people as a means of spiritual uplift and social harmony—salvation would have to be known directly, not through hearsay. Concurrently, though, the drive to exclusiveness which rested on the assumption that only the few were truly capable or inclined to devote their lives to science, demanded recognition of separate status. The latter need impelled both the drive against frauds and imposters and efforts to establish means of formal accreditation that characterized American science a hundred years ago. These proved to be difficult tasks. In anthropology, which straddled the classical curricula of moral and natural philosophy, character rather than expertise tended to count heavily. Current theories of perception taught that every man sees clearly and faithfully if not distorted by impure motives—the motives of the scrambling marketplace. Furthermore, desire for scientific coverage of a large continent before its destruction by heavy waves of population led to reliance on honesty rather than formal credentials. Under the circumstances, anthropological observation was necessarily a popular phenomenon.

And yet distinctions did gradually emerge. The scientific experience that the Smithsonian offered to the lay public was really limited to observation; the Institution heightened functional differences by emphasizing gatherers on one hand, theorizers on the other. It at once connected and distinguished among the elite and the democracy in science. Circular questionnaires from Henry King to Schoolcraft, Morgan, Gibbs, and Powell explicitly invited participation even while they directed and systematized, thereby channeling field work.

The Bureau of American Ethnology inherited these patterns and habits. The early BAE struggled to establish scientific criteria in the face of assumptions that resisted formal credentials. Employment in a government bureau had, by the 1890s, itself become a major index of scientific status. Indeed, one of the multiple purposes for which Powell astutely used his publications was the building of his staff. The emphasis varied with the individual. Cushing was the intuitive genius, Mallery the stalwart, honest investigator, J. O. Dorsey the conscientious, sympathetic Christian. There was room for all kinds, but that very flexibility meant that at root the Bureau's requirements remained simple and subjective: honesty and character.

Powell's categories guided the Bureau. His scientific philosophy was grounded in the conviction that most human thought was filled with delusion and error, usually caused by arrogant, unfounded speculation. The Major conceived of his Bureau as a tool for dissolving mystery, for reducing the puzzles of aboriginal America to understandable historical sequences. In theory this was to be accomplished through ever-greater accumulations of data. In the early years especially, the premium lay on new, exciting discoveries—for Cushing, Mallery, and McGee, in fact, the great discovery of profound significance became obligatory.

There was a palpable sense of excitement and promise in those years. The organization of science in Washington was informed by an evolutionary vision that anticipated a single world brotherhood of man, a unified, ecumenical cosmos. The image of American linguistic development—from many small groups speaking diverse, mutually unintelligible languages, to ever-greater concentrations of common culture—seemed to point the way. The multifarious inventions that Mason and Goode organized in the Museum, right up to the telephone and telegraph, seemed to bond men ever more tightly in a common fate. Perhaps most striking to the Washington men was the racial amalgamation already in the process of homogenizing all mankind into a single biological strain. As they looked into the future, they saw that the American Indian, like the Negro, was destined to be absorbed into a swelling stream of common mankind.

The visions of assimilation and of evolution to a world culture might have encouraged resignation and discouraged efforts to reform or aid the Indian. Indeed, the BAE was accused repeatedly by the Bureau of Indian Affairs and others of hampering efforts to educate and civilize the Indians. Powell did not seek, however, simply to preserve Indian customs for scientific study, but rather, as he had first argued in 1874, to provide scientific grounds for gradual, humane reform. But while wise public policy depended on scientific knowledge, he also aggressively insisted that man must take control and responsibility for his destiny, by discovering the laws of nature and employing them for man's welfare. The ambivalence between reform action and positive knowledge is clear in the following summary by McGee of BAE goals:

Ethnologists, like other good citizens, are desirous of raising the Indian to the lofty plane of American citizenship; but they prefer to do this constructively rather than destructively, through knowledge rather than ignorance, through sympathy rather than intolerance—they prefer to pursue in dealing with our immature race the course found successful in dealing with the immature offspring of our own flesh and blood. *Incidentally,* they desire to record those steps in mental and moral progress visible among our aborigines, with the view of tracing the mental and moral progress of all mankind, and thereby more wisely guiding efforts toward future betterment.[72]

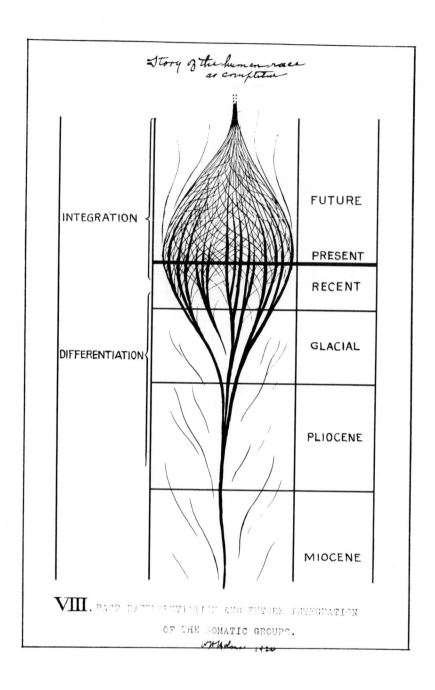

"Story of the Human Race as Completed," sketch by W. H. Holmes, 1920.

Acting on these beliefs, Powell and the Washington anthropologists helped to usher in a new era of government-supported, institutional science. But even as they "organized anthropologic research in America," they retained the contradictory expectations of an earlier period. Like their countrymen busily building the economic, social, political, and educational structures of twentieth-century America, they were ill-prepared for the implications of their acts. Their vigorous assertion of human control sprang from a profound fear that control had already been lost, or abdicated, not to a natural but to a technological, corporate environment that separated man from man.

Here lay the irony for Powell's generation: they molded the forms of modern society but were not modern men. Powell and McGee were interdisciplinary scientists in a sense that cannot be fully recaptured, since they looked for character and certain habits of thought before specific knowledge. Mason retained a piety and wonder toward his work, as well as a simplistic notion of taxonomic science—both revealed his antebellum roots. Powell provided an institutional environment in the Bureau that, in the end, began to alter anthropology in method and data by encouraging a sense of capacity and identity among some staff members. It was a major contribution, but largely unintended.

Unintended results: these more than anything else marked the course of Washington anthropology, as they characterize so much of our modern history. The contours of modern American anthropology formed beyond the borders of intention. They were never really mapped out ahead, even by Boas—though to be sure, he, like Putnam, Brinton, and Powell had his dreams and plans. On the contrary, while they celebrated man's powers of control, Powell and his Washington coworkers backed into the future, carrying into a new century the glorious experiences of one world even as they built another.

Notes

1. James K. Flack, *Desideratum in Washington: The Intellectual Community in the Capital City, 1870–1900* (Cambridge, 1975), p. 158.

2. Michael James Lacey, "The Mysteries of Earth-Making Dissolve: A Study of Washington's Intellectual Community and the Origins of American Environmentalism in the late Nineteenth Century," Ph.D. diss. (George Washington University, 1979), p. 3.

3. Jerry Israel, ed., *Building the Organizational Society: Essays on Associational Activities in Modern America* (New York, 1972).

4. Constance McLaughlin Green, *Washington: Capital City, 1879–1950* (Princeton, 1963):200–01. On the early years of the Carnegie Institution of Washington, see Nathan Reingold, "National Science Policy in a Private Foundation: The Carnegie Institution of Washington," in Alexandra Oleson and John Voss,

eds., *The Organization of Knowledge in Modern America, 1860–1920* (Baltimore, 1979), pp. 313–41.

5. Ibid., pp. 190, 195–96.

6. Ibid., p. 188.

7. Figures are taken from SI, *AR for 1900*, p. LVII.

8. Henry Adams, *The Education of Henry Adams: An Autobiography* (Boston, 1961), p. 331.

9. Boas judged that Powell lost control of the Bureau at an early date because the field of investigation was simply too vast and complex for the series of handbooks that Powell originally planned. Every worker went his own way, Boas thought; and this "chance development" intensified after about 1895. Boas to Robert S. Woodward, 13 January 1905, BP.

10. BAE-IN, p. 838, NAA. (Page numbers refer to the revised transcript of testimony.)

11. Ibid., pp. 288–89.

12. Ibid., pp. 279–83.

13. Ibid., p. 501.

14. Ibid., p. 386.

15. Mason to Langley, 23 June 1891, SIA.

16. E. W. Claypole, "Prof. G. F. Wright and his Critics," *Popular Science Monthly* 42 (1893): 776.

17. Regna D. Darnell, "The Development of American Anthropology, 1879–1920: From the Bureau of American Ethnology to Franz Boas," Ph.D. diss. (University of Pennsylvania, 1969), pp. 81–82.

18. BAE-IN, p. 881.

19. Ibid., pp. 927, 942.

20. Ibid., pp. 918–22.

21. Ibid., p. 922.

22. Ibid., pp. 915–17. For a fuller discussion, see C. M. Hinsley, Jr. and Bill Holm, "A Cannibal in the National Museum: The Early Career of Franz Boas in America," *American Anthropologist* 78 (1976): 306–16.

23. Boas to Walcott, 21 January 1902, BP.

24. George W. Stocking, Jr., "Franz Boas and the Founding of the American Anthropological Association," *American Anthropologist* 62 (1960): 1–17.

25. On museum-university conflicts, see Darnell, "Development," pp. 166–234; and Darnell, "The Emergence of Academic Anthropology at the University of Pennsylvania," *Journal of the History of the Behavioral Sciences* 6 (1970): 80–92.

26. Boas to Laufer, 11 February 1918, FMA.

27. On early Chicago anthropology, see George W. Stocking, Jr., *Anthropology at Chicago: Tradition, Discipline, Department* (Chicago, 1979).

28. Report to the Director [of the 1893 Exposition] for July 1893, FWP; Putnam to C. O. Whitman, 14 March 1894, FWP.

29. Putnam to Thompson, 19 May 1894, FWP.

30. Boas to F. J. V. Skiff, 2 March 1894, FMA.

31. Holmes to George A. Dorsey, 12 May 1897, FMA.

32. See, e.g., Dorsey to Skiff, 17 January and 18 January 1901, FMA.

33. Dorsey to Boas, 24 April 1907, FMA.

34. Boas to Walcott, 7 December 1903, BP. In this interesting letter Boas reviewed and individually evaluated virtually the entire anthropological community.

35. Laufer to Boas, 13 April 1908, BP; quoted in Darnell, "Development," p. 206. Alfred Kroeber has left the following commentary on this point: "George Dorsey once confided to me, in the Palace Hotel in San Francisco before the earthquake of 1906, that Boas was like a tree all over which there grew as fruits those whom he admitted to his friendship—to participation and identification, in modern terms. But those not so admitted would never be close to Boas, and Dorsey himself, for all his trying, remained wholly shut out. For those who remember Dorsey and his energy, self-reliance, competitiveness, and hard-boiled man-of-business manner, this will seem a strangely affecting confession. It shows Boas functioning as a powerful father figure, cherishing and supporting those with whom he identified in the degree that he felt they genuinely were identifying with him, but, as regards others, aloof and probably fundamentally indifferent, coldly hostile if the occasion demanded. A true patriarch, in short, with patriarchal strength and outlook." Kroeber, "The Place of Boas in Anthropology," *American Anthropologist* 58 (1956): 151–59.

36. Dorsey to Boas, 2 February 1906 and 2 March 1906; Boas to Dorsey, 7 March 1906, FMA. Relaying Boas's comment to Cole, Dorsey advised, "Don't let this worry you but do what you can to counteract this impression."

37. Dorsey to Boas, 24 September 1906; Boas to Dorsey, 1 October 1906, FMA.

38. Boas to Dorsey, 27 April 1903; Boas to Laufer, 28 November 1916, FMA.

39. Boas to Laufer, 26 February 1919 and 9 February 1920, FMA.

40. Swanton to Boas, 16 August 1903, BP.

41. BAE-IN, p. 352.

42. McGee to Walcott, 26 January 1910, GP.

43. Minutes of the annual meeting of the Board of Regents, 27 January 1904, SIA. The Langley proposal was actually drafted some months earlier by Holmes. See Holmes to Langley, in WHH 8, sec. 4.

44. Bell to Langley, 3 February 1904, SIA.

45. BAE, *AR for 1902*, pp. ix–xiv; McGee to Boas, 18 September 1903, SIA.

46. BAE-IN, pp. 253–57.

47. Franz Boas, "Organization of the Bureau of American Ethnology," n.d., BP. Boas outlined his ideas briefly before the investigating committee (pp. 933–36, 939–40), but this ms. is a fuller statement.

48. *Science* (21 November 1902), p. 828; Boas to Bell, 9 November 1902, BP; see also Boas to Charles P. Bowditch, 17 December 1903, BP.

49. Boas, "Organization," p. 9.

50. Virginia Noelke, "The Origin and Early History of the Bureau of American Ethnology," Ph.D. diss. (University of Texas at Austin, 1975), pp. 232, 322.

51. Holmes to Frederick Starr, 16 May 1905, NAA; Holmes to G. Stanley Hall, 25 April 1905, NAA. Both letters quoted in Noelke, "Origin and Early History," p. 313.

52. Mary Holmes to Aleš Hrdlička, 22 January 1933, Hrdlička Papers, NAA; W. H. Dall to Holmes, 20 April 1905, WHH 9: 136.

53. WHH 9: 108.

54. See, e.g., "The Place of Archeology in Human History," the introduction to Holmes's *Handbook of Aboriginal American Antiquities, BAE Bulletin* 60, Part I (Washington, D.C., 1919), pp. 1–8.

55. Putnam to Morgan, 18 December 1876, LHM.

56. Bandelier to Morgan, 13 March 1880, LHM.

57. W. H. Holmes, "Contributions of American Archeology to Human History" (21 August 1904), in WHH 9: 227–28.

58. Ibid., pp. 226–27.

59. Noelke, "Origin and Early History," pp. 271, 273. The following discussion of Fewkes draws on Noelke's treatment, pp. 271–77, though the interpretation is mine.

60. J. W. Fewkes, "The Prehistoric Culture of Tusayan," *American Anthropologist,* o.s. 9 (1896): 151–73.

61. Arthur H. Rohn, "The South and Intermontane West" in James E. Fitting, *The Development of North American Archaeology* (Garden City, 1973), p. 190.

62. Holmes to Hrdlička, 3 October 1932; Hrdlička to F. W. Hodge, 24 October 1932, Hrdlička Papers.

63. Frederick W. Hodge, ed., *Handbook of American Indians North of Mexico, BAE Bulletin* 30, Part I (Washington, D.C., 1907), pp. 433–37.

64. Holmes, *Handbook of Aboriginal American Antiquities,* p. xiii.

65. Hodge, *Handbook of Indians,* p. viii.

66. George W. Stocking, Jr., "The Basic Assumptions of Boasian Anthropology," in Stocking, ed., *The Shaping of American Anthropology, 1885–1911: A Franz Boas Reader* (New York, 1974), pp. 1–20.

67. Ibid., pp. 331–32.

68. Ibid., pp. 283–306, esp. 301–03.

69. Ibid., p. 332.

70. Ibid.

71. This nineteenth-century "culture of science" has been brilliantly elucidated by Edward Lurie in his *Nature and the American Mind: Louis Agassiz and the Culture of Science* (New York, 1974).

72. W J McGee, *The Red Man and Helper* (Carlisle, Penn., 1904), p. 2. Emphasis added.

Bibliography

BOOKS AND MONOGRAPHS

Abbott, Charles C. *Primitive Industry.* Salem, Mass.: George A. Bates, 1881.

Adams, Henry. *The Education of Henry Adams: An Autobiography.* Boston: Houghton Mifflin, 1961.

Atwater, Caleb. *Description of the Antiquities of Ohio and Other Historical States. Transactions and Collections of the American Antiquarian Society.* 1. Worcester: American Antiquarian Society, 1820.

Bancroft, George. *History of the United States.* 14th ed. Boston: Little, Brown, 1854.

Bartlett, John R. *The Progress of Ethnology, an Account of Recent Archaeological, Philological, and Geographical Researches in Various Parts of the Globe, tending to elucidate the Physical History of Man. Transactions of the American Ethnological Society* 2. New York: 1848.

Bell, Whitfield J., ed. *A Cabinet of Curiosities: Five Episodes in the Evolution of American Museums.* Charlottesville: University of Virginia Press, 1967.

Berkhofer, Robert F., Jr. *The White Man's Indian: Images of the Indian from Columbus to the Present.* New York: Random House, 1978.

Blackwood, Beatrice. *The Classification of Artifacts in the Pitt Rivers Museum, Oxford.* Oxford: Pitt Rivers Museum, 1970.

Bledstein, Burton J. *The Culture of Professionalism: The Middle Class and the Development of Higher Education in America.* New York: W. W. Norton, 1976.

Boas, Franz. *The Mind of Primitive Man.* New York: Macmillan Co., 1911.

Boller, Paul F., Jr. *American Thought in Transition: The Impact of Evolutionary Naturalism, 1865–1900.* Chicago: Rand McNally, 1969.

Brew, John O., ed. *One Hundred Years of Anthropology.* Cambridge: Harvard University Press, 1968.

Cappon, Lester, J., ed. *The Adams-Jefferson Letters.* Chapel Hill: University of North Carolina Press, 1959.

Carter, Paul A. *The Spiritual Crisis of the Gilded Age.* DeKalb: University of Northern Illinois Press, 1971.

Coulson, Thomas. *Joseph Henry: His Life and Work.* Princeton: Princeton University Press, 1950.

Croll, James. *Climate and Time in Their Geological Relations: A Theory of Secular Changes of the Earth's Climate.* New York: D. Appleton and Co., 1875.

Curtin, Jeremiah. *Creation Myths of Primitive America in Relation to the Religious History and Mental Development of Mankind.* Boston: Little, Brown and Co., 1898.

————. *The Memoirs of Jeremiah Curtin*. Madison: Wisconsin State Historical Society, 1940.

Cushing, Frank Hamilton. *My Life at Zuñi*. Santa Fe: Peripatetic Press, 1941.

————. *Outlines of Zuñi Creation Myths*. BAE, AR for 1892, pp. 321–447. Washington, D.C.: GPO, 1896.

————. *Zuñi Breadstuff*. New York: Museum of the American Indian, Heye Foundation, 1920.

————. *Zuñi Folk-Tales*. Introduction by J. W. Powell. New York: G. P. Putnam's Sons, 1901. Reissued with introduction by Mary Austin. New York: Knopf, 1931.

Dall, William H. *Spencer Fullerton Baird: A Biography*. Philadelphia: J. B. Lippincott Company, 1915.

Daniel, Glyn E. *A Hundred Years of Archaeology*. London: Duckworth, 1950.

Daniels, George H. *American Science in the Age of Jackson*. New York: Columbia University Press, 1968.

————. *Nineteenth-Century American Science: A Reappraisal*. Evanston: Northwestern University Press, 1972.

Darnell, Regna. *Readings in the History of Anthropology*. New York: Harper & Row, 1974.

Darrah, William Culp. *Powell of the Colorado*. Princeton: Princeton University Press, 1951.

Darwin, Charles. *The Descent of Man and Selection in Relation to Sex*. 2d ed. New York: D. Appleton and Co., 1922.

Deuel, Leo. *Conquistadores Without Swords: Archaeologists in the Americas*. New York: Schocken, 1967.

Dickens, Charles. *American Notes*. Philaldelphia: Nottingham Society, n.d.

Dupree, A. Hunter. *Science in the Federal Government: A History of Policies and Activities to 1940*. Cambridge: Harvard University Press, 1957.

Eiseley, Loren. *Darwin's Century: Evolution and the Men Who Discovered It*. Garden City: Doubleday & Co., 1958.

Ewers, John C. *Murals in the Round: Painted Tipis of the Kiowa and Kiowa-Apache Indians; An exhibition of tipi models made for James Mooney of the Smithsonian Institution during his field studies of Indian history and art in southwestern Oklahoma, 1891–1904*. Washington, D.C.: Smithsonian Institution Press, 1978.

Fitting, James E., ed. *The Development of North American Archaeology: Essays in the History of Regional Traditions*. Garden City: Doubleday, 1973.

Flack, James Kirkpatrick. *Desideratum in Washington: The Intellectual Community in the Capital City, 1870–1900*. Cambridge, Mass.: Albert Schenkman, 1975.

Fowler, Don D., and Fowler, Catherine S., eds. *Anthropology of the Numa: John Wesley Powell's Manuscripts on the Numic Peoples of Western North America,*

1868–1880. Smithsonian Contributions to Anthropology 14. Washington, D.C.: Smithsonian Institution Press, 1971.

Fowler, Don D., and Matley, John. *Material Culture of the Numa: The Powell Collection, 1868–1876.* Smithsonian Contributions to Anthropology. Washington, D.C.: Smithsonian Institution Press, 1975.

Frankel, Charles, ed. *Controversies and Decisions: The Social Sciences and Public Policy.* New York: Russell Sage Foundation, 1976.

Fredrickson, George M. *The Black Image in the White Mind: The Debate on Afro-American Character and Destiny, 1817–1914.* New York: Harper & Row, 1971.

Furner, Mary O. *Advocacy and Objectivity: A Crisis in the Professionalization of American Social Science, 1865–1905.* Lexington: University of Kentucky Press, 1975.

Gatschet, Albert Samuel. *The Klamath Tribe and Language of Oregon.* Contributions to North American Ethnology 2. Parts 1 and 2. Washington, D.C.: GPO, 1890.

Gerth, H. H., and Mills, C. Wright, eds. *From Max Weber: Essays in Sociology.* London: Routledge and Kegan Paul, 1948.

Gibbs, George. *The Memoirs of the Administration of Washington and Adams, edited from the Papers of Oliver Wolcott, Secretary of the Treasury.* New York: 1846.

Gilliland, Marion Spjut. *The Material Culture of Key Marco, Florida.* Gainesville: University of Florida Presses, 1975.

Goetzmann, William H. *Exploration and Empire: The Explorer and the Scientist in the Winning of the American West.* New York: Alfred A. Knopf, 1966.

Goldschmidt, Walter, ed. *The Uses of Anthropology.* Special Publication of the American Anthropological Association no. 11. Washington, D.C.: American Anthropological Association, 1979.

Goode, George Brown, ed. *The Smithsonian Institution, 1846–1896: The History of its First Half-Century.* Washington, D.C.: Devine Press, 1897.

Green, Constance McLaughlin. *Washington: Capital City, 1879–1950.* Princeton: Princeton University Press, 1963.

———. *Washington: Village and Capital, 1800–1878.* Princeton: Princeton University Press, 1962.

Green, Jesse, ed. *Zuñi: Selected Writings of Frank Hamilton Cushing.* Lincoln: University of Nebraska Press, 1979.

Guralnick, Stanley M. *Science and the Ante-Bellum American College.* Memoirs of the American Philosophical Society 109. Philadelphia: American Philosophical Society, 1975.

Harris, Marvin. *The Rise of Anthropological Theory: A History of Theories of Culture.* New York: Thomas Y. Crowell Co., 1968.

Haskell, Thomas L. *The Emergence of Professional Social Science: The American*

Social Science Association and the Nineteenth-Century Crisis of Authority. Urbana: University of Illinois Press, 1977.

Haven, Samuel F. *Archaeology in the United States.* Smithsonian Contributions to Knowledge 8. Washington, D.C.: GPO, 1856.

Hayes, E. N. and Hayes, T., eds. *Claude Lévi-Strauss: The Anthropologist as Hero.* Cambridge: MIT Press, 1970.

Hays, Samuel P. *Conservation and the Gospel of Efficiency: The Progressive Conservation Movement, 1890–1920.* Cambridge, Mass.: Harvard University Press, 1959.

Helm, June, ed. *Pioneers in American Anthropology: The Uses of Biography.* Seattle: University of Washington Press, 1966.

Henry, Joseph. *The Papers of Joseph Henry,* edited by Nathan Reingold. Vol. 1: December 1797–October 1832: The Albany Years. Washington, D.C.: Smithsonian Institution Press, 1972.

Hodge, Frederick W., ed. *Handbook of American Indians North of Mexico.* Part 1. *BAE Bulletin* 30. Washington, D.C.: GPO, 1907.

Holmes, William Henry. *Handbook of Aboriginal American Antiquities. BAE Bulletin* 60, Part 1. Washington, D.C.: GPO, 1919.

Hooker, Arthur, ed. *Official Proceedings of the Nineteenth National Irrigation Congress, held at Chicago, Illinois, U.S.A., December 5–9, 1911.* Chicago: R. R. Donnelly & Sons Co., 1912.

Huddleston, Lee Eldridge. *Origins of the American Indians: European Concepts, 1492–1729.* Austin: University of Texas, 1967.

Israel, Jerry, ed. *Building the Organizational Society: Essays on Associational Activities in Modern America.* New York: Free Press, 1972.

James, Edward T., ed. *Notable American Women, 1607–1950: A Biographical Dictionary.* Cambridge: Belknap Press of Harvard University Press, 1971.

Jefferson, Thomas. *Notes on the State of Virginia.* In Foner, Philip S., ed., *Basic Writings of Thomas Jefferson.* Garden City: Halcyon House, 1944.

John Wesley Powell: Proceedings of a Meeting Commemorative of his Distinguished Services, held in the Columbian University under the Auspices of the Washington Academy of Sciences, February 16, 1903. Proceedings of the Washington Academy of Sciences 5:99–187. Washington, D.C.: Judd and Detweiler, 1903.

Jones, Joseph. *Antiquities of Tennessee.* Smithsonian Contributions to Knowledge 22. Washington, D.C.: GPO, 1882.

Judd, Neil. *The Bureau of American Ethnology: A Partial History.* Norman: University of Oklahoma Press, 1968.

Kardiner, Abram, and Preble, Edward. *They Studied Man.* New York: Mentor Books, 1963.

Kolakowski, Leszek. *The Alienation of Reason: A History of Positivist Thought.* Translated by Norbert Guterman. Garden City: Doubleday & Co., 1969.

Kroeber, Alfred L., *et al. Anthropology Today: An Encyclopedic Inventory.* Chicago: University of Chicago Press, 1953.

Kuhn, Thomas. *The Structure of Scientific Revolutions.* Chicago: University of Chicago Press, 1962.

Laguna, Frederica de, ed. *Selected Papers from the American Anthropologist, 1888–1920.* Evanston, Ill.: Row, Peterson and Co., 1960.

Liberty, Margot, ed. *American Indian Intellectuals. 1976 Proceedings of the American Ethnological Society.* St. Paul: West Publishing Co., 1978.

Lowie, Robert H. *History of Ethnological Theory.* New York: Holt, Rinehart and Winston, 1937.

Ludewig, Hermann E. *The Literature of American Aboriginal Languages.* Edited by Nicolas Trübner, with additions and corrections by William W. Turner. London, 1858.

Lurie, Edward. *Nature and the American Mind: Louis Agassiz and the Culture of Science.* New York: N. Watson, 1974.

Lyell, Charles. *The Geological Evidences of the Antiquity of Man.* 4th ed., rev. London: John Murray, 1873.

McCulloh, James H. *Researches, Philosophical and Antiquarian Concerning the Aboriginal History of America.* Baltimore: F. Luces, Jr., 1817.

McGee, Emma R. *Life of W J McGee.* Farley, Iowa: privately printed, 1915.

McGee, W J, ed. *Proceedings of a Conference of Governors in the White House, Washington, D.C., May 13–15, 1908.* Washington, D.C.: GPO, 1909.

McGee, W J. *The Seri Indians of Bahia Kino and Sonora, Mexico. BAE, AR for 1896.* Washington, D.C.: GPO, 1898. Reprinted with introduction by Bernard L. Fontana. Florieta, N.M.: Rio Grande Press, 1971.

McGee Memorial Meeting of the Washington Academy of Sciences. Baltimore: Williams and Wilkinson Co., 1916.

McKusick, Marshall. *The Davenport Conspiracy.* Iowa City: The University of Iowa, 1970.

McVaugh, Rogers. *Edward Palmer: Plant Explorer of the American West.* Norman: University of Oklahoma Press, 1956.

Mallery, Garrick. *Picture-Writing of the American Indians. BAE, AR for 1889,* pp. 1–907. Washington, D.C.: GPO, 1893.

———. *Sign-language among the North American Indians, compared with that among other People and Deaf-Mutes. BAE, AR for 1880,* pp. 263–552. Washington, D.C.: GPO, 1881.

Manning, Thomas J. *Government in Science: The U.S. Geological Survey, 1867–1894.* Lexington: University Press of Kentucky, 1967.

Mardock, Robert W. *The Reformers and the American Indian.* Columbia: University of Missouri Press, 1971.

Mason, Otis T. *Aboriginal American Basketry: Studies in a Textile Art Without Machinery. USNM, AR for 1902,* pp. 171–548. Washington, D.C.: GPO, 1903.

Mayer, Brantz. *Mexican Archaeology and History.* Smithsonian Contributions to Knowledge 9. Washington, D.C.: GPO, 1857.

Mitra, Panchanan. *A History of American Anthropology*. Calcutta: University of Calcutta, 1933.

Mooney, James. *Calendar History of the Kiowa Indians*. BAE, *AR for 1896*. Washington, D.C.: GPO, 1898. Reprinted with an introduction by John C. Ewers. Washington, D.C.: Smithsonian Institution Press, 1979.

————. *The Ghost-Dance Religion and the Sioux Outbreak of 1890*. BAE, *AR for 1893*, Part 2. Washington, D.C.: GPO, 1896.

————. *Myths of the Cherokee*. BAE, *AR for 1898*, Part 1. Washington, D.C.: GPO, 1900.

————. *Sacred Formulas of the Cherokees*. BAE, *AR for 1886*. Washington, D.C.: GPO, 1891.

————. *Siouan Tribes of the East*. BAE Bulletin 22. Washington, D.C.: GPO, 1894.

Morgan, Lewis Henry. *Ancient Society: or, Researches in the Lines of Human Progress from Savagery through Barbarism to Civilization*. Edited by Eleanor Burke Leacock. Cleveland: World Publishing Co., 1963.

————. *Systems of Consanguinity and Affinity in the Human Family*. Smithsonian Contributions to Knowledge 17. Washington, D.C.: GPO, 1871.

Morton, Samuel George. *An Inquiry Into the Distinctive Characteristics of the Aboriginal Race of America*. Boston, 1842; Philadelphia, 1844.

————. *Crania Americana, or a Comparative View of the Skulls of the Various Aboriginal Nations of North and South America. To Which is Prefixed an Essay on the Varieties of the Human Species*. Philadelphia, 1839.

Murra, John V., ed. *American Anthropology: The Early Years. 1974 Proceedings of the American Ethnological Society*. St. Paul: West Publishing Co., 1976.

Nash, Roderick, ed. *The American Environment: Readings in the History of Conservation*. Reading, Mass.: Addison-Wesley, 1968.

Nott, J. C., and Gliddon, G. R. *Types of Mankind, or Ethnological Researches based upon the ancient monuments, paintings, sculptures, and crania of races, and upon their natural geographical, philological, and Biblical history*. Philadelphia: Lippincott, Grambo and Co., 1854.

Oehser, Paul H. *The Smithsonian Institution*. New York: Praeger Publishing, 1970.

————. *Sons of Science: The Story of the Smithsonian Institution and its Leaders*. New York: Henry Schuman, 1949.

Oleson, A., and Brown, S. C., eds. *The Pursuit of Knowledge in the Early American Republic*. Baltimore: The Johns Hopkins University Press, 1976.

Oleson, A., and Voss, J., ed. *The Organization of Knowledge in Modern America, 1860–1920*. Baltimore and London: The Johns Hopkins University Press, 1979.

Pearce, Roy Harvey. *Savagism and Civilization: A Study of the Indian and the American Mind*. Baltimore: The Johns Hopkins University Press, 1965.

Pilling, James C. *Proof-Sheets of a Bibliography of the Languages of the North American Indians.* Washington, D.C.: GPO, 1895.

Pinchot, Gifford. *Breaking New Ground.* New York: Harcourt, Brace, 1947.

Pott, P. H. *Naar Wijder Horizon: Kaleidscoop op ons beeld van de Buitenwereld.* The Hague: Mouton & Co., 1962.

Powell, John Wesley. *Truth and Error.* Chicago: Open Court, 1898.

Prichard, James C. *Researches in the Physical History of Man.* Edited by George W. Stocking, Jr. Chicago: University of Chicago Press, 1973.

Rau, Charles. *The Archaeological Collection of the United States National Museum, in Charge of the Smithsonian Institution.* Smithsonian Contributions to Knowledge 22. Washington, D.C.: GPO, 1876.

————. *Observations on Cup-shaped and other Lapidarian Sculptures in the Old World and in America.* Contributions to North American Ethnology 5. Washington, D.C.: GPO, 1882.

————. *Prehistoric Fishing in Europe and North America.* Smithsonian Contributions to Knowledge 25. Washington, D.C.: GPO, 1884.

Reingold, Nathan, ed. *Science in Nineteenth-Century America: A Documentary History.* New York: Hill and Wang, 1964.

Resek, Carl. *Lewis Henry Morgan: American Scholar.* Chicago: University of Chicago, 1960.

Schlesinger, Arthur M., Jr. *Robert Kennedy and His Times.* New York: Ballantine Books, 1978.

Schoolcraft, Henry Rowe. *Information regarding the history, condition and prospects of the Indian tribes of the United States: collected and prepared under the direction of the Bureau of Indian Affairs.* 6 vols. Philadelphia: Lippincott, Grambo & Co., 1851–57.

————. *Personal Memoirs of a Residence of Thirty Years with the Indian Tribes on the American Frontiers.* 1851. Reprint. New York: Arno Press, 1975.

Silverberg, Robert. *Mound Builders of Ancient America: The Archaeology of a Myth.* Greenwich: New York Graphic Society, 1968.

Silverstein, Michael, ed. *Whitney on Language: Selected Writings of William Dwight Whitney.* Cambridge: MIT Press, 1971.

Slotkin, Richard L. *Regeneration Through Violence: The Mythology of the American Frontier, 1600–1860.* Middletown, Conn.: Wesleyan University Press, 1974.

Smith, Henry Nash. *Virgin Land: The American West as Symbol and Myth.* New York: Random House, 1950.

Somkin, Fred. *Unquiet Eagle: Memory and Desire in the Idea of American Freedom, 1815–1860.* Ithaca: Cornell University Press, 1967.

Spencer, Herbert. *First Principles.* Reprinted from 5th London ed. New York: A. L. Burt, 1880.

————. *The Study of Sociology.* Introduction by Talcott Parsons. Ann Arbor:

University of Michigan, 1961.

Squier, Ephraim G. *Aboriginal Monuments of New York*. Smithsonian Contributions to Knowledge 2. Washington, D.C.: GPO, 1851.

————. *The Serpent Symbol and the Worship of the Reciprocal Principles of Nature in America*. New York: G. P. Putnam, 1851.

————. , and Davis, Edwin H. *Ancient Monuments of the Mississippi Valley: Comprising the Results of Extensive Original Surveys and Explorations*. Smithsonian Contributions to Knowledge 1. Washington, D.C.: GPO, 1848.

Stanton, William. *The Great United States Exploring Expedition of 1838–1842*. Berkeley: University of California Press, 1975.

————. *The Leopard's Spots: Scientific Attitudes Toward Race in America, 1815–1859*. Chicago: University of Chicago Press, 1960.

Stegner, Wallace. *Beyond the Hundredth Meridian: John Wesley Powell and the Second Opening of the West*. Boston: Houghton Mifflin, 1954.

Stevenson, Matilda Coxe. *The Zuñi Indians: Their Mythology. Esoteric Fraternities, and Ceremonies*. BAE, AR for 1902. Washington, D.C.: GPO, 1904.

Stocking, George W., Jr. *Anthropology at Chicago: Tradition, Discipline, Department*. Chicago: The University of Chicago Library, 1979.

————. *Race, Culture and Evolution: Essays in the History of Anthropology*. New York: Free Press, 1968.

————. , ed. *Selected Papers from the "American Anthropologist," 1921–1945*. Washington, D.C.: American Anthropological Association, 1976.

————. *The Shaping of American Anthropology, 1883–1911: A Franz Boas Reader*. New York: Basic Books, 1974.

Thomas, Cyrus. *Report on the Mound Explorations of the Bureau of Ethnology*. BAE, *AR for 1891*, pp. 3–730. Washington, D.C.: GPO, 1894.

Thoreson, Timothy H. H., ed. *Toward a Science of Man: Essays in the History of Anthropology*. The Hague: Mouton, 1976.

Trollope, Anthony. *North America*. New York: Harper & Brothers, 1862.

Van Tassel, David D., and Hall, Michael G., eds. *Science and Society in the United States*. Homewood, Ill.: Dorsey Press, 1966.

Weiss, John, ed. *The Origins of Modern Consciousness*. Detroit: Wayne State University Press, 1965.

Whitman, Walt. *Walt Whitman: Complete Poetry and Selected Prose and Letters*. Edited by Emory Holloway. London: Nonesuch Press, 1938.

Whitney, William Dwight. *Language and the Study of Language: Twelve Lectures on the Principles of Linguistic Science*. New York: Charles Scribner & Co., 1867.

Whittlesey, Charles. *Ancient Works in Ohio*. Smithsonian Contributions to Knowledge 3. Washington, D.C.: GPO, 1852.

Wiebe, Robert H. *The Search for Order, 1877–1920*. New York: Hill & Wang, 1967.

Willey, Gordon R., and Sabloff, Jeremy A. *A History of American Archaeology.* San Francisco: W. H. Freeman and Co., 1974. 2d ed., 1980.

Wissler, Clark. *The Relation of Nature to Man in Aboriginal America.* New York: 1926. Reprint. New York: AMS Press, 1971.

Wright, George Frederick. *The Ice Age in North America and its Bearings upon the Antiquity of Man.* Oberlin: Bibliotheca Sacra Co., 1889.

_____. *Man and the Glacial Period.* New York: D. Appleton, 1892.

Ziff, Larzer. *Puritanism in America: New Culture in a New World.* New York: Viking Press, 1973.

PERIODICALS

Abbott, Charles C. "Occurrence of Implements in the River Drift at Trenton, New Jersey." *American Naturalist* 7 (1873):204–09.

_____. "Second Report on the Paleolithic Implements from the Glacial Drift in the Valley of the Delaware River near Trenton, N.J." *Eleventh Annual Report of the Peabody Museum* (1878):225–57.

_____. "The Stone Age in New Jersey." *American Naturalist* 6 (1872):144–60, 199–229.

Adler, Cyrus. "Samuel Pierpont Langley." SI, *AR for 1906,* pp. 515–533.

Boas, Franz. "Museums of Ethnology and their Classification." *Science* 9 (1887):587–89.

_____. "The Occurrence of Similar Inventions in Areas Widely Separated." *Science* 9 (1887):485–86.

_____. "The Study of Geography." *Science* 9 (1887): 137–41.

Buettner-Janusch, John. "Boas and Mason: Particularism versus Generalization." *American Anthropologist* 59 (1957):318–24.

Bushnell, David I., Jr. "Drawings by George Gibbs in the Far Northwest, 1849–1851." Smithsonian Miscellaneous Collections 97, no. 8 (1938).

Chamberlin, Thomas C. "The Method of Multiple Working Hypotheses." *Science,* o.s. 15 (1890):92–96; later expanded in *Journal of Geology* 5 (1897):837–48.

Cockerell, T. D. A. "Spencer Fullerton Baird." *Popular Science Monthly* 68 (1906):63–83.

Collier, Donald, and Tschopik, Harry, Jr. "The Role of Museums in American Anthropology." *American Anthropologist* 56 (1954):768–79.

Cox, William VanZandt. "George Brown Goode: A Memorial Sketch." *American Monthly Magazine,* January 1897, pp. 1–11.

Cross, Whitney R. "W J McGee and the Idea of Conservation." *Historian* 15 (1953):148–62.

Cushing, Frank Hamilton. "Antiquities of Orleans County, New York." SI, *AR for 1874*, pp. 375–77.

————. "Exploration of Ancient Key Dwellers' Remains on the Gulf Coast of Florida." *Proceedings of the American Philosophical Society* 35 (1896):329–448. Reprinted, with introduction by Philip Phillips. New York: AMS Press, 1977.

————. "The Germ of Shore-Land Pottery." *Memoirs of the International Congress of Anthropology*, pp. 217–34. Chicago, 1894.

————. "The Need of Studying the Indian in Order to Teach Him." Albion, N.Y.: A. M. Eddy, 1897. Reprint of original in *Twenty-Eighth Annual Report of the Board of Indian Commissioners*. Washington, D.C.: GPO, 1897.

————. "A Study of Pueblo Pottery, as Illustrative of Zuñi Culture Growth." BAE, *AR for 1883*, pp. 467–521. Washington, D.C.: GPO, 1886.

Darnell, Regna. "The Emergence of Academic Anthropology at the University of Pennsylvania." *Journal of the History of the Behavioral Sciences* 6 (1970):80–92.

————. "The Powell Classification of American Indian Languages." *Papers in Linguistics* 4 (1971):79–110.

————. "The Professionalization of American Anthropology: A Case Study in the Sociology of Knowledge." *Social Science Information* 10, no. 2 (1972), pp. 83–103.

————. "The Revision of the Powell Classification." *Papers in Linguistics* 4 (1971):233–57.

Darton, N. H. "Memoir of W J McGee." *Annals of the Association of American Geographers* 3 (1912):103–10.

Dexter, Ralph W. "Putnam's Problems Popularizing Anthropology." *American Scientist* 54 (1966):315–32.

Dorsey, James Owen. "Siouan Sociology." BAE, *AR for 1894*, pp. 205–44. Washington, D.C.: GPO, 1897.

Duponceau, Peter Stephen. "Report of the Historical and Literary Committee to the American Philosophical Society, January 9, 1818." *Transactions of the Historical and Literary Committee of the American Philosophical Society* 1. Philadelphia, 1819.

Fewkes, Jesse Walter. "The Prehistoric Culture of Tusayan." *American Anthropologist*, o.s. 9 (1896):151–73.

Fletcher, Robert. "Brief Memoir of Colonel Garrick Mallery." Washington, D.C.: privately printed, 1895.

Fontana, Bernard L. "Pioneers in Ideas: Three Early Southwestern Ethnologists." *Journal of the Arizona Academy of Science* 2 (1963):124–29.

Fowler, Don D., and Fowler, Catherine S. "John Wesley Powell, Anthropologist." *Utah Historical Quarterly* 37 (1969):152–72.

Freeman, John F. "Religion and Personality in the Anthropology of Henry Schoolcraft." *Journal of the History of the Behavioral Sciences* 1 (1965):301–13.

————. "University Anthropology: Early Departments in the United States." *Kroeber Anthropological Society Papers* 32 (1965):78–90.

Gatschet, Albert S. "Analytical Report upon Indian dialects spoken in southern California, Nevada, and on the lower Colorado River, etc." *Annual Report of the U.S. Geological Survey West of the 100th Meridian for 1876.* Washington, D.C.: GPO, 1876.

————. "Report on the Pueblo Languages of New Mexico, and of the Moquis in Arizona: their affinity to each other and to the languages of the other tribes." *Annual Report of the U.S. Geological Survey West of the 100th Meridian for 1875.* Washington, D.C.: GPO, 1875.

Gibbs, George. "The Intermixture of Races." SI, *AR for 1864,* pp. 375–76.

————. "On the Language of the Aboriginal Indians of America." SI, *AR for 1870,* pp. 364–67.

————. "A Physical Atlas of North America." SI, *AR for 1866,* pp. 368–69.

Gilbert, Grove Karl. "John Wesley Powell." SI, *AR for 1902,* pp. 633–40.

Goode, George Brown. "The Genesis of the U.S. National Museum." USNM, *AR for 1891,* pp. 273–380.

————. "Museum-History and Museums of History." *Papers of the American Historical Association* 3 (1889):495–519.

————. "The Principles of Museum Administration." *Annual Report of the Museums Association of Great Britain for 1895.* York: Coultas & Volans, 1895.

Gore, J. Howard. "Anthropology at Washington." *Popular Science Monthly* 35 (1888):786–95.

Gould, Stephen Jay. "Morton's Ranking of Races by Cranial Capacity: Unconscious Manipulation of Data May Be a Scientific Norm." *Science* 200 (5 May 1978):503–09.

Gruber, Jacob. "Ethnographic Salvage and the Shaping of Anthropology." *American Anthropologist* 72 (1970):1289–99.

Haas, Mary. "Grammar or Lexicon? The American Indian Side of the Question from Duponceau to Powell." *International Journal of Anthropological Linguistics* 35 (1969):239–55.

Hallowell, A. Irving. "The Beginnings of Anthropology in America." In *Selected Papers from the American Anthropologist, 1888–1920,* edited by Frederica de Laguna. Evanston, Ill.: Row, Peterson and Co., 1960, pp 1–90.

————. "The History of Anthropology as an Anthropological Problem." *Journal of the History of the Behavioral Sciences* 1 (1965):24–38.

Henshaw, Henry W. "Autobiographical Notes." *The Condor,* vol. 21, no. 3 (1919), pp. 102–107; no. 4, pp. 165–171; no. 5, pp. 177–181; no. 6, pp. 216–222; vol. 22, no. 1 (1920), pp. 3–10; no. 2, pp. 55–60; no. 3, pp. 95–101.

Hinsley, Curtis M., and Holm, Bill. "A Cannibal in the National Museum: The Early Career of Franz Boas in America." *American Anthropologist* 78

(1976):306–16.

Hodge, Frederick Webb. "W J McGee." *American Anthropologist* 14 (1912):683–86.

Hoffman, Walter J. "The Menomini Indians." BAE, *AR for 1893,* pp. 11–328. Washington, D.C.: GPO, 1896.

Holmes, William Henry. "Museum Presentation of Anthropology." *Proceedings of the American Association for the Advancement of Science* 47 (1898):485–88.

———. "Primitive Man in the Delaware Valley." *Science,* n.s. 6 (1897):824–29.

———. "Report on the Ancient Ruins of Southwestern Colorado, examined during the summers of 1875 and 1876." *10th Annual Report of the United States Geological and Geographical Survey of the Territories.* Washington, D.C.: GPO, 1878.

Hough, Walter. "Otis Tufton Mason." *American Anthropologist* 10 (1908):661–67.

Hrdlička, Aleš. "Physical Anthropology in America." *American Anthropologist* 16 (1914):508–54.

Hymes, Dell H. "Kroeber, Powell, and Henshaw." *International Journal of Anthropological Linguistics* 3, no. 6 (1961), pp. 15–16.

Kayser, Elmer Louis. "Columbian Academy, 1821–1897: The Preparatory Department of Columbian College in the District of Columbia." *Records of the Columbia Historical Society* (1971), pp. 150–63.

Keyes, Charles R. "W J McGee, Anthropologist, Geologist, Hydrologist." *Annals of Iowa* series 3, vol. 2 (1913), pp. 6–10.

Knowlton, F. J. "Memoir of W J McGee." *Bulletin of the Geological Society of America* 24 (1912):18–29.

Kohlstedt, Sally. "A Step Toward Scientific Self-Identity in the United States: The Failure of the National Institute, 1844." *Isis* 62 (1971):339–62.

Kroeber, Alfred L. "Frank Hamilton Cushing." *Encyclopedia of the Social Sciences* 2 (New York, 1930–35):657.

———. "The Place of Boas in Anthropology." *American Anthropologist* 58 (1956):151–59.

———. "Powell and Henshaw: An Episode in the History of Ethnolinguistics." *International Journal of Anthropological Linguistics* 2, no. 4 (1960), pp. 1–5.

———. "The Seri." *Southwest Museum Papers* 6 (1931).

Lamb, Daniel S. "The Story of the Anthropological Society of Washington." *American Anthropologist* 6 (1904):564–79.

Langley, Samuel P. "Memoir of George Brown Goode." Washington, D.C.: National Academy of Sciences, 1897.

LeConte, Joseph. "The Factors of Evolution." *The Monist* 1 (1890–91):321–35.

Lowie, Robert H. "Reminiscences of Anthropological Currents in America Half a Century Ago." *American Anthropologist* 58 (1956):995–1016.

McGee, W J. "The Beginning of Agriculture." *American Anthropologist,* o.s. 8 (1895):350–75.

————. "The Beginning of Zooculture." *American Anthropologist*, o.s. 10 (1897):215–30.

————. "Cardinal Principles of Science." *Proceedings of the Washington Academy of Sciences* 2 (1900):1–12.

————. "The Course of Human Development." *Forum* 26 (1898):56–65.

————. "The Earth the Home of Man." *Special Papers of the Anthropological Society of Washington* 1, no. 2. Washington, D.C.: Anthropological Society of Washington, 1894.

————. "Expedition to Papagueria and Seriland: A Preliminary Note." *American Anthropologist*, o.s. 9 (1896):93–98.

————. "Fifty Years of American Science." *Atlantic Monthly* 82 (1898):307–20.

————. "Man and the Glacial Period." *American Anthropologist*, o.s.6 (1893):85–95.

————. "Man's Place in Nature." *American Anthropologist* 3 (1901):1–13.

————. "Necrology: Frank Hamilton Cushing." BAE, *AR for 1900*, pp. xxxv–xxxviii.

————. "Paleolithic Man in America: His Antiquity and Environment." *Popular Science Monthly* 34 (1888):20–36.

————. "The Science of Humanity." *American Anthropologist*, o.s. 10 (1897):241–72.

————. "The Siouan Indians: A Preliminary Sketch." BAE, *AR for 1894*, pp. 157–204. Washington, D.C.: GPO, 1897.

————. "The Trend of Human Progress." *American Anthropologist* 1 (1899):401–47.

Mallery, Garrick. "A Calendar of the Dakota Nation." *U.S. Geological and Geographical Survey of the Territories Bulletin* 3, no. 1. Washington, D.C.: GPO, 1877.

————. "Greeting by Gesture." *Popular Science Monthly* 38 (1890–91):477–90.

————. "Israelite and Indian: A Parallel in Planes of Culture." *Popular Science Monthly* 36 (1889–90):52–76, 193–213.

————. "A Philosophic Phantasy." Read before the Philosophical Society of Washington, 18 February 1893. Privately printed, n.d.

————. "Some Common Errors Respecting the North American Indians." *Bulletin of the Philosophical Society of Washington* 2 (1875–80):175–81.

Mark, Joan. "Frank Hamilton Cushing and an American Science of Anthropology." *Perspectives in American History* 10 (1976):449–86.

Mason, Otis T. "Aboriginal American Harpoons: A Study in Ethnic Distribution and Invention." USNM, *AR for 1900*, pp. 189–304.

————. "Aboriginal American Zootechny." *American Anthropologist* 1 (1899):45–81.

————. "Basket-Work of the North American Aborigines." USNM, *AR for 1884*, Part 2, pp. 291–316.

————. "The Birth of Invention." SI, *AR for 1892*, pp. 603–11.

_____. "Cradles of the American Aborigines." USNM, *AR for 1887*, pp. 161–212.

_____. "The Educational Aspect of the United States National Museum." *Johns Hopkins University Studies in Historical and Political Science* 8 (1890):505–19.

_____. "Ethnological Exhibit of the Smithsonian Institution at the World's Columbian Exposition." *Memoirs of the International Congress of Anthropology*, pp. 208–16. Chicago, 1894.

_____. "Influence of Environment upon Human Industries or Arts." SI, *AR for 1895*, pp. 639–65.

_____. "The Leipsic Museum of Ethnology." SI, *AR for 1873*, pp. 390–409.

_____. "North American Bows, Arrows, and Quivers." SI, *AR for 1893*, pp. 631–79.

_____. "The Occurrence of Similar Inventions in Areas Widely Apart." *Science* 9 (1887):534.

_____. "Primitive Travel and Transportation." USNM, *AR for 1894*, pp. 237–593.

_____. Review of *Korean Games* by Stewart Culin. *American Anthropologist*, o.s. 9 (1896):22–23.

_____. "The Scope and Value of Anthropological Studies." *Proceedings of the American Association for the Advancement of Science for 1884*: 365–83.

_____. "Technogeography, or the Relation of the Earth to the Industries of Mankind." *American Anthropologist*, o.s. 7 (1894):137–61.

_____. "Throwing-Sticks in the National Museum." USNM, *AR for 1884*, Part 2, pp. 279–91.

_____. "Traps of the Amerinds: A Study in Psychology and Invention." *American Anthropologist* 2 (1900):657–75.

_____. "The Ulu, a Woman's Knife, of the Eskimo." USNM, *AR for 1890*, pp. 411–16.

_____. "Vocabulary of Malaysian Basketwork: A Study in the W. L. Abbott Collections." *USNM Proceedings* 35 (1908):1–51.

_____. "What is Anthropology?" Washington, D.C.: Smithsonian Saturday Lectures, 1883.

Molella, Arthur, and Reingold, Nathan. "Theorists and Ingenious Mechanics: Joseph Henry Defines Science." *Science Studies* 3 (1973):323–51.

Mooney, James. "Albert Samuel Gatschet, 1832–1907." *American Anthropologist* 9 (1907):561–65.

_____. "In Memoriam: Washington Matthews." *American Anthropologist* 7 (1905):514–23.

Morton, Samuel George. "Account of a Craniological Collection." *Transactions of American Ethnological Society* 2. New York, 1848.

Osborn, Henry Fairchild. "Goode as a Naturalist." *Science*, n.s. 5 (1897):374–79.

Pandey, Triloki Nath. "Anthropologists at Zuñi." *Proceedings of the American Philosophical Society* 116 (1972):321–37.

Powell, John Wesley. "Competition as a Factor in Human Evolution." *American Anthropologist,* o.s. 1 (1898):297–321.

———. "Darwin's Contributions to Philosophy." *Proceedings of the Biological Society of Washington* 1 (1882):60–70.

———. "From Savagery to Barbarism." *Transactions of the Anthropological Society of Washington* 3 (1885):173–96.

———. "Human Evolution." *Transactions of the Anthropological Society of Washington* 2 (1883):176–208.

———. "Garrick Mallery." SI, *AR for 1895,* pp. 52–53.

———. "James Owen Dorsey." SI, *AR for 1895,* pp. 53–54.

———. "Museums of Ethnology and their Classification." *Science* 9 (1887):612–14.

———. "The Personal Characteristics of Professor Baird." *Philosophical Society of Washington Bulletin* 10 (1887):71–77.

———. "Sketch of Lewis H. Morgan." *Popular Science Monthly* 18 (1881):114–21.

———. "The Three Methods of Evolution." *Philosophical Society of Washington Bulletin* 6 (1884):27–51.

Rau, Charles. "Artificial Shell-Deposits in New Jersey." SI, *AR for 1864,* pp. 370–74.

———. "Indian Pottery." SI, *AR for 1866,* pp. 346–55.

———. "Memoir of C.F.P. von Martius." SI, *AR for 1869,* pp. 169–78.

———. "North American Stone Implements." SI, *AR for 1872,* pp. 395–409.

Reingold, Nathan. "The New York State Roots of Joseph Henry's National Career." *New York History* 54 (1973):132–44.

Royce, Charles C. "Cessions of Land by Indian Tribes to the United States: Illustrated by those in the State of Indiana." BAE, *AR for 1880,* pp. 247–62.

———. "The Cherokee Nation of Indians." BAE, *AR for 1884,* pp. 121–378.

———. "Indian Land Cessions in the United States." Introduction by Cyrus Thomas. BAE, *AR for 1897,* pp. 521–964.

Sherwood, John. "Frank Cushing, Boy Wonder of the Smithsonian's Old Bureau of Ethnology." *Smithsonian* 10, no. 5 (1979), pp. 96–113.

Starr, Frederick. "Anthropological Work in America." *Popular Science Monthly* 41 (1892):289–307.

Stevens, John Austin. "A Memorial of George Gibbs." SI, *AR for 1873,* pp. 219–25.

Stocking, George W., Jr. "Franz Boas and the Founding of the American Anthropological Association." *American Anthropologist* 62 (1960):1–17.

_____. "The History of Anthropology: Where, Whence, Wither?" *Journal of the History of the Behavioral Sciences* 2 (1966):281–90.

_____. "On the Limits of 'Presentism' and 'Historicism' in the Historiography of the Behavioral Sciences." *Journal of the History of the Behavioral Sciences* 1 (1965):211–17.

Sturtevant, William C. "The Authorship of the Powell Classification." *International Journal of Anthropological Linguistics* 25 (1959):196–99.

_____. "Does Anthropology Need Museums?" *Proceedings of the Biological Society of Washington* 82 (1969):619–50.

Swanton, John R. "William Henry Holmes." *National Academy of Sciences Biographical Memoirs* 17:223–52. Washington, D.C.: National Academy of Sciences, 1937.

Thoreson, Timothy H. H. "Art, Evolution, and History: A Case Study of Paradigm Change in Anthropology." *Journal of the History of the Behavioral Sciences* 13 (1977):107–125.

Trumbull, James Hammond. "On the Best Method of Studying the North American Languages." *Transactions of the American Philological Association* 1 (1869–70):55–79.

Washburn, Wilcomb E. "The Museum and Joseph Henry." *Curator* 8 (1965):35–54.

Wilson, Daniel. "Lectures on Physical Ethnology." SI, *AR for 1862–63*, pp. 240–302.

Wilson, Thomas. "The Smithsonian Institution and its Anthropological Work." *Journal of the Royal Anthropological Institute of Great Britain and Ireland for 1890:* 509–15.

Wissler, Clark. "W J McGee." *Encyclopedia of the Social Sciences* 5 (1930):652–53.

ADDRESSES, CIRCULARS, PAMPHLETS

American Ethnological Society. *Indian Languages of North America. AES Circular* 1. New York, June 1852.

Baird, Spencer F. *General Directions for Collecting and Preserving Objects of Natural History.* Washington, D.C., 1848.

Gibbs, George. *Instructions for Archaeological Investigations in the U.S.* SI, *AR for 1861*, pp. 392–96.

_____. *Instructions for Research Relative to the Ethnology and Philology of America.* Smithsonian Institution Miscellaneous Collections 7. Washington, D.C.: GPO, 1863.

_____. *Instructions relative to the Ethnology and Philology of America.* Appendix A: Physical Characters of the Indian Races; Appendix B: Numerical Systems. Smithsonian Contributions to Knowledge 15. Washington, D.C.: GPO, 1865.

Goode, George Brown. *Classification of the Collection to Illustrate the Animal Resources of the United States: A List of Substances Derived from the Animal*

Kingdom, with Synopsis of the Useful and Injurious Animals and a Classification of the Methods of Capture and Utilization. Washington, D.C.: GPO, 1876.

————. *The Organization and Objects of the National Museum. USNM Circular* 15. Appendix 4. *USNM Proceedings* 14. Washington, D.C.: GPO, 1881.

Henry, Joseph. "Address of Prof. Joseph Henry." *Fifth and Sixth Annual Reports of the American Museum of Natural History*: 44–50. New York, 1874.

Henshaw, Henry W., and Mooney, James. *Linguistic Families of the Indian Tribes North of Mexico, with a provisional list of the Principal Tribal Names and Synonyms.* Washington, D.C.: GPO, 1885.

Hunter, Alfred. *A Popular Catalogue of the Extraordinary Curiosities in the National Institute arranged in the Building belonging to the Patent Office.* Washington, D.C., 1859.

King, Henry. *Directions for Making Collections in Natural History, prepared for the National Institution for the Promotion of Science.* Washington, D.C., 1840.

Mallery, Garrick. *Introduction to the Study of Sign-language among the North American Indians as Illustrating the Gesture-speech of Mankind.* Washington, D.C.: GPO, 1880.

Mason, Otis T. *Ethnological Directions Relative to the Indian Tribes of the United States.* Washington, D.C., 1875.

Pilling, James C. *Proof-Sheets of a Bibliography of the North American Indians.* Washington, D.C.: Smithsonian Institution, 1885.

Poinsett, Joel R. *Discourse on the Objects and Importance of the National Institution for the Promotion of Science, established at Washington, 1840. Delivered at the First Anniversary.* Washington, D.C., 1841.

Powell, John Wesley. *Address Delivered at the Inauguration of the Corcoran School of Science and Arts, in the Columbian University, Washington, D.C., October 1, 1884.* Washington, D.C.: Gibson Bros., 1884.

————. *Introduction to the Study of Indian Languages with Words, Phrases and Sentences to be Collected.* Washington, D.C.: GPO, 1877. 2d ed., 1880.

Rhees, William J. *Guide to the Smithsonian Institution and National Museum.* Washington, D.C., 1859.

————. *Visitor's Guide to the Smithsonian Institution and National Museum.* Washington, D.C., 1880.

Schoolcraft, Henry Rowe. *An Address, Delivered before the Was-Ah-Ho-De-No-Son-Ne, or New Confederacy of the Iroquois, at its Third Annual Council, August 14, 1846.* Rochester, 1846.

————. *Incentives to the study of the Ancient Period of American History. Address to the New York Historical Society, 17 November 1846.* New York, 1847.

————. *Plan for the Investigation of American Ethnology: to include the facts derived from other parts of the globe, and the eventual formation of a Museum of Antiquities and the peculiar Fabrics of Nations: and also the collection of a library of the Philology of the World, manuscript and printed.* New York, 1846.

Yarrow, Harry Crécy. *Introduction to the Study of Mortuary Customs among the North American Indians.* Washington, D.C.: GPO, 1880.

UNPUBLISHED WORKS

Beckham, Stephen Dow. "George Gibbs, 1815–1873: Historian and Ethnologist." Ph.D. dissertation, University of California at Los Angeles, 1969.

Bieder, Robert Eugene. "The American Indian and the Development of Anthropological Thought in the United States, 1780–1851." Ph.D. dissertation, University of Minnesota, 1972.

Brandes, Raymond Stewart. "Frank Hamilton Cushing: Pioneer Americanist." Ph.D. dissertation, University of Arizona, 1965.

Colby, William L. "Routes to Rainy Mountain: A Biography of James Mooney, Ethnologist." Ph.D. dissertation, University of Wisconsin-Madison, 1977.

Darnell, Regna D. "The Development of American Anthropology, 1879–1920: From the Bureau of American Ethnology to Franz Boas." Ph.D. dissertation, University of Pennsylvania, 1969.

Erickson, Paul A. "The Origins of Physical Anthropology." Ph.D. dissertation, University of Connecticut, 1974.

Freeman, John F. "Henry Rowe Schoolcraft, 1793–1864." Ph.D. dissertation, Harvard University, 1960.

Jacknis, Ira. "The Field Columbian Museum Expedition to the Northwest Coast, 1897." Unpublished paper.

————. "Franz Boas and Museums of Anthropology in America, 1880–1920." Unpublished paper.

Lacey, Michael J. "The Mysteries of Earth-Making Dissolve: A Study of Washington's Intellectual Community and the Origins of American Environmentalism in the Late Nineteenth Century." Ph.D. dissertation, George Washington University, 1979.

Noelke, Virginia H. "The Origin and Early History of the Bureau of American Ethnology, 1879–1910." Ph.D. dissertation, University of Texas at Austin, 1974.

Poor, Robert. "Washington Matthews: An Intellectual Biography." Master's thesis, University of Nevada-Reno, 1975.

Tax, Thomas G. "The Development of American Archeology, 1800–1879." Ph.D. dissertation, University of Chicago, 1973.

ARCHIVAL MATERIAL

This study draws largely on unpublished archival material, some of it opened for the first time. In addition to the collections listed below, I enjoyed access to copies of the incoming and outgoing correspondence of Joseph Henry, gathered, from various collections, at the Joseph Henry Papers, Smithsonian

Institution, under the editorship of Nathan Reingold. These letters are cited in the notes by original collection.

Beloit.
Beloit College Archives.
Stephen D. Peet Papers.

Boston.
Harvard University Archives.
Peabody Museum Papers.
Frederick Ward Putnam Papers.
Peabody Museum Archives.
Papers of Frank Hamilton Cushing and the Hemenway South-Western Archaeological Expedition.

Chicago.
Field Museum Archives.
Franz Boas Files.
George A. Dorsey Files.

Los Angeles.
Southwest Museum.
Frederick Webb Hodge/Frank Hamilton Cushing Papers.
Charles F. Lummis Papers.

Madison.
Wisconsin State Historical Society.
George Gibbs Family Papers.
Increase Lapham Papers.

New Haven.
Yale University Library.
Elias Loomis Papers.
William Dwight Whitney Papers.

New Orleans.
Tulane University Medical Library.
Joseph Jones Papers.

Philadelphia.
American Philosophical Society.
Franz Boas Papers.
John Fries Frazer Papers.

Princeton.
Princeton University Library.
Joseph Henry Collection.

Providence.
John Carter Brown Library.
John Russell Bartlett Papers.

Rochester.
University of Rochester Library.
Lewis Henry Morgan Papers.

San Marino.
Henry E. Huntington Library and Art Gallery.
William J. Rhees Papers.

Santa Fe.
Museum of Navaho Ceremonial Art.
Washington Matthews Papers.

Washington, D.C.
George Washington University Archives.
Catalogues and Prospectuses of the Columbian College Preparatory
  School, 1861–84; GWU, Bulletins, 1871–84.
Library of Congress.
Anita Newcomb McGee Papers.
William John McGee Papers.
Gifford Pinchot Papers.
Ephraim George Squier Papers.
**Smithsonian Institution, Library of the National Museum of American
Art and the National Portrait Gallery.**
William Henry Holmes, "Random Records of a Lifetime Devoted to Science
  and Art, 1846–1931." 20 vols.
Smithsonian Institution, National Anthropological Archives.
William L. Abbott Papers.
Anthropological Society of Washington Papers.
Bureau of American Ethnology Letterbooks, 1879–1920.
Bureau of American Ethnology Letters Received, 1879–1910.
Aleš Hrdlička Papers.
Records of the 1903 Investigation of the BAE.
Matilda Coxe Stevenson Papers.

U.S. National Museum Papers (including papers of Otis T. Mason and Walter Hough).

Smithsonian Institution Archives.

Correspondence of the Assistant Secretary, 1850–1910.

Correspondence of the Secretary, 1846–1910.

Robert Kennicott Papers.

Otis T. Mason's Letters from Europe, 1889.

National Institute Papers.

Richard Rathbun Papers.

William J. Rhees Papers.

Smithsonian Institution Libraries.

Manuscripts of Otis T. Mason and Charles Rau.

Worcester.

American Antiquarian Society.

Samuel F. Haven Papers.

Index

This book was produced by the Smithsonian Institution Press, Washington, D.C.
Printed by Braun Brumfield, Inc.
Set in VIP Garamond by Photo Data, Inc.
The text paper is sixty pound Warren's Old Style
with Holliston Roxite C cover
and Colortext endpapers.
Designed by Elizabeth Sur.

ocial Development

e-to-eye contact.

mile of recognition.

ppearance of
ranger and separa-
on anxiety.

eak of stranger and
eparation anxiety.

tranger and separa-
on anxiety
iminishes.
eginning of peer
lay.
urn-taking with
eers.

iffuse crowds in
ames of "Cops and
obbers."

echnical skill in
rafts and sports, and
pecialized roles in
eam sports.

2. *Simple Exchange*

3. *Good Child*

4. *Law and Order*

5. *Representative
Government*
6. *Individual
Conscience*

3. *Phallic Stage*

4. *Latency*

5. *Genital Stage*

3. *Initiative versus
Guilt*

4. *Industry versus
Inferiority*

5. *Identity versus
Role Confusion*

6. *Intimacy versus
Isolation*

7. *Generativity versus
Stagnation*
8. *Ego Integrity
versus Despair*

ount and
create simple stories.

Social peer play;
writing own name;
size differences.

Reading readiness;
beginning of formal
schooling.

Formal logic in
mathematics and
science; search for
own values.

J Pollard

CHILDREN Behavior and Development

Contributors

David E. Barrett
National Institutes of Health, Bethesda, Maryland   Chapter 9

William R. Brassell
West Carolina Center, Morganton, North Carolina   Chapters 1, 4

Willard W. Hartup
University of Minnesota, Minneapolis   Chapter 10

Kenneth L. Hoving
Kent State University, Kent, Ohio   Chapter 6

James M. Larkin
University of Pennsylvania, Philadelphia   Chapter 3

C. Edward Meyers
University of Southern California, Los Angeles   Chapter 9

Philip Morse
University of Wisconsin, Madison   Chapter 8

David Schwartz
Chapter 3

Linda S. Siegel
McMaster University, Hamilton, Ontario, Canada   Chapter 7

Peter K. Smith
University of Sheffield, England   Chapter 2

Norman L. Thompson, Jr.
Macquarie University, Sydney, Australia   Chapters 3, 11

3rd edition

Holt, Rinehart and Winston   New York   Chicago   San Franciso   Atlanta
Dallas   Montreal   Toronto   London   Sydney

CHILDREN

Behavior and Development

Boyd R. McCandless
Robert J. Trotter

Senior Acquisitions Editor	Richard Owen
Senior Developmental Editor	Louise Waller
Managing Editor	Jeanette Ninas Johnson
Senior Project Editor	Francoise Bartlett
Production Manager	Victor Calderon
Photo Research	Peggy Middendorf
Designer	Bill Gray
Art Director	Robert Kopelman

Library of Congress Cataloging in Publication Data

McCandless, Boyd R.
  Children.

  Bibliographies.
  Includes index.
  1. Child psychology. I. Trotter, Robert J., joint
  author. II. Title.
  BF721.M12 1977   155.4   76-54683
  ISBN 0-03-089750-5

Special thanks to Science Service and to *Science News* magazine for providing the time and training needed to complete this project. Thanks to Susan Strasburger, Ruth Vogelsong, and Cherry Doyle for their help in preparing the manuscript. And, finally, thanks to the good people at Holt, Rinehart and Winston for all their help and encouragement. — R.J.T.

For permission to use copyrighted materials, the authors are indebted to the following:
CHAPTER 1: p. 1, photo by Iris Kleinman; pp. 5, 15, The Bettmann Archive; p. 7, The Granger Collection, New York; p. 9, Sigmund Freud Copyrights Ltd.; p. 20, photo courtesy of James B. Watson; p. 23, Harvard News Office photo; p. 27, Table 1-1 from Trotter, R. J. "East Side, West Side: Growing Up In Manhattan," *Science News*, 1976, 109, 20, 315.
CHAPTER 2: p. 43, The Bettmann Archive; pp. 46, 59, The Granger Collection, New York; p. 49, From *Child Development* by Sueann Robinson Ambron. Copyright © 1975 by Holt, Rinehart and Winston. Reprinted by permission of Holt, Rinehart and Winston; p. 50, Courtesy of the Upjohn Company, Kalamazoo, Michigan; pp.

64, 77, photos by Michael Weisbrot; p. 71, photo courtesy of M. Kawai; p. 74, photo by George Silberbauer.
CHAPTER 3: p. 89, photo courtesy of the Museum of Modern Art. Copyright © 1970, United Artists Corporation, all rights reserved; pp. 91-92, photos courtesy of H. F. Harlow, University of Wisconsin Primate Laboratory; p. 98, photo courtesy of Helen Malinowska Wayne; p. 104, United Nations photos; p. 106, left, Featherkill Studio; right, United Nations photo; pp. 110, 113, photos © 1976 by J. Brian King.
CHAPTER 4: p. 144, photo courtesy of Landrum B. Shettles, M.D., F.A.C.S., F.A. C.O.G.; pp. 147, 157, from *Fundamentals of Child Development*, second edition, by Harry Munsinger. Copyright © 1971, 1975 by Holt, Rinehart and Winston, Inc. Reprinted by permission of Holt, Rinehart and Winston; p. 148, Wide World Photos; p. 150, photo by Iris Kleinman; p. 160, photo courtesy of William Vandivert and *Scientific American*; p. 162, From *Understanding Human Behavior* by James V. McConnell. Copyright © 1974 by Holt, Rinehart and Winston. Reprinted by permission of Holt, Rinehart and Winston; pp. 168, 171, 175, Featherkill Studio.

(continued on page ix)

foreword

My first encounter with the original edition of this book came in 1961 as a graduate student at Indiana University. A short year later, its author, Professor Boyd R. McCandless, joined the faculty there. My positive impressions of his first book—strong in scholarship, insightful analysis, and clarity of style—were reinforced by meeting and coming to know the author and his family. During the next several years the course of my doctoral study was firmly charted by immeasurable intellectual stimulation and personal encouragement from Professor McCandless. After an appointment to the faculty at the University of Washington, my professional good fortune continued with an opportunity to assist in and prepare ancillary instructional materials for the second edition of the book I had so early admired. Still further collaboration followed, including the preparation of a separate, jointly written book. This indelible experience served as a beacon for continued professional alliance.

It was therefore both heartening and gratifying to be entrusted with a critique of the initial plans for the third edition of *Children: Behavior and Development*. These plans reached fruition and serious work was well underway when tragedy struck. Those of us who knew, respected, and loved Boyd McCandless were stunned and forever touched by his premature death on December 5, 1975.

Fortunately for his readership Professor McCandless had completed the basic conceptual framework and collated the substantive material for this revision just prior to his death. But the manuscript itself, in early draft form, was not ready for printer's ink. Equally fortunate, then, was the availability of a gifted and scientifically aware writer to prepare the manuscript for final publication. Robert Trotter has sculptured its basic anatomy to a point of excellence in readability. I salute him for dealing so successfully with this challenging task, especially since the spirit of Boyd McCandless' astute scholarship and warm humanism has been so well preserved.

In a formal sense, this book signifies the last milestone for Boyd McCandless' many achievements. Sadly, my congratulations to him must be given posthumously. But I can rejoice in his memory, the wealth of experiences that we and our families have shared together through the years, and the achievements that are certain to come in future years from the many students and colleagues whom he influenced. For a scholar whose life was dedicated to benefit others there is perhaps no more fitting legacy.

Seattle, Washington   Ellis D. Evans
October 1976

preface

In the ten years that have elapsed between the second and third editions of *Children*, research in developmental psychology has mushroomed. This has been particularly true of work with preadolescents; in fact, the field has changed so much since 1967 that the third edition has become virtually a new book.

An effort has also been made to lower the reading level of the text from that of the previous edition, thus increasing its comprehensibility for students taking the introductory course in child development.

The format of the third edition is markedly changed. Since today's students seem to be quite sophisticated in the field of general psychology, the old chapter called "Special Factors in Human Learning" has been dropped, as have the chapters entitled "Child-rearing Practices" and "Authoritarianism and Prejudice." Relevant material from these chapters has been included where appropriate in the book.

New information on language and on cognition has dictated separate chapters on these subjects in the third edition. The biology of behavior and a chapter on infancy have been included to strengthen the book. Moral, ethical, and social development is now treated, providing a more accurate coverage of developmental psychology as the field exists today. In addition, a separate chapter on psychosexual development has been written.

The Appendix gives an overview of development by chronological age and specific topics, such as perception, cognitive stages, and so on.

Part I describes the main theories of child development, then invites the reader to peruse two overview chapters—one dealing with biological perspectives of the growth of the child and the other with social development. The chapters of Part II return to biology and to cognition and discuss separate topics in more depth. The focus of Part III is the social growth of the child.

Important terms and words defined in the text appear in boldface type.

In order to draw on the widest possible research and knowledge in various aspects of child development, the author has included important contributions from the authorities listed below. Appreciation is extended to: William R. Brassell, West Carolina Center, Morganton, North Carolina, for Chapters 1 and 4; Peter K. Smith, University of Sheffield, England, for Chapter 2; Norman L. Thompson, Jr., Macquarie University, Sydney, Australia, for Chapter 11; Kenneth L. Hoving, Kent State University, Kent, Ohio, for Chapter 6; Linda S. Siegel, McMaster University, Hamilton, Ontario, Canada, for Chapter 7; Philip Morse, University of Wisconsin, Madison, for Chapter 8; David E. Barrett, National Institutes of Health, Bethesda, Maryland; and C. Edward Meyers, University of Southern California, Los Angeles, for Chapter 9; Willard W. Hartup, University of Minnesota, Minneapolis, for Chapter 10; Norman L. Thompson, Jr., Macquarie University, Sydney, Australia; David Schwartz; and James M. Larkin, University of Pennsylvania, Philadelphia, for Chapter 3; David Abrams for the Appendix. The basic book, however, remains the author's, who assumes liability for its weaknesses and credit for its strengths.

Some of the content of the new edition reflects events in the life of the author between 1967 and 1975—a wider perspective derived from cultures other than that of the United States. This period away from home includes more than half a year in Australia, deeply immersed in its culture, and a good bit of time in Jamaica, working with preschool urban and rural children.

Having spent much of a lifetime in the field of developmental psychology surrounded by exceptionally competent women, the problem of how to overcome the limits of the English language in relation to females has been studied by the author but not overcome. There is as yet no graceful way to deal with male-female pronouns. Although this has been in the author's mind and consciousness, the problem has not been solved.

The book has been written to aid the student in understanding of the child who is springboard to the adolescent, and, later, the adult. The author hopes students will learn from the book and will enjoy that learning.

B. R. McC.

Atlanta, Georgia
November 1975

acknowledgments

The author expresses gratitude to the reviewers of this edition—Ellis D. Evans of the University of Washington, A. J. H. Gaite of the University of Oregon, Lauren Jay Harris of Michigan State University, Brian Mac-

Whinney of the University of Denver, Sidney Rosenblum of the University of New Mexico, John W. Santrock of the University of Texas, Dallas, and Thomas D. Spencer of San Francisco State University. In addition, the following people are thanked for contributing the Research Reports: A. J. H. Gaite, University of Oregon, for Chapters 1, 2, and 5; John R. Stabler, Georgia State University, for Chapter 3; Helene Block, Oakton Community College, and Amado M. Padilla, University of California, Los Angeles, for Chapter 4; Mary Fulcher Geis, University of North Carolina, for Chapters 6 and 7; Janie D. Osborn, North Georgia College, for Chapter 8; Walter Hodges, Georgia State University, for Chapter 9; Toni Santmire, University of Nebraska, for Chapters 10 and 11; Thomas E. Cheshire, Central Piedmont Community College, and Rhoda Olenick, Loop College, for Chapter 12.

contents

PART 2   Biological and Cognitive Bases of Development 140

PART 3   Cultural and Social Bases of Development 408

the study of
child development

The history of childhood has changed over the years and continues to change because of information that has been gathered on human development. This information has been organized in theories that help explain and predict human behavior. Additional information is coming to light through the research methods being used by developmental psychologists. Chapter 1 offers a brief history of childhood and an introduction to the theories and methods of developmental psychology.

developmental psychology: its history, theory, and methods

Children are fascinating. But more than that, they are important. They are the key to the future. Surprisingly, however, children have not always been treated as if they were important or valuable. At various times throughout the history of Western civilization it was common practice to kill, abandon, abuse, and terrorize even the youngest of children. In fact, the history of childhood has been called "a nightmare from which we have only recently begun to awaken." This is the conclusion of Lloyd de Mause and his colleagues who have written one of the first comprehensive histories of childhood (2).

A thorough search of historical documents has revealed what de Mause sees as significant trends or stages in the history of childhood. The first such stage he calls infanticidal. It was characterized by **infanticide,** or the murder of infants, a practice that appears to have been socially accepted from prehistoric times until about the fourth century A.D. The writings of early Greeks and Romans, for instance, contain hundreds of references to infanticide. Among wealthy families the first-born child was usually allowed to live if it was healthy. But other children, especially if they were girls and almost always if they were illegitimate, were often thrown into rivers, "potted" in jars to starve, or exposed on a hill or roadside. Roman law did not even consider the killing of children as murder until A.D. 374. And infanticide was so common that historians of the time blamed it for the depopulation of both Greece and Rome.

When infants were allowed to live they were not always kept by their parents. Abandonment, says de Mause, characterized the second stage of the history of childhood (from the fourth to the thirteenth century). Records show that during this period many children in Western Europe were sold as slaves or servants, and many were given away or abandoned to monasteries and nunneries. Some were even mutilated and sold as beggars. A blind child or one with a crushed foot or amputated limb excited more pity and collected more money as a beggar.

The most common form of abandonment during the Middle Ages began with a wet nurse, a woman who suckles other women's children. Parents who could afford it usually sent their children to live in the home of a wet nurse for the first two to five years of life. After that the children were usually cared for by servants and were then sent off to school or to work. Parents spent a minimum of time rearing their offspring.

As depressing as this history may seem, de Mause sees a brighter side. The quality of child care appears to have improved progressively throughout history. Gradually, parents began to pay more attention to their children. In the seventeenth century, the British philosopher John Locke described the child's mind as a *tabula rasa*, or "clean slate," and parents and educators tried to write

English schoolmaster thrashing a pupil.

on that slate. In other words, they tried very hard to teach children or mold them into shape. The methods used, however, were sometimes severe. Discipline was thought to be necessary to learning, and de Mause's evidence on the disciplining of children leads him to believe that a large percentage of the children born prior to the eighteenth century were what would today be termed "battered children." Beatings began in infancy and were a regular part of a child's life. Beating instruments included whips of all kinds, shovels, canes, iron and wooden rods, and bundles of sticks as well as some special instruments that were designed to raise blisters. These instruments were especially popular in schools.

By the eighteenth century, a real change in the treatment of children was becoming apparent. In England, societies for the prevention of cruelty to children were created. Children were still struck and punished, but they were no longer subjected to regular whippings. Ideas about childhood also began to change. The thoughts of Locke were being replaced by those of Jean Jacques Rousseau, the influential French philosopher. Rousseau described the child as a "noble savage," unspoiled by the pressures of parents, teachers, and society. His philosophy suggested that children should be allowed to grow and develop in an atmosphere of freedom. In this manner, they would learn from their experiences and interactions with the environment. Unlike Locke,

Rousseau did not believe that education should be forced on children. Let them develop naturally, he urged, and eventually (at about the time of puberty when children begin to reach sexual and physical maturity) their minds would be prepared for a more formal type of education or training.

The eighteenth century, the Age of Reason, was also an age during which science made some important starts with regard to children. **Pediatrics,** the branch of medicine that deals with the care of infants and children, was born, and the infant death rate began to decline. In Switzerland, the educational reformer Johann Heinrich Pestalozzi published observations on the growth and development of his young son. The fact that such a work was published indicates that the importance of children and childhood was becoming apparent to a growing number of people.

In the nineteenth century, scientific interest in children continued to grow and even blossomed with a boost from one of the most important scientists of the day — Charles Robert Darwin. Like Pestalozzi, Darwin published a day-to-day record of the development of his son. But it was Darwin's major work, his explanation of evolution in *The Origin of Species,* that really had an effect on the study of children (and on almost every other area of science).

After making detailed observations and studies of a great many animals around the world, Darwin attempted to explain how evolution worked to produce new and different species or types of animals. In brief, he found that some animals inherit characteristics that help them adapt or fit better in their environment. Those animals that are the fittest survive and pass on their new adaptive characteristics to the next generation. Those that do not inherit the adaptive characteristics are less likely to survive, and eventually they die out. After many generations and after the inheritance of many characteristics, a new species is produced.

Darwin was studying and writing about animal species, but it seemed reasonable to apply some of his ideas to humans. Psychologists became very interested in studying the adaptive characteristics of humans, and a great many studies were made of the changing or developing characteristics of humans from infancy to old age. Near the end of the nineteenth century the study of children began to receive attention in the United States with the work of G. Stanley Hall, the first psychologist to investigate seriously the development of children. Hall was especially interested in childhood experiences and learning, and his books on the education of children were among the first to be used in colleges.

Since Hall's time, many more books about child development have been written, and the history of childhood has continued to change. Although child abuse and child neglect are still serious problems, child-rearing trends in the United States today bear almost no resemblance to those of several centuries ago. De Mause calls the second half of the twentieth century the helping stage

Naturalist Charles Darwin (1809–1882).

in the history of childhood. Parents, teachers, and even government policy are actively involved in helping children fulfill their needs as they grow and develop into adults. If the treatment of children has grown increasingly better, as de Mause and his colleagues suggest, it is because much has been learned about children in this century. A great many psychologists, educators, researchers, and other interested people have spent a lot of time studying children and collecting information on the behavior and development of children.

Almost every area of child development has been and is still being thoroughly examined: physical growth, from the moment of conception to adolescence; social development, including the effects of children's interactions with parents, teachers, other children, and society in general; and cognitive, or mental, development, including language ability, intelligence, creativity, and many other areas in which mental processes are involved.

All of the information that has been collected on children is important, but it does not really explain child development. For years, Darwin collected data on different types of animals, but that information did not really explain the development or evolution of different types or species of animals. It was only after Darwin put all of the information together in a systematic or organized manner that the real meaning of his findings became clear. A systematically organized body of knowledge is called a theory. Darwin put together the theory of evolution.

Putting together a theory is like putting together a jigsaw puzzle. Each piece represents a fact, and as the facts are pieced together the picture (the theory) becomes more complete. But even though theories are based on facts, theories are not necessarily true. As new facts are added, the picture (the theory) may change. Good theories do, however, help in the search for truth. As more and more pieces of a puzzle are found and fitted together properly it becomes easier to look for and find the remaining pieces that will complete the picture. Similarly, once some of the facts have been found and fitted together into a theory, it usually becomes easier to find more facts and fit them into their proper place. In this manner, good theories help explain the information that has been collected, and they predict what might be found in the future. Since science attempts to explain and predict the workings of the world, theories are an important part of the scientific method—facts are collected, a theory is proposed, and new facts are gathered in an attempt to prove or test the theory. As long as research continues to support a particular theory, the theory will stay in use. If new findings do not support it, the theory may have to be changed or even discarded. At present, there are several major theories that have been useful in explaining child development.

FREUD AND PSYCHODYNAMIC THEORY

The theory that revolutionized thinking about childhood in the twentieth century was put together by Sigmund Freud (1856–1939), an Austrian physician who received his medical degree from the University of Vienna, the city in which he lived most of his life. Freud began his professional career as a **neurologist,** or nerve specialist (a neuron is a nerve), and he was relatively successful in his studies of the human nervous system. As a neurologist, Freud saw many patients who suffered from what were thought to be disorders of the brain and nervous system, and in this way he eventually became interested in the study of mental illness.

Freud believed that human behavior, including most mental illness, is caused by **psychodynamic forces** (from the words for "mind" and "energy"). These energies of the mind, he believed, are constantly at work causing behavior and shaping the human personality. He further argued that this energy is present in everyone from the time of birth, and that it affects every stage of human development. Therefore, in order to understand human behavior Freud believed that it is necessary to understand the psychodynamic forces at work during infancy and early childhood.

At first, few people took Freud's theory seriously. For one thing, he empha-

Neurologist Sigmund Freud (1856–1939) founder of psychoanalysis.

sized the importance of sexual needs and drives, in children as well as in adults. But in nineteenth-century Vienna sex was a very private matter, and even physicians did not normally speak of sexual subjects in public. Eventually, however, Freud's theory was accepted by a great many people because it was useful in explaining and predicting human behavior, and because it was the only fully developed theory of the time. In fact, Freud's theory became immensely popular and has had a great impact on twentieth-century thinking. Because Freud stressed the importance of childhood, the study of childhood has become almost routine for anyone interested in understanding human behavior.

Libidinal Energy

One of the dynamic forces that shapes individual personalities, according to Freud, is **libidinal energy** (from the Latin word for "desire" or "lust"). This energy, he said, is constantly being produced from the time a child is born. It builds up in each individual much the way steam builds up in a pressure cooker or a boiler. If the steam or energy is not released, there is danger of an explosion. People don't physically explode, but Freud's theory says that high energy levels cause pain and discomfort, while low energy levels are associated with pleasure. Anything that increases libidinal energy leads to tension and unhappiness. Anything that decreases libidinal energy leads to feelings of contentment and well-being.

With his background in human biology, it is not surprising that much of

Freud's theory is based on human biological systems. Personality and human behavior, he believed, are shaped by the way infants and children learn to control and release libidinal energy. And this energy is released through three biological systems: the mouth (oral cavity) and eating, the anus and elimination, and the genitals (sex organs) and sexual behavior.

The Oral Stage

During the first few years of an infant's life the oral system is extremely important. Children's first experiences with satisfaction and discomfort and with pleasant and unpleasant human relations are associated with the mouth and the feeding process. During this **oral stage,** libidinal energy is pleasantly released through oral activities—eating, sucking, swallowing. Relaxed and generous treatment during the oral stage is thought to produce childhood and adult personalities characterized by cooperative, peaceful, friendly, optimistic, and sharing and giving traits.

Children who are deprived of food or otherwise harshly treated during the oral period seem to suffer from a build-up of libidinal energy and tend to be overwhelmed by fears and anxieties. According to Freudian theory, infants who are not sufficiently gratified or pleased during the oral stage tend in later life to spend a lot of time trying to compensate or make up for deficiencies suffered during the oral stage. Overeating, overdrinking, and excessive smoking are often thought of as forms of oral compensation. People who seem to devote an undue amount of energy defending against the anxiety and insecurity associated with oral deprivation are sometimes said to be fixed or fixated at the oral stage. In addition to the more obvious oral behavior, orally fixated adults are sometimes seen as miserly, arrogant, aggressive, impatient, competitive, suspicious, depressed, and cynical.

The opposite of deprivation, overprotection and overgratification, during the oral stage can also lead to **fixation.** Overprotecting parents sometimes tend to keep their children from moving on to later developmental stages. Without encouragement to develop, children may become orally fixated in a different way. Such people tend to be overly dependent. They put too much trust in others, expect others to do everything for them, and have unrealistic feelings of security and self-confidence. Orally deprived children, on the other hand, tend to become prematurely dependent on themselves and self-sufficient, while at the same time remaining insecure and uncertain. In this manner, Freudian theory explains how similar personality traits (dependence) may have completely different origins, just as very different-appearing behaviors may have similar origins.

The Anal Stage

The **anal stage** overlaps the oral stage and lasts from about 1 year or 18 months to around 4 years. During this period children are asked to submit to the will of their parents, to forego their own pleasure and learn to give in to the demands of society. This can be seen most vividly during toilet training (in Western societies). During the anal stage children begin to gain control over their muscles, including the muscles that control elimination. Release of libidinal energy in the anal stage is associated with muscle control, and pleasure is derived from activities like urinating and defecating. The trait of **autonomy** (self-determination or self-will) is thought to develop or be blunted during the anal stage.

The **anal character** (fixation at the anal stage) may, according to Freud, be the result of too early or overly strict and harsh toilet training. The anal personality is characterized by excessive orderliness, stinginess, and obstinacy. Too strict toilet training is also thought by some people to inhibit or hold back the natural exploratory interest of children by causing them to be filled with shame in matters related to the elimination of body waste. In such cases, children may regress, or move backward developmentally, to the oral, dependent stage and fail to develop self-confidence and independence. In children who never give in to parental training, adult traits of wastefulness, unpunctuality, extravagance, and vacillation (indecisiveness) are thought to occur.

Anal fixation, like oral fixation, is also thought to occur through either deprivation or overgratification. Such overgratification might be the result of parents not imposing limits and affectionately giving in to all of a child's demands. Fixation due to this type of indulgence might produce a personality with overpowering self-confidence, insensitivity to needs of others, and extreme social dominance. Fixation due to overindulgence during the anal stage probably occurs less often than fixation due to deprivation for two reasons. Parents almost always have to put some limits on their children in order to protect them from bodily harm. And even if parents are overindulgent, children soon learn that other adults and even other children require them to stay within certain limits.

The Phallic Stage

Between 3 and 5 or 6 years of age children become increasingly aware of their own sexuality. Young boys and girls find out that they are physically different from each other. The pleasant release of libidinal energy during this stage is often associated with self-manipulation or stimulation of the genitals (the male's penis, or phallus, and the female's vagina). Freud calls this the **phallic stage,** but he has often been criticized for overemphasizing the male aspects of development and minimizing the importance of female development. The changes that seem to take place during the phallic stage do, however, apply to both males and females. During this stage children are interested in their own sexuality as well as that of others, and they usually begin to build up a warm relationship with the parent of the opposite sex.

According to Freudian theory, overly harsh and restrictive treatment during the phallic stage may impair or damage self-confidence, curiosity, and ambition and produce anxiety about the body and its natural functions, particularly in the area of sexual behavior. Fixation due to overgratification at this stage is probably relatively rare in the United States because parents and society tend to discourage childhood sexuality.

The Oedipus Conflict

A child's attachment to the parent of the opposite sex results in what Freud saw as one of the most important aspects of development. If normal development is to continue, boys must give up the intense relationship they may have had with their mothers. Girls must do the same with regard to their fathers. Presumably, giving up this relationship represents a major struggle or conflict for young children. Freud called it the **Oedipus conflict.**

Oedipus was a tragic character in Greek mythology. As a child, he was separated from his parents and reared by other people. As a young man, he met his father (whom he did not know) and killed him in an argument. Later, Oedipus returned to his home kingdom of Thebes where he met his mother, the queen Jocasta. Not knowing she was his mother, Oedipus fell in love with and married her. For these mistakes, both Oedipus and his mother (wife) suffered terribly.

Freud used the story of Oedipus to symbolize the type of love-hate relationship he thought all children go through with their parents (even though children may not recognize what is happening, as Oedipus did not).

A resolution or solution to the Oedipus conflict usually takes place between 5 and 6 or 7 years of age. The conflict is resolved by a compromise. A young boy soon realizes that he cannot actually replace his father, but that he can capture a good deal of his mother's love by imitating the values and behavior of his father. Girls are supposed to follow the same developmental pattern, but Freud thought this happened later in girls than in boys. In resolving her conflict, a young girl will imitate much of her mother's behavior in an attempt to capture her father's love. In this manner, boys and girls begin to develop their own value systems and behavior patterns, borrowed in part from their parents. Boys tend to develop their father's type of masculinity, girls their mother's feminity.

When the Oedipus conflict is successfully resolved, boys presumably take a natural, easy, proud attitude toward their maleness, girls toward their femaleness. If, for one reason or another (such as unduly harsh, rejecting, or overprotective parents of either sex), the Oedipus conflict is not resolved, young children may continue their strong attachment to the parent of the opposite sex—perhaps at the expense of developing their own masculine or feminine identity. Failure to resolve the Oedipus conflict has been suggested as one explanation for homosexual behavior and for problems of sexual performance such as impotence on the part of the male and frigidity on the part of the female. Again, as with earlier stages, similar behavior may have very different origins: One girl may conceivably become homosexual because she had a strong, tender mother and a weak father; another because her father was harsh and rejecting but to a lesser degree than her mother.

The Latency Period

Following the resolution of the Oedipus conflict, infantile sexuality seems to recede or become less important. This marks the beginning of the **latency period** (from age 6 to 12). Latency, from the Latin word for "hidden," suggests that sexuality is still present but hidden by other interests. During this developmental stage much attention (libidinal energy) seems to be directed at learning skills and the further development of a set of values and standards. As children begin to leave the home more often, they start to learn from people other than their parents. Freud believed that during this period boys seek the company of other boys and find masculine models or heroes among older men. Similarly, girls tend to stick together during this period and begin to imitate and learn from older women other than their mothers. Freud called latency the "natural homosexuality period" that comes before the reawakening of sexual interest.

The Genital Stage

The period of latency ends when children begin to reach physical and sexual maturity during puberty. Secondary sex characteristics (including fully developed sex organs and breasts, facial hair for males and the monthly menstrual cycle for females) develop during puberty, and libidinal energy is once again focused on the genitals. During this **genital stage,** growing children become aware of the fact that relations with the opposite sex can be pleasant.

The genital stage brings with it several problems. As adolescents become aware of their own sexuality, they may become self-conscious about their growing bodies and secondary sex characteristics. They may worry that they are developing too slowly or too rapidly. They may also have trouble deciding between the comfortable existence of childhood and the responsibilities of adulthood. These and other problems during the genital stage sometimes lead to emotional upsets, moodiness, and rebellion against authority. But if the previous stages have been handled relatively well, adolescents will usually be prepared to make the adjustments required by the genital stage and move into adulthood.

Evaluating Psychodynamic Theory

One of the most important aspects of psychodynamic theory was that it forced psychologists for the first time to look carefully at childhood experiences for explanations of adult behavior. In addition, it forced researchers to consider, in a systematic way, the internal forces that seem to be involved in much human behavior. As important as these factors are, however, Freudian theory is not perfect. For one thing, the internal forces that Freud describes, like libidinal energy, cannot be seen or measured. Their existence cannot even be proved. Because of this, many of Freud's ideas have been difficult to verify or prove.

Another problem is that Freud did not have all of the facts when he put his theory together. Living and working with middle-class Europeans at the turn of the century, Freud was naturally influenced by the people with whom he was most familiar. He also worked with many people who were emotionally troubled, and their behavior and experiences probably had a great deal to do with his theory. Had Freud lived in another time, in another place, he might have produced a completely different theory. Anthropological studies, for instance, suggest that what Freud called the "latency period" probably does not exist in cultures that have a casual or permissive attitude toward sexuality in children. And the Oedipus conflict, which may sound reasonable when applied to middle-class children and their parents in the United States or Europe, does not seem to apply to cultures that have a different family structure, such as those in which children are reared in a community setting with a number of adults acting as parents. Freud's theory also suggests that as a resolution to the Oedipus conflict, young boys begin to imitate their fathers and thus develop masculine attitudes. Without a strong father, the theory maintains, young boys do not learn proper masculine behavior. But there are cultures in which fathers do not play an important role in family life and in which the mothers are dominant. Yet there is no evidence to indicate that young males in such cultures are any more mother-fixated or less masculine than boys in a typical U.S. family. These findings, as well as a variety of evidence, all show that Freud's theory is not universal—that is, it does not apply to all people in all places.

As these and other shortcomings of psychodynamic theory became obvious, theorists and researchers began to update and modify Freud's original theory. The neo-Freudians, or New Freudians, for example, have retained much of Freud's theory but have attempted to change it where necessary to account for facts of which Freud was not aware. Erik Erikson has been especially influential in the updating of Freudian theory. He describes personality development in stages similar to Freud's, but he emphasizes the importance of social relationships and cultural differences instead of purely biological and sexual influences. Others have attempted to strengthen psychodynamic theory in other areas. Psychodynamic theory is much more complex than can be seen from an outline of Freud's developmental stages. Because this theory is so complex and has been so important, the ideas of Freud and his followers will be further developed in various chapters throughout this book.

Psychologist Jean Piaget
(1896–   ).

PIAGET AND THE COGNITIVE APPROACH

The Swiss psychologist Jean Piaget is one of the most influential thinkers in the field of child development today. Instead of concentrating on physical growth or on social and emotional development, Piaget has focused on studying one of the most human of behaviors—**cognition.** All of the intellectual abilities of the mind (thinking, knowing, perceiving, remembering, abstracting, and generalizing) are included in the term "cognition."

Following the lead of Pestalozzi, Piaget began making detailed observations of children. He worked with preschool children at the Institute Jean Jacques Rousseau in Geneva, and followed closely the cognitive development of his own three children. From these observations, Piaget has constructed a theory of intelligence that outlines the cognitive development of children and the mental stages they seem to go through (5).

Assimilation and Accommodation

Adaptation, says Piaget, is the most important process in intellectual functioning. If it is cold, people adapt by putting on more clothes. If it is hot, they adapt by taking off some clothes. But the weather is only one condition to which people must learn to adapt. There are millions of sensations and experiences that we must learn to live with. While there are many specific ways of adapting, according to Piaget, there are only two basic forms of adaptation: assimilation and accommodation.

Assimilation means to take in. That is what infants do as they listen to people around them talking. They assimilate, or take in, the various sounds and parts of a language and gradually build up their own language ability.

Accommodation is an outgoing process by which people adjust or adapt to the environment. After children have assimilated a few words, they begin to use those words. The outgoing words are usually meaningless at first. In order to speak properly and communicate efficiently, children must learn to change the sounds they make. They must learn to accommodate and make their speech the same as that of the people around them. In this manner, through assimilation and accommodation, children learn to adapt to the particular language of their environment. According to Piaget, each assimilation and accommodation leads to mental growth and development.

The word "hot" is a good example. After touching something hot and hearing the word "hot" several times, most children, after a certain age, will assimilate the meaning of the word and will accommodate by not touching a hot object. The result is a useful adaptation that keeps children from getting burned. Through experience, children gradually learn that the word "hot" applies to more than one object, and that the world is full of things that are hot and should not be touched. In this manner, children begin to build up a mental concept or category of things that are hot. Similar concepts are gradually formed for such things as food, water, toys, and people.

In order to form concepts or ideas about the world, says Piaget, three things are necessary. The first is experience—touching something hot. The second is social transmission, or the passing along of information—"Don't touch that, it's hot!" And the third necessary factor in concept formation is maturation—a one-month-old child is just not mature or old enough to form a mental category of hot objects.

Mental ability, says Piaget, develops or matures through four stages or periods: the sensory-motor stage, the preoperational period, the concrete operational period, and the formal operational period. Piaget believes that all children go through each of the stages in the same order, no matter what culture the child is reared in or how much experience and training the child receives. Various parts of the stages may overlap, and some children may go faster than others (especially with more experience and training), but the steps must always be taken in the same order.

The Sensory-Motor Stage

During the **sensory-motor stage** (from birth to about the second year) the first noticeable signs of intelligence in children seem to be related to the senses and to motor activities (physical movements). At birth, infants are egocentric or self-centered. The only existence they are aware of is their own. They may follow a moving object with their eyes, but when the object is out of sight it ceases to exist as far as the child is concerned. Playing peek-a-boo with very young infants is almost useless, because they do not realize what the game is about. According to Piaget, very young infants have no idea of object permanence. In other words, when an object is out of sight, it does not exist.

Gradually, during the sensory-motor stage, the senses and motor movements help infants become aware of and make contact with the external world. After much sensory experience with moving objects (including people) they begin to realize that those objects continue to exist even when out of sight. As children learn to control their body movements and physical activities, they begin to reach out for objects. By 9 months of age (on the average) infants have had enough experience to begin to reach out for hidden objects, provided they have seen the object being hidden. At about this age, peek-a-boo becomes a fun game for children.

The sensory-motor stage is especially important for development. As infants reach out to objects and people in their world, they begin to build up a mental picture of a world that contains more than just themselves. And the sooner they become aware of the external world, the sooner they begin to learn from it. By the age of two, with the beginnings of language and the ability to communicate and use symbolism, children have usually had enough sensory-motor experience to realize that they are not alone in the world.

<table>
<tr><td>

The
Preoperational
Period

</td><td>

During the **preoperational stage** (from about 2 to 7 years) children begin to acquire the ability to perform internal mental activities or operations—as opposed to purely physical operations. During the sensory-motor stage, for instance, children will reach for a toy or object that they see and want. In the preoperational stage children learn to think and ask for toys even when the toys are not within sight. With this ability to imagine or symbolize the world, preoperational children begin to play at make-believe. In pretending or making believe that they are someone else (a parent, teacher, doctor, and so on), young children assimilate and begin to learn the customs and manners of people around them. By imitating other people, young children accommodate to new and strange experiences.

</td></tr>
</table>

No one can see the mind or its mental development, but some of Piaget's experiments with young children demonstrate rather vividly the mental changes that children seem to go through. Piaget, for instance, shows two balls of soft clay of equal size to children. Once the children agree that the balls are the same size, he rolls one of them out into a long sausage shape and then asks if the two pieces of clay are still the same size and if they still contain the same amount of clay. Preoperational children will usually say that the sausage shape contains more clay because it is longer. If the sausage is then rolled back into a ball, the children will once again agree that both balls contain the same amount of clay. The minds of preoperational children, explains Piaget, have not yet developed to the stage where they can grasp transformations or changes in shape.

By the time children reach the age of 6 or 7 (sometimes called the age of reason), transformations do not seem as hard to understand. If the sausage is rolled out very thin and long, the children may still say that it is bigger than the ball. But if the sausage is short and fat (closer to the shape of a ball), the children will usually realize that the sausage and the ball contain the same amount of clay.

The Concrete Operations Stage

During the next stage of development, the **period of concrete operations** (from about seven to eleven years of age), children's thinking begins to speed up. They can look at a ball of clay and realize that it will contain the same amount of clay no matter what shape it is in. During this stage, children gradually come to understand other types of transformations. A cup of milk in a bowl, for instance, seems to be the same amount of milk as a cup of milk in a tall, thin glass—even though the containers have different shapes.

During the stage of concrete operations, children begin to use their growing mental ability to think about what happens to concrete or solid objects without actually having to experiment with the objects. By skipping over the physical or sensory-motor parts of an experience in this manner, mental operations are greatly speeded up. Preoperational children might search through every room in a house for a lost toy. Children in the concrete operations stage can sit back and think about where the toy might be without having to go through all the motions of a physical search. Children in the concrete operations stage can usually think about any object they have had some experience with. The same children cannot usually extend such thinking to include non-concrete or abstract ideas.

The Period of Formal Operations

Abstract thinking develops during the period of formal operations (after the age of 11 or 12). Piaget calls this final period the **stage of formal operations** because during this stage adolescents learn to follow the form of thinking or reasoning. In the formal stage children think about thoughts (or mentally operate on mental operations). Piaget explains much of this stage in terms of mathematics. People in the formal operations stage, for instance, can understand terms like "a billion years," which must be thought of in abstract rather than concrete terms. People in this stage can generalize or form opinions about abstract concepts like love, honor, truth, and justice. By the end of the period of formal operations (at 14 or 15 years of age), mental development is usually complete. Any further mental ability comes only with continued thinking, learning, experience, and the acquisition of information.

Piaget and his followers have put together a unique theory, one that has been very useful in explaining certain areas of human development and in filling in some of the gaps in psychodynamic theory. Cognitive theory concentrates on understanding the origin, nature, methods, and limits of human knowledge—areas that have not been well developed in psychodynamic theory. But in doing so, cognitive theory has often overlooked the social, emotional, biological, and individual aspects of human development. Piaget borrowed from Freud, and his theory is subject to some of the same criticisms that have been leveled at psychodynamic theory. Like Freud, Piaget supposed that certain internal forces are responsible for human behavior. But these forces, even if they do exist, have yet to be measured scientifically. Also, like Freud, Piaget based much of his theory on observations of a select group of children, his own children in many instances. Had Piaget worked with children from a number of different cultures, he too might have come up with a different theory. So as useful as Piaget's theory is, there is evidence that does not support his outline of human developmental stages. Some children, for example, seem to be able to handle certain mental problems before Piaget's theory predicts they should. It may be that maturation and intellectual development take place as a continuous process rather than in stages. But even if there are no specific developmental stages, it is often easier to understand the process of mental development by following Piaget's stages.

BEHAVIORISM AND LEARNING THEORY

The theories of Freud and Piaget help explain human behavior and development, but both theories contain elements that cannot be proved. "Libidinal energy" may be a reasonable term for explaining the internal forces that seem to drive or force people to act, but libidinal energy cannot be seen or measured. Its existence cannot even be proved. Piaget talks about "mental concepts," and he attempts to demonstrate their existence in the way children answer questions or solve problems. The mental concepts themselves, however, cannot be seen or measured scientifically. What can be seen and measured are the behaviors produced by these supposed internal events and forces. **Behaviorism** is a third approach to the study of human beings. It attempts to be more scientific than the other theories by concentrating only on scientifically observable and measurable events—behaviors.

Behaviorism got its start in the United States early in this century with the work of John B. Watson. Watson believed strongly that psychology should not be involved in philosophy and mentalism (theories that contain unprovable assumptions about the mind) but should concentrate on scientifically observable natural events.

Human development, from a behaviorist point of view, is seen not as a

Behaviorist John B. Watson
(1878-1958).

series of stages or phases through which children must go, but as a learning
process and a gradual build-up of behavior patterns and habits. According to
behaviorist theory, behaviors are not the result of unseen, internal forces but
are learned through experience with the environment, including experiences
with people. Accordingly, children in the oral stage do not eat in order to release libidinal energy, but because they have learned that eating can be a
pleasant experience. Similarly, children avoid hot objects because they have
learned that touching hot objects can be a painful experience.

According to learning theorist Robert M. Gagné, stages of development are
not related to age, except in the sense that learning takes time (4).

**Classical
Conditioning**

One of the most exciting things about children is that they learn. Learning
ability is present at birth, and one of the most basic or classic types of learning
is **classical conditioning.** This type of learning involves making an association
between a **stimulus** and a **response.** A stimulus is anything in the environment
that causes an organism (child, adult, animal, or plant) to react or respond. A
loud sound, such as a bell, is a stimulus that may cause people to blink their
eyes. This responding to a stimulus is one of the most basic forms of human
behavior. But people do not always respond in the same manner to a stimulus.
Under different conditions, they learn to respond differently to the same stimulus. For fire fighters, a bell means it is time to go to work because a bell always
rings when there is a fire. For school children, a bell may mean it is time to eat

because a bell always rings before lunch. After enough experience with a stimulus (bell), people learn to make an association between the stimulus and the response (fighting a fire or eating). The differing responses of fire fighters and school children are the result of differing conditions. The way in which people form an association between a stimulus and a response is called classical conditioning.

Through classical conditioning people learn to respond to millions of stimuli—lights, bells, smells, food, smiles, kind words, and so on. Because there are so many different conditions, stimuli, and responses, classical conditioning can account for much human behavior. John Dollard and Neal Miller have used the stimulus-response theory to explain how children form habits and basic ways of responding during the earliest years of their lives (3). These conditioned habits may last for years and become basic parts of each personality.

Conditioned responses or habits, however, are not always permanent. They can be unlearned. The process by which conditioning wears off is called **extinction.** If a bell rings every day but the school children are not fed, the association between the stimulus (bell) and the response (getting ready to eat) will eventually be extinguished. The children will no longer be conditioned to respond to the bell.

Generalization and Discrimination

An experiment conducted by Watson and R. Raynor helps demonstrate the importance of classical conditioning (8). An eleven-month-old child known as Little Albert was shown a white rat. Albert seemed interested in the rat and attempted to play with it. But every time the child crawled toward the animal, the experimenters made a loud noise that frightened the child. After several attempts to reach the rat, Little Albert began to associate the animal with the loud, frightening noise. Through classical conditioning Albert had learned to fear the rat.

But something else happened. Albert was shown a white rabbit, and he reacted to it in the same manner he had learned to react to the rat. Apparently Albert's conditioned fear was not restricted to rats. He had learned to fear furry objects in general. A fur coat and a Santa Claus mask, for instance, both made Albert cry and react with fear. Through a process known as **generalization,** Albert's conditioned response had been expanded from a specific fear of white rats to a general fear of furry objects.

The opposite of generalization is **discrimination.** Once children have had enough experience with the environment, they will learn to discriminate or tell the difference between various stimuli. If a church bell rings and children are not fed, they will learn to discriminate between the church bell and the lunch bell. Through discrimination they eventually learn that all fruits are not oranges, that all animals are not dogs, and that all adults are not their parents.

Classical conditioning is a very simple type of learning that goes on in everyone's life, but classical conditioning does not explain all human behavior. A hungry child, for instance, does not always wait for someone to ring a bell. Instead of waiting for a stimulus in the environment to bring about a reaction, people sometimes stimulate or operate on their environment to get what they want. By stimulating the environment, including other people in the environment, it is possible to get the environment to react. Children cry when they are hungry, and parents usually react. Actions that operate on the environment are called operant behaviors. And just as stimulus-response behaviors are learned by classical conditioning, operant behaviors are learned by **operant conditioning.**

Operant conditioning is sometimes called **behavior modification** because it changes or modifies the behavior of an organism. Psychologist B. F. Skinner has used experiments with animals to show how behavior modification works. A rat in a cage has certain behaviors that appear to be natural and voluntary. It will sniff around, explore, stand up, sit down, and so on. If there is a button or a lever in a cage that can be pushed, the rat will probably get around to pushing it sooner or later. If immediately after the lever has been pushed a piece of food rolls down a chute into the cage, the rat will probably eat the food and then go back to exploring. After a while, the rat will probably hit the lever again; and if food drops into the cage again, the rat may begin to make an association between the lever and the food. If food drops into the cage every time the animal hits the lever, the rat will eventually learn a new behavior and will push the lever (operate on the environment) whenever it wants food. In a similar manner, children learn to put money in vending machines and push buttons to get what they want. They are operating on their environment.

In classical conditioning, a set of stimuli (sound and food) is used to elicit or bring forth a response. In operant conditioning, the response (rat pushing lever) is voluntary and is not elicited by a particular stimulus. Whether or not the animal repeats the response, however, is influenced by whatever stimulus is associated with the response. A rewarding stimulus (food) will influence the animal to respond. A punishing stimulus (such as an electric shock) will usually keep the animal from responding or pushing the lever in the future.

A special cage with a lever and feeding machine was designed by Skinner for use in operant conditioning experiments. By watching rats, pigeons, and other animals in such cages—now known as Skinner boxes—Skinner developed a set of principles to explain how operant behaviors are learned.

If the rat in Skinner's box had never hit the lever, it would never have learned how to use the lever to get food. A child who has never seen a candy machine might never put a coin in the slot. So the first thing a hungry rat or child must do is find out that a certain behavior—pushing a lever or putting a coin in the slot—can produce a desired result. Skinner allowed the rat to work

Psychologist B. F. Skinner
(1904–   ).

by trial and error, and the animal just roamed around the cage until it accidentally hit the lever. When this happened, the rat was fed and it began to learn the relationship between the lever and the food. A similar type of hit-or-miss technique can be seen in children as they learn a language. A child who knows only a few words, may try each word in an attempt to ask for a toy. When the child hits on the proper word, the parents know what the child wants and respond (sometimes) by giving the child the toy. The child begins to learn that one specific word will produce a desired result.

Modeling

    The hit-or-miss approach works, but it can be very slow. The rat might not get around to pushing the lever for a long time. It might be hours before a child comes out with the right word, or before a student comes up with the proper solution to a problem in mathematics. Experimenters and teachers, therefore, have ways of speeding up learning or the acquisition of proper responses. A child or a student can be told how to behave or told what the proper response should be. Parents repeat words over and over to young children in the hope that the infants will learn the words and learn how to use them. Teachers spend hours explaining a subject to students in the hope that the students will be able to come up with the proper response at test time.

    But all behaviors can't be explained verbally. An experimenter can't tell a rat how to push a lever, and parents have trouble explaining the behaviors necessary in riding a bicycle. And it is sometimes difficult to teach students how to solve a particular type of problem by explaining the solution. When verbal instructions don't seem to work, **modeling** is often used. A teacher or instructor models or acts out the desired behavior.

A rat in a Skinner box may play around for hours before hitting the lever, but if a rat that has already learned how to use the lever is put into the box, things are speeded up. The first rat watches the second rat push the lever for food, and before long the first animal catches on and starts pushing the lever. Parents speed up a child's learning by showing the child how to get on a bike and ride. Teachers use the blackboard to show students how to do long division.

Modeling is also called imitation or social learning. And because children are such great imitators, much of what they learn during the first years of life is a direct result of imitating the actions of parents and other people who serve as models. But even when adults are not purposely acting as models, much of what they do serves as a model to influence the behavior of children.

Albert Bandura and his colleagues arranged for young children to observe adults either attacking an inflated doll or sitting quietly next to the doll. Later, the children were put in the room with the doll. Those children who had seen the adults behaving aggressively toward the doll imitated that behavior. Those children who had seen the adults sitting quietly with the doll imitated that behavior (1). Other experiments have shown that aggressive behavior can also be learned from films or television. And according to behaviorist theory, every human behavior in every stage of development is a result of some type of learning.

Evaluating Behaviorist Theory

Behaviorism, because of its serious attempt to be completely scientific, avoids some of the problems of the other theories. By confining itself to observable, measurable facts (behaviors), every part of the theory can be verified or proved. By avoiding discussion of the "mental" aspects of being human, behaviorism avoids arguments about things that cannot be proved or disproved. Behaviorism also attempts to be universal by describing reactions that are common to all people rather than to a specific group of people. Stimulus-response experiments, for instance, have been performed with all sorts of organisms, from the most basic animals to the most complex humans. The principles of stimulus-response behavior can, therefore, be said to apply to all organisms rather than to a specific group (as in the cases of Freud and Piaget).

But it is precisely because behaviorism has attempted to be scientific that it has been criticized. For one thing, it is argued that behaviorism is based too much on animal studies, and that animal behavior cannot explain all human behavior. Second, by insisting on a purely scientific approach, behaviorists are forced to deny or at least avoid studying such things as thoughts, hopes, and aspirations. And many people believe these very things to be an important part of being human, even if they can't be seen or proved to exist. Finally, behaviorism insists that all human actions are the result of measurable, controllable environmental influences. And if all of these influences are known, then all human behavior can be explained, predicted, and controlled. But saying that a person's behavior can be completely predicted or controlled denies the existence of that person's free will. And free will is an important part of being human that most people are unwilling to give up, even for the sake of science. So behaviorism, like the other theories, has its shortcomings. But it does fill in gaps left by the other theories, and because behaviorism has made enormous contributions to the understanding of human behavior, it, like the other theories, will be more fully developed and discussed in later chapters.

With all of the criticisms (and there are many more for each of the theories) it is obvious that psychology has yet to come up with a universal theory capable of explaining all human behavior. The theories available, however, have proved their usefulness and will continue to do so because each theory concentrates on specific areas of human development. When one theory does not fully explain a certain type of behavior, one of the others usually will. If a more universal theory is produced that is capable of replacing what we have, it will probably be because more and better evidence has been found. And researchers are constantly at work searching for such evidence.

RESEARCH IN CHILD DEVELOPMENT

A major goal of research in child development has always been to observe and describe "normal" or average children as they grow. Normative research (from the word "normal"), for example, has pointed out that by the time most infants are three months old they can focus their vision on an object as well as adults can. With this type of information, parents and pediatricians can evaluate a child's developmental progress. Another goal of developmental research is to explain the processes involved in development, and a number of research plans or strategies (designs) have been designed to do this. The two basic types of research are **naturalistic** (observations of children under natural conditions) and **manipulative** (observations of children when conditions are changed or manipulated).

Naturalistic Research

The Family Research Project, directed by Thomas S. Langner and his co-workers at Columbia University's School of Public Health, is one example of naturalistic research (6). For this particular study, extensive information was gathered on more than 2,000 children and their parents living in New York City. Two groups were studied. The first consisted of 1,034 children aged 6 to 18 from a cross section of households. (A cross section of this type is a representative sample meant to be typical of all households.) This sample was

56 percent white, 29 percent Spanish-speaking, 14 percent black, and 1 percent of other races. The second group consisted of 1,000 children who were members of households receiving welfare. Each one-year age group made up about one-thirteenth of each sample, and males and females were equally represented.

Mothers in the selected households were interviewed at the start of the study and again five years later. They were asked to provide information on their family lives and their children. The children were examined by psychiatrists, and additional information was gathered from school and agency records (welfare agencies, social services, police, and so on).

From these data, 18 typical types of childhood behavior were drawn up. These included such things as conflict with parents, mentation problems (the child mixes up words or has trouble remembering things), isolation (plays alone, doesn't keep friends), and sex curiosity (masturbates often, likes to see parents undressed).

Using a computer, the children were classified according to their behaviors and placed in one of the 18 behavior groups. About one-third of the children from the typical cross-section group were found to be psychologically or mentally troubled in some way. More than 13 percent were rated by psychiatrists as being seriously impaired and in need of immediate psychological attention.

The next major part of the research project was to identify those factors in the children's family life, environment, and background that might be related to their behavior. Because the possible number of factors involved was much too large to be studied, the researchers concentrated on the characteristics of parents, their marriages, and child-rearing practices. By looking closely at these factors and relating them to the children's behaviors, it was possible to find out which particular factors were related to specific behaviors. The factors were then listed in order of their reliability as predictors of childhood behavior.

Because most of the factors involved had immediate as well as long-term effects, all factors were examined from both perspectives during the study. The children's behaviors were rated at the start of the study and again five years later. For instance, punitive parenting (parents spank children often and deprive them of privileges) ranked fourth as a predictor of the children's behavior at the time of the first interview. But when looked at for its effect five years later, punitive parenting was found to be the most important factor in terms of predicting long-term behavior (see Table 1-1).

The Family Research Project is a good example of many of the research strategies that are important to studies of child development. In the first place, it was naturalistic. This is the most traditional form of developmental research. Darwin used it in writing a diary of his son's development. Piaget used

Table 1-1

Predictor	Content	Behaviors Predicted
Punitive parents	Parents spank child with a strap or stick and often use deprivation of privileges	Fighting Conflict with parents Regressive anxiety Delinquency
Mother excitable-rejecting	Mother often screams at child, is very changeable in handling child and regards self as an excitable person when handling child	Conflict with parents Regressive anxiety Fighting Sex curiosity Isolation Self-destructive tendencies Conflict with siblings Mentation problems Competition Impairment of school functioning
Cold parents	Parents rarely hug and kiss the child or show affection easily to the child	Conflict with parents Fighting Conflict with siblings Undemanding Delinquency
Mother's physical and emotional illness	Mother's health is poor. Mother has periods when she can't get going, feels weak all over and is often bothered by nervousness	Regressive anxiety Fighting

naturalistic research (observed his own children) in developing his theory. In this type of research, children are observed going about their lives in their natural environment with little or no interference from researchers. While the New York study didn't actually spend a lot of time observing children, it was based on naturalistic observations made by parents, teachers, and others, and the children were not interfered with by the researchers.

The study was also **longitudinal.** It looked at the same group of children periodically over a long period of time. Long-term, or longitudinal, studies are perhaps one of the best strategies for studying behavior as it emerges and changes with time. This historical or longitudinal approach is aimed at understanding how past experiences are related to present behavior. Piaget's longitudinal study of his children helped him understand their development.

Longitudinal studies can be either prospective or retrospective. In **prospective studies,** facts are gathered about children being studied at different times during the study. In **retrospective studies,** parents, teachers, and others are asked to reconstruct from memory the children's history and early experiences. Most of Freud's patients gave him retrospective accounts of their childhood. Retrospective studies are not as reliable as prospective studies and are rarely used because the memory is not always accurate. This method is, however, used when no other record of a child's history is available.

In addition to being naturalistic and longitudinal, the Family Research Project was cross-sectional. This approach is sometimes used instead of a longitudinal study in an attempt to study developmental characteristics. In a typical **cross-sectional study,** groups of children from at least two age levels are studied at the same time and compared on specific characteristics, such as ability to solve a certain type of problem. By looking at the performance of both age groups, the researchers can draw conclusions about the effects of age. The Family Research Project studied children in 13 age groups. This approach is less precise than longitudinal research because it does not tell the researcher how the same child performed at each age level.

The cross-sectional approach is not always used to study differences between age levels. Other factors such as ethnic and economic background can also be studied. In the New York City study a cross section of children from the typical ethnic and economic groups in the city was selected. The effects of one particular family factor, such as punitive parenting, could thus be studied for its effect on children from different backgrounds.

A similar approach is cross-cultural research in which an attempt is made to study the effects of a specific factor on people living in different cultures. **Cross-cultural research** was used to show that what may have been true of the people Freud studied was not true of people in other parts of the world.

Another naturalistic strategy is **comparative research** in which comparisons of behavior are made between different species. Jane van Lawick-Goodall, for instance, is famous for her studies of chimpanzees in the wild. Ethology, the study of development and behavior of other species, sometimes helps to outline general principles of development that may apply to all species. Such studies also lead to an understanding of how human behavior may have emerged during the course of the development of the human species.

Much comparative research is naturalistic, but animals are also taken out of their environment and studied in the laboratory. Much of Skinner's research was done with animals, and animals are often used in research that humans cannot be subjected to. The development of vision, for instance, has been studied in kittens by raising them from birth in an environment that consists of only black and white vertical stripes. When these animals are later placed in a normal environment, they can see vertical lines but they are blind to horizontal lines. This is one example of manipulative research. Many more will be described in later chapters.

In many hospitals in the United States it is routine practice to separate a mother and her newborn infant for the first few days after birth. The infant is taken to a nursery, and the mother stays in a hospital room. The infant is then brought to the mother several times a day for feeding. Some researchers have suggested that future mother-child relationships can be affected by even such a short separation.

Marshal H. Klaus and his colleagues have designed an experiment to test this hypothesis (7). (An hypothesis is a proposition or assumption based on part of a theory. Research is designed to find facts that either prove or disprove the hypothesis.) Part of Klaus's hypothesis is based on behavioral studies of a number of animal species as well as on studies of human maternal behavior. These studies suggest that what happens in the period immediately following delivery may be critical to later maternal behavior. Goats, sheep, and cattle, for example, show disturbances of mothering behavior if they have been separated from their young for the first hour or so after delivery. After such a separation, the mothers may fail to care for their young and may even butt their offspring away.

Mice and rats show a lack of skill in caring for their young if mother and pup have been separated during the first few hours following delivery. Psychologist Harry Harlow's studies of rhesus monkeys show that mothers who are not allowed to touch their infants, but are allowed to see them through a window, soon lose interest in those infants.

Specific patterns of maternal behavior seem to be related to factors other than separation. Pregnant rats lick their genital areas during labor and just before birth. This behavior carries over to the pups after birth, when the mothers lick their pups. If the behavior pattern is changed, the result can be abnormal mothering. In one experiment, high collars were placed on the necks of pregnant rats to prevent self licking. The collars were removed shortly before birth, but the rats did not lick their infants clean in the normal fashion. Instead, the mothers ate some of the pups. The mothers even refused to suckle those pups that weren't eaten.

For a period after delivery, weeks or even months, most animal species show characteristic maternal behavior patterns such as licking, nesting, and grooming. Observations of humans suggest that such behavior patterns are also found in human mothers. In many societies, for instance, there is some regularized method of dealing with newborns. Anthropological studies show that in many cultures the mother and infant are secluded during the first three to seven days after birth while the navel heals. In Israeli kibbutzim (communes), separation does not usually occur until after the fifth day. In

Russia, mothers are not separated from their infants during the first weeks of life. Klaus and his colleagues point out that "routine complete separation of mother and infant in the first days after delivery exist only in the high-risk and premature nurseries of the Western world." Even after normal births, some degree of separation of mother and child is standard procedure.

It is this disruption of what appears to be a normal behavior pattern that is the subject of Klaus's research. Evidence of the danger of immediate separation of mother and child comes from studies of premature infants (those born early) who were taken away from their mothers for special treatment. At the turn of the century, Pierre Budin, a specialist in infant care, noted that "Unfortunately . . . a certain number of mothers abandon the babies whose needs they have not had to meet, and in whom they have lost all interest. The life of the little one has been saved, it is true, but at the cost of the mother."

Another example comes from the work of Martin Cooney, who, in 1896, displayed a "child hatchery" that was used to isolate and protect premature infants. Cooney traveled as an exhibitor to fairs in England and the United States where he exhibited premature infants in their "hatcheries." Significantly, Cooney sometimes had difficulty getting parents to take their children back.

Because the human infant is wholly dependent on its mother or caretaker for all physical and emotional needs, the strength of the attachment bond between the two is important in determining whether a child will survive and develop normally. The battered child syndrome, for instance, is one of the most dramatic examples of disturbed mothering. In one study of battered children, the incidence of prematurity or serious illness (problems such as diabetes may require immediate separation of mother and child) was 39 percent. Although many factors contribute to the battered child syndrome (such as the mother's own rearing), Klaus suggests that early separation may be a significant factor.

If the separation of mother and child immediately after birth, for medical reasons, can have such dramatic effects on the mother-child affection bond and on future behavior, then it is possible that any separation might have subtle, but still important, effects on the mother-child relationship.

In 1970, after reviewing the information on the separation of mothers and infants, Klaus and John H. Kennell concluded that "it would not be unreasonable to change many of our existing rules and regulations. However, no widespread change should take place until there is strong evidence that what we are doing is damaging, and that a change would be desirable." Since then, Klaus and his colleagues have been collecting that evidence.

They are studying the mothers of full-term, rather than premature, infants. They are testing the hypothesis that there is a period shortly after birth that is uniquely important for the mother-to-infant attachment in humans. For the study, 28 women were selected and placed in two groups. The 14 mothers in the first group had traditional contact with their infants: a glimpse of the baby shortly after birth, brief contact and identification at 6 to 12 hours, and then visits for 20 to 30 minutes every four hours for bottle feeding. In addition to this contact, the other 14 mothers, those in the extended-contact group, were given their nude babies for one hour within the first three hours of birth and also five extra hours of contact each afternoon on the first three days after delivery—a total of 16 hours of extra contact with their infants while in the hospital.

To determine if the additional contact altered later behavior, the mothers were asked to return to the hospital one month after delivery for three separate observations. They were interviewed, observed while the child was being examined, and filmed while feeding their infants. The extended-care mothers scored higher on questions related to caretaking and seemed to interact more with their infants. They were also more likely to sooth the child if it cried during the physical examination. Films showed that while feeding, the extended-contact mothers spent more time fondling and making eye-to-eye contact with their infants. The eye contact is thought to be especially important, and some researchers have even suggested that eye-to-eye contact between mother and child might be responsible for initiating maternal caretaking behavior.

The researchers concluded that the differences between the two groups in eye contact and tactile stimulation (petting and caressing) that probably occurred during the first month, in more than 200 feedings, and in numerous other encounters, may have definite effects on the infant. Studies show, for instance, that increased maternal attentiveness helps bring about exploratory behavior as well as the early development of cognitive behavior in infants.

The differences between the two groups of mothers were obvious, but still, the researchers said, "Caution is recommended before any drastic changes are made in hospital policies." But since that study was completed, the mothers have been seen again, at one year and at two years. One year after giving birth, the mothers in the two groups continued to be significantly different in their answers to interview questions and in their behavior during a physical examination of the child. The extended-contact mothers continued to display more fondling behavior and eye-to-eye contact behavior. Of the mothers who had returned to work or school, the extended-contact women were more preoccupied with their babies than were the other mothers. The researchers concluded that it was time for a thorough review and evaluation of present hospital delivery practices. And changes might even have to be made with regard to fathers. A study done in Sweden suggests that fathers who had extended contact with their infants during the first five days after birth were more likely to spend more time interacting with their children.

During the two-year follow-up, mother-child verbal interaction was observed and recorded. After an initial interview, each mother was left alone with her child for a "free play" period in a room containing toys. The situation was taped and analyzed, and several measures of verbal behavior were made: rate, length and variety of utterances, grammatical structure, form, class, and type or function of sentences.

The differences between the groups were again apparent. When talking with their children, the mothers in the extended-contact group had a verbal output distinctly greater in variety and elaboration. Their utterances were somewhat longer and contained more function words (that is, prepositions and conjunctions that are characteristic of more mature speech).

The extended-contact mothers used more appropriate forms for giving information, for getting a response from the child, and for explaining simple concepts. They addressed twice as many questions to their children and initiated more teaching behavior. The mothers in the other group used more content words, the type of speech one might use in giving basic information.

From these results, it appears that the extended-contact mothers have a greater awareness of the growing needs of their children. Such sensitivity and increased attention could have important effects on future cognitive and linguistic development. Thus, say the researchers, permission for a mother to spend a few additional hours with her newborn infant immediately following delivery may change the linguistic environment she provides for her child in its first years of life, and this, in turn, may affect the child's learning and language far into the future.

Maternal behavior is known to be determined by many complex factors, so it is surprising that just 16 hours during the first three days of life can have an effect that lasts for at least two, and perhaps many, years. And, as the researchers note, this extra contact is easily manipulated.

This experiment is one example of manipulative research. The experimenters manipulated or altered what would have been the natural course of events by giving one group of mothers extra contact with their children. The goal of manipulative research is to have control over specific factors in an experiment, such as the amount of time mothers spend with their infants. The factors or basic elements in such an experiment are called variables or independent variables because the researchers can vary them (by giving more or less contact time to the mothers and infants). **Independent variables** are factors that can be manipulated independently of other conditions.

The behavior under study (the later behavior of the mothers and children) is called the **dependent variable** because its occurrence depends on the effects of the independent variable. Another example of independent and dependent variables can be seen in the time of day school exams are given. Some students perform better in the morning than they do immediately after lunch. The independent variable (time test is given) can be changed, and the dependent variable (score on test) may change.

One method of ensuring that the independent variable is indeed responsible for changes in the dependent variable is to use an experimental design in which two or more groups are studied. The simplest type of group design involves one group that receives the experimental treatment (extended contact between mothers and infants) and a **control group** that does not. The control group in the mother-infant contact study was not manipulated in any way by the experimenters.

Single-subject designs are also used in manipulative research. Operant conditioning experiments, for instance, are often conducted with only one subject. In a Skinner box, a rat is taught to push a lever. Using the same theoretical approach, a child might be taught a useful behavior. A child who mumbles, for instance, might be taught to speak clearly. The usual operant experiment involves presenting a child with a positive reinforcer as an independent variable. A **positive reinforcer** is any stimulus that maintains or increases the frequency with which a response occurs. A piece of food dropped into a Skinner box is a positive reinforcer if it gets the animal to push the lever again. A piece of candy or a toy might be used as a reward every time the mumbling child speaks clearly. By manipulating the environment (with candy) the experimenter changes the child's behavior. If one type of candy doesn't work, further manipulation might be called for, and the experimenter will have to find a more suitable reinforcer or reward for the child. Material reinforcers, such as candy or money, are not the only rewards to which children respond. Social rewards, such as praise from parents, teachers, or friends is usually an effective reinforcer. Not only the type but the timing of a reward is important. If a reward comes immediately after a behavior, it is more likely that the child will make the association between the reward and the behavior. If the reward is put off for a long time, the child may forget what the reward is for and fail to make a strong association between the reward and the behavior.

To be sure that an experiment has produced the desired results, it is necessary to measure the subject's behavior before and after the manipulation. The first measurement of behavior is called the **baseline** (bottom line) **measurement.** Before the experiment begins, for instance, 70 percent of the mumbling child's words might be unintelligible. This baseline figure (70 percent) is then compared with the child's speaking behavior after the experiment. If the child speaks more clearly, more often, the experiment may be considered a success.

Of course, all research isn't successful. There are many problems that researchers must overcome in their attempts to produce reliable results, and there are many methods currently being used to overcome these problems. The research described in this chapter helps explain some of these methods. Other methods and research designs will be described throughout this book.

With the results of that research, old theories are being revised and new ones are being born. More and more is being learned about how children develop and about the factors that influence development. And the more that is learned, the more possible it becomes to change the history of childhood—for the better.

SUMMARY

The history of childhood has gone through several stages, from the earliest times when it was common practice to murder, discard, or give away children to the present time when most people believe that it is necessary to help children develop to their fullest potential. These changes came about as more and more information was gathered on children and their development. The information has been organized into theories that attempt to explain and predict human behavior.

Psychodynamic theory, formulated by Sigmund Freud, suggests that human behavior is influenced by internal energies or forces, such as libidinal energy. A build-up of libidinal energy causes discomfort. Behaviors that reduce the level of libidinal energy cause pleasure.

Libidinal energy is released through different biological systems during various stages of development—the oral, and phallic stages, the period of Oedipal conflict, latency and the genital stage.

During the oral stage (the first year or two) libidinal energy is released through oral behaviors such as eating. During the anal stage (ages 1 to 4) libidinal energy is associated with muscle control (as in toilet training), and pleasure is derived from activities like elimination of bodily waste. During this stage children learn self-control. During the phallic stage (ages 3 or 4 to 6) children become aware of their sexuality and usually develop a strong attachment to the parent of the opposite sex. This can lead to what Freud called the Oedipus conflict—jealousy of the parent of the same sex. The latency period (from 6 to 12 years) has been called the "natural homosexual period." This stage comes just before puberty and mature sexual development. During the genital stage (after 12 or 13 years) adolescents reach physical and sexual maturity. They must give up the pleasures of childhood and begin to face the responsibilities of adulthood.

Psychodynamic theory was the first fully developed theory of personality, and it has been important in shaping twentieth-century thinking, especially about the importance of childhood. But psychodynamic theory has shortcomings. It does not explain all human behavior, especially behavior in cultures other than the United States and Western Europe. Also, it is difficult to prove because internal forces and energies cannot be measured or even proved to exist. The complexity and importance of psychodynamic theory (including the followers of Freud) will be more fully developed in later chapters.

Cognitive theory concentrates on intellectual development, an area not well covered by psychodynamic theory. Jean Piaget has been influential in developing cognitive theory and the stages of intellectual development — the sensory-motor stage, the preoperational stage, the period of concrete operations, and the period of formal operations.

Adaptation is important to cognitive theory, and assimilation and accommodation are the basic methods of adaptation. Through assimilation, children take in information from the environment. Accommodation is an outgoing process through which people adapt.

When infants are born they are egocentric or self-centered. They are aware only of themselves and their own needs. During the sensory-motor stage (the first two years of life) infants use their senses and motor activities to become aware of, make contact with, and begin learning from the external world.

During the preoperational period (from 2 to 7 years) children begin to perform mental operations as well as physical operations.

During the concrete operations stage (7 to 11 years) children's thinking begins to speed up because they have a better understanding of the physical world. They can sit back and think about the physical world and understand such things as transformations.

During the stage of formal operations (from 11 to 15 years) children learn to handle abstract ideas. They can think about thoughts and understand concepts like love, honor, truth, and justice.

Cognitive theory offers a unique way of understanding intellectual development, but it overlooks social, emotional, biological, and individual aspects of development. Because of its significant impact on the understanding of human thinking, cognitive theory will be more completely described in later chapters.

Behaviorist theory avoids some of the problems of the other theories by concentrating on scientifically observable events (behaviors) instead of internal events (mental energies and mental operations). Behaviorism is based on learning. It says that personality development is the result of an accumulation of human behaviors.

The simplest form of learning is classical conditioning in which an association is made between a stimulus and a response.

Generalization is a method by which learning is extended. An association between a stimulus and a response can be extended or generalized to apply to other stimuli. The opposite of generalization is discrimination. Through experience people learn to discriminate or tell the difference between various stimuli.

Operant conditioning or behavior modification is a more complex form of learning that involves stimulating the environment in order to make it react (children cry in order to get their parents to feed them). Through operant conditioning children learn to modify or change their own behaviors in order to change the behavior of the environment (including the behavior of other people).

Modeling (imitation or social learning) is another important type of learning. Children learn by imitating many models in their environment—parents, teachers, friends, strangers, people on television. Modeling and the other forms of learning are so important to human development that they will be more completely described in the chapter on learning.

Behaviorism, like the other theories, does not explain all of human behavior. It overlooks some internal human behaviors which can't be measured but which seem to be important in human development. Each of the major theories has gaps, but because each theory concentrates on specific areas, much human behaviors can be explained by applying the strong points of each theory. If a more useful theory is ever developed, it will probably be because new facts about human development have been found by researchers.

Research in developmental psychology has two basic strategies or designs—naturalistic and manipulative.

Naturalistic research involves observing subjects in their natural environment as they go about their business with no interference from researchers. This research may be longitudinal (studying development as it occurs over time) or cross-sectional (studying several individuals in different stages of development).

Manipulative research involves changing the environment in order to observe the effect such changes will have on development. The effects of manipulation can best be seen if the environment of one subject or group of subjects (the experimental group) is changed while that of a similar subject or group (the control group) remains unchanged. Differences in development between the subjects can then be attributed to the changes (variables) in the environment. Developmental research will be described and explained throughout this book. Such research is changing the history of childhood.

The Child Development Movement

It is perhaps a sign of maturity when an area of study begins to take a serious interest in its history. There has been recently in child development a marked increase in articles which have looked back at the development of the movement and in so doing have traced the trends in theory and research that have emerged over time. Other articles have focused on the thinking, style, and personalities of those who made significant contributions to child development in its early years of research. For those who believe that an understanding and appreciation of the past in child development makes the present clearer and helps decision-making about the future, 1975 was a particularly good year. Two articles published in that year—one by R. R. Sears and one by M. J. Senn— examine in detail the history and growth of the child development movement in the United States.

Sears describes different sets of preconditions that, coming together, allowed child development to flourish. Thus, the influence of the eighteenth-century French philosopher Jean Jacques Rousseau and much later of Sigmund Freud stimulated interest in studying children. But also needed was the developing interest on the part of the scientific community to lead to the idea that the development of children was a proper subject for research. Needed particularly was acceptance of the notion that scientific study could be a base for social changes affecting children. Sears notes that the rise of the child development movement parallels the development of compulsory public education for all children. It does not seem unreasonable to suppose that teachers and educators—and indeed the general public—quickly discovered a need to know about children once it became universal to group them together in schools. The years following World War I were boom years in child development, with a proliferation of research, books on child development, and the founding of several institutes and study centers devoted to studying children. For example, the Institute of Child Development at the University of Minnesota was founded in 1925; at Yale University, Arnold Gesell's Psycho-Clinic, with its main concern child development, was greatly expanded, as was the Iowa Child Welfare Research Station which had begun in 1919; and in 1929 the Fels Research Institute was established in Yellow Springs, Ohio. The growth of the child development movement between the wars was perhaps culminated by the founding of the Society for Research in Child Development in 1933.

The growth of the movement slowed during World War II as researchers were turned to other problems, but since then the study of child development has flourished, with a sharp increase in research output that shows no signs of abating. Sears concludes his article by noting that while fierce arguments still rage within the movement over such matters as approaches and methods of research, these controversies probably reflect the good health of the movement rather than anything else.

Senn approaches the history of the child development movement through interviews with persons in the field. He interviewed more than 80 people and gathered their views on each other and on major figures with whom they had worked. He also explored with his subjects the relationship of child development to pediatrics and the relevance of the movement to better child care practices in the United States. Senn's work is not an attempt to quantify, but rather it presents a broad picture of the child development movement in terms of the personalities who formed it and of the important events that characterized its development. Thus, for example, Lawrence Frank is recalled as "the inspirational and organizing force behind the new institutes" established between the world wars which he was able to assist because of his connections with various private foundations and because he passionately believed that research and study was needed.

It would be hard not to conclude that the child development movement is strong today. Research on early childhood development, the learning of sex roles, early language learning, and a host of other topics continues to abound. Each year alone hundreds of studies investigate Piaget's ideas on cognitive development. It seems safe to say that if only because in our culture we are endlessly and tirelessly fascinated with ourselves, the study of children will continue to flourish.

Based on R. R. Sears, "Your Ancients Revisited: A History of Child Development." In E. M. Hetherington, ed., *Review of Research in Child Development*, Vol. 5. Chicago: University of Chicago Press, 1975; M. J. E. Senn, "Insights on the Child Development Movement in the United States," *Monographs of the Society for Research in Child Development*, 1975. 40 (serial no. 161).

RESEARCH REPORT 1.2

Some Difficulties with Research

To state the obvious, children are not the same as rats or monkeys, which makes for a major problem in conducting research in child development. Children are complicated organisms and they are *human beings*. So researchers cannot control and manipulate any part of their lives as freely as they do the lives of rats or monkeys. A major part of the problem is that it is often difficult to randomly assign human subjects in an experiment to conditions or groups. An example will serve to illustrate the problem. If you want to know if intelligence is mostly a matter of environment or heredity the ideal solution is to use sets of identical twins (each pair with the same genetic make-up). At birth you randomly distribute them to different environments. Then, over the years, differences in intelligence, if any, between the children in each pair can be observed. But it is an impossible study to carry out! It is the moral, ethical, and practical problems that test child development researchers perhaps most of all.

Brickell (1974) reported a study that took subjects from a school district.

The children participating in the study came from a systematically biased sample. If researchers want to deal with some districts from a state, the better districts are volunteered. Requests for some schools from a district gives researchers the "better" schools. Requests for some classrooms of students from a school gives researchers the "better" classrooms. Requests for some students from a classroom results in the "better" students. This kind of bias can seriously distort research findings. It also illustrates the kind of problem a researcher faces when getting study subjects. It is not always easy to persuade institutions of any kind to let researchers select the sample of subjects.

Labouvie, Bartsch, Nesselroade, and Baltes (1974) report a different kind of research problem, the validity of simple longitudinal research designs. In this type of design the researcher, for instance, identifies a sample of 10- or 11-year-old boys and studies their development through adolescence. The researcher interviews, measures, and tests the subjects periodically over the whole time span. The design seems to be the "obvious" way to study development. But, in fact, there are problems. Bias in sampling is one. In addition, a sample drawn from boys in school does *not* represent the total population of the age range (*all* 10- or 11-year-old boys in or out of public schools).

Labouvie and his colleagues identified other problems with this kind of design. Using a sample of 1,580 seventh-to-eleventh-grade students they investigated the influence of selective dropouts from the sample. A control sample was tested only in the second year, and dropouts from the original sample were identified. The results clearly showed that those who dropped out of the study were different from those who stayed in. We might conclude that the longer a study goes on, the more restricted and biased is the sample that remains with the study each passing year.

The Labouvie study also showed that when retesting on an ability measure is employed, this can confuse the results. The authors conclude that when sensitive measures are used in a retest, contrast groups must be employed to avoid artificial changes, those which do not truly reflect growth and development.

Cross-sectional designs also have their problems. Subjects in different groups of such a design do not, for example, necessarily have the same general life experiences.

The intent of this essay is not to suggest that research into child development is impossible or that it is all necessarily weak. But it should be noted that good research is difficult to design and execute, particularly when it involves human beings.

Based on J. Brickell, "Nominated Samples from Public Schools and Statistical Bias," *American Educational Research Journal*, 1974, *11* (4), 333–341; E. Labouvie, T. Bartsch, J. Nesselroade, and P. Baltes, "On the Internal and External Validity of Simple Longitudinal Designs," *Child Development*, 1974, *45*, 282–290.

REFERENCES

1. Bandura, A., D. Ross, and S. A. Ross. "Imitation of Film-mediated Aggressive Models," *Journal of Abnormal and Social Psychology*, 1963, *66*, 3–11.
2. de Mause, L., ed. *The History of Childhood*. New York: Psychohistory Press, 1974. See also Philippe Aries, *Centuries of Childhood: A Social History of Family Life*. New York: Knopf, 1962.
3. Dollard, J., and N. E. Miller. *Personality and Psychotherapy*. New York: McGraw-Hill, 1950.
4. Gagné, R. M. "Contributions of Learning to Human Development," *Psychological Review*, 1968, *75*, 177–191.
5. Pulaski, M. A. S. *Understanding Piaget*. New York: Harper & Row, 1971.
6. Trotter, R. J. "East Side, West Side: Growing Up in Manhattan," *Science News*, 1976, *109* (20), 315.
7. Trotter, R. J. "Changing the Face of Birth," *Science News*, 1975, *108* (7), 106–108.
8. Watson, J., and R. Raynor. *Journal of Experimental Psychology*, 1920, *3*, 1–14.

Today's children are the result of millions of years of physical and cultural evolution. In order to understand these children, it is necessary to understand the biological and evolutionary mechanisms that produced them.

the biology of behavior

Dawn, before the dawn of history—the sun comes up across East Africa. In the mountains, valleys, and plains, in the deserts, jungles, and grasslands, small groups of prehuman primates (the ancestors of the human race) begin to scratch and stir. For them it will be another day of what seems to be a never-ending battle for survival. Continually, wars must be waged against the harsh elements, the rugged terrain, the hungry predator animals, and increasingly, wars must be waged against similar groups competing for the same food and territory. For some of these primitive groups the battles seem to be less trying, success seems to come easier. These groups, the survivors, have met and defeated their enemies. They have learned from their past mistakes and are well prepared to do battle and survive again.

Who are these survivors? What makes them more likely to succeed? Why aren't they, like other bands, ever defeated, disbanded, or dispersed? Robert S. Bigelow, an anthropologist from New Zealand, has proposed a theory that attempts to answer these questions (22). His theory is based on the inheritance of two specific behavior patterns—cooperation and competition.

Cooperation within groups and competition between groups, says Bigelow, were necessary for survival during the time that the human race was evolving. A young child or a mother carrying her child, for instance, would have been easy prey for a leopard. But as long as children, or mothers and children, stayed within their social groups, they remained relatively safe. This type of group cooperation was probably necessary for survival and can still be seen today among baboons. A single baboon is unable to fight off a lion or leopard, but three or more baboons cooperating can usually persuade a large cat to withdraw. The early humans, like baboons, probably had to join forces and act as cooperative social units if they were to survive. But because hungry lions and leopards are not driven away by empty threats, the human groups had to back up their threats with powerful and effective aggressive responses. According to Bigelow's theory, the groups that learned the value of cooperation in conjunction with aggression grew larger and were more likely to survive.

Hungry cats were not the only enemies of early humans. As successful groups expanded and became more numerous, they came into contact with other groups more often and had to compete for the most favorable territories. Primitive human warfare began, and different kinds of survival tactics became necessary. Some human groups learned to make weapons of sticks and stones. Just as weapons became the tools of aggression, methods of communication became the tools of cooperation. Visual or vocal signals, for instance, could be used to warn group members of danger or to plan an attack. The groups who learned to use the tools of aggression and of cooperation were more effective and successful at survival. In battles for the best hunting grounds, the groups who were the most aggressive and the best organized usually won. The losers

Early humans who learned the value of cooperation along with aggression were more likely to survive.

were forced to abandon the more favorable territories and move to less hospitable environments. There, under harsher conditions, they became less healthy, produced fewer offspring, and were even less successful at survival than before.

Bigelow is talking about creatures who lived between two million and 100,000 years ago, during the time when the human brain was evolving and doubling in size. His theory suggests that the behaviors necessary for survival at that time helped shape the evolving human brain. The ability to use language and make tools, for instance, depends on the physical structure and organization of the brain. And the survivors from that period (the ancestors of today's human race) inherited a brain with a built-in capability not only for language and tool use but for cooperation and competition as well.

Bigelow's theory (and there are others like it) can help explain some human behaviors. It might explain the thousands of wars that make up human history, and it might explain why most researchers find that children seem to be naturally aggressive. In one study, for instance, 379 mothers reported that at one time or another they had been forced to put up with angry outbursts of quarreling on the part of their children, and almost all mothers (95 percent) reported instances of strong aggression directed by the child at the parents (18).

Another study, this one of nursery school children, found that some sort of aggressive behavior, ranging from fairly mild to violent, occurs during free play about every five minutes for boys and about every seven or eight minutes for girls (16). Numerous other studies report similar findings of aggression among even young children.

Theories like Bigelow's imply that humans are born with a natural tendency to be aggressive. But not everyone is willing to accept such a warlike picture of the human race. Another whole school of thought says that aggression is not inherited but is learned. Such theories suggest that warfare is not a part of our evolutionary heritage from two million years ago but is a relatively recent invention only 10,000 years old — after the human brain had reached its present stage of development. Such theories suggest that parents, teachers, friends, and society in general (including television) teach aggressive behavior.

These two theories of aggression have important implications. If aggressive tendencies are built into every human, then they probably cannot be eliminated or extinguished. They can only be controlled or perhaps channeled into activities that are more productive than fighting, such as hard work or sports. On the other hand, if aggressive tendencies are learned, they might be controlled and eventually eliminated by keeping society from teaching aggressive behavior to children. For example, taking unnecessary violence off the television screen has been suggested as one way of keeping children from learning aggressive behavior.

The cause of aggression is yet to be determined, but as important as this question may be, it is only one part of a much larger subject. This is the **nature-nuture question.** It asks which aspects of human behavior are a direct result of nature or biological inheritance and which are learned as a result of nurture or rearing (nurture is from the Latin word for "feed" or "suckle"). Not only aggression, but intelligence, creativity, personality disorders like schizophrenia, and a great many human personality characteristics have all been attributed to both nature and nurture by different theorists.

Actually, nature and nurture are probably both involved in most aspects of human development. Children inherit a brain capable of learning a language, but the way children are nurtured (the environment in which they are reared) seems to determine the extent and form of the language they learn. The same is true of most human behaviors and characteristics. Therefore, in order to understand human development, it is necessary to understand the effects of both nature and nurture. This has been a major concern of developmental psychologists.

In order to determine exactly how nature and nurture affect human development, psychologists have had to borrow information from other fields of science; and they have had to develop methods for investigating the effects of nature and nurture. Genetic theory and the field of biology, for instance, help explain how certain human characteristics are inherited. The fields of behavior genetics and ethology offer clues as to how and why behavior patterns may been inherited. Studies of individuals with very similar biological backgrounds (such as identical twins) and of people with very different biological backgrounds (people from different parts of the world and from different cultures) throw further light on the nature-nurture question. The theory of evolution and the history of human evolution help psychologists understand the causes and effects of both nature and nurture on human development. These and other lines of investigation are all helping to answer the still unanswered nature-nurture question.

GENETIC THEORY

Developmental psychologists have long been interested in the effects of both inherited characteristics and environmentally influenced or learned characteristics, but they have had to concentrate on environmental factors because those were the only ones over which they had any control. In other words, it is sometimes possible to control what a child learns or the environment in which a child grows up, but it is not possible to control what a child is or what a child inherits. In recent years, however, this situation has begun to change. The growing field of **genetics** (the biology of heredity) is making it increasingly possible to understand the mechanisms of heredity and to predict which characteristics will be inherited. The new field of behavior genetics attempts to understand how inherited characteristics are related to behavior. All of this has been made possible by the work of a monk, Gregor Mendel.

Mendelian Inheritance

Mendel, the son of a poor farmer, became a monk in order to get an education. Because he did poorly at the University of Vienna and did not qualify as a teacher, his superiors sent him off to a monastery in Brno, Moravia (now part of Czechoslovakia). There, Mendel went back to his boyhood interest—plants. Having had some training in biology, he decided to devote his time to biological experiments with plants. This was in 1856, and he spent the next eight years working with one particular type of plant, the common garden pea. Mendel selected seven different characteristics of the pea (shape of seed, color of seed, height of plant, and so on) and designed experiments to determine how these characteristics are passed on from generation to generation.

A look at one of these famous experiments demonstrates the basic idea of Mendel's theory. Some of Mendel's peas had round seeds; others had wrinkled seeds. Because the round seeds produced more plants with round seeds and the wrinkled seeds produced more plants with wrinkled seeds, it seemed obvious that the characteristics of round and wrinkled were inherited or passed on from generation to generation. Mendel asked what would happen if round and

Botanist Gregor Mendel (1822–1884).

wrinkled seed plants were crossbred or interbred with each other. He found out by using the pollen (the equivalent of sperm in an animal) of one type of plant to fertilize the other type of plant. The seeds produced by the fertilized plant were then sown and allowed to grow. The result was a **hybrid** (the offspring produced by breeding plants or animals of different varieties).

According to the theory of the time, the hybrid plants should have had characteristics that were somewhere between the characteristics of both parents. But the expected did not happen. After Mendel crossbred the round and wrinkled seed plants, the resulting plants all produced round seeds. There were no wrinkled seeds and no in-between seeds.

The next thing Mendel did was crossbreed the hybrid plants with each other. This time something else unexpected happened. Instead of getting all round seed plants again, he got 5,474 round seed plants and 1,850 wrinkled seed plants. This is very close to a ratio of three round seed plants to one wrinkled seed plant.

Mendel worked out a theory to explain this ratio. He supposed that the round or wrinkled characteristic of a plant is controlled by two particles (now called genes, from the Greek word for "birth"). Each parent plant contributes one of the genes. If the gene from each parent is the same, say for round, then round seeds will be produced. But if the genes are different, one for wrinkled and one for round, one gene would be **dominant** and the other **recessive** (tending to go backward or recede). The dominant gene would be the one that would make its effect seen. And this is just what happened in the first crossbreeding. A gene for round seeds was contributed by one plant and a gene for wrinkled seeds was contributed by the other. Because the gene for round seeds was dominant, its effects were seen. All of the first-generation hybrids had round seeds. But even though one gene was dominant, each of the plants still contained the nondominant, or recessive, gene for wrinkled plants. And this showed up in the next generation.

The hybrid plants contained both types of genes — r for round and w for wrinkled. When the hybrids were crossbred with each other, each plant contributed one gene, either r or w, to the next generation. With two possible genes to contribute, there was a fifty-fifty chance that either an r or w would be contributed. Each parent plant could contribute either of the two genes. The possible combinations of genes for a third-generation plant were therefore: rr, rw, wr, and ww. Since r is dominant over w, three of these combinations of genes produce plants with round seeds. In the ww combination wrinkled seeds are produced because the dominant gene is absent. This works out to Mendel's ratio of three to one. And many experiments have since confirmed Mendel's theory.

The rr and ww combination are called **homozygous** combinations. (Homo means "same," and zygous refers to a cell or organism that contains genes from each parent.) The rw combination is a **heterozygous** combination. ("Hetero," meaning "different," implies that two different types of genes have been inherited from the parents.) The particular combination of genes (such as rw or ww) is called a **genotype.** The characteristics they produce (round or wrinkled) are called the **phenotype.** As a rule, different genotypes produce different phenotypes. For example, the homozygous combinations rr and ww produce different phenotypes, or observed characteristics. Similar phenotypes, however, do not always indicate similar genotypes. The round phenotype could be the result of a heterozygous genotype *(rw)* or of a homozygous genotype *(rr).* The wrinkled phenotype can only be the result of a homozygous genotype *(ww)* because w is a recessive gene and will affect the phenotype only under homozygous conditions.

Mendel published his findings in 1866, but they did not receive much attention. People who saw Mendel's results seemed not to understand them or thought them unimportant. It was not until 1900, 16 years after Mendel's death, that several scientists rediscovered his findings. And with that, the field of genetics really got its start. Scientists have since been attempting to unravel the complexities of human heredity.

Human Heredity

The genetic make-up of humans is much more complex than that of garden peas; and it is not practical to attempt controlled crossbreeding experiments with humans the way Mendel did with peas. But even without such experiments, it is possible to see that the mechanism of human heredity does work the way Mendel had predicted.

Sickle cell anemia is a hereditary disease that affects a small portion of the black population (as well as some whites) in the United States. The disease is caused by the inheritance of genes that result in the production of an abnormal form of hemoglobin, the oxygen-carrying component of red blood cells. The red blood cells of people with the disease take on a characteristic crescent or sickle shape that deprives the cells of the ability to transport oxygen efficiently. This results in a severe and fatal form of **anemia** (any deficiency in the oxygen-carrying material in the blood). People with the disease have inherited the condition from both parents. This homozygous genotype produces the disease (phenotype), which usually results in death at an early age.

In the heterozygous condition the sickle-cell trait (but not the disease or phenotype) is inherited from only one parent, and genes for normal hemoglobin are inherited from the other parent. In this condition the disease does not show up because the gene for normal hemoglobin is dominant. About 10 percent of the black population has the trait, but a much smaller percentage actually has the disease. The trait and the disease, however, can be inherited if both parents have the disease. In such cases the chances of a child inheriting the disease are, as Mendel's theory predicts, one in four.

DNA

It is now known that **genes** are not actually individual particles but portions of chemical molecules of deoxyribonucleic acid, or **DNA. A molecule** is a unit of matter made up of atoms. The DNA molecule is one of the basic building blocks of the human organism. This complex molecule consists of two intertwining chains that spiral around each other. The way molecules are arranged along this double spiral represents a code; and the code contains the information that directs the synthesis or building of the body's cells. The codes, in other words, are genes. It is at this very basic molecular level that human development really begins. The code or gene for the production of the sickle cell, for instance, is located on a strand of DNA. It is estimated that human DNA contains at least 10,000 genes.

Chromosomes

In most organisms strands of DNA are arranged into larger units called **chromosomes.** This means "colored body." By means of a staining process chromosomes appear as colored bodies within a cell when seen under a microscope. A set of chromosomes is found in the nucleus or center portion of each cell (with the exception of red blood cells which do not have nuclei). In most organisms the chromosomes are arranged in pairs, and the number of pairs varies depending on the type of organism. Mendel's peas contained 14 chromosomes or 7 pairs. Human cells contain 46 chromosomes or 23 pairs. While similar, the members of each pair are not exactly alike. The two chromosomes of a pair contain genes for the same traits (shape of pea seed or type of hemoglobin), but the genes are not always the same (round or wrinkled peas, normal or sickle-cell hemoglobin). Genes that code for different versions of the same trait and are located on paired chromosomes are called **alleles,** or allelomorphs.

Alleles in Human Development

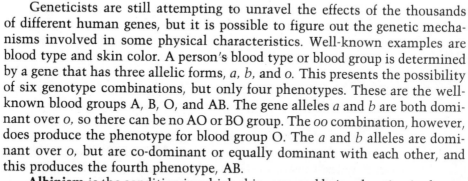

Geneticists are still attempting to unravel the effects of the thousands of different human genes, but it is possible to figure out the genetic mechanisms involved in some physical characteristics. Well-known examples are blood type and skin color. A person's blood type or blood group is determined by a gene that has three allelic forms, *a*, *b*, and *o*. This presents the possibility of six genotype combinations, but only four phenotypes. These are the well-known blood groups A, B, O, and AB. The gene alleles *a* and *b* are both dominant over *o*, so there can be no AO or BO group. The *oo* combination, however, does produce the phenotype for blood group O. The *a* and *b* alleles are dominant over *o*, but are co-dominant or equally dominant with each other, and this produces the fourth phenotype, AB.

Albinism is the condition in which skin, eye, and hair coloration is absent. This happens when melanin, the chemical responsible for skin coloration, is not produced by the body cells. A gene allele that controls coloration or pigmentation fails to initiate melanin production. This albinism allele is recessive, so when it occurs in the heterozygous condition pigmentation will be normal. But in the homozygous condition, with two recessive genes for albinism, a child will be an albino. As with other recessive gene conditions (sickle-cell anemia), both parents of an albino child will have had at least one gene allele for albinism.

Phenylketonuria (PKU) is another rare disorder thought to be the result of a recessive gene. A child born with PKU appears normal at birth, but within six months to a year symptoms begin to appear (the child's urine may have a peculiar odor, and the child may vomit a lot and have inflamed skin). In PKU, the body lacks the ability to break down a certain chemical, phenylalanine, that is present in protein foods. The phenylalanine builds up in the blood and damages the brain. The eventual result of the disorder is usually severe mental retardation.

PKU does not always lead to mental retardation, however. If the condition is detected early enough, it can be successfully treated (3). The existence of phenylpyruvic acid in the child's urine indicates the disorder. If this is detected during the first few months of life, before the brain is severely damaged, the disorder can be controlled by putting the child on a special diet low in

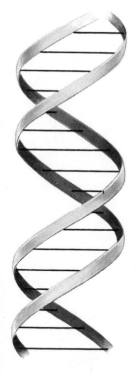

A portion of a DNA molecule.

phenylalanine (protein foods). In many cases such treatment results in normal development of the child.

PKU is a good example of how nature and nurture work together in human development. A particular genotype or combination of genes usually results in a particular phenotype (observed characteristics). Nature produces the genotype, but nurture can affect the phenotype. In the case of PKU, both parents contribute genes for the disease (phenotype). In this homozygous condition (two recessive genes) the phenotype would be expected to develop. But nurture, in the form of a special diet, also has an effect on the phenotype. The protein-free diet can keep the disease from developing even though the genotype for the disease is still present.

Sex-linked Genetic Traits

Sex has been especially helpful to geneticists and others studying inherited traits. Human chromosomes, which contain the genetic blueprint for development, also determine the sex of each individual. Two chromosomes, the 23rd pair, are responsible for this. They are known as the **sex chromosomes** and are slightly different from the other 44 chromosomes. Instead of always being similar to each other the 23rd pair can consist of two large X chromosomes or an X and a smaller Y chromosome. Individuals with the XX combination are females; those with the XY combination are males. A YY combination cannot normally occur because one chromosome in each pair is inherited from the mother, and females (XX) can contribute only an X chromosome. Males (XY) can contribute an X or a Y.

female or male   Human chromosome cells.

Because of this situation the effects of genes located on the sex chromosomes are easier to understand than the effects of other genes. The inheritance of genes located on the sex chromosomes will be linked to the sex of the parents and the offspring. A gene located on the Y chromosome, for instance, can be inherited only by males from their fathers. But the Y chromosome is small and seems to determine only a few traits other than the typical male pattern of bodily development. The larger X chromosome, however, is responsible for a number of sex-linked traits. The best-known example is probably **hemophilia** (blood-clotting failure).

The pattern of inheritance of sex-linked traits is not hard to work out. The rare recessive gene allele for hemophilia is located on the X chromosome. But the disease or phenotype usually shows up only in males. This is because there is no corresponding allele (recessive or dominant) on the Y chromosome. So in the XY (male) condition, the normally recessive hemophilia gene is dominant and always produces the disease in males. In the heterozygous XX (female) combination the normal allele is dominant and the phenotype is normal. The disease is not produced. Because a homozygous XX combination for the hemophilia allele is extremely rare, the disease does not normally appear in females.

A male with hemophilia cannot pass on the disease to his sons because he gives them a Y rather than an X chromosome (which has the hemophilia allele). But a male with hemophilia will always pass on the recessive gene to his daughters because he gives them an X chromosome. The daughters will not usually have the disease, however, because the hemophilia allele is recessive. Instead, having the genotype, they will be "carriers" of hemophilia and will pass on the trait (but not the disease) to half of their daughters. They will pass on the phenotype (the disease itself) to half of their sons. This does not mean that half of their sons will actually inherit the condition, but that each son will have a fifty-fifty chance of inheriting it—depending on which of the mother's two X chromosomes is inherited.

The hemophilia gene can be seen at work in the descendants of Queen Victoria of England. She was a carrier of the hemophilia gene, and a number of her male descendants contracted the disease.

REPRODUCTION

Sex is at the beginning of the history of childhood, and sex is the beginning of child development. But long before men and women produced any children or passed on any of their genes, there was a sexual revolution that made possible the many physical and psychological characteristics that are now a part of human development.

Three billion years ago the first life forms on earth reproduced asexually. No sexual union was necessary. Small, single-cell organisms reproduced simply by splitting in half. Sex and sex partners were unnecessary. At a certain stage in its life each cell would divide into two new cells that were each exact duplicates of the parent. The new cells, in turn, divided to produce more duplicates of the original. Every once in a while a mistake in the process caused a physical change, or **mutation,** that may have resulted in a slightly different type of organism. But for the most part life went on unchanged for about two billion years.

Then came the revolution. Less than one billion years ago simple organisms began to reproduce sexually (perhaps because of a mutation). The first to do so were probably blue-green algae (a primitive form of plant life that lives in water and still exists today). Two of these cells came together and produced an egg that developed into a third cell. This type of sexual union not only represented a new type of reproduction, it introduced a greater chance for change in the system. In asexual reproduction the new cells are duplicates of the parents. In sexual reproduction the new cell can inherit different characteristics from each parent cell and can therefore be different from either of them. This speeded up the rate of change in life forms and eventually produced the millions of types of creatures that inhabit the earth.

Mitosis and Meiosis

Sex did not replace asexual reproduction, which is still the method of reproduction in some lower organisms. It is also the basic process of all physical growth and development. During development body cells (hair, skin, bone, and so on) divide and multiply asexually and produce more similar cells.

The process of asexual cell reproduction is called **mitosis** (from the Greek word for "thread"). Chromosomes look like small pieces of thread inside each cell. It is the action of these threads, or chromosomes, that controls mitosis. What seems to happen is that the DNA double helix, which makes up each chromosome, splits down the middle and unwinds into two strands. Each single strand then collects from within the cell the chemicals necessary to reform as a double helix strand of DNA. The result is another set of chromosomes, exactly like the original set. All chromosomes in a particular cell go through this replication or duplication process at the same time. The two sets of chromosomes then draw apart and the cell divides.

Meiosis (from the Greek word for "less") is the process by which sex cells (sperm and eggs) are produced. These cells have less than the normal number of chromosomes. The sperm cell of the male and the ova, or egg cell, of the female have exactly half the normal number of chromosomes. Each human sex cell has 23 rather than 46 chromosomes. During sexual reproduction the male and female sex cells are joined to form a new cell with the normal number of chromosomes. It is this new cell, which inherits half of its chromosomes from the mother and half from the father, that grows and develops into a new organism.

Mutations

During sexual reproduction each parent contributes hundreds of thousands of genes to the new individual. This vast number of genes, in numerous combinations, gives rise to the millions of specific characteristics that are seen in the development of each individual and leads to tremendous possibilities of variation. But the fact that so many genes are involved in this delicate process also gives rise to the possibility of a great many mistakes or **mutations** in the process. It is probable that most humans have one or a few mutations in their genotype. If the mutations are on recessive genes, their presence is unlikely to show up in the usual heterozygous condition. They would appear, however, in the homozygous condition, and the effects could be harmful as in PKU and other inherited diseases. The fact that such diseases can be inherited is considered to be an argument against breeding between close relatives. Cousins who have inherited a mutation (such as hemophilia) from one of their grandparents, for instance, could produce a child with a homozygous genotype for the mutation (the disease). While inbreeding or breeding between close relatives is probably not harmful in most cases, there is some evidence that conception between closely related individuals leads to a greater likelihood of miscarriages, still births, or early infant deaths (17). These deaths could be the result of inherited mutations.

Many mutations can be harmful or even fatal in their phenotypic effects (still births, PKU, sickle-cell anemia, hemophilia), but occasionally a mutation can be beneficial. Sickle-cell anemia has both beneficial and harmful effects. Normally, a dangerous genetic mutation like the one responsible for sickle-cell anemia, would be expected to disappear after a few generations because the affected individuals often die before they are old enough to have children and pass on the disease. But sickle-cell anemia has not died out, and researchers have found that under certain circumstances this particular mutation can be beneficial.

Sickle-cell anemia is most common in certain parts of Africa in which a particularly dangerous type of malaria is also common. A similar type of hemoglobin disorder is found in areas of Italy, Sicily, and Asia where malaria is common. In these areas the sickled hemoglobin protects people against the effects of malaria. People with the sickle-cell trait, therefore, are better off than people without it in areas where malaria is common. Although individuals with the relatively rare homozygous condition (and the disease) are at a disadvantage, those with the trait (but not the disease) are at an advantage. They will be more likely to live and reproduce than those who do not have the sickle-cell trait.

In the United States, where malaria is not a problem, the abnormal hemoglobin is less useful, and geneticists predict that within the next several generations the numbers of people with the trait and the disease will be greatly reduced.

In addition to genetic mutations, chromosome mutations are possible in humans. None seems advantageous, and most result in serious developmental problems.

Down's syndrome, which is sometimes known as mongolism, is a serious disorder characterized by slanting eyes and a flat, broad face and nose. In addition to several other abnormal physical characteristics, Down's syndrome produces moderate mental retardation (5). The condition was originally thought to be genetic, but researchers have found that it does not usually run in families. In 1959 a number of French scientists found an extra chromosome, 47 instead of 46, in several Down's syndrome cases. The reason for the extra chromosome is unknown, but about 12,000 Down's syndrome children are born in the United States every year (1). Because the risk of having a child with Down's syndrome is greater among older women (about 1 in 50 for a woman in her forties compared with 1 in 2,000 for a woman in her twenties), some researchers have suggested an environmental cause. Radiation, for instance, like that produced by an X-ray machine, is thought to damage genes and chromosomes. If so, then the older a woman is, the greater chance she will have had of being exposed to radiation. In one part of India where environmental radiation is exceptionally high (because of the presence of a radiation-producing mineral in the soil), researchers found the rate of Down's syndrome and other forms of mental retardation and chromosomal abnormalities to be four times higher than would be expected (14). Whether or not the cause is radiation, the chromosomal abnormality associated with Down's syndrome results in an irreversible disruption of the process of human development.

Klinefelter's syndrome is a rare condition in which a male is born with an extra sex chromosome. The result is XXY instead of XY. In such males the reproductive organs tend to be small, and the body chemicals associated with masculine development are reduced.

Turner's syndrome is a rare condition in which a female is born with only one sex chromosome, X instead of XX. These individuals have a female body but cannot reproduce because of incomplete feminine development.

While geneticists have outlined the probable mechanisms involved in the inheritance of some human characteristics, researchers are far from understanding all of the complexities of the genetic process. In the first place the effects of any one gene can often be changed by environmental effects, as in the case of PKU. In addition to such environmental effects there are other complexities. A single gene can have a specific effect on a person's phenotype, but most genes probably influence many different aspects of development. Human characteristics (such as height, facial expression, intelligence, aggression) are affected by more than one gene. Furthermore, the effects of any particular gene often depend on the other genes in the genotype. So a particular gene in one person may have different or no effects in another person.

Does genetic theory answer the nature-nurture question? Can aggressive tendencies (or any human personality trait) be inherited through one's genes? Knowledge of how genes and chromosomes are passed on from generation to generation helps explain how nature works in determining human development, but genetic theory does not fully explain the roles of nature and nurture in human development. In fact, research in genetics is raising additional questions. This can be seen in studies of human aggression.

There does not seem to be a particular gene for aggressive behavior, but one type of chromosome abnormality has been linked to violent and antisocial behavior. In 1965, Patricia A. Jacobs and her colleagues at the Western General Hospital in Edinburgh, Scotland, reported that there were more XYY males than would be expected among patients classified as criminally insane (12).

Males born with an extra Y chromosome (XYY) appear to be normal in many respects, but the extra chromosome does have some effects. It seems to produce an extra amount of "maleness" (just as the extra X chromosome in Klinefelter's syndrome seems to result in reduced masculinity). Males with the XYY condition are usually taller and more impulsive than average males, and they reach sexual maturity at an earlier age than do normal XY males. Investigations made with animals suggest one way in which nature and biology could work to produce such aggressive tendencies. Male hormones (the bodily chemicals responsible for male physical and sexual development) have been found to be related to aggressive behavior in rats and monkeys. Animals with high levels of male hormones tend to be more aggressive than animals with low levels of male hormones. Even female rats become more aggressive when injected with male hormones. Since the production of these hormones is partially controlled by the genes, it is possible that genetic influences could result in higher levels of aggression in XYY males. Although the condition is rare (perhaps as low as 1 in 1,000), it did offer an explanation for some aggressive behavior.

More recent research, however, has pointed out that only a small fraction of the total number of XYY individuals ever appear in a mental institution (6). And closer study suggests that environmental and social factors, rather than heredity or the extra chromosome itself, may be responsible for the aggression that is sometimes seen in XYY males. Because these individuals are physically different and have different needs (including increased sexual needs at an early age), they may be treated as "different" by society and may suffer from the fact that their needs are not always met. This could result in emotional problems and psychological disturbances that lead to criminal or aggressive behavior.

Much more research will have to be done before any positive relationship between aggressive behavior and heredity is worked out, but the XYY example has raised other questions — ethical or moral ones.

It is now possible to determine an individual's chromosome makeup at the time of birth by a simple blood test. Chromosome abnormalities, such as XYY, can be tested for. But should every male child be examined for the condition? What should be done about those who have it? Such examinations are not now done on a regular basis, and many people feel that it would be ethically wrong to do so. If a child were labeled as XYY at birth, for instance, it is possible that he would be subjected to different and possibly damaging treatment by society and even by his parents. Parents and those close to the child who would be told that he is "likely to be criminally insane" may not give that child the loving care he needs. Parents may even be afraid of their own children. This type of treatment could be more damaging to the child's development than the XYY condition itself.

Another example has to do with sickle-cell anemia. **Amniocentesis** is a process by which the genetic makeup of an unborn child can be determined. A long needle is inserted into the womb of a pregnant woman, and some of the fluid (amniotic fluid) that surrounds the unborn child is withdrawn. Researchers have found that an examination of this fluid can determine whether or not the unborn child will have the sickle-cell trait or sickle-cell anemia (24). If the child is "different," there is the possibility that it will be treated differently. Parents who know that their child will have a serious disorder, like sickle-cell anemia or Down's syndrome, have a serious ethical decision to make. Should they allow the child to be born or should the woman have an abortion?

This question can also be asked in regard to the birth of a normal child. In China, sons have traditionally been responsible for the care of their parents; and Chinese parents have, therefore, always wanted to be sure they had at least one son. Infanticide was practiced to get rid of unwanted female children. But now amniocentesis and other methods are available for determining the sex of an unborn child, and abortion, rather than infanticide, can be used to avoid having female children.

The ethical questions involved are serious. Of 100 pregnant women recently screened in China to determine the sex of their unborn children, a female **fetus** (unborn child) was detected in 46. Of these mothers, 29 (more than 60 percent) decided to have an abortion. Of 53 women found to be carrying a male child, only one chose to have an abortion (4). The importance of the ethical question here is obvious.

Even though the field of human genetics raises some important ethical questions, geneticists are gradually outlining the mechanisms of heredity and are learning more and more about the way in which physical characteristics and even some human behaviors might be controlled by genes. But many questions remain unanswered. For this reason it is necessary to turn to a related field of study. Instead of looking at the basic biological mechanisms of heredity, it is possible to get an understanding of present patterns of human behavior (such as aggression and intelligence) by examining how such behaviors may have developed. This can be done by looking at human evolution, by looking at the development of our ancestors from millions of years ago, and by looking at their ancestors from billions of years ago.

THE THEORY OF EVOLUTION

In the 1850s, before Mendel began his pea experiments and long before anyone ever heard of genes or genetic theory, a theory of evolution was proposed. Not one, but two men working independently came up with the exact same theory. One was Charles Darwin; the other was Alfred Russel Wallace. Both were British.

In 1831, Darwin took a job as a **naturalist** (observer of plants and animals) aboard a ship called the *Beagle* which was setting out on a five-year voyage to map the coast of South America. Darwin was amazed at the enormous variety of plants and animals he saw in South America, and he began to wonder how so many species came to be. Traditional thinking in the nineteenth century held that the world, with all of its plants and animals (including humans), had been created at one time—perhaps in six days as the Bible says. But seeing such a variety of life, Darwin soon became convinced that the world was not created with a single set of unchanging species. Instead, he reasoned, plant and animal species develop differently (**evolve**) when they are isolated from each other. A particular type of plant growing in England, for instance, might inherit some specific characteristics (perhaps through genetic mutation, which Darwin called random change) and evolve into a very different type of plant after many generations. The exact same type of plant growing in a different environment, such as South America, might inherit a different set of characteristics and evolve into a type of plant completely different from the one growing in England.

But why would one plant evolve in one direction while another evolved in a different direction? Darwin worked out an answer to this question after reading an essay on population by the famous English economist Thomas Malthus. Malthus said that populations grow faster than their food supplies, and that because of overpopulation, people must compete for food. (This was quite obvious from looking at the overcrowded, overworked, and underfed population of the slums of nineteenth-century London.) Darwin applied this line of thought to populations of plants and animals.

In a very crowded forest trees throw a lot of shade and cut each other off from one of their basic food supplies (sunlight). But if through a lucky mutation a particular tree has inherited a genotype for tallness, that tree will grow above the others and get more sun. It will have inherited a characteristic that helps it to survive more efficiently in its particular environment. If it survives, it will be likely to pass on its genes and produce more tall trees. Eventually the shorter trees will be starved out, and the taller species will be all that is left.

For trees growing in a different environment, such as South America where the sun shines more often than it does in England, evolution may take another direction. The gene for tallness may not be as important as it is in English forests, and trees that inherit such a gene may not have a particular advantage in the competition for survival. Broader branches or a different type of root system, however, may be important, and genes for these characteristics might be the ones that are passed on.

The same is true for animal species. In a situation where there are too many animals and not enough food, the animals must compete for food. Those that may have inherited characteristics that help them in the competition are most likely to survive. They will pass on their genes to their offspring. In this way nature acts as a selective force to kill off the weakest and produce a new species from the survivors. (This is the theory Bigelow and others use to explain how competition and aggressive characteristics may have been inherited by the human species.)

In the 1840s Darwin wrote out a complete explanation of his theory and then deposited it in a bank with a sum of money to have it published after he died. It seems that Darwin did not want to become involved in the controversy and argument he knew his theory would produce. The theory not only goes against the biblical account of creation by suggesting that every plant and animal that ever existed could have evolved over billions of years from only one life form, it suggests that humans might have evolved from lower forms of life—monkeys and apes. Darwin realized that many people would be unwilling to accept such a suggestion.

But Darwin could not avoid the controversy. He was forced to publish his theory because another naturalist was about to publish the exact same thing. During the 1840s and 1850s Alfred Wallace traveled as a naturalist through South America and southeastern Asia. After reading Malthus, he too came up with a theory of evolution. Knowing that Darwin would be interested, Wallace wrote to him. Darwin was more than interested, and he decided not to let someone else take all the credit (or blame) for something he had worked on for 20 years. An agreement was made, and both theories were read at the same scientific meeting in London. Little attention was paid at first, but in 1859 when Darwin published his famous book *The Origin of Species*, the expected controversy arose. And it hasn't completely died down yet.

Regardless of the controversy, the theory of evolution has survived. It has survived because it has been extremely useful in explaining not only the origin of species but the development of the human species. Together with Mendel's

A nineteenth-century British cartoon satirizing Darwin's theory of evolution. The naturalist showing an ape its close resemblance to man.

theory and more recent work in genetics, the **theory of evolution** explains how both physical and behavioral characteristics may have evolved.

Environmental Changes

Evolution is going on constantly with every new generation of plant and animal life, but most major evolutionary changes took place during the billions of years before recorded history. In fact, more than 99 percent of the species that ever existed are **extinct** (no longer existing in living form). These species became extinct, in most cases, because they were no longer successful at reproduction. This success is determined by several factors. Individual animals will have different rates of success at reproduction according to their success in surviving to sexual or reproductive maturity, their success in finding a mate and having offspring, and their success in helping the offspring through the rearing stage. All of these factors are under genetic influence, but success is also measured with respect to the environment.

The **ecological niche,** the specific environmental area occupied by an organism, contains many of the elements that determine successful reproduction. Particularly important are ecological factors such as supplies of food, water, and oxygen; the type of food available; possible dangers from natural hazards and predators; and the reactions of other animals of the same and different species.

When animals are well adapted to an ecological niche their needs are being met and they usually reproduce successfully. But ecological niches do not always remain stable. They may change for any of several reasons, and changes in an ecological niche can change the reproductive success of a species. Climatic changes, for instance, can affect the temperature as well as water and plant life distribution. Also, as species evolve, new ecological niches become available. The first primates evolved and adapted to life in the forests; but as the climate changed, the forests grew smaller. Some primates were probably forced to move out of the forests and adapt to conditions in a different ecological niche.

Animals themselves change their environment. One species may kill off another and in this way change the ecological niche by eliminating either predators or prey. Animal species also change the plant life and physical environment. The most dramatic example is that of the human species. Much of the face of the globe has been changed by the felling of forests, damming of rivers, cultivation of fields, and the building of cities. All of these environmental changes affect the species (including humans) that share the environment.

If a species has inhabited an ecological niche for a long time, and if the niche itself is stable, evolutionary change within the species will be relatively slow. Most of the individuals in the niche will have been selected because they have the characteristics that lead to successful survival and reproduction in that niche. In such a case the pressures of natural selection are said to be "weak," and change is slow. **Natural selection** will simply weed out those few individuals who, through disadvantageous mutations or an unlucky combination of genes, are unsuccessful at reproduction.

The situation will be different if the ecological niche is changing for some reason or if a species has moved into a new niche. Some members of the species will have characteristics that help them adapt more successfully to the new or changing conditions. These individuals will be more likely to survive and reproduce. Their **adaptive characteristics** will be passed on. Other members of the species will be weeded out. In this case selection pressures are said to be "strong," and evolutionary change will be relatively rapid.

Most of the major environmental changes that shaped the earth and its species took place millions of years ago. Mountains rose and fell. Continents split apart and came together again. Forests turned into deserts and back into forests again. Several times, large areas of the earth were covered by ice. During all of these drastic changes selection pressures were strong. But even under the most severe conditions, evolutionary change is a slow process. It takes generations and generations. Because evolution is such a slow process, it is difficult to find a well-documented case of evolutionary change in progress. Even so, there is much evidence to support Darwin's theory. One case in particular does show the process of physical change through evolution.

In Great Britain, a particular type of moth (*Biston petularia*) has been known for many years. When they were first found, these moths had rather light-colored wings, but in 1845 a specimen was discovered with dark wings. It was found near Manchester, one of the growing industrial centers of England. Fifty years later, by 1895, almost all (99 percent of these moths in the area around Manchester had dark wings. This 50-year period was a time of rapid industrialization around Manchester, and industrialization brought with it pollution of the air and surrounding vegetation by dirty smoke and coal dust. The ecological niche of the moths was changing rapidly, and selection pressures were strong. The result of these pressures can be seen in the changing color of the moths' wings.

The coloring of a moth's wings is very important to its survival in a particular environment. If the foliage (leaves of plants and trees) in an area is relatively light-colored, a moth with light-colored wings will be able to sit on a leaf without being easily spotted (and eaten) by a bird. But a light-colored moth on a dark leaf will be easily spotted. So it seems that genes for dark wings would be an advantage for moths in an area that has been darkened by pollution.

Since the turn of the century it has been found that many species of moths in the United States and Great Britain have shown similar changes in the coloring of their wings when they live in industrial areas. This darkening is called **industrial melanism.** (**Melanin** is the body chemical whose absence causes albinism in humans.) The ecological niche of these moths changed, and the processes of evolution helped them change with it through natural selection over several generations. The darker moths were selected for survival. By contrast, moths in nonpolluted rural areas have not changed color.

This seems like a nice explanation, but can it be proved? Experiments done by releasing light- and dark-colored moths in selected areas have helped confirm the theory. In polluted areas with darker vegetation, light-colored moths were spotted and eaten by birds more often than dark-colored moths. In country areas, more dark-colored moths were eaten.

Physical Evolution in Humans

The same type of selective pressures that produced moths with dark wings are at work in human evolution, but the process is much slower because humans are able to adapt to a great many environmental conditions without the need for genetic changes. Certain human characteristics, however, can be understood (though not completely) in evolutionary terms. Skin color, body size, and blood type (as in sickle-cell anemia) are examples.

Skin color is one of the most obvious of human traits. It is controlled in part by the amount of melanin in a person's skin and is believed to be an adaptive characteristic. Evidence for this is the fact that skin color varies according to geography. People in tropical regions tend to have dark skin, while those in the northern parts of the world tend to have lightly pigmented skin. One explanation for this is that melanin acts to protect the skin from the sun's damaging ultraviolet radiation. People with more melanin (and darker skin) may have been selected in tropical areas where solar radiation (sunlight) is strongest. Melanin and dark skin do keep out ultraviolet radiation, but some radiation is necessary because it helps the body to produce vitamin D. Therefore, people with less melanin (and lighter skin) may have an adaptive advantage in northern lands where ultraviolet radiation is relatively weak.

Certain human body types also seem to be the result of natural selection and adaptation to environmental conditions (11). The Eskimo body, for instance, tends to be short, squat, and compact, while bodies of people from northeastern Africa tend to be long and lean. These differences could be the result of adaptation. A short, compact body tends to conserve heat and would be advantageous under cold, arctic conditions. A long, lean body tends to disperse heat quickly and keeps people cooler. This characteristic might be selected for in the hot climate of Africa.

Human Races

The major physical differences seen between members of the human species (skin color, body shape, hair texture) have led to attempts to classify the human species into subspecies or races. The three basic classifications are: Mongoloid, or Asiatic; Caucasoid, or European; and Negroid, or African. The **Mongoloid** is usually described as having straight hair, a flat face, a flat nose, and spread nostrils; the **Caucasoid** as having pale skin, a narrow nose, and variable eye color and hair texture; and the **Negroid** as having dark skin, thick lips, a broad nose, and kinky hair.

Presumably racial classifications were originally made in an attempt to define and understand the differences between humans. But racial classifications have not proved to be very helpful in explaining human differences. For one thing, a great many people don't fit into any one of the three basic racial classifications. American Indians, Australians, and Polynesians are examples. For another thing, the classification system does not account for some obvious differences within categories. Arabs, Hindus, and Europeans are physically different, yet they are all called Caucasians. Attempts at more precise classifications have led to descriptions of as many as twenty-nine different human races. But again, even this wide variety of physical types does not explain the many differences among humans.

In spite of the many attempts to classify the human species into races, no distinctly different genetic human types have been discovered. Most studies that have examined behavioral differences among racial groups have concluded that the differences among individuals within one group are greater than the differences among groups (10). When differences are found among groups, they can usually be explained by environmental or social forces. An obvious example is the way blacks have been treated in the United States. Social and economic pressures as well as **racism** (the belief that one race is superior to another) have kept many blacks in inferior neighborhoods, jobs, and schools. This sort of treatment (rather than genetic differences) can explain the behavioral differences that may exist between white and black populations. It can also explain why blacks sometimes perform less well than whites on tests of intelligence.

Racism is part of the nature-nurture question. How much of human development and behavior is determined by genetic makeup and how much is determined by the way people are nurtured and treated by society and the environment? This question is still unanswered, but much information has been collected on physical and genetic differences and their effects on human behavior. Because this information helps explain human development, it will be discussed in relation to various aspects of development throughout this book. Because intelligence is such an important part of human development, the possibility of a relationship between genes and intelligence raises some especially important questions. These issues will be examined in the chapter on intelligence.

BEHAVIOR GENETICS

Geneticists and biologists may eventually answer parts of the nature-nurture question by identifying specific genes or genetic combinations related to human characteristics like aggression and intelligence. But they haven't done so yet. Researchers in related fields are tackling the question from a different direction. Instead of investigating the basic biological mechanisms that determine heredity, it is possible to investigate what is inherited, including behavior patterns. Different species of animals inherit different physical characteristics, but they also inherit different behavior patterns. A pig doesn't behave like a cat and lap up milk or chase birds, even though it is not physically prevented from doing so. Like physical characteristics, some behavior patterns are inherited. They are related to genotypes, and they are the result of generations of evolution. Behavior patterns that are appropriate for a particular environment are selected, and genes associated with these behaviors are passed on. The study of inherited behavior patterns, however, is much more difficult than the study of inherited physical characteristics, because behaviors can be changed by learning. And it is often difficult to tell whether a particular behavior pattern (such as aggression) is the result of genes or of environmental influences such as learning. In order to understand human development, it is important to know which behaviors may have been inherited and which are learned. One relatively new and growing field of study attempts to do this. It is **behavior genetics,** the study of genetic factors in behavioral characteristics.

One method of examining the effects of genes on behavior is to look for similarities in behavior in members of a particular species. If all cats chase birds without having been taught to do so, it can be assumed that such behavior has been inherited, especially if the behavior seems to help the individual or species survive. Careful observation of human infants points out some behaviors that seem to be common to all members of the species. If it can be shown that such behaviors have not been influenced by learning, it can be assumed that these behaviors are at least partially the result of inheritance.

Smiling by babies is at least partly the result of inheritance.

Smiling, laughing, and crying are examples. These behaviors are present in all normal children very early in life before the infants have had much opportunity to learn them from others. Because of that, these behaviors are thought to be at least partially **innate** (built-in) rather than **acquired** (learned). This belief is strengthened by the fact that smiling, laughing, and crying are seen in blind and deaf children who would have had almost no opportunity to learn such behaviors (7). Since infants have very few methods of communicating their wants and needs, it is easy to see why behaviors like crying and laughing might be adaptive and might be selected.

Selective Breeding

Another way of looking for inherited behaviors is to examine differences among members of a species. Some cats are tame; others are wild. The difference could be due to inherited behavior characteristics. The many species of domestic (bred for the home) animals that have been associated with humans during the past several thousand years are a good example of how different behaviors can be inherited by members of the same species. Domestic dogs, cats, pigs, horses, cows, and sheep are behaviorally as well as physically different from members of the same species living in the wild. The domestic animals have been bred over generations for tameness—lack of aggression and willingness to associate with humans. These animals are the result of selective breeding. Those that had the desired characteristics (tameness, speed, endurance, rapid growth, high milk production, or whatever) were kept for breeding purposes. The less tame animals may have escaped or may even have been eaten. Their genes were not passed on. In this type of selective breeding humans rather than the forces of nature do the selecting.

Attempts to selectively breed humans like animals have been made—usually with disastrous consequences. In the 1930s Adolf Hitler and the Nazi Party of Germany attempted to establish a genetically pure master race through selective breeding. Part of the plan included the destruction of so-called "impure racial types," and millions of Jews and other non-German people were murdered.

Because of the ethical questions involved (Who should be allowed to breed? Who should be allowed to be born?), selective breeding experiments are not usually done with humans. There is evidence, however, to suggest that some human characteristics are inherited. One study (20), based mainly on parents' reports of their children, suggests that infants inherit a specific temperament or disposition. The researchers found that distinct styles of behavior are evident during the first few weeks of life. These included activity level, sensitivity to new stimuli, and the ease with which a child is calmed after an outburst.

In another study (8) behavioral responses of children were examined during the first few days of life. Caucasian (white) and Chinese children in the

United States were studied. The white children struggled immediately to remove a cloth that had been placed over their faces. The Chinese children remained relatively calm and did not struggle to remove the cloth. In both studies the observed differences were attributed to genetic causes, but there may be other explanations. A child's diet, for instance, or even a mother's diet during pregnancy, could have an effect on a child's activity level and responsiveness.

Twin Studies

Another method of examining the effects of genes on behavior is to compare the behavior patterns of individuals known to have similar genotypes. Twins are the best example. Identical twins develop from only one egg. Such twins look almost exactly alike, are always of the same sex, and have the same genotype. Fraternal twins, on the other hand, develop from two eggs that were fertilized at the same time. Fraternal twins don't always look alike, are not always of the same sex, and have different genotypes. Studies of identical twins are often made in attempts to determine whether a specific behavior pattern is genetically influenced. Behavior patterns shared by identical twins could be the result of their similar genetic background. Schizophrenia is an example.

Schizophrenia is a severe psychological and behavioral disturbance that may be at least partially determined by genes. The fact that both members of pairs of identical twins develop schizophrenia more often than do pairs of fraternal twins supports this belief. But this evidence is not conclusive because identical twins usually have much more in common than their genetic makeup. They usually grow up together, have a very close relationship, and are treated much alike. In other words, their environments are very similar, and some factor in the environment could be the cause of schizophrenia. Twins, for instance, share their mother's womb for nine months. It is possible that environmental factors in the womb (rather than genetic factors) could result in schizophrenia for both twins. A shortage of oxygen shortly before or during the birth process is one such factor that has been suggested as a cause of schizophrenia.

Because strong environmental influences are present from the moment of conception when the egg is fertilized, most methods of studying the effects of genes on behavior can be questioned. Even so, there is good evidence that some individual differences in behavior are due to genetic influences. But until geneticists have worked out the exact relationship between genes and behavior, other methods will have to be used to determine which behaviors are inherited and which are acquired. The theory of evolution can be of some help here. Just as physical characteristics (skin color, blood type, body build, and so on) have been selected for their adaptive advantages, behavioral characteristics have undoubtedly been selected in the same way.

Two million years ago when our ancestors were scratching and stirring in the forests and deserts of East Africa, they had already inherited many specific behavior patterns. These were the result of billions of years of evolution, beginning with the simplest life forms.

The most basic behaviors are seen in the most basic life forms. Even plants have a sort of limited type of behavior. Their growth and movement are controlled by sources of external stimulation, such as light, heat, and water. Simple one-celled animals have slightly more complex behaviors. They can move around in response to the environment. If it is too hot for them, they will attempt to move away from the source of heat. If they survive better in darkness, they will attempt to move away from light.

Reflexes and Instincts

Higher up the evolutionary ladder more complex organisms like jellyfish have sense organs and a simple nervous system. In such animals a net of nerve fibers carries information from the sense organs and helps coordinate the total movement of the organism as it reacts to environmental stimuli. Unlearned, automatic responses to external stimuli are called reflexes. The blink of an eye when a light is flashed and the withdrawing of a hand from a hot stove are reflex responses controlled by the nervous system.

In more advanced species, with a better-developed nervous system, more complex patterns of response are possible. Such built-in response patterns are called **instincts** (from the Latin word for "urge"). Probably the best-known example of instinctive behavior is the maternal behavior of some animals, such as the urge of some animal mothers to build nests and nurse and clean their young. Web-spinning in spiders, swimming in tadpoles, and mating patterns in rats and other lower animals are also believed to be instinctive behaviors. They are unlearned, automatic, specific to a species, and appear once the animal has reached a certain level of maturity. But even behaviors that appear to be completely instinctive may, in fact, be dependent on learning. Cats will not usually kill rats unless they have seen one being killed or have accidentally drawn blood from a rat while playing with it (15). Even maternal behavior in some animals seems to be partially the result of learning. When female rats are not allowed to work with or handle material of any kind during their early lives, they fail to build nests or adequately take care of their young later in life (9).

In some of the most famous animal experiments, psychologist Harry Harlow raised monkeys in isolation (without mothers, fathers, or monkey friends). The female animals of this group did not learn mother love from their own mothers and did not display mother love when they had infants. They either ignored the infants or, in some cases, killed them. These and other experiments suggest that what may seem to be one of the most basic and important instincts, mother love, does not develop normally without learning.

Many human behaviors have been attributed to instinct—"Children instinctively know their mothers," or "Humans have a killer instinct." But humans, with a greater ability to learn than animals, may have no instincts. Even if humans do have instincts, these behavior patterns are usually so weak or have been so modified or changed by learning and experience that they cannot be detected. If instincts are truly a genetically controlled part of the human heritage, then they would be built into all members of the species. But many women do not have an urge to nurse or care for their children. So if a maternal instinct does exist in humans, it is weak enough to be cancelled out by learning and experience. Some human reflexes can even be overridden by the brain. It is possible, for instance, to keep from withdrawing a hand from a hot stove. It is probable that complex human behavior patterns are not innate but are the result of training and experience.

When evolution finally produced animals with a complex central nervous system, spinal cord, and brain, more complex behavior patterns became possible. These animals are called **vertebrates** (vertebrae are the bones that make up the spinal cord and protect the nerves that run through it from all parts of the body to the brain). In the lower or less-developed vertebrates (such as some of the smaller species of fish) behavior seems to be mostly instinctive. In the higher vertebrates, those with a larger and more complex nervous system and brain, a greater amount of learning is possible. These animals do not simply respond to the environment in a set, instinctive way. Their responses are controlled by both the immediate environmental stimulation and by previous experiences that have been recorded or remembered in the brain. Cats and dogs remember which humans have befriended them in the past or which foods have made them ill. With this remembered information, their present behavioral responses may be different than they were earlier. And with a different set of experiences, each animal may have different rather than the same instinctive behaviors.

By careful observation of animals it is sometimes possible to determine which behaviors are instinctive and which are acquired. **Ethology** (from the Greek word for "trait") is the scientific study of animal traits and behaviors. By observing animals in their natural environment, ethologists attempt to understand the innate or built-in behavior patterns that evolution has produced.

Imprinting

The work of a German ethologist, Konrad Lorenz, has helped explain some of the complex relationships between innate and acquired behavior. In some of his most famous experiments Lorenz raised geese that had been hatched in an incubator. The first moving object the geese saw after they hatched was not their mother but Lorenz. Instinctively, the young geese began to follow the scientist around. They behaved as if he were their real mother. Later, when the geese were placed with their mother, they ignored her and ran back to Lorenz for protection. Lorenz found that young geese instinctively follow the first moving object they see after they are hatched, no matter what is is. They attach themselves to an object and (according to Lorenz's theory) the image of that object is stamped or **imprinted** on their brains. Lorenz experimented with the imprinting process and even imprinted geese to balloons by having a balloon move around in front of them shortly after they were hatched.

The imprinting process has an obvious adaptive advantage. Young geese must have a model to learn appropriate goose behavior from. Since the first moving object geese would normally see is the mother, she usually becomes the imprinted model. The geese who became attached to Lorenz or to balloons did not learn proper goose behavior, and as adults were not prepared for life as geese.

The exact timing of imprinting has been found to be important or critical. The "critical period" for imprinting in geese seems to be between 16 and 24 hours after hatching. In other words, imprinting works best if it takes place during that period. If geese are hatched in a dark incubator and not allowed to see any moving object during the first two or three days of life, imprinting does not normally occur. What seems to happen is that a stronger instinct overrides the urge to imprint to a moving object. The newly developed instinct is fear of strangers. Under normal conditions this would keep young geese safely near their mothers, and keep them from imprinting on strangers. This fear of strangers, however, does not extinguish the imprinting instinct. The geese hatched in the dark incubator were just too frightened of strangers to imprint on anything. When these geese were given drugs to calm them and make them less fearful, they did imprint up to a week after hatching. This suggests that the critical period may not be as critical as was originally thought.

Since imprinting was first described, researchers have spent a good deal of time studying it. Imprinting has been found in many (but not all) species of birds and in sheep and seals. There is no strong evidence, however, for imprinting in humans.

Imprinting is an example of how instincts and environmental learning can work together to produce adaptive behavior in some animals. Once a certain behavior has been identified as instinctive, the next step is to find out what triggers or sets off the behavior. Any moving object can start the process of imprinting in geese. A small red dot on the adult herring gull's beak triggers or releases pecking behavior in young herring gulls. When the young gulls see the red spot on the adult beak, they peck at it. This gets the adult gulls to open their beaks and feed the infants. The behavior is so instinctive that the young gulls will peck at any red spot they see, whether it is on an adult's beak or not.

Other signs in the environment, such as the weather or the position of the sun, control the homing and migration instincts of some animals. Such signs are called **releasing mechanisms** because they release the innate behavior patterns the animal was born with.

Mammal
Behavior

Next highest on the evolutionary scale after vertebrates come mammals (from the Latin word for "breast"). **Mammals** are warm-blooded, fur-bearing vertebrates that give birth to live infants (instead of laying eggs). Female mammals have breasts or milk-producing mammary glands with which to feed their young. Mammals became important as a life form after the extinction of the dinosaurs, nearly 100 million years ago. And now there are more than 15,000 mammal species.

In most mammals after the female's egg is fertilized by the male, it grows for some time in the mother's womb, getting food and oxygen from her bloodstream. After birth the infant continues to feed from the mother's breasts and is protected by one or both parents until it reaches a certain stage of maturity. During pregnancy and breast-feeding (the juvenile stage) the young mammal's nervous system and brain begin to learn the many behaviors that will be necessary for survival.

Mother-child attachment behavior is seen in all mammal species, but the period of attachment is much longer in some. Horses, cattle, deer, and sheep, for instance, are constantly on the move looking for food and running from their enemies. The young of these animals must be up on their feet and ready to follow the herd shortly after birth. In other species—including wolves, foxes, lions, tigers, and most mammals that live in social groups—the period of attachment and physical dependency is much longer. For the young of these species there is usually much more time for exploratory behavior and play. This type of activity provides learning experiences that are probably responsible for the wider range of behavior patterns seen in the adults of these species (2).

Primate
Behavior

The longest mother-child attachment period is seen in **primates,** the group of mammals that includes monkeys, apes, and humans. For primates there is one important factor that makes possible the long period of infancy. This is the fact that most primate species tend to live in social groups. While a mother is feeding and protecting her infant, other members of the group help protect and feed the mother. Group members warn each other of dangers, help fight off predators like lions and tigers, and help each other find food and water.

Unselfish behavior aimed at helping others is called **altruism** (from the Latin word for "other"), and altruistic behavior seems to be an important part of successful group living. But in evolutionary terms, altruism does not at first glance appear to be a behavior pattern that would be passed on with one's genes. If altruistic individuals are the ones most likely to go out and fight the lions and tigers, they are also the most likely to get killed and the least likely to pass on their genes (including any genes for altruism). In 1975, in his book *Sociobiology,* Edward O. Wilson provided evidence to support a theory of how altruistic behavior patterns might be inherited (23). The theory is based, in part, on kin or relative selection. Parents, by protecting and caring for their own children, are actually increasing the chances that their genes will survive and be passed on (through their children). Members of a social group are not as closely related as parents and their children, but they do share similar genetic combinations because they are usually related to each other in some way. Therefore, group members who die in an attempt to protect the group are actually increasing the chances that their genes (or similar ones) will survive and be passed on by their kin or relatives.

In addition to offering protection, social groups offer another very important advantage. In general, the more complex an organism is, the less likely it is that behavior patterns will be transmitted genetically. Without built-in or inherited behaviors to guide them, the higher species, like primates, must learn most of the behaviors that will help them survive. During a long infancy primates learn through social experience. They may learn such things as where to find food and water; skills and information are learned and passed on from one member of the group to others and from one generation to the next. Chimpanzees, for instance, do not reach maturity until about eight or nine years of age. Prior to that they spend most of their time with their mothers and with other young chimps. During this juvenile period the young chimps

Young chimpanzees imitate their mothers' choice of food and use of simple tools.

learn many of the behaviors they will need as adults. Most of these behaviors are probably learned through imitation. Young chimps imitate their mothers' choice of food and the use of simple tools. They can learn to use leaves to wipe themselves and twigs to dig up ants and termites. They learn social behaviors, such as how to treat each other and how eventually to care for their own off-spring, as Harlow's experiments showed. These and many more behaviors are learned during a long childhood and can be passed on to succeeding generations (19). It was from generations and generations of primates capable of learning a great many adaptive behavior patterns that humans probably evolved.

HUMAN EVOLUTION

The story of human evolution is long, complex, and incomplete; but enough evidence has been found in recent years to suggest an outline of the major steps in human evolution. The skeletal remains of early human and prehuman primates have been found, and together with knowledge of genetic and evolutionary theory they tell the story of human development as a species. It appears that between 10 and 20 million years ago primate species began to evolve in different directions. Some primates evolved into the present-day species of apes and chimpanzees. Others evolved into humans. This probably makes chimpanzees the closest living relatives of the human species. Recent evidence shows that the chromosome structure of humans is closer to that of chimpanzees than it is to any other primate species (13).

What first caused the evolutionary split between these primate groups is unknown, but it is possible that the hominids (those that eventually evolved into humans) moved out or were forced out of their forest homes and began to spend time in open country. Most wild apes still live in forests, for they are well adapted to that type of life. But overpopulation, or perhaps a change in the climate which reduced the size of the forests, may have forced the early hominids into an ecological niche for which they were not adapted. With a new and different set of environmental forces at work, natural selection slowly changed these creatures and helped them adapt to their new world. Instead of swinging from branches, they had to move long distances over open territory. Those who were best at this survived and evolved into a species that could walk upright and use their hands for gathering food and using simple tools. There is good evidence that upright-walking, tool-using creatures were living in Africa four million years ago. These **hominids** were about 4 feet tall and had a brain slightly larger than that of present-day chimps.

By a little less than two million years ago hominids had developed much more efficient tools (stone spears and knives) and were probably becoming effective hunters. They also learned to use fire for warmth and to cook their meat. This added protein and better nutrition to their diet, and they continued to grow stronger and taller. The remains of these creatures (found with their tools, fire pits, and the bones of the animals they probably ate) show that they were about 5 feet tall and had a brain more than twice as large as that of a chimpanzee and only slightly smaller than that of today's human brain.

The Hunter-Gatherer Life

Hunting was necessary for the early hominids because there is much less to eat in open country than in forests. But not all hominids could hunt. Chasing an antelope across the hot African plains can be a strenuous task. Probably only the most healthy group members went out hunting, while the very old and mothers with infants waited at a camp site. Because the hunters probably came home empty-handed quite often, those who remained in camp had to find other methods of supplying food for the group. They did this by gathering nuts, fruits, and whatever vegetables could be found. This **hunter-gatherer way of life** was probably necessary to the first humans; it can still be seen in some parts of the world. The Bushmen of the Kalahari desert in Africa are hunter-gatherers. They move around in small groups. The men hunt, while the women gather what food they can and take care of their children. When the hunters return, all members of the group share the food.

Communication is an important part of successful group hunting. Individual hunters must signal each other when they spot an animal. The hunters must then communicate their plans to each other, such as how to surround and trap an animal. Because communication is controlled in the brain, those individuals whose brains were best equipped to communicate were probably the most effective hunters. They were more likely to get enough food and to survive and pass on their genes (including the genes involved in brain development and communication).

As genes for a larger brain were selected, women began to give birth to infants with larger heads. Even though women's hips are generally wider than those of men, they are not wide enough to permit the birth of a child with a fully developed human brain. If evolution had continued to select women with wider and wider hips, it might have eventually interfered with women's ability to walk upright. Instead, natural selection went in another direction. Human infants are born with a brain that is not fully developed. The size of a human infant's brain is only one fourth that of an adult brain (with newborn chimpanzees it is one half). This adaptation increased the helplessness of newborn humans and extended the period of infancy, giving the brain time to reach its full size, and giving the infant time to learn the many behaviors necessary for survival.

As the human brain continued to evolve to its present size, humans became capable of more learning. They learned to make clothing and shelter.

The Bushmen of the Kalahari Desert hunt while the women gather food and take care of the children.

With such skills they were able to adapt to climates colder than that of Africa. They were able to move north and gradually spread across the face of the earth. By 40,000 years ago true human populations with fully evolved brains were living in parts of Africa, Europe, and Asia.

Cultural Evolution

As the human species evolved, a body of knowledge grew and was passed on from generation to generation. This body of knowledge, the **culture** of the species, contained information about tool-making, hunting, and communication. Because this information was necessary to survival, natural selection would have favored those individuals capable of learning and communicating cultural skills. Those with the largest brains and the most flexible hands, for instance, would have been the best equipped to learn and communicate their culture and to use the skills of their culture. They were the[...] vive and pass on their genes. Today, newborn humans inherit[...] cal characteristics necessary to learn and use the skills of their c[...] survive in their environments.

The gradual building up of cultural information has continued and [...] erated throughout human history. The hunter-gatherer culture led to sett[...] agriculture, to city life, to industrialization, and finally to today's technological culture. By creating these cultures, humans have, in effect, created their own environments. They are no longer completely at the mercy of what nature offers but are capable of shaping the environment to fit their needs. With centuries of physical evolution behind them, the early hominids were finally equipped to survive in cold northern climates. With centuries of cultural evolution behind them, technology-controlling humans no longer have to wait for natural selection to reshape and adapt their bodies. They can reshape the environment and survive in the coldest parts of the world, under the sea, or in outer space. These technological adaptations are the result of cultural evolution, the most recent trend in human evolution.

Implications of Our Biological Past

More than 99 percent of all humans now live in a different kind of environment from that in which the species evolved. The hunter-gatherer way of life, the way in which our human ancestors lived during much of the time the species was evolving to its present state, is now the way of life for only a few tens of thousands of people in isolated parts of the world. Methods of child-rearing and the experiences of childhood have changed in many ways during the transition to modern urban life. Although human children are especially adaptable and have been able to survive successfully in changing physical and cultural environments, there are limits to adaptability. An understanding of our biological past can help define these limits and possibly can suggest the types of experiences and environments that will be best for child development as the species continues to evolve.

The future of human evolution is unknown, and our knowledge of past evolution is incomplete; but what is known can help explain the present and can even help prepare for the future. **Ethologists,** the scientists who study animal and human behavior from a biological and evolutionary point of view, have made some discoveries that do help explain human behavior. Their study of mother-child attachment in various species is one example.

Most young children between 6 and 12 months of age become very anxious and disturbed when they are left alone by their mothers. This disturbance is known as **separation anxiety.** It is similar to the instinctive fear seen in young geese, and it is seen in some children of up to three years of age. In the 1950s mother-child attachment was thought to be based on children's dependence on their mothers for food; the loss of a food source was thought to

of separation anxiety. But ethologists like Lorenz have studied
discovered much more complex forms of attachment such as
ome of Harlow's work with monkeys showed that providing an
od source when the mother is absent does not reduce separation
t appears that food is not the major reason for mother-child attach-

n ethological and evolutionary point of view, the close mother-
onship can be explained as an inherited behavior pattern designed
thers near their children. This behavior is seen in primitive hunter-
ocieties as well as in modern technological societies (21). But if
mother-child attachment is seen as an inborn human behavior, the next question is, what is its biological cause? The answer seems to be warmth and
protection. Infants need to stay near their mothers to keep their body tempera-
tures up to normal. In heated environments this may not be as important as
it once was, but protection is still necessary. Thousands of years ago infants
needed protection from wild animals. Today they need protection from automobiles and from other technological dangers. For these reasons attachment
behavior is necessary for survival and was probably selected.

These and other ethological studies suggest that mothers should stay near
their infants and respond to their needs. But it has also been suggested that
mothers should not overprotect their children and "spoil" them by responding
to every cry for food and attention. Such overprotection is supposed to keep
children from developing independence. One study has found the opposite to
be true (24). In this study a naturalistic, longitudinal approach was used to
observe 26 infant-mother pairs. The effects of crying were studied for the first
year of life. During the first few months the mother's responsiveness to her
child's crying seemed to have no effect on the amount of crying. Because the
infants sometimes kept on crying even after the mothers responded, some
mothers became less responsive. They began to pay less attention to their
infants and just let them cry. Other mothers continued to respond every time
the child cried.

After one year the researchers found that those children whose crying had
not been responded to regularly were still crying a lot. Those infants who had
been answered were crying much less and had learned other methods of communication. These children seemed to have developed a feeling of trust and
safety. Knowing that someone is going to be there when needed, such children
are likely to develop more, not less, independence. And many studies have
shown that independent children are usually high achievers as adults.

From these studies it can be seen that a knowledge of our biological and
evolutionary heritage can help explain present human behavior (attachment
and crying) and might even affect the future by changing present behaviors

Attachment behavior helps assure that infants will be protected from the dangers of modern society.

(such as child-care behavior). But ethologists have isolated only a limited number of possibly inherited behavior patterns, and it is not likely that they will ever explain all of the behaviors the human brain is capable of producing. Even so, ethologists believe it is better to understand our biological heritage and attempt to work with it rather than against it.

What about aggression? Do genes and the theory of evolution explain human aggression? In a sense they do. It is easy to see how aggression may have been a necessary part of our evolutionary development and how the tendency to be aggressive may have become a built-in part of our brain and nervous systems. But if we inherited aggression we might also have inherited tendencies to be socially cooperative and altruistic. So the nature-nurture question becomes a complicated one. Almost every human behavior that seems to be innate can be explained as a result of learning and conditioning. And behaviors that seem to have been inherited by some people seem to be nonexistent in others. This is true of aggression.

In 1971, on the island of Mindanao in the Philippines, a tribe of Stone Age people was discovered. These people, known as the Tasadays, had been almost completely isolated from the rest of the world for at least 600 years. When they were found, the Tasadays were living much as our hunter-gatherer ancestors did. One outstanding characteristic of the Tasadays is that they are completely lacking in aggression. Their language has no words for "weapon," "hostility," "anger," or "war." From this small isolated sample it can be argued that the human species is not marked by an inherited instinct for aggression. But because the Tasadays have been isolated for so long, it can be argued that they are genetically different. They have evolved in an ecological niche in which aggressive behavior does not seem to have been necessary. In either case, whether we have inherited our aggression or whether we have learned it, the fact remains that we have inherited a brain capable of learning and controlling our aggressive tendencies. In the case of aggression, as in most aspects of human development and behavior, nature and nurture work together.

SUMMARY

The nature-nurture question asks which aspects of behavior are inherited and which are learned. Aggressive behavior in humans is an example. Some theories say it is inherited; others say it is learned. An understanding of genetics and evolution may help answer questions about the causes of aggression and lead to a better understanding of how both nature and nurture influence human development.

Genetic theory, developed by Gregor Mendel, explains the mechanisms involved in the transmission of traits from one generation to the next. Mendel's experiments with garden peas helped confirm his theory.

Inheritance is controlled by genes. Genes for specific traits are inherited from each parent. The combination of genes inherited is called a genotype. The observable effects of the genes is called a phenotype.

Genes are either dominant or recessive. A homozygous genotype exists when two dominant or two recessive genes are inherited for the same trait. A heterozygous genotype exists when a dominant and a recessive gene are inherited for the same trait. In the homozygous condition, the effects of the genotype are always seen in the phenotype (observed characteristics). In the heterozygous condition, only the dominant gene usually has an effect on the phenotype.

Sickle-cell anemia is an hereditary disease caused by a recessive gene. If an individual's genotype is homozygous for the disease, the recessive sickle-cell gene will have been inherited from both parents, and it will affect the phenotype (cause the disease). If the genotype is heterozygous, the normal gene will be dominant and the effects of the sickle-cell gene will not be seen in the phenotype (the disease does not appear). Individuals who have the heterozygous genotype are said to have the sickle-cell trait (rather than the disease).

DNA is the basic building block of living organisms. The way chemicals are arranged in the complex DNA molecule represents a code. The codes are what we call genes. Human DNA contains at least 10,000 genes.

Chromosomes are strands of DNA. Each human cell (except the sex cells) contains 46 chromosomes arranged in pairs. The two chromosomes of each pair contain genes for the same trait. Genes that code for different versions of the same trait (normal or sickle-cell hemoglobin) and are located on paired chromosomes are called alleles. PKU, a condition controlled by allelic forms of genes, is one example of how nurture can sometimes overcome the effects of nature. The genotype for PKU will not affect the phenotype if the condition is recognized soon enough and treated with a special diet.

The 23rd pair of human chromosomes contain the sex chromosomes. Females have two X chromosomes in their 23rd pair. Males have an X and a smaller Y chromosome. The effects of genes located on the sex chromosomes can be seen because they are linked to the sex of parents and offspring. Hemophilia is an example of a sex-linked genetic trait.

Sexual reproduction helps bring about change within a species. Genes from parents are combined during sexual reproduction to produce a third individual with a different genotype. Asexual reproduction is called mitosis. During mitosis chromosomes reproduce themselves, and the cell divides into two new cells exactly the same as the parent cell. Meiosis is the process by which sex cells (sperm and egg) are produced. Sex cells have half the normal number of chromosomes. When they come together the result is a new cell with the normal number of chromosomes.

Mutations are mistakes. They can result in faulty genes or chromosomes. Most mutations are probably harmful (hemophilia and PKU), but some can be beneficial (the sickle-cell trait protects people against some forms of malaria).

Advances in genetics raise ethical questions. There is some evidence, for instance, that males with an extra Y chromosome (XYY) are overly aggressive (perhaps due to excess male hormones). Should infants with this condition be identified and given special treatment? The treatment may be more harmful than the condition. Sickle-cell anemia can be detected in unborn children. Should such children be aborted?

Darwin's theory of evolution explains how the various species of plants and animals (including humans) came to exist. Those individuals who have beneficial mutations in their genotype will be better able to adapt to their environment and will be more likely to survive and pass on their genes to succeeding generations. Those individuals who have harmful mutations or do not have the genes necessary for adaptation will be less successful at survival and reproduction.

The ecological niche in which an organism lives has powerful effects on evolution. Evolutionary pressures for change will be weak on organisms well adapted to their ecological niche. If the environment changes or if the organism moves into a different ecological niche, pressures for change will be strong because different adaptations to the environment will be called for. The wing color of one species of moth changed during a 50-year period. This is believed to have been caused by pollution of the moths' ecological niche.

Human skin color and body shape also seem to have evolved as adaptations to the environment. Dark skin and a tall thin body may be adaptations to a hot, bright climate. Light skin and a squat body may be adaptations to a dark, cold climate.

Physical differences among groups of humans have led to classification of the species into subspecies or races. Racial distinctions, however, are not very useful in describing individuals. The differences among individuals of any one race are usually greater than the differences among races. Differences that may exist among races can usually be explained by nurture (the way people are treated) rather than nature (genetic differences).

Behavior genetics is the field of science that attempts to understand how behavior evolved and is inherited. Cats and pigs, for instance, have inherited different behavior patterns. Selective breeding can even produce different behavior patterns within a species. Tame and wild pigs have different inherited patterns of behavior.

The study of inherited behavior is complicated by the fact that behaviors are learned as well as inherited, and it is often difficult to tell the difference between the effects of nature and nurture. The study of identical twins (with identical genotypes) is one method of investigating the effects of genes on behavior.

Ethologists study animal behavior and its evolution. The simplest animal species have the simplest behaviors, such as reflexes and instincts. More advanced species, with a more complex nervous system and a greater ability to learn, have many acquired behaviors.

Imprinting is another example of how nature and nurture work together in development. Geese instinctively imprint or attach themselves to the first moving object they see after hatching. This instinctive or natural behavior keeps geese near their mother (usually), and then nurture takes over as the geese begin to learn goose behavior patterns from their mother.

Mammals and primates have much more complex nervous systems and behavior patterns than animals of the lower species. Some mammals and most primates (including humans) live in social groups, and much of their behavior is the result of social learning. Even mother-infant attachment behavior in primates seems to be the result of learning rather than instinct (nurture rather than nature).

Altruism is unselfish behavior aimed at helping other members (including relatives) of a social group. Altruistic individuals who attempt to protect their social group may not survive to pass on their genes. One theory, however, suggests that by helping the group survive, altruism helps ensure that the group's genes will survive (including the genes for altruism) and be passed on.

Between 10 and 20 million years ago, primate species began going through changes that probably led to the evolution of the human species. Climate changes may have forced some primates to leave their ecological niche in the forests and begin living as hunter-gatherers in more open territory.

Evolutionary processes selected primates with larger brains capable of more learning. By 40,000 years ago, true human populations with fully evolved brains were living in Europe, Asia, and Africa.

Much of what the early humans were able to learn (tool use, hunting skills, communication methods) formed a body of knowledge that represented the culture of the species. This body of cultural knowledge has been added to, modified, and passed on from generation to generation through the process of cultural evolution. A gradual build-up of culture has led to today's technological culture.

An understanding of the biological background and the evolutionary development and adaptations of the human species can suggest the types of experiences and environments that will be best for human development. Mother-child attachment behavior is an example. Ethologists and other researchers suggest that a close mother-child relationship is a biological and behavioral adaptation that provides infants with the warmth, protection, and opportunity for social learning necessary for normal development.

Human aggressive behavior, an example of the nature-nurture question, may have been inherited because it was probably a necessary adaptation during the evolution of the species. But aggression, like most human behaviors, is also a learned behavior. Even though the cause of aggression cannot be precisely determined, and the nature-nurture question cannot be fully answered, an understanding of both nature and nurture reveals the importance of both in human development.

Genetic Factors in Schizophrenia and Alcoholism

Studies that have attempted to investigate the influence of genetic, or biological, inheritance upon behavior have been particularly popular in the last 10 years. When dealing with human beings, however, the kinds of experiments that could be conducted to help in distinguishing the relative influence of biology and the environment are necessarily limited by ethical considerations. Obviously we cannot randomly assign human infants to different environmental conditions, and this lack of randomness in experimental designs weakens the certainty or confidence that we can have in our findings. Nevertheless, using studies that investigate identical twins (who share the same genetic make-up) and studies that examine children and parents, researchers have accumulated evidence suggesting that genetic factors do play a part in causing some human behavior.

Heston (1966) reported on a study investigating schizophrenia that used two matched groups of children. The first group included 47 adopted children whose biological mothers were schizophrenic but not their adopted mothers. The second group of children was almost identical to the first group but consisted of 47 adopted children who did not have schizophrenic biological mothers. When Heston examined these two groups of children he found that of the group with schizophrenic biological mothers, 5 of the children were themselves schizophrenic. Of the control group children—those whose biological mothers were not schizophrenic—none were schizophrenic. Clearly, these kinds of results suggest that there may well be a genetic factor in schizophrenia.

Schuckit, Goodwin, and Winokur (1972) reported on a study that looked at possible genetic factors in alcoholism. Defining alcoholism as "drinking in a manner that interferes with one's life" (leading to divorce, job loss, arrests, hospitalization), Schuckit et al. identified 69 persons who matched their definition and who also had half-siblings, that is, sisters or brothers with one parent in common but not both. The researchers then interviewed relatives of this group and compared the incidence of alcoholism among their relatives with the incidence of alcoholism among the relatives of their half-siblings. The results showed that "of children who had alcoholic biologic parents, those raised by nonalcoholic parent figures and those raised by alcoholic parent figures experience an almost identical rate of alcoholism." The data showed that among half-siblings with an alcoholic biologic parent and raised with an alcoholic parent figure, 46 percent were alcoholic; 50 percent of similar half-siblings were alcoholic when raised *without* an alcoholic parent figure. The percentage for half-siblings *without* an alcoholic biologic parent were 14 and 8 percent, respectively.

The study by Schuckit et al. strongly suggests that the consistent predictor of alcoholism in half-siblings is a biological factor—having an alcoholic biologic parent. It should be noted that the study does not *prove* that environmental factors are not important—they may very well be. But it does suggest, as does the Heston study, that biological factors may well be involved in schizo-phrenia and alcoholism.

Based on L. L. Heston, *British Journal of Psychiatry*, 1966, *112*, 819; M. Schuckit, D. Goodwin, and G. Winokur, "A Study of Alcoholism in Half Siblings," *American Journal of Psychiatry*, March, 1972, *128*, 9.

RESEARCH REPORT 2.2

Extra Y Chromosome and Human Criminality

This chapter has mentioned the possible linkage between certain kinds of behavior and chromosomal abnormalities in males, particularly the possible elevated crime rate for males with an extra Y chromosome. Here we will look at a recent piece of research which has examined this suggested relationship in some detail.

Witkin et al. (1976) recently reported on an involved and careful follow-up study of a population of 31,436 male Danish citizens born to women who were residents of Copenhagen, between January 1, 1944, and December 31, 1947. Previous research involving the possible link between criminality in men and abnormal chromosomal make-up (XYY) was usually done on very selected populations, but as Witkin et al. noted, the subject caused a considerable stir. Earlier research and commentary suggested that if such a link were firmly established, society should perhaps take preventive measures with persons identified as having that particular chromosomal abnormality. The importance of the topic and the possible far-reaching consequences of such a link between criminal behavior and chromosomal abnormality, as well as the inadequacy of previous research, led to this particular study.

The study was done in Denmark because of the presence of two necessary characteristics: (1) the availability of complete birth records for the population, and (2) a relatively stable society so that there was an expectation that not too many people in the sample would be lost.

Since it is well established that men with the abnormal chromosome make-up XYY tend to be taller than normal men, the authors did chromosomal determinations from blood samples and buccal smears on all men in the top 15.9 percent of the height distribution of their Danish male population of 31,436. Taking a height cut-off of 184 centimeters, the authors obtained a group consisting of 4,591 men. Deaths during the case-finding period further reduced the number to 4,588. In fact, chromosome determinations were made for 4,139 men, 90.8 percent of the starting group of 4,558 living, tall men. Information on criminal convictions was obtained from penal registers, and information on the intelligence of the sample from intelligence test results in draft board records. Further evidence of intellectual functioning was obtained by assessing the educational level achieved by the individuals in the sample.

The data the authors collected suggested that their find rate of 2.9 per thousand XYY's and 3.9 per thousand XXY's among the tall men sampled in the study was about what would be expected. It is worth quoting the authors' conclusions since they state their findings very clearly:

> As to the rate of criminality, our finding is consistent with past findings from studies of institutionalized populations in that the XYY's we identified had a higher mean rate of criminal conviction than the XY controls. With regard to the possible correlates of the elevated XYY crime rate, the hypothesis we considered that height may be an intervening variable was not confirmed. In fact, within our tall XY group, height showed a small but statistically significant negative relation to criminality. On the other hand, the evidence from this study is consistent with the second hypothesis we considered, the intellectual dysfunction hypothesis. The XYY's had an appreciably lower mean on [intelligence test scores] than did the XY's, and they also had a substantially lower mean on the relative index of educational achievement level attained, although some of the XYY's were within or nor far out of the normal range on these variables. Moreover, in our XY sample, criminality showed a substantial relation to both measures of level of intellectual functioning. While intellectual functioning is clearly implicated as an important mediating variable, we cannot at this time say whether it is the only factor involved.

The authors go on to note that the notion of the relationship between aggression and abnormal chromosomes is not supported:

> Among all the offenses committed by XYY's, there was only a single incidence of an aggressive act against another person, and in that case the aggression was not severe. *Thus, the frequency of crimes of violence against another person was not statistically significantly higher in the XYY's than in the XY's.* [Italics added.] The elevated crime rate in our XYY sample reflects an elevated rate of property offenses. This picture is in keeping with the results of previous studies, most of which have also found that XYY's are not more likely to commit crimes against people than are XY's.

This study is interesting not only for the substance which it reports—its examination of the matter of criminality and abnormal chromosomal make-up—but also because it illustrates the complexity and detail involved in a careful pursuit of this topic, and because it recognizes that even with this large-scale, detailed study a certain amount of uncertainty remains. However, the study strongly suggests that persons with the abnormal chromosomal make-up XYY are not likely to be more aggressive than the normal population of XY's. It also implies that if this group does tend to commit more crimes than a normal population, this seems to be attributable to lower intellectual levels of functioning rather than to higher levels of aggression or to the fact that XYY males are taller than normal XY males.

H. Witkin, S. Mednick, F. Schulsinger, E. Bakkestrom, K. Christiansen, D. Goodenough, K. Hirschtorm, C. Lundsteen, D. Owen, J. Phillip, D. Rabin, and M. Stocking, "Criminality in XYY and XXY Men," *Science*, August 13, 1976, *193*, 547–555.

REFERENCES

1. Benda, C. "Down's Syndrome: Beginning of End," *Roche Reports*, 1970, 7 (15), 1–5.
2. Bruner, J. S. "The Nature and Uses of Immaturity," *American Psychologist*, 1972, *27*, 1–28.
3. Centerwall, W. R., and S. A. Centerwall. *Journal of the History of Medicine*, 1961, *16*, 292–296.
4. *China Medical Journal*, March 1975, *1*, 117.
5. Coleman, J. C. *Abnormal Psychology and Modern Life*. Glenview, Ill.: Scott, Foresman, 1972, 569–570.
6. Editorial. *Lancet*, 1974, *II*, 1297.
7. Eibl-Eibesfeldt, I. *Ethology: The Biology of Behavior*. New York: Holt, Rinehart and Winston, 1975.
8. Freedman, D. G. *Human Infancy: An Evolutionary Perspective*. New York: Wiley (Halsted Press), 1974.
9. Goldenson, R. M. "Instinct," *The Encyclopedia of Human Behavior*. New York: Doubleday, 1970.
10. Goldenson, R. M. "Race Differences," *The Encyclopedia of Human Behavior*. New York: Doubleday, 1970.
11. Haviland, W. A. *Anthropology*. New York: Holt, Rinehart and Winston, 1974, 151–156.
12. Jacobs, P. A., Brunton, M., McClemont, W. F. *Nature*, 1965, *208*, 1351.
13. King, M. C., and Wilson, A. C. Evolution at two levels in humans and chimpanzees. *Science*, 1975, *188*, 107–116.
14. Kochupillai, N., et al. *Nature*, 1976, *262*, 60–61.
15. Kuo, Z. Y. "The Genesis of the Cat's Response to the Rat," *Journal of Comparative Psychology*, 1930, *11*, 1–36.
16. McCandless, B. R., Carolyn B. Bilous, and Hannah L. Bennett. "The Relation between Peer Popularity and Dependence on Adults in Preschool-age Socialization," *Child Development*, 1961, *32*, 511–518.
17. Morton, N. E. "Morbidity of Children from Consanguineous Marriages," *Progress in Medical Genetics*, 1961, *1*, 261–291.
18. Sears, R. R., Eleanor E. Maccoby, and H. Levin. *Patterns of Child-Rearing*. Evanston, Ill.: Row, Peterson, 1957.
19. Teleki, G. "Chimpanzee Subsistence Technology: Materials and Skills," *Journal of Human Evolution*, 1974, *3*, 575–594.
20. Thomas, A., Chess, S., Birch, H. G. "The Origin of Personality," *Scientific American*, 1970, *223*, 102–109.
21. Trotter, R. J. "Human Behavior: Do Animals Have the Answer?" *Science News*, 1974, *105* (17), 274–279.
22. Trotter, R. J. "War," *Science News*, 1973, *104* (16), 250–251.
23. Wilson, E. O. *Sociobiology*. Cambridge, Mass.: Harvard University Press (Belknap Press), 1975.
24. Yuet, Wai Kan, et al., and Blanche P. Alter, et al. *New England Journal of Medicine*, 1976, *124* (19), 1039–1040.

Children are provided by nature with a blueprint for biological development. Nurture provides them with a social and cultural heritage. Chapter 3 examines some of the major cultural and social influences in development.

culture and development

What would happen if human infants were reared in the wild by wolves? Would they be more like humans or animals? Would they learn a language? Would they develop like normal human beings? A partial answer to these questions came in the 1940s after several people in India reported that they had seen small, naked children running along on all fours with a family of wolves. An Anglican missionary named Singh heard the reports and decided to investigate. In *Wolf Children and Feral Men* he tells the story of two young girls who had been living with a pack of wolves (45).

"Feral" means "wild," and that's what these children turned out to be. After their capture, they were taken to an orphanage run by Singh and his wife. Singh reported that the girls knew no language and howled like wolves. Their eyes "glared in the dark like blue lights," their hearing was extremely good, they could smell meat from a distance of 70 yards, and their teeth were sharp. At the orphanage they ate like animals, lapping up food from a pan and devouring raw meat as if they were starving.

The younger of the two girls was believed to be about 1½ years old at the time of capture. She made some progress in learning to walk upright, but died about a year after she was brought to the orphanage. The older girl was about 8 years old. She never did learn to walk upright, but she did stop howling like a wolf and eventually learned to use about 50 words. She died after eight years at the orphanage.

Scientists have long wondered how much could be learned about human development from infants reared in isolation from other humans. Cases like that of the wolf girls provide some answers, but nothing was known of their background and little was learned from them during their stay at the orphanage. In order to really examine the effects of being reared away from all other humans, a controlled experiment would have to be set up in which children would be separated from their parents and examined closely as they developed in isolation. An experiment of this type might help answer parts of the nature-nurture question and help explain how much of human development is a result of learning from other humans and how much stems from biological inheritance. Since such an experiment would be cruel and dangerous for the children involved, researchers have had to wait for cases like that of the wolf girls to answer their questions. One of the most famous and well documented of these cases took place in nineteenth-century France. It involved a young boy who has since come to be known as the Wild Boy of Aveyron. Psychologist Harlan Lane has recently reexamined the facts in the case (28).

In the winter of 1799, a naked boy was seen running through the forest of southern France. Hunters captured this "wild child" on several occasions and exhibited him like an animal in a cage, but he was usually crafty enough to escape. After several captures and escapes, French authorities finally sent the

Still from a movie based on the story of the wild boy of Aveyron.

boy from Aveyron in southern France to Paris where he could be examined and studied by scientists. The child is believed to have been about 11 years old when captured, and he had apparently lived alone in the woods for six or more years. Like the Indian girls, the French boy seemed to be more animal than human. Experts, including Philippe Pinel (who is known as the father of psychiatry), examined the boy and concluded that he was an incurable idiot. The experts suggested that this was probably why the boy had been abandoned by his parents in the first place.

Jean Itard, a young French physician, had a different idea. He thought that the wild behavior of the child was the result of being isolated from human contact for a long time. Itard named the boy Victor and spent five years trying to educate him.

When Victor was captured he walked and ran more like an animal than a human. When alone he sat and rocked back and forth. When allowed out he roamed around in freezing weather without clothes. He could grab food out of a pot of boiling water or out of a hot fire without showing signs of pain. He had a highly developed sense of smell, but was unable to focus his eyes on anything for more than a few seconds. Victor could hear well, but appeared to hear only those sounds associated with food. He would turn toward the sound of a nut cracking, but he paid no attention to the sound of human voices. He made no attempts to communicate and seemed to view other humans as little more than obstacles to his wants and needs.

After more than five years with Itard, Victor had changed little. He did learn to live in a house and sleep in a bed as well as eat with a fork and knife. He also learned to wear clothes and to focus his eyes, but he never learned to communicate very well. Itard managed to teach Victor to read, write, and understand a few simple words, but no more. Social development was almost nonexistent. Victor seemed to have some affection for Itard and for the woman who cared for him, but he never learned to socialize with other people. He continued to live a simple life and died at about the age of 40.

As was seen in Chapter 2, nature provides each child with a blueprint for biological development. Cases like that of Victor and the wolf girls, however, make it quite clear that nature does not provide everything that is necessary for what is considered to be normal human development. Nurture, in the form of human social contact, also plays an extremely important role in human development. The results of millions of years of biological evolution are built into each newborn infant, but the results of millions of years of cultural evolution must be acquired by each infant through social interactions. Because Victor and the wolf girls were isolated from this type of social contact during a major part of their childhood, both their physical and social development were seriously affected.

Although both nature and nurture are involved in human development, the nature-nurture question asks how much of each is involved in the various aspects of development. The case of the wild child offered scientists a good chance to study this question, but unfortunately the results of those studies are still unclear. It is not known whether Victor's inability to talk was the result of some physical damage he may have suffered, or whether it was due to the fact that he had been isolated from human speech for so long. It is also unclear whether Victor's wild behavior was the result of a serious mental problem (such as brain damage) or of prolonged isolation. What does seem to be clear is the fact that prolonged isolation during childhood can have serious effects on human development.

LOVE AMONG THE MONKEYS

Because it is impractical and inhumane to study the effects of long-term social isolation on human infants, psychologists have turned to the study of animals for further clarification of the nature-nurture question. Some of the best-known and most important studies in this area are probably those conducted by Harry Harlow and his colleagues at the Wisconsin Regional Primate Center (18).

Psychologist Harry
Harlow with subject.

Harlow began working more than 40 years ago with rhesus monkeys—small, brownish animals from India that are often used in biological and psychological experiments. He originally set out to investigate how these monkeys learn, and he and his wife set up a monkey breeding program so that they would have plenty of animals to work with. They soon learned, however, that infant monkeys in captivity often catch diseases from their mothers and die. To avoid this problem, the Harlows separated the infants from their mothers a few hours after birth and reared them in individual cages where they could be hand fed by humans. This led to other problems. The infants were provided with cheesecloth diapers to serve as baby blankets, and they soon developed such strong attachments to the blankets that it was, as Harlow says, hard to tell where the blanket stopped and the baby began. Furthermore, the infants became greatly disturbed when the diapers were removed from the cage for cleaning. They screamed and cried just as if their own mothers had deserted them.

The researchers decided that what the monkeys needed was an artificial or **surrogate** (substitute) **mother** that they could cling to as they would their own mothers. After several different designs were tried out, Harlow finally came up with a model for a monkey mother that the infants seemed to like. It was a hollow wire cylinder wrapped with a terrycloth towel and topped with a wooden head. These surrogate mothers could also be provided with breasts by placing a milk bottle inside so that the nipple stuck through at the appropriate place.

Harlow became so involved with the infant monkeys and their apparent

An infant monkey clinging to its surrogate mother.

love for these strange wire and cloth mothers that he switched from studies of learning to studies of love. He has since described five types of social attachment or love that are seen in most primates, including humans:

1. **Infant-mother love.** This is the type of love that infants usually show for their mothers. Harlow's infant monkeys showed this kind of love by clinging tightly to their cloth mothers.
2. **Peer love.** As infants grow older and leave their mothers more often, they usually develop strong feelings of love or affection for their peers, or age mates.
3. **Heterosexual love.** As young primates near the age of **puberty,** or sexual maturity, another type of love becomes possible. This is heterosexual love, or love for members of the opposite sex.
4. **Mother-infant love.** This type of love, the love of a mother for her offspring, is seen in most adult females who have children.
5. **Father-infant love.** This is the type of love that is possible between a father and his children.

Infant-Mother Love

Babies need to be fed, and it was originally believed that this need for milk was the most important factor in an infant's love for its mother. Harlow's use of surrogate mothers has shown that warmth and comfort are perhaps even more important than food in the development of a strong infant-mother attachment. The Harlows discovered this by offering infant monkeys a choice between two types of surrogates, one wrapped in terrycloth and one of bare wire. If the two mothers were kept at the same temperature, the infants would always cling to the cloth mother. During the first few weeks of life, if the wire mother was heated while the cloth mother was cool, the infants would cling to the warm wire mother. When they were several weeks old, they switched and spent most of their time on the more comfortable cloth mother. Even when the wire mother contained the milk, the infants would only go to it for feeding and then return to the cloth model.

Why would infant monkeys prefer a cloth-covered mother to a wire one? Harlow suggests that **"contact comfort"** is one of the most powerful influences in the lives of infant monkeys. In the wild, and even living in captivity with their natural mothers, infant monkeys spend much of their time rubbing against their mothers and staying in close contact with them. Whenever infant monkeys are frightened, disturbed, or annoyed, they usually run to their mothers and cling tightly. A wire mother just doesn't provide as much contact comfort as a cloth-covered one does.

According to Harlow, one of the basic qualities of an infant's love for its mother is trust, and prolonged contact comfort, even from a surrogate mother, helps infants develop feelings of security, confidence, and trust. This has been seen in experiments in which an infant monkey is put into a play room without its mother. The infant will usually ignore the toys—no matter how interesting they are—curl up in a ball, and screech in terror. If the cloth mother is then put into the room, the infant will rush to it and cling tightly. After a few minutes of contact comfort, the infant seems to regain some confidence and gradually begins to explore the toys. Even then, however, the infant will usually stay close to the mother and run back to it often as if for reassurance.

The Harlows found that once infant monkeys have developed a sense of trust in their mother (real or surrogate), they will usually love that mother no matter what she does. In one set of experiments the researchers attempted to determine whether **maternal rejection** might result in abnormal behavior patterns similar to those seen in human infants whose mothers ignore or punish them severely. They did this by building "monster mothers." Four types of rejecting mothers were used. One occasionally blasted the clinging infant with compressed air; another shook so violently that the infant would fall off; a third contained a device that would fling the infant across the cage; and a fourth, a real monster, had sharp spikes that poked through the cloth from time to time making it impossible for the infant to hold on.

The infants brought up with these monster mothers did show a brief period of disturbance when the mothers threw them off or poked them. They would cry for a while, but as soon as the mothers went back to normal, the infants would return. The only artificial mother that really kept the infants away was one designed by Stephen Suomi. This surrogate mother had ice water running through its wire frame. Newborn monkeys would hold on to the cold mother for a brief period of time, but would then retreat into a corner and reject her forever.

After many such experiments, Harlow concluded that the love of the infant for its mother is dependent on several things. Warmth is the most important thing a mother provides for an infant monkey during the first few weeks of life. After that, contact comfort becomes most important. Food and gentle shaking or rocking are also important, but less so than warmth and comfort in the development of love.

Peer Love and Heterosexual Love

The warmth and comfort provided by the mother represent a very basic type of social contact. As primate infants grow older, they need more and more social stimulation. This was shown in other experiments with the surrogate-reared monkeys. In some respects these animals appear to be fairly normal. When tested for certain types of learning abilities, for instance, they perform about as well as do monkeys reared with real mothers. However, when groups of surrogate-reared monkeys were first put in a cage with each other, they displayed abnormally high amounts of aggression. Usually young monkeys will chase each other around and play with each other. These surrogate-reared animals, however, had never seen other monkeys and didn't know how to react. The initial aggressive reactions eventually disappeared, but the surrogate-reared monkeys were found to have other problems. Many of them showed stereotyped or repetitive and meaningless behavior, or they would freeze into a strange posture and stare off into space for hours on end. A few would even become paralyzed with fear whenever another monkey approached.

In addition to these strange behaviors, the surrogate-reared monkeys had another problem. They seemed to know nothing about sex. The Harlows had reared these animals in the first place so they could start a breeding colony. But when the animals were put with each other on a small island, nothing happened. Even when an experienced male was put on the island with them, none of the females got pregnant.

Rats and most lower species of animals reared in isolation will mate soon after they are released from isolation if they are sexually mature. Their sex lives are controlled by their hormones, and they seem to know instinctively how to perform the sex act. Heterosexual love among primates does not come as easily. It seems to develop out of peer love, and if monkeys have had no peers to experiment with, they don't learn how to respond sexually.

Monkeys mate with the female crouching on all fours and the male mounting her from behind. The male supports himself by clinging to the female's hind legs. If the female does not assume the proper position or does not allow the male to cling to her, sex is impossible. During much of normal peer play monkeys chase each other around and practice the mating position, even though they are not mature enough to actually copulate. If they don't get this practice, they don't seem to be able to perform sexually as adults. This may also have been the case with the Wild Boy of Aveyron. He spent much of his childhood without mother love or peer love and presumably learned nothing of sex. When he reached sexual maturity he showed no inclination to respond sexually.

In another set of experiments monkeys were reared in total isolation for six months. They had neither surrogate mother nor peers, and when they were later put into cages with normal monkeys, they refused to interact or play. They spent most of their time huddled in corners rocking back and forth. The wild boy showed similar behaviors when he was first captured.

Mother-Infant Love

The Harlows finally found two ways of getting their sexless surrogate-reared females pregnant. One way was to confine the female in a small cage with a highly experienced male. Another way consisted of using an apparatus known as the "rape rack." When these animals finally did get pregnant and give birth to their first infants, they turned out to be real "monster mothers." Having had no contact with their own mothers or with other animals as they grew up, they did not know how to respond to their own infants. At first they totally ignored the infants. Only if the infant was persistent would the mother allow it to cling to her. Those who did eventually begin to respond to their infants gradually became good mothers and were much better with their later children. Some of the motherless mothers, however, showed no maternal affection at all. To these mothers the infants were no more than toys. These monster mothers stepped on their infants, crushed their faces into the floor of the cage, chewed off fingers and feet, and one even popped her infant's head into her mouth and crushed it like an eggshell.

Most people tend to think of mothers as having some sort of **maternal instinct** that makes them love their children no matter what. While most female primates do have a tendency to be interested in and care for their offspring, Harlow's experiments suggest that this tendency is strongly influenced by the mother's past experiences. Since human parents are also strongly influenced by their past experiences, Harlow's research may help explain why perhaps as many as 250,000 children in the United States suffer physical abuse from their parents each year (34). Of these "battered babies," almost 40,000 receive serious injuries. The number of children killed by their parents each year is not known, but it may be in the thousands. Parents have locked their children in cages, burned them, boiled them, slashed them with knives, shot them, and broken almost every bone in their bodies.

Harlow's research suggests that parents who abuse their children may be individuals who never learned proper parenting as children. Studies have shown that parents who beat and neglect their children were often beaten and neglected themselves as children (35). Battering parents have also been described as being socially isolated, as having trouble adjusting to marriage, and as being unable to build up warm relationships with other people, including their children. This suggests that parents who did not learn how to love from their own parents may not have acquired the social skills necessary for bringing up their own infants in a healthy fashion.

Father-Infant Love

Harlow's studies weren't all done with isolated monkeys, and they weren't all done with rhesus monkeys. In another set of experiments Harlow worked with families of macaque monkeys living in a specially designed arrangement. A large, four-family cage was used in which four pairs of male and female monkeys lived with their offspring. Each male had physical access to his own mate and to all of the infants of the other families. The males, however, could not get to each other or to the mates of the other males because of the size of the openings in the cage. This arrangement gave the Harlows an opportunity to study paternal, or father, love.

The fathers all played special protective roles in their families. They did not allow the mothers to abuse or abandon the infants. They showed varying degrees of affection for all of the infants, and some fathers spent more time playing with the infants than the mothers did. During this social play the fathers ignored aggression from the infants, including pinching, biting, tail- and ear-pulling—behaviors they would never accept from adolescents or adults of either sex. The older male infants and juveniles seemed to be practicing fathering behavior as they cradled, carried, and protected the young infants. The exact role of fathers and father love in monkey families is not completely understood, and Harlow admits that "We have still much to learn about the variables in the development of paternal behavior." It does seem, however, that male monkeys play a role in protecting their own and other infants.

These studies and the experiments with surrogate-reared and isolated monkeys give a good indication of the importance of social relationships in the lives of primates. Real monkey mothers, for instance, teach their infants such things as how to understand gestural (sign language) and vocal communication and where to leave their feces. By separating their clinging infants from their bodies, mothers also initiate exploratory behavior in their infants while still providing a comfortable and secure base for them to return to. During early peer play mothers regulate and control aggression. This leads to the formation of effective peer relationships and to later heterosexual love. These and many of the social behaviors necessary to normal development were not learned by those monkeys reared without mothers, fathers, or peers.

Monkeys, of course, aren't human, and Harlow warns that great caution must be taken in drawing conclusions about humans from studies of animals. Even so, Harlow's research helps demonstrate the importance of various types of social interactions in primate development and shows the serious effects of lack of nurturing and social stimulation.

HUMAN CULTURE AND DEVELOPMENT

Monkeys are born into a relatively sophisticated society that they learn from and must learn to live with. Humans are born into an even more complex social setting that is the result of millions of years of cultural evolution. Unlike biological evolution, cultural evolution is not built into the genes. It must be acquired through cultural and social interaction. Except for the wild child, the wolf girls, and a few other special cases, all children are born into a cultural setting that influences the language they learn, the thoughts they think, and many of the behaviors they will perform throughout their lives. Because culture influences so much of each individual's life, it must be studied as a major factor in human development.

Culture is defined as the behavior patterns, beliefs, acts, institutions, and all other products of human work and thought that are learned and shared by a particular group of people and are passed on from generation to generation. A **cultural group** may be as large and complex as that of the United States or it may be as small and basic as that of a hunter-gatherer group. But whatever the size, it is the group's culture that influences much of what its infants learn and how they will develop. This includes intellectual and psychological development as well as physical development. Culture, for example, usually determines what people eat, and diet helps determine physical development.

A **society** is a group of individuals who share a common culture. The process by which culture is passed on to new members of a group or society is called **socialization.** This process must take place in order for the new members to know what behaviors are expected of them as well as what they may expect from their **cultural environment.** Children in a large, busy city are taught to watch out for automobiles. Children in a rural African village might be taught to watch out for dangerous animals. In either case the socialization process is necessary. It begins at birth and is a learning process that continues throughout life and affects every stage of development.

Because culture and socialization are so important to human development, researchers have long been interested in determining the exact effects of culture on development. To do so they have often found it necessary to compare the effects of two or more different cultures. Freud, for instance, was searching for basic truths that would apply to all people. But he had to base much of his theory on what he knew of his own European culture, and, in some instances, he has since been proved wrong.

Anthropologist Bronislaw Malinowski (1884–1942).

In the case of the Oedipus conflict (see Chapter 1), Freud explained that hostility between a father and son develops as a result of the mother-child attachment. Because the mother-child attachment is biologically necessary for the child, Freud thought that a son would instinctively become jealous of his father and see the father as a threat to the mother-child relationship. Because the mother-child relationship is basic to all cultures, Freud reasoned that the Oedipus conflict would show up in all cultures.

Until the 1920s, the study of culture was mainly the job of **anthropologists** (those who investigate the physical, social, and cultural development of humans). It was an anthropologist, Bronislaw Malinowski, who showed that Freud's idea of the Oedipus conflict might not be true for all cultures (31). Malinowski lived for two years with the natives of the Trobriand Islands, a small group of islands off the coast of New Guinea. In this culture the role of the father is not the same as it is in Western societies. After marriage a Trobriand couple lives in the home of the wife's brother. From the child's point of view, all family authority and control of property are in the hands of the mother's brother, the child's uncle. The uncle also serves as the family disciplinarian. In this type of family Malinowski found no evidence of conflict, hostility, or rivalry between fathers and sons. So it seems that the Oedipus conflict shows up only in certain cultural situations.

Malinowski's work did not prove that Freud's theory was completely wrong. It just showed that part of the theory was limited and did not apply to all people in all cultures. Malinowski's findings, which were published in

1953, did more than challenge Freudian theory. They suggested that all theories based on knowledge of only one culture might also be limited. Since that time much more emphasis has been placed on **cross-cultural studies,** or studies that compare different cultures.

Cross-Cultural Studies of Socialization

Victor and the wolf girls had no form of human socialization while they lived on their own. As a result, they were completely unsocialized in any human sense at the time of their capture. It seems obvious, then, that the lack of a culture and a socialization process can have drastic effects on human development. But as the anthropologists have pointed out, it is not just the presence or absence of a culture that is important, but the type of culture. Hundreds of different cultures can have hundreds of different effects on human development, and these cultures each arose as an adaptive response to a particular environment. The cold, artic environment in which the Inuit people (Eskimos) have lived for thousands of years, for instance, has produced its own particular set of cultural adaptations:

> The wick of moss floating in the melting blubber of the lamp began to sputter, sending black coils of smoke toward the opening in the ceiling and calling her attention to the trimming, but she ignored it. She got up, removed the hides from the floor and with a garment scrapper gouged out a hole in the snow. She knelt over it, let her pants down to her knees and waited resting on one elbow on the couch and the other in the snow block. . . . And in the dark, Asiak's child dropped head first into the snowhole. Where there was something tugging at her she bent forward and chewed through it, and as soon as her child was free, a wail filled the igloo and she hurriedly lit the lamp to see what she had brought forth. . . . She licked the soft heap of pale brown flesh till it gleamed immaculate except for the blue mongolic spot at the base of the spine, then mopped it with a foxskin, smeared it with blubber, and quickly tucked it away into her deerskin bag because the pangs of afterbirth were assailing her (42).

This description of an Inuit mother giving birth shows how important adaptation to an environment can be in producing cultural behavior patterns.

The availability of resources is another aspect of the environment that has a strong influence in cultural patterns of socialization. This can be seen in a comparison of the child-rearing practices of the Inuits of Baffin Island in northeastern Canada and those of the Temne people of the Sierra Leone on the west coast of Africa (5). The hunting life of the Inuits requires that they travel widely across a barren, snow-covered environment in search of food. To be prepared for these environmental demands, the children are strongly encouraged from a very early age to be self-reliant and independent. Their parents do not watch over them constantly, and children are given a great deal of freedom to develop the skills that will prepare them for the solitary life of hunting. In contrast, the Temne, who must work hard to raise a single yearly crop, exercise strict control over their children. Temne parents emphasize dependence, reliance, and strong group membership. These characteristics are valued and necessary if tribe members are to work well together taking care of their food supply throughout the year. It seems that cultural patterns influenced by the environment produce Inuit adults who tend to be independent and individualistic. The Temne, on the other hand, tend to rely heavily on each other and are group-oriented rather than individualistic.

Parental Practices around the World

Parents, or some care-giving group, probably represent the most important factor in the environment of young children. Parents, who are themselves the product of a particular culture, are usually the first socializers of their infants, and they tend to pass on to their children much of what they themselves learned as children. For this reason parental practices and parent-child interactions can account for many of the behavioral and developmental differences seen among children of different cultures.

Mary Salter Ainsworth has examined and attempted to explain some of these differences by studying mother-child attachment in Uganda in East Africa (1). She found that Ganda infants respond to their mothers by crying, whereas infants in the United States usually respond to their mothers by smiling. Ainsworth believes this difference comes about because adults in the United States, more so than those in Uganda, often interact with infants by trying to make them smile. Ganda mothers, on the other hand, spend more time holding their infants and attend to them more promptly and consistently when they cry. These differences in social interaction help explain why Ganda infants often cry in the presence of their mothers, and U.S. infants smile in the presence of their mothers. Because the environmental setting of Uganda presents more potential dangers than does the typical home in the United States, the Uganda crying response can be seen as a useful adaptive behavior that is encouraged by mothers.

Other important differences have also been noted between the treatment of infants in Western and non-Western cultures (29). Western cultural groups tend to isolate infants physically, particularly in sleeping arrangements, and they wean (stop breast-feeding) and toilet train infants at a earlier age than is the case in non-Western, traditional societies. Cultural groups also differ in feeding practices, the amount of parent-infant contact and other practices that have an effect on learning opportunities for the infant.

Learning opportunity is not the only factor leading to differences among infants from various cultures. Two thirds of the world's children are born in technologically underdeveloped countries in which a majority of the population live at or below the poverty level. A significant number of these children experience serious **malnutrition** during their early years. This malnutrition is thought to be responsible for more deaths among young children than all other causes combined. When malnourished infants do survive, they are usually smaller in size, more vulnerable to infection, and exhibit more limited intellectual development than well-nourished children (7, 22, 37).

Although seriously malnourished children perform less well in later childhood on behavioral and intelligence tests than do children who have had adequate nutrition, it is usually impossible to separate the nutritional factors from social and psychological factors. This is partially due to the association of malnutrition with infection. Children subject to infection are sick much of the time and are less likely to be exposed to environmental learning situations (such as school).

The possibility of confusing the effects of malnutrition with those of a poor social environment have been pointed out in a study of severely malnourished children in South Africa (47). Two groups of children were studied for several years. One group had been malnourished during infancy. The second group had received adequate nutrition during early life. Those children who had suffered from severe malnutrition scored significantly below the well-nourished group on intelligence tests. In fact, this group scored consistently lower on intelligence tests than the adequately nourished group for a period of more than 10 years. This may have been due to the fact that the malnutrition occurred during the first year of life when brain growth is most rapid.

The study did show that less-privileged children perform less well on tests, but it did not separate nutritional from other possible environmental and social factors. The living conditions of the two groups, for instance, differed as much as did their diets. The poorly nourished children tended to be from broken homes in which alcoholism and unemployment were serious problems. The other children lived in brick houses with plumbing, and their parents were employed. It is possible that the environment of the malnourished children offered fewer learning situations (including interactions with parents) than did the environment of the adequately fed children.

Another subject of cross-cultural studies of infant development has been comparisons of overall growth and sensorimotor development (which has to do with physical or motor responses resulting from the reception of information from the senses). Particular attention has been paid to parental practices that may contribute to the rate of growth in these areas. One researcher (52) has compared the findings of 50 such studies that were made of children up to age 2 in Europe; North, Central, and South America; the Near East; Asia; and the Pacific Islands. These studies showed a distinct speeding up of motor development among infants reared in traditional, nonindustrial communities. This accelerated growth was most evident during the first six months of life. An important factor seems to be that all of the infants from preindustrial societies shared certain cultural experiences during their first year of life. Most of these children were reared in large families with many care-givers, including parents, grandparents, brothers, sisters, aunts, uncles, and in-laws. In these large or extended families, infants are usually given constant physical stimulation. Relatives spend a lot of time handling the infants, picking them up, and carrying them on their backs or hips. In these cultures children attend most adult activities where they receive a great deal of sensorimotor stimulation. In addition to this physical stimulation, these children were usually breast-fed whenever they cried for food, night or day, and they were not required to stick to a strict routine for sleeping or toilet training. Those in the warmer climates were also freer to move about because they did not wear restrictive clothing. All of these factors seemed to be involved in bringing about rapid physical and sensorimotor development.

By contrast, the wild boy of Aveyron and the wolf girls probably received very little stimulation when they lived in the wild. As a result, neither their senses nor their motor development were normal. The wild boy, for instance, seemed to hear only those sounds associated with food or survival. It took years for him to learn to distinguish human voices. When he was captured he was insensitive to extremes of heat and cold. In an attempt to develop the boy's senses, Itard gave him extra sensory stimulation. He spent hours massaging the boy's body and putting him in and out of hot baths. The treatment worked. Victor, who originally loved to run around naked in the snow, and who never caught a cold, eventually began to enjoy extremely hot baths. He also needed warm clothes when he went out, and after he became sensitive to the cold, he began to catch colds.

The speeded-up sensorimotor development of the children studied in nonindustrialized countries did not appear to continue after the first six months of life. In fact, it began to slow down in the children of rural communities of Africa, Asia, and South America. This slowing down first becomes apparent when breast milk is no longer adequate for the needs of the growing child at about 6 months (41). At the time of weaning, usually in the second year of life, the slowing down becomes even more apparent.

The slowing down of sensorimotor development may be due to the change in diet, especially in areas where adequate nutrition is not available. But there seems to be another reason. When breast-feeding stops, children get less physical stimulation from their mothers. Breast-feeding often stops because the mother has given birth to another child. The mother must then devote most of her attention to the newborn, and the older child receives less stimulation. In Western societies children at this age usually begin to experience an increase in freedom to move around and explore their environment. This gives them a chance for increased sensory stimulation.

Another cross-cultural study of infant development has been carried out by Terry Brazelton and his associates (8, 9). They worked with an isolated group of Mayan Indians in southeasten Mexico, the Zinacantecos. This study shows not only the effects of culture on infants but the effects infants can have on a culture.

The Zinacantecos are a culturally distinct tribe living in relative isolation in scattered mountain villages. They are farmers who have refused to become part of the dominant Mexican culture, and they rarely intermarry with other Indian groups. The Zinacantecan cultural emphasis is on uniformity and conformity of behavior. That is, they cling to their traditional customs and behavior patterns, and there is very little acceptance of individualistic behavior.

Brazelton and his colleagues studied three aspects of infant development: the characteristics of the newborn child at birth and during the first week of life, mother-child interaction, and development during the first year of life. They found that the newborn Zinacantecos differ from North American children at birth. Although they were the size of premature infants in the United States, they had none of the jerky movements characteristic of premature infants. Beginning at birth Zinacantecan infant motor activity is smooth and fluid, without the tendency to overreact that is often seen in North American infants. In short, unlike North American newborns, these Indian infants were better coordinated during the first few days of life, and they were able to maintain quiet, alert states for long periods with slow, smooth transitions from one state to another.

Because the Zincantecos rarely intermarry with other Indian groups, and because they have been isolated for a long time from other human populations, it is possible that the initial calm disposition and quiet behavior pattern of their infants is due to some genetic factor. In other words, Zinacantecan children may be born with a tendency to be less reactive to stimulation than are other children (see Chapter 2).

Developmental testing by Brazelton and his group indicated that the Zinacantecan infants seemed to lag consistently one month behind the average North American child in motor and mental development during the first year of life. The lag did not increase with age, which is an indication that these infants experienced the same sequence of development at about the same rate as North American children. In contrast to North American infants, the Zinacantecos are very quiet, they rarely "mouth" their hands, and never suck their fingers.

Perhaps the developmental lag is due in part to the limited social and visual stimulation experienced by the Zinacantecan infants as a result of cultural practices and beliefs. Soon after birth the infants are clothed in a long, heavy skirt that extends beyond the feet. Then they are wrapped in additional

The heavy wrapping of this Mexican infant's legs restricts activity and slows motor development.

layers of blankets. According to the Indian belief, this protects the children from "losing parts of their souls." This heavy wrapping, however, severely restricts motor activity, such as kicking and moving the arms and legs. Also, during the first three months of life, Zinacantecan infants' faces are kept covered except during feeding. The Indians believe this practice protects their children from "the evil eye." The practice also restricts visual stimulation. After close confinement with their mothers during the first month of life, the infants are carried on the mother's or another woman's back in a shawl large enough to hold and completely enclose them. So the infants remain relatively confined and restricted.

As close as the mother and child may be, mother-child interaction is still infrequent in Zinacantecan society. Mothers rarely attempt to get responses from their children by looking at them or talking to them. Breast-feeding is frequent, as high as nine times during a four-hour period and usually in response to the slightest disturbance or restlessness on the infant's part. But in general, Zinacantecan mothers pay very little attention to the other needs of their infants.

Brazelton and his associates found that the quiet, inactive Zinacantecan children are well adapted to their culture's emphasis on conformity. They believe that the infants' quiet behavior is due in part to their early treatment. But they also believe that the child-rearing practices of the Zinacantecos may have been affected or shaped by the behavior of the quiet, alert infants. Quiet children get little attention or stimulation from their parents, and with little stimulation, they tend to remain relatively calm and inactive. So it may be that the customary manner of dealing with Zinacantecan infants did not develop by chance, but in response to the original characteristics of the newborn infants. They, in turn, develop in a particular way in response to the treatment they receive.

These and a great many other cross-cultural studies show the wide variation of infant treatment that exists from culture to culture. Such studies are not always conclusive because other variables, such as nutrition, play important roles in development, but cross-cultural studies do strongly suggest that the course of development of infants is affected by their early experiences, which are often the result of cultural patterns which vary from culture to culture.

PARENTAL PRACTICES IN THE UNITED STATES

Cultures vary because environments vary and because people have found different methods of adapting to their environments. In the United States, as in every other culture, certain behavior patterns, beliefs, attitudes, and values have arisen in response to the environment. Parents pass on these beliefs and values in order to prepare their children for survival in a particular environment.

The effects of child-rearing practices in the United States can be seen more clearly when they are compared with child-rearing practices of another culture. One study has compared maternal care and infant behavior in U.S. families and in traditional Japanese families (12). In general, the researchers were interested in the importance of particular cultural differences in understanding human behavior. Specifically, they investigated categories of infant behavior (including play, wakefulness, and happy and unhappy vocalization or noise-making) and categories of care-giver behavior (including feeding, dressing, positioning, rocking, looking at, playing with, and lulling the infant).

The sample studied consisted of 30 Japanese and 30 North American infants 3 to 4 months old. Both parents were present in each family. They all lived in large urban centers and were neither very rich nor very poor. Even after controlling for all of these factors, the researchers admit that some of their findings could be the result of differences in the rates of physical growth or of genetic differences (as with the Zinacantecos). But the most important difference between the groups was cultural.

The researchers measured the behaviors of the two groups by using a time-sampling procedure to observe the mother-infant pairs in their homes. This procedure consists of taking note of the behaviors being studied on a regular basis, such as every 15 seconds. Then, after a longer period of time, all of the behaviors are counted and comparisons can be made. For this particular study, four observations per minute were made during certain periods of the day. A total of 800 observations indicated that both groups were the same as far as basic biological needs were concerned. Both groups of children cried to be fed or changed about the same number of times, and mothers in both groups responded to their children's needs about the same number of times. Other than biological needs, the researchers found significant differences between the two cultural groups in terms of both maternal and infant behavior. North American infants were more physically active, happily vocal, and more involved in the exploration of their bodies and environments than were the Japanese infants. In regard to these behaviors the Japanese infants seemed to be more passive than active. They tended to lie quietly. They also displayed occasional episodes of unhappy vocalization or crying, which appeared to be their method of attracting the attention of their mothers.

The differences between the two groups seemed to be a result of care-giving practices. Japanese mothers engaged in more lulling, carrying, and rocking of their infants. They concentrated on soothing and quieting their children through physical rather than verbal means. The U.S. mothers, on the other hand, looked at their children and chatted actively with them in what seemed to be an attempt to get the infants to respond verbally and physically.

On the basis of these observations it appears that Japanese and North American mothers have different cultural attitudes or beliefs about their children. The Japanese behave as if their infants are basically active, and it is the

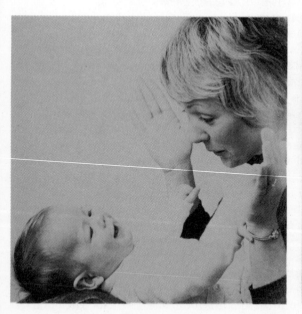

Differences in parental attitude which affect care-giving practices can be seen in these photos of an American and a Japanese mother with their children.

mother's job to soothe and calm them. The North American mothers behave as if their children are basically passive, and it is the mother's job to stimulate them and make them more active. The children naturally respond differently to these varying types of treatment. The researchers found that a great deal of cultural learning takes place within the first three to four months of life. By this age it can be seen that the infants are already learning to be either Japanese or North American. This continues as the infants increasingly react to the attitudes and expectations of their mothers.

In order to see just how much of an effect genetic influences may have had on these two groups, the exact same procedure was followed with Japanese women whose families had been in the United States for three generations (11). After several generations in the United States, the Japanese families had lost some of their traditional values and had become somewhat Westernized. This showed up in their attitudes and child-rearing practices. These Japanese women spent a greater amount of time chatting to their infants than did the traditional Japanese mothers. The third-generation children, in turn, responded with more happy vocalization and physical activity. The Japanese women in the United States did not, however, lose all of their cultural heritage. They still spent more time than U.S. mothers playing with, lulling, and carrying their infants in their arms. This extra attention helps explain why Japanese infants tend to spend less time than North American infants in solitary play.

In addition to cross-cultural studies of parenting, a great many studies have been made of specific parental practices in the United States. These studies concern the closest and some of the most important relationships between infants and parents. They include studies of feeding practices, toilet training, and sex training.

Feeding Practices

For more than 40 million years mammals have **breast-fed** their young. Most of the more than 4 billion people alive today have been breast-fed, and most of today's women are breast-feeders. As traditional and as natural as breast-feeding may be, increasing numbers of mothers have turned to **bottle feeding** during the past 50 years, and a great many questions have been raised about the consequences of this less intimate form of feeding.

One of the major studies of child-rearing practices, including breast-feeding, was conducted by Sears, Maccoby, and Levin (43). Of the 379 mothers of 5-year-olds who were interviewed, 39 percent had breast-fed the child who was the subject of the study. In a majority of cases the child had been breast-fed for less than three months. Other studies have found that about half of all mothers in the United States try breast-feeding with their children, but most give up the practice by about three months (19).

It seems logical that the decision to breast-feed may be linked with other decisions about "closeness" or "intimacy" with the newborn infant. In one study it was predicted that a choice to breast-feed would be associated with a choice to "room in" with the newborn (24). Under the rooming-in plan the infant is placed in the mother's hospital room shortly after birth. In the more conventional nursery plan new infants are kept in the hospital nursery and brought to their mothers for feeding at regular intervals. Nurses assume care for the newborns other than feeding (see the discussion of rooming in and mother-child intimacy in Chapter 1).

The researchers interviewed 1,251 women about their rooming-in and feeding preferences prior to the birth of their babies. Of these women, 53 percent chose to breast-feed, 40 percent to bottle feed, and the rest were undecided. The difference of 14 percent between this study and the Sears, Maccoby, and Levin study of breast-feeding may be due to the difference in time at which the question was asked. In the Sears study mothers remembered what they had done five years earlier. In the second study the mothers predicted what they would do. In addition, the women in the second study had been officially encouraged by the hospital staff to both breast-feed and room in.

Rooming in was chosen by 54 percent of the mothers. Thirty-one percent preferred the nursery, and 15 percent were undecided at the time of the interview. As predicted, the choice of rooming in was closely associated with the choice of breast-feeding. Of the mothers who preferred the rooming-in plan and its intimacy with the child, 64 percent chose breast-feeding, which also demands close, intimate contact with the child. Of those who preferred the hospital nursery, only 35 percent chose breast-feeding, while 60 percent selected bottle feeding. The undecided mothers were in between. About half selected the breast, the others selected the bottle. The results of this study suggested that a woman's decision to breast-feed her child is closely associated with her desire to be close to and intimate with the child. As was seen in Chapter 1, this sort of intimacy, even during the first few days of life, can have long-lasting effects on the future of the mother-child relationship and on the child's development.

Another study has found a relationship between maternal attitudes toward breast-feeding and actual success at breast-feeding (38). Some women are unsuccessful at breast-feeding for various physical reasons, and others have more or less success at it. In this study, 91 mothers who had just given birth were interviewed and asked about their feelings toward breast-feeding. The mothers were rated as positive, doubtful, or negative. They were then observed to see how much milk they were giving to their infants and how much milk they actually had available. Based on these observations, the women were classified as successful, unsuccessful, or abortive breast-feeders. The successful ones were those whose infants required no supplemental or extra feeding

in addition to the mother's milk after the fourth day of █████
classified as unsuccessful if, after the fourth day, their babies ██████
mental feedings. The abortive feeders were those who gave up br████
entirely before they left the hospital.

Of the 91 mothers, 51 were classified as showing positive attitudes to█████
breast-feeding. Of these, 74 percent were successful breast-feeders. Only one
mother with a positive attitude toward breast-feeding fell into the abortive
category. Of the 23 mothers who expressed negative attitudes, only 26 percent
were successful. Thirty-three percent were included in the abortive group. The
17 mothers who had doubtful attitudes included 35 percent who were successful, 47 percent who were unsuccessful, and 18 percent who were abortive.

Mothers with positive attitudes give their infants an average of 59 grams
(slightly more than 2 ounces) of milk at each fourth-day feeding; mothers with
doubtful attitudes, 42 grams; and mothers with negative attitudes, only 35
grams of milk at each fourth-day feeding. The researchers further report that
there were no real differences among the three groups in the amount of milk
actually available for the infants, and that such factors as experience with
previous children and experience of actually putting the infant to the breast
did not affect the results.

From these and other studies, most of which were based in part on the interview method and on remembered behaviors (rather than actual observations
of mother-child interactions, which are more accurate), a few conclusions can
be drawn: half or fewer of the mothers studied actually breast-feed their infants, and positive attitudes toward breast-feeding seem to be associated with
it and with other types of intimate mother-infant relations.

Scheduling of Infant Feeding

Whether mothers breast-feed or not, feeding is one of the first forms of
nurturing and social contact infants have. Should these first contacts be made
as pleasant and as gratifying as possible by feeding infants whenever they seem
hungry? Or should infants be fed on a strict schedule? Pediatricians have answered this question differently, but in recent years most have favored the **self-
demand schedule.** That is, feed the infants when they seem to be hungry.

Evidence favoring self-demand schedules is seen in a study of 668 demand-
fed babies up to their first birthday (2). These infants eventually set up realistic
feeding schedules for themselves, although during early infancy they ate more
frequently than the usual every four hours. About 70 percent of them had
switched to a schedule of three meals per day by the time they were 10 months
old. At 1 year of age they were well within generally accepted standards for
height and weight, and fewer than 1 percent had severe feeding problems. Only
7 percent showed some resistance to feeding and required coaxing.

Other studies of individual children and of twins also support the idea

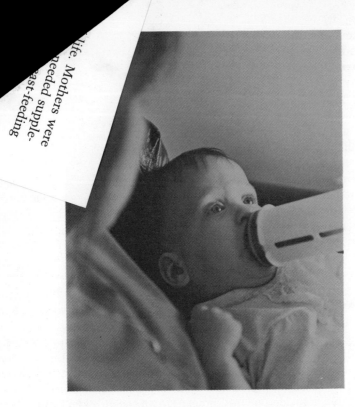

...life. Mothers were ...needed supple- ...ast-feeding ...ard

Whether by breast or bottle, feeding is one of the first forms of social contact infants have.

of self-demand schedules (44, 49). One study found that children who have more **rigid feeding schedules** are less active in their first years than children fed more flexibly (55). But in this study mothers who scheduled feedings strictly also engaged in a wide range of other restrictive practices, so it is difficult to evaluate the influences of strict feeding schedules apart from other factors.

Freudian theory suggests that feeding practices during the oral stage (see Chapter 1) are related to later personality development. Restrictive and severe treatment is supposed to lead to distrust of other people, while permissive treatment is supposed to help establish feelings of trust. Several studies have found some evidence to support this theory. One, for instance, found that oral deprivation, including severe weaning practices (stopping breast-feeding abruptly), reduces trust in other people (53).

Other studies, however, such as the one done by Sears, Maccoby, and Levin, found very few relationships between early feeding practices and later personality development (43). Feelings of pleasure or displeasure over the pregnancy, the degree of warmth in the mother-child relationship, and feelings of competence or inadequacy concerning child care were not related to mothers' decisions about breast-feeding. The only variable that was significantly related to a decision about breast-feeding was **sex permissiveness** (that is, the mother's feelings about her child's sex behavior). Mothers who were not sex permissive were least likely to breast-feed. It is likely, the authors point out, that such attitudes are related to the mother's personal modesty.

Breast-feeding or the lack of it had no effect on such child behaviors (as reported by the mothers) as aggression, dependence, feeding problems, bed-wetting, or disturbance over toilet training.

As far as the scheduling of feeding was concerned, nearly half (48 percent) of the mothers were relatively relaxed. They partially or completely followed the infant's rhythm and made no real effort to impose a strict schedule. Another 22 percent followed fairly rigid or inflexible feeding schedules, but according to the mothers' reports, type of scheduling and weaning did not affect the personalities of the children at 5 years.

About two thirds of the mothers began weaning before their children were 11 months old, and most of them finished the process within about four months. Infants whose weaning was started latest were most quickly weaned. Fifteen percent of the infants were not weaned by 2 years of age. There was some tendency for late, severely, or very permissively weaned children to show upset more frequently than early, gently, but decisively weaned babies. However, nearly as many babies weaned between 5 and 8 months showed upset as did those weaned after they were 16 months old (30 percent and 35 percent, respectively).

Fifty-five percent of the mothers reported that their children had only very mild or no feeding problems. Only 17 percent reported severe feeding problems. The presence or absence of such problems was not related to whether a child had been breast-fed, scheduled or fed on demand, or to the child's age at weaning. Feeding problems did accompany such parental behaviors as the following: severe toilet training, strong suppression of the child's aggression toward the parents, being negative toward or rejecting the child's dependency (resenting clinging or attention demands), using much physical punishment, and showing little warmth toward the child.

In other words, these mothers' reports of their children's behavior do not demonstrate effects on personality of infant feeding and weaning practices, but do suggest instead that feeding problems may be associated with general restrictiveness on the part of the parents.

What then can be said of feeding practices? The best conclusion about the specifics of feeding seems to be that mothers who are well-meaning and who try in a relaxed way to do what they sincerely believe is best for their children—particularly when this is in harmony with the cultural ways of the community with which they are most closely associated—obtain the best results with their children.

Although **toilet training** has been a matter of consideration and necessity in all cultures since the dawn of civilization, and although a vast amount of material has been published on the subject, the number of careful studies of just what mothers and fathers do, how it works, and what, if anything, happens to the child as a result of it is small. The Sears, Maccoby, and Levin study, however, does provide a good picture of how toilet training is actually carried out in the United States in the twentieth century.

Most child-development specialists ordinarily encourage parents to postpone bowel training until some time in the second year, when children have fairly good postural control, can voluntarily control their sphincters, and can be expected to learn to make some signal about their needs. But the average age at which parents in the Sears study began bowel training was 11 months. The average age of completing it was 18 months. Thus, the training procedure on the average required seven months, although some parents managed it in a few weeks and others took as long as 18 months. Almost half (47 percent) of the mothers started toilet training before their children were 9 months old; fewer than 8 percent waited to begin until the second half of the child's second year. Those whose training started late learned most quickly.

Another study found that only 43 percent of parents start their children's bowel training by the time they are 18 months old (19). More than half of the parents in this study reported that their babies had completed bowel training by 30 months of age. The average was 22 months, and girls were faster than boys. All figures on times of toilet training, however, are perhaps less than accurate. Both wetting and soiling are looked down on in our culture, and parents have been made to think that late toilet training represents both faulty child adjustment and improper child-rearing practices. Therefore, the pressure to report children as dry and clean at an early age is great.

In order to study severity of toilet training, Sears and his colleagues worked out a 5-point rating system. Ratings of 1 and 2 were considered mild (child more or less trains self . . . mild disapproval for some accidents), and 52 percent of the mothers were characterized as mild in their training methods. Ratings of 4 and 5 were considered severe (mother clearly shows disapproval; child may be left on toilet for fairly lengthy periods . . . child punished severly for deviations; mother angry over them), and 18 percent of the mothers were characterized as severe in their methods.

A number of other attitudes and practices were found to be associated with severity of toilet training. Mothers who trained severely also put relatively great pressure on their children to use good manners, be neat and orderly, be careful around the house and with furniture, keep quiet, and do well in school. They were more likely than lenient mothers to use physical punishment and deprivation of privileges and reasoned less with their children. In other words, this study suggests that toilet training is not an isolated factor, but is accom-

Today both fathers and mothers may be involved in the toilet training of their children.

panied by a whole set of other child-rearing practices affecting many phases of the child's social and sexual behavior. If this is true, it is impossible to single out toilet training as a determiner of personality. Sears and his colleagues suggests that a more general, overall factor of permissiveness–restrictiveness, rather than specifics like toilet training, may be responsible for a child's behavior and personality development.

As mothers described them, the severely toilet-trained children were more emotionally disturbed by the training than those who were trained mildly. However, the degree of warmth the mothers injected into the process was also important. Mothers who were warm in their attitudes but severe in their training produced fewer emotional upsets as a result of training than mothers who were relatively cold and severe.

The problem of a child's learning to sleep dry at night is a major one for parents. The mothers in the Sears, Maccoby, and Levin study most frequently trained their children by getting them up a night to go to the bathroom, and many of them attempted to limit the amount of late afternoon and evening liquids. Some used more severe methods, such as making the children wash out their pajamas or bedclothes, and many parents also offered rewards for night dryness. Almost half (44 percent) reported that their children were dry at night by the time they were 2 years old. About 80 percent of the children were night-dry by the time the study was conducted (when the children were 5 years old), leaving about 20 percent still having an occasional or frequent accident at the age of 5 or 6. Children tended either to be bed-wetters or to have feeding problems, not both.

The age of beginning bladder training made no difference in the age at which the children gained full bladder control, but mothers who had high anxiety about sex, were relatively cold and undemonstrative toward the child, and used severe toilet-training procedures were, as the researchers report, "most efficient for producing prolonged bed wetting."

Warm, permissive mothers with anxiety about sex got their children dry at night earliest. This relationship is an interesting one. An area of behavior that is extremely important to the mother, but about which she is punitive and cold, may be one in which children refuse to conform, thus expressing rebellion and resentment. This may be one way children have of "training" or punishing their parents. When the behavior is extremely important to the mother, but she is gentle and warm in her training, the child rewards her by taking note of her wishes.

Freudian, or psychoanalytic, theory suggests that bed-wetting is children's way of getting back at or punishing their parents. The Sears study offers some support for this point of view since there was some relationship between overall severity of punishment and bed-wetting, particularly when the severity was combined with a cold, rejecting manner toward the child.

In one study of factors that are related to slow physical or motor development, rigid toilet training (like rigid feeding scheduling) was associated with relatively slow motor development (55). A number of other factors in parental practices were also found to be related to slowed or retarded motor development. Children who were relatively slow in motor development were weaned earlier, toilet trained earlier, handled more punitively, and were more restricted in play space and experimentation. They had less bodily contact and time with others and were less frequently breast-fed and for a shorter time.

Conclusions about toilet training are, for the most part, more clear-cut than those for feeding and weaning. This may be because children are older and therefore better able to learn when toilet training begins.

Studies of toilet training do not in any consistent way support Freudian theory (see the discussion of the anal stage in Chapter 1), but they suggest that psychoanalytic theory may be correct in emphasizing the importance of toilet training on later development. Parents in the United States tend to start toilet training earlier than the "experts" advise. The earlier toilet training is started, the longer it takes to complete. The more severe the training, the more upset the child is by it. Rigid toilet training, when combined with a number of other practices that might be called restrictive, also seems to slow down motor development. (Motor development is discussed in Chapter 5.)

Mothers high in anxiety about sex start toilet training earlier than mothers who are more relaxed about sex. The most successful mothers in early training for night dryness are high in sex anxiety, but use mild training procedures and show much warmth to their children. The least successful mothers also have high sex anxiety, but combine it with severe training procedures and relatively cold attitudes and emotions toward their children.

Finally, and probably most important, the rigidity with which toilet training is carried out is related to a number of other childrearing practices, almost all of which may be thought of as being restrictive. It cannot be said definitely that toilet training alone is important in shaping a child's personality, but it can be said that toilet training is one of a number of indicators of the type of relationship parents have with their child, and all of these taken together have important and perhaps lasting effects on personality.

Sex Training

The wild child, without a social environment to learn from, and Harlow's monkeys, reared in isolation, did not develop normal sexual behavior as adults. These examples suggest that competent adult sexual behavior in the higher primates — including humans — is dependent to a great extent on social learning during childhood. Such learning may come in a variety of ways: through the examples of adults and older children; through experimentation, alone or with others; from information passed on from adults and other children; and from information passed on through the communications media, including radio, television, books, and movies.

Freud suggested that sexuality in infancy and childhood is primarily associated with gratification during the oral, anal, and genital stages. Children who are mishandled during these stages, Freud suggests, may devote an abnormal amount of time and behavior in later years to making up for what happened during childhood. Mishandling may occur through deprivation, overly strict and punitive training, or through overgratification.

Freud's views about **infantile sexuality** provoked a great deal of controversy and strong emotional reactions when they were first expressed. Some of this emotionality has died down in recent years, but infantile sexuality is still a subject that is not often openly discussed and has not been thoroughly examined. Experimental testing and research that might prove or disprove Freud's theory has been limited. Much of what is known about childhood sexuality has come from clinical practice (having to do with observation and treatment of patients) and anecdotal reports of adults about the sexuality of their children. Major studies of human sexuality, like Alfred Kinsey's, have revealed much about adult and adolescent sexuality but little about that of children (23). Almost all that is known about children in this area is that they are interested in sex, experience orgasms earlier than is commonly thought, and from early childhood show much more interest and participation in sexual matters than the average adult guesses (or remembers).

The most comprehensive survey of child-rearing practices in the area of sexual behavior is probably that provided by Sears, Maccoby, and Levin. They found that there are four goals of **childhood sex training** in the United States. The first, and one that is found in many modern societies, has to do with the taboo or strong social restriction against **incest,** or sexual relations between close relations. The second goal is one that is found in some but not all cultures. It has to do with training against **masturbation** (training that almost always breaks down during adolescence, particularly among males). The third is to teach children to avoid **sex play** with other children, and the fourth is to control **sex information.** "Information control," say the researchers, "is one of the methods by which adults attempt to induce the growing child to postpone sex gratification and limit sex activities in the early years."

Sears and his colleagues point out that there are substitute gratifications for things children give up as they are weaned and toilet trained: solid foods are found to be tasteful and pleasant; parents reward one for cleaning one's plate; being dry and clean have their own rewards. But for sex, there are no substitutes until the time of adolescence. This leaves parents with little possibility of guidance through substitute rewards. Instead, they often attempt to inhibit or shut off sexual behavior. To do this, they usually try to prevent genital stimulation (for example, they supervise play carefully, dress children in loose, nonbinding clothing, and observe modesty in the home). Parents also attempt to distract children (for example, by changing activity if children seem to be getting "sexy"), scare children (such as telling them that if they run around without clothes they will catch cold, or telling them that if they manipulate their genitals they will hurt themselves), and avoid precise labeling (such as using euphemisms or inoffensive terms for the genitals). Parents attempt to control information by making up stories such as, "I found you under a rose bush."

Much control of sex is accomplished through training for modesty. Sears, Maccoby, and Levin asked 379 mothers how permissive they were about their children's going around indoors without clothes, and how severe was the pressure they exerted toward indoor modesty. Again using the two highest of 5-point rating scales to define permissiveness (little or no restraint on nudity, for example), about one third (36 percent) of the mothers were permissive. Almost half (44 percent) fell at the other end of the scale, believing that the "child must be clothed at all times," or being only very slightly permissive. On the other hand, the mothers were not very severe in enforcing their ideas about modesty. If mild pressure is defined as doing nothing more drastic than teasing children about nudity, then three fifths (61 percent) of the mothers used mild pressure only. If severe pressure is defined as scolding, warning, punishing, and becoming angry and emotional, only 7 percent of the mothers used severe pressure.

Children "playing with themselves" brought fourth considerable emotional reaction from the mothers. Fewer than a fifth (18 percent) felt that "a certain amount is to be expected," or that "it's natural, just curiosity"; while one half (49 percent) considered it wrong or harmful or "might not do anything if it happened just once, but wouldn't like it." As with nudity, however, they did not back up their strong opinions with strong action, since 45 percent of them used mild or no pressure against masturbation, and only about 5 percent were classified as using severe pressure against masturbation.

The picture of permissiveness about sex play among children is similar. Fewer than a sixth (16 percent) of the mothers believed in permissiveness, and almost three fifths (57 percent) of them expressed firm attitudes against it. But again, opinions were not backed up by strong action. Almost half (46 percent) of the mothers said that so far as they knew, no incidents had occurred. When mothers mentioned that such incidents had occurred, 45 percent had been quite permissive in their actions, and only 13 percent had behaved severely and forbiddingly. Interestingly enough, more mothers who were rated high on their tendency to keep a close check on their children *did not know* of sex-play incidents.

Even though the mothers seemed to "talk loudly and carry a little stick" concerning children's sexual behavior, there was a strong relationship between mothers' disapproval of a certain behavior and their taking definite steps to prevent it. That is, mothers who were not permissive about a given type of behavior did punish when it occurred.

The mothers in this study who were not permissive about sex permitted relatively little aggression toward parents on the part of their children. They were more likely than permissive mothers to toilet train their children severely, keep a close watch on their whereabouts, use physical punishment fairly often, and be strict about noise, table manners, and care of household property. They were also relatively cold emotionally toward their children, did not like it when the children clung to them or made attention demands, and put much emphasis on their daughters being feminine, their sons masculine. In other words, these mothers fell toward the restrictive extreme of the behavioral factor of permissiveness–restrictiveness.

Data from the Sears study suggest that permissiveness in sexual matters is closely related to general permissiveness. Mothers in the United States who have been studied seem to have generally negative attitudes toward children's sexual behavior, but they do not exercise very strong open pressure against it (perhaps because they themselves are guilty, uneasy, and uninformed in the area). When they punish they punish for the things they and the culture generally disapprove of.

Clinical evidence about the effects of sex training suggests that both harsh and restrictive sex training and overly permissive training, including overexposure to sexual information and experiences, may leave a child sexually disturbed. Chapter 10 includes a more complete discussion of sexual development and the consequences of direct and indirect sex training.

Feeding, toilet training, and sex training are only three of the many ways in which children and parents interact. It is in these and a variety of other social interactions that many of the social and cultural values of the parents are passed on to the children. Chapter 11 gives a more complete description of socialization practices and social development.

SOCIAL AND CULTURAL EFFECTS ON DEVELOPMENT

The parental practices described in the Sears, Maccoby, and Levin study were based on the attitudes and behaviors reported by mothers from two large East Coast suburbs. While these findings represent an overview of parental practices in the United States, there are many important differences in behavior patterns that exist from family to family. Some of the most important of these differences are related to social, economic, racial, and ethnic differences among families.

Social Class
Social equality may be one of the basic goals of society, but true economic and social equality is found only in the smallest and least complex societies. In most large cultures, like the United States, social distinctions are made between various groups. So even though children are born into a specific overall culture, they are also born into a particular part or class of society. The values and practices of these various **social classes** have different effects on development. Children growing up in the slums of New York, on a farm in Iowa, or in a mansion in California all experience quite different social environments. Social scientists have devoted much time to research on the characteristics of different social classes and the development of children in these classes in order to better understand the effects of the social environment in which children learn the values, attitudes, and behaviors expected of them.

While there is disagreement over the exact definition of "social class" and even on the usefulness of the term, it is generally agreed that most societies are divided so that some individuals occupy higher positions than others. Children, for instance, usually rank lower than adults, and in some societies women have a lower rank or status than men. The basic characteristic of a class system, however, is the ranking of families rather than individuals. The members of a family share many characteristics that affect their relationships with outsiders, including the same home, income, values, and status. Social classes, therefore, are made up of large groups of families that occupy a similar position in a society.

These social class systems are not the same in every society. Cultures differ in the numbers and types of classes that are recognized, as well as in the amount of mobility or movement that is possible between classes. The most rigid class structure is called the **caste system.** "Caste" is from the Latin word for "pure," and in caste systems the various social groups maintain their purity by associating with members of other castes only when necessary. This sort of social organization existed legally in India until recently. In that country a number of uniquely separate social communities existed side by side. People were born into a caste and lived out their lives in that group with little possibility of moving into a higher caste. Members of one caste were not allowed to marry members of another caste, and the only communication among the castes was usually on an economic level. Members of the lowest class were called Untouchables. They were considered to be impure, and members of higher castes would not even touch them.

In contrast to the rigid caste system that still exists to some degree in India, the industrialized countries of the West have a more **open social system.** In the United States, for instance, no legal distinction is made among social groups. However, individuals in the United States do differ with respect to social power, economic resources, access to educational and job opportunities, and the amount of prestige or status associated with their jobs. "Social class," "social status," and "socioeconomic status" are interchangeable terms used to refer to a person's social position.

Because there appear to be no sharp dividing lines between the social classes in a changing system like that of the United States, it is difficult to define the various social classes. One review of studies done on socialization and socioeconomic status in the United States (20) found that different researchers have used from two to ten distinct categories of social status in their studies. But even though the class groupings used to define social structure in the United States are not exact, class structure has been found to be associated with important differences in the socialization of children.

Upper, middle, working, and lower class are the most often used names for the various social groups in the United States. The **upper class** is made up of the nation's most influential families, those with a lot of money, good education, and political and economic power.

The **middle class** is sometimes divided into **upper-middle** and **lower-middle classes.** Professionals, such as physicians, lawyers, bankers, university professors, and business executives make up the upper-middle class. Small business owners, clerical and other white-collar workers, successful skilled workers, and owners of small farms are usually thought of as part of the lower-middle class.

The **working class** is made up of blue-collar workers, skilled and semi-skilled workers, and small trades people. At the bottom of the social structure in the United States is the **lower class.** Its members often live in deteriorated or run-down sections of the community. They are usually unskilled workers who often can't find work and are poorly educated. The lack of money and education can obviously have serious effects on behavior patterns and attitudes.

Regardless of how socioeconomic status is defined or measured, a number of differences among classes have been found that provide information about the social environment within which children are reared. However, it is important to recognize that the class structure in the United States is not rigid, and that there is a considerable amount of overlap in characteristics among the various groups. There are also wide differences among families within any one class, so statements such as, "The values of working-class parents are different from those of middle-class parents" are not always exact or correct.

Child-rearing Values

While many values may exist within any one class, some general socioeconomic status differences in parental values and goals for children have been found. One study (25) has examined the characteristics that middle- and working-class parents want to develop in their children. It was found that mothers and fathers in the United States, regardless of social class, believe it is important for their children to be honest, happy, well mannered, and considerate. However, parents from these two social classes differ in some of the qualities and characteristics that are considered to be desirable.

A major goal for middle-class parents is to rear children who are self-directed or who can think for themselves and who want to act in a socially acceptable manner, not because it is required by authorities but because that is the way they truly want to behave. Working- and lower-class parents tend to be more interested in conformity, obedience, respect for authority, neatness, and cleanliness. Working-class parents tend to feel that such characteristics will help their children secure a respectable social position. Obedient children in this social class are expected to follow parental orders rather than develop their own internal guidelines for behavior.

This relationship between social class and child-rearing values does not seen to be confined to the United States. For example, although there are some differences between parents in the United States and parents in Italy in characteristics considered desirable in their children, the link between social class and parental values seems to be much the same in the two countries (39). In both Italy and the United States, middle-class mothers and fathers are likely to emphasize the development of self-direction in their children. Working-class parents tend to stress children's conformity to external rules and authority.

This particular difference between middle- and working-class parents may be the result of the parent's occupation (26). The researchers point out that a person's experiences at work may influence that person's view, not only of the occupational world but also of the broader social world. Individuals holding jobs for a long period of time during which they are able to display initiative, thought, and independent judgment tend to develop a set of values that includes a concern for the development of self-direction in their children. Jobs that provide such opportunities are usually associated with the middle class. Working-class jobs, on the other hand, are usually closely supervised, and there is little or no room for self-reliance or independent judgment. People in such jobs learn to value obedience and respect for authority and tend to foster development of these attitudes in their children.

Parents and other care-givers do not always act in accordance with their values, but values are influential in guiding behavior in many situations. Uri Bronfenbrenner (10) has reviewed the early research on the relationship between social class and child-rearing practices. He found that working-class parents, with their emphasis on strict obedience, tend to use physical power as a form of punishment to control their children. Middle-class parents, emphasizing independence, were more likely to use less physical techniques of punishment—reasoning, isolation, appeals to guilt, and other methods that involved the threat of a loss of emotional support and love.

More recent studies (16), based on actual observations of parent-child interactions rather than on reports by care-givers, support the view that middle-class mothers are more attentive and responsive to their children, as well as more aware of their children's feelings, than are working- and lower-class mothers. These studies also point out that techniques of control tend to differ by class, with care-givers from lower classes using physical power more often.

The differences between social-class values and behaviors may be smaller than they appear, and there is a great deal of overlap in the values and behaviors among the social levels of society in the United States. But it is important to recognize and understand those differences in socialization goals and methods that still do exist between the middle- and lower-class groups. Even though the differences among social classes in the United States may be disappearing—due to such factors as education, rapid communication, and upward movement within the social system—it is obvious that the equalizing process is not yet complete.

Racial and Ethnic Groups

Social class distinctions represent some of the most important differences among major groups in the United States, but there are other distinct groups whose practices and beliefs can have differing effects on child development. Some of the most obvious group distinctions made are based on race. As discussed in Chapter 2, "race" refers to subdivisions of the human species based on distinct physical characteristics that are passed on from generation to generation. In addition to **racial groups,** there are **ethnic groups** (from the Greek word for "nation"). Italian-Americans and Puerto Ricans, for example, are two large ethnic groups that exist within the overall culture of the United States. Ethnic distinctions are usually based on cultural heritage, religion, and language rather than on physical characteristics. People of different racial and ethnic backgrounds are represented in all social or economic classes. Some have maintained much of their distinct ethnic and cultural heritage. Others have adopted many of the cultural traditions of the larger society.

How much do ethnicity and race affect development? There is no clear answer, but it is probable that social and economic differences have more important effects on development than do either race or ethnicity (34). There is good evidence to support this belief (50). For example, when social and economic factors are carefully controlled, commonly reported differences between black and white children do not appear. These differences include such characteristics as self-esteem, goal-setting behavior, and beliefs about the possibility of controlling one's own destiny. When social and economic factors are not taken into account, sharp differences in these characteristics appear, usually in favor of middle- and upper-class white children.

While there is no solid evidence to suggest inherited differences in psychological development among ethnic and racial groups, physical and motor development may be a different matter. During the early years of life, for instance, black children are generally more advanced than whites in motor development. This may have an effect on psychological development, but if inborn psychological differences do exist, they have not been recorded.

The apparent physical differences between blacks and whites can be seen in athletic activities. Blacks seem to excel in activities that require agility and bursts of speed, such as jumping events and sprints in track. Black athletes are also overrepresented (when compared with their percentage in the overall population) in professional sports such as baseball, football, and basketball. On the other hand, with a few exceptions, whites tend to do better in sports that involve buoyancy and endurance, such as swimming and long-distance track events. Even these differences in athletic abilities, however, may be more the result of social factors than of physical factors. Blacks have suffered educational and economic disadvantages for years, mainly because of racial prejudice. But in recent years prejudice against blacks and other minority groups has decreased as far as participation in most sports is concerned. Perhaps because of this, a greater number of blacks than would be expected have concentrated on athletic abilities and therefore are overrepresented in such activities when compared with whites. Whites, because they have not been discriminated against, have had a wider choice of occupational areas which they could enter.

Blacks, of course, aren't the only discriminated-against or disadvantaged group in the United States. These general categories of such groups can be made (34):

1. Prejudiced-against groups with common ways of behaving that do not equip them to function very well according to the conventional standards of success in the United States. Such groups include blacks (particularly poor blacks); some of the Spanish-speaking peoples (particularly the Chicanos—those of Mexican descent, the Puerto Ricans, and poor but not middle-class Cuban immigrants); many of the most recent wave of Chinese immigrants; almost all American Indians; and many who have Eskimo and Hawaiian heritage. There are other prejudiced-against and disadvantaged minorities, but those that have been mentioned are the most numerous.
2. Disadvantaged groups that are not victims of any specific racial or ethnic prejudice. A very large number of Appalachian and poor white children belong to this group.
3. Prejudiced-against groups that get along adequately or well according to U.S. standards (low crime rate, good education, vocational success, and so on). The Japanese-Americans, a large proportion of the older Chinese-Americans and their descendants, and the Jews belong to this group. Strictly speaking, "Jew" refers to religion rather than ethnicity, but this distinction is not always made.

Religion

As with ethnic and cultural heritages, **religious background** can have an effect on child-rearing practices. Unfortunately, not much is known about the exact effects of religion on human behavior. The reason for this is that people are often sensitive about discussing their religious feelings with researchers. It may also be that researchers are not very seriously interested in religion and its effects on development because most people spend relatively little time in church. Also, it is difficult to separate the possible effects of religion on development from other related factors such as ethnic and social background (34).

When the effects of religion in behavior have been measured, the results have not always been clear-cut (33, 36). In general, those who claim to be religious appear to be less forgiving, more prejudiced, and more rigid than those who are less religious. However, further study of church-going suggests that those who attend frequently and regularly and those who do not attend at all are less prejudiced than those who attend sometimes, but still claim to be religious.

Research findings on religious beliefs and behavior may not be clear, but religion can affect child development in some obvious ways: educational experiences (for example, parochial versus public schooling), social activity (for example, church groups and clubs), intergroup relations (such as anti-Catholicism or anti-Semitism). All of these religiously based activities can contribute to differences in knowledge, attitudes, and ways of thinking and behaving. Differences in methods and goals of child training have been seen in families with different religious beliefs (54). These differences range from the degree to which disciplinary practices are used by parents to the emphasis parents place on self-reliance. A belief in a powerful and punishing God, for instance, has been related to a more punitive approach to child rearing (27). Similarly, differences in attitudes toward achievement among children have been linked to the religion of their parents (14, 15). Children from Jewish homes frequently rate higher in their desire for achievement than their Catholic peers. Religious background may also be related to attitudes toward such things as drug use. In one study of marijuana users, 60 percent of the users reported no religious affiliation (48). Of those users who did report a religious affiliation, 11 percent were Protestant, 11 percent were Jewish, and 4 percent were Catholic.

Another, perhaps more indirect, way in which religion may affect human behavior is its possible relationship to broader political and economic factors, which are extremely powerful in shaping both the culture and its individual members. One work concerning political, economic, and religious interactions relates the Protestant ethic to the rise of capitalism (51). According to this work, the Protestant personality (which represents a major portion of the population of the United States) is characterized as individualistic, thrifty, and self-sacrificing, an efficient user of time, strong in personal responsibility, and committed to the supreme value of personal productivity. These characteristics, in turn, are related to personal salvation. They also happen to be necessary for the successful practice of capitalism. Thus, achievement motivation in entire societies may be traced, in part, to a religious base.

No matter what a person's religious or ethnic background may be, all individuals share some of the cultural views of the overall society. This is important because individual survival often depends on knowledge of the culture's beliefs about what is done and what ought to be done. It is important, for instance, to know the group's solution to problems raised by the environment as well as the rules of justice and morality that serve as a guide for the behavior of group members with respect to each other. This information is passed on to children by parents, but other institutions, such as schools and churches, also play a role in the socialization process. Other factors, such as radio, television, newspapers, motion pictures, and even music, are also influential parts of the overall social environment that help shape a culture. So even though there are many ethnic groups and smaller cultures (**subcultures**) in the United States, there is still a basic cultural pattern that affects the development of children reared in the United States.

THE FAMILY AND SOCIALIZATION

The setting into which each child is born can be seen as a within circles with the child in the center. The outer circl child's cultural heritage. It varies from community to co country to country, and from one broad area of the world to an innermost circle represents the family's socioeconomic statu .... is affected by the outer circle, and it, in turn, has an effect on many aspects of the family's relationship with the child. The innermost circle, the one closest to the child, represents the family or care-giving group in which the child will be reared. All three circles influence each other and have an effect on the child, but it is the inner circle, the **family,** that has the greatest impact on how the child will develop. Not only the people in the family, but the very structure of the family plays an important role in human development

Family Structure

The most important functions of the family with regard to child rearing probably have to do with socialization and the provision of emotional support for newborns. In most parts of the industrialized world these functions are performed by a family that consists of a mother, father, and their children — the **nuclear family.** But the nuclear family is not the only child-rearing arrangement.

One variation of the nuclear family that has been occurring more frequently in the United States is the **single-parent family** — a mother or father and the offspring. Most of the single-parent families are of the mother-child type rather than the father-child type. In 1974, there were approximately nine million children under the age of 18 being reared by one parent. Only 800,000 of these were in father-headed homes. While some single-parent families are due to either the death of one parent or to the birth of children out of wedlock,

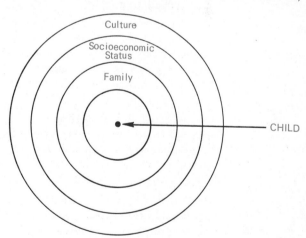

The setting into which a child is born can be seen as a series of circles.

the increase in single-parent families is due largely to an increasing number of divorces and separations. But because most people who divorce eventually remarry, the single-parent family is often a temporary arrangement. The effects of mother absence and father absence are discussed in Chapter 11.

Probably the oldest family arrangement, and one that is still common in more traditional societies, is the **extended family.** These family groups usually consist of three generations of family members—children, parents, and grandparents. For example, such a group might include all the male descendants of the oldest man of a family and their wives and children, orphaned cousins, nephews and nieces, and widowed aunts and sisters. Household responsibilities, including child care, are usually shared. The extended family is considered to be a safeguard against poverty for its less fortunate members and a source of great security and love for young children. Because of the size of most extended families and the number of available care-givers, children are usually never long without needed attention.

The extended family is seen less and less in the United States because few people can afford this type of arrangement. In recent years, however, more and more people have been experimenting with variations of the extended family. Group marriages, artificially extended families (in which not all members are related), and various types of communal living arrangements have been proposed as methods of giving both adults and children the support and attention they might not otherwise receive.

Large communal organizations exist in China, Russia, and Israel, and a few have been established in the United States. The effects of growing up in such an arrangement have been closely studied in the Israeli communes—the kibbutzim. In these communes children are usually considered to belong to the group and are reared by adults who are not their parents. At birth infants are placed in the Infant's House to be cared for by trained care-givers. The mothers visit their children regularly for nursing until weaning is completed at around the age of nine months. After a year in the Infant's House, the children are moved into children's houses which are organized according to age level. Nurses and teachers are responsible for the socialization parents would normally provide. Children in the kibbutzim do, however, spend some time with their parents—usually several hours each evening and most of Saturday.

Studies of the effects of kibbutz rearing have found kibbutz-raised children to be mature, well socialized, cooperative, and above average in mental development (40). Other studies, however, have found that kibbutz children may have some personality problems, including some difficulty in establishing close relationships and showing deep emotional feelings (6, 46). These problems may be due to the fact that kibbutz children do not have the opportunity to form strong attachments to their parents in early life.

Personality Patterns of the Family

The size and structure of families varies, and this has an effect on the amount of attention and stimulation, opportunities for peer play, and the number of adult models children have to imitate and learn from. Most families in the United States, however, still consist of two parents and their children. It is during thousands of interactions with the parents, including those involving feeding and toilet training, that children acquire many of the values, attitudes, and behaviors that will affect their lives for years. This is not surprising, considering the closeness of most parent-child relationships, especially during the early years. It is also not surprising that children sometimes develop personality patterns similar to those of their parents. This is seen most dramatically in studies showing that the parenting behavior of emotionally disturbed parents can lead to emotional and behavioral problems in children.

In one such study researchers charted the characteristics of the families of 25 children who were not in need of clinical services (for behavior problems) and of the families of 32 children who were in need of such services (3). The children were between 6 and 12 years of age at the time of the study. The family groups were well matched in variables other than the child's adjustment.

Analysis of the data indicated that the maladjusted children fell into two major groups. For purposes of convenience the authors labeled the first of these the "conduct-problem" group, made up of children who showed uncontrollable or highly aggressive behavior. The second group was called the "personality-problem" group. Its members showed such symptoms as shyness, undue sensitiveness, and feelings of inferiority. Both labels, of course, reflect personality problems, but they are applied in accordance with a widely used classification of children with behavior disturbances: those who act out their unhappiness (conduct problems); and those who "take it out on themselves" (the personality-problem group). They might also be called the "attackers" and "withdrawers."

The researchers found that the parents of the conduct-problem group, typically, were maladjusted and inclined to be arbitrary with their children, and were themselves likely to give vent violently and unpredictably to their emotions. The mother was likely to be active and tense, very free with suggestions, dictatorial, and stubborn. But the fathers, apparently rather withdrawn from the situation, tended not to enforce regulations. Such a situation, obviously, can easily become a vicious spiral: the mother, frustrated by the father, becomes shriller and shriller; the father, frustrated by the mother, withdraws more and more, and the child is left in the middle, with an antagonist parent on the one hand and a nonsupportive and withdrawn one on the other.

For the group of children with personality problems, the role of the father appeared to be significantly more important than that of the mother. None of her behaviors was particularly related to such symptoms; but the fathers were revealed to be maladjusted and thwarting of the child.

The authors conclude their study with the following statement: "The many important associations between father and child behavior lead to the conclusion that future research, and perhaps therapeutic practice, should *give more consideration to the role of the father in child development.*" A closer look at the effects of fathers on their children is presented in Chapter 11.

In another study (30) personality-test data from 49 sets of parents of children referred for psychiatric help were compared with the test data of 49 carefully matched parents of normal children. Most of the families were lower-middle-class people.

On the personality test (the Minnesota Multiphasic Inventory, usually referred to as the MMPI), the fathers of the disturbed children showed up as more concerned with body complaints and illness; they were gloomier in their outlook on life, yet at the same time appeared to be less mature and more impulsive; and they were more tense and anxious. The mothers, too, were more impulsive and less mature, and more depressed and anxious. They laid blame on other people for their problems, were less honest, and were inclined to act out their aggressions and unconventional impulses.

Although these findings are based on a paper-and-pencil test and do not directly represent real-life behavior, they fit well enough with the results obtained in the previously mention study. Both of these studies, then, suggest that disturbed fathers and mothers have disturbed children. Children who might be described as "attackers" have mothers who are dominating and demanding and fathers who are unusually lax and withdrawn. The mothers of "withdrawers" do not differ as a group from the mothers of nonproblem children, but the fathers of "withdrawers" appear to be more dominating and restrictive than the other group of fathers.

Birth Order and Family Size

Not only parents, but children make up the structure of a family. The number of children, their sexes, the order in which they are born, and the spacing between children all seem to have important effects on development. First-born children, for instance, have been compared with their siblings (brothers and sisters) and have been found to be different from them in several ways. First-born children tend to do better on intelligence tests, are more likely to go to college, are usually less aggressive, and are more stubborn than later-born children. These findings relate to first-borns in general, but do not predict that every first-born will have these characteristics.

The effects of **family size** have also been studied and, in general, it seems that having a large number of children can have negative effects on individual development (13). A study of Canadian boys found that the greater number of siblings they had, the lower were their scores for verbal and number abilities on IQ tests (32). This effect was stronger in the lower socioeconomic groups than in the higher ones. A study of Dutch boys also found that as family size increases, the level of children's intellectual ability declines (4). Other studies have found that children from smaller families tend to be taller, stronger, and more energetic than those from larger families (13, 17, 56).

Robert Zajonc has proposed a theory that helps explain the intellectual differences seen between **first-born** and **later-born children** and between children from small and large families (57). The theory is based on the idea that within a family the intellectual growth of every member is dependent on that of all other members. This can be illustrated mathematically, based on what Zajonc calls the intellectual level of parents and children. Since adults obviously have much more knowledge and experience, they are given an intellectual level of 30 units. This number is not related to age or to IQ scores, but is an arbitrary number used to compare the intellectual level of adults with that of children. In this system a newborn would have an intellectual level of zero. The intellectual environment into which a child is born can be seen as the average of the intellectual levels of all members of the family, including that of the child. The intellectual environment of a two-parent family at the birth of the first child, then, would have an average value of 20 [(30 + 30 + 0) ÷ 3 = 20]. If a second child is born when the intellectual level of the first-born child reaches 4, the second child enters an intellectual environment that has an average value of 16 [(30 + 30 + 4 + 0) ÷ 4 = 16]. If a third child is born when the intellectual level of the first has reached 7 and that of the second child is 3, the family intellectual environment will be reduced to 14 [(30 + 30 + 7 + 3 + 0) ÷ 5 = 14].

These figures suggest that intellectual environment should decline with birth order, but **child spacing** must also be considered. If the second child is not born until the first has reached an intellectual level of 24, the newborn will enter an environment with an intellectual average of 21 [(30 + 30 + 24 + 0) ÷ 4 = 21], which is even more favorable than the 20 entered by the first-born. So with large enough age gaps between children, the negative effects of birth order may be erased or even reversed.

What this theory suggests is that children from large families spend more time in a world of small-sized minds and therefore are slower in intellectual development than are children from small families who have more contacts with grown-up minds. This could also explain some of the differences in intelligence seen between children from different social classes. Lower-class families tend to have more children than middle- and upper-class families. (See Chapter 9 on Intelligence.)

"Just as the twig is bent, the tree's inclined." This line is often quoted in reference to human development. It implies that early environmental experiences have a lasting effect on a child's development. And this certainly seems to have been the case with the wild boy of Aveyron. Without a culture, a society, or a family, he had severe problems with physical, social, and mental development. Even with a great deal of training, this boy never fully recovered from what seem to be the effects of severe social isolation. But a bent twig does not always have to grow into a crooked tree.

Newborn Indian children in some rural areas of Guatemala in Central America undergo a form of physical and social isolation that seems, in some ways, almost as severe as that undergone by the wild boy. These children live in areas where disease is widespread and medical help is hard to find. As a result, many children die before they are 2 years old. The Indians of Guatemala have attempted to adapt to these severe environmental disadvantages by isolating newborn infants for the first year of life. Parents try to protect their children from disease by keeping them away from all other human beings. The infants are kept shut up in their dark huts where they are cut off from most types of environmental stimulation. They get very little attention or affection and have almost no chance to explore their environment.

As would be expected, such isolation has an effect on the Guatemalan infants. Jerome Kagan has studied these infants and found that most of them are seriously retarded or slowed down in development (21). By the time they are 2 years old, their intellectual development is almost a year behind that of normal, healthy 2-year-old children in the United States or even those in Guatemalan cities. But Kagan has found that these children do not appear to have been permanently retarded by their early social isolation.

By the time the Guatemalan children are 11 years old, they are lively, active, alert, and their intellectual abilities are almost equal to those of middle-class 11-year-olds in the United States. They appear to have overcome the effects of their early isolation and have caught up with other children of the same age. Kagan concludes that there is less relationship between early experiences and later development than has been traditionally assumed. The human infant is a very plastic or flexible creature that can adapt well to many physical and social factors in the environment.

The fact that human development is flexible suggests that many of the cultural and social effects on development discussed in this chapter need not be permanent. A change in the environment appears to have had dramatic effects in the course of development of the Guatemalan Indian infants. When they were released from their early isolation and put into a more stimulating social environment, they began to develop more rapidly and even seem to have caught up with other children their age who had more normal early environ-

Guatemalan children do not seem to be permanently affected by their early isolation.

ments. Similarly, children reared in one cultural or social class can often become successful members of another culture or class. But as flexible as human development is, this does not mean that the early experiences of children should be ignored. The wild child never recovered from what were probably the effects of prolonged social isolation. Many children who have received severe and harsh treatment never fully recover from the effects of the treatment (as Harlow's experiments with monkeys suggest). So even if children can recover from the effects of a poor physical, cultural, or social environment, it is probably best to try to nurture them with as rich and as stimulating an environment as possible.

SUMMARY

Chapter 2 discussed the basic biological and genetic mechanisms that influence development. Chapter 3 is an overview of the cultural and social influences on development. Cases like that of the wild child and the wolf girls demonstrate the extreme importance of nurture and social influences. Without a social environment, these children were socially, emotionally, and physically abnormal.

Social isolation experiments are not performed with human infants, but Harry Harlow's research with isolated and surrogate-reared monkeys illustrate some of the basic social interactions that seem to be necessary for normal primate development. These include infant-mother love, peer love and heterosexual love, mother-infant love, and father-infant love. Lack of one or more of these may have serious effects on development.

Cross-cultural studies provide another method of investigating the effects of cultural influences on human development. Some of the earliest cross-cultural studies showed that the Oedipus conflict described by Freud does not exist in all cultures. Many other cross-cultural studies have shown how the physical environment and availability of resources affect cultural development and parental practices.

Cross-cultural studies have shown that cultural practices affect such things as the amount of physical and social stimulation children receive from their parents and other adults. This stimulation, in turn, influences the physical and social development of children. It also seems that the physical characteristics of infants (which may be genetic) have an influence on cultural and parental practices. Cross-cultural studies are not always conclusive because of other variables, such as malnutrition, play an important role in development, but cross-cultural studies do suggest that the course of infant and child development is strongly influenced by early cultural and social experiences.

Some of the most important early social experiences children have come during feeding, toilet training, and sex training. The way these and other parent-child interactions are handled may have long-lasting effects on physical, emotional, and social development, but one major study suggests that it is the amount of parental permissiveness or restrictiveness in all parent-child interactions (rather than in any one specific area) that influences development. In general, cold, restrictive, rigid, and punitive parenting seems to lead to more childhood behavior problems and emotional upsets than does warm, permissive, flexible, and loving parenting.

Parents influence children, but parents themselves are influenced by a number of cultural and social factors that affect their behavior and child development. The most important of these factors is social class. Social class in the United States is not always clearly defined, and there are large overlaps between social groups as far as values and behavior are concerned, but there do appear to be important differences among social classes in the way they rear their children. In general, middle- and upper-class parents have been found to be more attentive and responsive to their children as well as more aware of their children's feelings than working- and lower-class parents tend to be.

Differences among racial and ethnic groups may also be responsible for differences in parenting, but psychological differences among such groups seem to be the result of social and economic rather than racial or ethnic factors. Religious beliefs can also affect parental practices and child development, although the exact relationship is not always clear. Religious affiliation does, however, provide children with social experiences (schools, clubs, and so on) that they might not otherwise have, and these can influence thoughts and behavior.

Within the overall culture are social groups. Within social groups are families, the basic units of society and the basic unit for the socialization of infants and children. The structure of a family influences development by providing children with more or less opportunities for social interactions and different types of social interactions. The personality of parents, as well as the number and spacing of children, affect the types and amounts of social interaction children will have.

Throughout this chapter, cultural and social factors have been shown to be powerful influences on human development. Studies like that done by Jerome Kagan in Guatemala suggest that such influences need not always be permanent. The human organism is flexible and adaptable enough to survive and develop in a wide variety of environments. Even so, the importance of the early environment should not be ignored. Children should probably be provided with as rich and as stimulating an environment as possible.

RESEARCH REPORT 3.1

The Ik

How much of what is considered to be human nature in Western culture can be lost under conditions of extreme adversity? Some light can be shed on this question by looking at the plight of the Ik (pronounced eek) of northern Uganda in Africa. The history of the Ik goes back at least 2000 years. They lived as nomadic hunter-gatherers, a way of life that was destroyed shortly before World War II when the government of Uganda decided to make a national park out of the Kidepo Valley, the main hunting ground of the Ik. The Ik were crowded together at the edges of the park and were encouraged to become farmers on dry, steep mountain slopes. Hunting in the Kidepo Valley was forbidden.

Colin M. Turnbull, an anthropologist, lived among the Ik for a period of 18 months during the 1960s and later described the devastating effects that moving their homes, crowding, drought, and famine had had on "The Mountain People." For example, the family as such simply ceased to exist. Children were "put out" at about 3 years of age to sleep in open courtyards. They formed age bands in which each child sought another close to him or her in age for defense against older children. By 12 or 13 children, if they survived, had learned the wisdom of acting on their own and for their own good. They, in turn, later put *their* children out at age 3.

Homemaking deteriorated, doorsteps and courtyards were littered with feces, and adultery and incest replaced old taboos against such practices. Turnbull wrote: "If there was such a thing as Icien morality I had not yet perceived it, though traces of a moral past remained." Goodness for the Ik meant to have enough food for oneself. A good person was one who had a full stomach. To withhold food from children or the aged was regarded as an accomplishment to brag about. If persons obtained government rations, they would stop on the way home and gorge themselves, even though this might cause vomiting. There was indifference and no planning for the future. "Every Ik knew that trying to store anything was a waste of time."

Persons who collapsed from weakness were objects of laughter and derision. For example, when a blind widow who tried to make her way down a mountainside fell and rolled to the bottom, the feeble thrashing of her arms and legs provoked laughter in the community. When Turnbull attempted to give her food and water, he was informed that food and medicine were for the living, not the dead. The Ik recognized what they accepted as the human's natural determination to survive before all else.

"The Ik do not value emotion above survival, and they are without love." Love was dismissed as idiotic and even dangerous. They believed in a god who had created them, abandoned them, and then retreated to his domain somewhere in the sky. Qualities looked on as positive in Western cultures such as kindness, consideration, affection, honesty, and compassion were now no longer functional. Turnbull concluded that "Far from being basic human qualities, they are luxuries we can afford in times of plenty."

These people provide a clear lesson, summed up by Turnbull: "The Ik teach us that our much vaunted human values are not inherent in humanity at all, but are associated only with a particular form of survival called society and that all, even society itself, are luxuries that can be dispensed with." "If man has any greatness it is surely in his ability to maintain these values, clinging to them to an often very bitter end, even shortening an already pitifully short life rather than sacrifice his humanity. But that too involves choice, and the Ik teach us that man can lose the will to make it."

"There is a positive trend to human affairs," as Bronowski says in *The Ascent of Man*, but our genes do not guarantee us a glorious and noble future. The experience of the Ik people can serve to warn us that if we do not take care of the quality of the world environment, there is a chilling possible end for humankind as we know it.

Colin M. Turnbull, *The Mountain People*. New York: Simon & Schuster, 1972.

Children Judge the Colors Black and White

Regardless of language or culture, human beings feel positively about the color white and negatively about the color black. This was verified with cross-linguistic measuring instruments (semantic differentials) which "probed" the "brains" of 23 cultures (Osgood, May, and Miron, 1975). Although there was wide variation within and between cultures in preferences for the colors blue, green, yellow, and red, the color white was universally ranked either first or second (blue sometimes outranked white) while the color black was universally ranked lowest.

This phenomenon can be seen throughout the United States, and some idea of its strength can be appreciated by trying to think of words or phrases which use the color white in a *negative* way and the color black in a *positive* way. A survey of dictionaries (the Oxford Dictionary and others) and books of slang noted 40 cases in which white is used in a positive way, 23 cases in which white is used in a negative way, 65 cases in which black is used in a negative way, and only 15 cases in which black is used in a positive way (Stabler and Goldberg, 1973). Folk heroes come dressed in white and villains wear black. Brides dress in white, and black is the color associated with death. Though our sins are said to be black, they can become "white as snow."

Several lines of investigation have shown that this symbolism influences children (Williams and Stabler, 1973). Williams developed a Color Meaning Test consisting of pictures of pairs of animals which were identical except that one was white and one was black. He would tell a child a story about an animal, and the child would then be asked to point to the "naughty kitten," the "good horse," the "bad dog," or the "smart rabbit." Williams found that by age 6, 89 percent of the Euro-Americans (whites) and 80 percent of the Afro-Americans (blacks) showed the white-is-good, black-is-bad concept.

Stabler asked preschool children to evaluate 40 objects (candy, plastic vomit, a rubber snake, a nickel, a dirty tissue, a cigarette butt, and so on). He showed the objects to the children one at a time and asked them to guess which box—a black box or a white box—held an object "just like" the one in front of them. The children were encouraged to shake the boxes and listen for auditory clues. They usually guessed that the pleasant objects were in the white box and the unpleasant ones were in the black box.

In a related procedure, tape recorder speakers were placed in black and white boxes, and children were asked to point to the box which was broadcasting such statements as, "I am good," "I am bad," "I am good-looking," "I am ugly," "I am the winner," "I am the loser," "I am smart," "I am stupid." Actually, except for some neutral statements, the sound was broadcast with equal intensity from both speakers. Again, color made a difference, and the children more often chose the white box as the source of positive statements than they did the black box. Other children heard the boxes broadcast statements like "You are good," "You are bad," "You are good-looking," "You are ugly"; they made similar choices.

In these three studies Euro- and Afro-American children responded similarly, but the Afro-American children did so less consistently.

On the basis of stimulus and semantic generalization, one might expect that the color symbolism of black and white would influence children's perception of racial differences. There is evidence that this is so. Children who have such color attitudes, as measured by the "talking boxes" procedure, show more positive play behavior with Euro-American children and more negative play behavior with Afro-American children ($r = .53$) (Stabler, Zeig, and Rembald, 1976).

Altering children's attitudes toward the colors black and white might reduce their prejudgments on the basis of race. However, the origins of such color attitudes are difficult to identify. Williams speculates that fear of the dark may have been an adaptive characteristic that increased the likelihood of our ancestors' survival, and that, therefore, a genetic predisposition exists for the formation of such attitudes. The common experience of the day–night cycle, with accompanying development of positive feelings for day and negative for night, might also account for the universal and early development of the white–black perceptions. Perhaps this phenomenon is only validated by the symbols prevalent in the general culture.

From: C. E. Osgood, W. H. May, and M. S. Miron, *Cross-Cultural Universals of Affective Meaning*. Urbana, Ill.: University of Illinois Press, 1975; J. R. Stabler and F. J. Goldberg, "The Black and White Symbol in Matrix," *International Journal of Symbology*, 1973, *4*, 27–35; J. E. Williams and J. R. Stabler, "If White Means Good, then Black . . . ," *Psychology Today*, 1973, *7*, 50–55; J. R. Stabler, J. A. Zeig, and A. B. Rembald, "Children's Evaluation of the Colors Black and White and Their Interracial Play Behavior," *Child Study Journal*, 1976, *10*, 157–162.

REFERENCES

1. Ainsworth, M. D. S. *Infancy in Uganda: Infant Care and the Growth of Love.* Baltimore, Md.: The Johns Hopkins Press, 1967.
2. Aldrich, C. A., and E. W. Hewitt. "A Self-regulating Feeding Program for Infants," *Journal of the American Medical Association*, 1947, *135*, 340–342.
3. Becker, W. C., et al. "Factors in Parental Behavior and Personality as Related to Problem Behavior in Children," *Journal of Consulting Psychology*, 1959, *23*, 107–118.
4. Belmont, L., and F. A. Marolla. "Birth Order, Family Size, and Intelligence," *Science*, 1973, *182*, 1096–1101.
5. Berry, J. W. "Temne and Eskimo Perceptual Skills," *International Journal of Psychology*, 1966, *1*, 207–229.
6. Bettelheim, B. *The Children of the Dream.* New York: Macmillan, 1969.
7. Birch, H. G. "Health and the Education of Socially Disadvantaged Children." In H. Bee (ed.), *Social Issues in Developmental Psychology*. New York: Harper & Row, 1974.

8. Brazelton, T. B. "Implications of Infant Development among the Mayan Indians of Mexico." *Human Development*, 1972, *15*, 90–111.

9. Brazelton, T. B., J. S. Robey, and G. A. Collier. "Infant Development in the Zinacanteco Indians of Southern Mexico," *Pediatrics*, 1969, *44*, 274–293.

10. Bronfenbrenner, U. "Socialization and Social Class through Time and Space." In E. E. Maccoby, T. M. Newcomb, and E. L. Hartley (eds.), *Readings in Social Psychology*, 3d ed. New York: Holt, Rinehart and Winston, 1958.

11. Caudill, W., and L. Frost. "A Comparison of Maternal Care and Infant Behavior in Japanese-American, American, and Japanese Families." In U. Bronfenbrenner and M. A. Mahoney (eds.), *Influences on Human Development*, 2d ed. Hinsdale, Ill.: Dryden Press, 1975.

12. Caudill, W., and H. Weinstein. "Maternal Care and Infant Behavior in Japan and America," *Psychiatry*, 1969, *32*, 12–43.

13. Clausen, J. A., and S. R. Clausen. "The Effects of Family Size on Parents and Children." In J. T. Fawcett (ed.), *Psychological Perspectives on Population*. New York: Basic Books, 1973.

14. Elder, G. H., Jr. "Adolescent Socialization and Development." In E. F. Borgatta and W. W. Lambert (eds.), *Handbook of Personality Theory and Research*. Chicago: Rand McNally, 1968, 239–364.

15. Elkind, D. "The Developmental Psychology of Religion." In O. H. Kidd and J. L. Rivoire (eds.), *Perceptual Development in Children*. New York: International Universities Press, 1966, 193–225.

16. Erlanger, H. S. "Social Class and Corporal Punishment in Childrearing: A Reassessment," *American Sociological Review*, 1974, *39*, 68–85.

17. Fogelman, K. R. "Developmental Correlates of Family Size: A Report from the National Child Development Study," *British Journal of Social Work*, 1975, *5*, 43–57.

18. Harlow, H., M. K. Harlow, and S. J. Suomi. "From Thought to Therapy," *American Scientist*, 1971, *59*, 538–549.

19. Heinstein, M. "Child Rearing in California." Berkeley, Calif.: Bureau of Maternal and Child Health, State of California Department of Public Health, 1966.

20. Hess, R. D. "Social Class and Ethnic Differences upon Socialization." In P. H. Mussen (ed.), *Carmichael's Manual of Child Psychology*, Vol. 2, 3d ed. New York: Wiley, 1970.

21. Kagan, J., and R. E. Klein. "Cross-cultural Perspectives on Early Development," *American Psychologist*, 1973, *28*, 947–961.

22. Keusch, G. T. "Malnutrition and Infection: Deadly Allies," *Natural History*, 1975, *84*, 27–34.

23. Kinsey, A. C., W. B. Pomeroy, C. E. Martin, and P. H. Gebhard. *Sexual Behavior in the Human Female*. Philadelphia: Saunders, 1953.

24. Klatskin, E. H., A. G. Lethin, and E. B. Jackson. "Choice of Rooming-in or Newborn Nursery," *Pediatrics*, 1950, *6*, 878–889.

25. Kohn, M. L. "Social Class and Parental Values," *American Journal of Sociology*, 1959, *64*, 337–351.

26. Kohn, M. L., and C. Schooler. "Occupational Experience and Psychological

Functioning: An Assessment of Reciprocal Effects," *American Sociological Review*, 1973, *38*, 97–118.

27. Lambert, W. W., L. M. Triandis, and M. Wolf. "Some Correlates of Beliefs in the Malevolence and Benevolence of Supernatural Being: A Cross-societal Study," *Journal of Abnormal and Social Psychology*, 1959, *58*, 162–169.

28. Lane, H. *The Wild Boy of Aveyron*. Cambridge, Mass.: Harvard University Press, 1976.

29. LeVine, R. A. "Cross-cultural Study in Child Psychology." In P. H. Mussen (ed.), *Carmichael's Manual of Child Psychology*, Vol. 2, 3d ed. New York: Wiley, 1970.

30. Liverant, S. "MMPI Differences Between Parents of Disturbed and Nondisturbed Children," *Journal of Consulting Psychology*, 1959, *23*, 256–260.

31. Malinowski, B. *Sex and Repression in Savage Society*. London: Routledge & Kegan Paul, 1953.

32. Marjoribanks, K., H. J. Walberg, and M. Bargen. "Mental Abilities: Sibling Constellations and Social Class Correlates," *British Journal of Social and Clinical Psychology*, 1975, *14*, 109–116.

33. McCandless, B. R. *Adolescents: Behavior and Development*. Hinsdale, Ill.: Dryden Press, 1970.

34. McCandless, B. R., and E. D. Evans. *Children and Youth: Psychosocial Development*. Hinsdale, Ill.: Dryden Press, 1973.

35. McConnell, J. V. *Understanding Human Behavior*, 2d ed. New York: Holt, Rinehart and Winston, 1977.

36. Medinnus, G. R., and R. C. Johnson. *Child and Adolescent Psychology*. New York: Wiley, 1969.

37. Meredith, H. V. "Body Size of Contemporary Groups of One-year-old Infants Studied in Different Parts of the World," *Child Development*, 1970, *41*, 551–600.

38. Newton, N. R., and M. Newton. "Relationship of Ability to Breastfeed and Maternal Attitudes toward Breastfeeding," *Pediatrics*, 1950, *5*, 869–875.

39. Pearlin, L. I., and M. L. Kohn. "Social Class, Occupation and Parental Values: A Cross-national Study," *American Sociological Review*, 1966, *31*, 466–479.

40. Rabin, A. I. *Growing Up in the Kibbutz*. New York: Springer, 1965.

41. Rebelsky, F., and P. A. Daniel. "Cross-cultural Studies in Infant Intelligence." In M. Lewis (ed.), *Infant Intelligence*. New York: Wiley Interscience, 1976.

42. Reusch, H. *Top of the World*. New York: Harper & Row, 1950.

43. Sears, R. R., E. E. Maccoby, and H. Levin. *Patterns of Child-rearing*. New York: Harper & Row, 1957.

44. Simsarian, F. P., and P. A. McLendon. "Further Records of the Self-demand Schedule in Infant Feeding," *Journal of Pediatrics*, 1954, *27*, 109–114.

45. Singh, J. A. L., and R. M. Zingg. *Wolf Children and Feral Men*. New York: Harper and Brothers, 1942.

46. Spiro, M. E. *Children of the Kibbutz*. Cambridge, Mass.: Harvard University Press, 1958.

47. Stock, M. B., and P. M. Smythe. "Does Under-nutrition During Infancy Inhibit Brain Growth and Subsequent Intellectual Development?" *Archives of the Diseases of Childhood*, 1963, *38*, 546–552.

48. Tart, C. T. *On Being Stoned*. Palo Alto, Calif: Science and Behavior Books, 1971.
49. Trainham, G., G. J. Pilafian, and R. M. Kraft. "Case History of Twins Fed on a Self-demand Regime," *Journal of Pediatrics*, 1945, 27, 97–108.
50. Tyler, L. E. *The Psychology of Human Differences*, 3d ed. New York: Appleton, 1965.
51. Weber, M. *The Protestant Ethic and the Spirit of Capitalism*, T. Parsons, trans. New York: Scribner, 1958.
52. Werner, E. "Infants Around the World: Cross-cultural Studies of Psychomotor Development from Birth to Two Years," *Journal of Cross-Cultural Psychology*, 1972, 3, 111–134.
53. Whiting, J. W. M., and I. L. Child. *Child Training and Personality*. New Haven, Conn.: Yale University Press, 1953.
54. Whiting, J. W. M., I. L. Child, W. W. Lambert, A. M. Fischer, J. L. Fischer, C. Nydegger, W. Nydegger, H. Maretzki, T. Maretzki, L. Minturn, K. Romney, and R. Romney. *Field Guide for a Study of Socialization*, Vol. 1. New York: Wiley, 1966.
55. Williams, J. R., and R. B. Scott. "Growth and Development of Negro Infants," *Child Development*, 1953, 24, 103–121.
56. Wray, J. D. "Population Pressure on Families: Family Size and Child Spacing," *Reports on Population/Family Planning*. New York: Population Council, August, 1971, No. 9.
57. Zajonc, R. B., and G. B. Markus. "Birth Order and Intellectual Development," *Psychological Review*, 1975, 82, 74–88.

2

biological and cognitive
bases of development

Infancy, the first two years of life, has come to be regarded as one of the most important stages of development. Environmental factors beginning at the time of conception as well as the treatment a child receives during infancy can have lasting effects on development.

infancy

Imagine stepping out of a cool, dark movie theater into a hot, glaring, sunny afternoon.

Imagine being wakened from a quiet, restful sleep by the blaring noise of a brass band.

If your reflexes and senses are normal, these drastic changes would be not only shocking, they might be extremely painful.

Now, imagine what it would be like to experience all of these violent sensory changes if you were a naked, newborn infant. Such shock is what greets most infants at the moment of birth in many modern hospitals in the Western world. They are faced with blinding lights, noise, cold air, and fabrics that might feel harsh against their tender skin. They are held aloft by their feet and snapped into an erect position. They are slapped on the rear end and made to cry. These are part of what French physician Frederick Leboyer calls the violence of birth as it takes place in many of the clean, efficient delivery rooms of Europe and the United States.

But there might be a more soothing way to be born. In *Birth Without Violence* (40), Leboyer describes what he believes to be the pain infants suffer being born. "What more proof do we need?" he asks.

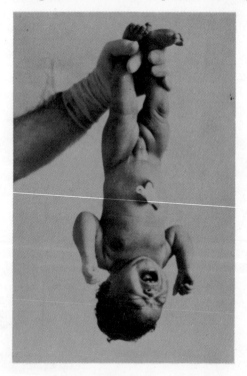

Violent sensory shock greets newborn infants at the moment of birth in most modern hospitals in the Western world.

That tragic expression, those tight-shut eyes, those twitching eyebrows . . . that howling mouth, that squirming head trying desperately to find refuge . . . those hands stretching out to us, imploring, begging, then retreating to shield the face—that gesture of dread. Those furiously kicking feet, those arms that suddenly pull downward to protect the stomach. The flesh is one great shudder. . . . Every inch of the body is crying out: "Don't touch me!" And at the same time pleading: "Don't leave me! Help me!" Has there ever been a more heartrending appeal?

In answer to this appeal, Leboyer offers a method of making birth less painful and shocking to the infant. It is a slow, quiet birth in which everything is done to protect the infant from shock. For example, the infant's sensitive eyes are spared the glare of delivery room lights and floodlamps. "Of course," admits Leboyer, "some light is necessary to watch over the mother, so that she will not be injured when the child's head emerges." But then, he says, extinguish all light, except a small night light. "And this is all to the good, since newborn infants are almost always ugly. . . . It is better that the mother discover her child by touching it."

Unnecessary noise is avoided. The Leboyer method calls for complete silence in the delivery room, instead of the loud commands, such as "Push, push," that might possibly upset the mother and that might be painful to the infant.

Once the child's head appears, the birth can be eased along by the doctor's finger under each of the infant's armpits. Supported so, the infant is gently settled onto the mother's abdomen. There, for several minutes, the child is allowed to adjust slowly to its new environment while it continues to receive warmth and comfort from its mother.

The Leboyer method also eliminates the traditional holding up of the child. The infant's spinal column, while in the mother's womb, has never been completely straight. Holding the infant up by the feet snaps the spine into the straight position. This, Leboyer says, may be as shocking and painful to the infant as the slap on the rear that usually follows.

The traditional slap is meant to make the infant cry and thus take its first breath and begin using its lungs for breathing. The Leboyer method does not use the slap, but instead allows the infant to lie quietly on the mother's abdomen with the umbilical cord attached. Through this cord the infant continues to receive blood and oxygen from its mother as it did before birth. Gradually, after several minutes, the child's lungs and breathing system begin to function on their own, and the umbilical cord stops operating. Then, after perhaps 5 minutes, the cord can be cut. The child will have been continually fed oxygen and will not have been slapped.

Next, instead of placing the infant on a cold metal scale to be weighed, it is gently lowered into water that has been warmed to near body temperature. Here the infant is rinsed and will eventually open its eyes and begin to move its limbs freely. The result of such a nonviolent birth, concludes Leboyer, is not a screaming, kicking, terrified infant but a relaxed and even smiling child.

Because of its gentle and humane approach to birth, the Leboyer method has received a great deal of attention in recent years. Another reason for this attention is the fact that severe shock or trauma during the birth process can have serious and lasting effects on development, as will be seen in this chapter. The Leboyer method not only attempts to avoid all shock or trauma but suggests that a calm, easy birth may be beneficial for development. As yet, there is no evidence to suggest that this is so or that the thousands of children who have been delivered by the Leboyer method are any different from those born the usual delivery-room way. Carefully controlled longitudinal studies will have to be conducted in order to determine if the gentleness of the Leboyer method actually has a beneficial effect on infants and their development.

Whether or not the Leboyer method proves to have positive effects on development, the attention it has received is an indication of the increasing importance attached today to infancy and the early stages of development. Freud originally suggested that adult emotional health is linked to early childhood experiences. Today, scientists are concluding that early experiences, including the birth process, significantly influence many areas of development. Not only social and emotional development but physical and mental development are influenced — perhaps permanently — by events and encounters during infancy, which spans approximately the first two years of life. Indeed, development is influenced by factors operating as early as conception.

CONCEPTION AND PREGNANCY

Approximately nine months before an infant faces the lights of the delivery room, social and genetic forces will have combined to start the development process. Social forces determine which man and woman will contribute their genes to the child. When the genes join conception takes place, and the complex process of development begins.

The female's **ovum,** or egg, and the male's **sperm** begin their long journey before conception takes place. The ovum leaves its **follicle,** or capsule, in the **ovary** where it was produced and travels to the **fallopian** tube. The sperm, which have been deposited in the **vagina,** swim through the **uterus,** or **womb,** to the fallopian tube where they surround the ovum. Only the strongest of the sperm cells will complete this journey, and if the timing is perfect and the egg is ready to be fertilized, several sperm cells will penetrate the surface of the egg. One of these sperm cells will complete the process of fertilization by moving to the **nucleus,** or center, of the egg. There, the 23 chromosomes of each

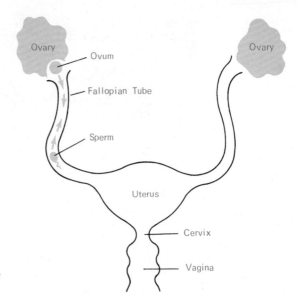

A diagram of the female
reproductive system showing how
conception occurs.

Labels in diagram: Ovary, Ovum, Fallopian Tube, Sperm, Uterus, Cervix, Vagina, Ovary

sex cell (see Chapter 2) will come together to form one cell with 46 chromosomes, the normal number for a human cell. This fertilized ovum is called a
zygote (from the Greek word meaning "to join").

Shortly after fertilization, the zygote begins to undergo mitosis—cell
division. During the next few days, this growing body of cells leaves the
fallopian tube and eventually **implants,** or attaches itself, to the upper lining
of the uterus.

The uterus, a thick-walled, pear-shaped organ, is lined with material that
will nourish the **embryo** (the organism in its early stages of development). If
fertilization and implantation do not take place, the lining of the womb is
discharged during menstruation, and a new cycle begins—on an approximately
monthly basis. If the implantation does take place, the new organism will continue to develop in the womb for the duration of the pregnancy. Normal pregnancies last between 266 and 270 days, or about nine months. The time of
birth can be estimated by adding seven days to the date of the first day of the
last menstrual period and then counting forward nine months.

Prenatal Stages

During the **prenatal** (before birth) **period,** the original fertilized egg divides and multiplies into an organism that consists of 200 billion cells at birth.
This rapid growth and development follows an orderly and predictable schedule that is usually divided into three stages. The first prenatal stage, the **period
of the ovum,** lasts one or two weeks. During this time, the ovum moves from
the fallopian tube to the uterus. As it continues to divide and grow, it receives

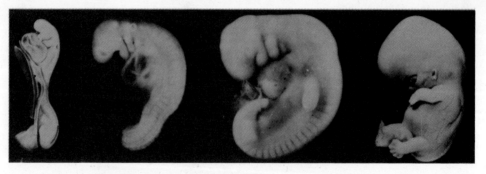

Four stages in the development of a human embryo; from left, at about 2 weeks, 4 weeks, 6 weeks, and 8 weeks.

its nourishment from its own yolk. When the human ovum has grown to about the size of a pinhead (after 10 to 14 days), it attaches itself to the wall of the uterus (as previously mentioned). From then on, it receives all of its nourishment from the mother's body.

The next prenatal stage, the **period of the embryo,** lasts until the end of the second month of pregnancy. During this time, growth is rapid. By the end of the third week, when the embryo is only one fourth of an inch long, the heart starts to beat. Between the fourth and eighth weeks the eyes, ears, nose, and mouth become recognizable. Fingers and toes begin to appear between the sixth and eighth weeks. By the end of two months, the face, fingers, and toes are well formed and the sex organs are beginning to form.

The embryo's life-support system is also formed during this period. It consists of the placenta, the umbilical cord, and the amniotic sac. The **placenta** is an organ that lines the wall of the uterus and partially surrounds the growing embryo. The **umbilical cord** connects the embryo, at the **navel,** to the placenta. The mother's bloodstream opens into the placenta, and the umbilical cord carries blood from the placenta to the embryo and back again. This provides the embryo with nourishment and oxygen and allows for waste material to be sent back to the mother's bloodstream. The **amniotic sac** surrounds the embryo and is filled with a watery fluid (**amniotic fluid**) that helps cushion the embryo from bumps and shocks experienced by the mother. This fluid contains the cells that are examined during amniocentesis, the process used to test for such deficiencies as sickle-cell anemia and chromosomal abnormalities (see Chapter 2).

The third prenatal period, the **period of the fetus,** lasts from the end of the second month until birth. By the start of this period, the fetus already has most of its human features. During the period of the fetus, these features continue to develop and begin to function.

Fetal development takes place in two directions: from the head downward and from the inside outward. In other words, the head develops before the legs, and the internal organs reach full development before the external organs, such as the hands and feet. By the fifth month, the head, stomach, and most internal organs are well developed. By the seventh month, the fetus is well enough developed to have a chance of survival if it is born then.

Development that proceeds from head to tail is called **cephalocaudal** (meaning "head" and "tail"). Development that proceeds from the center of the body outward is called **proximodistal.** Development along these general lines continues after birth, as will be seen in Chapter 5.

By the third or fourth month, the fetus is capable of some movement, and by the fourth or fifth month, the head, arms, and legs begin to move independently. The amount of movement varies from fetus to fetus, with some being almost inactive and others moving as much as three fourths of the time. They may squirm, kick, or have hiccups. Fetuses that have been very active tend to be underweight at birth, having used up a lot of energy. Those that have been very inactive sometimes take longer to develop coordinated motor activity after birth (23), having had less exercise.

Pregnancy

While the fetus is going through its many dramatic developmental stages, the woman carrying the fetus is also undergoing obvious changes. **Pregnancy,** which is usually discussed in terms of three-month periods called **trimesters,** is often first suspected when a sexually active woman misses her monthly **menstrual period.** Although some women (perhaps 20 percent) may continue to experience monthly bleeding or "spotting" during pregnancy, a missed period is an indication that conception has taken place. There are, however, other reasons for missing a menstrual period. Women younger than 20 and older than 40 sometimes skip a period for no apparent reason. Illness and emotional upset may result in a missed period, and women who have recently had a child, especially if they are breast-feeding, may not menstruate for several months. Because of such irregularities, a missed period is not always a sure sign of pregnancy, but there are other indications of pregnancy during the first trimester.

One early symptom of pregnancy is enlargement and tenderness of the breasts. The **hormones** associated with pregnancy stimulate the **mammary glands,** or milk-producing organs, and the woman may become aware of a feeling of fullness in her breasts. This may be accompanied by a tingling in the breasts, with the nipples becoming especially sensitive to the touch in early pregnancy.

"Morning sickness," or a feeling of nausea, is experienced by many women during the first six to eight weeks of pregnancy. It often consists of a queasy feeling in the stomach upon awakening and may result in vomiting and feelings of illness at the sight or smell of certain foods. Some women experience morning sickness in the evening, some have only a very mild form of nausea with no vomiting, and a very few women experience vomiting so severe that they must be hospitalized and treated. Excessive tiredness and a need for sleep are also felt by many women during the early stages of pregnancy.

More frequent urination is another early sign of pregnancy. During the first trimester this is related to swelling of the uterus, which puts increased pressure on the bladder. Later, after the uterus expands and moves upward into the abdomen, this symptom may disappear, but in the final stages of pregnancy, when the head of the fetus descends into the pelvic area, pressure may again be exerted on the bladder.

Women can usually continue to work and participate in most activities during the second trimester of pregnancy.

The second trimester is usually the most peaceful and pleasant period of pregnancy (36). The nausea and tiredness of the first trimester are generally less noticeable, and during these months pregnant women can be quite active. They can continue to work and participate in most activities (including sex), though physicians generally warn against overexertion.

During the final three months of pregnancy the increased activity of the fetus and the swelling abdomen make expectant mothers much more aware of the growing child they carry. The woman's weight during this stage may become a problem. Hormonal changes usually result in an increased appetite, but most physicians suggest that pregnant women try not to gain more than about 20 pounds (36). The average infant at nine months weighs 7.5 pounds. The rest of the woman's weight gain is accounted for by the placenta (about 1 pound), the amniotic fluid (2 pounds), enlargement of the uterus (2 pounds), enlargement of the breasts (1½ to 2 pounds) and additional fluids and fat tissue accumulated by the woman (about 6 pounds). Women who gain weight excessively during pregnancy may put a strain on their hearts and may begin to suffer from high blood pressure. They also tire more easily and become more awkward in their movements.

By the ninth month, most pregnant women are anxious to see their child, to find out if it is a boy or a girl, and to know that it is normal. In the vast majority of cases women give birth to healthy, well-formed infants. In a few cases there are complications, some of them serious.

PRENATAL INFLUENCES ON DEVELOPMENT

It used to be said that unborn children could be affected by the thoughts and experiences of their mothers. A mother frightened by a dog was supposed to produce a child afraid of dogs. A mother who listened to a lot of music supposedly would give birth to a musical child. There is no evidence to support such claims, but many studies have shown that human development can be seriously affected by conditions in the womb and by the mother's health.

Radiation

Six months after the atomic bomb was dropped on Hiroshima, Japan, in 1945 the serious effects of **atomic radiation** in the human fetus were apparent (52). Many women who were less than 20 weeks pregnant and who were within a half mile of the explosion gave birth to badly deformed children. While atomic radiation is not a widespread problem, other types of more common radiation can be harmful to the fetus. **X-rays,** for example, are used to take photographs of bone structures and to treat some types of cancer. The fetus does not appear to be affected by small amounts of such radiation, but larger amounts can result in serious physical and mental abnormalities (48). Another type of radiation, **ionizing radiation,** has also been found to be harmful. If a woman receives this type of radiation in heavy enough doses at certain times during pregnancy, she could be in danger of giving birth to a child with an incompletely developed head and brain (35). As was seen in Chapter 2, radiation may also be the cause of chromosomal abnormalities resulting in Down's syndrome and other developmental problems.

Drugs

The fetus receives nutrition from its mother by way of her bloodstream. But the mother's blood does not go directly to the fetus. It is filtered first by the placenta. In recent years it has become apparent that drugs in the mother's bloodstream are not all filtered out by the placenta, and some that get through can harm the fetus. For example, women addicted to heroin during pregnancy have been known to give birth to infants addicted to the drug (36). These infants go through the same withdrawal pains after birth that an adult experiences when taken off the drug.

A more common drug, alcohol, has also been linked to serious developmental problems. This has been known since the 1800s when it became obvious in England that some gin-drinking women were giving birth to dwarfed children. A recent study has found that facial, limb, and heart defects are common among children of women who drink heavily during pregnancy (32). In one investigation one female child was found to have an underdeveloped and crooked jaw, was unable to extend her elbows, and had dislocated hips. Her fourth and fifth fingers overlapped, she had a heart defect, her ears and genitals were not fully developed, and a tumor was found on her right leg. All of the children studied were less than average size at birth, and none showed any catch-up growth even after hospital admission. The researchers concluded that the deformities were due to alcoholism (or to poisonous agents in the alcohol) and suggested that perhaps as many as 20 percent of alcoholic mothers may give birth to deformed children. Studies done with mice and with men suggest that a man's drinking can also cause damage to his future children (2). It may be that heavy drinking can lead to birth defects by damaging the genes in the male's sperm cells. It is difficult, however, to say positively that alcohol is the primary cause in such cases because conditions closely associated with alcoholism, such as malnutrition, may be involved.

Maternal Diseases

German measles, or **rubella,** is a disease that can be harmful to a fetus. If a woman contracts German measles during the first month of pregnancy, there is a 50 percent chance that her child will be born with severe disorders of the eyes, ears, and heart. By the third month the risk of such disorders is reduced to 10 percent. Since 1969, however, a vaccine that protects women against rubella has been available in the United States.

Syphilis can also be passed on to the fetus from the mother during pregnancy. Such a child may be born deformed or mentally retarded or may begin to show the symptoms of syphilis many years after its birth (66).

One of the most serious complications of pregnancy, if untreated, is a condition called **toxemia** (from the Latin word for "poison"). In fact, much modern prenatal care has come about because of the research done on the cause and treatment of this disease. The cause of toxemia is still unknown, but it seems that a **toxin,** or poison, produced by the body causes the symptoms—high blood pressure, protein in the urine, and the retention of fluids by the body. The disease occurs only in pregnant women, and if it is not treated successfully the result can be death for both the mother and child.

Maternal Diet

One of the most common causes of death of a fetus and of incurable damage to infants is prolonged nutritional deficiency, or **malnutrition,** on the part of pregnant women. Less serious malnutrition has been shown to have harmful effects on the infant's later intellectual performance. A major function of the placenta and umbilical cord is the transfer of nourishment from the mother to the unborn child. If the mother does not have an adequate diet, the fetus will not receive proper nourishment. In one study women living in poverty were given vitamins during pregnancy and while they were nursing their infants (28). Their infants' IQ's averaged eight points higher at age 4 than those of children whose mothers had similar diets but no vitamins. Other studies have concluded that maternal malnutrition during pregnancy can have harmful effects on children in such areas as body weight, rate of growth, number of brain cells at birth and in later life, and learning ability as measured in adulthood (69). Some evidence indicates, however, that the negative effects on learning ability produced by malnutrition are not always permanent.

Spontaneous Abortion

Drugs, disease, radiation, and maternal diet can result in birth defects, but in some cases a **miscarriage,** or spontaneous abortion, occurs before the fetus is mature enough to survive on its own. About 10 or 15 percent of all pregnancies end in miscarriage, with most occurring during the first trimester. A first sign that a woman may miscarry is **vaginal "spotting"** or bleeding. If the symptoms of pregnancy disappear and the woman develops cramps in the area of the pelvis, the fetus may be expelled. About 50 percent of miscarried fetuses are defective in some way (36). About 15 percent of miscarriages are caused by illness, malnutrition, or some physical shock to the pregnant woman, but the reason for the remaining 85 percent of miscarriages is not known.

Even though the development of the fetus is a delicate and complex process during which many things can go wrong, most women who have had good care and an adequate diet during pregnancy give birth to normal, healthy children. During the birth process and in the time immediately before and after birth, however, several more complications may arise that can affect development.

Complications During the Birth Process

Leboyer's concern with keeping the umbilical cord intact during the first few minutes after birth represents a response to one of the most common complications of the birth process—**anoxia,** or a shortage of oxygen. The complete lack of oxygen can result in death, but even a short-term interruption in the oxygen supply can have long-term effects on development. This is because the immature brain of the newborn child is still growing and needs a continuous supply of oxygen. Brief periods of anoxia may have only temporary effects, but severe anoxia can result in permanent physical and mental damage.

There are several possible causes of anoxia during the time surrounding birth. The most obvious one is cutting off the oxygen supply from the mother's bloodstream by cutting the umbilical cord before the infant is able to begin breathing. The infant's oxygen supply can also be limited by severe bleeding or **hemorrhaging** by the mother during labor and delivery. In some instances, severe contractions of the uterus during labor can also cause brief periods of anoxia.

If the anoxia is severe, the brain will be damaged and the result can be **cerebral palsy,** a problem characterized by defective muscle power and coordination. Studies have also shown that brain damage due to anoxia can cause permanent mental problems and may be related to such conditions as schizophrenia (54). Brief periods of anoxia can lead to other mental problems, but the exact effects of anoxia may differ from child to child.

In addition to anoxia, there are other possible complications of the birth process that can damage the child. Pressure in the birth canal, for instance, can cause bone fractures and brain hemorrhages. Such hemorrhages may have temporary or long-lasting effects, depending on the damage they cause in the brain.

The drugs used to control the mother's comfort during childbirth may also affect development. Evidence indicates that these drugs can pass through the placenta and enter the child's bloodstream (43). When this happens, the infant's later activity level and alertness may be affected. One pediatrician (11) suggests that such drugs can interfere with reactions that occur naturally between mother and child during the first few hours after birth (such as touching). If the first contacts between a mother and child are important in the formation of a strong mother-child attachment, as some researchers believe (see Chapter 1), then drugs that interfere with the first contact might be harmful to the mother-child attachment.

Prematurity

One obstacle to the formation of a mother-child relationship immediately after birth is **prematurity.** Normal pregnancies last about 40 weeks. Premature infants are those born three, four, or more weeks ahead of schedule. Because the body temperature of these infants is not yet stable but changes with the temperature of the external environment, they are often kept isolated in incubators where the temperature can be carefully regulated. This reduces the frequency and variety of stimulation they encounter and limits social and physical contact with parents.

About 7 percent of all infants are born premature. Toxemia, maternal infections, and a few other conditions are known to bring about premature births in some cases, but the reasons for most premature births are still unknown.

The immediate problems facing premature infants depend on the degree of immaturity—the less mature the infant, the greater the problems. For one thing, premature infants are sick more often than **full-term infants.** Premature infants tend to get infections and are subject to various respiratory or breathing difficulties. They are more sensitive to maternal medication during the birth process, and feeding is difficult, especially for the smallest "preemies" who sometimes lack the strength to suck at the bottle or breast. Their immature swallowing mechanisms may also cause choking, gagging, or breathing in of liquids.

Because of all these problems, premature infants have a poorer chance of surviving than do full-term infants. If premature infants do survive, there is a chance that they may have developmental problems—lower intelligence, learning difficulties, poor hearing and vision, physical awkwardness or clumsiness, and certain types of cerebral palsy (19). Apparently, the problems associated with prematurity are greater for males than females, though the reasons for this are not understood. Even when they are born with about the same degree of maturity, more males than females fail to survive, and those who do survive show evidence of more severe damage to the brain and nervous system (10). Although prematurity may present special complications during infancy, many premature infants who have had good care do catch up (physically and mentally) with full-term children during the preschool years.

THE INFANT'S FIRST ABILITIES

The glaring lights, loud noises, and other environmental shocks that the Leboyer method attempts to avoid during the birth process are not usually considered to be damaging to the newborn child. But severe shocks (like anoxia) can have serious effects, so it is possible that milder shocks (like bright lights or loud noises) might have subtle or slight effects. These could, as Leboyer suggests, be harmful to development, but because newborns are limited in their ability to communicate, it is not always easy to determine whether or not they have a developmental problem.

Habituation

As helpless as human infants are, they do have a number of abilities and ways of adapting and responding to the environment. Methods have been devised for testing these abilities and for determining developmental progress. One such method has to do with **habituation**—getting used to a stimulus. Failure to notice the background noise of an air conditioner is an example of habituation. In habituation experiments with infants, a **stimulus** (such as a ringing bell) is presented. At first infants will respond by turning their heads or looking in the direction of the sound. Even newborns, shortly after birth, will respond if the stimulus is strong enough. After the stimulus has been presented many times, infants seem to become bored with it and respond less often. Eventually, as habituation takes place, they will not respond at all. Then if the stimulus is changed in some obvious way (a louder bell or one that makes a different sound), the original response will usually reappear. In a sense, this is the infant's way of saying yes or no—"Yes, I recognize that this is a different sound," or "No, I cannot tell the difference between these sounds." An infant that does not respond may have a problem. Classical and operant conditioning experiments (see Chapter 1) are also used to test the ability of infants to learn, as will be seen later in this chapter. Learning is more fully examined in Chapter 6.

Reflexes

The presence or absence of certain inborn reflexes, such as sucking and rooting, can also be used as a test of development. With the proper stimulation, these reflexes can be produced in healthy newborns. Infants will exhibit the **sucking reflex** if the inside of their mouths are touched. Even sleepy infants will begin to suck if the soft palate (the fleshy rear part of the roof of the mouth) is stimulated. When they are awake and hungry, infants will turn their mouths toward the source of a stroke on the cheek. This is the **rooting reflex.** It helps infants locate food, even when their eyes are closed and even before they have learned that the nipple is the source of milk. Human infants will also reflexively keep their air passages clear. They twist their heads or wave their arms across their face in an attempt to remove an object that has been placed over their nose or mouth. This **antismothering reflex** is so efficient that it is unlikely that infants will smother in their bedding or clothing.

The sucking, rooting, and antismothering reflexes have obvious survival value. Other reflexes seem less related to survival, but may have been important earlier in the evolution of the species. The **Moro** and **grasp reflexes,** for example, seem to protect infants from falling. In the Moro response, a loud noise or sudden change of position, especially one related to falling, results in reflexive movements of the arms and legs. They move outward, upward, and then inward, while the hands open and then close tightly in a clenched fist. In the grasp reflex, pressure on the palms results in a fist so tight that newborns can be lifted and supported by their own grasp. These reflexes are very important to young monkeys, who must hold on to their mothers as they move about in the trees.

The **Babinski reflex** (named for the French scientist who first described it) does not seem to have any survival value, but can be used to test an infant's nervous system. The Babinski response is stimulated by lightly stroking the sole of the foot. In infants younger than eight months of age this results in an upward extension of the toes, especially the big toe. It is commonly used to test whether the motor area of the brain is functioning properly.

Some reflexes last throughout life, while others, like the Babinski, disappear as infants mature. With continued development, nonreflexive behaviors appear that can be used as measures of development. By the end of the first

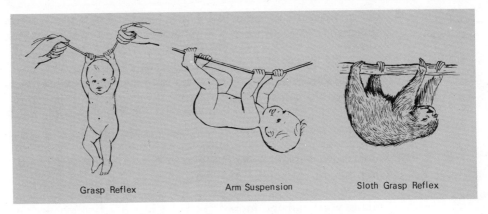

| Grasp Reflex | Arm Suspension | Sloth Grasp Reflex |

The grasp reflex in a human infant is similar to that of young jungle mammals.

year, researchers can examine such responses as smiling, vocalization, eye movement, and various types of eye-hand coordination, as well as the developing perceptual, cognitive, and social-emotional abilities of infants.

PERCEPTUAL ABILITIES OF INFANTS

Unlike the young of many other species, human infants are almost completely helpless. They can survive only if others provide for them. Even in this helplessness, however, remarkable adaptability can be seen. Behavior patterns are not rigidly set. Instead, human infants are flexible and capable of adapting to a wide variety of environments. But infants do more than simply respond to environmental stimuli; their interactions with the environment are complex rather than one-way. Infants respond to all sorts of stimuli (sights, sounds, smells, and so on), and their responses result in changes in the environment. If parents or caretakers are pleased by an infant's responses, they are likely to provide more of the same type of stimuli. If caretakers are displeased by the responses, an attempt may be made to remove or reduce the stimuli causing the displeasure. Through their own behavior, even at an early age, infants have considerable success at getting more of what they want and less of what they don't want. Very tiny babies, for example, can control their food intake by stopping sucking, by dropping off to sleep at the breast or bottle, by sucking vigorously, or by crying to signal that they are hungry. As they grow older, their control of the environment becomes even greater, partly because they begin, in a primitive way, to solve problems, such as reaching for or moving toward an object that they want. The steadily increasing control of their own bodies aids infants in the process of selecting stimuli. They are eventually able to roll from side to side to seek or avoid a stimulus. They can "shift scenes" by rolling from their stomachs to their backs, or vice versa. Sitting up, creeping, standing, and walking enable them more and more to obtain stimuli they want or avoid those they dislike or are tired of. (Motor development and the ability to control the body are discussed in Chapter 5.)

Obviously, infants cannot react to the environment or act on it in any meaningful manner if they are not aware of it. This awareness of the environment comes through the **sense organs.** At the beginning of life, sense organs receive stimulation, and infants respond in rather simple, almost automatic ways. Light rays, for example, strike the eyes and are transmitted to the appropriate areas of the nervous system and brain. The reaction is simple: in bright light the **pupils** (the dark spots at the center of the eyes) contract or close down and shut out some of the stimulation; in dim light the pupils dilate or expand and more light is let in. Shortly after birth infants will blink as stimuli approach their eyes rapidly. Later, more complex responses are made to visual stimuli. Meaning is gradually added to visual stimuli (and all others). A three-sided figure is eventually distinguished from a circle and labeled as a triangle. Certain faces will eventually become "Mommy" and "Daddy." Visual clues will be used to recognize "a place I may fall off of," and so on.

All of this—awareness of stimuli, attention to them, and attachment of at least some meaning to them—is known as **perception.**

In the simplest terms, it can be said that people function well or poorly, succeed or fail, depending on the way they manage their behavior in terms of their perception of themselves and the world around them, and on the way their perceptions fit in with those of the people among whom they live.

Perception and all that it involves begins with the infant's awareness of the environment. The infant's senses and all of the stimuli the senses react to are basic to everything that happens, from infancy through adulthood.

Vision

From birth infants are capable of receiving and reacting to stimulation of their senses, and **vision** is one of the most important of the senses. At birth all of the major features of the senses are present, though they are only half as large as they will be at maturity, and some features are less well developed than others. This means that infants, until they are about 1 year old, see the world differently than adults do. Just exactly what they see is not completely known, but clues have been found by observing infants' reactions to various visual stimuli.

One stimulus that brings about an immediate reaction is a sudden increase in brightness. When this happens, most infants are startled. They close their eyes and throw back their heads. In general, very young infants seem to be most comfortable in dim light, as Leboyer suggests. One reason is that the eyes of infants react rather slowly to changes in light during the first few days of life. The pupils, as was mentioned earlier, control the amount of light that enters the eyes by opening and closing. This is a reflexive action, but it works slowly during the first days of life. Until it is fully developed, children tend to have trouble adjusting to bright lights.

Although infants do not seem to like brightly lighted rooms, they can **fixate** on (stare at) a light source. Within the first few hours of life infants can usually fixate at least one eye on a light source. By the second or third day they show the ability to fixate both eyes on a light. Shortly after birth infants also respond to moving objects within their visual field. This can be seen as infants follow or track moving objects with their eyes. Most can do this within 96 hours of birth (27). **Tracking** is made possible by the six muscles that control each eye. These muscles enable the eye to move up and down, sideways, and in a circular pattern. But at first the two eyes do not always move in the same direction at the same time. One eye may look upward or outward, while the other is looking downward. By the third month, however, better muscle control has developed and both eyes begin to track in the same direction at the same time (42).

Reception of and reaction to environmental stimuli is influenced by the parts of the environment that have special appeal for the infant. In general, infants tend to look longer at complex patterns. They even seem to prefer certain patterns over others. As they get older, they seem to prefer more complex patterns (12, 65). This evidence is not completely clear, because some researchers have found that a **preference for complexity** does not increase with age but is already present in the newborn (30). In either case, the preference for complexity would appear to be a good thing: The more complex the stimuli investigated (looked at in this case), the richer the experience and the more to be learned.

There is clear evidence that infants do have a preference that increases with age for new and different stimuli and for representations of the human face (34). Very young infants are as likely to smile at a circle containing two dots as at a real human face with two eyes or to fixate on a face with scrambled instead of normal features (20). Up to the age of 3 months or so, a single facial feature will usually get a child to smile as easily as an entire face will, but by 5 or 6 months, the whole face must be presented before the infant will smile at it (8). From this evidence it seems that ability to recognize the human face is not inborn but has to be learned through experience.

Visual perception of depth is important in several ways. If infants have not yet developed **depth perception,** they cannot manage the reaching and manipulating behavior that is necessary for them to learn about the world around them. One study showed that infants prefer to fixate on three-dimensional figures of heads rather than on flat or two-dimensional pictures of heads (19). This suggests that infants can perceive depth or distance. An experiment performed by Eleanore Gibson made it quite obvious that by at least 6 months infants have an understanding of depth (18). Gibson's experiment used what is now known as a **visual cliff.** It consisted of a flat center board with a solid surface on one side and a drop off, or "cliff," on the other side. Infants old enough to crawl (6 months and older) were placed on the center board and then called by their mothers from different sides of the board. The infants could see over the "cliff," but they could not fall because a flat piece of glass extended out from the center board.

When mothers called from the solid side of the center board, the infants crawled toward them. When the mothers called from the "cliff" side, the infants would not move out on the glass surface. The children could feel the solid glass surface, but they could also see the "cliff." Apparently, the infants were able to understand or perceive the height and would not crawl over the edge.

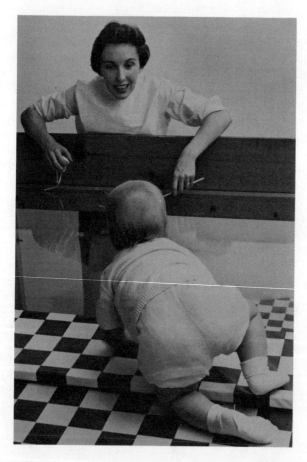

This infant will not cross the "deep" side of the visual cliff.

Children younger than 6 months of age did not take part in the visual cliff experiment because they could not crawl, but there is evidence that even newborns may have depth perception. Newborn animals able to crawl were tested on the visual cliff, and they refused to crawl out on the glass. Gibson believes that development of depth perception, at least of this self-protective sort (keeping oneself from falling off things), does not depend on having had experiences in stepping down, climbing up, or walking into things. But as anyone who has ever cared for infants knows, their depth perception is by no means accurate enough to keep them from falling off things. One of the parent's most constant jobs is to keep infants from doing exactly that.

Scientists as well as parents have long wondered what the world really looks like to infants. No one can answer this question directly, of course, since infants are not able to describe their visual world. Indirect evidence about a child's first visual experiences with the world is available. It comes from observations and reports of people who, after a lifetime of blindness, have had their sight suddenly restored (29). These newly sighted people cannot tell cubes from squares nor squares from triangles without handling them and checking and rechecking their visual images with their familiar sense of touch. While in the hospital following surgery, some learned color names that they remembered 11 months later, whereas they forgot the names of geometric forms. They were shown an egg, a potato, and a cube of sugar until they could name them promptly; but when these objects were put into colored light, they were not recognized. A cube of sugar could be named easily when placed on a table or in another person's hand, but not when hung by a thread with a changed background.

For normal older children and adults, the perception of squares, cubes, circles, and so forth is so prompt that it seems to be almost automatic or inborn. This does not seem to be the case, as the observation of formerly blind individuals suggest. Recognition of even very common figures seems to be the result of much perceptual learning that comes through interaction with the environment. During the four months following early infancy, visual perception and response become increasingly acute or accurate, and enormous amounts of learning occur. Six-month-old children can usually distinguish between their mothers and fathers, between familiar and strange adults, and between expressions of approval and disapproval. They form clear images, reach for things, and grasp them with moderate accuracy. They definitely possess the ability to distinguish colors, and their judgment of distances is fair, although they often make efforts to reach things outside their grasp. Six-month-olds have usually outgrown the tendency to be least active in the light and most active in the dark. They recognize certain toys as favorites and often show a degree of alarm when placed in strange situations. In general, by 6 months of age, infants have become exceedingly complex visual receptors and reactors. Observations of the development of infants in their first year suggests that they are attempting to become acquainted with all of their environment through all of their senses: they poke, fondle, clutch, taste, rub, smell, manipulate with both hands and feet, stare long and quietly, observe things far away and near. It is as though they were trying to coordinate each sense with every other as well as with all the objects (including people and animals) they can sense. Piaget, as will be seen in Chapter 7, offers an interesting analysis of this behavior.

Hearing

Unlike the eye, the human ear is believed to be completely ready to work at birth—and even before, in the womb. **Sound energy** (movement or vibrations in the air) enters the **ear canal** and strikes the **eardrum.** This, in turn, activates three small bones in the **middle ear** which pass on the vibrations to the **inner ear.** There, the vibrations stimulate the endings of nerve fibers that lead to the brain.

The infant ear may be fully developed, but it is smaller than an adult ear, a fact that has several important consequences. The **Eustachian tube,** for example, connects the air-filled middle ear to the upper part of the throat and helps equalize air pressure between the ear canal and the middle ear by opening and closing (the familiar "popping" sensation experienced as air pressure changes in a rapidly ascending or descending elevator). The Eustachian tube also helps drain liquids from the middle ear to the throat, but because infections can travel from the throat to the middle ear through the Eustachian tube, infants are more likely than adults to get ear infections. The Eustachian tube is shorter in infants than in adults, so infections have a shorter distance to travel in infants. Such infections can cause temporary hearing loss and, if untreated, permanent damage.

Not only is the Eustachian tube shorter in infants, the ear canal is shorter

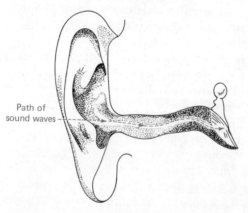

Path of
sound waves

The outer ear.

than that of adults and therefore reacts differently to sound vibrations. This means that infants hear slightly different sounds than adults do. In general, infants seem to respond best to low-frequency or low-pitched sounds like a human whisper (as opposed to a high-pitched sound like a shrill whistle), while high-frequency noises seem to shock them and cause distress reactions (16). The common use of the lullaby may be based on the infant's preference for low-pitched sounds.

Until the 1930s, it was generally believed that newborns could not hear at all. This may be because for the first few days or so, fluid in the ear canal (from the amniotic sac) sometimes interferes slightly with hearing. But even with this interference, researchers have found that infants are nearly as sensitive to loudness as adults are (17). The reactions of infants to sounds are not always easy to see, but changes in heart rate, breathing rate, and general body movements indicate hearing ability. Habituation experiments show this, as discussed earlier. In one study changes in newborns' breathing pattern and leg movements were seen when there was a shift from a higher- to a lower-pitched sound (41).

The **ability to determine the location of a sound source** is also seen in infants and is probably as important as the ability to fixate or track with the eyes. Even while in the delivery room, infants will look in the correct direction in response to a sound coming from the left or right (70). They probably cannot, however, locate the exact position of a sound source. Sound from directly in front of a person hits both ears at the same time. Sound from the right side hits the right ear first. The difference in time between when a sound enters the two ears gives the brain a clue to the exact direction from which the sound is coming. Because the ears of infants are closer together than those of adults, the time difference is shorter. This means that infants have less of a clue to work with in detecting the location of a sound source. With growth and experience, however, the ability to locate sounds improves.

By the end of the third month, infants are usually able to locate quiet sounds like a human whisper (6). By the sixth month, the ability to locate sounds is well established (14), and from then on infants will look most frequently in the direction of sounds that are meaningful to them. The wild boy of Aveyron (Chapter 3) had little experience with human voices and no interest in them, so he paid no attention to human voices when he was first captured. But for most infants **the sound of human speech** is the most meaningful sound in their environment. From the earliest days of their lives, infants pay more attention to human speech than they do to other sounds. This phenomenon is related to the way they eventually learn a language, as will be seen in Chapter 8.

Films of young infants (some only 12 hours old) show that they are aware of adult speech patterns (15). When the films are slowed down, it can be seen that the movements of infants listening to adult speech correspond exactly to the rhythm of the speech. They appear to be almost dancing to the pattern of the adult speech. If the child is in motion before the talking starts, its movements soon lock into the speech sound. Head, elbows, shoulders, feet, hips, and toes all pick up the rhythm. Infants seem to follow the rhythm of any human language (English or Chinese) but not of disconnected or meaningless sounds. By getting in rhythm with the speech patterns of a particular culture, it seems that infants are practicing (millions of times) the form and structure of the language they will eventually learn.

Hearing human speech is so important to infants that they will work for it. In one experiment, 1-year-old children were allowed to hear nursery songs if they would flip certain switches (67). These infants worked the switches up to 5,000 seconds a day. As infants grow older, they become more selective. For example, they will work harder to hear a brightly inflected voice (one that changes pitch) or a recording that changes its message often than they will to hear a dull, flat voice or a recording that says the same thing over and over. As with vision, it seems that infants prefer complex and changing experiences.

By the end of the first half year, infants react with pleasure to the parental voice; can apparently distinguish scolding or threatening sounds from comforting or loving and protective sounds; frequently show pleasure in music; demonstrate by moving their heads that they can follow a sound stimulus, such as a ticking watch; may react to street noises, such as fire sirens or dogs barking; and, in general, have developed a way of responding to sound similar to an adult's.

Taste and Smell   Compared with vision and hearing, little is known about the development of the chemical senses, **taste** and **smell.** These senses are known as **chemical senses** because the taste and smell receptors react to chemical stimuli in the environment. The chemical senses are important, but perhaps not as important as they may have been earlier in human evolution. When people lived off the land, they had to know what to eat and what to avoid. Sweet-tasting substances in nature are usually nutritious, bitter-tasting substances are often poisonous. Infants and adults still prefer sweet over bitter.

A good sense of smell was also necessary to survival. It helped hunters track down animals, and it probably helped to warn against approaching enemies. The smell of smoke still serves to warn people of fire, and there is evidence that 6-week-old infants can identify their own mothers by their odor (56).

From birth the infant appears to be well supplied with **taste receptors** on the tongue (37). In fact, in children the taste receptors are occasionally found in other parts of the mouth as well, but these "extra" receptors disappear by adulthood. The receptor cells are contained in about 10,000 **taste buds,** which are located on small projections on the tongue. Contrary to earlier belief, the individual cells are not specialized to react to one of the four basic taste qualities (**sweet, salty, bitter,** and **sour**). Instead, they are sensitive to chemicals in general, and the individual cells possess varying degrees of sensitivity to tastes included in two or more of the four basic categories.

Infants prefer sweet tastes, as do older children, adults, and most animal species. Within days of birth they will increase their sucking responses more for sugar solutions than for solutions with sour or salt tastes. Sour solutions are the second most preferred; salty, the third; bitter solutions are actively avoided. From their responses to different tastes, it seems clear that newborns are sensitive to taste, perhaps more so than at any other time in life.

In humans the sensation of smell is produced by molecules moving through the air and interacting with receptor cells in the uppermost section of the **nostrils.** The receptors are so highly sensitive and numerous—in the tens of millions—that even some solid substances can be detected by smell. **Smell receptors,** however, adapt quickly so that people are not constantly aware of odors in the environment.

The smell receptors are not activated unless they are actually in contact with the molecular or chemical stimuli; therefore air must flow through the nostrils for stimulation to occur. For this reason the sense of smell is more efficient when an individual sniffs in the air. Air breathed in normally does not always reach the receptors, but sniffing changes the usual airflow and sends currents of air upward into the region of the smell receptors. Babies breathe through the nose from birth, thus chemical stimuli are constantly within close range of the receptor cells. In addition, the breathing pattern of newborns is rather irregular, so that changing air currents are quite likely to occur.

Babies in the first few weeks of life show avoidance of certain foods. Whether this is due to the taste, smell, or texture of the food is not known, but each of the three factors probably enters into the reaction. Many foods will be rejected at the first feeding, apparently without prior learning.

The sense of taste is central in the adjustment of the older child and the adult, but taste is so interwoven with the sense of smell and food texture that it is difficult to say just which sense is associated with later food preferences or rejections. Studies of adults suggest a relationship between good personal adjustment and lack of food dislikes: people who have few dislikes for certain reasonably common and basic foods show better personal adjustment than those with many food dislikes. Such a finding, of course, holds for groups but not necessarily for any given individual. Since food is essential to life, and since the senses of taste and smell are closely related to eating, it is probably important to build up predominately pleasant associations with these senses and with the entire process of eating.

The Skin Senses The **skin senses** provide information about the external environment in direct contact with the surface of the body. The sensations aroused by **cutaneous** or, skin, stimulation are **pressure, pain, heat,** and **cold.** The skin receptors do not appear to be as specialized as was once thought. In fact, there is no clear evidence linking specific structures to temperature sensitivity, nor have receptors for pain been identified. More is known about **tactile,** or touch, **receptors.** Infants are responsive to **tactile stimulation** very early in life, as is seen by the Babinski, rooting, and grasping reflexes. Apparently, sensitivity to touch increases during the first few days following birth. Infants are relatively insensitive to pain at birth, but sensitivity increases rapidly, judging from experiments that showed increased reactions over the first five days to pinpricks and to mild electric shock (59).

Temperature changes also cause reactions in newborns. Several reflexes are triggered by rapid changes in temperature, including a recoiling of the head in response to cold or warm stimulation to the forehead (37). In addition, general activity level tends to change in response to the surrounding temperature. Newborns are more active in cooler environments and less active in warmer ones (53).

The young infant's sensitivity to pain and temperature have obvious survival value. Their early tactile sensitivity plays an important developmental role. The sense of touch provides young infants with much of their information about the world. As they grow older, touch is an important and necessary part of grasping and manipulating. Bodily contact with the mother or caretaker is believed to be necessary for a sense of trust or security to develop (18). Indeed, in extreme cases, a lack of contact can lead to retardation of mental, emotional, and physical development—and perhaps even to death, as will be seen later in this chapter.

The Body Senses An awareness of the body is necessary in all areas of development. Infants must know where the various parts of the body are and how they move if they are to control their posture and movements. Obviously, this awareness is necessary for the development of the most basic motor abilities, such as balance and muscular coordination. Even speech would be impossible if the child received no information about the relative positions of the tongue and lips. Two sensing systems provide this information.

The **vestibular** system conveys information about spatial movement and the spatial orientation of the body as a whole, including balance. Its receptors are in a small area, or **vestibule,** of the inner ear. The **kinesthetic** system also provides information about movement, including the movement of individual body structures. Its receptors are located in the muscles, joints, tendons, and perhaps around the blood vessels.

From a practical standpoint, the effects of movement are difficult to separate from other forms of stimulation. For example, rocking, a soothing technique in most cultures, provides not only movement stimulation but skin stimulation (including touch and warmth). In one study (39) newborns were exposed to tactile stimulation and movement for 30-second periods. It was found that crying could be reduced or stopped by both types of stimulation, but that motion had a more powerful effect.

Some forms of movement have been shown to be more effective than others in soothing infants. Rocking infants upward and downward (in a mechanically driven bassinet) is more effective than side-to-side motion (50). The more vigorous the rocking, the greater its effectiveness as a soother of infants (51). These studies suggest that movement may foster mother-infant attachment because it provides the mother with a method for soothing her infant promptly and effectively. In this manner, stimulation from movement during early infancy may contribute to the infant's social development. Also, contact comfort resulting from movement, as well as touch, may contribute to the development of trust and security, as was seen with Harlow's monkeys in Chapter 3 and as some research with humans suggests (18).

MENTAL ABILITIES OF INFANTS

It may appear at first glance that during the first two years of life infants do little more than eat, sleep, cry, and respond almost automatically or reflexively to stimuli in the environment. While the abilities of infants are limited during this period, many things are happening and much development is taking place that lays the foundation for later abilities. In addition to perceptual abilities, the first signs of learning, language, and cognitive abilities are all evident during the first two years of life.

Attention

In order to learn about the environment, infants must be able to direct their sensory systems toward selected portions of the environment. Without this ability to select stimuli, infants would be hopelessly flooded with information. Perception, learning, and functioning on any level would be impossible without the ability to focus on limited segments of the environment.

Apparently the human organism has a built-in tendency to scan the environment selectively. Even premature infants in the newborn nursery are capable of giving simple "orienting responses" to visual and auditory stimulation (44, 58). These **orienting responses,** as they are usually defined, consist of several things: dilation of the pupils; changes in respiration, heart rate, and activity level; and orientation, or turning of the head, toward the source of stimulation.

Such orienting responses are considered to be the first signs of **attention,** if not a necessary part of it. Orienting is brought about by changes in the quality or intensity of stimulation. Its purpose is to heighten the organism's sensitivity to changing conditions in the environment—in effect, it is a "What's-going-on?" response.

Although orientation is seen in newborns, the orienting response occurs only rarely during the first few weeks of life, and even then in an undeveloped form. It is gradually refined, however, as the infant matures. For example, 16-week-old infants are more likely than 6-week-old infants to show the orienting response (5).

Much of what is known about attention in infancy has come from studies of attentiveness to visual events. In these studies visual fixation (orientation of the head and eyes toward a picture or some other visual stimulus) is usually seen as attention. The usual method in such studies involves presenting two different visual patterns to the infant. Using a television or movie camera, or viewing through a peephole, the investigator records the infant's fixation—for example, how long the infant fixates on or stares at each of the two targets. In general, research suggests that very young infants pay attention to change in the environment. Babies are much more likely to respond to a blinking light than to a steadily shining light, or to a sound presented intermittently rather than continuously. Later, experience plays a major role in influencing the direction of the infant's attention. As infants gain experience with events in their environment, they build up mental representations of them called **schemas.** A schema is a memory pattern that is the basis for recognizing and recalling stored information. Without a schema or some sort of mental pattern, for example, infants would not recognize faces. The actual structure of a schema has never been fully explained, but the concept of the schema has proved useful in explaining how infants distribute their attention.

Toward the end of the second month, attention to a particular stimulus depends upon an infant's experience with that stimulus and its schema. If the

Even newborn infants show orienting responses to outside stimulation.

stimulus is somewhat different from the schema, infants will pay more attention to it than if it is exactly the same as or completely different from the schema. In other words, a stimulus is not attractive to infants if it is either too complicated or unusual for them to understand or if it is too simple or dull.

Attention to differences seems to be the major factor in attention until the end of the first year. At this point infants begin to interpret stimulus events, a step beyond merely recognizing them. In effect they form hypotheses to help in their interpretations. Five-year-olds, for example, will hypothesize that their mother has had a shower when they see her in a bathrobe and shower cap. At the age of 8 or 9 months an infant will merely notice her changed appearance but not try to explain it.

Habituation

The newborn baby's tendency to pay attention to change is clearly useful, because changing stimuli are those most likely to contain new information at any given moment. Such a tendency would be completely useless, however, if children were not able to turn off their attention to some stimuli. Background noises, for example, would interrupt concentration if they could not be ignored or filtered out. One process through which humans filter out insignificant stimulation is habituation. As mentioned earlier, habituation in infants is seen in their responses to repeated, unchanging stimulation—specifically, fewer and fewer responses are made until they cease altogether. (Decrease in response to stimulation can also occur because of fatigue—either general fatigue or fatigue of a specific sense receptor. This, however, represents a loss of ability to respond, not the process of habituation.)

Like attention, habituation improves with age. Younger infants tend to show less habituation to repeated stimulation than older infants. In other words, the more mature infants are, the more quickly they stop responding to an unchanging stimulus. It is as if the older infants have a better memory and/or become bored more easily.

Language Ability

Although infants usually utter no meaningful words before their first birthday, they make sounds from birth onward. At first, newborns engage mostly in reflexive crying. At about 6 weeks of age they begin to engage in vocal play—cooing, gurgling, and babbling—apparently for the fun of it. At 5 or 6 months of age, as visual fixation and grasping abilities become established, they enter a stage called **lalling.** At this time they seem to begin to understand the relationship between sounds they make and the noises they hear. They echo back the sounds they make. They also begin to use sounds to communicate—to attract attention and to express desires. At 9 or 10 months the baby's sounds begin to resemble adult speech, and by that time they also imitate sounds made by others. True speech is usually produced between 12 and 18 months. Language development will be described more fully in Chapter 8.

Infantile cognition, the processes through which infants acquire knowledge and understanding of their environment, has received a great deal of attention in recent years because of Piaget's work (see Chapter 1). According to Piaget, infants do not engage in true **ideation,** what can be called thinking, until about the age of 24 months. Before that time the infant's behavior reflects a kind of sensorimotor intelligence in which they appear to be sensing-acting organisms with little or no mental activity taking place between sensing and acting. In other words, they simply respond to stimuli. Nonetheless, much takes place intellectually during the first 18 months of life—for example, the growing understanding of **object permanence,** the fact that things out of sight do not necessarily cease to exist. Crude notions of **what causes things to happen** as well as early **concepts of time** develop during this period. In addition, infants learn **spatial relationships** and acquire **means-end behaviors:** that is, they learn responses that will help them reach desired goals. Piaget's sensorimotor stages and cognitive development are discussed in Chapter 7.

Most of the research dealing with **learning** in infants has been done in the laboratory and has involved classical conditioning and operant conditioning (see Chapter 1). Although conditioning may be too limited a process to explain the full variety of learning that takes place in infants (33), demonstrations of conditioning in newborn children suggests that learning is possible throughout life. Clearly, newborn infants possess at least some ability to learn or to change their behavior as a result of experience.

The two most common responses in studies of early conditioning have been head-turning and sucking. In one study, 30 percent of the 2- to 4-day old infants tested turned their heads to the side on which their cheek was stroked (60). The percentage of infants who turned was increased, however, to more than 80 percent by rewarding the babies for head-turning with a sweet-tasting solution. This indicates that learning has taken place because the increase was greater than might be expected by chance and greater than that found in a control group exposed to the same procedure, except that reinforcement did not follow head-turning.

In the same series of studies the researchers found evidence of discrimination learning in newborns. Head turns preceded by a buzzer (the positive stimulus) were reinforced with the sweet solution, but those preceded by a tone (the negative stimulus) were not reinforced. During the first part of the experiment the infants showed that they had learned to respond to the positive stimulus and not to the negative one. After 60 trials, the cues were reversed: the tone became the positive stimulus and the buzzer the negative stimulus. Once again, head-turning responses to the positive stimulus exceeded responses to the negative stimulus. Clearly the newborns had learned which cues signaled a reward. The infant's sucking response has also been modified through conditioning, and a great many studies have demonstrated learning ability during the first weeks of life. Other types of learning, as well as learning in older children, are described in Chapter 6.

SOCIAL-EMOTIONAL ABILITIES IN INFANTS

By the end of the child's first year, a more or less permanent relationship has usually been formed with the mother. This relationship is known as an **attachment.** Although it seems obvious that infants should become attached to the person who provides their care, the conditions that lead to this attachment are not completely understood. There is agreement, however, that the formation of an attachment to the mother represents the beginning of the child's social life.

According to Freudian theory, the infant's attachment to the mother is believed to be related to her role in feeding and her provision of gratification through the opportunity to suck. While the relationship to the mother is focused first on her breast, it extends to include her whole person. Indeed, the child's efforts to sustain the attachment relationship have been called **oral dependence** (see Chapter 1).

Learning theorists have discribed the development of attachments in a somewhat different manner. Specifically, stimulation and reinforcement occurring between a mother and her baby are believed to be responsible for attachment. From birth onward, the infant gives signals (cries, for example)

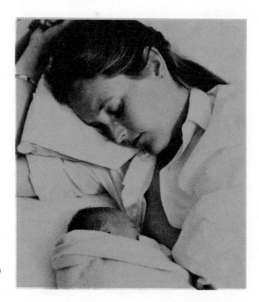

The infant's relationship to the mother is focused first on her breast, and extends to include her whole person.

which bring the mother nearer and which result in care-giving by the mother. This care-giving provides the infant with necessary reinforcers such as food and water, temperature regulation, and tactile stimulation. By her presentation of such reinforcers, the mother becomes a reinforcing stimulus, and simultaneously her behavior increases the regularity with which the child uses attachment signals.

Each mother and infant develop their own characteristic ways of interacting. Some mothers talk a great deal to their infants; some stroke their infants with great regularity; some poke and stimulate their babies more than others. Individual differences in the nature of the infant's attachments are presumed to be the result of these differences in the nature of mother-infant interaction.

Psychologist John Bowlby has described mother-child attachment in terms of various psychological and evolutionary factors (9). According to his theory, attachment development passes through four phases: (1) the first two or three months of life, a period during which the infants show a genetically preprogrammed tendency to direct their attention and certain other behaviors (smiling, for example) to human beings; (2) the second quarter of the first year, a period during which infants begin to focus their responses on one figure (usually the mother); (3) the third quarter of the first year, during which infants intensify their attachment and learn to seek proximity (nearness) with the mother by crawling or moving toward her as well as by means of signals; (4) finally, the last quarter of the first year, a period during which the various aspects of attachment—visual, clinging, following, babbling, and crying—begin to operate as a "feedback system," and the relationship between mother and child can be described as a "partnership."

The infant's goal in this feedback system is proximity to mother, a goal which is believed to be established through evolutionary processes. Attachments serve to protect infants from dangerous predators, and they increase the chance of survival by increasing the availability of food and the opportunity to learn from the mother. Once this system is fully developed, child and mother act as partners. In some circumstances both child and mother realize that they should stay close; in others one or both partners invite separation. In all cases, however, the interaction is mutually regulated.

Research has confirmed the general outline of attachment development suggested by Bowlby's theory. For example, preferences for social stimulation in contrast to nonsocial stimulation are apparent among babies between 2 and 4 months of age. These preferences, however, do not depend on the identity of the social object. Young babies are as happy to look at unfamiliar caretakers as they are to look at their mothers. Somewhere between 6 and 9 months of age, most babies begin to manifest a specific attachment. At about this time separation from the mother has a greater impact on the infant than separation from other persons (57), and smiling and physical contact-seeking are directed more to the mother than to strangers. There may be individual differences in the timing of attachments, but the third quarter of the first year seems to be the time during which this event occurs for most babies.

Other changes in social behavior occur at this same time. **Fear of strangers,** although not seen in all babies, occurs a month or so later than the first signs of specific attachments. Such fears increase gradually from 4½ to 12½ months of age (46). Young infants, when approached by a stranger, reach out, smile, and coo. Older infants, however, frown, cry, and turn away.

The nature of the situation makes a definite difference in the interaction of young infants with both strangers and familiar persons. Being put down by the mother often results in crying among younger babies, but not among older infants. In contrast, being left alone in a room, being left with others, or being left in a carriage outside the house brings about increasingly frequent protest throughout the first year of life (57). It has also been shown that when the mother sits quietly in an empty room with her 10-month-old infant by her side, the baby will soon begin to fuss and pull at the mother. In contrast, the presence of a single attractive toy (for example, a plastic telephone) will usually interest the child and result in decreased interaction with the mother.

The intensity of a child's fear of strangers is partly influenced by the infant's nearness to the mother. Fearfulness is seen much less frequently when the infant is held by the mother than when the baby is seated on the floor or held by a stranger (1). It has also been reported that the entrance of a stranger into a room causes 1-year-old children to stay nearer their mothers than they otherwise would and reduces their exploratory activity (1). Thus, there is a kind of dual relation between fear and attachment: Fear intensifies attachment activity, and contact with the mother reduces the child's fear. Overall, the mother's proximity functions as a "secure base" for the infant, as was seen with Harlow's monkeys (Chapter 3).

Hypotheses suggesting that methods of feeding and weaning are important to mother-child attachment have not, in general, been supported by research, as seen in Chapter 3. On the other hand, it has been shown that the amount of sensory stimulation that mothers provide to their babies is related to the intensity or closeness of the mother-child attachment. In fact, both the amount of interaction between a mother and her infant and the speed of her responses to distress signals were found to be greater in instances of intense attachment than in instances of less intense attachment (57). From these and other studies it seems that maternal stimulation contributes to the formation of specific attachments, but it may also be that some infants are particularly good at bringing forth affectionate behavior from their mothers. In all likelihood, then, the relation between maternal stimulation and attachment development works two ways: individual differences in maternal behavior may result in individual differences in infant attachment, but at the same time variations in the infant's attachment behavior may be responsible for variations in the caretaking activity of mothers (1).

INDIVIDUAL DIFFERENCES IN INFANCY

Newborn infants may all seem to be pretty much alike, and they all develop along the same general lines, but no two are ever exactly alike. Those who have genetic damage, those who were harmed during pregnancy or the birth process, and those who have been exposed to a severely disadvantaged environment may be dramatically different in abilities and development. Even among normally developing infants, however, there are subtle and sometimes obvious differences in temperament, reaction to stimulation, activity level as well as in a number of other physical and psychological characteristics. These differences, which are both inherited and acquired, affect the course of development and make each infant a distinct individual.

Behavioral differences among infants are usually measured by **developmental tests.** Although these infancy tests are useful in screening for developmental problems, they are not particularly useful for predicting later intelligence or abilities, except in cases where severe abnormalities exist. For infants in the normal or superior range, scores on developmental tests given during infancy have very little relationship to later abilities (3). In fact, before the age of 12 months, the social and economic status of the child's parents is better at predicting a child's future abilities than are developmental tests. In any case, infancy tests measure sensorimotor and perceptual abilities, while intelligence tests for older children and adults emphasize language abilities. The score from an infancy developmental test is usually called a **DQ,** or a **developmental quotient** (as opposed to IQ, or intelligence quotient). The relationship between DQ and IQ is discussed further in Chapter 9.

Sex Differences

Perhaps the most obvious difference among infants is the sexual one. This difference begins at conception when the father contributes either an X (female) or Y chromosome, but the difference does not really begin to show up until about the eighth week of fetal life (45). Before that every fetus develops as if it were going to be a female. After the seventh or eighth week the effect of the Y chromosome can be seen. If the Y chromosome is present, it causes the production of **male hormones,** the body chemicals that control sexual development. These hormones cause the fetus to begin developing male sex organs. If the male hormones are not present, the fetus will continue to develop as a female. Experiments with animals have shown that even an XY (male) fetus will develop the physical appearance of a female if, just after conception, the pregnant mother is given drugs that make the male hormone inactive (49).

Hormonal influences have an immediate effect on development. Although newborn males are larger and stronger than females in some respects, they are less mature at birth and less likely to survive. Males, more than females, suffer from anoxia and infections. More male fetuses fail to survive through pregnancy; more die during birth; and, in the United States, almost one third more males than females die during the first year. The fact that more males than females are conceived helps to keep the male and female populations about equal.

It is obvious that males and females are different physically, but hormones don't tell the whole story. From the moment of birth **environmental differences** begin to play an important role in development. "It's a boy!" or "It's a girl!" say the excited parents, and from then on, the newborn child will usually be treated in a certain way because of its gender. This treatment, along with physical differences caused by hormones, has a great deal to do with infant development and behavior.

It is not known whether hormones are more or less important than social treatment in the development of infant behavior, but both factors are involved. One study has shown how physical characteristics (possibly due to hormonal differences) can affect the way parents treat their infants (47). Thirty first-born infants and their mothers were observed. By the time the infants were 3 weeks old it could be seen that males and females were being cared for and

Mothers of male babies at first tend to be more attentive to their infant's needs because the males place more demands on them. Less attention is given when it is found to have little effect on infant behavior.

treated differently. The mothers of males were much more involved with their infants—holding them more, attending to them, petting and touching them, and looking at them. At 3 months of age, these differences were still present but to a much smaller degree. It seems that the mothers were more responsive to male infants at first because the males placed more demands on them. Male infants were awake more, they were more irritable, and they looked at their mothers more. But by the age of 3 months, the mothers had become less responsive to the male infants because their attention and care had little effect on the male irritability and crying. These mothers apparently began to see the crying of their infants as typical male behavior rather than as a distress signal.

Just as mothers of males tended to become less involved with their infants, mothers of females tended to become more involved. They began to react more and more to the females' earlier smiling and happy vocalization by talking to and looking at their babies. This difference in treatment can have immediate as well as long-term effects on a child's behavior, just as does almost everything in a child's early environment. Sex differences are discussed more fully in Chapter 11.

THE EARLY ENVIRONMENT

With few exceptions the setting into which a child is born has as great an influence on development as do genetic and inherited factors. At birth each child enters a unique cultural, social, and family setting that helps determine perceptual, cognitive, social, emotional, and physical development. Exactly how much influence each of these environmental factors has on development is not always easy to determine because they are all so closely related. Infants deprived of mothering, for instance, are also often deprived of social and sensory stimulation. Children in orphanages are deprived of close parental relationships, but they are also often restricted in their freedom to explore and interact with the environment (although orphanages are much better in this respect than they were 30 years ago). Even though the exact influence of such variables is not known, it is generally believed that the experiences of the first two years of life are extremely important for developing infants (31).

Not only social experiences but visual and other sensory experiences during infancy can affect development, as has been seen in studies of children reared in different visual environments. Children in North America and European cities live in an environment that consists mostly of straight lines—straight streets and square buildings and rooms. The Cree Indians of Canada live in a traditional setting made up of lines and curves running in all directions. Researchers have tested the visual ability of people from both environments and found slight differences (68). People from the cities could see vertical and horizontal strips very well, but they could not see lines running in other directions quite as well. When the Crees were tested, they could see lines running in all directions equally well. Since there was no evidence for genetic differences that could account for this, the researchers concluded that the visual ability of the Crees was a result of being reared in a more visually varied or stimulating environment.

Since all knowledge comes through the senses, intellectual development depends on having adequate sensory perception. It seems that the senses, like muscles, develop best with a good deal of exercise or experience. This may explain why infants almost always pay attention to changes in the environment and why they tend to seek out complex or stimulating experiences as soon as their senses are ready to handle them.

Environmental Deprivation

Thirty or 40 years ago, most orphanages and institutions for children were dull, dreary places that few people would want to visit, much less grow up in. But many children were reared in such places, and studies of these children have dramatically shown the effects of **environmental deprivation** — growing up in an unstimulating environment.

One of the first of these studies was conducted by René A. Spitz (63, 64). He observed, worked with, and tested two groups of infants. One group was being reared in a prison nursery where they were fed, cared for, and played with by their mothers (and other women, in some cases), who were delinquent girls. The other group of infants was being reared in a home for foundlings, children abandoned by their parents. In the foundling home each infant was cared for by a nurse who also had responsibility for six other infants. The foundlings spent all of their time in cribs with no toys and with bed sheets hung over the railings. The result was that each infant was in solitary confinement until old enough to stand up in the bed. The only thing the infants could see was the ceiling. Probably as a result of lack of environmental stimulation, these infants spent most of their time lying on their backs. After months like this, a hollow was worn in the mattresses. By the time they reached the age when they should have been able to roll over on their sides, the hollow in the mattress was so deep that the infants were actually prevented from turning in any direction. As a result, Spitz found most infants, even at 10 or 12 months, lying on their backs playing with the only objects available, their own hands and feet.

The developmental progress of the prison-reared infants and foundlings was quite different. Developmental tests at the start of the study showed that the foundlings were slightly ahead of the prison infants. But when all the children were tested at 2 years of age, the foundlings were far behind the others and seemed to be mentally retarded. In contrast, the prison-reared infants showed a gradual increase in development and seemed to be about normal. Spitz claimed that the lack of development seen in the foundlings was due to maternal deprivation, but it could just as easily have been the result of sensory and environmental deprivation.

In another study adopted infants who had spent most of their first three years in an orphanage were compared with children who had been placed in foster homes during early infancy (24, 25, 26). There were significant personality and intellectual differences between the two groups. Those who had spent three years in the orphanage were impulsive, had short attention spans, caused trouble at home and in school, were socially immature, and had few friends.

Environmental
Enrichment

Studies done in orphanages have been important for several reasons. They have helped explain infant development, and because the findings have been so dramatic, they have changed the way most orphanages are run. Few are as dreary and as unstimulating as they were in the 1930s. But these studies have shown something else—that it is sometimes possible to change the course of development by providing children with an **enriched environment.**

In the 1930s H. M. Skeels shocked many people by claiming that he had been able to increase the intelligence of apparently mentally retarded children by placing them in an unusual environment. This was especially surprising to the many people who believed that intelligence was genetically inherited. To make matters more complicated, the unusual environment in which Skeels had placed the children was an institution where they were cared for by retarded women (61, 62).

Skeels had been working at an orphanage in Iowa. The buildings used to house the children were old, some dating back to the Civil War. Inside the buildings conditions were bleak, similar to those seen by Spitz. Infants were kept in cribs with sheets draped over the sides. They had few toys, and their only human contacts were with nurses who did little more than feed and change them on schedule. At the age of 2 the children were moved to cottages where they ate and slept according to rigid schedules. At the age of 6 they received a minimal sort of schooling on the orphanage grounds. In every respect their environment was unstimulating.

One day Skeels noticed two young girls. He described these infants as "pitiful little creatures" who were undersized, sad, inactive, and spent most of their time rocking back and forth on their beds. Intelligence tests available at the time suggested that these girls had IQ's of 50 or less (100 is average). Because of their extremely poor mental and physical condition, it was not likely that they would be adopted. They were, therefore, transferred to a home for the mentally retarded.

Some time later, Skeels began to work at the home for the retarded. There he was surprised to find "two outstanding little girls. They were alert, smiling, running about, responding to the playful attention of adults and generally behaving and looking like any other toddlers." They were the same two girls who had previously been considered to be mentally retarded. Skeels tested them and found their IQ's to be normal. He didn't believe his findings at first, so he waited a year and retested the girls. They were still average.

What had happened to these children who had been placed (separately) with groups of retarded women? Skeels found that each child had been sort of adopted by a woman who had time to devote to a child. Other women in the home began to consider themselves as "aunts" and shared in caretaking responsibilities. Even the nurses and attendants (unlike those in the orphanage) devoted time to the children — who no longer spent time just rocking back and forth on their beds.

Skeels was convinced that moving the infants to a more challenging and exciting environment where they were given more attention was responsible for their improvement. In an attempt to prove this, he set up an experiment. During the next several years a total of 13 infants were eventually removed from the orphanage and placed in an institution for the mentally retarded. All showed signs of improvement. Marie Skodak Crissey, who worked with Skeels, has kept in touch with many of these individuals for 40 years. Of this group who began life with a major developmental delay, but who experienced a highly stimulating environment for some period of their lives, none is retarded. All are living on their own. The same is not so for another group who had been normal in infancy, but who for one reason or another were not adopted and remained in orphanages during their formative years. Of this group of 12, 10 ended up spending nearly all of their lives in institutions for the mentally retarded.

A number of other studies have shown that even a few weeks of extra stimulation can have important effects on infant development. One researcher fed, changed, played with, and talked to 6-month-old institutionalized infants (55). This treatment was provided eight hours a day for eight weeks, and the infants who had received this special treatment were found to have become more socially responsive than those who received regular institutional care. In another experiment, institutionalized infants received tactile (touch) stimulation in two 10-minute sessions, five days a week (13). The experimenter merely stroked the infants and spoke to them every 60 seconds. After 10 weeks, these infants showed developmental advances not seen in infants at the same orphanage who had received the exact same treatment except for the stimulation.

If even this small amount of extra stimulation can have important effects on development, then a carefully designed program of stimulation and environmental enrichment should have even greater effects. This does seem to be the case. A stimulating and enriched home life probably offers the best environment for development, but because not all homes can provide this, special programs have been set up in some day-care centers and nursery schools. In most cases these projects produce increases in mental, physical, and social development as long as the children continue to attend. Such studies, which are discussed in Chapter 9, as well as almost everything that is known about infant development, show the extreme importance of environmental effects. Human development, from the time of conception through the birth process and infancy, follows a pattern laid down by the genes. But at every stage of this development, environmental influences are at work, and they can have lasting effects on the course of development. Poor nutrition, drugs, and other factors can harm the fetus. Anoxia and other problems during the birth process (possibly including those mentioned by Leboyer) can damage the newborn infant. Severe or long-term environmental deprivation during infancy can have lasting effects. A full and rich environment, on the other hand, can help infants develop and reach their fullest potential.

SUMMARY

The Leboyer method of "birth without violence" attempts to make the birth process as gentle and soothing as possible for the infant. This method has not been proved to be beneficial for development, but its humane approach to birth is an indication of the importance early experiences are believed to have on future development. Environmental experiences during infancy have been found to have lasting effects on development. These experiences begin to have their effects at the time of conception.

During the nine months following conception, the human organism follows a predetermined pattern of growth and goes through three stages of development: the ovum, the embryo, and the fetus. From the pregnant woman's point of view, pregnancy is divided into three-month periods called trimesters. Most women give birth to normal, healthy children, but factors including radiation, drugs, disease, and diet can cause complications. Such complications, as well as problems during the birth process and a number of genetic factors, can result in miscarriages, premature births, and later developmental problems.

Infants are quite helpless at birth, but they have a number of abilities. Habituation responses and reflexive responses, for instance, are seen in newborns. Testing for these abilities helps determine whether or not developmental problems exist.

As helpless as newborns are, they are able from the earliest days to react to stimuli and behave in certain ways that affect their environment (they cry in order to get fed.) This is possible because of the infant's developing perceptual abilities—awareness of stimuli, attention to them, and attachment of meaning to them.

Studies of infant perception and their sensing abilities show that by at least 6 months of age infants are sensing the world in much the way adults do. Vision, hearing, taste, smell, and the skin and body senses provide infants with information about their environment. By actively seeking increasingly complex stimuli, infants learn more and more about the world.

In addition to perceptual and sense abilities, infants show the first signs of developing mental and cognitive abilities. Attention, habituation, early language abilities, thinking, and learning are all evident in infants. Rich and numerous experiences with the environment lay the foundation for further development of these abilities.

The mother-child attachment in most cases is an infant's first real social experience and is the beginning of social and emotional development. By staying near their mothers, infants stay close to their source of food, comfort, protection, and attention. The physical and social stimulation infants receive as a result of the mother-child attachment are necessary for continued normal physical and social development.

Because of an enormous variety of differences in genetic background and environmental experiences, no two infants are ever exactly the same. The differences among infants can be measured by developmental tests. These tests are useful in screening for developmental problems but have little relation to later abilities.

Perhaps the most obvious difference among infants is the sexual one. Genes and hormones determine sexual development, but a child's gender often has a great influence on the treatment that child receives. This treatment is responsible for some of the developmental differences seen between the sexes.

The environment into which a child is born probably plays as important a role in development as do genetic factors. Infants deprived of social and emotional stimulation are often slowed or retarded in some or all areas of development. A full and rich environment can help infants reach their fullest potential.

Darwin: An Early Child Psychologist

Darwin's *The Origin of Species* (1859) had a profound impact on scientific thought. Not unaffected by Darwin's careful observations of the evolutionary process was the science of psychology, which was just beginning to take form in Europe. One aspect of Darwin which is less well known is his astute observation and recording of his own child's development, completed in 1840, but not published until 1877. In the following passage on the child's early efforts to communicate Darwin the scientist describes what he observed 37 years earlier. Interestingly, the passage ends with Darwin the child psychologist wishing that he had made more observations, a common concern of those who try to describe child development.

Means of Communication. The noise of crying or rather of squalling, as no tears are shed for a long time, is of course uttered in an instinctive manner, but serves to show that there is suffering. After a time the sound differs according to the cause, such as hunger or pain. This was noticed when this infant was eleven weeks old and I believe at an earlier age in another infant. Moreover, he appeared soon to learn to begin crying voluntarily, or to wrinkle his face in the manner proper to the occasion, so as to show that he wanted something. When 46 days old, he first made little noises without any meaning to please himself, and these soon became varied. An incipient laugh was observed on the 113th day, but much earlier in another infant. At this date I thought, as already remarked, that he began to cry to imitate sounds, as he certainly did at a considerably later period. When five and a half months old, he uttered an articulate sound "da" but without any meaning attached to it. When a little over a year old, he used gestures to explain his wishes; to give a simple instance, he picked up a bit of paper and giving it to me pointed to the fire, as he had often seen and liked to see paper burnt. At exactly the age of a year, he made the great step of inventing a word for food, namely, *mum,* but what led him to it I did not discover. And now instead of beginning to cry when he was hungry, he used this word in a demonstrative manner or as a verb, implying "Give me food" . . . he also used a *mum* as a substantive of wide signification; thus he called sugar *shu-mum,* and a little later after he had learned the word "black," he called liquorice *black-shu-mum,*—black-sugar food.

I was particularly struck with the fact that when asking for food by the word *mum* he gave to it (I will copy the words written down at the time) "a most strongly marked interrogatory sound at the end." He also gave to "Ah," which he chiefly used at first when recognizing any person or his own image in a mirror, an exclamatory sound, such as we employ when surprised. I remark in my notes that the use of these intonations seemed to have arisen instinctively, and I regret that more observations were not made on this subject.[1]

[1] Charles Darwin, "A Biographical Sketch of an Infant," *Mind,* 1877, *11,* 286–294.

Investigating Fear of Strangers

You may have noticed that newborn infants are often startled by a sudden loud noise or movement. Do they also have an inborn fear response to strangers?

Studies indicate that newborns do not show any fear of strangers, in fact anyone may pick them up or play with them. Infants seem to respond to the attention, not to the person. In most cases, however, infants eventually begin to display a fear of strangers, usually around the age of 8 months.

Researchers Hebb and Hunt state that there are definite perceptual experiences in an infant's life which must precede the fear response. They explain fear as the difference between what the infant expects and what happens to it. If there is too much difference between what it is used to and what it sees, the infant is unable to deal with this and becomes afraid.

Another researcher, H. R. Schaffer (1966) argues that the fear response is more complex and is not just automatic or based on the infant's perceptions and maturation. His research delves into early encounters that build up to the stranger anxiety.

In a study of social encounters of young infants Schaffer found that 69 percent of the infants demonstrated a fear of strangers by the time they were 36 months old and 94 percent by the time they were 48 months old. Eventually all infants in this study demonstrated a fear of strangers.

Schaffer points out that attachment behavior develops in stages. A change occurs in the infant's intellectual structure during the second half of the first year. The infant begins to organize its perceptions around permanent objects (object concept) with an independent existence in time and space. Now the infant is able to form permanent relationships to others. In a similar fashion, Schaffer says, fear behavior is also built up. By the second half of the first year the infant can distinguish known from unknown persons. But not until the emergence of the object concept is the child able to compare one individual with another in terms of, for example, familiarity.

Nature of the Infant Study

Thirty-six infants (18 boys and 18 girls) were chosen for a short-term longitudinal study of early social behaviors. They were born full term, lived at home, and were considered normal in every way. During the first year the infants were seen at home every 4 weeks after the initial contact (from 6 to 14 weeks of age). The children were seen again at 18 months of age. All contacts were made by a female investigator.

At the beginning of every visit the investigator related to the infant in a series of steps designed to move her physically closer to the child: (1) The investigator appeared in the infant's visual range, stood still, looked at the infant, but did not stimulate it in any way. (2) She smiled and talked to the infant, but did not move any closer. (3) She approached the infant, smiled, and talked. (4) She made physical contact with the infant, taking its hand and stroking its arm. (5) She offered to pick up the infant by holding out her hands. (6) She picked up the infant and sat it on her knee.

Stranger anxiety was defined as the age at which the infant initially showed a fear response. Fear reactions could be crying, facial expressions, hiding of the face, drawing back, and so on. If an infant did not respond or just stared, this response was not included. The mother stood nearby at all times, and the infant could reach her.

Other social interaction variables were considered. These were maternal availability, maternal responsiveness, maternal interaction, and the number of children in the infant's family. Variables used to measure opportunities to become acquainted with people other than mother were the number of caretakers and the number of people contacted.

Result of the Study

This study bears out the findings of other researches that the mean age of fear of strangers is around 8 months of age, although a wide range of individual differences must be considered.

In the initial weeks of life all infants showed automatic responsiveness; that is, they smiled almost immediately and showed no signs of unfamiliarity. But from 13 to 19 weeks a lag in the smile for the stranger appeared, while Mother received an immediate smile and response. In many infants ambivalent patterns of behavior were observed; they would alternately stare, smile, and stare again. With an increase in age the infants' smiles decreased. During the month just before the onset of fear, 14 infants turned away from the stranger totally, remaining "frozen" throughout the contact.

It should be noted that fear was rarely evoked by the sight of a nonmoving stranger who did not interact with the infant. Furthermore, it is not necessarily the case that once an infant has shown a fear of strangers the child will continue to exhibit ths response. Thirty to 50 percent of the infants studied did not have any recurrence of fear during the entire study.

The only socially significant variables in this study were (1) the number of children in the family and (2) the number of people normally seen. No supporting evidence could be found to define the intensity of the maternal relationship. There was a correlation between the number of people encountered and the age of stranger anxiety. The greater the number of contacts, the later was the onset of fear of strangers.

Schaffer's data considered the extent to which age of onset of fear of strangers is related to previous social encounters. It is interesting to note that the data imply that multiple mothering can delay or even eliminate the stranger anxiety response. Is this desirable? Can or should the fear of strangers response be totally eliminated? If so, what are the developmental implications? Further research is needed to clarify this interesting and challenging aspect of growth.

Based on H. R. Schaffer, "The Onset of Fear of Strangers and the Incongruity Hypothesis," *Child Psychologist*, 1966, 7, 96–106.

Watson: "Give Me a Dozen Healthy Infants"

One of the significant figures in U.S. psychology was John B. Watson. Watson was in the vanguard of the behavioristic revolution with his argument that psychology could only be the study of stimuli and responses, not mentalistic ideas and images or psychodymanic processes such as those proposed by Freud. So convinced was Watson of his ideas that he often offered practical advice to the lay person about a large number of matters, including child-rearing practices. Watson maintained that with proper control of the stimuli or the environment he could produce the responses or behaviors he wanted in children. In one well-known passage Watson asserted:

> Give me a dozen healthy infants, well-formed, and my own specified world to bring them up in and I'll guarantee to take any one at random and train him to become any type of specialist I might select—doctor, lawyer, artist, merchant, chief and, yes, even beggar-man and thief, regardless of his talents, penchants, tendencies, abilities, vocations, and race of his ancestors. I am going beyond my facts and I admit it, but so have the advocates of the contrary and they have been doing it for many thousands of years. Please note that when this experiment is made I am to be allowed to specify the way the children are to be brought up and the type of world they have to live in.[1]

This quotation demonstrates the fervor of Watson's behaviorism. He was an extreme environmentalist who believed that children are shaped by their parents and the circumstances around them. Watson's ideas in modified form are still held today by some psychologists. The best example are those psychologists who advocate behavior modification techniques in their work with children. Two simple principles form the basis for all behavior modification operations. First is the principle of reinforcement, which says that a child will learn to repeat an act for which it is rewarded and to avoid one for which it is ignored or punished. The second principle, that of learning by successive approximations, says that complicated behavior patterns, especially those requiring skill, are learned gradually, in small steps that come closer and closer to an optimal level of performance.

Are these the principles that Watson meant when he said that given his "own specified world" he could take any infant and train it to become any type of specialist? Would you agree with Watson's behaviorism?

[1] John B. Watson, *Behaviorism*. Chicago: The University of Chicago Press, 1924, p. 104.

REFERENCES

1. Ainsworth, M. D. S., S. M. V. Bell, and D. J. Slayton. "Individual Differences in Strange-situation Behavior of One-year-olds." In H. R. Schaffer (ed.), *The Origins of Human Social Relations.* London: Academic Press, 1971.
2. "A Man's Drinking May Harm His Offspring," *Science News,* 1975, *107* (8), 116.
3. Bayley, N. "Development of Mental Abilities." In P. H. Mussen (ed.), *Carmichael's Manual of Child Psychology.* New York: Wiley, 1970.
4. Bell, R. Q. "Contributions of Human Infants to Caregiving and Social Interaction." In M. Lewis and L. A. Rosenblum (eds.), *The Effect of the Infant on Its Caregiver.* New York: Wiley, 1974.
5. Berg, W. K. "Cardiac Orienting Responses of 6- and 16-week-old Infants," *Journal of Experimental Child Psychology,* 1974, *17,* 303–312.
6. Bergman, M. "Screening the Hearing of Preschool Children," *Maico Audiology Library Series,* Report 4, 1964.
7. Bower, T. G. R. "The Visual World of Infants," *Scientific American,* 1966.
8. Bower, T. G. R. *Development in Infancy.* San Francisco: Freeman, 1974.
9. Bowlby, J. *Attachment and Loss,* Vol. 1, *Attachment.* New York: Basic Books, 1969.
10. Braine, M. D. S., C. B. Heimer, H. Wortis, and A. M. Freedman. "Factors Associated with Impairment of the Early Development of Prematures," *Monographs of the Society for Research in Child Development,* 1966.
11. Brazelton, T. B. "Influence of Parinatal Drugs on the Behavior of the Neonate," *American Journal of Psychiatry,* 1970, *126,* 1261–1266.
12. Brennan, W., E. W. Ames, and R. W. Moore. "Age Differences in Infants' Attention to Patterns of Different Complexities," *Science,* 1966, *155,* 354–356.
13. Casler, L. "The Effects of Extra Tactile Stimulation on a Group of Institutionalized Infants," *Genetic Psychology Monographs,* 1965, *71,* 137–175. (a)
14. Chun, R. W. M., R. Pawsat, and F. R. Forster. "Sound Localization in Infancy," *Journal of Nervous and Mental Disorders,* 1960, *130,* 472–476.
15. Condon, W. S., and L. W. Sander. "Neonate Movement Is Synchronized with Adult Speech: Interactional Participation and Language Acquisition, *Science,* 1974, *183,* 99–101.
16. Eisenberg, R. B. "The Organization of Auditory Behavior," *Journal of Speech and Hearing Research,* 1970, *13,* 461–464.
17. Eisenberg, R. B., D. B. Coursin, E. J. Griffin, and M. A. Hunter. "Auditory Behavior in the Human Neonate: A Preliminary Report," *Journal of Speech and Hearing Research,* 1964, 7, 245–269.
18. Erikson, E. H. "The Problem of Ego Identity," *Journal of the American Psychoanalytic Association,* 1956, *4,* 56–121.
19. Feinbloom, R. I. "Prematurity." In J. H. Durston (ed.), *Pregnancy, Birth and the Newborn Baby.* Boston: Delacorte Press/Seymore Lawrence, 1972. (b)
20. Frantz, R. L., and S. Nevis. "Pattern Preferences and Perceptual-cognitive Development in Early Infancy," *Merrill-Palmer Quarterly,* 1967, *13,* 77–108.
21. Friedlander, B. Z. "The Effect of Speaker Identity, Voice, Inflection, Vocabulary, and Message Redundancy on Infants' Selection of Vocal Reinforcement," *Journal of Experimental Child Psychology,* 1968, 6, 443–459.

22. Gibson, E. J., and R. D. Walk. "The 'Visual Cliff,'" *Scientific American*, 1960, *202*, 64–71.

23. Goldbarb, W. "Rorschach Test Differences between Family-reared, Institution-reared, and Schizophrenic Children," *American Journal of Orthopsychiatry*, 1949, *19*, 625–663

24. Goldbarb, W. "Variations in Adolescent Adjustment of Institutionally Reared Children," *American Journal of Orthopsychiatry*, 1947, *17*, 449–457.

25. Goldbarb, W. "Effects of Psychological Deprivation in Infancy and Subsequent Stimulation," *American Journal of Psychiatry*, 1947, *102*, 18–33.

26. Goldenson, R. M. "Prenatal Development," *The Encyclopedia of Human Development*. New York: Doubleday, 1970.

27. Greenman, G. W. "Visual Behavior of Newborn Infants." In A. J. Solnit and S. A. Provence (eds.), *Modern Perspectives in Child Development*. New York: Hallmark, 1963.

28. Harrel, R. F., E. Woodyard, and A. I. Gates. *The Effects of Mothers' Diets on the Intelligence of Offspring*. New York: Bureau of Publications, Teachers College, Columbia University, 1955.

29. Hebb, D. O. *The Organization of Behavior: A Neuropsychological Theory*. New York: Wiley, 1949.

30. Hershenson, M., H. Musinger, and W. Dessen. "Preference for Shapes on Intermediate Variability in the Newborn Human," *Science*, 1965, *147*, 630–631.

31. Hunt, F. McV. *Intelligence and Experience*. New York: Ronald Press, 1961.

32. Jones, K. L., et al. "The Deformed Children of Alcoholic Mothers," *Science News*, 1973, *104* (1), 6.

33. Kagan, J., and N. Kagan. "Individuality and Cognitive Performance." In P. H. Mussen (ed.), *Carmichael's Manual of Child Psychology*, Vol. 1. New York: Wiley, 1970.

34. Kagan, J., and N. Lewis. "Studies of Attention in the Human Infant," *Merrill-Palmer Quarterly*, 1965, *11*, 95–128.

35. Kappelman, M. M. "Prenatal and Parinatal Factors Which Influence Learning." In J. Hellmuth (ed.), *Exceptional Infant: Studies in Abnormalities*, Vol. 2. New York: Bruner/Mazel, 1971.

36. Katchadourian, H. A., and D. T. Lunde. *Fundamentals of Human Sexuality*, 2d ed. New York: Holt, Rinehart and Winston, 1975.

37. Kaye, H. "Sensory Processes." In H. W. Reeses and L. P. Lipsitt (eds.), *Experimental Child Psychology*. New York: Academic Press, 1970.

38. Kaye, H., and L. P. Lipsitt. "Relation of Electrotactual Threshold to Basal Skin Conductance," *Child Development*, 1964, *35*, 1307–1312.

39. Korner, A. F., and E. B. Thoman. "The Relative Efficacy of Contact and Vestibular-Proprioceptive Stimulation in Soothing Neonates," *Child Development*, 1972, *43*, 443–453.

40. Leboyer, F. *Birth Without Violence*. New York: Knopf, 1975.

41. Leventhal, A. S., and L. P. Lipsitt. "Adaptation, Pitch Discrimination, and Sound Localization in the Neonate," *Child Development*, 1964, *35*, 759–767.

42. Ling, B. C. "A Genetic Study of Sustained Visual Fixation and Associated

Behavior in the Human Infant from Birth to Six Months," *Journal of Genetic Psychology*, 1942, *61*, 227–277.

43. Marx, G. F. "Placental Transfer and Drugs Used in Anesthesia," *Anesthesiology*, 1961, *22*, 294.

44. Miranda, S. "Visual Abilities and Pattern Preferences of Premature Infants and Full-term Neonates," *Journal of Experimental Child Psychology*, 1970, *10*, 189–205.

45. Money, J., and A. Ehrhardt. *Man and Woman. Boy and Girl.* Baltimore, Md.: The Johns Hopkins Press, 1973.

46. Morgan, G. A., and H. N. Ricciuti. "Infants' Responses to Strangers During the First Year." In B. M. Foss (ed.), *Determinants of Infant Behavior*, Vol. 4. London: Methuen, 1969.

47. Moss, H. A. "Sex, Age, and State as Determinants of Mother-Infant Interaction," *Merrill-Palmer Quarterly*, 1967, *13*, 19–36.

48. Murphy, D. P. "The Outcome of 625 Pregnancies in Women Subjected to Pelvic Roentgen Irradiation," *American Journal of Obstetrics and Gynecology*, 1929, *18*, 179–187.

49. Neuman, F., and W. Elger. "Antiandrogens," *Research in Reproduction*, 1970, *2* (3), 3–4.

50. Pederson, D. R., L. Champagne, and L. Pederson. "Relative Soothing Effects of Vertical and Horizontal Rocking." Paper presented at the meeting of the Society for Research in Child Development, Santa Monica, Calif., March 1969.

51. Pederson, D. R., and D. TerVrugt. "The Influence of Amplitude and Frequency of Vestibular Stimulation on the Activity of Two-month-old Infants," *Child Development*, 1973, *44*, 122–128.

52. Plummer, G. "Anomalies Occurring in Children Exposed *in Utero* to the Atomic Bomb in Hiroshima," *Pediatrics*, 1952, *10*, 686.

53. Pratt, K. C. "Note on the Relation of Temperature and Humidity to the Activity of Young Infants," *Journal of Genetic Psychology*, 1930, *38*, 480–484.

54. "Prenatal and Birth Complications Linked by Schizophrenia," *Science News*, 1970, *98* (1), 15–16.

55. Rheingold, H. L., L. J. Gewirtz, and H. W. Ross, "Social Conditioning of Vocalizations in the Infant," *Journal of Comparative and Physiological Psychology*, 1959, *52*, 68–73.

56. Russell, M. J. "Human Olfactory Communication," *Nature*, 1976, *206* (5551), 520–522.

57. Schaffer, H. R. "The Onset of Fear of Strangers and the Incongruity Hypothesis," *Journal of Child Psychology and Psychiatry*, 1966, *7*, 95–106.

58. Schulman, C. A. "Effects of an Auditory Stimulus on Heart Rate in High-risk and Low-risk Premature Infants." Paper presented at the Eastern Psychological Association, Washington, D.C., 1968.

59. Sherman, M., and I. C. Sherman. "Sensorimotor Responses in Infants," *Journal of Comparative Psychology*, 1925, *5*, 53–68.

60. Siqueland, E. R., and L. P. Lipsitt. "Conditioned Headturning in Human Newborns," *Journal of Experimental Child Psychology*. 1966, *3*, 356–376.

61. Skeels, H. M. "Adult Status of Children from Contrasting Early Life Experiences," *Monographs of the Society for Research in Child Development,* 1966, *31,* Serial No. 105.
62. Skeels, H. M., and H. B. Dye. "A Study of the Effects of Differential Stimulation on Mentally Retarded Children," *Proceedings and Addresses of the American Association on Mental Deficiency,* 1939, *44,* 114–136.
63. Spitz, R. A. "Hospitalism: An Inquiry into the Genesis of Psychiatric Conditions in Early Childhood," *Psychoanalytic Study of the Child,* 1945, *1,* 53–74.
64. Spitz, R. A. "Hospitalism: A Follow-up Report," *Psychoanalytic Study of the Child,* 1946, *2,* 113–117.
65. Thomas, H. "Visual Fixation Responses," *Child Development,* 1965, *36,* 629–638.
66. Thompson, W. R., and J. E. Grusec. "Studies of Early Experiences." In P. H. Mussen (ed.), *Carmichael's Manual of Child Psychology,* Vol. 1. New York: Wiley, 1970.
67. Turnure, C. "Response to Voice of Mother and Stranger by Babies in the First Year," *Developmental Psychology,* 1971, *4,* 182–190.
68. "Vision: Effects of Early Variation," *Science News,* 1973, *104* (20), 312.
69. Vore, D. A. "Prenatal Nutrition and Postnatal Intellectual Development," *Merrill-Palmer Quarterly,* 1973, *19,* 253–260.
70. Wertheimer, M. "Psychomotor Coordination of Auditory and Visual Space at Birth," *Science,* 1961, *134,* 1692.

E very aspect of children's development is affected by their bodies and physical growth. In order to understand children in their behavior it is necessary to know how they grow, develop, and acquire physical skills.

5.

physical development

If you are **left-handed,** you are discriminated against and at a definite disadvantage. Musical instruments, gum wrapper tabs, scissors, can openers, playing cards, and slot machines are all designed to favor right-handed individuals. Since biblical times, at least, the left-handed minority have been looked down upon. In the Book of Judges, left-handedness is associated with warlike tendencies. The Israelites were twice defeated by an army of left-handed soldiers. And in many cultures around the world the words for "left" or "left-handed" also have negative meanings. *Gauche* is French for left, but it also means "awkward." *Mancino* is the Italian word for "left" or "deceitful." *Nolevo* is Russian for "left" or "sneaky." In English, the word "sinister" means "wrong," "dishonest," "corrupt," or "evil." It also means "on or toward the left hand."

Is there any reason to believe that left-handed people are different in other ways from right-handed people? Perhaps. Estimates of the extent of left-handedness range from 6 to 11 percent of the general population. Theodore H. Blau, who has evaluated thousands of psychologically troubled children, has found that 16 percent of his patients are left-handed (18). After observing and testing such children for years, he has come up with some findings about left-handedness and mixed-handedness (a tendency to use either hand):

Left-handed children are more likely to be reported as having significant physical and behavior problems during the first five years of life than are right-handed children.

They are more likely to have preschool adjustment problems and first-grade achievement problems.

They are more likely to have reading, arithmetic, and speech problems.

The age at which bed-wetting stops is likely to be later among left-handed children.

Left-handed children are more likely to show certain socially unacceptable behavior traits, including stubbornness, difficulty in completing projects, difficulty in following directions, impulsiveness, difficulty in learning from experience, and oversensitivity.

Left-handed children are more likely to show symptoms of poor sleep, headaches, and dizziness.

Left-handed children are more likely to be imaginative and creative.

Why do some left-handed children develop behavior patterns that are different from those of most right-handers? Blau believes it has to do with the fact that left-handed children are subjected to a special set of experiences. The Romans developed the right-handed handshake, the right-handed salute, and the word "sinister." Ever since, and probably even before the time of the Romans, society has worked against left-handed children. Although not all parents force their left-handed children to become right-handed, there is pressure on left-handed children to do what doesn't come naturally (use the right hand for writing, eating, and so on). This pressure can possibly explain some of the behavioral problems of left-handed children. A child who overcomes the pressures of society, for instance, and remains left-handed, may indeed develop a streak of stubbornness. The human brain, which controls handedness, may also be responsible for some of the behavioral differences seen between left- and right-handed individuals, as will be seen later in this chapter.

Many questions remain to be answered about handedness, but one of the most important has to do with child-rearing practices. Blau suggests strongly that left-handed children should be accepted. They should not be treated as if they were unusual, and they should not be forced into the right-handed system. Instead, he says, they need to be given continual reassurance and help as they learn to get along in a right-handed society.

Left-handedness is a special condition, but it points out the fact that every area of social and personal development is affected by the body. Being left-handed, red-headed, tall, fat, loud, attractive, hairy, clumsy—all of these physical characteristics can have an effect on the way people are treated. And the way they are treated, in turn, has an effect on the way they behave. So in order to understand human behavior, it is necessary to understand physical and motor development and their effects on behavior.

Developmental Norms

Human development is usually discussed in terms of what is normal or average. Thousands of growing children have been observed, measured, and tested, and **"norms,"** or averages, have been established for almost every stage of development. Norms do not explain either growth or behavior, but they are often useful in charting the progress of both normal and abnormal children.

The word "normal," when it is used to describe children, refers to one or more of their characteristics that are average. "Normal" does not mean "ideal" or "optimal," though it is often used as though it had that meaning. Using "normal" as "optimal" or "ideal" can lead to mistakes in prediction. For example, if the "normal" age of puberty for boys is around 14 years, then it should be ideal to reach puberty at that age. But as will be seen later in this chapter, early-maturing boys sometimes have advantages over late- and average-maturing boys. From this example, it can be seen that "normal" means "average," but it does not necessarily mean "ideal." Throughout this chapter, norms, or averages, will be used to describe development. It should be remembered that norms are not always ideal, and that children are more likely to be slightly above or below the norm than to be average.

Are left-handed people
psychologically different?

PRINCIPLES OF PHYSICAL GROWTH
AND MOTOR DEVELOPMENT

Being left-handed involves much more than picking up a pencil, a spoon, or anything else with the left instead of the right hand. It involves the development of the visual system and the ability to look at and recognize a pencil (see Chapter 4). It involves the physical growth and development of the arm and hand, including bone structure and muscles. It involves the development of the brain and nervous system and the ability (motor ability) to coordinate sensory inputs from the eyes with the delicate and precise muscle movements necessay for holding a pencil and writing. All of these complex abilities are the result of genetic and environmental influences, which determine the rate and direction of physical development. The physical maturity necessary to hold a pencil develops with time and is determined to a great extent by the genes. The motor ability necessary to control and use a pencil develops with time (and genes) as well as with practice. All of these factors, working together, determine which hand will eventually be used for writing.

But before it is possible to write, much physical and motor development must have taken place. This development follows the principles or guidelines seen in fetal development. The first principle is called **cephalocaudal,** meaning "from head to tail" in Latin. Growth and motor development proceed, in general, from the head to the tail end of the body. At birth, for instance, the head is much nearer its adult size than are the legs. The body muscles that come under control first are also those near the head. Infants in a prone position (on their backs) first develop the muscle control necessary to lift their heads off the surface. Later, arm, shoulder, and stomach muscles develop, and infants can raise the torso or upper part of the body. Later still, leg and thigh muscles develop so that infants can raise their hips off the surface.

The second principle of physical growth and motor development is called **proximodistal,** meaning "from near to far." Development proceeds, in general, from the center of the body outward. In the womb, for instance, the internal organs are fully developed before the fingernails. The body muscles that come under control first are those near the center of the body. This can be seen in reaching ability. At first, reaching movements are controlled by shoulder muscles, and the arm and hand move as a unit. By the end of the first year, after motor control has moved outward from the center of the body, infants can use their hand muscles and make independent finger movements.

The third principle of development is **from general to specific.** The fetus can be seen to have a general shape before any specific organs have developed. General, or overall, motor control is present before specific muscles can be used. This can be seen when infants are pricked on the foot with a pin. There

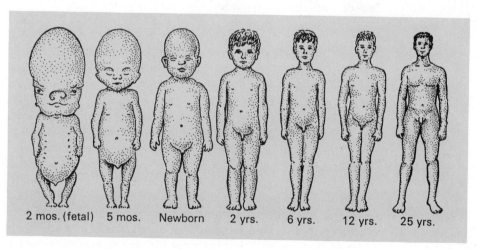

2 mos. (fetal) 5 mos. Newborn 2 yrs. 6 yrs. 12 yrs. 25 yrs.

The pattern of human body growth from before birth through maturity.

is an immediate general body reaction—crying, kicking and arm waving. At six months, infants react much more specifically and adaptively—they may cry, but they will also withdraw their feet quickly from the pin prick. Early grasping attempts are also general rather than specific. They originate from the shoulder and often involve awkward heaving and movement·of the entire body. By one year of age, most infants can pick up and manipulate even small objects with well-coordinated and specific movements of the wrist and fingers. The rest of the body is not involved, except for head movements and coordination of the eyes with whatever is being done by the hands.

Motor control becomes more specific with practice. As an infant learns to connect the necessary muscle movements in the proper order to perform a specific act, such as walking, unnecessary or inappropriate movements drop out, and those that remain become smoother and more effective. At 18 months, for example, children seem to walk for the sake of walking (practice). They are quite awkward and seem to have no goal or direction in mind. By the time they are 2 years old, they usually walk for a reason (to get somewhere), and their movements have become quite automatic and smooth.

There are exceptions to the three basic developmental principles. The cephalocaudal principle (from head to tail) suggests that control of the feet should come relatively late. But some infants can use their feet almost as well as they use their hands. Many 6-month-olds, for instance, hold a bottle efficiently with their feet as they feed themselves. This ability to manipulate and grasp with the feet is soon lost, however, as infants begin to use their feet for more important things—walking. There are other exceptions to these developmental principles, but the most obvious development does seem to be cephalocaudal, proximodistal, and from general to specific.

PATTERNS OF PHYSICAL GROWTH

In addition to the three principles of growth, three general patterns of growth have been identified. The first is **neural growth** (a **neuron** is a nerve cell), and it includes the development of the nervous system, the head, brain, spinal cord, and eyes. Neural growth is most rapid during infancy and slows down considerably during early childhood.

The second pattern of growth is **sexual,** or reproductive. It takes place in two phases and includes development of the primary and secondary sex characteristics. The **primary sex characteristics**—the genitals, the female's egg-producing ovaries, and the male's sperm-producing testes—develop during fetal life and immediately after birth. There is almost no sexual development between infancy and late childhood, but just before and during puberty rapid growth takes place with the development of **secondary sex characteristics**—fully developed genitals, pubic and underarm hair, female breasts, and male

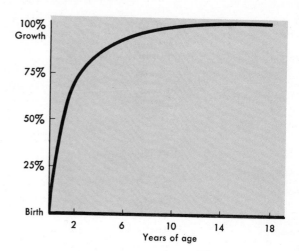

The pattern of neural growth.

facial hair. Sexual growth tapers off during adolescence, although the testes continue to grow until men are in their middle twenties.

The third and most obvious growth pattern is the **somatic pattern** (from the Greek word for "body"). **Somatic growth** includes such things as length of arms and legs, size of chest and abdomen, weight and height, and width of shoulders and hips. Some internal organs, such as the liver and kidneys, also follow this pattern. Somatic growth is rapid during infancy (following a loss of weight immediately after birth) and moderately slow during childhood. It speeds up again during puberty (approximately a year earlier for girls than for boys) and is followed by a slow year-by-year increase in later adolescence.

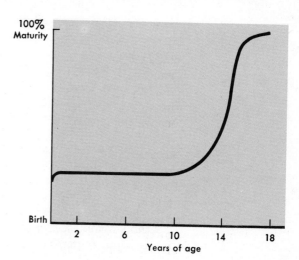

The development of primary sex characteristics.

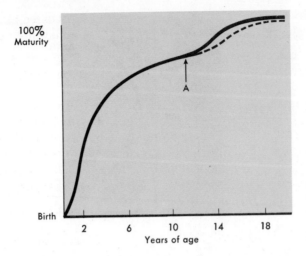

Growth curve for body dimensions of some major internal organs. From point A the solid line represents girls' growth; the dotted line, boys .

Neural, sexual, and somatic growth are genetically determined, and if the necessary environmental factors are present, development will proceed normally until the fullest genetic potentials or possibilities are reached. In general, children need sunlight, sufficient sleep, fresh air, exercise, and a diet that includes milk, fruits, and vegetables. In the United States, where proper nutrition and health care are available, it appears that most people do reach their genetic potential — the fullest amount and type of physical growth possible.

For more than 100 years people in the United States have been growing slightly taller with each generation. But in 1976, the National Center for Health Statistics reported that physical growth in the United States may have reached the limit of its genetic potential (14). More than 20,000 children were studied from infancy to adolescence. The results show that males and females aren't maturing any earlier. Successive generations in the United States have continued to show increases in weight, especially during adolescence, but the average height for males has leveled off at slightly more than 5 feet 9 inches and at 5 feet 4½ inches for females. The average onset of puberty for females, which had been going down in age, seems to have stabilized at 12 years 9½ months. It is about 14 years for males. The researchers concluded that environmental factors, such as health care and nutrition, are probably making their maximum contribution to human growth in the United States. This may have happened in the higher socioeconomic groups during the 1930s, and it now appears to be true for 95 percent of the U.S. population.

Although adolescence is not considered to be a part of childhood, adolescence is a major period of physical growth and development. Some of the changes that take place during adolescence will be discussed in this chapter in order to provide more complete coverage of physical development.

Changes in Kind

As growth and development proceed, various types of changes occur. Life starts with a change in kind. The union between the sperm and ovum produces a completely different kind of being, the **zygote.** This simple structure continues to change during prenatal life to eventually include blood cells and bone cells, muscle tissue and fat tissue, the nervous system and the skeletal system. Most of the **cartilage** (gristle) that makes up the skeletons of infants changes into bone during childhood and adulthood. The bones of the aged are more brittle than those of the young. All of these changes are examples of changes in kind.

Changes in Number

During adolescence the number of bones in the human body drops from about 350 to less than 220. One reason for this is hardening of the cartilage that links certain bones, making one bone of two. Another reason is the loss of teeth. Five-year-olds have between 48 and 52 teeth in one stage or another of development. By the time they are 15, they have usually lost 20 temporary teeth. With increasing age, more teeth are likely to be lost, with the wisdom teeth usually going first because of decay or because the jaws are not large enough to hold them.

Five-year-olds have between 48 and 52 teeth in one stage or another of development.

Changes in Size

Children always seem to be changing in size, particularly in height or weight, but there are periods of negative growth (or decrease) as well as positive growth. For example, the **ligaments,** or connective tissue, from the testes to the floor of the **scrotum,** the sac that contains the testes, increase in length during the first six months of prenatal life. In the seventh month these ligaments shorten by 50 percent and continue to shorten another 25 percent by the time of birth.

For the first few days after conception there is no change in the size of the zygote, but it soon begins to grow rapidly in size. Following birth almost all infants lose some weight and then begin to grow again until about 18 years of age. From around 20 to 30 years of age there is a small change in height, and after that height decreases steadily, although not rapidly, during the mature years and old age. Height actually decreases between one quarter and one half inch from the time of getting out of bed in the morning to the time of going to bed at night. This loss, however, is only temporary, due to the weight of the body on itself all day. The height is recovered during sleep.

The **thymus gland** — a regulator of growth — increases in weight almost until puberty, then decreases strikingly in size. For both sexes, the genitals remain at approximately their infantile size until shortly before puberty. At this time and throughout adolescence, the male's penis and testicles and the female's breasts, vagina, and uterus grow to their adult size.

Changes in Shape

The most dramatic changes in shape take place before birth, but there are also changes in shape that take place between childhood and adolescence. Most preschool children, for instance, are pot-bellied. Following puberty, this condition usually changes, with most people having a flat stomach. After about the age of 30, the pot-belly may begin to reappear.

Adolescence brings other changes in shape. The "winged" shoulder blades of children usually pull in and the back becomes flat. The shoulder width of males increases more rapidly than hip width, leading to the typical masculine figure. The opposite is true of females, whose hips widen to make childbirth easier.

With the growth of permanent teeth and the loss of baby fat, the face takes on a different shape. When the teeth are lost the face again takes on a different shape.

Changes in Position

After birth there are only a few changes in the physical positions of the various parts of the body. The most obvious position changes involve the teeth. During childhood, as the permanent teeth grow into place, they move upward or downward, depending on which jaw they are in. At birth the big toe is more widely spaced from the others than it will be later. During its development the stomach moves from a vertical to a transverse, or cross-wise, position. The ribs change from a forward to a lateral position and from open to closed.

The skin progressively darkens with age, and the iris, or colored part of the eye, sometimes becomes lighter. The hair of many infants darkens during childhood and then changes to gray during middle or old age. The hair also goes through changes in distribution, number, and texture. The hair around the genitals begins to grow, darken, and change in texture during adolescence, until by the time of the middle or late teens the adult type of relatively thick, coarse, and curly pubic hair surrounds the genitals. The appearance of coarse and curly hair in the armpits follows the appearance of pubic hair. Next, for males, comes the thickening and coarsening of facial hair. There are, however, racial differences in hairiness. Caucasians tend to be the hairiest, Negroids less hairy, and those of Mongolian descent (including American Indians) less hairy. When facial hair does develop, it is first noticeable on the upper lip. It extends outward, upward, and downward with time until, in his middle twenties, the average male is bearded over his lower and lateral face and the upper throat region. Females also develop facial hair, but it is much finer than that of males. Last comes thicker, coarser, and longer hair on the arms and legs, as well as on the chest and shoulders of some males.

At about the time pubic, facial, and bodily hair has reached its fullest distribution for the male, the process begins to reverse itself. By the time they are 30, many men have begun to lose their hair. Women's hair also begins to thin with age, though not as much as men's. This loss of hair is a continuous process that seems to be genetically determined and irreversible.

Changes in
Texture
The "sponge-rubber" texture of 6-month-old infants changes as they lose their baby fat. Females tend to regain some of this softness after adolescence because their bodies contain more fatty tissue than the bodies of males. Males become harder after adolescence as fatty tissue is replaced by muscle. From the time of early maturity, the skin gradually loses its softness and elasticity, and wrinkles begin to develop.

PATTERNS OF MOTOR DEVELOPMENT

Motor development, including muscular coordination and the control necessary for physical activities, also follows predictable patterns (8). But before motor development can begin, a certain amount of maturity and physical growth is necessary. The nerves, muscles, and skeleton, must be developed before coordinated activity is possible. Brain growth is especially necessary. Infants can't sit, stand, or walk properly until the **cerebellum,** the area of the brain that controls balance, is developed. This growth takes place rapidly dur-

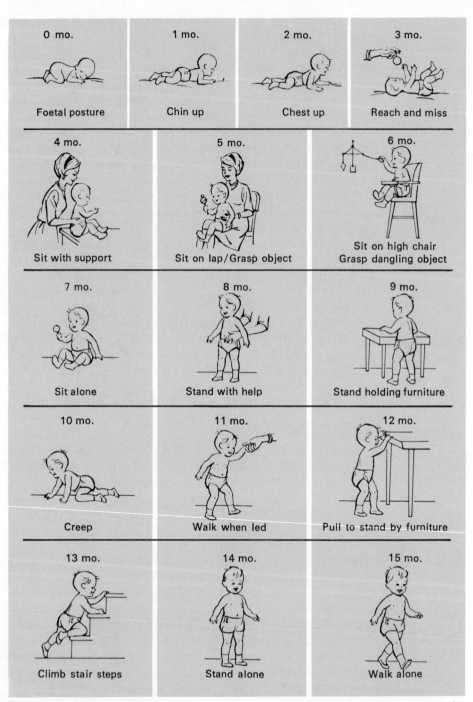

The pattern of motor development.

ing the first 18 months of life. But motor development does not just come with time and maturation. Learning and practice are necessary.

Researchers have spent much time trying to determine which is more important, **maturation or learning.** In some of the most famous of these experiments, identical twins were studied because genetic differences in the rate of maturation would not interfere with the results. In one study, one twin was given early training in such tasks as stair climbing and button fastening (5). The other twin received training at a later (more mature) time, and then both were tested. The trained twin did better on the tasks at first, but the other twin, with much less training and practice, caught up rapidly. Within a short time both twins were doing equally well at the tasks. The conclusion was that maturation is more important to motor development than learning. In other words, training will not help much if the child does not have the necessary physical maturity. But without the training and practice, neither twin would have been able to perform the developmental tasks. Thus both maturation and practice are necessary. But patterns of motor development are not exactly the same in all children, because some children mature faster than others and because some are exposed to different amounts and types of training than others.

Head and Body Control

Most infants can lift their heads for a few seconds, but they can't usually hold their heads in an upright position until they are about 3 months old.

Infants cannot turn their bodies immediately after birth, but usually by the second month they can turn from side to back. By 6 months they can roll over completely.

By 4 months most infants can pull themselves into a sitting position. By 5 months they can usually sit upright with some support. And by 9 or 10 months they can sit up without support for 10 minutes or so.

Arm and Leg Control

Poorly coordinated arm movements are usually seen during the first few days of life, but accurate reaching and grasping are not possible until after the sixth month. A 4-month-old child will make backhanded or circular sweeps at an object, but will not make a direct approach until the end of the first year. The grasping reflex is present at birth, but thumb-finger opposition (touching the thumb to the tips of the fingers) is not possible until the fourth month. After about another month most infants are able to accept and hold objects that are handed to them.

Shortly after birth infants held off the ground will perform reflexive walking movements, but the complex coordination necessary for walking does not develop for another 9 to 15 months. This development begins as infants kick their legs and strengthen their muscles. By about the sixth or seventh month they are strong enough to push themselves along backwards in a sitting position, and forward by crawling on their stomachs. During the ninth month, infants usually begin creeping movements. They raise their shoulders and abdomen off the ground and push themselves along with one leg. A month later, they are usually able to stand with support. By about their first birthday they can stand alone. Shortly after this comes the first step and then independent walking. Smooth, automatic walking is usually achieved between 2 and 3 years of age. Smoothness and strength in all motor activities continue to develop, with the greatest increase in strength coming after puberty when the muscles grow rapidly in size.

The Mouth and Sphincters

As physical and motor development proceed, there are changes in function, or use, as well as changes in shape, size, and so on. For the first seven or eight months of life, for example, the major motor function of the mouth is sucking. Between the sixth and eighth months, as the teeth begin to come in, the mouth begins to have other functions. As incoming teeth irritate the gums, infants begin to mouth and chew various objects such as their fingers and hands. When the teeth actually appear, nipping and biting are possible. At this point the relationship between a mother and child may begin to change.

The **sphincters,** the ringlike muscles that control elimination of urine and feces, also play an important role in parent-child relationships during toilet training. At birth the sphincters operate involuntarily. But as muscle control develops, with time and practice, voluntary, predictable control is achieved. This usually takes place after about 18 months, but may not be achieved until the second or third year. Even in adulthood, under conditions of stress or extreme tension, sphincter control may be lost.

Hand Skills

The human hand is one of the most important of all evolutionary developments. A hand capable of making and using tools was responsible for much of cultural evolution. A hand able to manipulate a pencil or to build bridges, trains, and computers can be credited for much of our technological culture. A hand that is capable of reaching out and manipulating the world is one of the most important tools every child has. Precise hand control is therefore one of the most necessary of all motor abilities.

At 1 year of age most children have enough motor control to hold a pencil and to remove a hat. At 2 they can scribble and open boxes. At 3 they can copy circles and dry dishes. At 4 they can copy squares, trace diamonds, draw recognizable human figures, and tie knots. But human hands can do much more than this. By the age of 6 children can build crude tables or boats out of wood, and they can model clay, make cookies, sew, and feed themselves (8).

Feeding follows set developmental patterns based on hand control. At 8 months infants can hold a bottle to their mouth. At 1 year they begin trying to drink from a cup or feed themselves with a spoon. At 2 they use forks, and by 3, they can spread jam with a knife.

Hand coordination also enables children to dress themselves. At 1½ years they can pull off their shoes and socks. By 5 they can dress themselves completely, except perhaps for tying their shoes. Between 4 and 5 children also learn to bathe themselves, brush their teeth, and comb their hair.

Writing skills also follow a predictable pattern. Three-year-olds scribble, but by 3½ they can print large capital letters. At 5 they print their names in capitals—many of which may be backward. At 6 they can print the entire alphabet as well as numbers from 1 to 20. Between 8 and 9 they give up printing, begin to write smaller, and gradually develop an individual style. The ages mentioned in relation to these and other motor abilities are based on norms or averages. Individual children may be slightly ahead or behind others of the same age in these abilities.

Handedness and the Brain

During the first year, most infants are **ambidextrous**—they can use both hands equally well. But by the second year most children have developed a preference for one hand over the other. By the end of the preschool period about 9 out of 10 children in the United States have developed a preference for the right hand. This preference, however, does not necessarily extend to all activities. Some people eat with one hand and write with the other. Some play tennis with one hand and paint with the other. And a few are completely ambidextrous in all activities. These are signs of **mixed-handedness,** or **mixed dominance.** And this, like most other aspects of motor control, is determined in the brain.

The **human brain** is a round or spherical organ that sits atop the **spinal column.** It continually receives information about the external world and the body from the eyes, ears, and other senses. This information is interpreted

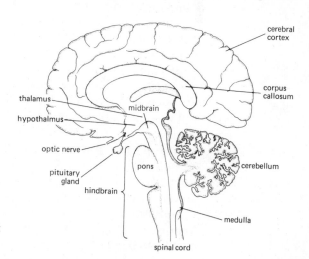

The human brain and its most important areas.

and decisions are made about how to deal with incoming information. If action is required, the brain sends out signals to the muscles and body to coordinate motor activity.

The human brain is divided into two nearly equal halves, like many other parts of the body (two eyes, two hands, and so on), and each **hemisphere,** or half, controls the motor activity of the opposite half of the body. This situation could result in very uncoordinated activity if the hemispheres of the brain sent out different messages to the body. If, for example, the left hemisphere was telling the right hand to begin writing while the right hemisphere was telling the left hand to begin writing, the result could be utter confusion. But this does not happen, because one hemisphere is usually **dominant** over the other, at least in certain motor activities. When the dominant hemisphere sends a message to one hand, it also sends a message to the other hemisphere, and through it to the other hand. In this way the left hand knows what the right is doing, and confusion is avoided. The result is **coordinated motor activity,** and in most people the left hemisphere—exemplified by the mastery of the right hand—is dominant.

Left-hemisphere dominance is the rule, but there are exceptions. Some people seem to be born with **right-hemisphere dominance.** This could be a genetic trait or it could be due to environmental causes. If part of the left hemisphere is damaged (perhaps due to **anoxia,** or a shortage of oxygen before or during birth), the right hemisphere has the capability of taking over some of the functions of the left hemisphere. This could result in right-hemisphere dominance. Whatever the cause, genetic or environmental, right-hemisphere dominance leads to left-handedness, or possibly to mixed dominance.

One reason for mixed dominance, or mixed-handedness, is that most parents train their children to be right-handed. With this training the naturally left-handed child begins to become right-handed, and the left hemisphere takes over some control that would normally be in the right. This can lead to mixed dominance in the brain as well as mixed-handedness. This sort of mixed dominance could explain some of the problems that have been seen in mixed- and left-handed children, as discussed earlier in this chapter in reference to the work of Theodore Blau. Bed-wetting, Blau suggests, could be one result of mixed dominance. In mixed-dominance children the sphincter that controls urination might be getting two signals from the brain—one from each hemisphere. Such a situation could possibly result in some motor-control confusion and cause mixed-dominance children to have more than the normal amount of difficulty in learning to control bed-wetting. Not enough direct evidence is available as yet to confirm Blau's theory, but his proposals do help explain some of the difficulties that mixed-dominance children sometimes have. Headaches, dizziness, poor sleep, and reading and speech problems could all be related to mixed dominance in the brain. But not all of the problems seen in mixed-dominance children are the direct result of confusing signals from the brain. Some personality traits, such as stubbornness, seem to stem from the social treatment mixed-dominance children receive. And these children get this treatment, initially, because they are different physically.

PERSONALITY AND PHYSICAL DEVELOPMENT

"Left-handed people are sinister." "Fat people are jolly." "Close-set eyes indicate a criminal mentality." These and many other similar sayings have been around for a long time. And for just as long people have tended to believe that personality traits are determined by body types. In the nineteenth century it was even claimed that the shape of the human skull was an indication of personality. Phrenology, the method of interpreting the bumps and depressions on a human skull, was a popular area of study then. But phrenology didn't prove to be very accurate at explaining or predicting human behavior, and few phrenologists are still in business. Similarly, many of the old sayings about personality are no longer believed. Few people actually believe that left-handers are sinister, that fat people are always jolly (especially if they are trying to lose weight and can't), or that close-set eyes have anything to do with criminality.

But there is a link between physical development and personality. In an extreme case, like Down's syndrome (see Chapter 2), a **defective genetic make-up** results in a distinctive body type as well as reduced mentality. **Hormones** provide another link between the body and the personality. **Genes** help determine hormone production, and hormones can affect areas of development related to personality. Hormones control such things as body size, sexual development, and activity and metabolism (the overall rate of the body's physical activities). A person with a large body, extra amounts of sex hormones, and a high rate of metabolism may be an aggressive and overactive personality type. Someone with a large body but a low rate of metabolism may be overweight, sluggish, and dull. With evidence to link the body type with some personality traits, entire theories of personality have been produced.

Biological Theories of Personality

In 1925, Ernst Kretschmer, a German psychiatrist, published his claim to have found a clear link between body types and personality (13). His findings were based on his understanding of hormones and his work with mental patients. He measured the shapes and sizes of many patients and attempted to fit them all into three basic body types. For each type, said Kretschmer, there are specific personality characteristics.

Kretschmer's theory did not hold up very well. There are just too many people who don't fit exactly into any of the categories he described. Even those who do fit into a specific body type don't always have the personality characteristics Krestchmer said they should have.

In the 1940s, W. H. Sheldon of Harvard University updated Kretschmer's work and attempted to develop a more precise classification system for body types (16, 17). Sheldon worked mostly with male college students. Nude front, side, and back photographs were taken of these adolescents, and from 4,000 photographs Sheldon identified three basic body types:

1. **Endomorph:** A soft, round person with a large stomach and underdeveloped muscles and bones.
2. **Mesomorph:** A hard, rectangular person with a strong athletic build.
3. **Ectomorph:** A thin, fragile person with a large brain.

But Sheldon didn't stop with three body types. He identified seven degrees of each type and said combinations of all types and degrees are possible. In other words, each person can be rated from 1 to 7 on each of the three basic body types. An almost pure case of endomorphy, for instance, would be rated as 7 3 1. That is, 7 on the endomorph scale, 3 on the mesomorph scale, and 1 on the ectomorph scale. An equally pure rating of ectomorphy would be 1 3 7. Since each person is rated on three scales of seven, the result is 343 possible body types ($7 \times 7 \times 7 = 343$).

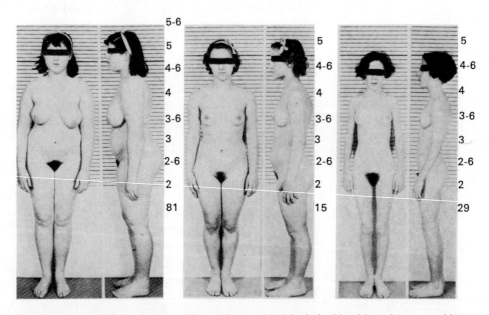

Sheldon's three basic body types. All are 16-year old girls. *Left:* this girl conforms roughly to the endomorphic type and may be designated 7 1 1 on Sheldon's scale. *Center:* this girl conforms roughly to the mesomorphic type and may be designated 1 7 1. *Right:* this girl is an ectomorphic type, though she should be taller to be Sheldon's typical 1 1 7 type.

Next, Sheldon selected a number of personality traits that seemed to represent most human characteristics. After observing a group of young men closely for one year, Sheldon attempted to relate combinations of personality characteristics with specific body types. Many of the relationships he found seemed to be at least partially correct. Some highly endomorphic people (soft, round) do tend to be jolly and sociable. Some highly mesomorphic people (hard, muscular) do tend to be aggressive and dominant, and some ectomorphic people (thin, large brain) tend to be quiet and intellectual.

Biological theories of personality, like Kretschmer's and Sheldon's, are based in part on the assumption that the genes responsible for physical development are also responsible for personality development. This may be true to some extent, but few direct relationships between genes and personality have been found. Theories of personality development based solely on genetic or inherited differences have never been taken very seriously or become very popular by psychologists in the United States. One reason for this is that such theories emphasize inherited differences between individuals. This is opposed to the democratic ideal that says all people are created equal. The way people are treated (as with left-handers) and the way people treat and think of themselves (their cognitive awareness of themselves) are probably more important than genes in determining personality development. Fat or overweight people, for example, might not like to take part in physical activities. But in order to remain part of a group, such people might attempt to be especially sociable and jolly. The social group might reward this trait by always expecting fat people to tell jokes and be life-of-the-party types. Such people are sometimes called extroverts (meaning "to turn outward") because they tend to direct their interests outward, toward other people.

Endomorphs (thin people), on the other hand, might see themselves as physical weaklings. To make up for what they see as a deficiency, they might concentrate on intellectual power. If such people avoid physical activities and stick to their books, society might respond by avoiding them. The result could be a quiet, intellectual loner or an introvert. Such people tend to direct their interests inward toward themselves.

Mesomorphs (muscular and well-built) may see themselves as physically competent and able. Because they know they are good at physical contests — whether it be football or a beauty contest — they tend to get involved in such activities. Society sometimes sees this aggressiveness as bravery or courageousness and often turns to such people for leadership.

Several studies have confirmed that many people do think of others in terms of physical stereotypes (oversimplified beliefs based on widely held opinions rather than on facts). In one study silhouettes, or outline drawings, of basic male body types were made up (1). A questionnaire was then used to determine people's feelings about these specific body types. More than one third of the college students who looked at the silhouettes and answered the questionnaire did have very definite ideas about what type of person each body type represented.

The endomorph silhouette was described as the man who eats the most, eats the most often, will make the poorest athlete, will make the worst soldier, will be the poorest professor of philosophy, can endure pain the least well, will make the least successful military leader, will be least likely to be chosen leader, will make the poorest university president, will be the least aggressive, will drink the most, will be least preferred as a personal friend (but would have many friends), will make the poorest doctor, and will put his own interests above those of others.

This is an almost totally negative stereotype. But stereotypes are not based on fact, so they are not necessarily true. Probably no endomorph has all of the negative traits attributed to the silhouette, and many may have none of those traits. Even so, if people believe the stereotype, they will tend to treat endomorphs accordingly. This treatment can have an effect on the way endomorphs behave and think of themselves.

The mesomorph has an almost completely opposite stereotype. When the silhouette of the male mesomorph was rated, people said that such a man would make the best athlete, the most successful military leader, and the best soldier. He was chosen as the man who would assume leadership, as well as the man who would be elected as leader. He was judged not to smoke at all and to be self-sufficient in the sense of needing friends the least. However, he was most preferred as a friend and was judged to have many friends. People filling out the questionnaire also judged the mesomorph to be the most aggressive, to endure pain the best, to be least likely to have a nervous breakdown, and to drink the least.

The stereotype of the ectomorph is less desirable than that of the mesomorph, but in general more favorable than that of the endomorph. The ectomorph was judged to be the most likely to have a nervous breakdown before the age of 30, to eat the least and the least often, to smoke three packs of cigarettes a day, to be the least self-sufficient in the sense of needing friends the most (but was judged to have the fewest friends), to hold his liquor the worst, to make a poor father, and, as a military leader, to be likely to sacrifice his men.

Children's Body Build and Behavior

Studies relating body type to personality do not really say much about the way people are, but they do give a good indication of how people think of each other, especially where body type is concerned. Studies of children show many of the same things.

One researcher, following Sheldon's procedure, used photographs of young children (2-, 3-, and 4-year-olds) to judge whether they were endomorphs, mesomorphs, or ectomorphs (21). More girls were rated as endomorphs and more boys as mesomorphs, though boys showed more variability. Nursery school teachers then rated the behavior of the children. Male endomorphs were judged to have more socially undesirable qualities, such as revengefulness. Mesomorphs were the most socially acceptable—leaders in play, ambitious, daring; they were judged to be energetic, noisy, and self-confident. Ectomorphs were rated as introverts—quiet, unsocial, and self-reliant. Female mesomorphs were found to be more aggressive than other girls, and female endomorphs were found to recover more easily from upsets. Other than that, no strong relationships were found between female body type and personality.

Studies using silhouettes found that children are aware of physical characteristics in themselves and others (20). Most of the children rated the silhouettes just as adults had done. They did so with silhouettes of both adults and children. This indicates that even young children have learned the stereotypes associated with body image. These children were aware of their own body image and were able to pick out the silhouette most like their own. When asked which they would most like to resemble, most picked the mesomorph figure.

Not only body type but physical attractiveness plays an important role in the way children are treated. This is evident even in nursery school, especially among boys. In one study school children were asked to rate their school mates (4). The unattractive boys were often considered to be more aggressive and "scary" than the attractive boys. In another study physical beauty was found to affect adults' attitudes toward children (3). Women were shown reports of a severe classroom disturbance. When a photograph of an attractive girl was attached to the report, the women tended to excuse the bad behavior. In describing this attractive child, one woman said, "She plays well with everyone, but like anyone else, a bad day can occur. Her cruelty . . . need not be taken too seriously." When the same behavior was described and a picture of an unattractive girl was shown, another woman said, "I think the child would be quite bratty and would probably be a problem to teachers. She would probably try to pick a fight with other children her own age." Attractive children, it seems, are given the benefit of the doubt and are probably given more favorable treatment than are unattractive children.

Rates of Physical Maturity and Personality

Physical attractiveness and body shape and size do have important effects on the way children see themselves and each other. But young children do not differ as much physically as they will later. When they begin to reach puberty and their bodies begin to mature, physical differences between individuals become quite noticeable. This is because children do not all reach physical maturity at the same time. Between the ages of 11 and 13 girls are, on the average, taller and heavier than boys. Also, most girls reach physical maturity earlier than boys by about two years. This can have important effects on behavior and personality development. When most girls are becoming inter-

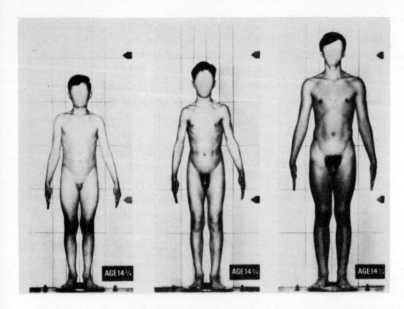

If children mature much earlier than their friends, they may face special treatment that influences their personality development.

ested in dating, their male school mates are usually a head shorter, physically immature, and still uninterested in heterosexual (male-female) relationships. The girls end up spending time with boys who are several years older, or the boys end up with girls who are larger and more mature.

There are differences in rates of physical maturation not only between the sexes but within the sexes. Some children are late maturers, and some are early maturers. If children mature much earlier than their friends, they may face special treatment that relates to personality development.

A longitudinal study conducted in California has followed up on the development of early- and late-maturing children (10). From a group of 90 boys, the 16 earliest maturers and the 16 latest maturers were selected for study. Observations and ratings were made by adults as well as the friends of the boys.

At the age of 14, ratings of physical maturity made from photographs showed almost no overlap between the two groups. The physically mature boys were taller, heavier, and had more pubic hair and larger genitals. From 13 to 15 years of age the physically immature boys tended to be long-legged, of slender build, and relatively weak during the period when they were farthest behind in size. These boys were rated by adults as being lower in physical attractiveness, less masculine, less well-groomed, and more "child-like." However, they did not differ from the more advanced group in ratings of popularity, leadership, self-assurance, cheerfulness, or social effect on the group.

When rated by their friends the physically immature boys showed up about the same as when rated by adults, but the differences between them and the advanced group were not as severe. Their friends rated the physically less mature boys as being more restless, talkative, and bossy. They believed that they were more attention-seeking and less inclined to have self-assurance in school. They were also regarded by friends as being less popular and less likely to be leaders. They were also rated as being less likely to have older friends, as having less of a sense of humor about themselves, and as having a less attractive general appearance.

In addition to ratings by adults and friends, personality tests have been used to determine the effects of early and late maturity (11). The **Thematic Apperception Test** (TAT) is one personality test that has been used (though not all psychologists agree that it is very useful or valid). In this test subjects are shown a series of pictures and asked to make up a story to go along with each picture. They are asked to tell who the people in the pictures are, how they got into the situation pictured, and what will happen to them. This test is called a **projective test** because the people telling the stories tend to project their own needs and ideas onto the main character in the story. The actions of the main character, then, are assumed to be seen as reasonable or desirable to the story-teller. This isn't always the case, and projective tests sometimes have very little to do with the true personality of the person taking the test. But if the stories are examined with care by a skilled professional, valid clues can sometimes be found to the test taker's personality.

When the TAT was given to early- and late-maturing 17-year-old boys, it was found that more of the late- than early-maturers used TAT themes that reflected negative images of themselves. The heroes of their stories were often described as unintelligent weaklings. They were rejected, scorned, or disapproved of by their parents and other authorities. Many of the main characters in these stories left home or defied their parents. They often fell in love or had a romance and were helped, encouraged, or given something by someone other than their parents. The late-maturers also tended to describe the hero as feeling helpless and seeking aid or sympathy.

These themes suggest that late-maturing boys have negative self-concepts. They seem to blame their parents for their condition, although perhaps unconsciously. And they feel relatively weak, alone, and helpless. Therefore, they seek assistance from others—perhaps by falling in love.

The physically advanced group tended to tell stories in which the hero was aggressive in a physical and antisocial fashion. They also tended, more often than the others, to say they couldn't think of anything to say about the pictures. This can be seen as an indication of self-confidence—a finding that they can get away with aggressive behavior if they feel like it. It also suggests a tendency to be rather matter of fact and unimaginative (as has been found in other studies).

The TAT did suggest that the two groups of boys have some similarities.

Several themes showed up about equally in the stories of both groups. These included: stories in which the hero is prevented by his parents from doing something he wants to do; in which he establishes good relations with his parents; attempts to gain a high goal or do something important, or seeks fame and fortune. From these themes it seems that although late-maturing boys may have more hostility toward their parents, they have about the same amount of positive feelings as do early maturers. Both groups seem to want to be successful.

Effects of Early Maturity

In the United States, where physical maturity and athletic ability are respected, early maturers, especially males, seem to have a definite advantage. It is not unlikely, for example, that positions of leadership will be given by adults to the most mature of a group of young boys. Such boys may develop into more responsible and mature adults with a great deal of self-confidence because that has been expected of them more often than of late-maturing boys, and because by the time they are adults, they will have had more experience at leadership.

Athletics offer early maturers another advantage. Because of their superior height, weight, and strength they usually excel at athletics and achieve a high degree of social status among their friends. This prestige and status may continue into adult life even though the late maturers catch up in terms of physical size and ability.

Early-maturing males also have an advantage in their relations with females. Maturing at about the same time as the girls in their classes, they have a several-year advantage over late-maturing boys. They are well matched with girls the same age and are able to take out girls without the embarrassment of being the smaller member of the pair.

Even though late-maturing boys eventually catch up in height and weight, they undergo a long period of social disadvantage during an important period. This could have serious effects on their later social and emotional lives, especially if they do not receive reassurance that they are normal and will eventually catch up.

Effects of Early and Late Maturity on Females

The rate of maturation varies in females as it does in males, but the effects of early and late maturity seem to be much less important among females. In some ways the effects are even the opposite of those seen in boys.

For one thing, until recently, leadership qualities and athletic abilities have not been stressed for young girls. Early-maturing girls, therefore, would not have had the same advantages as early-maturing boys. Because social, rather than physical, abilities have traditionally been stressed during the development of young girls, the stereotypes associated with body type have not had as much impact on females as on males.

Athletics offer early maturing boys
a definite advantage.

Not only does body type seem to count for less with females, early maturity can be a drawback rather than an advantage for females. Several years may go by before an early-maturing girl can go out with boys in her class without feeling conspicuous because she is more mature than the boys. Early-maturing girls, if they are not psychologically mature, may get into social and sexual complications by dating older boys.

One researcher has reported that late-maturing girls were judged by adult observers as having higher prestige and more leadership qualities than early maturers (9). Late-maturing girls were found to have been mentioned more often in high school newspapers and to have been elected to more high school offices (12). TAT stories told by these girls at age 17 revealed few differences between early- and late-maturing girls.

Many of these studies of early- and late-maturing males and females were conducted in the 1940s and 1950s, and few of them have been updated or repeated in recent years. Because cultural and social values have changed quite a bit since then, it is difficult to say whether or not rates of maturing have the same effects they may have had a generation ago. In any case, such studies do suggest the importance of physical development in determining the way individuals think of themselves and others.

Developmental Deviations and Handicaps

An almost infinite number of possible genetic combinations and environmental conditions are responsible for the fact that no two people are ever exactly alike physically. Because of physical differences, no two people ever receive the exact same treatment. And the treatment they do receive can be harmful or helpful to future development. Left-handed children may receive training that goes against their natural tendencies. This could result in confusion and learning problems. Early-maturing children may receive special treatment that could result in the development of aggression or of leadership qualities. In both cases, however, these children would usually be considered to be within the range of normal physical development. But not all children are physically normal.

Medical progress has done much to improve the survival rate of premature infants and many other infants and children suffering from conditions that would previously have been fatal. This progress, as well as genetic defects, accidents, and diseases, has resulted in an increasing number of physically handicapped children. Various studies suggest that between 5 and 20 percent of all children have serious physical handicaps, and about one third of these children will have psychological problems as a direct result of their physical condition (15).

Sensory disabilities (such as blindness and deafness) account for about 20 percent of all handicaps. Of about 100,000 cases of blindness in the United States, 20 percent are due to genetic causes, 15 percent to accidents, and the rest to disease (7). **Blindness,** like any other physical disability, can keep children from taking part in physical and social activities. This can hamper both physical and social development, and blindness itself can cause delay in learning. All of these factors can result in psychological problems. One study has found, however, that most of the psychological problems blind children experience are due to the attitudes of other people (19). In a school for the blind, 143 adolescents were interviewed. Most complained that they were particularly disturbed when people pitied them, treated them like helpless children, and put too much emphasis on their limitations.

Deafness brings with it another set of problems that can interfere with development. Deaf infants miss out on the cooing and reassuring sounds made by parents. These sounds are especially important to the development of emotional security. Because of their handicap, deaf infants are usually less responsive to their parents than are infants who can hear. Parents who do not realize their child is deaf may, in turn, react negatively to what they see as aloofness on the part of the child and give that child less positive treatment than they would give a child who can hear.

Physical deformities (loss of a limb, a crippling disease, and so on) and chronic or long-term illness in children can also cause severe problems in psychological development. Such children miss out on many normal physical and social activities and may develop problems similar (but more severe) to those seen in late-maturing males. In addition, researchers have found that physically handicapped and chronically ill children tend to have problems in school (15). These problems may be due to frequent absences, lack of strength, or general discouragement, but no matter what the cause, the result can be delayed intellectual achievement and development. This can lead to a dislike of school and even more problems. Chronically ill children, when compared with healthy children, are more frequently truant (absent without permission), more often troublesome in school, more often socially isolated, and more likely to be described by teachers as having poor attitudes toward their work.

The degree of seriousness of personality problems seen in physically handicapped children varies. Some become severely disturbed, while others seem to be well adjusted. It depends not only on how such children are treated but on the way they accept their condition. Extreme feelings of inferiority, self-pity, fear, and hostility as well as an acceptance of the role of "helpless cripple" can all be damaging to personality development (2). While these children may be at a special disadvantage because of their physical condition, it does appear that they can be helped toward normal personality development with encouragement and reassurance from parents, teachers, friends, and, in more severe cases, specialists like social workers, guidance counselors, and psychologists (15). It has been found that children can adjust to almost any physical defect (except, perhaps, cases that involve severe mental retardation) without serious consequences to personality development (6). In most instances, the family can be of great help by encouraging the development of skills and abilities that will offset the physical disability. The same holds true for the almost infinite number of differences seen in physical and motor development. Fat, tall, hairy, clumsy, late-maturing, and left-handed children can all have normal personality development if they are encouraged to develop their abilities, and if they are not constantly made to feel that something is wrong with them.

SUMMARY

Being left-handed, tall, fat, loud, attractive, hairy, clumsy—all of these physical characteristics can have an effect on the way people are treated. This, in turn, can have an effect on the way people behave. Therefore, in order to understand children and their behavior, it is necessary to understand physical development.

There are three general principles of physical development: cephalocaudal (from head to tail), proximodistal (from the center outward), and from general to specific. Three general patterns of physical growth have also been identified: neural (including development of the head, brain, spinal cord, and eyes); reproductive (development of the primary sex characteristics and reproductive organs), and somatic, or body growth.

Among the major changes that take place during physical development are changes in kind, number, size, shape, position, color, and texture. These changes as well as all physical growth are genetically determined, but environmental influences, including stimulation, exercise and practice, influence all areas of physical development.

Motor development also follows predictable patterns. With a certain degree of environmental stimulation and practice, infants gradually gain the ability to control their bodily movements. The brain is especially important in motor development. It interprets information from the environment and coordinates actions and interactions with the environment.

Physical development has been found to affect personality development in several ways. Studies have shown that the way individuals behave and think of themselves and others is influenced by physical appearances. Even children's behavior is influenced by physical appearances.

Rates of maturity have also been found to have effects on personality development, but probably the most obvious instances of physical development influencing personality have to do with handicapped children. While such children may be seriously disadvantaged, in most cases they can have normal personality development if they acquire skills and abilities that offset their physical disabilities.

Physical Attractiveness, Sex, and Adult Punitiveness

Various studies have shown that physical attractiveness is an important personal characteristic which influences the judgments and behaviors of others and the inferences that they make about another person. For example, Clifford and Walster (1973), in a study that examined the effect of physical attractiveness on teacher expectations, showed that elementary school teachers thought that attractive children had greater intellectual potential than did unattractive children, even when they had identical information on both groups of children. A child's sex has also been shown to influence people's judgments and inferences about him or her; for example, some evidence suggests that a parent is more permissive with a child of the opposite sex. Dion (1974) reported on two studies that examined the relationship of both a child's sex and attractiveness to punishing behavior on the part of an adult.

In her first study Dion had 52 adult females (chosen because in our culture women are the primary socializers of young children) view an interaction between the experimenter and a child on what the female subjects thought was closed circuit TV but what was in fact a video tape. This procedure allowed the child to have his or her attractiveness manipulated or altered. On the video tape children performed a picture-matching task and on all tapes always made 15 correct and 15 incorrect responses. The adult subjects watched the performance and then rated the child's performance on a questionnaire following the tape. The subjects also responded to questionnaire items designed to show how they felt about the child they had observed and were asked to rate their assessment of the child's general personality. The study used one 8-year-old white male and one similar female child in the video tapes. Make-up and hair style changes were employed to alter attractiveness, but the children always wore the same clothes. In her second study Dion repeated the same kinds of procedures, but on this occasion used adult males as the subjects.

The results of the studies showed, first, that both female and male adult subjects did perceive differences in the attractiveness of the children. Thus, the manipulation of the children's physical appearance was successful. Second, the *male* subjects were *not* influenced by either a child's attractiveness or sex when it came to evaluating the child's performance and abilities at the task. *Female* subjects were influenced, for they tended to be more lenient toward an attractive boy than toward an attractive girl; they also tended to penalize an unattractive boy more than an attractive boy, but reversed this with girl children. Finally, in rating the children's personalities and motivation on the questionnaire, male subjects were more positive toward boys than they were toward girls. Female subjects showed no sex differences in their ratings.

Taken overall, the results of Dion's studies suggest that, particularly for boys, it is an advantage to be perceived by adult females as being attractive. However, it should be remembered that these studies had a task/activity/performance as the central activity of the child, and Dion cautions that perceptions, judgments, and actions by adults might be centered around the task activity, and thus they might behave or react differently in more social or less structured situations.

Based on M. Clifford and E. Walster, "The Effect of Physical Attractiveness on Teacher Expectation," *Journal of Personality and Social Psychology*, 1973, 9, 183–188; K. E. Dion, "Children's Physical Attractiveness and Sex as Determinants of Adult Punitiveness," *Developmental Psychology*, 1974, 10 (5), 772–778.

RESEARCH REPORT 5.2

Physical Appearance and Interpersonal Attraction

We know that some important aspects of physical growth and development as well as variability in growth may influence the life and times of a person. Evidence suggests, for example, that the life experiences of early-maturing adolescents are different from those of later-maturing adolescents. In addition, there is a link between the value judgments that people make about a person and the stereotypes of physical characteristics which exist within our culture. A person's physical characteristics are important because they can influence the judgments and assumptions that others will make about him or her.

Kleck, Richardson, and Ronald (1974) investigated the relationship between physical appearance and interpersonal attraction in two studies. The authors noted at the outset that other researchers had found consistent results suggesting a connection between physical characteristics and social acceptance. However, this early research was not clear with regard to whether particular physical characteristics were important because they influenced the *initial interaction* between people or whether they were of *continuing* importance during long-term social interactions. Kleck and colleagues speculated that distinctive physical characteristics might be important because it is on the basis of physical characteristics—attractiveness or unattractiveness—that initial interactions between children are or are not made. Further, it might be that in situations where the opportunity exists for a longer-term interaction, the importance of physical characteristics in judgments and behavior might diminish.

In their first study, carried out with boys from 9 to 14 years at a three-week vacation camp, the authors obtained social-acceptance ratings on each child based upon interview data in which children indicated the extent to which they liked, or found acceptable and wanted as friends, other children in the camp. The authors then selected five children from the two extreme groups—that is, five children judged to be very socially *acceptable* and five children judged to be very *unacceptable.* (The only restriction was that each group was of similar racial composition.) The researchers then asked 73 other male children who were attending a different section (in time) of the vacation camp to look at photographs of the 10 boys selected earlier. The children had no knowledge of or contact with the original group and were asked to rate the children in the photographs on the basis of social acceptance. The results showed that the children much preferred the high socially accepted children over those low in social acceptance.

In the second study the authors proceeded in a similar manner, but instead of selecting children from the very extreme groups of social acceptance or unacceptance they selected larger groups from less extreme positions. In addition, in the second study the subjects or judges were both male and female campers drawn from the same setting, and they viewed the photographs a year later. Once again the results were striking. The authors stated, "The results clearly support the proposition that differences in perceived physical attractiveness systematically relate to social acceptance." They also found the results of their two studies to be consistent with the findings of other researchers. In conclusion Kleck noted that their results suggest that physical appearance variables continue to be important for boys even after significant periods of interaction.

These studies are a neat demonstration of the extent to which human beings are influenced by the physical characteristics of others. They clearly show that physical characteristics significantly influence the decisions and judgments human beings make about each other. It seems that we often do not respond to the inner man or woman but to his or her appearance.

Based on R. Kleck, S. Richardson, and L. Ronald, "Physical Appearance Cues and Interpersonal Attraction in Children," *Child Development*, 1974, *45*, 305–310.

REFERENCES

1. Brodsky, C. M. *A Study of Norms of Body Form-Behavior Relationships.* Washington, D.C.: Catholic University of America Press, 1954.
2. Coleman, J. C. *Abnormal Psychology and Modern Life*, 4th ed. Glenview, Ill.: Scott, Foresman, 1972.
3. Dion, K. "Physical Attractiveness and Evaluations of Children's Transgressions," *Journal of Personality and Social Psychology*, 1972.
4. Dion, K., and E. Bersheid. "Physical Attractiveness and Socioeconomic Choice in Nursery School Children," Research Report, 1971. In E. Aronson, *The Social Animal.* San Francisco: Freeman, 1972.
5. Gesell, A., and H. Thompson. "Learning and Growth in Identical Twins," *Genetics and Psychology Monographs*, 1929, *6*, 1–123.
6. Goldenson, R. M. "Body Image," *The Encyclopedia of Human Behavior.* New York: Doubleday, 1970.
7. Goldenson, R. M. "Blindness," *The Encyclopedia of Human Behavior.* New York: Doubleday, 1970.
8. Goldenson, R. M. "Motor Development," *The Encyclopedia of Human Development.* New York: Doubleday, 1970.

9. Jones, H. E. "Adolescence in Our Society." In *The Family in a Democratic Society.* New York: Columbia University Press, 1949, 70–82.
10. Jones, M. C., and N. Bayley. "Physical Maturing among Boys as Related to Behavior," *Journal of Educational Psychology,* 1950, *41,* 129–148.
11. Jones, M. C., and P. H. Mussen. "Self-conceptions, Motivations and Interpersonal Attitudes of Late- and Early-maturing Boys," *Child Development,* 1957, *28,* 242–256.
12. Jones, M. C., and P. H. Mussen. "Self-conceptions, Motivations, and Interpersonal Attitudes of Early- and Late-maturing Girls," *Child Development,* 1958, *29,* 491–501.
13. Kretschmer, E. *Physique and Character.* New York: Harcourt, Brace & World, 1925.
14. "Limits to Growth," *Science News,* 1976, *109* (25), 393.
15. Pless, I. B., and K. J. Roghmann. "Chronic Illness and Its Consequences." In *Annual Progress in Child Psychiatry and Child Development, 1972.* New York: Bruner/Mazel.
16. Sheldon, W. H. *The Varieties of Human Physique,* New York: Harper & Brothers, 1940.
17. Sheldon, W. H. *The Varieties of Temperament,* New York: Harper & Brothers, 1942.
18. "Sinister Psychology," *Science News,* 1974, *106* (14), 220–222.
19. Sommers, V. S. "The Influence of Parental Attitudes and Social Environment on the Personality of the Adolescent Blind." New York: American Foundation for the Blind, 1949.
20. Staffieri, J. R., and B. R. McCandless. "A Study of Social Stereotype and Body Image in Children." Paper presented at the 50th Annual Meeting of the American Educational Research Association, 1966.
21. Walker, R. N. "Body Build and Behavior in Young Children," *Monographs of the Society for Research in Child Development,* 1962, *27,* Ser. No. 84.

H uman development consists of physical growth and maturation as well as changes in behavior over time. Most of these changes in behavior come about as a result of learning through interaction with the environment, including people in the environment. Learning is the process by which new information, habits, and abilities are acquired. If learning were not possible, human development and survival itself would not be possible.

learning

In the 1950s juvenile delinquents were famous for their greasy ducktail hair-cuts, black leather jackets, and gang wars. This particular stereotype is seen less often in the 1970s, but juvenile delinquency still exists and remains a problem. **Juvenile delinquents** are children whose antisocial behavior is considered to be beyond parental control and are therefore subject to legal action. Auto theft, robbery, burglary, assault, truancy, arson, vandalism, drug abuse, and running away from home are the offenses most often associated with juvenile delinquency. When legal action is brought against juveniles for such offenses, the result is usually confinement in a state institution. This gets the offenders off the streets, but it does little to correct delinquent behavior or to teach socially acceptable behavior. Researchers in Lawrence, Kansas, have attempted to change this situation by reeducating delinquent children in a controlled environment specially designed to overcome behavioral difficulties (29).

The environment they are using is called **Achievement Place.** It consists of a residential home, two trained "teaching parents," and seven or eight youthful offenders (11 to 16 years old) who have been sent there by the Juvenile Court of the Department of Social Welfare in the local community. The home is run according to the principles of behavior modification (see Chapter 1), and its goal is to educate youths in academic, social, and self-care or vocational skills.

Most children sent to Achievement Place have had trouble in school. Truancy, tardiness, and disruptive behavior have usually led to suspension or dropping out. A great many factors are involved in producing such behavior, but lack of motivation or desire is often a major problem. Most of these students don't seem to care about getting an education and see no connection between doing well in school and achieving success in later life. One way to change this situation is to make the rewards of doing well in school more immediate and understandable. Students at Achievement Place go back to school or remain in their community school – but with a difference. Each student has a daily report card on which teachers in each class note whether or not the student has behaved in class, completed homework and other assignments, or performed adequately on tests and exams. Back at Achievement Place the teaching parents give students a certain number of points for each desired behavior. These points can be used by the children to purchase a variety of privileges – free time, trips, spending money.

Elery Philips, Dean Fixen, and Montrose Wolf of the University of Kansas helped design and put Achievement Place into operation. They found that before using the daily report card students spent about 25 percent of their study time in appropriate study behavior. Using the card and point system increased

A lack of motivation or desire leads some students to drop out of conventional school systems.

this figure to almost 90 percent. An average of one letter-grade increase was common for most students after a nine-week period.

For many delinquents, however, school is only part of their problem. In the Achievement Place home teaching parents, who are trained in human development, instruct the children in such areas as positive social interaction, personal cleanliness, and community involvement. Specific behavior goals for each youth are set, based on behavior that members of the family, school, and community as well as the teaching parents believe should be changed. Desired behavior earns points. Undesirable behavior—speaking aggressively, arguing, disobeying, being late, stealing, lying, and cheating—loses points. When self-control, responsibility, and the ability to work productively at the home and in school are demonstrated, the child is ready to return to the community.

Follow-up data indicate that the effects on behavior of Achievement Place are long-lasting. Most youths who have attended Achievement Place continue to go to school, and very few get into trouble with the law again. The researchers reported that after two years only 19 percent of the graduates had to be sent back to Achievement Place, compared with 53 percent who had been

Fred S. Keller (1899–   ), designer of the
Personalized System of Instruction (PSI).

in a state institution and had been sent back. Because Achievement Place has
had such good results, it has become a model for dozens of similar homes
across the country.

The point system used at Achievement Place is not new to educators. For
years teachers have been giving gold stars and other prizes and awards for good
grades and good behavior. Research on behavior and learning, however, suggests additional methods of improving teaching. One method in particular—
based on behavior modification techniques and learning theory—is gaining
increasing acceptance in schools. Designed by Fred S. Keller, it is known as
the **Personalized System of Instruction (PSI).**

In the early 1960s Keller was asked by the government of Brazil to study
the educational system of that country and make recommendations for
change. The traditional lecture system was in use there. Keller saw major
drawbacks in the system and proposed methods of overcoming them. The
lecture system, for example, assumes that all students have the same capability and can learn at the same rate. Grading often depends on whether the
student understands the material at the rate it is given.

The lecture system has other drawbacks. In some ways it is too unstructured. Some lecturers follow a text or outline, but many discuss whatever comes to mind at a particular time of day. In other ways the lecture system is too structured. Students are required to be in a certain place at a specific
time to hear the lecture. Final exams for all courses are usually scheduled
within a short period of time, and few exceptions are made for any outside
problems or commitments (financial, social, personal) a student may have.

The lecture system can be troublesome in other ways. Some lecturers are admittedly brilliant entertainers, but most are simply not able to hold the attention of a class for an hour, much less for three hours a week. Even if students are interested, note-taking detracts from concentration, and concentration detracts from note-taking. Finally, almost anything a lecturer can say is already written down somewhere.

With these problems in mind Keller devised a system of teaching that allows students to proceed at their own rates. He decided that information should be presented in small sequential steps. Objectives should be clearly defined and stated prior to each step, and students should demonstrate complete mastery of material before moving on to the next step.

Following the Keller method, an instructor selects course material from a textbook, a variety of texts, or any other appropriate source. On the semester system the material is divided into 20 subunits — each representing a little less than one week's work. The instructor tells the student to learn the material and indicates the objectives, study questions, and important points to be aware of. Upon completing each section the student asks to be tested. If the test indicates that the material has been learned, the student goes on to the next section. If not, more study is indicated, and a different form of the test is given when the student again requests it. In this manner a student takes the course in whatever amount of time is required.

Short essay questions are usually used as tests in this type of course, and students are allowed to defend any errors or mistakes. One year is often allowed to complete a semester's work. Those who do not complete it are not further penalized with an F, but are allowed to withdraw from the course. All those who complete the material get an A. Anyone who finishes ahead of time can devote more hours to other courses or can move on to the next course.

In the PSI system no lectures are given. The instructor merely designs the course — and continually redesigns it as necessary — and is available to answer questions. PSI provides immediate feedback, since tests are graded on the spot, and positive reinforcement, since complete mastery always earns an A. Progress is charted in a public place, such as a study hall bulletin board, and students are encouraged to compete and interact with each other.

Upon his return from Brazil, Keller and J. G. Sherman put PSI to use at several universities in the United States. Teachers who have used the system say students learn more and enjoy courses more when they are taken under the Keller method (29) than when they are taken under the traditional method. PSI not only works but works impartially for all students. Students evaluated in one study had better recall five weeks after a PSI-administered course than those who took the same course given in the traditional method. The individualized approach also gives weaker students the necessary structure to improve study skills, and continued success serves as a motivator.

The Keller method and similar approaches to learning do, however, have some drawbacks. Students who are not highly motivated or who do not particularly care about learning or mastering the material do not always do well when they are allowed to work (or not work) at their own pace. Brighter students tend to speed up, while slower and less motivated students tend to slow down. This leads to a high rate of incompletions and drop-outs in such courses. One evaluation of a "self-paced" math course, for example, found that students who completed the course made great gains, but the number who actually finished was lower than when the same course was taught by more traditional methods (7).

Even with these drawbacks, the Keller method has been found to be extremely promising in courses where a large body of information is to be conveyed. It is especially useful in the physical sciences, but is also used in sociology, economics, psychology, and introductory courses in all fields. In 1973 more than 1,000 courses were being taught in the United States by the Keller method.

Behavior modification as used at Achievement Place and in PSI is not very mysterious or complicated. It is simply the systematic application of what has been learned about learning. When this knowledge is used it is possible to modify or change many human behaviors into more effective or positive social patterns. Achievement Place and PSI are only two examples of how learning technology has been put to work in recent years. With behavior modification techniques delinquents can be taught socially acceptable behaviors, and students can be taught a variety of subjects, including how to learn more efficiently. But long before this type of learning takes place, much learning has already occurred. Delinquents have learned delinquent behavior; students have learned to be students. From infancy learning is one of the most important functions of the human organism. Learning is the key to human development. Without it survival is not possible.

SIMPLE LEARNING

"A blooming, buzzing confusion" greets newborn infants upon their arrival into the world, according to William James, one of the first influential U.S. psychologists. What he meant was that infants are faced with millions of sights, sounds, tastes, smells, and other environmental stimuli that are completely new and meaningless to them. Infants must learn to make sense of this confusion if they are to survive and develop. But learning takes time and experience.

With little or no learning infants begin life by responding to the environment in a set or reflexive manner (see Chapter 4). They blink at bright lights, withdraw from pain, and turn their heads toward the touch of their mother's nipple on their cheeks. These and other reflexive behaviors necessary for survival are the result of preexisting connections in the infant's nervous system and brain. These connections are part of the genetic blueprint of each newborn child.

Reflexes may be necessary for infant survival, but they are not enough to help infants make sense of the environment, and they are not enough for complete human development. In many lower species, such as bees, reflexes and instinctive behaviors are all that are necessary. Bees are born with a set of behaviors that do not change much throughout their lives. Bees behave like bees and remain bees. If infants continued to rely on their reflexive behaviors, they would remain infants. But this does not happen. The connections in the human nervous system and brain can be changed. New connections can be made. When the connections are changed, new behaviors emerge. The new and changing connections are the result of learning.

Learning is the process by which new information, habits, abilities, and behaviors are acquired. In general, learning is a modification of behavior due to contact with the environment, but three requirements must be met before learning can be said to have taken place (10). First, contact with the environment must bring about a change in the way an individual thinks, perceives, or reacts to the environment. Second, the change must be the result of observation, repetition, practice, study, or some other activity. (Behavior changes brought about by fatigue, drugs, illness, or maturation are not thought of as learned changes.) The third important requirement necessary for learning is that the change in behavior must be lasting. A fact or a behavior pattern that is forgotten immediately after it has been acquired has not really been learned.

Associations

The first step in making sense of the world is making **associations,** or connections, among different aspects of the world. Things that are experienced together will be linked, or associated, in the memory. One of the first such associations infants make has to do with nipples and milk.

Infants will make reflexive sucking movements if a nipple is placed in their mouth. Experiments using two types of bottles and nipples show that infants also make associations (20). If a bottle of milk with a large, smooth, flesh-colored nipple is presented along with a bottle of lemon juice with a small, rough, green-and-yellow-striped nipple, infants will usually try both nipples. After several attempts, however, they begin to be able to tell the difference, or discriminate, between the sweet- and sour-tasting nipples. This can be seen in their reaction to the two bottles. Infants will begin to make sucking motions when they see the smooth nipple, even before it touches their lips. They will not make sucking movements when they see strangely colored, sour-tasting nipples. They will usually turn away from the touch of the small, rough nipple.

One of the first associations infants make has to do with nipples and milk.

These reactions indicate that an association has been made between the large, soft nipple and the pleasant-tasting milk and between the strange-looking nipple and its unpleasant taste. Learning has taken place. The three requirements for learning have been met. Contact with the environment (nipple) has brought about a change in the way the infant reacts (to the nipple). This change is the result of repetition or practice. The infant will usually have to experience the sweet- and sour-tasting nipples several times before the association is made. The change in behavior is lasting. The infant will usually remember to avoid the green and yellow nipple in the future.

The formation of associations is an important part of any type of learning, from the simplest to the most complex. Associations, however, do not fully explain learning. Even the most basic kinds of learning are influenced by **cognitive processes,** or mental activities (24). In other words, when an association is made some sort of mental activity takes place inside the organism. Cognitive processes may not always be obvious in simple types of learning (such as when an infant learns almost automatically to refuse a sour-tasting nipple), but in more complex kinds of learning mental activity is apparent. The influence of cognitive processes is seen whenever behavior is affected by thinking or by making a decision. When someone reflects on or thinks about the solution to a problem or chooses among alternative solutions, cognition is involved.

In this chapter the processes involved in learning will be described and the influences of cognition on learning will be mentioned. A more complete description of cognitive development follows in Chapter 7.

The Russian psychologist Ivan Pavlov was one of the first to describe **classical conditioning.** He was investigating the process of digestion in dogs, and because digestion begins in the mouth with the production of saliva, Pavlov attempted to measure the amount of saliva produced by his laboratory animals. Usually, as soon as a dog sees its food saliva is produced. Similarly, hungry people's mouths begin to water at the sight of food, and infants begin to make sucking motions at the sight of a nipple. But Pavlov ran into a problem with his experiment. The dogs sometimes began to salivate before they even saw the food. If the dogs heard their keepers rattling the food dishes, for instance, they would begin to salivate. At first this response upset Pavlov because he was interested in studying salivation in connection with digestion, not in connection with the sounds of dishes rattling. But eventually Pavlov came to realize that something interesting was happening.

In dogs and humans food usually stimulates or activates the salivary glands. But Pavlov's dogs were reacting to a type of stimulation that should not normally cause salivation. Pavlov called this **psychic stimulation** and de-

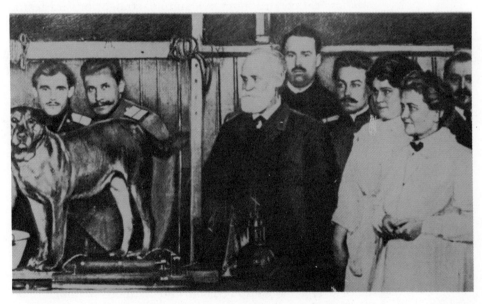

Russian psychologist Ivan Pavlov (1849–1936), one of the first researchers to describe classical conditioning.

signed experiments to study it. He used a musical note as a stimulus and played it just before the dogs were given a bit of food. The food naturally caused salivation, but before long the dogs began to salivate at the sound of the musical note. They had apparently learned that the sound meant food was on the way. They had made an association between the sound and the food.

Under normal conditions food is a **stimulus** (S) that causes salivation as a **response** (R). Because food will cause salivation unconditionally (under most circumstances or conditions), the food in Pavlov's experiment is called an **unconditioned stimulus** (US). The salivation response is called an **unconditioned response** (UR) for the same reason. It occurs unconditionally or under almost any conditions when food is presented. When Pavlov introduced a special condition, the musical note, it was called a **conditioned stimulus** (CS). Usually a conditioned stimulus is neutral. In other words, musical notes do not normally cause salivation because they are not usually associated with food. With training, however, Pavlov's dogs learned to associate the CS (music) with the US (food). These conditioned dogs eventually got to the point where the CS (music) always produced the UR (salivation). When this happens the unconditioned response is called a **conditioned response** (CR), and in classical conditioning a conditioned stimulus (music) always results in a conditioned response (saliva).

Classical conditioning is a simple, straightforward learning process that everyone experiences from the first days of life. Conditioning experiments with infants have shown that classical conditioning operates in humans in the same manner it does in animals (17, 18). This is seen in studies in which a sound or a tone is presented seconds before infants are fed. After several trials the infants begin making sucking motions at the sound of the tone, before the food is presented. Such experiments have been successful with infants as young as 2 days old. Through classical conditioning infants can learn to associate a sound with food just as they learn to associate the sight of a nipple with food. School children salivate at the sound of a lunch bell. As they grow and interact with the environment they learn conditioned responses to all sorts of stimuli. But all people do not receive the same conditioning, and differences in conditioning lead to differences in behavior.

Factors in Conditioning

Numerous experiments by Pavlov and others have demonstrated the various factors involved in making conditioning work. The strength of the conditioned stimulus (music in Pavlov's experiment) is important. Pavlov's dogs would not have learned to respond to a specific sound if that sound were not loud or strong enough to be heard and distinctive enough to be separated from other sounds in the laboratory environment. The order in which the conditioned stimulus (music) and the unconditioned stimulus (food) are presented is also important. Conditioning works best if the CS (music) comes before the

US (food). If the dogs are fed before the musical note is sounded, they will have trouble making the proper association and will probably not learn to associate the sound with the food. The amount of time between the conditioned stimulus and the unconditioned stimulus is another factor. If the note is sounded 20 minutes before the food is presented, the association between the sound and the food will probably not be made. And, finally, repetition is important. The first time a dog hears a musical note before being fed the sound probably means little to the animal. After the sound and food are presented in association several times, however, a connection between the two begins to be made. In other words, the more experience an organism (animal or human) has with a set of stimuli and responses, the more likely the organism will be to associate the stimulus with the response.

Conditioning is not always permanent. Conditioned responses can be unlearned by a process known as **extinction.** The training Pavlov gave his dogs could be extinguished by presenting the music over and over again without presenting the food. Eventually the association between the music and the food was broken. Even reflexive behaviors can sometimes be extinguished. The infant, who reflexively sucks on a nipple, will lose that reflexive behavior if the nipple is always sour tasting.

Avoiding Conditioning

Classical conditioning has been found to be most effective with young children and to become less effective as children grow older (11). This may be because it is an automatic process that seems to depend on only the most basic nervous system connections. Neither insight nor thinking is necessary. An infant does not think: "There's the good-tasting nipple, now I begin sucking." The infant doesn't have to think at all. Once the association has been made between the nipple and the food, the sucking reflex occurs every time the stimulus is presented. This type of conditioning may work less well with older children because they do think about what is happening. Chapter 1 discussed a well-known experiment in which a small child, Little Albert, was taught to fear white rats through classical conditioning. The experimenters taught Albert to fear rats by presenting the rat and a loud, frightening noise at the same time. Albert soon began to associate the rat with the frightening noise and learned to fear white rats. An older child or an adult can usually resist this type of conditioning. A child who realizes that the noise is not harmful may just ignore it and go on playing with the white rat.

Although classical conditioning is a relatively simple type of learning that is most effectively used to teach associations between stimuli and already-existing behaviors (such as reflexes), it is a powerful type of learning that accounts for much human behavior. A young child who has been bitten by a dog may form a strong association between dogs and pain and never overcome a fear of dogs. Many adults gag and begin to feel sick at the sight and smell of vomit. It is possible that as children they learned a strong association between vomit and sickness. The adult reaction (vomiting) may be a conditioned response that was learned very early in life.

Operant Conditioning

Infants are usually active little creatures. They laugh, cry, and wave their arms and legs around. Many of these behaviors are in response to stimuli in the environment. But even young infants do much more than respond to the environment. They may cry or smile in response to something, and as they do so they gradually begin to learn that their behavior can have an effect on the environment, including people in the environment. Infants cry to get fed or to get attention. In such cases they are stimulating the environment rather than being stimulated by it. If the environment (parents) responds in a manner that pleases the infant, the child is likely to repeat the behavior that caused the response. Infants quickly learn that crying helps them get what they want, whether it is food or attention. This type of learning is called **operant conditioning** (see Chapter 1).

In operant conditioning the organism doing the learning, rather than the environment, provides the stimulus. The stimulus causes the environment to react, and if the reaction is pleasant or desirable, the organism is likely to repeat the initial behavior (stimulate the environment again). Eventually an association will be made between the behavior and the reaction of the environment (crying results in attention). This type of learning is called operant conditioning because the organism doing the learning or being conditioned is operating on the environment. Behaviors learned through this type of conditioning are called **operant behaviors.** Operant conditioning is also called behavior modification because the behavior of the person doing the operating is changed or modified in some way after reacting with the environment. The initial behavior is more or less likely to be repeated, depending on the response (desired or undesired) of the environment.

Like classical conditioning, operant conditioning has been a basic method of learning throughout human history. Hungry infants have always cried (stimulated or operated on the environment) when they wanted their parents to respond. Parents have stimulated children with such things as attention, praise, candy, or toys when they wanted their children to respond or repeat a certain behavior. Through operant conditioning both parents and children learn those behaviors that will most effectively get them what they want.

Some of the principles of operant conditioning can be seen at work in the Achievement Place program. If children at Achievement Place do what they are supposed to do (study, take care of their belongings, stay out of fights), the environment (teachers, caretakers, and friends) responds in a positive manner. Children earn praise and points for good behavior. The points earned can be used for special privileges. The theory is that if the children appreciate the rewards and know that the rewards will be given for good behavior, they will be more likely to repeat the desired behavior.

**Factors in
Operant
Conditioning**

Research on the mechanisms of operant conditioning has pointed out some of the factors that make this type of learning so effective. In classical conditioning the strength and timing of the stimulus are important. A powerful conditioned stimulus (such as a loud noise) presented in close association with an unconditioned stimulus (food) **reinforces,** or strengthens, the association between the unconditioned stimulus and the response (salivation). In operant conditioning it is the power and timing of the response that reinforces the stimulus (the initial behavior). If parents respond quickly and positively to a child's cry, the crying behavior will be reinforced, or strengthened. Many children cry at bedtime because they don't want to go to bed. If the parents respond by giving the child attention and letting the child stay up a little longer, the child will be likely to cry again in order to bring about the same response from the parents.

Reinforcement in operant conditioning is sometimes called **feedback.** The results of a behavior are fed back to the child in the form of a response from the environment — such as being allowed to stay up. With this information or feedback, the child knows exactly what response a behavior is having and can modify behavior accordingly. If the parents do not allow the child to stay up, the child knows through feedback (or the lack of it) that the crying behavior is not having the desired effect.

Report cards provide feedback. An A on a report card is usually a good reinforcer of the behavior that earned the A. If parents, teachers, and friends

Positive feedback from teachers may encourage a child to work harder.

congratulate a child for earning an A, and if the child appreciates the attention and feeling of accomplishment, the child will usually work hard to earn another A.

In instances where children have had trouble learning, the type and timing of the reinforcement can be manipulated in an attempt to improve learning behavior. If a child works hard to earn an A, for instance, but does not receive a report card (feedback) for several weeks or months, the child will not know what result the behavior produced. The association between the hard work and the A may not be made. If a child does not receive any reinforcement (congratulations and attention), the association may not be made. By manipulating the timing of the feedback and the type of reinforcement it is sometimes possible to strengthen the associations and to modify a child's behavior. This is what Achievement Place attempts to do. With daily report cards (immediate feedback) the children know exactly what results their behavior has had. The close timing of the behavior and its results increases the chances that a strong association will be made. Keller's Personalized System of Instruction also employs the principles of operant conditioning. Tests are graded right after they are taken, and students receive immediate feedback. They are told which questions they answered correctly and which they missed. With this feedback they can attempt to modify future behavior.

The timing and type of feedback are important, but immediate positive reinforcement does not always yield the best results. If children get a candy bar or some other reinforcement for every good behavior, they may eventually grow tired of candy bars. The reinforcer will have lost its power to bring about a certain behavior. One of the most important findings in the field of learning has been that reinforcement is most powerful when it is **intermittent,** or does not come on a regular schedule. B. F. Skinner demonstrated this in an experiment with a pigeon (25).

A pigeon in a Skinner box (see Chapter 1) learned to peck at a button for food. Once the pigeon learned that the pecking produced food, Skinner stopped feeding the animal after every peck. But the bird had been conditioned, so it kept on pecking. If the pecking never produced more food, the pecking behavior would have been extinguished. But just before this happened the bird was fed again. The original behavior was strengthened, and the pigeon started pecking again with new enthusiasm. By finding out exactly how much reinforcement the bird needed, Skinner was able to work out a precise schedule of reinforcement that would increase the probability of the pecking behavior during a long period of time. The bird pecked at a rate of 6,000 times per hour for several hours even though it was rewarded only every five minutes.

Intermittent reinforcement can also be used with humans. Children do not usually need to be rewarded for every good behavior if they know their behavior will eventually be rewarded. But they must be rewarded before the behavior is extinguished, so schedules of reinforcement are often used. Report cards come on a regular schedule, and students know when they are coming—just as Skinner's pigeon knew that food was coming every five minutes. One schedule, however, does not suit all individuals. The children at Achievement Place, for instance, seem to need a lot of immediate reinforcement at first (report cards every day). Once they have learned the behavior patterns that their teachers and caretakers require of them, the schedule can usually be changed. The report cards can be scheduled intermittently. Gradually these children work up to a regular schedule of reinforcement. They learn to wait for their rewards if they know rewards are coming.

Just as there are schedules of reinforcement, there are different types of reinforcement. Young children often work and learn for toys, candy, and other material rewards. But once they have mastered a useful behavior, such as telling time or tying their shoes, the material rewards may no longer be necessary. The learned behavior becomes its own reward in many cases. Young children love to feel that they have accomplished something. They love to show off their newly learned behavior to their parents and friends. This feeling of accomplishment and pride in learning becomes its own reward. Many of the children who have trouble learning seem to be those who do not respond to this type of reinforcement, perhaps because they have failed often and have had little experience with feelings of accomplishment. At Achievement Place

Once they have mastered a useful behavior, children may no longer require material rewards as reinforcement.

material reinforcement in the form of points for privileges is used until the children begin to make positive accomplishments. When they have had some experience with the type of reinforcement that such accomplishments can produce, they usually begin to learn the value of the reinforcement. Gradually personal and social rewards replace material rewards.

Behavior Therapy

In addition to shedding light on how simple learning occurs, knowledge of the processes involved in conditioning has led to the development of **therapies,** or treatments, for some types of behavior problems. Such treatments are called **behavior therapies,** and they have been found to be especially effective with children who have learning problems. The case of Patti K., a 4-year-old girl who was born with brain damage, is a good example (26).

In addition to brain damage, Patti had numerous physical problems during infancy and early childhood. At about 18 months of age she became seriously ill and lost almost a quarter of her body weight. For a while the left side of her body seemed to be partially paralyzed, and she had trouble learning to walk and run. Because of these physical problems Patti's early behavior patterns were never normal. A family physician attempted to treat the child's physical problems, but because of her behavior problems, including an inability to communicate effectively and to adjust to nursery school, she was put in the care of two behavior therapists, Donald E. P. Smith and Timothy Walter.

Patti had a number of bad habits. First of all, she was something of a little "pig" as far as eating was concerned. At various times during the day she would open the refrigerator, take out several dishes of food, and eat as much as she could. Nothing her parents did, including appeals to reason and spankings, had much effect on this behavior. When Patti was taken out in public she would embarrass her parents by heading for the nearest supply of food and digging into it as if she feared she would never get a chance to eat again.

A second set of unacceptable behaviors involved screaming. When Patti failed to get what she wanted, she would let out a series of sharp, loud cries that would usually convince people around her to give her what she wanted.

A third problem involved toilet training. Often when Patti did not get her way, especially at nursery school, she would say, "Oh! Oh! B.M." (meaning bowel movement). Then she would soil her pants. By the time her clothes were changed and she was cleaned up, the argument had usually been resolved in Patti's favor.

After observing Patti for some time as well as talking to her parents and teachers, the therapists decided that Patti's major problem was that she had somehow learned many inappropriate ways of getting what she wanted. The screaming and the soiling of her pants were operant behaviors that she had learned to use because they helped her get her way. Because these behaviors were successful once or twice, she used them over and over. Each time the screaming or soiling produced the desired reaction, the more likely it became that Patti would use that behavior again. Her overeating was a little more difficult to analyze, but Smith and Walter decided that it occurred because Patti had never learned to talk very well. She couldn't communicate the fact that she was hungry, nor could she explain what kind of food she was hungry for. She simply took whatever she could get whenever it was handy.

Many of Patti's troublesome behaviors were apparently learned rather than a result of her brain damage. In order to help Patti and her parents get along better, and to make it more likely that the child would succeed in school, Smith and Walter decided to help her learn more appropriate and socially pleasing ways of getting what she wanted. This involved, first of all, helping her unlearn some of her unpleasant habits.

According to learning theory, habits are learned because they are rewarding or reinforcing or because they help one to avoid unpleasant or threatening situations (20). If Patti saw another child at school playing with a toy she wanted, she would try to take it away from the other child. If the child resisted, Patti would scream loudly and keep screaming until the other child dropped the toy or the teacher came over and gave the toy to Patti in order to put a stop to the screaming. In this manner the teacher would reward or reinforce the screaming behavior. Because of such reinforcement, it is not surprising that Patti developed a habit of screaming to get her way. If someone tried to get Patti to do something she didn't want to do, she would soil her pants. The mess she created usually helped her avoid doing something she considered unpleasant. Avoiding an unpleasant stimulus can also be rewarding and reinforcing in the formation of a habit.

As mentioned earlier, conditioned behaviors and habits need not be permanent. They can be unlearned through a process known as extinction. If a habit or a behavior is never rewarded or reinforced, it will usually disappear or be extinguished. Smith and Walter used **extinction training** as part of their therapy for Patti by trying to make sure that her inappropriate behaviors were never reinforced. Their observations of Patti had convinced them that her parents, teachers, and the other school children were actually helping maintain Patti's bad habits by unknowingly rewarding her whenever she misbehaved. Teachers, for example, insisted that they had punished Patti when she screamed. The punishment, however, was usually very mild and probably not strong enough to outweigh the rewarding aspects of the screaming. When Patti screamed she got a lot of attention, which was reinforcing. In addition, she usually got the toy that she wanted or got out of doing something she didn't want to do. When Patti raided the refrigerator her parents would get upset and spank her; but she usually got the food she wanted as well as the undivided attention of her parents for a significant period of time simply by eating too much.

The therapists decided to attempt to extinguish Patti's unpleasant behaviors as well as teach her more acceptable ways of getting what she wanted. The extinction training consisted of ignoring all of Patti's antisocial behaviors. The teaching of new behaviors was somewhat more complex. Part of Patti's problem was the fact that she didn't know the names of most of the foods she wanted to eat. Another part of her problem was that she had difficulty keeping her impulses under control. When she saw something she wanted she did not want to wait to get it. She wanted it immediately. Smith and Walter set up a training program to help Patti increase her vocabulary and help her learn to accept delays in getting the rewards she wanted. They knew that they couldn't expect her to change overnight. But they hoped to make a little progress each day by teaching her a few words at a time and by teaching her to wait a few seconds longer for her rewards. This technique is called **successive approximations toward a goal.** It consists of moving in very small steps from the behavior a person exhibits at the beginning of therapy toward the new behaviors that are considered to be the goal of the therapy (20). Each movement, no matter how small, that the person makes toward the goal is rewarded. Each incorrect response that is not aimed in the right direction is ignored.

Since not all people are rewarded by the same things, Smith and Walter had to find out what Patti wanted as a reward for the progress she made. They found that she was fond of sweet cereals and cookies, and they made use of these in Patti's training. The therapists began by pointing to an object and saying its name: "Milk, Patti, this is milk. Can you say milk?" She couldn't, but if she uttered any sound at all the therapists would give her a piece of sweet cereal or a bite of cooky. After she had learned to make a noise whenever they asked her to, they began selectively rewarding noises that sounded like "milk," such as "meek" or "mik." They ignored any sounds that were not close to "milk." Soon "milk" sounds were made by Patti more often, and the therapists could get her to come closer and closer in her approximations of the word before they rewarded her. Using this technique, Smith and Walter were able to teach Patti new words in only a few minutes. They began taking her on walks and got her to name many of the things she saw; and eventually they took her to supermarkets and taught her to name most of the common foods she saw there.

While this verbal training was going on the therapists also worked on Patti's impulse control. Her parents agreed to stop giving her attention when she overate. If they caught her at the refrigerator, they would take the food away without saying anything and make her leave the kitchen for five minutes. Once her vocabulary had increased, Smith and Walter taught Patti to ask for the foods she wanted and to say "please." She was rewarded for these behaviors with a piece of what she wanted. If she opened the refrigerator door without saying "please," they would shut the door until she did say it. After Patti had learned to do this she was taught to wait longer and longer between the time she first asked for something and the time she received it. But because Patti knew that if she waited she would be rewarded, she learned to control her impulses. Still using the technique of successive approximations, the therapists taught Patti to wait before eating her reward until she was told she could eat it.

At the start of the therapy if Patti had seen a cooky, she would not have waited more than a few seconds before screaming that she wanted it. After only a few weeks of training, however, she could hold a cooky in her hand for several minutes and not eat it until told to do so. After six months of training Patti's parents took her to a party where the success of the training was proved by her behavior. Instead of heading for the refreshment table and stuffing herself, Patti, at her parents' suggestion, passed around plates of food to the other guests and waited until everyone was served before she ate.

Reinforcers and Punishers

Patti's therapists worked at changing her behaviors by giving and withdrawing various types of rewards or reinforcement. The giving or withdrawing of reinforcement is used in operant conditioning to bring about an increase or decrease in the response rate of a specific behavior. These conditions—giving versus withdrawing and increase versus decrease in response rate—can be used to define four types of stimuli in operant conditioning (24):

1. If presenting the stimulus after the response leads to an increase in the rate of response, the stimulus is called a **positive reinforcer.** Cookies and sweet cereal were used with Patti as positive reinforcers to increase the probability that she would say "milk."
2. If presenting the stimulus after the response leads to a decrease in the rate of response, the stimulus is called a **punisher.** The therapists could have given Patti a spanking (punisher) after she soiled her pants in the hope of decreasing the response rate of that behavior, but, as will be seen, punishment is not always an effective teacher.
3. If withdrawing the stimulus results in an increase in the rate of the response, the stimulus is called a **negative reinforcer.** This is *not* the same as a punisher. A punisher is supposed to decrease the rate of behavior. A negative reinforcer is supposed to increase the rate of a behavior. The therapists ignored Patti's soiling of her pants in the hope that this would increase the probability of her staying clean. In this case "ignoring" can be considered a negative reinforcer because it increased the probability of a desired behavior.
4. If withdrawing the stimulus results in a decrease in the rate of the response, the stimulus is called a **response cost.** When the therapists ignored Patti's screaming they were, in effect, withdrawing attention from her. Because this eventually led to a decrease in screaming behavior, the withdrawal of attention, in this case, can be called a response cost.

In general, it would seem that any pleasant stimulus could be used as a positive reinforcer or response cost and that any painful or aversive stimulus could be used as a punisher or negative reinforcer. But these stimuli are defined in terms of the response they bring about (increase or decrease) rather than according to their pleasing or displeasing properties. For example, praise is usually thought of as being pleasing, and therefore it should serve as a positive reinforcer when presented after a behavior. But teachers and researchers who work with children have found that after many presentations the praise may change from a positive reinforcer to a punisher (24). Children sometimes reach the point where they begin to say, "Don't say 'Good!' anymore" and begin to reduce their response rate as if to avoid hearing the words of praise. Not only can positive reinforcers prove to be punishers, but confusion sometimes exists between negative reinforcers and punishers. A negative reinforcer, when it is withdrawn, leads to an *increase* in the rate of response of a behavior. A punisher, when it is applied, leads to a decrease in the rate of response. Because punishers bring about a decrease in a behavior, punishers are sometimes effective in getting someone to break a habit or unlearn a behavior. A bitter or sour-tasting substance, for instance, may be put on a child's thumb in order to keep the child from sucking that thumb. The child sucks, the punisher is presented (sour taste), and if the child stops sucking, the punisher has worked. Punishers are less useful in getting someone to learn a new behavior. Research with animals, for example, has shown that punishers suppress a behavior only temporarily. When the punisher is withdrawn the undesired behavior often returns. In other words, if a thumb-sucking child hasn't learned a new behavior to replace the undesired behavior, the thumb-sucking may return once the punisher is withdrawn. Punishment has other drawbacks as far as learning is concerned. It may inhibit the expression of a habit, but it often has very unpleasant side effects. Punishment often leads to frustration, which may be followed by aggression and hate expressed toward the person doing the punishing (20).

Even though it has not been found to be effective in teaching new skills, attitudes, or behaviors, punishment has been a teaching tool throughout the history of childhood. In 1970, 62 percent of those questioned in a national survey favored spanking and similar forms of punishment in the lower grades. In 1969, more than 65 percent of the teachers questioned by the National Education Association favored the use of corporal (physical) punishment in elementary schools (28).

Even though physical punishment is still used by many teachers and parents, there is evidence that in many cases it may be more harmful than helpful. For one thing, punishment often comes too late after the undesired behavior. A child may fail an exam but not be punished until several weeks later when the report card arrives. In such a case it may be too late for the child to form a strong association between the behavior and the punishment. The only effect may be to frustrate the child. Children who are punished often may learn to associate their parents, teachers, and learning with pain.

Even if punishment is administered at the time of the undesired behavior, it still may not be effective. If a child is trying to work through the various steps of a long division problem, for example, and the teacher continually interrupts and scolds (verbal punishment) for mistakes, the child may become so nervous and overanxious that the problem never gets solved. In this way punishment actually interferes with learning. If the problem does get solved, there is a chance that the child may learn to associate the problem—rather than the mistakes—with the pain.

Not only does punishment often fail to teach desired behaviors, it sometimes teaches undesired behaviors. Physical punishment becomes a source of frustration and pain and may stimulate anger and aggressive tendencies. Many studies, for example, have found a relationship between punishment and later aggressive behavior on the part of the child, often leading to delinquency (see the relationship between punishment and later aggressive behavior found in the Family Research Project, Chapter 1). Researchers working with delinquent children have found that most of these children were harshly punished when young (28). Even verbal violence and name calling by parents and teachers have been found to be related to delinquency. Children who are constantly told that they are bad, hateful, and unloved sometimes begin to believe that they are bad, hateful, and unloved. They may begin to behave in a bad and hateful manner.

With much evidence to show that physical punishment is not an effective teaching method, several groups, including the National Education Association, have published a resolution stating:

> The use of physical violence on school children is an affront to democratic values and an infringement of individual rights. It is a degrading, dehumanizing and counter productive approach to the maintenance of discipline in the classroom and should be outlawed from educational institutions as it has already been outlawed from other institutions in American society (28).

OBSERVATIONAL LEARNING

"Children need people in order to become human. . . . To relegate children to a world of their own is to deprive them of their humanity, and ourselves as well." This statement, made by developmental psychologist Urie Bronfenbrenner, emphasizes the importance of learning by observing the behavior of others (5). A dramatic example of Bronfenbrenner's point can be seen in the case of the wild child who spent most of his early years alone in the forests of

Social learning theorist Albert Bandura
(1926–   ).

France (see Chapter 3). Without other human beings to observe and learn from, this child developed no human social behaviors. He learned how to find food, which foods to eat, and which to avoid, and he learned many other behaviors necessary for his survival. Such learning can be explained in terms of classical and operant conditioning. The wild child did not, however, learn to be truly human. Learning to be human comes to a great extent through observation of other humans. As Bronfenbrenner says, "Children need people in order to become human."

Learning is the modification of behavior that comes through contact with the environment. The wild child did not learn truly human behavior because his environment did not contain other humans. Most children do grow up in a social or human environment, and a great deal of learning takes place as a result of observing and imitating people in the environment who serve as models. This is **observational learning.**

Social learning theorist Albert Bandura has described the processes involved in observational learning (3). The most important factors are **attention, retention, motor reproduction,** and **reinforcement** or **motivation.**

Attention

"Pay attention!" is a command children and students hear often. It is an important command as far as observational learning is concerned because children cannot learn from another person's behavior if they do not see or are not aware of that behavior. In other words, they must pay attention.

Although it is not always easy to hold a child's attention, certain individuals seem to be better than others at drawing and holding attention. Persons who have high status, power, high levels of competence, and are interesting and attractive tend to be the ones who attract the most attention. Because such people can usually attract and hold the attention of others, they are more likely to influence the behavior of others than are low-status, incompetent, and unattractive individuals. In addition, those behaviors of high-status individuals that seem to be directly responsible for their status are the behaviors most likely to be attended to and imitated.

As children go through life different people in the environment hold their attention and serve as models. At first parents are the most powerful and influential models in a child's life. Children usually spend a great part of the first years of their lives with their parents and learn many attitudes and behaviors from them. As children grow older and leave their homes more often, other people in their environment begin to attract attention. Teachers and friends are usually influential models. The first child in the neighborhood who learns to ride a bicycle, for example, may attract a lot of attention and serve as a model for other children. As different behaviors become important (at home, in school, business, marriage, child-rearing), people who have been successful at these behaviors serve as models. In this manner the most successful behaviors of the species are passed on from generation to generation.

Retention

Children can watch other people, but if they don't remember what they have seen, no learning takes place. Not only the model's behavior but the context in which it took place and the reason for the behavior must usually be remembered if the model is to influence the child's behavior. If children don't understand what a model is doing, or don't know why a behavior is being performed, they are not likely to remember or repeat the behavior.

Behaviors can be recalled most effectively if they have been represented in the memory in the form of descriptive verbal symbols or **codes.** A young child learning to ride a bicycle, for example, might have a verbal code or set of instructions: Hands on the grips, left foot on the pedal, lean forward, push down, throw the right leg over, and so on. Once such a code — which usually requires some language ability — has been placed in the memory, it can be recalled and used as a guide by children (and adults) as they attempt to imitate the steps of a behavior.

Experiments with young children have been used to demonstrate the importance of verbal coding in the recall of modeled behaviors. In one study children aged 4 and 7 were shown a short movie of a model performing 20 behaviors (16). These behaviors were novel, or new, and not likely to be already known by the children. The experimenter told the children before the film was shown that they would be asked to repeat what the model had done. After the film, the 4-year-olds were able to repeat, or reproduce, on the average only 6 of the 20 behaviors. The 7-year-olds were able to reproduce 14 of the behaviors. It seems that the 4-year-olds, with less language ability, had not been able to use word symbols to describe the behavior to themselves. Without this description or code they were less likely to recall and repeat the behaviors. Children older than 6 usually have enough verbal ability to form a symbol system for recall. The 7-year-olds, with their language ability and practice at coding things for the memory, were able to recall more of the model's behaviors. The performance of two additional groups of 4- and 7-year-olds seems to support these conclusions.

For one group the experimenter described each act of the model and then asked the children to repeat the description. The second group was not given a description, but was asked to describe for the experimenter what the model was doing. The performance of the 4- and 7-year-olds in these two groups helps demonstrate the importance of verbal coding for the recall of modeled behaviors. When the 4-year-olds were asked to describe what the model was doing, and therefore to form a verbal code of the behavior, they were later able to recall and reproduce 10 of the 20 behaviors. When they were given a description by the experimenter and then asked to repeat that description, thereby strengthening the code, they were able to reproduce 12 of the 20 behaviors.

The 7-year-olds, with more language ability, did not need the experimenter's description and did not seem to make use of it. They did no better than when they had heard no description. They were able to reproduce 14 of the 20 behaviors. They did much worse, however, when they were asked to describe what was going on. Being asked to provide a description of what the model was doing actually seemed to interfere with their own ongoing process of coding and memory storage.

These experiments suggest that providing a symbol system (description) for children under 6 aids them in the ability to store and recall modeled behaviors. Providing such information for children older than 6 may interfere with their memory processes.

Motor Reproduction

No matter how well children pay attention, and no matter how good a memory they may have of a modeled behavior, they will not be able to reproduce that behavior if they do not have the necessary motor skills. Riding a bicycle, for example, requires a certain amount of physical maturity and motor ability. A young child may pay attention and remember every step in the process, but if he or she does not have the necessary physical ability, the bicycle riding behavior of the model will not be reproduced. With physical maturity and practice most children are eventually able to handle a bicycle. But practice does not always make perfect. Some people never learn to ski or play golf or tennis as well as their favorite models of these behaviors do.

"A person can acquire, retain and possess the capabilities for skillful execution of modeled behavior, but the learning may rarely be activated into overt performance if it is negatively sanctioned or otherwise unfavorably received," explains Bandura in reference to the fourth necessary factor in observational learning (3). The first three, as has been mentioned, are attention, retention and motor ability. The fourth is reinforcement, one of the most important aspects of observational learning or any type of learning. A modeled behavior that is positively reinforced — that brings about a pleasant or desired reaction — is more likely to be imitated and learned than a behavior that is punished — that brings about an unpleasant reaction.

Positive reinforcement for the model not only increases the chances that an observed behavior will be repeated but it helps in all stages of observational learning. Children pay more attention to a behavior for which the model is well rewarded. If they pay attention, they are more likely to remember the behavior. Children are also more likely to work hard to reproduce a behavior that has been rewarded. If children do imitate and learn a modeled behavior, it is usually because they want the same reward the model has received.

Much of what has been learned about observational learning in recent years has come about as a result of experiments with children and live or filmed models. In most such experiments children are shown a model and experimenters observe the effects of the model's behavior on the children's behavior. Some of Bandura's most well-known experiments have dealt with the effects of aggressive behavior by models. In an experiment that shows the power of reinforcement Bandura had children watch a filmed model behave in an aggressive manner (2). One group of children saw the model punished for aggressive behavior; a second group saw the model rewarded for the same behavior; and a third group saw no consequences occur for the model's behavior. Children who saw the aggression rewarded displayed more imitative aggressive responses than either of the other groups. However, when all three groups were offered rewards for each modeled behavior they could accurately reproduce, there was no difference between the groups. All had learned or could at least reproduce an equal amount of the observed aggressive behavior.

Aggression has been emphasized in research on observational learning because in recent years many people have voiced concern about the effects of televised violence on human behavior. These is good reason for this concern, as many examples have shown. Several years ago, for example, a television drama, "The Doomsday Flight," told the fictional story of a man who had placed a bomb on a crowded commercial airliner. The bomber then proceeded to phone the airline office and give hints about the whereabouts of the bomb. This kept up the suspense of the television show, but it also seems to have put some ideas in the heads of a few viewers. Before the telecast ended one airline

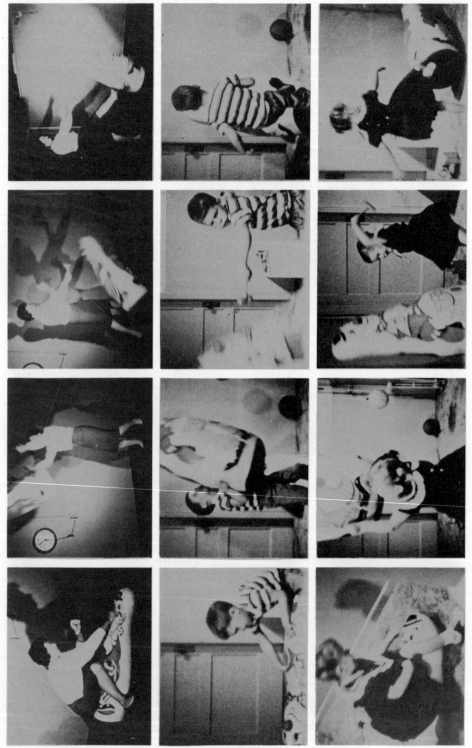

Bandura's aggression experiment shows the effects of modeling on aggressive behavior.

received a bomb threat. Within 24 hours four more threats were reported. By the end of the following week a total of eight bomb threats had been made, twice the number of threats recorded for the entire month preceding the broadcast.

Because of such incidents a government committee made up of 12 behavioral scientists was formed to investigate the effects of televised violence on human behavior. The committee reported in 1972 that 96 percent of all homes in the United States have one or more television sets, and that the average home set is on more than six hours a day. About eight violent episodes per hour were being shown. The investigators concluded, based on 23 research projects, that this violence can cause some people to act aggressively under some circumstances. Impressionable young children, who rely on television for much of their knowledge of the world, are probably the most strongly affected. It was found, for example, that children use the aggressive behavior they see on television as a model for their games. It was also found that children who liked violent programs the most had more fights with their parents (30).

Television isn't all bad, and it isn't all violence. Shows like "Sesame Street" suggest that television can be an important teaching tool. Preschoolers have learned to count and even to read with the help of "Sesame Street." Television is not the perfect teacher, but surveys have shown that regular viewers of "Sesame Street" have made substantial learning gains over nonviewers (31).

MOTIVATION

If children learn anything from observing the models they see on "Sesame Street" and other television programs, it is due in part to the fact that the behavior of the characters is reinforced. If the reinforcement seems appropriate and desirable, children may be **motivated,** or driven, to imitate and learn the behavior.

Motivation is much more than just a reason for learning. It is an important part of most human behaviors. In many cases motivation is obvious. People work for money, fame, power, friendship, a feeling of accomplishment, and for far-off and abstract goals, such as "going to heaven." But not all goals and motives are obvious. Because of different backgrounds, environments, and learning experiences, people have learned to appreciate different rewards and strive for different goals. It would be difficult to understand everything that motivates an individual without knowing everything about that person, but theories of motivation have been developed that attempt to explain the basic motives of human behavior.

Motives, or **drives,** are often classified as either primary or secondary. A **primary drive** is considered to be one related to the inborn biological needs that must be satisfied if life and the species are to continue. Hunger, thirst, and sex are examples of inborn primary needs. When deprived of them, animals and humans are motivated to perform the behaviors that will reduce the drive or satisfy the need. In addition, curiosity seems to be a primary drive. According to some theories, curiosity results from a lack of variety of environmental stimulation (24).

The primary drives are necessary for survival, but they do not explain all human motivation. Humans have many **secondary drives** that are learned, often during attempts to satisfy the primary needs. Dependency and the need for mastery and achievement are examples of secondary drives. They are learned rather than innate, or inborn. Even curiosity in humans seems to be partially learned. It is generally believed that the learned motives, or secondary drives, are the major source of motivation for human behavior (24).

The Energizing and Sensitizing Functions of Motivation

How does motivation function in regard to learning? One theory suggests that a motive or drive performs one or more of these functions: it **energizes,** or **sensitizes, selects,** and **directs** (8, 22). When a drive energizes it puts the organism into a state of heightened activity "designed" to encounter the maximum stimulation in the "hope" of finding stimuli that will reduce the drive. When the drive acts as a sensitizer stimuli related to reducing the drive are more likely to be noticed than when the drive is not operating. Of course, some learning must have taken place before a motive can sensitize a person to a stimulus. An individual must have learned that the stimulus is related to or will help to satisfy the drive. In the beginning of a child's life the energizing function of a drive is entirely, or at least partially, unlearned. This can be seen in the behavior of 2-week-old infants. An hour after they have been fed and changed, they are usually very relaxed and are breathing evenly and deeply. Their hands, arms, legs, necks, and heads—indeed, the whole body—are still, almost limp. Observed at the second hour after feeding, they remain relaxed but occasionally clench and unclench their hands. This motion is not an intense one. During the third hour after feeding their hands grow more active; they flutter them. Presently they make motions with their arms; their heads turn; their mouths pucker; they move their feet and legs. Then, as the third hour draws to a close, they are in motion "all over." They move their heads restlessly; arms and hands and legs move; skin color heightens. Then the eyes open, and after a moment of adaptation to the light, their bodies come to even more vigorous motion. They vocalize, whimper, cry—first noisily, then whiningly, with total body action and deeply flushed features accompanying the crying. Every parent recognizes the symptoms: the baby is hungry. The only thing that will stop this feverish activity for more than a few seconds is food. The intensity of the baby's hunger drive is directly related to the "time of deprivation" (the amount of time that has gone by since the child was last fed).

Thus drive, in its energizing sense, puts the whole body in motion so that infants may make contact with a maximal range of stimulation in the "hope" that one of the stimuli encountered by these many responses will reduce the drive or satisfy the need (in this case, supply the hungry child with the breast or bottle). The responses of sucking and head-turning to the bottle are the ones that eventually put infants in touch with the nipple.

The sensitizing function of a drive is similarly adaptive. When a drive energizes, the organism is more active and presumably more likely to encounter drive-reduction stimuli. The sensitizing function of a drive depends more on learning than the energizing function. All of the learning processes discussed earlier in the chapter may well have contributed to this sensitizing function. In some cases it has been affected by classical conditioning, in others by operant conditioning.

The added alertness that goes with the sensitizing function of a drive puts the organism (child) in touch with the stimuli appropriate for satisfying whatever drive is operating.

At three o'clock in the afternoon, a 3-year-old may run happily through the kitchen a dozen times, at no time attending to any of the stimuli that room provides. But at four-thirty or five o'clock a trip through the kitchen is suddenly halted; the child stops, cries, "I'm hungry," and begins to yank at the cupboard where the cookies are or the drawer where the bread and crackers are kept. The child is suffering from "time of deprivation." Heightened hunger drive makes the child more sensitive to stimuli that earlier had made no impression: the cupboard and drawer where cookies, bread, and crackers are kept.

Adults may work cheerfully all morning in a room close to a restaurant kitchen or bakery and at no time notice the odors. But at eleven-thirty the smell stimuli suddenly become more noticeable, and they begin to feel ravenously hungry. This too is an example of the sensitizing function of a drive.

Social or learned drives and motives may work in a similar manner. Preschool children who have been deprived of adult attention for a brief period of time will achieve more in an apparent attempt to gain attention, or satisfy their heightened dependency needs, than preschoolers not so deprived (14). This result is similar to the energizing function of drive. The young child in an institution reacts with exaggeration to the smallest attention of the visiting adult—perhaps an illustration of the sensitizing function of a drive. For children of any age *curiosity* has a sensitizing and an energizing function: children work harder if they are curious, and they are more sensitive to intellectual stimulation of all sorts.

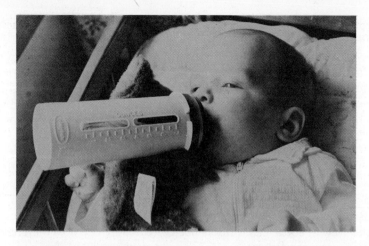

Sucking and head-turning movements eventually put infants in touch with the nipple.

The Selective Function of Motivation

Infants, as they become progressively more restless with the passage of time since their last feeding, exhibit a number of different behaviors. They cry, thrash with their arms and legs, agitate their bodies, roll their heads, intermix crying with sucking movements, and agitate their legs. When the bottle is between their lips all these movements except sucking diminish or disappear. As they grow a little older the touch of the bottle or breast on the face terminates all these responses except an adaptive head-turning in the direction of the nipple, seeking motions with the lips, and eventual sucking responses. Still later the mere sight of the bottle ends the random behavior and causes infants to get ready for the nipple. In other words, the reward (food) that reduces the drive helps infants to *select* appropriate responses: first sucking, then seeking, and, later, grasping.

This selective function of a drive, then, is the one that helps to eliminate useless or inefficient responses, and it assists in establishing efficient ways of behaving. Teachers can use it to help children learn to learn.

The Directive Function of Motivation

The energizing function of a drive is probably innate, serving to increase the probability of an organism's coming into contact with stimuli that will reduce the drive and thus enable it to survive. More learning accompanies the sensitizing than the energizing function, but it too is directed toward survival. The selective function of a drive is similar to learning, in the sense that it results in greater efficiency in satisfying a drive, but the directive function is completely learned. For one drive plus a given stimulus, one type of behavior is appropriate; for another drive and the *same* stimulus, another behavior is chosen, as a result of past experience or learning. This function of a drive enables the individual to choose one of two or more behaviors already available, each of which is equally appropriate to the stimulus (when "stimulus" is considered only as an objective event or thing). The drive provides information to the individual about how to behave: it is, itself, an informative stimulus.

As an example, consider 3-year-old Sally. Sally has been up very late on Tuesday night and awakens to go to nursery school on Wednesday somewhat the worse for wear. She arrives, passes the nurse's inspection, and enters the playroom. She sees a blue blanket (the stimulus) in the corner and approaches it. Her drive (avoidance of the unpleasant symptoms of fatigue), coupled with the blanket, suggests to her that she pick up the blanket, take it to a cot, and lie down with it to rest. The drive, in other words, interacts with the objective stimulus and directs her behavior. But on Wednesday night Sally goes to bed early and arrives at school rested and bursting with energy. Her drive is for exploration and play. This drive, coupled with the same blue blanket, now leads to using the blanket as a prop in a game.

In the same fashion the lonely adult may welcome a large, formal social function; on the other hand, after a week filled with social activities the notion of attending a similar function may be repugnant. The kitchen smells that were so hunger-arousing before lunch may be mildly unpleasant after a heavy meal. In each case different drives coupled with the same objective stimuli have directed the individual to choose very different responses from among those available.

The same general stimulus, "teacher," may evoke very different types and intensities of behavior from a child. Teacher A, who is firm, warm, and competent may secure from a child efficient effort and hard work. Teacher B, indecisive, vague, and ill-prepared, possibly harsh and unfair, may produce the opposite behavior: the child daydreams or sulks or misbehaves and accomplishes little as far as school learning is concerned.

Although it is not accepted by all that a drive must be reduced if learning is to occur, it is generally agreed that learning typically occurs when drive is reduced. The agent or thing that reduces the drive is commonly referred to as the *reward*. There may be cases where more stimulation or greater drive is sought (1). In such a situation increased stimulation or drive may be thought of as the reward. In any event, reward coupled with drive usually results in learning.

Self-actualization

The energizing, sensitizing, selective, and directive functions of primary and secondary needs explain much behavior, but some psychologists have suggested that higher goals are involved in directing or motivating human behavior. Among these are the needs for such things as justice, order, love, goodness, beauty, and truth. Some theories suggest that these are secondary or learned needs, others suggest that they are inborn and unique to humans. Psychologist Abraham Maslow suggests that humans have an inborn desire to progress toward what he calls **self-actualization** (19). According to Maslow, self-actualization involves achieving the highest level of fulfillment or human potential in every area of life.

Most factors influencing human behavior are external. That is, they are the result of environmental factors. The lack of food, for example, puts infants into an agitated state after several hours. This lack may have different effects on adult behavior, but it, as well as the other primary needs, can be seen as a powerful motivating force in most human behaviors. What Maslow is talking about has to do with internal or self-directing forces that seem to be at least partially independent of the environment. His theory says that when an individual's biological and physical needs, including needs for physical activity and sensory stimulation, are being met adequately, that individual will then be motivated to fulfill even higher goals. Among these are the need to love and be loved, the needs for achievement, competence, independence, freedom, and prestige. Whether these goals are explained as the result of internal or external forces, they are usually considered to be among the most important of human goals. They are not easy to achieve, but once they have been reached it becomes possible, according to Maslow, to move toward the highest human goal—self-actualization. For a happy, well-fed, well-loved child self-actualization may mean the chance to explore a room full of exciting toys. Self-actualization on the adult level is more difficult to define, even for Maslow. He does, however, offer examples of prominent individuals who seem to have achieved a high degree of self-actualization. Among them are Lincoln, Eleanor Roosevelt, Einstein, and Beethoven.

Eleanor Roosevelt is an example of an individual who achieved a high degree of self-actualization.

Classical and operant conditioning are basic mechanisms by which the behavior of children is changed. But even the addition of observational learning does not explain the changes necessary to produce a Lincoln, Einstein, Eleanor Roosevelt, or Beethoven. More complex forms of learning are necessary to explain such changes.

Generalization

There would be little point in learning if it were not possible to transfer what is learned in one situation to another situation. A child who learns to ride one bicycle should be able to ride a similar bicycle. What is learned in school should have applications and be useful in situations outside school. The method by which learning is transferred from one situation to another is called **generalization** (see Chapter 1). If generalization were not possible, children would have to learn a new way of reacting every time they entered a new situation.

Stimulus generalization is the tendency to make the same response to new but similar stimuli. Studies of stimulus generalization have attempted to define the degree to which the new situation (or stimulus) can differ from the one in which learning originally occurred and still have a transfer of learning take place. The first such studies were done with animals that had been conditioned to respond to a particular stimulus. As would be expected, the greater the difference between the original conditioned stimulus and any new stimulus, the less likely was the chance of a transfer of learning. A dog conditioned to respond to a 10-inch black square, for example, is more likely to generalize and respond to an 8-inch black square than to a 10-inch green triangle. A small child who has just learned that a cow is a large, four-legged animal might respond to a horse by saying, "cow." The same child, however, is less likely to say "cow" when a chicken walks by.

Another kind of generalization consists of making similar responses to the same stimulus. A dog conditioned to lift its left paw at the sound of a bell will not be able to respond correctly if its paw is held down. In such cases the conditioned dog will often lift its right paw (4). This is not the conditioned response, but it is similar to the original response. Responding in this manner is called **response generalization.**

Stimulus and response generalization represent shortcuts to learning and are responsible for much human behavior. Generalization can, however, sometimes be more harmful than helpful. Children who have learned that a bad, punishing, rejecting parent is "the boss," and who have learned that teachers are "bosses," may transfer the negative and fearful feelings they have toward their parents to the first teacher they encounter. In this instance generalization, or the transfer of learning, has been brought about by a **verbal mediator**—something that brings about a result or conveys information to

A small child who has learned that a cow is a large, four-legged animal may generalize and apply this label to all large, four-legged animals.

others. The word "boss" is the verbal mediator. Having been applied to parents as well as to teachers, it helps to make these two different stimuli (parents and teachers) similar in the child's mind. Being similar, they can elicit or bring about the same response (fear).

A typical way of studying generalization in children consists of asking them to press a button when a light in the center of a horizontal row of lights comes on. After several trials with the center light, other lights in the display are turned on once in a while. Young children tend to overgeneralize and respond (push the button) sometimes when these other lights are flashed, especially if the light flashed is close to the center. The frequency of responses decreases, however, the farther the light is from the center.

Some investigators using the horizontal light setup have reported that as children grow older they are less likely to generalize in such a situation. That is, after a certain age children will respond only to the center light (15, 16, 21, 27). Similarly, as children grow older they are less likely to call a horse a cow. One reason for this may be that older children pay better attention and are more motivated than younger children. In one experiment designed to test this theory, experimenters gave rewards for correct responses and took away rewards for incorrect responses (16). The rewards had little effect on the performance of 9- to 12-year-olds. This suggests that older children will make the correct response in this type of situation whether they are rewarded or not. Six- and 7-year-olds who were not rewarded did overgeneralize. But 6- and 7-year-olds who were rewarded performed as well as the 9- to 12-year-olds. Apparently, even young children will not overgeneralize (call a horse a cow) if they have learned the proper responses and are sufficiently motivated to use them.

Discrimination

Calling a horse a cow is not a very serious mistake for a young child, but generalization can sometimes go too far and have far-reaching consequences. A child who has been bitten by one dog may, through generalization, learn to fear all dogs. Children who are punished often may learn to fear or even hate their parents. This response, as already mentioned, may generalize to a fear of all authority figures, including such people as teachers and police. **Discrimination** is the process that helps prevent incorrect responses to similar stimuli. It is the ability to respond differently to similar situations or stimuli.

A dog that has learned to respond to a black, 10-inch square can usually be taught, with some extra training, to discriminate between the square and a similar but slightly different object. With a little extra training and practice, children eventually learn to discriminate between cows and horses.

Discrimination is usually taught by presenting two similar stimuli and then rewarding the child for selecting the correct one. This can be seen in the early stages of learning to read, when discrimination is especially important. For example, children must learn to respond one way to s - a - w and another way to w - a - s; one way to l - a - d and another way to l - a - p. Much practice is necessary in such cases before the stimulus, l - a - d, is correctly identified and discriminated from l - a - p. But with the help of television shows like "Sesame Street" and much teacher and parent reinforcement ("Yes, right" and "No, wrong"), quick, effortless discrimination among letters and words becomes possible, usually by the age of 6 or 7.

Incidental
Learning

When people speak of learning they often mean such things as going to school, studying, solving problems, and taking tests. This type of learning is called **intentional learning.** It involves observation, attention, retention, generalization, and many of the aspects of learning already discussed. There is another type of learning that usually goes along with intentional learning and is a part of a child's everyday experiences. This is **incidental learning.**

Intentional learning can be seen as children tackle a specific problem or attempt to master a skill. This type of learning involves concentration or focused attention. Incidental learning (from the Latin word for "to happen") does not require concentration on a particular problem. It just happens.

Incidental learning may happen as a child is concentrating on a problem, or it may happen as a child is playing or just going about the business of life. A student learning to spell, for example, may be told to read a short story and correct all of the spelling mistakes in it. The child may be sharpening and reinforcing spelling skills in this way, but if the story is in any way interesting,

Intentional learning involves concentration or focused attention.

the child may just happen to learn something other than spelling. Whenever a learning task involves more than one stimulus, as most do, there is a chance that incidental learning will take place.

The role of attention is especially important in incidental learning. The amount and variety of stimulation children and adults receive is fantastic. If they were to respond to all stimuli, they would be flooded with a great deal of irrelevant information, and useful responses would be crowded out or disturbed by unnecessary responses to irrelevant stimuli. In order to be efficient and effective in their responses, humans must learn to be selective in their attention to the stimuli that are important to them. Increased ability to pay attention to relevant stimuli leads to more efficient intentional learning, but increased attention to relevant stimuli also results in decreased attention to irrelevant stimuli. This would suggest that as children grow older and more selective, incidental learning should decrease. This does seem to be true and has been demonstrated in a number of studies.

In one experiment a series of cards, each containing a drawing of an animal and a household object, were shown to children (12). From four to six of the cards were displayed to each child in individual testing situations. The cards were then placed face down on a horizontal row before the child. Another card, identical to one of those displayed, was then presented, and the child was asked to locate the matching card from the face-down cards. Children from grades 1, 3, 5, and 7 were tested. Half were asked to locate the animals and half the household objects. Intentional learning was measured by the number of times the child correctly located the item requested. Incidental learning was measured after the completion of the location tests by showing the children the animal or object used to solve the location problem and asking them to recall the animal or object that had been paired with it. The results showed that intentional learning (and selective attention) increased with age, but incidental learning did not increase after about the age of 11 or 12. After that, children's improved selective attention seems to result in less incidental learning.

In another study, researchers used stimuli that were not as easily separable or identifiable as the animals and household objects (13). They used outlines of shapes on colored paper, with the color present both within and outside the outline shape. Under these conditions there was an increase in incidental learning from the ages of 8 to 12 years. This suggests that when relevant and irrelevant stimuli cannot be easily separated, children may find it more efficient to pay attention to both, leading to improvement of both intentional and incidental learning at least up to the age of 12. This finding illustrates an extremely important point: the nature of the task used in studying behavior plays an important role in determining the results. This study suggests that as children mature they do not use an increasingly more selective approach to *all* learning situations. Rather, they become more flexible in how they focus their attention, discriminating between situations in which it is more efficient to pay attention selectively and those in which it is more efficient to pay attention to several types of stimulus information at the same time.

MEMORY

Children play and explore their world constantly. They seek out new experiences and stimuli and have the ability to learn from almost every experience. If the experiences of one situation have an effect on a child's behavior in a later situation, learning has taken place. But if the experiences of the first situation are not remembered, they will have no effect on future behavior. **Memory,** already discussed in relation to observational learning, is an important and necessary part of all types of learning. Without it learning is impossible. With it each experience a child has can influence future behavior.

If the experiences of one situation are to influence future behavior, several things must happen. The events of the first situation must be transformed or put into a form suitable for memory storage. The formation of **mental images** and **verbal codes** or **symbols** is especially important if an event is to be stored in the memory. These images and codes must be retained or held during the time separating the original situation and any later situation in which behavior is to be affected. If the second situation is recognized as being similar to the first, behavior in the second situation will be influenced if the stored material can be recalled and used. These are the basic steps of memory, a very complex human ability.

Sensory-information Store

Three types of memory have been studied in humans: sensory-information store, short-term memory and long-term memory. The first, as its name implies, has to do with the senses.

All information comes through the senses. The senses code the information and send it into the brain where it can be interpreted or made sense of. Sometimes the brain needs a second or more to decide whether or not information is important enough to be paid attention to. Because there is this short delay, the senses have a mechanism for holding on to some stimuli. The senses, in other words, have a sort of memory. When a flash bulb goes off in someone's eyes, for instance, the image of the flash is held or stored in the image receptors of the eyes for several seconds or longer. Even less noticeable stimuli are also held in the senses for very brief periods of time. This type of memory is called the **sensory-information store.**

Under normal circumstances the senses do not hold on to information for very long, but research has shown that the sensory information store can last for up to several minutes (20). Subjects in a dark room were shown a bright color slide for only one fiftieth of a second. The room remained dark, and some of the subjects were able to hold the image of the slide and actually see it in front of their eyes for several minutes. In some cases it is even possible, by slightly pressing on the eyeballs, to bring back an image up to 30 minutes after the image was shown. The sense receptors continue to send the most recent message to the brain. But an image can be retained in this manner only if the subject has stayed in a dark room or if no other images have been seen. Whenever a new piece of information comes along the first image is erased from the sensory-information store and the sense receptors immediately send off a different message to the brain. As long as an image is being held in the sensory-information store the brain can extract information from that image and decide if more attention must be paid to the information.

Under normal circumstances the sensory-information store cannot hold a stimulus for very long, so the interpretation of a stimulus must be sent from the senses to the brain if it is to be further interpreted. When a bit of information reaches the brain, it is held in the **short-term memory** while a more thorough interpretation is made. The short-term memory can hold information for only a few seconds longer than the sensory-information store usually does. Those few seconds, however, are usually long enough for the brain to decide whether or not to send the information to the third and most important part of the memory — the **long-term memory.**

Short-term Memory

The short-term memory is like a small bucket with a hole in it. Information which is poured in constantly leaks out of the bucket within a few seconds. The short-term memory can hold only about five to nine items of information at one time, but as long as an item is in the short-term memory it can be remembered or pulled out for further use.

Most people are familiar with the workings of the short-term memory. You are reading a book, for example, when someone walks in and asks you a question. You look up and say, "What?" But before the question is repeated, your brain has fished the question out of the short-term memory and is already preparing an answer. If six questions are asked, however, you probably won't be able to remember or to answer all of them. Some will have leaked out of the bucket in the length of time it takes you to answer.

The short-term memory is almost always in use. In many cases—such as the immediately recalled question—the short-term works on its own without any conscious help. There are many instances, however, when something must be remembered for longer than a few seconds. In these instances there are a few ways of getting around the shortcomings of the short-term memory. You need a phone number, so you look the number up, dial it, and wait for an answer. In most cases the number will leak out of the bucket within a few seconds. But what if the phone is busy? You have to look the number up again and redial. After this happens several times most people decide to memorize the number or consciously hold it in the memory. Usually a phone number can be held in the short-term memory for quite a while by simply concentrating on the number. But if you are trying to hold on to a number and someone comes up and asks you a question, you will probably forget the number while you are answering the question. For such cases there is a method for holding on to information more permanently. Most people can retain information by reinserting that same information into the short-term memory over and over several times, silently or out loud. Rehearsal or repetition is one of the best ways to keep information in the short-term memory.

Long-term Memory

Most people can hold at least five items in the short-term memory. If a grocery list contains 15 items to be remembered, however, there is usually a problem remembering everything on the list. One method of solving this problem and remembering more than five or six items is called **chunking.** By dividing the 15-item list into three 5-item chunks, more than the usual five or six items can be inserted into the memory. For example, divide the grocery list into three or more major categories. The categories may be something like fruits, vegetables, and meats. Next, organize the entire list by putting several items into each category. Once this is done only the major categories need usually be remembered. As each major category or chunk is recalled the items that belong in that category can usually also be recalled.

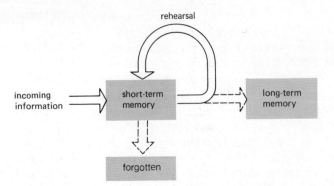

Short- and long-term
memory diagram.

A grocery list can usually be divided into easily remembered categories. There are other lists, however, that cannot be organized so easily. In difficult cases artificial categories or devices can sometimes be used. **Mnemonics** (from the Greek word for "memory,") is the name given to devices that aid the memory. If a list of words is to be remembered, it is sometimes possible to take the first letter of each word and form a new word that can be used as a mnemonic or memory device. The mnemonic, or new word, can be easily recalled from the short-term memory, and after a couple of readings of the list, most people can recall the entire list from the mnemonic. The first letter of each word is contained in the mnemonic, and the first letter is usually enough of a hint to bring back the entire word. Each word of the list can be recalled in the same way. "STM," for instance, is a mnemonic for short-term memory.

An example of another type of mnemonic is the jingle that many people use to remember how many days are in the months of the year. "Thirty days hath September," and so on. The rhythm and rhymes of the jingle help people remember the entire sequence of months and days.

Organization and mnemonics can extend the life of information in the memory for minutes or hours and sometimes even longer. These tricks do not, however, explain how people remember phone numbers for years. Not only phone numbers but incredibly vast amounts of information are remembered and recalled by everyone without any tricks. Names, faces, songs, mathematical formulas, historical facts—all of these and millions of different types of information are stored away in the normal human brain and remembered or recalled for years. The portion of the human memory that is able to hold so much information for so long is called the long-term memory (LTM).

The long-term memory seems to be limitless. That is, it is large enough to contain as much information as anyone can put into it. Unlike the short-term memory, the long-term memory does not have a leak in it. The long-term memory not only holds vast amounts of information but seems to be able to hold information forever.

The long-term memory can be pictured as a vast library with many books and a well-organized and cross-referenced card catalogue. For each book (piece of information to be stored) an index card is filled out (symbols, codes, or images are formed). The book is cross-referenced (associations are made between new and existing information in the memory). The book is then placed on its proper shelf (storage), and the index card is filed. The book can be found (recalled) by searching through the card catalogue under any one of the cross-references with which the book may be associated. The more associations or cross-references a book has, the easier it is to find. Children can recall the faces of their parents easily because they have usually seen those faces thousands of times in hundreds of situations. The face of a distant relative, which may have been seen at only a few family gatherings, has fewer associations and is usually much more difficult to recall. In general, the more associations a piece of information has, the easier it is to recall. Coding, organization, and the formation of associations takes time and practice. With practice, as children grow older, the ability to store and recall information from the long-term memory becomes better.

Memory Development

The ability to use the long-term memory may increase with age, but even young children have memory ability. Tests of this ability usually consist of asking children to recall something they have seen or heard or asking them to recognize something they have seen or heard. Children tend to perform much better when they have to recognize something than when they have to recall something. They may be able to recall (describe from memory) only 3 of 50 pictures they have seen, but will usually be able to recognize (remember having seen before) all 50 pictures. The young child's ability to recall events or stimuli may be less efficient than that of adolescents and adults because they have had less practice at forming images, codes, symbols, and associations. Language ability is often necessary in the formation of codes and symbols. It is also possible that the brain mechanisms necessary for good memory are not fully developed in young children.

Some research on the development of memory suggests that differences between children and adults depend to some extent on whether or not a conscious attempt is being made to use the memory. Recognition, for example, is usually an involuntary process at which children often perform as well as adults. Children seem to be less efficient at conscious attempts to retain and recall information.

Conscious attempts to remember often employ memory tricks or strategies, such as "Thirty days hath September. . . ." Most students are familiar with such strategies, but young children are not. Rehearsal, for instance, is one of the most often used memory aids. Older children use it all the time, but younger children must learn to use it. In one study when kindergarten children were told to repeat or rehearse the information to be remembered, their ability to recall improved (9). The ability to use this strategy all the time, however, does not seem to come easy. Many children in the study stopped rehearsing when no longer instructed to do so. Another study showed that fourth graders do use rehearsal, but the manner in which they do so differs from that used by college students (23).

As the amount and type of rehearsal (and other memory strategies) change, children tend to become more efficient in their ability to store and recall information. As their memory improves, their learning ability improves. With improved learning, children are capable of becoming Lincolns, Einsteins, Eleanor Roosevelts, or Beethovens.

LEARNING TECHNOLOGY

The importance of learning cannot be overemphasized. Along with physical growth and maturation, learning can account for most aspects of human development. But knowledge about learning does more than help explain human development. **Learning technology** (the application of what has been learned about learning) can be used to solve many learning and behavior problems.

Learning problems can be seen in delinquents who have learned socially unacceptable behavior, in children who have learning handicaps, and in average children who are having trouble mastering difficult subjects in school. Learning technology has been successfully applied to all of these problems.

At Achievement Place the principles of observational learning are applied when teaching parents act as models for socially acceptable behaviors. The principles of behavior modification are used to help extinguish undesired behaviors and motivate children to learn new behaviors.

Children with learning handicaps benefit perhaps even more from learning technology than delinquents. Because of their handicaps such children may be capable of only the most basic type of learning. For years very little attempt was made to teach such children. Now that research on learning has defined the basics of learning, educators are able to apply this knowledge and teach even the most severely handicapped children useful behaviors. The case of Patti K. is an example.

When these basics of learning are applied to normal students, as in Keller's Personalized System of Instruction, it is possible to teach even the most difficult subjects. As more and more is learned about learning, better teaching and more learning may be possible.

SUMMARY

Learning is the modification of behavior due to contact with the environment. It is the process by which new information, habits, abilities, and behaviors are acquired. Along with physical growth and maturation, learning can account for most aspects of human development. Without the ability to learn, survival would not even be possible.

At its most basic or simple level, learning consists of the formation of associations among different aspects of the environment. Infants, for instance, learn to associate nipples with milk. This can be seen in conditioning. In classical conditioning an association is made between a stimulus and a response. In operant conditioning organisms learn an association between their own behavior and its effects on the environment. In classical conditioning the strength and timing of the stimulus as well as the order in which the stimulus and response occur help determine whether or not an association will be made. In operant conditioning it is the type and timing of the response that strengthen or reinforce the stimulus (initial behavior). In operant conditioning reinforcement is sometimes called feedback. By manipulating the timing of feedback and the type of reinforcement, it is sometimes possible to strengthen associations and modify behavior. Behaviors that have been learned through conditioning can sometimes be unlearned through a process known as extinction.

Observational or social learning, learning from the behavior of others, accounts for a great deal of human behavior. According to social learning theorist Albert Bandura, attention, retention, motor reproduction, and reinforcement or motivation are the most important processes in observational learning.

Motivation is one of the major reasons for learning. In most cases the behaviors performed in attempts to reduce a drive or fulfill a need result in learning. Motivation is usually defined in terms of primary (biological) and secondary (learned) needs. In respect to learning, motivation performs one or more of several functions. It energizes and sensitizes an organism to important aspects of the environment. It also selects the behaviors and directs an organism in ways that will reduce a need or drive.

Generalization and discrimination are examples of complex learning. Generalization allows for the transfer of learned behaviors from one situation to another. Discrimination is the process that helps prevent incorrect responses to similar stimuli. Incidental learning is the type of learning that sometimes takes place along with intentional learning. Whenever a learning task involves more than one stimulus, as most do, there is a chance that incidental learning will take place.

Memory is an important process in most types of learning. If experiences and information from one situation are not remembered, they will not usually affect future behavior. Three types of learning are seen in humans: sensory-information store, short-term memory, and long-term memory.

Learning helps explain many aspects of human behavior and human development. In addition, what has been learned about learning can be applied in attempts to modify human behavior and to make learning more effective and efficient.

RESEARCH REPORT 6.1

Memory in Young Children: Transitive-inference Problems

The red stick is taller than the blue stick.
The blue stick is taller than the green stick.

If you were presented these premises, you could quickly and correctly conclude that the red stick must also be taller than the green stick. This type of transitive-inference problem is, however, very difficult for young children. Although Piaget believes that young children fail transitive-inference problems because of their inability to think logically, some researchers argue that deficiencies in other basic information-processing capabilities are involved. Bryant and Trabasso (1971) suggest that the young child fails because of an inability to remember the information which he or she is asked to reason about.

To test this possibility, fifty 4- and 5-year-olds were required to learn four premises before they were presented transitive-inference problems involving them. Five sticks, each of a different color and length, were used. The sticks could be ordered by length such that red > (taller than) blue > green > yellow > white. In the learning phase the experimenter showed the child pairs of sticks in a special container and asked him or her to indicate which stick in each pair was taller. The child was told whether or not the answer was correct. The container was constructed so that the sticks protruded one inch from the top, regardless of their actual length. Thus, the child could not answer correctly by visually comparing the sticks; he or she had to learn and remember the color of the taller stick in each pair. The children were presented the same four pairs (red and blue, blue and green, green and yellow, and yellow and white) until they consistently remembered which stick in each pair was taller. The learning phase insured that the children mastered the four premises: red > blue, blue > green, green > yellow, yellow > white.

The experimenter then presented the critical transitive-inference problems. The child was asked to indicate which stick in each of six new pairs was taller. The test pairs were red and green, red and yellow, red and white, blue and yellow, yellow and white, and green and white. Because the pairs were presented in the special container, the child could not base an answer on visual comparisons of length; he or she could answer correctly by making the appropriate inferences from the premises the child had mastered earlier.

On the critical problems both age groups correctly selected the taller stick more often than expected by chance. The children's accuracy exceeded chance expectations even on the blue and yellow pair which demanded the most complex inference because both sticks were the taller stick in one premise and the shorter stick in another premise. The researchers concluded that young children's memory deficits should not be mistaken for reasoning deficits. Preoperational children may be able to make transitive inferences when precautions are taken to insure that they remember the relevant information.

Based on P. E. Bryant and T. Trabasso, "Transitive Inferences and Memory in Young Children," *Nature*, 1971, 232, 456–458.

RESEARCH
REPORT 6.2

How Are Children Affected by Watching Television?

What effects does television watching have on children? In a study by Liebert and Baron (1972) which investigated this topic each of 136 children, aged 6 to 9 years, was asked to watch a television program until the experimenter was ready for him or her. As the children waited, half of them viewed a three-and-a-half–minute violent segment from the television series "The Untouchables." The segment included a chase scene, two fist fights, two shootings, and a knifing. The other half of the children watched for the same length of time a nonviolent film about a sports event. The experimenter then escorted the child to the next room where he or she was shown a panel containing a white light, a red button with the word *hurt* beneath it, and a green button with the word *help* beneath it. Each child was told that the white light would come on whenever a child playing a game in the adjoining room tried to turn a handle. Each child was further told that he or she must press either the red or the green button when the white light came on. The experimenter explained that pressing the green button helped the other child by making the handle easier to turn, but that pressing the red button hurt the other child by making the handle too hot to touch. Another child was not actually playing a game in the adjoining room; instead, the apparatus was rigged so that the white light came on 20 times during a five-minute period.

The amount of time that each child pressed the red button was used as a measure of his or her willingness to hurt another child. The results indicated that children who had watched the violent film pressed the *hurt* button for a longer amount of time than did children who had watched the nonviolent film. The researchers concluded:

> The overall results of the present experiment provide relatively consistent evidence for the view that certain aspects of a child's willingness to aggress may be at least temporarily increased by merely witnessing aggressive television episodes. . . . The present results emerged despite the brevity of the aggressive sequences (less than 4 minutes), the absence of a strong prior instigation to aggression, the clear availability of an alternative helping response, and the use of nationally broadcast materials rather than specially prepared laboratory films. (p. 474)

Similar research has also been conducted to determine whether the content of television programs can increase desirable rather than undesirable behavior (Sprafkin, Liebert, and Poulos, 1975). Thirty first-graders watched one of three half-hour programs: a "Lassie" episode containing a dramatic helping scene in which the main character Jeff risked his life to rescue Lassie's puppy; a "Lassie" episode in which the same characters were involved but the plot concerned violin lessons for Jeff; or a "Brady Bunch" episode about a family who did not have a dog. After the television show each child was given a game in which he or she could win prizes by pressing a button that would light a bulb. The experimenter also placed earphones on the child. The child was told that if puppies at a nearby kennel cried, their cries could be heard through the earphones. The experimenter explained that if the child heard the cries while playing the game, he or she could help the puppies by pushing a special *help* button that alerted the keeper who lived near the kennel. The experimenter then left the room, and a two-minute tape of puppies crying was played to the child.

The researchers reported that children who had seen the "Lassie" program with the helping scene pressed the *help* button longer than did the children who had seen either of the other programs. This finding is especially impressive, because children who pressed the *help* button lost time from the game in which they were winning prizes for themselves. As the researchers suggested, their findings imply that "it is possible to produce television programming that features action and adventure, appeals to child and family audiences, and still has a salutary rather than a negative social influence on observers" (p. 125).

Based on R. M. Liebert and R. Baron, "Some Immediate Effects of Televised Violence on Children's Behavior," *Developmental Psychology*, 1972, 6, 469–475; J. N. Sprafkin, R. M. Liebert, and R. W. Poulos, "Effects of a Prosocial Televised Example on Children's Helping," *Journal of Experimental Child Psychology*, 1975, 20, 119–126.

REFERENCES

1. Baer, D. M., and J. A. Sherman. "Behavior Modification: Clinical and Educational Applications." In H. W. Reese and L. P. Lipsitt (eds.), *Experimental Child Psychology.* New York: Academic Press, 1970.
2. Bandura, A. "Influence of Model's Reinforcement Contingencies on the Acquisition of Imitative Responses," *Journal of Personality and Social Psychology,* 1965, *1,* 589–595.
3. Bandura, A. *Aggression: A Social Learning Analysis.* Englewood Cliffs, N.J.: Prentice-Hall, Inc., 1973.
4. Bekhtever, V. M. *General Principles of Human Reflexology.* New York: International Publishers, 1932.
5. Bronfenbrenner, U. *Two Worlds of Childhood: U.S. and U.S.S.R.* New York: Simon and Schuster, 1972.
6. Coates, B., and W. W. Hartup. "Age and Verbalization in Observational Learning," *Developmental Psychology,* 1969, *1,* 556–562.
7. Douglas, J. H. "Learning Technology Comes of Age," *Science News,* 1976, *110* (11), 170–174.
8. Farber, I. E. "The Role of Motivation in Verbal Learning and Performance," *Psychology Bulletin,* 1955, *52,* 311–327.
9. Flavell, J. H. "Developmental Studies of Mediated Memory." In H. W. Reese and L. P. Lipsitt (eds.), *Advances in Child Development and Behavior,* Vol. 5. New York: Academic Press, 1970.
10. Goldenson, R. M. "Learning," *The Encyclopedia of Human Behavior.* New York: Doubleday & Company, 1970, 686–690.
11. Goldenson, R. M. "Conditioning," *The Encyclopedia of Human Behavior.* New York: Doubleday & Company, 1970.
12. Hagen, H. W. "The Effect of Distraction on Selective Attention," *Child Development,* 1967, *38,* 685–694.
13. Hale, G. A., and R. A. Piper. "Developmental Trends in Children's Incidental Learning: Some Critical Stimulus Differences," *Developmental Psychology,* 1973, *8,* 327–335.
14. Hartup, W. W. "Nurturance and Nurturance-Withdrawal in Relation to Dependency Behavior of Preschool Children," *Child Development,* 1958, *29,* 191–201.
15. Hebb, D. O. "Drives and the C.N.S.," *Psychology Review,* 1955, *62,* 243–254.
16. Jeffery, W. E., and R. W. Skager. "Effect of Incentive Conditions on Stimulus Generalization," *Child Development,* 1962, *33,* 865–870.
17. Lipsitt, L., and H. Kaye. "Conditioned Sucking in the Human Newborn," *Psychonomic Science,* 1964, *1,* 29–30.
18. Marquis, D. P. "Can Conditioned Responses Be Established in the Newborn Infant?" *Journal of Genetic Psychology,* 1931, *39,* 479–492.
19. Maslow, A. H. *Toward a Psychology of Being.* New York: Van Nostrand Reinhold Company, 1962.
20. McConnell, J. V. *Understanding Human Behavior,* 2d ed. New York: Holt, Rinehart and Winston, 1977.

21. Mednick, S. A., and L. E. Lehtinen. "Stimulus Generalization as a Function of Age in Children," *Journal of Experimental Psychology*, 1957, *53*, 180–183.
22. Melton, A. W. "Learning." In W. S. Monroe (ed.), *Encyclopedia of Educational Research*, 2d ed. New York: The Macmillan Company, 1950, 668–690.
23. Ornstein, P. A., and C. Liberty. "Rehearsal Processes in Children's Memory." Paper presented at the meeting of the Society for Research in Child Development, Philadelphia, 1973.
24. Reese, H. W. *Basic Learning Processes in Childhood.* New York: Holt, Rinehart and Winston, 1976.
25. Skinner, B. F. "Are Theories of Learning Necessary?" *Psychological Review*, 1950, *57*, 193–216.
26. Smith, J. M., and D. E. P. Smith. *Child Management.* Ann Arbor, Mich.: Ann Arbor Publishers, 1966.
27. Tempone, V. J. "The Nature of the Stimulus in Primary Stimulus Generalization," *Canadian Journal of Psychology*, 1968, *22*, 244–251.
28. Trotter, R. J. "This Is Going To Hurt You More Than It Hurts Me," *Science News*, 1972, *102* (21), 332–333.
29. Trotter, R. J. "Behavior Modification: Here, There and Everywhere," *Science News*, 1973, *103* (16), 260–263.
30. "TV and Violence: A Modest Relationship," *Science News*, 1972, *101* (4), 55.
31. "Who Wants To Live on Sesame Street?" *Science News*, 1973, *103* (12), 183.

Children are not miniature adults, as was once thought. They think and understand the world differently than adults do. Studies of cognitive development have helped emphasize this point and have helped explain the way children understand the world. Without an understanding of cognitive development, it is not possible to understand children.

cognitive development

INTRODUCTION: THINKING MACHINES

Robots and mechanical monsters lumbered across the pages of science fiction novels for years before technological advances such as transistors, television, and computers made it possible for these mechanical marvels actually to step into the world of scientific reality. Even when they did, in the 1950s and 1960s, many people considered them nothing more than expensive toys. But this didn't discourage the inventors of such toys. The field of **artificial,** or machine, **intelligence** has grown steadily during the past 20 years, and attempts to design a "thinking" machine have continued. Mathematicians and engineers at the Massachusetts Institute of Technology's Artificial Intelligence Laboratory, for example, have combined a computer, a television camera, and a mechanical arm into a system with enough artificial intelligence to recognize blocks of various sizes, colors, and shapes and to assemble them into structures without step-by-step instructions from an operator. For more complex tasks an advanced arm has been developed with eight movable joints that can reach around obstacles. A similar mechanical arm at Stanford University has been programmed to pick up the pieces of a water pump, assemble them, and screw them together. Such machines will eventually be able to perform mechanical tasks too minute or too delicate for human hands. But so far these machines don't do much of what would be called thinking. Other machines, however, do seem to have a basic sort of intelligence.

A computer designed by Bell Laboratories has a vocabulary of almost 2,000 words. It can read stories and speak them aloud. The U.S. Air Force is working on machine translation of German into English, Chinese into English, and Russian into English. During the Vietnam war a computer was programmed to translate English into Vietnamese. Programming took 18 months, but eventually the machine was able to translate an average U.S. Army manual into Vietnamese in less than two hours.

Checker- and chess-playing machines even have the ability to learn from their mistakes. One at MIT has been rated as a better-than-average chess player in tournament chess. Such research has been attacked as a useless and frivolous waste of time because machines will probably never be able to really think. But artificial intelligence researchers say robots are only tools for the study of intelligence. Getting a machine to learn English, for example, demonstrates the problems and methods humans have in learning a language. Such problems don't always show up in a language laboratory. Seymour Papert, codirector with Marvin Minsky of the Artificial Intelligence Laboratory at MIT, compares the study of intelligence to the study of flight (26). He points out that just as flight couldn't be analyzed until the principles of aerodynamics were worked out, human intelligence can't be thoroughly studied until the basic principles of intelligence are formulated. Jean Piaget (see Chapter 1) is investigating principles of intelligence by observing the mental development of children. Papert and his co-workers are doing the same thing by finding out how machines learn. The end result, Papert says, will be theories of intelligence that apply to humans and machines.

Papert and Minsky believe that enough is already known about machine intelligence to use it as a basis for planning new learning environments for children. One of their projects demonstrates how artificial intelligence technology can be used in education. The idea is not to use machines as teachers; instead, computers are being used to give children practice in thinking. To do this it is not sufficient merely to have a computer. It is necessary to develop situations in which the computer can be used by a child to solve real problems. Several computer-controlled devices have been designed to do this. One is a music generator that enables a child to produce songs and to experiment in music composition. Another is a graphic system with the ability to produce animated cartoons. The computer can be programmed to compose stories or poems. There is also a mechanical animal called "the turtle" that can be programmed to do a number of things, including move around a classroom and leave a track or draw a picture on the floor. By learning to program the computer to generate music, pictures, or physical activities, the student is supposed to develop the mental tools to think about such things as time, space, sound, and physical matters.

This approach can be seen in many projects as the children program machines to imitate some aspects of their own behavior. To understand how

Machine technology may be used as a basis for planning new learning environments for children.

to make the turtle move, for example, the children look at their own motions. To make the computer produce grammatical English, they look at their own sentences. By programming a computer to play games of skill, children begin to understand the processes involved in improving their own mental skills. Work with music may lead to a child's being able to think clearly about time as it applies to things other than music. Eventually, Papert and his co-workers hope to use computer technology and what they have learned about intelligence to develop methods of helping children learn in such areas as physics, linguistics, biology, and psychology.

COGNITION

The complicated process that goes on inside a computer is similar to what goes on inside the human brain. Like a computer, the brain takes in information, processes it, and gives back an answer. In humans the processing of information is called **cognition.**

Cognition is, without a doubt, one of the most important behaviors of the human organism. Attempts to understand cognition, however, have been hampered by the fact that what happens in the brain can't be seen. Without this inside information theories of cognition have had to rely on external signs of cognition as exemplified in behaviors, many of which take the form of language. From these signs attempts are made to determine what is really happening inside the human brain.

Learning Theory

Learning theory and all of the aspects of learning discussed in Chapter 6 offer one way of understanding cognition and thought processes. Recall the infant who refused to suck on a green and yellow nipple. The child received a piece of information (color of nipple), processed the information, and gave back an answer (refused to suck). Learning theory suggests that through previous experiences the infant had formed an association between the strangely colored nipple and its unpleasant taste. With this learned association the child knew to avoid the unpleasant experience. Through continued experience with the environment, and the gradual accumulation of millions of associations, each child builds up a set of learned behaviors. Through conditioning, observational learning, generalization, discrimination, and all of the other factors involved in learning, a child's thinking processes and behaviors gradually become more complex.

While **learning theory** helps explain human behavior, children always seem to be doing something unexpected. Operant conditioning, for example, can explain some aspects of how children learn a language. Parents reinforce children as they learn and begin to use new words. But once children have acquired a number of words, they begin to use these words in new and novel ways. They say things for which they may not have been reinforced, and they talk about things they may never have experienced. It seems, then, that more is going on in the child's mind than the formation of associations between stimuli and responses. Learning theory does not shed a great deal of light on the complex behavior known as cognition, so we turn to other theories for more complete explanations.

Information-processing Theory

Computers are a long way from achieving human intelligence, but in some ways computers are like the brain. This analogy can help us to understand cognition. Computers can be opened up and examined. Because they are built and programmed by humans, it is possible to know exactly what processes are going on inside them. A computer, for example, can be programmed with a set of instructions or rules, such as the rules for playing chess. The rules tell the machine exactly how to process incoming information. When an opponent's move is fed in, that information is processed, and a new situation exists to which the computer must respond. Knowing all the rules, the computer will be able to select the move most likely to achieve its programmed goal.

Some computers, while they are going through a decision-making process, print out the steps in that process. From such print outs it can be seen that the machine goes through the same steps a human would in thinking about how to solve a problem. If the steps taken by the machine are incorrect, or if a mistake has been made, the computer can be reprogrammed with new rules. If a problem is too complex, new information-processing rules can be inserted. As computer technology advances, it becomes possible to use more sophisticated rules and programs.

Explanations of cognition based on **information-processing** suggest that children, like computers, learn certain basic rules or strategies for dealing with incoming information. As more rules are learned, more complex problems can be handled. Gradually children develop the sophisticated set of rules necessary for the type of thinking seen in adults.

Psychologist Jerome Bruner has described some of the basic information-processing strategies or rules that seem to appear at different stages in a child's development (2).

1. The Enactive Stage In the first stage infants code events in the world and think in terms of motor responses or physical activities. When infants reach for, hold, or put things in their mouths, they are exploring the physical environment and learning certain rules about it. Bruner calls this the **enactive stage** because infants enact, or physically act out, their understanding of the

Psychologist Jerome S. Bruner (1915–   )

environment. Hungry infants, for example, might hold out their arms and make sucking motions. With no language and very little experience with the environment, infants may have no other way of representing to themselves that they are hungry and that they want to be fed. In other words, they are actually thinking with their physical motions.

2. The Ikonic Stage As infants gain more experience with their world they develop a method of representing the world without specific motor responses or activities. By about the first birthday, according to Bruner, infants begin to represent objects and events with images and visual perceptions. An ikon is an image, and Bruner calls this second stage of cognitive development the **ikonic stage.** With the ability to use images instead of physical actions, an infant's cognitive processes are greatly expanded. Although infants continue to use enactive representation during the first year or two, ikonic representation helps them think about objects and events that are not physically present.

Ikonic representation does expand children's ability to think about the world, but images help represent only the physical qualities of an object. They do not contain information about the object's functions or general properties. For example, children will usually sort objects or pictures on the basis of their visual qualities. This can be seen in one experiment in which children and adults were asked to describe the similarities among several objects (12). The children grouped the objects according to how they looked. A 4-year-old was likely to say that a banana, a peach, and a potato are alike because they are all "sort of yellow." Adults tended to group these same objects together because they are all food. Adults, with a more sophisticated set of rules, can think about the functions and qualities of objects. Children in the ikonic stage are dominated by their perceptions.

3. Symbolic Representation As children begin to use language to interpret and represent the world, they enter what Bruner calls the stage of **symbolic representation.** Words are symbols that can be used to think about almost anything. With such symbols children are not limited to thinking about objects that have to be visualized or sensed. Symbolic representation is another important step that greatly expands cognitive abilities, but it is a difficult step that takes several years.

4. Logical Thinking At the most mature level of cognitive functioning older children and adults are capable of processing information according to the rules of logic. Put simply, **logical thinking** allows for the use of two pieces of information in the processing of a third and new bit of information. If, for example, A is larger than B, and B is larger than C, the rules of logic say that A is larger than C. The new information (A is larger than C) is arrived at without actually having to experience A and C together. With this and the other rules of logic perceptual experiences (as in ikonic and enactive representation) are not necessary in the processing of information. Symbols are manipulated according to the rules, and new information is processed.

Through experience with the environment children gradually learn the rules of logic. Once the rules have been learned they can be applied whenever necessary, even in situations that have not been previously experienced. It is these rules of logic that make computers seem almost human in some of their information processing.

With logic and a vast memory bank, computers are usually faster and sometimes more accurate than the people who built and programmed them. As impressive as computers are, however, they still lack some very important human qualities. They don't have human creativity or true insights (the ability to see a situation or problem in new and meaningful ways). Computers can be programmed to write stories and draw pictures, but they can't produce a real work of art. Even if they did, they wouldn't know that they had. Computers do only what their human programmers tell them to do.

Information-processing theory and work with computers help to explain some basic cognitive processes, but human programmers don't yet know enough about their own thought processes to design a computer capable of human thinking. Until that happens, information-processing theory won't be able to answer all of the questions about human cognition.

Structural Theory

The nature-nurture question enters into discussions of cognition as it does all areas of human development (see Chapters 2 and 3). Both learning theory and information-processing theory stress nurture. That is, they emphasize the importance of learning through interaction with the environment. Mental associations and rules are learned, they are not provided by the genes or nature. A third major theory of behavior and cognitive development says that nature provides each human infant with certain basic biological structures that make cognition possible. **Structural theory,** particularly that of Piaget, suggests that cognitive development is related to the development of internal structures. Infants and children continually attempt to adapt or adjust to the environment (see the discussion of assimilation and accommodation in Chapter 1). As they do so preprogrammed internal structures unfold and become available for use in cognition. These structures, which develop as a result of interactions between experience (both physical and social) and maturation, provide the growing child with the organizational processes necessary for human cognition.

A basic assumption of structural theory is that as internal structures unfold or develop, children pass through a series of unique and distinctive stages. These stages build upon each other and lead to adult cognition. Each of the four stages described by Piaget (see Chapter 1) is characterized by a distinct type of cognition.

The stages are distinct, but they are not discontinuous. In other words, a child does not suddenly wake up one morning with a completely different type of thinking ability. The stages develop quite gradually, and they may overlap. This can be seen as the behaviors and thought processes of the early stages continue to appear in later stages—though they may have been altered due to learning and mental development. Even though the stages do overlap, Piaget's theory says the order in which they appear is the same in every child.

1. The Sensory-Motor Stage During the first stage of cognitive development, which spans the first two years of life, children understand the world in terms of their own actions and motor behaviors. They think and understand the world with their movements. (This is what Bruner calls enactive representation.) An example of **sensory-motor stage** behavior is seen in an incident that Piaget relates about his daughter Jacqueline when she was 9 months old. She clearly demonstrated her feelings about certain aspects of the environment by her acts:

> She discovers more complex signs during a meal than previously. She likes the grape juice in a glass but not the soup in a bowl. She watches her mother's activity. When the spoon comes out of the glass she opens her mouth wide, whereas when it comes from the bowl her mouth remains closed. Her mother then tries to lead her to a mistake by taking the spoon from the bowl and passing it by the glass before offering it to Jacqueline. But she is not fooled.

2. The Preoperational Stage As children pass out of the sensory-motor stage they begin to represent things internally and no longer have to act out their thoughts. (In Bruner's terms they are beginning to use ikonic representation.)

But because infants at this stage don't yet have the ability to perform mental operations, Piaget calls this the **preoperational stage,** and it lasts from about age 2 to age 7.

During this stage children's thoughts are still closely related to their own bodily movements and their perceptions. They don't seem to have an understanding of an objective or independent reality outside themselves. Piaget says they are egocentric. Ego means "self," and infants seem to understand the world with themselves at the center of everything. They understand little other than their immediate consciousness and cannot at first distinguish themselves from the rest of the world.

Piaget has demonstrated egocentric thinking by showing a child a three-dimensional scene with a doll in it. As the doll is moved to various positions around the scene, the child is asked to point to one of several pictures and select one that represents what the doll would see. In the preoperational stage children often fail to select the correct picture. They seem to understand the world from their own egocentric point of view only and fail to realize that other people would have a different perspective. This kind of thinking is of a more mature type that develops gradually during the next stages.

3. Concrete Operations During the next stage, from about 7 to 11 years, when children are able to represent the physical world with images and symbols, they gradually develop the ability to perform mental operations with those symbols. Piaget terms this the stage of **concrete operations.** Children begin to use numbers (symbols), for example, to count objects. They begin to show the first signs of thinking logically about the physical or concrete world rather than accepting surface appearances. Even so, children in the concrete operations stage are frequently fooled by external appearances.

Piaget and his colleagues have developed many tests that help characterize a child's mental operations at this stage. In one such test Piaget shows a child two balls of soft clay, making sure that the child agrees that they are equal (18) in size. He then rolls one out into a fat sausage shape and asks the child if the amount of clay is still the same in each piece. Children in the preoperational stage may be fooled by appearances and say that the rolled-

Children in the preoperational stage may say that the rolled-out piece contains more clay than the round piece because it is longer.

out piece contains more clay than the round piece because it is longer. At the beginning of the concrete operations stage the child may still be fooled by appearances, but later in this stage the child will come to realize that the amount of clay remains the same, no matter how it is shaped.

4. Formal Operations The final period of cognitive development described by Piaget appears in early adolescence, at about age 11, and lasts through adulthood. At this stage thinking is no longer restricted to images and symbols of concrete objects. This stage is called the period of **formal operations** because the mental abilities that develop during this stage allow an individual to understand the form of logical thinking and reasoning. With such abilities the adolescent and adult mind is capable of understanding theories and designing computers. The period of formal operations, according to Piaget, is the goal toward which all earlier stages are directed.

SIMILARITIES AND DIFFERENCES IN COGNITIVE THEORIES

Unlike computers, children and their thought processes cannot be taken apart and thoroughly examined. So human cognition, which is much more complex than the workings of any machine, must be explained in terms of theories instead of solid facts. Children's behaviors are observed, and attempts are made to explain those behaviors and the thoughts responsible for them by using one theory or another. Learning theory, information-processing theory, and structural theory are all based on observations of the same subject— human children. But because each approach views the developing child from a slightly different angle, each comes up with an explanation of cognition that is slightly different from the others. Since the three theories look at the same subject from slightly different perspectives, a combination of all of them probably offers a more well-rounded explanation of cognitive development than any single theory does.

The most important difference among the theories has to do with the age at which children are able to solve certain problems. Learning theory and information-processing theory suggest that any subject can be taught to any child if the child has had the necessary background or experience and if the subject matter is presented in the appropriate form. According to these theories, there are no definite stages of cognitive development. Children think differently at different ages because it takes time to learn new behaviors and rules for thinking. Structural theory, on the other hand, suggests that some things just cannot be understood until a child's mind has reached a certain stage of biological development, no matter how much experience or training the child receives.

This basic difference among the theories can have important implications for education. Learning theory has developed some highly sophisticated teaching technology based on the principles of operant conditioning or behavior modification (see the discussion of Keller's PSI in Chapter 6). Computerized learning programs are used to present material and schedule reinforcement in a highly organized manner. Such methods have proved to be quite successful with many students and with certain types of subject matter. Structural theory, on the other hand, says that as the biological structures of the mind unfold, children need to exercise their developing cognitive powers. They do this by constantly experimenting with the environment and discovering new things about it. At each stage of cognitive development children discover more and are able to understand more. This theory has led to what is called the discoverist approach to education. An example can be seen in the way Papert and his colleagues allow children to experiment with computers and discover how they function. These students not only begin to learn about computers, they begin to understand their own cognitive functioning.

The differences among the approaches can be seen more clearly by looking at how a course is taught in the traditional manner. Chemistry students, for example, memorize formulas and perform classic experiments that have been performed by thousands of students before them. Learning technology can help make this type of learning easier. Operant conditioning can be used to help students memorize formulas and chemical reactions. But according to Piaget, this type of learning can be damaging to active, lively minds, especially if they aren't ready to learn the material. Memorizing formulas is an almost useless task if the principles of how to use those formulas are not understood. Structural theory suggests instead that students should learn the basic principles of chemistry by being allowed to develop their own experimental projects. Discovery through doing, says Piaget, not only teaches but can awaken original thinking (25).

Although learning theory and the discoverist approach to education differ, they have both been found useful in the classroom, and a combination of the two often produces the desired results. Both approaches are useful because the similarities among the theories of cognitive development are probably greater than the differences. The most important similarity is that all major theories of cognitive development stress the importance of the environment. The associations and rules of learning theory and information-processing theory, for example, are learned as a child continually interacts with and learns about the environment. Theories that stress this type of development are on the nurture side of the nature-nurture question. Structural theory, because it emphasizes the importance of biological development, is usually thought of as being on the nature side of the nature-nurture question. But structural theory also points out the importance of the environment. It says that cognitive structures develop as children continually attempt to adapt to the environment. An environment that encourages creative experimentation, Piaget maintains, helps a child learn to use the biological structures as they gradually unfold. An especially challenging environment, but one that is not too far beyond the child's abilities, Piaget suggests, can even speed up this development. Because it stresses the importance of both biological structures and the environment, Piaget's theory has been called both a nature and a nurture theory (3).

THE INFANT'S WORLD

Jacqueline looks at my watch, which is 10 cm. from her eyes. She reveals a lively interest, and her hands flutter as though she were about to grasp, without however discovering the right direction. I place the watch in her right hand without her being able to see how (the arm being outstretched). Then I again put the watch before her eyes. Her hands, apparently excited by the contact just experienced, then proceed to move through space and meet violently, subsequently to separate. The right hand happens to strike the watch; Jacqueline immediately tries to adjust her hand to the watch and thus manages to grasp it. The experiment is repeated three times: it is always when the hand is perceived at the same time as the watch that the attempts become systematic. The next day I resume the experiment. When the watch is before her eyes, Jacqueline does not attempt to grasp it although she reveals a lively interest in this object. When the watch is near her hand and she happens to touch it, or it is seen at the same time as her hand, then there is searching, and searching directed by the glance. Near the eyes and far from the hands the watch is again simply contemplated. The hands move a little but do not approach each other. I again place the object near her hand: immediate searching, and again success. I put the watch a third time a few centimeters from her eyes and far from her hands: these move in all directions but without approaching each other. In short there are still two worlds for Jacqueline, one kinesthetic [related to bodily reactions] and the other visual. It is only when the object is seen next to the hand that the latter is directed toward it and manages to grasp it. That evening, the same experiment with various solid objects. Again and very regularly, when Jacqueline sees the object facing her without perceiving her hands, nothing happens, whereas the simultaneous sight of object and of hand (right or left) sets prehension [grasping] in motion. Finally it is to be noted that, that day, Jacqueline again watched with great interest her empty hand crossing the visual field: the hand is still not felt to belong to her (16).

With hundreds of carefully recorded observations like this, Piaget has managed to paint a clear and understandable picture of the developing cognitive abilities of his own children. With such observations he has made it quite obvious that infancy is not just a time for eating, sleeping, and crying but is a period during which the awareness of objects and the relationship between events in the world begins.

Although Piaget's observations of cognitive development almost completely revolutionized the study of cognition in children, a few details of his theory are still considered as hypotheses yet to be proved. For one thing, Piaget's observations are based on a small number of children. While his findings may be accurate, they cannot definitely be said to apply to all children in all cultures. For another thing, Piaget's findings are based on motor responses, and there are many factors other than cognition that can affect such responses. Lack of motivation, distraction, or fear in a strange situation are a few reasons why motor responses may not accurately reflect cognition. Even with these possible drawbacks, there is a great deal of evidence from research done with thousands of children that generally confirms Piaget's theory. His description of cognitive development is considered by many psychologists to be one of the most thorough and important available. Through Piaget many people have come to a real understanding of the child's world (13, 14, 18).

Much of this world can be seen in Piaget's description of the six substages of the sensory-motor period (the first two years). Each of these substages is characterized by a different type of interaction with the environment, and each of the interactions represents an increasing understanding of the world. Throughout these stages Piaget studied the development of what are called **schemata.** A schema (singular of "schemata") is a mental structure or pattern of behavior. Children have schemata for such things as food, hand waving, and looking. These schemata or mental concepts develop as children use them. According to Piaget, schemata are like muscles that develop and become firm with exercise. Schemata are exercised during repeated sensory-motor reactions with the environment.

After many attempts Jacqueline managed to grasp her father's watch. She was exercising the schema for accurate grasping. These repeated sensory-motor reactions are called circular reactions by Piaget because they consist of a back-and-forth or circular interaction with the environment. These circular reactions, which begin in the first stage, lead to the development of new schemata.

Six Stages of the Sensory-Motor Period

Stage 1 (from birth to one month) involves exercising the sensory-motor schemata. The first stage of development in the sensory-motor period is characterized by reflexive movements (see Chapter 4) and otherwise unorganized or gross bodily reactions and movements. The reflexive reactions provide the basis for more organized movements that develop throughout the sensory-motor period. Piaget has proposed two mechanisms to account for the gradual modification of reflexive reactions and the change of gross bodily movements to more meaningful and controlled reactions. These mechanisms are assimilation and accommodation.

Assimilation is the process by which an organism takes in information about the world. With this information schemata are gradually modified as children adapt to changes in the environment. Piaget describes three types of assimilation. In generalizing assimilation a schema that has been formed through reaction to one aspect of the environment is applied to other aspects of the environment. Jacqueline, for example, experimented with grasping her father's watch. Through generalizing assimilation she began to grasp other objects. This is quite similar to the process of generalization described in connection with learning in Chapter 6.

In recognitory assimilation children recognize and discriminate between objects that belong to a particular schema and those that do not. This is similar to the discrimination discussed in learning theory. Examples of these two types of assimilation are seen in one of Piaget's observations of his son Laurent:

> Laurent [at 9 days of age] is lying in bed and seeks to suck, moving his head to the left and to the right. Several times he rubs his lips with his hand which he immediately sucks. He knocks against a quilt and wool coverlet and each time he sucks the object, only to relinquish it after a moment and begins to cry. When he sucks his hand he does not turn away from it as he seems to do with the woolens, but the hand itself escapes him through lack of coordination. He then immediately begins to hunt again.

Laurent sucked his hand reflexively. Through generalizing assimilation he began to suck other objects, such as a terrible-tasting wool blanket. Recognitory assimilation helped him discriminate between his hand and the blanket. With the ability to recognize the difference between the two he continued to suck his hand but turned away from the taste of the blanket.

Laurent didn't know to avoid the blanket after the first taste; he needed to repeat the reaction several times. Piaget calls this functional assimilation because it has to do with the function or use of assimilated schemata. As schemata are used over and over they become assimilated. When fully assimilated, behaviors are more useful, and this usefulness serves as a sort of positive reinforcement for continued repetition of the behavior. But changes in the environment call for changes in behavior. The ability to change a behavior or a schema in response to a changing world is called **accommodation** (see Chapter 1). An example of accommodation is seen in Jacqueline's different reactions to a spoon coming out of a glass and a spoon coming out of a bowl. She accommodated, or modified, her reaction by not opening her mouth for the spoon from the bowl.

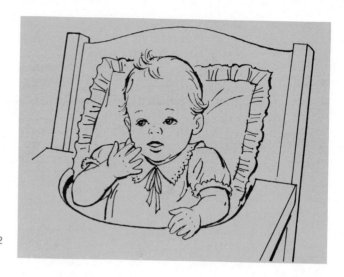

Hand-watching by a Stage 2 infant.

Stage 2 (from 1 to 4 months) is characterized by the primary circular reaction. During this stage new response patterns are formed by chance from combinations of primitive or earlier reflexes. These responses, such as arm waving and sucking, happen over and over (**circular reaction**) and are characterized by attempts to prolong satisfying and pleasant events in the environment. But at this stage responses occur only by accident. There is no apparent planning on the part of the infant. Responses during this stage usually consist of a simple motion or a series of movements that are not intended to have any consequences in the environment or to make something happen. They are merely done for the pleasure of doing them. This can be seen in Jacqueline's attempts to look at her hands for the pleasure of looking at them, even though she cannot yet intentionally bring them into her visual field:

> Jacqueline seems not to have looked at her hands before (two months and 30 days). But on this date and the following she frequently notices her moving fingers and looks at them attentively. At three months and 13 days when her hands move into her visual field she looks fixedly at them just as she looks at the folds of the quilt when they appear before her but, if her eyes attempt to see the hands, the hand movements do not yet depend on the vision at all.

Stage 3 (from 4 to 8 months) is dominated by secondary circular reactions. As infants continue to react with the environment they accidentally discover behaviors that affect the environment. They begin to repeat these behaviors intentionally. Such behaviors are called **secondary circular reactions.** They differ from the primary circular reactions of the previous stage in several ways. The primary reaction refers to activities that affect the infant's own body. Secondary circular reactions are those that affect the external environment. In primary circular reactions infants appear to be interested primarily in activity. In secondary circular reactions they seem to be interested in the results of the activity. Piaget's daughter Lucienne provides an example:

> Lucienne is lying in her bassinet. I hang a doll over her feet which immediately sets in motion the schema of [shaking]. . . . But her feet reach the doll right away and give it a violent movement which Lucienne surveys with delight. Afterward she looks at her motionless foot for a second, then recommences. There is no visual control of the foot, for the movements are the same when Lucienne only looks at the doll or when I place the doll over her head. On the other hand, the tactile control of the foot is apparent: after the first shakes, Lucienne makes slow foot movements as though to grasp and explore. For instance, when she tries to kick the doll and misses her aim, she begins again very slowly until she succeeds (without seeing her feet). In the same way I cover Lucienne's face or distract her attention for a moment in another direction; she nevertheless continues to hit the doll and control its movements.

At this stage, unlike later ones, there is little response to novelty for its own sake. When infants are presented with a new object they do not try to find out in what way it is new. Piaget's son's first reactions to a paper knife show this:

> He grasps it and looks at it, but only for a moment. Afterward he immediately swings it with his right hand as he does all objects grasped. He then rubs it by chance against the wicker of the bassinet and tries to reproduce this sound heard, as though it were a rattle. . . . It then suffices that I place the object in his left hand for him to shake it in the same way. He ends by sucking it. The novelty of the object has therefore in no way interested the child, except for a brief glance at the beginning.

The response to novelty in this stage and the preceding ones is almost pure assimilation (taking in of information). No accommodation or change of behavior is made in response to new stimuli.

Stage 4 (8 to 12 months) marks the beginning of coordination of the secondary schemata. At this stage infants begin actively to try to understand relationships between objects. They begin to understand what effects their behaviors will produce, and they begin to coordinate behaviors in order to bring about desired effects. In other words, with more complex coordinations of previous behavior patterns they are able to manipulate the environment in order to achieve their goals. They will push obstacles aside or use their parent's hand as a means to an end:

I present a box of matches above my hand, but behind it, so that he cannot reach it without setting the obstacle aside. But Laurent, after trying to take no notice of it, suddenly tries to hit my hand as though to remove or lower it; I let him do it to me and he grasps the box. I recommence to bar his passage, but using as a screen a sufficiently supple cushion to keep the impress of the child's gestures. Laurent tries to reach the box, and, bothered by the obstacle, he at once strikes it, definitely lowering it until the way is clear.

If the desired object is hidden, however, the infant acts as if it no longer existed. Piaget explains that at this stage infants have no idea of object constancy. That is, they do not realize that objects exist in the environment even when they are not seen. This type of thinking is what Piaget calls egocentrism, in which infants are aware only of their own immediate experience. It is only gradually, after repeated experience with objects that swing, drop, or roll out of sight, that infants begin to realize that the objects still exist and begin to look for them. Such experience helps establish the idea of **object constancy** or permanence, one of the most important achievements of the sensory-motor period.

Stage 5 (12 to 18 months) is characterized by directed groping. At this stage infants begin real experimentation with the environment. They no longer attempt only to reproduce behaviors discovered by accident. They try to find new means of achieving ends. Their movements are directed. Piaget describes seeing his son break off one piece of bread at a time and drop it to the floor, watching with great interest to see where it lands. According to Piaget, this was not just a repeated behavior, as in earlier stages, but a serious attempt to find out what happens to the dropped bread. It is through such experimentation that infants gradually learn how to behave in order to achieve a desired goal:

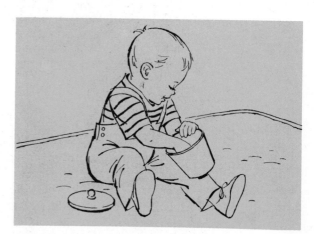

Directed groping by a
Stage 5 infant.

In Jacqueline's presence I place my watch on the floor, beyond her field of prehension. I put the chain in a straight line in Jacqueline's direction but place a cushion on the part which is nearest the child. Jacqueline at first tries to grasp the watch directly. Not succeeding, she looks at the chain. She notes that the latter is under the cushion. Then Jacqueline removes the latter at one stroke and pulls the chain while looking at the watch. The movement is adapted and quick. As soon as the watch is within reach, Jacqueline lets go of the chain in order to grasp the object directly. There is, consequently, no interest in the chain itself; it is the watch that is wanted.

Stage 6 (18 months to about 2 years) is marked by internalization of sensory-motor schemata. At this final stage of the sensory-motor period infants begin to represent things internally (ikonic representation), instead of using the trial and error behavior of earlier stages. Another of Piaget's observations illustrates the difference between sensory-motor (or enactive) representation and the internal awareness and representation of relationships in the environment:

I put the chain back into the box and reduce the opening to 3 mm. It is understood that Lucienne is not aware of the functioning of the opening and closing of the matchbox and has not seen me prepare the experiment. She only possesses the two preceding schemata, turning the box over in order to empty it of its contents, and sliding her finger into the slit to make the chain come out. It is of course this last procedure that she tries first; she puts her finger inside and gropes to reach the chain but fails completely. A pause follows during which Lucienne manifests a very cautious reaction, bearing witness not only to the fact that she tries to think out the situation and to represent to herself through mental combination the operations to be performed, but also to the role played by imitation in the genesis of representations. Lucienne mimics the widening of the slit. She opens and shuts her mouth . . . she uses simple motor indications as "signifier" or symbol. . . . Lucienne, by opening her mouth, thus expresses, or even reflects, her desire to enlarge the opening of the box. This schema of imitation with which she is familiar constitutes for her the means of thinking out the situation. . . . Lucienne unhesitatingly puts her finger in the slit and, instead of trying as before to reach the chain, she pulls so as to enlarge the opening. She succeeds and grasps the chain.

MAJOR ACHIEVEMENTS IN COGNITION

By the end of the sensory-motor period, with the beginnings of logical thinking, children have made major advances in cognitive development. But they still have much more to achieve before they truly understand the world the way adults do. At first they are still egocentric. They see the world from their own point of view and believe that everyone else sees it the same way. But as Piaget has shown, children do see the world differently. There are major cognitive achievements they must make and important concepts they must come to understand before they see the world in a mature way.

Space

Piaget presents his son with an upside down bottle, but the child "no longer tries to suck the wrong end . . . he immediately displaces the wrong end with a quick stroke of the hand while looking beforehand in the direction of the nipple." This child is showing the first signs of understanding the idea of physical space. The **concept of space** includes such things as the relationships of objects to each other in the environment, direction, distance, perspective, and movement. Understanding these concepts is obviously important for such things as learning to walk, getting food from the plate to the mouth, and for most activities that require physical movement.

The understanding of the placement and orientation of objects in space is one of the earliest conceptual skills acquired by children, but it takes time and a great deal of experience with the physical world. Several experiments show the gradual development of spatial skills. In one such experiment children between 18 months and 5 years of age were observed performing a variety of tasks that tested the development of spatial skills. Until the age of 2 or 2½ years the children showed little understanding of how to put boxes of different sizes into one another. The usual response was to try to bang the closed ends together or fit the larger box into the smaller one. The children occasionally succeeded by trial and error, but until the age of 4 they did not show any evidence of planning in their attempts.

In another task the children were asked to put blocks of different shapes into similarly shaped holes. The youngest children merely banged the blocks against the holes. They did not try to adjust the block so that the proper shape would fit into the hole. They sometimes succeeded by accident, but as with the boxes, they did not try to repeat the accidently discovered relationship. They did not yet have a systematic approach to the problem.

In another task the children were asked to reach for a stick from behind a fence. The bars of the fence were too close together for the stick to fit through, but until the age of 4 the children tried to get it through. They did not seem to realize that the bars of the fence were too close together, and they did not think of lifting the stick over the fence. The understanding of spatial and size relationships necessary to perform these tasks does not seem to develop until at least the age of 4.

Piaget and his colleagues studied the concept of space in children by studying children's drawings, their recognition of objects by touch, how children copy pictures, and how they recognize objects from another's point of view. Piaget found five aspects of physical space to which children gradually become sensitive. The first of these is proximity, or nearness of objects to each other. A typical 3-year-old's drawing of a human body usually shows

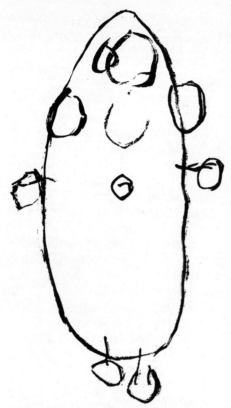

The drawing of a child under 4 may reflect a failure to understand proximity and order in space.

an incomplete understanding of proximity. The arms may be too near the head, for example, or the eyes too near the mouth.

Another feature of space that young children often fail to understand is separation. A child drawing a cross may realize that a vertical and a horizontal line are necessary, but may not draw them so that they cross or touch each other. Failure to understand order in space may result in a drawing of a face with the mouth and nose in the wrong order (mouth above nose). Failure to understand what Piaget calls continuity may result in a drawing of a person floating above the ground rather than positioned on it.

When children were asked to recognize forms by touch, Piaget found that they can easily tell the difference between a circle and an open ring, but they have more difficulty telling the difference between a circle and a square.

By the time children are 6 or 7 years old they begin to understand direction in space. By this age they can usually identify their own left and right hands and feet, the right and left of a doll, and objects to the left and right of each other on a table. Earlier, when their conceptions were more egocentric, they could identify their own right and left but not that of a doll.

Piaget has also studied the idea of distance in space. Before children can understand this, they must develop a concept of what is called distance conservation, the idea that the distance between two points is fixed or constant no matter what is placed in that space. Piaget tested children's concept of distance conservation by placing two dolls on a table about 50 centimeters apart. A model of a brick wall was then placed between the dolls, and children were asked whether the dolls were still as far apart as before the wall was put between them. Children younger than 7 often said, "They're nearer than before. It's farther when the screen wasn't there because when it is it's only half as far." Older children realize that the distance between the dolls remains the same even when the wall is there.

The idea of a stable or fixed unit of space must occur before children are able to measure distance. Until children have mastered the idea of distance conservation they cannot usually understand such things as the equal area of two different-shaped rectangles or the locations of objects in two-dimensional space. These abilities, like other concepts related to physical space, continue to develop as children continue to experiment with the environment.

Time

Many of Piaget's investigations of the concept of space also involved the **concept of time.** For example, experimenters would move cars along two tracks of unequal length, and the children would often insist that the car that moved the greater distance was faster. This was because they seemed to have an incomplete concept of time and did not understand the relationship between space and time.

Not only relationships between space and time but concepts of past, present, and future are vague for young children. Because of their egocentric thinking, young children have no understanding of past or future. They seem to understand only the present, their own time. This confusion can be seen in the statements of a typical 2½-year-old: "I had a bath tomorrow and I even washed my ears." A 3½-year-old reports: "I'm not going to take my nap yesterday." For young children all events that have already taken place are often grouped into one category—yesterday. An egocentric concept of time is also seen in the fact that it is difficult for children to understand how it can be night at home and day in a different part of the world.

In addition to being egocentric, children's concepts of time are usually linked to concrete events. A study of 2- to 6-year-olds found that they measured the passage of time in terms of activities and concrete events: Bath time is after supper, bedtime comes after the story, and so on (1).

This and other studies have shown that children need a great deal of experience with time before they begin to understand correctly differences among past, present, and future. This ability comes at about the age of 4, but children usually cannot correctly name the day of the month until about age 8. The slow development of an accurate sense of time is seen in the fact that between the ages of 10 and 16 children reduce their error in estimating a five-minute period by only 79 seconds. They still make about a 90-second error at age 16.

It is possible, however, that television is helping to speed up the development of concepts of time in children. The desire to watch a particular program at a specific time stimulates their interest in time. Because most children's programs last 15 minutes or a half hour, and most commercials last 30 seconds or a minute, children who watch a lot of television begin to get a sense of these units of time. This helps speed up their already developing concept of time (5).

Number and Quantity

Many children, some as young as 18 months, can count by rote. That is, they can correctly say the names of numbers in a perfect sequence. But this counting is not always the same as having a **concept of number** or quantity. It is not uncommon, for example, to find children who can say the numbers in order, but who cannot count a set of objects and arrive at the correct answer. A 4-year-old asked to count nine pennies might say, "One, two, three, four hundred, seven, nine, fifteen, eleventeen, thirty." Three-year-olds counting their fingers may come up with a different answer each time. This is because they may skip one or more fingers or may count some more than once.

The concept of numbers takes a long time to develop, and Piaget says there is no sense in trying to rush the process. Young children can deal only with small numbers. A 3-year-old can usually count and deal with numbers only up to three, a 4-year-old up to four, and a 5-year-old up to five. The concept of an indefinite series of numbers and the ability to add, subtract, multiply, and divide usually comes after the age of 7. One of the reasons it takes so long for a concept of numbers to develop is that children often confuse cardinal and ordinal numbers. Cardinal numbers refer to quantity (3 cows, 14 oranges, and so on). Ordinal numbers refer to order or position (the first cow, the fourteenth orange, and so on). It is only after a great deal of experience that children begin to understand this double concept of numbers.

Before children develop a complete concept of numbers, they must first understand the concept of quantity. They must, for instance, learn about size. By about 3 or 3½ years children can usually correctly select the larger or smaller of two objects. Before then they may have only a vague idea of big and little, but no understanding of gradations of size between big and little.

The ability to add, subtract, multiply, and divide usually comes after the age of 7.

Once children have a concept of quantity they must learn the idea of conservation of quantity. Piaget's experiment with two arrangements of the same number of coins showed the trouble children have understanding that the number of coins remains the same (is conserved) no matter how the coins are arranged. They come to this understanding at first by counting the coins in each row. Later, children develop the concept of equivalence, or the idea of a one-to-one relationship. They can look at two rows of coins and realize that they have the same number of coins without counting them. Through continued experience with quantities and numbers children gradually develop an understanding of numbers and eventually learn to perform mental operations with numbers.

Piaget continually stresses the importance of experimenting with and experiencing the environment in the development of concepts. This, he says, is necessary not only for the development of concepts of numbers but for the development of all concepts. The idea of experimenting with numbers, however, brings up questions with regard to the use of pocket calculators by schoolchildren. Some educators believe that children who rely on calculators will not get enough experience with numbers and will not develop an adequate concept of numbers. These educators argue that students won't even know how to add, much less perform more complex operations, if their calculator batteries ever go dead. Other educators argue that calculators stretch a student's interest and increase motivation. With calculators students can solve more interesting problems and work out solutions to problems that they might otherwise avoid. As with most such arguments in which both sides have valid points, a compromise might offer a better solution than either side does. Once children have developed a good concept of numbers through practice and experimentation, they can go on to more complex concepts of mathematics and more complicated problems with the use of a calculator.

Causality

How does a child come to understand what causes things to happen in the physical world? Piaget studied children's concepts of the physical world by asking them questions about how things work, whether or not certain things are alive or dead, and what causes various natural phenomena, such as night and day. Questions about causes helped him work out a **theory of causality** in children. Piaget found that children have a tendency to engage in animistic thinking. In this type of thinking children attribute life (animism) to inanimate objects (those that have no life). They may say, for example, that the sun is alive because it moves. Being alive is a cause for its action.

Some examples of animistic thinking can be seen in the answers children give to a set of questions designed to test Piaget's theory of animism in children (20). Twenty objects are named, and children are asked to say whether each object is alive or dead and why it is alive or dead:

1. Stone—Alive, because it moves.
2. Pencil—Alive, because it writes.
3. Button (broken)—If it's broken, it's no use. It's dead.
4. Watch—It's alive if it tells time, but it's dead if it can't tell time.
5. Dish (chipped)—It's just as dead as a broken button.
6. Candle—Only if it is lit. (What would happen if the light went out, and then came on again?) It would die, then it would come back to life.
7. Bicycle—Alive, because it runs.
8. Chair—Alive, because people sit on it.
9. River—Alive, when people go in it.
10. Clouds—Alive, because they're moving all the time.
11. Tree—Alive, because it's waving and growing.
12. Sun—It's always alive, because God helps it.
13. Wind—Alive, because it blows. But when it does not blow, it's not dead; it's just asleep.
14. Automobile—Alive, because it runs.
15. Bird—Alive, because it flies. When they are shot, birds are dead.
16. Fire—Alive, because it goes.
17. Dog—Alive, because it walks.
18. Grass—Alive, because it grows.
19. Bug—Yes, alive, because it runs.
20. Flower—Alive, because people water it a lot.

From such responses Piaget has described four stages of animistic thinking. At first children tend to believe an object is alive if it is intact and in good condition. If the object is damaged or broken, it is dead. A broken dish, for example, is dead. Later, children say a thing is alive if it moves. If it is stationary, it is dead. In the third stage of animistic thinking a thing is believed to be alive if it moves under its own power (the sun is alive but a bicycle is not). At the most mature level of animistic thinking only animals and plants are thought of as being alive.

A number of experiments have confirmed the existence of animistic thinking in children, some as old as 16. But by school age and even before most children know that animals are alive and airplanes are not.

Like most of Piaget's theories, the idea of animistic thinking in children is based on children's responses, not on a firsthand knowledge of what is going on inside of their heads. Because of this researchers are continually attempting to either prove or disprove Piaget's theories. While much of his work has been confirmed, some of his theories have been found to be less than completely accurate. Animism, for example, may be an important aspect of causality in the minds of most young children, but it has not been found in all children. Margaret Mead, the famous anthropologist, tested for animistic thinking among the Manus children of the Admiralty Islands of the western Pacific. She found very little evidence of animism except in cases where the children had been taught to believe that a certain object (like the sun) was alive. Other researchers have also found that animism is not universal or not found in all children.

Magical thinking has also been found to be related to causality in children. They sometimes believe things happen—especially things that they haven't had much experience with—because of some magical powers or forces. Another aspect of causality in children is artificialism, or the tendency to believe that human beings cause all natural phenomena. Piaget's daughter saw clouds of smoke coming out of her father's pipe and assumed that the clouds in the sky were made by her father.

As children become more and more familiar with events in the natural world, and as they develop more logical thinking, fewer and fewer animistic, magical, and artificialistic explanations are given for why things happen.

Humor

An infant's first smile, which usually occurs some time during the first week, is a reflexive action. By about 3 months of age children begin showing their pleasure by smiling at other people. By the end of the first year a real appreciation of comic and humorous things begins to appear. Children at this age not only laugh while being tickled, they laugh at unusual sounds, funny faces, and games like peek-a-boo. This, and the further development of a

sense of humor, is a result of many factors, including learning and social influences, but it can also be seen to be related to cognitive development.

Not all forms of humor are completely understood, but several studies have shown that one of the most important elements of humor, especially in children, is incongruity. Incongruity exists when the parts of a situation or event do not fit together in the expected way. Very young children, with their egocentric outlook and limited experience with the world, may find incongruity in anything they have never experienced before. They may find humor in the clothing or customs of a foreign country. In older children and adults this type of novelty is not usually considered as humorous, but incongruity still is. The television show "Sesame Street" has made effective use of incongruity in its attempts to entertain and educate children.

In order to understand incongruity children must have built up cognitive expectations of the world so that they can understand deviations from their expectations. It is such deviations that are often presented in jokes, riddles, or cartoons. In one experiment children were shown cartoons based on novelty and incongruity. The younger children could say what was funny about the novelty cartoons but not about the incongruity cartoons (9). Similar studies with riddles found the same thing. Riddles ("What does a giraffe have that no other animal has? Baby giraffes.") and nonriddles ("What does a giraffe have that no other animal has? A long neck.") were presented to children of different ages. First-graders found the riddles and nonriddles equally funny. They did not seem really to appreciate the incongruities of the riddles.

With continued cognitive development, however, children not only appreciate incongruities but increasingly subtle incongruities. Older children and young adults gradually begin to find humor in witty remarks, stories that build to an unexpected climax, and humor that takes serious matters lightly (17).

The fact that children do not always laugh at jokes or understand humor the way adults do may seem to be a relatively minor point as far as understanding children is concerned, but it is another important indication of the many differences that exist between the cognitive processes of children and adults. Parents, teachers, and adults who deal with children and who do not realize that these differences exist may cause frustration and confusion in children by using basic concepts (of space, time, number, causality, or humor) in ways that children are not yet ready to handle. Adults frequently communicate with children (give directions, provide verbal explanations, and so on) in ways that are ill-suited to the cognitive readiness of the children. Adults often assume that children's comprehension of certain basic concepts is the same as their own. A good teacher or an adult who wants to communicate meaningfully and effectively with a child will first find out how complete the child's conceptual development is.

A sense of humor is important to growing children, as are the concepts of space, time, number, and causality. But if children are to develop the ability to operate on or manipulate their mental structures and become logical thinking machines, as Piaget says they do, several other important concepts must be developed. Piaget and his colleague Barbel Inhelder have described these concepts and the development of logical thinking in children (17).

Transformations

Coming out of the sensory-motor stage children often have trouble understanding changes in the physical world because their egocentric, preoperational minds tend to concentrate or "center" on one thing at a time. They use their perceptions to understand the world as it is, but they often ignore the changes, or **transformations,** that make the world the way it is. This has been demonstrated in a very simple experiment. When two identical containers filled to the same height with liquid are shown to preoperational children, they will admit that the containers have equal amounts of liquid. If one of the containers is then poured into a tall, thin container and the other is emptied into a short, wide one, preoperational children will insist that the tall, thin one has more liquid than the short, wide one. This is because they center on one aspect of the liquid at a time. They see the liquid in its original state and in its final state and make a judgment based on their perceptions of these two states. The tall, thin container looks as though it has more liquid, so to the preoperational mind, it must have more. Children at this stage do not understand the transformation by which the liquid in one state was gradually changed to another state. The ability to "decenter," or to comprehend transformations by focusing on more than one aspect of the environment at a time, is an indication of the passage or transition from preoperational to concrete operational thought.

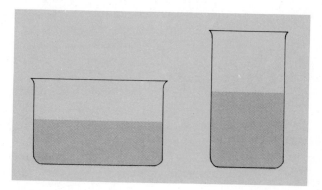

The amount of water in both glasses is the same, but for the preoperational child, the tall, thin glass appears to have more water in it than the wide, short glass.

Psychologist Harry Munsinger explains this in terms of information processing (11). The preoperational mind is limited in the amount of information it can process. Therefore, children in this stage of cognitive development concentrate on the most obvious bits of information available to them, the original and final states of the liquid. Later, with more complex information-processing rules, children can include both the initial state and the transformation in one thought. With this and other more advanced information-processing rules comes a gradual understanding of the logical notion of transformations. In the concrete operational stage children simply watch the liquid being poured (transformed) from one container to another and realize that the amount of liquid has remained the same.

Reversibility

Another important mental operation necessary to the development of logical thinking is **reversibility.** According to Piaget, reversibility is the ability to follow a train of thought (watch the liquid being poured from one container to another) and then reverse that thought process (think of the water being poured back into its original container). Preoperational children's thoughts are usually not reversible because they concentrate on single states rather than on transformations from state to state. If children do not understand the transformation, they will not be able to follow the process backwards and be able to think of the original state. In other words, they just don't think of what would happen if they poured the liquid back into its original container. As children near the concrete operations stage (around 7 years of age) their minds become more flexible and they can usually reverse their thoughts. They realize that pouring the liquid back into the original container cancels the first transformation and leaves the liquid in its original state.

Classification

Children's minds become even more flexible during the stage of concrete operations as they develop still more mental structures necessary for logical thinking. One of these structures is the idea of **classification.** Children must have an understanding of classes and subclasses if they are to understand a statement such as, "All dogs are animals, but not all animals are dogs." In this instance, animal is a larger class that can include the smaller subclass, all dogs. The subclass, however, cannot include all of the larger class, all animals.

Inhelder and Piaget have developed a number of tasks that test children's understanding of classes and subclasses. They found that children begin the process of classification by grouping things together, but not on a consistently logical basis. For example, a 4-year-old was given a group of geometric shapes and instructed to put the ones that were the same together. The child began by putting rectangles together. But one of the rectangles was yellow, so the child put some yellow triangles and semicircles into the pile. After the yellow semicircle, the child put some other colored semicircles into the pile. The confusion of classes and subclasses was obvious.

Class Inclusion and Multiple Classification

Even when children have mastered the basics of classification and can sort objects into classes consistently, they still have not mastered all the aspects of classification. In another experiment children were shown four red triangles and two blue triangles. Each object belonged to one of two subclasses (red or blue). They all belonged to the higher or superordinate class (triangles). The children were then asked whether there were more red ones (subclass) or more triangles (superordinate class). Children younger than 7 or 8 years of age confused the subclass with the superordinate class and answered that there were more red ones. They did not realize that the superordinate class included the subclass. Without this concept of **class inclusion,** they answered on the basis of the subclass (color) instead of on the basis of the superordinate class (triangles).

The questions Inhelder and Piaget used in testing for the concept of class inclusion are tricky. Even children older than 10 or 11 may not understand what is required of them when such a question is asked. Other researchers have demonstrated that when simpler and less confusing questions are used even 4-year-olds have some understanding of class inclusion. But no matter at what age this concept develops, it is necessary for logical thinking.

In addition to class inclusion, another important concept in logical reasoning is **multiple classification,** or the ability to classify objects simultaneously in two or more categories. People, for example, can be classified by skin color (black, yellow, white), by where they live (rural, urban, suburban), or by sex (male, female). Piaget and others have found that 8-year-old children can usually operate with and understand systems of classification that include two categories. A few years later they are able to understand multiple classifications that include three or more categories.

Asymmetrical Relations

Not all classification systems are based on similarities. Some deal with differences, or asymmetries. An ability to understand **asymmetrical relations** and classify objects according to a regular sequence of differences is another important factor in logical thinking. A basic concept in this ability is called **transitivity.** It has to do with understanding asymmetrical relationships such as: If A is larger than B, and B is larger than C, then A must be larger than C.

An understanding of transitivity and asymmetrical logical relationships can be seen in tests of seriation, or the ability to order objects of different dimensions in a series. Tests of seriation consist of giving children a set of blocks or sticks of different sizes and asking them to put the objects in order from the smallest to the largest. To solve this type of problem children must have a

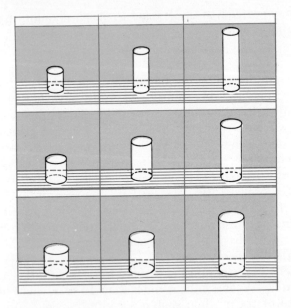

Glasses of different sizes and shapes arranged on shelves are used to test children's concepts of multiple asymmetrical relations.

concept of transitivity. They must realize that if stick *A* is larger than stick *B*, it is also larger than sticks *C, D,* and *E*. Children younger than 4 may get only two or three sticks in the right order, but 4- and 5-year olds can usually perform the task using a trial and error method. Older children, with a more firmly developed concept of asymmetrical relations and an understanding of transitivity, can usually put the sticks in logical order without having to check each stick against all the others.

Piaget tested children's concepts of multiple asymmetrical relations (two or more different types of asymmetry) with glasses of different sizes and shapes. A box with shelves was used to arrange the glasses in a horizontal series by height and in a vertical series by width. Height increased across the top and width down the side. A glass was then removed from one of the shelves, and children were asked to select from several glasses of different sizes and shapes the one that would complete both the horizontal and vertical series.

Jerome Bruner used a similar test but made it more complex. He not only asked the children to replace a few glasses but he took out all the glasses and asked the children to put them back in the proper order. Then he made it even more complicated by putting the shortest, widest glass in the corner where the tallest, thinnest glass had been and asked the children to reproduce the multiple series in the reverse order. Bruner found that the 3-year-old children relied on their perceptions and could replace some of the glasses in the original order. They could not, however, put them back in reverse order. Seven-year-olds could. They seemed to understand the logical order of the glasses and could reverse that order.

PROBLEM-SOLVING

The entire process of cognitive development has one basic goal—problem-solving. Almost every human behavior is in some way related to problem-solving, whether it is an infant trying to find out which end of the bottle to suck, a child sorting red and blue triangles, a student taking a test, or a scientist designing a computer. These and millions of problems are faced throughout life, and most of them are solved with the use of the logical reasoning abilities that, in computer terminology, have been programmed into each growing child.

No matter what type of problem a child is faced with, there are four basic steps that must usually be taken before a solution is reached. The first involves **motivation** and **recognition** of the fact that a problem exists. Throughout life people are motivated to fulfill certain needs (see Chapter 6). Each need represents a problem that must be solved. Infants, for example, are motivated by the need for food. They must find ways to solve the problem of hunger. When they are well fed they can turn their attention to other needs, such as the need for exercise or attention. The motivation or desire to meet these and other needs means that a problem has been recognized and a solution must be sought.

Before a problem can be solved it must be **defined.** In other words, the exact aspects of the problem must be understood before a proper solution can be reached. A mechanic working on a car might realize that a problem exists and be motivated to solve it, but will have little success in doing so until the exact difficulty is defined. Similarly, a child sorting red and blue blocks must realize that the problem involves color, not shape or size.

Once a problem has been defined, the next step consists of looking for a solution or **forming an hypothesis.** A child faced with the task of arranging a set of glasses by height and width may think of several possible solutions or hypotheses. Do the thin glasses go across the top, for example, or do they go down the side? The next and final step in problem-solving consists of testing the hypothesis. Four-year-olds trying to arrange a set of glasses might test several hypotheses by rearranging the glasses over and over until they look right. Older children, with more logical reasoning ability and a more flexible mind capable of performing complex mental operations, may be able to visualize the problem and test each hypothesis mentally rather than physically.

Going through the various steps of problem-solving may be easy or difficult, depending on the problem. Simple problems, such as sorting blocks, may be easily recognized and defined and are almost automatically solved without a lot of hypothesis testing. More difficult problems may require a great deal of effort, first in defining the problem, then in coming up with and testing various hypotheses. But these aren't the only problems involved in problem-solving. There are several factors that can interfere with the various steps of problem-solving.

Mental Set

The easiest problems to solve are those that have been solved before. Through practice and experience children learn ways to approach many problems, and once they have come up with a successful solution, they can apply that solution over and over to similar problems. An infant who has discovered that crying brings attention will continue to apply that solution as long as it works. In other words, the infant has a set, or ready-made, solution to a certain type of problem. The existence of this type of **mental set** greatly increases problem-solving ability. A child who has developed a mental set for arranging glasses, for example, will approach similar problems with a set solution and be able to arrange cups, dolls, coins, or other objects. A basic function of education is the teaching of mental sets. Through repetition, practice, and experience in school children develop mental sets for solving mathematical, reading, and many other types of problems. The mental sets that children develop in school can then be applied to problems outside school.

Mental sets are like information-processing rules that have been programmed into a computer. As useful and necessary as they are, however, they can be a drawback when applied to the wrong problem. This can be seen in infants who have learned that crying helps solve one type of problem and then apply that solution to all sorts of other problems. This kind of mental inflexibility is not only seen in infants. Older children and adults also have mental sets that hamper their problem-solving ability. This has been demonstrated in a variety of experiments.

In one study subjects were presented with seven problems in which they were asked to measure out a certain amount of water by using jars of different sizes (7); for example: "If you have a 29-quart jar and a 3-quart jar, how can you obtain 20 quarts?" The first five such problems could be solved in several steps by pouring water from one jar to the other several times. The sixth and seventh problems could be solved in a similar manner involving several steps, but these two problems could also be solved in a more direct manner. By the time the people solving the problems had completed the first five, they had developed a mental set. Most of them went on to solve the last two problems in the more complex or involved manner. They kept on pouring water back and forth and did not seem to see the more simple and direct solution. They solved the problems correctly, but their mental set had resulted in less efficient problem-solving.

The experimenter found two ways of breaking this habit, or mental set. A second group of people worked on the same seven problems, but they did the first five one day and the last two several days later. Separating the problems by time seemed to weaken the mental set, and most of these people did see the more direct solution to the final two problems. Another group was simply cautioned several times and encouraged to "Look sharp" and "Don't be blind." This encouragement helped them stay mentally alert, and most of them saw the simpler solution. With encouragement children too can develop flexible thinking and learn to use set solutions only when they apply.

Functional Fixedness

A similar example of mental inflexibility involves the function of tools used to solve problems. People tend to use certain objects in set or fixed ways and don't always realize that a tool may have other uses. The function of a hammer, for example, is fixed in the minds of most people. With this **functional fixedness** people know that hammers are used to drive nails. But functional fixedness, like mental set, can sometimes keep people from finding the best solution to a problem.

One of the most well-known examples of functional fixedness came in an experiment in which people were asked to tie the ends of two ropes together (10). The solution to this problem was not easy because the ropes were hanging from a ceiling about 15 feet apart. The set way of approaching this problem would be to take the end of one rope, walk with it to the other rope, and tie the two together. In this particular problem, however, the ropes were too far apart. A person holding on to one rope could not reach far enough to grab the second rope without letting go of the first. But there was another solution to the problem. A hammer had been placed on the floor in the corner of the room. Because of functional fixedness, most people did not realize that the hammer could be used to solve the problem. By simply tying the hammer to the end of one rope and swinging that rope in a wide arc, it is possible to walk over to the second rope and wait for the rope with the hammer to swing by.

Creative Problem-solving

Mental set and functional fixedness are usually aids to problem-solving. With the ready-made solutions they provide, many problems are solved quickly and efficiently. But as has been seen, not all problems can be solved in set ways with established rules. People are constantly being challenged by problems that call for new or original solutions. The type of thinking that produces new and original solutions is called **creative thinking.**

Creativity is a highly prized quality that is usually attributed to a few great thinkers, such as inventors, scientists, or artists, who have produced truly original and useful solutions to old problems. But creativity is not a quality that is limited to only a few. It exists to a greater or lesser degree in all people. Children, because of their limited experience, are constantly meeting problems they have never faced before. In many cases they come up with original solutions. These solutions may be the same ones that millions of children before them have discovered, but that does not mean the solution is not new to them. Whenever a child discovers an original solution to a problem some degree of creative thinking has been involved. Some children may display creative abilities more often than others, but no children are without some degree of creativity. At first this may show up in simple behaviors, such as finding novel ways to play with toys. With continued cognitive development and an increased store of knowledge and information, increasingly complex types of creative thinking become possible.

Even though creativity exists in all people, studies of creativity have usually concentrated on the type of thinking involved in scientific discovery. These studies suggest four general steps that seem to be involved in the creative process (27). **Preparation** is the first step. Scientists who have made great discoveries have usually done so only after years of intensive study and preparation. After this comes a **period of incubation** (from the Latin word for "to hatch" or "to lie down on"). During this incubation period very little seems to happen. The scientist who has spent years gathering facts and information seems to let that information sit for a while. Then, at some later time, comes the third step in the creative process. It is usually called an **insight.** An insight is a new way of looking at an old problem. As mentioned earlier, computers don't have insights or creative abilities. It is probable that much unconscious mental activity during the incubation period has in some way rearranged the facts and information so that it could be seen in a new light. This insight may come in a flash or it may come very slowly. It may be quite clear, or it may be just a vague notion. The final stage of the creative process consists of **testing the insight.** Many ideas that at first seem to be the result of creative thinking may prove, when tested, to be incorrect rather than creative. A novel answer is not truly creative unless it proves to be useful as well as original.

These four steps, preparation, incubation, insight, and testing, suggest a general way in which the creative process may operate, but no one knows for sure. It is likely that creativity is a much more complex process.

Even though children are not likely to make great scientific discoveries, most people agree that creativity is a valuable cognitive tool. Creative individuals have made valuable contributions to society, and creative problem-solving can be useful to any individual. For these reasons researchers have devised ways of measuring what appears to be creative thinking. The *Unusual Uses Test* consists of asking children to propose reasonable but unconventional uses for common objects such as a brick, a light bulb, or a piece of paper. The *Plot Titles Test* consists of asking children to write as many appropriate titles as possible for two stories during an allotted time. A wide range of individual differences in creativity during childhood and adolescence have been found by using these and similar tests (8). It has also been discovered that test conditions make a difference in creative performance. Creativity seems to flourish when time limits are removed, when a gamelike atmosphere exists, when children are allowed to share ideas, and in situations where stress and anxiety are at a minimum (23, 24).

Personality differences between creative and less creative children have also been found. Many studies have been conducted in this area, and a good deal of evidence is available suggesting that creative individuals are similar in many ways. In general, creative children are often highly self-confident, intellectually curious, independent in judgment and behavior, less concerned than most with social convention or conformity, genial and friendly (although not necessarily intimate with their parents), interested in complex and novel activities, persistent, sensitive to problems, willing to entertain and sometimes express impulses, and likely to value and have a strong sense of humor (8). These findings suggest that creativity and the characteristics usually associated with positive development and personality adjustment go together. This does not mean that "good" personality adjustment is a guarantee of creativity, or vice versa. It does, however, suggest that the popular idea of creative individuals being "mad" or in some way mentally "unbalanced" or maladjusted is not correct.

Studies of the parents and home lives of creative and less creative children

Certain parental attitudes and child-rearing practices are associated with the development of creativity in children.

have found certain parental attitudes and child-rearing practices to be associated with the development of creativity. In one study, for example, parents of highly creative children were found to be comparatively less critical of their children and their schools, more liberal and tolerant in general outlook, interested in their children's values, and open to experiences, interests, and enthusiasms (4). It has also been found that a low degree of punishment in the home, low pressure for conformity, and emotional support of and satisfaction with the children are related to higher rates of creative thinking in children (21).

As with personality factors, home conditions and parental attitudes cannot be said to guarantee creativity in children. It is even possible that the parental attitudes mentioned may have come about in response to a child's creativity rather than before the child displayed such behavior. No one knows for sure what factors in the home foster creativity, but in general the overall attitude toward child-rearing seen in these studies of creative children do appear to be closely related to the development of creativity.

Not only parents and homes but teachers and schools have been examined with respect to the development of creativity (22). As would be expected, classrooms in which creative output seems to be low are those in which challenging activities are seldom pursued, children are rarely allowed to ask questions or explore, a strong division is made between work and play (for example, "The fun's over now, children; it's time for arithmetic"), and pressures for absolute intellectual and social conformity are applied (for example, "Johnny, only girls write love stories in English composition. Why don't you write about football or deep-sea diving?" or "Whoever heard of a green Santa Claus? Do your picture over again and color Santa red!").

Piaget has suggested that the basic goal of education is to produce individuals who are capable of creativity, invention, and discovery (15), and many people agree with him. For this reason researchers have attempted to find ways of fostering creativity among students. While much more needs to be learned about creativity, at least three methods have been found useful in increasing creative thinking (19). The first has to do with encouragement and instructions to be original, such as: "Try to think of things that no one else will think of." This type of encouragement helped keep people from being inflexible with regard to mental sets, and it also seems to help increase creative thinking.

A second method involves practice. In a word association test, for example, a list of 12 words was presented one at a time to students 6 times. Each time through the list they were asked to respond to each word with a different but associated word. This type of exercise seems to help in the ease with which people form new and possibly original associations. A third method of increasing creative thinking involves training and experimentation in problem-solving strategies. For example, students might be encouraged to think about transformations or different actions that can be performed on common objects. This type of training might help increase flexibility and avoid functional fixedness. Whether or not this or any type of training can help increase individual creativity to any significant degree is unknown, but the training itself is probably valuable. The factors found to be useful in increasing creativity are the same factors that seem to be useful and necessary in all types of cognitive development — encouragement, practice, and experimentation.

COGNITIVE STYLE

While most children seem to go through the same or similar stages of cognitive development, the end result is not always the same. Each child seems to develop a slightly different **cognitive style,** or approach to problem-solving. Physical differences, especially brain damage resulting in mental retardation, can account for some of the variation in cognitive style, but personality and intellectual differences are also involved. These will be examined in later chapters (see Chapter 9). Cultural differences have also been found to be important. Cross-cultural studies comparing North American and European children with those from other parts of the world have found differences in the ages at which children begin to understand concepts like conservation and classification. In most of these studies the differences have been found to be related to environmental and social factors, such as the amount and type of schooling and experience a child has had. In addition to these differences, some other important findings have been made with regard to cognitive style.

Reflectivity versus Impulsivity

Probably the most obvious difference in cognitive style between children is the manner in which they respond to a problem. Some children are characteristically deliberate and reflective in their problem-solving activities. They examine new information and situations carefully and systematically before they make a decision. Others respond more quickly without thinking through a situation or problem. They do not take sufficient time to think about the information available and the different possible solutions. This difference in **reflectivity** and **impulsivity** in children has been found to appear as early as age 2, but all children tend to become more reflective with age.

The change in reflectivity as children grow older has been demonstrated by Jerome Kagan of Harvard University and his colleagues (6). They used what is called the *Matching Familiar Figures Test.* In this test children are asked to select from six similar familiar figures the one that matches a standard figure presented separately from the rest. Reflectivity and impulsivity are rated according to how long it takes a child to make a decision and whether or not the decision is correct. Between 5 and 12 years of age children show a dramatic decrease in errors, but an increase in decision-making time. In other words, reflectivity increases with age. But even though most children become

An example from the Matching Familiar Figures Test.

more reflective, the difference among children remains. Impulsive children may become more reflective, but they are still usually more impulsive than the reflective children who have also increased in reflectivity.

A child's metabolism or general rate of bodily activity may account for some of the reflectivity-impulsivity difference. Some children are just quicker to respond than others. But other factors, such as social experiences, are involved. Some teachers and parents tend to place greater emphasis on speed than on accuracy. This could reinforce impulsivity. Others may reinforce accuracy, leading to greater reflectivity. Fear of making mistakes is also involved. Those children who are most anxious about making mistakes are generally more reflective.

Modeling has also been shown to be involved in children's tendencies to be reflective or impulsive (28). Teachers (models) were given an adult version of the *Matching Familiar Figures Test*. Children from their classes were tested at the beginning and again at the end of the school year to determine if the teacher's style had influenced them. It was found that children do tend to model their cognitive behavior after their teachers. Children with impulsive teachers tend to become more impulsive, and children with reflective teachers tend to become more reflective. This was especially true for impulsive boys with reflective teachers. They showed the greatest increase in decision-making time during the year.

In another study a deliberate attempt was made to modify children's cognitive style. Impulsive children were simply told to wait before answering on the *Matching Familiar Figures Test*. After several sessions of this type of training the children exhibited more reflectivity when responding to other situations. While this and other studies suggest that it is possible to increase reflectivity in some cases, it is probably more difficult to train children to increase their impulsivity. This is because an increase in impulsivity would lead to more incorrect responses in most situations, and children are not usually reinforced or rewarded by incorrect answers.

Human versus Machine Intelligence

Throughout this chapter the computer has been used to illustrate the basics of cognitive development. A computer, with its millions of electrical circuits and connections, is in some ways like the human brain with its 10 billion cells, each connected to others in a variety of ways. In much the same way that logic circuits are built or programmed into a computer, logical concepts develop in children (either through experience, as learning theory and information-processing theory say, or through experience and biological development, as Piaget's structural theory says). Computers demonstrate their ability to use their logic circuits by sorting blocks, playing chess, or solving complex mathematical equations. Piaget's insightful descriptions of children's behavior show how they too use their growing logical abilities to sort blocks, play chess, and eventually solve complex equations.

As useful as the computer is in helping explain human cognition, in helping children learn to think (as at MIT's Artificial Intelligence Laboratory), and in solving problems for humans, the computer is not a thinking machine like the human brain. Its cognitive style is that of a machine, not of a human. It may have concepts (or rules) of space, time, and number, and it may perform operations involving transitivity and class inclusion, but it lacks human qualities like a sense of humor and creativity. Computers may eventually duplicate the delicate movements of a child's hand, and they may solve many problems quicker than humans can, but they will never duplicate the cognitive ability of the human brain. It is human cognitive abilities that have created computers, not the other way around.

SUMMARY

The human brain takes in information, processes it, and gives back an answer or response. All of the activities involved in the processing of information by the human brain make up what is known as cognition, one of the most important of human activities.

Learning theory suggests that cognitive development is the result of an accumulation or build-up of learned behaviors. Information-processing theory suggests that humans, like computers, acquire certain rules for dealing with and processing incoming information. Structural theory, like that of Piaget, suggests that cognitive development is related to the unfolding of internal structures. As a result of experience and maturation, these structures become available for use in cognition. Because all three theories stress the importance of interaction with the environment, and because all three have valid points, a combination of the three probably offers the most well-rounded approach to the understanding of cognitive development.

Piaget's vivid descriptions of his own children's progression have helped him outline the major stages of cognitive development. These are the sensory-motor stage, the preoperational stage, the stage of concrete operations, and the stage of formal operations or logical thinking. Piaget's descriptions of the six substages of cognitive development in the sensory-motor stage have made it quite clear that infancy is a time during which important advances in cognitive development are made.

Infants are egocentric. They understand the world from their own point of view, but through various types of assimilation and accommodation they begin to understand the world and their relation to objects in it. They begin to understand the effects of their behaviors on objects, and they begin to develop an understanding of object permanence.

In addition to object permanence, children must develop other basic concepts before they are able to understand the world the way adults do. Among these are the concepts of space, time, number, quantity, causality, life, death, and humor. Adults who communicate most effectively and meaningfully with children are usually those who realize that children's basic concepts of the world may differ from their own.

The final stage of cognitive development consists of acquiring the ability to think logically. Piaget and others have described the development of a number of logical thinking abilities. They include the ability to operate logically with concepts such as transformations, reversibility, classification, class inclusion, multiple classification, and asymmetrical relations.

Since most human behaviors are directed toward the solution of problems, problem-solving can be seen as the major goal of cognitive development. Through experience and practice children develop mental sets that provide them with set ways of approaching problems. Mental sets and functional fixedness are helpful, but they can also be harmful when applied to the wrong problems.

Not all problems can be solved with set rules. Many require creative or original solutions. Because creativity is such a valuable cognitive tool, many researchers have investigated creativity and attempted to find ways of fostering its development. In addition, some studies suggest that creativity may be associated with "good" personality adjustment.

While children do seem to go through the same stages of cognitive development, the result is not always the same. The most obvious difference in cognitive style seen between children probably has to do with the manner in which they respond to problems. Some tend to be impulsive while others tend to be more reflective. These ways of responding may be the result of genetic differences or they may be the result of learning. Attempts to teach or modify cognitive style suggest that it is easier to teach children to be more reflective than it is to teach them to become more impulsive.

RESEARCH
REPORT 7.1

Rehearsal Strategy and Children's Learning

Adults often rely on a rehearsal strategy as a memory aid. All of us have repeated—either aloud or to ourselves—phone numbers, addresses, or locker combinations in an attempt to remember them. Research has been conducted to determine whether young children also use a rehearsal strategy in learning tasks where it would help them.

Sixty kindergarten, second-grade, and fifth-grade children participated in the study (Flavell, Beach, and Chinsky, 1966). Each child was shown a set of seven pictures of familiar objects. On each trial of the task the experimenter pointed to several of the pictures. The child's job was to point to the same pictures in the same order as the experimenter. Each child received at least three trials in which recall of the pictures was tested immediately and three trials in which recall was tested after a 15-second delay. Because the children might have been reluctant to rehearse the picture names aloud if the experimenters were watching them, each child wore a toy space helmet. The helmet's opaque visor was lowered during the delay, so only the child's lips were visible. An experimenter trained to read lips recorded the occurrence of rehearsals; for example, softly whispering the names of the pictures or moving the lips was scored as a rehearsal. The results indicated that 12 second-graders and 17 fifth-graders rehearsed, as compared to only 2 kindergarteners.

Researchers (Keeney, Cannizzo, and Flavell, 1967) then asked whether young children could be taught a rehearsal strategy. The same recall task was used to identify 24 first-graders who spontaneously rehearsed and 17 first-graders who failed to rehearse. The nonrehearsers were taught to rehearse by the experimenter repeatedly whispering the picture names; and they received additional trials during which the experimenter constantly reminded them to rehearse. Then, on later trials, the experimenter allowed them to choose whether they wanted to rehearse or not.

Before the nonrehearsers were taught this strategy they recalled fewer of the pictures than did the children who rehearsed spontaneously. However, when the nonrehearsers were shown how to rehearse and were reminded, their memories improved. Unfortunately, when the children were no longer reminded to use the strategy they stopped using this new memory aid. The authors suggested that young children show a production deficiency in the use of rehearsal. That is, young children are able to use rehearsal successfully when they are prompted, but they still fail to use the strategy when they are left to their own devices.

How can we get children to continue to use this beneficial strategy? Eighteen 6- and 7-year-old children who did not spontaneously rehearse were taught to do so and were reminded to do so, as in the preceding study (Kennedy and Miller, 1976). Half of the children were also given a reason for using the strategy. The experimenter told them: "My goodness, you did so much better when you whispered those names over and over. I guess whispering helped you remember the pictures. Right?" (p. 567). Then the children received recall trials during which they chose whether they wanted to continue to use the strategy. The results showed that nonrehearsers who received teaching and also were told the reason for it continued to rehearse; children who received only the teaching dropped the strategy. The authors concluded:

Persistent use and utility of a newly acquired rehearsal strategy may depend, at least in part, on having a rationale for engaging in such activity. . . . Given that rehearsal has merit in a learning task, and the child proves capable of using it, the present data most directly suggest that relevant production deficiency may be overcome through training in the strategy which includes information about its benefits. (p. 568)

Adapted from J. H. Flavell, D. H. Beach, and J. M. Chinsky, "Spontaneous Verbal Rehearsal in a Memory Task as a Function of Age," *Child Development*, 1966, *37*, 283–299; T. J. Keeney, S. R. Cannizzo, and J. H. Flavell, "Spontaneous and Induced Verbal Rehearsal in a Recall Task," *Child Development*, 1967, *38*, 935–966; R. A. Kennedy and D. J. Miller, "Persistent Use of Verbal Rehearsal as a Function of Information about its Value," *Child Development*, 1976, *47*, 566–569.

**RESEARCH
REPORT 7.2**

Cognitive Achievements before the Acquisition of Language

Piaget is one of the first developmental psychologists to describe the important cognitive achievements that occur before the child acquires language. Newborn children's egocentrism is great: They are not aware that the world and its objects continue to exist even when they cannot see them and are not acting on them; they do not understand that they themselves are only single objects within a world of objects. In the passage below Piaget (1967) describes some of the milestones that occur as sensorimotor children gradually acquire knowledge of themselves and of an external world that exists apart and distinct from them:

The period that extends from birth to the acquisition of language is marked by an extraordinary development of the mind. Its importance is sometimes underestimated because it is not accompanied by words that permit a step-by-step pursuit of the progress of intelligence. . . . This early mental development nonetheless determines the entire course of psychological evolution. In fact, it is no less than a conquest by perception and movement of the entire practical universe that surrounds the small child. At eighteen months to two years this "sensorimotor assimilation" of the immediate external world effects a miniature Copernican revolution. At the starting point of this development the neonate grasps everything to himself— or, in more precise terms, to his body—whereas at the termination of this period . . . he is for all practical purposes but one element or entity among others in a universe that he has gradually constructed himself, and which hereafter he will experience as external to himself. (pp. 8–9)

At birth, mental life is limited to the exercise of reflex apparatuses. . . . They have none of the mechanical passivity that might be attributed to them. On the contrary, from the very outset, they manifest genuine activity. . . . The sucking reflexes, for example, become refined, and the neonate sucks better after one or two weeks than during the first days. At a somewhat later age, these reflexes lead to practical discriminations and recognitions that are easily observed. Still later, and most important, these reflexes give rise to a kind of generalization of activity. The infant is not content to suck only when he nurses; he also sucks at random. He sucks his fingers when he encounters them, then whatever object may be presented fortuitously, and finally he coordinates the movement of his arms with the sucking until he is able to introduce his thumb into his mouth systematically. . . . In short, the infant assimilates a part of his universe to his sucking to the degree that his initial behavior can be described by saying that for him the world is essentially a thing to be sucked. In short order, this same universe will also become a thing to be looked at, to listen to, and, as soon as his movements allow, to shake. (pp. 9–10)

Intelligence actually appears well before language. . . . It is an entirely practical intelligence based on the manipulation of objects; in place of words and concepts it uses percepts and movements organized into "action schemata." For example, to grab a stick in order to draw up a remote object is an act of intelligence (and a fairly late developing one at that: about eighteen months). Here, an instrument, the means to an end, is coordinated with a pre-established goal. In order to discover this means, the subject must first understand the relationship between the stick and the objective. A more precocious act of intelligence consists in bringing the objective closer by means of pulling the support on which it is resting. This occurs toward the end of the first year. (p. 11)

Early behavior becomes increasingly elaborated and differentiated to the point where the infant acquires sufficient behavioral facility for him to notice the results of his actions. In these "circular reactions" the baby is not content merely to reproduce movements and gestures that have led to an interesting effect. He varies them intentionally in order to study the results of these variations and thus gives himself over to true explorations or to "experiments in order to see." This is exemplified by the behavior of the twelve-month-old child who throws objects on the ground in one direction or another in order to see how and where they fall. (pp. 11–12)

The result of this intellectual development is in effect to transform the representation of things to the point of completely changing ... the subject's initial position with respect to them. At the outset of mental evolution there is no definite differentiation between the self and the external world, i.e., impressions that are experienced and perceived are not attached to a personal consciousness sensed as a "self," nor to objects conceived as external to the self. ... In other words, consciousness starts with ... egocentricity, whereas the progress of sensorimotor intelligence leads to the construction of an objective universe in which the subject's own body is an element among others and with which the internal life, localized in the subject's own body, is contrasted. (pp. 12–13)

Excerpted from J. Piaget, *Six Psychological Studies*, (D. Elkind, ed., and A. Tenzer, trans.). New York: Random House, 1967 (originally published, 1964).

REFERENCES

1. Ames, L. B. "The Development of the Sense of Time in the Young Child," *Journal of Genetic Psychology*, 1946, 68, 97–125.
2. Bruner, J. *Processes of Cognitive Growth: Infancy*. Worcester, Mass: Clark University Press, 1968.
3. Elkind, D. *Children and Adolescents: Interpretive Essays on Jean Piaget*. New York: Oxford, 1970.
4. Getzels, J. W., and P. W. Jackson. *Creativity and Intelligence*. New York: Wiley, 1962.
5. Goldenson, R. M. *The Encyclopedia of Human Behavior: Time Sense*. New York: Doubleday, 1970.
6. Kagan, J., and N. Kagan. "Individual Variation in Cognitive Processes." In P. Mussen (ed.), *Carmichael's Manual of Child Psychology*. New York: Wiley. 1970, 1273–1365.
7. Luchins, A. S. "Mechanization in Problem Solving: The Effect of *Einstellung*," *Psychological Monographs*, 1942, No. 248.
8. McCandless, B., and E. Evans. *Children and Youth: Psychosocial Development*. Hinsdale, Ill.: Dryden Press, 1973.
9. McGhee, P. E. "Development of the Humor Response," *Psychological Bulletin*, 1971, 76, 328–348.

10. McKeachie, W. J., and C. L. Doyle. *Psychology*, 2d ed. Reading Mass.: Addison-Wesley, 1970.
11. Munsinger, H. *Fundamentals of Child Development*, 2d ed. New York: Holt, Rinehart and Winston, 1975.
12. Olver, R. R., and J. R. Hornsby. "On Equivalence." In *Studies in Cognitive Growth*. New York: Wiley, 1966, 68–85.
13. Piaget, J. *The Origins of Intelligence in the Child*. New York: Norton, 1952.
14. Piaget, J. *The Construction of Reality in the Child*. New York: Basic Books, 1954.
15. Piaget, J. "Development and Learning." In R. E. Ripple and V. N. Rockcastle (eds.), *Piaget Rediscovered*. Ithaca, N.Y.: Cornell University Press, 1964, 7–20.
16. Piaget, J. *Six Psychological Studies*. New York: Random House, 1967.
17. Piaget, J., and B. Inhelder. *The Early Growth of Logic in the Child*. New York: Basic Books, 1958.
18. Pulaski, M. A. S. *Understanding Piaget*. New York: Harper & Row, 1971.
19. Ridley, D. R., and R. C. Birney. "Effects of Training Procedures on Creativity Test Scores," *Journal of Educational Psychology*, 1967, *58*, 158–164.
20. Russell, R. W., and W. Dennis. "Studies in Animism: A Standard Procedure for the Investigation of Animism," *Journal of Genetic Psychology*, 1939, *55*, 389–400.
21. Sears, P. S. "The Study of Development of Creativity: Research Problems in Parental Antecedents," *ERIC: ED 021 279*, 1969.
22. Torrance, E. P. *Education and the Creative Potential*. Minneapolis: University of Minnesota Press, 1963.
23. Torrance, E. P. "Curiosity of Gifted Children and Performance on Timed and Untimed Tests of Creativity," *Gifted Child Quarterly*, *13*, 155–158, Autumn 1969.
24. Torrance, E. P. "Stimulation, Enjoyment, and Originality in Dyadic Creativity," *Journal of Educational Psychology*, 1971, *62*(1), 45–48.
25. Trotter, R. J. "Discoverists vs. Behaviorists," *Science News*, 1973, *103*(12), 192.
26. Trotter, R. J. "Robots Make Intelligent Teachers," *Science News*, 1973, *104*(5), 76–77.
27. Wallas, G. *The Art of Thought*. New York: Harcourt, Brace, 1926.
28. Yando, R. M., and J. Kagan. "The Effect of Teacher Tempo on the Child," *Child Development*, 1968, *39*, 27–34.

L anguage, a unique characteristic
of the human species, is closely
related to such things as learning,
memory, and cognition. An
understanding of the basics of
language and its development is
central to any understanding of
human nature and of children.

8

language

"It is by language that we trace with the greatest certainty, the progress of the human mind," said Lord Monboddo, an eighteenth-century British anthropologist. In his major work, *The Origin and Process of Language*, he discussed (before Darwin) an evolutionary link between orangutans and humans and went on to describe the "natural history" of the human race through the development of language. Great thinkers, before and since Lord Monboddo, have almost all found the question of the **origin of language** to be central to any understanding of the human species. The **possession of language and speech** has always been considered the chief characteristic that distinguishes humans from all other animals, and language has always been closely associated with fundamental questions about human nature, such as learning, cognition, social behavior, and the possibility of possessing and passing on information.

Attempts to understand the origin and evolution of language, however, have been hampered by the lack of solid evidence. We can't go back a million years or so and watch our ancestors evolving, so a certain amount of speculation will probably always be involved in our understanding of language. Even so, there is a long history of attempts to study the origin of language.

One of the first known experiments with language was described by the Greek historian Herodotus nearly 2,500 years ago. An Egyptian king, wanting to find out which nation was the oldest on earth—hoping that his own would be the one—had two children isolated at birth from all human speech. The idea was to find out which language the children would speak if left to their own devices. That language, it was thought, would be the "true" or "natural" human language. The first word uttered by the children was not Egyptian but sounded like something from the Phrygian language (Phrygia was a country in Asia Minor). This proved to the king that the Phrygians, not the Egyptians, were the oldest nation on earth. Similar experiments have been recorded throughout history, often with the result that the first word spoken sounded like a word from the Hebrew language. As late as the eighteenth century, the same experiment was still being proposed. By then, however, it was generally admitted that such experiments should not be undertaken because of the harm such isolation could do to the children.

Attention next turned to the so-called wolf children, children who for some reason had been abandoned and had grown up with animals (the most familiar case is that of the wild boy of Aveyron, discussed in Chapter 3). But these examples offered few clues to a "natural language." The search for a universal language was eventually given up when it was realized that if children don't learn to use language during their early years, they will probably never be capable of more than the crudest forms of communication. More recently it has been found that the babbling of infants during the first years of life contains all of the sounds necessary for the development of any language, including ancient Phrygian, Egyptian, Hebrew, and English (32, 28).

Another approach was made by Condillac, an eighteenth-century French psychologist who was interested in the philosophy of language (43). He asked: How have humans gained knowledge? He answered that language, or the use of signs, is the indispensable instrument without which humans would have remained in the condition of animals. Condillac's account of the origin of language begins with natural cries, or what he calls the language of action. These consist of reflexive gestures or movements of the head, hands, eyes, and every other part of the body. But most important in this language of action, said Condillac, were the vocal gestures, the natural cries that express some inner passion (screams of fear, sighs of pleasure, and so on). The situations that trigger these involuntary vocal gestures or sounds would happen over and over. Through repeated use of these sounds early humans eventually gained the power to recall some of them and use them at will, without relying on external triggering mechanisms. Such sounds could then be reproduced for the information of other people. For example, a sign indicating fright at the approach of a lion could, by a person who was not directly threatened, be reproduced to warn another who was in danger. In such a manner early humans would gradually, by very slow degrees and in the long process of time, come to do voluntarily what they had previously done by reflex alone. Condillac believed the deliberate use of a few simple signs would extend the operations of the human mind and the ability to think. The signs would in time be improved, increased in number, and made more familiar. The further extension of this natural language would in turn lead to deliberately created verbal symbols — language.

With Condillac and those like him the tradition of linguistic philosophy came to a temporary dead end. During the nineteenth century the study of the origin of language was, at times, even prohibited for religious reasons. Since language was thought to be a gift from God, it was considered blasphemy to speak of the evolution rather than the divine origin of language. But after Darwin and by the twentieth century the study of language and its origin had begun to reestablish itself, this time as a science rather than a philosophy. The scientific study of the nature and structure of language is known as **linguistics,** but many other areas of research are currently adding to our understanding of language. They include archaeology, anthropology, biology, animal behavior, brain research, and psychology.

Anthropologist Ashley Montagu, for instance, suggests that a detailed study of early human tool-making may yield clues to the cognitive processes of early humans and to the origin and evolution of language and speech. His theory is that speech originated in the process of tool-making, and he says that the variety of tools made by our ancestors indicates an ability to communicate

Psychologist Julian Jaynes (1923–   ).

on a symbolic level that would have required speech. Not only tool-making but big game hunting, Montagu says, was probably related to the development of speech. Hunting is much more successful if hunters can verbally signal to each other changes in plans and strategies. The three — tool-making, big game hunting, and spoken language — says Montagu, would probably have evolved together with a sort of three-way feedback relationship leading to the further development of each. If this tool-making hypothesis is correct, some form of human speech may have been in use one or two million years ago, the age of some of the oldest human stone tools.

Psychologist Julian Jaynes of Princeton University disagrees (44). He says that speech was not necessary for transmission from generation to generation of such simple skills as tool use and tool-making:

> It is almost impossible to describe chopping off flints into simple choppers and hand axes in language. This act was transmitted solely by imitation in exactly the same way chimpanzees transmit the trick of inserting vine stems into ant hills to get ants. . . . In our own culture, it is doubtful if language is at all necessary in the transmission of such skills as swimming or riding a bicycle.

Jaynes believes that speech and language evolved much more recently than one or two million years ago. They must have developed, he says, during a time when some portion of the human population was being persistently forced into a new ecological niche (see Chapter 2) to which it was not fully adapted. Any trait as universal in a species as language is, he says, must have developed during an age when it would have had a great survival value.

The most dramatic ecological changes to which the human species was subjected were probably the great glacial or ice ages, during which major portions of the earth were covered with ice. These glaciations would have forced severe changes in living conditions and habits and could have resulted in sufficient environmental pressures to provide language with a necessary survival value. Jaynes says that language probably developed during the most recent ice age, which lasted from 70,000 to 10,000 years ago. Prior to that, he says, members of the human species probably communicated just like all other primates, with an abundance of visual, vocal, and tactile (touch) signals that were very far removed from the syntactical language we practice today. (**Syntax** has to do with the way words are arranged to form meaningful phrases and sentences.)

How did language begin? Jaynes says it may have begun, as Condillac suggested, with the "language of action." This ability is seen in many species and often consists of visual-gestural (sign language) communication. But as early human populations migrated out of Africa into the northern climates, visual signals became less effective for a variety of reasons. Dark caves and hunting by night made visual signals almost useless. Tool use made it important to free the hands and body for increasingly complicated activities. It is possible that under such pressures incidental (reflexive) vocal signals took on the intentional or voluntary function that was formerly the property of visual signals only. This was a momentous step, says Jaynes, and it probably had a long evolution that was not complete until the start of the last ice age. By then, he says, our ancestors may have been ready to begin talking.

The first real elements of speech, suggests Jaynes, were the endings of intentional cries. Imagine a cave dweller screaming "Wahee!" at the close approach of a saber-toothed tiger. The intensity of such a scream would probably depend on the intensity of the danger, or the nearness of the tiger. A tiger further away for example, might result in a cry of much less intensity, such as the more relaxed "Wahoo." It is these endings, "ee" and "oo," that may have become the first modifiers meaning "near" and "far."

The next step toward syntactic language would be separating the endings from a particular cry and attaching them to another cry with the same indication. For example, "Wahee" could mean "close tiger," while "Yahee" could mean "close lion." Modifiers separated from their cries could also have become commands. The cry of "EE!" shouted at someone could mean "come near," while "OO!" could mean "go farther." This type of signal would have been advantageous for hunting groups.

Jaynes goes on to explain how inflective questioning and negation may have developed. From those, the development of nouns for animals, nouns for things, and then to names for people are discussed. The theory also includes the development of verbs, prepositions, other parts of speech, and syntax and an explanation of how all of these could have developed during the relatively short time span of 70,000 years.

Jaynes's theory of the evolution of language is based on a mixture of available evidence and conjecture, or speculation, about the past. Like any theory, it is not considered to be the final word. As new evidence is accumulated the theory may have to be modified. The value of such a theory, however, is that it offers a framework within which it is possible to think about the nature of language and all that it implies about the nature of humanity.

For centuries theories of language and humanity have been closely related, and as will be seen in this chapter, language is closely related to such human abilities as learning, remembering, and cognition. In addition, an understanding of the origin of language helps explain the development of language in infants and children.

LANGUAGE STUDIES

A child asks for a cracker. Does that indicate language ability? A parrot asks for a cracker. Is that language? A chimpanzee moves its hands in a certain way or manipulates plastic symbols in a way that its trainers understand. Is that language? In order to answer these questions it is necessary to know what language is and what it is not. As a general definition, **language** is a system of symbols with commonly recognized meanings. Manipulation of these symbols (verbally or in written form) enables humans to communicate with each other. But birds and bees use symbols (sounds and movements) and have the ability to communicate. In fact, every species, from the simplest to the most complex, has some form of communication system. The higher a species is on the evolutionary scale, the closer its communication system is to that of humans. But if human language ability is truly unique, it must have some characteristics that set it apart from animal communication. A great deal of thought has gone into defining such characteristics, and several qualities have been listed that seem to make human language ability unique (21).

One seemingly unique characteristic of the human language is that it uses a **small number of sounds** to produce a large number of meanings. The basic units of sound are called **phonemes.** Some languages use as few as 15 phonemes. Others use as many as 85. The English language is based on about 45 phonemes or sounds. They correspond to the way vowels and consonants are pronounced.

Combinations of phonemes are used to produce **morphemes,** the basic units of meaning. There are more than 100,000 morphemes in the English language (19). They consist of root words, prefixes, and suffixes. Combinations of morphemes, arranged according to the rules of grammar, are used to produce meaningful messages. With only 45 basic sounds, a user of the English language can produce an almost infinite number of meaningful messages. Compared with this, animal communication is extremely limited. Even animals that can produce a great variety of sounds, such as parrots, produce only a very limited number of messages. Birds warn each other of danger, call their mates, or tell each other to stay out of their territory. They do not produce novel messages the way a child might tell its parents what happened at school.

Speech, which is closely related to language, is not the same as language. **Speech** refers to actual utterances and the ability of humans to manipulate or verbally produce the phonemes that make up a language. Language is generally viewed as the complex system of grammatical rules that give meaning to speech. (See Figure 8-1.)

Figure 8–1   Definition of Terms Pertaining to Language

A number of terms that are used throughout this chapter are defined here for future reference:

1. **Phoneme:** One of the set of the smallest units of speech that distinguish one utterance from another in a given language. The *b* in *boy* and the *g* in *girl* are two English phonemes.
2. **Morpheme:** A combination of phonemes or sounds that yields a relatively stable unit of language that cannot be divided into smaller meaningful parts. *Boy, girl,* and *most* are morphemes. Meaningful parts of words, including prefixes and suffixes such as *al* and *ly,* are also morphemes, as are *almost* and *mostly.*
3. **Morphology:** Having to do with the form and structure of words. *Boy* and *girl* are singular nouns. *Boys* and *girls* are the plural forms. *Most* is an adjective. *Mostly* is the adverb form.
4. **Phonology:** Having to do with the pronunciation of words.
5. **Semantics:** Pertaining to the meanings of words. Some words, like *boy* and *girl,* have rather obvious meanings. Other words, such as *equality, democracy,* and *happiness,* have more subtle and complex meanings. As will be seen in the discussion of vocabulary development, children seem to begin by attaching the most obvious meanings to the words they use and then gradually learn the more subtle meanings of words.
6. **Syntax:** Having to do with the way words are put together to form meaningful phrases or sentences. Syntactically, "baby comes" has a specific meaning, but "comes baby" has no accepted meaning in the English language.

---

7. **Grammar:** That aspect of language that includes all of the rules for the construction of words (morphology), the arrangement of words into phrases and sentences (syntax), the meanings of words (syntax), and the pronunciation of words (phonology).

The acquisition of these complex rules systems by children is accomplished with amazing ease, but the course of children's learning of grammar is marked by characteristics that clearly distinguish "early" from mature language construction (27). For example, compare the following common expressions of infants and preschool children with their mature versions:

Child's Utterance

(a) "Allgone cooky."
(b) "That a nice kitty was."
(c) "I are here!"
(d) "Lookit mine feets in the water."

Mature Version

(a) "The cooky is all gone."
(b) "That was a nice kitty."
(c) "I am here!"
(d) "Look at my feet in the water."

The examples of typical children's utterances represent a mix of normal and grammatical construction related to sentence and word form. Examples (a) and (b) involve sentence form (syntax), while examples (c) and (d) involve word form (morphology). By adult standards these utterances represent "errors," but such constructions are normal and typical for the young child's system of language. As indicated in this chapter, during the early years of life children rapidly incorporate the rules of grammar into their language system.

Formerly, it was widely believed that children's language is basically an incorrect form of adult language that results from children's "handicaps" in memory, attention, and thinking (27). It is now generally realized that children do not simply speak a "garbled version" of adult language. Piaget's work (see Chapter 7) has shown how children's cognitive abilities differ from those of adults, and now research on language suggests that children's language (which is closely related to cognition) also has unique structural patterns that develop in what seem to be distinct stages. In most cases children's grammatical development is well advanced by school age and closely resembles the adult form by the middle elementary grades. However, it is during the preschool years that the most dramatic advances in grammatical development are made. For this reason, this chapter will focus on the early stages of language development.

Another important characteristic of human language is **displacement,** the ability to communicate about objects and events not actually present in space or time. Animals, like infants, seem to be egocentric (as described in Chapter 7) and dominated by their perceptions. They communicate only about things that concern them in the present time. They don't communicate about the past or the future or about things they haven't experienced. Because animals communicate only about the present state of the environment and about the way they experience the environment, they cannot tell lies. They communicate only what they experience. The **ability to tell lies, make up stories, or create great literary works,** as Shakespeare did, is another characteristic that is unique to humans.

"Learnability" and reflectiveness are also qualities thought to be unique to humans. **Learnability** means that users of one human language can learn to use another language. **Reflectiveness** indicates that humans can reflect on or think about what they are communicating. They can communicate about communication. While these and the other qualities mentioned are characteristic of human language, there is not complete agreement that they are all unique to humans. It can be argued that many species have the ability to use one or more of these features (41). Research with chimpanzees, especially, has called into question the uniqueness of the human communication ability.

Animal Studies and Language

"An infinite number of monkeys pecking away at an infinite number of typewriters, will eventually produce the complete works of Shakespeare." Even if this old saying is true, the process might take an infinite amount of time. While no one actually expects monkeys to write plays, various researchers have attempted to teach primates methods of communicating with humans. Chimpanzees, because they have a more highly developed brain than the lower primates, have been the students of most of these experiments. Such experiments are fascinating in themselves (What would a chimpanzee have to say?), but they are also scientifically important for a variety of reasons. Attempts to teach chimps to communicate with humans have led to a better understanding of language, have helped define what is truly unique about human language, have shed light on the complexities of human language, and have demonstrated how difficult it is for chimps as well as for children to learn a language.

In the 1930s Winthrop and Luella Kellog raised a female chimpanzee with their infant son. The chimp never learned to talk, but after 16 months it was able to recognize and respond to almost 100 words. In the 1940s Keith and Cathy Hayes repeated the feat and even taught their chimp to speak or mouth the words "mamma," "papa," and "cup." Progress stopped there, however, because the mouths and throats of chimpanzees are not able to reproduce human speech sounds. Realizing this, researchers have turned to other modes or methods of communication.

R. Allen and Beatrice T. Gardner knew that in the wild chimps use their hands and arms to communicate with each other. Taking this as a cue, the Gardners taught a young female chimp to communicate with her hands. The chimp, Washoe, learned American Sign Language, the sign language used by the deaf in the United States. After four years of training Washoe was able to use 140 signs. She could ask for things, apologize for mischief, and talk (or make signs) to herself (42).

In another experiment Ann and David Premack taught a chimp to use plastic symbols as words for communication (34). The colored plastic pieces with metal backing could be placed on a magnetic board and moved around in various ways to form sentences. The chimp, Sarah, learned to use almost 130 words. "Her understanding," said the Premacks, "goes beyond the meaning of words and includes concepts of class and sentence structure."

Does this sort of behavior on the part of a chimpanzee represent true language ability? Not everyone agrees. It is possible that Sarah and the other chimps were just conditioned to respond for a reward. Given enough bananas it is possible that any chimp could learn to do tricks or put signs together in a certain way. Real language capability, it is argued, requires a demonstration of knowledge of sentence structure and syntax along with the ability to use this knowledge for something other than the promise of a material reward. Researchers at the Yerkes Regional Primate Center in Atlanta are trying to demonstrate these abilities in a chimpanzee with the aid of a computer. They are attempting to teach a chimp named Lana to read and write.

In order to teach Lana to communicate, a special language called Yerkish was designed. It is made up of simple geometric figures that can be combined to stand for various concepts. These symbols are displayed on a typewriter-like computer keyboard that Lana has learned to use to type out grammatically correct requests for food or entertainment. Within five months Lana had learned to use 40 of the Yerkish symbols. By the time she was 4 years old, she could use 75 symbols and was asking to learn more. She could use the computer keyboard to ask questions, such as the names of objects.

In order to use these words Lana must first pull a bar above the computer. She then punches out the proper signs in the proper order. In Yerkish, word order is decided by classes of words. "Banana," for instance, is in the class of words that can follow "eat," but it cannot follow "drink." Above the computer console are seven small projection screens on which the symbols appear in the order in which they were punched. If the sequence is completed correctly, the computer automatically triggers a dispenser and gives the chimp what she asked for. If there has been a mistake, the computer sounds a buzzer, erases all images on the screen, and Lana must begin again.

Lana operating her language computer.

Does all of this mean that Lana is learning a language, or does it mean that she is being conditioned to perform for a reward? Duane Rumbaugh, who is in charge of the project, says Lana has reached a very advanced stage of conditioning, but he says there are encouraging signs that much more is happening. It is known, for instance, that Lana hasn't simply memorized the proper sequence to punch on the keyboard, because when the positions of the symbols are changed she can still find the proper ones and use them in order to make a request. Proof that she reads and understands the visual symbols is shown when Lana accidentally hits the "please" key. She recognizes the symbol and does not hit the key again, but goes on to add a request to it, such as "Please machine open window." If one of the researchers punches the first two or three keys of a sentence, Lana can finish it correctly. The researchers hope eventually to use the screens to ask Lana questions and engage her in conversation.

Attempts to communicate with chimps have shown that these animals do have the capability of acquiring a vocabulary and, perhaps, that they are able to use words in novel ways. The Yerkes project even goes beyond word learning. "Our situation," explains Rumbaugh, "has a grammar and a syntax and we want to see if the animal can learn to use words in novel ways to be productive linguistically." But why would anyone want to do this? The Gardners explain that they were examining the extent to which another species might be able to use language as a study in comparative psychology and as a way of looking at what language is. The Premacks were also attempting to better define the nature of language and the brain that produces it. "Ultimately," they said, "the benefit of language studies will be realized in an understanding of intelligence in terms not of scores on tests but of the underlying brain mechanism." The researchers at Yerkes give similar reasons. They want to find out if, in a controlled environment, chimps, gorillas, and orangutans can be taught to communicate spontaneously through the use of a language-like system for their own purposes. In addition, they hope to find out something about the basic problems many children have in learning language.

The Brain and Language

Research with animals may produce important information about the nature of language and how it is learned, but even if animals can learn some language, they do not have a brain capable of using language the way humans do. **Brain research** is another important area of study that is adding greatly to our knowledge of human language ability.

The vocal cries of most lower primates have been found to be produced by an area deep in the center of the brain known as the **limbic system.** Electrical stimulation of various parts of the limbic system in rhesus and squirrel monkeys, for instance, can cause these animals to produce their entire range of vocal cries. It is possible that the involuntary vocal signals of early humans

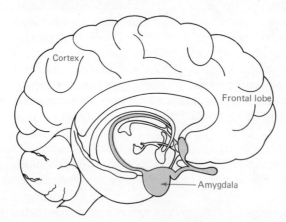

Cortex

Frontal lobe

Amygdala

The limbic system.

were controlled by the limbic system, but during the process of evolution the control of vocalization was eventually transferred to the **cortex,** or thick outer layer of the brain. When certain areas of the human cortex are damaged, the ability to speak is lost. When the same areas of the cortex of a monkey are damaged vocalization is not lost. This suggests that human speech is not simply an elaboration or extension of the vocal responses of lower primates but that it evolved quite independently and serves a different purpose (44).

The areas of the cortex that evolved in connection with speech appear to be mainly in the **left hemisphere,** or half, of the brain. To the naked eye the halves of the brain look almost like mirror images of each other, but for more than 100 years it has been known that the right and left hemispheres function differently (see Chapter 5). In 1861, Pierre Broca, a founder of modern brain surgery, discovered the area of the brain that controls spoken language. It is in the left cortex and is now known as **Broca's area.** In 1874, Carl Wernicke discovered another speech center in the left hemisphere. It is concerned with the understanding of language and is known as **Wernicke's area.** Lesions (wounds or injuries) in these two parts of the left hemisphere have been found to cause various types of **aphasia,** or the loss or impairment of the ability to use words as symbols or ideas.

Speech is only one ability that the hemispheres do not have in common. People who have suffered damage to one or the other hemisphere of the brain show a number of behavioral differences. An accident involving the left hemisphere can impair speech or produce aphasia, but it can also lower performance in logical and mathematical thought processes and in such things as reading, writing, and naming. Damage exclusively to the **right hemisphere** does not usually disrupt linguistic abilities, but it can lower performance in spatial tasks (such as perceiving distances), simple musical abilities, recognition of familiar objects and faces, and bodily self-awareness (45).

The specialization of the hemispheres for different tasks seems to be advantageous in humans. If the left hemisphere is damaged, the right can sometimes take over the linguistic abilities of the left side. This is especially true if the damage occurs early in life. Recent research suggests that specialization of the hemispheres for different functions does not begin until about the age of 5. Before that both hemispheres seem to have equal abilities with regard to most cognitive functions. After that language specialization is thought to begin in the left hemisphere while other types of specialization begin in the right. So if a child younger than 5 suffers damage to the linguistic left hemisphere, the right, which has not become specialized yet, can usually take over the language capabilities. If use of the left hemisphere is lost after the age of 13 or so, much less compensation takes place, and the child will not usually recover more than minimal speech abilities (38).

There may also be a difference between the sexes with regard to the time of hemisphere specialization. Tests of spatial abilities suggest that specialization of the hemispheres may not begin until the age of 13 in females (46). If the female brain does not become specialized until adolescence, young girls may be at an advantage over young boys in several ways. The brains of females, particularly the right hemisphere, may have greater plasticity or flexibility for a longer period of time. If so, language functions could transfer more easily to the as yet unspecialized right hemisphere following left hemisphere damage (perhaps due to anoxia, or inadequate oxygen at birth; see Chapter 4). Such plasticity in the female brain could explain why males have more language development problems (such as aphasia) than females.

THEORIES OF LANGUAGE DEVELOPMENT

Human language is a complex system of sounds, words, phrases, and sentences arranged according to the rules of grammar (which are not always easy to understand). The complexity of language is demonstrated not only by the difficulty chimps have learning a language but by the difficulty most people have learning a second language. If the process is so difficult, even for adults, how then do children acquire a first language? How do they acquire such a large vocabulary as well as an understanding of grammar and syntax by the time they are 6 years old? Theories similar to those used to explain cognition are also helpful in explaining language development.

Learning Theory   Learning is obviously one way of acquiring a language. Through classical and operant conditioning, with feedback and reinforcement, chimps can almost learn a language. Through these same methods students can learn a second language. Imitation and modeling are also involved. This is seen in the fact that children from different cultures acquire different languages. Without the opportunity to hear and process language spoken by other people, children wouldn't learn any language, much less a particular language.

According to B. F. Skinner, the processes involved in learning (see Chapter 6) are all that are necessary to explain language development in children (35). Children, according to Skinner's theory, begin by making a variety of sounds. Through selective reinforcement of certain sounds they gradually learn to produce more meaningful sounds or words. Following the example of people around them, children gradually learn to arrange words in a meaningful way, and through continued reinforcement from parents, teachers, and friends, they eventually learn the rules of grammar.

Learning theory explains how people learn a second language, especially if they set out to do so and use all of the learning methods available. But infants don't set out to learn a language, they just do (unless they are handicapped). A child's acquisition of a first language may be the result of a dif-

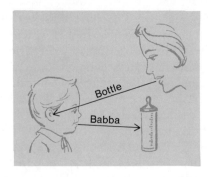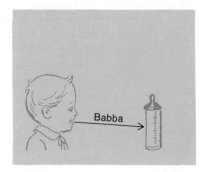

Through selective reinforcement of certain sounds children gradually learn to produce more meaningful sounds or words.

ferent and much more complex process that learning theory does not fully explain.

Some studies, for instance, suggest that imitation may be a method of strengthening language abilities rather than a method of acquiring a first language. In one study the speech of six children was examined during the time they were first beginning to combine two words in a grammatical manner (5). Of the six children studied, two did not imitate what they heard. It is not hard to imagine, for example, a verbal interaction between a parent and a child repeated 15 times with no change in the child's response: Parent: "Baby went." Child: "Baby goed." Parent: "No, baby went." Child: "Baby goed." Parent: "No, baby went." Child: "I see, baby goed," and so on.

The children in the study who did show some imitation did so only in cases where the grammatical construction in question had already appeared in their speech. Children who know to say "baby went," for instance, might slip up and say "baby goed" once in a while. If they are corrected after they have shown knowledge of the correct construction, they will usually imitate this response. In this manner imitation can help strengthen a child's language abilities. Imitation does not, however, explain how the correct construction was acquired in the first place.

There is even evidence that adults imitate children's language instead of the other way around. Studies of parent-child verbal interactions show that adults adjust their own speech to fit the needs of their children. A study of mothers and their 1- and 2-year-old children showed that the mothers use a smaller vocabulary and much less complex sentences when talking to their children than when talking to older children or adults (18). They also tend to avoid broken sentences and giving confusing information. In general, their speech to 2-year-olds is much simpler, less confusing, and more repetitious than the speech they use with 10-year-olds (36). Parents also tend to exaggerate the tone or rhythm of sentences addressed to young children, stress the last words of sentences, place well-marked pauses at the end of sentences, and often speak to children in a slightly higher voice (closer to that of a child's voice). Not only do adults sometimes modify the complexity of their speech when talking to young children, even children as young as 3 years of age simplify their speech and repeat sentences when talking to younger children compared with their speech to adults (37). From such observations it appears that children use certain levels of complexity in their speech before their parents do so in talking to them. In other words, parents seem to learn from their children the level of speech that is appropriate to use with them. As a child's language ability continues to develop, parents begin to increase the complexity of their speech with the child. In doing so they help to strengthen the language ability that the child has already acquired and present models of speech that the child will eventually begin to use.

Reinforcement and operant conditioning also seem to be more useful in strengthening or adjusting language abilities than in helping a child acquire a first language. This is seen in the fact that no matter what type of reinforcement they receive, almost all children show the same basic knowledge of syntax and **semantics,** or the meaning of words, at about the same time of life in a wide variety of language environments (10). Research with mentally retarded children has shown that the principles of operant conditioning or behavior modification can be of great value in helping such children develop language abilities (20, 29), but the exact role that conditioning plays in normal language development is not known. At present there is no evidence to suggest that the acquisition of syntax and semantics is dependent on the presence of an adult trainer who actively reinforces the child for correct verbal responses.

Even if imitation and reinforcement do not fully explain the acquisition of a first language, this does not mean that social learning is unimportant in the process of language development. Parents are usually very sensitive to the development of their children's language abilities, and through continued interactions with their children parents play an important role in helping children adjust their language as it becomes more adultlike. This can be seen especially as parents correct mistakes and repeat and extend the utterances of their children. For example, a child might say, "Here come bus," and the parent might respond, "Here comes the bus." Such extensions of a child's early speech help children remember the correct forms they have already learned and help them adjust their growing language ability so that it will eventually match that of their parents.

The Biology of Language

The fact that learning theory does not completely explain the complexities of language development has led some researchers to conclude that human language ability may be the result of **biological connections or structures in**

the brain. As the brain develops during infancy and early childhood, these structures would provide a child with certain basic rules of language that would, therefore, not have to be learned. Psychologist Eric Lenneberg, for instance, says there are several characteristics of language that lead to the assumption that it has a biological basis (24). Language is a form of behavior found in all cultures of the world. It begins at about the same age in children from all cultures. It is based on the same formal operating characteristics (phonemes, morphemes, and syntax) no matter what its outward form may be (English, Spanish, Russian). Throughout recorded history these operating characteristics have been the same. And finally, language is a behavior that can be impaired by specifically located brain lesions that leave other mental and motor skills relatively unaffected. Any human behavior that has all of these characteristics, says Lenneberg, may likewise be assumed to have a rather specific biological basis.

Not a great deal is known about the brain structures that are related to language or about how they might help produce language, but the existence of language areas in the brain does suggest that humans might be prewired or programmed with some special language abilities that do not have to be learned. Biologists are still trying to find out exactly how the brain's language areas function in this regard, but linguists have taken another approach to the study of language and the brain. By studying the basic form of languages, linguists hope to find certain elements or rules that are common to all languages. These common or universal rules might help explain the brain structures responsible for language. Noam Chomsky of the Massachusetts Institute of Technology explains: "The language faculty may be regarded as a fixed function, characteristic of the species, one component of the human mind, a function which maps experience into grammar." If this is so, then it might be possible, through the study of language and grammar, eventually to isolate this "fixed function." There might, for instance, be a specific property of grammar (Chomsky calls this "property P") that is unlearned and universal to all grammars, a precondition of learning (43). If a property P can be discovered, it would suggest the existence of a genetically determined language ability (an ability that would not have to be learned). It would also suggest that language might have a partially determined structure as a matter of biological necessity, much as the general character of bodily organs is fixed for the species. "In my view," says Chomsky, "work of the past years has provided considerable support for a conception of the language faculty along these lines. . . . Thus it seems to me not unreasonable to approach the study of language as we would the study of some organ of the body." So far a property P has not been found, but the search for it has led to a great deal of valuable linguistic research and to some interesting findings about the nature of language.

A less biological approach, but one that is closely related to Chomsky's theory, has resulted in an explanation of the human language ability based on what is called "**generative grammar.**" This theory, which is similar to the information-processing theory of cognition, suggests that children produce or generate novel sentences after they have acquired certain basic rules about language. Whether these rules are the result of biological structures in the brain or whether they are learned is not known. But the existence of such rules would help explain language development in children. Roger Brown, who is well known for his investigations of language development in children, says that

> in acquiring a first language, one cannot possibly be said simply to acquire a repertoire [a list or supply] of sentences, however large that repertoire is imagined to be, but must instead be said to acquire a rule system that makes it possible to generate a literally infinite variety of sentences, most of them never heard from anyone else (9).

This does not mean that children acquire the rules of language construction in any formal manner or that parents try to teach children their language according to the rules of sentence structure. Preschool children usually do not know any linguistic rules, and chances are that a good many parents don't know most of the formal rules of language. One must suppose, says Brown, that what happens is that preschool children are able to extract from the speech they hear a set of construction rules, many of them very complex and abstract, which neither they nor their parents know in any clearly defined form.

Not only children and parents but psychologists and linguists have been stumped by these complex and abstract rules of language. Brown and others have attempted to determine what universal rules might be involved in language acquisition by taping the spontaneous speech of children and analyzing how it changes as they grow older. So far they have not been able to find a full set of construction rules that explain language, but their research has helped outline the stages through which children go as their language ability develops. Throughout this development the various types of learning, the special abilities of the human brain, and the acquisition of rules can be seen to be at work. It is the exact contribution of each that is still in question.

LANGUAGE DEVELOPMENT

The constant jumble of sounds, words, phrases, and sentences that surrounds an infant must be extremely confusing, even more confusing than the sounds of a foreign language are to an adult. The adult at least knows that the foreign language has meaning. Infants don't even know that at first. Before infants begin to make sense of these sounds, and before they can be said to have any language ability, they must do several things. They must develop their own sound-making ability, and they must crack the codes that give meaning to all of the sounds they hear. They must then find out how to use the codes to give meaning to their own speech sounds. The codes include **phonetics** (the meaning of phonemes or sounds), **morphology** (the meaning of morphemes and words), and **syntax** (the meaning of combinations of words). With these codes broken, children go on in the development of a vocabulary and a style of speaking.

Vocal Development

Infants begin life with the ability to make noise. They cry. This, however, is only the beginning. During the first year of life an infant's sound-making ability goes through some dramatic changes that result, finally, in the ability to produce recognizable human speech. The changes that take place during the first year can be seen in four distinct stages. The first stage of vocal development is **crying** (0 to 3 weeks). What may sound like meaningless cries during this period are actually the beginnings of organized speech. First of all, infant's cries show that they have the ability to use their sound-making equipment (1). By applying constant pressure to the vocal cords and by forcing air past the vocal cords and through the mouth, infants can produce a continuous cry. This ability, which is seen in all normal, healthy children, is a necessary first step toward speech. The lack of this ability or any abnormality in the infant's cry may even be an indication of brain damage (23).

The first indication of the ability to produce different sounds is evident in crying. The pitch or tone of an infant's cry tends to drop off at the end of a cry. This is probably because the infant runs out of air in the process of crying and must take another breath. This, in turn, leads to a drop in pressure on the vocal cords and a lowering of pitch (25). Finally, by the end of the first stage of vocal development, infants begin to use variations in the basic cry to communicate pain or anger. These messages, which most parents recognize, are expressed primarily in the turbulence or intensity of the cry (26).

The second stage of vocal development (3 weeks to 5 months) is characterized by the **pseudocry,** or fake cry, and **cooing** (comfort sounds). The pseudocry and cooing are made possible by changes in the vocal equipment. The position and size of the **larynx,** which contains the vocal cords, changes as the child grows, allowing the infant to produce a greater variety of sounds.

The third stage of vocal development (5 to 12 months) is characterized by an even greater variety of speech sounds, more variations in the combinations of sounds, and, for the first time, systematic variations in the tone or pitch of speech sounds. At about 5 or 6 months, for instance, infants begin to end some of their utterances with rising as well as falling tones. Eventually these rising intonations will be used to signal questions.

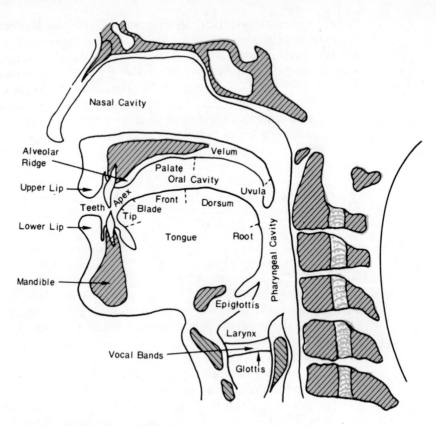

Human sound-making equipment.

Perhaps the most important aspect of the third stage of vocal development has to do with the multisyllabic (many syllables) vocalizations known as **babbling.** It has been suggested that this babbling stage is a practice period during which infants become familiar with the sounds they can produce and perfect the production of those sounds. It is also possible that during this stage infants discover the relationship between what they are doing with their vocal equipment and what they are hearing. Hearing their own sounds may provide feedback that helps them change and refine their speech sounds. Evidence for this is seen in the fact that infants born deaf usually babble only during the first part of the babbling stage. Perhaps because they do not hear and do not realize that they are making sounds, they are not encouraged to continue.

The fourth stage of vocal development (after 9 months of age) is characterized by the beginning of **patterned speech.** It is at this stage that infants usually begin to produce their first recognizable words. Practice with the pronunciation of phonemes continues for several years until all of the sounds of the language are mastered, but after about 9 months of age, children usually begin to attempt to produce meaningful words. These attempts are not always successful, however, for several reasons. At this stage children have not completely developed the use of their speech-producing equipment, including full control of the tongue and lower jaw. Although children can hear and distinguish the different phonemes that make up words, they cannot always reproduce those sounds (27). This is illustrated by the following exchange between a 2½-year-old and a babysitter:

> Child: I having chitchun choop!
> Babysitter: You're having what?
> Child: Chitchun choop?
> Babysitter: Chitchun choop?
> Child: No! *Chitchun choop!*
> Babysitter: Oh! Chicken soup?
> Child: Yah! Chitchun choop!

The child could obviously hear the correct pronounciation and would not accept the mispronunciation from someone else. Even so, the child could not say "chicken soup." This and other pronunciation problems are common for the first several years. Children may leave out syllables ("away" becomes "way"), repeat syllables ("Da" is "Dada" and "Ma" is "Mama"), or replace more difficult sounds with simpler ones ("spoon" becomes "boon"). Difficult consonant combinations such as *st, str, dr,* and *fl* are usually the last ones mastered, and pronunciation problems with these and other sounds may continue until age 7 or 8. Even though they may still mispronounce a few sounds, most children are speaking clearly by the age of 5 (27).

Single-word Utterances

A child's first word is usually seen as a milestone in development and is a great moment for proud parents. This is because a child's first purposefully produced word signifies more than the organization of sounds into a meaningful word. These first words, usually called **single-word utterances**, represent the beginning of a knowledge of semantics (meaning) and syntax and demonstrate some important aspects of cognitive development.

For many years it was thought that children's first words were actually short sentences, or "holophrases." This was because a single-word utterance like "cooky" could be understood as a complete sentence: "I want a cooky." In addition, children sometimes use different tone patterns (rising or falling) at the ends of words, as if to signal the difference between questions and direct statements. This, plus the fact that children who use only single-word utterances sometimes show an understanding of more complex utterances (two or more words), suggested that children at this very early stage of speech know something about syntax and sentence structure. It has even been suggested that children are born with some syntactic knowledge, but for some reason or other can produce only one word at a time.

Recently investigators have suggested that when children say a single word like "cooky," they are not necessarily referring to the object in a sentence, such as "I want a cooky." It may be that at this single-word stage children have some knowledge of the meaning of words (22), but this does not mean that they have any knowledge of sentence structure (4, 31). Instead, it may be that single-word utterances can best be understood in terms of cognitive development.

According to Piaget, most of the first two years of life make up the sensory-motor stage of cognitive development (see Chapter 7). During this time children explore the consequences of their actions on the surrounding world and organize their understanding of the relationship among themselves, objects, and events. At the end of the sensory-motor stage they discover that objects have a permanent existence. Once children have discovered the permanence of objects they can begin to represent or symbolize those objects. Images are one method of cognitive representation (**ikonic representation**), but language offers children a more flexible method of symbolic representation. Therefore, major milestones in the development of a child's first verbal symbols (single-word utterances) could be related to cognitive development in the sensory-motor stage and to the concept of object permanence. This can be seen as single-word utterances gradually become more complex (two words used together).

Several investigations have found that when children first produce words (9 to 12 months) they do not use those words to name just any objects in the environment, but instead refer to objects that they themselves act upon in daily experience (30) or refer to certain relationships among objects, persons, and events (4). At about 16 to 18 months of age most children show a rapid increase in the number of new words added to their vocabulary. It is at this time that they begin to **label** many more of the objects about them and begin to form **concepts** of those objects. For example, when children say "ball" in the early part of the single-word–utterance stage the meaning of the word may be limited to one aspect of a child's relationship to a ball. It is the child who rolls or bounces the ball in the living room, thus "ball" may mean "something to play with in the living room." Later in the sensory-motor stage, with more fully developed concepts, the meaning of "ball" is no longer restricted to the child's actions on it. The ball may take on distinctive features ("red ball," "blue ball"), it may be seen as something that others act on ("Mommy ball," "Daddy ball"), or it may be seen in relation to its own actions ("bounce ball," "roll ball").

This growing complexity of children's speech (from single- to two-word utterances) does not have to be seen in terms of **syntactic development** (knowledge of how words are related to each other), but can be seen as a result of the developing concept of object permanence and a more complete understanding of objects and their characteristics, relationships, and actions. According to Piaget, this type of thinking develops between 18 and 24 months of age and corresponds to the growing complexity of language. This growing complexity in the single-word–utterance stage leads to two-word utterances and more complex forms of speech and may provide the foundation for syntactic development.

Two-word Utterances

"Cooky!" might mean "Baby wants a cooky," "The cooky is big," or any one of a number of things, depending on when, where, and how the word is used. But a child's meaning is not always clear from a single-word utterance. Once children begin to combine two or more words, the meaning of their utterances becomes much more understandable, and their ability to communicate increases greatly. The code by which words are combined is called syntax, but it may be that children use a simpler code before they really begin to use syntax. The simpler code is based on the meaning of words (semantics) rather than on the way words are used in a sentence (syntax).

The syntactic interpretation of children's first word combinations is seen in an experiment in which a researcher observed and recorded children as they produced **two-word utterances** (3). By carefully recording not only what the children said but the situation in which they said it, it was possible to discover different meanings for children's two-word utterances. "Mommy sock," for instance, could mean "Mommy put on my sock" in one situation and "This is mommy's sock" in another situation. By making use of knowledge of the situation in which an utterance was made to find out what the utterance seemed to mean, the researcher concluded that children use syntactic rules, such as *subject-object*, *verb-object*, and *subject-verb*, in producing their two-word utterances. It was also suggested that at this stage children understand and use more complex syntactic structures, such as *subject-verb-subject*, in generating sentences, even though they may be able to use only two of the three parts of the sentence.

Although this interpretation of children's early word combinations fits in with the way adults use syntax in word combinations, it may be that children at this stage still do not have an understanding of syntax. Abstract categories, such as *subject* and *verb*, and abstract relationships, such as *subject-verb*, are not taught to 2-year-olds, and they may even be too complex to be understood by such young children. Instead, it is possible that children's first word combinations are based on their understanding of words (semantics) rather than on the rules of syntax (6).

The **semantic code**, which includes classes and relationships of words, might be a simpler code for children to break than the more abstract **code of**

syntax. This is similar to the code that the chimpanzee, Lana, is being taught. The syntactic class *verb*, for instance, is broken down into the simpler semantic classes of *action verb* and *nonaction verb*. *Hit, push, take,* and *kick* are action verbs. *Want, need,* and *like* are nonaction verbs. If children treat all of these words as belonging to the syntactic class *verb*, then both action and nonaction verbs should be seen in children's first utterances. But this is not the case. Action verbs are used more often, and for some children the use of action verbs seems to be a necessary development before they begin to use nonaction verbs or show an understanding of the syntactic class *verb* (7).

The syntactic classes *subject* and *object* also seem to be preceded by less abstract semantic classes of nouns, such as *agentive* (one who initiates an action) and *dative* (object or person affected by an action verb). These simpler noun classifications might then develop into the broader, abstract classifications of *subject* and *object*. In this manner the more concrete semantic classifications could be the basis for later development of the more abstract syntactic classifications. This explanation of the beginning of syntactic development fits in with Piaget's description of cognitive development from the early concrete thinking stage to the more abstract thinking of later stages.

Syntactic Development

Neither cognitive development nor language development follow the same timetable in all children. Some children say their first word at 12 months of age and begin to combine words at 18 months. Others may be slightly ahead or a month or more behind this schedule. Therefore, age does not appear to be the best way to judge children's syntactic development. One solution to this problem is to group children according to their average or **mean length of utterance** (MLU). This is usually calculated by the number of morphemes in an utterance. For example, *birthday* and *hits* contain two morphemes each (the *s* sound is considered a morpheme, as are other word prefixes and suffixes). *Cooky, is,* and *Connecticut* contain one morpheme each. So if a child utters "Want cooky" and "See doggy," the average or mean length of utterance would be $(2 + 3)/2 = 2.5$ MLU.

Roger Brown has used mean length of utterance as a method of grouping children into five stages of syntactic and semantic development (10).

Stage I	1.0 to 2.0 MLU
Stage II	2.0 to 2.5 MLU
Stage III	2.5 to 3.0 MLU
Stage IV	3.0 to 3.75 MLU
Stage V	3.75 to 4.50 (and beyond) MLU

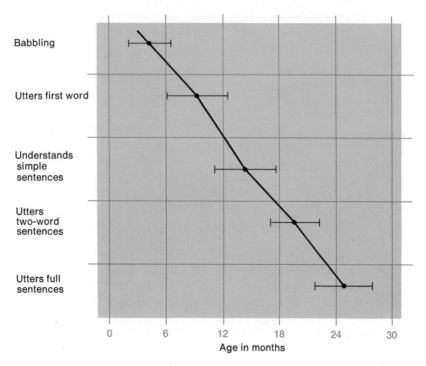

The range and average age for several landmarks of verbal behavior.

Children may differ slightly in the time which they reach these stages, but Brown and others found that within a given stage children seem to use the same set of rules in generating sentences.

Early Stage I children use mostly simple semantic rules such as *agent + action* ("Baby push") and *action + object* ("Bite finger"). Other important developments in Stage I are the increased use of subjects that, semantically, are not agents ("Tower fall down"), Wh-questions ("Where cookie?"), and negatives ("No bed").

Having acquired a basic set of semantic rules and possibly some syntactic rules, children in Stage I still have trouble making themselves understood, especially by people other than their parents or those close to them. In Stage II they begin to use some grammatical morphemes (see Table 8-1) that allow them to be much more precise and to communicate more efficiently. Stage II also marks the beginning of noun and verb inflections (meaningful changes of tone at the ends of words), prepositions, and use of the verb *to be* in its various forms and articles. The use of these morphemes begins in Stage II, but

Table 8–1 The 14 Basic Grammatical Morphemes and the Developmental Order in Which They Generally Emerge, Beginning in Stage II

Forms	Examples
1. Present progressive	eat-*ing*
2. *In*	*in* chair
3. *On*	*on* floor
4. Plural	hat-*s*(/s/), ball-*s*(/z/), house-*s*(/iz/)
5. Past irregular	*broke, came, got*
6. Possessive	cat's(/s/), dog's(/z/), horse's(/iz/)
7. Uncontractible copula	*am, is, are, be*
8. Articles	*a, the*
9. Past regular	roll-*ed*(/d/), walk-*ed*(/t/), wait-*ed*(/id/)
10. Third person regular	want-*s*(/s/), tell-*s*(/z/), push-*es*(/iz/)
11. Third person irregular	*does, has*
12. Uncontractible auxiliary	*is, are*
13. Contractible copula	I'*m*, it's(/s/), he's(/z/), we're(/r/)
14. Contractible auxiliary	I'*m* pushing, it's pushing, he's pushing, we're pushing

continues to increase through Stage V as children show more and more knowledge of syntax.

In the later stages of syntactic development children gradually learn to change the basic sentence structures of Stage I and Stage II to form, in Stage III, yes-no questions ("Are you sleeping?"), complex Wh-questions ("Who was sleeping after we left?"), imperatives, or commands ("You sleep right now!"), and negatives ("You can't sleep now."). Even more complicated sentences are constructed in Stage IV. By Stage V children know enough about semantics and syntax to produce an utterance such as, "Although we have been rained upon, our spirits are not dampened!". Such a verbal (as well as cognitive) accomplishment is a long way from the simple *agent + action* utterances of Stage I.

Considering the amazing accomplishments children make as they progress from a cry to single-word utterances to the production of semantically correct complex sentences, it is not surprising that some theories have suggested that children begin their language development with some advance knowledge of the basic rules of the game. But recent studies of language development suggest that the advanced syntax of older children seems to be based on the acquisition of basic semantic rules that, in turn, are closely related to cognitive development.

From a single-word utterance to a semantically correct sentence is a long way, but most children have acquired the major rules of their language by the time they are 4 years old. Language development does not stop there, however. More complex syntactic rules continue to be acquired through the age of 10, and another necessary part of language, the **vocabulary,** continues to grow long past the age of 4.

One way to study vocabulary development is to count the increasing number of words children use as they grow older (see Table 8-2). This method shows that children's knowledge of words increases steadily and rapidly, but it does not explain how the vocabulary develops. In other words, it does not explain the process by which children acquire new words and organize the meanings of those words in their vocabularies.

Several recent studies suggest that children's knowledge of words and their meanings changes in several important ways before they are able to assign the same meanings to words that adults do. It seems that children begin by using only one or two obvious features of a word's meaning. Thus, a child's utterance, "bow-wow," might mean almost any animal. The child's definition of "bow-wow" seems to contain only its major feature—animal. Later, when other features begin to be added—such as shape—"bow-wow" might mean

Table 8-2   Vocabulary Growth as a Function of Age

Age (Years, Months)	Number of Words	Increment
0; 8	0	
0; 10	1	1
1; 0	3	2
1; 3	19	16
1; 6	22	3
1; 9	118	96
2; 0	272	154
2; 6	446	174
3; 0	896	450
3; 6	1222	326
4; 0	1540	318
4; 6	1870	330
5; 0	2072	202
5; 6	2289	217
6; 0	2562	273

Table 8–3 A Sample Instance of Overgeneralization and Restructuring[a]

		Word	Semantic Domain	Possible Criterial Feature(s)
Stage I		bow-wow	dog(s)	shape
Stage II		bow-wow	dogs, cows, horses, sheep, cats	shape
Stage III	(a)	bow-wow[b]	dogs, cats, horses, sheep	
	(b)	moo	cows	sound (horns?)[c]
Stage IV	(a)	bow-bow	dogs, cats, sheep	
	(b)	moo	cows	sound
	(c)	gee-gee	horses	size (tail/mane?)
Stage V	(a)	bow-wow/doggie	cats, dogs	size
	(b)	moo	cows	
	(c)	gee-gee/horsie	horses	
	(d)	baa	sheep	sound
Stage VI	(a)	doggie	dogs	
	(b)	moo	cows	
	(c)	gee-gee/horsie	horses	
	(d)	baa lamb	sheep	
	(e)	kitty	cats	shape, sound

[a] Cf., e.g., data in Ament (1898), Grégoire (1937), Leopold (1948), Lewis (1937), Perez (1892) and Shvachkin (1948).
[b] There may be some overlap in the use of the two words if *new* animals are seen at this point.
[c] Size may be an important factor: e.g. Shvachkin (1948) found that *vava* was used for dogs and *mu* for cows and big dogs.

any of several animals of a particular shape, including dogs, cows, horses, sheep, and cats. Eventually more specific features (size and sound) are added to the definition. These features narrow down the semantic category, and fewer animals are called "bow-wow." As other words are added to the child's vocabulary (cow, horse, sheep, cat), only those features that are specifically doglike are contained in the child's definition of "bow-wow" (see Table 8–3). This "semantic-features" hypothesis for the acquisition of a vocabulary suggests that children begin by using only one or two general semantic features in defining a word and then go on to add more and more features until the child's definition matches that of adults (13, 14).

The gradual acquisition of semantic features helps explain the overgeneralizations that most young children make as well as the confusion they exhibit in learning terms that have to do with relationships (*more* versus *less*), prepositions (*in, on, under*), verbs (*ask* versus *tell*), and complex nouns (*brother* and *sister*). In learning to use these words children usually begin with a large semantic category (in which a word is defined by few features) and gradually add those features that bring the word into the smaller category used by adults.

The first relational objectives that children begin to apply correctly are usually the most general pair, *big–small*. They use these words by about the age of 4, but often use them in a general manner to represent the contrasting aspects (positive versus negative) of more specific adjective pairs, such as *long–short, thick–thin, deep–shallow, tall–short, wide–narrow, young–old,* and *high–low* (12, 39).

Studies of children's understanding of relational adjective pairs show how children progress from a general to a more specific semantic definition of such words. Three- to 7-year-olds, for instance, were shown two cardboard apple trees that had different numbers of apples on them (17). The children were asked, "Does one tree have more or less apples on it than the other?" Most of the 3-year-olds thought that *less* and *more* both meant *more*. These children seemed to be defining both words according to a single meaning (quantity). Older children were able to understand *less* and *more* because, it seems, they were able to focus on the specific factors of contrast between the words rather than on the general factor of quantity (33). Similar results have been found for other relational adjective pairs (18). In each case, 3-year-olds appear to identify the member of each pair that could serve as a dimensional name, usually the positive member of the pair. For example, *tall* is usually used to refer to the dimension of height. People ask "How tall are you?" not "How short are you?" Children tend to use *tall* first in their definition of dimension or height and later learn the meaning of the negative or contrasting word, *short*.

Even more confusing than relational adjectives for young children are the conjunctions *before* versus *after* and verbs such as *come* versus *go* and *bring* versus *take*. This confusion is seen in an experiment in which 3- to 5-year-olds were asked if they knew what was happening first in sentences such as, "Before I patted the dog, I jumped over the fence" and "I patted the dog after I jumped over the fence." Younger children understood neither word (*before* or *after*) but simply relied on the order of words in the sentence to interpret what had happened first (11).

Before they distinguish the semantic features of *before* and *after*, children also go through a stage in which they think that before and after mean the same thing. The same type of confusion seems to exist with regard to the meanings of *come* and *bring* and *go* and *take* (15). Six-year-olds believe that *go* and *take* mean *come* and *bring*, respectively. It is not until approximately 9 years of age that children have sorted out all of the necessary semantic features to distinguish between *come* and *go* and *bring* and *take*.

A final example of vocabulary development is seen in the acquisition of features used to define *brother* and *sister*. At first, children treat *brother* the same as *boy* and *sister* the same as *girl* (see Table 8–4). Later, children recog-

Table 8-4   Two Early Stages in the Development of the Semantics of "Brother"

Stage I	*Lo* [aged 5; 0]
	   What is a sister?
	      A sister is a girl you know.
	   Are all the girls you know sisters?
	      Yes, and all the boys are brothers.
	
	Kan [aged 7; 6]
	   What's a brother?
	      It's a boy.
	   Are all boys brothers?
	      Yes.
	   Is your father a brother?
	      No, because he's a man.
	
	Sob [aged 7; 0]
	   Is your father a brother?
	      Yes, when he was little.
	   Why was your father a brother?
	      Because he was a boy.

Stage II	*So* [aged 8; 0—an only child, not sure if he himself is a brother]
	   A brother is when someone has a child, well the child who comes next
	   is a brother.
	
	Hal [aged 9; 0]
	   What's a brother?
	      When there's a boy and another boy, when there are two of them.
	   Has your father got a brother?
	      Yes.
	   Why?
	      Because he was born second.
	   Then what is a brother?
	      It is the second brother that comes.
	   Then the first one is not a brother?
	      Oh no, the second one that comes is called brother.

nize that the meanings of *brother* and *sister* require other children in the family and that age is not related to the definition of either. The final determining feature in the definition of these words is related to cognitive development and the concept of reversibility ("If Jimmy has a brother named Johnny, then Johnny has a brother named Jimmy"; or "If Susie has a sister named Sally, then Sally has a sister named Susie"). This reversible relationship is learned at about age 10 or 11 when, according to Piaget, the cognitive operation of reversibility has been mastered.

From these examples it can be seen that throughout early childhood and adolescence vocabulary development depends on the continuing changes in the organization of the semantic factors that define words. This process is closely related to the acquisition of semantic and syntactic rules and to cognitive development.

LANGUAGE AND COGNITION

In this chapter language development has been linked in various ways to cognitive development. This is because there are some quite obvious links between language and cognition. Most people, for instance, use some sort of "inner speech" or "self-communication" in their thinking and cognitive processing. In fact, people are so dependent on the language-thought relationship that it is almost impossible to think about certain things without relying on language. (Try to think about everything that happened yesterday without using words.) In addition to thinking, many aspects of learning are related to language. Children learn from what they are told, and they eventually begin to learn from what they read. They then use language to think about what they have been told or what they have read. Memory, too, is dependent on language in many ways. Information can be more easily remembered if it is translated into symbols (words) and then mentally rehearsed (see Chapter 6).

Even though the link between language and thought may be obvious, the exact relationship between the two is not known. Language, for instance, is not necessary for all types of thought. Musicians can think about music without using words, and artists are usually very good at thinking in images. In fact, all people use both of these types of thinking in their daily activities. Infants, before they have any language ability, show signs of cognition; and deaf people, with very little language ability, can think and solve problems mentally.

The fact that language seems to be necessary for some but not all types of cognition has led to the proposal of different theories to explain the link between language and thought. At one extreme are theories suggesting that language determines thought processes. For example, if a language has eight different words for different types of snow (wet snow, dry snow, driven snow, fallen snow, and so on), the people who use that language will be able to think more precisely about snow than people who have only one or two words for snow. Such a theory suggests that language actually controls what people are able to think about and how they understand the world. On the other hand, if a group of people who had never seen snow before and had no words for it were suddenly stranded at the North Pole, they would probably begin to think very seriously about snow, with or without words. This represents the opposite extreme in the language-thought question. According to Piaget, cognitive development does not depend on language. Thought, says Piaget, exists independently of language. This can be seen in the fact that cognitive development begins early in life, long before children have uttered their first word. But even if thought and language are independent, it cannot be denied that language is an important tool in many types of cognition. This also seems to be the conclusion of recent brain research.

It is becoming increasingly clear that language and verbal abilities are mainly controlled in the left hemisphere of the brain, while musical and spatial types of cognition are controlled by the right hemisphere. This would suggest that language is extremely important for some types of thinking but not necessary for others. But since both hemispheres and both types of cognition (verbal and spatial) are important, neither should be neglected.

SOCIAL FACTORS AND LANGUAGE

Because language is so important to cognition, it has been suggested that children who are deficient or inferior in language abilities for one reason or another may be deficient in thinking abilities and, therefore, may be lower in intelligence than children who have well-developed language abilities. The most dramatic example of this is probably seen in comparisons of middle- and lower-class children. Middle-class children tend to be more advanced than lower-class children in vocabulary development, sentence structure, and pronunciation (40). Some educators and psychologists feel that this might contribute to the poor performance of lower-class children in school as compared with that of middle-class children.

Several researchers have attempted to determine exactly how middle- and lower-class language differs. Two hypotheses have been developed. One suggests that **lower-class language** is actually deficient or less well developed than **middle-class language.** The other hypothesis suggests that the two styles of language are equally useful but different (in the way that the Chinese and English languages are equal but different).

Studies conducted in Great Britain demonstrate the **deficiency hypothesis** (1, 2). The different speaking styles of lower- and middle-class people were compared, and two general styles of language were defined—**restricted** and **elaborated.** The researcher found that lower-class speech tends to use a restricted code consisting of simple, concrete statements that are limited in expressiveness and the amount of information they contain. Middle-class speech, on the other hand, tends to be more varied and complex and often contains references to feelings and logic. Examples of these styles of speech might be a middle-class parent who says: "Would you keep quiet for a minute? I want to use the phone" and a lower-class parent who says: "Shut up." This does not mean that middle-class parents never say "shut up"; it just means that they tend to use a more elaborated style of speech more often than do some lower-class parents. Since a child's language environment is believed to be important to the rate of progress in using language, constant exposure to a restricted type of language might lead to a language deficiency and to the use of a restricted style of speech by the child. (See Figure 8–2.) Considering the fact that success in school (especially on tests) is often dependent on elaborated language, social-class differences in language could have far-reaching effects.

Figure 8–2 Restricted versus Elaborated Language Styles

One of the most important differences in individual language styles is seen in the degree to which language is used for elaborative (versus restrictive) purposes (27). The following example illustrates this point: The situation involves 5-year-olds who have discovered a jack-in-the-box in the corner of a day care center.

1. Restricted Style

Caregiver	*First Child*
(a) "What's that you have?"	(a) "I got this thing!"
(b) "What?"	(b) "This thing!"
(c) "What?"	(c) "You know. This thing in that box."
(d) "What is it?"	(d) "I dunno."
(e) "Can you do anything with it?"	(e) "I dunno."
(f) "Have you tried turning the handle?"	(f) "Hey!"
(g) "What happened?"	(g) "This man come out!"
(h) "Do you like it?"	(h) "Yeh."

2. Elaborated Style

Caregiver	*Second Child*
(a) "What's that you have?"	(a) "A box from the toy chest."
(b) "What?"	(b) "This box. I think it's a toy."
(c) "What is it?"	(c) "A box with different colors on it."
(d) "Can you do anything with it?"	(d) "Well—I's'pose I could use it to build something with maybe."
(e) "Have you tried turning the handle?"	(e) "Look! When you turn this little handle a tiny clown pops up!"
(f) "Do you like it?"	(f) "S' funny, but I was kinda scared at first 'cause it 'prized (surprised) me. I think I'll go and scare someone else." (*Child leaves*)

These illustrations demonstrate the degree to which children differ in the manner in which they describe their impressions. The comments of the first child are relatively restricted. Although this does not mean that the child's actual thinking about the jack-in-the-box is lacking, it would be difficult for an observer to tell just what the child's impressions were. By contrast, the impressions of the second child are expressed much more elaborately and completely.

While the relationship between social class and language style is not clear, it seems likely that the kind of early language environment a child encounters will strongly affect how that child learns to use language. Because of this, language models—adults and older children who elaborate ideas and feelings for children—are probably extremely important in the development of a style of speaking (27). To illustrate further, consider the following example. The situation involves mothers and their children riding together on a bus in heavily congested traffic. In each case the mother is holding her 3-year-old child on her lap (2).

1. Restricted

Mother	Child
"Hold on tight."	"Why?"
"Hold on tight."	"Why?"
"You'll fall."	"Why?"
"You'll get hurt!"	"Why?"
"I told you to hold on tight, didn't I?"	

2. Elaborated

Mother	Child
"Hold on tightly."	"Why?"
"If you don't, you will be thrown forward and fall."	"Why?"
"Because if the bus suddenly stops, you'll jerk forward onto the seat in front of you."	"No, I won't."
"You won't if you hold on tightly."	

As can be seen, the "styles" represented above differ in degree of elaboration in syntax and vocabulary, in focus on clarifying ideas, particularly cause-effect relationships, and in amount of unnecessary repetition. The mother using the more elaborated style is perhaps more consistent with the style usually associated with formal language, particularly the language of most classrooms in the United States.

This social deficiency hypothesis helps explain why some children do poorly in school, but what it is saying, in effect, is that one language is better than another. It is like saying that Chinese-speaking children are less intelligent than English-speaking children because they can't pass a test given in English. This line of thinking has led to an alternate hypothesis based on differences rather than deficiencies in language usage. It has been argued, for example, that the restricted code does not indicate deficiencies in lower-class children but deficiencies in the tests used to measure the abilities of such children (16). Just as a test written in English is not the best way to assess the abilities of Chinese-speaking children, a test written in elaborated language may not be a fair way of testing children who use a restricted code. According to this argument, the poor performance of lower-class school children is the result of language differences, not of language or cognitive deficiencies. Since most school tests use middle-class language as a standard, there is little chance that lower-class speech could prove to be anything but deficient on such tests.

The **difference hypothesis** suggests that lower- and middle-class speech are basically equivalent. That is, both are effective systems of communication within their respective environments. Applying this theory, however, does little to help people who use a restricted code. They are at a disadvantage not only in the school system but in the legal system and many areas of the business and economic world, where the elaborated code is used.

Attempts to change this situation have been based on both the deficit and the difference hypotheses. The deficit approach suggests that an effort should be made to teach all children middle-class language. Because the most important language achievements occur during the preschool years, this approach calls for systematic language training beginning at an early age.

The difference hypothesis suggests that greater social recognition should be given to the fact that lower-class language is not deficient. Lower-class speech, instead, should be encouraged in certain areas, such as the lower grades. But since middle-class language is likely to remain the standard in most areas of life, it too should be part of all educational programs. In other words, the educational system should be flexible in its encouragement of different language codes.

One area of confusion that exists in discussions of language ability is that between social differences and ethnic differences. **Black English,** the ethnic dialect or variety of English used by many blacks in the United States, is not the same as lower-class or restricted English. Studies of black English have found it to be the functional equivalent of standard English rather than a collection of errors and omissions made by people who have failed to learn standard English or who fail to understand it. Black English, however, is not the language of the school system, so children who use it, no matter what social class they belong to, would be expected to be at a disadvantage in school.

This is a serious problem for many children. Whether this problem is due to language deficiencies, language differences, or other language problems is not completely understood. These and other questions about language and its special role in human development are being answered, however, as research continues on the evolution of language, the ability of animals to use language, the role of the brain in language, the link between cognition and language, and the semantic and linguistic properties of language.

SUMMARY

The possession of language and speech has always been considered one of the chief characteristics that distinguishes humans from all other species, and language has always been closely associated with questions about human nature, such as learning, cognition, social behaviors, and the possibility of possessing and passing on information. While the evolution and origins of language are not completely understood, what is known serves as a basis for understanding the development of language in children.

Language is a system of symbols with commonly recognized meanings. Manipulation of these symbols enables humans to communicate with each other. The basic units of sound used in a language are phonemes. The basic units of meaning are morphemes. Syntax has to do with the way words are arranged to form meaningful phrases and sentences. The rules of grammar consist of all the rules for the construction of words, phrases, and sentences as well as the meaning and pronunciation of words.

The complexities and uniqueness of human language have been demonstrated in a number of serious attempts to teach chimpanzees to communicate with humans. Through such experiments researchers hope to find out more about the nature of language and about the problems many children have learning a language.

Brain research is another area that is leading to a better understanding of language ability. In most humans the left hemisphere of the brain controls speech and language abilities. Damage to the language areas of the left hemisphere can result in disruption of language abilities. If such damage occurs early in life, there is a chance that the right hemisphere can take over some of the language functions of the left hemisphere.

Theories of language development are similar to those used to explain cognitive development. Learning theory suggests that the processes involved in learning (including conditioning, imitation or modeling, and reinforcement) can account for the rapid development of language in children. A second theory, based on the existence of language areas in the brain, suggests that humans may be genetically programmed with basic language abilities that do not have to be learned. A third theory suggests that children produce or generate novel sentences after they have acquired certain basic rules about language.

The first sign of speech development is evident immediately after birth when infants demonstrate their ability to vocalize by crying. During the first year of life infants go through several stages of vocalization (including the pseudocry, cooing, babbling, and, finally, patterned speech sounds). By about 9 months of age they usually begin to attempt to produce meaningful words, and most children speak clearly by the age of 5.

Studies of single-word and two-word utterances suggest that children's first meaningful words and word combinations may be based on the concrete rules of semantics (the meanings of words) rather than on the more abstract rules of syntax (the rules for combining words). This explanation of the early stages of language development fits in with Piaget's description of cognitive development, from early concrete stages to the more abstract thinking of later stages.

Studies of the mean length of utterances of children have helped outline five stages of syntactic development in children. Children progress from single-word utterances to syntactically correct utterances of four or more words by the time they are 4 years old.

Vocabulary development increases steadily and rapidly during childhood. Some researchers have suggested that this increasing knowledge of the meanings of words develops as children gradually add more specific semantic features to the meanings they give to words.

Language and cognition are closely related, as is seen in the fact that most people use words or "inner speech" in many of their cognitive processes. Some theories suggest that language actually determines thought processes. Others (including that of Piaget) suggest that cognitive development does not depend on language. In either case, language is an important tool in such things as learning, memory, and most types of cognition.

Social factors are also important in language development. Middle-class children tend to be more advanced in vocabulary development, sentence structure, and pronunciation. Studies also suggest that lower-class language may be more restricted than middle-class, elaborated language. Lower-class children who do use a restricted form of English are probably at a disadvantage as far as schooling is concerned because most schools use the elaborated form of language with which they may not be familiar. This may lead to learning problems that could be far-reaching.

Semantic Development in Children

"Semantics" refers to the development of meaning. The progression of language meaning is closely related to cognition. Initially children use words holophrastically. (In infant speech a "holophrase" refers to a single word or a phrase used to express a sentencelike meaning. Examples are "Daddy" may mean "I see Daddy" or "Daddy is in bed and I see him.") McNeill (1970) points out that the child develops a "holophrastic dictionary." This dictionary is cumbersome, since the infant may pair a specific word to several meanings, and the word is thus susceptible to ambiguity. This ambiguity can be reduced when the child creates a "sentence dictionary," in which a word is paired with a single sentence interpretation. With additional experiences, however, the "sentence dictionary" also becomes too burdensome for the child. At this point, according to McNeill, the child moves to construct a "word dictionary." The move to a "word dictionary" necessitates a complete reworking of the child's semantic system. In the holophrastic stage the child stores undifferentiated information; with the "word dictionary" the child begins to elaborate a system of semantic features.

For example, when children are at the stage of constructing the holophrastic or sentence dictionary, they may learn the word "doggie." Since the children have no other word for animals, they will say "doggie" whenever they see a cat, a horse, a cow, and so on. At a later stage, with the acquisition of the word dictionary children will observe that the *dog* is an *animal;* the *cat* is an *animal;* and so on.

In learning a language children must learn the attributes that belong to a given concept, as well as the attributes that do not belong. According to McNeill, this process is known as *horizontal vocabulary expansion.*

Most of the words preschool children acquire are learned in this fashion. Thus, for children to acquire a fixed meaning for a term they must learn that a dog has hair, four legs, a tail; but it does not say "meow," and it cannot contract its claws.

As children learn the specific attributes for a concept (dog) they also master other related concepts (cat, lion) and form a word group (animal). This word grouping (animal) is called a *semantic cluster.* Having constructed a semantic cluster, it is fairly easy to add additional concepts (horse, guinea pig, cow) to this grouping. McNeill refers to this process as *vertical vocabulary expansion.* Vertical acquisition occurs much faster than horizontal acquisition and may involve learning fewer words during the early years.

By 6 to 8 years of age children will have mastered phonetic and syntactic development. At age 7 sentence structure will be similar to that of adults, and generally the 44 phonemes will have been acquired. Semantic development continues throughout the life of the individual.

Semantic development is an important part of language development and cognition. Language is practically the only way in which to assess cognitive thought. Language promotes thought and develops along with cognitive growth.

From D. McNeill, *The Acquisition of Language.* New York: Harper & Row, 1970; D. McNeill, "The Development of Language." In P. H. Mussen (ed.), *Carmichael's Manual of Child Psychology.* New York: Wiley, 1970.

**RESEARCH
REPORT 8.2**

Norms in Language Development

Age	Vocabulary	Syntax	Phonology	Semantics
0–3 wks.	—	Crying	Capable of producing front vowel sounds	—
3 wks–5 mos.	—	Pseudocry, cooing	Vocal cords changing to allow greater variety of sounds	Communicates pain, anger, hunger
6 mos.	—	Babbling, multisyllables	P, M, A	Uses holophrases
1 yr.	3 words	First words often "MaMa" or "PaPa," repetition of syllables	T, K, G, I, U	Holophrastic dictionary
2 yrs.	270 words	Holophrastic speech, telegraphic speech, 2–3 words (MLU), negative sentences, Wh- questions		Addition of sentence dictionary
3–4 yrs.	1,500 words	3–4 words (MLU), "ing" and "ed" verbs, "to be" verb forms (copula), inflections	B, M, W, H, D, N, G, NG, Z (as in *azure*), th (as in *thick*)	Addition of word dictionary, sentence dictionary partially remains
4–5 yrs.	2,000 words	Major rules of language now acquired, complex sentences, rhyming	V, R, CH, J, SH (as in *shut*)	Horizontal language expansion
5–6 yrs.	2,500 words	"If" and "so" clauses, play (pun) sentences.	F, L, HW, ZH, TH (as in *that*)	Semantic clusters
6–7 yrs.		Iteration, sentence structure similar to adults	Full mastery of 44 phonemes, continues to learn rules of phonology	Vertical language expansion

Adapted from J. Osborn and D. Osborn, *Cognitive Tasks: An Approach for Early Childhood Education.* Athens. Ga.: Education Associates, 1974.

REFERENCES

1. Bernstein, B. "Social Class and Linguistic Development: A Theory of Social Learning." In A. H. Hakey, J. Floud, and C. A. Anderson (eds.), *Education, Economy and Society*. New York: Free Press, 1961.
2. Bernstein, B. "Social Structure, Language and Learning." In J. P. DeCecco (ed.), *The Psychology of Language, Thought, and Instruction*. New York: Holt, Rinehart and Winston, 1967.
3. Bloom, L. *Language Development: Form and Function in Emerging Grammars*. Cambridge, Mass.: MIT Press, 1970.
4. Bloom, L. *One Word at a Time*. The Hague: Mouton, 1973.
5. Bloom, L., L. Hood, and P. Lightbrown. "Imitation in Language Development: If, When, and Why?" *Cognitive Psychology*, 1974, *6*, 380–420.
6. Bowerman, M. "Structural Relationships in Children's Utterances: Syntactic or Semantic?" In T. Moore (ed.), *Cognitive Development and the Acquisition of Language*. New York: Academic Press, 1973, 197–213.
7. Bowerman, M. "Relationship of Early Cognitive Development to a Child's Early Rules for Word Combination and Semantic Knowledge." Paper presented at the American Speech and Hearing Association meetings, Las Vegas, Nev., 1974.
8. Broen, P. "The Verbal Environment of the Language-learning Child," *American Speech and Hearing Association Monograph*, 1972, *17*.
9. Brown, R. "Development of the First Language in the Human Species," *American Psychologist*, 1973, *28*, 97–106.
10. Brown, R. *A First Language: The Early Stages*. Cambridge, Mass.: Harvard University Press, 1973.
11. Clark, E. "On the Acquisition of the Meaning of 'Before' and 'After'," *Journal of Verbal Learning and Verbal Behavior*, 1971, *10*, 266–275.
12. Clark, E. "On the Child's Acquisition of Antonyms in Two Semantic Fields," *Journal of Verbal Learning and Verbal Behavior*, 1972, *11*, 750–758.
13. Clark, E. "What's in a Word? On the Child's Acquisition of Semantics in His First Language." In T. Moore (ed.), *Cognitive Development and the Acquisition of Language*. New York: Academic Press, 1973, 61–110.
14. Clark, E. "Some Aspects of the Conceptual Basis for First Language Acquisition." In R. Schiefelbusch and L. Lloyd (eds.), *Language Perspectives: Acquisition, Retardation, and Intervention*. Baltimore, Md.: University Park Press, 1974, 105–128.
15. Clark, E., and O. Garnica. "Is He Coming or Going? On the Acquisition of Deitic Verbs," *Journal of Verbal Learning and Verbal Behavior*, in press.
16. Cole, M., and J. S. Bruner. "Cultural Differences and Inferences about Psychological Processes," *American Psychologist*, 1971, *26*, 867–876.
17. Donaldson, M., and G. Balfour. "Less Is More: A Study of Language Comprehension in Children," *British Journal of Psychology*, 1968, *59*, 461–472.
18. Donaldson, M., and R. Wales. "On the Acquisition of Some Relational Terms." In J. Hayes (ed.), *Cognition and the Development of Language*. New York: Wiley, 1970, 235–268.
19. Goldenson, R. M. "Language." In *The Encyclopedia of Human Behavior*. New York: Doubleday, 1970, 671–675.

20. Guess, D., W. Sailor, and D. Baer. "To Teach Language to Retarded Children." In R. Schiefelbusch and L. Lloyd (eds.), *Language Perspectives: Acquisition, Retardation, and Intervention*. Baltimore, Md.: University Park Press, 1974, 529–563.

21. Hockett, C. F., and S. A. Altman. "A Note on Design Features." In T. A. Sebok (ed.), *Animal Communication*. Bloomington: Indiana University Press, 1968.

22. Ingram, D. "Phonological Rules in Young Children," *Journal of Child Language*, 1974, *1*, 49–64.

23. Karelitz, S., R. Karelitz, and L. Rowenfeld. "Infants' Vocalizations and Their Significance." In P. Bowman and H. Mantner (eds.), *Mental Retardation: Procedures of the International Medical Conference*. New York: Grune & Stratton, 1960, 439–446.

24. Lenneberg, E. H. "On Explaining Language," *Science*, 1969, *164*, 635–643.

25. Lieberman, P. *Intonation, Perception, and Language*. Cambridge, Mass.: MIT Press, 1967.

26. Lind, J. "Newborn Infant Cry," *Acta Paediatrica Schandinavica*, 1965, Suppl. *163*.

27. McCandless, B., and E. Evans. *Children and Youth*. Hinsdale, Ill.: Dryden Press, 1973.

28. McNeill, D. "The Development of Language." In P. Mussen (ed.), *Carmichael's Manual of Child Psychology*, Vol. 1. New York: Wiley, 1970, 1061–1161.

29. Miller, J., and D. Yoder. "An Ontogenetic Language Strategy for Retarded Children." In R. Schiefelbusch and L. Lloyd (eds.), *Language Perspectives: Acquisition, Retardation, and Intervention*. Baltimore, Md.: University Park Press, 1974, 505–528.

30. Nelson, K. "Structure and Strategy in Learning to Talk," *Monographs of Social Research in Child Development*, 1973, *38* (1–2).

31. Nelson, K. "Concept, Word, and Sentence: Interrelations in Acquisition and Development," *Psychological Review*, 1974, *84*, 267–285.

32. Osgood, C. E. *Method and Theory in Experimental Psychology*. New York: Oxford University Press, 1953.

33. Palermo, D. "More about Less: A Study of Language Comprehension," *Journal of Verbal Learning and Verbal Behavior*, 1973, *13*, 211–221.

34. Premack, D. "Language in Chimpanzees?" *Science*, 1971, *172*, 808–822.

35. Skinner, B. F. *Verbal Behavior*. New York: Appleton-Century-Crofts, 1957.

36. Snow, C. "Mother's Speech in Children Learning Language," *Child Development*, 1972, *43*, 49–565.

37. Snow, C. "Mother's Speech Research: An Overview." Paper presented at the Conference on Language Input and Acquisition, Boston, Mass., Sept. 1974.

38. "Talking to the Quiet Brain," *Science News*, 1975, *108*(2), 22.

39. Tashiro, L. "On the Acquisition of Some Non-comparative Terms." Senior honors thesis, Stanford University, 1971.

40. Templin, M. C. *Certain Language Skills in Children*. Minneapolis: University of Minnesota Press, 1957.

41. Thorpe, W. H. "The Comparison of Vocal Communication in Animals and

Men." In R. A. Hinde (ed.), *Non-verbal Communication*. Cambridge: Cambridge University Press, 1972, 27–47.

42. Trotter, R. J. "I Talk to the Animals," *Science News*, 1973, *103*(22), 360–361.
43. Trotter, R. J. "From Language to Linguistics and Beyond," *Science News*, 1975, *109*(21), 332–334.
44. Trotter, R. J. "Language Evolving," *Science News*, 1975, *109*(24), 378–383.
45. Trotter, R. J. "The Other Hemisphere," *Science News*, 1976, *109*(14), 218–223.
46. Witelson, S. F. "Sex and the Single Hemisphere," *Science*, 1976, *4251*, 425–427.

I ntelligence is one of the most prized of all human characteristics. Attempts to define and measure intelligence have not always been successful, but as more is learned about intelligence it becomes increasingly clear that environmental stimulation is an important factor in fostering the intellectual development of children.

intelligence

INTRODUCTION: THE MILWAUKEE PROJECT

"Amazing." That's what was said about the achievements of John Stuart Mill, the eminent nineteenth-century English philosopher and economist. What was amazing was the fact that by the time he was 8 years old he had read the Greek and Latin masters in the original and was teaching them, as well as geometry and algebra, to other children. These enormous mental accomplishments and Mill's subsequent intellectual fame were apparently the result of the intensive early training he received from his father.

"Amazing" is a term that has also been applied to a more recent intensive training program—the Milwaukee Project. In the 1960s, infants from one of the worst slum areas of Milwaukee were selected as subjects for an early intervention and enrichment program. The idea was to enrich the lives of these children by providing them with a variety of experiences that they would not normally have. It was hoped that such **intervention,** or outside interference, would have a beneficial effect on the development of the children.

In 1971, director of the program Rick Heber of the University of Wisconsin released some preliminary results. The children in the experimental program (at 42 months of age) were scoring more than 30 points higher on intelligence tests than a similar group of children (the control subjects) who had not taken part in the program. Some of the experimental children scored as high as 135 on the intelligence tests (100 is normal or average on an IQ or intelligence test).

Psychologist Rick F. Heber (1932–   ).

"Amazing," said some people. Others were more skeptical. They said the follow-up period hadn't been long enough. Many expected the apparent intellectual gains of the experimental group to vanish, especially after they entered school. Five years later, in 1976, another follow-up report was made. The children of the Milwaukee Project had been in school for three years, and their intellectual gains had not vanished. They were still scoring between 20 and 30 points higher than the control children (33).

The Milwaukee Project grew out of Heber's concern that virtually the entire national research effort in the field of mental retardation was being directed at that aspect of the problem associated with obvious physical abnormalities (see the discussion of chromosomal abnormalities and mental retardation in Chapter 2). Heber, former director of President John F. Kennedy's Panel on Mental Retardation, believed that too little effort was being directed toward the most common form of mental retardation, so-called sociocultural or cultural-familial retardation—mental retardation (IQ range of 50 to 75) that exists in the absence of any identifiable nervous system disorder and is found to run in families from economically depressed areas. Of all individuals defined or classified as mentally retarded, nearly 80 percent fall into the cultural-familial category. The neglect of this type of retardation could be attributed, says Heber, "to the long-held and widely accepted view that cultural-familial mental retardation was genetic in its origin and, therefore, nonpreventable save through socially unacceptable measures to limit reproduction."

In order to find a more acceptable method of reducing the rate of this type of retardation, Heber and his colleagues attempted to discover whether the condition was caused by genetic or environmental factors. They did this by conducting a series of surveys in a section of Milwaukee characterized by census data as having the city's lowest average family income and education level and the highest rate of unemployment and population density per living unit. It was the typical urban slum of the 1960s. Though the area contained less than 3 percent of the city's population, it accounted for about 35 percent of the total number of children classified as "educable mentally retarded"— mildly retarded but still capable of learning.

Since many children born and reared in the slums do develop and learn normally in the intellectual sense, the researchers concluded that something other than economic conditions must be responsible for the high rates of mental retardation. Survey data revealed that mothers with IQs below 80 (less than half of those tested) accounted for almost 80 percent of the children with IQs below 80. In addition, the lower the maternal IQ, the greater the probability of offspring scoring low on intelligence tests.

The survey results convinced the researchers that the very high prevalence of mental retardation associated with slums is concentrated within individual families who can be identified on the basis of maternal IQ. In other words, the source of the high degree of sociocultural mental retardation appeared to be the retarded parent residing in the slum environment rather than the slum itself in any general sense. Says Heber: "Our simple casual observation suggested that the mentally retarded mother residing in the 'slum' creates a social environment which is distinctly different from that created by the 'slum-dwelling' mother of normal intelligence."

To test this hypothesis Heber and his colleagues began a long-term intervention program in the survey area. During a period of more than one year, 40 newborn infants and their mothers (with IQs below 75) were selected and put in either experimental or control groups on a month-by-month basis. The sample was confined to black families because of the substantially lower mobility of black families in that particular section of Milwaukee. The researchers didn't want to begin work with families who were likely to leave the city.

The experimental families began an intense rehabilitation program with two primary emphases: the vocational rehabilitation of the mothers and a personalized enrichment program for the newborns that began in the first weeks of life. In addition to vocational help, the mothers received some training in homemaking and child-care skills.

The infant program began in the home with daily visits from a teacher. When the children reached about 3 months of age, the program continued in a special education center on a year-round basis, five days a week, seven hours a day until the children were eligible to enter first grade at age 6.

John Stuart Mill's special education program was successful in many respects, but his father, James Mill, was criticized for neglecting his son's social and physical development. The boy was sickly. The Milwaukee Project attempted to avoid such problems. The general goal of its education program was to provide an environment and a set of goals that would allow the children to develop to their fullest potential intellectually, socially, emotionally, and physically. Language development and cognitive skills, however, were emphasized.

In order to assess the effects of the program the children were tested often on a variety of measures—medical evaluation, general intelligence tests, experimental learning tasks, measures of mother-child interactions, and a number of measures of language development. They were tested bimonthly during the first two years and then monthly through age 6. Both groups took identical tests on a schedule keyed to birth dates. No significant differences were found between experimental and control groups on medical or physical evaluations, but on every other measure the experimental children did much better. Differences in problem-solving ability and language development were especially significant. The experimental children were able to enter school, says Heber,

The Milwaukee Project began with a personalized enrichment program which allowed the experimental children to enter school with the language skills and aptitudes needed for learning.

"with the language skills and aptitudes which they need for learning, and which could so easily have remained dormant."

Language skills also played an important role in the differences noted in mother-child interactions between the groups. In mother-child interactions sophisticated behavior, such as the initiation of problem-solving behavior by verbal clues or prods and the organization of tasks with respect to goals, is usually fostered by the mother. But when the mother has a low IQ, the interaction is often more physical than verbal and less organized. This was the case with the control children and their mothers. The experimental children, however, when interacting with their mothers, took responsibility for guiding the flow of information and provided most of the verbal information and direction. They often structured the interaction by questioning or by teaching their mothers. In turn, the mothers of these children began imitating or modeling some of the behaviors of their children and consequently, began to use more verbal reinforcement and more verbal response. The experimental children seem to have become "educational engineers" in interactions with their low-IQ, low-verbal mothers.

A variety of intelligence tests were used throughout the study to measure intellectual gains and to compare the groups. The findings of these tests can be questioned, admits Heber, because repeated practice with the tests (for both groups) will have had some effect on the results. But what is more important, he says, is the continued difference between the two groups. From 24 to 72 months, the experimental group maintained a 20- to 30-point advantage over the control group (120.7 compared with 87.2 at 6 years of age). At 9 years of age, three years after entering school, the experimental group was still performing at or above normal and maintaining more than a 20-point IQ advantage. After entering school the performance of both groups did drop, as expected, but not as much for the experimental group as had been predicted. The drop for these children can be explained as an adjustment problem, as one case shows. One little girl tested well above average in reading on a pre-first-grade test, but during the first two months of first grade she decided that she did not want to talk. Possibly she was angry about no longer being with her preschool teachers. Because of the child's refusal to speak, her teacher decided to put her back in kindergarten. But just before the change was to be made, the child walked up to the teacher's desk, opened a book, and read fluently from it. A shocked teacher called in her supervisors to witness the event. From then on the child was a model student.

No John Stuart Mills have been produced by the Milwaukee Project, but what has been accomplished can be described as amazing. The researchers correctly identified a group of children who were likely to become mentally retarded. This is seen by the fact that at 96 months of age, one third of the control group scored below 75 on IQ tests, even after repeated practice with the tests. Presumably, the experimental children would have scored about the same if it had not been for the intervention. Not only were the researchers able to identify children who might later be classified as mentally retarded; it appears that they were able to do something to prevent that retardation. None of the experimental children scored below 75, and only two scored as low as 88.

These results are impressive, but some questions remain to be answered. Why, for example, did some of the experimental children do better than others? Were the original selection procedures strict enough to ensure that all of the children were physically equal at the start of the study? Was the intervention treatment the same for all of the children? Also, because the researchers intervened in so many areas of the children's lives, it is not possible to determine exactly which of the intervention procedures may have affected the intellectual development of the children. Some of these questions may be answered as follow-up continues with the children and as more data are released, but similar studies with larger numbers of children will probably have to be conducted before all of the questions are answered. In the absence of such studies, the results of the Milwaukee Project will have to be considered as tentative or preliminary. Even so, the data so far have impressed many people.

Whether or not the results of the Milwaukee Project are seen as amazing depends on one's point of view. Many people believe that every child is born with a certain predetermined intellectual potential and that intelligence does not change much throughout life. If that is the case, then it is surprising that the experimental children should have been able to do so well and score so much higher than the control children.

On the other hand, many people believe that intelligence is not determined at birth and that the way children are reared has a great deal to do with their intellectual achievements. Psychologist J. McVicker Hunt, for example, has for many years been examining the effects of the environment (or "life history," as he calls it) on early development. Long ago he came to the conclusion that the environment plays an extremely important role in intellectual development and that there is a great deal of plasticity or flexibility in early development. Hunt wasn't surprised at all by the results of the Milwaukee Project. "What did happen," he says, "is just a demonstration of what can happen."

The Milwaukee Project suggests what can happen, but in order to understand what did happen several questions must first be answered:

What is intelligence?

How is intelligence measured?

Why do some children seem to be brighter or more intelligent than others?

How much of a person's intelligence is determined by inherited genes and how much by the environment?

Does intelligence change during a person's lifetime or is it static and unchangeable?

INTELLIGENCE

Throughout the years of the Milwaukee Project the researchers charted the progress of the children in several areas of development and made many measures of what is commonly called **intelligence.** But in order to measure something, that something must first be defined. This has not proved to be an easy task with regard to intelligence. Almost everyone has some idea of what intelligence is, and most people agree that intelligence is an extremely important and valuable human characteristic. Few people agree, however, as to exactly what intelligence is. In fact, the more thoroughly intelligence is investigated, the more complex it seems to be.

Intelligence has, first of all, a genetic component. That is, intelligence depends to some degree on the physical equipment each child is born with. This includes the brain, nervous system, sense organs, and so on, the development of which is determined to some extent by genetic factors. For example, if environmental conditions have been the same or nearly the same for two children and intellectual differences are found between the children, these differences can be assumed to be due in part to genetic differences.

The best evidence that genetic heritage makes a difference in intelligence probably comes from studies of twins. Identical twins possess what amounts to identical heredity with each other (see the discussion of twin studies in

Chapter 2). IQ tests administered to identical twins who have been reared together show that they are usually similar in measured intelligence. Nonidentical twins, those who have slightly different genetic backgrounds, do not exhibit as much similarity in measured intelligence as do identical twins.

Since many carefully controlled studies have demonstrated that similar genetic heritage usually results in similar intellectual abilities, there is little doubt that genes do play a role in intellectual development. What is in doubt is exactly how much of a role genes play in determining intelligence. A great deal of research time and effort has gone into attempts to determine the influence of genes on intelligence, but so far no conclusive evidence has been found that says exactly how much genes affect intelligence. All that is known for sure is that both nature and nurture—genes and the environment—contribute to the development of intelligence, as they do to all areas of human development. It is also known, or at least suspected, that the more complex the human structure or function under consideration, the more likely it is that the environment or nurture plays an important role in shaping it. The environment has little to do with eye color, for example. It has more to do with weight and height. It is almost certain that it has much more to do with intellectual functioning.

There is little that can be done about nature or heredity. As was mentioned in Chapter 2, selective breeding and attempts to control reproduction lead to serious ethical and moral questions.

There is much that can be done about nurture or the environment, as the Milwaukee Project suggests. Therefore, it is probably better to concentrate on the environmental effects on intelligence (as this chapter does) until such time as more is known about the facts of the relative contributions of nature and nurture to the development of intelligence.

Defining Intelligence

Early in this century intelligence was believed by some people to be a unique type of energy or force that each individual had more or less of. Charles Spearman, a pioneer in work with the concept of intelligence, suggested that intelligence could be represented by one general or *g* factor that influenced all conscious behavior (28). The more one had of this *g* factor, the more intelligent one was supposed to be. Because not all intelligent people have the same abilities, Spearman proposed the existence of several special or *s* factors related to specific areas of intelligence. These *s* factors included such things as mathematical, musical, artistic, and motor abilities.

Spearman's two-factor theory of intelligence (*g* and *s*) was only the starting point. Investigators who followed him found human intelligence far too complex to be explained by only two factors. In 1938, L. L. Thurstone proposed a model of intelligence based on seven pure or primary factors, each relatively independent of the others (32). His primary mental abilities were **numerical**

ability, word fluency, verbal meaning, memory, reasoning, spatial relations, and **perceptual speed.** There is little doubt that these seven abilities are important aspects of intelligence, but even seven seems too small a number to define intelligence. Continued research has led to more complex explanations of intelligence involving many interrelated factors.

Guilford's Structure of Intellect

One of the most influential explanations of intelligence to be proposed in recent years is that of J. P. Guilford (8). He sees intelligence as problem-solving ability but says this ability is made up of 120 factors. These factors can be pictured as a three-dimensional cube. This model represents what Guilford calls the **structure of intellect (SI).**

According to Guilford's model an intelligent behavior consists of three things: an **input** of information (which he calls **content**), **processing** of that information (**operations**), and an **output** (**product**). In order to account for the complexity of the human intellect, Guilford proposes several types of content, operations, and products.

The four classes of content are **figural, semantic, symbolic,** and **behavioral.** Figural relates to information that can be dealt with in its physical or concrete form, such as visual or auditory (sound) input. This can be seen in a test of spatial relations or memory for musical themes. Semantic content has to do with meanings in language and also in other forms of representation, such as

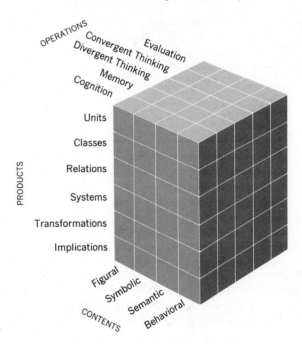

Guilford's structure of intellect.

diagrams or cartoons that tell a story. Symbolic content deals with symbols of meaning apart from semantics, such as the symbols in algebra, musical notation, or electronic diagrams. Behavioral content refers to matters of "social intelligence," such as the ability to interpret gestures or facial expressions.

Guilford's operations refer to the ways in which the mind processes the four types of input. The first type of operation is called **cognition,** which consists of knowing or identifying a specific input. Another operation is **memory,** the ability to store and retrieve information. In addition to these, Guilford lists three more complex operations. **Convergent production** consists of the ability to bring together (converge) a variety of information in the production of a new piece of information. The operations of logic and arithmetic, for instance, require the use of various inputs in order to reach an answer (see the discussion of logical thought in Chapter 7). **Divergent production** is the opposite type of operation. It consists of producing several correct responses to one input. A test of divergent production might consist of asking children to give several possible titles for a story or captions for a photograph. This type of operation is related to hypothesis formation and creativity (see the discussion of creativity tests in Chapter 7). **Evaluation** is the fifth of Guilford's mental operations. It is similar to hypothesis testing in which the value of a product (the solution to a problem) is judged. Evaluation goes on in all stages of intelligent behavior as inputs, operations, and products are constantly being evaluated.

In addition to the four classes of content and the five mental operations, Guilford lists six types of product or output. These are the results of operations on inputs. The products may be **simple units** (such as the name of an object), **classes** (a category name, such as fruit), **relations** (connections between units and classes), **systems** (including such things as outlines or mathematical equations), **transformations** (changes in relations), and **implications** (results of combinations, transformations, and so on).

As can be seen, Guilford's structure of intellect offers a complex explanation of intelligence. Any of four classes of content can be operated on in five different ways to produce six types of product. The result of this ($4 \times 5 \times 6$) is 120 factors of intelligence. These factors, and perhaps several others yet to be discovered, can provide a more precise meaning of the thing people call intelligence.

Intelligence As Problem-solving Ability

Learning abilities, cognitive abilities, language, memory, motivation, perception, motor skills—all of these factors, as well as the ability to use them efficiently in a variety of different situations—are included in attempts to understand intelligence. But since intelligent behavior almost always comes about as an attempt to solve some sort of problem, it is often convenient to think of intelligence simply as **problem-solving ability.**

Different environments, however, present different types of problems. Therefore, intelligence must be understood as a relative concept. What is intelligent behavior in one environment, culture, or part of society may not be appropriate or intelligent under a different set of circumstances. The problems faced by children in the slums of Milwaukee, the deserts of Australia, and the suburbs of Los Angeles are different, and each requires a different type of intelligence or problem-solving ability. For children going through the school system in the United States, intelligence is probably most often defined as the ability to solve the problems on intelligence tests.

MEASURING INTELLIGENCE

Some children are obviously quicker, brighter, or more intelligent than others, and for years attempts have been made to measure what appear to be differences in intelligence. Some of the first attempts to measure mental abilities were based on physical reaction times. In 1816, F. W. Bessel, a German astronomer, was working with a group of people who were using telescopes to observe celestial events, such as comets. Bessel found that certain individuals took longer to react to what they were observing. A sort of mental quickness seemed to be involved, and attempts were made to measure this quickness as a factor in intelligence. In 1883, Sir Francis Galton, a younger cousin of Charles Darwin, suggested that a variety of other mental reactions could also be measured. He set up a laboratory and invented machines to test all sorts of sensory reactions. In 1890, J. McKeen Cattell, an experimental psychologist, brought Galton's test to the United States and began testing his college students. These students, in turn, helped spread the idea of mental testing throughout the United States. In most cases what these early psychologists were measuring were sensory reactions rather than what are today considered to be mental abilities or intelligence.

The Binet-Simon Test

The first important measures of intelligence began in France in 1905. Alfred Binet, a prominent psychologist of the time, began studying thought processes by having his two young daughters solve simple problems and report on how they had reached their solutions. Next, Binet began to investigate the approaches to problem-solving used by several famous artists, mathematicians, and chess players, as well as a number of people who were mentally retarded. His findings led him to the conclusion that the sensory reactions being studied by Cattell and others were not enough to explain such complex mental powers as imagination, memory, and comprehension. Binet began to design a number of test problems that would help explain these higher mental abilities known as intelligence.

While Binet was involved in these studies, he was asked by the French government to develop a test that could discriminate between schoolchildren

Psychologist Alfred Binet (1857–1911).

who were mentally deficient and those who had normal mental abilities. He began this project with the assumption that retarded children learn very slowly and therefore would not know as much as normal children of the same age. What was needed, Binet decided, was a test that most French children of a certain age could pass. Any child of the age group being examined who could not pass the test might possibly be retarded. Working with Théophile Simon, Binet developed a set of tests of verbal and numerical abilities that could discriminate among children of various ages. One test, for example, contained a group of simple questions that most normal 5-year-old French children should be able to answer. Another set of problems was developed for 6-year-olds, another for 7-year-olds, and so on. A 5-year-old, for example, should be able to count up to four and draw a square. An 8-year-old should be able to count backward from 20 to 0. All of these tests were given to a great many children until Binet and Simon knew exactly which questions should be answered by the average children of each age group.

With the **Binet-Simon tests,** French schoolteachers were able to tell a child's **mental age.** If a 5-year-old could answer all of the questions on the test for 6-year-olds, that 5-year-old would be considered to have a mental age of 6 (as opposed to a **chronological,** or actual, **age** of 5). By comparing a child's mental age and chronological age, teachers were able to tell which children were having problems. If the tests showed that a 10-year-old had a mental age of only 5, the teachers could assume that the child was mentally retarded in some way or had some other serious problem.

These first tests of intelligence proved to be accurate enough to do more than test for mental retardation. With them, teachers could tell how poorly or how well students were doing in school, and they could predict how children would perform in future years. If a 7-year-old could pass the tests for 7-year-olds, that child would be considered normal. If the same child could only pass the test for 6-year-olds, then extra help might be called for. If the 7-year-old solved all of the problems on the test for 9-year-olds, that child was considered to be doing better than average and could be predicted to continue performing above average in many cases.

IQ

The Binet-Simon tests proved to be so useful with French schoolchildren that L. M. Terman and a group of psychologists translated them into English and made them appropriate for use with schoolchildren in the United States. The test they developed, the **Stanford-Binet,** has since become one of the most widely used intelligence tests in the United States.

In addition to translating the tests and otherwise strengthening them, Terman introduced the term **IQ,** or **intelligence quotient.** This numerical designation of intelligence was originally derived by dividing mathematical age by chronological age and multiplying by 100. A 7-year-old, for example, who passes the test for 7-year-olds has a mental age of 7 and an IQ of 100 $(7 \div 7 \times 100 = 100)$. Whenever mental age and chronological age are equal, the IQ will be 100, and this is considered to be normal or average. If a 7-year-old and a 9-year-old both receive scores of 100, this does not mean that they are equal in intelligence. The 9-year-old will have had to pass a more difficult test. So IQ tells only how well a child is doing with respect to that child's age group. IQ does not give a general or overall measure of intellectual capacity.

Because general mental development, except for vocabulary growth and specific intellectual skill learning, slows down after late adolescence, mental age ceases to be meaningful after the age of 16 or 18. For example, an 18-year-old might score 100 on an intelligence test for 18-year-olds and be considered normal. But if the same formula were used to rate a 36-year-old who solved exactly the same number of problems on the same test, the 36-year-old would score only 50 $(18 \div 36 \times 100 = 50)$, well below average. Such a score would be quite misleading, since both individuals, having solved the same problems, would be well within the range of normal for adults. Because the use of mental age can lead to this type of confusion, most test designers now use a slightly different formula to calculate IQ. Instead of using mental age, a standard or average score is arrived at after many people within an age group have taken the test. Each individual's score is then divided by the average score, and the resulting number is multiplied by 100.

Standardization

In order to test accurately the intelligence of anyone, a test must be used that takes into account that particular person's background. A test for children who have lived on a farm all of their lives, for example, might have to be different from a test for children reared in the city. But no two people are ever exposed to the exact same set of experiences, so in order to be completely accurate, a different test would have to be designed for each individual. Making a new test for each person, however, would be impractical. Binet got around this problem by designing a test that was **standardized,** or based on the standards of a large group of children with similar (but not quite the same) backgrounds. He included questions that children from each different segment of French society should be able to answer. On such a test a few exceptional children could be expected to do better than others, and a few would do poorly, but most should score in the standard, or average, range.

When the Binet test was used with children in the United States, it not only had to be translated, it had to be altered in certain ways to account for the differences in background between French children and those in the United States. Some questions had to be taken out and others put in. Then the test could be given to a large number of children, and their scores would indicate whether or not the test was accurately standardized. Any test that is standardized for a particular group should yield what is known as a **normal distribution** of scores for that group. In other words, most children being tested should score in the normal range, near 100 IQ. Only a few children should score very much above or below the norm. When the scores of a test with a normal distribution are plotted on a graph, the result is a curve shaped like a bell. If we can accept the assumption that intelligence is a normally distributed

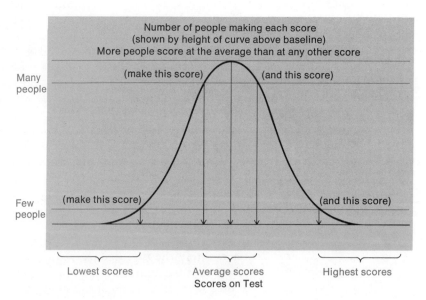

A bell-shaped curve of intelligence.

characteristic, any IQ test that does not yield a bell-shaped curve when given to a large group of people is probably not a valid indicator of intelligence for the people of that group.

IQ has become almost a key to certain types of success in the United States. Even though a high IQ does not necessarily mean that a person will be a success in later life, IQ does open certain doors that lead to high-paying careers. IQ often determines what college a person goes to and whether or not he or she qualifies for medical, law, or some other graduate school. Because IQ tests are often used to make decisions that can influence a person's entire life, **psychometricians,** the experts who design intelligence tests, take special care to construct tests that will be fair and accurate for all who take them.

Standardization and use of the bell-shaped curve of normal distribution help to ensure that a test is relatively fair and accurate, but there are two other factors that are taken into account when IQ tests are designed. The tests are supposed to be reliable and valid.

A yardstick is a reliable measure of distance. A yardstick is always 36 inches long, and every inch is always exactly the same length. If a football field is 100 yards long the first time it is measured, it will still be 100 yards long the second, third, and fourth times it is measured. IQ or related scholastic aptitude scores should be reliable enough to give the same results time after time. Someone who has an IQ of 110 on Monday should be able to take the same test on Tuesday, Wednesday, and Thursday and still score 110. A test that gives such results would presumably be reliable.

Unfortunately, IQ tests are not as reliable as yardsticks. The person who scored 110 on Monday might have some personal problems or a headache on Tuesday. Such problems might interfere with concentration and cause that person to score 100 on Tuesday. The same person might be highly motivated and feel much better and score 120 on Wednesday. By Thursday, that person might score even higher after having practiced with and gotten used to the test. Or, the test taker might be bored with the same test and do worse than on Monday.

Test designers examine their tests for **reliability** by having people take the same test two or more times. Even so, a completely reliable test is difficult to design. There are just too many factors involved, such as motivation, health, and experience. Each can affect the reliability of a test. Unlike yardsticks, IQ tests don't always give exactly the same results.

Validity is almost as difficult to achieve as reliability as far as IQ tests are concerned. A valid test is one that accurately measures what it says it will measure. IQ tests should measure intelligence. But, as has been seen, there is little agreement as to exactly what intelligence is. Even when intelligence is broadly defined as problem-solving ability there are different types of problems that must be faced and solved by people from different backgrounds. For people from each of these environments, intelligence might mean something slightly different. Because intelligence can mean so many things to so many people, a completely valid measure of intelligence is not easy to design.

If IQ tests are neither completely reliable nor totally valid, why does almost every schoolchild in the United States take these tests, and why is so much attention paid to the results? IQ tests have been found useful because they can sometimes indicate a child's potential for achieving success in the present school system. Most IQ tests are designed by people who have gone through the school system for children in that system. They are usually standardized on the intellectual norms of middle-class children who are a major part of the school system in the United States. Being designed by the people who are products of a certain system and constructed for people in that system, IQ tests reflect the values of that system. In other words, most IQ tests measure those mental abilities that are especially valuable or useful for success in the middle-class schools of the United States.

Because they are designed for a particular group (middle-class students), IQ tests are most reliable and valid when applied to that group. They are less useful when applied to minority groups—blacks, Spanish-speaking people, Orientals, and lower-class children of all races. Blacks, for example, usually score lower on IQ tests as a group than do middle-class whites. Orientals usually perform better than whites.

The fact that middle-class children usually outperform lower-class and some minority children does not mean that middle-class children are more intelligent than children from these other groups. It does mean, however, that most middle- and upper-class children are better prepared to succeed in middle-class schools than are most lower-class and minority children.

One explanation for the success of the experimental children in the Milwaukee Project is that they were taught many of the problem-solving behaviors necessary for success in IQ tests and for later success in school during their intensive day-care training. If these children had spent their early years at home with their families (like the control children), they probably would not have developed the kinds of abilities necessary for success on IQ tests.

Group Tests

IQ tests have proved to be accurate at predicting school success for a large group of children, so even though complaints are made that these tests are unfair to minority groups, the use of IQ tests has become widespread. Since the Binet test was first introduced, a number of intelligence tests have been designed, and many of them are now being used (Table 9–1). Most schoolchildren have taken at least one and probably several of these tests. The Binet tests, however, were designed to be given on an individual, or on a one-to-one, basis. An examiner sits down with a child and goes through each question.

Table 9–1 Commonly Used Intelligence Tests

Individually (clinically) Administered Tests	Group-administered Tests, Mostly Verbal
A. Entirely or largely verbal (use language in testing and also test language skills)	Cooperative School and College Ability Tests (SCAT)
All "Binet" tests, especially the Stanford-Binet	California Test of Mental Maturity (CTMM)[1]
Illinois Test of Psycholinguistic Abilities[2]	Primary Mental Abilities Test (PMA)[2]
The Merrill-Palmer Scales	Differential Aptitude Tests (DAT)[2]
Peabody Picture Vocabulary Test	IPAT Culture Fair Intelligence Test
McCarthy Scales of Children's Abilities[1]	Lorge-Thorndike Intelligence Tests
Wechsler's Tests[1]	
Wechsler Intelligence Scale for Children (WISC-R)	
Wechsler Preschool and Primary Scale of Intelligence (WPPSI)	
Wechsler Adult Intelligence Scale (WAIS)	
B. Nonverbal or "performance"	
Columbia Test of Mental Maturity	
Raven Progressive Matrices	
Pintner-Patterson Scale	
Leiter International Performance Scale	
Bender-Gestalt	
Wechsler's Tests (same list as above)[1]	

[1] Has nonverbal component.
[2] Yields multiple scores based on psycholinguistic or factor theory.

Today most children are more familiar with **group tests** in which an examiner administers a test to a whole classroom. This method of testing saves a lot of time, but group tests present several problems. Individual tests allow for close contact and communication between the examiner and the person being tested. Group tests, which are often scored by machine, do not offer such personal contact. Children who do not understand the instructions or who have some other difficulty may have trouble getting their problems taken care of. The case of a 6-year-old named Myrna illustrates the type of problem that group testing sometimes presents.

Individual tests allow for close contact and communication between the examiner and the person being tested.

In the group test Myrna was taking several items required that a mark be made on a drawing. For example, in one item a hen was pictured in the left-hand margin of the test booklet. The hen was separated from four other objects by a vertical line. The objects pictured to the right of the line included a baseball, a palm tree, a square, and a hen. All of the 6-year-olds in this particular group setting were asked to "make a mark on the one to the right that is like the one to the left." In this case the hen to the right was exactly like the one to the left, so a mark was to be made on the right-hand drawing of the hen. Myrna, a careful child who had been taught to do things neatly, misunderstood the directions. She had been taught never to mess up drawings. Thus, for the hen item and all others like it in the test, she carefully blocked in the entire outline of the drawing. This took so much time that she finished only a few items, while most of the other children completed the test. When the tests were graded the teacher considered only the overall number of answers each child got correct. Myrna, for obvious reasons, did not get very many right.

Myrna's parents were called in the next day and told that their daughter was "rather slow" and should probably be held back. There was even a possibility that she would have to be put into a class for slow-learning children. Myrna's parents were surprised because they were sure that their daughter was not a slow learner. They convinced the teacher, who reexamined Myrna's test booklet and found out what had gone wrong. On a retest, clearly understanding that it was permissible to make checkmarks on the drawings, Myrna did quite well. If Myrna's parents had not intervened, she might have been put into a special class. Such classes can usually be a great deal of help to children who are having learning problems, but such classes can also cause problems for the children assigned to them. Myrna's friends and other teachers might have begun to regard her as a "slow learner" and treated her as such. This treatment can result in a loss of self-confidence and cause even greater problems to the individual.

When IQ tests are properly administered and properly scored, they can be quite useful. But because testing errors can have serious consequences, and because IQ tests seem to be unfair to lower-class and some minority groups, it has been argued that such tests should not be used at all. This argument has not stopped the use of IQ tests, but it has alerted people (including test designers and test users) to the fact that IQ tests do have some shortcomings and that they must be used and interpreted with great care and caution.

Verbal and Performance Tests

The two abilities most often evaluated by intelligence tests are **verbal** and **performance,** or nonverbal, abilities. IQ tests usually examine language abilities in several ways. They often call for spoken or written responses to spoken or written directions; and they usually call for some sort of demonstration of cognitive abilities based on language. Verbal tests may include vocabulary items (What is an orange?), likenesses (In what way are wood and coal alike?), analogies (Birds fly, fish _____.), memory (Repeat back a sentence or list of numbers.), and arithmetic reasoning (If three pencils cost 24¢, how much does each pencil cost?).

Other items that do not test language abilities directly may still call for some kind of verbal manipulation, such as a test item that calls for the rearranging of cartoons into a story sequence. Purely nonverbal or performance tests attempt to avoid all use of language. In a performance test a child may have to point to a missing part of a bicycle, assemble a puzzle, find the odd object among three or four similar objects, or sort a variety of shapes into categories.

In addition to verbal and performance tests, IQ tests may sample mental speed (a higher score for more completed problems), intellectual power (problems ranging from quite simple to extremely difficult), and breadth or scope of intelligence (a wide range of information is asked for). The two most commonly agreed-on factors in intelligence, however, are verbal and performance.

What Do IQ Tests Measure?

There is little doubt that IQ tests are good measures of problem-solving ability. There is some question, though, as to whether or not measures of problem-solving ability add anything to our understanding of what intelligence is. According to some researchers, the concept of IQ has not helped identify the types of information involved, the learning conditions that govern information processing, or the motives to process information (13, 16). Nor has the concept of IQ served to show how the structures of intellectual ability build upon each other in psychological development. It has also been argued that IQ tests do not offer useful information on the nature of learning, concept formation, and reasoning processes, and that they do not relate closely to socially valued adult skills (35). In other words IQ tests only give an indication of "what" a child can do. They provide little understanding of "how" the child does it, and this is seen by some people as a major restriction on our full understanding of intellectual processes (5).

Because IQ tests are better at measuring the quantity of information a child has than the quality of the child's intellect, many psychologists have called for a new approach to the assessment of intelligence, one that will provide information on the developmental processes involved. J. McVicker Hunt, for one, has suggested that Piaget's theory and methods of research offer a means of assessing intelligence by characterizing a child's cognitive organization rather than simply placing the child on a numerical scale (14). Several researchers have followed Hunt's suggestion and combined traditional IQ test items with tasks originally used by Piaget in his experiments on cognitive development (see Chapter 7). Others have explored the relationships between Piaget-type tasks and mental abilities of various kinds (5). These approaches seem promising and may eventually lead to a better understanding of intelligence and to better measures of intellectual processes. In the meantime, traditional IQ tests continue to be useful in measuring problem-solving abilities in children and adults, but particularly for predicting achievement in academic settings.

TESTS FOR AGE GROUPS

There are different types of intelligence tests (individual and group, verbal and performance) and different versions of each type. But since Binet's tests were first developed, IQ tests have usually been classified according to the age group for which they were designed. There are infant tests, preschool tests, elementary school tests, as well as tests for adolescents and adults.

Because IQ tests are often used to predict how well a child will do in school, one method of evaluating the accuracy or predictability of IQ tests has been to measure how well the results of an early test relate to or correlate with the results of later tests. A statistical formula is used to calculate the correlation between the results of two tests. A **correlation coefficient** is the numerical expression of this relation. The relation between height and weight in a group of children helps explain how a correlation coefficient is used. First the children are lined up according to height, with the tallest at one end and the shortest at the other. A simple observation will show a tendency for the taller children to be the heaviest and the smaller to be the lightest. There may be a few children who are heavier than those taller than they are, and vice versa. But for the group as a whole greater height will go with greater weight. In other words, height and weight will be positively correlated.

Correlation coefficients, theoretically, can range from a perfect positive correlation (expressed as +1.00) to a perfect negative correlation (−1.00). The condition of a perfect positive correlation between height and weight would be met if the tallest child was also the heaviest, and so on down the line to the shortest and lightest. The more variation between height and weight within the group (such as the third from the tallest being the fifth from the heaviest), the lower the correlation will be. If there is no relationship between height and weight in the group, but simply a chance arrangement, the correlation will be zero. In the unlikely circumstance that the tallest child proves to be the lightest, the next tallest the next lightest, and so on until the shortest child is the heaviest, the conditions for a perfect negative correlation (−1.00) would be met.

Correlation coefficients, when supplied to the results of early and later IQ tests, give a quick indication of how well the early test predicts later performance. The closer the correlation coefficient is to +1.00 (as in an exact one-to-one relationship), the better the predictive power of the early test. A correlation of 0.85, for example, is rather high. A correlation of 0.05 is rather low. A perfect correlation (+1.00) between IQ tests is rare. This would occur only if all children who took the test received the exact same scores on a later test.

Tests of Infant Intelligence

To anyone who knows infants it is obvious that finding test items to sample an infant's intelligence or problem-solving ability is difficult. A problem involves finding the way to a goal. Infants do have goals (they want to be full, dry, warm, and, when awake, they seek various types of stimulation), but they have few direct methods of reaching these goals. Infants depend on adults for the solutions to most of their problems. How then can an intelligence test be designed for infants?

Designers of infant intelligence tests have found several methods of sampling infant behaviors that seem to be related to intelligence. They generally test for sensorimotor responses to changes in the environment, behaviors that indicate social responsiveness, and relatively simple problem-solving activities. Examples of these are, respectively, turning the head in the direction of a bell or light; smiling in response to the smile or voice of an adult; and dropping one or two items in order to grasp a third. In addition, verbalizations in

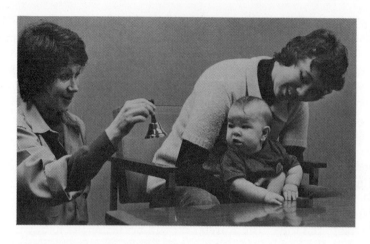

Turning the head in the direction of a bell by an infant is often used as a predictor of later intelligence.

infancy (crying, babbling, and speech sounds) have also been used as predictors of later intelligence. One researcher found a surprisingly high correlation (0.45) between the frequency of outbursts in infants' crying and scores on the Stanford-Binet test at age 3 (20).

Even though some tests of infant abilities do show a slight correlation with later intelligence, there is some doubt as to whether infant tests actually measure intelligence. Most of the items sampled in such tests seem to be related to sensorimotor abilities rather than to purely mental abilities. A child who is advanced in sensorimotor abilities earns a high score, while a child who is retarded or behind in sensorimotor development earns a low score. Sensorimotor alertness, however, plays little part in intelligence items designed for children older than about 40 months. Because infant tests usually measure sensorimotor development (though not necessarily intellectual development), the results of these tests are usually given in terms of **DQ,** or **developmental quotient,** rather than IQ.

In general, measures of DQ taken during the first few months of life do not correlate highly with IQs obtained after 36 or 42 months. It has been found, for example, that scores from one commonly used infant test (the Bayley Mental Test) obtained at 8 months of age cannot distinguish between unusually early-developing or precocious children (IQ greater than 140 at 4 years of age) and children of normal intelligence (IQ of 108). Within the precocious or high-intelligence group correlations between Stanford-Binet IQs and Bayley Mental test scores ranged from −0.08 to +0.4 (34). Other studies have found slightly higher but still relatively poor correlations between infant test scores and later IQ scores.

It is not until infants reach 18 or 20 months of age that their test scores begin to show a promise of relating to later IQ. Only in cases of serious developmental impairment do early DQs accurately predict later IQs in the retarded range. Mild mental retardation of the type seen in the Milwaukee Project is rarely predicted from infant tests given before 18 months.

What is the meaning of the lack of correlation between early DQ and later IQ? Some researchers have suggested that what is "mental" has not sufficiently developed in infants to the point where it can be tested. But according to Piaget, "the structures that characterize thought have their roots in sensorimotor mechanisms" (24). If Piaget is correct, then sensorimotor activities should be a relatively good indicator of later intelligence, and children who are advanced in sensorimotor abilities should have a head start in cognitive development over those whose sensorimotor abilities are less well developed.

Why doesn't this head start show up? Piaget's theory has an answer that has to do with the environment. According to Piaget, cognitive abilities emerge as infants interact with the environment. In a rich and varied environment infants are exposed to different stimuli that they attempt to deal with in terms of their present stage of development. As they do so, they evolve more sophisticated methods of interpreting the environment and move on to more advanced stages of cognitive development. As long as the environment is rich enough to continually challenge an infant, cognitive development will progress through the stages described by Piaget. On the other hand, according to Piaget, if the environment is not stimulating and challenging, cognitive development will be slowed or retarded. If this theory is correct, then DQ and IQ would be expected to correlate closely only if an infant has been kept in a relatively stable environment throughout the stages of development. For example, infants kept in a restricted environment that offers little in the way of stimulation might develop slowly as far as sensorimotor abilities are concerned. If the environment does not change much, these infants would also be expected to develop slowly as far as cognitive and intellectual abilities are concerned. In such a case DQ and IQ would have a high correlation. Under slightly different circumstances infants might be born into an environment that offers just enough stimulation and variety to foster normal physical and sensorimotor development, but not enough to continue challenging the infants as they progress through the later stages of cognitive development. In this case the infants would probably have a normal DQ but a low IQ.

This environmental explanation of cognitive and intellectual development helps explain the lack of correlation between DQ and IQ as well as some individual differences in IQ. Few people are ever exposed to exactly the same environmental experiences, so differences would be expected. Jerome Kagan's study of Indian children in Guatemala (discussed in Chapter 3) is a good illustration of how changes in the environment can affect the course of mental development (19). Kagan and his colleagues compared the early development of Indian infants with later intellectual abilities of children from 5 to 11 years old. The infants were tested for attention to changes in the environment, object permanence, and stranger anxiety, or fear of strangers. The older children were tested on a number of problem-solving tasks. The researchers found the infants to be passive and deficient in most areas of development. The older children showed normal or nearly normal abilities (as compared with the abilities of middle-class children in the United States).

What was most significant about this study was the fact that the Guatemalan infants had been kept in a state of almost total environmental isolation during the first year or so of life. This was done to protect the infants from disease, but the lack of stimulation resulted in what would be considered developmental retardation (as compared with middle-class children in the United States). However, between the ages of 1 and 2 years there was a drastic change in the variety of experiences and opportunities for exploration to which these Indian infants were exposed. From this time on they encountered environmental and cultural demands that seemed to foster rapid intellectual growth, rapid enough for these children to catch up with the norms of middle-class U.S. children by the age of 11 or so. This could not have been predicted from the relatively low DQs of the infants.

Although the methods used to test the Guatemalan children were not quite the same as are usually used in the United States, and the researchers used a cross-sectional rather than a longitudinal approach (they tested different children at different ages instead of the same children at different ages), the results do seem to confirm the importance of the environment in cognitive development. They suggest that sensorimotor abilities are not a good indicator of later cognitive functioning because the powerful effects of the environment can change the course of development. In other words, differences between early and later levels of cognitive functioning (and perhaps between early and later measured intelligence) may be attributable largely to differences in the richness of the environment to which individuals must accommodate at various stages of development. This is also seen in the results of the Milwaukee Project. The experimental children were exposed to a variety of stimulating and challenging experiences beginning shortly after birth and lasting through six years of carefully planned day care. The intellectual development of these children appears to have progressed along normal lines. The control children who were not exposed to an enriched environment on a continual basis seem to have fallen behind in intellectual development.

Infant intelligence tests, as well as studies like those done in Guatemala and Milwaukee, suggest several things. First, it seems clear that a certain "minimal" environment is sufficient for infants to develop cognitively in a quite normal and even advanced way, perhaps up to the time they are 15 or 18 months old. What is minimal? Infants need food, warmth, comfort, and some degree of environmental stimulation. Exactly how much stimulation is needed is not known, but to be on the safe side it is probably best to provide infants with as rich a variety of experiences as is possible, including a good deal of social interaction.

The second thing that is seen from the results of infant intelligence tests is that physically normal children, even in a rather minimum environment like that of the Guatemalan Indian infants, develop basic cognitive skills that they need for coping with their particular environments, although they may be slowed down in later intellectual development.

Third, it seems clear that infant intelligence tests are poor predictors of what a child's cognitive abilities will be at 10 or 11 years of age, although serious retardation can probably be predicted. All in all, it is probably safest to regard infant intelligence tests in much the same way one regards a physical examination: If infants pass a physical examination, it means they are all right then and there, but it is no guarantee that they will continue to stay in good health. A high DQ does not indicate a high IQ any more than a clean bill of health guarantees that an infant will not catch pneumonia within a week or so after the physical exam.

Preschool-age Tests

Once children reach about 2 years of age it becomes possible to test for more of what is usually considered to be intelligent behavior. Verbal test items at the preschool level might include such things as asking children to identify toy objects (miniature cars, dogs, dishes, and the like) or pictured objects such as birds or ships. Performance items for preschoolers include building a low tower from one-inch blocks and fitting simple geometric shapes (circles, squares, triangles) into similarly shaped holes in a flat piece of wood known as a form board. Another item, partly verbal and partly performance, is to identify different parts of the body by pointing to them. These tests, like those for infants, are almost always given on an individual basis. Group tests are not usually used until children are 5 or 6 years old.

Although these intelligence tests for preschoolers do more than measure sensory-motor alertness, they still measure only a limited type of intelligence. Even so, the tests generally used for preschoolers have been found to be more reliable predictors of later intelligence than infant tests. Predictions made from such tests are valuable for such problems as placing children in ability groups, deciding whether or not to let an underage child into kindergarten, and diagnosing mental retardation.

As might be expected, the older children are, the more accurately their preschool test scores predict their intelligence test scores as adolescents and young adults. The increasing correlation can be seen in the results of a longitudinal study that tested children from 6 months of age through 18 years (1). Intelligence tests given at 6 months actually had a slight negative correlation with tests given at 18 years, but after the first birthday correlations became increasingly higher. At 1 year of age the correlation was about 0.25. By 2 and 3 years of age the correlation was up to 0.50, and it continued to increase to more than 0.70 for children at 5, 6, and 7 years of age. In other words, tests given in the early preschool years predict later intellectual development relatively well, although extreme individual variations in mental growth can and do occur from the preschool ages to maturity.

If preschool test scores are a good indication of later intelligence, then the scores of the children in the Milwaukee Project would be expected to hold up. Some studies, however, have indicated that intelligence is not always stable from childhood to adulthood. In one such study 252 children took numerous intelligence tests between the ages of 21 months and 18 years (12). The researchers found that between the ages of 6 and 18 years almost 60 percent of the children changed 20 or more points in IQ. Some children moved rather consistently upward or downward as much as 50 points in score, and their changes tended to be in the direction of the intellectual level of their families. If the home environment was intellectually stimulating and challenging, the scores of the children were more likely to increase than decrease. If the home environment did not provide much in the way of stimulation, scores were likely to go down. The home conditions affected some but not all children, so it is possible that the intellectual gains made by the experimental children in the Milwaukee Project may not hold up for all of the children.

Another major reason why preschool tests don't always accurately predict later performance has to do with the conditions under which a test is taken. As mentioned in the discussion of test reliability, there are a great many factors that can affect test results. Examples of conditions that may produce variations in test scores are tenseness, anxiety, fatigue, and illness on the part of the children being tested. All of these things can interfere with concentration, memory, and test performance in general. Different degrees of relaxation, expertness, familiarity with the child, and warmth on the part of the examiner can also influence test scores. Young children are easily made insecure; their language is not always clear; their attention span is short; and they easily grow tired. An examiner who is not particularly sensitive to such problems in young children may create conditions under which a child will not perform well.

Three separate tests given to the same child illustrate this point: A 3½-year-old girl was tested one morning while she was fresh and alert and in familiar surroundings. The test was administered by an examiner who was warm and leisurely and who was well known to the child. Under these conditions the child did well and scored 163 on the IQ test. As a result she was placed in a kindergarten class for 4-year-olds. A year and a half later the child was reexamined by a brusque, businesslike examiner who was rather bored by the whole process of test administration. The test was given in noisy circumstances near the main playroom of the kindergarten in which the child was enrolled. This test result showed an IQ of 120, and it was recommended that the child be held back for another year in kindergarten. This recommendation was not followed, however, partly because of the earlier test results. Throughout all later schooling the child behaved more in line with predictions based on the 163 IQ than the 120 IQ, so it is probably well that she was not held back. A third test was given under routine circumstances when the child was in the fourth grade, and she scored 150. This example demonstrates both the extreme fluctuations in IQ a child may show under different circumstances as well as the consequences of taking action on the basis of a single intelligence test, particularly one given when the child is more at the mercy of the environment than in later years.

Intelligence Tests for Elementary Schoolchildren, Adolescents, and Adults

As soon as children reach an age when they can follow instructions, concentrate well enough to keep from being distracted, and use a pencil, group intelligence tests can be used. Most intelligence tests are of the group type, although individual tests are sometimes used with older children and adults as well as infants and preschoolers.

Tests for schoolchildren and adults fall into the same general categories as those for younger children: verbal and performance. On verbal tests older children may be asked to define words, ranging from such simple ones as *letter* to such complex ones as *indefatigable;* or to unscramble sentences against a time limit. For example, one minute might be allowed to make sense of the following: *"Town little followed the to dog me."* Adults and older children, in a test of concentration and memory, may be asked to repeat as many as nine numbers read monotonously by the examiner at the rate of one per second; or to give in reverse order as many as seven or eight numbers read in the same fashion. Analogies of different levels of difficulty are often used. A relatively simple example is: *"Sharp* is to *blunt* as *tall* is to _____." Riddlelike situations are also used; and schoolchildren are often asked to read a passage against a time limit and give back as many ideas as they can from the passage.

Performance items consist of such things as assembling elaborate formboard or jigsaw-puzzle tasks against a time limit; running complicated paper-and-pencil mazes; or planning a route to search for an object lost in a field. These are commonly said to be nonverbal or performance tasks, although it has been pointed out that this is probably not an accurate description. From early childhood on children tend to give verbal tags to the tasks on which they are working, even though they do not say the words aloud. This is consciously used verbal mediation, as discussed in relation to memory (see

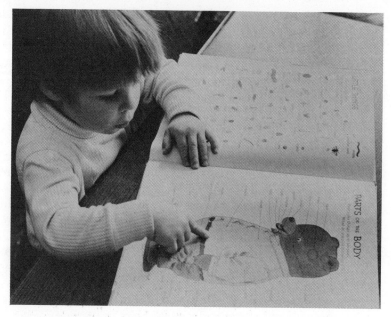

A young child identifying the parts of the body as part of a standardized intelligence test.

Chapter 6). On a maze task, for example, children may say to themselves: "A left turn—no, that's a blind alley—better try a right turn." In other words, there is no clear distinction between verbal and performance items on most intelligence tests, although factors of efficiency, speed, and spatial relationships enter into performance items that do not enter into verbal items. Rather than performance items, some group tests concentrate on the use of numbers, both in computation and reasoning problems. Such tests are usually referred to as quantitative rather than verbal tests of intelligence.

Most tests show that there is a correlation of about .65 between verbal and performance test items. This means that there is a clear tendency for those who do well on one type of test to do well on the other. This correlation can be useful. There is some evidence, for instance, that children of average or near-average verbal IQ, whose performance quotients are much higher, may have reading difficulties more often than would be suspected from their verbal IQ alone.

One reason that group IQ tests are used so often with school-age children is that group tests probably predict school success better than individual tests do. This is because group tests have more in common with school-learning tasks than individual tests do. Schoolchildren ordinarily read or do arithmetic or spelling in groups, and a test taken in a group setting would be more likely than an individual test to predict later group or school performance. Anxious children, for example, may not perform up to their best level on a group intelligence test, just as they may not perform well in a group reading or arithmetic session. Therefore, group test scores would accurately predict school performance, although at a lower level than the child may be capable of without the distraction of anxiety. Calm, efficient children who like competition tend to do well in both types of situations, so either group or individual tests would predict their school performance accurately.

Predicting school success, however, is not the only goal of intelligence testing. Such prediction suggests only how a child is likely to perform, not how well a child could perform. A good school is interested in more than prediction of academic achievement. A common school aim is to help children perform up to their abilities. Individual tests can be of help in achieving this goal. In such tests the examiner reassures the child and attempts to draw the very best performance from the child. If a child scores 20 points higher on an individual test than on a group test, there is an indication that the child may be capable of doing better in school. Special efforts can then be made to help the child become a more efficient student. These efforts may include extra coaching, reassurance, counseling, or a combination of these and other measures.

PATTERNS OF INTELLECTUAL GROWTH

Millions of children and adults have taken IQ tests at various times throughout their lives. The results of these tests give some indication of the rate of growth, the time of leveling off, and the beginning of decreases in all sorts of human behaviors that are roughly classified as "intelligent." Findings vary widely, but there are some general trends of intellectual growth that seem to hold true for most people. Intelligence appears to grow less rapidly with increasing age. More than 40 percent of mature intellectual status has been achieved by 10½ years, for example, and intellectual growth from then on is progressively slower. Some researchers have concluded that no more "intellectual power" is added after about 20 years of age, although individuals can add almost limitlessly to personal skills of all sorts. There is also evidence that intellectual growth may continue longer for bright and superior individuals and stop earlier for individuals of lower intelligence (17). Still other researchers report that intellectual development continues well into maturity for almost all people (2). One reason for confusion on this point has to do with the fact that what is being called intelligence is not always clearly defined. Another reason may be that IQ tests are unfair in some ways to older people. Younger people are probably more tuned in to the particular

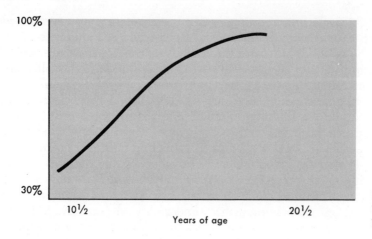

Intellectual growth from 10½ to 20½ years of age.

skills that are asked for on most intelligence tests than are people who have been out of school for many years. This could account for decreasing levels of performance by some individuals as they grow older. One recent study, however, has found that if the same people are followed up for a long period of time, their intelligence seems to increase or stay stable until at least age 60 (25). Even thereafter increases are often observed as long as people are not affected by serious diseases or confined to nonstimulating settings.

During infancy and the early preschool years intelligence increases faster as children grow older (positively accelerated growth). At school age increases in intellectual growth begin to be smaller each year (negatively accelerated). From the teens on intellectual growth is very gradual. These findings represent the regularities or established patterns of intellectual growth and decline. There are, however, individual variations in intellectual development that range from mental retardation at one extreme to genius at the other.

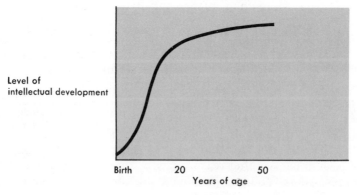

A hypothetical composite age curve representing the growth of intelligence from birth to middle years.

Mental retardation is a general term referring to a condition of inadequate mental development that impairs some people's ability to adjust normally to life. The condition varies by degrees as well as causes and, depending on definitions and age levels, is identified in about 1.5 to 2 percent of the population of the United States (23).

Mental retardation is usually divided into three classes. **Educable mental retardation** or **handicap** (EMR, EMH) is used to signify a mild degree of retardation in children who are otherwise normal and for whom an academic education leading to literacy and the attainment of employment skills is expected. Most children classified as educable mentally retarded get along well as adults and are usually no longer labeled as retarded once they get out of school. This group represents about 80 percent of all mentally retarded individuals, as was mentioned in the discussion of the Milwaukee Project.

Children who are not expected to become fully self-sufficient but who are capable of some education and partial independence as adults are classified as **trainable mentally retarded** or **handicapped** (TMR, TMH). Members of this group can earn wages but often have to live under some sort of sheltered conditions, as in a group home with trained personnel who will help them with various problems that they may not be able to handle on their own. Beyond these two general levels of retardation is a third classification that identifies individuals who have a still greater degree of retardation. Terms such as **developmental disability** are often used to refer to these individuals.

Table 9-2 gives the approximate IQ range and maximum mental ages associated with various levels of retardation. However, it is usual practice not to classify individuals as retarded on the basis of IQ or any other single indicator alone. Only if individuals show serious social incompetence as well as intellectual deficiency are they characterized as mentally retarded. Overdependence on IQ, especially in the educable mentally retarded range, may result in the making of a "false positive" diagnosis and the labeling of indi-

Table 9-2 Common Terminology Related to IQ and MA in Mental Retardation

Typical IQ Range	Approximate Maximum MA Expected	School Terminology	Clinic and Hospital Terminology
50 to 70	10	EMR, EMH	Mildly mentally retarded
25 to 50	7	TMR, TMH	Moderately mentally retarded
Up to 25	4	Developmental disability	Severely or profoundly retarded

viduals as retarded who, though limited, are capable of independent and reasonably competent functioning in life.

Recently there has been an increase in care exercised in taking steps that lead to identifying slow learners as educable mentally retarded and placing them in special school classes. Previously it was the custom to make a special placement of all children with learning problems whose IQs were at or below 80. In theory a **special education** program may provide the best opportunity for such children, but special placement is also a source of social rejection by other children. Because of this rejection, special placement may do more harm than good. For this reason most schools are now reluctant to label children as retarded unless they have a serious disability.

The fact that children with lower IQs are not always labeled as retarded does not mean that these children do not have learning problems. Even children whose mental functioning is at a so-called low-normal level (IQ range 85 to 90) will usually be found to have learning problems of one kind or another that prevent them from keeping up with their classmates. Most of these individuals will be successful in adult life in the sense of securing employment and demonstrating economic independence. Their single greatest problem in childhood and adult life may be the tendency to look down on themselves because of their academic failures.

For the most part children with IQs below 50 or 55 (those in the trainable range and below) have distinguishing physical characteristics in addition to their mental problems. Most of them will have an identifiable abnormal physical condition that often includes dwarfed or stunted stature, other unusual body features, susceptibility to disease, and a short life span. These problems may be the result of genetic or chromosomal abnormalities as in PKU or Down's syndrome (see Chapter 2), or they may be the result of drugs, injuries, or diseases, such as German measles, that affect the unborn child (see Chapter 4). In general, the lower the IQ, the more likely the condition will be complicated by problems other than limited mentality, and the more likely there will have been a specific cause that affected the body and its processes in addition to affecting mental development. The higher the IQ, especially IQ above 50, the less likely that the condition will be complicated by any bodily or physiological abnormality and the more doubt that the label "retarded" should be used.

When mental retardation does exist, no matter what the cause, mental growth will be slow and limited in maximum attainment. In general, severely or profoundly retarded children are not expected to reach beyond the competency level of normal 4-year-olds at their highest level of mental development. This means that they will not be expected to learn to read or develop complex mental concepts. Moderately retarded, or trainable mentally retarded, children can acquire useful concepts and some reading abilities, and their highest level of development is usually equivalent to that of normal children in the first grade. Children in the educable mentally retarded range (IQ 50 to 70) may reach a mental age of about 10 years. They can learn to read, though their language development will be slow. When other children can understand complex sentences and verbal logic, these children will still be coping with simple sentences. In terms of Piaget's theory these children reach the level of concrete operations, but not the level of formal thinking.

Such slow cognitive development affects not only intellectual growth but personality and moral and social development as well. This is because retarded children are limited in their ability to understand subtleties and make discoveries that are easy for normal children. These limitations make necessary special considerations in parenthood and educational practice. A principle to guide parents and teachers is that retarded children will not be as able as nonretarded children to learn by observing and imitating and will have trouble forming useful generalizations by themselves. What can be taken for granted in nonretarded children cannot be taken for granted with the retarded, who must be directly taught many extra things. Most retarded children, however, have a great capacity to acquire information and skills if they are given assistance and practice. Another principle to be remembered is that children who see themselves as not fulfilling their learning role and as disappointing their parents may acquire negative personality traits, such as a lack of drive toward success and a tendency to give up. It has been demonstrated that many of the factors generally assumed to be directly related to retardation may be due instead to the fact that retarded children often develop a negative self-image and low self-expectancy (38).

The Intellectually Gifted

If John Stuart Mill and Sir Francis Galton had taken IQ tests, they would probably have scored higher than 180. Abraham Lincoln would have scored between 125 and 140, Benjamin Franklin 145, and Napoleon between 135 and 140 (7). These estimates of IQ are based on studies of the biographies of famous individuals, most of whom have been called geniuses on the basis of their achievements. Young children of extraordinary intellectual power who have not had the time or opportunity to make great achievements have also been called geniuses, but the term "potential genius" is probably more correct. In one of the best-known studies of potential geniuses, Lewis Terman selected 1,000 children with IQs of 140 or higher and followed their progress for more than 30 years (30, 31). He found that most of these highly intelligent individuals turned out to be well adjusted and successful, but very few of them ever achieved the type of success that is usually associated with the word "genius." Other researchers have used an IQ of 180 or higher to designate a potential genius, but even these children have only one or two chances in ten of ever making the contributions or achievements that would justify calling them geniuses (11). Since few people ever prove to be true geniuses, the term "gifted" is usually used to designate children of exceptionally high intelligence. **Gifted children of the first order** are said to be those in the upper 0.1 percent of the general population. **Gifted children of the second order** are those in the upper 10 percent of the remaining population.

Many studies of gifted children have been conducted. One possible explanation of their increased mental abilities is that they have learned to learn more rapidly than average children (10). Jerome Bruner speaks of the informational habit of early learning as "readiness." By this he does not mean readiness to learn to read or work with numbers, but readiness involving receptivity and capability for later and more effective acquisition of things that are ordinarily thought of as intellectual skills (4). It may be that this informational habit or readiness comes about partially because of early stimulation. It seems that, within normal limits, the more stimulation young infants receive, the more they will demand as older children.

In addition to intellectual capabilities, gifted children have generally been found to be taller, stronger, healthier, show fewer behavior problems, and do better work in school than average and below-average children. Even though bright or gifted children do usually outperform children of average intelligence, the academic achievement of gifted children in public schools in the United States is far lower than would be expected on the basis of their IQ scores. One researcher followed the progress of gifted boys and girls from 6 to 12 years of age and found that their educational achievements were consistently behind what their IQs would have predicted (21). At age 7, for example, the 40 boys in the study averaged a mental age of 9 years and 3 months, but their overall educational age was only 7 years and 2 months. The 42 girls in the study also performed at that level. At 12 years of age the boys averaged 17 years and 11 months in mental age, but only 15 years and 8 months in intellectual age. The girls averaged 17 years and 5 months in mental age but only 15 years in educational age.

This type of **underachievement** is seen among slow learners and those at the lower end of the IQ scale as well as among gifted children. The reasons for underachievement, however, seem to be different for each group. Gifted children are probably victims of underexpectation. The slow learners are victims of frustration, defeat, and overexpectation.

Because public schools are geared to the average child, gifted children, like the retarded, are often singled out for special education. The most often used forms of special education for gifted children are enrichment and acceleration. Julian Stanley of The Johns Hopkins University has worked with hundreds of gifted children. He defines **enrichment** as any educational procedure beyond the usual ones that does not accelerate or retard the student's placement in the subject or grade (29). In other words, enrichment is some-

Psychologist Julian Stanley (left) heads the Study of Mathematically Precocious Youth at The Johns Hopkins University. The study, begun in 1971, has identified hundreds of exceptionally talented seventh- and eighth-graders in Maryland schools.

thing added to normal school work. Stanley further defines four types of enrichment: busy work, irrelevant academic enrichment, cultural enrichment, and relevant academic enrichment. Busy work is probably one of the most often-used forms of enrichment. It consists of giving the student more of the same subject material than is required of the average student. Irrelevant enrichment refers to special subject matter that is meant to enrich the educational lives of intellectually gifted students but is not directed at the specific talents of these students. Cultural enrichment has to do with supplying aspects of the performing arts—such as music, art, drama, dance, and creative writing—that are often overlooked in public schools. When students are given advanced material or higher-level treatment of topics in an area in which they have special abilities, the enrichment is said to be relevant to their abilities.

Most forms of enrichment, says Stanley, represent a horizontal approach to education. That is, they broaden a student's experience within a particular grade level or age range but do little to help the student advance. By contrast, academic **acceleration** is vertical. It consists of moving students up into a higher school level of a subject in which they excel or to a higher grade level than the chronological age of the student would ordinarily call for. If a seventh-grader is allowed to take algebra, usually at least an eighth-grade subject, that is subject-matter acceleration. If a student is allowed to skip a grade, that is grade acceleration.

Stanley's years of work with gifted children and data from the Johns Hopkins program for gifted children have led him to the conclusion that academic acceleration can be much more educationally profitable and intellectually challenging than enrichment, especially for those children who want to be accelerated. He offers an example of an eighth-grade boy with an IQ of 187 who was superior in mathematics. The boy had already skipped a grade, but instead of letting him move on to advanced mathematics, his Algebra I teacher used the type of enrichment that Stanley calls "busy work." The boy was asked by his teacher to work every problem in each chapter rather than just the odd-numbered problems that the other students worked. He could have completed the entire course with distinction in a very few hours without working many of the problems, but his teacher wanted to hold him for 180 50-minute periods. It is a pity, says Stanley, that at the beginning of the school year the gifted child was not allowed to take a standardized algebra test, learn the few points he didn't already know, and move on to Algebra II within a few days.

There is a happy ending to the story of the boy oppressed by busy work in his beginning algebra course. After the eighth grade he studied mathematics part time at the college level for credit. He went through college algebra and trigonometry, calculus, advanced calculus, and linear algebra with an initial grade of B and then all A's. He also completed an introductory course in computer science at Johns Hopkins with a grade of A when he was 12 years of age. Furthermore, he completed his college chemistry through two semesters of organic chemistry with A's. At the age of 15 years and 2 months he became a full-time student at Johns Hopkins, having sophomore status because of the 39 credits he had already earned.

"Though this boy did manage to turn the usually stultifying effects of busy work into great motivation to detour further such obstacles and forge ahead," says Stanley, "it would seem quite difficult to make any general positive case for this type of enrichment."

This case is not that of a typical youngster, but in only three years of mathematical talent searching in Maryland alone, Stanley and his colleagues have found more than 200 similarly superior boys and girls. For most of them acceleration, rather than enrichment, seems to provide the type of challenging work that helps them continue to advance in their studies. Some of the gifted children who are part of the Johns Hopkins program not only skipped grades but skipped most or all of high school and went directly into college. It is clear, says Stanley, that this type of radical acceleration can work much better than academic enrichment for those students who really want it. They benefit greatly from the time saved, frustration avoided, and stimulation gained. Although most of the gifted children in the Johns Hopkins study were boys, most other studies of academic acceleration have contained more girls than boys and have found acceleration to be beneficial for both girls and boys (6).

One question that is often brought up in connection with academic acceleration has to do with the social and emotional development of children who are suddenly put into a class with older students. The researchers at Johns Hopkins have found, after six years of studying the social and emotional development of intellectually gifted children who have been accelerated, that if the acceleration is by their own choice, they have few if any social or emotional problems. Many people automatically assume that one's social and emotional peers (equals) are one's age mates. Personality studies of the gifted children in the Johns Hopkins program, however, show that emotionally these children are more like bright persons several years older than themselves than they are like their own age mates. There is considerable variability, says Stanley, but on the average they are better matched socially and emotionally with able students who are older.

If this is true, then academic acceleration would be beneficial to gifted children socially and emotionally as well as intellectually. Terman's study of gifted children reached similar conclusions (30). He found that the most successful gifted adults were those who had been accelerated a year or more in school. No social or emotional problems resulted from such acceleration.

Another study of academic accelerations conducted by D. A. Worchester in the 1950s uncovered similar findings (37). Worchester said of acceleration:

> It is interesting that, although acceleration has undoubtedly been used far more than any other method of providing for the rapid learner, and although there has been more research as to the outcomes of acceleration than there has been for any other method, and although almost all of the research has shown results favorable to acceleration with hardly any study showing negative values, still a large proportion of teachers and administrators will have little or none of it.

Worchester further comments that acceleration is "a sort of daylight saving. We get the chores of the world done early in the day so that there may be more opportunity for the real joys of living a little later." He estimates that "if we got the top 3 percent of our gifted into their life work a year earlier, the country would have the advantage of some million years additional use of its best brains, and it could probably find use for them. Only good effects, in general, have been found for up to two years of acceleration."

Sex Differences in Intelligence

Throughout the many years that intelligence has been studied and intelligence tests have been given, there have always been findings that males and females differ in intelligence. Males have been found to excel slightly in numerical reasoning and spatial judgment, females in verbal fluency and rote memory (34). In addition, girls have been found to gain less than boys in intelligence between adolescence and adulthood, with the brightest girls at adolescence making the least gains (3). Those girls who do continue to make gains have sometimes shown signs of personal and social maladjustment, while boys who continue to gain are better adjusted than those who stand still or decline in intelligence (9).

The difference in spatial and verbal abilities between males and females may eventually be explained in terms of brain-hemisphere specialization (as discussed in relation to language development in Chapter 8), but it seems that most of the intellectual differences between males and females are a result of sex-role stereotyping that has traditionally penalized competent women in the United States (22). Competent and intellectual females have not generally been well received, while competent males have been richly rewarded. Consequently, bright females may hide their intellectual abilities or stop pursuing intellectual goals when they find that such achievements in females are not well regarded. This may be especially true during adolescence when personal popularity becomes important. It could account for the slow-down in intellectual gains seen in some girls at adolescence.

Although sex-role stereotyping has decreased in recent years, and the doctrine of male superiority is not as widespread as it used to be in the United States, certain of these attitudes remain that can negatively affect female students. For example, one 11-year-old girl who, during her first five years of grade school, was consistently the best in her class in work with numbers, fell to just about average in the sixth grade. When asked why this happened, she shrugged and said matter-of-factly, "Girls just aren't supposed to be that good in arithmetic."

Race and Social Class Differences in Intelligence

Darwin's theory of evolution emphasized individual differences and the ability of different members of a species to meet the challenge of the environment and survive to pass on their genes. The fittest individuals of a species would be more able than the others, and they would survive. Their genes would ensure that the species continued in the form best suited for survival in a particular environment. It was because of this theory that intelligence testing first began.

Francis Galton developed a variety of methods for accurately measuring individual differences between humans. These first measures focused on differences in strength, memory, and such things as sensitivity to pain. These measurements eventually led to intelligence testing. The aim of such testing was to determine who was the fittest and most likely to survive. Galton believed that the "best" individuals should be identified through tests and allowed to have children. Less fit individuals, he believed, should not be allowed to pass on their genes. In this way the direction of human evolution could be consciously controlled with only the "best" of human characteristics being passed on to succeeding generations. **Eugenics,** which means "good genes" or "good birth," is the term used to refer to the selection of superior individuals who should be allowed to survive. Galton believed that through the use of eugenics the human race would become better and better.

Galton's plan to allow only certain individuals to reproduce was not well received and was never put into practice for obvious reasons. Similar eugenic plans, however, have been proposed from time to time, and IQ tests have been suggested as the best way to select superior individuals. Such a plan, for example, might call for all individuals with an IQ of 85 or lower to be sterilized. While it is not likely that any form of eugenics will be socially acceptable in the United States, many researchers have used the results of IQ tests to suggest that one race or group of humans is superior to another.

Hundreds of studies of group or race intelligence have been done in recent years, often with the result that blacks as a group score lower on IQ tests than whites. One such study tested the intelligence of children at about 4 years of age (27). Four groups of children were examined: lower-class blacks, lower-class whites, middle-class blacks, and middle-class whites. The average IQ of the entire group was 93. For all lower-class children it was 84; for all middle-class children it was 101. A difference of 15 points in favor of white children was found between the black and white groups (the white average was 100, the black average was 85), but this difference is exaggerated because more of the black children were from the lowest social class. When the various aspects of the intelligence tests were examined, the only race difference that consistently favored the white children was their performance on tests that demanded an ability to use standard English. Black children, despite the fact that their social class was lower than that of the whites, were superior to the whites in "memory for symbolic systems," or **memory span.**

Hundreds of similar studies have found similar or only slightly different results, and some researchers have interpreted these results to mean that blacks as a racial group are genetically inferior or deficient in intelligence. Others have concluded that blacks score lower on IQ tests because of cultural and environmental differences. The cultural setting in which many black children are reared is different from that of middle-class white children for whom most IQ tests are designed. Differing cultures require different types of intellectual functioning, and tests standardized on middle-class white children may not be an adequate measure of the intellectual functioning of black children. Language abilities, especially, differ from one social or cultural group to another, and most intelligence tests rely heavily on the use of standard, middle-class English (see the discussion of difference versus deficiency in regard to language abilities in Chapter 8). Social influences and expectations also influence the intellectual development of various groups. The sixth-grade girl who stopped studying arithmetic was just doing what she thought was expected of her. Black children who are expected to be less intelligent than white children might also decide to do what is expected of them. In this manner social influences rather than genetic influences could account for some of the differences in intelligence seen between blacks and whites.

While studies of race and intelligence may eventually show some genetic differences in intelligence between social groups, or may lead to a better understanding of exactly what percentage of intelligence is determined by heredity and what percentage is determined by the environment, such matters are far from being settled. A statement issued by the Genetics Society of America at its annual meeting in 1976 sums up the current state of affairs with regard to race and intelligence (26):

RESOLUTION OF INTELLIGENCE

Preamble

Recent years have seen a revival of concern about the relative importance of genes and environment in determining differences in intelligence among individuals, social classes and races. The controversy and the extreme views expressed are not new. The excesses of the early eugenics movement show the pitfalls of naive hereditarian assumptions. Equally unsupportable is the doctrinaire environmentalism that denies any significant role of heredity in important human behavioral traits. Since even well-meant social policies may be harmful if based on error or inadequate knowledge, we believe that the views of many geneticists should be considered in trying to resolve the current controversy.

Statement of GSA Members on Heredity, Race and IQ

Measurement of intelligence. Because of their reproducibility and wide-spread use, IQ scores have been the basis for most analyses of genetic and environmental contributions to intelligence. Nevertheless, their limitations as measures of intelligence are widely recognized. Indeed, intelligence has never been defined to the satisfaction of all social scientists. The interpretation of IQ scores is especially troublesome when comparisons are made between different cultural groups. These limitations must be borne in mind in any genetic analysis.

Factors influencing IQ. IQ scores are attempts to measure the quantitatively varying character of intelligence; such characters are usually influenced by both genetic and environmental factors whose effects and interactions are often difficult to separate unambiguously. Although there is substantial agreement that genetic factors are to some extent responsible for differences in IQ within populations, those who have carefully studied the question agree on the relative magnitudes of genetic and environmental influences, and on how they interact. Moreover, in general, even if the variation in a trait is largely genetic, this does not mean that the degree of expression of that trait cannot be significantly altered by environmental manipulation. Nor does a large environmental component in variation necessarily imply that we can easily change it.

Racial and class differences in IQ. It is particularly important to note that a genetic component for IQ score differences *within* a racial group does not necessarily imply the existence of a significant genetic component in IQ differences *between* racial groups; an average difference can be generated solely by differences in their environments. The distributions of IQ scores for populations of whites and of blacks show a great deal of overlap between the races, even in those studies showing differences in average values. Similar although less severe complexities arise in consideration of differences in IQ between social classes. It is quite clear that in our society environments of the rich and the poor and of the whites and the blacks, even where socioeconomic status appears to be similar, are considerably different. *In our views, there is no convincing evidence as to whether there is or is not an appreciable genetic difference in intelligence between races.*

Implications for Society

All human populations have a vast store of genes in common; yet within populations, individuals differ in genes affecting many characters. Each population contains individuals with abilities far above and below the average of the group. Social policies, including those affecting educational practice, should recognize human diversity by providing the maximum opportunity for all persons to realize their potential, not as members of races or classes but as individuals. We deplore racism and discrimination, not because of any special expertise but because they are contrary to our respect for each human individual. Whether or not there are significant genetic inequalities in no way alters our ideal of political equality, nor justifies racism or discrimination in any form.

The Role of Geneticists

It is our obligation as geneticists to speak out on the state of current knowledge on genetics, race and intelligence. Although the application of the techniques of quantitative genetics to the analysis of human behavior is fraught with complications and potential biases, well-designed research on the genetic and environmental components of human psychological traits may yield valid and socially useful results, and should not be discouraged. We feel that geneticists can and must also speak out against the misuse of genetics for political purposes, and the drawing of social conclusions from inadequate data.

THE WANDERING IQ

Why were the results of the Milwaukee Project so surprising to some people? Because they represent one more piece of evidence in a growing body of data that is challenging some long-held views on the nature of intelligence. J. McVicker Hunt has described some of these changing beliefs (15). One of the most important changes in regard to intelligence is the idea that intelligence is fixed or stable. Another is the idea that intelligence is predetermined. Galton's eugenic approach was based on these ideas. He and many others since his time believed that each individual is born with a certain predetermined and fixed amount of intelligence that does not change throughout life. According to this theory, some people were born with more genes for intelligence than others. Those who had less of these genes would never become intelligent, no matter how much training or education they received.

This attitude or belief in a fixed and predetermined intelligence was widely held as recently as 1939. That was when H. M. Skeels reported that a group of retarded children had shown great gains in intelligence after being removed from an orphange and placed in a home for mentally ill women (see the description of the Skeels study in Chapter 3). When Skeels reported that the retarded children had shown an increase in intelligence after a change of environment, many people actually ridiculed his findings and laughed at the idea of a "wandering IQ." They refused to believe that IQ could change much as a result of an environmental change. Hundreds of tests and retests had shown that the intellectual position of individuals in a group remained fairly constant. A third-grader who scored 100 on an IQ test was likely to score very near 100 a year later and even five or more years later. But this evidence, explains Hunt, concerned children of school age. When investigators began to examine the constancy of the developmental quotient in preschool children, the degree of constancy proved to be very much lower. Now, a good many studies have shown that the "wandering IQ" is a reality. These studies, says Hunt,

> suggest strongly that lack of constancy is the rule for IQ or DQ during preschool years and that the IQ is not at all fixed unless the culture or the school fixes the program of environmental encounters. . . . In fact, trying to predict what the IQ of an individual child will be at eighteen from a DQ obtained during the first or second year is much like trying to predict how fast a feather might fall in a hurricane. The law of falling bodies holds only under the specified and controlled conditions of a vacuum. Similarly, any laws concerning the rate of intellectual growth must take into account the series of environmental encounters which constitute the conditions of that growth (15).

The Milwaukee Project is one of the studies that shows how intelligence changes during infancy and childhood. By manipulating and enriching the environmental encounters of a group of children, the researchers were able to provide these children with the type of challenging experiences that lead to normal intellectual development. What seems to have happened is that the children were continually stimulated and challenged by their day-care environment. As they gained the intellectual skills necessary to meet each challenge, they moved on to other challenges and more advanced intellectual achievements. If the environment had ceased to challenge (as was probably the case with the control children), intellectual growth might have slowed or even stopped. But this does not seem to have happened with the experimental group, and as the Milwaukee Project suggests, it need not happen.

SUMMARY

Most people agree that intelligence is an extremely important and valuable human characteristic. Few people agree, however, as to exactly what it is. Definitions of intelligence have suggested that it may consist of anywhere from 2 to 120 factors, but the most important factors in intelligence probably have to do with learning abilities, cognitive abilities, language, memory, motivation, perception, and motor skills as well as the ability to use all of these factors efficiently. Because intelligent behavior almost always comes about as an attempt to solve some sort of problem, it is probably convenient to think of intelligence as problem-solving ability.

Tests have been designed to measure intelligence. The score on such tests is usually called an IQ, or intelligence quotient. IQ is not an absolute measure of intelligence, but rather a relative concept that can be used to compare the intellectual performance of one child to that of others of the same age and background. The average IQ is 100. Those who score above or below 100 are rated as higher or lower than average.

Various types of IQ tests have been designed. There are tests for use with individuals and tests for groups, tests for different age groups and tests of verbal and nonverbal abilities. Such tests do not help explain what intelligence is or how it comes about, but they do measure problem-solving ability and have proved to be fairly accurate at predicting school performance, especially for middle-class children. This is because IQ tests are designed for and standardized on middle-class children.

Tests designed to measure the mental abilities of infants yield a score known as a DQ, or developmental quotient. Most of the items sampled in such tests seem to be related to sensorimotor abilities rather than purely mental abilities. DQs obtained before the age of 18 or 20 months usually do not predict later intelligence, except in the case of serious developmental impairment. The older children are, the more accurately IQ tests predict intellectual performance. There are many factors, however, that can affect test performance, including such things as tenseness, anxiety, fatigue, and illness on the part of the child being tested. The conditions under which a test is being taken and the attitude of the examiner are also important.

During infancy and the early school years, intellectual growth increases faster as children grow older. At school age increases in intellectual growth begin to be smaller each year. From the teens on intellectual growth is very gradual, though it may continue well into old age.

Extremes in intellectual development range from mental retardation on the one hand to genius or giftedness on the other. When mental retardation exists intellectual growth is slowed and limited in maximum attainment. Special consideration and training is usually necessary to help such children achieve their fullest intellectual potential. Intellectually gifted children are those who seem to have learned to learn more rapidly than average children. Academic acceleration has proved to be one of the most effective methods of helping gifted children achieve their maximum intellectual potential.

Differences in spatial and verbal abilities between males and females may eventually be explained in terms of differences in brain-hemisphere specialization, but it seems that most of the intellectual differences seen between males and females are a result of different social pressures on the sexes and sex-role stereotyping that has traditionally penalized competent and intellectual females. Measured differences in intelligence between the races also seem to be the result of social rather than genetic factors.

Intellectual development, like all other areas of human development, is dependent on genetic and environmental factors. Although both factors are involved, little is known about the exact effects of heredity on intelligence, and little can be done about one's heredity. On the other hand, it is becoming increasingly clear that the environmental factors that influence intellectual development are not only powerful but can sometimes be controlled. The Milwaukee Project is one example of how important environmental factors are in stimulating intellectual development in children.

RESEARCH REPORT 9.1

Early Experiences and Adult Intelligence

Does early experience make a difference in adult intelligence?

In the 1930s a number of investigators in Iowa were studying the effects of different experiences on children's development. At that time most psychologists thought of intelligence as a characteristic fixed by heredity that would unfold as the child matured. Differences in life experiences were thought to influence intelligence little, if at all.

The study by Skeels, presented here in abbreviated form, provides some reasons for being skeptical about the fixed and predetermined nature of intelligence. Skeels discovered by accident that two young girls transferred from an orphanage to a home for the mentally retarded consistently improved in their performance on tests of intelligence though they had been far behind their chronological age in development at the time of their transfer. Each later evaluation showed normal mental development.

No one knows for sure what happened, but these two girls had been placed on a ward where older, brighter girls and women were housed in the institution for the retarded. These older persons had provided a mother and "adoring aunts" for the infants. Skeels was later to say that the single most important factor in the girls' development appeared to be the close, loving, stimulating relationship between each infant girl and one of the inmates of the institution.

Because of this experience and the inability to find adoptive placements for developmentally delayed children in the orphanage, 11 additional children were eventually transferred to the institution for the retarded. These 11 plus the two original girls became known as the experimental group, while another 12, who remained in the orphanage and were still there at age 4, became the contrast group. The transfer group was reared for some period of time in two different institutions in the state of Iowa.

Individual children in the experimental group were placed on wards in an institution for the retarded with older, brighter girls. Only one or two children from the orphanage were placed on any given ward. The 11 children who came after the original two girls also became the objects of affection and attention from the ward inmates. Attendants, as well as inmates, spent much time with "their children," gave them attention, took them out, bought them gifts.

The contrast group lived in a bleak environment which provided little in the way of individual attention or direct love and affection. There was no one to "adopt" these children. The contrast between the two group experiences must have been truly great.

What happened to the children after the experimental period? Of the 13 experimental children, one remained in the institution for the retarded until grown, 5 were adopted straight from the institution, 6 went back to the orphanage and then were adopted, and 1 went back to the orphanage and then was placed in the institution for the retarded.

Six contrast children were transferred permanently to an institution for the retarded but did not gain the attention the experimental children had because they were older. Two contrast children were transferred to the same school as the experimental children but at an older age. They experienced an environment similar to that of the experimental children. Three contrast children remained in the orphanage. The twelfth contrast child was paroled to the marginal home of his grandparents.

In summary, 11 of the experimental children escaped the state institutions, whereas 11 of the contrast children grew to adulthood within one or another state institution.

About 21 years later all of these children (now adults) were found, or accounted for, and their adult status was documented. The two groups showed differing patterns of competence in adulthood: all of the 13 experimental children were self-supporting; five of the contrast children were still wards of the state; the average education of the experimental children was twelfth grade; and the average education of the contrast group was below third grade. In addition, the experimental children were significantly higher in social class status when compared to the contrast group and also compared favorably to the 1960 U.S. Census figures. Eleven of the 13 experimental children were married; two of the 12 contrast children were married; nine experimental children had a total of 28 children; and one contrast child had one child and had been divorced. Offspring of the experimental group scored from 86 to 125 on IQ tests, with an average of 104. The one offspring of the contrast child showed marked mental retardation. The experimental group cost the state less than one fifth of what it cost to provide custodial care for the contrast group.

The dramatic results of this rather naturalistic look at two small groups of children over a long period of time certainly leads one to suspect that drastic differences in environment do lead to differing expressions of competence. Are environments of less contrast associated with significant differences? Just what experiences affect what behaviors is not at all clear.

Based on H. M. Skeels, "Adult Status of Children with Contrasting Early Life Experiences," *Monographs of the Society for Research in Child Development*, 1966, *31*, 1–65. The following sources also served as references: H. M. Skeels and H. B. Dye, "A Study of the Effects of Differential Stimulation on Mentally Retarded Children," *Proceedings and Addresses of the American Association on Mental Deficiency*, 1939, *44*, 114–136; H. M. Skeels, "A Study of the Effects of Differential Stimulation on Mentally Retarded Children: A Follow-up Report," *American Journal of Mental Deficiency*, 1942, *46*, 340–350.

**RESEARCH
REPORT 9.2**

Social Class and Cultural Influences on Mental Abilities

Do children of different social classes and cultural groups demonstrate different levels and patterns in mental abilities?

Lesser, Fifer, and Clark (1965) studied the patterns of four mental abilities of first-grade boys and girls from four different cultural groups. Each of these cultural groups was represented by children who came from both the lower class and the middle class. The four mental abilities were (1) verbal ability, (2) reasoning, (3) number facility, and (4) space conceptualization. The four cultural groups were (1) Chinese, (2) Jewish, (3) black, and (4) Puerto Rican.

The investigators were interested in the extent to which sex, social class, and cultural group were associated with the scores on the measures of mental abilities. They reasoned that there would be differences among the various cultural groups, the two social classes, and between boys and girls on each of the measures. They also thought that children from different social classes and cultural groups would have different patterns of scores. Finally, the investi-

Development. New York: Holt, Rinehart and Winston, 1968, 293–330.

16. Hunt, J. McV., and G. E. Kirk. "Social Aspects of Intelligence." In R. Cancro (ed.), *Intelligence, Genetics, and Environmental Influences.* New York: Grune & Stratton, 1971, 262–306.

17. Jones, H. E. "The Environment and Mental Development." In L. Carmichael (ed.), *Manual of Child Psychology.* New York: Wiley, 1954, 631–696.

18. Jones, H. E., and H. S. Conrad. "Mental Development in Adolescence," *National Society of the Study of Education, Thirty-ninth Yearbook,* 1940, 207–222.

19. Kagan, J., and R. E. Klein. "Cross-Cultural Perspectives on Early Development," *American Psychologist,* 1973, *28,* 947–961.

20. Karelitz, S., et al. "Relation of Crying Activity in Early Infancy to Speech and Intellectual Development at Age 3," *Child Development,* 1964, *35,* 769–777.

21. Ketcham, W. A. "Growth Patterns of Gifted Children," Merrill-Palmer *Quarterly,* 1957, *3,* 188–197.

22. McCandless, B. R., and E. D. Evans. *Children and Youth: Psychosocial Development.* Hinsdale, Ill.: Dryden Press, 1973.

23. Mercer, J. R. *The Eligible and the Labeled.* Berkeley and Los Angeles: University of California Press, 1973.

24. Piaget, J. "Language and Thought from the Genetic Point of View." In P. Adams (ed.), *Language in Thinking.* Middlesex, England: Penguin Books, 1972.

25. "Revising Limits to Intellectual Growth," *Science News,* 1976, *109*(25), 393.

26. Russell, E. S. "Resolution on Intelligence." Issued at the Annual Conference of the Genetics Society of American, Salt Lake City, Utah, Sept. 1976.

27. Sitkei, E. D., and C. E. Meyers. "Comparative Structure of Intellect in Middle- and Lower-Class Four-year-olds of Two Ethnic Groups," *Developmental Psychology,* 1969, *1,* 592–604.

28. Spearman, C. *The Abilities of Man.* New York: Macmillan, 1927.

29. Stanley, J. S. "The Case for Extreme Education Acceleration of Intellectually Brilliant Youths," *The Gifted Child Quarterly, 20*(1), 1976, 66–75.

30. Terman, L. M., and M. H. Oden. *Genetic Studies of Genius.* Vol. 4, *The Gifted Child Grows Up.* Stanford, Calif.: Stanford University Press, 1947.

31. Terman, L. M., and M. H. Oden. *The Gifted Group at Midlife.* Stanford, Calif.: Stanford University Press, 1959.

32. Thurstone, L. L. "Primary Mental Abilities," *Psychometric Monographs, 1,* 1938.

33. Trotter, R. J. "The Milwaukee Project," *APA Monitor,* September 1976.

34. Tyler, L. E. *The Psychology of Human Differences,* 3d ed. New York: Appleton-Century-Crofts, 1965.

35. Vernon, P. E. "Intelligence." In W. B. Dockrell (ed.), *On Intelligence.* Toronto: Ontario Institute for Studies in Education, 1970, 99–117.

36. Willerman, L., and M. R. Fiedler. "Infant Performance and Intellectual Precocity," *Child Development,* 1974, *45,* 483–486.

37. Worchester, D. A. "Acceleration: Good or Bad?" Paper presented at the APA Division of School Psychologists, Midwestern Psychological Association Meeting, 1959.

38. Zigler, E. "Familial Mental Retardation: A Continuing Dilemma," *Science,* 1967, *155,* 292–298.

3

**cultural and social
bases of development**

Children are social creatures. They are born into a social world, and every aspect of their development, including physical, intellectual, and cognitive development, is affected by society. At first, infants are completely dependent on society; later, as they become more social, they learn many basic skills from society. Finally, as truly social human beings, they are relied upon by others and are expected to be useful members of society. Because human development and survival itself would probably not be possible without society, it is necessary to understand the basics of social development.

social development

10

What would you do if you heard screams of terror and pleas for help coming from outside your bedroom window?

What would you do if you looked out the window and saw a young woman being brutally attacked and stabbed?

Nothing—that's what 38 of Kitty Genovese's neighbors did the night in 1964 when she was murdered outside her New York City apartment. What might have been "just another murder" made headline news when the conditions surrounding the murder became known. Although many of Kitty Genovese's neighbors saw and heard what was happening, not one lifted a finger to help her. No one came to her rescue or even called the police. This shocked many people, especially those who believe that humans are basically good and will, when possible, lend a helping hand.

Why did so many people refuse to help? Social psychologists began trying to answer this question after the Genovese case received so much publicity. **Conformity,** or doing what everyone else does, appears to be one answer. In the Genovese case it was as if each neighbor was thinking: "Why should I get involved if all these others aren't doing anything?" Researchers at Princeton University have come up with another interesting answer (61). In an attempt to find out why **altruism,** or concern for the welfare of others, seems to be increasingly rare in our society, the researchers recruited 40 volunteers from the Princeton Theological Seminary and involved them in an experiment designed to find out if the seminarians practice what they preach. Each seminarian was asked to prepare a brief talk. Then one by one in 15-minute intervals they were sent to another building to record their talks.

Lying in an alley between the two buildings was a young man coughing, groaning, and apparently in pain. He had been planted there as part of the experiment. Of the 40 seminarians only 16 stopped to help. Twenty-four did not swerve from their path, and one even stepped over the planted victim.

Some of the volunteers had been told that they would be early for the recording session and that they should take their time. A second group had been told that it was time to go and they would have to hurry. Those in a third group had been told that they were late and that they should rush. Of those in the first group 63 percent stopped to help. In the second group 45 percent stopped, and in the third group only 10 percent stopped.

The researchers concluded that altruism exists, but is demonstrated only under certain circumstances. The seminarians stopped to help not because of any personality or character trait but because they had time to spare. In other words, it appears that people are often just in too much of a hurry to help each other.

People may be in too much of a hurry to help each other all of the time, but without some helping behavior human life would probably not be possible. We rely on and are relied upon by other people. Infants are born into a social world, a world inhabited by millions of other people. Only a few of these people will have a direct influence on the young child, but without them and their help normal development and survival would be in danger. Under normal conditions social interactions play an important role in all stages of development. People protect infants from danger, help them fulfill their bodily needs, and stimulate the growth of important skills such as language. Later, as children mature, it is people toward whom they direct most of their attention, energy, and effort. In other words, they become social creatures. They come to realize that other people are necessary, important, and even deserving of help.

The child's growing understanding that people are necessary, important, and have unique significance is one of the most important achievements of human development. It is the goal of social development.

Erikson's Eight Stages

Moments after birth children have their first social encounter. This marks the beginning of **social development,** which continues throughout life as more and more encounters take place and as children become involved in different types of social interactions. Although no two individuals ever have exactly the same experiences, and social development is different for each person, it is possible to define major stages of social development. Perhaps the most influential theory in this area is the one proposed by Erik Erikson, who has described eight stages of development (13).

Erikson, a close follower of Freud, has based his theory on the types of learning and social interaction that take place at different age levels rather

Psychologist Erik Erikson
(1902–   )

than on the development of biological systems as Freud did (see Chapter 1). Because Erikson's eight stages are directly related to forces in society, he calls them **psychosocial stages.** During each stage individuals are faced with a particular type of crisis or conflict that must be resolved before it is possible to move on to the next stage of social development. Depending on whether or not the crisis is resolved, certain social characteristics—or their opposites—will be learned.

1. Trust versus Mistrust The first of Erikson's psychosocial stages is the **sensory stage** (during the first one or two years of life). Similar to Freud's oral stage, it is the time during which infants must rely on other people in the social environment for all of their needs. If children receive a good quality of care and nurturing during this period, they will learn to trust and rely on their caretakers and will feel secure and dependent. The crisis comes when children do not receive good care during the sensory stage, or if parents give inconsistent care. Children who do not receive good care may not learn to trust people in their environment. Mistreated children may become frustrated and angry and may even be mistrustful, suspicious, and fearful as adults. In extreme cases mistrust can lead to depression and even paranoia—an exaggerated fear of everyone and everything.

2. Autonomy versus Shame and Doubt The second stage of psychosocial development is called the **muscular** or **anal stage** (from 1½ or 2 to 3½ or 4 years). Like Freud, Erikson points out that this is the time during which children learn to control their own muscular movements. They learn to crawl and then to walk and to make use of their newfound powers. Growing awareness of their physical ability results in a feeling of autonomy or independence. Attempts at autonomy, at least during the early part of this psychosocial stage, may show up in the form of tantrums, stubbornness, and negativism. Two-year-olds, for example, may do such things as resolutely fold their arms in order to prevent an adult from holding their hands as they cross a street. A loud, ringing "No!" is often heard from children at this age.

The crisis during the muscular stage is often brought about because parents are afraid to let their children show independence. Some parents become overanxious or overprotective when their children begin to show signs of independence. If children are not allowed to gain some autonomy at an early age, they may begin to feel ashamed of themselves and begin to doubt their powers. In adulthood the lack of autonomy can show up not only as shame and doubt but as timidity. People who have not developed sufficient autonomy sometimes feel they have no control over their lives and are afraid to make a choice.

3. Initiative versus Shame and Guilt The third stage is called the **locomotor** or **genital stage** (ages 4 and 5). It combines Freud's phallic and Oedipal stages. During this time children's awareness begins to extend beyond their own bodies to the people and things around them. They learn to use their imagitions and to broaden their skills through active play of all sorts, including fantasy. They learn to cooperate with others and to lead as well as follow. Children are naturally curious about other people, places, and things. During the locomotor stage they begin to take the initiative and to follow through on their natural feelings of curiosity. They begin to talk to friends, neighbors, and relatives and to explore their physical surroundings.

Social training is important during the locomotor stage. Children's initiative and curiosity should probably be encouraged, but children must also begin to learn what things are not to be explored. Children are not usually allowed to run up to every stranger they see, and they are not allowed to explore the middle of a busy street. Too much control by parents, however, can destroy a child's natural spontaneity and curiosity. Children who are not allowed to follow some of their instincts may begin to feel guilty about what are only natural feelings. Immobilized by guilt, they may become fearful, hang on the fringes of groups, continue to depend unduly on adults, and be restricted in the development of play skills and imagination. As adults, children whose initiative has not developed may be inhibited or afraid to explore anything new — including new people, new foods, or new ideas.

4. Industry versus Inferiority The period of **latency** (from years 6 to 11) usually takes in the first years of school when children begin to learn the values and skills of their society. In this period, especially at school, children learn to master the more formal skills of life: relating to peers according to rules; progressing from free play to play that has rules and may demand formal teamwork; mastering social studies, reading, arithmetic, and so on. Homework becomes a necessity, and the need for self-discipline increases yearly. Children who have successfully resolved the earlier psychosocial crises will, according to Erikson, be trusting, autonomous, and full of initiative. They will learn easily enough to be industrious and will be ready to try out new skills. If they are naturally curious, for instance, children may become intellectually curious. If they have learned not to be timid about meeting people, they should be able to make friends at school and compete in physical and intellectual contests — such as games, sports, and school work.

During this stage the crisis has to do with failure. If young children fail at everything they try, they might lose any industriousness or competency they may have been developing. Continued failure may make children feel inferior. Parents and teachers who realize that young children need to be successful as often as possible do not force children into situations where success is not possible.

5. *Identity versus Role Confusion* During the **stage of puberty and adolescence** (from 12 to 18) every individual goes through a crisis that is not as easily solved as the previous psychosocial crises. The problem consists of integrating, or gathering together, into one **identity** or personality all of the traits of the first four stages. During puberty and adolescence young people must find out who they really are. They are not just their parents' children or their teachers' students. They should be young males or females who have developed specific sexual identities (see Chapter 11). They should have developed certain skills, talents, and social identities that will point them toward college or a career. They should have developed meaningful goals and beliefs. All of these things should come together in one identity.

For children who have not successfully resolved the crises of the earlier psychosocial stages, establishing an identity is sometimes difficult. Older children often experience "role confusion." In other words, they don't know exactly who they are or what they should be. Self-doubts, experimentation with different roles (including delinquency), and rebellion are seen in some older children as they attempt to establish a firm identity and a role that will be most suitable for them.

6. *Intimacy versus Isolation* Unlike Freud, Erikson believes that development continues after adolescence. Continued psychosocial development, however, depends to a great extent on successful resolution of the crises of childhood and adolescence according to Erikson. Individuals who have not become fixated or stuck at a lower level have usually gained a sense of trust and identity that allows them to move into the stage of young adulthood and to begin to form meaningful relationships with other adults. These meaningful relationships, according to Erikson, usually lead to an **intimate** and lasting **partnership** with a member of the opposite sex. Two truly mature adults, he says, should—once they have found each other—be able to love and trust each other and share equally in everything from sex to work to play. Two people who have found themselves and each other are then able to provide the necessary social setting for rearing children successfully.

7. *Generativity versus Stagnation* The crisis in **middle age** comes about when people sit back and do not continue to grow and develop socially. **Generativity** means the ability to reproduce, generate, or be productive. Successful adults do more than produce children. They should be able to generate works and ideas. People who continue to be productive show concern for themselves, their families and society in general. People who do not continue to produce

or who produce only what they need are usually self-centered. They are often complacent and do not continue to grow and develop in a social sense. Such people become stale or stagnant, according to Erikson.

8. *Integrity versus Despair* **Maturity** comes with the pulling together or integration of the first seven stages of development. Those few people who have been successful in solving all of life's crises or conflicts reach what Erikson calls **ego integrity.** They can look back on their lives with a sense of achievement. Those people who have not been so successful often look back and feel that their lives have had no meaning or were useless and wasted. Those people who look back on an incomplete life often look ahead to death with a feeling of despair.

Considering the number of conflicts and crises that must be faced during the various stages of development, it seems almost impossible for anyone ever to achieve maturity or what Erikson calls ego integrity. But most people do reach some degree of maturity.

Erikson's eight psychosocial stages provide a useful outline for examining social development in children, but they do little to explain what sort of environment will produce trust, autonomy, initiative, and industry. Recent research, however, is clarifying these points, as will be seen in this chapter. The major areas of research include children's interactions with their parents and peers, pro-social behaviors, antisocial behaviors, and moral development.

ATTACHMENT AND DEPENDENCY

Wars probably represent the worst failure of social functioning on a group level. Delinquency, crime, and antisocial behavior are examples of individual breakdowns in social functioning. Because these social problems are so serious and potentially destructive, adequate social development is probably one of the most important accomplishments of human beings. As Erikson's theory suggests, childhood is an especially important time in social development. Abnormal social functioning often originates in early childhood when, according to the theory, failure to resolve the psychosocial crises of one stage prevents satisfactory progression through the next stages.

Moving satisfactorily through Erikson's stages obviously requires guidance, and it is logical that, at least during the first four stages (to age 11), this guidance must come primarily from the child's caretakers, the family. During these early stages children gradually learn that their parents and (through generalization) other people are important and that they are dependent on them. **Dependency,** in a theoretical sense, is not the same as dependent *behavior.* In the first sense it refers to a child's realization of the necessary and rewarding characteristics of parents and others. This understanding presumably comes through a combination of good mothering and good fathering, coupled with the child's anxiety about the loss of this nurturance. In the second and more common sense dependency refers to the clinging, lap-sitting, affection- and assistance-seeking behavior usually referred to as dependent.

Those parents who have helped their children acquire dependency (in the theoretical sense of the word) have provided a powerful tool for later, more complicated socialization. That is, if parents are important and generally rewarding to children, then through the process of generalization other adults, children, and social rules also become important.

Social development, as discussed in regard to infants in Chapter 4, begins with the establishment of a strong **attachment** bond between the infant and the primary caretaker, usually the mother. By the end of the first year a more or less permanent attachment exists between the infant and mother. In the following years different types of attachments develop, and other persons become objects of the child's attachments.

Beyond Infancy

Although attachment and dependency appear to be the foundation of social development, dependency behaviors change greatly during the developmental process. The sort of dependency typically shown by infants, for instance, would be inappropriate in the preschool years. It is typical of 2-year-olds to cling to their mothers, to be shy with strangers, and openly to seek affection; but 4-year-olds are expected to have grown out of this "babyish" behavior.

The changes in attachment and dependency behavior during the time following infancy have been demonstrated in a longitudinal study of 48 children who were observed in a laboratory setting on three different occasions —at ages 2, 2½, and 3 (45). On each occasion the children were observed in several situations: For a few minutes the child was observed alone with the mother; next, a stranger entered; then the mother returned and the stranger left. Each session also included a time during which the child was observed alone.

The children's behavior during these sessions was related to both age and the situation. At all ages the most crying occurred when the child was left entirely alone and the next most when the child was left with the stranger. The older the children were, however, the less crying there was. Being left alone also tended to inhibit or keep the children from handling the toys in the room. Being left with a stranger produced this effect too, but to a smaller degree. There were age differences as well. Play with toys was more frequent in the "alone" condition at age 3 than at the younger age levels.

Younger children tended to stay near their mothers when they were left alone with them. Older children were more likely to move around the room, but the entrance of a stranger erased this age difference. When the stranger

Play is more frequent in the "alone" condition at age 3 than at younger age levels.

entered, all children stayed near their mothers. Similar differences were seen in the number of times children spoke, smiled at, or showed things to their mothers. These behaviors were more frequently seen at the older age levels; but when the stranger entered mother-directed behaviors decreased, and age differences were no longer apparent. This, as well as other studies, indicates that separation of mother and child brings about clinging and crying, but with decreasing frequency as children grow older. The forces responsible for this change in attachment behavior are not well understood. It is probable that children's growing interest in the world around them as well as their past history of interactions (pleasant or unpleasant) with their mothers are involved.

Beyond the Third Year

By the age of 3 most children are spending less and less time with their parents and more and more time with other people, especially other children. Social relationships have usually been formed with siblings (brothers and sisters) and peers (other same-age children) by this time, and those relationships are different from those between children and adults. The change from adult-oriented to **peer-oriented behavior,** as well as the differences in types of social interactions, can be seen in the behavior of children in nursery schools and day-care centers. In one study 20 2-year-olds and 20 4-year-olds were observed (32). Affection-seeking was the most often seen dependent behavior in younger children, and it was usually directed at the nursery school teacher. Older children directed most of their dependent behavior (attention-seeking and approval-seeking) toward other children.

It is not known whether the original mother-child relationship leads to the development of later peer relationships or whether these two types of social interactions develop independently, but even very young children respond differently to adults than they do to other children. Researchers presented strangers (either an adult or a 4-year-old child) to 8- and 12-month-old infants and found that the infants reacted more positively to the children than to the adults (23). These different reactions may be due to genetic preprogramming, or it may be that even infants have some sort of self-concept. An unknown child, being more similar to this self-concept than an unknown adult, would be expected to produce a more favorable reaction. In either case children do direct different behaviors toward adults and peers. Children follow one another around, engage each other in conversation, and sometimes offer help. Rarely, however, do they express affection verbally, hug one another, or cling to each other, even though such behaviors are commonly used with adults. Rarely does a child cry or fuss because of the absence of another child. Such behavior is usually only seen after separation from an adult. Children will, however, cling tightly and stay close to each other under exceptional circumstances. One report on the behavior of six young children reared together in a concentration camp during World War II described much clinging, mutual affection, and fear at being separated from each other (18). Psychologist Harry Harlow also found that infant monkeys reared together without their parents cling tightly to one another (see Chapter 3). Ordinarily, however, physical contact is something that children seek with adults rather than with other children.

The conditions that bring about attachment activity also differ according to whether a child is with other children or with adults. When both adults and peers are present fear tends to trigger running to an adult rather than to age mates. Only when adults are not available does fear result in physical contact directed toward peers.

Another difference between parent-child and child-child interactions has to do with play. Parents may engage in play periods with their children for a few minutes at a time, but usually they act as observers or supervisors. On the other hand, long periods of playful interaction between peers are common. These probably provide children with important training periods for social development in many ways. Among these are increased ability in taking the role of others and controlling aggressive drives (28).

Beyond Early Childhood

There is little evidence to suggest that overly attached infants become highly dependent children or that highly dependent children become weak and dependent adults. There is some evidence, however, that individual differences in dependency continue through childhood, especially among girls. Girls who are passive and dependent at one time tend to be passive and dependent during later periods of development (37). This does not appear to be as true of boys. While biological differences (such as the higher activity level of boys) may be partially responsible for this difference between the sexes, a large part is probably due to the fact that girls are generally under more pressure than boys in our society to be passive and dependent.

While early attachment behaviors are not necessarily linked to later behaviors, they are linked to a number of social behaviors involving both adults and peers. In one study preschool children who had been rated by their teachers as highly dependent worked harder at a test that led to social approval than did children who were rated as less dependent (12). Other aspects of this apparent need for social approval on the part of highly dependent children include tendencies to be conforming and compliant (36). That is, they are more likely than independent children to conform, or follow the lead of others, and to comply or give in to the will of others, particularly in interactions with peers (8). Dependency has also been linked to children's willingness to express sympathy and offer assistance to peers, while independence has been linked to the development of aggression. A study of delinquent boys found that they were more independent and tended to seek both affection and assistance less often than more dependent boys, even in situations where it would ordinarily have been reasonable to do so (2).

Situational Factors

Four-year-olds may cry long and hard the first time they are left at a nursery school. Homesickness is seen in many children. These are rather obvious examples of the effects the immediate situation can have on attachment behavior, but even less obvious situational factors, such as a brief separation or a reduction in social contact, can affect attachment activity.

In one study preschool children were given paints and brushes and asked to make paintings (21). Some children completed their paintings with the researcher sitting close by, being attentive to them. Others painted while the researchers sat in a far corner of the room attending to other work. Bids for attention were made more frequently under the "low availability" conditions than under "high availability." In a similar study preschool children were observed while their mothers were either attentive to them or busy filling out a questionnaire. More dependent behavior—clinging, tugging at the mother, and asking for attention—was shown when the mother was busy than when she was attentive.

Various kinds of stress also increase attachment behavior. Two groups of preschool girls and their mothers were observed under different conditions: high anxiety (waiting in a room containing a variety of strange sights and noises) and low anxiety (waiting in a pleasant environment). Some, but not all, attachment behaviors increased under the high-anxiety condition. The children stayed closer to their mothers, but attention-seeking behaviors did not increase (55). This suggests that only those behaviors that have the potential for reducing anxiety or that offer protection to the child are increased by stress. Attachment activity that does not have much stress-reducing potential (for example, attention-seeking) is not influenced by stress.

Socialization Factors

Of all the factors involved in the development of dependency in children, **socialization practices,** especially parental attitudes and practices, are probably the most important (see the discussion of socialization and parental practices in Chapter 3).

Parental rejection has been found to be the most powerful predictor of childhood dependence. Rejection has been reported to be related to dependency in preschool-aged children, preadolescent children, and adolescents (59, 64, 46). Presumably the conflict and anxiety produced in children by rejecting parents causes the children to seek even more attention and become even more dependent. Children who are overly dependent, the clinging-vine types, may be rejected in part because they *are* so dependent. Many parents simply do not enjoy a dependent child, so the clinging leads to increased rejection rather than the other way around.

Parental discipline is another important factor in childhood dependence, but its effects seem to be related to the overall relationship that exists between parents and children. Some parents use a great deal of control with their children but maintain a warm and friendly relationship. Others use a high degree of control but do not stay close (emotionally) to their children. These approaches to parenting result in different amounts and types of dependence in children, as one researcher has demonstrated (4).

Preschool children were rated and classified as one of three types:

Parental discipline is an important factor in childhood dependence.

energetic-friendly (children who were self-reliant, self-controlled, explorative, and content with themselves); *conflicted-irritable* (children who were discontented, withdrawn, and distrustful); and *impulsive-aggressive* (the least self-reliant children, least controlled, and most impulsive). Interviews with the children's parents revealed distinct patterns of parent-child interactions for each group of children. Parents of the most self-reliant children (energetic-friendly) were controlling and demanding of independence, but also were warm, reasonable, and understanding of the child's feelings and points of view. This combination of positive reinforcement for autonomous or independent behavior plus warmth and high parental control is called **authoritative behavior.** Parents of the conflicted-irritable children were forceful or coercive but detached and less warm than the other parents, a combination that is called **authoritarian.** Parents of the most dependent, least inquisitive, and least self-controlled children (impulsive-aggressive) were themselves noncontrolling and nondemanding, but warm. They were **permissive.**

In this study the children were classified and then the characteristics of the parents were studied. To check the results a second study was conducted in which the characteristics of parents were investigated first and predictions were made about the children's behavior (5). The same relationships were found. It seems, then, that the most effective balance between children's self-reliance and dependence comes from a background of authoritative parent behavior rather than a background of excessive control or excessive permissiveness. As the famous child specialist Benjamin Spock has put it:

> I am making the point that independence comes from security as well as from freedom, because a few people get it twisted around backward. They try to "train" independence into children by keeping them in a room by themselves for long periods even though they are crying for company. I think that when the issue is being forced this hard, a child is not learning anything very good.
>
> So babies at around a year are at a fork in the road. Given a chance, they gradually become more independent: more sociable with outsiders (grown-ups and children), more self-reliant, more outgoing. If they're confined a great deal, kept away from others, used to having only parents, often just one parent, hovering over them, they are apt to become tied to that parent, more timid with strangers, wrapped up in themselves (59).

PEER RELATIONS

What would childhood be without friends and playmates? Social development begins in the home with the parents, but for most children it continues with other children. These child-child relationships are very important, and numerous studies show that they have lasting effects on social development and behavior. In fact, failure to engage in peer activities and failure to occupy a relatively comfortable place in peer groups are among the best indicators of difficulties in development.

Although adult-child relations and peer relations represent different social systems, experiences in the home do have an influence on the development of peer relations. Children whose attachments to their mothers are rated as "secure," for example, tend to be more responsive to other children in nursery school (42). Satisfactory home lives, in which comfortable attachment relations with both parents continue from early childhood through later childhood, usually result in good peer relations.

What Is a Peer?

In general, **peers** are children of more or less the same age, even though age is not always the best indicator of a child's developmental status. Children of the same age often differ greatly in size, intellectual ability, and physical skill. Therefore, it is probably more accurate to say that peers are those children who interact at about the same behavioral level. And peerlike behavior is social activity in which the actions of one child represent a developmental status that is similar to that of the other child (41). Accordingly, children may be peers in one setting (such as the classroom) but not in another (the playground).

Development of Peer Relations

Peer relations begin in infancy with babies showing an intense interest in each other (11). At first this interest is expressed by looking at other infants when they are active or crying, but there is no real two-way interaction. The looked-at infant doesn't respond. Later, during the second half of the first year, peer interactions are seen. Older infants approach each other and mutually explore eyes, mouths, and ears. Occasional sharing behavior occurs toward the end of the first year along with increased vocalizing.

Once infants begin responding to each other, social differences begin to appear. Some children are more popular than others. One researcher's observation of five children in a day-care center, for instance, found that one was socially popular while another was avoided (39). Detailed observations of these infants showed that the popular infant responded more often to the interest shown by others than did the unpopular infant. Although infants do respond to each other in a social manner, there is little evidence that strong, focused relationships occur, except under unusual circumstances (as mentioned in regard to the children reared in a World War II concentration camp). Actually, 1-year-old infants will interact with adults rather than other infants when given a chance. By the end of the second year, however, interest in other children increases. Two-year-olds, as compared with 1-year-olds, will spend more time interacting with other babies than with their mothers when given the opportunity. This trend toward greater and greater interest in peer relations continues through childhood and adolescence. Such changes reflect children's increased feelings of security in exploring the environment while separated from their parents, but also demonstrate that children provide increasingly novel and varied stimulation for each other as they grow older.

Not only the quantity but the quality of peer relations changes as children grow older. In the 1930s one investigator observed the interactions of nursery school children who ranged in age from 2 to 5 years (50). The behavior of the youngest children was described as "solitary." Children tended to play alone at this age, and social interaction was likely to consist of merely looking at someone else. Among children who were slightly older, social behavior consisted of "parallel play." These children played side by side and engaged in similar activities, but displayed little direct communication. Among the oldest children social behavior was "associative." Cooperation, conversational exchanges, and give-and-take interactions were common. This developmental sequence does not capture all of the subtle changes that occur in peer relations during the preschool years; but it has been reported by many investigators and is as characteristic of children in the 1970s as it was in the 1930s (3).

An important aspect of the increasing interactions between children is the development of friendships. These relationships between children are apparent early in the preschool years. Friendships at this stage are not as lasting as they are among older children, but by the age of 3 children do show preferences for certain other children. In most but not all cases friendships are based on shared interests and similar personality traits. Friendships also often involve children of the same sex. This preference for friends of the same sex is more common during middle childhood than either before or after and

Friendship between young children often involves children of the same sex.

is probably the result of shared interests rather than an avoidance of the opposite sex.

Mechanisms of Peer Influence

One of the reasons that peer relations are so important in development is that children have a great influence on each other's behavior. Most children worry about what their friends will think and try to behave in a manner that friends will approve. Two of the mechanisms involved in children's influence on each other's behaviors are modeling and reinforcement (see Chapter 6). Children tend to imitate each other and reinforce each other for appropriate behaviors.

Peer Modeling Various experiments have shown that **peer modeling** exerts a powerful influence on children in a wide range of intellectual and social activities, including behaviors that are usually difficult to change. Impulsive third-graders, for instance, tend to become more reflective on problem-solving tasks after watching reflective sixth-graders perform the same tasks (10). Peer models have also been shown to be effective in teaching solutions to simple problems and in teaching basic behaviors to severely retarded children (48). Preschool children who are fearful of dogs have been shown to become less fearful after being exposed to films of "fearless" 4-year-old models (1).

Other studies show that peer modeling can increase children's sociability. Severely withdrawn nursery school children participated in one such study (49). Half of the children were shown a movie about peer interaction in a nursery school. Interaction in the film began slowly with toy-sharing and then increased in both rate of social interaction and the number of children involved. Children were first shown watching other children play, then joining the group and being rewarded for joining in. Social involvement was accompanied by much talking, smiling, and approval, and a narrator called attention to these events. The other group of withdrawn children saw a film of equal length about dolphins. Social interaction was measured after the children returned to their classrooms. Dramatic increases were seen among the children who had been exposed to the peer models, but practically no increase occurred among the children who had watched the dolphins.

Peer Reinforcement Children who make fun of their teachers, start fights, or disrupt their classrooms will be likely to repeat those behaviors if they receive encouragement and approval from their peers—and children are usually quite obvious in giving such social rewards and reinforcement. Pro-social behaviors can also be encouraged by peer reinforcement, even in very young children. In one experiment five nursery school children were selected as targets for special treatment by their peers (63). The children's peers were instructed to behave toward them in a carefully programmed manner. The target children were to be ignored when they behaved in an inappropriate manner and to be given attention when their behavior was what the experimenters wanted. Surprisingly, the children's peers (who were themselves only 4 and 5 years of age) were able to follow the rules and ignore the target children when their behavior was inappropriate but give attention when their behavior was what was wanted. The behavior of each of the five target children changed in the desired direction during this experiment.

A long history of social reinforcement seems to increase the effectiveness of other forms of social influence. For example, a child's history of interactions with peers affects the child's tendency to imitate other children. Children who are used to positive interactions with their peers will be more likely to copy rewarding models than models who are not rewarding (29). Children who have had little positive interaction with their playmates tend to imitate nonrewarding children more often than they imitate rewarding children. A child's long-term relation with the child supplying reinforcement also alters the effects of peer approval and disapproval. If, for example, praise is given by one preschool child to another in a simple task, that approval will be more effective if given by a nonfriend than by a friend (25). Peer reinforcement is also more powerful when the reinforcing child is older or younger than the subject, but less powerful when the children are the same age.

These results suggest that conditions that are strange to a child or that are a bit different from ordinary conditions in which peer interactions take place increase the effectiveness of peer reinforcement. Positive feedback from peers that occurs in an unexpected setting seems to be more powerful than feedback that occurs when and where it is expected.

GROUP RELATIONS

One situation in which a good deal of peer imitation and reinforcement is seen is in social groups. A social group is a structured and organized collection of individuals who share common goals and interests. Children in nursery school share common interests, follow group rules, and sometimes have group leaders; but close-knit social groups are not usually formed in the preschool years. Later, group membership and social acceptance become very important to children. Those who belong to a social group are usually proud of being a part of the group; identify strongly with the group; and share group ideas, interests, and attitudes. Group members often copy each other's style of dress, manner of speaking, and way of behaving.

Studies of group formation suggest that the sharing of a common goal is one of the most important aspects of group formation. In one experiment 22 fifth-grade boys at a summer camp in two separate camp sites were observed during the time that social groups were formed (58). Opportunities were provided for the children to engage in various activities (crafts, sports, cookouts, movies, and so on), but some of the activities (preparing a meal from raw materials) required that the children work together with a common goal. Under these conditions the children organized themselves into groups in a very short time. Some children became group leaders, and others had specific jobs and positions within the group. Group attitudes developed and group pride was seen. When the groups accidentally discovered each other group pride increased and group names were adopted.

In an attempt to study conditions that affect group harmony and tension, experimenters manipulated the groups in several ways. First, they arranged a series of athletic competitions between the groups. These games were rigged so that neither group won or lost all of the time. This increased group competition and resulted in increased hostility between the groups. Intergroup fights were common, and name calling and vandalism (raiding each other's camps) were frequent. Intergroup friendships ceased while friendships between group members became stronger. Competition was thus shown to be a major factor in intergroup conflict.

The final stages of the experiment consisted of attempts to reduce this hostility. Contact alone did not accomplish this. In fact, joint trips to the movies and sharing the dining hall resulted in pitched battles and increased hostility rather than reduced tensions. Later, the researchers engineered instances in which members of both groups were required to work cooperatively on very important problems. On one occasion the water supply for both camps gave out; on another the food truck broke down. It was expected that this enforced cooperation would reduce intergroup conflict and increase friendliness between the groups, and this proved to be the case.

This experiment makes several important points about children's social development. First, efforts to reduce intergroup tensions that involved bringing hostile groups together and communicating favorable information about one group to the other are relatively ineffective. Sometimes these methods work and sometimes they don't. Second, the achievement of intergroup harmony depends on opportunities to work toward common goals. Hostile groups must work toward important goals that affect both groups in order for lasting changes in intergroup attitudes to take place.

Social Acceptance

Studies of social functioning within groups have also been made, with emphasis on social structure. Social organization in children's groups is usually quite obvious, with the most popular children being the leaders and others each having a recognized position or status within the group. In general, popular children are those who are friendly and open in their behavior toward other children and adults. They also tend to be less anxious, better adjusted, brighter, and to have more skills than their less popular peers. As was mentioned in Chapter 5, physical attractiveness also plays a role in popularity. Children tend to attribute higher social status to children they rate as attractive than to children they rate as less attractive. It has also been found that popular children have more conventional names than less popular children. A study of elementary school children, for instance, found the highest number of unconventional names (such as Hepzibah and Percy) among the least popular children, with the children themselves rating the unconventional names as being less desirable (47).

The fact that physical attractiveness and social status often go together is probably due to social stereotyping. There seems to be a widely held belief in the United States among both children and adults that "to be beautiful is to be good." Children who know that they are attractive or have a socially desirable name probably have a higher self-concept than children who know they are unattractive or have an undesirable name. And it is known that children's self-concept or attitude toward themselves can affect their social behavior. Children who feel they are unattractive, for instance, may be unwilling to join in social activities where their unattractiveness will be seen by all. Attractive children may be eager to join in and show off their good looks. This type of behavior can, in turn, affect the attitudes of others toward the child, with the non-joiners being further avoided and the eager joiners being readily accepted.

It is also possible that children who have been reinforced for their good looks ("Look at that beautiful child!") may work harder at keeping themselves attractively groomed and dressed in order to increase such reinforcement. If this is so, the correlation between physical attractiveness and popularity runs in two directions. Physical beauty may increase the chances of social acceptance, but social acceptance may also encourage children in attempts to increase their physical attractiveness.

A similar interpretation can be applied to the other characteristics of popular children. Friendliness and low levels of anxiety may increase a child's popularity, but at the same time popularity itself may lead to increased friendliness and better regulation of anxiety.

Conformity

Regardless of popularity, group members usually display many of the same attitudes and behaviors. Peers exert a great deal of pressure on each other to conform or give in to the customs and rules of the group. Some children are more independent than others, but most show strong tendencies to conform under peer pressure. Children who are well-liked or who are disliked, however, have been found to conform less than children who are of middle social status. There even seems to be a particular status position that is associated with the highest degree of conformity.

When group leaders, second-ranking members, and lowest-ranking members were studied in a peer-pressure situation, the most conformity was seen in the second-ranking individuals—those who had almost made it to the top of the peer group (31). It may be that second-ranking individuals are among the most ambitious children in the peer group and are those who believe that conformity will help them get to the top.

Older children and teenagers are often described as being highly conformist, probably because they stick so closely together, tend to like the same things, dress alike, and even wear their hair in similar styles. It may be, however, that older children only conform in certain obvious areas and are actually less conforming and more independent than younger children. As Piaget explains it, children go through three stages related to conformity. Preschool children are egocentric. That is, they think mainly about themselves, their own needs and wants. They may follow rules or imitate adults, but they are not certain of the reasons for doing so and usually care little for social rules and regulations. Later, there is increased conformity in children's peer interactions. They adhere strictly to group-endorsed rules and claim that any change in the rules is wrong. Finally, children's behavior becomes less conformist, and they will admit that changes in the rules are sometimes possible.

Research suggests that conformity decreases with increasing age, depending on the type of situation involved. Children of all ages, for instance, are

Older children and teenagers can be highly conformist.

more likely to conform in a strange situation than in one with which they are familiar. When faced with a new game or an unfamiliar environment, they will usually wait and see how their friends handle the situation.

The manner in which age is related to conformity also depends on the difficulty of the task. In one study children in grades 2, 5, and 8 were requested to determine which of two diagrams shown by a slide projector for a few seconds contained the greater number of dots (34). Sometimes both diagrams contained 15 dots, and it was rather difficult for the children to determine whether one contained more or less than the other. They weren't allowed time to count the dots. In a second, less difficult, task one diagram contained 15 dots and the other 16. In the third and easiest to distinguish condition one diagram had 15 and the other 17 dots. The children being studied heard two classmates respond first and then had to give their own answers. There was increasing conformity with age on the most difficult task (15 and 15 dots). That is, the older the children were, the more likely they were to follow the lead of their classmates who answered first (even though the classmates sometimes gave the wrong answers). On the medium-difficulty task (15 and 16 dots) there was increasing conformity from the second to the fifth grade, but decreasing conformity from the fifth to eighth grade. On the easiest task there was decreasing conformity with age throughout the three groups.

From these and other studies it appears that no definite statement can be made about whether conformity decreases or increases with age. It is known, however, that in relatively straightforward situations older children and adolescents are more willing to trust their own judgments and withstand peer pressure than are younger children.

Are children more likely to conform to adult or to peer pressure? Again, it depends on the situation. When conformity is related to children's behavior (as in children's games or choice of friends) peers seem to have a greater influence than adults. When a difficult judgment or problem is involved (such as plans for the future or achievement in school), an older, "wiser" model appears to be the most influential (6).

ALTRUISM

Peer and group interactions, as well as family life, provide children with numerous opportunities to learn and practice social behavior. While it is difficult to classify all social behavior as either good or bad, two basic types of social behavior have been studied in children—pro-social behavior, or altruism, and antisocial behavior, or aggression. Learning to control aggressive impulses and aggressive behavior is an important and necessary part of growing up, but learning to do good for others is just as important. Children are expected to become useful members of society, and they are expected to learn to share, to do favors for others, to express sympathy, and to "pitch in during times of crises." These are all altruistic behaviors.

Two types of altruism have been identified: normative and autonomous altruism. **Normative altruism** is egocentric. It is the "What's in it for me?" or "I'll help you if you help me" type of behavior. This self-centered, or egocentric, altruism is seen in most children. They are willing to help or do something for others if they know they will be rewarded. Social rewards, such as praise ("Wasn't it nice of you to help your friend.") are often enough to encourage normative altruism. Certain acts of sympathy, such as helping a hurt friend, demonstrate the egocentric aspect of some altruism. Researchers found that children who were active in seeking affection and attention from others were also likely to give sympathetic attention to others (30). This suggests that children give sympathy to each other for reasons that are similar to those for which they seek sympathy.

Not all altruistic behavior is based on the expectation of a reward. **Autonomous altruism** is the type of pro-social, or helping, behavior that occurs in the absence of any obvious social pressure and appears to be autonomous or independent of rewards. It is the "I'll help you because you need help" type of behavior. Autonomous altruism is common among children, but certain types of altruism, such as generosity, are more common among older rather than younger children. Most preschoolers, for instance, will share their possessions if they have more than one item, but the proportion of items shared increases with age. The reasons for this behavior are not completely understood, but sharing behavior is more common among children who are secure in their social relationships and who have experienced success and

Helping behavior is common among children, but may decrease with age in certain cases.

personal fulfillment than among insecure children who have experienced many failures.

In one experiment two groups of children experienced either success or failure in a bowling game (35). A third group played a similar game that did not provide much opportunity for success or failure. During a lull in the game someone came around collecting funds for "children who have no toys." The children were approached when they were alone so that peer pressure would not influence their decisions. More of the children who had recently experienced success in the bowling game contributed than the children in either of the other two groups. The sum of the contributions of the successful children was also greater than that given by children in the other groups.

Development of Altruism

Primitive forms of self-sacrifice are seen in many children, beginning in the second year. Toddlers will spontaneously share their cookies with strangers, offer their toys to visiting relatives, and perform other pro-social acts. Such behaviors do not seem to be directly traceable to early learning or modeling, so the conditions that produce them at these early stages remain unknown. It may be, however, that an altruistic tendency has been built into the human species during the course of evolution (as discussed in Chapter 2), based on survival of the species rather than survival of the individual.

Whatever its basis, the simple sharing seen among young children, which has many of the characteristics of autonomous altruism, is usually replaced by nonaltruistic behavior during the preschool years. Observations of nursery school children show that spontaneous sharing of toys, space, and other possessions is relatively infrequent. Sympathy, too, is a relatively rare event at this stage. Observations of one group of children between the ages of 4 and 5 showed the following frequencies of sympathetic behavior during a 100-minute period: giving affection—an average of .42 times per 100 minutes; giving reassurance—.95; giving positive attention—6.9; giving protection—1.05 (30). These very low frequencies of altruistic behavior do not change much from the early to the late preschool years.

Attempts to teach or encourage altruistic behavior in children have proved to be relatively difficult. Exposure to sharing models and direct reinforcement of altruistic behavior work in some circumstances but not always. There is evidence that it is easier to increase normative than autonomous altruism. In one experiment young children would not share their marbles with others when the outcome was the experimenter's approval, but they would share when the reward was a piece of bubble gum (17).

Between the kindergarten years and the years of preadolescence sharing behavior increases in most children, but by the elementary school years it is apparent that altruism is not a generalized characteristic. In other words, all forms of sharing, caring, and helping are not seen in the same children; and all forms of altruism do not follow the same developmental course.

Expressions of sympathy and sharing of possessions increase during the preadolescent period, but willingness to help another person in distress follows a different course. When children from kindergarten through the sixth grade were exposed to sounds of distress and cries of help from an adjoining room, their behaviors differed according to age (61). The children, who were alone at the time, had been told to stay in their rooms. Both kindergarten and sixth grade children showed a tendency not to give help. The children from the second and fourth grades did help. It may be that the low level of helpfulness shown by the youngest children was a result of their limited social experience and cognitive development; they may not have fully understood the situation or known what to do about it. The older children may have refused to help for different reasons. Perhaps they thought they would be regarded as disobedient if they helped, since they had been told to stay in their rooms. Whatever the reason, the development of altruistic behavior differs according to the type of altruism involved.

Social Factors in Altruism

In the early 1960s persons who had been active in the civil rights movement were interviewed (54). Two groups of activists were identified: a fully committed group who had given up their homes, jobs, and educational goals for activist causes and a partially committed group who had occasionally participated in freedom rides but had not given up their other pursuits. There were two main differences in the parent-child relationships of these groups. First, the fully committed activists recalled that they had parents who had been deeply involved in activist causes—protesting religious discrimination, taking part in the Spanish Civil War in the 1930s, and so forth. The parents of the partially committed activists had only been verbal supporters of prosocial causes and, not infrequently, had been hypocritical about them. They preached one thing, but did another. Second, the fully committed subjects had had much more positive relationships with their parents during childhood and continuing through the time of the interviews. In fact, the partially committed activists frequently expressed anger because their parents' behavior did not always fit their words. Similar findings have come from carefully controlled studies. This suggests that the models provided by parents are extremely important in the development of altruism in children.

Not only parents but peers are influential in the development of prosocial behavior, as seen in studies of nursery school children. In one experiment children were individually exposed to a peer model who was giving out trinkets to another child (29). The children being studied were either very sociable or very nonsociable, and the models were children from the same school who had either been quite rewarding to the subjects (had given many social rewards) or who had not rewarded them at all. After observing the model, when both the model and the experimenter were gone, altruistic behavior was much more frequent than when no model had been observed. The sociable children were more influenced by models who had been kind to them than by those who had not. The unsociable children imitated models who had not been rewarding more often than they imitated those who had. So the relationship of the child to the altruistic model is critical in peer interactions relating to altruism, just as it was in parent-child interactions relating to individual involvement in civil rights causes.

Other studies indicate that the consistency between what models say and do influences the altruism of children. While most parents are in favor of pro-social behavior and good conduct, not all practice what they preach. The old saying "Do as I say, not as I do" is often heard from parents. The effects of this discrepancy between word and deed have also been examined by researchers (7). Third- and fourth-grade children were exposed to filmed models who were either generous or greedy in terms of sharing with the March of Dimes their winnings in an experimental game. The models were either charitable, selfish, or neutral in what they had to say about their actions. Some models were consistent in practicing and preaching charity, or practicing and preaching selfishness, while others were hypocritical (they practiced one thing and preached another). Whatever the variation, these studies showed clearly that moral preachings have less effect on behavior than do moral practices. The models' actions were more powerful than their words in affecting the child's sharing.

The model's preachings were found to have an impact on the attractiveness of the model as rated by the children. Models who preached charity were better liked than were those who preached greed, regardless of the behavior they practiced. Just as the model's preaching had little effect on the children's behavior, the model's practices had little effect on the children's evaluation of the model. Work with slightly older children indicates that there is increasing criticism of hypocritical models as children grow older. Just like the partially committed civil rights workers, selfish-behaving, generous-sounding models are less likely to draw approval from older children than from younger children.

Nurturance and warm, supportive social experiences, as the study of the activists suggests, also seem to be related to the development of altruism. These effects have also been demonstrated in experiments with children (65). In one experiment 104 nursery school children were divided into various experimental groups according to the type of interpersonal experience provided by a teacher and the type of altruistic training the children received. Half the children had experience with a nurturant caretaker, one who "initiated friendly interaction, offered help and support freely, was sympathetic and protective, expressed confidence in the children's abilities, gave praise frequently and responded to their bids for attention." This experience was provided in half-hour sessions, five days a week for two weeks. The other half of the group were exposed to a nonnurturant adult, one who "maintained a reserved attitude and who generally ignored requests for attention and help." Later, these same adults presented either of two types of altruistic training: Type A—portrayal of situations involving misfortune and expressions of sympathy, help, and relief with three-dimensional play materials called dioramas; or Type B—direct modeling of altruism in addition to the dioramas. Both Type A and Type B training led to increased altruism on the part of the children in later exposure to diorama presentations of misfortune. The most interesting results, however, came during observations in a nonschool situation two weeks later. Expressions of sympathy and offers of help were most frequent among the children who had had Type B training (diorama and modeling) from a nurturant adult.

While much remains to be learned about the social factors that lead to the development of pro-social behavior, this experiment suggests that the best conditions for development of sympathetic, helpful behavior are those in which children see adults involved in altruism at every level—in principle and in practice, both toward the child and toward others in distress.

AGGRESSION

The opposite of altruism is antisocial behavior, and the most common form of antisocial behavior is **aggression.** Because aggression is so noticeable in children (especially in some of their rough-and-tumble play) and because it is so potentially destructive, a great deal of research effort has gone into attempts to understand and control aggression.

Aggression, in the antisocial sense, is violent and destructive behavior that is purposely directed against other people or the environment. It comes in many forms (including name calling, shoving one's way to the head of the line, slugging someone, breaking another child's toys, and rejecting a friendly gesture) and is seen in most children—but in some more than others.

Literally dozens of studies conducted in many different cultures show that boys are more aggressive than girls (44). This difference between the sexes appears as soon as peer interaction becomes a significant part of a child's life, usually during the third year. Boys are more aggressive than girls throughout childhood and adolescence; men are more aggressive than women, at least until middle age in the United States. Sex also affects the choice of targets in children's aggression. Girls are less often victimized or picked on than boys. These sex differences in aggression are seen not only in humans but in many other species as well. It is likely that they are partially the result of biological factors, such as differences in body size and structure and in hormones and other body chemicals. Even so, social conditions probably have a great deal to do with the development of different levels of aggression in boys and girls. In the United States it is young boys, not girls, who are taught and expected to be aggressive.

Studies of social-class differences in the United States show that lower-class children tend to be more aggressive than middle-class children. A number of social factors seem to be involved in producing this difference. First, lower-class families tend to be more severe in their child-rearing practices than are middle-class families. Second, exposure to aggressive models, including parents and peers, is more likely in lower-class families. Third, encouragement of aggression in certain settings, such as the peer group, is more likely in lower-class situations. And fourth, general levels of frustration and deprivation are likely to be greater in lower-class than middle-class children.

Other conditions that play a role in the development of aggression in children are birth order and body shape. In general, males born later are more aggressive than first-born males, with this difference being seen less often among females (16). Single children have also been reported to be more aggressive than those who have brothers and sisters. Mesomorphic children (muscular, broad shouldered), as mentioned in Chapter 5, are also more likely to be aggressive and assertive in both socially appropriate ways (competitive in sports) and inappropriate ways (delinquency). Whether this difference in levels of aggression is due to biological or social factors is not known, but most research suggests that social factors (the way children are treated) play a greater role in aggression than genetic factors.

No matter what the cause, high levels of aggression in children of either sex have been found to be a drawback to social development. Overly aggressive children, for instance, are often rejected by their peers (26). The most common reason given by children for disliking another child is "he hits" or "she's mean." These results are based on studies of antisocial aggression and do not imply that willingness to protect oneself or to respond to frustration with socially acceptable aggression is associated with abnormal social development.

Frustration

The most widely studied cause of aggression is the condition known as frustration. To frustrate means to prevent from accomplishing a purpose or fulfilling a desire. Anger in children often comes about as a result of interference with an on-going activity. Taking away toys, making them come in from play, making them get up from the television set in order to take a bath—all of these things can frustrate children and can cause anger and aggression in some.

Although there are many possible causes of frustration in a child's life, frustration does not always lead to aggression. Numerous experiments have shown that children can learn through reinforcement to be either aggressive or constructive in the face of frustration. That is, they can scream and kick when they don't get their way, or they can take a more constructive attitude and attempt to do something about the source of frustration. Depending on the type of reinforcement children have received, they will tend to be either more or less aggressive in frustrating circumstances. Children whose parents always give in to screaming and kicking will be reinforced for that behavior and will be likely to use it again.

Reinforcement affects aggression even when the training is not directly pointed at frustration. In one nursery school experiment an aggressive child was singled out for special treatment by the teachers (57). They were instructed to ignore the child's aggressive outbursts and to interfere only to protect the other children. This procedure—ignoring rather than reinforcing—produced significant decreases in the child's aggressive activity. Similar experiments with entire nursery school classes have also resulted in decreases in aggression.

Development of Aggression

The tantrums of infancy may be the beginnings of aggression. These rages occur early in life and are seen in most children. The relation between infant tantrums and the outbursts of older children is not clear, but tantrum behaviors do change with age. Early rage is usually undirected flailing about and screaming. Anger in the preschool years is more directly focused. It usually has an obvious cause and a definite target.

Other changes in aggressive interactions are also seen as children grow older. One very detailed study, for instance, found that between the ages of 1 and 3 there is an increase in certain physical aspects of aggression (stamping and hitting), but after the third year physical aggression declines and the activity becomes more symbolic (22). Angry talk comes more and more to accompany physical violence or to substitute for it.

Another change that occurs during the preschool years is the increased frequency of "after reactions." These behaviors follow a hostile outburst, but are relatively nonviolent. After reactions include sulking, whining, and brooding. As most parents who have had to deal with a pouty child probably know, the frequency of these behaviors continues to increase after the age of 4, even though the overall frequency of aggressive behavior declines during the elementary school years (27).

The development of aggression is also marked by changes in the factors that bring about aggressive outbursts. In infancy most angry outbursts follow instances of physical discomfort and needs for attention (22). During the second and third years such episodes are often brought on by "habit training"—efforts on the part of the parents to change the child's behavior. During the preschool years conflicts with peers play an increasingly important role in aggression and are the most common cause of aggression in the following years. These aggressive interactions with peers not only increase but change with regard to the cause of aggression. Conflicts involving possessions are the most common cause of aggression at every age level from 18 months through the sixth year, but one study found that up to 78 percent of younger children's quarreling is over possessions, while only 38 percent of older children's quarrels begin this way (9).

Similar findings have come from a study of 4- to 8-year-olds (27). Observations were made during a five-week period in three day-care centers for the purpose of studying two types of aggression: **instrumental aggression** — which is aimed at the retrieval of an object, territory, or privilege; and **hostile aggression** — which is directed at other people. Interfering with a child's on-going activity resulted in a higher percentage of instrumental aggression among the younger children than the older children. A lower percentage of hostile aggression occurred overall among the younger children than the older ones. Most of the aggression among the preschool-aged children was instrumental or object-directed. The aggression of the older children was a mixture of both object- and person-directed harmful behavior. These findings suggest the influence of cognitive development on aggressive behavior. It appears that younger, more egocentric children are interested only in their toys, territory, and so on. Aggression is likely to appear, therefore, when their personal needs are interfered with. Older children, with a greater degree of social and cognitive development, react not only in order to achieve personal needs but can also act purposely to harm other people.

Older children may act aggressively not only to achieve personal needs but also to harm someone.

Cognitive abilities are also involved in children's evaluations of aggression in others. Researchers studied children's reactions to stories in which the consequences of "naughty" aggression were either serious or less serious (56). Some stories ended with the victim of the aggression falling down and getting a scratch on the leg, while others ended with the victim suffering a broken leg because of the fall. The aggression leading to serious injury was judged to be more naughty by the 8-year-olds than the aggression leading to less serious injury. Twelve-year-olds judged the aggressive activities to be equally serious, even though the outcome was not the same. Either children care less about serious injury as they grow older (which is possible) or, as Piaget suggests, their attitudes toward aggression change and their ability to make moral judgments based on the aggressor's intention rather than on the outcome increases.

The Family and Aggression

Basic attitudes toward aggression are formed in many ways in many circumstances. One of the first and most influential situations in the formation of aggression is obviously the family. Families most likely to produce aggressive children are those in which there is a good deal of violence (mothers and fathers and sisters and brothers often arguing and fighting). Observations of families show that the behaviors most often responsible for aggression in children are acts of aggression by other family members (51). In other words, aggression begets aggression.

Violence in the family often comes in the form of punishment. Punishment for aggression, if administered on a consistent basis, does inhibit or reduce aggression *in the setting in which punishment occurs* (33). Most children know enough to stop their hostile activity when they are faced with strong and consistent counteraggression (punishment). They know, for instance, not to pick on someone bigger, stronger, and more aggressive who always hits back. This does not mean that punishment inhibits aggression in all circumstances. In fact, punishment can actually lead to increased aggression. A great deal of evidence shows that severe parental punishment is associated with high levels of aggression *outside the setting in which the punishment occurs.* A child who has been severely punished may cease hostile activity and not attack the punisher, but that same child may then go outside the home (or classroom or wherever the punishment occurred) and be even more aggressive, possibly as a result of the frustration associated with being punished. The fact that high degrees of parental punishment lead to high levels of aggression outside the home has been confirmed in many studies. In one, all third-grade children in one county in upstate New York were rated by their peers as being more or less aggressive (15). The most aggressive boys and girls were those from homes in which parental punishment was frequent.

Aggressive delinquents have also been found to have more punitive or punishing parents than nonaggressive children (2).

Along with punishment, parental rejection, lack of warmth and affection, and lack of supervision are associated with children's aggressiveness (2). This does not mean that these parental qualities actually cause aggression in children. In many cases there is probably a two-way relationship. It is possible that parental punishment and rejection contribute to the occurrence of aggressive behavior by causing frustration and by providing models of aggression. At the same time aggressiveness on the part of children may encourage parents to be punitive, hostile, and rejecting.

Peers and Aggression

The peer group is probably as important as the family in the development of attitudes toward aggression. Observations of nonhuman primates (monkeys and apes) show that the rough-and-tumble play of peers leads to aggression in many instances, but also teaches young primates how to handle and control aggression and eventually leads to nonaggressive social interactions (24). During the rough-and-tumble experiences of childhood young primates (including humans) learn a number of things, including who they are allowed to play roughly with and what levels of aggressive behavior are acceptable to what individuals. They also learn methods of coping with aggression and the emotional outcomes of aggressive interactions.

Whether parents alone can teach children these things is doubtful. First, the rough-and-tumble experiences necessary for learning how to handle aggression are not usually part of parent-child relationships. The family, for instance, is supposed to protect children from danger, insure an adequate food supply, and provide children with opportunities to learn certain skills. Parent-child attachments help families accomplish these things, but attachments cannot be maintained in the presence of unlimited aggression. Parents cannot carry out their duties as parents when children cannot restrain their rage; at the same time, children cannot withstand uncontrolled parental abuse. Such aggression weakens attachments and breaks the bonds that make it possible for the family to serve its basic purpose.

The peer group, on the other hand, seems to be the most appropriate place for children to learn how to use and control aggression. The peer group provides an escape from parental disapproval of aggression as well as a social ground on which children can experience and learn from aggressive interactions with their equals. What chance, after all, does a child have in a fist fight or shouting match with a full-grown adult?

When children do meet equal or near-equal terms in peer groups they have a chance to experiment with aggressive behaviors, and this experimentation is probably necessary in learning about aggression. Children who have never been the victims of aggression, for instance, may not understand the effects their own aggression can have. In general, successful aggression leads to more aggression. Unsuccessful aggression leads to less aggression. In other words, reinforcement for both aggression and counteraggression (fighting back) helps teach children attitudes toward aggression. Nursery school children's responses to peer aggression provide a good example.

In one study bodily attack and attacking with objects were positively reinforced between 75 percent and 97 percent of the time through crying and passive or defensive behavior on the part of the victim (52). In such cases continued aggression was likely, especially against the same victim. Counteraggression on the part of the victim, however, was usually followed by a change in the response of the aggressor (less aggression) or a change in victims, or both. Children who were victimized and who counterattacked successfully tended to become more aggressive. Those who were not victimized or who counterattacked unsuccessfully showed no change in aggressive behavior.

The Media and Aggression

Much peer interaction takes place in school, and children learn a lot about aggression (and other things) from their peers. Yet, in general, children in the United States spend more time watching television than going to school during the first 15 years of their lives (43). So it is not surprising that children also learn a lot from television. About 80 percent of the television shows in the United States contain violence (20). Since the most violent programs on

In general, children in the United States spend more time watching television than going to school during the first 15 years of their lives.

television are those designed for children, especially cartoons, it is not surprising that children learn a lot about aggression from television.

The effects of all this televised violence have been demonstrated many times. In one typical study 9-year-olds were rated by their classmates with respect to aggressive behavior (14). The children's parents were interviewed with regard to the children's television-viewing habits. The boys who preferred violent television shows were found to be the most aggressive, regardless of how much time they spent watching television. No relation was found between viewing habits and aggression for girls. In a follow-up study of the same boys 10 years later a positive correlation was found between exposure to violence on television at age 9 and aggressive behavior at age 19 (40). These findings strongly suggest that watching violence on television leads to increases in aggressive behavior. It is possible to argue, however, that it is the children who are already aggressive who choose to watch television violence. But this seems not to be the case, as a number of experiments show.

One of the experiments showing that children learn aggressive behaviors from exposure to televised violence was conducted with nursery school children during a summer session (19). The children were observed for three weeks during which the frequency of aggressive behaviors was counted. Then, for four weeks, some children watched aggressive programs ("Superman," "Batman"). Others watched "Misterogers Neighborhood." A third group watched neutral films of farm scenes and circuses. Observations made in the nursery school showed that exposure to the aggressive programs did affect social behavior, but the level of aggression shown during the first observation period was an important factor. Children who were initially high in aggression showed more aggression after exposure to aggressive programs than after either of the other types of programs. Children who were not very aggressive during the first observation were not influenced, as far as aggression is concerned, by any of the programs. These and numerous other studies suggest strongly that television is an important factor (along with the family and peers) in the development of aggression.

Regulation of Aggression

Since there are so many ways to learn aggressive behavior and since aggression is so widespread, the regulation of aggression is an important area in dealing with children. The regulation of aggressive behavior involves two main processes: moment-to-moment control of children's actions and long-term self-control. A teacher, for instance, might give a child a reward during an aggressive outburst in order to stop the problem quickly. This type of reaction may stop the immediate aggression, but it probably also reinforces the child's aggressive behavior and therefore does little in the way of helping the child develop long-term control of aggression.

Typical parental reactions to children's aggressive behavior and both the

Table 10–1
Parental Reaction and Children's Aggression

Parental Reaction	Effective in Reducing Aggression?	
	Immediately	Long-term
1. Diverting child's attention	Yes	Yes
2. Remove source of trouble	Yes	No
3. Isolation	Yes	Yes
4. Ignoring	Yes	Yes
5. Provide substitute activity	Yes	No
6. Bribery	Yes	No
7. Grant child's desire	Yes	No
8. Coaxing	No	No
9. Soothing	No	No
10. Reasoning	No	Yes

immediate and long-term effects are presented in Table 10–1. These results are based on logs kept by a group of parents (22). Close examination of the results shows that three main tactics produced immediate reduction of the angry outbursts: removing the cues associated with the aggressive behavior (this included removing the source of trouble, diverting the child's attention, and isolation); providing a substitute activity (this included bribery); and providing the goal of the aggression or giving in to the child's desire. Punishment of any kind was not effective in the immediate reduction of aggression, nor were parental behaviors that drew attention to the child's aggression but that did not clearly involve substitute behaviors (such as coaxing and soothing). Only removal of aggressive cues was effective in promoting both immediate and long-term control. Providing competing activity and yielding to the child were not effective in long-term training, even though they worked toward the immediate reduction of anger. Reasoning, which did not usually help end specific instances of anger, proved effective in the long term but not in the short term.

Most of the methods used in this study continue to be the methods most often used by adults in their efforts to socialize children's aggression, which is not always an easy task. As has been seen, no single factor seems to be responsible for the development of aggressive behavior, and no one regulatory method can be used in every situation to reduce it. Reduction of aggression to zero is probably not an appropriate goal in most cultures anyway. Rather, the appropriate aims of childhood socialization are to establish clear moral values with regard to the expression of aggression and to provide appropriate training within such a moral framework.

MORAL DEVELOPMENT

Just as the main achievement of infant socialization is the formation of specific attachments, the main achievement of childhood socialization is the attainment of a mature moral outlook. Infants react in a manner that will get them what they need to survive. They seem to neither know nor care for the needs of others. By adolescence, however, most individuals have learned to respect the needs of others and to behave in accordance with social rules and regulations. Moral adults are those who have developed personal standards of behavior, a social conscience, and respect for the rights of others.

While the particular rules that govern the individual's behavior may differ from culture to culture, all societies possess some sort of ethical system. Certain actions have the word "right" attached to them, while others are identified as "wrong." Children are expected to learn right from wrong, to behave in accordance with these values, and, if they do not do so, to have a good explanation for their behavior. Reaching this stage is the goal of **moral development.**

Behavior during the first year of life is essentially amoral, or without morals. During infancy social control comes from external forces—as it does to a great extent throughout life. No appeal to higher-order ethical principles, for instance, will prevent a toddler from snatching a toy from another child. Prevention can be achieved only by (1) removing the child from the situation; (2) distraction or substitution; (3) punishment; or (4) the introduction of a stimulus, such as an authority figure whom the child has learned to model on or obey through past experience.

These preventative measures are seen in almost all systems of justice or morality. Murderers are removed from society and imprisoned. People are encouraged to act out hostility through participation in violent sports (distraction or substitution). Fines and other punishments are administered when people disobey the law. Most people learn to be responsive to a variety of social cues, ranging from stern looks to the presence of the police.

But all moral behavior is not dependent on external forces. During the preschool years children's behavior increasingly comes to be controlled by internal cues. Mental operations and biological processes, including those associated with anxiety and distress, begin to influence moral action. Children who are about to do something they know is wrong, for instance, may begin to feel nervous, anxious, frightened, or even ill. When such internal activities become important considerations in "good" behavior, children are sometimes said to have developed **internalized standards.**

It is important to understand that the existence of internal standards is not something that can be proved. Even if they do exist, they are rarely total and rarely permanent. Standards of moral conduct depend to a greater extent on external forces, as is seen by the fact that they vary from situation to situation. The same children who cheat on arithmetic tests will not necessarily cheat in a game; and cheating in play does not always involve the same children who cheat on tests of athletic skill.

Whether moral controls are internal or external, they do exist, and theories of moral development have been proposed to explain them. Freudian or psychoanalytic theory views the social process as being mainly concerned with the development of controls over "dangerous" inborn drives—especially sex and aggression. This theory is a modern expression of the doctrine that says the child is "innately evil" or possessed of "original sin." Learning theorists, on the other hand, tend to view morality as an accumulation of learned responses (avoidance of "wrong" and tendencies to do what is "right") that result from social interactions in which some behaviors are punished and others are rewarded. This theory is similar to the doctrine that says the mind of the child is a *tabula rasa*, or "clean slate," which is written on by parents, teachers, and the rest of society (see Chapter 1). In other words, all behaviors are learned; none are innate. Finally, cognitive theory suggests that moral development is guided by so-called higher mental processes that emerge naturally during the give-and-take of peer interactions rather than as a result of guidance or pressure from authoritarian adults. This image of the child is similar to Rousseau's description of the child as a "noble savage" of "innate purity." It says that children are basically good and will discover for themselves what is "right" and "wrong."

While each of these theories have useful things to say about moral development, cognitive theory, because it emphasizes a step-by-step emergence of moral thinking, probably presents the clearest picture.

Cognitive Development and Morality

Two major theories of moral development from a cognitive point of view have been proposed, one by Piaget (53) and, more recently, one by Lawrence Kohlberg (38). The theories are similar and are closely related to general cognitive theory (see Chapter 7). According to these theories, moral development, like cognitive development, comes about as children pass through a series of stages. As one stage is replaced by another, the quality of moral thinking changes. These changes represent mental structures that are "integrated" or "generalized." That is, they consist of more than the mere sum of learned avoidances or learned rules. According to this theory morality is not "stamped in" from external sources nor transmitted "ready-made" from adults. Instead, children contribute actively to the working out of new types of moral thought as they interact daily with other people, particularly their peers. The stages of moral development, according to this theory, are the same for every child and follow in the same unchanging order, though the rate of progression through the stages may vary from child to child depending on the quality and quantity of social experiences.

For Piaget, morality consists of both an understanding of social rules and a sense of social justice — commitment to principles of equality and reciprocity (mutual give and take) on which most Western systems of social ethics are based. Piaget's theory is concerned with the changes that occur during childhood related to these two elements in moral thinking. He studied these changes in moral thinking by examining children's conceptions of rules in ordinary games.

During the preschool years, according to Piaget, children are essentially premoral — they do not yet have their own conception of morality and possess no clear understanding of social rules, except for the regulations laid down by adults. Rules are regarded casually at this stage. Organized social activity is likely to be chaotic, with everybody behaving according to different rules, as anyone knows who has ever managed a birthday party for 3-year-olds. Piaget's term "egocentrism" applies to this stage. Children take great pleasure in imitating the ordered activities of their elders, but have no understanding of the reason for doing so. They play, says Piaget, essentially for themselves, just for the fun of running about or hiding or whatever.

After this premoral stage true moral development begins, and goes through two broad stages. The first, called the **stage of moral realism,** usually begins late in the preschool period and is marked by an increase of interest in formal rules and a rigid adherence to them. Compliance with social rules becomes all-important to children at this stage, with children believing that all people should comply with rules because they are sacred and unalterable. Everyone is understood to share the same conceptions of rules and is expected to abide by them. Moral wrong at this stage is measured in terms of the consequences of rule violation rather than in terms of the intention of the wrongdoer, and is accompanied by a belief in "immanent justice" — the notion that wrongdoing will be punished by some externally caused misfortune.

"This second stage," says Piaget, "sets in from the moment when the child, either through imitation or as a result of verbal exchange, begins to want to play in conformity with certain rules received from outside." From the moment children begin to imitate the rules of others, he says, no matter how egocentric their play may be, they regard the rules of the game as sacred and untouchable. Piaget questioned children about the rules for playing marbles and found that at about age 7 or 8 children tend to believe such rules came from God or from their parents. Children at this stage express great respect for such rules. They refuse to alter them and claim that any change, even if accepted by general opinion, would be wrong.

The next stage in moral development, according to Piaget, can be called the stage of **autonomous morality,** or the **morality of reciprocity.** Children begin to understand that rules are made by humans, and that they come from a variety of persons, including the individual members of one's own peer group. Once children understand this, they begin to comprehend that rules can be changed or adjusted according to the situation. This different attitude toward rules is seen in Piaget's questioning of children older than about 10. These children are likely to say that rules are made so that children will not quarrel while playing, but that the rules can be changed as long as most of the others in the game agree. Conformity at this stage is related to the expectations of peers rather than the demands of authority figures. Wrong-doing is measured in terms of intentions rather than outcome. Punishment is understood to come from human sources rather than from impersonal external forces.

Kohlberg has extended and modified Piaget's theory on the basis of interviews with children. The interviews involve the presentation of a series of moral dilemmas about which the child must make a judgment. One frequently used dilemma is this:

> In Europe, a woman was near death from cancer. One drug might save her, a form of radium that a druggist in the same town had recently discovered. The druggist was charging $2,000, ten times what the drug cost him to make. The sick woman's husband, Heinz, went to everyone he knew to borrow the money, but he could only get together about half of what it cost. He told the druggist that his wife was dying and asked him to sell it cheaper or let him pay later. But the druggist said "No." The husband got desperate and broke into the man's store to steal the drug for his wife. Should the husband have done that? Why?

Kohlberg, like Piaget, believes that moral development is related to the general course of cognitive development and that it occurs in sequential stages, except that all individuals do not necessarily pass through every stage nor reach the highest levels of moral thought. He believes that the sequential stages of moral thinking are the same from culture to culture, but that the stages are not necessarily related to age. Assignment to a stage is based on children's answers to the interview dilemmas and on the reasons offered by children in support of their answers.

Kohlberg's description of moral development is more detailed than Piaget's. Kohlberg has described three levels of moral development, each containing two distinct stages (38). At the first level children are said to be premoral. In other words, no true moral development has yet taken place. The behaviors of infants are based on attempts to avoid pain or seek pleasure with no understanding of "goodness" or "badness."

Within this **premoral level** are two stages of primitive morality. Stage 1

During Kohlberg's "good boy"/"good girl" stage of moral development, children act in ways pleasing to those around them.

has to do with punishment and obedience. A young child at this stage is likely to reason thus: "I should not hit the baby because I will get a spanking." Gradually, if moral development proceeds on schedule, the child moves into a second stage in which moral behavior is based on rewards. The child is good in order to receive a reward (rather than to avoid punishment as in the previous stage). This type of "good" behavior is egocentric and reflects no true moral understanding of right and wrong.

The next level of moral development, which Kohlberg calls **conventional morality,** also consists of two stages. The first is the "good boy" and "good girl" stage in which moral behavior consists of behaving in a manner that will help a child avoid disapproval or dislike by others. Behavior at this stage is considered by the child to be moral if it pleases other people or results in the approval of parents, peers, and others important to the child. This type of behavior is gradually replaced by the "law and order" stage. Children at this stage have usually developed great respect for authority and the value of fixed rules (as Piaget found out). The tendency to obey rules by children at this stage appears to be more than a desire to avoid punishment. It seems to be related to a true belief in society's rules and a desire to preserve social order.

Up to and through these four stages morality, according to Kohlberg, is conventional. That is, it is pretty much related to the conventional or accepted rules of society. The final level of moral development is called **post-conventional morality.** It involves the development of a set of personal moral principles rather than acceptance of the principles of one's social or cultural group. The first stage at this level, says Kohlberg, involves the morality of contract, of individual rights, and of democratically accepted law. The individual who has reached this stage considers contracts with others to be morally binding.

Moral action is considered in relation to individual rights and the standards of behavior that have been set up through democratic action. There is also the realization that these rules can be changed by democratic action. People who have reached this stage obey the law not because they want to avoid punishment or receive a reward but because they do not want to lose the respect of society and do not want to be thought of as immoral. Morality by this stage has become more a matter of personal conviction than simply a matter of following rules.

The final and most advanced stage of moral development involves morality of individual principles and conscience. At this highest stage of moral development abstract ethical principles (such as the golden rule) are selected and used to guide individual behavior. These principles are self-selected in the sense that they represent the individual's belief in the sacred nature of human life and the ultimate values of the individual. People who have reached this stage follow their principles in order to avoid self-condemnation ("I couldn't live with myself if I did . . ."). In other words, they have developed a true moral conscience and a true understanding of right and wrong.

Not all of the evidence supports the cognitive explanation of moral development. There are questions, for instance, about whether or not the stages are the same for each child or for each culture. There is no question, however, about the importance of moral development. The possession of a social conscience is one of the most important goals of social development and is necessary if people are to live together in any sort of harmony. When social consciousness does not exist, social life—and society—disintegrate.

SUMMARY

A child's growing understanding that people are necessary, important, and have unique significance is one of the most important achievements of human development. It is the goal of social development. Social development begins moments after birth when infants have their first social encounter and proceeds, according to the theory Erik Erikson, through eight stages. During each stage individuals are faced with a particular type of social crisis or conflict that must be resolved before it is possible to move on to the next stage. Depending on whether or not the crisis is resolved, certain social characteristics or their opposites will be learned.

Moving through the eight stages of psychosocial development requires guidance, and during the first four stages this guidance usually comes from the family. Attachment and dependency behaviors represent the social bond between infants and parents and appear to be the foundation of social development. Numerous situational and social factors have been found to be related to attachment and dependency behavior at various ages and to the development of self-reliance. A workable balance between dependence and self-reliance probably develops as a result of authoritative parenting (a combination of positive reinforcement for independent behavior plus warmth and high parental control).

Social development begins in the home, but as children mature and become more independent it continues outside the home in peer relations, which have lasting effects on social development and behavior. Peer relations are especially influential because children care what their friends think and try to behave in a manner that their friends will approve. Peer modeling and peer reinforcement are two mechanisms by which children influence each other's behavior.

Organized social groups are also important aspects of social development, with common goals being the social glue that holds groups together. Group acceptance is an important part of children's lives, and conformity (displaying the same attitudes and behaviors as others) is one method children have of gaining group acceptance. Although independence is seen in many situations, conformity is especially evident when children are in strange or unfamiliar situations.

Peer and group interactions as well as family life provide children with numerous opportunities to learn and practice social behaviors. Altruism is one of the most important classifications of social behavior. While much remains to be learned about the factors that lead to the development of pro-social behaviors such as altruism, experiments suggest that the best conditions for the development of sympathetic, helpful, and altruistic behavior are those in which children see adults involved in altruistic behavior at every level.

The opposite of altruism is antisocial behavior, the most common form of of which is aggression. Numerous studies have shown that boys are more aggressive than girls. Biological factors may be responsible for this, but social factors are also involved (boys, not girls, are expected to be aggressive in our society).

The most widely studied cause of aggression is frustration, which is usually the result of interference with an ongoing activity. Studies show, however, that frustration need not always lead to aggression and that children can learn to behave constructively in the face of frustration.

The tantrums of infancy may be the beginnings of aggression, which tends to become more physical up to about the age of 3 and then becomes more symbolic and verbal. The media, especially television, appear to be influential in teaching children aggressive responses, and the most aggressive children tend to be those from families in which there are high levels of aggression. Peer-group interactions also stimulate aggression in children, but such interactions are probably necessary if children are to learn methods of controlling and coping with aggression.

The main achievement of socialization is the attainment of a mature moral outlook. From the cognitive development point of view moral development proceeds through three broad stages. During the premoral stage behavior is egocentric and based on pleasure seeking and the avoidance of pain. The stage of conventional morality is based on acceptance of the rules of society. The post-conventional stage of morality, the highest level of moral thinking, is achieved when an individual has developed personal ethical principles and a strong social conscience.

RESEARCH REPORT 10.1

Socialization Practices and Sex Differences

In most societies there are observable personality differences between males and females. The question of whether these differences are a function of innate biological differences or of differences in the way boys and girls are reared has important implications. One involves the extent to which changes in child-rearing practices can induce changes in personality characteristics. To shed light on this question investigators examined the child-rearing practices of different cultures with regard to differentiation by sex to determine whether certain personality characteristics are universal, or found in all human societies. To the extent that a characteristic is universal, the assumption is that it is a result of biological factors rather than factors peculiar to certain cultures.

The study gathered data on the socialization practices of 110 different cultures around the world, most of which were aboriginal. Six different areas of socialization were assessed in terms of whether or not the culture differentiated between the pressures exerted on girls and boys. When no difference was found the culture was given a "no sex difference" rating on that area. When differences were found the direction of the pressure was determined—whether boys were being encouraged to develop the characteristic in question, or girls. The six areas in which socialization practices were evaluated were (1) attention and indulgence toward infants; (2) training for responsibility; (3) nurturance training; (4) obedience training; (5) self-reliance training; and (6) training for achievement.

On the first area, attention and indulgence toward infants, no sex differences were found in 92 percent of the cultures evaluated. That is, infants were not clearly differentiated by sex with respect to these practices in most cultures. On the other five variables sex differences in socialization were much more common. In nurturance training, 82 percent of the cultures evaluated provided stronger socialization for girls, and none provided stronger socialization in nurturance for boys. Eighteen percent showed no sex differences in this area. Self-reliance training was stronger for boys in 85 percent of the cultures studied, and was stronger for girls in none of them. Fifteen percent of the cultures showed no sex differences in training in this area. Training for achievement was stronger for boys in 87 percent of the cultures studied and stronger for girls in 3 percent, and there were no sex differences in 10 percent of the cultures. Responsibility training was stronger for girls in 61 percent of the cultures and stronger for boys in 11 percent; no sex differences on this variable were found in 28 percent of the cultures. Only obedience training showed a higher percentage of cultures having no sex differences (62 percent) with 35 percent showing stronger socialization for girls and 3 percent for boys.

The observed sex differences in the areas of nurturance, self-reliance, and achievement training are generally consistent with some almost universal trends in adult sex role differentiation. The economic roles of men have traditionally more frequently involved tasks in which the man leaves home and needs high skill levels, tasks for which self-reliance and achievement training are good preparation. The economic roles of women have more frequently involved ministering to the needs of others, which requires nurturance skills and responsibility in carrying out routines.

These differentiations go beyond the mere economic, however. Warfare, the prerogative of the aggressive male, also demands self-reliance and achievement. Child bearing and infant care, the biological tasks of the woman, demand nurturance and responsibility.

Further analysis of the data indicated that large sex differences in socialization practices are associated with economic structures that require the superior strength and motor skill development of the male—for example, cultures based on hunting and farming. In addition, large sex differences in socialization practices are associated with social customs related to large family groups (extended families) and high cooperative interaction.

These generalizations are consistent with trends in the more technological cultures toward less differentiation in sex roles in the adult population, particularly in the middle and upper classes. This is seen as the result of the fact that mechanized, technological cultures are less dependent on the physical strength and aggressiveness of the male, leading to less training for these characteristics. Too, the rise of the nuclear family and its isolation from others in the culture means that the male must assume some housekeeping tasks when the woman is ill or not at home. Again, training for the male in nurturance and responsibility could be a help in these functions.

In conclusion, the study data support the generalization that most cultures do differentiate in their socialization pressures toward greater nurturance, obedience, and responsibility for girls and more self-reliance and achievement for boys. The exceptions to this pattern, however, confirm the fact that cultural factors, rather than biological ones, are responsible for the personality differences between the sexes.

Summarized from H. Barry, M. K. Bacon, and I. L. Child, "A Cross-cultural Survey of Some Sex Differences in Socialization," *Journal of Abnormal and Social Psychology*, 1957, 55, 321–332.

RESEARCH REPORT 10.2

The Unique Capabilities of Women

Erik Erikson, one of the first psychologists to study identity formation (see Chapter 11), believes that women need to integrate their biological uniqueness with the new cultural opportunities being made available to them today by occupying roles more traditionally associated with men. This is essential, Erikson argues, because the unique resources of women, which stem from their biological function, must be tapped if we are to resolve the social crises of our times.

In his article "Womanhood and the Inner Space" he states:

There are a great number of economic and practical reasons for an intensified awareness of woman's position in the modern world. But there are also more elusive and darker reasons. The ubiquity of nuclear threat, the breakthrough into outer space, and increasing global communication are all bringing about a total change in the sense of geographic space and historical time, and thus they necessitate nothing less than a redefinition of the identity of the sexes within a new image of man. . . . It is clear that the danger of man-made poison dropping invisibly from outer space into the marrow of the unborn in the wombs of women has suddenly brought one major male preoccupation, namely, the solution of conflict by periodical and bigger and better wars, to its own limits. . . .

The dominant male identity is based on a fondness for what works and for what man can make, whether it helps build or destroy. For this very reason the all too obvious necessity to sacrifice some of the possible climaxes of technological triumph and of political hegemony for the sake of the mere preservation of mankind is not itself an endeavor enhancing the male sense of identity. . . . Maybe if women would only gain the determination to represent publicly what they have always stood for privately, in evolution and in history (realism of householding, responsibility of upbringing, resourcefulness in peacekeeping, and devotion to healing) they might well add an ethically restraining, because truly supranational, power to politics in the widest sense.

But standing in the way of achieving this objective, Erikson points out, is the fact that "self-made man, in 'granting' a relative emancipation to women, could offer only his self-made image as a model to be equalled, and much of the freedom thus won by woman now seems to be spent in gaining access to limited career competition, standardized consumership, and strenuous one-family homemaking." Women are thus at a disadvantage, according to Erikson, because their singular concerns cannot be given the opportunity for expression in roles set up by men for men.

On the other hand, he argues that "the unborn" differences between human males and females can be shown to have a meaningful function within an ecology which is built . . . around the fact that the human fetus must be carried inside the womb for a given number of months, and that the infant must be suckled, or, at any rate, raised within a maternal world best staffed at first by the mother. . . . It makes sense, then, that the little girl . . . tends to survive her birth more surely and turns out to be a tougher creature, to be plagued, to be sure, by many small ailments, but more resistant to some man-killing diseases (for example, of the heart) and with a longer life expectancy. It also makes sense that she is able earlier than boys to concentrate on details immediate in time and space, and has throughout a finer discrimination for things seen, touched, and heard. To these she reacts more vividly, more personally, and with greater compassion. More easily touched and touchable, however, she is said also to recover faster, ready to react again and elsewhere. That all of this is essential to the biological task of reacting to the needs of others, especially weaker ones, is not an unreasonable interpretation; nor should it, in this context, seem a deplorable inequality that, in the employment of the larger muscles, woman shows less vigor, speed, and coordination.

Erikson is quick to point out, however, that these special qualities do not preclude women from taking on men's roles and performing well in them. He warns that

There will be many difficulties in a new joint adjustment of the sexes . . . but they do not justify prejudices which keep half of mankind from participating in planning and decision making, especially at a time when the other half, by its competitive escalation and acceleration of technological progress, has brought us and our children to the gigantic brink on which we live.

Adapted from Erik H. Erikson, "Womanhood and the Inner Space," in Erik H. Erikson, *Identity: Youth and Crisis* (New York: Norton, 1968), pp. 261–294.

REFERENCES

1. Bandura, A., J. E. Grusec, and F. L. Menlove. "Vicarious Extinction of Avoidance Behavior," *Journal of Personality and Social Psychology*, 1967, 5, 16–23.
2. Bandura, A., and R. H. Walters. *Adolescent Aggression.* New York: Ronald Press, 1959.
3. Barnes, K. E. "Preschool Play Norms: A Replication," *Developmental Psychology*, 1971, 5, 99–103.
4. Baumrind, D. "Child Care Practices Anteceding Three Patterns of Preschool Behavior," *Genetic Psychology Monographs*, 1967, 75, 43–88.

5. Baumrind, D. "Current Patterns of Parental Authority," *Developmental Psychology*, 1971, *4*, 1–103.
6. Brittain, C. V. "Adolescent Choices and Parent-Peer Cross Pressures," *American Sociological Review*, 1963, *28*, 385–391.
7. Bryan, J. H., and N. H. Walbek. "Preaching and Practicing Generosity: Children's Action and Reactions," *Child Development*, 1970, *41*, 329–353.
8. Crandall, V. C., W. Katkovsky, and V. J. Crandall. "Children's Beliefs in Their Own Control of Reinforcements of Intellectual-Academic Achievement Situations," *Child Development*, 1965, *36*, 91–109.
9. Dawe, H. C. "An Analysis of Two Hundred Quarrels of Preschool Children," *Child Development*, 1934, *5*, 139–157.
10. Debus, R. L. "Effects of Brief Observation of Model Behavior on Conceptual Tempo of Impulsive Children," *Developmental Psychology*, 1970, *2*, 22–32.
11. Durfee, J. T., and L. C. Lee. "Infant-Infant Interaction in a Daycare Setting," paper presented at the meeting of the American Psychological Association, Montreal, Canada, August 1973.
12. Endsley, R. C., and W. W. Hartup. "Dependency and Performance by Preschool Children on a Socially Reinforced Task," *American Psychologist*, 1960, *15*, 399.
13. Erikson, E. H. *Childhood and Society*. New York: Norton, 1950.
14. Eron, L. D. "Relationship of T.V. Viewing Habits and Aggressive Behavior in Children," *Journal of Abnormal and Social Psychology*, 1963, *67*, 193–196.
15. Eron, L. D., L. O. Walder, L. R. Huesmann, and M. M. Lefkowitz. "The Convergence of Laboratory and Field Studies of the Development of Aggression." In J. de Wit and W. W. Hartup (eds.), *Determinants and Origins of Aggressive Behavior*. The Hague: Mouton, 1974.
16. Feshbach, S. "Aggression." In P. H. Mussen (ed.), *Carmichael's Manual of Child Psychology*, Vol. 2. New York: Wiley, 1970.
17. Fischer, W. F. "Sharing in Preschool Children as a Function of Amount and Type of Reinforcement," *Genetic Psychology Monographs*, 1963, *68*, 215–245.
18. Freud, A., and S. Dann. "An Experiment in Group Living," *The Psychoanalytic Study of the Child*, Vol. VI. New York: International Universities Press, 1951.
19. Friedrich, L. K., and A. H. Stein. "Aggressive and Prosocial Television Programs and the Natural Behavior of Preschool Children," *Monographs of the Society for Research in Child Development*, 1973, *38* (Serial No. 151).
20. Gerbner, G. "Violence in Television Drama: Trends and Symbolic Functions." In G. A. Comstock and E. A. Rubinstein (eds.), *Television and Social Behavior*. Vol. 1: *Media Content and Control*. Washington, D.C.: Government Printing Office, 1972, 28–187.
21. Gewirtz, J. L. "Three Determinants of Attention-seeking in Young Children," *Monographs of the Society for Research in Child Development*, 1954, *19*(2) (Serial No. 59).
22. Goodenough, F. L. *Anger in Young Children*. Minneapolis, Minn.: University of Minnesota Press, 1931.
23. Greenberg, D. J., D. Hillman, and D. Grice. "Infant and Stranger Variables Related to Stranger Anxiety in the First Year of Life," *Developmental Psychology*, 1973, *9*, 207–212.

24. Hamburg, D. A., and J. van Lawick-Goodall. "Factors Facilitating Development of Aggressive Behavior in Chimpanzees and Humans." In J. de Wit and W. W. Hartup (eds.), *Determinants and Origins of Aggressive Behavior*. The Hague: Mouton, 1974.

25. Hartup, W.W. "Friendship Status and the Effectiveness of Peers as Reinforcing Agents," *Journal of Experimental Child Psychology*, 1964, *1*, 154–162.

26. Hartup, W. W. "Peer Interaction and Social Organization." In P. H. Mussen (ed.), *Carmichael's Manual of Child Psychology*, Vol. 2. New York: Wiley, 1970.

27. Hartup, W. W. "Aggression in Childhood: Developmental Perspectives," *American Psychologist*, 1974, *29*, 336–341.

28. Hartup, W. W. "Peer Interaction and the Behavioral Development of the Individual Child." In E. Schopler and R. J. Reichler (eds.), *Psychopathology and Child Development*. New York: Plenum, 1976.

29. Hartup, W. W., and B. Coates. "Imitation of a Peer as a Function of Reinforcement from the Peer Group and Rewardingness of the Model," *Child Development*, 1967, *38*, 1003–1016.

30. Hartup, W. W., and E. D. Keller. "Nurturance in Preschool Children and Its Relation to Dependency," *Child Development*, 1960, *31*, 681–689.

31. Harvey, O. J. and C. Consalvi. "Status and Conformity to Pressures in Informal Groups," *Journal of Abnormal and Social Psychology*, 1960, *60*, 182–187.

32. Heathers, G. "Emotional Dependence and Independence in Nursery School Play," *Journal of Genetic Psychology*, 1955, *87*, 37–57.

33. Hollenberg, E., and M. Sperry. "Some Antecedents of Aggression and Effects of Frustration in Doll Play," *Personality*, 1951, *1*, 32–43.

34. Hoving, K. L., M. Hamm, and P. Galvin. "Social Influence as a Function of Stimulus Ambiguity at Three Age Levels," *Developmental Psychology*, 1969, *1*, 631–636.

35. Isen, A. M., N. Horn, and D. L. Rosenhan. "Success, Failure and Altruistic Behavior," unpublished manuscript, Stanford University, 1971.

36. Jakubczak, L. F., and R. H. Walters. "Suggestibility as Dependency Behavior," *Journal of Abnormal and Social Psychology*, 1959, *59*, 102–107.

37. Kagan, J., and H. A. Moss. *Birth to Maturity*. New York: Wiley, 1962.

38. Kohlberg, L. "Stage and Sequence: The Cognitive-Developmental Approach to Socialization." In D. A. Goslin (ed.), *Handbook of Socialization Theory and Research*. Chicago: Rand McNally, 1969.

39. Lee, L. C. "Social Encounters of Infants: The Beginnings of Popularity," paper presented at the biennial meetings of the International Society for the Study of Behavioral Development, Ann Arbor, Mich., 1973.

40. Lefkowitz, M. M., L. D. Eron, L. O. Walder, and L. R. Huesmann. "Television Violence and Child Aggression: A follow-up study." In G. A. Comstock and E. A. Rubinstein (eds.), *Television and Social Behavior*. Vol. 3: *Television and Adolescent Aggressiveness*. Washington, D.C.: Government Printing Office, 1972, 35–135.

41. Lewis, M., and L. A. Rosenblum (eds.). *Friendship and Peer Relations*. New York: Wiley, 1975.

42. Lieberman, A. F. "The Social Competence of Preschool Children: Its Relation to

Quality of Attachment and to Amount of Exposure to Peers in Different Preschool Settings," unpublished dissertation, The Johns Hopkins University, 1976.

43. Liebert, R. M. "Television Violence and Children's Aggression: The Weight of the Evidence." In J. de Wit and W. W. Hartup (eds.), *Determinants and Origins of Aggressive Behavior.* The Hague: Mouton, 1974.

44. Maccoby, E. E., and C. N. Jacklin. *The Psychology of Sex Differences.* Stanford, Calif.: Stanford University Press, 1974.

45. Maccoby, E. E., and S. S. Feldman. "Mother-attachment and Stranger-reactions in the Third Year of Life," *Monographs of the Society for Research in Child Development,* 1972, 37(1) (Serial No. 146).

46. McCord, W., J. McCord, and P. Verden. "Familial and Behavioral Correlates of Dependency in Male Children," *Child Development,* 1962, 33, 313–326.

47. McDavid, J. W., and H. Harari. "Stereotyping of Names and Popularity in Grade-school Children," *Child Development,* 1966, 37, 453–459.

48. Miller, N. E., and J. Dollard. *Social Learning and Imitation.* New Haven, Conn.: Yale University Press, 1941.

49. O'Connor, R. D. "Modification of Social Withdrawal Through Symbolic Modeling," *Journal of Applied Behavioral Analysis,* 1969, 2, 15–22.

50. Parten, M. B. "Social Participation among Preschool Children," *Journal of Abnormal and Social Psychology,* 1932, 27, 243–269.

51. Patterson, G. R., and J. A. Cobb. "Stimulus Control for Classes of Noxious Behaviors." In J. F. Knutson (ed.), *The Control of Aggression.* Chicago: Aldine, 1973.

52. Patterson, G. R., R. A. Littman, and W. Bricker. "Assertive Behavior in Children: A Step Toward a Theory of Aggression," *Monographs of the Society for Research in Child Development,* 1967, 32 (Serial No. 113).

53. Piaget, J. *The Moral Judgment of the Child.* Glencoe, Ill.: Free Press, 1932.

54. Rosenhan, D. "The Natural Socialization of Altruistic Autonomy," In J. R. Macaulay and L. Berkowitz (eds.), *Altruism and Helping Behavior.* New York: Academic Press, 1970.

55. Rosenthal, M. K. "Effects of a Novel Situation and of Anxiety on Two Groups of Dependency Behaviours," *British Journal of Psychology,* 1967, 58, 357–364.

56. Rule, B. G., and P. Duker. "Effects of Intentions and Consequences on Children's Evaluation of Aggressors," *Journal of Personality and Social Psychology,* 1973, 27, 184–189.

57. Scott, P. M., V. Burton, and M. R. Yarrow. "Social Reinforcement under Natural Conditions," *Child Development,* 1967, 38, 53–63.

58. Sherif, M., O. J. Harvey, B. J. White, W. R. Hood, and C. W. Sherif. *Intergroup Conflict and Cooperation: The Robbers Cave Experiment.* Norman: University of Oklahoma Press, 1961.

59. Smith, H. T. "A Comparison of Interview and Observation Measures of Mother Behavior," *Journal of Abnormal and Social Psychology,* 1958, 57, 278–282.

60. Spock, B. *Baby and Child Care.* New York: Pocket Books, 1976.

61. Staub, E. "A Child in Distress: The Influence of Age and Number of Witnesses

on Children's Attempts to Help," *Journal of Personality and Social Psychology,* 1970, *14,* 130–140.

62. Trotter, R. J. "Is Altruism Dead?" *Science News,* 1971, 3(99), 387.

63. Wahler, R. G. "Child-Child Interactions in Free Field Settings: Some Experimental Analyses," *Journal of Experimental Child Psychology,* 1967, *5,* 278–293.

64. Winder, C. L., and L. Rau. "Parental Attitudes Associated with Social Deviance in Preadolescent Boys," *Journal of Abnormal and Social Psychology,* 1962, *64,* 418–424.

65. Yarrow, M. R., P. M. Scott, and C. Z. Waxler. "Learning Concern for Others," *Developmental Psychology,* 1973, *8,* 240–260.

Children are sexual creatures, and a great deal of their lives will be spent in sex-related activities. Much of the behavior directed at them will be as a result of their maleness or femaleness. "Psychosexual development" is the term used to refer to the manner in which one adjusts to one's sex. Because sex plays a role in many areas of human development, children who are poorly adjusted in this area may suffer a great deal of unhappiness.

psychosexual development

11

INTRODUCTION: CONUNDRUM

I was 3 or perhaps 4 years old when I realized that I had been born into the wrong body, and should really be a girl. I remember the moment well, and it is the earliest memory of my life.

And please, God, let me be a girl. Amen.

It was also worrying for me, for though my body often yearned to give, to yield, to open itself, the machine was wrong.

Sometimes I considered suicide, or to be more accurate, hoped that some unforeseen and painless accident would do it for me, gently wiping the slate clean.

It was a marriage that had no right to work, yet it worked like a dream, living testimony, one might say, to the power of mind over matter—or of love in its purest sense over everything else.

We produced five children, three boys, two girls, but by the nature of things sex was subsidiary in our marriage. It was a friendship and a union of equals, for in our house there could be no dominant male or female place. If we divided our responsibilities, we did it along no sex lines, but simply according to need or capacity.

My quandry was becoming obsessive, however hard I tried to concentrate upon my work, however comforting the consolations of family and friendship. The strain was telling on me—not only the strain of playing a part, but the strain too of living in a male world.

But it could not work forever. The instinct to keep moving played itself out, as I grew older, and as a cat expecting kittens prepares herself a nest in barn or chimney, so there came a time for me when the wandering had to stop. My time was approaching. My manhood was meaningless. With Elizabeth's loving help I abandoned the attempt to live as a male, and took the first step towards a physical change of sex . . . a slow-motion Jekyll and Hyde.

But I do not for a moment regret the act of change. I could see no other way, and it has made me happy . . . I would search the earth for surgeons, I would bribe barbers or abortionists, I would take a knife and do it myself, without fear, without qualms, without a second thought.

If society had allowed me to live in the gender I preferred, would I have bothered to change sex? . . . I hope so . . . But I think not, because I believe the transsexual urge, at least as I have experienced it, to be far more than a social compulsion, but biological, imaginative, and essentially spiritual, too.

These are the words of Jan Morris, a well-known British journalist who was born a male but who remembers always wanting to be female. In her biography, *Conundrum*, which means riddle or unanswerable question, Morris tells the story of her confusing life (69). As a young man named James Morris, he served in the army and then began a successful career as a foreign cor-

James Morris

respondent. In 1953, at the age of 26, he achieved world-wide fame as a reporter on an expedition up Mt. Everest. James Morris married, fathered five children, and lived as a male. Throughout all of this Morris was convinced that he should really be a woman, and he decided to do something about that conviction.

In 1964 Morris began eight years of hormone treatments. Hormones are the body chemicals that help control sexual development (see Chapter 5). During this time Morris took about 12,000 hormone pills that gradually changed his body chemistry and gave him the outward appearance of a woman. He began dressing as a woman, and in 1972 went to Casablanca in Morocco to have a sex-change operation. Since that time Jan Morris (see page 464) has been living as a woman in all ways.

PSYCHOSEXUAL DEVELOPMENT

One of the first questions asked by anyone interested in a newborn infant is whether the baby is a boy or a girl. The answer to this question will have profound significance for the child because the most basic category into which human beings are placed is that of sex—female or male. But as can be seen in the case of Jan Morris, there is much more to being male or female than biological characteristics. In addition to the physical or biological dif-

Jan Morris, after 1972.

ferences between the sexes there are important psychological or social factors involved in being a boy or girl, man or woman. These factors are probably more important in individual psychosexual development than are the biological differences between the sexes.

In order to be happy in most societies it is essential that biological maleness or femaleness be accompanied by psychological and social maleness or femaleness to some degree. Certainly it is possible to be happy while deviating from the expected sex-related behaviors of a society. Many males and females who live a homosexual life-style, for example, do achieve a personally comfortable and socially adequate adjustment in the United States, although this adjustment is sometimes achieved only with great difficulty. On the other hand, children who display those characteristics and behaviors held by society to be appropriate to their sex are likely to achieve an easy and satisfying adjustment to their sexuality.

The fact that society often determines what is or is not appropriate sex-related behavior does not mean that this is "the way things should be." In fact, current sex-role stereotypes in the United States have been found to be rather restrictive for both males and females, and the ongoing movement to de-emphasize sex differences is to the advantage of both sexes. There are real differences between the sexes, and to ignore these differences, especially those on the biological level, would be a potentially serious mistake for a parent, educator, or anyone who deals with children. Instead, a more thorough knowledge of the differences that exist will lead to a better understanding of children and their psychosexual development.

Basic Concepts in Psychosexual Development

"**Psychosexual development**" is the term used to refer to the manner in which one adjusts psychologically to a sex role and learns about one's sexuality (62). Psychosexual development involves both a behavioral *product* and certain psychological *processes*. Concepts such as sexual identity, homosexual, and masculine and feminine usually refer to a set of behavioral products or responses that characterize a person's social and sexual relationships with others. Processes in psychosexual development have to do with the way in which one acquires psychosexual characteristics. The processes include hormonal action and the various mechanisms involved in social learning (see Chapter 6).

Sex, or **gender,** is the biological distinction between male and female, including chromosomal, hormonal, and structural differences between men and women. A **sex role** has to do with the behaviors expected of an individual because of his or her assignment to one or the other sex. Thus a child who is assigned to the category "female" is usually expected to engage in certain behaviors that are different from those expected if the child were a male. **Sex-role stereotype** refers to a particularly strong opinion or belief held by a group of people regarding the behaviors expected of males and females and the extent to which sanctions or rules should be applied to maintain those standards. In all cultures there are individual differences in the degree to which sex-role standards are achieved (20). In the United States, for example, it is important for women to possess some characteristics considered to be stereotypically masculine, and for men to possess certain characteristics that are feminine. In fact, few women can be considered "completely feminine," and few men can be considered "completely masculine." And there is great variation in the degree to which individual men and women conform to the sex-role stereotype.

Sexual identity, or **gender identity,** is the degree to which a person has taken on the behaviors, attitudes, and values associated with the masculine or feminine role (15, 67). Some psychologists (10) have found it helpful to distinguish three aspects of sexual identity: (1) **sex-role orientation** — one's perceptions and evaluations of the degree to which one's internal standards and external behaviors correspond to others' expectations concerning maleness and femaleness; (2) **sex-role preference** — the sex role that one would most like to follow if given free choice; and (3) **sex-role adoption** — the actual behaviors that one exhibits. These three aspects of sexual identity are not always in harmony within an individual. For example, a little boy may prefer to be a little girl, as Jan Morris did, but social pressure usually causes him to adopt the behaviors of a boy. Unless he changes his sex-role preferences, it is unlikely that he will achieve a natural and sincere masculine orientation, although he may be able to live his life as a socially acceptable male. As will be seen later in the chapter, more little girls apparently prefer to be little boys than vice versa, but homosexuality is estimated to be higher among males than among females (32).

Age Progression in Psychosexual Development

Almost everyone who comes in contact with a child acts differently depending upon whether the child is a boy or a girl. Some time roughly between 18 and 36 months of age the child acquires a basic sexual identity (68) and begins to label himself or herself as a boy or as a girl. Between the ages of 2 and 7 the child develops **gender constancy** — the understanding that one's gender does not change from time to time or from situation to situation. Three stages have been identified in the acquisition of gender constancy (78). They are **gender identity, gender stability,** and **gender consistency.** Children are able to label themselves and others as either boys or girls (gender identity) before they realize that it is impossible to change from being a girl to a boy at different times in life (gender stability). These two events, in turn, occur before the child comes to realize that one's sex cannot change from situation to situation or because one wants it to change (gender consistency).

At about the time a basic sexual identity has been established, sex-typed behavior begins to be seen in children. Sex differences in play behavior, with boys being more rough-and-tumble, have been observed among children as young as 2 years old, and play differences between girls and boys are well established by the age of 3 years (22, 25). Although both boys and girls show sex-typed behavior (attitudes, feelings, values, and thought processes considered to be appropriate to one sex or the other) in early childhood, boys are more obviously sex-typed in their activities at this stage than girls are (37). Throughout childhood and even into adolescence boys tend to avoid behaviors they think inappropriate to their sex and prefer their own sex role to a greater extent than girls do. The greater degree of stereotyped sex-role preferences and behavior among boys than among girls, however, may be based on the recognition by both sexes of the higher status and greater number of privileges associated with being a male in the United States (56).

The sex-typing of behavior becomes stronger as children grow older. Elementary school boys are seen to display more masculine attitudes than preschoolers, and by late childhood girls prefer activities considered feminine to a greater extent than at earlier periods. Overall, those children who are most appropriately sex-typed during the early school years maintain a more stereotypic orientation in later life than children showing less stereotyped preferences (47).

BEHAVIORAL DIFFERENCES

There is little doubt that young boys and girls do behave differently. Just how different are the sexes, and what processes are responsible for these differences? Researchers have answered these questions in different ways. Some believe that there are many important personality and cognitive differences between males and females and that these differences are innate or inborn. It has been suggested, for example, that certain characteristics have been biologically built into females as a result of evolution and that these characteristics are directly related to the female's "primary role"—the maternal role (45). It has been further suggested that where sex differences do exist they should be emphasized in the education and socialization of children (33). In this way children will learn behaviors that work with, rather than against, their biological heritage.

Not all researchers agree with this point of view. Psychologist Eleanor Maccoby and C. N. Jacklin examined a great deal of data on the subject, concluding that there are sex differences in only a few areas of development and that many of the observed differences between the sexes are the result of socialization practices and learning rather than of innate processes (57). Because decisions about the rearing of boys and girls are made partially on the basis of what is known about differences between the sexes, it is important to find out which of these differences are truly innate, which are questionable, and which are definitely learned.

Differences at Birth

One of the first obvious differences between the sexes is apparent at birth. Newborn females tend to be more mature than males and more resistant to stress. Newborn males are usually larger, but they are more vulnerable to infections and noninfectious diseases (31). As mentioned in Chapter 4, this susceptibility to stress, infection, and disease results in a higher death rate for infant males than for females.

Researchers have also found that newborn males tend to be fussier, sleep less, and cry more than females. These behaviors could be related to the lower toleration of stress among males, but when they are found during the first years of life they may be due to the widespread custom of circumcising males in the United States (52). One researcher, for example, found that circumcised males were more agitated and slept less than females and uncircumcised males (11). There were no such differences between females and uncircumcised males. The results of this study illustrate the point that documented evidence of behavioral differences between the sexes during the first days of life does not necessarily mean that the differences are innate.

Differences through Childhood

Maccoby and Jacklin reviewed the research evidence related to 19 additional areas in which there are commonly believed to be perceptual and **psychological sex differences.** The results of the studies generally support the following conclusions: girls have greater verbal ability than boys; males are superior to females in visual-spatial and mathematical abilities; and males are more physically and verbally aggressive than females. Although the verbal ability of girls appears to develop more quickly during early childhood, the sexes are similar from preschool years until about age 11. In early adolescence the sexes begin to differ once more, with girls becoming increasingly superior in verbal abilities (including comprehension of difficult written material, creative writing, and verbal fluency). As in all areas in which sex differences have been found, however, there is considerable overlap in the performance of groups of girls and boys in their scores on verbal tests.

Sex differences on visual-spatial tasks have been examined in many ways. Skills involved in these tasks are seen in such activities as detecting spatial relationships among parts of a design despite background camouflage ("hidden figures"), having a good sense of direction, and arranging objects according to two-dimensional patterns (44). While it is not known whether boys or girls (or neither) are superior on these types of tasks in the preschool years, there appear to be no differences between the ages of 5 and 11 years. From early adolescence through high school, however, boys become increasingly better than girls on visual-spatial tasks, a superiority that is maintained until old age. With respect to mathematical skills, the sexes seem to be equal until adolescence when boys begin to surpass females. The superiority of males does not appear to be due entirely to the number of math courses taken.

The most clearly documented sex difference in social behavior is the greater degree of aggression among boys, as mentioned in Chapter 10. Although aggressive attacks are triggered by similar circumstances among boys and girls, the social play of males contains more frequent aggressive activity than the social play of females. Such differences occur in the early preschool years as well as in middle childhood (36). These differences are clearest with respect to physical aggression; the evidence is inconsistent about sex differences in verbal aggression (26).

On the basis of their review Maccoby and Jacklin conclude that there is no evidence to support the following beliefs about sex differences commonly held in the United States: girls have lower self-esteem than boys; girls are more social; girls are more suggestible; girls are better at rote learning and simple repetitive tasks, while boys are better at higher-level tasks; boys are more analytic or logical; girls are affected more by heredity, boys are affected

Cultural and Social Bases of Development   468

more by the environment; girls lack achievement motivation; and girls are auditory while boys are visual. Beliefs about sex differences for which the evidence is lacking or ambiguous include the notion that girls are more fearful, timid, anxious, compliant, and nurturant than boys; and boys are more dominant, active, and competitive than girls.

While there is still much to be learned about which sex differences are innate and which are learned, it is probable that both biological factors and child-rearing practices interact to produce many of the observed differences between boys and girls.

How are maleness and femaleness defined biologically? At least five factors are involved (14):

1. Chromosomal composition (XX for the female and XY for the males).
2. Composition of the gonads or sex glands (ovarian tissue for females and testicular tissue for males).
3. Hormonal composition (the estrogen-androgen balance, estrogens being the female hormone and androgens the male hormone).
4. Internal structures (vagina, uterus, ovaries, and fallopian tubes for females; seminal vesicles and prostate gland for males).
5. External genitals (clitoris and labia for females; penis and scrotum, containing testicles, for males).

Two other genetically controlled reflexive actions accompany maleness and femaleness (62). The first is the capacity for **tumescence,** or a swelling and enlargement of the sex organs. This is seen in both sexes but is more obvious in males. For example, complete male genital erection is possible during the earliest days of life. This reaction may be the result of pressure from a full bladder or of penile manipulation.

A second reflex in sexual behavior is orgasm and ejaculation. **Orgasm,** or **sexual climax,** can be produced in human infants of either sex, although the male's ability to ejaculate is not acquired until puberty. The production of eggs by the female and normal sperm by the male is usually delayed until later in the cycle of puberty.

Additional biological sex differences include body size and shape, distribution and amount of fatty and muscular tissue, and distribution and amount of body hair. While some of these differences become more obvious after puberty, they are usually plain enough so that a child's biological sex can be seen at a glance.

For most individuals the factors involved in biological sex are either male or female (chromosomal composition, hormonal composition, gonads, and so forth, are all either male or female). This is not true, however, in all cases. John Money, a psychologist at The Johns Hopkins Hospital, has worked with a number of children and adults for whom the factors involved in sexual development were not all male or all female. Money's work with these individuals has aided in the understanding of the processes involved in psychosexual development, including the role that biological factors play in these processes (66).

Money's investigation of psychosexual development begins with the human **embryo,** the organism in one of its first stages of development (see Chapter 4). Early in the life of the embryo undifferentiated gonads (neither male nor female) and both Mullerian and Wolffian ducts develop (these ducts are the structures that will develop into female or male internal sex organs, respectively). The sex chromosomes (XX for female and XY for males) are responsible for the development of the gonads in the unborn child. If a Y chromosome is present, testes develop; if a Y chromosome is not present, ovaries grow. In turn, the hormones produced by the testes stimulate development of the Wolffian ducts into internal male structures, while the Mullerian ducts wither away. If testicular hormones are not present, the Mullerian ducts develop into internal female structures while the Wolffian ducts wither away. Thus tissues exist in the embryo for a short period during pregnancy which can lead to the formation of a child with either male or female internal genital organs or, in very rare instances, structures of both sexes (hermaphrodites). In order to have masculine development, something must be added: a Y chromosome for masculine gonads and testicular hormones for internal male genitalia. Without these additions female development takes place. This has led some investigators to say that the basic developmental pattern is female (66).

There is a critical or important period for the development of the external genital organs around the end of the third month of pregnancy. During the first weeks of prenatal life the external genitalia have the capacity to develop into either male or female forms. Again, something must be added in order for masculine development to occur. If **androgen,** the male sex hormone, is present in sufficient quantities during the critical period, the fetus will develop a penis and scrotum. In the absence of androgen the external genitalia will grow into a clitoris, labia minora, and labia majora.

Money and his colleagues studied genetic females who received extra androgen during the critical period for external genitalia development. The extra amount of androgen was due either to overactive or malfunctioning glands in the fetus or the mother, or because the mother was receiving an androgen-like drug to prevent miscarriage. Although the infant girls had internal female organs, many were born with external genitals indistinguishable from those of males, and they were labeled as boys at birth. If the mistake in sex assignment was discovered prior to the age of 18 months or so, it usually was possible to correct the external organs surgically and reassign the child as a female. Naturally, the parents and other relatives often needed considerable counseling and support at such a time. After the age of 3 years, however, reassignment was almost impossible due to the child's classification of himself as a boy. Based on these findings, Money and his co-workers have hypothesized that there is a critical, or sensitive, period between approximately 18 months and 3 years of age for the development of a child's basic sexual identity.

A situation similar to this exists among genetic males. Due to a genetic abnormality, some individuals do not respond to the effects of the androgen. Genetic males born with this **"androgen-insensitivity syndrome"** have internal male sexual organs and external female genitals. These infants are almost always labeled female at birth and reared as girls. The incongruence or mismatch between chromosomal sex and internal structures on the one hand and external structures and assigned sex on the other often is not discovered until adolescence when the girl does not menstruate. In other instances the discovery is not made until adulthood when sexual intercourse is difficult due to a short vagina or when the woman is unable to conceive a child.

In addition to its role in the development of genital structures, androgen also affects the organization of the hypothalamus (a part of the brain that controls certain biological activities). Parts of the hypothalamus become organized in males and females in such a way that they react differently to later hormonal discharge, particularly at puberty. These differences in sensitivity to androgen are thought to be factors that influence later social development. For example, female monkeys that have been masculinized by prenatal injections of androgen show male play behaviors, including elevated levels of rough-and-tumble play (89). Similarly, in human beings, Money and his colleagues found that fetally androgenized girls (those who had received too much androgen before birth), in comparison with normal girls, were more masculine in their behavior (19). The androgenized girls who had been surgically corrected early in life so their external genitals could not be distinguished from those of normal girls preferred to play with boys, saw themselves as tomboys, and preferred outdoor sports over other activities considered to be more feminine. In contrast, individuals with the androgen-sensitivity syndrome (genetic males with external female genitalia) were described as fitting the stereotyped feminine role very closely (59). These women whose brains presumably were not affected by androgen during the critical period were unmistakenly feminine.

From such evidence it appears that androgen, which is responsible for certain physical structures in the male, is also a factor in the development of certain behavior patterns among human beings. Androgen affects the hypothalamus before birth so that most male and female brains are different. The hypothalamus in males is sensitive to the small quantities of androgen circulating in the body during childhood, as well as the increased amounts that are produced after puberty. This sensitivity to androgen may be a factor in the greater degree of aggression observed among males. However, there are very complex interactions between biological and sociocultural factors in determining social behavior. While it would be a mistake to ignore biological factors in human development, especially those factors that may influence male and female behavior patterns, most sex differences do not come from biological sources. As Money and his co-workers clearly have shown, the sex to which a child is assigned (even if the assignment is wrong) is important for the development of the individual's sexual identity.

**Sex Reassign-
ment: A Case
Study**

The importance of **assigned sex** can be seen dramatically in the case of one child treated by Money. The parents of the child had a normal set of male identical twins whom they had had circumcized at the age of 7 months. The electric current used in the circumcision was too strong, and the entire tissue of the penis on one boy was burned. The tissue then decayed and the penis fell off.

The parents were understandably upset and saw a number of medical people in hope of finding some answer for their son's problem. Finally they consulted with a plastic surgeon who was familiar with the principles of sex reassignment (from male to female, or vice versa), and this doctor recommended the boy be reassigned as a girl. After months of agonizing over the decision, the parents changed the child's name, clothing, and hair style and allowed doctors to begin surgical reconstruction of the child's genitalia at the age of 21 months. The construction of a fully-functioning vagina will take place when the child's body is fully grown.

Money and his colleagues have kept track of the child for approximately six years, beginning at the time of the first surgical reconstruction of the child's genital organs. The mother was able to report in great detail the differences between the twins, as well as the reactions of family members to the two children.

The first aspects of change for the child were clothes and hairdo. The mother began to let the girl's hair grow and dress her in pink slacks and frilly blouses. Soon the mother made a special effort to keep her daughter in dresses, hair ribbons, bracelets, and even "granny gowns" for night wear. Within a year or so the child had a clear preference for dresses over slacks, and she took pride in her long hair. In contrast to her twin brother, she soon acquired a strong dislike for being dirty.

Boys and girls receive different socialization and treatment from parents with respect to genital functioning, sex, and reproduction. According to the mother, the young girl learned to sit down to urinate, although she often tried to copy her brother and made "an awful mess." The children began to learn their future reproductive roles, the little girl planning to be a mother and the boy a father, with the parents pointing out the desirability of each role for their children. The twins also modeled the role behavior of their parents. The mother reported instances of the little boy copying his father's behavior in relation to his sister: "Like he'll bend over and give her a kiss on the cheek or he'll give her a hug—and if he (my husband) gives me a swat on the fanny, he'll go and give her a swat on her fanny, too." The boy clearly imitated his father's behavior, and most of the time the girl copied her mother's responses.

Although the daughter developed interests in domestic activities and wanted and received dolls, a doll house, and a doll carriage for Christmas, she had many tomboyish traits, such as abundant physical energy, a high activity level, and dominance in a girls' group. The mother attempted to discourage such behavior, reporting that she was trying, without great success when the girl was about 6 years old to train her to be more quiet and ladylike.

This case demonstrates the possible effects of early biological factors influencing the tomboyish behavior of this little girl (and it is completely appropriate to call her a girl because this is the category to which she has been clearly assigned). However, the strong influences of the child's assigned sex on her behavior, her parents' socializing attempts, and the reactions of her brother toward her as a girl can also be seen. If she follows the typical pattern reported by Money in similar cases, she will continue to develop a comfortable and satisfying identity as a female (67).

Social and Cultural Factors

A look at the wide range of differences in sexual development and sexual behavior around the world demonstrates clearly that human sexual behavior is strongly influenced by cultural factors. The form and timing of sexual development vary greatly within and between cultures (62). So do the style and frequency of sexual practices and the degree of tolerance of sexual "deviation." This wide **cross-cultural variation in sexual practices** indicates not only the importance of social factors or cultural learning on sexual behavior and attitudes, it illustrates the plasticity or changeability of human behavior and the power of social forces to change a basic human drive.

In one anthropological analysis of sexual behavior societies have been rated on a scale of restrictiveness-permissiveness about sexual practices and the socialization of sexual behavior (28). In the most extreme societies, for example, ultrasecretive and limited sexual contact usually occurs between adults; young children and adolescents are denied access to sexual knowledge and are prevented from expressing sexual interests in any form. Methods of enforcement of this restriction include such things as strict separation or segregation of the sexes until marriage, continuous adult chaperonage of girls, and threats of severe disgrace, physical punishment, or even death.

Societies at the other end of the scale take an extremely permissive approach to sexuality. Sex play among children may be allowed in public. Children are not kept from observing adult sexual activity in the home and may even be sexually stimulated by their parents or caregivers through masturbation. In addition to a wide variety of sexual practices, widely different beliefs are usually associated with restrictive or permissive approaches to human sexuality. Belief in a vengeful god and fear of social retribution are often associated with restrictiveness. Where open sexuality among the young is encouraged, beliefs include the idea that children must have sexual exercise early in life in order to achieve fertility, or that girls will not mature without the benefit of sexual intercourse.

While cross-cultural differences in sexual behavior are numerous, there are also certain regularities surrounding sex and marriage from culture to culture. In fact, no culture is without laws, both written and "unwritten," that relate to sexuality, regardless of how permissive or restrictive the culture may be (62). For example, sanctions against rape, incest, and sexual relations between adults and children exist in virtually every organized society (58). Values apparently related to preservation of the family unit can be seen in still other cross-cultural regularities. These include the widely held beliefs that mothers should be married; that marriage is not taken on for a short-term period; and that mothers should live with their children. In the United States these beliefs may not be as strong as they once were; but no matter what attitudes are held by a society, it is usually these attitudes that will affect child-rearing practices and will be passed on from generation to generation.

Sex-role Stereotypes in the United States

Beliefs about sexual behavior and what is expected of males and females are so widespread that most U.S. parents have a good idea of what to expect of their sons and daughters. These expectations, in turn, affect parental perceptions of and behavior toward their children, with sons and daughters being seen and treated differently even in areas where no difference exists. In one study, for example, parents were asked to describe their first-born child's behavior (75). The researchers interviewed both the mothers and fathers of 15 male and 15 female infants within the first 24 hours of life. Although the male and female infants did not differ in birth length, weight or on measures of general health, both mothers and fathers described their infant daughters and sons differently. Daughters were seen as softer, finer-featured, smaller, and more inattentive than the sons. Mothers and fathers agreed with one another in their descriptions, except that both fathers of sons and fathers of daughters rated their children more extremely than did the mothers. Sons were rated as firmer, larger-featured, better coordinated, more alert, stronger, and hardier by their fathers than by their mothers. Likewise, fathers rated their daughters as softer, finer-featured, more awkward, more inattentive, weaker, and more delicate than did the mothers. In other words, although the parents had had very little time for interaction with their offspring, and there were no apparent differences between the infants except for sex, the parents perceived the qualities and behaviors of the boys and girls differently.

In another study researchers examined the contents of the rooms of 48 boys and 48 girls among upper middle-class families in a university town (73). The ages of the children ranged from 1 month to almost 6 years of age. The rooms of boys often had animal decorations, contained more vehicles, educational-arts materials, sport equipment, toy animals, machines, live animals, and military toys. The girls' rooms were more likely to have a floral design with lace, fringe, and ruffles. There were no differences in the number of books, musical instruments, or stuffed animals in the rooms of the children. The children may have had some role in determining which toys were bought for them, but considering their ages, the differences in the content of boys' and girls' rooms most likely reflected the attitudes of their parents about what was appropriate for little girls and boys. Apparently, parents in the mid-1970s are behaving in accordance with very definite sex-role stereotypes.

There is much additional evidence that strong and consistent sex-role stereotypes among children and adults are being maintained in the United States. A number of studies have shown that school-aged children of all social classes can state which toys and activities are preferable for a child their age (27, 60). Elementary school children state that aggression, independence, competence, and dominance are characteristic of males, while female traits include affection, nurturance, and passivity (35). In one of several studies with college students and adults in the northeastern United States, there was almost perfect agreement between men and women about the content of male and female sex-role stereotypes, as well as the characteristics considered socially desirable for the population at large (74). The male-valued and female-valued behaviors are given in Table 11–1. As can be seen, more of the valued traits for an adult in this country are classified as male than female. When asked about themselves, most of the people in the study revealed self-concepts that were less extreme than the stereotypes but were sex-typed nevertheless. Individuals of both sexes, especially women, included characteristics they considered negative in their self-concepts. These stereotypes were independent of sex, age, religion, educational level for younger people, and marital status (13). There seems to be considerable agreement among people of varying backgrounds about the different characteristics associated with the adult male and female social roles.

In general the masculine role in the United States can be described as "instrumental" and the feminine role as "expressive" (70). In other words, the masculine (father) role is one of making decisions, mastering environ-

Table 11-1
Male- and Female-valued Stereotypic Sex-role Characteristics

Male-valued Characteristics

Aggressive	Feelings not easily hurt
Independent	Adventurous
Unemotional	Makes decisions easily
Hides emotions	Never cries
Objective	Acts as a leader
Not easily influenced	Self-confident
Dominant	Not uncomfortable about
Likes math and science	being aggressive
Not excitable in a	Ambitious
minor crisis	Able to separate feelings
Active	from ideas
Competitive	Not dependent
Logical	Not conceited about appearance
Worldly	Thinks men are superior
Skilled in business	Talks freely about sex with men
Direct	

Female-valued Characteristics

Does not use harsh language	Interested in own appearance
Talkative	Neat in habits
Tactful	Quiet
Gentle	Strong need for security
Aware of feelings of others	Appreciates art and literature
Religious	Expresses tender feelings

mental problems, getting the job done, and dispensing rewards and punishments. The expressive (mother) role is directed toward handling the social and emotional needs of other people with supportive, concerned, affectionate, and conciliatory behaviors. The beliefs that many people hold about the female and male roles are very similar to these descriptions whether or not the behaviors of males and females actually conform to the stereotypes.

Sex-typing and Social Class

As discussed in Chapter 3, there are important differences among the social classes in the United States, especially in child-rearing practices. Therefore, it is not surprising that there appears to be a relation between sex typing and social class. While stereotypic notions about the sexes may be similar among people from the various social classes, especially for younger people, it seems that individuals from the lower socioeconomic groups in this country may be more strict in enforcing sharply defined sex-typed behavior (39).

In one investigation children were studied separately in various sex and social class groups (72). Lower-class boys were the first clearly to identify themselves with masculine interests, whereas middle-class girls were the last to take on a pattern of feminine interests. Lower-class girls and middle-class boys were between these two extremes. The average lower-class boy showed sex-typed behavior quite clearly (choice of masculine rather than feminine toys) by the time he was about 4 or 5; not until some three or four years later did the average middle-class girl show similarly sex-typed behavior.

A study with 8- to 10-year-old boys and girls also found that lower-class boys had a stronger masculine sex-role preference than upper-middle-class boys (34). There were no differences between the lower- and upper-middle-class girls. These studies used a measure of sex-role preference called the "It Test" (15). "It" is a stick figure without features that vaguely resembles the human shape. The assumption behind the test is that children will consider or "identify" themselves as "It," and that the sex role and activities they choose for "It" are actually those that they would choose for themselves. The testing procedure consists of having "It" indicate a preference for being a boy or a girl; choose between a number of pairs of toys, one of which is clearly masculine, the other clearly feminine; and indicate a friendship preference for one of several differently drawn figures, ranging from boyish boys through girlish girls. There is strong evidence that the "It" figure objectively resembles a boy more than a girl (27, 80). Thus, while some children may make choices for themselves, others will make realistic choices for the sex they think the figure to be. If the boys tested were making choices based on their knowledge of what was considered appropriate activities for males, it appears that these lower-class boys perceive the permissible role for a boy in a more restricted way than do upper-middle-class boys.

Speculations about the causes of social class differences in sex-role development are various. It seems likely that masculine and feminine roles are more clear-cut among the lower- or working-class population than they are in the middle class, and that the masculine role is more attractive than the feminine. It has also been found that lower-class mothers make a greater distinction between boys and girls in their reported views of what is desirable for children of each sex (51). Working-class men do heavy work on their jobs and assume little care for their children or the house. Working-class women, when employed, usually take such traditionally feminine jobs as housekeeping, cooking, or laundering. But the middle-class group, both father and

Sex-roles are usually not as rigid for middle-class children.

mother, may be teachers or lawyers or work in the family business. Middle-class wives frequently handle the family finances and drive the automobile with equal or greater frequency than the husband. Middle-class fathers help with the dishes and may do the shopping as they come home from the office. So, models for the middle-class child's behavior are often less distinctive and more flexible than those of lower-class children. This is especially true when the mother works outside the home. It is also likely that lower-class parents have less tolerance for individual differences on the part of their children than do middle-class parents (39). The peer group (the child's same-age friends) may be especially important for sex-typing among lower-class children. The sanctions for sex-typed behavior are mercilessly enforced in many peer groups, leading to relatively exaggerated masculinity and femininity.

THEORIES OF PSYCHOSEXUAL DEVELOPMENT

The formation of a firm and comfortable sexual identity is an important developmental task for the growing child. Behavioral scientists have devoted much effort to understanding and explaining the processes by which children acquire their sexual identity. Several major theories have been influential in guiding research in the area of psychosexual development.

Classical
Psychoanalytic
Theory

Freudian theory, as discussed in Chapter 1, has had a major impact on the study of personality development, and his concept of "identification" has been especially influential in explaining psychosexual development (29). **Identification** in this sense has to do with the tendency to incorporate or adopt the behavior of other individuals or groups. Freud's ideas about identification continued to change throughout his writings, but he basically discussed two processes in the development of sexual identity. The first is called **anaclitic identification.** "Anaclitic" is from the Greek word meaning "to lean on" or "to depend on" and has to do with the tendency to depend on another person for emotional support. According to Freud, anaclitic identification is the primary method by which females are thought to acquire feminine characteristics. It consists of a strong dependency and emotional attachment based on fear of the loss of love from a nurturant or giving parent. Both boys and girls form an intense initial attachment in infancy with their major caregiver, who usually is the mother. As the infant experiences separation from the mother, which must happen at some time to all children as the mother goes about routine matters and imposes schedules on her infant, the child becomes fearful about permanently losing the support and nurturance of the mother. In order to defend against the tension and anxiety caused by possibly losing the mother's love, as well as making an effort to please her, the child begins to take on various personality aspects of the mother. Through such activities as imitation of maternal behaviors, it is believed, the tension and anxiety provoked by a possible withdrawal of maternal love are reduced. Continued imitation and adoption of the mother's behaviors and attitudes lead to the development of a feminine identity similar to that of the mother.

The major process involved in the development of a masculine identity has been called **defensive identification,** or identification with the aggressor. During the Oedipal stage of development (see Chapter 1), which occurs approximately between the ages of 3 and 5 years, the boy sexually desires his mother and becomes intensely hostile toward his father, who is reviewed as a rival. These incestuous wishes directed toward the mother and hostility directed toward the father are kept under control by the child's fear of his father's strength and the possibility of punishment, especially castration. Since this fear is great and the loss of his genitals is unthinkable, the young boy copes with his father's strength by "internalizing" aspects of the paternal character — that is, he acts out fantasies of being the father. This serves the dual purposes of convincing the father that his son is an ally rather than an enemy and allows the boy to possess his mother (in thought) once he has taken on parts of his father's personality. The Oedipal conflict is resolved for the boy by repressing both his incestuous sexuality and feelings of aggression along with adopting personality characteristics of his father. At the end of the Oedipal stage the little boy supposedly has become more like his father and, thus, appropriately masculine.

Freud's theory has been influential, but it has been attacked for several reasons. These include his statements that women have weaker consciences than men, since the identification process is supposedly less harsh for girls, and his explanation of female psychology in terms of the woman's **penis envy,** or her realization that she lacks a penis. There is no convincing evidence to support the idea of weaker consciences among women. In fact, most investigators find that in experimental situations girls show greater resistance to temptation than do boys (57). In regard to penis envy, it is probable that Freud confused biology and culture. Social stereotypes are more important to understanding the psychology of women than are the genital differences between males and females. In U.S. culture being a boy usually carries with it more prestige than being a girl. Any "envy" seen on the part of females is probably due to differences in social prestige rather than differences in genitals.

Role Theory

The **role theory** of psychosexual development suggests that the father is important in producing appropriate sexual identities in both boys and girls (instead of just boys, as Freudian theory suggests). According to this theory, fathers play different "roles" with their male and female children, and these roles lead to differences in psychosexual development between males and females (46). The initial identification for both sexes is with the expressive mother who uses love-oriented techniques of control, a method that is thought to be important for the development of internal controls (conscience). Unlike the father, the mother tends not to discriminate between her children because of differences in sex. While the expressive mother may be important in the formation of a conscience in both boys and girls, the father teaches his daughter the expressive role by rewarding her for being attractive and "feminine," and his son the instrumental role by demanding that the boy act like a man. In other words, the father plays the role of a teacher to his son and a husband to his daughter.

Results from numerous studies tend to support various aspects of the role theory of psychosexual development. As the theory suggests, there does seem to be a relation between mothers' level of moral judgment and the children's, but not between fathers' and children's (50). Many investigators have also found evidence supporting the idea that the father is a crucial person in the development of a typical and comfortable sexual identity for both boys and girls. Fathers do appear to treat their sons and daughters differently, more so than mothers do (75); and father-identified males and females tend to be better adjusted than mother-identified individuals (10). Adolescent girls from father-absent homes, for example, are less comfortable and less appropriate in their behavior toward males than are girls from father-present homes (42). Furthermore, while the behavior of mothers may be one factor in the formation of a homosexual identity for males, father-child interactions play a central role in the establishment of a homosexual life-style for both male and female homosexuals (82).

Social Learning Theory

As mentioned in Chapter 6, the principles of **learning theory** can be helpful in explaining almost any category of an individual's behavior and, thus, can be used to describe the acquisition of sex-typed behavior (2). The major learning principles involved include reinforcement, punishment, and modeling, or imitation. As has been seen, very early in life children learn what their sex is, what is expected of people of that sex, and the behaviors that are valued for boys and girls. Children are given positive reinforcement for behavior appropriate to their sex, while inappropriate behavior is either punished or ignored. In addition, children learn a great deal by observing others in their environment without directly experiencing the consequences of performing the behaviors. Social learning theorist Albert Bandura stresses the importance of observational learning, pointing out that if children had to learn *everything* through direct experience, their life spans would be very short (3).

Boys appear to receive greater social pressure to engage in sex-typed behavior than do girls. Both parents, but especially fathers, place fewer restrictions on girls engaging in cross-sex activities than they do on boys (24). This is seen in the fact that boys are rewarded for masculine behavior and punished for feminine behavior, while young girls typically are not punished for masculine behavior (62). Early in life parents and other family members are the primary dispensers of rewards and punishments; but as the child grows older other people, especially peers and teachers, are important in reinforcing and punishing sex-related behaviors.

Very early in life children acquire the ability to imitate, and parents, siblings (brothers and sisters), peers, teachers, textbooks, and television characters all serve as models for children of both sexes. The ability to imitate these models becomes an increasingly useful method for learning new skills, acquiring information, and learning to solve problems. The act of modeling is itself often rewarded ("You are acting like a little man, just like your father" or "You're going to make someone a good wife"), and behaving like a model often brings the same rewards for the child that it brought for the model. The characteristics of the model are important in determining whether or not a child will imitate the modeled behavior. Imitation occurs more often, for example, when children see the model as being similar to themselves—high in competence, expert in some area that is important to them, warm and nurturant, and the controller of valued resources (1).

Cognitive-Developmental Theory

Cognitive-developmental theory, based on the work of Piaget, suggests that structural patterns of thought change as children mature and increase the range of their interactions with their environment (49). For example, as stated earlier in the chapter, there seems to be an orderly sequence in the development of gender constancy, with gender identity and gender stability occurring prior to gender constancy. These sequential stages could be related to the stages of cognitive development described by Piaget (see Chapter 7). Children's basic sexual identity starts with their achievement of a simple cognitive self-categorization early in life as a boy or girl. Once this categorization is stabilized or made permanent, it is usually irreversible and serves as the basic organizer of sex-role attitudes and values throughout life. Such a stabilization of sexual identity may correspond to the stages of cognitive development, specifically to the concept of object permanence (realization that physical objects continue to exist even though out of sight), which usually occurs by about the second birthday.

The child's self-categorization as a boy or girl is an important determinant of basic preferences and values. For example, once a girl has classified herself as a female, she prefers the feminine role and all the trappings associated with it. She seeks out same-sex models in order to learn appropriate behavior, and reinforcement for modeling on other females serves as informational feedback that she is correctly adopting the feminine role. In other words, sex-typed behavior is neither the product of incorporating elements of the same-sex parent nor the direct consequence of the long processes of reinforcement and modeling. Rather, according to cognitive theory, it is the result of children actively seeking out behaviors that are associated with their own sex.

Comparing the Theories

Classical psychoanalytic theory has been influential in stimulating thought about and research in the entire area of psychosexual development. In fact, before Freud little or no attention had been paid to psychosexual development. However, many aspects of the theory are difficult to test, and some parts of it have not been supported by research findings. The role theory of sexual identification fits with many of the findings in the gender-identity research, but by equating expressiveness with the mother's (feminine) role and instrumentality with the father's (masculine) role, this theory overlooks the variability and flexibility in behavior among modern men and women. Cognitive theory has stimulated both interesting research and new ways of looking at the process involved in psychosexual development, but the attention it pays to universal sequences of cognitive development leads to a neglect of both the individual variations in gender identity and the cultural pressures that bear on psychosexual development.

While all of these theories have been useful, it is the powerful processes discussed in social learning theory that are probably the most useful in understanding the formation of gender identity in the child, as long as the role of cognitive structuring is also recognized (65).

ROLE OF SOCIALIZING AGENTS IN PSYCHOSEXUAL DEVELOPMENT

From the moment of birth, when sex assignment takes place, children experience a different sort of treatment than they would have received if they had been assigned to the opposite sex. Most of the people in the child's world will come to expect different types of behavior from the baby, depending on its

In the United States the father plays an important part in the sex-typing of both boys and girls.

sex. The names of children usually depend on their sex; infant boys still are often dressed in blue and girls in pink, and different behaviors are looked for and reinforced in the two sexes very early in life ("He's so active, just like a boy," "She's so sweet and cuddly, just like a girl"). Because of this, the roles played by family members, peers, teachers, and the mass media are extremely important in sex-typing and the development of gender identity.

The Family and Psychosexual Development

In the United States the father plays a very important part in the sex-typing of both boys and girls, especially for his sons, as we have seen. While the mother has some influence on the development of femininity in girls, she appears to have little effect on the acquisition of male characteristics among boys, except that she may weaken her son's masculinity if she is too dominant (40). The actual masculinity of the father and femininity of the mother, however, have been found to be relatively unrelated to sex-typing behavior of their same-sex offspring (50). If a father scores high on some measure of masculinity, his son will not necessarily score high in masculinity as well. Instead, it appears that the attitudes of parents and their treatment of their children are related to the development of masculinity and femininity. Both parents encourage "sex-appropriate" behavior in their children and discourage that which is "inappropriate," especially for their sons. The father, however, appears to be more insistent in expecting sex-typed behavior among his off-spring than the mother, and several studies have found the strongest relations to be between the fathers' encouragement of sex-typing behaviors and their daughters' femininity (46, 77). The lack of relation between the fathers' encouragement of "sex-appropriate" behavior and their sons' masculinity may be because most boys are so strongly masculine that the fathers' encouragement of sex-typing would not appear to be necessary—other members of society, in addition to fathers, exert pressure on boys to be masculine.

The most important parental characteristics relating to the masculinity of sons and femininity of daughters appear to be warmth, nurturance, and dominance (41). Nurturance and warmth of the same-sex parent enhance the learning of "sex-appropriate" qualities in both boys and girls. In addition, there is a clear tendency for children to adopt the adult who controls those things children value, such as a weekly allowance or permission to stay up late at night (3). This finding is related to the results of studies showing that children imitate more often and are more similar to the dominant (controlling) than the passive parent. When the father is the dominant parent, both boys and girls tend to identify with him. This situation has been found to be related to increased masculinity in boys, but not in girls. Girls still tend to retain their femininity, even when they identify closely with a dominant father. When the mother is the dominant parent, both boys and girls tend to identify with her. As mentioned earlier, this situation can lead to decreased masculinity in boys (40).

Dominance patterns in U.S. families are changing—at least in middle-class families—and there may be still greater changes in the future. In fact, it seems that major changes are occurring in society that may lead to expectations of different role relationships between the sexes, both inside and outside the family. It is difficult to say what these changes will bring, but research suggests that a complete reversal of the traditional dominance pattern with the mother clearly dominant to the father may lead to adjustment problems for both sons and daughters (82). Since the family is a social system that functions through the contributions of both the father and mother, any imbalance of roles resulting in either maternal or paternal dominance may cause serious malfunctioning in the family's ability to produce "healthy" offspring.

Extreme cases of maternal or paternal dominance probably disrupt normal psychosexual development because in either case children are exposed to, and learn from, an unbalanced family situation. A similarly unbalanced situation occurs when children are reared without one or the other parent, and in most cases of parental absence it is the father who is absent from the home. The most common reason for father absence, and one that is occurring increasingly often, is divorce. If the current trend continues, 40 percent of all new marriages in the United States will end in divorce. In more than 90 percent of the divorces involving children, custody of the children goes to the mother (83).

Father Absence

The effects on boys and girls of being reared in a home without a father have been investigated by many researchers (6, 7, 42). In general, **father absence** has been found to have negative effects on the psychosexual development of children, particularly when it occurs early in life, and the effects are apparently more serious for boys than for girls. In comparison with father-present boys, father-absent boys are generally more dependent, less aggressive, less competent in peer relationships, less efficient in school, less advanced in moral judgment, and have a weaker masculine identity.

Not only boys but young girls seem to need a father figure to learn from and interact with. Girls, by watching and by interacting with their fathers, learn how to react to males and how males will react to their sexuality. The effects of father absence on girls appear to be minimal in childhood, but such effects show up more clearly in early adolescence, as can be seen in a study conducted by psychologist Mavis Hetherington (42).

Hetherington examined the behavior of 72 teenage girls from three different types of family background. One group of 24 girls had been deprived of a father because of divorce. The second group of 24 had been reared by their widowed mothers; and those in the third group were from families with both a mother and father. Few of these young women had any noticeable behavior problems, and all were doing reasonably well in school. There were, however, definite differences in the way the girls from each group reacted to males.

As part of the study each girl was shown into an office where she was interviewed by a man. There were three chairs in the office for the girls to use. Girls reared by divorced mothers tended to sit in the chair closest to the interviewer and to adopt an open and sprawling posture. They leaned forward toward the man, looked into his eyes often, smiled often, and were talkative. The girls whose fathers had died acted quite differently. They sat stiffly upright in the chair farthest from the male interviewer, tended to turn their shoulders away from him, and did not smile, establish eye contact, or talk as much as the other girls did. Girls from two-parent homes acted in a manner between the two extremes and were much more at ease with the man than were both groups of father-absent girls, who tended to pluck at their clothes, pull at their fingers, and twirl their hair. The differences among the groups did not show up when the girls were interviewed by females.

Hetherington found that the attitudes displayed by the girls during the interviews also showed up in the girls' social relationships with males. Girls from divorced families sought more attention and praise from males than did girls in the other two groups. They were also more likely to spend much of their time hanging around places where young men could be found—gymnasiums, carpentry and machine shops, and near the stag line at community or school dances. In their search for attention these girls tended to use their bodies to attract boys. They dated more often and tended to be sexually promiscuous, engaging in sexual intercourse more often and at an earlier age than did girls of the other two groups. Girls whose fathers had died tended to avoid males. They started dating much later than the others and seemed to be sexually inhibited. At one dance observed by the psychologists these girls avoided the male areas of the dance floor, and two even hid in the ladies' room for the entire evening. The differences among the girls were not due to popularity, says Hetherington, because the girls received equal numbers of invitations to dance when they were in the dance hall.

Hetherington's study suggests that a girl's sexual behavior can be related to father absence or neglect. It also shows that a child's attitude toward males is influenced by the reason for father absence. Interviews with the girls indicate that the daughters of divorced parents tended to dislike their fathers, perhaps because of the mother's negative attitude toward her ex-husband and perhaps because the girls felt that their fathers had abandoned them. Girls whose fathers had died were more likely to remember their fathers as idealized images or models of masculinity, which no other male could live up to. Though they expressed it differently, both groups of father-absent girls were insecure in their dealings with men. This insecurity was greatest in the girls who had lost their fathers before the age of 5.

Hetherington's studies, like Harry Harlow's research with monkeys (see Chapter 3), suggest that children who do not have the opportunity to learn social and sexual roles from their parents may suffer psychological damage. But for many reasons—death, war, prison, divorce, desertion—it is sometimes

Boys from fatherless homes can develop adequate masculine sex-role behavior when they have strong, competent mothers who show respect for the masculine role.

impossible to avoid the loss of one or both parents. The possible damage caused by such a loss need not always occur. In father-absent homes, for example, other people can sometimes help prevent the negative effects of being reared without a father. It appears that boys from such homes can develop adequate masculine sex-role behavior when they have mothers who are strong, competent, and show respect for the masculine role (9). Additionally, the presence of an older brother may be a very important factor in the development of masculine behaviors among boys with no other father figures in the home. When an older brother is available, father-absent boys are more masculine than are boys who have only older sisters or no siblings (87).

Mother Absence   Certainly the father is not the only important agent in the psychosexual development of children, but because there are so few instances of **mother absence** or homes without a maternal figure, there are little data on the effects of children being reared without a mother (or mother surrogate). In recent years, however, there has been increased interest in the effects of **working mothers** on their children's development, including sex-typing. This is important because of the large numbers of mothers who are employed in this country (in 1971, according to U.S. Census figures, approximately 30 percent of mothers with preschool children and 50 percent of mothers with school-age children were working).

Two fairly recent reviews of the large body of data on the relation between maternal employment and development of the child demonstrated that it is difficult to give conclusive answers to questions about the effects of working mothers on their children (21, 43). Many factors must be considered. For example, the effects may depend on the reason for the mother working, her type of employment, the family circumstances, whether employment is full or part time, the age and sex of the child, the kinds of child care arrangements that can be made, the social class of the parents, and so on. As expected, when a mother works because she enjoys her career, there appear to be fewer negative effects on her children than when her employment is motivated by the desire to escape from family responsibilities and child care. The findings of the various studies generally support the conclusions that children of working mothers perceive smaller differences between male and female roles, believe that men and women should share responsibilities inside and outside the home equally, and have higher evaluation of female competence. In addition, daughters of working mothers appear to be more independent, probably because of modeling on their independent mothers.

There can be problems when mothers work outside the home. One study found that 10 percent of the children from lower socioeconomic families in the United States had no supervision when their parents were absent from the home (84). One researcher studied the effects of presence or absence of supervision on more than 100 fifth-grade children of working mothers in a lower-class neighborhood (88). It was found that more girls than boys were unsupervised and that the negative effects of lack of supervision were less severe for boys than for girls. Unsupervised girls had lower achievement and intelligence test scores in comparison to those girls who had adult supervision. Supervised children appeared to be more self-reliant, with a greater sense of personal freedom. It was also found that full-time maternal employment was related to better social adjustment and high intelligence test scores than was sporadic, part-time employment.

The Role of Peers

One of the most obvious behavior differences between the sexes is the fact that boys prefer to be with boys and girls prefer other girls as companions as early as 3 years of age (37). This **preference for same-sex friends** increases throughout childhood and appears to peak just before adolescence. Adolescents begin to choose opposite-sex friends with increasing frequency, and peer relations change considerably with respect to sex. This preference for same-sex friends is an important source for the support of sex-role standards (20). Prior to adolescence both boys and girls tend to believe they should act more positively toward same-sex peers than to those of the opposite sex. Boys identify more with other boys during middle and late childhood in adopting sex-typed patterns than with parents or girls, while girls identify more with parents. Although the peer group is important for both sexes, it is probably more important for boys than girls.

An observational study of 3-year-old children in two nursery schools found that boys reinforced other little boys a total of 359 times during the

A preference for same-sex friends increases throughout childhood and peaks just before adolescence.

observational periods, but reinforced girls only 71 times (25). The girls reinforced other girls 463 times and boys only 63 times. Almost all the **peer reinforcement** was for sex-appropriate behavior. One boy in the study was decidedly feminine in his activities. His peers criticized him more than they did other children and played with him less. This and a number of other studies show clearly that children reinforce their same-sex peers early in life for behavior preferred for their sex and, at least for boys, punish peers who deviate from the norm.

Experiments have also demonstrated the importance of peers serving as models for sex-typed behavior beginning in early childhood. For example, young children usually avoid toys they think inappropriate for their sex. But when kindergarteners saw same-sex peers playing with toys considered inappropriate for their sex, they later showed a tendency to play with those same toys (48). Observation of a model who resisted temptation to play with such toys led to less interaction with the toys. These effects were seen in both boys and girls, but were stronger in boys.

One researcher working with lower-class adolescents has pointed out that teenage gangs provide the first opportunity for many boys who come from female-dominated homes to learn some aspects of the male role (64). It has also been seen that many boys who appear to have acquired a "shaky" masculine identity in early childhood because of the lack of paternal figures or because of cold and distant fathers show exaggerated masculine behavior, especially of an aggressive-destructive type (4). The overly stereotyped masculine sex roles of such boys probably are due to pressures from the peer group to "act like real men."

The Role of Schools

Parents and peers probably represent the strongest influences on sex roles, but schools and teachers also play an important part in psychosexual development. There is evidence, however, that teachers reinforce mostly feminine behaviors and values, at least through the early grades. Psychologists who have investigated the subject have found that female preschool teachers overwhelmingly reinforce both boys and girls for engaging in feminine behavior (22, 25). Since it appears that most young boys maintain their masculine interests and behaviors in the face of teachers' preference for girlish activities, it is probable that peer and parental reinforcement for male conduct, as well as the boys' own knowledge of what "is right for a boy," cancel out the influence of these teachers. The mixed signals boys get from women teachers (who make up the majority of preschool and elementary teachers in this country) on the one hand, and parents and peers on the other, probably place boys in conflict and teaches them that school is "a place for girls." In fact, it has been found that boys and girls in elementary school do associate school with the female sex role (71).

Educational values in many U.S. schools influence teachers to promote "feminine" characteristics among their students.

This preference of teachers for activities considered feminine may be due to the structure and organization of the classroom in this country rather than the fact that most teachers are women. Schools are supposed to give students training in specific skills and to teach them the basic values and beliefs of the culture. In order to do this, schools are structured to encourage pupil achievement. In numerous schools dependency is encouraged, since dependent behavior makes it easier for teachers to maintain the discipline and obedience many administrators and teachers believe necessary for efficient learning and academic achievement. Aggression, running, loud activity, and so on, are discouraged and are seen as disruptive to the well-ordered classroom. Therefore, it is reasonable to expect teachers of both sexes to reinforce quiet, dependent, polite, "feminine" behavior.

Investigators studying male and female preschool and female primary school teachers found that these groups liked and approved of dependency more than aggression among both boys and girls (23, 53). Male preschool teachers approved of dependent behavior (which is considered a feminine characteristic) among all children even more than female teachers did. Preschool teachers of both sexes approved of dependency in boys more than in girls, which may mean they are eager to encourage this behavior among the group of children (boys) least likely to display it. Such evidence strongly suggests that the educational values in many U.S. schools influence teachers to promote characteristics among their students that are considered to be feminine by the wider society.

Several researchers have also reported that preschool girls receive more instruction than boys. This could be related to the fact that some teachers believe girls to be more dependent and conforming than boys, as well as to the running battles between certain teachers and more aggressive boys. Since boys receive reinforcement for behavior associated with the feminine role, and since more academic instruction is given to girls in the early school years, it is not surprising to find that there are approximately three to four boys with severe reading problems for every girl. Girls also demonstrate greater academic achievement in elementary school, while the school drop-out rate among boys is higher than for girls (61).

This situation has led some educators and psychologists to suggest hiring more male teachers for the early school grades in order to combat the so-called feminization of the schools. While it appears that male teachers do make some difference in the types of experiences children receive in their early years of formal schooling, the general cultural situation is probably even more important. For example, several studies have compared reading achievement among elementary school children in Germany and the United States (71). It was found that the presence of a male or female teacher for the first four years of school in Germany is not related to differences in reading achievement between boys and girls, and *there is no difference between the sexes in reading problems.* This is a surprising finding in view of the much larger number of boys with reading problems and the poorer reading achieve-of boys in the United States. It may be that the findings of reading studies among boys and girls in Germany (and those conducted by other investigators in Great Britain and Holland) can be attributed to the much higher status given to scholarship and reading in European countries. It appears that reading, books, and general academic achievement are not "just for sissies" but rather are the subject of considerable prestige for all people. It is probable that more male teachers in the preschools and primary grades in the United States will have only minimal effect unless there are broader changes in cultural values.

The Role of the Mass Media

Although children find important models among members of their families, peers, teachers, and other people with whom they have frequent contact, these are not the only influential sources of imitation. Considering the amount of time most children spend reading in schools and at home, as well as the hours they spend watching television each day, it is not surprising that the mass media in the United States provide many influential models for sex-role development.

There is now much evidence that children's picture books, story books, and school texts have tended to reinforce the sex-role stereotypes that are dominant in this country (12, 16, 76). Boys outnumber girls as the major characters in children's stories, for example. A majority of girls are shown as emotional, dependent, domestic, passive, subordinate, and incompetent in many activities, while boys usually are shown as clever, creative, active, capable, strong, and independent.

Even the future work roles presented to children are sex-typed. Children's books show women either at home or in jobs typically considered female, such as secretaries, librarians, stewardesses, nurses, and so on. Boys are shown in a wider variety of vocational possibilities, including President, baseball player, executive, explorer, scientist, and fireman. Male occupations usually are more prestigious and glamorous.

Television probably is an even more influential model of behaviors for children than books, since it is estimated that the average child spends more time watching television than in any other activity except sleep (54). The sex roles on television are similar to those found in children's books. When researchers looked at the 10 most popular programs for children according to the ratings for one season, they found that four did not regularly contain even one female character, though all had male characters (79). In those shows that had at least one female and one male figure, there were more males (67 percent) than females (33 percent). Males were portrayed as more aggressive, constructive, and dependent than females. The finding that the male characters were more dependent than the females may seem surprising, since dependency is considered a part of the female sex-role stereotype. However, the investigators included in the dependent category behaviors in which the actor requested information in order to carry out a task (instrumental dependency), which is not a sex-typed characteristic. Males also engaged in more behaviors and were more often rewarded for their actions. Females were played as yielding individuals who were punished for high levels of activity. There was a tendency for the actions of the female characters to have no environmental consequences—nothing at all happened.

With the strong sex-role stereotypes presented on children's television programs, it is not surprising to find a relation between the amount of time boys and girls spend watching television and their degree of sex-typing. Researchers studied a group of middle-class children who were enrolled in kindergarten through the sixth grade. They found that children of both sexes who watched television about 25 hours a week made more sex-typed choices on a test of sex-role preference than did children who watched television

10 hours a week or less (30). The results were repeated in a follow-up study of the same children 15 months later (63). While these findings do not prove that television causes sexist attitudes, they do show a strong association between the amount of time spent watching television and the extent of sex-role preference of young viewers.

In general, the picture of males and females presented by children's books and television programs is very similar to the sex-role stereotypes discussed earlier in this chapter. These portraits probably are influential in the socialization of children. The feminine role in our society is shown as inferior in status; the girl or woman is depicted as emotional, domestic, passive, and fairly incompetent. On television more of the female characters use magic than do males (79). It is almost as if a female in our society can only have an impact on the world through the supernatural! The masculine role is not only given greater prestige, the male is seen as better able to cope with his environment. However, there are negative aspects to the male role. While there is excitement in the life of the stereotypically active, striving male, there is little room for gentleness, self-expression, or sensitivity toward others.

SEXUAL IDENTITY AND ADJUSTMENT

The devaluation of the feminine role in the United States appears to be changing, but the position of women has been poor in many areas of the world throughout recorded history. Jean Jacques Rousseau's prescription for the education of women, for instance, written in eighteenth-century Europe at the height of the "Enlightenment," would produce a female who would fit the feminine stereotype in the United States in the twentieth century.

> The whole education of women ought to be relative to men. To please them, to be useful to them, to make themselves loved and honored by them, to educate them when young, to care for them when grown, to counsel them, to console them, and to make life sweet and agreeable to them—these are the duties of women at all times and what should be taught them from their infancy.

If a young girl accepts and adopts the feminine role, she is accepting a position that she will discover at some point is considered inferior and secondary. If she does not adopt the role, at least outwardly, she will experience a certain amount of rejection in society. A tomboyish girl does not receive the scorn given to an effeminate boy in childhood, but she will experience an increasing amount of ridicule if she does not begin to adopt more feminine characteristics beginning in late childhood. At the very least, the assertive, striving girl may have few dates in high school and be labeled as castrating as she enters adulthood.

The results of studies with males, from the preschool years into adulthood, show that conspicuous masculinity is associated with good personal adjustment and femininity with poor adjustment. For example, highly masculine preschool boys have been found to be more outgoing, competent, and socially adjusted than boys low in masculinity (85). Masculine adolescent boys have been found to exhibit higher self-esteem and lower anxiety than less masculine boys (18). Masculinity in late adolescent and adult males is related to reported better personal adjustment, greater self-confidence, and more favorable self-attitudes (81).

While masculinity in males is usually associated with good adjustment, some studies have found that a very high level of masculinity is related to high anxiety (86). This may be because some boys who have very masculine preferences are insecure in their sex-role orientations (8). In order to defend against the fear, and sometimes even panic, of not being "really masculine," some boys overcompensate and behave in a hyper- or super-masculine manner. Indirect support for this hypothesis comes from studies of adult men with feminine sex-role orientations and masculine preferences (55). These men were more likely than any other males in the study to find a defendant guilty in a simulated trial situation if nonessential evidence about earlier homosexual activity by the defendant was brought into the case. It appears that sexual behavior which does not fit the typical male role is threatening to men with less firm masculine identities. These men defend against the threat by reacting in a punishing manner toward those who deviate.

As would be expected, the relation between femininity and personal adjustment among females is more complex than that between masculinity and adjustment among males. A few investigators have reported a positive relation between the degree of femininity in girls and certain measures of personal adjustment. Some, for example, have found that the most feminine preschool girls tend to be more socially adjusted and competent than the least feminine girls (85). However, most studies of girls and women of various ages have found no relation between femininity and adjustment, and a few have found that femininity in females is associated with poorer adjustment (38). Many competent girls and women in the United States probably feel frustrated as they learn they must hide their abilities to fit the definitions of their sex role (17). While some are able to adjust well, others experience considerable conflict and anger, and some women completely reject major aspects of the feminine role.

Androgyny

It is said that sex-role differentiation has outlived its usefulness and serves only to prevent both men and women from developing as full and complete human beings. This charge is made by supporters of the women's movement, who claim that people should no longer be taught to conform to outdated standards of masculinity and femininity but should be encouraged to be

androgynous, that is, to have both female and male characteristics. A psychologically androgynous individual, it is claimed, would be able to employ such so-called masculine characteristics as ambition, dominance, and self-reliance and so-called feminine traits like affection, gentleness, and understanding. The ability to respond with either masculine or feminine characteristics would help the androgynous individual in adapting to a variety of situations without regard for stereotyped sex-role behavior.

Psychologist Sandra Bem has attempted to test the hypothesis that androgyny can lead to greater adaptability or that sex-role typing can seriously restrict the range of behaviors available to individuals as they move from situation to situation. More than 700 subjects took part in her study (5).

A sex-role questionnaire was used to score men and women according to masculinity, femininity, and androgyny. Of those tested, 34 percent of the males and 27 percent of the females were rated as androgynous. These people showed an equal endorsement of both masculine and feminine attributes. Masculine, feminine, and androgynous individuals of each sex were then subjected to various situations. In an experiment designed to test for "independence from social pressure" (a behavior rated as significantly masculine), masculine males and females and androgynous males and females displayed the most independence. When asked to take part in a "significantly feminine behavior" (playing with a kitten), feminine and androgynous males and females displayed the greatest ability for overall involvement. It was the purely masculine and purely feminine types (especially feminine females) that showed the least adaptability from situation to situation.

Bem concludes:

> The current set of studies provides the first empirical demonstration that there exists a distinct class of people who can appropriately be termed androgynous, whose sex role adaptability enables them to engage in situationally effective behavior without regard for its stereotype as masculine or feminine. Accordingly, it may well be—as the woman's movement has urged—that the androgynous individual will some day come to define a new and more human standard of psychological health.

SUMMARY

"Psychosexual development" is the term used to refer to the manner in which one adjusts psychologically to one's sexuality. It is one of the most important areas of human development and is closely related to personal happiness.

Biology plays a major role in sexual development, with the sex chromosomes determining the type of genitalia that develop and the genitalia controlling the production of sex hormones.

As important as biological factors are, social and psychological factors are probably more important in individual psychosexual development. By the time they are 3 years old most children have developed a basic sexual identity, and sex differences in behavior are well established. Some of these differences (such as the higher rates of activity, aggression, and rough-and-tumble play) may be due to sex-related biological differences (such as body size and hormones), but many of the observed differences between the sexes appear to be the result of social influence.

The fact that sexual behavior differs greatly from culture to culture is one indication of the influence social and cultural factors have on psychosexual development. In the United States, for example, beliefs about sexual behavior are so widespread that most parents have a good idea of what to expect from their sons and daughters. These expectations, in turn, affect parental behaviors, with sons and daughters being treated differently. Sex-role stereotypes are seen at all levels of society, but sex-typing is perhaps stronger in the lower class where masculine and feminine roles are usually more clear-cut.

Four theories have been influential in explaining psychosexual development. Freudian, or psychoanalytic, theory suggests that identification with the same-sex parent is the primary method by which children acquire the characteristics of their sex. Role theory suggests that fathers are important in producing sexual identities in both sons and daughters (rather than just in sons, as Freud suggested). Social learning theory emphasizes the importance of reinforcement, punishment, and modeling in the acquisition or learning of sexual attitudes and behaviors. Finally, cognitive theory relates psychosexual development to changing thought structures that emerge as children mature cognitively. While psychoanalytic theory was influential stimulating research in the area of psychosexual development, learning theory is probably the most useful in explaining psychosexual development (as long as the importance of cognitive structuring is recognized).

Learning of one's sex role begins in the home, and research suggests that the parental characteristics related to the development of masculinity in sons and femininity in daughters are warmth, nurturance, and dominance in the same-sex parent.

An imbalance in parental roles, which may be due to extreme dominance by one parent or the other or absence of one parent or the other, can have negative effects on psychosexual development. Father-absent boys (especially if the absence occurs early in a child's life) are generally more dependent, less aggressive, less competent in peer relations, less efficient in school, less advanced in moral judgment, and have weaker masculine identities than father-present boys. Father absence appears to have less serious effects on girls, but father-absent girls have been found to have difficulties in relating to males. Mother absence, a less common occurrence, probably also has negative effects on psychosexual development, but such studies have been rare. Children of working mothers, however, have been found in some cases to be more independent and less rigid in sex-role stereotyping than children of nonworking mothers.

Sex-role stereotypes have probably been restrictive to both males and females in the United States. If a young girl accepts the stereotyped feminine role, she is accepting a position that she will discover at some point to be inferior and secondary. If she rejects it, she risks rejection by society. Males who accept the masculine role aren't put in such a bind because U.S. society does not devalue the masculine role. There is evidence, however, that high levels of masculinity are related to poor adjustment. One solution to the adjustment problems of males and females with regard to sex-role stereotypes may be psychological androgyny (having both female and male characteristics). A psychologically androgynous individual, it is claimed, would be able to employ such so-called masculine characteristics as ambition, dominance, and self-reliance as well as so-called feminine traits like affection, gentleness, and understanding.

RESEARCH REPORT 11.1

Children's Diminishing Egocentrism with Age

The decreasing egocentrism of a child with age is related to an increasing ability on the part of the child to take the point of view of another person and then relate his or her own behavior to that of the other person. That this ability increases steadily with age was demonstrated in an ingenious and readily replicable study.

Children in grades two to eleven were brought individually into a room in which there were two adults. One adult showed the child two plastic cups placed upside down on a board. One cup had one nickel glued to the bottom while the other had two nickels similarly attached. The child was told that one experimenter was going to leave the room. While the experimenter was gone, the child was to remove the money from under one of the cups. On returning, the experimenter would choose one of the cups. If the one with the money still under it was chosen, the experimenter could keep the money. The child was told that the task was to fool the experimenter—to guess which cup would be chosen and take the money out of that cup. The experimenter then left the room. The child was asked to take the money from under one cup and to offer a rationale for the choice.

Three strategies were identified for deciding which cup to take the money from.

Strategy A: In this strategy the child simply asserted that the experimenter wanted the most money or that the cup used in the demonstration would pay off again, attributing a simple egocentric motive to the experimenter. There was no recognition that the experimenter knew that the child is trying to fool him. For example:

> "Do you want me to tell you?" (Umhum. Which one do you think he'll choose?) "The dime." (You think he'll choose the dime cup. Why do you think he might choose that one?) "He'll get more money — if the money is under there."

This strategy was used by 85 percent of the grade two children, and the percentage using this strategy steadily decreased with age.

Strategy B: Here the child clearly attributed social cognitions to the experimenter in addition to the egocentric motives of Strategy A. The child recognized that the experimenter knew that the child would try to fool him, and modified his behavior accordingly:

> (S chooses the one-nickel cup.) (Why do you think he'll take the one-nickel cup?) "Well, I figured that, uh, if it was me I'd take this one (two-nickel cup) because of the money I'd get to keep. But he's gonna know we're gonna fool him — or try to fool him — and so he might think that we're gonna take the most money out, so I took the small one (the one-nickel cup). I'd go for the small one."

This strategy was used by only 5 percent of the grade two children, and its use increased steadily with age.

Strategy C: This strategy was even more complex and less egocentric. The child here predicted not only a change in the behavior of the experiment based on the latter's expectations of what the child would do, but that the experimenter would expect the child's behavior to change further based on the experimenter's modification. That is, the child was seeing the beginning of an infinite series of "The experimenter will think that I'll think . . .," and so on. For example:

> "Uh, when we were, he chose the dime cup the first time . . . and, uh . . . well, let's see . . . I think, uh, that he would think that we would choose the opposite cup." (Opposite cup from what?) "From the, in other words, this cup, the nickel cup, but then might, he might, he might feel that we, that we know that he thinks that we're going to pick this cup so therefore I think we should pick the dime cup, because I think he thinks, he thinks that we're going to pick the nickel cup, but then I think he knows that we,

that we'll assume that he knows that, so we should pick the opposite cup."
(Okay, so we should pick the dime cup?) "Yes."

This strategy did not appear at all until grade six when 10 percent of the children utilized it. It was not seen again until grade eleven when 10 percent of the children also used it.

These trends are consistent with trends in children's abilities to behave consistently with rules and the expectations of others. The ability of children to understand the needs of others and to modify their own behavior accordingly may be an important component both of conformity and of altruistic behavior.

Summarized from J. H. Flavell *et al.*, *The Development of Role-taking and Communication Skills in Children* (New York: Wiley, 1968).

The Development of Morality

Piaget would begin his interview by presenting the child with some marbles and a piece of chalk and asking the child to explain the rules of the game of marbles. After the child had explained the rules, Piaget either played the game with the child or brought in another child to play the game. Piaget then observed the play to determine whether the child used the rules explained earlier. After the play had continued for a while, Piaget interviewed the child to determine if the child thought the rules could be changed, where they had come from, and whether or not they had always been the same.

From the children's responses to explaining the rules and observing their actual play Piaget was able to identify four steps in the child's knowledge of and ability to play the game. These four steps are systematically related to the premoral, moral realism, and morality of reciprocity stages of moral development.

Step 1: Children of 2 or 3 years of age have no knowledge of the game of marbles. They observe rules in the sense that they do repeated or regular things with the marbles, but the rules are individual rules and are not related to those of the game as played by older children.

Step 2: Between the ages of 3 and 5 children discover that there are regular features of the game played by older children. They begin to be aware that there is a square within which the marbles are placed, that one shoots at the marbles in the square from behind a line, and so on. When explaining the rules, however, they fail to coordinate these features into a coherent set of rules that will make a game. When playing they imitate some of these features, but they fail to coordinate their behavior with that of the others and are unconcerned with winning in the usual sense. Their interest in the game lies with the skill of knocking marbles out of the square rather than with what others are doing. Also, a rule used at one minute in the game is forgotten the next.

Step 3: Around 7 or 8 years the child begins to compare his or her achievement with that of others and to recognize that winning means doing better than the others. Now the interest in the game becomes doing better than the others, and the rules are used as a means to establish initial equality. At this step children do not know all of the rules, nor do they explain them as a coherent set making a game. They all are motivated to learn the rules, however, and do this more through active imitation of the behavior of children who appear to know the rules than by verbal transmission. In actual play they often ignore rules they cite in explaining how to play, they continue to use rules they appear to make up on the spur of the moment, and simply omit rules in dispute with other players.

Step 4: By age 11 or 12, the child knows the rules as a coordinated set which all the players know and use exactly as stated. Each child knows many variations of specific rules, and when a group plays together they spend time at the beginning to decide which rules will be used. Interest is centered more on the game itself than on winning, and much time is spent adjudicating disputes or anticipating what disputes may arise and setting up rules for them beforehand.

It is easy to see that only the child who has attained Step 4 would be considered a truly moral adult in the sense that he or she both knew and obeyed the rules of conduct.

These steps in the learning of games have direct relations to the stages of moral development. The relation between the premoral child and the Step 1 and early Step 2 child is clear. The premoral child has no real conception of rules as a social reality and, at best, imitates adults or older children in behavioral ways. This corresponds directly to the child who does not even know that there is a game called marbles and who proceeds to carry out whatever actions come to mind.

The relation between the child who is a moral realist and the child in Steps 2 and 3 is much more paradoxical. Here the child asserts that the rules cannot be changed, that even if one could think up a rule that was not in use, it would not be fair to play with that rule and that the game has always been played as it is now. This child views the rules as absolute and to be obeyed in all circumstances. What a contrast this is to what the child does when playing the game! Here he or she does not know all the rules, does not play according to them consistently, and makes up rules basically to suit his or her own purposes. According to Piaget, this paradox arises out of the fact that the rules initially arise from outside the child and are imposed on the child's mind by the example of others. Thus, while intending to conform to the rules in a genuine way, the child does not have exact knowledge of them and so cannot follow them. In addition, the very respect the child has for the rules leads to the thinking that any rule that comes to mind must be a real rule, so he or she does not understand that the rules that are made up are any different from those imposed from outside.

By the end of Step 3 the child has gained a reliable and complete knowledge of the rules of the game as played in his or her own neighborhood. As the practice of the rules becomes better and better, the child's belief in the intrinsic and absolute truth of specific rules diminishes. He or she becomes aware of the fact that others sometimes use different rules and that these rules could also be used to make a game. Thus the child moves to Step 4 in the practice of rules and to the morality of reciprocity in relation to the rules. Rules now are viewed as the outcome of a free decision and are worthy of respect insofar as they obtain mutual consent of all participants. More important, since the child now knows why the rules exist in relation to the game, and since he or she chooses to participate using those rules, obedience to them is exact. The rules are no longer imposed from without, but come from the child's own understanding. This represents true respect for the rules and truly moral behavior.

Summarized from Jean Piaget, *The Moral Judgment of the Child* (New York: Crowell Collier and Macmillan), 1962.

REFERENCES

1. Bandura, A. *Principles of Behavior Modification*. New York: Holt, Rinehart and Winston, 1969.
2. Bandura, A. "Social-learning Theory of Identificatory Processes." In D. A. Goslin (ed.), *Handbook of Socialization Theory and Research*. Chicago: Rand McNally, 1969.
3. Bandura, A. *Social Learning Theory*. Morristown, N.J.: General Learning Press, 1971.
4. Bandura, A., and R. H. Walters. *Adolescent Aggression*. New York: Ronald Press, 1959.
5. Bem, S. L. "Sex-role Adaptability: One Consequence of Psychological Androgyny," *Journal of Personality and Social Psychology*, 1975, *31*, 634–643.
6. Biller, H. B. "Father-absence, Maternal Encouragement, and Sex-role Development in Kindergarten-age Boys," *Child Development*, 1969, *40*, 539–546.
7. Biller, H. B. "Father-absence and the Personality Development of the Male Child," *Developmental Psychology*, 1970, *2*, 181–201.
8. Biller, H. B. *Father, Child, and Sex Role*. Boston: D. C. Heath, 1971.
9. Biller, H. B. "The Mother-Child Relationship and the Father-absent Boy's Personality Development," *Merrill-Palmer Quarterly*, 1971, *17*, 227–241.
10. Biller, H. B., and W. Barry. "Sex-role Patterns, Paternal Similarity, and Personality Adjustment in College Males," *Developmental Psychology*, 1971, *4*, 107.
11. Brackbill, Y. "Continuous Stimulation and Arousal Level in Infancy: Effects of Stimulus Intensity and Stress," *Child Development*, 1975, *46*, 364–369.
12. Britton, G. E. "Sex Stereotyping and Career Roles," *Journal of Reading*, 1973, *17*, 140.
13. Broverman, I. K., S. R. Vogel, D. M. Broverman, F. E. Clarkson, and P. S. Rosenkrantz. "Sex-role Stereotypes: A Current Appraisal," *Journal of Social Issues*, 1972, *28*, 59–78.
14. Brown, D. C., and D. B. Lynn. "Human Sexual Development: An Outline of

Components and Concepts," *Journal of Marriage and the Family*, 1966, *28*, 155–162.

15. Brown, D. G. "Sex-role Preference in Young Children," *Psychological Monographs*, 1956, *70*(14, Whole No. 421).

16. Child, L. L., E. H. Potter, and E. M. Levine. "Children's Textbooks and Personality Development: An Exploration in the Social Psychology of Education," *Psychological Monographs*, 1946, *60*(3, Whole No. 279).

17. Coleman, J. S. *The Adolescent Society*. New York: Free Press, 1961.

18. Connell, D. M., and J. E. Johnson. "Relationships Between Sex-role Identification and Self-esteem in Early Adolescents," *Developmental Psychology*, 1970, *3*, 268.

19. Ehrhardt, A., R. Epstein, and J. Money. "Fetal Androgens and Female Gender Identity in the Early-treated Andrenogenital Syndrome," *The Johns Hopkins Medical Journal*, 1968, *122*, 160–167.

20. Emmerich, W., K. S. Goldman, and R. E. Shore. "Differentiation and Development of Social Norms," *Journal of Personality and Social Psychology*, 1971, *18*, 323–353.

21. Etaugh, C. "Effects of Maternal Employment on Children: A Review of Recent Research," *Merrill-Palmer Quarterly*, 1974, *20*, 71–98.

22. Etaugh, C., G. Collins, and A. Gerson. "Reinforcement of Sex-typed Behaviors of Two-year-old Children in a Nursery School Setting," *Developmental Psychology*, 1975, *11*, 255.

23. Etaugh, C., and V. Hughes. "Teachers' Evaluations of Sex-typed Behaviors in Children: The Role of Teacher Sex and School Setting," *Developmental Psychology*, 1975, *11*, 394–395.

24. Fagot, B. I. "Sex Differences in Toddlers' Behavior and Parental Reaction," *Developmental Psychology*, 1974, *10*, 554–558.

25. Fagot, B. I., and G. R. Patterson. "An *In Vivo* Analysis of Reinforcing Contingencies for Sex-role Behaviors in the Preschool Child," *Developmental Psychology*, 1969, *1*, 563–568.

26. Feshbach, S. "Aggression." In P. H. Mussen (ed.), *Carmichael's Manual of Child Psychology*, Vol. 2. New York: Wiley, 1970.

27. Fling, S., and M. Manosevitz. "Sex Typing in Nursery School Children's Play Interests," *Developmental Psychology*, 1972, *7*, 146–152.

28. Ford, C. S., and F. A. Beach. *Patterns of Sexual Behavior*. New York: Harper & Row, 1951.

29. Freud, S. *An Outline of Psychoanalysis*. New York: Norton, 1949.

30. Freuh, T., and P. E. McGhee. "Traditional Sex Role Development and Amount of Time Spent Watching Television," *Developmental Psychology*, 1975, *11*, 109.

31. Garai, J. E., and A. Scheinfeld. "Sex Differences in Mental and Behavioral Traits," *Genetic Psychology Monographs*, 1968, *77*, 169–299.

32. Gebhard, P. H. "Incidence of Overt Homosexuality in the United States and Western Europe." In J. M. Livingood (ed.), *Homosexuality: Final Report and Background Papers*. Rockville, Md.: National Institute of Mental Health, 1972.

33. Goldberg, S. *The Inevitability of Patriarchy*. New York: Morrow, 1973.

34. Hall, M., and R. A. Keith. "Sex-role Preference among Children of Upper and Lower Social Class," *Journal of Social Psychology*, 1964, *62*, 101–110.

35. Hartley, R. E. "Children's Concepts of Male and Female Roles," *Merrill-Palmer Quarterly*, 1960, 6, 83–91.
36. Hartup, W. W. "Aggression in Childhood: Developmental Perspectives," *American Psychologist*, 1974, 29, 336–341.
37. Hartup, W. W., and E. A. Zook. "Sex-role Preferences in Three- and Four-year-old Children," *Journal of Consulting Psychology*, 1960, 24, 420–426.
38. Heilbrun, A. B. "Parent Identification and Filial Sex-role Behavior: The Importance of Biological Context." In J. K. Cole and R. Dienstbier (eds.), *Nebraska Symposium on Motivation, 1973*. Lincoln: University of Nebraska Press, 1974.
39. Hess, R. D. "Social Class and Ethnic Influences upon Socialization." In P. H. Mussen (ed.), *Carmichael's Manual of Child Psychology*, Vol. 2. New York: Wiley, 1970.
40. Hetherington, E. M. "The Effects of Familial Variables on Sex Typing, on Parent-Child Similarity, and on Imitation in Children." In J. P. Hill (ed.), *Minnesota Symposia on Child Psychology*, Vol. 1. Minneapolis: University of Minnesota Press, 1967.
41. Hetherington, E. M. "Sex Typing, Dependency, and Aggression." In T. D. Spencer and N. Kass (eds.), *Perspectives in Child Psychology*. New York: McGraw-Hill, 1970.
42. Hetherington, E. M. "Effects of Father Absence on Personality Development in Adolescent Daughters," *Developmental Psychology*, 1972, 7, 313–326.
43. Hoffman, L. W. "Effects of Maternal Employment on the Child: A Review of the Research," *Developmental Psychology*, 1974, 10, 204–228.
44. Hutt, C. *Males and Females*. Baltimore, Md.: Penguin, 1972.
45. Hutt, C. "Sex Differences in Human Development," *Human Development*, 1972, 15, 153–170.
46. Johnson, M. M. "Sex-role Learning in the Nuclear Family," *Child Development*, 1963, 34, 319–333.
47. Kagan, J., and H. Moss. *Birth to Maturity*. New York: Wiley, 1962.
48. Kobasigawa, A. "Inhibitory and Disinhibitory Effects of Models on Sex-appropriate Behavior in Children," *Psychologia*, 1968, 11, 86–96.
49. Kohlberg, L. "A Cognitive-Developmental Analysis of Children's Sex-role Concepts and Attitudes." In E. E. Maccoby (ed.), *The Development of Sex Differences*. Stanford, Calif.: Stanford University Press, 1966.
50. Kohlberg, L. "Stage and Sequence: The Cognitive-Developmental Approach to Socialization." In D. A. Goslin (ed.), *Handbook of Socialization Theory and Research*. Chicago: Rand McNally, 1969.
51. Kohn, M. L. "Social Class and Parental Values," *American Journal of Sociology*, 1959, 64, 337–351.
52. Korner, A. F. "Methodological Considerations in Studying Sex Differences in the Behavioral Functioning of Newborns." In R. C. Friedman, R. M. Richart, and R. L. Vande Wiele (eds.), *Sex Differences in Behavior*. New York: Wiley, 1974.
53. Levitin, T. E., and J. D. Chananie. "Responses of Female Primary School Teachers to Sex-typed Behaviors in Male and Female Children," *Child Development*, 1972, 43, 1309–1319.

54. Liebert, R. M., and R. A. Baron. "Some Immediate Effects of Televised Violence on Children's Behavior," *Developmental Psychology*, 1972, 6, 469–475.
55. Lipsitt, P. D., and F. L. Strodtbeck. "Defensiveness in Decision Making as a Function of Sex-role Identification," *Journal of Personality and Social Psychology*, 1967, 6, 10–15.
56. Lynn, D. B. *Parental and Sex Role Identification: A Theoretical Formulation*. Berkeley, Calif.: McCutcheon, 1969.
57. Maccoby, E. E., and C. N. Jacklin. *The Psychology of Sex Differences*. Stanford, Calif.: Stanford University Press, 1974.
58. Marshall, D. S., and R. C. Suggs. *Human Sexual Behavior: Variations in the Ethnographic Spectrum*. New York: Basic Books, 1971.
59. Masica, D. N., J. Money, and A. A. Ehrhardt. "Fetal Feminization and Female Gender Identity in the Testicular Feminizing Syndrome of Androgen Insensitivity," *Archives of Sexual Behavior*, 1971, 1, 131–142.
60. Masters, J. C., and A. Wilkinson. "Consensual and Discriminative Stereotypy of Sex-type Judgments by Parents and Children," *Child Development*, 1976, 47, 208–217.
61. McCandless, B. R. *Adolescents: Behavior and Development*. Hinsdale, Ill.: The Dryden Press, 1970.
62. McCandless, B. R., and E. D. Evans. *Children and Youth: Psychosocial Development*. Hinsdale, Ill.: Dryden Press, 1973.
63. McGhee, P. E. "Television as a Source of Learning Sex-role Stereotypes," unpublished paper presented at the Society for Research in Child Development, Denver, 1975.
64. Miller, W. B. "Lower Class Culture as a Generating Milieu of Gang Delinquency," *Journal of Social Issues*, 1958, 14, 5–19.
65. Mischel, W. "Toward a Cognitive Social Learning Reconceptualization of Personality," *Psychological Review*, 1973, 80, 252–283.
66. Money, J. *Sex Errors of the Body*. Baltimore, Md.: The Johns Hopkins Press, 1968.
67. Money, J., and A. A. Ehrhardt. *Man and Woman, Boy and Girl*. Baltimore, Md.: The Johns Hopkins Press, 1972.
68. Money, J., J. C. Hampson, and J. L. Hampson. "An Examination of Some Basic Sexual Concepts," *Bulletin of Johns Hopkins Hospital*, 1955, 97, 301–319.
69. Morris, J. *Conundrum*. New York: Harcourt Brace Jovanovich, 1974.
70. Parsons, T. "Family Structures and the Socialization of the Child." In T. Parsons and R. F. Bales (eds.), *Family, Socialization and Interaction Process*. Glencoe, Ill.: Free Press, 1955.
71. Preston, R. C. "Influence of Sex of Teacher, Social Climate of the School, and Adult Readership Patterns upon Reading Achievement of Boys and Girls," paper presented at the New York University Conference on Sex Stereotyping in Language and Reading, New York, May 1974.
72. Rabban, M. "Sex-role Identification in Young Children in Two Diverse Social Groups," *Genetic Psychology Monographs*, 1950, 42, 81–158.
73. Rheingold, H. L., and K. V. Cook. "The Content of Boys' and Girls' Rooms as an Index of Parents' Behavior," *Child Development*, 1975, 46, 459–463.

74. Rosenkrantz, P., S. Vogel, H. Bee, I. Broverman, and D. M. Broverman. "Sex-role Stereotypes and Self-concepts in College Students," *Journal of Consulting and Clinical Psychology*, 1968, *32*, 287–295.

75. Rubin, J. Z., F. J. Provenzano, and Z. Luria. "The Eye of the Beholder: Parents' Views on Sex of Newborns," *American Journal of Orthopsychiatry*, 1974, *44*, 512–519.

76. Saario, T. N., C. N. Jacklin, and C. K. Tittle. "Sex Role Stereotyping in the Public Schools," *Harvard Educational Review*, 1973, *43*, 386–416.

77. Sears, R. R., L. Rau, and R. Alpert. *Identification and Child Rearing*. Stanford, Calif.: Stanford University Press, 1965.

78. Slaby, R. G., and K. S. Frey. "Development of Gender Constancy and Selective Attention to Same-sex Models," *Child Development*, 1975, *46*.

79. Sternglanz, S. H., and L. A. Serbin. "Sex-role Stereotyping in Children's Television Programs," *Developmental Psychology*, 1974, *10*, 710–715.

80. Thompson, N. L., and B. R. McCandless. "IT Score Variations by Instructional Style," *Child Development*, 1970, *41*, 425–436.

81. Thompson, N. L., and B. R. McCandless. "The Homosexual Orientation and Its Antecedents." In A. Davids (ed.), *Child Personality and Psychopathology: Current Topics*, Vol. 3. New York: Wiley Interscience, 1976.

82. Thompson, N. L., D. M. Schwartz, B. R. McCandless, and D. A. Edwards. "Parent-Child Relationships and Sexual Identity in Male and Female Homosexuals and Heterosexuals," *Journal of Consulting and Clinical Psychology*, 1973, *41*, 120–127.

83. Trotter, R. J. "Divorce: The First Two Years Are the Worst," *Science News*, 1976, *110*(15), 237–238.

84. U.S. Department of Labor. "Child Care Arrangements." Washington, D.C.: Government Printing Office, 1965.

85. Vroegh, K. "Masculinity and Femininity in the Preschool Years," *Child Development*, 1968, *39*, 1253–1257.

86. Webb, A. "Sex-role Preferences and Adjustment in Early Adolescents," *Child Development*, 1963, *34*, 609–618.

87. Wohlford, P., J. W. Santrock, S. E. Berger, and D. Liberman. "Older Brothers' Influence on Sex-typed Aggressive and Dependent Behavior in Father-absent Children," *Developmental Psychology*, 1971, *4*, 124–134.

88. Woods, M. B. "The Unsupervised Child of the Working Mother," *Developmental Psychology*, 1972, *6*, 14–25.

89. Young, W. C., R. W. Goy, and C. H. Phoenix. "Hormones and Sexual Behavior," *Science*, 1964, *143*, 212–218.

Children's self-concepts—their personal awareness and evaluation of themselves—are private areas of experience, but they affect all facets of human behavior. Since children will have to spend their whole lives with themselves, it is probably best that they learn to like themselves.

12.

self-concept

Sybil was perplexed. She sat there in what she knew to be the fifth-grade class-room, but couldn't understand why she was there instead of in the third grade where she belonged. When the teacher asked Sybil to work a multiplication problem, she was at a loss. She had learned to add and subtract in the third grade but knew nothing of multiplication. Another thing Sybil knew nothing of was her own multiple personality.

The last thing Sybil remembered was attending her grandmother's funeral two years earlier. But gradually, as she looked around and began to recognize her classmates, it dawned on her that she must have been having another one of her memory lapses, or memory blackouts. What she didn't realize was that these seeming losses of memory were much more than that. While Sybil was "gone," or blacked out, for two years, several totally different personalities had been doing things and had been in complete control of her mind and body.

Sybil is a real person, and this is only one of the many bizarre incidents that make up her life story, the story of a woman with 16 complete and totally different personalities. The book *Sybil* (26) reads like fiction, but according to the author, the only facts that have been changed are those that would iden-tify the woman called Sybil (30). The real Sybil helped supply information for the book, as did Cornelia Wilbur, the psychiatrist who treated Sybil for 11 years.

Sybil began seeing the psychiatrist in 1954. She realized that she had a problem—in the form of blackouts that lasted anywhere from minutes to years—but felt guilty about it and could not bring herself to tell the analyst. Then one day Sybil went through a change in the psychiatrist's office. The usually shy, timid young woman flew into a rage, ran across the office, and broke a window. She began speaking like a young girl, pronounced words differently, moved differently, and called herself Peggy. A few minutes later she returned to her chair, seemed to calm down, and asked about the broken window. Sybil had returned and knew nothing of what Peggy had been up to. She did not even know that Peggy existed, but under questioning she admitted that she had been experiencing time lapses for as long as she could remember.

This was Dr. Wilbur's first indication of what Sybil's problem might be. She thought that perhaps Sybil was two people, a dual personality. Before the psychiatrist could confront Sybil with this, she was shocked to meet a third and completely different person in Sybil's body. This third woman, who called herself Vicky, was sophisticated, warm, and friendly. She knew all about Sybil and Peggy and was willing to talk about them. During the next several years and with the help of Vicky, the psychiatrist met and got to know all of the 16 personalities who were taking turns using Sybil's body.

Each self, when in control of Sybil, was a whole person. These personalities came in various ages and sexes—infants, adolescent boys, and mature women—and each had a distinct voice and vocabulary. Each carried herself (or himself) in a distinct manner and had a different body perceptions. Some saw themselves as thin, others as plump; some were tall, others short; some said they were blond, others brunette. Each had a personal philosophy and lifestyle, but all shared a rather strict morality.

Using hypnosis, Dr. Wilbur was able to speak to all of Sybil's selves. The conversations while Sybil was under hypnosis were extraordinary. Two, three, or more of Sybil's selves would emerge to talk with the analyst or with each other. The details of these conservations helped the psychiatrist piece together the details of Sybil's harsh childhood.

Sybil's mother had been an extremely disturbed woman who sexually abused and tortured her. Sybil was regularly beaten, locked in closets, and almost killed by her mother on several occasions. Sybil's father was a stern man who kept himself emotionally distant from Sybil and never questioned her bruises or broken bones.

While it is difficult to know what was actually going on in the mind of young Sybil, Dr. Wilbur offers a theory to explain how the numerous personalities came to be. By the time Sybil was 3 years old she realized, at least unconsciously, that she was not loved by her parents. This discovery was so emotionally shocking to the child that it forced her first dissociation, or personality separation. According to the theory, what Sybil did—even though she was not conscious of doing so—was create another person, a person who would suffer abuse and punishment in her place. Whenever there was trouble Sybil would let this other person take over. In this way she was protecting her basic self from her parents. The tactic worked so well as a defense mechanism that it was used over and over, and 16 personalities were born.

Under hypnosis each personality told what experience was responsible for his or her existence. Each was the instrument for coping with a specific emotion, while Sybil herself remained free of all emotions. Peggy, for instance, was assertive and enthusiastic. She came out whenever Sybil was angry and needed those characteristics. Mary was thoughful and home-loving. Sid and Mike, patterned after Sybil's father and grandfather, were carpenters and handy around the house. Nancy and Clara were religious. Vicky—who knew everything about all of the others—was the self-assured type of woman Sybil seemed to want to be.

Eventually, after years of sessions with her psychiatrist, Sybil began to understand the conditions associated with her problem. She finally became a seventeenth personality—a completely new Sybil with all the emotions, memories, and feelings of her former selves. She remembers the cruelty of her mother, the multiplication tables someone else learned, and the piano lessons someone else took. Sybil has become a whole person and is now a respected artist and teacher at a Midwestern university.

SELF-CONCEPT

Who am I? What am I? How did I come to be this way? Why am I?

Sybil may have had trouble answering these questions, or the different aspects of her personality may have answered them in different ways, but Sybil's case is extraordinary and rare. Most individuals have some understanding of who they are. This self-understanding is closely related to many important aspects of human behavior. Even though the self is essentially private, it is translated into action by most of the things we say and do, by the attitudes we express. Because the self enters into all areas of behavior, questions about the self have been at the heart of philosphical thought for centuries and are a major concern of psychology.

As children grow and develop they learn about the world, their place in it, and about themselves. **Self-concept** is the term usually used to refer to this area of private experience and self-evaluation. Self-concept, which is the sum total of personal awareness, evaluations, and expectations, comes from how one has been dealt with by others, how one has dealt with others, and how well one has coped with life. In formulating a self-concept one goes through the same stages and is subject to the same laws of learning (see Chapter 6) as in the formation of any other concept or idea. Such learning, which is intensely personal and in large part private, is of vital importance to both private happiness and public behavior.

Who am I?

Beginnings of the Self-concept

Children are aware of their characteristics and attributes and the ways in which they are both like and unlike others. This awareness probably begins some time during the first year of life when infants first show signs of knowing that they are separate from the rest of the environment. They become aware of *me* and *not me*. By the end of the first year most children show genuine self-recognition. They can recognize themselves, for example, in a mirror (13). As this self-awareness develops, children begin to think of themselves in specific terms—as tall, strong, talkative, healthy, slow, dull, awkward, dirty, and so on.

Preschool-aged children do not usually have firmly developed ideas about individual characteristics and differences, but there is no doubt that by the time they are 2 or 3 years old they each see themselves as being distinct from their parents and from other children (20). They use words such as "me," "mine," "you," "yours," and sometimes "we" and "ours." Some researchers believe that the use of the first person singular—"I"—indicates that true self-consciousness has been achieved (1). At this stage children begin to have an understanding of how they differ from others. By the age of 3 most children know their sex (see Chapter 11) and understand the physical characteristics that distinguish boys from girls. By age 3 children also show signs of understanding that racial differences exist and may begin to think of themselves in terms of their skin color (28). They begin to identify with others and recognize that they are part of a group, compete with others, and make self-judgments.

Self-esteem

The ability to recognize and describe oneself is an indication of the developing self-concept. Self-descriptive behavior (which is usually relatively objective and free of value judgments) is not the same as self-evaluative behavior—how children rate or judge the worthwhileness of their appearance, abilities, and so on. This evaluative behavior, which contributes greatly to the self-concept, is related to what is known as self-esteem.

Self-esteem refers to the value children place on themselves and their behaviors. It has to do with how they feel about themselves and whether they rate themselves as "good" or "bad." Such judgments, which are not always accurate, are frequently the result of what children learn about themselves from others. It is unlikely, for instance, that young children separate objective fact from subjective evaluations when they hear such things as: "Say, aren't you a big boy!" "Where did you get all that red hair?" "Look at how that little scamp climbs that tree." "I sure wish you looked more like your mother." "Algernon? What an odd name for a little boy!" "When are you going to learn that little girls just don't do that?"

Many studies suggest that individual differences in self-esteem are apparent as early as kindergarten age (31). As children grow older and become more objective with regard to themselves, their self-evaluations may tend to become less positive (18). This may be related to the child's wider range of social experiences (having a greater number of children to compare oneself with), increases in cognitive development, school factors (such as negative teacher evalutations), and peer evaluations.

Theories of Self-concept

Because the self-concept is private and internal it is difficult to know exactly how it changes with age. The major theories of human development can, however, be useful in explaining some of the factors involved in the growth of the self-concept. Psychoanalytic theory (as presented by Erikson; see Chapter 10) and cognitive theory (as presented by Piaget; see Chapter 7) see changes in the self-concept as a result of progression through stages. Learning theory sees it as an accumulation of learned behaviors and attitudes toward the self.

It is doubtful that infants possess what adults would call a self-concept during the first two years of life (Piaget's sensorimotor stage; Erikson's stage one, trust versus mistrust). If there is a self-concept in the infant or toddler, it is probably a dimly recognized sort of self-confidence. It is possible, for example, to watch a 1-year-old struggling to walk and imagine that the child is thinking: "I can do it and I have the courage to try." Other behaviors of infants also suggest a sort of self-concept with regard to people around them, or at least an awareness that other people are different from themselves. Some behave as if they were thinking: "People can be trusted and I will depend on them." Others seem to have a different attitude with regard to themselves and those around them: "People are no good and cannot be depended on." This is only speculation based on the behaviors of infants. It is not possible to know what really goes on concerning the self-concept in children before they become verbal, thoughtful beings.

A second stage in the development of self-concept may coincide with Piaget's preoperational stage, from about 2 to 4 or 5 years of age. This is about the time also of Erikson's stage of autonomy versus shame and doubt (see Chapter 10). Children at this state tend to have a not-very-confident "I am the center of the universe" attitude. Their own personal needs still dominate their behavior even if they do not always express these needs verbally. They are capable of rather complicated social efforts on behalf of their own needs —their belief that they are the center of the universe. Consider a 3-year-old who is getting less attention from a parent because of the arrival of a new baby in the family. Instead of shouting, "I want to sit in Mommy's lap," the child may suggest, "Baby wants to sit in Daddy's lap now." If the suggestion is accepted, the infant will be passed from the mother to the father, and the 3-year-old can take over the mother's lap. Preoperational children, like the

Three-year-olds are capable of complicated social efforts in order to meet their own needs.

one in this example, are beginning to learn how their behavior affects the environment. This contributes to their growing self-concept.

At about 4 or 5 years children are thought to move into a stage of thinking that Piaget calls concrete operations (see Chapter 7). This stage, usually reached by the age of 6 or 7, will extend through the elementary school years (until about age 11 or 12). Erikson divides this period into two stages: the third, initiative versus shame and guilt; and the fourth, industry versus inferiority. During these years children develop a sense of their own worth—self-esteem. Their judgments, however, are likely to be at one extreme or the other: "I can" or "I can't," or "I'm bad" or "I'm good." These rather concrete or extreme evaluations are gradually modified and become more realistic in the next stage.

The highest of Piaget's cognitive stages is the stage of formal operations. Although the evidence is not clear, many children in the United States apparently enter this stage shortly before the time of puberty at ages 11 or 12. Others may not reach this stage until much later, if at all. If and when they do, a major characteristic of the stage of formal operations is the ability to stand apart and look at oneself—to think about one's thoughts, as it were. At this stage children's self-concepts are no longer so extreme, nor are they based completely on the words and actions of others. In the formal operations stage children evaluate not only themselves but evaluate their evaluations of themselves. Only when this happens is it possible to have a real understanding of the self and a true self-concept. According to Erikson, this understanding develops slightly later (during adolescence) in stage five, identity versus role confusion. The self-concept is a central theme throughout Erikson's eight stages of psychosocial development, but it is during stage five, he suggests, that older children and adolescents face an identity crisis. This crisis refers to a period of decision-making about basic life commitments, particularly regarding ideological (moral and political) and occupational concerns. With the help of numerous social inputs and the ability to evaluate these inputs, most children confirm their commitments, resolve their identity crises, and go on to develop a firm understanding of who they really are and what they want to be.

Child-rearing Practices   Although the development of the self-concept can be seen as a progression through stages and may be related to cognitive maturity, it is likely that most of the attitudes one holds toward oneself are the result of social learning. If this is so, it can be assumed that one will develop a good self-concept about behaviors or characteristics that have been rewarded by parents and other important persons during childhood. A poor concept will develop with reference to traits that were punished or criticized. Research findings support this assumption. One study found that children's self-concepts develop according to the pattern of parental rewards and punishments. When this pattern is one in which objective success is stressed, rather than the needs of the developing child, the child's self-concept may suffer (2). Researchers measured what they called "extrinsic valuation." By this they mean that parents show excessive concern over the child's school (and other) achievements and presumably view the child as someone who enhances the parents' status. Children (10-year-old boys and girls) in such families tend to see their parents as overmotivating them, as planning in grand terms for their careers, and as displaying their school and other achievements excessively. Children from such families were themselves excessive in their ambitions. They were unrealistically persistent in believing that, next time, they would do well on a task at which they had failed many times already. Teachers rated these children as being low in social maturity. In short, this study suggests that children who are loved for themselves alone do better than those whose parents count them as showpieces (this does not mean that parents should not be proud of what their children accomplish).

Other researchers have also looked for the roots, or antecedents, of self-esteem in parental attitudes. Stanley Coopersmith, well known for his studies of self-esteem, asserts:

> The most general statement about the antecedents of self esteem can be given in terms of three conditions: total or nearly total *acceptance* of the children by their parents, clearly defined and enforced *limits*, and the *respect* and latitude

for individual action that exists within the defined limits. . . . These relationships indicate that definite and enforced limits are associated with higher rather than low self esteem; that families which establish and maintain clearly defined limits permit *greater* rather than less deviation from conventional behavior, and freer individual expression, than do families without such limits; that families which maintain clear limits utilize less drastic forms of punishment; and that the families of children with high self esteem exert greater demands for academic performance and excellence. Taken together, these relationships indicate that, other things being equal, limits and rules are likely to have enhancing and facilitating effects and that parental performance within such limits is likely to be moderate, tolerant, and generally civilized (11).

In addition, Coopersmith reports that parents of high self-esteem children are themselves high in self-esteem. One presumes, then, that these parents are able to survive the hassles that most parents go through when they set limits, however reasonable, for their children.

MEASUREMENT OF THE SELF-CONCEPT

Each of us knows that we exist as individuals. Because there is no way that everything about the personal self can be communicated to others, even if we wished to do so, it has been difficult to investigate thoroughly or explain what the self-concept is. Attempts to measure the self-concept, for example, get confused with social desirability. Children describing themselves are likely to mention only those characteristics they believe will place them in a favorable light or bring approval from other people. Willingness to be frank and honest is another problem. Children may feel that they are fat or ugly or even that they are better than others, but be unwilling to admit to such feelings. Because of these and other problems, including the definition of self-concept, some researchers have given up on the whole area of study (31). But most people will admit that the self-concept exists, no matter what it is called. They realize that the nature of the self-concept has a lot to do with whether or not one enjoys or is burdened by life and whether or not one succeeds at the things one tries.

Since the self-concept exists, and since it is so important to personal happiness and development, a number of attempts have been made to investigate and measure it. While none of these measures capture the whole idea of the self-concept, most catch enough of it to demonstrate that it is an important part of the personality.

Desirability

Most measurements of the self-concept include the idea of **desirability** and **undesirability.** Desirability may be evaluated by one investigator according to an abstract social norm. To be good or to be pretty or to be intelligent is ordinarily something that society values positively. To be bad or to be ugly or to be stupid is something that society thinks of as a negative quality. Some investigators measure desirability and undesirability in terms of the evaluations of the subjects themselves. For one child to be vivacious may be "good"; another may be indifferent to the vivacity. For still another this quality may have negative connotations: vivacious people flit around and are silly. One child may think of sophistication as something valuable; another may think of it as a phony and undesirable quality.

Measurements of self-concept vary, then, in relation to the values one holds. In most measures of the self-concept a number of terms, traits, values, or characteristics is presented to a subject. Some researchers list adjectives such as *good, brave, beautiful, strong,* and *honest,* and ask the subjects of their study to estimate the degree to which each term applies to them. Ordinarily, a rating of 1 means "Very much like me" or "Very characteristic of me." A rating of 5 carries with it the idea of "I am almost never like this" or "This is not at all like me." The adjectives listed are characterized by the *social* notion of desirability.

Another list might include *vivacious, ambitious, nonchalant, sophisticated, self-contained.* Here, the social value of the words is less clearcut. Some people will think of *vivacity* as meaning alive, glancing, scintillating; whereas others will think of it as jittery, artificial, birdlike. To some, *ambitious* means hard-working, sober, wanting to advance. Others think of it as implying pushiness, disregarding the rights of others. It is probable that no two people see a self-concept test in quite the same way. For such a list of adjectives the subjects of any given study are ordinarily asked, as with the first list, to estimate the degree to which the adjective is characteristic of them. After they have gone through the list of adjectives, they are requested to estimate the desirability of the quality they have just rated. Again, a rating of 1 for desirability ordinarily means that they think the quality is desirable; a rating of 5 indicates that they dislike it.

Regardless of the system of evaluation used, every choice of every subject is given a positive, neutral, or negative value. Ordinarily, these are added algebraically, and the resulting figure is thought of as an "index of the self-concept."

There are other ways of getting at the self-concept. Some investigators use lists of traits more elaborate than simple adjectives. Examples are: "I go out of my way to look after people who are in trouble"; "I am particularly fond of animals"; "I think poorly of people who get ahead by questionable methods." Subjects make a rating of how characteristic of themselves the statement is and of how desirable the trait is.

Still other investigators use paired but opposite adjectives, such as *warm and outgoing* versus *cool and self-contained; constantly on the go* versus *relaxed and a little lazy.* Such investigators may ask their subjects to check where they think they stand on a line drawn between the adjectives of a pair. Subjects are then asked to estimate the value of each of the qualities.

"Who Am I?" Some research workers ask their subjects simply to answer the question "Who am I?" The answers indicate a positive or negative self-concept. Or subjects are asked to go back over their answers and indicate with a plus all those they think are socially or personally desirable, with a zero those they think are neutral, and with a minus those they see as socially or personally undesirable.

Another common variation of the method is to have the subject do a Q-sort. In this technique a large number of statements or adjectives is given to subjects on separate slips of paper. They are then asked to rate these slips on, for example, a seven-point scale. They then distribute the slips. Of 100 such statements, subjects are allowed to place only seven on the figure 1, meaning "most like me," and only seven others on the figure 7, "least like me." In second and sixth positions, they may place 12 statements each; in third and fifth place, 19; and in the middle or fourth place, 24 statements. These statements may be judged positive or negative, or may be rated for desirability by each subject.

A less frequently used method of measuring the self-concept consists of having the subjects take a personality test, such as the Thematic Apperception Test. This test consists of a number of pictures. For each picture, the subject is asked to tell who the characters are, what has happened to them before, what is happening at the time the picture was taken, and what the outcome will be. Researchers then decide with whom the subject is most closely identified (who "stands for" the subject, or who is the "hero"). They then rate the attributes of this character in the story as positive, neutral, or negative. From these ratings a judgment of the self-concept of the subject is made.

Some of these techniques, such as the Q-sort, are rather complicated when used with children, but variations of all of them have been employed with children as well as adults. Compared with the number of adult studies, however, there are few studies of the self-concept in children. Those studies that have been done with children ordinarily employ a simple technique of listing a series of adjectives or traits. They then ask the children to indicate whether these are "like them" or "unlike them." After this the request is made that the children indicate by a plus whether they think the quality is a "good" one; by a zero whether they do not care one way or another; and by a minus if they do not like this aspect of themselves. This is a simplified version of the "Who am I?" test described earlier. The "Who am I?" technique has also been used with children old enough to write.

Self-concept studies of children younger than about fourth-grade age are rare, since (because of reading and writing difficulties) each child must be examined individually. An individual examination in an area such as this is likely to affect the results. Children are likely to respond not according to the way they feel or believe but according to the way they think the adult tester wants them to feel or believe.

While the most often used measures of self-esteem tend to be self-report measures, researchers are working to perfect alternatives that may add something valuable to our understanding of self-concept and its development. Alternatives include such things as ratings by others of attitudes thought to be connected to the self-concept (confidence, initiative, goal-setting behavior, and so forth); observations of actual self-reference behavior ("I" statements); and shows of emotion in self-oriented situations.

One of the first questions that must be asked of any measuring technique, or of any behavioral indicator of a concept, is: Are its results repeatable—are they stable over time? If they are not, one is forced to question either the measures or the long-run scientific usefulness of the concept. In general, measures of the self-concept have demonstrated moderate stability over time. In one study (14) researchers tested a group of sixth- and eighth-graders on a self-concept measure. After two years they repeated the same test (a Q-sort). The results of both tests were quite similar. The younger children showed as high a level of stability as the older, and boys were no different from girls in measured stability. In other words, even in the presumably unstable period of adolescence, a self-concept measure will probably yield results close to a measure made two years earlier.

THE SELF-CONCEPT AND PERSONAL ADJUSTMENT

Are measurements of self-concept useful? Do they help in the understanding or predicting of human behavior? The answer is yes. Good self-concepts, as measured by tests, tend to be reflected in behavior that represents good personal and social adjustment. Poor self-concepts are often associated with poor adjustment. While changes in self-concept do not necessarily lead to changes in behavior, in general, persons with good self-concepts are less anxious, more effective in group interactions, and more honest with themselves than those who have poor self-concepts (20).

Self-concept and Anxiety

Anxiety is a feeling of dread or apprehension about some unknown danger. Unlike fear, which is a response to a clearcut danger, anxiety is a feeling of uneasiness that develops for no obvious reason. Like fear, anxiety often produces certain physical changes, including rapid breathing, increased heart rate, and muscular tension. All people are subject to anxiety, and most learn

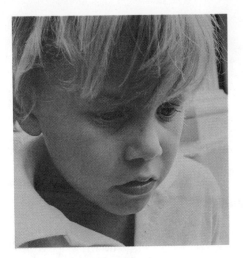

Studies indicate a relation between self-rejection, or negative self-concepts, and increased levels of anxiety.

to live with moderate levels of it. Constant high levels of anxiety can lead to emotional and physical exhaustion.

Not all of the factors associated with anxiety are known, but studies of both adults and children indicate a relation between self-rejection, or negative self-concepts, and increased levels of anxiety. One study asked a large number (about 300) of fourth-, fifth-, and sixth-grade boys and girls to indicate whether each of a series of adjectives was "very like them" or "very unlike them" (19). The subjects were then asked whether each of the traits was personally desirable or undesirable. This provided an overall index of the good-bad dimension of their self-concepts. These same children also took an anxiety test. Both boys and girls with poor self-concepts were found to be more anxious than children with good self-concepts.

Another study utilized the same anxiety scale for a group of 102 fifth- and sixth-grade children, but used a different measure of self-concept (10). The accuracy of the self-concept measurement is seen in the fact that the children's judgments of themselves were similar to their teachers' judgments of them. Children who had high self-esteem were found to be significantly less anxious than those with low self-esteem. Youngsters with high self-esteem were also found to be more popular than those with low self-esteem, and to be better at recalling their past failures. This presumably enables them to correct past mistakes. Children with low self-esteem, on the other hand, tend to suppress or deny past failures.

Effectiveness in Groups

The way people see themselves can have an effect on the way they behave in social groups. Those who are most sure of themselves speak up and take leadership roles. Those with lower degrees of self-esteem tend to be less forceful and more likely to be followers (23). In one study students took part in free-wheeling, or leaderless, discussion groups. Those with high feelings of adequacy and with favorable self-concepts were rated by others in the groups as being generally *more* effective than those who expressed feelings of inadequacy and negative self-concepts. The criteria that the group members— all of whom were initially unacquainted with each other—used in making their judgments of group effectiveness were, among others: contributing the best ideas to the group, degree of activity in the group, amount of intellectual stimulation provided to other members of the group, adequacy in explaining their ideas and clarifying the ideas of others, most influential in the group, and most appealing in that the rater desired to become better acquainted with that person.

This study supports the idea that self-concepts *are* translated into action, and contributes further support to the finding that good self-concepts are related to generally adequate social functioning, including popularity.

In another study subjects were led to believe that they were rejected by the group. Others were given the impression that they were accepted (12). Not surprisingly, the researcher found that "persons made to feel well-accepted in a group found the group more attractive than did those made to feel poorly accepted." But an individual's rating of the attractiveness of the accepted group varied according to self-concept. The group was rated significantly more attractive by those with low self-esteem. This may be related to a strong need for acceptance among such people. Other studies have uncovered similar findings. A general conclusion seems to be that while people with poor self-concepts are less popular than those with high self-esteem, and while they are generally rated as less effective in groups, they have a stronger need for groups and may overreact to group acceptance.

Self-concept, Race, and Social Class

In the 1940s psychologist Kenneth Clark conducted an experiment which suggested that black children, some as young as 3 years, felt that being black was not a good thing (8). These children rejected black dolls in favor of white ones, saying that white dolls were prettier and generally superior. These choices were taken as an indication of low self-esteem among black children. In the 1950s and early 1960s studies of the racial preferences of children continued to show black children choosing white dolls and rejecting black ones. From such studies it was concluded that black children in the United States had damaged self-concepts simply because they were black instead of white. Considering the way the white majority of society has tended to discriminate against and look down on blacks, these conclusions were not surprising.

In the 1970s the situation seems to have changed. Self-concept measurements of black children who have grown up since the early 1960s show a dif-

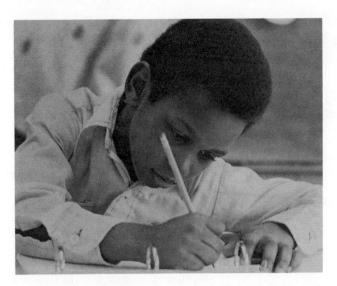

The current relationships between self-esteem and racial preference may signal a new spirit of dignity in the lives of black children.

ferent picture. In one study 60 black boys and girls between the ages of 7 and 8 were tested (6). Thirty were from a middle-class suburban school; 30 others were from a lower-class inner-city school. Each was administered a self-esteem test and then questioned about a black and a white doll. Unlike the earlier studies, this one found that more black children preferred the black doll. Those children with the highest self-esteem almost all chose the black doll. There were no significant sex or social class differences. It is possible, concluded the researchers, that the relationship between self-esteem and racial preference may signify a new spirit of dignity in the lives of black children.

Being reared in a poor part of town under disadvantaged conditions — a life-style that is looked down on by the majority of society — would also be expected to produce low self-esteem, but this may not be the case. Recent studies, including the previously mentioned large-scale study conducted in Iowa, have found significant differences in self-acceptance favoring disadvantaged children. In that study lower-class children scored higher in self-esteem than middle-class children at all ages, of both sexes, in black and other races, and in rural as well as urban areas. The lower-class children, like those of average intelligence, tended to be comfortable with their peers, thought they were easy to like, and saw themselves as popular. The middle-class children, like those of high intelligence, did not think as much of themselves, especially in terms of school. They tended to think that teachers perceived them as less able than they were. One reason for these findings, say the researchers, may be that lower-class children have a lower level of ambition than middle-class children and therefore are happy with their level of achievement and place in life. Middle-class children have usually been taught that school is important, meaningful, and relevant, and they may lose self-esteem when they do not achieve success. Another reason may be that lower-class children are forced to develop a strong self-concept in order to protect themselves in a middle-class environment.

What does it mean if children see themselves as being very similar to what they would ideally like to be or, on the other hand, as being much inferior to their idealized selves? Research findings are not in complete agreement on this question, but there are indications that really sharp differences between one's self-concept and what one wants to be (the ideal self) are related to personal unhappiness. There is also evidence that excessive self-satisfaction (no difference between the perceived and the ideal self) has its disadvantages. A certain amount of restless discontent or dissatisfaction may act as a constructive force (ambition) urging individuals to better themselves.

Many of these findings are based on studies that, in addition to asking subjects to indicate how they feel about themselves, ask subjects to go through the same set of items again and indicate how they would like to be ideally. Since almost everyone would like to be "better," the ideal self is usually judged to be at least as good and almost always better than the perceived self. The difference between the scores for the perceived self and the ideal self is the **discrepancy score.** The larger the discrepancy, the more dissatisfied with themselves people are presumed to be.

Most studies of this type have used adults as subjects, but the findings have implications for children, and a few studies have been made of children. In one, 78 adolescents were given a personality test and then asked to do a Q-sort of 100 self-evaluating items, both for their perceived and ideal self-concepts (17). The discrepancy scores were then related to the overall adjustment scores on the personality test. The findings were significant, with the lower levels of discrepancy (higher levels of self-satisfaction) being related to better adjustment.

Another study, conducted with 184 sixth-graders, found the self-dissatisfied youngsters to be more anxious and less secure than those who were more self-satisfied (5). In a study in which self-rejecting subjects were interviewed, it was found that they were more likely to say such things as they give up more easily than others; are more sensitive than others; are less happy, less calm, and more restless than others; and that things pile up on them (22). They tended to believe that they were more distractible and high-strung, that life is a strain, and that they cannot live up to their parents' expectations of them. These subjects were also more anxious, but as a group did as well in school as those who were more self-accepting.

These studies all indicate that a large discrepancy between the perceived self and the ideal self can be associated with poor overall adjustment. Yet as mentioned previously, excessively high degrees of self-satisfaction (low discrepancy) do not necessarily indicate good adjustment. Highly self-satisfied individuals, for example, have been found to be overly defensive and unwilling to admit to undesirable traits (3). The highly dissatisfied individuals from the same study were judged to be confused and despairing and to have unrealistic and contradictory goals. Those with only a moderate degree of dissatisfaction appeared to be the most reasonable and accepting of their self-appraisals and were comfortable in their relations with others. They may have their problems, say the researchers, but they neither despair nor deny their traits.

Not all other studies have confirmed these findings. One found, for example, that both high and low degrees of self-satisfaction are related to better adjustment than is a moderate degree of self-satisfaction (7). This difference in results may be due to the fact that the researchers used different measures of self-esteem or to some unknown factor. Since the findings do not all agree, a question remains unanswered: When does self-dissatisfaction cease to be a "desire to improve oneself" and become a serious handicap? There is a very real difference between individuals who see themselves as being imperfect, yet manage to live comfortably with themselves, and those who torture themselves with inferiority feelings and self-doubts.

Self-concept and the "Real Self"

Just as discrepancies between the perceived self and the ideal self are related to measures of adjustment, discrepancies between the perceived self and the "real self" seem to be related to adjustment. There is no concrete way of knowing the "real self." The closest approximation that can be made is to compare statements of individuals about themselves with judgments of people who know them well. Such studies have been infrequent, but teachers are usually in a good position to make *relatively* reliable judgments about their students.

Coopersmith (10) measured the self-concepts of fifth- and sixth-grade children in one such study and then obtained teacher judgments about the children (the "real selves"). Some of the children rated themselves high, others low in self-concept. Although the youngsters were generally accurate—in the sense that the teachers agreed with their self-estimates—disagreements between child and teacher judgments did occur. From the total population of self- and teacher judgments, Coopersmith selected a group of high self-esteem children whose teachers thought poorly of them (these were called the high-low, or HL, group) and another group of children who thought poorly of themselves but who were highly regarded by their teachers (the low-high, or LH, group). When these children were compared those who were successful in school but who regarded themselves poorly (the LH's) were found to be more popular and better academic achievers, although more self-critical and more ambitious. These youngsters appear to "take it out on themselves," yet they are well regarded by both teachers and peers.

Coopersmith also selected two other groups for special study. In one of these the good self-concepts of the children agreed with the favorable "real self" ratings of their teachers. These youngsters made up the high-high, or HH, group. Another group of children had poor self-concepts with which the teachers agreed (the low-low, or LL, group). The LL's were found to be less popular and more anxious than the HH's. They achieved less and had lower ideal concepts of themselves (but were still overly self-critical). In other words, humble yet successful children seem to do better than less humble but equally favorably rated children. Children who neither thought they were doing well nor were actually doing well were those who were relatively unidealistic about themselves. Yet they failed to meet even their own relatively low standards.

SELF-CONCEPT AND SCHOOL ACHIEVEMENT

It would seem logical that a poor self-concept, which implies a lack of confidence in facing and mastering the environment, would be related to deficiency in one of the most important areas of accomplishment for children —their performance in school. It is not surprising then that numerous studies have documented a significant relationship among such things as academic achievement, school satisfaction, and self-concept (24). This relationship has been reported for children at all grade levels, from the primary grades through college (20). In general, it is the child with low self-esteem whose academic progress is hindered.

Under-achievement

The link between self-concept and school achievement is probably best illustrated by studies of underachievement. Such studies usually involve a comparison of pupils who are achieving close to their potential with children who are not. While the achieving pupils may certainly feel inadequate in some areas, it is the underachievers who are likely to report more general feelings of inadequacy (27).

Self-concept and school achievement do seem to be related, but the connection is not as straightforward as might be expected. It may be that some children with poor self-concepts do poorly in school because they don't try as hard as children with more confidence and better self-concepts. On the other hand, it may be that these children with poor self-concepts have experienced failure so often that they learn to think of themselves as failures.

Other complexities in the link between achievement and self-esteem were pointed out in a large-scale study of schoolchildren in Iowa (29). The self-esteem measurement developed by Stanley Coopersmith was used to evaluate 3,800 children between the ages of 8 and 13. One of the first findings concerned the relationship between self-concept and intelligence. The researchers discovered that children with the highest scores on a group intelligence test had significantly lower self-concepts than the students of average intelligence. Responses to the self-esteem test indicated that children of average intelligence feel they are easy to like, that other children usually follow their ideas, that they are popular with their peers, and that they are fun to be with. The children of high intelligence tended to feel that teachers expect too much of them because of their high intelligence. They also reported that their parents expect too much of them. These findings further illustrate the point that the relation between self-concept and academic achievement is a complex one. As important as a positive self-concept may be to achievement, it is not all that is necessary for academic success. School achievement depends on a variety of factors and cannot be traced to the existence of a single personal characteristic.

Even though the relationship between self-concept and school achievement is complex, there is little doubt that success in school plays an important role in the development of self-esteem. School offers children their first opportunity outside the home to test their abilities. If they are successful in school they are likely to grow in self-esteem. If they suffer repeated failures they are likely to lose self-confidence.

Because self-concept and school achievement are so closely related, numerous attempts have been made within the school setting to find ways of increasing the self-esteem of students, or at least of avoiding those factors that may be harmful to a student's self-concept. Few hard facts have been reported concerning exactly what can be done to keep from damaging the self-images of students, but several factors have been considered. Individualized instruction, for example, sometimes helps minimize frustration and reduce

Success in school plays an important role in the development of self-esteem.

failure (see the discussion of Keller's personalized system of instruction in Chapter 6). Efforts have also been made to deemphasize rigid student evaluation and grading systems based on competition, in which someone is always doomed to failure. Counseling to help build self-confidence, acceptance, and understanding has also been found to be helpful, as have attempts to cultivate positive teacher-pupil relationships (20). As important as these factors and the entire field of educational psychology are, only a few of them can be represented here. One of the most important has to do with frustration and failure.

Frustration and Failure: The Child's View

No one, no matter how bright, succeeds at everything on the first try. Consequently, frustration and failure are a part of life, and they are especially common in the school setting where children are constantly challenged by new situations. **Frustration,** or the feeling that one is somehow prevented from attaining a purpose, comes about when children, for one reason or another, are kept from doing what they want to do. **Failure,** of course, is when they do not get anything done at all. These two conditions bring about responses that range all the way from giving up immediately and leaving the situation to becoming very angry, throwing oneself around, or breaking things. Frustration and failure also bring about cognitive behavior that ranges from blaming oneself entirely to blaming others entirely.

Because frustration and failure are a part of life, children need to learn many things about facing and dealing with them. Much has been written on this subject, and a great deal of research has been done. Instead of describing the research, methods of helping children cope with both frustration and failure are presented here.

Children need to be able to look at the situation in which they are being frustrated or are failing. The wise adult helps them see as many dimensions of the situation as possible and check their role in it as accurately and extensively as they can. This is likely to involve them in talking with parents, teachers, or friends. No harm is done by asking people: "How did I do?" and "What did I do wrong?" Frustration and failure are as much a part of life as success. No one ever hesitates to ask another, "What was it about my performance that was good?" By the same token, asking about the reasons for frustration and failure are legitimate and probably even more helpful. Those who have succeeded at something already know how to do it. Those who have failed obviously need the secret of success.

Help children not to expose themselves to impossible situations, but rather to avoid them if possible and get out of them gracefully if they have entered them and cannot possibly succeed. For example, a girl who is already 5 feet 5 inches tall at age 11 is not likely to make it as a ballerina. In such a case forewarning is in order.

Help children look for alternatives in important endeavors they are undertaking. It is possible in most situations to behave in manners (a), (b), (c), and (d). If (a) does not work, then try (b), and so on. Encourage children to try them all and then to think of other possibilities if they still are not successful.

Children should be helped to recognize their characteristic ways of reacting to failure. When situations resemble each other responses to them are likely to resemble each other. Since failure is failure whenever it may occur, responses to failure are likely to be similar from one failure to another. The intensity of the response may differ from situation to situation (depending on the type of failure involved), but parents and teachers should try to make a judgment of the characteristic ways children in their charge react to failure and help them develop responses that are as constructive as possible.

Some children give up easily. Teachers and parents should talk with them once they are sure that this is a characteristic strategy, help them understand situations and their own behavior, and then encourage them to plan for the next time. If they are inclined to give up after a first unsuccessful attempt, help them plan to try twice next time, then three times on the next occasion, and so on up to some reasonable limit. (But if one has tried four times between the ages of 25 and 50 to climb Mt. Everest and failed each time, it seems unrealistic to try again at age 60.)

Some children "blow up" in the face of frustration and failure. They should be helped to look at themselves and their feelings and to leave the situation just before their limits are reached.

Help children plan for situations in which they may be frustrated or fail, or both—"Forewarned is forearmed." If children have some idea about the situation they are getting into, they are likely to act more adaptively than if they have no potential strategies at hand.

Finally, children should be helped to realize that their own patterns of behavior are likely to evoke similar responses: a grin evokes a grin; a fist is likely to be met by a fist; when one cooperates with someone the other person is also likely to cooperate; the same holds for competition. Children must also realize that none of these "rules" works all the time, but that they are more useful than no plan at all.

Frustration and Failure: The Adult's View

Always remember that children can think, and whatever their age or sex, having an intellectual grasp of a situation will help them cope with it. In other words, help children come to recognize and understand what it is that produces frustration, and how failures can occur. This is a matter of encouraging self-evaluation in light of the demands that may be made of the child from one situation to the next.

Similarly, try to guide children out of impossible situations. In situations that threaten frustration or failure help them gain a realistic sense of what they can and can't do. When a situation is impossible help them learn how to escape gracefully. Children need not be made to feel guilty or ashamed because they do not have a "right" answer or a perfect way of performing a task.

It follows, then, that frustration should be kept at the lowest possible level for children. For example, 5- and 6-year-olds often find that learning to write is difficult. The difficulty can create tension even under the best of circumstances. Unfortunately, adults often create additional tension. This sometimes happens by accident when equipment which is beyond their developmental stage is given to children. Thin, finely pointed pencils are a case in point. These are hard to grasp and pressure on the pencil can break the lead. That is why the standard, thick, heavy-leaded "kindergarten" pencil is used. A poorly selected instrument can add to frustration that has nothing to do with the task of writing. In this example children should be given an instrument that is least likely to add to the difficulty of writing and printing skills.

Help children generalize across situations. As mentioned earlier, there are elements in common among most frustration-failure situations. Techniques that are useful in one are likely to be useful in another, just as techniques that fail for one situation are likely to fail for others. Children can learn to decide when to ask for help, clearer directions, additional information, and the like. They can also be helped to tell the difference in the many moods expressed by adults and peers. These moods can affect the quality of how children and adults will get along together in high demand situations.

Help children learn the rules of the social "games" they must play in as much detail as they can understand. Coach them in these rules, and keep watch on their understanding of such rules. These games will range from the neighborhood play group through adult organized play. They include how to act in class, how to take tests, and spread to a wide variety of social experiences. This does not mean that children must always obey the rules that have been set up. On the contrary, there are occasions when the rules need to be changed. In general, children who are aware of the social standards by which their behavior is judged usually feel secure. If they know how to participate in peer group activity they can be self-confident about their own behavior and how to predict the behavior of others.

Allow children to experience progressively greater degrees of frustration and possible failure from early childhood on. A child for whom everything is done learns little about life, just as children faced with tasks beyond their skills learn nothing about mastery and success. Progressive experience with frustration and failure may be a necessary "toughening process," although little is known about this phenomenon. It is tempting for adults to protect or shield children. But eventually children act on their own in a society that values independence. Really bad experiences should be avoided in any humane approach to child-rearing and education. Unfortunately, this is a major problem for some, if not many children. How can we eliminate hopeless poverty, brutality, and other evils?

Try to help children avoid having too much motivation, such as anxiety or fear, that could interfere with a good performance. Some motivation is essential, or nothing will be tried. Most children will try most things at least once because they are curious, but some children will try too hard or become overly fearful about the consequences of not doing well. Very few things in day-to-day living are matters of life and death. Children need to be helped to develop perspective. If something cannot be learned today, maybe it can be learned tomorrow or next week. Too much motivation tends to exaggerate responses, and these do not work very well.

A child is overmotivated if the consequences of a particular behavior are so strongly valued that failure to gain those consequences brings about other types of behaviors that interfere with the child's chances of ever gaining the particular goal that is so much desired. Parents and teachers should help children attach more value to some consequences—such as efficiency in reading —and decrease value for others—"You will live your whole life long even though you did not get the chance to play the lead role in the third-grade play." Reshaping motivation is difficult, but it is often a necessary part of helping children learn to live with frustration and failure. Children need to find out that there are many times when it will probably be necessary to shrug one's shoulders and say and mean, "So what?"

Providing for Individual Differences

The wide variation among children in a typical classroom provides many learning experiences in human relations and can add interest to a teacher's job, but it can also be a source of frustration and failure for children and their teachers.

Consider, for example, a small-town fifth-grade class. The children are usually 10 or 11 years old, although some who have been held back will be older, and there will be an occasional 9-year-old. The teacher is likely to have 30 to 40 children in the class, about half boys and half girls. Some of the girls will have already reached puberty, but most of them will be in their pre-puberty growth spurt. Two of the boys in the class have reached puberty. They are the oldest members of the class, and both of them have previously repeated grades.

The social and economic status of the children ranges from very low to quite high. Two of the children come from poor farm families. They come to class shabbily dressed after almost an hour's ride on the school bus. The child from the top of the social ladder is the daughter of a prominent physician in the town and walks the two blocks from her large, handsome home to the school.

The class members have all had group intelligence tests (see Chapter 9). The lowest IQ in the class is 77, the highest 145. One child in the room reads at the second-grade level; another reads at about the level for high school seniors. Ability in mathematics ranges from the second- to the ninth-grade level. Some of the children have never had a daily newspaper in their homes. One family takes both a morning and an evening paper and drives a long distance each week to pick up the Sunday *New York Times*. Some children have traveled no farther than a few miles outside the town limits, but the doctor's daughter has toured Europe.

One child in the room is black; another, whose parents speak almost no English, is chicano. The children belong to a variety of churches or no church at all, even though the town is mostly Protestant. One of the older boys spent a year in a school for delinquents.

This is an extreme picture, but it illustrates the range of pupil experiences teachers are likely to encounter in many U.S. schools. If children are to have appropriate opportunities to learn, such classes must be very flexible. With a population like the one described, a teacher would need almost to be a genius and have eight arms to meet the individual needs of the pupils. In such cases most teachers are forced, or choose, to aim their teaching at or a little below the middle level of the class. They must spend a disproportionate amount of time working with "slow-learning" and "difficult" children. Typically, the top fifth of a class partially teaches itself, while pupils in the bottom fifth mainly meet frustration and failure. The top-fifth children are bored and experience frustration; those in the bottom fifth are lost and are victims of both frustration and failure.

Children should be instructed in different subject matters according to their ability to help each other.

Such a system produces two results. First, many of the brighter students probably learn not to work. Second, children in the bottom fifth, plus those who spend their elementary and secondary school years in boredom, may generalize their experiences and learn to dislike all education.

As serious as this situation may seem, the U.S. educational system is not failing at its task. The dream of universal education is being realized to some degree. The literacy rate in the United States is high, although not the highest in the world. Almost all children believe that school is worthwhile, and many enjoy it. Most teachers do their best to understand the problems of the different children in their classes, and methods are available to them for overcoming individual differences within a classroom.

The most important tools for accommodating to individual differences are knowledge and understanding of the children's backgrounds and flexible strategies for fitting teaching and learning experiences to these backgrounds. Second, school systems should supply a wide range of work materials for each class so that no child goes unchallenged and every child can succeed at some things. Third, teaching should be done according to our best knowledge about creating productive and satisfying group experiences. In other words, children can be instructed in different subject matters according to their skills in self-help and cooperation with others. A math group, for example, might include the top third of the class in number ability; but a reading group might contain a few of the top and a few of the bottom, with the top children acting as teachers or tutors for the slower group. Insofar as possible, children who like each other should work together. In some cases grouping should be arranged so that children who are social leaders help social loners learn skill in relating to others. Teachers should also learn about the social structure in their classes. "Who likes whom?" (an intimacy or simple friendship measure) "Who respects whom?" (a peer judgment about competency). An understanding of these peer relationships will help teachers in their judgments of students. Children are usually better judges of the eventual outcome of other children's lives than are parents or teachers. Those in charge of the development of children can too easily overlook the rich store of knowledge that children possess about each other.

Reporting to Children and Their Parents

Some researchers have found that no single factor contributes as much to a student's sense of self-esteem as does a good report card, or damages it so severely as do poor grades (25). Accordingly, teachers' reports to children and their parents are extremely important and should be made with as much precision as possible.

Children should probably take achievement tests annually to find out where they stand with regard to the skills and information that are judged to be necessary for getting along in U.S. society. In particular, knowing how pupils

All children are graded more or less informally in their classes.

compare to the national standard can be important for decision-making about necessary educational experiences. For example, some years ago, the first author of this book served as a consultant to a remote school in Hawaii. The morale in this school was good; children were learning; and they seemed to be happy. The population was mobile, and many children left the school and went to more cosmopolitan schools on the large island of Oahu or on the mainland. A surprisingly high number of them failed in such schools, became disturbed, and dropped out entirely as soon as they were able to do so. The problem seemed to be that children in this geographically and culturally isolated school were judged by their teachers only relative to the performance of their own peer group. For example, a child might have been first in the class from kindergarten through fifth grade, but when moved to a more complex and sophisticated setting might have ranked only in the middle of the class. In such cases children often suffered severe and even crippling blows to self-esteem.

In addition to national achievement tests, all children are graded more or less informally in their classes. Grades are given according to results from teacher-made tests, teachers' reactions to the behavior of students, students' personalities, and so on. These teacher grades, however, do not necessarily reflect how much a child really knows, as judged from results on standardized achievement tests. Teachers seem to grade some children in school as much by the way they behave socially as by how much they learn (21). For many years school performance, as judged by teachers' grades, is the main source of information available to children about their competency. For this reason those who educate teachers should perhaps give more attention than is

Evaluations should not be confined to formal school subjects, but should include all the important areas in which children function.

usually given to training future teachers in how to evaluate pupil performance fairly, accurately, and for maximum information to the child.

Perhaps most meaningful of all is a third type of evaluation: helping children to determine how they are doing in relation to their own previous performance. If they are showing greater improvement month by month in the third grade than they had in the second grade they can be helped to recognize and get a positive sense of accomplishment from this fact.

Instructive feedback to children in school should not be confined to formal school subjects. It should include all the important areas in which children function—art, music, skill at physical play, and so on. Talent is by no means limited to reading, writing, and mathematics. Children who have an accurate understanding of their talents and abilities would seem better able to develop a realistic self-concept. The important guideline here is to provide constructive, specific, and supportive feedback. Unguarded criticism, especially that which occurs in a cold or hostile manner, has no place in the classroom.

CHANGING THE SELF-CONCEPT

No matter what experiences a child has in school, the self-concept is bound to change with age. Infants change their images from "immobile self" to "mobile self" when they start walking. Self-concepts change again when children enter school and become students and part of a peer group. As new skills are learned and as more information is acquired, the self-concept becomes increasingly complex. With continued physical and sexual maturation, and especially with the dramatic biological changes that come during puberty, the self-concept undergoes even further changes.

While most of these changes come about naturally during the course of growing up as children interact with and learn from their social and physical environments, some changes in self-concept are purposely brought about. In fact, it is the job of some people to change the self-concept of others. Remedial reading teachers want to change the self-concepts of their pupils from "I can't read" to "I can read." Psychotherapists want to change the self-concepts of their parents from "I am not any good and might as well be dead" to "I am a worthwhile person and life is worth living." Television ads are meant to change the self-concepts of viewers from "I never buy brand X" to "I always buy brand X." Politicians want to change the self-concepts of voters in the direction of the political party under whose banner they are running.

If, as discussed earlier, unrealistically low self-concepts or large discrepancies among the perceived self, the ideal self, and the "real self" can lead to unhappiness and poor personal adjustment in school and out, then successful attempts to change an individual's self-concept may result in increased happiness for that individual. Therefore, it is important to have some understanding of the processes involved in changing the self-concept.

One theory related to changes in the self-concept has been proposed by psychologist Leon Festinger (15). Basically, Festinger's theory is concerned with changes in attitude, but because the self-concept has to do with the attitudes one holds toward oneself, his theory has important implications for changing the self-concept.

Festinger suggests that when individuals hold inconsistent perceptions, either about themselves or the environment, they are placed in a state of tension. Festinger calls this **cognitive dissonance** ("dissonance" meaning a harsh or disagreeable combination). This is an uncomfortable state of affairs that individuals try to relieve by bringing their own perceptions closer together. A child might have a self-concept with regard to spinach ("I hate spinach"), but for some reason may be induced to eat spinach and finds out that it isn't so bad. In such a case the child will have conflicting perceptions—"I hate spinach" and "spinach isn't so bad." If the tension or dissonance set up by these conflicting perceptions is great enough, the child will usually change one perception or the other.

A number of experiments have supported Festinger's hypothesis. They suggest mechanisms by which attitudes, including those having to do with the self-concept, may be changed. In one such experiment college students were asked to take part in an extremely dull and boring task (16). The task involved spending a half hour putting 12 spools on a tray, emptying the tray, refilling it with spools, and so on. The students were allowed to work at their own speed using only one hand. Then, for the second half hour, they were asked to work with a board containing 48 square pegs. The task involved turning the pegs a quarter turn, one at a time, and then beginning all over again, again using one hand and working at their own speed. It is difficult to imagine that anyone enjoyed these tasks, but the students were all asked to report favorably on them to the person next in line to begin the tasks. Such reports, of course, would be inconsistent with the students' true feelings about the tasks.

Some of the students were simply asked to make a favorable report. A second group, the minimal-reward group, was offered $1 per person to make the inconsistent report. A third group, the maximal-reward group, was offered $20 per person to make the favorable report. Members of all three groups were then asked by the experimenters to give a report of their true feelings about the boring tasks. Those who received no money for giving the favorable report gave the tasks a mildly negative rating. They were probably showing good manners in being so mild. The maximal-reward group ($20) gave the tasks a neutral rating. The minimal-reward group ($1) rated the tasks as moderately enjoyable. They even stated that they would be willing to go through the procedure again, while those in the other two groups were unwilling to repeat it.

These results fit with Festinger's hypothesis: If people are induced to say or do something contrary to their private opinions or attitudes, they will be likely to change their opinions in order to bring them more in line with what they have said or done — and thereby reduce their level of cognitive dissonance. But as the experiment demonstrates, the greater the pressure used to bring about the dissonant behavior, the less likely people are to change their opinions. In other words, the greater the pressure, the more likely it is that people will be able to separate their behaviors from their personal convictions. Those who received $20, for example, might say to themselves, "I just did it for the money; it doesn't affect my real feelings about the boring task." Those who received only $1 had less of an excuse for their behavior and, therefore, were more likely actually to change their opinions about the boring tasks, and even to say they would repeat them.

These findings have implications for changing the self-concept. If through mild pressure or reward individuals can be induced to say or do something contrary to their self-concepts, they will alter their self-concepts in the direction of the spoken opinion or behavior. If someone who has a poor self-image with regard to public speaking were in some low-pressure fashion induced to make a good speech, that person's self-concept might improve with regard to public speaking.

In another study college students were given an option of listening to or not listening to a propaganda session on a topic about which they held strongly opposing opinions (9). A second group was subjected to strong pressure to listen to the propaganda. The low-pressure group moved almost four times as far as the high-pressure group in the direction of agreeing with the propaganda. The suggestion for self-concept change is obvious: One is more likely to induce individuals to make changes in self-concept by nonforceful, low-pressure methods than through high social pressure.

Not only social pressure, but the opinions of others—especially important others such as parents—are often involved in changes in self-concept. This is seen in an experiment in which like–dislike ratings were obtained from eighth-graders for 34 vegetables (4). Once the opinions were taken, the researcher, posing as a nutrition worker, asked the youngsters to take part in a food-tasting program. The program was designed so that the students each ended up tasting the vegetable they liked least. They were told they could eat it or not, as they wished. If they ate it, however, they would be given a choice of either two free movie tickets or two records. For the low-consequences group nothing more was said. In the high-consequences group the experimenter mentioned casually (when the youngsters had almost finished eating the dish of vegetables), "Oh, I almost forgot to mention that one of the reports we plan to put out from this study will simply be a letter to the parents of each person who takes part, just indicating which vegetable the person ate." The parents, in other words, would know that the children were eating something they usually refused to eat at home.

After the food-tasting part of the experiment the youngsters were asked to rate the 34 vegetables again. They were also told that some people change their opinions while others do not. The high-consequences group—those whose parents were to be informed—changed significantly more in their ranking of the previously disliked vegetable than the low-consequences group, although this group also gave slightly higher ratings to the test vegetables after having tasted them. The implications for self-concept change are again obvious: If the behavior contrary to the self-concept is likely to be known by important others (is going to become public), then the predicted self-concept change will be greater than if the consequences remain private.

OTHER QUALITIES OF THE SELF-CONCEPT

The extremely personal aspects of the self-concept have kept researchers from thoroughly examining it. Most research in this area has been concerned with only the most obvious aspect or quality of the self-concept, its positive or negative balance. There are, however, other qualities of the self-concept that deserve attention.

Complexity and Breadth

The self-concept is much more than a set of attitudes reflecting an individual's view of the self as either good or bad. It usually consists of a wide array of complex attitudes related to one's experience. Average adults, for example, almost certainly have more complex and broader self-concepts than do children. Highly educated adults probably have more complex and broader self-concepts than those who have had little education and a narrow range of experiences. The person who lives only for work can be expected to have a narrower self-concept than one who has many interests and activities. Married people and parents develop areas of self-concept that unmarried individuals and those without children do not have or need.

Congruency and Accuracy

The self-concept, as research suggests, should conform to a person's actual situation in life. There are times during life, however, when the self-concept is out of line with reality. Some early-maturing children, for example, continue to think of themselves as "little" after their teachers and other adults have begun to react to them as mature. Boys and girls who have been either obese or underweight sometimes carry with them negative self-concepts after they have achieved normal weight. Such incongruities of self-concept are helpful to no one.

Clarity and Articulateness

People who are very self-aware or inner-directed may be more able than others to articulate their self-concepts to themselves and others. These self-concepts may not, however, be more accurate or positive than those of other people.

Consistency

During the course of normal development, as maturity is gained, behavior in general becomes better organized and more stable. So it is with an individual's self-concept. As knowledge about oneself is acquired, including insights concerning one's relative strengths and limitations with regard to various activities and traits, certain expectations come about and are reflected in estimates of what one can or cannot do. This kind of thinking usually leads to consistency between one's self-concept and one's behavior. Children who know they are good at some game, for example, will be likely to take part in and enjoy that game. They will be less likely to participate in or enjoy the games in which they know they will do poorly. Many poorly adjusted children and adults are those who carry with them inconsistent and contradictory self-concepts.

Flexibility

Consistency with regard to the self-concept is important, but the self-concept should also be flexible. An individual should have the ability to change roles and shift from one appropriate self-concept to another as the occasion demands. A person should be able to be a leader in one situation and a follower or helper in another, a teacher in one situation and a student in another. Adults may have to change from having a high degree of personal freedom and independence to being responsible parents. Or they may change from being parents of preschoolers to being parents of adolescents. They are members of the family circle at one time and of the social circle at another, and then change back again. There are other changes — from the security of the home to the excitement and unfamiliarity of a vacation; from being with an intimate circle of friends to occasions when the group is made up of strangers.

Self-acceptance   Different from self-esteem is **self-acceptance,** whether self-esteem is measured according to a good-bad dimension or according to the discrepancy between an actual and an ideal self-concept. Some children and adults can regard themselves accurately, facing the fact that they are not all they would like to be, yet living comfortably and constructively with this awareness. Others are in constant turmoil because they are not all they think they should be. Self-acceptance should not be merely complacency. A moderate degree of personal discomfort probably functions constructively to motivate people toward higher achievements, but everyone should at times be able to say, "Oh, well, that is the way I am and I'll live with it."

SUMMARY

The self-concept, which is the sum total of one's personal awareness, evaluations, and expectations, is an essentially private area of experience, but it is translated into action by most of the things people do and say. Because the self enters into all areas of human behavior, questions about the self are a major concern of psychology.

Self-awareness probably begins some time during the first year of life, and by the second or third year children see themselves as being distinct from their parents and from other children.

Both Piaget and Erikson see development of the self-concept as a progression through stages, but it is likely that most of the attitudes children hold toward themselves are the result of social learning.

Most of what young children learn about themselves comes from their parents. It is probable that children develop good self-concepts about behaviors and characteristics that have been rewarded by parents and important others and develop poor self-concepts with reference to traits that were punished or criticized.

Numerous tests or measures of the self-concept have been designed and used. None captures the whole idea of self-concept, but most capture enough of it to demonstrate that it is an important part of the personality. In general, self-concept measures consist of having subjects estimate the degree to which various adjectives characterize them. Subjects are also often asked to rate the adjectives as desirable or undesirable.

Measures of self-concept have been found especially useful as indicators of personal adjustment. Low self-concepts, for example, have been related to high levels of anxiety, poor group effectiveness, and poor school performance—although the relationship here is complex. There is also evidence that sharp differences between one's self-concept and what one *wants* to be are related to personal unhappiness, but a certain amount of self-dissatisfaction probably serves as a constructive force urging individuals to better themselves.

School offers children one of their first chances outside the home to test their abilities. What happens in school, whether a child meets success or failure, has a great deal to do with the development of the self-concept. Because no one succeeds at everything on the first attempt, frustration and failure are bound to be a part of life, especially school life. There are methods, however, of helping children cope with frustration and failure.

One difficult task facing teachers is meeting the varied needs of children in their classes who often come from a wide range of backgrounds. The better prepared teachers are to provide for the individual needs of their students, the less likely they and their students are to face frustration and failure.

Because the self-concept is so important to personal happiness, successful attempts to change the self-concept can possibly result in increased happiness. One theory suggests that if through mild pressure or reward individuals can be induced to do or say something contrary to their self-concepts, they will alter their self-concepts in the direction of the spoken opinion or behavior.

The intensely personal and internal aspects of the self-concept have kept researchers from thoroughly examining it, but several qualities of the self-concept (in addition to the positive-negative balance) deserve consideration. They include its complexity, congruency, clarity, consistency, flexibility and, finally, self-acceptance.

RESEARCH REPORT 12.1

Changing Self-concepts in Elementary School Children

Low self-concept has long been closely related to behavior that is not well adapted to many areas of living. Educational specialists have discovered that self-concept is a large factor in educational achievement.

Many theorists of human behavior have wondered how the self-concept can be changed. The behavioral approach attempts to change what children say to and about themselves. The idea is that if a change in a specific behavior can be produced, usually through rewarding the behavior, the attitudes surrounding that behavior will also change.

Hauserman, Miller, and Bond selected 30 boys and girls from kindergarten through fourth grade as participants in an experiment designed to study self-concept change. All the children selected had low self-concepts. The principal testing instrument used for both student selections and pretest conditions was the Pictorial Self-concept Scale. This test consists of 50 picture cards showing cartoonlike drawings of various children's activities, with some positive and some negative activities. The child's task was to sort the cards into piles of "like me," "sometimes like me," and "not like me." The self-concept score was the result of the weighted value of each pile.

Prompters—teachers, aides, and student assistants—singled out activities in which the child displayed some behavior that was appropriate or successful in a situation. The teacher then requested the child to "tell me something good about yourself." Immediately after this the student was given feedback—a hug, a wink, a pat on the back, or was told "I am proud of you." Eight such reinforcements were made each day. If the child was unable to give a positive statement about himself or herself, the adult would model one which the child would then repeat.

After 40 days the Pictorial Self-concept Scale was given again as a past test. A four-week "no prompted positive statement" period followed, and then the Scale was given. A matched control group received no treatment. All testing was carried out by one of the researchers who did not participate in any prompting sessions. A significant difference was found between the experimental and control groups. Even after the four-week followup, the differences remained significant, showing change between the two groups. The reinforced students showed a rise in their self-concepts.

Were the results the direct result of the attention given to the low self-concept students? Some people do not believe that the test used was a proper one for reflecting attention given, and feel the results were questionable.

Much additional study is needed, and future research of this type should be done. Meanwhile, social scientists are beginning to discover and report on new, simple ways for enlarging emotional and academic growth in the classroom.

Based on N. Hauserman, J. S. Miller, and F. T. Bond, "A Behavioral Approach to Changing Self-concept in Elementary School Children," *The Psychological Record*, 1976, *26*, 111–116.

RESEARCH REPORT 12.2

Is There a Self-fulfilling Prophecy?

An experiment was designed to test the idea that favorable expectations by teachers would lead to an increase in pupils' intellectual achievement. The experiment was done at a public elementary school in a lower-class community of a medium-size city. Each of the six grades in the school is regularly divided into one fast, one medium, and one slow class. Reading ability is the most important factor that is considered in making class assignments.

All of the children in school were pretested with a standard nonverbal intelligence test. Teachers were led to believe that this test would predict intellectual "blooming." At the beginning of the school year each of the 18 teachers of grades 1 through 6 were given the names of those children in the classroom who would show dramatic intellectual growth in the year ahead. About 20 percent of the school population were so named. Such predictions were supposed to be based on the results of the intelligence test. Actually, the children were randomly selected. The only difference between "bloomers" and other children was in the teachers' minds.

All the children were given the same test again after one semester, after a full academic year, and after two full academic years. For the first two retests the children were in the same room with the teacher who had been told who the "bloomers" were. For the final testing all the children had been promoted to classes of teachers who had not been told any of the children were "bloomers."

Expectancy advantage was defined by the degree to which IQ gains by the "special" children exceeded gains made by control group children. After the first year of the experiment a significant expectancy was found, especially among second- and third-grade children. Only 19 percent of the control group children gained 20 or more IQ points, while 47 percent of the "special" children gained 20 or more IQ points.

During the follow-up year the younger children lost this expectancy advantage. Upper-grade children showed an increase in IQ points. The younger children, who seemed to be influenced easily, needed continued contact with the teacher who expected them to succeed in order to maintain IQ gains. Older children, who were hard to influence at first, were better able to maintain the IQ gain once it had been achieved. Children of the medium track showed the greatest expectancy advantage, especially after two years.

The children were rated by their teachers. "Bloomers" in reading ability were also rated as more intellectually curious, happier, and less in need of social approval. The younger children, and children in the medium track, showed greater expectancy advantage in terms of their teachers' perceptions of classroom behavior and in reading scores.

Rosenthal and Jacobson believe that teachers who had higher standards for grading the "special" children brought about their higher achievement simply by expecting them to do well. Perhaps what the teacher said, how it was said—by voice, touch, facial expressions—communicated expectations of improvement to these children. Possible changes in teaching technique helped the children learn new self-concepts, expectations, and motivation.

No remedial or crash programs were given to the children in the school. Only the belief that the children bore watching, that they had intellectual abilities that would "bloom," caused the gains in IQ.

If indeed teacher expectancies can bring about dramatic improvement in pupil competence without formal changes in teaching methods, chances for children's success in school might be greatly enhanced.

Based on Robert Rosenthal and Lenore Jacobson, *Pygmalion in the Classroom*. New York: Holt, Rinehart and Winston, 1968.

REFERENCES

1. Ausubel, D. P. *Theory and Problems of Child Development.* New York: Grune & Stratton, 1958.
2. Ausubel, D. P., et al. "Perceived Parent Attitudes as Determinants of Children's Ego Structure," *Child Development,* 1954, *25,* 173–183.
3. Block, J., and H. Thomas. "Is Satisfaction with Self a Measure of Adjustment?" *Journal of Abnormal Social Psychology,* 1955, *51,* 254–259.
4. Brehm, J. W. "Increasing Cognitive Dissonance by a *Fait Accompli,*" *Journal of Abnormal Social Psychology,* 1959, *58,* 379–382.
5. Bruce, P. "Relationships of Self-acceptance to Other Variables with Sixth-grade Children Oriented in Self-understanding," *Journal of Educational Psychology,* 1958, *49,* 229–238.
6. "Changing Racial Preference," *Science News,* 1972, *102* (6), 88.
7. Chodorkoft, B. "Self-perception, Perceptual Defense and Adjustment," *Journal of Abnormal Social Psychology,* 1954, *49,* 508–512.
8. Clark, K., and M. Clark. "Racial Identification and Preference in Negro Children." In T. M. Newcomb and E. L. Hartley (eds.), *Readings in Social Psychology.* New York: Holt, Rinehart and Winston, 1947.
9. Cohen, A. R., H. I. Terry, and C. B. Jones. "Attitudinal Effects of Choice in Exposure to Counterpropaganda," *Journal of Abnormal Social Psychology,* 1959, *58,* 388–391.
10. Coopersmith, S. "A Method of Determining Types of Self-esteem," *Journal of Educational Psychology,* 1959, *59,* 87–94.
11. Coopersmith, S. *The Antecedents of Self-esteem.* San Francisco: Freeman, 1967.
12. Dilles, J. E. "Attractiveness of Group as Function of Self-esteem and Acceptance by Group," *Journal of Abnormal Social Psychology,* 1959, *59,* 77–82.
13. Dixon, J. C. "Development of Self-recognition," *Journal of Genetic Psychology,* 1957, *91,* 251–256.
14. Engle, M. "The Stability of the Self-concept in Adolescence," *Journal of Abnormal Social Psychology,* 1959, *58,* 211–215.
15. Festinger, L. *Theory of Cognitive Dissonance.* New York: Harper & Row, 1957.
16. Festinger, L., and J. M. Carlsmith. "Cognitive Consequences of Forced Compliance," *Journal of Abnormal Social Psychology,* 1959, *58,* 203–210.
17. Hanlon, T. E., P. R. Hofstaetter, and J. P. O'Connor. "Congruence of Self and Ideal Self in Relation to Personal Adjustment," *Journal of Consulting Psychology,* 1954, *18,* 215–218.
18. Katz, P., and E. Zigler. "Self-image Disparity: A Developmental Approach," *Journal of Personality and Social Psychology,* 1967, *5,* 186–195.
19. Lipsitt, L. P. "A Self-concept Scale for Children and Its Relationship to the Children's Form of the Manifest Anxiety Scale," *Child Development,* 1958, *29,* 463–472.
20. McCandless, B. R., and E. D. Evans. *Children and Youth: Psychosocial Development.* Hinsdale, Ill.: Dryden Press, 1973.
21. McCandless, B. R., A. Roberts, and T. Starnes. "Teachers' Marks, Achievement Test Scores and Aptitude Relations by Social Class, Race and Sex," *Journal of Educational Psychology,* 1972, *63,* 153–159.

22. Mitchell, J. V., Jr. "Goal-setting Behavior as a Function of Self-acceptance, Over- and Underachievement, and Related Personality Variables," *Journal of Educational Psychology*, 1959, *50*, 93–104.
23. Mussen, P. H., and L. W. Porter. "Personal Motivations and Self-conceptions Associated with Effectiveness and Ineffectiveness in Emergent Groups," *Journal of Abnormal Social Psychology*, 1959, *59*, 23–27.
24. Purkey, W. W. *Self-concept and School Achievement*. Englewood Cliffs, N.J.: Prentice-Hall, 1970.
25. Rosenberg, J. *Society and the Adolescent Self-image*. Princeton, N.J.: Princeton University Press, 1965.
26. Schreiber, F. R. *Sybil*. Chicago: Regnery, 1973.
27. Shaw, M. C. "Underachievement: Useful Construct or Misleading Illusion?" *Psychology in the Schools*, 1968, *5*, 41–46.
28. Stevenson, H. W. "Studies of Racial Awareness in Young Children." In W. W. Hartup and N. L. Smothergill (eds.), *The Young Child*. Washington, D.C.: National Association for the Education of Young Children, 1967.
29. Trotter, R. J. "Self-image," *Science News*, 1971, *100* (8), 130–131.
30. Trotter, R. J. "Sybil," *Science News*, 1973, *101* (21), 344–345.
31. Wylie, R. C. *The Self-concept*. Lincoln, Nebr.: Univ. of Nebraska Press, 1961.

appendix

age norms for developmental changes

Developmental psychology is still in its infancy. Most research in the field has been done on small numbers of children in a largely middle-class, Western culture. It is, therefore, very important to remember these points:

1. Large numbers of children need to be sampled before we can know if the *age norms* given in the following tables are accurate even for our own culture.
2. More cross-cultural studies are needed to determine whether the *sequence of stages* is the same for all children in all cultures.
3. Age norms must not be used to decide if an individual child is retarded or slow in developing. Just because a boy or girl does not sit up alone by 6 months, walk and talk by 1 year, start reading at 6 years, or deal with the question of identity by age 14 or 15 does not mean the child has a problem.

Each child is different and special—both to his or her parents and to society. We need much more research before developmental psychology comes of age.

The time tables that follow go beyond the age range covered in this text so that stages and theoretical positions are presented in as complete a form as possible. The reader can thus see the events of a normal human life through the adult years in abbreviated form and at a quick glance.

Table 1 Stages of Prenatal Development (Chapter 4)

Age	
0	1. *Conception* During sexual intercourse, male sperm cells pass through the female organs (vagina, cervix, uterus) and into the Fallopian tube, where one unites with the female's ovum cell. If a sperm cell reaches the nucleus of the ovum, the two cells unite to form a *zygote*.
0–2 weeks	2. *Germinal Period* Zygote progresses through the Fallopian tube to the uterus for 3 days, floats there for 4 or 5 days, then becomes attached to the wall of the uterus. Cell divides into embryo and supporting membranes.
1 month	3. *Embryonic Period* Organ systems begin to appear—brain, kidneys, liver, digestive tract, beginning umbilical cord—and heart starts to beat. Embryo is about one fifth of an inch long.
2½ months	Embryo is about 1 inch long. Eyelids, ears, nose, tongue, teeth, arms, and legs begin to form. Reflexes also begin to appear.
3 months	4. *Fetal Period* First bone cells appear. Fetus is about 3 inches long. Ribs and vertebrae turn into hard, bonelike cartilage. Buds for all 20 temporary teeth are formed; vocal cords, fingernails, and toenails begin to appear. Fetus can kick its legs, turn its feet and head, close its fingers, bend its wrists, and open and close its mouth.
4 months	Lower body growth speeds up. Fetus is about 6 or 7 inches long. Reflexes begin to be more pronounced. Mother begins to feel movement of the fetus, which is called *quickening*.
5 months	Fetus is about 1 foot long and weighs about 1 pound. Skin structures reach final form and sebaceous glands (which give off a greasy substance) begin to function. Fetus alternates between sleep and wakefulness and lies in a "favorite" position.
6 months	Fetus is about 14 inches long and weighs about 2 pounds. Eyelids are open; taste buds, eyebrows, and eyelashes appear; body hair *(lanugo hair)* is evident. Slight muscular breathing movements, hiccuping, and the grasp reflex also appear at this time.
7 months	Fetus is now capable of independent life outside the womb. It is about 16 inches long and weighs about 3 pounds. Hair appears on its head.
8–9 months	Fat forms over body. Heart rate is much more rapid than before, and fetus increases its overall activity. At birth, infant may weigh about 7 pounds and measure about 20 inches.

Table 2   Stages of Perceptual Development (Chapter 4)

Age	
1 month	Infant responds to sudden brightness by closing eyes. Lens of eye adjusts to object of vision. Baby appears to prefer patterns to colors and moving objects to stationary ones. Infant will smile at any nodding object the size of a human head, even if it has no eyes, nose, or mouth. Size constancy (seeing an object from any distance more or less accurately as to its size) functions. The infant tends to watch boundaries (angles and edges) of objects rather than center areas.
1½ months	Eyes in a model of a head are important, but any two blobs can make the baby smile.
2½ months	Only a face with eyebrows can get the baby to smile. Shape constancy functions. Infants now watch both the edges of objects and the center areas.
3 months	To produce a smile, a head model now must have realistic eyes.
5 months	A combination of eyes, eyebrows, and mouth are necessary to produce a smile. Faces without mouths will cause the child to withdraw rather than to smile.
6–7 months	A broadly smiling face produces more smiling than a pursed mouth. Child has ability to distinguish mother from father and familiar from strange adults. Depth perception is firmly established. Child will not crawl over a glass with a drop below, as in Gibson's "visual cliff" experiment.
8 months	Ability to distinguish a real face from a model now appears, along with ability to follow moving objects that pass behind a screen and reappear on the other side.

Table 3   Stages of Physical Growth and Development (Chapter 5)

Age	General Physical Norms	Stages of Hand Control
0–1 month	Lifts chin up. Holds head upright.	Reflex grasp when palm is stimulated.
2 months	Lifts chest up.	
3 months	Reaches and misses. Supports weight on elbows.	Neither reflexive nor voluntary grasp.
4 months	Sits with support. Shakes rattle in hand and stares at it. Turns from stomach to back.	
5 months	Sits in lap.	Touches object with palm, but no firm grasp.

Table 3 Stages of Physical Growth and Development (Chapter 5) (Continued)

Age	General Physical Norms	Stages of Hand Control
6 months	Sits in high chair. Bends forward using hands for support. Turns from back to stomach.	Begins to be able to squeeze object.
7 months	Stands with help.	Hand-palm grasp without thumb.
9 months	Stands holding on to solid object.	Palm grasp with thumb. Picks up pellet with thumb and fingertips.
10 months	Crawls.	
11 months	Walks when led. Takes side steps holding on. Creeps.	
12 months	Rests on knees. Pulls to stand.	Begins to grasp with forefinger.
13 months	Climbs stairs. Throws a ball.	
14 months	Stands up alone.	
15 months	Starts walking.	Grasps with fingers and thumb together.
18 months	Full walking. Has difficulty building tower of 3 cubes. Creeps downstairs backward.	
24 months	Hand preference appears. Runs, but falls in sudden turns. Climbs stairs up and down.	Picks up pellet between thumb and index finger.
3 years	Average height is about 3 feet. Weight is around 33 lbs. Child generally has protruding stomach, short legs, and large head. Can stack 10 blocks, scribble with crayons, and fold paper.	
4 years	Legs now work independently of each other and the rest of the body. Can broad jump from both running and standing starts.	
6–12 years	Child's body shape looks like that of adult—stomach recedes, legs are longer, finer muscles develop, and chest enlarges. Growth is slower and steadier than at periods of infancy and toddler-hood.	

Table 3 Stages of Physical Growth and Development (Chapter 5) (Continued)

Age	General Physical Norms	Stages of Hand Control
12–16 years	Changes of puberty include adolescent growth spurt, emergence of menstruation in females, appearance of secondary sex characteristics (breasts, underarm and pubic hair, and widening of pelvis in females; facial, body, and pubic hair, nocturnal ejaculations, and voice change in males).	

Table 4 Stages of Cognitive Development (Chapter 7)

Age	Piaget	Bruner
0–1 month	*Substages of Sensory-motor Intelligence* 1. *Reflexive Movements and First Schemes* Exercise and construction of reflexes into schemes of grasping, sucking, looking, and so on through assimilation and accommodation.	*Enactive* "Thinking" is only with actions. Infant indicates hunger by holding out arms or making sucking motions.
1–4 months	2. *Primary Circular Reactions* Combination of simple schemes, such as arm waving and sucking.	
4–8 months	3. *Secondary Circular Reactions* Actions intentionally repeated for pleasurable effects, such as kicking the crib to hear noise of rattle. Infant applies established action schemes to novel objects, but does not accommodate behavior to them (shakes a toy gun as if it is a rattle).	
8–12 months	4. *Coordination of Secondary Schemes* Actions coordinated to effect results (pushing away a pillow to reach ball). If object is hidden, infant acts as if it has disappeared.	

Table 4   Stages of Cognitive Development (Chapter 7) (Continued)

Age	Piaget	Bruner
12–18 months	5. *Directed Groping* Search for new means to achieve goals. Curiosity in testing how unfamiliar objects behave (dropping bread crumbs on the floor to see how they land).	*Ikonic* Ability to mentally represent objects that are not physically present. Ability to classify objects by perceptual qualities— banana, peach, and potato are all yellow.
18–24 months	6. *Internalization of Schemes* Infant begins mentally to represent actions and objects in the sense of images and symbols. If an object is hidden, child searches for it as if retaining a permanent image of it in the mind, an achievement Piaget calls "object permanence." Infant may also indicate a desire to open a matchbox by opening and closing the mouth.	
2–7 years	*Stage of Preoperations* Child is now able to use symbols in language, drawing, symbolic play, and problem-solving. Symbols are all based on ego-centric view of the world (the sun is alive, because I'm alive. Night comes when I go to sleep.). Child judges amount of water in a glass based on appearance or shape of container (a tall glass has more water; a piece of clay shaped like a sausage has more clay than the same clay shaped as a ball).	*Symbolic Representation* Ability to use words and represent thoughts with symbols in pretend play, drawing, and everyday gestures.
7–11 years	*Stage of Concrete Operations* Child is now able to understand that a change in the shape of an object does not alter the amount (the piece of clay can be turned into several shapes, but it's still the same piece of clay). Logical reasoning is still limited to problems involving *concrete* (actual) objects.	*Logical Thinking* Ability to solve logical problems and to organize thoughts sequentially.

Table 4 Stages of Cognitive Development (Chapter 7) (Continued)

Age	Piaget	Bruner
11–adulthood	*Stage of Formal Operations* Ability to construct theories independent of concrete reference. Child now concerned with ideals of conduct and thinks of the future. Ability to solve problems of formal logic.	

Table 5 Stages of Language Development (Chapter 8)

Age	
0–1 month	*Crying Stage* Exercise of vocal equipment in crying. Pitch drops off at end of cry and different crying sounds indicate pain and hunger.
1–5 months	*Cooing Stage* Cooing is pitch-modulated, vowel-like, and can be sustained for 15–20 seconds. It tends to have a falling, glissando (or up or down the music scale) sound. Seems associated with pleasure such as while watching someone smile or after eating.
5–12 months	*Babbling Stage* Differences between vowels and consonants begin to be heard. Seems to alternate them into something like syllables, adding pitch and stress patterns. Strings of babbling sounds often have the shape of rising and falling sounds similar to those used in adult speech.
12–18 months	*One-word Utterance Stage* First meaningful words appear. These words contain only one or two vowels and consonants ("mamma," "papa," "bye-bye"). Infant seems to use these words to comment on actions and immediate perceptions ("up," "down," "mine," "doggy").
18–30 months	*Two-word Utterance Stage* Words are now combined grammatically ("up there" or "go up"). Child seems to relate words according to the meaning intended, not by their syntax.
3 years	*Syntactic Speech* Child now acquires ease in speaking native language with some grammatical correctness and a large vocabulary.

Table 6 Social Development (Chapter 10)

Age	
0–1 month	Makes eye-to-eye contact. Begins to smile back at adult's smile. Shows excitement and distress.
2 months	Quiets down when held. Begins to smile when someone other than own parents are recognized (smile of recognition).
3 months	Decrease in crying, but cry is different when mother is seen. Appears to recognize many different people.
4 months	Begins to show interest in mirror image. Becomes much more sociable. Vocalizes different moods of enjoyment, protest, and frustration.
5 months	Discriminates self and parent in mirror. Stops crying when spoken to. Resists adult's attempt to take away toy. Raises arms to be picked up. Begins to show fear and anger.
6 months	Begins to show fear of unfamiliar (stranger anxiety). May cry in presence of unknown people. Shows increased anxiety when in an unfamiliar situation without parents (separation anxiety).
7 months	Enjoys playing peek-a-boo or hiding head in blanket. This indicates the infant is beginning to deal with separation and stranger anxieties. Turns when hears own name. Distinguishes friendly and angry talking.
8 months	Fear of strangers and of separation from parents becomes strongest. Shouts for attention and pushes away what isn't wanted.
9 months	Initiates play with balls and small toys. Repeats act if applauded by audience.
10 months	Increased dependence on parents or caretakers. Learns meaning of "no." Shows guilt at wrongdoing. May imitate play of another child. Clings to parent when afraid of stranger.
12 months	Increase in negativism and defiant independence—refuses eating, resists napping, and has tantrums. Shows strong preferences for certain individuals. Begins to compete with brothers and sisters and peers for toys.
1–2 years	Begins to play with other children—to imitate their actions, to run when chased, and pretend social situations with toys.
2–7 years	Highly symbolic solitary play with blocks and toys. Some simple turn-taking in play with one or two other children, as in tag or hide-and-seek. Group play is mostly ritualistic activity done by many children, as in "Ring-Around-a-Rosy" and "Simon Says."
7–12 years	Exercise of new skills of logical thinking as in collecting and classifying stamps. Competitive game strategy as in marbles. Physical and verbal skill, as in jump rope. Group play is group versus group as in cowboys and Indians. Peer-group power relationships begin and are reinforced in games such as "King of the Mountain."
12–18 years	Technical skill grows in individual activities such as pottery making or music. Ability to coordinate physical and mental skills in specialized roles of team sports. Reinforcement of peer-group power relationships in verbal insults, as in name calling. Kissing games also emerge.

Table 7 Kohlberg's Stages of Moral Judgment (Chapter 10)

Age	
1–3 years	1. *Obedience and Punishment Orientation* Absolute yielding to powerful adults in order to avoid punishment.
3–5 years	2. *Simple Exchange* Child conforms in order to gain rewards by bartering—"I'll lend you my toy soldier, if I can play with your toy car." Child thinks goodness is giving something in exchange.
6–12 years	3. *Good Child Morality* Child wants to conform to standards of friends and family. Bases judgments of morality on what others think. "If I do what the teacher says, I'm a good child."
13–16 years	4. *Law and Order Stage* Blind obedience to community rules. Pre-adolescents may obey rigid social conventions of dress and may exclude those who do not fit into their group.
16–19 years	5. *Morality of Democratic and Representative Government* Based on agreement of individuals to follow accepted behavior, which respects the basic rights of everyone else regardless of different beliefs, races, or social classes.
19–25 years	6. *Morality of Individual Conscience* Individual follows principles of own conscience, even when this goes against laws and standards of the society. Does not set self above others. What is just for oneself must be that which is just for everyone. The Golden Rule is followed ("Do unto others as we would have others do unto us").

Table 8   Stages of Psychosexual Development (Chapters 10–12)

Age	Freud	Erikson
0–1 year	1. *Oral Stage* Gratification from around mouth by sucking nipples, bottles, fingers, and other objects. Child very dependent on others for needs. Operates on pleasure principle of immediate satisfaction. *Id* dominates.	1. *Trust versus Mistrust* Infant learns to *trust* caretakers who feed and protect child. Also learns to *mistrust* dangerous places (falling from a high place) or things that hurt (teeth or fingers).
1–3 years	2. *Anal Stage* Pleasure shifts to anus and retaining and eliminating feces. Parents try to socialize child to eliminate in acceptable place and according to a regular schedule (toilet-training). Child may become overly clean and rigidly organized, or extremely messy and defiantly independent. *Ego* mechanisms of control of impulses emerge.	2. *Autonomy versus Shame and Doubt* Parents try to "break will" of child by toilet-training. This makes child *ashamed* of body and its products, and *doubtful* of ability to function on his or her own. At the same time the child wants to be *autonomous* (or independent) and insists on doing things unassisted.
3–5 years	3. *Phallic Stage* Pleasure develops in genitals. Boy develops sexual attachment to mother; fears father will punish him by castration. Girl desires father and becomes rival of mother. This is resolved by repressing sexual interests and by identifying with same-sex parent, which brings about birth of *superego*.	3. *Initiative versus Guilt* Child begins to feel new powers and to *initiate* actions. This also causes some *guilt*. The child fears its own strength, for example, and begins to feel some regret for certain actions.
5–12 years	4. *Latency Stage* Repression of erotic impulses toward same-sex parent extended to sexual energy in general. This can then be expressed in school activities and learning.	4. *Industry versus Inferiority* Child *industriously* learns new skills and social rules and works on extended projects until they are completed. Feelings of *inferiority* may develop if a lot of failure occurs.

Table 8 Stages of Psychosexual Development (Chapters 10–12) (Continued)

Age	Freud	Erikson
Adolescence	5. *Genital Stage* At puberty sexual interest in opposite sex reappears and lasts throughout adulthood. Ability to have sexual intercourse and to love another intimately brings about true genitality, the goal of Freud's psychosexual stages.	5. *Identity versus Role Confusion* One plays many roles— student, sibling, game-player, lover. Out of this social mix of *role confusion*, one must locate one's true *identity*.
Adulthood		6. *Intimacy versus Isolation* With a firm sense of identity, one can become *intimate* with another without losing oneself in the relationship and without ending up feeling alone and *isolated*.
Middle Age		7. *Generativity versus Stagnation* A time of caring for the next *generation* as a parent, teacher, doctor, and so on. One actively transmits skills and values of the culture to others, if one practices *generativity*. Otherwise one is unproductive and *stagnant*.
Old Age		8. *Ego Integrity versus Despair* Old age brings either the wisdom of *ego integrity*, where one feels that everything in life has its special place and that one's life was necessary and good, or it brings an overwhelming feeling of *despair* that there is no more time left to do what one wanted in earlier years.

Table 9 Educational Milestones (Chapters 6, 7, and 12)

Age	
2–3 years	Child has enough command of language to learn to count, identify pictures, and create simple stories and rhymes.
4–5 years	Child can play with peers, write own name, and draw pictures that represent animals, people, and objects. Child can benefit from nursery school instruction, learning to recognize and write letters, understanding the difference between big and little or light and heavy, and understanding and creating complete stories.
6 years	Reading readiness age. Formal instruction in reading, writing, and mathematics can begin due to child's new abilities in perception and logical thinking. For example, the child can do what Piaget calls "concrete operations." The child adds and subtracts. The child can carry out addition and then reverse the process by subtraction, a process Piaget calls "reversibility."
9–12 years	Child can be given long-term projects, such as social studies reports or simple scientific experiments. Child can also cooperate with others on class projects and group games (see Erikson's stage of Industry versus Inferiority).
14–17 years	The adolescent begins to understand relationships of formal logic that are critical in learning advanced mathematics and in understanding the complexities of scientific methodology. There is also an attempt to master difficult technical skills in mathematical computation, sports, and the arts; to understand the idea of different forms of government and different historical styles in art and music; and to formulate one's own values and philosophy of life (*see* Piaget's Stage of Formal Operations, Erikson's Stage of Identity versus Role Confusion, and Kohlberg's Stages of Representative Government and Individual Conscience).

name index

Ainsworth, M. S., 100

Bacon, M. K., 452–454
Bakkestrom, E., 84n
Baltes, P., 39
Bandura, A., 24, 244, 481
Baron, R., 268–269
Barry, H., 452–454
Bartsch, T., 39
Beach, D. H., 311–312
Bee, H., 476
Bem, S. L., 495
Bessel, F. W., 369
Bigelow, R. S., 42–44, 58
Binet, A., 369–370, 372
Blau, T. H., 192–193, 206
Bowlby, J., 172
Brazelton, T. B., 103
Brickell, J., 38–39
Broca, P., 329
Bronfenbrenner, U., 121, 243–244
Broverman, D. M., 476
Broverman, I., 476
Brown, R., 334, 340–341
Bruner, J. S., 275–277, 300, 392
Bryant, P. E., 266–267
Budin, P., 30

Cannizzo, S. R., 311–312
Castaneda, A., 540, 541
Cattell, J. M., 369
Child, I. L., 452–454
Chinsky, J. M., 311–312
Chodorkoft, B., 539–540
Chomsky, N., 333
Christiansen, K., 84n
Clark, D. H., 404–406
Clifford, M., 219–220
Condillac, E. B. de, 319
Cooney, M., 30
Coopersmith, S., 514–515, 523–524
Crissey, M. S., 179

Darwin, C. R., 6, 7–8, 26, 57–58, 182
de Mause, L., 4–8
Dion, K. E., 219–220

Dollard, J., 21

Elkind, D., 314n
Erikson, E. H., 14, 413–417, 454–455, 512–514

Festinger, L., 534–535
Fifer, G., 404–406
Fixen, D., 224
Flavell, J. H., 311–312, 497–499
Frank, L., 38
Freud, S., 8–14, 98, 110, 115, 146, 171, 185, 413, 414, 478–480, 482

Gagné, R. M., 20
Galton, F., 369, 396–397, 400
Gardner, B. T., 326, 328
Gardner, R. A., 326, 328
Gesell, A., 37
Gibson, E. J., 159–161
Goldberg, F. J., 135
Goodenough, D., 84n
Goodenough, F. L., 444
Goodwin, D., 82–83
Guilford, J. P., 367–368

Hall, G. S., 6
Harlow, H., 29, 67, 72, 76, 90–97, 115, 131, 167, 173, 420, 486
Hayes, C., 325
Hayes, K., 325
Hebb, D. O., 183
Heber, R. F., 360–365
Herodotus, 318
Heston, L. L., 82–83
Hetherington, E. M., 38n, 485–486
Hirschtorm, K., 84n
Hitler, A., 65
Horowitz, F. D., 540–541
Hunt, J. Mc V., 183, 365, 378, 399, 400

Inhelder, B., 297, 298
Itard, J., 89–90, 102

Jacklin, C. N., 467, 468–469
Jacobs, P. A., 55

James, W., 228
Jaynes, J., 320–322

Kagan, J., 130, 307, 381–382
Keeney, T. J., 311–312
Keller, F. S., 226–228, 236, 264, 526
Kellog, L., 325
Kellog, W., 325
Kennell, J. H., 30
Kinsey, A. C., 115
Klaus, M. H., 29–30
Kleck, R., 220–221
Kohlberg, L., 446, 448–450
Kretschmer, E., 207–208

Labouvie, E., 39
Lane, H., 88–90
Langner, T. S., 25
Leboyer, F., 144–146, 153, 158, 180
Lenneberg, E. H., 333
Lesser, G. S., 404–406
Levin, H., 107–109, 110, 112–113, 116–117
Liebert, R. M., 268–269
Lipsitt, L. P., 540, 541
Locke, J., 4–5
Lorenz, K., 68–69, 76
Lundsteen, C., 84n

Maccoby, E. E., 107–109, 110, 112–113, 116–117, 467, 468–469
Malinowski, B., 98–99
Malthus, T., 57, 58
Maslow, A. H., 253–254
May, W. H., 135
McCandless, B. R., 540, 541
McNeill, D., 354–355
Mead, M., 295
Mednick, S., 84n
Mendel, G., 45–47, 48
Mill, J. S., 360, 362
Miller, N. E., 21
Minsky, M., 272–274
Miron, M. S., 135
Money, J., 472–473
Montague, A., 319–320

Morris, J., 462–463, 464
Munsinger, H., 298
Mussen, P. H., 355n

Nesselroade, J., 39

Osborn, D., 355n
Osborn, J., 355n
Osgood, C. E., 135
Owen, D., 84n

Palermo, D., 540, 541
Papert, S., 272–274
Pavlov, I., 231–233
Pestalozzi, J. H., 6, 15
Philips, E., 224
Phillip, J., 84n
Piaget, J., 15–19, 26–27, 162, 170, 266, 272, 278–280, 281, 282–300, 306, 309, 312–314, 324, 340, 346, 347–348, 378, 381, 430, 440, 446–448, 481, 499–501, 512–514
Pinel, P., 89
Poulos, R. W., 268–269
Premack, A., 326, 328
Premack, D., 326, 328

Rabin, D., 84n
Raynor, R., 21
Rembald, A. B., 136
Richardson, S., 220–221
Ronald, L., 220–221
Rosenkrantz, P., 476
Rousseau, J-J, 5–6, 446, 493
Rumbaugh, D., 327–328

Schaffer, H. R., 183–184
Schuckit, M., 82–83
Schulsinger, F., 84n
Sears, R. R., 33–38, 107–109, 110, 112–113, 116–117
Senn, M. J., 37–38
Sheldon, W. H., 208–209
Sherman, J. G., 227
Simon, T., 370
Singh, J. A. L., 88
Skeels, H. M., 178–179, 400, 402–404

Skinner, B. F., 22–24, 28, 236–237, 330
Smith, D. E. P., 238–241
Spearman, C., 366
Spitz, R. A., 177, 178
Spock, B., 423
Sprafkin, J. N., 268–269
Stabler, J. R., 135, 136
Stanley, J. C., 392–395

Stocking, M., 84n
Suomi, S. J., 93

Tenzer, A., 314n
Terman, L. M., 371, 391, 395
Thurstone, L. L., 366–367
Trabasso, T., 266–267
Turnbull, C. M., 133–134

van Lawick-Goodall, J., 28
Vogel, S., 476

Wallace, A. R., 57, 58
Walster, E., 219–220
Walter, T., 238–241
Watson, J. B., 19–20, 21, 185
Wernicke, C., 329
Wilbur, C., 508–510

Williams, J. E., 135
Wilson, E. O., 71
Winokur, G., 82–83
Witkin, H., 83–84
Wolf, M., 224
Worchester, D. A., 395

Zajonc, R. B., 129
Zeig, J. A., 136

subject index

Physical development, anatomical changes, 199–201
  deviations and handicaps, 216–217
  hand skills, 204–205
  handedness and the brain, 205–207
  and learning, 246
  left-handedness, 192–193
  locomotion, 203–204
  motor patterns, 201–207
  mouth, 204
  norms for, 193
  patterns of, 196–201
  and personality, 207–217
  principles of, 194–196
  rate of, and personality, 211–216
  sphincter control, 204
Physical stereotypes, 209–210
Piaget, cognitive theory, 282–300
  developmental stages, 278–280
Pocket calculators, 293–294
Positive reinforcement, 33
Pregnancy, 146–151
  disease during, 152
  prenatal influences on development, 151–155
Premature babies, 30, 154–155
Prenatal development, 147–149
Preoperational stage of development, 17–18, 278–279
Primate behavior, 70–72
  and social attachment, 90–97
Problem-solving, 301–307
  creative, 303–307
  intelligence as, 368–369
  and mental set, 302–303
Proximodistal development, 149, 195
Psychic stimulation, 231–232
Psychoanalytic theory, 478–480
Psychodynamic theory, 8–14
  evaluation of, 13–14
Psychosexual development, 463–467
  age progression in, 466–467
  basic concepts in, 465–466
  behavioral differences, 467–478
  biological factors, 469
  and father absence, 485–487
  hormonal influences, 469–472
  and mother absence, 487–488
  sex reassignment, 472–473
  sexual identity and adjustment, 493–495
  social and cultural factors, 473–474
  and socialization, 482–493
  theories of, 478–482
Puberty, 13, 200, 416

Punisher, stimulus as, 241–243
Punishment, and aggression, 440–441

Q-sort, 517

Race, and behavior, 65–66
  and child development, 121–123
  and color prejudice, 135–136
  as genetic classification, 62–63
  and intelligence, 396–399
  and language, 351–352
  and self-concept, 520–522
Radiation, and prenatal period, 151
Recessive gene, 47
Reflectivity, vs. impulsivity, 307–309
Reflexes, 228–229
  and instincts, 67–68
  of newborns, 156–157
Reinforcement, 235–238
  intermittent, 236–237
  by peers, 426–427
  positive, 33
  and punishers, 241–243
Releasing mechanism, 70
Religion, and child-rearing, 123–124
Reproduction, 51–54
  asexual, 51–52
  mitosis and meiosis, 52
Research, on animals, and speech, 325–328
  comparative, 28
  cross-cultural, 28, 99–102
  cross-sectional study, 28
  dependent and independent variables, 32–33
  difficulties of, 38–39
  longitudinal, 27–28, 39
  manipulative, 29–34
  naturalistic, 25–29
  prospective study, 28
  retrospective study, 28
  single-subject design, 33
  twin studies, 365–366
Response cost, 241
Response generalization, 255
Retention, 245–246
Reversibility of thought, 298
  and language, 346
Reward, 253
Role theory, 480

Schema, 168, 283
Schizophrenia, and anoxia, 154
  and genetics, 66, 82–83
Schools, achievement, and self-concept, 524–533

Schools (cont.)
  and psychosexual development, 489–491
  report cards, and self-concept, 531–533
Selective breeding, 65–66
Self-acceptance, 537–538
Self-actualization, 253–254
Self-concept, 510–515
  and anxiety, and popularity, 540–541
  beginnings of, 511
  changing of, 533–536
  and child-rearing practices, 514–515
  and defensiveness, 539–540
  index of, 516
  and individual differences, 529–531
  measurement of, 515–518
  and personal adjustment, 518–524
  and the "real self," 523–524
  satisfaction with, 522–523
  and school achievement, 524–533
  and school reporting, 531–533
  theories of, 512–514
  unexamined qualities of, 536–538
Self-esteem, 511–512
Semantic code, 339–340
Sensory disabilities, 216–217
Sensory-motor stage of development, 16–17, 278, 283–288
Sensory psychosocial stage, 414
Separation anxiety, 75–76
Sesame Street, 249
Sex chromosomes, 50–51
Sex differences, in aggression, 436–437
  behavioral, 467–478
  in dependency, 421
  infants, 467–468
  in intelligence, 395–396
  in physical maturity rate, 211–212
  psychological, 468–469
  and socialization, 452–454
Sex role, 465
  orientation to, 465–466
  stereotypes, in United States, 474–476
Sex training, 115–118
Sex-linked traits, 50–51
Sexual development, 196–197
  See also Psychosexual development
Sexual identity, 465–466
  and adjustment, 493–495
Sexual relations, cross-cultural variation, 473–474

Sexual relations (cont.)
  and social isolation, in monkeys, 94–95
Sickle cell anemia, 48, 53
Single-parent family, 125–126
Skin senses, in infants, 166
Skinner box, 22–24, 33, 236
Smell, sense of, 164–165
Social acceptance, 428–429
Social attachment, in monkeys, 90–97
Social class, and aggression, 437
  and child-rearing values, 120–121
  definition of, 118–120
  and intelligence, 404–406
  and intelligence tests, 374
  and language, 348–351
  and self-concept, 520–522
  and sex typing, 476–478
Social development, 413–417
  and aggression, 436–445
  altruism, 412, 431–436
  attachment and dependency, 417–423
  group relations, 427–431
  peer relations, 423–427
  and women's capabilities, 454–455
Social groups, 70–72
Social isolation, 88–90
  and development, 130
Social learning (see Modeling)
Socialization, 97
  cross-cultural studies of, 99–102
  and dependency, 422–423
  and the family, 125–129
  and psychosexual development, 482–493
  and sex differences, 452–454
Society, 97
  values of, and survival, 133–134
Somatic growth, 197–198
Space, concept of, 289–291
Special education, 390
Speech, 323
  infant's response to, 163–164
  patterned, beginnings of, 336–337
Stimulus generalization, 255
Stimulus-response learning, 20–21
Stress, and attachment, 421–422
Structural theory, and cognition, 277–280
Successive approximations, 240–241
Survival, 42–44, 58
Sybil, 508–510
Symbolic representation, 277
Syntactic code, 339–340

Age Norms for Developmental Changes

Age	Perception	Physical Development	Piaget's Stages	Bruner's Stages	Language Development
0 months	Responds to movement and watches edges of objects.	Fetal posture.	Sensory-motor Stages 1. Reflexes.	1. Enactive	1. Crying Stage
1 month		Chin up; reflex grasp.			
2 months	Watches center areas of objects and edges.	Chest up.	2. Primary circular reactions.		
3 months		Reaches and misses.			2. Cooing Stage
4 months		Sits with support.	3. Secondary circular reactions.		
5 months		Sits in lap.			
6 months	Depth perception: "visual cliff."	Sits alone.			3. Babbling Stage
7 months		Palm grasp.			
8 months	Follows object behind screen.	Stands; holding on.			
9 months			4. Coordination of secondary schemes.		
10 months		Creeps.			
11 months					
1 year		Pulls to stand. Walks alone.	5. Directed groping.	2. Ikonic	4. One-word Stage
2 years		Hand preference established.	6. Internal schemes.		5. Two-word Stage
3 years			Preoperational Period	3. Symbolic Representation	6. Syntactic Speech
4 years					
5 years					
6 years			Concrete Operations	4. Logical Thinking	
12 years			Formal Operations		
14 years					
16 years					
18 years					
Adulthood					
Middle Age					
Old Age					

See Appendix for details.